PC Cumulative Title Index, Vols. 1-61

"A***" (Char) **56**:128
"A" (Zukofsky) **11**:337-40, 345-46, 351, 356-58, 361-67, 369-73, 383, 385-93, 395-99
"A" 1-9 (Zukofsky) **11**:380
"A" 1-12 (Zukofsky) **11**:343-44, 367-68
"A celle qui est trop gaie" (Baudelaire) **1**:44, 60-2
"A Colón" (Darío) **15**:84, 115
"A Félix Guiliemardet" (Lamartine) **16**:284
"A Francisca" (Darío) **15**:107, 111
"A Jenn de la Peruse, poète dramatique" (Ronsard) **11**:246
"A la Forest de Gastine" (Ronsard) **11**:228
"A la promenade" (Verlaine) **32**:349, 390
"A la santé" (Apollinaire) **7**:44, 46-7
"A l'intérieur de l'armure" (Péret) **33**:203
"A l'Italie" (Apollinaire) **7**:22
"A lo lejos" (Jiménez) **7**:199
"A los poetas risueños" (Darío) **15**:95
"A mi alma" (Jiménez) **7**:194
"A Philippes des-Portes Chartrain" (Ronsard) **11**:269-70
"A Roosevelt" (Darío) **15**:77, 81, 90, 106, 115
"A son ame" (Ronsard) **11**:244
"A ti" (Darío) **15**:99
"A une heure du matin" (Baudelaire) **1**:59, 72
"A une Malabaraise" (Baudelaire) **1**:49
"A une passante" (Baudelaire) **1**:45, 73
"A Verlaine" (Darío) **15**:93
"Aaron" (Herbert) **4**:102, 114, 130
"Aaron Hatfield" (Masters) **36**:184, 191
"Aaron Stark" (Robinson) **1**:460, 467; **35**:367
"Abacus" (Seifert)
See "Počitadlo"
"Abandon" (Li Po) **29**:177
"The Abandoned" (Abse) **41**:9
"The Abandoned Newborn" (Olds) **22**:329
"The Abandoned Observatory" (Yau) **61**:329
ABC of Economics (Pound) **4**:328
"ABCs" (Olson) **19**:267, 271, 316
"The Abduction" (Kunitz) **19**:181-82
"The Abduction of Saints" (Walker) **30**:354
"L'abeille" (Valéry) **9**:353, 387-88, 393-94
"Abel" (Stein) **18**:316
"Abel and Cain" (Baudelaire)
See "Abel et Caïn"
"Abel et Caïn" (Baudelaire) **1**:68
"Abel's Bride" (Levertov) **11**:175
"Abend" (Stramm) **50**:170-71, 174, 198, 201, 207, 221
"Der Abend" (Trakl) **20**:237-38, 244, 251, 258
"Abendgang" (Stramm) **50**:171, 175-76, 202
"Abendland" (Trakl) **20**:231-32, 235, 240-44, 251, 269
"Abendländisches Lied" (Trakl) **20**:231, 236, 248-49, 251, 258, 269
"Abendlied" (Trakl) **20**:239, 269
"Abendmahl, Venezianisch, 16. Jahrhundert" (Enzensberger) **28**:165
"abgelegenes haus" (Enzensberger) **28**:140
"Abigail" (Silverstein) **49**:333
"Abishag" (Glück) **16**:126, 141
"Abnegation" (Rich) **5**:365
"Aboard the Santa Maria" (Illyés) **16**:248
"Abode" (Milosz) **8**:215
"The Abominable Lake" (Smith) **12**:353
Abondance viendra (Char) **56**:127-28, 187
"An Abortion" (O'Hara) **45**:162
"The Abortion" (Sexton) **2**:349
"About Almonds and Ambergis" (Goodison) **36**:158
"About Money" (Ignatow) **34**:273
"About Opera" (Meredith) **28**:195, 206
"About Poetry" (Meredith) **28**:193-94
"About the House" (Auden) **1**:21, 24
"About the Phoenix" (Merrill) **28**:239
"About These Verses" (Pasternak) **6**:251
Above the Barriers (Pasternak)
See *Poverkh barierov*
"Above the Gaspereau" (Carman) **34**:225
Above the River: The Complete Poems of James Wright (Wright) **36**:360-61, 370-71, 379, 391, 397-400
"Above These Cares" (Millay) **6**:235
"Abraham and Orpheus" (Schwartz) **8**:306, 308-09
"Abraham Lincoln Walks at Midnight" (Lindsay) **23**:275, 280, 284, 288, 294-95
"L'Abri rudoyé" (Char) **56**:152
"Abril sus flores abría" (Guillén) **23**:125
Abrojos (Darío) **15**:94
Absalom and Achitophel (Dryden) **25**:82-3, 88, 106-08, 113-14
"Abschied" (Benn) **35**:82, 83, 85
"Der Abschied" (Sarton) **39**:338
"abschied von einem mittwoch" (Enzensberger) **28**:136
"Absence" (Borges)
See "Ausencia"
"Absence" (Gozzano) **10**:178
"Absence" (Sarton) **39**:369
"L'absence, ny l'oubly, ny la course du jour" (Ronsard) **11**:246
"The Absence of Little Wesley" (Riley) **48**:340, 360
"Absence Proves Nothing" (Stone) **53**:247-48, 257
"Absences" (Larkin) **21**:249-51
"Absences I" (Éluard) **38**:70-71
"Absences II" (Éluard) **38**:70-71
"L'Absent" (Char) **56**:153
"The Absent Girl" (Ní Chuilleanáin) **34**:357
"The absent One" (Senghor)
See "L'Absente"
"Absent With Official Leave" (Jarrell) **41**:201
"L'Absente" (Senghor) **25**:255, 258
"Absentia animi" (Ekeloef) **23**:59-60, 63, 76, 86
"Absent-Minded Professor" (Nemerov) **24**:266
"Absolute Clearance" (Ashbery) **26**:124
"Absolute Retreat" (Finch)
See "The Petition for an Absolute Retreat"
"Absolute Zero" (Parra) **39**:308-10
"Absolution" (Brooke) **24**:52
"Absolution" (Sassoon) **12**:241, 250, 252, 261, 276, 278, 280
"Abt Vogler" (Browning) **2**:37, 75, 80, 88, 95
"El abuelo" (Guillén) **23**:134-37
"Abur Don Pepe" (Guillén) **23**:126
"The Abyss" (Roethke) **15**:270
"The Abyss of Mr. Cogito" (Herbert) **50**:19
"The Abyss of War" (Owen) **19**:343
"Abzählreime" (Celan) **10**:124-25
"Academic" (Roethke) **15**:246
"Academic Discourse at Havana" (Stevens)
See *Ideas of Order*
Academic Squaw: Reports to the World from the Ivory Tower (Rose) **13**:233, 238
"Acceptance" (Sassoon) **12**:259
"Accepted" (Patmore) **59**:230
"Accès" (Tzara) **27**:229-31
"Accidentally on Purpose" (Frost) **1**:213
"Accomplishment" (Gallagher) **9**:59
"An Account of a Visit to Hawaii" (Meredith) **28**:171, 189
An Account of a Weatherbeaten Journey (Matsuo Bashō)
See *Nozarashi kikō*
"Accountability" (Dunbar) **5**:133, 146
"An Accounting of All Her Men" (Ríos) **57**:325
"Accroupissements" (Rimbaud) **57**:203, 253, 289, 293-95
"Les accroupissements" (Rimbaud) **3**:284
"The Accusation" (Wright) **36**:343
"Accused Cherub" (Rimbaud)
See "L'Angelot maudit"
"The Accuser" (Milosz) **8**:204
"Acevedo" (Borges) **32**:88
"Ach das Erhabene" (Benn) **35**:36
"Ach, um deine feuchten Schwingen" (Goethe) **5**:247
"The Ache of Marriage" (Levertov) **11**:169
"Achieving a Poem while Drinking Alone" (Tu Fu) **9**:327
"The Achill Woman " (Boland) **58**:7, 15-16, 27, 30, 55, 57-58, 66, 68
"Achilles and Deidamia" (Gower) **59**:98-99
"Achille's Song" (Duncan) **2**:115
"Acknowledgment" (Lanier) **50**:55
"Acon" (H. D.) **5**:273
Aconsejo beber hilo (Fuertes) **27**:10-12
"Acquainted with the Night" (Frost) **1**:197, 205-06, 208; **39**:246
"Acquamorta" (Quasimodo) **47**:285-86
Acque e terre (Quasimodo) **47**:270, 274-75, 300-302
"An Acre of Grass" (Yeats) **51**:142, 152
"Across Lamarck Col" (Snyder) **21**:288
"Across the Bay" (Davie) **29**:110
"An Acrostic" (Poe) **1**:446
"Act III, Sc. 2" (Graham) **59**:175
"The act of madness" (Char)
See "L'extravagant"
"Act of Union" (Heaney) **18**:196
"Acta de independecia" (Parra) **39**:277
"Acteon" (Gower) **59**:88, 92
"Actfive" (MacLeish) **47**:191-92, 259
Actfive, and Other Poems (MacLeish) **47**:176, 178-79, 191, 197, 246, 260

"The Action of the Beautiful" (Sarton) **39**:325, 333, 365
"Acto completo'" (Guillén) **35**:227
"Acts and Monuments" (Ní Chuilleanáin) **34**:359, 363, 380-81
Acts and Monuments (Ní Chuilleanáin) **34**:348, 350-51, 355, 359, 363
"Ad Alessandro d'Ancona" (Carducci) **46**:52
"Ad Angelo Mai quand'ebbe trovato i libri di Cicerone della Repubblica" (Leopardi) **37**:111, 147-49
"A.D. Blood" (Masters) **36**:170, 230
"Ad Castitatem" (Bogan) **12**:117
"Ad Libitum" (Elytis) **21**:132-33
"Ad Mariam" (Hopkins) **15**:159, 164, 166
Ad Patrem (Milton) **29**:241
"Adam" (Brathwaite) **56**:62
"Adam" (Tomlinson) **17**:316, 342
"Adam" (Williams) **7**:350, 354
"Adam and Eve" (Shapiro) **25**:284-85, 287, 290-91, 301, 320
Adam & Eve & the City (Williams) **7**:350, 402
"Adam Is Your Ash" (Borges)
See "Adán es tu ceniza"
"adam thinking" (Clifton) **17**:30, 36
"The Adamant" (Roethke) **15**:272, 291
"Adam's Curse" (Yeats) **20**:338
"Adam's Dream" (Muir) **49**:260-61
"Adam's Way" (Duncan) **2**:103
"Adán es tu ceniza" (Borges) **32**:67
"The Addict" (Sexton) **2**:364
"Addition" (Cavafy) **36**:53
Additional Poems (Housman) **2**:176-77, 190
"address" (Alurista) **34**:32
"Address for a Prize-Day" (Auden) **1**:8, 37
"Address of Beelzebub" (Burns) **6**:83-4, 88-9
"Address to a Lark" (Clare) **23**:39
"Address to a Louse" (Burns)
See "To a Louse, on Seeing One on a Lady's Bonnet at Church"
"Address to Imagination" (Wheatley) **3**:335
An Address to Miss Phillis Wheatly (Hammon) **16**:179, 187-89
"Address to My Soul" (Wylie) **23**:303, 305, 310, 313, 322, 333
"Address to Saxham" (Carew) **29**:7-8, 41-43
"Address to the Angels" (Kumin) **15**:204
"Address to the De'il" (Burns) **6**:49, 78, 83-4, 87
"An Address to the Muse" (Abse) **41**:8
"Address to the Scholars of New England" (Ransom) **61**:289
"An Address to Weyerhauser, the Tree-Growing Company" (Wagoner) **33**:352
"Adelaide Abner" (Smith) **12**:310, 326
"Adelaide Crapsey" (Sandburg) **41**:241
The Adi Granth (Kabīr) **56**:343-46
"L'adieu" (Apollinaire) **7**:48
"L'adieu" (Lamartine) **16**:277, 299
"Adieu" (Rimbaud) **3**:273; **57**:172, 247, 249, 251-52, 254, 276, 279
"Adieu á Charlot" (Ferlinghetti) **1**:181-82, 188
"Adieu, Mlle. Veronique" (Brodsky) **9**:2, 5
"Adieu to Norman, Bon Jour to Joan and Jean-Paul" (O'Hara) **45**:133, 138, 141, 145, 147, 160-61, 219
"Adieux a la poesie" (Lamartine) **16**:273
"Adieux à Marie Stuart" (Swinburne) **24**:313
"The Adirondacs" (Emerson) **18**:76-77, 111, 113
"Adivinanzas" (Guillén) **23**:106
"Adlestrop" (Thomas) **53**:338-41, 344
"The Admiral's Ghost" (Noyes) **27**:121, 134
"Admonition" (Wagoner) **33**:369-70
"admonitions" (Clifton) **17**:31
"Adolescence" (Dove) **6**:106
"Adolescence—III" (Dove) **6**:109
"Adolescencia" (Jiménez) **7**:183, 209
"The Adolescent" (Jiménez)
See "Adolescencia"
"Adolescent" (Tsvetaeva)
See "Otrok"
"Adonais" (Arnold) **5**:7
"Adonais" (Wylie) **23**:323
Adonais: An Elegy on the Death of John Keats (Shelley) **14**:164, 171, 174, 178, 183, 186-89, 197, 211, 218, 233-34, 236-37, 239-40
"Adonis" (H. D.) **5**:269, 304, 308
"Adonis" (Ronsard) **11**:251
"Adowa" (Brathwaite) **56**:12
Adq1Sled Burial, Dream Ceremony" (Dickey) **40**:155
Adrastea (Herder) **14**:171, 173, 178, 192, 211-12, 217, 221-24, 233-37, 239
"Adult Bookstore" (Shapiro) **25**:306-307, 322
"Adultery" (Dickey) **40**:181, 197, 226-27, 232, 258
"Adulthood" (Giovanni) **19**:110, 139
"Adulto? Mai" (Pasolini) **17**:261
"An Advancement of Learning" (Heaney) **18**:187, 190, 200
"El advenimiento" (Borges) **32**:49-50
"Advenimiento" (Guillén) **35**:187
"Advent" (Kavanagh) **33**:72, 85, 94, 134, 138, 161
"Advent" (Merton) **10**:340
"Advent" (Rossetti) **7**:290, 297
Advent (Rilke) **2**:280
"Advent, 1966" (Levertov) **11**:176
"Advent Calendar" (Schnackenberg) **45**:338, 341
"Adventures" (Pavese) **13**:205
"Adventures in the Bohemian Jungle" (Kavanagh) **33**:86, 95, 117-8, 121
"Adventures of a Frisbee" (Silverstein) **49**:331
"Adventures of Isabel" (Nash) **21**:265
Adventures While Preaching the Gospel of Beauty (Lindsay) **23**:278, 295
"Adventures While Singing These Songs" (Lindsay) **23**:282
"Adversity" (Gray)
See "Ode to Adversity"
"Advertencia" (Fuertes) **27**:26
"Advertencia al lector" (Parra) **39**:296, 305-8
"Advertisement" (Jackson) **44**:13
"Advertisement for the Waldorf-Astoria" (Hughes) **53**:115
"The Advice" (Raleigh) **31**:212, 214, 236
"The Advice" (Roethke) **15**:274
"Advice about Roses" (Stein) **18**:313
"Advice to a First Cousin" (Ríos) **57**:323
"Advice to a Girl" (Teasdale) **31**:332, 341, 349
"Advice to a Hamilton (Ont.) Laby About to Travel Again" (Birney) **52**:16, 36, 96
"Advice to a Prophet" (Wilbur) **51**:208, 218, 227, 229, 231, 237, 248, 287
Advice to a Prophet and Other Poems (Wilbur) **51**:202, 214, 232, 235, 273-74, 287, 289, 291, 293, 301
"Advice to the Girls" (Harper) **21**:207, 216
"Advice to the Orchestra" (Wagoner) **33**:327
"Advice to Young Ladies" (Hope) **56**:303
"Advocates" (Graves) **6**:144
"Ae Fond Kiss" (Burns) **6**:97
"Aedh Hears the Cry ofthe Sedge" (Yeats) **20**:347
Aeginetan Odes (Pindar) **19**:406
"Aeneas and Dido" (Brodsky) **9**:7
"Aeneas at New York" (Tate) **50**:322
"Aeneas at Washington" (Tate) **50**:231, 244, 250-51, 270, 272, 274, 280, 295, 304, 306-7, 321-22
The Aeneid (Vergil) **12**:358, 361, 364-68, 371-73, 375-78, 380-99, 401-08
"The Aeolian Harp" (Coleridge) **11**:51, 63, 73-4, 81-2, 88, 91, 97, 106-07, 109; **39**:180, 221
"Aesthetic" (Tomlinson) **17**:327, 344
"The Aesthetic Point of View" (Auden) **1**:12, 15
"Aesthetics II" (Ignatow) **34**:204
"Aesthetics of the Shah" (Olds) **22**:314
"Aeterna Poetae Memoria" (MacLeish) **47**:145
"Aether" (Ginsberg) **4**:81
"Afar" (Reese) **29**:336
"Afelpado" (Storni) **33**:260;
"Affliction" (Herbert) **4**:118, 131
"Affliction" (Mistral)
See "Tribulación"
"Affliction I" (Herbert) **4**:111-12, 128, 131-32
"Affliction IV" (Herbert) **4**:112, 120
"The Affliction of Margaret—of—" (Wordsworth) **4**:402
"The Affliction of Richard" (Bridges) **28**:88
"Afflictions Sanctified by the Word" (Cowper) **40**:84
"Affres, détonation, silence" (Char) **56**:155, 190-91
"Afin qu'àtout jamais" (Ronsard) **11**:242
"Afinamiento" (Storni) **33**:271;
"Afoot" (Carman) **34**:197, 217
"Afraid" (Hughes) **53**:83-84
"Afraid of the Dark" (Silverstein) **49**:347
"Africa" (Angelou) **32**:28
"Africa" (Giovanni) **19**:141
"Africa" (McKay) **2**:221
Africa (Blake) **12**:13
Africa (Petrarch) **8**:239-42, 246, 258, 260, 266-68, 278
"Africa and My New York" (Viereck) **27**:278, 282
"Africa on the Mind Today" (Goodison) **36**:158
"The African Chief" (Bryant) **20**:4
"An African Elegy" (Duncan) **2**:103
"African Images: Glimpses from A Tiger's Back" (Walker) **30**:347
"Africa's Dark Face" (Hughes) **53**:85
"Afro-American Fragment" (Hughes) **53**:84, 121
"After" (Reese) **29**:330
"After 1984" (Muir) **49**:223, 256
"After a Childhood Away from Ireland" (Boland) **58**:53
"After a Death" (Tomlinson) **17**:336
"After a Departure" (Abse) **41**:3, 12
"After a Flight" (Montale) **13**:158
"After a Flight" (Montefiore)
See "Dopa una fuga"
"After a Hypothetical War" (Muir) **49**:223, 258
"After a Journey" (Hardy) **8**:88, 93, 118, 135
"After a Long Illness" (Duncan) **2**:119
"After a Rain" (Pasternak) **6**:271
"After a Tempest" (Bryant) **20**:37-8
"After a Train Journey" (Sarton) **39**:290
"After a Visit (At Padraic Colum's Where There Were Irish Poets)" (Cullen) **20**:60, 69
"After an Accident" (Davie) **29**:129
"After an Illness, Walking the Dog" (Kenyon) **57**:6
After and Before the Lightning (Ortiz) **17**:245
"After Another Reading of Dante" (Corso) **33**:37
"After Apple-Picking" (Frost) **1**:193, 221-22; **39**:230, 235, 237, 246-47
"After Aspromonte" (Carducci)
See "Dopo Aspromonte"
"After Beckett" (Mahon) **60**:225
"After Catullus" (Hacker) **47**:80
"After Consulting My Yellow Pages" (Wagoner) **33**:327
"After Dark" (Rich) **5**:364
"After Death" (Rossetti) **7**:269, 280, 287
"After Death" (Teasdale) **31**:325, 336
"After Dinner" (Curnow) **48**:20
"After Drinking All Night with a Friend, We Go Out in a Boat at Dawn to See Who Can Write the Best Poem" (Bly) **39**:75-6
After Every Green Thing (Abse) **41**:6, 10, 33
"After Everything" (Cisneros) **52**:148
"After Forty Years of Age," (Kavanagh) **33**:121, 162
"After Grace" (Merrill) **28**:234, 250

"After great stormes the cawme retornes" (Wyatt) **27**:311
"After Hearing a Waltz by Bartok" (Lowell) **13**:84
"After Keats" (Levine)
See "Having Been Asked 'What Is a Man?' I Answer"
"after Kent State" (Clifton) **17**:17, 35
"After Long Silence" (Yeats) **20**:328-29; **51**:106, 136
"After Love" (Teasdale) **31**:321
"After Making Love We Hear Footsteps" (Kinnell) **26**:259, 292
"After Many Days" (Dunbar) **5**:137
"After May" (Kavanagh) **33**:117
"After Mecca" (Brooks) **7**:63, 81
"After My Chronology by Peter Lorre" (Yau) **61**:337
"After My Last Paycheck from the Factory" (Chin) **40**:3
"After Nerval" (Mahon) **60**:136, 139
"After Paradise" (Milosz) **8**:209
"After Parting" (Teasdale) **31**:363
After Parting (Bely)
See *Posle razluki*
"After Rain" (Page) **12**:168, 178, 190
"After Rain" (Thomas) **53**:268
"After Reading Mickey in the Night Kitchen for the Third Time before Bed" (Dove) **6**:121
"After Reading Sylvia Plath" (Clampitt) **19**:99
"After Reading Two Towns in Provence" (Carver) **54**:12
After Russia (Tsvetaeva)
See *Posle Rossii*
"After School" (Carman) **34**:224
"After Smiling" (Jackson) **44**:6
"After the Agony" (Atwood) **8**:6
"After the Alphabets" (Merwin) **45**:94
"After the Ball" (Merrill) **28**:270
"After the Cleansing of Bosnia" (Kumin) **15**:224
"After the Crash" (MacNeice) **61**:179
"After the Cries of the Birds" (Ferlinghetti) **1**:173-74, 176
"After the Dancing" (Cruz) **37**:11
"After the Deluge" (Rimbaud)
See "Après le déluge"
"After the Dinner Party" (Kenyon) **57**:13, 40
"After the Dinner Party" (Warren) **37**:377
"After the Fire" (Merrill) **28**:221-22, 225, 258, 263-64
"After the Flood, We" (Atwood) **8**:12
"After the Funeral" (Abse) **41**:14
"After the Funeral: In Memory of Anne Jones" (Thomas) **2**:390; **52**:213, 217, 226, 235, 255, 265, 269, 271, 273, 276, 281, 314
"After the Gentle Poet Kobayashi Issa" (Hass) **16**:196
"After the Harvests" (Merwin) **45**:74
"After the Last Bulletins" (Wilbur) **51**:187, 206, 212-13, 220, 222, 297
"After the Last Dynasty" (Kunitz) **19**:179
"After the Opera" (Lawrence) **54**:238-39
"After the Persian" (Bogan) **12**:107, 118, 124-25, 129
"After the plague, the city-wall caked with flies, the smoke's amnesia" (Walcott) **46**:258
"After the Release of Ezra Pound" (Abse) **41**:16
"After the Sentence" (Brutus) **24**:106
"After the Solstice" (Merwin) **45**:20
"After the Storm" (Sarton) **39**:367
"After the Storm" (Stryk) **27**:203
"After the stubbornly cheerful day" (Brutus) **24**:118
"After the Surprising Conversions" (Lowell) **3**:202-03
"After the Winter" (McKay) **2**:228
"After Troy" (H. D.) **5**:268
"After Twenty Years" (Rich) **5**:384
"After Waking" (Bly) **39**:7
"After wards" (Stein) **18**:313
"After Whistler" (Mueller) **33**:176-77
"After Work" (Snyder) **21**:288
"After Working" (Bly) **39**:4, 76, 84
"After Working Long on One Thing" (Kenyon) **57**:45
"After You Speak" (Thomas) **53**:271
"Afterglow" (Carver) **54**:19
"Afterimages" (Lorde) **12**:155
"Afterlives" (Mahon) **60**:132, 134-35, 140, 142-43, 153, 168, 178, 185-86, 192, 234
"Aftermath" (Longfellow) **30**:42
"Aftermath" (Plath) **1**:389; **37**:177
"Aftermath" (Sassoon) **12**:269, 289
Aftermath (Longfellow) **30**:47
"An Afternoon" (Carver) **54**:21-22
"Afternoon" (Parker) **28**:362
"An Afternoon in June" (Bly) **39**:115
"Afternoon in the House" (Kenyon) **57**:13, 17, 26, 39
Afternoon of a Faun (Mallarmé)
See *L'après-midi d'un faune*
"Afternoon of Sand" (Wagoner) **33**:365-66
"Afternoon on a Hill" (Millay) **6**:235-36; **61**:213
"Afternoon Rain in State Street" (Lowell) **13**:79
"Afternoon Sleep" (Bly) **39**:79
"The Afternoon Sun" (Cavafy) **36**:42
"Aftersong" (Carman) **34**:225
"The After-thought" (Smith) **12**:329-32
"An Afterward" (Heaney) **18**:243
"Afterward" (Warren) **37**:326
"Afterwards" (Hardy) **8**:101, 131
Afterwhiles (Riley) **48**:290, 322
"Afterword" (Atwood) **8**:11
"Afterword" (Brodsky) **9**:25
"Afterword" (Carruth) **10**:71
"(Afterword)" (Graham) **59**:136
"An Afterword: For Gwen Brooks" (Madhubuti) **5**:346
"Afton Water" (Burns)
See "Sweet Afton"
"Again" (Kavanagh) **33**:151
"Again" (Nemerov) **24**:291
"Again Again" (Viereck) **27**:265
"Again and Again and Again" (Sexton) **2**:353
"Again at Zima Station" (Yevtushenko) **40**:340, 347
"Again I Visited" (Pushkin)
See "Vnov' Ya Posetil"
"Again, the River" (Hacker) **47**:118-19
"Against a comely Coistroun" (Skelton)
See *Agaynste a Comely Coystrowne*
"Against Absence" (Suckling) **30**:123
"Against Botticelli" (Hass) **16**:198
"Against Dullness" (Szirtes) **51**:158
"Against Elegies" (Hacker) **47**:103, 105-7, 116
"Against Fruition II" (Suckling) **30**:123, 129, 140-41, 147
"Against System Builders" (Goethe) **5**:229
"Against That Day" (Brown) **55**:74, 114
Against the Evidence: Selected Poems 1934-1994 (Ignatow) **34**:341-43
"Against War, Against Watchtower" (Chin) **40**:29
"Agamemnon" (Cavafy) **36**:54
"Agape" (Kinnell) **26**:287
"Agatha" (Eliot) **20**:101, 123
"Agatha" (Valéry)
See "Agathe; ou, La sainte du sommeil"
"The Agatha Christie Books by the Window" (Ondaatje) **28**:335
"Agathe; ou, La sainte du sommeil" (Valéry) **9**:357, 400-01
Agaynste a Comely Coystrowne (Skelton) **25**:339
"Age" (Larkin) **21**:227, 236, 248
"The Age" (Mandelstam) **14**:121
"Age" (Teasdale) **31**:380
L'Age cassant (Char) **56**:112, 115, 117-18
"L'Age de la vie" (Éluard) **38**:65
"The Age Demanded" (Pound) **4**:320
"Age d'or" (Rimbaud) **57**:243, 250, 253
The Age of Anxiety: A Baroque Eclogue (Auden) **1**:14, 23, 33-4, 39
"The Age of Innocence" (Hope) **56**:266
"The Age of Reason" (Graham) **59**:147, 155-56, 179, 187
The Age of Reason (Hope) **56**:290-91, 297
"Aged Man Surveys the Past Time" (Warren) **37**:275, 284, 288, 331
"The Agent" (Wilbur) **51**:215, 231
"The Ages" (Bryant) **20**:4, 35
"The Ages of Man" (Bradstreet)
See "The Four Ages of Man"
The Ages of the Year (Cassian) **17**:6
"Aggression" (O'Hara) **45**:223
"Aging Refugee from the Old Country" (Viereck) **27**:280
"Agitato ma non troppo" (Ransom) **61**:269, 280
"Agli amici della Valle Tiberina" (Carducci) **46**:51, 70-71, 74, 80
"Agli Italiani" (Carducci) **46**:51
"An Agnostic" (Smith) **12**:352
"The Agony" (Herbert) **4**:100
"An Agony. As Now" (Baraka) **4**:16, 24
"Agora que conmigo" (Juana Inés de la Cruz) **24**:187
"Agosta the Winged Man and Rasha the Black Dove" (Dove) **6**:109
"Agraphon" (Sikelianos) **29**:366, 374-75
"Les Agréments et l'utilité" (Éluard) **38**:91
"Agrio está el mundo" (Storni) **33**:246;
"Agrippina in the Golden House of Nero" (Lowell) **3**:222
"Agua" (Mistral) **32**:161
"Agua sexual" (Neruda) **4**:306
"Aguadilla" (Cruz) **37**:33-34
"Ah, Are You Digging on My Grave?" (Hardy) **8**:131
"Ah, me!" (Storni)
See "¡Ayme!"
"Ah Natercia cruel" (Camões) **31**:29
"Ah! Sun-Flower" (Blake) **12**:34
"Ah, 'Tis Vain the Peaceful Din" (Thoreau) **30**:254
"Ahasuerus" (Nemerov) **24**:257, 295
"Ahmad" (Thumboo) **30**:305, 333
"Ahora habla Dios" (Fuertes) **27**:28
"Ahvan" (Tagore) **8**:415
"Ai critici cattolici" (Pasolini) **17**:258
"Ai fratelli Carvi, alla loro Italia" (Quasimodo) **47**:287
"Aigeltinger" (Williams) **7**:370
"L'aigle du casque" (Hugo) **17**:56
"Aiguevive" (Char) **56**:152, 156
Aika (Nishiwaki) **15**:238
"The Aim, The Best that Can be Hoped For: The Magician" (Piercy) **29**:325
"The Aim Was Song" (Frost) **1**:194
"Aimless Journey" (Tagore)
See "Niruddesh yatra"
"Air" (Merwin) **45**:15
"Air" (Toomer) **7**:333
"Air" (Walcott) **46**:321, 325
"Air and Fire" (Berry) **28**:11
L'air de l'eau (Breton) **15**:51-2
"Air de sémiramis" (Valéry) **9**:365, 391-92
"Air Hostess" (Amichai) **38**:19
"Air Liner" (Shapiro) **25**:296
Air mexicain (Péret) **33**:220, 231
Air Raid (MacLeish) **47**:148-49, 152, 164, 210-11, 242, 257
"Air Raid Over Harlem" (Hughes) **53**:114
"El aire" (Guillén) **35**:231
"El aire" (Mistral) **32**:161, 168
"Aire and Angels" (Donne) **1**:130, 149
Aire nuestro (Guillén) **35**:185, 186, 187-88, 225-32, 234, 237, 238, 239
"Airen" (Hagiwara) **18**:167, 180
"Los aires" (Guillén) **35**:157
"Airman's Virtue" (Meredith) **28**:182-83
"Airone morto" (Quasimodo) **47**:278
"Airoplain" (Cruz) **37**:36
Airs & Tributes (Brutus) **24**:110-11, 117

"The Airy Christ" (Smith) **12**:295, 330-31, 333
"Aix-en-Provence" (Rexroth) **20**:209
"Ajanta" (Rukeyser) **12**:204, 214, 219, 224
"Ajedrez II" (Borges) **22**:84-5
"Ajudah" (Mickiewicz) **38**:166
"Akatsuki no kane" (Ishikawa) **10**:214
"Akerman Steppes" (Mickiewicz)
See "Stepy Akermańskie"
Akhshav bara'ash (Amichai) **38**:23, 26
'Akhshav 'vayamim ha'aherim (Amichai) **38**:33
Akogare (Ishikawa) **10**:194, 212-16
"Al Aaraaf" (Poe) **1**:437, 449
"Al adquirir una Enciclopedia" (Borges) **32**:91
"Al amor cualquier curioso" (Juana Inés de la Cruz) **24**:184, 234
"Al Conte Carlo Pepoli" (Leopardi) **37**:112
"Al coronel Francisco Borges" (Borges) **32**:57
"Al iniciar el estudio de la gramática anglosajona" (Borges) **22**:99
"Al lector" (Darío) **15**:105
"Al maragen de mis libros de estudios" (Guillén) **23**:97
"Al margen de Mallarmé" (Guillén) **35**:202
"Al margen de un cántico" (Guillén) **35**:201
"Al margen de un contacto" (Guillén) **35**:229
"Al mio grillo" (Montale) **13**:138
"Al mismo individuo" (Guillén) **23**:126
"Al oído de Cristo" (Mistral) **32**:155, 174
"Al pintor Swaminathan" (Paz) **1**:354
"Al poeta español Rafael Alberti, entregándole un jamón" (Guillén) **23**:134
"Al que ingrato me deja, busco ama" (Juana Inés de la Cruz) **24**:183
Al que quiere! (Williams) **7**:344-45, 348-49, 377-79, 387-88, 398, 405-10
"Al soneto con mi alma" (Jiménez) **7**:192
"Al tuo lume naufrago" (Quasimodo) **47**:278
"Ala bāb al-haykal" (Gibran) **9**:78
"Alaba los ojos negros de Julia" (Darío) **15**:114
"Alabama Poem" (Giovanni) **19**:140
"Alabaster" (Merrill) **28**:283
Al-ajnihah (Gibran) **9**:78
"Las alamedas" (Guillén) **35**:193
"Alas, a Prince" (Tu Fu) **9**:317
"Alas the While" (Wyatt) **27**:318
"Alaska" (Benn) **35**:45, 46
"Alaska" (Snyder) **21**:300
"Alaska Passage" (Birney) **52**:28, 82
"Alastor; or, The Spirit of Solitude" (Shelley) **14**:171, 173, 178, 192, 211-12, 217, 221-24, 233-37, 239
"Alatus" (Wilbur) **51**:249
Al-'awāsif (Gibran) **9**:79-81
"Al-bahr" (Gibran) **9**:80
"Albaniad" (Elytis) **21**:115
"L'albatros" (Baudelaire) **1**:65
"Albero" (Quasimodo) **47**:272
"A Albert Durer" (Hugo) **17**:94-95
"Albert Schirding" (Masters) **36**:170, 182
Albertine Disparue (Enzensberger) **28**:156
"Albertus" (Gautier) **18**:142-43, 151-54, 160-64
Albertus, ou l'âme et le péché; légende théologique (Gautier) **18**:147, 149-51, 154
"Albino" (Komunyakaa) **51**:29
"Albinus and Rosemund" (Gower) **59**:88, 108
"Album" (Szymborska) **44**:269
Album de vers anciens, 1890-1900 (Valéry) **9**:363, 365, 386-87, 390-91, 395
Album zutique (Rimbaud) **57**:204, 246, 252-53
"Alcestis" (Gower) **59**:58
"The Alchemist" (Bogan) **12**:98, 103, 114
"The Alchemist" (Meredith) **28**:187
"The Alchemists" (Hogan) **35**:259
"Alchemy" (Corso) **33**:37
"Alchemy of the Logos" (Rimbaud)
See "Alchimie du verbe"
"Alchemy of the Word" (Rimbaud)
See "Alchimie du verbe"
"Alchimie du verbe" (Rimbaud) **3**:261, 267, 274; **57**:174, 227, 238, 243, 245, 247-49, 254, 273, 280
"Alcohol" (MacNeice) **61**:141
"The Alcoholic Love Poems" (Alexie) **53**:30
"An Alcoholic's Death" (Hagiwara)
See "Death of an Alcoholic"
Alcools (Apollinaire) **7**:6, 9-10, 12, 14-15, 38-46, 48-9
"Alegorí a de la primavera" (Storni) **33**:294-96;
"Alejamiento" (Borges) **22**:92
"Aleksandru" (Pushkin) **10**:421
"Aleluja" (Pasolini) **17**:256
"Alessandria" (Carducci) **46**:9, 24, 64
"Alessandrina" (Carducci)
See "Alessandria"
"Alewives Pool" (Kinnell) **26**:238
"Alexander Jannaeus and Alexandra" (Cavafy) **36**:22
"Alexander Throckmorten" (Masters) **36**:221
"Alexander's Feast; or, The Power of Musique. An Ode, in Honour of St. Cecilia's Day" (Dryden) **25**:72-5, 88
"Alexandria" (Carducci)
See "Alessandria"
"Alexandria" (Doty) **53**:52
"Alexandria" (Shapiro) **25**:295
"Alexandrian Kings" (Cavafy) **36**:3, 8, 29-32, 40, 50
"An Alexandrite Pendant for My Mother" (Hacker) **47**:119
Alexis und Dora (Goethe) **5**:240
"Alf Burt, Tenant Farmer" (Warren) **37**:319, 331
"Alfansa" (Forché) **10**:134, 169-70
"Alfonso" (McKay) **2**:205
"Alfred the Great" (Smith) **12**:296, 316
"Algae" (Wagoner) **33**:356
"Algernon, Who Played with a Loaded Gun, and, on Missing His Sister, Was Reprimanded by His Father" (Belloc) **24**:26
Algiers in Wartime (Viereck) **27**:265
"Al-hurūf al-nāriyah" (Gibran) **9**:78
Alí dagli occhi azzurri (Pasolini) **17**:264-65
"Alice" (Graves) **6**:139
"Alice Du Clos" (Coleridge) **11**:106
"Alice Fell" (Wordsworth) **4**:404, 415
"Aliénés" (Char) **56**:137, 157
"Alive" (Harjo) **27**:56
Alive: Poems, 1971-1972 (Wright) **14**:372, 375
"Alive Together" (Mueller) **33**:175
Alive Together: New and Selected Poems (Mueller) **33**:195, 197
"Al-jamāl" (Gibran) **9**:81
"All, All Are Gone the Old Familiar Quotations" (Nash) **21**:273
"All Alone Along the Road I Am Walking" (Lermontov)
See "Alone I Go along the Road"
"All along the Watchtower" (Dylan) **37**:49, 56, 61
"All and Some" (Ashbery) **26**:124, 127, 135
"All Clowns Are Masked and All Personae" (Schwartz) **8**:305
"All Comes" (Ignatow) **34**:318
"All Elegies are Black and White" (Guest) **55**:185, 212
"All for You" (Ní Chuilleanáin) **34**:369
"All God's Children" (Brathwaite) **56**:19
"All Gone" (Char)
See "Tous partis"
"All Gray-Haired My Sisters" (Guest) **55**:208, 213, 218
"All Guilt and Innocence Turned Upside Down" (Schwartz) **8**:285
"All Hallows" (Glück) **16**:126-27, 132, 140-43, 148-49
"All I Gotta Do" (Giovanni) **19**:108, 112
"All in Green Went My Love Riding" (Cummings) **5**:87
"All Is Mine" (Guillén)
See "Tengo"
All Is Mine (Guillén)
See *Tengo*
"All Kinds of Caresses" (Ashbery) **26**:139
"All kings and all their favourites" (Donne)
See "The Anniversarie"
"All Life in a Life" (Masters) **1**:326, 328, 335-36, 342; **36**:175
"All Life Is a Rotary Club" (Corso) **33**:48
All Love (Seifert)
See *Samá láska*
"All Morning" (Roethke) **15**:271
"All Mountain" (H. D.) **5**:305
All My Pretty Ones (Sexton) **2**:346-47, 349-50, 353, 355, 360-61, 370
"All Nearness Pauses, While a Star Can Grow" (Cummings) **5**:109
"All of Us Always Turning Away for Solace" (Schwartz) **8**:305
All of Us: The Collected Poems (Carver) **54**:25-29
"All Our Yesterdays" (Borges) **32**:90
"All Over Again" (MacNeice) **61**:125
"All Quiet" (Ignatow) **34**:277, 207, 323
"All Revelation" (Frost) **39**:233
"All Souls" (Sarton) **39**:326
"All Souls' Day" (Sassoon) **12**:258
"All Souls' Night" (Yeats) **51**:151
"All Sounds Have been as Music" (Owen) **19**:336
"All That Was Mortal" (Teasdale) **31**:341
"All the Beautiful Are Blameless" (Wright) **36**:282, 396
All: The Collected Short Poems, 1923-1958 (Zukofsky) **11**:348-49, 351, 354-56, 393-94
All: The Collected Shorter Poems, 1956-64 (Zukofsky) **11**:349, 353, 356, 383, 390
"All the Dead Dears" (Plath) **1**:388, 407; **37**:186, 199, 214, 245
"All the Earth, All the Air" (Roethke) **15**:286
"All the Fancy Things" (Williams) **7**:394
"All the Spirit Powers Went to Their Dancing Place" (Snyder) **21**:291
"All the Way Back" (Jackson) **44**:107
"All the World Moved" (Jordan) **38**:119
"All These Birds" (Wilbur) **51**:188, 305
"All Things Are Current Found" (Thoreau) **30**:181, 204, 213-14
"All Things Conspire" (Wright) **14**:338
"All We" (Muir) **49**:200, 250
"All Worlds Have Halfsight, Seeing Either With" (Cummings) **5**:111
"allá ajüera" (Alurista) **34**:32-3
"Alla città di Ferrara" (Carducci) **46**:52
"Alla croce di Savoia" (Carducci) **46**:51, 56
"Alla Francia" (Pasolini) **17**:295
"Allá lejos" (Darío) **15**:93
"Allá lejos" (Guillén) **23**:126
"Alla Libertà rileggendo le opere di Vittorio Alfieri" (Carducci) **46**:51
"Alla Luna" (Leopardi) **37**:82, 84, 102, 109, 124-34
"Alla memoria di D.C." (Cannan) **46**:64
"Alla mia terra" (Quasimodo) **47**:301-2
"Alla primavera o delle favole antiche" (Leopardi) **37**:141, 165, 167
"Alla Regina d'Italia" (Carducci) **46**:52
"Alla rima" (Carducci) **46**:74, 80-81
"Alla Stazione in una Mattina d'Autunno" (Carducci) **46**:6-7, 25, 51, 56, 86
"Alla sua donna" (Leopardi) **37**:144-45
"Alla Tha's All Right, but" (Jordan) **38**:118, 125
"Alla Vittoria" (Carducci) **46**:52
"All'amor suo" (Leopardi) **37**:144
"All'Aurora" (Carducci) **46**:54
"All-destroyer" (Tagore)
See "Sarvaneshe"
"an alle fernsprechteilenhmer" (Enzensberger) **28**:134, 136, 140
"Alle fonti del Clitumno" (Carducci) **46**:7, 16, 29, 37, 39, 42, 54, 65, 76, 81-84, 88
"Alle fronde dei salici" (Quasimodo) **47**:281
"Alle Valchirie" (Cannan) **46**:26
"L'allée" (Verlaine) **32**:348-49

"Allégeance" (Char) **56**:155
"Allégorie" (Baudelaire) **1**:56
"Allegre" (Walcott) **46**:272
"L'Allegro" (Milton) **19**:201-02, 226, 228-34, 249, 254-56; **29**:220, 232, 239
L'Allegro (Milton) **29**:220, 239
"Alley Rats" (Sandburg) **2**:304
"The All-Golden" (Riley) **48**:289
"Alliance of Education and Government" (Gray)
See "Essay on the Alliance of Education and Government"
"Allie" (Graves) **6**:141
"The Allies" (Lowell) **13**:76, 78
"Allison Beals and Her Twenty-Five Eels" (Silverstein) **49**:341
"All'Italia" (Leopardi) **37**:81, 98-104, 107, 150
"Allmacht" (Stramm) **50**:169, 175, 189, 192-93, 198, 206
"Allô" (Péret) **33**:201, 206, 214, 231
"Allons adieu messieurs tachez de revenir" (Apollinaire) **7**:22
"Allora e Ora" (Carducci) **46**:5
"Alloy" (Rukeyser) **12**:210
"The Ally" (Cervantes) **35**:116
"Alma" (Storni) **33**:251;
"Alma desnuda" (Storni) **33**:237;
"Alma Mater" (Robinson) **35**:367
"Alma minha gentil" (Camões) **31**:24-25
"Almanac" (Sandburg) **41**:308
"Almanac" (Swenson) **14**:268
"Almanach pour 1'année passée" (Verlaine) **32**:399-402, 405
"Almansor" (Heine) **25**:145, 160
"Almas de Duralex" (Fuertes) **27**:23
Almas de violeta (Jiménez) **7**:199
Al-mawakib (Gibran) **9**:79-81
"Almond" (McGuckian) **27**:92-93, 105
"Almond Blossom" (Lawrence) **54**:220
"The Almond of the World" (Elytis) **21**:132
"The Almond Trees" (Walcott) **46**:284-85
"Almost a Fantasy" (Montale) **13**:151
Almost Everything (Kavanagh) **33**:74
"Almost Last Judgement" (Borges)
See "Casi Juicio Final"
"Almost Perfect" (Silverstein) **49**:333
"Alms" (Storni)
See "Limosna"
"Almuerzo al sol" (Mistral) **32**:185
"Alone" (Bly) **39**:71
"Alone" (Niedecker) **42**:100, 121, 127, 138
"Alone" (Poe) **1**:442-44
"Alone" (Teasdale) **31**:360
"Alone for a Week" (Kenyon) **57**:15
"Alone I Go along the Road" (Lermontov) **18**:281, 298, 303
"Alone in a Shower" (Hongo) **23**:197
"Along History" (Rukeyser) **12**:228
"Along the Field as We Came By" (Housman) **2**:183
"Alonso Quijano Dreams" (Borges) **32**:66
"Alpha" (Brathwaite) **56**:50, 96
"The Alphabet" (Shapiro) **25**:283, 291, 298-99
Alphabet (Cage)
See *Marcel Duchamp, James Joyce, Erik Satie: An Alphabet*
"Alphabet of Ahtt" (Mackey) **49**:57
"Alphabets" (Heaney) **18**:230-31, 237
"alphabirney" (Birney) **52**:32
"Alphonso of Castile" (Emerson) **18**:71
Alpine (Oppen) **35**:311
"Alpine Noontime" (Carducci)
See "Mezzogiorno alpino"
"Alpuhara" (Mickiewicz)
See "Alpujarra"
"Alpujarra" (Mickiewicz) **38**:174
"Alquimia" (Borges) **22**:94
"Al-shā'ir" (Gibran) **9**:79
"Altar" (Chin) **40**:12-13
"The Altar" (Herbert) **4**:114, 120, 130
"The Altar" (MacLeish) **47**:182
"The Altar of Righteousness" (Swinburne) **24**:350-54
The Altar of the Past (Gozzano)
See *L'altare del Passato*
L'altare del Passato (Gozzano) **10**:177
"Altarwise by Owl-light" (Thomas) **2**:388-89, 403, 406; **52**:237, 240-41, 245, 247, 296-301, 304, 314, 331
"Einem alten Architekten in Rom" (Brodsky) **9**:2, 4
"Alternate Thoughts from Underground" (Atwood) **8**:40
"Although I had a check" (Surrey) **59**:297
"Altitude: 15,000" (Meredith) **28**:173
"L'alto veliero" (Quasimodo) **47**:303
Alturas de Macchu Picchu (Neruda) **4**:282, 284-85, 292-93
"Al-umm wa wahīduha" (Gibran) **9**:78
"Aluroid" (Birney) **52**:85
"Ałushta at Night" (Mickiewicz)
See "Ałuszta w nocy"
"Ałushta in Daytime" (Mickiewicz)
See "Ałuszta w dzień"
"Ałuszta at Day" (Mickiewicz)
See "Ałuszta w dzień"
"Ałuszta at Night" (Mickiewicz)
See "Ałuszta w nocy"
"Ałuszta w dzień" (Mickiewicz) **38**:166
"Ałuszta w nocy" (Mickiewicz) **38**:166
"Always a Rose" (Lee) **24**:247-48, 251
"Always and always the amaranth astir" (Villa) **22**:346
"Always I did want more God" (Villa) **22**:352
"Always the Mob" (Sandburg) **2**:302; **41**:240, 274, 329
"Always to Love You America" (Viereck) **27**:279-80
"The Alyscamps at Arles" (Swenson) **14**:255
"Alysoun" (Snyder) **21**:288
"am or" (Bissett) **14**:14
"Am Rand Eines alten Brunes" (Trakl) **20**:265
"Am Saum des nordischen Meers" (Benn) **35**:23-25
"Am/Trak" (Baraka) **4**:39
"Am Was. Are Leaves Few This. Is This a or" (Cummings) **5**:107
"Ama tu ritmo..." (Darío) **15**:101
"Amado dueño mío" (Juana Inés de la Cruz) **24**:181
"Amām 'arsh al-jamāl" (Gibran) **9**:79
"Amanda Barker" (Masters) **36**:181
"Amanece, amanezco" (Guillén) **35**:195
"Amanecer" (Borges) **32**:81, 124
"Amante dulce del alma" (Juana Inés de la Cruz) **24**:189
"Los amantes" (Guillén) **35**:180, 183
"Los amantes viejos" (Aleixandre) **15**:5-7
"Les Amants de Montmorency" (Vigny) **26**:391, 411-12
"Amaranth" (H. D.) **5**:305
Amaranth (Robinson) **1**:477-78, 482-83; **35**:368
"Amazing Grace" (Mueller) **33**:174-75
"Amazing Grace in the Back Country" (Warren) **37**:312, 336
"Ambarvalia" (Nishiwaki) **15**:238
Ambarvalia (Nishiwaki) **15**:228-29, 232-41
"The Ambassador" (Smith) **12**:330, 339
"Ambassadors of Grief" (Sandburg) **2**:308
Ambit (Aleixandre)
See *Ambito*
"Ambition" (Thomas) **53**:287-88
Ambito (Aleixandre) **15**:9, 16, 27, 29-32
Ambitus (Cassian) **17**:6
"Ambulances" (Larkin) **21**:229-30, 234
"Ambush" (Mickiewicz)
See "Czaty"
"Ame" (Nishiwaki) **15**:228
Amelia (Patmore) **59**:213, 215-16, 218, 222-23, 257
"Amelia Garrick" (Masters) **36**:188
"Amen!" (Rossetti) **7**:268
"Amen" (Trakl) **20**:248
Amen (Amichai)
See *Me-horei Kol Zeh Mistater Osher Gadol*
"El amenazado" (Borges) **22**:80-1
Amenities of Stone (Wright) **36**:389, 391
"America" (Angelou) **32**:28
"America" (Ginsberg) **47**:3, 5, 8, 10, 38, 66
"America" (McKay) **2**:212
"America" (Merrill) **28**:267
"America" (Wheatley) **3**:363
America: A Prophecy, 1793 (Blake) **12**:13, 25-7, 63
"America America" (Ignatow) **34**:318
"AMERICA BUILDS MORE / buildbores to bill more—" (Birney) **52**:79
"America Historia Politica" (Corso) **33**:27
"America, I Do Not Invoke Your Name in Vain" (Neruda)
See "América, no invoco tu nombre en vano"
"América, no invoco tu nombre en vano" (Neruda) **4**:292
"America Politica Historia, in Spontaneity" (Corso) **33**:35, 49
"America Was Promises" (MacLeish) **47**:158, 165, 167, 237
America Was Promises (MacLeish) **47**:191, 201, 243, 245, 257
"The American" (Kipling) **3**:161
"The American Cemetery" (Yevtushenko) **40**:345
"American Change" (Ginsberg) **4**:53, 84
"The American Dream" (Wright) **36**:390
"American Heartbreak" (Hughes) **53**:150
"The American Hegemony" (Corso) **33**:44
"American Journal" (Hayden) **6**:188-89, 191-92, 195
American Journal (Hayden) **6**:194-96
"American Letter" (MacLeish) **47**:126, 135, 145-46, 188
"American Milk" (Stone) **53**:253
"American Miscellany" (H. D.) **5**:268
"American Portrait, Old Style" (Warren) **37**:312, 337
American Scenes and Other Poems (Tomlinson) **17**:309, 317-18, 325-26, 333, 335, 337, 341-42, 348, 352
"American Triptych" (Kenyon) **57**:14, 39, 43
"American Twilights, 1957" (Wright) **36**:337
"The American Way" (Corso) **33**:27, 44, 49
Americana (Viereck) **27**:263
Amers (Perse) **23**:217, 221, 223, 233, 237-47, 249-56
"Ametas and Thestylis Making Hay-Ropes" (Marvell) **10**:269, 271, 294, 304
"L'amica di nonna speranza" (Gozzano) **10**:177, 181-82
"L'amico che dorme" (Pavese) **13**:229
Les amies (Verlaine) **2**:432
"L'Amiral" (Péret) **33**:210
L' Amitié du Prince (Perse) **23**:217, 246
Amitié d'un Prince (Perse) **23**:211, 221, 230, 249-50
L'Amitié se succède (Char) **56**:115-16
"Amnaid" (Dafydd ap Gwilym) **56**:225-29
"Amnesia in Memphis" (Corso) **33**:40
"Amnesiac" (Plath) **37**:256
"Amo amor" (Mistral) **32**:152
"Among Ourselves" (Meredith) **28**:216
"Among School Children" (Yeats) **20**:316, 326, 328, 330, 332, 336-38, 340-42; **51**:76, 120, 128, 143, 151
"Among Sunflowers" (Wright) **36**:370
"Among the Gods" (Kunitz) **19**:149, 173
"Among the Red Guns" (Sandburg) **41**:339
"Among the Tombs" (Kinnell) **26**:256
"Among the Trees" (Bryant) **20**:14, 47
"Among the Worst of Men" (Thoreau) **30**:233, 235-36
"Among Those Killed in the Dawn Raid Was a Man Aged a Hundred" (Thomas) **2**:388; **52**:278

"Amor a Silvia" (Guillén) **35**:201
"Amor e'l cor gentil" (Dante) **21**:73
"Amor mundi" (Rossetti) **7**:282
"El amor que calla" (Mistral) **32**:152, 176
"Amore e Morte" (Leopardi) **37**:92, 111, 123, 125, 138, 171
Amores (Lawrence) **54**:162, 231, 233-35, 240
Amores (Ovid) **2**:234-35, 237-38, 242-43, 245, 251, 253-54, 258-59, 261
Amoretti (Spenser) **8**:329, 388-89
Amoretti and Epithalamion (Spenser) **8**:388
"Amos (Postscript 1968)" (Walker) **20**:278-79
"Amos Sibley" (Masters) **36**:182
"Amos-1963" (Walker) **20**:278-79
"L'amour" (Char) **56**:168
"L'Amour" (Éluard) **38**:96
"Amour" (Verlaine) **2**:416-17, 425
Amour (Verlaine) **32**:359, 370, 386
"L'amour et le crâne" (Baudelaire) **1**:45
"L'Amour la mort la vie" (Éluard) **38**:79
L'amour la poésie (Éluard) **38**:61, 67, 80, 83-6
"L'amour par terre" (Verlaine) **32**:351, 390, 393
"Amour parcheminé" (Breton) **15**:52
"L'amoureuse" (Éluard) **38**:69, 73
"L'amoureuse en secret" (Char) **56**:171
"Les amours" (Laforgue) **14**:74
Amours (Ronsard) **11**:220-21, 246, 250, 254, 256, 258, 275, 277-78, 293
Amours de Cassandre (Ronsard) **11**:247-48
"Amours d'Eurymedon et de Calliree" (Ronsard) **11**:241
Amours diverses (Ronsard) **11**:270
"Amphibian" (Browning) **2**:80
Amplitude: New and Selected Poems (Gallagher) **9**:57-62
"Amravan" (Tagore) **8**:416
"Amsterdam" (Merrill) **28**:223
Amubaruwaria (Nishiwaki) **15**:232, 240
"Amusing Stanzas to Don Juan" (Storni)
See "Divertidas estancias a don Juan"
"Amy's Cruelty" (Browning) **6**:23, 28, 32
"An den Knaben Elis" (Trakl) **20**:226, 234-35, 246
"An den Wassern Babels" (Celan) **10**:127-28
"An einen Frühverstorbenen" (Trakl) **20**:230
"L'an trentiesme de mon eage" (MacLeish) **47**:125, 127, 156, 186, 197
"Ana María" (Guillén) **23**:102
Anabase (Perse) **23**:209-14, 216-18, 221-23, 225-28, 230-31, 233-34, 241-43, 246, 248, 250, 253, 256-59, 261
"Anabasis" (Merwin) **45**:23-4, 74
Anabasis (Perse)
See *Anabase*
"Anacreontica romantica" (Carducci) **46**:78
"Anactoria" (Swinburne) **24**:308, 310-11, 322, 325-26, 343, 360-61
"Anahorish" (Heaney) **18**:201-2, 241, 251
"Ananse" (Brathwaite) **56**:47, 69, 86, 100
"Ananta jivan" (Tagore) **8**:406
"Ananta maran" (Tagore) **8**:406
"Anaphora" (Bishop) **3**:37, 56; **34**:124, 127-28
"L'anapo" (Quasimodo) **47**:278
"Anasazi" (Snyder) **21**:295-96
"Anashuya and Vijaya" (Yeats) **20**:343
An Anatomie of the World (Donne)
See *The First Anniversarie. An Anatomie of the World. Wherein By Occasion of the untimely death of Mistris Elizabeth Drury, the frailtie and decay of this whole World is represented*
"Anatomy" (Muir) **49**:237
"An Anatomy of Migraine" (Clampitt) **19**:92
"Ancestors" (Pavese) **13**:204
"The Ancestors" (Tate) **50**:255, 257, 280
"The Ancestors" (Wright) **14**:353
Ancestors (Brathwaite) **56**:100
"Ancestral Houses" (Yeats) **20**:349
"Ancestral Photograph" (Heaney) **18**:200
"Ancestry" (Corso) **33**:50
"Anchar" (Pushkin) **10**:373
"Anchorage" (Harjo) **27**:55, 58, 63, 65-66
"The Anchored Angel" (Villa) **22**:348-49
The Ancient Acquaintance (Skelton)
See *Auncient Aqueyntaunce*
"The Ancient Briton Lay Ynder His Rock" (Hughes) **7**:147
Ancient Days (Cavafy) **36**:53
"Ancient discipline" (Pavese)
See "Disciplina antica"
"An Ancient Gesture" (Millay) **6**:232, 240
"The Ancient Heroes and the Bomber Pilot" (Hughes) **7**:132
"Ancient History" (Sassoon) **12**:258
"Ancient Lament" (Carducci)
See "Pianto antico"
"the ancient lord laydee un th univers" (Bissett) **14**:27
"The Ancient Mariner" (Coleridge)
See *The Rime of the Ancient Mariner: A Poet's Reverie*
The Ancient Mariner (Coleridge)
See *The Rime of the Ancient Mariner: A Poet's Reverie*
"Ancient One" (Montale)
See "Antico, sono ubriacato della tua voce"
"The Ancient Sage" (Tennyson) **6**:407
"An Ancient Song" (Muir) **49**:237
"An Ancient to Ancients" (Hardy) **8**:121
"Ancient tragedy" (Cavafy) **36**:54
"Ancient Tuscan Poetry" (Carducci)
See "L'Anitca Poesia Toscana"
"Ancient Wisdom Speaks" (H. D.) **5**:307
"Ancora ad Annecy" (Montale) **13**:138
"Ancora dell'inferno" (Quasimodo) **47**:289
Ancora dell'inferno (Quasimodo) **47**:289
And (Cummings)
See *&*
& (Cummings) **5**:75, 92-3, 95, 104-05
"And a Few Negroes Too" (Madhubuti)
See "A Message All Blackpeople Can Dig (& A Few Negroes Too)"
"And a Wisdom as Such" (Duncan) **2**:115
"And All I Have is Tu Fu" (Chin) **40**:30-1, 33-4
"And Another Thing" (Giovanni) **19**:118
"& Co." (Shapiro) **25**:295
"And Death Shall Have No Dominion" (Thomas) **2**:379, 385, 389-90, 397
"And Did Those Feet in Ancient Time Walk upon England's Mountains Green?" (Blake) **12**:45
"And Forty-second Street" (MacLeish) **47**:126, 145
"And God a Me" (Goodison) **36**:158
"And I" (Abse) **41**:19
"And I" (Jackson) **44**:97, 99
"And I Lounged and Lay on their Beds" (Cavafy) **36**:76
"And if an eye may save or slay" (Wyatt) **27**:354
"And in the Hanging Gardens" (Aiken) **26**:24
And in the Human Heart (Aiken) **26**:22
"And now a soft commentaries from Angelo Solimann Africanus the Neumann" (Brathwaite) **56**:54
"And One for My Dame" (Sexton) **2**:363
"And Pass" (Toomer) **7**:332
"And So Goodbye to Cities" (Merton) **10**:334, 344
"And So Today" (Sandburg) **2**:307-08; **41**:249, 255, 260, 271
"And Socializing" (Ashbery) **26**:163
"And Step" (Ignatow) **34**:318
"And Still I Rise" (Angelou) **32**:3, 23, 28
And Still I Rise (Angelou) **32**:2-3, 11
"And the Children of Birmingham" (Merton) **10**:334, 341
". . .And the Clouds Return after the Rain" (Smith) **12**:331
"And the Earth Grow Young Again" (Birney) **52**:37
"and the green wind is mooving thru the summr trees" (Bissett) **14**:33
"And the Head Began to Burn" (Storni)
See "Y la cabeza comenzó a arder"
"And The Land Is Just As Dry" (Ortiz) **17**:227
"And the Stars Were Shining" (Ashbery) **26**:164-166
And the Stars Were Shining (Ashbery) **26**:164-166
"And the Trains Go On" (Levine) **22**:224
"And Their Winters and Their Nights in Disguise" (Oppen) **35**:337
"And then you said the words" (Shvarts) **50**:145
"And There Was a Great Calm" (Hardy) **8**:119
"And They Call This Living!" (Stryk) **27**:203
"And This is Your Praise" (Amichai)
See "Vehi tehillatekha"
"and Tuesday III" (Hacker) **47**:94
"And Ut Pictura Poesis Is Her Name" (Ashbery) **26**:118, 123, 135
"And What About the Children" (Lorde) **12**:139
"And with What Bodies Do They Come?" (Dickinson) **1**:102
"And You as Well Must Die" (Millay) **6**:211
"And You, Helen" (Thomas) **53**:290-91, 293
Æneid (Surrey) **59**:284-87, 289, 298, 312, 339, 341, 343-44, 347-49, 353
"Ætna and the Moon" (Patmore) **59**:201, 228, 233
"El andaluz universal" (Jiménez) **7**:205
"&" (Wilbur) **51**:295
"The Andean Flute" (Mahon) **60**:148
"Andenken" (Hölderlin) **4**:172, 178
"der andere" (Enzensberger) **28**:139
"¡A probiña qu' esta xorda . . . !" (Castro) **41**:89
"¡Ayme!" (Storni) **33**:276;
"¡Do íntimo!" (Castro) **41**:88
"¡Hojas nuevas! risa siento" (Castro) **41**:115
"¡No pasarán" (Paz) **48**:178-79, 243
"¡Silencio!" (Castro) **41**:115
"¿... Qué?" (Storni) **33**:251;
"¿Para quién escribo?" (Aleixandre) **15**:41
"¿Qué Te?" (Castro) **41**:95
"¿Qué tiene?" (Castro) **41**:116
"Andraitix—Pomegranate Flowers" (Lawrence) **54**:172
"André Masson" (Éluard) **38**:71
"Andrea del Sarto" (Browning) **2**:37, 86, 88, 95; **61**:5, 88
"Andrée Rexroth" (Rexroth) **20**:206-07
"Andromeda" (Hopkins) **15**:134, 148
"Andromeda Chained to Her Rock the Great Nebula in her Heart" (Rexroth) **20**:196
"Anecdote" (Parker) **28**:360
"Anecdote for Fathers" (Wordsworth) **4**:425-28
Anecdote of Rain (Zagajewski) **27**:389, 399
"Anecdote of the Jar" (Stevens) **6**:309, 326-27
"Anecdote of the Prince of Peacocks" (Stevens) **6**:309
"Anelida and Arcite" (Chaucer) **19**:10, 74
"Aneurin's Harp" (Meredith) **60**:250
"Anew" (Ignatow) **34**:335
Anew (Zukofsky) **11**:342, 347, 382-83
"L'ange du méridien" (Rilke) **2**:275
"L'ange, fragment épique" (Lamartine) **16**:266
"Das angebrochene Jahr" (Celan) **10**:124
"Angel" (Lermontov) **18**:274, 276, 279
"Angel" (Merrill) **28**:248
"The Angel" (Wright) **36**:280, 289
Angel (Graham) **59**:166
"Angel Atrapado XXI" (Yau) **61**:336
"Angel Atrapado XXII (The Elements)" (Yau) **61**:336
"Angel Boley" (Smith) **12**:352
"Angel Butcher" (Levine) **22**:222-23
"Angel/Engine" (Brathwaite) **56**:70, 97
"An Angel in Plaster" (Carman) **34**:226
The Angel in the House (Patmore) **59**:200, 203-6, 209-14, 218-19, 221-27, 229-30, 232-35, 237, 239-40, 243-45, 247-51, 253-55, 258-62, 264-65, 267, 269, 271, 274
"The Angel of Death" (Lermontov)
See "Angel smerti"
The Angel of History (Forché) **10**:160, 169

"Angel smerti" (Lermontov) **18**:300
"The Angel Sons" (Lindsay) **23**:281
"Angel Surrounded by Paysans" (Stevens) **6**:304
"Los Angeles Poems" (Davie) **29**:99
"Angelic Love" (Meredith) **60**:244
"L'angelo nero" (Montale) **13**:134
Angelos Sikelianos: Selected Poems (Sikelianos) **29**:368
Angels and Earthly Creatures (Wylie) **23**:303-304, 307, 309, 313-14
"The Angels at Hamburg" (Jarrell) **41**:195-96
"The Angels of Fate" (Amichai)
See "Mal'akhei goral"
"Angels of the Love Affair" (Sexton) **2**:365, 367
"Angels Surrounded by Paysans" (Paz) **48**:261
"Angelus" (Fuertes) **27**:39
"Angel-Volk" (Shvarts) **50**:135
"The Angel-Wolf" (Shvarts)
See "Angel-Volk"
"The Anger of the Sea" (Ishikawa)
See "Umi no ikari"
"Anger's Freeing Power" (Smith) **12**:295, 311, 330
"Angina" (Dickey) **40**:196, 213-14, 256
"Anglais Mort à Florence" (Stevens) **6**:311
Angle of Ascent (Hayden) **6**:188, 190, 194
Angle of Geese, and Other Poems (Momaday) **25**:187, 188-89, 193
"An Anglican Lady: in memoriam Margaret Hine" (Davie) **29**:116
"Angling A Day" (Kinnell) **26**:260
"Anglo-Mongrels and the Rose" (Loy) **16**:316, 322
"Anglosaxon Street" (Birney) **52**:8-10, 14, 21, 27, 37, 44, 46, 56, 79
"Angoisse" (Rimbaud) **57**:178, 246, 275, 285-86, 293
"L'Angoisse" (Verlaine) **32**:386-87
"Angriff" (Stramm) **50**:208, 218
"The Angry God" (Ferlinghetti) **1**:183
"Angry Love" (Aleixandre) **15**:19
"Angry Samson" (Graves) **6**:151
"Angry Young Men" (Yevtushenko) **40**:345
"Angststurm" (Stramm) **50**:172, 205, 208-9, 222
"The Anguish" (Millay) **6**:217
"Anguish" (Rimbaud)
See "Angoisse"
"Anillo" (Guillén) **35**:179, 180, 181, 183
"Anima" (Carruth) **10**:85
"De Anima" (Nemerov) **24**:289
"Anima hominis" (Yeats) **20**:327
"Anima mundi" (Yeats) **51**:151
Animadversions upon the Remonstrants Defence (Milton) **29**:238
Animal de fondo (Jiménez) **7**:183-84, 203, 211, 214
"Animal de luz" (Neruda) **4**:289
Animal of Depth (Jiménez)
See *Animal de fondo*
Animal of Inner Depths (Jiménez)
See *Animal de fondo*
"Animal of Light" (Neruda)
See "Animal de luz"
"Animal, Vegetable, and Mineral" (Bogan) **12**:92, 99, 107, 125
"Animal-Flower" (Shvarts)
See "Zver'-tsvetok"
"The Animals" (Merwin) **45**:21, 25, 42
"The Animals" (Muir) **49**:196, 271, 273
"Animals Are Passing from Our Lives" (Levine) **22**:213
The Animals in That Country (Atwood) **8**:3-4, 12, 15-16, 23
"Animula" (Eliot) **31**:120
"Animula" (Oppen) **35**:343
Animula (Eliot) **5**:194, 197-98, 203
"Animus" (Shvarts) **50**:135, 142
"L'Anitca Poesia Toscana" (Carducci) **46**:52
"Anklage" (Goethe) **5**:248
"Ankor Wat" (Ginsberg) **4**:61
"Anna" (Wyatt) **27**:345
"Anna Comnena" (Cavafy) **36**:33, 90, 93
"Anna Comnene" (Cavafy)
See "Anna Comnena"
"Anna Imroth" (Sandburg) **41**:239, 243, 336
"Anna Liffey" (Boland) **58**:20, 22, 28, 37-38, 50
"anna speaks of the childhood of mary her daughter" (Clifton) **17**:37
"Annabel Lee" (Poe) **1**:425, 429, 434, 438, 441, 444, 447-48
"Annandale Again" (Robinson) **1**:476
"Anne" (Valéry) **9**:374, 392
"Anne Boleyn's Song" (Sitwell) **3**:315
"Anne Hay" (Carew)
See "Obsequies to the Lady Anne Hay"
"Anne Rutledge" (Masters) **1**:334, 348; **36**:174, 183, 191-92, 199
"The Annealing" (Piercy) **29**:314
"L'anneau de la licorne" (Char) **56**:138
L'année terrible (Hugo) **17**:55-56, 65, 97-99, 101
Les Années funestes (Hugo) **17**:65
"Annetta" (Montale) **13**:138
"The Anniad" (Brooks) **7**:53, 58, 61, 80, 102, 104
Annie Allen (Brooks) **7**:53-4, 56-8, 60-2, 68, 75, 78, 80-1, 85, 91, 96, 102, 104-05
"Annie Hill's Grave" (Merrill) **28**:248
"Annie Pengelly" (Goodison) **36**:155
"Annie's Arctic Snake" (Wakoski) **15**:334
"Annihilation" (Aiken) **26**:24
"The Anniversarie" (Donne) **1**:130
The Anniversaries (Donne) **1**:145-48, 155-56, 158
"Anniversario" (Montale) **13**:110
"Anniversary" (Abse) **41**:8
"An Anniversary" (Berry) **28**:12-13
"Anniversary" (Elytis) **21**:118-19, 134
"The Anniversary" (Lowell) **13**:66, 97
"Anniversary" (Marvell)
See "The First Anniversary of the Government under O. C."
"Anniversary" (Montale)
See "Anniversario"
"The Anniversary" (Stryk) **27**:204
"Anniversary Poem" (Oppen) **35**:286, 295, 339
"Anno domini MCMXLVII" (Quasimodo) **47**:284
Anno Domini MCMXXI (Akhmatova) **2**:3, 13-14, 18
"Annual" (Swenson) **14**:284
"The Annunciation" (Merton) **10**:339
"The Annunciation" (Merwin) **45**:11-12, 14, 16, 29
"The Annunciation" (Mueller) **33**:180
"The Annunciation" (Muir) **49**:196, 200, 205, 273, 298
"Annunciation" (Sarton) **39**:326, 328, 323, 342-43
"Annunciation Eve" (Tsvetaeva)
See "Kanun Blagoveshchen'ia"
"Annunciation with a Bullet in It" (Graham) **59**:137-38
Annunciations (Tomlinson) **17**:359-60
"Annus Mirabilis" (Larkin) **21**:237
"Annus Mirabilis, 1789" (Cowper) **40**:97-8, 120
"Annus Mirabilis: The Year of Wonders, 1666" (Dryden) **25**:90-1, 93, 95, 99, 115-16
"El año lírico" (Darío) **15**:95, 117
"anodetodalevy" (Bissett) **14**:31
"Anodyne" (Komunyakaa) **51**:52, 55
"Anonymous Signature" (MacLeish) **47**:126
"Anorexic" (Boland) **58**:37, 72-75, 77
"Another Animal" (Swenson) **14**:284
Another Animal (Swenson) **14**:246, 251-52, 260, 264, 267, 274, 277, 282-83
"Another August" (Merrill) **28**:221
"Another Dark Lady" (Robinson) **35**:368
"Another dreadful job about Mother Ireland" (Kavanagh) **33**:77
"Another Letter to My Husband" (Bradstreet) **10**:28
Another Life (Walcott) **46**:232, 235-36, 239-42, 244-45, 259, 266-67, 269, 271, 273, 276-80, 287-89, 308, 321-22
"Another Mystery" (Carver) **54**:18
"Another New-yeeres Gift; or song for the Circumcision" (Herrick) **9**:118, 120
"Another Poem for Me—After Recovering from an O.D." (Knight) **14**:39, 43, 53
"Another Poem of Gifts" (Borges) **32**:58, 66
"Another Poem of Thanksgiving" (Borges) **32**:131
"Another Ride from Ghent to Aix" (Riley) **48**:340
Another Side of Bob Dylan (Dylan) **37**:60
"Another Son" (McGuckian) **27**:100
Another Song (Cage) **58**:201
"Another Space" (Page) **12**:180, 190, 197-98
"Another Spring" (Levertov) **11**:169-70
"Another Spring" (Rexroth) **20**:207
"Another Sunday Morning" (Mahon) **60**:147-48
"Another Time" (Auden) **1**:18-19, 30, 34
"Another Time" (Soto) **28**:402
"Another Version" (Mueller) **33**:188
"Another Week-end at the Beach" (Curnow) **48**:39
"Another Word on the Scientific Aspiration" (Lindsay) **23**:269
"Another Year" (Williams) **7**:370
"Anoukis and later Jeanne" (Char)
See "Anoukis et plus tard Jeanne"
"Anoukis et plus tard Jeanne" (Char) **56**:157, 171, 177
A'nque (Alurista) **34**:15, 26
"anrufung des fisches" (Enzensberger) **28**:136
"Anselmo" (Riley) **48**:300
"Answer" (Finch)
See "Ardelia's Answer to Ephelia"
"Answer!" (Guillén)
See "Responde tú"
"The Answer" (Herbert) **4**:130
"The Answer" (Jeffers) **17**:129, 131
"The Answer" (Sandburg) **41**:242, 314
"The Answer" (Teasdale) **31**:321-22, 325
The Answer (Montagu) **16**:340-41, 346
"Answer to a consul" (Paz)
See "Respuesta a un cónsul"
"An Answer to Another Perswading a Lady to Marriage" (Philips) **40**:297
"An Answer to Some Verses Made in His Praise" (Suckling) **30**:156-57
"An Answer to the Rebus" (Wheatley) **3**:363
"Answer to Voznesensky and Evtushenko" (O'Hara) **45**:118, 165
"Answering a Layman's Question" (Li Po) **29**:142
"Answering a Question in the Mountains" (Ashbery) **26**:129
"Answering Magistrate Chang" (Wang Wei) **18**:364-65
"Antaeus" (Heaney) **18**:203, 207-9
"Antaeus: A Fragment" (Owen) **19**:354
"Antarctica" (Mahon) **60**:217
Antarctica (Mahon) **60**:192-94, 196, 199
"Antaryami" (Tagore) **8**:408
"Ante Aram" (Brooke) **24**:62
"Ante Lucem" (Blok) **21**:2, 23
"Ante Mortem" (Jeffers) **17**:117, 141
"An Antebellum Sermon" (Dunbar) **5**:120, 123, 133, 147
"Antecedents" (Tomlinson) **17**:302-04, 306, 311, 323, 338
Antechinus: Poems, 1975-1980 (Hope) **56**:282
"Antediluvian" (Ní Chuilleanáin) **34**:351
"Antelación de amor" (Borges) **32**:83
"Ante-Natal Dream" (Kavanagh) **33**:147
"Antenati" (Pavese) **13**:217, 220, 225-26
"Antéros" (Nerval) **13**:181, 191-92, 194, 198
"Anthem for Doomed Youth" (Owen) **19**:326, 332, 336, 346, 360-63, 365-67, 369-70
"Anthem for Man" (Wagoner) **33**:326

"The Anthill" (Cervantes) **35**:114, 134
Anthology (Jiménez)
See *Antolojía poética (1898-1953)*
Anthology for a Thousand Ages (Yakamochi)
See *Man'yōshū*
The Anthology of Magazine Verse (Braithwaite) **52**:106-7
"An Anthropological Guide to the Customs of the Country" (Shvarts)
See "Antropologicheskoe stranovedenie"
"Antico inverno" (Quasimodo) **47**:275
"Antico, sono ubriacato della tua voce" (Montale) **13**:115, 141
"Anti-Desperation" (Arnold) **5**:7
"Antigone" (Arnold) **5**:8
"The Antigone Riddle" (Mahon) **60**:150, 192
"Antigua casa madrileña" (Aleixandre) **15**:34, 36
The Antilles: Fragments of Epic Memory (Walcott) **46**:260
"Antilógica" (Guillén) **35**:146
"Antinous" (Pessoa) **20**:165, 169
"Antiphon" (Herbert) **4**:103
"The Antiphon" (Levertov) **11**:198
"Anti-poem" (Shapiro) **25**:316, 321
"Antipoema?" (Fuertes) **27**:48
Antipoems: New and Selected (Parra) **39**:291-92, 306-9
"Antipolis" (Dickey) **40**:176, 178
"Antique" (Rimbaud) **57**:230, 254
"Antique Harvesters" (Ransom) **61**:268-69, 275
"The Antiquity of Freedom" (Bryant) **20**:43, 47
L'Antitête (Tzara) **27**:234-37
Anti=Thelyphthora (Evans) **40**:71
"Anti-Vietnam War Peace Mobilization" (Ginsberg) **4**:76
Antología mayor (Guillén) **23**:142
Antologia personal (Borges) **32**:93
Antología poética (Storni) **33**:235, 245;
Antología total (Aleixandre) **15**:32
Antología y poemas (Fuertes) **27**:10-1
Antología y poemas del suburbio (Fuertes) **27**:10, 18
Antolojía poética (1898-1953) (Jiménez) **7**:183-84
"Antonio Machado" (Guillén) **35**:201
"Antrim" (Jeffers) **17**:117
"Antropologicheskoe stranovedenie" (Shvarts) **50**:162
"Anvil" (Brathwaite) **56**:12
The Anxiety of the Rose (Storni)
See *La inquietud del rosal*
"Any Human to Another" (Cullen) **20**:60
"Any Porch" (Parker) **28**:353-54
"Any Time Now" (Curnow) **48**:38-39
"anyone lived in a pretty how town" (Cummings) **5**:81
"Anywhere is a Street into the Night" (Momaday) **25**:202, 212
Aoneko (Hagiwara) **18**:170, 172-73, 175-77, 181-83
"Apá" (Alurista) **34**:28
"Apache Love" (Ortiz) **17**:224
"Apache Red" (Ortiz) **17**:228
"El aparecido" (Guillén) **35**:187
"The Apartment Is as Silent as Paper" (Mandelstam) **14**:149
"Apegado a mí" (Mistral) **32**:200-02
"El apellido" (Guillén) **23**:131
"The Apennines" (Bryant) **20**:16-17
"Apes and Ivory" (Noyes) **27**:114
"Aphasia" (Mueller) **33**:192
"Aphorisms, I" (Villa) **22**:355
"Aphorisms, II" (Villa) **22**:353, 355
"Aphorisms, III" (Villa) **22**:355
"Aphorisms on Futurism" (Loy) **16**:311-13, 316, 322, 324
"Aphrodite" (Glück) **16**:150
"Aphrodite Goes Away for Saturday Night" (Shvarts) **50**:143
"Aphrodite Ode" (Sappho)
See "Ode to Aphrodite"
"Aphrodite Rising" (Sikelianos) **29**:367, 369
"Apocalipsis" (Cardenal) **22**:112, 125, 129
"Apocalypse" (Cardenal)
See "Apocalipsis"
"Apocalypse: Umbrian Master, about 1490" (Enzensberger) **28**:151
"Apogee of Celery" (Neruda)
See "Apogeo del apio"
"Apogeo del apio" (Neruda) **4**:277
"Apollo" (Dickey) **40**:189, 199-200, 220, 237
"Apollo and Marsyas" (Herbert)
See "Apollo i marsjasz"
"Apollo at Pheræ" (Masters) **1**:329; **36**:176
"Apollo i marsjasz" (Herbert) **50**:3, 5, 34
"Apollo in New York" (Viereck) **27**:278
"Apollo of the Physiologists" (Graves) **6**:152-53
"An Apollonian Elegy" (Duncan) **2**:105
Apollonius of Tyana (Olson) **19**:282, 298
"Apollonius of Tyre" (Gower)
See *Confessio Amantis*
"Apollo's Edict" (Swift) **9**:252
"Apologia pro poemate meo" (Owen) **19**:329, 334-35, 344, 348, 353-55, 370
"Apologies to All the People in Lebanon" (Jordan) **38**:127, 145
"Apologies to the Federal Bureau of Investigation" (Giovanni) **19**:108
"Apology" (Morris) **55**:242, 253, 285, 291-97, 325, 329
"Apology" (Wilbur) **51**:188
"Apology for Bad Dreams" (Jeffers) **17**:129-30, 142, 147
"The Apology of Demetrius" (Masters) **1**:343
"Apology of Genius" (Loy) **16**:308, 321
"An Apology to the Lady Cartaret" (Swift) **9**:296
Apophoreta (Martial) **10**:230, 241
"Apostrophe to a Dead Friend" (Kumin) **15**:218-20
"The Apostrophe to Vincentine" (Stevens) **6**:309
"apoteos" (Ekeloef) **23**:75
"The Apotheosis of the Garbagemen" (Wagoner) **33**:337
"The Apotheosis of Tins" (Mahon) **60**:136, 138, 149, 155, 174, 189-90
"Apparent Failure" (Browning) **2**:68; **61**:49
"The Apparition" (Donne) **1**:130, 152
"The Apparition of His Mistress Calling Him to Elizium" (Herrick) **9**:93, 103, 133, 138-39
"Apparition of Splendor" (Moore) **49**:126-28, 131, 136, 139, 161
"The Apparitions" (Yeats) **20**:351
"Appeal to Dwynwen" (Dafydd)
See "Galw ar Ddwynwen"
"Appeal to a Lady with a Diaper" (Birney) **52**:28, 63, 79
"An Appeal to the American People" (Harper) **21**:190
"Appearances" (Glück) **16**:157, 161
"The Appeasement of Demeter" (Meredith) **60**:330
Appendice (Pasolini) **17**:279
"Appendix Form in Poetry" (Viereck) **27**:287
"Appendix to the Anniad Leaves from a Loose-Leaf War Diary" (Brooks) **7**:61
"L'Appennino" (Pasolini) **17**:270
"Appetite" (Smith) **12**:310
"The Apple" (Kinnell) **26**:261
"The Apple" (Page) **12**:168, 170
"Apple" (Soto) **28**:398
Apple (Yevtushenko)
See *Yabloko*
"The Apple Blossom Snow Blues" (Lindsay) **23**:264
"Apple Dropping into Deep Early Snow" (Kenyon) **57**:35
An Apple from One's Lap (Seifert)
See *Jablko z klína*
An Apple From the Lap (Seifert)
See *Jablko z klína*
An Apple from Your Lap (Seifert)
See *Jablko z klína*
"An Apple Gathering" (Rossetti) **7**:260-1, 280
"Apple Peeler" (Francis) **34**:255
"Apple Tragedy" (Hughes) **7**:143, 159
"The Apple Tree" (Berry) **28**:5
"The Apple Tree" (Parker) **28**:364
"The Apple Trees" (Glück) **16**:126-27, 132, 140, 142
"The Apple Woman's Complaint" (McKay) **2**:210
"Apples" (Merwin) **45**:87, 95-7
"Apples and Water" (Graves) **6**:141
"Appleton House" (Marvell)
See "Upon Appleton House"
The Applewood Cycles (Viereck) **27**:286, 289
"The Applicant" (Plath) **1**:394, 400-01; **37**:232, 255
"Applies" (Reese) **29**:335
"The Appointment" (Kenyon) **57**:17
"The Appointment Card" (Ignatow) **34**:318
"The Appology" (Finch) **21**:140, 159, 162, 167, 178
"Appraisal" (Teasdale) **31**:349
"Apprehensions" (Duncan) **2**:110, 112
"An Apprentice Angel" (MacDiarmid) **9**:155
"l'Appressamento della morte" (Leopardi) **37**:170, 172
"Approach to Thebes" (Kunitz) **19**:156, 161, 168, 173-74
"The Approaches" (Merwin) **45**:45
"Approaching Prayer" (Dickey) **40**:163, 175, 192, 208-9, 248
"The Approaching Silence" (Illyés) **16**:248
"Approaching Winter" (Bly) **39**:7, 85
Approximate Man (Tzara)
See *L'Homme approximatif*
"Appuldurcombe Park" (Lowell) **13**:84
"Après le déluge" (Péret) **33**:230
"Après le déluge" (Rimbaud) **3**:261; **57**:173, 177, 221, 236, 239, 249, 275, 282, 285, 293
"Après une lecture de Dante" (Hugo) **17**:96-97
L'après-midi d'un faune (Mallarmé) **4**:186, 188, 190, 197, 207-08
"April" (Glück) **16**:171
"April" (Kavanagh) **33**:109, 162
"April" (Merwin) **45**:20
"April" (Ransom) **61**:294
"April 5, 1974" (Wilbur) **51**:284
"April 1885" (Bridges) **28**:83
April Airs (Carman) **34**:205, 211, 228
"April Fables" (Nishiwaki) **15**:231
April Galleons (Ashbery) **26**:162, 174
"April in November" (MacLeish) **47**:210
"April in Paris" (Komunyakaa) **51**:33
April in Sydney (Komunyakaa)
See *February in Sydney*
April Interval (Hacker) **47**:112
"April Is the Saddest Month" (Williams) **7**:351, 354, 400
"April on Toronto Island" (Mahon) **60**:195
"April Treason" (Ransom) **61**:272
"April Walk" (Kenyon) **57**:45
"April was Opening its Flowers" (Guillén)
See "Abril sus flores abría"
"April Weather" (Carman) **34**:223
"Aprilian" (Carman) **34**:202
"Aquarelles" (Verlaine) **2**:415
"L'aquarium" (Laforgue) **14**:72
"The Aquarium" (Lowell) **13**:79
"Aquatre heures du matin" (Rimbaud) **3**:274
"Aquél" (Borges) **32**:56
"Aqui" (Paz) **48**:248
"Aquí estoy expuesta como todos" (Fuertes) **27**:25
"Aqui Nomas" (Alurista) **34**:47
"Arabel" (Masters) **1**:328; **36**:175
"Aran" (Mahon) **60**:198
Arap Petra Velikogo (Pushkin) **10**:394
Ararat (Glück) **16**:157-64, 168, 170
"Araucanian and Latin" (Parra) **39**:277
"El árbol" (Aleixandre) **15**:22

Arbol adentro (Paz) **1**:374, 376-77; **48**:192, 261
"Arbol muerto" (Mistral) **32**:178
"Arboreal Cathedral" (Shvarts) **50**:147
Arbre des voyageurs (Tzara) **27**:234
"Les Arbres" (Bonnefoy) **58**:170
Arbuthnot (Pope)
See *An Epistle to Dr. Arbuthnot*
"L'Arc" (Perse) **23**:228
"The Arc Inside and Out" (Ammons) **16**:12, 61
"L'arca" (Montale) **13**:113
Arcadia (Sidney)
See *The Countess of Pembroke's Arcadia*
"La Arcadia perdida" (Cardenal) **22**:132
"Arcady Unheeding" (Sassoon) **12**:240, 275
Archaeologist of Morning (Olson) **19**:268, 282, 306, 308
"Archaic Figure" (Clampitt) **19**:92
Archaic Figure (Clampitt) **19**:91-3
"Archaics" (Guest) **55**:212
"Archduchess Anne" (Meredith) **60**:251, 262-63
"The Arched Instant" (Shvarts) **50**:132
The Archeology of Movies and Books (Wakoski) **15**:372-73
Archer (Viereck) **27**:285, 288-89, 291-92
Archer in the Marrow (Viereck) **27**:287-88, 292
Archer in the Marrow The Applewood Cycles 1967-1987 (Viereck) **27**:285-86
"Archibald Higbie" (Masters) **1**:333
"Der Archipelagus" (Hölderlin) **4**:147-8, 164
"Architectural Image" (Sarton) **39**:320
"The Architectural Metaphor" (Ní Chuilleanáin) **34**:368-69
"Architecture" (Alexie) **53**:40
"An Architecture" (Berry) **28**:4, 7
"Architecture" (Stevens) **6**:293
"The Architecture: Passages 9" (Duncan) **2**:107
"El arco-iris" (Mistral) **32**:169
"The Arctic Ox (or Goat)" (Moore) **49**:143
"Arcturus" (Teasdale) **31**:360
"Arcturus in Autumn" (Teasdale) **31**:338
"Ardelia to Melancholy" (Finch) **21**:146, 150, 152, 157, 165, 168, 177-80
"Ardelia's Answer to Ephelia" (Finch) **21**:148, 154-55, 163, 165
The Ardent Slingsman (Neruda)
See *El hondero entusiasta, 1923-1924*
"Ardilla de los tunes de un katu" (Cardenal) **22**:131
"La arena traicionada" (Neruda) **4**:292-93
"Arethusa" (Shelley) **14**:167
"The Argonauts" (Lawrence) **54**:199
"The Argument" (Aiken) **26**:24
"Argument" (Char) **56**:114, 190
"The Argument" (Kenyon) **57**:27, 37
"Argument" (Lawrence) **54**:173, 207, 212
"Argument 1" (Hughes) **53**:115
"The Argument of His Book" (Herrick) **9**:85, 95, 97, 101, 105, 107-10, 116, 132-34, 138-39, 141
"Ariadne" (H. D.) **5**:304
Arias tristes (Jiménez) **7**:199, 209
"Ariel" (Plath) **1**:381, 409, 413; **37**:234, 240-41, 260
Ariel (Plath) **1**:379-80, 383-84, 387, 389-91, 393-96, 405-07, 410-11; **37**:175-76, 187, 193, 196-98, 260-61, 263-65
Ariel Poems (Eliot) **31**:156
"Ariettes oubliées" (Verlaine) **2**:431
"Arion" (Eliot) **20**:123, 125, 134-35, 145
"Arion" (Herbert) **50**:3
"Arion on a Dolphin to his Marjestie in his passadge into England" (Philips) **40**:318
"Ariosto" (Carducci) **46**:52
"Ariosto" (Mandelstam) **14**:144
"Ariosto and the Arabs" (Borges) **22**:92
"Arisbe" (Howe) **54**:119-21, 149-50
"Ariso" (Ishikawa) **10**:215
"Aristoboulos" (Cavafy) **36**:34
Aristophanes' Apology (Browning) **2**:96
"Arizona Desert" (Tomlinson) **17**:331, 341
"The Ark" (Montale)
See "L'arca"
The Arkansas Testament (Walcott) **46**:259, 266, 323
The Arm and the Flame (Seifert)
See *Ruka a plamen*
"The Armada" (Swinburne) **24**:312
"The Armadillo" (Bishop) **34**:78, 80
"Armageddon" (Ransom) **61**:308, 324
"Armageddon" (Tennyson) **6**:407-08, 413, 415-18
Armand Schwerner (Schwerner) **42**:204
"Armed with the vision of narrow wasps" (Mandelstam)
See "Vooruzhennyi zren'em uzkikh os"
"Armenia" (Mandelstam) **14**:118
"Les armes miraculeuses" (Césaire) **25**:8, 29
Les Armes Miraculeuses (Césaire) **25**:15, 18, 21, 29-30, 44
"Armgart" (Eliot) **20**:101, 116, 124, 131, 133-36, 144
"Una armonía*** (Guillén) **35**:181
"Armor" (Dickey) **40**:150, 175
"Armor's Undermining Modesty" (Moore) **4**:267; **49**:126, 128, 132, 134, 157
"Arms" (Tagore)
See "Bahu"
"Arms and the Boy" (Owen) **19**:336, 354, 358
The Arms of Venus (Seifert)
See *Ruce Venušiny*
"Army" (Corso) **33**:25, 47-8
"Army Song" (Wang Wei) **18**:367
"Arnold, Master of the Scud" (Carman) **34**:202
Ārogya (Tagore) **8**:424, 426
Aromates chasseurs (Char) **56**:130, 136-38, 140, 145, 173, 184, 187-89
Aromatic Hunters (Char)
See *Aromates chasseurs*
"Aromos" (Parra) **39**:285
"Around Pastor Bonhoeffer" (Kunitz) **19**:158
"Arp" (Éluard) **38**:71
"Arrabal" (Borges) **32**:126
"Arrabal en que pesa el campo" (Borges) **32**:84
"Arrangements with Earth for Three Dead Friends" (Wright) **36**:336
"Arras" (Page) **12**:168, 170, 178, 180, 189-90, 197
"Arremba sulla strinata proda" (Montale) **13**:116
"Arrest of Antoñito the Camborio" (García Lorca)
See "Prendimiento de Antoñito el Camborio"
Arrière-histoire du poème pulvérisé (Char) **56**:112
"Arrival" (Brathwaite) **56**:7, 49, 86
"Arrival" (Guillén) **23**:105
"The Arrival" (Merwin) **45**:52, 55, 86
"Arrival and Departure" (MacLeish) **47**:197
"The Arrival and Departure of Adam and Eve at Dover" (Abse) **41**:33
"Arrival at Santos" (Bishop) **3**:44; **34**:78, 94, 116, 189
"The Arrival of the Bee Box" (Plath) **1**:410-13; **37**:233
"Arrivals" (Birney) **52**:16, 45
"Arrivals and Departures" (Stone) **53**:228
"Arrivals, Departures" (Larkin) **21**:236
"Arrivals Wolfville" (Birney) **52**:34, 36
The Arrivants (Brathwaite) **56**:26, 32-33, 36, 41, 43-45, 49-51, 53, 59, 61, 65-66, 72-77, 82, 84, 86, 88-89, 94-96, 98-100
"Arrivée des voyageurs" (Éluard) **38**:91
"Arriving at the Frontier on a Mission" (Wang Wei) **18**:367, 389
"Arriving in the Country Again" (Wright) **36**:326
"An Arrogant Bagpiper" (Castro)
See "Un arrogante gaitero"
"Un arrogante gaitero" (Castro) **41**:110
"El arrorró elquino" (Mistral) **32**:180
"The Arrorró of Elqui" (Mistral)
See "El arrorró elquino"
"Arrow" (Dove) **6**:123
"The Arrow That Flieth by Day" (O'Hara)
See "Ode (to Joseph LeSueur) on the Arrow That Flieth by Day"
"The Arrow That Flieth by Night" (O'Hara) **45**:154
"Arrows of Flowers" (Bissett) **14**:7
"Arrullo patagón" (Mistral) **32**:180
Ars Amandi (Ovid)
See *Ars amatoria*
Ars amatoria (Ovid) **2**:233-34, 238-39, 241-47, 253-55, 261
"Ars poetica" (Borges) **32**:42, 62, 65
"Ars Poetica" (Cavafy) **36**:112
"Ars poetica" (Dove) **6**:121-22
"Ars Poetica" (MacLeish) **47**:125, 181, 186, 195, 212-14
"Ars poetica?" (Milosz) **8**:197, 201
Ars Poetica (Cavafy) **36**:54, 55-56
Ars Poetica (Horace) **46**:97, 99, 101, 104-5, 114, 124-25, 132, 138, 140-42, 145-47, 157, 159, 222
"Ars Poetica: A Found Poem" (Kumin) **15**:216
"Ars Poetica: Some Recent Criticism" (Wright) **36**:317, 373, 377
"Ars vivendi" (Guillén) **35**:197-98
Arsenal (Char) **56**:112, 126-27, 168
"The Arsenal at Springfield" (Longfellow) **30**:21, 27, 46
"Arsenio" (Montale) **13**:107, 120, 124-25, 147, 164
"Arsinoë" (Ekeloef) **23**:59, 61
"Art" (Emerson) **18**:98
"L'art" (Gautier) **18**:128, 156-57, 164
"An Art Called Gothonic" (Olson) **19**:305
L'Art d'être grand-père (Hugo) **17**:65, 86
"Art Is Either A Complaint Or Do Something Else" (Cage) **58**:220
"Art McCooey" (Kavanagh) **33**:81, 94-95, 102, 152-4, 157
"The Art of Forgetting" (Mueller) **33**:193
Art of Love (Ovid)
See *Ars amatoria*
"The art of poetry" (Dalton) **36**:137
"Art of Poetry" (Verlaine)
See "L'Art poètique"
The Art of Poetry (Horace)
See *Ars Poetica*
"The Art of Response" (Lorde) **12**:140
The Art of Worldly Wisdom (Rexroth) **20**:179, 181-83, 192, 198, 203, 211, 213
"Art Poétique" (Bonnefoy) **58**:132
"L'Art poètique" (Verlaine) **2**:416-18, 428, 430-34; **32**:340-43, 353, 355, 360, 363, 368-69, 374, 376, 385-86, 396, 398-99, 401-04, 412
Art the Herald (Noyes) **27**:140
"Arte poética" (Guillén) **23**:128
De Arte Poetica liber (Horace)
See *Ars Poetica*
"L'arte povera" (Montale) **13**:138
"Artémis" (Nerval) **13**:173, 179, 181, 184-87, 195-96, 198
"Artemis Orthia" (Sikelianos) **29**:367
"Artemis Prologuises" (Browning) **2**:26
"An Artesian Well" (Sarton) **39**:321, 339
"Arthur Mitchell" (Moore) **49**:146
"The Articles of War" (Francis) **34**:243
"Articulation of Sound Forms in Time" (Howe) **54**:93-95, 97, 100-101, 124-25, 128-30, 133
Articulation of Sound Forms in Time (Howe) **54**:38, 41, 43, 45-48, 51-52, 54, 59-62, 64, 66-69, 87, 110, 112, 114-16
"Artificer" (Milosz) **8**:191
"Artificial Flowers" (Cavafy) **36**:105
"Artillerie" (Herbert) **4**:101, 129
"Artillery" (Herbert)
See "Artillerie"
Artine (Char) **56**:126-27
"The Artist" (Blok) **21**:16
"An Artist" (Heaney) **18**:215
"An Artist" (Jeffers) **17**:141
"The Artist" (Kunitz) **19**:161, 168, 173-75

"The Artists' and Models' Ball" (Brooks) **7**:107
"An Arundel Tomb" (Larkin) **21**:229-30, 234, 238-39, 258
"Der Arzt" (Benn) **35**:50
"As a Possible Lover" (Baraka) **4**:16
"As a World Would Have It" (Robinson) **1**:460
"As Any (Men's Hells Having Wrestled with)" (Cummings) **5**:108
"As Bad as a Mile" (Larkin) **21**:233-34
"As Children Together" (Forché) **10**:144, 156-57, 168-69
"As Created" (Riley) **48**:302
"As de Pique" (Péret) **33**:217
As Does New Hampshire (Sarton) **39**:338-9, 342, 360
"As Eagles Soar" (Toomer) **7**:340
"As Envoy to the Barbarian Pass" (Wang Wei) **18**:362
As Fine As Melanctha (Stein) **18**:327
"As Flowers Are" (Kunitz) **19**:155, 162
"As for Fame I've Had It" (Ammons) **16**:44
"As for me, I sing and sing" (Castro)
See "Yo cantar, cantar, canté"
"As Hermes Once" (Keats) **1**:279
"As I Ebb'd with the Ocean of Life" (Whitman) **3**:396-97, 421
"As I Grow Older" (Hughes) **1**:251; **53**:122
"As I Lay with My Head on Your Lap Camarado" (Whitman) **3**:379
"As I Remember" (Stone) **53**:222
"As I Sat Alone by Blue Ontario's Shore" (Whitman) **3**:377, 387
"As I Step over the Puddle at the End of Winter, I Think of an Ancient Chinese" (Wright) **36**:340, 374
"As I Was Saying" (Parra) **39**:310-11
"As I Went Down to Havre de Grace" (Wylie) **23**:305, 310, 324
"As I Went Out One Morning" (Dylan) **37**:55-6
"As in a rose the true fire moves" (Villa) **22**:351
"As in their Time" (MacNeice) **61**:177
"As Is the Sea Marvelous" (Cummings) **5**:104
"As It Should Be" (Mahon) **60**:142, 152, 183
"As John to Patmos" (Walcott) **46**:272
"As kingfishers catch fire" (Hopkins) **15**:169
"As Lovers Do" (MacDiarmid) **9**:156
"As Loving Hind" (Bradstreet) **10**:35-6
"As Many Questions As Answers" (Jackson) **44**:6
"As Miracles Go" (Stone) **53**:223
"As My Blood Was Drawn" (Hayden) **6**:194
"As My Uncle Ust to Say" (Riley) **48**:300
"As One Does Sickness Over" (Dickinson) **1**:94
"As One Put Drunk into the Packet Boat" (Ashbery) **26**:120
"As one who hath sent forth on bold emprise" (Belloc) **24**:10
"As Seen by Disciples" (Brooks) **7**:63
As Ten, as Twenty (Page) **12**:163-64, 167, 173, 193
"As the Dead Prey upon Us" (Olson) **19**:321, 323
"As the Team's Head-Brass" (Thomas) **53**:298, 305, 308, 346, 350
"As Thyself" (Lawrence) **54**:249
"As virtuous men pass mildly away" (Donne)
See "A Valediction: forbidding mourning"
"As viudas d'os vivos e as viudas d'os mortos" (Castro) **41**:88
"As We Desired" (Guillén)
See "Como quisimos"
"As We Know" (Ashbery) **26**:136-138, 141, 156, 172
As We Know (Ashbery) **26**:131-132, 135-137, 140
"As Weary Pilgrim" (Bradstreet) **10**:8, 15, 28, 34, 36-7
"As Well as Any Other" (Jackson) **44**:73, 103-4
"As You Leave Me" (Knight) **14**:41, 43, 52
"Asa Gray wrote Increase Lapham" (Niedecker) **42**:152
"Asahya bhalobasa" (Tagore) **8**:405
"Ascending the Mountain on Double Nine" (Li Po) **29**:183-84, 186
"Ascensão de Vasco da Gama" (Pessoa) **20**:155
"Ascent" (Merwin) **45**:90-1
"Ascent into Hell" (Hope) **56**:266, 271, 278, 288
"Ascetic" (Kavanagh) **33**:69, 92, 96, 120, 161
"aschermittwoch" (Enzensberger) **28**:134
"The Ash Grove" (Thomas) **53**:310
"Ash Snow or Moonlight" (Lee) **24**:240
"The Ash Tree" (Marie de France)
See "Le Fraisne"
"Ash Wednesday" (Seifert) **47**:323
"Ashar nairashya" (Tagore) **8**:405
"Ashes" (Teasdale) **31**:335
Ashes (Bely)
See *Pepel'*
"Ashes, ashes, all fall down" (Piercy) **29**:315, 318, 320
"The Ashes of Gramsci" (Pasolini) **17**:258, 284, 288-89
The Ashes of Gramsci (Pasolini)
See *Le ceneri di Gramscí*
"Ashes of Life" (Millay) **6**:206; **61**:212
"Ashes on Saturday Afternoon" (O'Hara) **45**:167, 231
Ashes: Poems New and Old (Levine) **22**:218-19, 223-24
"Ashurnatsirpal III" (Sandburg) **2**:323
Ash-Wednesday (Eliot) **5**:162-64, 170, 174, 186, 192, 194, 197-206, 209-10; **31**:119, 156
"Asia" (Carver) **54**:23
"Asian Birds" (Bridges) **28**:51, 85
"Asian Figures" (Merwin) **45**:61
Asian Figures (Merwin) **45**:62
"Asian Peace Offers Rejected Without Publication" (Bly) **39**:91
"The Asians Dying" (Merwin) **45**:9, 23, 34, 43, 49, 52
"Aside" (Shapiro) **25**:295
"Ask Me No More" (Tennyson) **6**:366
"Ask me no more where Jove bestows" (Carew) **29**:5
Ask the Bloody Horse (Abse) **41**:31
"Ask the Roses" (Levine) **22**:224
"Ask Your Mama" (Hughes) **53**:115
Ask Your Mama: 12 Moods for Jazz (Hughes) **1**:249, 251-53, 261, 268, 270; **53**:94, 108, 145, 164, 178
"The Asking" (Soto) **28**:400-01
"Asking for a Reconciliation" (Dafydd)
See "Gofyn Cymod"
"Asleep" (Owen) **19**:336, 354, 359, 368
Asolando (Browning) **2**:96
Asolando: Fancies and Facts (Browning) **2**:66-7, 88
"Aspasia" (Leopardi) **37**:92, 103, 109, 123
"An Aspect of Love, Alive in the Fire and Ice" (Brooks) **7**:82, 88, 91, 94
"Aspecto" (Storni) **33**:237;
"The Aspen and the Stream" (Wilbur) **51**:220, 229, 231
"Aspen Tree" (Celan) **10**:112-13
"Aspens" (Thomas) **53**:275, 294-96, 330
Asphalt Georgics (Carruth) **10**:77, 91
"An Asphodel" (Ginsberg) **47**:6
"Asphodel, That Greeny Flower" (Williams) **7**:371, 375, 390-92, 402-03
"Aspic Surmise" (Mackey) **49**:75-76
"Aspirations" (Verlaine) **32**:384
"Ass" (Cisneros) **52**:162
"The Ass" (Smith) **12**:302-6, 319
"The Assabet" (Thoreau) **30**:195
"Assassin" (Hass) **16**:195
"The Assassin" (Sexton) **2**:365
"Assassin" (Tomlinson) **17**:318, 322, 325-27, 341, 345-46
"Assassination Raga" (Ferlinghetti) **1**:173
"Assault" (Millay) **6**:236, 238
"Assay of the Infinite Man" (Neruda)
See *Tentativa del hombre infinito*
"An Assent to Wildflowers" (Meredith) **28**:192
"The Assertion" (Day Lewis) **11**:146
"The Assignation" (Wright) **36**:280, 343
"Les assis" (Rimbaud) **57**:184, 203, 210, 212, 216, 293-94, 289289
"Assommons les pauvres" (Baudelaire) **1**:59
"The Assumption" (Noyes) **27**:136
Assumptions (Hacker) **47**:80-81, 105, 119
"Astern" (Benn) **35**:67
"Astigmatism" (Lowell) **13**:84
"Astrea Redux. A Poem on the Happy Restoration and Return of His Sacred Majesty Charles the Second" (Dryden) **25**:99-101, 103-06
"the astrologer predicts at mary's birth" (Clifton) **17**:37
"Astrometaphysical" (Frost) **39**:233
"Astronauts" (Hayden) **6**:194
"The Astronomer Poems" (Wakoski) **15**:348, 365
"Astrono-mía" (Cervantes) **35**:132
"Astrophel" (Swinburne) **24**:313
"Astrophel: A Pastoral Elegy" (Spenser) **8**:365, 367, 387
Astrophel and Stella (Sidney) **32**:216-17, 224, 227, 231-34, 237-44, 248-53, 267-68, 270, 272-93, 298, 303, 307, 310-11, 315, 318, 320-26, 329-34
Astrophil and Stella (Sidney)
See *Astrophel and Stella*
"The Asylum" (Carruth) **10**:71, 82-4
"At a Bach Concert" (Rich) **5**:352, 387, 393
"At a Calvary near the Ancre" (Owen) **19**:334, 341, 362-63
"At a Concert of Music" (Aiken) **26**:24, 72
"At a Country Funeral" (Berry) **28**:16, 29
"At a Country Hotel" (Nemerov) **24**:260
"At a Glance" (Tomlinson) **17**:333
"At a Hasty Wedding" (Hardy) **8**:85
"At a Loose End" (Lawrence) **54**:244
"At a Lunar Eclipse" (Hardy) **8**:89
"At a March against the Vietnam War" (Bly) **39**:12
"At a Motel near O'Hare Airport" (Kenyon) **57**:46
"At a Party" (Bogan) **12**:106
"At a Potato Digging" (Heaney) **18**:200
"At a Solemn Music" (Milton)
See "On a Solemn Music"
At A Solemn Music (Milton) **29**:238-40
"At a Solemn Musick" (Schwartz) **8**:289
At A Vacation Exercise (Milton) **29**:241
"At a Wayside Shrine" (Owen) **19**:362
"At a Window" (Sandburg) **2**:300; **41**:225, 243, 268
"At Algeciras—A Meditation upon Death" (Yeats) **20**:342
"at any hour" (Alurista)
See "a cualquier hora"
"At Auden's Grave" (Shapiro) **25**:322
"At Baia" (H. D.) **5**:267
"At Barstow" (Tomlinson) **17**:353, 355
"At Candle-Lightin' Time" (Dunbar) **5**:122
"At Castle Boterel" (Hardy) **8**:118
"At Cedar Creek" (Wright) **14**:375
"At Cooloolah" (Wright) **14**:344, 371
"At Darien Bridge" (Dickey) **40**:191
"At Dawn" (Milosz) **8**:210
"At Daybreak" (Sassoon) **12**:247
"At Daybreak" (Zagajewski) **27**:389
"At Dead Low Water" (Curnow) **48**:6
At Dead Low Water, and Sonnets (Curnow) **48**:3, 12
"At Delphi" (Sarton) **39**:339, 341
"At Dusk" (Cummings) **5**:93, 106
"At Easterly" (Clampitt) **19**:100
"At First" (Walker) **30**:355
"At First, at Last" (Swenson) **14**:262, 288
"At Grass" (Larkin) **21**:229, 238-39, 244, 251, 257
"At Hanratty's" (Tomlinson) **17**:361
"At Holwell Farm" (Tomlinson) **17**:326, 341, 349, 352, 354

"At Ithaca" (H. D.) **5**:268
"At Joan's" (O'Hara)
See "Poem Read at Joan Mitchell's"
"At Last" (Walcott) **46**:236, 248, 274, 278, 289
"At Lindos" (Sarton) **39**:343
"At Luca Signorelli's Resurrection of the Body" (Graham) **59**:148, 155-56
"At McDonald's in Rutland" (Stone) **53**:258
"At Melville's Tomb" (Crane) **3**:90, 103
"At Midnight" (Teasdale) **31**:360, 370
"At Midnight's Hour I Raised my Head" (Thoreau) **30**:254
"At Muzot" (Sarton) **39**:326, 342
"At My Father's Grave" (MacDiarmid) **9**:156
"At My Hospital Window" (Viereck) **27**:294, 296
"At Night" (Ekeloef) **23**:85
"At Night the Salmon Move" (Carver) **54**:28
"At North Farm" (Ashbery) **26**:159-160
"At Odd Moments" (Brutus) **24**:116
"At One O'Clock in the Morning" (Baudelaire)
See "A une heure du matin"
"At Rest in the Blast" (Moore) **49**:112, 126, 129, 136
"At School" (Smith) **12**:330, 333
"At Sea" (Carman) **34**:199
"At Sea" (Teasdale) **31**:360
"At Sea" (Toomer) **7**:336
"At Sea" (Wagoner) **33**:357
"At Su Terrace Viewing the Past" (Li Po) **29**:145
At Terror Street and Agony Way (Bukowski) **18**:23
"At That Hour" (Joyce)
See "III"
"At the Ball Game" (Williams) **7**:368, 385
"At the Birth of an Age" (Jeffers) **17**:111, 130,141-42, 144
"At the Bottom of the Green field She Lies" (Sarton) **39**:323
"At The Brink" (Curnow) **48**:24
"At the Caberet-Vert" (Rimbaud)
See "Au caberet-vert"
"At the Cabaret-Vert, 5 p.m." (Rimbaud)
See "Au Cabaret-Vert cinq heures du soir"
"At the Café Door" (Cavafy) **36**:67
"at the cemetary walnut grove plantation south carolina 1989" (Clifton) **17**:30
"At the Center" (Stone) **53**:230
"At the Centre" (Gunn) **26**:226
"At the Chelsea Arts Club" (Mahon) **60**:237
"At the Close" (Meredith) **60**:250
"At the Corner of the Field" (Amichai) **38**:22
"At the Désespérade" (Char)
See "À la désespérade"
"At the Dime Store" (Kenyon) **57**:45
"At the Edge" (Tomlinson) **17**:343, 345
"At the End of Sirmione" (Wright) **36**:378
"At the Executed Murderer's Grave" (Wright) **36**:291, 303, 315, 324, 337, 353, 362, 373-74, 399
"At the Fall of an Age" (Jeffers) **17**:141, 144
"At the Faucet of June" (Williams) **7**:382-83, 387-89, 410
"At the Feeder" (Kenyon) **57**:39
"At the feet of others I did not forget" (Lermontov)
See "U nog drugikh ne zabyval"
"At the Ferocious phenomenon of 5 O'clock I find Myself" (Cummings) **5**:93
"At the Fillmore" (Levine) **22**:224
"At the Fishhouses" (Bishop) **3**:42, 46, 48; **34**:57-8, 61, 97, 101, 105-05, 133-34, 144, 181-85, 189
"At the Funeral of Great-Aunt Mary" (Bly) **39**:11
"At the Gare Bruxelles-Midi" (Ferlinghetti) **1**:183
"At the Gate of the Valley" (Herbert) **50**:34
"At the Gates of the Tombs" (Sandburg) **2**:307; **41**:271, 314
At the German Meetingplace (Éluard)
See *Au rendez-vous allemand*
"At the German Writers Conference in Munich" (Dove) **6**:109
"At the Granite Gate" (Carman) **34**:213
"At the Grave of Henry Vaughan" (Sassoon) **12**:246-47
"At the Great Release" (Carman) **34**:226
"At the Hairdresser's" (Brooks) **7**:58, 68, 86, 102
"At the Head of This Street a Gasping Organ is Waving Moth-" (Cummings) **5**:93
"At the Hemingway Memorial" (Wagoner) **33**:348
"At the Hour of the Breaking of the Rocks" (Warren) **37**:331
"At the IGA: Franklin, New Hampshire" (Kenyon) **57**:45
"At the Indian Killer's Grave" (Lowell) **3**:202
"At the Lincoln Monument in Washington, August 28, 1963" (Walker) **20**:277-78
"At the Loom: Passages 2" (Duncan) **2**:107
"At the Mouth of a Creek" (Wagoner) **33**:374
"At the Museum, 1938" (Stone) **53**:257
"At the Museum of Modern Art" (Swenson) **14**:265
"At the National Black Assembly" (Baraka) **4**:28, 38
"At the Old Place" (O'Hara) **45**:115, 126
"At the Piano" (Hardy) **8**:93
"At the Pool" (Mahon) **60**:190
"At the Public Market Museum: Charleston, South Carolina" (Kenyon) **57**:6, 23
"At the Railroad Station on an Autumn Morning" (Carducci)
See "Alla Stazione in una Mattina d'Autunno"
"At the River Charles" (Viereck) **27**:282
"At the Screen Door" (Komunyakaa) **51**:24-25
"At the Slackening of the Tide" (Wright) **36**:281-82, 299, 324
"At the Sources of the Clitumnus" (Carducci)
See "Alle fonti del Clitumno"
"At the Station on an Autumn Morning" (Carducci)
See "Alla Stazione in una Mattina d'Autunno"
"At the Summer Solstice" (Kenyon) **57**:4
"At the Theatre" (Cavafy) **36**:41, 42
"At the Tomb of the Czech Kings" (Seifert) **47**:326
"At the Tourist Centre in Boston" (Atwood) **8**:5, 23
"At the Town Dump" (Kenyon) **57**:39-40
At the Very Edge of the Sea (Akhmatova)
See *U samovo morya*
"At the Voice of a Bird" (Carman) **34**:210
"At the Well" (Piercy) **29**:300
"At The-Place-of-Sadness" (Gallagher) **9**:64
"At This Point" (Montale)
See "A questo punto"
"At Tintagel" (Teasdale) **31**:335
"At Utter Loaf" (Riley) **48**:334
"At Waking" (Hardy) **8**:104
"At Welsh's Tomb" (Wakoski) **15**:353
"At Zime Junction Once More" (Yevtushenko) **40**:351-52
Atalanta in Calydon (Swinburne) **24**:340
"Atalanta's Race" (Morris) **55**:242, 249
Atarashiki yokujō (Hagiwara) **18**:175
"Atardeceres" (Borges) **32**:60, 102-03, 124
"Atavism" (Wylie) **23**:301, 307
"Atavismo" (Pavese) **13**:209, 214
Atemwende (Celan) **10**:96-7, 105, 110
"AThe Miracle" (Bukowski) **18**:5
"Athena in the front lines" (Piercy) **29**:313, 317
"Athene's Song" (Boland) **58**:42
"Atherton's Gambit" (Robinson) **1**:466
"Ations" (Silverstein) **49**:331, 335
"Atlanta in Camden Town" (Carroll) **18**:46
Atlanta Offering Poems (Harper) **21**:189
"The Atlantic" (Tomlinson) **17**:333
"Atlantic City Waiter" (Cullen) **20**:52, 64
"Atlantic Coast Reggae" (Jordan) **38**:132
"Atlantic Door" (Birney) **52**:35, 92
"Atlantic Oil" (Pavese) **13**:223
"The Atlantides" (Thoreau) **30**:203
"Atlantis" (Crane) **3**:90, 97, 106, 110-11
"Atlantis" (Szymborska) **44**:300
Atlantis (Doty) **53**:47, 49, 51, 53-55, 61, 63, 65-66
"An Atlas of the Difficult World" (Rich) **5**:398
An Atlas of the Difficult World: Poems, 1988-1991 (Rich) **5**:398-99
Atta Troll: Ein Sommernachtstraum (Heine) **25**:132-34, 137-38, 164
"Attack" (Sassoon) **12**:266, 283-84, 286
"An Attempt at a Room" (Tsvetaeva)
See "Popytka komnaty"
"An Attempt at Jealousy" (Tsvetaeva)
See "Popytka revnosti"
"Attention, Attention" (Baraka) **4**:24
"Attibon Legba" (Brathwaite) **56**:75
"The Attic" (Mahon) **60**:141, 155, 187, 228
"Attic" (Sikelianos) **29**:368
"The Attic Which Is Desire" (Williams) **7**:351, 399
"Attis" (Tennyson) **6**:363
"Atumpan" (Brathwaite) **56**:100
"Atys, the Land of Biscay" (Housman) **2**:179, 181
"Au Cabaret-Vert cinq heures du soir" (Rimbaud) **57**:203, 241, 244, 253
"Au caberet-vert" (Rimbaud) **3**:283
"Au Clair de la lune" (MacDiarmid) **9**:191
"Au Comte d'Orsay" (Lamartine) **16**:267
"Au cœur de mon amour" (Éluard) **38**:70
"Au lecteur" (Baudelaire) **1**:46, 57, 67, 70
"Au platane" (Valéry) **9**:365, 394-96
"Au Rendez-vous allemand" (Éluard) **38**:63
Au rendez-vous allemand (Éluard) **38**:79
"Au revoir" (Éluard) **38**:67
"Au Rossignol" (Lamartine) **16**:280
"Au Roy" (Ronsard)
See "Discours au Roy"
"Au Salon" (Pound) **4**:364
"Aubade" (Glück) **16**:133
"Aubade" (Larkin) **21**:259
"Aubade" (Lowell) **13**:93
"Aubade" (Sitwell) **3**:297
"Aubade" (Smith) **12**:331
"Aubade for Hope" (Warren) **37**:282-84, 366, 377
"Aubade: Harlem" (Merton) **10**:340
"Aubade: Lake Erie" (Merton) **10**:333, 340, 350
"Aubade: Opal and Silver" (Doty) **53**:54
"Aubade—The Annunciation" (Merton) **10**:339
"Aube" (Rimbaud) **3**:261-62, 264; **57**:174, 228, 239, 244, 250, 275, 284
"L'Aube a l'envers" (Verlaine) **32**:378
"Aube, fille des larmes, rétablis" (Bonnefoy) **58**:167
"L'aube spirituelle" (Baudelaire) **1**:56, 63
"Aubépine" (Char) **56**:120
"L'Auberge" (Verlaine) **32**:375-76
"The Auction" (Kinnell) **26**:286
"Audacity of the Lower Gods" (Komunyakaa) **51**:30
"Auden and MacNeice: their Last Will and Testament" (MacNeice) **61**:171
Au-Dessus du vent (Char) **56**:117
"Auditors In" (Kavanagh) **33**:62, 99, 121-2, 137, 148, 161
"Audley Court" (Tennyson) **6**:365
"Audubon" (Niedecker) **42**:152
Audubon, A Vision (Warren) **37**:307-8, 310, 313, 326-28, 330, 334, 340, 345-50, 358-59, 361, 363, 366, 371, 373, 381, 384
"Auf dem See" (Goethe) **5**:255
"Aufblick" (Benn) **35**:50
"The Augsburg Adoration" (Jarrell) **41**:180, 197
"Auguri per Proprio Compleanno" (Ungaretti) **57**:376

"Auguries of Innocence" (Blake) **12**:35-6
"Augurios" (Paz) **1**:361
"August" (Belloc) **24**:29
"August" (Rich) **5**:371
"August" (Riley) **48**:309
"August" (Wylie) **23**:319, 322, 332
"August 9th 1" (Thumboo) **30**:332
"August 9th 2" (Thumboo) **30**:333
"August 19th..." (Hughes) **53**:114
"August 22, 1939" (Rexroth) **20**:195
"August First" (Carruth) **10**:91
"August Journal" (Hacker) **47**:104, 106, 116
"An August Midnight" (Hardy) **8**:112
"August Night" (Swenson) **14**:266, 284
"August Night" (Teasdale) **31**:335
"August on Sourdough, A Visit from Dick Brewer" (Snyder) **21**:288
"August Rain, After Haying" (Kenyon) **57**:11, 41, 43
"August Revival: Crosby Junction" (Warren) **37**:331
"August Sun" (Bly) **39**:70
"August Was Foggy" (Snyder) **21**:288
Aujourd'hui (Hugo) **17**:80
"Aul Bastundzi" (Lermontov) **18**:300
"The Auld Farmer's New Year Morning Salutation" (Burns)
See "The Auld Farmer's New Year's Day Address to His Auld Mare Maggie"
"The Auld Farmer's New Year's Day Address to His Auld Mare Maggie" (Burns) **6**:78
"Auld Lang Syne" (Burns) **6**:59, 75, 98-9
"AÚN" (Darío) **15**:98
Aún (Neruda) **4**:289
Auncient Aqueyntaunce (Skelton) **25**:345, 351
"Aunque cegué de mirarte" (Juana Inés de la Cruz) **24**:187
"Aunt Chloe's Politics" (Harper) **21**:200, 202, 213
"Aunt Sue's Stories" (Hughes) **53**:82, 118
"Aunts" (McGuckian) **27**:95
"La aurora" (García Lorca) **3**:141
"Aurora Borealis" (Dove) **6**:110
Aurora Leigh (Browning) **6**:2, 6-7, 10-13, 21-3, 25-6, 31-2, 34-8, 40, 44, 46
"The Auroras of Autumn" (Roethke) **15**:280
"The Auroras of Autumn" (Stevens) **6**:338
Auroras of Autumn (Stevens) **6**:303, 335
"Aurore" (Valéry) **9**:356, 363, 365, 367-68, 371, 394, 396
"Aus der Harzreise" (Heine) **25**:139
"Aus einer Sturmnacht" (Rilke) **2**:277
"Auschwitz" (Quasimodo) **47**:287
"Ausencia" (Borges) **22**:94; **32**:60, 82
Ausgewahlte gedichte (Celan) **10**:102
"Auspice of Jewels" (Jackson) **44**:12
"Aussenminister" (Benn) **35**:58
"Aussi bien que les cigales" (Apollinaire) **7**:18, 22
"Aussöhnung" (Goethe) **5**:250-51
"Australia" (Hope) **56**:266, 283
"The Author to her Book" (Bradstreet) **10**:7, 18, 27, 34
"The Author upon Himself" (Swift) **9**:295-96, 304, 306, 308-09
The Authors Dreame to the Ladie Marie the Countesse Dowager of Pembrooke (Lanyer) **60**:5, 79, 97, 111-12, 115
"The Author's Earnest Cry and Prayer" (Burns) **6**:78-9
"The Author's Manner of Living" (Swift) **9**:295
"Author's Note on Marabouts and Planted Poets" (Viereck) **27**:259, 262
"Author's Prologue" (Thomas) **52**:226, 237, 263, 277, 290, 303-4
"Auto Wreck" (Shapiro) **25**:279, 288, 297, 312, 319, 325
"Autobiografía" (Fuertes) **27**:49
"Autobiographia literaria" (O'Hara) **45**:177
"Autobiographies" (Mahon) **60**:160
"Autobiography" (Ferlinghetti) **1**:177-80, 183-84, 187
"Autobiography" (Gunn) **26**:205, 208
"Autobiography" (Harjo) **27**:71
"Autobiography" (MacLeish) **47**:193
"Autobiography" (MacNeice) **61**:110, 135, 168-69
Autobiography (Zukofsky) **11**:365
"Autobiography of the Present" (Jackson) **44**:96
"Autochthon" (Masters) **1**:333; **36**:177
"Automatism of Taste" (Tzara) **27**:235
"The Automaton" (Jarrell) **41**:127
"Automne" (Apollinaire) **7**:42
"L'automne" (Lamartine) **16**:277, 290, 298, 301
"Automne" (Verlaine) **32**:400-02, 404-06
"Automne malade" (Apollinaire) **7**:39, 42-3
"Autoprólogo" (Fuertes) **27**:23
"Autopsicografia" (Pessoa) **20**:172
"The Autopsy" (Elytis) **21**:123
"The Autopsy Room" (Carver) **54**:14
"Autopsychography" (Pessoa)
See "Autopsicografia"
"Autoretrato" (Parra) **39**:270, 300
"Autorretrato barroco" (Storni) **33**:293-94, 296;
"Autre complainte de Lord Pierrot" (Laforgue) **14**:81, 97
Autre complainte de Lord Pierrot (Laforgue) **14**:62, 88
"Autre complainte de l'orgue de barbarie" (Laforgue) **14**:81, 98
"Une autre voix" (Bonnefoy) **58**:174
Autrefois (Hugo) **17**:80
"Autumn" (Dickey) **40**:186
"Autumn" (Ignatow) **34**:322
"The Autumn" (Lamartine)
See "L'automne"
"Autumn" (Lowell) **13**:97
"Autumn" (Neruda)
See "Otoño"
"Autumn" (Pasternak) **6**:266
"Autumn" (Paz)
See "Otoño"
"Autumn" (Smith) **12**:345
"Autumn" (Thoreau) **30**:286
"Autumn" (Tomlinson) **17**:339
"Autumn 1980" (Hacker) **47**:105
"Autumn Begins in Martins Ferry, Ohio" (Wright) **36**:324, 339-40, 374, 389-90
"An Autumn Burning" (Berry) **28**:9
"Autumn Cellars" (Montale) **13**:149-50
"Autumn Cove Song # 5" (Li Po) **29**:145
"Autumn Equinox" (Rich) **5**:351-52, 393
"Autumn Evening" (Merwin) **45**:88
"Autumn Forest" (Pasternak) **6**:267
"Autumn Gold: New England Fall" (Ginsberg) **4**:54
"Autumn I" (Ignatow) **34**:306
"Autumn in California" (Rexroth) **20**:194, 214
"Autumn in Funland" (Abse) **41**:30
"Autumn in Prague" (Muir) **49**:228, 238
"Autumn Journal" (MacNeice) **61**:144-45
Autumn Journal (MacNeice) **61**:106-7, 109-10, 115, 123-26, 134, 148-55, 161, 163-66, 172-73, 175, 180-82, 185-86
"Autumn Lament" (Mallarmé)
See "Plainte d'automne"
"Autumn Meditation" (Wang Wei) **18**:343
"Autumn Movement" (Sandburg) **41**:313
"Autumn (Parc Monceau)" (Teasdale) **31**:339
Autumn Sequel (MacNeice) **61**:127-28, 162-66, 181-82
"Autumn Sequence" (Rich) **5**:363, 382
"Autumn Song" (Darío)
See "Canción otoñal"
"Autumn Song" (Verlaine)
See "Chanson d'automne"
"The Autumn Sonnets" (Sarton) **39**:340, 360-1
"Autumn Valentine" (Parker) **28**:365
"Autumnal" (Darío) **15**:117
Autumnal Leaves (Hugo) **17**:44
"Autunno romantico" (Carducci) **46**:48, 77, 80
"Auvergnat" (Belloc) **24**:34
"Aux arbres" (Bonnefoy) **58**:130-33
"Aux Chrétiens" (Lamartine) **16**:280
"Aux Ecluses du vide" (Césaire) **25**:12
"Aux ruines de Montfort-L'Amaury" (Hugo) **17**:89
"Avant-dernier mot" (Laforgue) **14**:95
"L'avant-Glanum" (Char) **56**:177
"Avanti! Avanti!" (Carducci) **46**:28, 50
"Avarice" (Herbert) **4**:102, 130
"Ave" (Rossetti) **44**:207-8
"Ave atque Vale" (Swinburne) **24**:321, 330-35, 337
"Ave Imperatrix!" (Kipling) **3**:190
"Ave Maria" (Crane) **3**:84, 86
"Ave Maria" (O'Hara) **45**:115, 147, 171-74, 207-8, 218
"Avec Ardeur" (Moore)
See "Occasionem Cognosce"
"Avenel Gray" (Robinson)
See "Mortmain"
"Avenue" (Pinsky) **27**:175
"The Avenue Bearing the Initial of Christ into the New World" (Kinnell) **26**:236-37, 239, 241, 257, 262, 264, 289
"Avenue of Limes" (Pasternak) **6**:267
"The Avenue of Poplars" (Williams) **7**:382
"Averroes's Search" (Borges)
See "La busca de Averroes"
"L'Aveugle Prédestiné tourne de lex dos aux passants" (Éluard) **38**:91
"Aviary" (McGuckian) **27**:81, 98
"Avila 1" (Yau) **61**:333
"Avila 4" (Yau) **61**:331
"Avis de tirs" (Césaire) **25**:29
"Aviso" (Parra) **39**:272
"Aviso a los gobernantes del mundo" (Fuertes) **27**:2
"Avisos" (Pessoa) **20**:162
"Avocado Lake" (Soto) **28**:375, 379
"Avoiding News by the River" (Merwin) **45**:21, 60
"Avon" (Carman)
See "Low Tide on Avon"
"Avondale" (Smith) **12**:352
"Avondall" (Smith) **12**:352
Avon's Harvest (Robinson) **1**:465-66, 468-69, 483
"Avtobus" (Tsvetaeva) **14**:325, 327
Awake in the Red Desert (Bissett) **14**:12, 14, 18-19
"Awake, my heart, to be loved: awake, awake" (Bridges) **28**:53, 63, 87
"Awakening" (Bly) **39**:11, 84, 90
"The Awakening" (Brathwaite) **56**:8
"Awakening" (Herbert) **50**:19
"Awakening" (Stryk) **27**:184, 186-87, 189, 206, 213
Awakening (Stryk) **27**:181, 195-98, 202-3, 213-16
"Awakening of the Waterfall" (Tagore)
See "Nirjharer svapnabhanga"
"Away!" (Frost) **39**:237
"Away" (Riley) **48**:289, 325
"Away! Away! Away! Away!" (Thoreau) **30**:203, 240, 265
"Away, Melancholy" (Smith) **12**:333
"Awe and Devastation of Solomos" (Elytis) **21**:135
"Awful Music" (Merton) **10**:337
The Awful Rowing Toward God (Sexton) **2**:360, 367-68, 371-73
"AWOL" (Abse) **41**:31
"The Awthorn" (Clare) **23**:46-7
"Axe Handles" (Snyder) **21**:308
Axe Handles (Snyder) **21**:299-302, 307-10, 320
"The Ax-Helve" (Frost) **1**:215; **39**:235
The Axion Esti (Elytis) **21**:118, 120-30, 133
"Axis" (Paz) **48**:188
"Axum" (Brathwaite) **56**:29
"Ay negra, si tu supiera" (Guillén) **23**:111, 142
"Ay qué tristeza que tengo!" (Guillén) **23**:119-20, 127

"Aye, Black Lover, If You Only Knew" (Guillén)
See "Ay negra, si tu supiera"
"Ayer Biru" (Thumboo) **30**:321
"Ayer me dijeron negro" (Guillén) **23**:142
"Ayíasma" (Ekeloef) **23**:64
"Aylmer's Field" (Tennyson) **6**:362
"Aymerillot" (Hugo) **17**:58
"The Azalea" (Patmore) **59**:209, 215, 239
Ázma iroikó ke pénthimo yia ton haméno anthipolohaghó tis Alvanías (Elytis) **21**:115, 120, 124, 127-29
"Azrail" (Lermontov) **18**:300
"Azucena" (Alurista) **34**:22
Azul (Darío) **15**:78, 86-7, 91-2, 94-6, 102-03, 105-07, 115, 117-18, 120
"L'azur" (Mallarmé) **4**:199-200, 208, 213
"The Azure" (Mallarmé)
See "L'azur"
"Azure and Gold" (Lowell) **13**:60
"Babbitry" (Stryk) **27**:211
"The Babe" (Olson) **19**:319-20
"Babi Yar" (Yevtushenko) **40**:339, 343-46, 350, 352, 368, 370
Babi Yar (Yevtushenko) **40**:356, 359, 365
"Babočka" (Brodsky) **9**:29
"Babord pour tous" (Péret) **33**:230
"Babushka" (Yevtushenko) **40**:340
"The Baby" (Nash) **21**:278
"Baby" (Sexton) **2**:367
"Baby Boom Che" (Alexie) **53**:16
"The Baby Carriage Forgotten near a Shop" (Shvarts)
See "Koliaska, zabytaia u magazina"
"Baby Face" (Sandburg) **41**:296
"Baby Picture" (Sexton) **2**:370
"Baby song" (Gunn) **26**:210
"Baby Tortoise" (Lawrence) **54**:187
"Baby V" (Levine)
See "Baby Villon"
"Baby Villon" (Levine) **22**:213
"Babyhood" (Swinburne) **24**:323
"Babylon Revisited" (Baraka) **4**:18
"Baccalaureate" (MacLeish) **47**:182
"The Bacchae" (H. D.) **5**:305
"The Bacchae Sonnets" (Schwerner) **42**:196
"Bacchanales" (Ronsard) **11**:230-32, 234
"Bacchanalia" (Pasternak) **6**:267
"Bacchic" (Cavafy) **36**:52
"Bacchus" (Emerson) **18**:85, 99, 103, 106
"Bacchus and his crew" (Cavafy) **36**:57
"Bacchus and the Pirates" (Noyes) **27**:121, 124-25, 133
"Bachelor" (Meredith) **28**:189
"Bachelor Uncle" (Wright) **14**:348
"Back" (Kenyon) **57**:36
"Back Again, Home" (Madhubuti) **5**:324, 329, 338
The Back Country (Snyder) **21**:288, 291-92, 296, 300
"Back from a Walk" (García Lorca)
See "Vuelta de paseo"
"Back from the City" (Kenyon) **57**:4, 39
"back in th city" (Bissett) **14**:30
"The Back o' Beyond" (MacDiarmid) **9**:196
"Back Then" (Komunyakaa) **51**:30
"Back to Life" (Gunn) **26**:192, 212
"Back to the Mother Breast" (Jackson) **44**:61
"The Back-Again" (MacNeice) **61**:121
"Backdrop Addresses Cowboy" (Atwood) **8**:4, 16, 41
"Background Noises" (Szirtes) **51**:171
"Background with Revolutionaries" (MacLeish) **47**:189, 240-41, 255
"The Backlash Blues" (Hughes) **1**:251, 257
Backpack Notes (Matsuo Bashō)
See *Oi no kobumi*
"The Backside of the Academy" (Rukeyser) **12**:236
"Backtracking" (Wagoner) **33**:339
"Backward Bill" (Silverstein) **49**:327
"The Backward Look" (Nemerov) **24**:287, 301
"Backyard" (Ignatow) **34**:306, 309
"Backyard" (Wright) **14**:377
"The Bacterial War" (Nemerov) **24**:298
"A Bad, Bad Man" (Brown) **55**:102, 104, 122
"Bad Blood" (Rimbaud)
See "Mauvais sang"
Bad Boys (Cisneros) **52**:156
The Bad Child's Book of Beasts (Belloc) **24**:12, 23-6, 35
"Bad Dreams" (Browning) **2**:59
"Bad Dreams" (Pinsky) **27**:145
"Bad Faith" (Cavafy) **36**:86, 117
"The Bad Glazier" (Baudelaire)
See "Le mauvais vitrier"
"Bad Man" (Hughes) **1**:270; **53**:82, 138-39
"Bad Morning" (Hughes) **1**:241
"Bad Ol' Stagolee" (Walker) **20**:287
"The Bad Old Days" (Rexroth) **20**:218
The Bad Parents' Garden of Verse (Nash) **21**:264-65
"Bad Penny" (Levine) **22**:218
"The Bad Season Makes the Poet Sad" (Herrick) **9**:89, 103, 109, 115
"Bad Times" (Oppen) **35**:289
"Bad War: a New Year's Card" (Warren) **37**:306
"Badger" (Clare) **23**:7
"The Badgers" (Heaney) **18**:219, 244
"Bad-Man Stagolee" (Walker)
See "Bad Ol' Stagolee"
"Bagabonds" (Rimbaud) **57**:191
"The Bagel" (Ignatow) **34**:204, 207, 305, 308
"Bagpipe Music" (MacNeice) **61**:133-34, 137, 157
"Baha'u'llah in the Garden of Ridwan" (Hayden) **6**:185-86, 196, 198
"Bahia, Brazil" (Carver) **54**:22, 24
"Bahnhofstrasse" (Joyce) **22**:137
"Bahu" (Tagore) **8**:407
"Baignée" (Valéry) **9**:392
"La bailerina de los pies desnudos" (Darío) **15**:80
"Le baiser" (Char) **15**:138, 144, 171
"Le Baiser" (Éluard) **38**:62
"Bajdary" (Mickiewicz) **38**:166
Bajo tu clara sombra y otros poemas sobre España (Paz) **48**:179-81, 244
"Bakche-Sarai" (Mickiewicz)
See "Bakczysaraj"
The Bak-Chesarian fountain: A Tale of the Tauride (Pushkin)
See *Bakhchisaraiski Fontan*
"Bakczysaraj" (Mickiewicz) **38**:149
The Bakhchisarai Fontan (Pushkin)
See *Bakhchisaraiski Fontan*
Bakhchisaraiski Fontan (Pushkin) **10**:358, 365, 386-88, 411, 417, 419, 421
"Bakhchisaray by Night" (Mickiewicz) **38**:223
"Le Bal" (Vigny) **26**:410-11
"Bal des pendus" (Rimbaud) **3**:281, 283; **57**:243, 289, 291-92
"Balada" (Mistral) **32**:152, 176
"Balada arrítmica para un viajero" (Storni) **33**:268;
"La balada azul" (Guillén) **23**:100, 140
"Balada de los dos abuelos" (Guillén) **23**:103, 132, 138
"Balada del güje" (Guillén) **23**:131-2
Baladas de primavera (Jiménez) **7**:184
Balākā (Tagore) **8**:413-15, 418, 427
"Balakhana" (McGuckian) **27**:82, 93
"The Balance" (Wagoner) **33**:369
"A Balanced Bait in Handy Pellet Form" (Curnow) **48**:16, 18, 38
"Balanchine's" (Merrill) **28**:254
"Le balcon" (Baudelaire) **1**:45, 63
"Los balcones del Oriente" (Guillén) **35**:233, 234
"The Balcony" (Baudelaire)
See "Le balcon"
"Balcony Scene" (Shapiro) **25**:316
"Balder Dead" (Arnold) **5**:35, 37, 58-9, 62
"Balin and Balan" (Tennyson) **6**:376-77
"Balkan Ballad" (Shvarts) **50**:148
"Ball" (Benn) **35**:50
"Ballad" (Ammons) **16**:25
"Ballad" (Mistral)
See "Balada"
"Ballad" (Oppen) **35**:324
"Ballad" (Pasternak) **6**:270
"A Ballad" (Suckling)
See "A Ballade. Upon a Wedding"
"A Ballad about Benkendorf, Chief of Gendarmerie, and Lermontov's Poem 'Death of a Poet'" (Yevtushenko) **40**:352
"Ballad Fourth: The Trogger" (Burns) **6**:78
"Ballad of a Sweet Dream of Peace" (Warren) **37**:332
"Ballad of a Thin Man" (Dylan) **37**:51
"Ballad of a Willful Woman" (Lawrence) **54**:204-5
"Ballad of Army Wagons" (Tu Fu) **9**:330
"The Ballad of Ballymote" (Gallagher) **9**:42
"The Ballad of Beautiful Words" (Nash) **21**:273
"A Ballad of Beauty and Time" (Boland) **58**:45, 98-99
"The Ballad of Billie Potts" (Warren) **37**:286-89, 312, 324-25, 331-34, 340, 348, 370, 376, 379-80, 382
"A Ballad of Boding" (Rossetti) **7**:271
"Ballad of Carmilhan" (Longfellow) **30**:25
"The Ballad of Chocolate Mabbie" (Brooks) **7**:57, 68, 102, 104
"The Ballad of East and West" (Kipling) **3**:157, 182-83, 188
"The Ballad of Eternal Life" (Muir) **49**:238
"The Ballad of Everyman" (Muir) **49**:257
"Ballad of Faith" (Williams) **7**:363
"The Ballad of Father Hudson" (Carman) **34**:225
"The Ballad of Father O'Hart" (Yeats) **20**:349
"the ballad of Francie Canoye, proofreader" (Niedecker) **42**:101
"A Ballad of François Villon" (Swinburne) **24**:324
"The Ballad of Frankie Lee and Judas Priest" (Dylan) **37**:55
"Ballad of Hector in Hades" (Muir) **49**:204, 213-14, 228-29, 234, 237, 264, 277, 287
"The Ballad of Jakko Hill" (Kipling) **3**:187
"The Ballad of Joe Meek" (Brown) **55**:101, 113, 121-23, 150, 154-55
"The Ballad of Late Annie" (Brooks) **7**:102-04
"The Ballad of Launcelot and Elaine" (Masters) **1**:328; **36**:175
"The Ballad of Margie Polite" (Hughes) **1**:241, 243, 247
"Ballad of Missing Lines" (Rukeyser) **12**:228
"Ballad of Mister Dutcher and the Last Lynching in Gupton" (Warren) **37**:305, 384
"The Ballad of Moll Magee" (Yeats) **20**:337
"Ballad of Mr. Chubb" (Birney) **52**:8, 22, 25, 27-28
"The Ballad of Nat Turner" (Hayden) **6**:176, 178-80, 186-87, 194-95, 198
"A Ballad of Negro History" (Hughes) **53**:115
"Ballad of Oedipus Sex" (Abse) **41**:22
"A Ballad of Past Meridian" (Meredith) **60**:252, 279-80, 330, 334
"Ballad of Pearl May Lee" (Brooks) **7**:57, 68, 86, 103-04
"Ballad of Rebirth" (Muir) **49**:237-38
"A Ballad of Remembrance" (Hayden) **6**:200
A Ballad of Remembrance (Hayden) **6**:183, 188, 194-95
"Ballad of Roosevelt" (Hughes) **53**:115
"The Ballad of Rudolph Reed" (Brooks) **7**:62, 96
"A Ballad of Sark" (Swinburne) **24**:313
"Ballad of Simón Caraballo" (Guillén) **23**:106
The Ballad of St. Barbara and Other Verses (Chesterton) **28**:96-97
"The Ballad of Sue Ellen Westerfield" (Hayden) **6**:196

"The Ballad of the Big Stamp" (Yevtushenko) **40**:369-70
"Ballad of the Black Sorrow" (García Lorca)
See "Romance de la pena negra"
"The Ballad of the Bolivar" (Kipling) **3**:164
"The Ballad of the Brown Girl" (Cullen) **20**:55, 64, 85-86
"Ballad of the Brown Girl" (Walker) **30**:347, 365
The Ballad of the Brown Girl: An Old Ballad Retold (Cullen) **20**:61, 77, 79, 86
"The Ballad of the Children of the Czar" (Schwartz) **8**:302, 305, 309
"Ballad of the Dark Trouble" (García Lorca)
See "Romance de la pena negra"
"Ballad of the Five Senses" (MacDiarmid) **9**:157, 193
"Ballad of the Flood" (Muir) **49**:211-12, 217, 224, 228, 237, 287
"Ballad of the Free" (Walker) **20**:276, 284, 292
"Ballad of the Girl Whose Name Is Mud" (Hughes) **53**:124
"Ballad of the Güije" (Guillén)
See "Balada del güje"
"The Ballad of the Harp-Weaver" (Millay) **6**:211, 225, 233
"Ballad of the Hoppy Toad" (Walker) **20**:290-92
"Ballad of the Jollie Gleeman" (Viereck) **27**:259
"The Ballad of the King's Jest" (Kipling) **3**:182
"Ballad of The Ladies of Past Times" (Villon)
See "Ballade des Dames du Temps Jadis"
"Ballad of the Landlord" (Hughes) **1**:258, 267; **53**:191
"Ballad of the Little Square" (García Lorca)
See "Ballada de la Placeta"
"The Ballad of the Lonely Masturbator" (Sexton) **2**:352, 370
"The Ballad of the Long-Legged Bait" (Thomas) **2**:382, 393, 402; **52**:255
"Ballad of the Moon, the Moon" (García Lorca)
See "Romance de la luna, luna"
"The Ballad of the Red Earl" (Kipling) **3**:181-82
"Ballad of the River Spirit" (Guillén)
See "Balada del güje"
"Ballad of the Seven Songs: A Poem for Emancipation Day" (Hughes) **53**:114
"Ballad of the Sixties" (Sarton) **39**:344
"Ballad of the Soul" (Muir) **49**:214-15, 217, 228, 238
"Ballad of the Spanish Civil Guard" (García Lorca)
See "Romance de la Guardia Civil Española"
"Ballad of the Summoned Man" (García Lorca) **3**:147
"The Ballad of the True Beast" (Hayden) **6**:196-97
"Ballad of the Two Grandfathers" (Guillén)
See "Balada de los dos abuelos"
The Ballad of the White Horse (Chesterton) **28**:93, 100, 105-08, 119-28
"Ballad of the World Extinct" (Celan)
See "Ballade von der erloschenen Welt"
"The Ballad of Trees and the Master" (Lanier) **50**:56, 81, 93, 101
"The Ballad of Valès-Dunes" (Belloc) **24**:11
"Ballad upon a Wedding" (Suckling)
See "A Ballade. Upon a Wedding"
"A Ballad Upon a Wedding" (Suckling)
See "A Ballade. Upon a Wedding"
"Ballad Written in a Clinic" (Montale)
See "Ballata scritta in una clinica"
"Ballada de la Placeta" (García Lorca) **3**:125
"Ballade" (Dunbar) **5**:139-40
"Ballade" (Gautier) **18**:348-51
"Ballade" (Stryk) **27**:191
The Ballade (Suckling)
See "A Ballade. Upon a Wedding"
"Ballade de bon conseil" (Villon) **13**:394-95
"Ballade de bonne doctrine à ceux de mauvaise vie" (Villon) **13**:394-95, 404-05
"Ballade de conclusion" (Villon) **13**:417
"Ballade de la Grosse Margot" (Villon) **13**:389-90, 393
"Ballade de mercy" (Villon) **13**:399, 413
"Ballade des contre verites" (Villon) **13**:414
"Ballade des Dames du Temps Jadis" (Villon) **13**:374, 405, 409-10
"Ballade des femmes de Paris" (Villon) **13**:380, 390, 413
"Ballade des Langues Envieuses" (Villon) **13**:404
"Ballade des menus propos" (Villon) **13**:409
"Ballade des Pendus" (Villon)
See "Epitaphe Villon"
"Ballade des proverbes" (Villon) **13**:404, 414
Ballade des seigneurs du temps jadis (Villon) **13**:410
"Ballade du concours de Blois" (Villon) **13**:392, 414
"La ballade du Mal Aimé" (Apollinaire)
See "La chanson du mal-aimé"
"Ballade d'une grande dame" (Chesterton) **28**:117
"Ballade for the Duke of Orleans" (Wilbur) **51**:221-22, 262, 273, 293, 301, 311
"Ballade of a Talked-off Ear" (Parker) **28**:363
"Ballade of Big Plans" (Parker) **28**:354
"Ballade of Dead Ladies" (Villon) **13**:387, 390-91
"Ballade of Fat Margot" (Villon)
See "Ballade de la Grosse Margot"
"Ballade of Hell and Mrs Roebeck" (Belloc) **24**:49
"A Ballade of Interesting News" (Belloc) **24**:42
"A Ballade of Suicide" (Chesterton) **28**:99
"Ballade of the Critic" (Shapiro) **25**:281
"Ballade of the Hanged" (Villon)
See "Epitaphe Villon"
"Ballade of the Women of Paris" (Villon)
See "Ballade des femmes de Paris"
"Ballade of Unfortunate Mammals" (Parker) **28**:351, 363
"Ballade pour prier Nostre Dame" (Villon) **13**:403, 405, 413
"Ballade pour Robert d'Estouteville" (Villon) **13**:395, 415
"Ballade to Our Lady" (Villon) **13**:390-91
"A Ballade. Upon a Wedding" (Suckling) **30**:119-20, 122, 148, 151-53, 155-56
"Ballade vom Auszug der drei" (Celan) **10**:126
"Ballade von der erloschenen Welt" (Celan) **10**:125
Ballades en Jargon (Villon) **13**:404, 406
"Ballads" (Hughes) **53**:101
Ballads, and Other Poems (Longfellow) **30**:107
Ballads and Poems of Tragic Life (Meredith) **60**:263, 292, 294, 327
Ballads and Romances (Mickiewicz)
See *Ballady i Romanse*
Ballads for Sale (Lowell) **13**:76, 84-5
Ballads of Lost Haven (Carman) **34**:205, 207, 211-13
Ballads of Spring (Jiménez)
See *Baladas de primavera*
"Ballads of the Traveler" (Sarton) **39**:345-46
Ballady i Romanse (Mickiewicz) **38**:157, 162, 164, 189
"Ballata Dolorossa" (Carducci) **46**:23
"Ballata scritta in una clinica" (Montale) **13**:108, 131, 167
"The Ballet" (Meredith) **28**:193, 215
"Ballet" (Pavese)
See "Balletto"
"Ballet" (Stone) **53**:228
"Balletto" (Pavese) **13**:205, 226
"Balloon" (Ní Chuilleanáin) **34**:350
"Balloon Faces" (Sandburg) **41**:276
"Balloons" (Plath) **1**:391; **37**:258
"The Ballroom at Sandover" (Merrill) **28**:235
"Balsa Wood" (Carver) **54**:12
"Baltasar Gracián" (Borges) **32**:132
"Baltazar" (Alurista) **34**:22
Balustion's Adventure (Browning) **2**:85-6, 95
"Bamberg" (Jarrell) **41**:197
"Bamboo" (Hagiwara)
See "Take"
"The Bamboo Flute" (Hope) **56**:291
"Bamboo Lodge" (Wang Wei) **18**:382
Banabani (Tagore) **8**:416
"Banane" (Benn) **35**:8, 50
"Banaphul" (Tagore) **8**:405
"Le Banc d'ocre" (Char) **56**:155
"Band Concert" (Sandburg) **41**:240
"The Bandaged Shoulder" (Cavafy) **36**:39, 41, 42
"La Bande Noire" (Hugo) **17**:87-88
"Bandi" (Tagore) **8**:407, 412
"Bandot" (Stryk) **27**:204-5
"The Bands and the Beautiful Children" (Page) **12**:169, 177
Bandusia Ode (Horace) **46**:127
"Banga bir" (Tagore) **8**:407
"Bangkok Boy" (Birney) **52**:60-61, 69
"The Bangkok Gong" (Kumin) **15**:213
"The Bangs" (Montale)
See "La frangia dei capelli"
"The Banished Gods" (Mahon) **60**:151, 190, 207
"Banishment" (Sassoon) **12**:267, 288
"A Banjo Song" (Dunbar) **5**:146
"A Banjo Song" (Johnson) **24**:136, 141
"Bankashi" (Yakamochi) **48**:133, 137-39
"The Banker's Daughter" (Lowell) **3**:218, 221
"Banking Coal" (Toomer) **7**:333
"Banking Potatoes" (Komunyakaa) **51**:23
"The bankrupt Peace Maker" (Lindsay) **23**:269
"Bankruptcy" (Carver) **54**:29
"Banks of a Stream Where Creatures Bathe" (Merrill) **28**:223, 255
"Banneker" (Dove) **6**:105, 109
"The Banner Bearer" (Williams) **7**:389-90
"The Banners" (Duncan) **2**:102
"Bannières de mai" (Rimbaud) **57**:174, 238, 250
"Banquet" (Gozzano) **10**:183
"The Banquet" (Herbert) **4**:134
The Banquet (Dante)
See *Convivio*
"Bantams in Pine-Woods" (Stevens) **6**:293, 303, 327
"Banyan" (Swenson) **14**:273
"The Banyan Tree, Old Year's Night" (Walcott) **46**:279
"Baptism" (Erdrich) **52**:191
"Baptism" (Herbert) **4**:100; **50**:24
"Baptism" (McKay) **2**:211
Baptism of Desire (Erdrich) **52**:186-87, 189-90, 193-94
"A Baptist Childhood" (Davie) **29**:101, 112
"Bar" (Benn) **35**:71
"A Bar in Manhattan" (Mahon) **60**:146
"Bar Orient" (Yau) **61**:334
Barabajan Poems (Brathwaite) **56**:62
"Barbare" (Césaire) **25**:23-25, 28, 31, 37
"Barbare" (Rimbaud) **3**:261; **57**:175, 228, 232, 240, 247, 253, 284
Barbare (Césaire) **25**:10
"Barbarian" (Rimbaud)
See "Barbare"
Barbaric Odes (Carducci)
See *Odi barbare*
Barbarous Odes (Carducci)
See *Odi barbare*
"Barbecue" (Stryk) **27**:208
"El barco" (Paz) **48**:179-80, 183
"Barco de refugiados" (Cervantes) **35**:108, 130, 132
"The Bard" (Gray) **2**:134-35, 139, 143-44, 146, 148, 151-54
Barddoniaeth Dafydd ab Gwilym (Dafydd ap Gwilym) **56**:232
"The Bards" (Graves) **6**:140, 144
"Bards of Passion and of Mirth" (Keats) **1**:312
"Bare Almond-Trees" (Lawrence) **54**:187

"The Bare Deal Board" (Ní Chuilleanáin) **34**:360
"Bare Fig-Trees" (Lawrence) **54**:187, 194
"Barefoot" (Sexton) **2**:352
A Barefoot Boy (Riley) **48**:340
"The Barefoot Dancer" (Darío)
See "La bailerina de los pies desnudos"
Barely and Widely, 1956-1958 (Zukofsky) **11**:348
"Bargain" (Stone) **53**:229
Barking at the Moon (Hagiwara)
See *Tsuki ni hoeru*
"Barking Hall: A Year After" (Swinburne) **24**:318-19
"Barmaids Are Diviner than Mermaids" (Nash) **21**:265
"The Barn" (Heaney) **18**:194, 200
"The Barn" (Thomas) **53**:329
"Barney Hainsfeather" (Masters) **36**:182
"Barnsley, 1966" (Davie) **29**:102
"Barnsley and District" (Davie) **29**:111
"The Baron of St. Castine" (Longfellow) **30**:62
"Baroque Comment" (Bogan) **12**:90, 92, 97, 101
"A Baroque Sunburst" (Clampitt) **19**:90
"A Baroque Wall-Fountain in the Villa Sciarra" (Wilbur) **51**:192, 195, 217, 250, 300, 314
"Barrabas. Eine Phantasie" (Trakl) **20**:239
Barrack Room Ballads and Other Verses (Kipling) **3**:155-56, 159-60, 163, 165, 167-69, 177, 182, 187-89
"Barrack Street" (Ní Chuilleanáin) **34**:349, 381
"Barrancas del Plata en Colonia" (Storni) **33**:261, 294;
"Barranquilla Bridge" (Birney) **52**:18
"A Barred Owl" (Wilbur) **51**:336
"The Barrel Organ" (Noyes) **27**:115-16, 133, 136-38
"Barren Spring" (Rossetti) **44**:173
"The Barrier" (McKay) **2**:212
"Bar-Room Matins" (MacNeice) **61**:139
"Barry Holden" (Masters) **36**:230
"Barter" (Teasdale) **31**:332, 340, 356, 388
"Bartok" (Illyés) **16**:231
"Baruch Spinoza" (Borges) **32**:68-72
"Basaleg" (Dafydd ap Gwilym) **56**:233
"Basant" (Kabīr) **56**:342, 346
"Base Details" (Sassoon) **12**:268, 277, 280
"The Base Stealer" (Francis) **34**:246, 255
"Baseball and Writing" (Moore) **4**:242, 256, 259-60; **49**:146-47
"Baseball Canto" (Ferlinghetti) **1**:183
"Basement Apartment" (Shapiro) **25**:316
The Basement Tapes (Dylan) **37**:60
"Básežn nejpokornější" (Seifert) **47**:330
Basic Work (Parra)
See *Obra gruesa*
"A Basin of Eggs" (Swenson) **14**:250
"The Basket" (Lowell) **13**:84, 95-6
"Baskets" (Glück) **16**:152
"The Basket-Weaver's Companion" (Char)
See "La compagne du vannier"
"Bas-Relief" (Sandburg) **41**:285
"A Bastard Peace" (Williams) **7**:369
"The Bastille" (Brooke) **24**:66, 80, 84, 89
"The Bat" (Kenyon) **57**:4, 37
"Bat" (Lawrence) **54**:170, 225
"Bateau ivre" (Hugo) **17**:65
Le bateau ivre (Rimbaud) **3**:249, 257-58, 268-70, 272-74, 282, 286; **57**:171-72, 197, 199, 202, 214, 216, 235, 239, 245-47, 249, 251-52, 299-300
"The Bath" (Ríos) **57**:325
"Bath" (Sandburg) **41**:365
"The Bath" (Snyder) **21**:292, 297
"A Bather" (Lowell) **13**:93-6
"The Bathers" (Shapiro) **25**:304
"Bathos" (Pope) **26**:357
"Batjushkov" (Mandelstam) **14**:118
"Batouque" (Césaire) **25**:29
"Bats" (Jarrell) **41**:208
"Battalion-Relief" (Sassoon) **12**:269
"The Battle" (Brooks) **7**:67
"The Battle of Brunanburh" (Tennyson) **6**:363, 369
"The Battle of Lowell's Pond" (Longfellow) **30**:20
The Battle of Marathon: A Poem (Browning) **6**:19
"Battle of Murfreesboro (1862-1922)" (Tate) **50**:306
"The Battle of Osfrontalis" (Hughes) **7**:123, 142, 160-61
"Battle Problem" (Meredith) **28**:172, 189
"The Battlefield" (Bryant) **20**:5
"Battlewagon" (Meredith) **28**:174
Battre tout bas (Char) **56**:115
"Baudelaire" (Schwartz) **8**:311, 319
"Baudelaire Irritates Nietzsche" (Char)
See "Baudelaire mécontente Nietzsche"
"Baudelaire mécontente Nietzsche" (Char) **56**:196, 198-202
"Bauxit" (Benn) **35**:70
"Bavaria" (Schnackenberg) **45**:342, 345
"Bavarian Gentians" (Lawrence) **54**:168-69, 172, 179, 181, 186-87, 197-202, 220, 226-27
Bay (Lawrence) **54**:173, 238
"Bayn al-kharā'ib" (Gibran) **9**:79
"Bayonne Turnpike to Tuscarora" (Ginsberg) **4**:54
"Bayou Afternoon" (Clampitt) **19**:102
"Bazook" (Stone) **53**:228-29, 236
Be Angry at the Sun and Other Poems (Jeffers) **17**:123, 135
"Be Grave, Woman" (Jackson) **44**:29-30
"Be Nobody's Darling" (Walker) **30**:339, 353, 365
Be Seated, Thou: Poems, 1989-1998 (Abse) **41**:32
"Be Still, My Soul, Be Still" (Housman) **2**:184, 192
"Beach at Versilia" (Montale)
See "Proda di Versilia"
"Beach Glass" (Clampitt) **19**:88
"The Beach Head" (Gunn) **26**:218
"The Beach Women" (Pinsky) **27**:162
"The Beachcomber" (Stryk) **27**:185-86
"Beachhead" (Walcott) **46**:247
"Beachy" (Sandburg) **2**:300; **41**:225
"The Beacon" (Wilbur) **51**:187
"The Beaks of Eagles" (Jeffers) **17**:145
"Beale Street Love" (Hughes) **1**:269
"The Bean Eaters" (Brooks) **7**:55-6, 62, 69, 100
The Bean Eaters (Brooks) **7**:56-8, 62-3, 67, 81, 86, 95-6, 98-9, 101-02, 105, 107
"Beans with Garlic" (Bukowski) **18**:23
"The Beanstalk" (Millay) **6**:237, 239
"The Bear" (Frost) **1**:203-04
"The Bear" (Kinnell) **26**:241-42, 244, 252, 257, 262-63, 273, 291
"The Bear" (Momaday) **25**:185-86, 188, 191, 193-95, 201-202, 209-10, 220
"Bear" (Wagoner) **33**:373
"The Bear and the Garden-Lover" (Moore) **4**:261
"Bear Fat" (Hogan) **35**:259
"The Bear on the Delhi Road" (Birney) **52**:44-46, 60-61, 87
"Bearded Oaks" (Warren) **37**:276, 288, 301, 307, 322, 332
"The Bearer of Evil Tidings" (Frost) **1**:202
"Bears" (Herbert)
See "Niedzwiedzie"
"The Beast and Burden" (Komunyakaa) **51**:34
Beast in View (Rukeyser) **12**:231-32
"Beasts" (Wilbur) **51**:206, 221, 331
"The Beast's Confession to the Priest" (Swift) **9**:281, 295
"The Beaters" (Gunn) **26**:198, 201, 220
"Beato sillón" (Guillén) **35**:156, 228
"Beatrice" (Teasdale) **31**:343
"Le beau navire" (Baudelaire) **1**:60
"Le Beau Navire" (Char) **56**:197
"Beau sang giclé" (Césaire) **25**:44-5
"La beauté" (Baudelaire) **1**:61, 65
"Beauté de femmes, leur faiblesse, et ces mains pâles" (Verlaine) **2**:416
"The Beautiful American Word, Sure" (Schwartz) **8**:302, 315
"Beautiful and Kind" (Ignatow) **34**:277, 287
"Beautiful Are the Delights of Early Years" (Yevtushenko) **40**:347
"Beautiful Black Men (with compliments and apologies to all not mentioned by name)" (Giovanni) **19**:106-7, 112
"The Beautiful Changes" (Wilbur) **51**:193, 198, 204, 214, 242
The Beautiful Changes and Other Poems (Wilbur) **51**:203-4, 226, 237, 254, 257, 263-64, 267, 269, 289-90, 292-93, 295-96, 314, 324, 330, 333
"Beautiful Lofty Things" (Yeats) **20**:307
"The Beautiful Man—France" (Cisneros) **52**:162
"Beautiful Ohio" (Wright) **36**:321, 360, 368
"The Beautiful Pauses" (Sarton) **39**:309
"A Beautiful Young Nymph Going to Bed. Written for the Honour of the Fair Sex" (Swift) **9**:257, 262, 267-69, 279, 281, 283-84, 286, 291, 295, 298, 301-03
"A beautifull Mistris" (Carew) **29**:9
"The Beauty" (Pushkin) **10**:371
"Beauty" (Storni)
See "La belleza"
"Beauty" (Teasdale) **31**:359
"Beauty" (Thomas) **53**:284, 286, 288-89, 292
"Beauty" (Wylie) **23**:300, 313, 327, 333
Beauty (Jiménez)
See *Belleza*
"Beauty and Beauty" (Brooke) **24**:56, 62
"Beauty and Sadness" (Song) **21**:341, 347
"Beauty and the Beast" (Dove) **6**:108
"Beauty and the Beast" (Tomlinson) **17**:323
"Beauty and the Illiterate" (Elytis) **21**:123
"The Beauty of the Head" (Swenson) **14**:281
"Beauty Shoppe" (Brooks) **7**:59, 102
"Beauty Who Took Snuff" (Pushkin) **10**:407
"The Beaver Pool in December" (Kenyon) **57**:14
"Bebop Boys" (Hughes) **1**:267; **53**:192
"Becalmed" (Longfellow) **30**:31
"Because" (Teasdale) **31**:356, 369, 388
"Because I Could Not Stop for Death" (Dickinson) **1**:84, 86
"Because I Deeply Praised" (Sikelianos) **29**:368
"Because I Love You (Last Night)" (Cummings) **5**:105
"Because I Sit Here So" (Jackson) **44**:29-30
"Because I Was Not Able to Restrain Your Hands" (Mandelstam) **14**:114, 118
"Because la Raza is Tired" (Alurista) **34**:23
"Because of Clothes" (Jackson) **44**:6
"Because One Is Always Forgotten" (Forché) **10**:138, 142, 144, 153, 155
"Because What I Want Most is Permanence" (Sarton) **39**:323, 338, 365
"Because,thy,smile,is,primavera" (Villa) **22**:356, 358
Beckonings (Brooks) **7**:84, 94
"Becoming new" (Piercy) **29**:301
"Becoming Strangers" (Piercy) **29**:309
"The Bed" (Hope) **56**:287
The Bed and the Table (Éluard)
See *Le lit la table*
"The Bed by the Window" (Jeffers) **17**:131
"The Bed in the Sky" (Snyder) **21**:289
"Bed Time" (Hughes) **1**:255
"Bedazzled" (Komunyakaa) **51**:65
"Bedfordshire" (Davie) **29**:116
"The Bedouin" (Riley) **48**:323
"The Bedpost" (Graves) **6**:141
"Bedrock" (Wagoner) **33**:367
"Bedspread" (Goodison) **36**:141-42, 148, 153
"A Bedtime Story" (Hughes) **7**:159
"Bedtime Story" (Mueller) **33**:193

"Bedtime Story" (Stone) **53**:218
"Bedtime Story" (Yamada) **44**:333-34, 346
"The Bee" (Dickey) **40**:229, 253
"The Bee" (Lanier) **50**:77
"The Bee Meeting" (Plath) **1**:394, 410-13; **37**:211
Bee Time Vine (Stein) **18**:316-34, 336, 341-42, 344, 349-54
"Beech" (Frost) **1**:197
"Beech, Pine, and Sunlight" (Lowell) **13**:64
Beechen Vigil and Other Poems (Day Lewis) **11**:148
"Beehive" (Toomer) **7**:311, 320, 334
"The Beekeeper Speaks" (Nemerov) **24**:262, 274
"The Beekeeper's Daughter" (Plath) **1**:389, 410-12; **37**:220, 241, 246, 248
"Beeny Cliff" (Hardy) **8**:136
"Bees Stopped" (Ammons) **16**:46
"Beethoven Attends the C Minor Seminar" (Tomlinson) **17**:320
"Beethoven Opus 111" (Clampitt) **19**:82, 85, 89
"Beetles" (Cervantes) **35**:119
"Before a Blue Light" (Kumin) **15**:211
"Before a Cashier's Window in a Department Store" (Wright) **36**:341, 345, 365, 375
"Before a Midnight Breaks in Storm" (Kipling) **3**:183
"Before an Old Painting of the Crucifixion" (Momaday) **25**:186, 188, 190, 197-98, 211, 219
"Before Glanum" (Char)
See "L'avant-Glanum"
"Before, If I Remember Well . . ." (Rimbaud)
See "Jadis, si je me souviens bien . . ."
"Before I Knocked and Flesh Let Enter" (Thomas) **2**:383, 402; **52**:227, 237, 290, 293-95, 302, 309-10, 313
"Before Knowledge" (Hardy) **8**:89
"Before March" (MacLeish) **47**:190
"Before San Guido" (Carducci)
See "Davanti San Guido"
"Before That" (Merwin) **45**:64
"Before the Altar" (Lowell) **13**:69, 83
"Before the Battle" (Sassoon) **12**:262
"Before the Birth of one of her Children" (Bradstreet) **10**:12, 18
"Before the Dance" (Tomlinson) **17**:319, 328, 330
"Before the Flesh in Bones" (Alurista) **34**:25, 47
Before the Flood (Dylan) **37**:63
"Before the Judgment" (Duncan) **2**:116
"Before the Look of You" (Reese) **29**:331
"Before the Old Castle of Verona" (Carducci)
See "Davanti il castel vecchio di Verona"
"Before the Statue of Endymion" (Cavafy) **36**:73
"Before the Storm" (Lowell) **13**:60-1
"Before the Trip" (Montale)
See "Prima del viaggio"
"Before Time Altered Them" (Cavafy) **36**:74
"Before We Mothernaked Fell" (Thomas) **2**:402
"Before We Sinned (Incarnate Devil)" (Thomas) **2**:402
"Before You Go" (Cervantes) **35**:104
"Begat" (Sexton) **2**:366
"Begegnung" (Stramm) **50**:175, 189
"Begegnungen" (Benn) **35**:69
"The Beggar to Mab, the Fairies' Queen" (Herrick) **9**:86
"The Beggars" (Wordsworth) **4**:377
"The Beggar's Valentine" (Lindsay) **23**:286
"The Beginner" (Kipling) **3**:183
"Beginner's Guide" (Nemerov) **24**:285
"Beginning" (Brathwaite) **56**:23-24, 88
"The Beginning" (Brooke) **24**:56, 82
"The Beginning" (Glück) **16**:164, 167
"Beginning" (Wright) **36**:286, 399-400
"Beginning a Poem of These States" (Ginsberg) **4**:81
"The Beginning and the End" (Jeffers) **17**:128, 132, 141
The Beginning and the End and Other Poems (Jeffers) **17**:114-15, 123, 128, 136
"The Beginning of September" (Hass) **16**:199, 210
"The Beginning of the End of the World" (Clifton) **17**:29
Beginning With 1914 (Mueller) **33**:197
"Beginnings" (Hayden) **6**:190
"The Beginnings" (Kipling) **3**:192
"Behind the Arras" (Carman) **34**:202
"Behind the Arras" (Dunbar) **5**:133
Behind the Arras: A Book of the Unseen (Carman) **34**:200, 205, 211-13, 218, 237-38
"Behind the Façade" (Stone) **53**:252
"Behind the Mirror" (Gunn) **26**:210-213
"Bei Hennef" (Lawrence) **54**:187, 195, 206-8, 224
"Beijing Spring" (Chin) **40**:9
"Beiname" (Goethe) **5**:248
"Being a Woman" (Stone) **53**:231-32, 236
"The Being as Memory" (Carruth) **10**:71
"The Being as Moment" (Carruth) **10**:71
"The Being as Prevision" (Carruth) **10**:71
"Being Beauteous" (Rimbaud) **3**:261, 263-64; **57**:234, 248, 282, 286-87
Being Here: Poetry, 1977-80 (Warren) **37**:313, 325, 329, 335-36, 345, 350, 357, 359-60, 365-67, 373, 380, 382
"Being of Beauty" (Rimbaud) **3**:263
"Being Shot" (Wagoner) **33**:337, 339, 345
"Being Young and Green" (Millay) **6**:236
"Le Bel oiseau déchiffrant l'inconnu au couple d'amoureux" (Breton) **15**:49
Belaia staia (Akhmatova)
See *Belaya staya*
Belaia staja (Akhmatova)
See *Belaya staya*
Belaya staya (Akhmatova) **2**:3, 6, 11-12, 18
"Beldams of Tepoztlán" (Birney) **52**:97
"Belderg" (Heaney) **18**:203
"Belfast" (MacNeice) **61**:106, 124, 170
"Belfast on a Sunday Afternoon" (Davie) **29**:106-08
"Belfast on a Sunday Morning" (Davie) **29**:119
"Belfast Tune" (Brodsky) **9**:28
The Belfry of Bruges (Longfellow) **30**:21, 27, 46
"Belgravia" (Guest) **55**:227
"Beli" (Kabīr) **56**:342
"Believe History" (Jeffers) **17**:141
"Bell" (Brathwaite) **56**:51, 96
"La bell au bois dormant" (Valéry) **9**:392
"Bell Buoy" (Merwin) **45**:7
"The Bell of Atri" (Longfellow) **30**:62
"Bell Speech" (Wilbur) **51**:187
Bella adrede (Guillén) **35**:175, 176, 177
"La Belle au Bois Dormant" (Jarrell) **41**:145, 175, 208
"La belle dame sans merci" (Keats) **1**:279, 282, 304-05
"La belle Dorothée" (Baudelaire) **1**:49
"La belle époque" (Milosz) **8**:211
"La Belle Hequmière aux filles de joie" (Villon) **13**:389
"Belle lecon aux enfants perdus" (Villon) **13**:394-95
"Bellerophon in Argos" (Morris) **55**:336
"Bellerophon in Lycia" (Morris) **55**:329, 331
"La belleza" (Storni) **33**:279, 300;
Belleza (Jiménez) **7**:202
"The Bells" (Poe) **1**:430-31, 439, 441; **54**:276, 321
"The Bells" (Sexton) **2**:359
Bells and Pomegranates (Browning) **61**:11
Bells and Pomegrantes (Browning) **2**:27, 70
"Bells for John Whiteside's Daughter" (Ransom) **61**:261, 263, 267-69, 287, 296, 301, 307, 318, 320
"Bells in the Rain" (Wylie) **23**:328-29
"Bells in Winter" (Milosz) **8**:189, 205
Bells in Winter (Milosz) **8**:174
Bells of Lombardy (Stryk) **27**:214-15, 218
"The Bells of San Blas" (Longfellow) **30**:47
"Bells of Winter" (Milosz)
See "Bells in Winter"
Bells on the heart (Char)
See *Les cloches sur le cœur*
"The Bells that Signed" (Day Lewis) **11**:144
"Belly Song" (Knight) **14**:46, 48
Belly Song and Other Poems (Knight) **14**:41-2, 48, 52
"A Beloved" (Lawrence) **54**:237
"Beloved" (Schnackenberg) **45**:338
"Beloved, Sleep" (Yevtushenko) **40**:347
"Below" (Celan) **10**:118
"Below Tintern" (Tomlinson) **17**:334, 336
"Belsazar" (Heine) **25**:140
"Belsen, Day of Liberation" (Hayden) **6**:194
"Belts" (Kipling) **3**:162
"Ben Jonson Entertains a Man from Stratford" (Robinson) **1**:462, 468, 487; **35**:362
"Benares" (Borges) **22**:72; **32**:80-1
"Bending the Bow" (Duncan) **2**:107
Bending the Bow (Duncan) **2**:104, 107, 113-116, 119, 125, 127
"Bendita Suerte" (Alurista) **34**:45
"Bendito sea tu Vientre" (Alurista) **34**:46
"Beneath a Cool Shade" (Behn) **13**:15
"Beneath My Hand and Eye the Distant Hills, Your Body" (Snyder) **21**:288
Beneath the Fortinaria (Bukowski) **18**:21
"Beneath the Shadow of the Freeway" (Cervantes) **35**:104, 106, 108, 110, 112, 117, 124, 133, 134, 135
"Bénédiction" (Baudelaire) **1**:54, 70
"Benediction" (Kunitz) **19**:148
"Bengali Heroes" (Tagore)
See "Banga bir"
"Benjamin Pantier" (Masters) **1**:347; **36**:169, 182, 230
"Bennie's Departure" (McKay) **2**:225
"Ben's Last Fight" (Merton) **10**:345
"Beowulf" (Wilbur) **51**:189
Beowulf (Anonymous) **22**:1-65
Beppo: A Venetian Story (Byron) **16**:83, 115-20
"Berck-Plage" (Plath) **1**:390; **37**:198-205, 232
"Bereavement" (Smith) **12**:351
"Bereft" (Frost) **39**:232
"Bereft" (Hardy) **8**:131
"Bergidylle" (Heine) **25**:145
"Berkeley Eclogue" (Hass) **16**:217
"Berlin" (Ferlinghetti) **1**:167
"Berlin in ruins" (Gunn) **26**:211-212
"Berlin Is Hard on Colored Girls" (Lorde) **12**:142
The Berlin Songbook (Bely)
See *Berlinsky pesennik*
Berlinsky pesennik (Bely) **11**:7
"Bermudas" (Marvell) **10**:268-69, 271, 275, 289, 311, 313-14
"Berry Holden" (Masters) **1**:324
"Bert Kessler" (Masters) **36**:182
"Bertha in the Lane" (Browning) **6**:17
Beside the River Sar (Castro)
See *En las orillas del Sar*
"The Besieged" (Paz) **48**:273
"Los besos" (Aleixandre) **15**:38
"Bessey of the Glen" (Clare) **23**:25
The Best American Poetry (Graham) **59**:184
"The Best Daddy" (Silverstein) **49**:349
"The Best Days" (Wright) **36**:360
"The Best of It" (Sassoon) **12**:248, 260
"Best Year's" (Soto) **28**:398-99
Le bestiaire; ou, Cortège d'Orphée (Apollinaire) **7**:48
A Bestiary (Wilbur) **51**:189-91
Bestiary/Bestiario (Neruda) **4**:286-87
"A Bestiary for My Daughters Mary and Katharine" (Rexroth) **20**:187, 190, 195, 218
"Bestiary U.S.A." (Sexton) **2**:367

"Besuch bei Ingres" (Enzensberger) **28**:150
"Besy" (Pushkin) **10**:413
"Betancourt" (Baraka) **4**:15
Betäubung (Benn) **35**:5, 8, 68
Bethlehem in Broad Daylight (Doty) **53**:47, 62
"Betraktelse" (Ekeloef) **23**:76
"Betrayal" (Lanier) **50**:56, 67
"Betrayal" (Muir) **49**:228, 237, 248, 297
"Betrayal" (Pavese)
See "Tradimento"
"The Betrothal" (Apollinaire)
See "Les fiançailles"
"The Betrothal" (Millay) **6**:211
The Betrothal (Patmore) **59**:227, 244
"Betrothed" (Bogan) **12**:127-28
"A Better Resurrection" (Rossetti) **7**:290
"Between Going and Staying" (Paz) **48**:273
"Between Our Selves" (Lorde) **12**:139
Between Our Selves (Lorde) **12**:137, 156
Between Stone and Flower (Paz)
See *Entre la piedra y la flor*
"Between the Porch and the Altar" (Lowell) **3**:200, 203-04, 206
"Between the Worlds" (Sandburg) **41**:330
"Between Two Hills" (Sandburg) **41**:243
"Between Two Prisoners" (Dickey) **40**:175, 258
"Between Us" (Merrill) **28**:252
"Between Walls" (Williams) **7**:399, 402
"Between What I See and What I Say" (Paz)
See "Entre Lo Que Veo y Digo..."
"Beucolicks" (Herrick) **9**:89
"Beverly Hills, Chicago" (Brooks) **7**:81
"Beware!" (Wylie) **23**:322
"Beware, Madam!" (Graves) **6**:163
"Bewick Finzer" (Robinson) **1**:467
"The Bewildered" (Rimbaud)
See "Les Effarés"
"Beyond" (Guillén)
See "Más allá"
"Beyond" (Jackson) **44**:103
"Beyond Delinquency" (Corso) **33**:25
"Beyond Even Faithful Legends" (Bissett) **14**:6, 24, 31
Beyond Even Faithful Legends (Bissett)
See *Selected Poems: Beyond Even Faithful Legends*
"Beyond Harm" (Olds) **22**:325, 341
"Beyond Howth Head" (Mahon) **60**:133-34, 142, 147, 164-65, 168, 196, 203-9, 214, 233
"Beyond Sharp Control" (Brutus) **24**:116
"Beyond the Alps" (Lowell) **3**:205, 211, 218, 221
"Beyond the Gamut" (Carman) **34**:202, 212
"Beyond the Last Lamp" (Hardy) **8**:125
Beyond the Mountains (Rexroth) **20**:185-86
"Beyond the Pleasure Principle" (Nemerov) **24**:260
"Beyond the Question" (Sarton) **39**:328-29, 342, 365, 367
"Beyond What" (Niedecker) **42**:147
"Beyond You" (Merwin) **45**:48
"Bez nazvaniya" (Pasternak) **6**:288
"Bezverie" (Pushkin) **10**:409, 411
"Bhagna mandir" (Tagore) **8**:415
"Bhairavi gan" (Tagore) **8**:407
"Bhakti" (Kabīr) **56**:331
Bhānu singha (Tagore) **8**:403
Bhanusingh Thakurer padavali (Tagore) **8**:405
"Bhar" (Tagore) **8**:412
"Biafra" (Levertov) **11**:176, 194
"Bianca among the Nightingales" (Browning) **6**:23-4, 28, 32, 38, 40
"The Bible Business" (Dalton) **36**:127
"The Bible Defense of Slavery" (Harper) **21**:190, 208, 217
"Bible Stories" (Reese) **29**:330
"bibliographie" (Enzensberger) **28**:137
"A Bibliography of the King's Book, or, Eikon Basilike" (Howe) **54**:89, 106, 125
A Bibliography of the King's Book or, Eikon Basilike (Howe) **54**:72-73, 76, 102, 105
La Bibliothèque est en feu (Char) **56**:113-14
"Bickford's Buddha" (Ferlinghetti) **1**:186-87
"Bicocca di San Giacomo" (Carducci) **46**:52
"The Bicycles and the Apex" (Oppen) **35**:321
"Bien loin d'ici" (Baudelaire) **1**:49
"Bien pudiera ser" (Storni) **33**:252, 276, 311;
"Bien que le trait de vostre belle face" (Ronsard) **11**:250
"Biens égaux" (Char) **56**:150
"Bienvenue" (Char) **56**:154
"Bifurcation" (Tzara) **27**:229-31
"The Big Baboon" (Belloc) **24**:24
"Big Bastard with a Sword" (Bukowski) **18**:13
"Big Bessie Throws Her Son into the Street" (Brooks) **7**:63, 81
"Big Boy" (Brown) **55**:72
Big City Primer (Yau) **61**:330-31
"Big Elegy" (Brodsky)
See "The Great Elegy for John Donne"
"Big Fat Hairy Vision of Evil" (Ferlinghetti) **1**:167
"The Big Graveyard" (Viereck) **27**:262
"The Big Heart" (Sexton) **2**:368
"Big Island Notebook 11" (Yau) **61**:331
"Big John Henry" (Walker) **20**:287
"Big Momma" (Madhubuti) **5**:326, 344
"The Big Timer" (Hughes) **53**:114
"Big Wind" (Roethke) **15**:276, 279
"The Bight" (Bishop) **3**:50, 52-4; **34**:97, 116, 118, 130, 158
Bījak (Kabīr) **56**:341-42, 344-46
The Bijak of Kabir (Kabīr) **56**:342-43
"Les bijoux" (Baudelaire) **1**:61
"Bilbea" (Sandburg) **41**:240, 312
"Bi-Lingual Education" (Cruz) **37**:35
"Bill of Fare" (Enzensberger) **28**:142
"The Billboard Painters" (Ferlinghetti) **1**:183
"Billboards" (Ondaatje) **28**:328, 331
"Billboards and Galleons" (Lindsay) **23**:287
"Billboards Build Freedom of Choice" (Birney) **52**:16, 21, 25, 63, 79
Billy the Kid (Ondaatje) **28**:293-94, 296-97
"Bimini" (Heine) **25**:167
"Binding the Dragon" (Sarton) **39**:365
"Bingu mondo no uta" (Yakamochi) **48**:102-3, 111-12, 129, 136
"Bío-Bío" (Mistral) **32**:166
Biograph (Dylan) **37**:59, 64-5
"The Biographer's Mandate" (Nemerov) **24**:289
"Biography" (Birney) **52**:58
"The Biography of a Myth" (Jackson) **44**:74, 89
"The Biology of Art" (Merwin) **45**:98
"Il Biondomoro" (Pasolini) **17**:264
"Biotherm (for Bill Berkson)" (O'Hara) **45**:120, 127, 131, 166-70, 245
"Birahulī" (Kabīr) **56**:342
"Birches" (Frost) **1**:196, 221, 225, 227-28, 230; **39**:230, 253, 256
"Birches" (Wylie) **23**:326
"Bird" (Brathwaite) **56**:45, 75
"Bird" (Harjo) **27**:72
"The Bird" (Muir) **49**:232
"The Bird and the Arras" (Finch) **21**:157, 160, 172
"The Bird Auction" (McGuckian) **27**:94
"Bird Ave" (Cervantes) **35**:134
"Bird Call Valley" (Wang Wei) **18**:381-82, 391
"The Bird Frau" (Dove) **6**:108
"Bird of Air" (H. D.) **5**:287
"Bird Sanctuary" (Mahon) **60**:166-67
"The Bird with the Coppery, Keen Claws" (Stevens) **6**:293, 304
"Birdbrain!" (Ginsberg) **4**:62, 76
"Birdcage Walk" (Merton) **10**:351
"Birdcries Stream" (Wang Wei)
See "Bird-Singing Stream"
"The Birdnesters" (Szirtes) **51**:157
"The Birds" (Belloc) **24**:5, 8
"Birds" (Césaire) **25**:46
"Birds" (Jeffers) **17**:147
"Birds" (Wright) **14**:347, 349, 353, 366
Birds (Perse)
See *Oiseaux*
Birds (Wright) **14**:348-49, 354
Birds, Beasts, and Flowers (Lawrence) **54**:170, 173, 187, 189, 191, 197, 200-201, 207, 212, 218, 227-28, 232, 236
"Birds for Janet" (Ondaatje) **28**:318, 332
"Birds in the Night" (Verlaine) **2**:415; **32**:396, 408-09, 411
"Birds in Winter" (Ignatow) **34**:306
"Birds' Nests" (Thomas) **53**:328
"The Birds of Killingworth" (Longfellow) **30**:62
"Birds of Passage" (Longfellow) **30**:27
"Birds of Prey" (McKay) **2**:212
"The birds that sing on Autumn eves" (Bridges) **28**:84
"Birds Walking" (Merwin) **45**:28
"Birds without Descent" (Aleixandre)
See "Pajaros sin descenso"
"Bird-Singing Stream" (Wang Wei) **18**:360, 376, 380-81, 386, 390
"Bird-Witted" (Moore) **49**:101
"The Biretta" (Heaney) **18**:256
"Birmingham" (MacNeice) **61**:116-17, 119-20, 124, 131, 138
"Birmingham" (Walker) **20**:283, 287
"Birmingham Sunday" (Hughes) **1**:252; **53**:150
"A Birth" (Dickey) **40**:181
"Birth and Death" (Jeffers) **17**:141
"Birth and Death" (Swinburne) **24**:324
"The Birth in a Narrow Room" (Brooks) **7**:54, 80
"Birth of a Fascist" (Viereck) **27**:280
"Birth of a Genius among Men" (MacDiarmid) **9**:153
"Birth of a Smile" (Mandelstam)
See "Rozhdenie ulybki"
"The Birth of Christ" (García Lorca)
See "Nacimiento de Cristo"
The Birth of Kumara (Kālidāsa)
See *Kumārasambhava*
"Birth of Love" (Warren) **37**:308, 360
"The Birth of Potchikoo" (Erdrich) **52**:193
The Birth of the Prince (Kālidāsa)
See *Kumārasambhava*
"Birth of the Virgin" (Swenson) **14**:285
The Birth of the War-God (Kālidāsa)
See *Kumārasambhava*
"Birthday" (Aleixandre) **15**:16
"Birthday" (Benn)
See "Der Geburtstag"
"Birthday" (Jeffers) **17**:141
"A Birthday" (Muir) **49**:233, 250-51
"A Birthday" (Rossetti) **7**:276, 278, 280
Birthday (Corso)
See *The Happy Birthday of Death*
The Birthday (Merrill) **28**:270
"A Birthday Cake for Lionel" (Wylie) **23**:321-22
"The Birthday Dream" (Dickey) **40**:154, 158
"A Birthday Kid Poem" (Ortiz) **17**:228
"Birthday on the Acropolis" (Sarton) **39**:327, 341
"Birthday on the Beach" (Nash) **21**:270
"Birthday Poem" (Shapiro) **25**:263
"A Birthday Present" (Plath) **37**:232, 255
"Birthday Sonnet" (Wylie) **23**:315
"Birthmarks" (Song) **21**:341
"The Birthplace" (Heaney) **18**:214
"Birthplace" (Oppen) **35**:297
"Birthplace Revisited" (Corso) **33**:23, 41
"Bisclavret" (Marie de France) **22**:258, 260, 268, 272, 282-84, 286, 298-99
"Biscuit" (Kenyon) **57**:41
"La bise se rue à travers" (Verlaine) **32**:363
"Bishop Blougram" (Browning) **2**:37
"Bishop Blougram's Apology" (Browning) **2**:43, 73
"The Bishop Orders His Tomb at St. Praxed's" (Browning) **2**:37, 48, 82, 94
"El bisonte" (Borges) **32**:90
"The Biting Insects" (Kinnell) **26**:288

"The Bitter River" (Hughes) **1**:251
"Bituminous?" (Silverstein) **49**:342
Bixby Canyon to Jessore Road (Ginsberg) **4**:89
Black & Blues (Brathwaite) **56**:34, 54, 60-62, 88-89
"Black and Unknown Bards" (Johnson) **24**:137, 142
"The Black Angel" (Montale)
See "L'angelo nero"
Black Armour (Wylie) **23**:301-302, 307, 309-10, 324, 332
"Black Art" (Baraka) **4**:10, 19, 25, 40
"The Black Art" (Sexton) **2**:373
Black Arts (Baraka) **4**:18
"Black Bill's Honeymoon" (Noyes) **27**:123, 134
"A Black Birch in Winter" (Wilbur) **51**:283
"Black Blood" (Blok) **21**:5
"Black Buttercups" (Clampitt) **19**:83, 86, 91
"The Black Christ" (Hughes) **53**:94
"The Black Christ" (Madhubuti) **5**:339-40
The Black Christ and Other Poems (Cullen) **20**:59, 62, 64, 68
"The Black Christ (Hopefully Dedicated to White America)" (Cullen) **20**:59, 64-66, 68, 71, 73-75, 87
"The Black Clown" (Hughes) **53**:114
"Black Cock" (Montale)
See "Gallo cedrone"
"The Black Cottage" (Frost) **1**:193, 198
"BLACK DADA NIHILISMUS" (Baraka) **4**:9, 14
"Black Dancer in the Little Savoy" (Hughes) **1**:246
"The Black Day" (MacLeish) **47**:246, 260
"Black Eagle Returns to St. Joe" (Masters) **1**:344
"Black Earth" (Mandelstam)
See "Chernozem"
"Black Earth" (Moore)
See "Melancthon"
"Black Easter" (Shvarts)
See "Chernaia Paskha"
Black Feeling, Black Talk (Giovanni) **19**:133, 135, 139
Black Feeling, Black Talk, Black Judgement (Giovanni) **19**:107-8, 110-11, 114, 118, 120-22, 124, 128, 136
"The Black Goddess" (Graves) **6**:154
"Black Hair" (Soto) **28**:379-80
"Black Harmonium" (Hagiwara)
See "Kuroi fūkin"
"Black Hawk held: In reason" (Niedecker) **42**:151
"The Black Hood" (Francis) **34**:254
Black Hosts (Senghor)
See *Hosties noires*
"Black Jackets" (Gunn) **26**:201
Black Judgement (Giovanni) **19**:135, 139, 143
"The Black Knight" (Thoreau)
See "Independence"
"Black Leather Because Bumblebees Look Like It" (Wakoski) **15**:326
"Black Love" (Madhubuti) **5**:342
"Black Magdalens" (Cullen) **20**:56, 62, 64
"Black Magic" (Sanchez) **9**:223, 234
Black Magic: Sabotage, Target Study, Black Art; Collected Poetry, 1961-1967 (Baraka) **4**:6, 8, 16-18, 24, 26
"Black Mail" (Walker) **30**:339, 352
"Black Majesty" (Cullen) **20**:64
"The Black Mammy" (Johnson) **24**:142
"The Black Man Is Making New Gods" (Baraka) **4**:19
"Black March" (Smith) **12**:300-01, 308, 319, 326
"Black Mesa" (Baca) **41**:47
"The Black Mesa" (Merrill) **28**:223, 255
Black Mesa Poems (Baca) **41**:47, 61, 63
"Black Money" (Gallagher) **9**:36, 53
"Black Mother Woman" (Lorde) **12**:154, 156-57
"A Black November Turkey" (Wilbur) **51**:218
"Black Nude" (Tomlinson) **17**:311
"Black Panther" (Hughes) **1**:251-52; **53**:111, 151
"Black People!" (Baraka) **4**:19, 25-6
"The Black Pit" (Hayden) **6**:187
"Black Power Chant" (Baraka) **4**:19
Black Pride (Madhubuti) **5**:321, 336, 338-41, 346
"Black Pudding" (Gallagher) **9**:64
"Black Rook in Rainy Weather" (Plath) **37**:237-38, 241
"Black Sampson of Brandywine" (Dunbar) **5**:129, 131, 138
"Black Shroud" (Ginsberg) **4**:90
"Black Silk" (Gallagher) **9**:50, 59, 62
"Black Sketches" (Madhubuti) **5**:337
"Black Snake Visitation" (Mackey) **49**:3
"Black Song" (Guillén)
See "Canto negro"
"Black String of Days" (Komunyakaa) **51**:35
"The Black Swan" (Jarrell) **41**:171, 173, 179, 191-92
"Black Tambourine" (Crane) **3**:98
The Black Unicorn (Lorde) **12**:137-38, 141-42, 144, 148, 151, 153-55, 157-58, 160
"The Black Virginity" (Loy) **16**:322
"Black/White" (Wright) **14**:366
Black white (Illyés)
See *Fekete feher*
"The Black Winds" (Williams) **7**:383-85, 388-89
"Black Woman" (Senghor) **25**:224-30
"Blackberrying" (Plath) **1**:407-09; **37**:238-39
"Blackberry-Picking" (Heaney) **18**:192
The Blackbird (Zagajewski) **27**:396
"Blackgirl Learning" (Madhubuti) **5**:344
"Blacklash Blues" (Hughes) **53**:111, 151
"Blackman/An Unfinished History" (Madhubuti) **5**:326, 343, 345
Blacks (Brooks) **7**:105
"Black-Shouldered Kite" (Wright) **14**:344
"Blacksmith" (Rimbaud)
See "Le Forgeron"
"The Blacksmith's Serenade" (Lindsay) **23**:264
"The Blackstone Rangers" (Brooks) **7**:88, 90-1
"Blackstudies" (Lorde) **12**:147, 158
"Blake" (Borges) **22**:97
"Blake" (Moore) **49**:114
"Blame not my lute" (Wyatt) **27**:315, 324
"Blanc" (Valéry) **9**:392
"Blanco" (Soto) **28**:375
"Lo blanco" (Storni) **33**:272;
Blanco (Paz) **1**:355-56, 358, 363, 368-69, 372, 374, 376-77; **48**:181, 194, 206, 214-16, 228, 232, 267, 274
The Blasted Pine (Birney) **52**:17
"Blasting from Heaven" (Levine) **22**:223
"Blaubeuren" (Tomlinson) **17**:360
"Bleeding" (Swenson) **14**:269-70, 285
"Blenheim Oranges" (Thomas) **53**:294, 318
"Blessèd Accident" (Warren) **37**:337
"Blessed are They that Mourn" (Bryant) **20**:6
"The Blessed Damozel" (Rossetti) **44**:164-65, 173, 184, 195, 202-3, 205, 236, 238
"The Blessed Damozele" (Rossetti) **44**:164-65, 173, 184, 195, 202-3, 205, 236, 238
"Blessed Is the Man" (Moore) **49**:126, 134, 139
"Blessed Sleep" (Johnson) **24**:159
"The Blessed Virgin, Compared to the Air We Breathe" (Hopkins) **15**:166
"The Blessed Virgin Mary Compared to a Window" (Merton) **10**:330, 338
"A Blessing" (Wright) **36**:285, 294, 325, 327-28, 334, 344, 350, 352, 356-57, 364, 369, 372, 374, 392, 394-96, 398, 403
"A Blessing in Disguise" (Ashbery) **26**:129, 143
"Blessing Myself" (Ignatow) **34**:276, 318
Blew Ointment (Bissett) **14**:5
blew trewz (Bissett) **14**:7-8
"Blighters" (Sassoon) **12**:263, 277, 282
"Blind Bartimeus" (Longfellow) **30**:13, 64
"The Blind Child's Story" (Dickey) **40**:177
"Blind Curse" (Ortiz) **17**:246
"The Blind Doge at 83" (Viereck) **27**:280
Blind Fireworks (MacNeice) **61**:180
"The Blind Leading the Blind" (Mueller) **33**:197
"Blind Man" (Alurista)
See "Hombre Ciego"
"The Blind Man" (Wright) **14**:337, 369
"Blind Man's Holiday" (Curnow) **48**:60
"Blind Panorama of New York" (García Lorca)
See "Panorama ceigo de Nueva York"
"Blind Spring" (Shvarts) **50**:148
"Blind William's Song" (Merwin) **45**:18
"Blind Willie and the Talking Dog" (Silverstein) **49**:349
"Blind Willie McTell" (Dylan) **37**:59, 65-66
"Der blinde junge" (Loy) **16**:309, 316
"Der blinde Sänger" (Hölderlin) **4**:147
"The Blinded Bird" (Hardy) **8**:98
Blindenschrift (Enzensberger) **28**:133-35, 138-40, 143, 150
"Bliss" (Pushkin) **10**:407
Bliznets v tuchakh (Pasternak) **6**:263, 275
"Blizzard" (Sarton) **39**:368
"blk/chant" (Sanchez) **9**:204, 225, 234
"blk / wooooomen / chant" (Sanchez) **9**:225
"Block 4 Barrack 4 'Apt' C" (Yamada) **44**:340, 342
"Blockade Portrait Via Genre, Still Life, and Landscape Painting" (Shvarts)
See "Portret blokady cherez zhanr, natiurmort, i peizazh"
"Blocks" (O'Hara) **45**:114, 160
"Blödigkeit" (Hölderlin) **4**:148
Blonde on Blonde (Dylan) **37**:44, 47, 50-52, 54
Blood (Quintana)
See *Sangre*
"Blood and the Moon" (Yeats) **20**:313; **51**:106
"Blood Feud" (Wylie) **23**:301
Blood for a Stranger (Jarrell) **41**:127-28, 139, 146, 159, 179, 184
"Blood from a Stone" (Oppen) **35**:320, 321, 342
Blood on the Tracks (Dylan) **37**:54, 56, 58-60
"Bloodbirth" (Lorde) **12**:157
"Bloodsmiles" (Madhubuti) **5**:337
"Bloody Absurdities" (Rimbaud)
See "Conneries"
"The Bloody Sire" (Jeffers) **17**:139
The Bloomingdale Papers (Carruth) **10**:78-84
"Bloomingdale's I" (Hacker) **47**:94, 97
"The Blossom" (Blake) **12**:7, 23, 33
"The Blossom" (Donne)
See "The Blossome"
"The Blossome" (Donne) **1**:126, 130, 147
"The Blow" (Hardy) **8**:94
"The Blow" (Neruda)
See "El golpe"
"Blow and Counterblow" (Montale)
See "Botta e riposta"
"Blow Up Tight to Fly" (Alurista) **34**:42
"The Blow-Fly" (Graves) **6**:163
"Blowin' in the Wind" (Dylan) **37**:49-50, 56, 71
"Blowing Boy" (Page) **12**:177
"Blue" (Brathwaite) **56**:55
Blue (Darío)
See *Azul*
"Blue and White Lines after O'Keeffe" (Song) **21**:331, 334, 336, 340-41
"Blue Bag" (Moore) **49**:146
"Blue Bayou" (Hughes) **53**:108
"The Blue Birds" (Thoreau) **30**:192, 194-95, 242, 257
"The Blue Bouquet" (Paz)
See "El ramo azul"
"The Blue Cat" (Hagiwara) **18**:181
Blue Cat (Hagiwara)
See *Aoneko*
Blue Chicory (Niedecker) **42**:98, 101, 106
"The Blue Closet" (Morris) **55**:238, 240, 279-84, 301-3, 323
"Blue Cockerel" (Merwin) **45**:6

The Blue Estuaries: Poems, 1923-1968 (Bogan) **12**:96-7, 100-03, 107, 112, 120-21
"Blue Evening" (Brooke) **24**:57-8, 76
"Blue Farm" (McGuckian) **27**:95
"The Blue from Heaven" (Smith) **12**:302, 304, 319, 331, 333
"Blue Gem Creeper" (Tagore)
See "Nilamanilata"
"Blue Girls" (Ransom) **61**:271, 288, 307, 313, 321-22
"Blue Lantern" (Song) **21**:331, 338-40, 343
"Blue Light Lounge Sutra for the Performance Poets at Harold Park Hotel" (Komunyakaa) **51**:14, 63
"Blue Lizard Lounge" (Yau) **61**:334-35
"The Blue Meridian" (Toomer) **7**:309, 311-12, 324-26, 328-29, 336,-37, 340
"Blue Moles" (Plath) **1**:389; **37**:188, 190
"Blue Monday" (Wakoski) **15**:325, 348
Blue Notes (Komunyakaa) **51**:62-64
The Blue Pencil (Bishop) **34**:95
"A Blue Ribbon at Amesbury" (Frost) **1**:196
"The Blue She Brings with Her" (McGuckian) **27**:81-82
"Blue Sky Rain" (McGuckian) **27**:82, 93
"Blue Squills" (Teasdale) **31**:358
The Blue Stairs (Guest) **55**:213, 217-19
"The Blue Swallows" (Nemerov) **24**:300
The Blue Swallows (Nemerov) **24**:260-63, 274, 277, 281, 289, 291
"The Blue Tower" (Stryk) **27**:214
"Blue Winter" (Francis) **34**:259
"A Blue Woman with Sticking out Breasts Hanging" (Cummings) **5**:99, 103
"Bluebeard" (Millay) **6**:205
"Bluebells" (MacNeice) **61**:119
"Bluebells for Love" (Kavanagh) **33**:102, 157
"Blueberries" (Frost) **1**:225
"A Bluebird in March" (Carman) **34**:203
"The Blue-Flag in the Bog" (Millay) **6**:233
"Bluejay" (Francis) **34**:256-57
"Blues" (Meredith) **28**:187
"Blues" (Walcott) **46**:230, 285
"Blues at Dawn" (Hughes) **1**:266; **53**:158
A Blues Book for Blue Black Magical Women (Sanchez) **9**:207, 211-16, 218-20, 228-29, 234, 238-41, 243
"Blues Chant Hoodoo Revival" (Komunyakaa) **51**:34, 46
"Blues for Ladies" (Hughes) **53**:101
"Blues for Men" (Hughes) **53**:101
"Blues for Ruby Matrix" (Aiken) **26**:29
Blues for Ruby Matrix (Aiken) **26**:24
"Blüte" (Stramm) **50**:170, 189, 208
"Boa Constrictor" (Silverstein) **49**:310
"Boädicea" (Tennyson) **6**:360, 363
"Boadicea. An Ode" (Cowper) **40**:115-16
"Boast of Quietness" (Borges)
See "Jactancia de quietud"
"Boasting of stillness" (Borges)
See "Jactancia de quietud"
"The boat" (Paz)
See "El barco"
"The Boat" (Sexton) **2**:365
"The Boat of Life" (Ishikawa)
See "Inochi no fune"
The Boat of Quiet Hours (Kenyon) **57**:3-4, 6, 9, 11, 19, 22-24, 35-37, 39-40, 45
"The Boat of the White Feather Bird" (Ishikawa)
See "Shiraha no toribune"
"Boat Ride" (Gallagher) **9**:50-1, 58-60
"Boats on the Marne" (Montale) **13**:146
Bob Dylan at Budokan (Dylan) **37**:64
"The Bobby to the Sneering Lady" (McKay) **2**:226
"Bobo's Metamorphosis" (Milosz) **8**:187
"Bob's Lane" (Thomas) **53**:305
Le Bocage (Ronsard) **11**:246
"Boccaccio: The Plague Years" (Dove) **6**:109
"THE BODY" (Bissett) **14**:9, 34
"Body" (Tagore)
See "Tanu"
"Body and Soul: A Mediation" (Kumin) **15**:206
"The Body as Braille" (Cervantes) **35**:132
"The Body of God" (Lawrence) **54**:199, 250
"Body of Summer" (Elytis) **21**:115
Body of This Death (Bogan) **12**:85-7, 103-04, 116, 119-20, 126-28
"Body of Waking" (Rukeyser) **12**:217, 220
Body of Waking (Rukeyser) **12**:217, 219-21, 224
Body Rags (Kinnell) **26**:240-42, 244, 246, 257, 261, 290-91, 293
"Body, Remember" (Cavafy) **36**:74, 75
"Body's Beauty" (Rossetti) **44**:253
"Boeotian" (Frost) **39**:254
"'Boes" (Sandburg) **41**:347
"Bog Oak" (Heaney) **18**:201
"Bog Queen" (Heaney) **18**:188, 195, 211
"Bogland" (Heaney) **18**:188, 195, 201, 205, 209, 211
"Bohemia" (Parker) **28**:363
"The Bohemian" (Dunbar) **5**:125
"Boire" (Éluard) **38**:71
"Le bois amical" (Valéry) **9**:391
"Le bois de l'epte" (Char) **56**:108, 113, 182
"La Boîte aux lumières" (Péret) **33**:230
Bojarin Orša (Lermontov) **18**:279, 300
"Bokardo" (Robinson) **1**:468; **35**:367
Boke of Phyllyp Sparowe (Skelton) **25**:330, 332-33, 335, 343-44, 346, 348, 353-54, 356-60, 367, 369, 374, 380-82, 384, 393-94, 396-400
"Bologna: A Poem about Gold" (Wright) **36**:367
"Bolshevik Epic" (Borges) **32**:121
"Bomb" (Corso) **33**:5-6, 9, 36, 43-4, 47-8
"Bomba" (Fuertes) **27**:39, 45
"Bomba atómica" (Guillén) **23**:124
"Bombardment" (Lowell) **13**:78
"Une bombe aux Feuillantines" (Hugo) **17**:100
"Bombed Train Station, 80 Killed" (Corso) **33**:50
"Bombinations of a Chimera" (MacDiarmid) **9**:193
"Bombings" (Niedecker) **42**:151
"Bon Voyage" (Robinson) **35**:368
"Bonaparte" (Lamartine) **16**:277, 291
"Bond and Free" (Frost) **39**:233
"Bone Dreams" (Heaney) **18**:188, 204
"The Bones" (Merwin) **45**:7, 9
"Bones" (Sandburg) **41**:360
"The Bones of My Father" (Knight) **14**:43,52
Bones of the Cuttlefish (Montale)
See *Ossi di seppia*
"The Bones of the Dead" (Mistral)
See "Los huesos de los muertos"
"The Bones Speak" (Wright) **14**:337, 339
"Bonfire" (Gallagher) **9**:61-2
"Bongo Song" (Guillén)
See "La canción del bongo"
Bonheur (Verlaine) **2**:417; **32**:386
La bonne chanson (Verlaine) **2**:413-14, 419, 431-32; **32**:353, 368, 375, 385, 393-94, 396, 399, 401, 407
"The Bonnie Broukit Bairn" (MacDiarmid) **9**:156, 160, 187
"Bonr" (Rimbaud) **57**:247, 251
"Les bons chiens" (Baudelaire) **1**:58-9
"Bonsal" (Guillén) **23**:126
"Boogie 1 a.m." (Hughes) **53**:92; **53**:123
"Boogie Segue to Bop" (Hughes) **53**:190
"The Book" (Darío)
See "El libro"
"A Book" (Stein) **18**:325, 348
"Book Buying in the Tenderloin" (Hass) **16**:195
The Book of Ahania (Blake) **12**:13
"Book of Ancestors" (Atwood) **8**:28-9, 42
"The Book of Annandale" (Robinson) **1**:460-61
The Book of Earth (Noyes) **27**:130, 132-3, 135
The Book of Elizabethan Verse (Braithwaite) **52**:106, 124
"The Book of Ephraim" (Merrill) **28**:224-25, 227-31, 235-37, 243, 245, 260-61, 263, 266, 271-75, 278
Book of Fame (Chaucer)
See *House of Fame*
The Book of Folly (Sexton) **2**:355-56, 360, 365, 368
The Book of Georgian Verse (Braithwaite) **52**:106
Book of Gypsy Ballads (García Lorca)
See *Primer romancero gitano*
"The Book of Hours of Sister Clotilde" (Lowell) **13**:84
"Book of Joyous Children" (Riley) **48**:296, 303
The Book of Light (Clifton) **17**:31
The Book of Los (Blake) **12**:62-4
The Book of Medicines (Hogan) **35**:259, 265, 276, 277, 279
"The Book of Myths" (Harjo) **27**:66-67
The Book of Nightmares (Kinnell) **26**:241-45, 247-49, 252-58, 261, 264-67, 271-75, 283, 291-93
Book of Pictures (Rilke)
See *Buch der Bilder*
The Book of Purgatory (Marie de France)
See *L'Espurgatoire Saint Patrice*
Book of Questions (Neruda)
See *Libro de las preguntas*
The Book of Restoration Verse (Braithwaite) **52**:106
Book of Saint Valentines Day of the Parlement of Briddes (Chaucer)
See *Parlement of Foules*
Book of Songs (García Lorca)
See *Canciones*
Book of Songs (Heine) **25**:153-54
"The Book of the Dead" (Rukeyser) **12**:203, 207, 213
The Book of the Dead (Rukeyser) **12**:210
Book of the Duchess (Chaucer) **19**:6, 10, 13, 21, 23, 38, 64-9, 71-4, 76; **58**:352
Book of the Duchesse (Chaucer)
See *Book of the Duchess*
Book of the Five and Twenty Ladies (Chaucer)
See *Legend of Good Women*
"A Book of the Unseen" (Carman) **34**:212
The Book of Thel (Blake) **12**:19, 33-5, 37, 51
Book of Troilus (Chaucer)
See *Troilus and Criseyde*
The Book of Urizen (Blake) **12**:15, 19, 35, 38, 60, 62
Book of Vagaries (Neruda)
See *Extravagario*
Book of Verse (Masters)
See *A Book of Verses*
Book of Verse (Morris) **55**:340
A Book of Verses (Masters) **1**:332, 342; 200, 221
"Booker T. Washington" (Dunbar) **5**:131
The Books of the Polish Nation and the Polish Pilgrimage (Mickiewicz)
See *Księgi narodu polskiego i pielgrzymastwa polskiego*
"Boom!" (Nemerov) **24**:266, 278
"Boom" (Stone) **53**:257
"A Boon" (Meredith) **28**:174
"Boone" (Berry) **28**:28, 38
"A Boone County Pastoral" (Riley) **48**:332
"Boop-Boop-Adieup Little Group!" (Nash) **21**:265
"A Boor" (Bukowski) **18**:15
"Boot Hill" (Ondaatje) **28**:304
The Bootleg Series Volumes 1-3 (Dylan) **37**:65
"Boots" (Kipling) **3**:192
"Boots of Spanish Leather" (Dylan) **37**:54, 58
"Booz endormi" (Hugo) **17**:65, 85
"Bora Ring" (Wright) **14**:335, 340, 374
"Border Line" (Hughes) **53**:122
The Borderers (Wordsworth) **4**:416
Borderland (Tagore)
See *Prāntik*

The Borderland (Tagore)
See *Prāntik*
"Bored" (Silverstein) **49**:330
"Bored on a Greyhound" (Stone) **53**:228
"Borges" (Borges)
See "Borges y yo"
"Borges and I" (Borges)
See "Borges y yo"
"Borges and Myself" (Borges)
See "Borges y yo"
"Borges y yo" (Borges) **32**:61, 77, 95, 133
"Boris Karloff in *The Mummy* Meets *Dr. Fu Manchu* " (Yau) **61**:346
"Born in December" (Rukeyser) **12**:224
"Born of a Shade" (Meredith) **60**:330
Born of a Woman: New and Selected Poems (Knight) **14**:37-9, 41-2, 46, 49, 51-2
"Borodinó" (Lermontov) **18**:278, 283, 290, 297, 304
"Borrowed Love Poems" (Yau) **61**:358
Borrowed Love Poems (Yau) **61**:337, 348, 357-58
"Bosque y bosque" (Guillén) **35**:155
"The Boss" (Ignatow) **34**:286
"Boston" (Moore) **49**:142
"Boston" (Stryk) **27**:203
"A Boston Ballad" (Whitman)
See "Poem of Apparitions in Boston in the 73rd Year of These States"
"The Boston Evening Transcript" (Eliot) **5**:153
"The Boston Hymn" (Emerson) **18**:77, 113, 119-20
"The Botanic Garden" (Noyes) **27**:129
"The Botanic Gardens" (Boland) **58**:43
"Botanical Gardens" (Masters) **1**:330
"Botanical Gardens" (Wright) **14**:341
"A Botanical Trope" (Meredith) **28**:190
"Bothering Me at Last" (Ignatow) **34**:273
"Boticelli's Spring" (Corso) **33**:26, 41
"Botta e riposta" (Montale) **13**:129, 131, 134, 147, 165
"Bottle Green" (Smith) **12**:333
"The Bottle in the Sea" (Vigny)
See "La bouteille à la mer"
"A Bottle of 1848 Vintage Valtellina" (Carducci)
See "A una Bottiglia di Valtellina del 1848"
"Bottled Water" (Stone) **53**:257
"Bottleneck" (MacNeice) **61**:141
"Bottom" (Rimbaud) **57**:234, 254, 285
"Bouche usée" (Éluard) **38**:70
"Boudaries" (Wright) **14**:374
"Le Bouge de l'historien" (Char) **56**:134
The Bouge of Court (Skelton)
See *The Bowge of Courte*
"Bound No'th Blues" (Hughes) **1**:254; **53**:82, 119, 136-37
"A Boundless Moment" (Frost) **1**:218
The Bounty (Walcott) **46**:258-59
"Bouquet" (Darío) **15**:113
The Bourgeois Poet (Shapiro) **25**:287-90, 292-94, 297, 299, 301-302, 308-11, 314-17, 321-22, 325
"Bournemouth" (Verlaine) **2**:416
"La bouteille à la mer" (Vigny) **26**:367, 371, 380-83, 391-92, 397, 402-404
"Bova" (Pushkin) **10**:407
The Bow and the Lyre (Yevtushenko) **40**:341
The Bowge of Court (Skelton)
See *The Bowge of Courte*
The Bowge of Courte (Skelton) **25**:329, 336-37, 340, 343, 349-50, 352, 361-62, 364-65, 367
"The Bowl and the Rim" (Graves) **6**:128
"The Bowl of Blood" (Jeffers) **17**:123, 144
"Bowls" (Moore) **4**:265; **49**:90
"A Box" (Stein) **18**:320-31, 349-50, 353
"A Box and Its Contents" (Ashbery) **26**:133
"The Box of Beads" (Kenyon) **57**:46
"The Boy" (Hacker) **47**:117
"The Boy" (Tagore) **8**:417
The Boy and the Stars (Seifert) **47**:326
"Boy at the Window" (Wilbur) **51**:230, 243, 266
"Boy by the Waterfall" (Sarton) **39**:323, 331
"Boy Driving his Father to Confession" (Heaney) **18**:243
"A Boy Drowns" (Thumboo) **30**:332
"A Boy Named Sue" (Silverstein) **49**:346-48
"Boy Riding Forward Backward" (Francis) **34**:242, 257
"Boy Wandering in Simms' Valley" (Warren) **37**:336
"Boy with a Sea Dream" (Page) **12**:168, 170
"Boy with Book of Knowledge" (Nemerov) **24**:287
"Boy with His Hair Cut Short" (Rukeyser) **12**:223
The Boyar Orsha (Lermontov)
See *Bojarin Orša*
"The Boyg, Peer Gynt, The One Only One" (Jarrell) **41**:174
"Boyhood in Tobacco Country" (Warren) **37**:318
"Boy-Man" (Shapiro) **25**:279, 297, 319
"Boys. Black." (Brooks) **7**:84
"Boys in Dresses" (Komunyakaa) **51**:23
"The Boys of Summer" (Thomas)
See "I See the Boys of Summer"
"A Boy's Summer Song" (Dunbar) **5**:138
A Boy's Will (Frost) **1**:192, 195, 197, 207, 213-14, 223-24; **39**:230-32, 235, 240, 246, 256
"Bracken Hills in Autumn" (MacDiarmid) **9**:197
"Brahma" (Emerson) **18**:83, 85, 88
"Braid Scots: An Inventory and Appraisement" (MacDiarmid)
See "Gairmscoile"
"Braiding" (Lee) **24**:247
"The brainsick race that wanton youth ensues" (Raleigh) **31**:201
"Brainstorm" (Nemerov) **24**:257, 268
"Braly Street" (Soto) **28**:375, 378-79, 384-85
"A Branch from Palestine" (Lermontov) **18**:298
A Branch of May (Reese) **29**:330, 335-337, 339, 345-346, 351-352
The Branch Will Not Break (Wright) **36**:283, 292-96, 298, 300, 302-5, 307-8, 313-14, 316-17, 319, 325-31, 338, 341-42, 344-45, 348, 350-52, 355, 362, 364-65, 371, 373-75, 378-79, 385-86, 389-91, 396, 399
"La branche d'amandier" (Lamartine) **16**:278
"Branches" (McGuckian) **27**:105
"Brancusi's Golden Bird" (Loy) **16**:321
"A Brand" (Johnson) **24**:160
"Brandons Both" (Rossetti) **7**:271
"Le brasier" (Apollinaire) **7**:47
"Brasilia" (Plath) **37**:204, 230, 233
"Brass Keys" (Sandburg) **2**:329
"Brass Spittoons" (Hughes) **1**:241, 263, 265; **53**:82, 143
"Bratsk Hydroelectric Station" (Yevtushenko) **40**:347, 350-53, 368
Bratsk Hydroelectric Station (Yevtushenko)
See *The Bratsk Station*
The Bratsk Power Station (Yevtushenko)
See *The Bratsk Station*
The Bratsk Station (Yevtushenko) **40**:356
Bratskaya G.E.S. (Yevtushenko) **40**:364
Bratya Razboiniki (Pushkin) **10**:358, 365, 386
"Bravado" (Frost) **39**:233
"A Brave and Startling Truth" (Angelou) **32**:30
"The brave combatants keep on falling" (Castro)
See "Cayendo van los bravos combatientes"
"Brave New World" (MacLeish) **47**:191, 246, 260
Braving the Elements (Merrill) **28**:220-23, 228-29, 244, 254, 256, 258-59, 281
"Brawl" (García Lorca)
See "Reyerta"
The Brazen Serpent (Ní Chuilleanáin) **34**:361-63, 367-69, 373, 383-84
"The Brazier" (Apollinaire)
See "Le brasier"
"Brazil, January 1, 1502" (Bishop) **3**:56; **34**:109, 139
"Brazil-Copacabana" (Guillén) **23**:117
"Brazilian Fazenda" (Page) **12**:178, 183, 190
"Brazzaville 22 Feb 72" (Brutus) **24**:123
"Bread" (Olds) **22**:328
"Bread" (Pasternak) **6**:267
"Bread Alone" (Wylie) **23**:311, 324
"Bread and Apples" (Mueller) **33**:197
"Bread and Music" (Aiken) **26**:24, 72
"Bread and Wine" (Cullen) **20**:62
"Bread and Wine" (Hölderlin)
See "Brot und Wein"
"Bread at Midnight" (Merwin) **45**:22, 49
Bread in the Wilderness (Merton) **10**:352
The Bread of Time (Levine) **22**:231
"The Break" (Pasternak) **6**:280-82
"The Break" (Sexton) **2**:352-53
"Break, Break, Break" (Tennyson) **6**:358
"A Break from the Bush" (Komunyakaa) **51**:41, 60
"Break of Day" (Brown) **55**:102, 105-6, 120, 122
"Break of Day" (Sassoon) **12**:244, 277
"Breake of Day" (Donne) **1**:152
"Breakfast" (Stauffer) **18**:322-23
"Breaking Camp" (Piercy) **29**:308
"Breaking Camp" (Wagoner) **33**:335, 344
Breaking Camp (Piercy) **29**:307
"Breaking Green" (Ondaatje) **28**:331
"The Breaking of the Rainbows" (Nemerov) **24**:288
"Breaking Open" (Rukeyser) **12**:221, 224, 230
Breaking Open (Rukeyser) **12**:220, 224-25, 230
"Breaking Out" (Ammons) **16**:45, 63
"Breaklight" (Clifton) **17**:35
"The Breast" (Sexton) **2**:352, 364
"Breasts" (Tagore)
See "Stan"
"the breath" (Bissett) **14**:19, 24, 29, 34
"The Breath of Life" (Lawrence) **54**:250
"The Breath of Night" (Jarrell) **41**:137
"The Breathing" (Levertov) **11**:171
Breathing Exercises (Parra)
See *Ejercicios respiratorios*
"Breathing Landscape" (Rukeyser) **12**:209
"The Breathing Lesson" (Wagoner) **33**:327
"The Breathing, the Endless News" (Dove) **6**:122
Breathing the Water (Levertov) **11**:200, 202-05, 209-10
Breathing Tokens (Sandburg) **41**:322-24
Breath-Turning (Celan)
See *Atemwende*
"Brebeuf and His Brethren" (Birney) **52**:36
"Brecht in Svendborg" (Mahon) **60**:177-78
"Bredon Hill" (Housman) **2**:160, 182-83, 185
"The Breeze's Invitation" (Thoreau) **30**:258
"Brendel Playing Schubert" (Mueller) **33**:197
"Brennan" (Wright) **14**:375
"Brennende liebe, 1904" (Glück) **16**:128
"Brer Rabbit, You's de Cutes' of 'Em All" (Johnson) **24**:142, 163
"Breton Walks" (Mahon) **60**:163
"Breton Walks, 1: Early Morning" (Mahon) **60**:191
"Breton Walks, 2: Man and Bird" (Mahon) **60**:191
"Breughel's Two Monkeys" (Szymborska) **44**:281, 286, 311-13
"Brevity" (Wright) **14**:375-76
"Brian Age 7" (Doty) **53**:69
"Brian the Still-Hunter" (Atwood) **8**:19
"The Briar Rose" (Boland) **58**:92
"Briar Rose (Sleeping Beauty)" (Sexton) **2**:354, 365, 368
"The Bridal Ballad" (Poe) **1**:428, 432, 445, 447
"Bridal Birth" (Rossetti) **44**:169, 203
The Bridal of Triermain (Scott) **13**:297, 301-02, 311-12, 314, 317, 320
"Bridal Piece" (Glück) **16**:127
"The Bride" (Lawrence) **54**:167, 245

"Bride and Groom Lie Hidden for Three Days" (Hughes) **7**:165, 168
"The Bride in the Country" (Montagu) **16**:338
"The Bride of Abydos: A Turkish Tale" (Byron) **16**:91, 109
"Bride Song" (Rossetti) **7**:264
"The Bridegroom" (Kipling) **3**:183
"The Bride-Night Fire" (Hardy) **8**:99
"The Brides" (Hope) **56**:266, 303
Brides of Reason (Davie) **29**:92-95, 107, 111, 116-17
"Bridge" (Ammons) **16**:40-1,54
"The Bridge" (Longfellow) **30**:18, 26, 46
"The Bridge" (Paz) **48**:273
"The Bridge" (Walcott) **46**:237
The Bridge (Crane) **3**:84-5, 87-90, 93-8, 100-01, 105-10
"The Bridge of Cloud" (Longfellow) **30**:18
"The Bridge of Estador" (Crane) **3**:100
"Bridge Passage" (Szirtes) **51**:169
Bridge Passages (Szirtes) **51**:167, 171
"Bridging" (Piercy) **29**:302
"Brief Elegy" (Ignatow) **34**:272, 276
"Briefings" (Ammons) **16**:31
Briefings: Poems Small and Easy (Ammons) **16**:10, 21-23, 28, 45-6
"Briefly It Enters, and Briefly Speaks" (Kenyon) **57**:37, 40
The Brigand Brothers (Pushkin)
See *Bratya Razboiniki*
"The Bright Field" (Walcott) **46**:233-34
"Bright Star! Would I Were Steadfast as Thou Art" (Keats) **1**:279
"Bright Sunlight" (Lowell) **13**:64
"Bright-Cut Irish Silver" (Boland) **58**:24
"Brighton Beach" (Mahon) **60**:147, 210
"The Brigs of Ayr" (Burns) **6**:78
"Brilliant Sad Sun" (Williams) **7**:396, 409
"Brindis cotidiano" (Fuertes) **27**:39
"Brindisi funebre" (Carducci) **46**:23, 69
"Bring Down the Beams" (Bukowski) **18**:4
"Bring in the Wine" (Li Po) **29**:145
"Bring the Day" (Roethke) **15**:252, 273-74, 301-02
"Bring Your Own Victim" (Curnow) **48**:16-17, 49
The Bringer of Water (Berry) **28**:35
"Bringers" (Sandburg) **2**:316-17, 324; **41**:261
"bringing home th bacon" (Bissett) **14**:34
"Bringing in New Couples" (Hughes) **7**:166
Bringing It All Back Home (Dylan) **37**:44, 50
"Bringnal Banks are Wild and Fair For a' That" (Scott) **13**:278
"Brise marine" (Mallarmé) **4**:208
"The British Church" (Herbert) **4**:100
"The British Museum Reading Room" (MacNeice) **61**:116, 138-39
"Brittle Beauty" (Wyatt) **27**:302
"Broadcast" (Larkin) **21**:237
"The broad-leaved Arrow-head . . ." (Niedecker) **42**:98, 102, 152
"The Broadstone" (Jeffers) **17**:117
"Broadway" (Sandburg) **41**:248, 340
"Broadway" (Teasdale) **31**:331
"Broagh" (Heaney) **18**:202, 241
"Broceliande" (Hacker) **47**:119
"Broke" (Hughes) **53**:114
"A Broken Appointment" (Hardy) **8**:88, 110
"The Broken Balance" (Jeffers) **17**:144
"Broken Chord Sequence" (Chin) **40**:36
"The Broken Dark" (Hayden) **6**:181, 193-95
"Broken Dreams" (Yeats) **20**:328
Broken English (McHugh) **61**:207
The Broken Ground (Berry) **28**:2-5, 14, 31
"The Broken Home" (Merrill) **28**:221, 227, 230, 253
"Broken Jar" (Paz)
See "El cántaro roto"
"The Broken Man" (Wylie) **23**:321
"The Broken Oar" (Longfellow) **30**:51
"Broken Off By The Music" (Yau) **61**:329
"The Broken Pitcher" (Paz)
See "El cántaro roto"
"Broken Promise" (MacLeish) **47**:190
"The Broken Tower" (Crane) **3**:90, 103, 111
"The Broken Wings" (Gibran) **9**:75
"Broken-Face Gargoyles" (Sandburg) **41**:313-14
"The Bronco That Would Not Be Broken" (Lindsay) **23**:269, 273, 286
Bronwen, the Traw, and the Shape-Shifter (Dickey) **40**:233-34
"Bronz Trumpets and Sea Water" (Wylie) **23**:301, 315
"Bronze" (Walcott) **46**:273, 322
Bronze (Merrill) **28**:247-68, 272
"The Bronze David of Donatello" (Jarrell) **41**:208
"bronze fruit" (Alurista)
See "fruto de bronce"
"A Bronze Head" (Yeats) **20**:332
The Bronze Horseman (Pushkin)
See *Medny Vsadnik*
"The Bronze Horses" (Lowell) **13**:60, 62, 64, 73, 80, 82
"Bronze Rape" (Alurista) **34**:46
"Bronze Tablets" (Lowell) **13**:76, 78
"Bronzes" (Sandburg) **41**:314
"Bronzeville Man with a Belt in the Back" (Brooks) **7**:106
"A Bronzeville Mother Loiters in Mississippi. Meanwhile a Mississippi Mother Burns Bacon" (Brooks) **7**:56, 62, 81, 86, 96, 98-9
"Bronzeville Woman in a Red Hat" (Brooks) **7**:58, 62
"Brooding" (Ignatow) **34**:282
"The Brook" (Tennyson) **6**:357, 359
"The Brook" (Thomas) **53**:327-28
"Brook Farm" (Toomer) **7**:323
"Brooklyn Bridge Nocturne" (García Lorca)
See "Ciudad sin sueño"
"Broom Weed" (Goodison) **36**:142
"Brot und Wein" (Hölderlin) **4**:146-51, 161, 166, 169, 171, 176
"A Brother" (Thumboo) **30**:300
"The Brother" (Walcott) **46**:278, 291
"Brother and Sister" (Eliot) **20**:102, 124
"Brother and Sisters" (Wright) **14**:336, 340, 351
"Brother, Do Not Give Your Life" (Yosano Akiko)
See "Kimi Shinitamô koto nakare"
"Brother Fire" (MacNeice) **61**:160-61
Brother to Dragons (Warren) **37**:290-92, 294, 300, 304, 310, 312, 326-29, 332-33, 339-40, 348, 361, 369-70, 377, 380, 382-83
"Brother Where Dost Thou Dwell" (Thoreau) **30**:180
"Brotherhood in Pain" (Warren) **37**:309
"Brotherly Love: A Little Letter to the White Citizens of the South" (Hughes) **53**:115
"Brothers" (Hughes) **53**:193
"Brothers" (Johnson) **24**:130-31, 138, 142, 161, 170
"The Brothers" (Muir) **49**:219, 296
"The Brothers" (Wordsworth) **4**:374, 380, 381, 393, 402, 414
The Brothers Highwaymen (Pushkin)
See *Bratya Razboiniki*
Brothers, I Loved You All: Poems, 1969-1977 (Carruth) **10**:69-70, 72-3, 91
"Brought from Beyond" (Clampitt) **19**:102
"A Brown" (Stein) **18**:3312
"Brown Boy to Brown Girl" (Cullen) **20**:64
"A Brown Girl Dead" (Cullen) **20**:55, 62
"The Brown Menace or Poem to the Survival of Roaches" (Lorde) **12**:154-55, 158
"The brown muskrat, noiseless" (Niedecker) **42**:151
"Brown River, Smile" (Toomer) **7**:324
"Browning resuelve ser poeta" (Borges) **22**:98; **32**:50-1
"Brown's Descent" (Frost) **1**:195
"Bruce's Address" (Burns) **6**:55
"A Bruised Reed Shall He Not Break" (Rossetti) **7**:290
"Una brújula" (Borges) **32**:75
"Brush Fire" (Wright) **36**:365, 369
"Brussels: Merry-Go-Round" (Verlaine) **32**:370
"Bruto Minore" (Leopardi) **37**:79, 102, 118
"Bruxelles" (Rimbaud) **57**:252
"Bruxelles: Simple fesques" (Verlaine) **32**:411
"Bryan, Bryan, Bryan, Bryan" (Lindsay) **23**:265, 270, 273-74, 279, 287-88, 294-95
"Bubba" (Sanchez) **9**:240
Buch der Bilder (Rilke) **2**:266-67
"Buch der Lieder" (Bridges) **28**:88
Buch der Lieder (Heine) **25**:129-131, 139-41, 143, 145-46, 157-58, 161, 164
"The Buck in the Snow" (Millay) **6**:238
The Buck in the Snow, and Other Poems (Millay) **6**:213-14
"Buck Lake Store Auction" (Ondaatje) **28**:335
"Buckdancer's Choice" (Dickey) **40**:213
Buckdancer's Choice (Dickey) **40**:151, 155, 157, 160, 187, 192-97, 200, 212, 215-16, 231-32, 257, 261-62
"Buckin' Bronco" (Silverstein) **49**:335
Buckthorn (Akhmatova)
See *Podorozhnik*
Bucolic Comedies (Sitwell) **3**:293, 302-04, 307-08, 319, 322
"Bucolics" (Auden) **1**:23
Bucolics (Vergil)
See *Georgics*
The Budapest File (Szirtes) **51**:173, 175-79
"The Buddhist Painter Prepares to Paint" (Carruth) **10**:89
"Budgie" (MacNeice) **61**:178, 182
"The Buds Now Stretch" (Roethke) **15**:288
"Buenos Aires" (Borges) **32**:57-8
"Buenos Aires" (Lowell) **3**:214
"Buenos Aires: 1962" (Birney) **52**:42, 97, 100
"La bufera" (Montale) **13**:113, 131
La bufera e altro (Montale) **13**:103-04, 107, 113-14, 117-18, 122, 125, 131-33, 141, 148-49, 156, 160, 165-67
"The buffalo" (Borges)
See "El bisonte"
"Buffalo. 12.7.41" (Howe) **54**:45
"Buffalo Bill" (Sandburg) **41**:259
"Buffalo Bill's Defunct" (Cummings) **5**:93
"Le buffet" (Rimbaud) **3**:271, 283; **57**:253
"The Bugler-Boy" (Hopkins) **15**:138
"The Bugler's First Communion" (Hopkins) **15**:136, 144
"Buick" (Shapiro) **25**:288, 295, 297, 319, 322, 325
"Build Soil: A Political Pastoral" (Frost) **1**:196, 199, 203, 217
"Builder Kachina" (Rose) **13**:236-37
"Builders" (Cavafy) **36**:53, 57
"The Building" (Larkin) **21**:255
"The Building of the Long Serpent" (Longfellow) **30**:20
"The Building of the Ship" (Longfellow) **30**:20, 27, 37, 48-50, 82
"The Building of the Skyscraper" (Oppen) **35**:309
"The Building of the Trophy" (Rose) **13**:235
"Buildings" (Birney) **52**:28, 46
"The Bull" (Wright) **14**:333, 359
"The Bull Moses" (Hughes) **7**:131, 140, 158
"Bull of Bandylaw" (Plath) **37**:260-65
"The Bull of Bendylaw" (Plath)
See "Bull of Bandylaw"
"Bull Song" (Atwood) **8**:25
"Bullfrog" (Hughes) **7**:165
"Bullocky" (Wright) **14**:336, 340, 345, 349, 351, 357, 360, 368
"Bulwarked Against Fate" (Moore) **49**:136
"Bumming" (McKay) **2**:226
"Bums, on Waking" (Dickey) **40**:255
"The Bunch of Grapes" (Herbert) **4**:123, 125
"Buques" (Storni) **33**:239;

"Burbles" (Mahon) **60**:225
"The Burden" (Kipling) **3**:183
"A Burden" (Rossetti) **7**:286
"Burden" (Tagore)
See "Bhar"
"The Burden of Ninevah" (Rossetti) **44**:204, 260-61
"The Burden of Nineveh" (Rossetti) **44**:204, 260-61
"The Burghers" (Hardy) **8**:99
"The Burghers' Battle" (Morris) **55**:340
"The Burglar of Babylon" (Bishop) **3**:48, 56; **34**:78, 82, 116, 188
"Burial" (Walker) **30**:340, 349, 365
"The Burial-place" (Bryant) **20**:3
"The Buried City" (Chesterton) **28**:101
"The Buried Lake" (Tate) **50**:281, 290, 292, 294-96, 329, 332-34, 336
"The Buried Life" (Arnold) **5**:37-8, 41-5, 47, 49-50, 59, 64
"Buried Love" (Teasdale) **31**:336, 387-88
The Buried Port (Ungaretti)
See *Il Porto Sepolto*
"Burliuk" (Shvarts) **50**:132, 153
"The Burly Fading One" (Hayden) **6**:196
"The Burn" (Kinnell) **26**:290
"Burn and burn and burn" (Bukowski) **18**:24
"Burned" (Levine) **22**:220-21, 227-28, 232
"The Burning" (Momaday) **25**:200-201
"The Burning Child" (Clampitt) **19**:83
"A Burning Desire to Be Explicit" (Moore) **49**:144
"Burning Hills" (Ondaatje) **28**:327, 332-33
Burning in Water Drowning in Flame: Selected Poems 1955-1973 (Bukowski) **18**:21
"Burning Mountain" (Merwin) **45**:8
"The Burning of Paper Instead of Children" (Rich) **5**:371, 393-95
"Burning Oneself Out" (Rich) **5**:360
"The Burning Passion" (MacDiarmid) **9**:153
The Burning Perch (MacNeice) **61**:110, 125, 175-79, 182
"Burning River" (Ortiz) **17**:233
"Burning the Christmas Greens" (Williams) **7**:360
"Burning the Letters" (Jarrell) **41**:137-38, 171, 173-74, 177-79
"Burning the Letters" (Plath) **37**:260-65
"Burning the Tomato Worms" (Forché) **10**:132, 134, 142
"The Burnt Bridge" (MacNeice) **61**:128
"Burnt Lands" (Pavese) **13**:205
"Burnt Norton" (Eliot) **5**:164, 166-68, 171, 174, 177-85, 201, 210
"The Burnt-Out Spa" (Plath) **1**:389; **37**:185-87
"Burque" (Baca) **41**:42
"Bury Me In a Free Land" (Harper) **21**:185, 187, 190, 192
"Burying Ground by the Ties" (MacLeish) **47**:146, 189
"Burza" (Mickiewicz) **38**:149
"A Bus along St. Clair: December" (Atwood) **8**:40
"Bus Stop" (Silverstein) **49**:349
"Busby Berkeley in the Soviet Union" (Szirtes) **51**:172
"La busca de Averroes" (Borges) **32**:48, 50
"Búscate plata" (Guillén) **23**:142
"The Buses Headed for Scranton" (Nash) **21**:271
"The Bush Garden" (Atwood) **8**:38-9
"Bushed" (Birney) **52**:22, 32, 44-45, 47-48
"Busie old foole" (Donne)
See "The Sunne Rising"
"The Business Life" (Ignatow) **34**:273, 305, 316, 323
"The Business Man of Alicante" (Levine) **22**:213
The Business of Fancydancing (Alexie) **53**:4, 10-11, 23, 25-26, 29-31, 34, 39-40
"Busker" (Stryk) **27**:208
"A bust of Janus speaks" (Borges)
See "Habla un busto de Jano"
"The Busy Man Speaks" (Bly) **39**:14, 94
"But Also" (Warren) **37**:326
"But Born" (Aleixandre) **15**:5
"But for the Grace of God" (Robinson) **35**:367
"But He Was Cool; or, He Even Stopped for Green Lights" (Madhubuti) **5**:329, 341
"But I Do Not Need Kindness" (Corso) **33**:41, 43
"But I say unto you: love one another" (Lawrence) **54**:249
"But Not Forgotten" (Parker) **28**:362
"But Not to Me" (Teasdale) **31**:379
"But We've the May" (Cummings)
See "Song"
"'Butch' Weldy" (Masters) **1**:324
"The Butcher's Wife" (Erdrich) **52**:172, 174-77, 189
"Buteo Regalis" (Momaday) **25**:186, 188, 193, 195, 199, 210, 220
Butterflies (Gozzano)
See *Le farfalle*
"Butterflies Over the Map" (Warren) **37**:332
"The Butterfly" (Brodsky)
See "Babočka"
"The Butterfly" (Giovanni) **19**:112
"Butterfly" (Lawrence) **54**:200
"Butterfly Piece" (Hayden) **6**:194, 198
"Butterflyweed" (Ammons) **16**:4
"Buttons" (Sandburg) **41**:236, 269, 351
"Buveuse" (Char) **56**:137
"Buying Loveliness" (Teasdale) **31**:356
"Buying the Dog" (Ondaatje) **28**:335
"by 3/6/51" (Olson) **19**:316
"By a Lost Riverside" (Wagoner) **33**:361
"By a Reactionary" (Chesterton) **28**:114
"By a River" (Wagoner) **33**:374
By Avon River (H. D.) **5**:302
"By Disposition of Angels" (Moore) **49**:102, 126-27, 129
"By God I Want above Fourteenth" (Cummings) **5**:94
"By Lamplight" (Kunitz) **19**:171
By Lingual Wholes (Cruz) **37**:10-13, 16, 25, 35
"By Moonlight" (Sarton) **39**:325
"By Night When Others Soundly Slept" (Bradstreet) **10**:62
"By Rugged Ways" (Dunbar) **5**:131
By the Aurelian Wall, and Other Elegies (Carman) **34**:205, 211, 220
"By the Cloud Path" (Merwin) **45**:48
By the Earth's Corpse (Hardy) **8**:121
"By the Fireside" (Browning) **2**:76, 78-9, 88
"By the Hoof of the Wild Goat" (Kipling) **3**:186
"By the Lake" (Sitwell) **3**:325
"By the North Sea" (Swinburne) **24**:313-17, 319, 327, 329, 343
"By the Road" (Williams) **7**:382-83
"By the Rosanna" (Meredith) **60**:250
"By the Ruins of a Gun Emplacement: Saint-Benoît" (Wright) **36**:313
"By the Sea" (Teasdale) **31**:358
By the Seashore (Akhmatova)
See *U samovo morya*
"By The Stream" (Dunbar) **5**:127
"By the Waters of Babylon" (Celan)
See "An den Wassern Babels"
"By Twilight" (Swinburne) **24**:317
"By Wauchopeside" (MacDiarmid) **9**:197, 199
"By Way of Explanation" (Cisneros) **52**:162-64
"By-pass" (Wright) **14**:373
"Bypassing Rue Descartes" (Milosz) **8**:200
"The Byrnies" (Gunn) **26**:186
Býti básníkem (Seifert) **47**:320, 323, 326-27, 340
"A Byzantine Nobleman in Exile Composing Verses" (Cavafy) **36**:94, 96, 98-99
"Byzantium" (Yeats) **20**:308, 310, 316, 327, 334-35; **51**:71, 77-80, 82, 86-87, 90, 93-94, 97-100, 105, 108, 115, 150
"a C." (Montale) **13**:138
"C Minor" (Wilbur) **51**:283
"Ça ira" (Carducci) **46**:47, 55
"Ça le creux" (Césaire) **25**:33
"Ca' the Yowes to the Knowes" (Burns) **6**:76
"Cabala" (Swenson) **14**:288
"Cabaret" (Brown) **55**:71, 76, 95, 102, 114, 151
"Cabaret" (Hughes) **1**:237
"Cabaret Girl Dies on Welfare Island" (Hughes) **1**:247
Cabbage Gardens (Howe) **54**:40, 52, 107
"Cabellera" (Paz) **48**:175, 243
"A Cabin in the Clearing" (Frost) **1**:212
"A Cabin Tale" (Dunbar) **5**:120
Cables to Rage (Lorde) **12**:140
"Cables to Rage, or I've Been Talking on This Street Corner a Hell of a Long Time" (Lorde) **12**:155
"Cables to the Ace" (Merton) **10**:337
Cables to the Ace; or, Familiar Liturgies of Misunderstanding (Merton) **10**:338, 345, 348, 351, 354
"Caboose Thoughts" (Sandburg) **2**:302; **41**:240, 270, 280, 282
"Cabra" (Joyce) **22**:149
"Le cacot" (Lamartine) **16**:284
Cadastre (Césaire) **25**:12, 15, 17, 30-2, 35-6, 38-9
"Cadenas rotas" (Alurista) **34**:27, 38
"Cadenus and Vanessa" (Swift) **9**:253-55, 296
"A Cadenza" (Clampitt) **19**:102
"Cadenza" (Hughes) **7**:159
"Cadore" (Carducci) **46**:52
Caelo tonantem (Horace) **46**:97
"Caerulei Oculi" (Gautier) **18**:125
"Caesar" (Merwin) **45**:22, 49
"Caesar when that the traytour of Egipt" (Wyatt) **27**:339
"Caesarion" (Cavafy) **36**:20, 75, 86, 87-89
Caesar's Gate (Duncan) **2**:101
"Café" (Milosz) **8**:175
"Café: 3 A.M." (Hughes) **53**:115, 127, 177, 192
"Café at Rapallo" (Montale) **13**:148
"Cafe Atarah" (Amichai) **38**:27
"Cafe du neant" (Loy) **16**:312-13, 328
"Café Tableau" (Swenson) **14**:275
A Cage of Spines (Swenson) **14**:247-48, 252, 260, 277, 284
"Caged Bird" (Angelou) **32**:7
"The Caged Bird" (Sarton) **39**:324
"Cages" (Kenyon) **57**:3
Cahier d'un retour au pays natal (Césaire) **25**:2-3, 5-7, 10-11, 13-16, 18-19, 29-33, 41-4, 47-9, 51-6, 58-61, 63, 65
"Caída de Europa" (Mistral) **32**:188
"Cain" (Coleridge)
See "The Wanderings of Cain"
"Cain" (Nemerov) **24**:261
Cain (Byron) **16**:86, 88, 90, 103-05, 108, 111
"Caino" (Ungaretti) **57**:369
"La cajita de Olinalá" (Mistral) **32**:179
"Cake" (Stein) **18**:322
"A Calder" (Shapiro) **25**:291
"Calendar" (Warren) **37**:331
The Calender (Spenser)
See *The Shepheardes Calender: Conteyning Twelve Æglogues Proportionable to the Twelve Monethes*
"Calendrier" (Char) **56**:154, 157
"Calendrier lagunaire" (Césaire) **25**:33, 45
"Caliban" (Brathwaite) **56**:87, 100
"Caliban upon Setebos" (Browning) **2**:58-9, 88, 95
"The Calico Cat" (Lindsay) **23**:281
"Calidus Juventa?" (Tate) **50**:306, 319, 325
"California" (Oppen) **35**:284
"The California Water Plan" (Snyder) **21**:291
Californians (Jeffers) **17**:134-35, 138
"The Call" (Akhmatova)
See "Zov"
"The Call" (Brooke) **24**:57, 82
"The Call" (Dickey) **40**:175-77, 184
"The Call" (Herbert) **4**:130

"The Call" (Kenyon) **57**:47
"Call" (Lorde) **12**:139, 141
"The Call Across the Valley of Not-Knowing" (Kinnell) **26**:251, 269, 273-75
"Call It Fear" (Harjo) **27**:54, 61
"Call it love" (Enzensberger) **28**:139
"Call Me Back Again" (Tagore)
See "Ebar phirao more"
"Call me Ishmael" (Cage) **58**:219
"The Call of the Wild" (Snyder) **21**:292-93, 297
Call Yourself Alive? (Cassian) **17**:4, 6, 13
"La calle" (Paz) **48**:230
"Calle" (Storni) **33**:239, 246, 283;
"Calle con almacén rosado" (Borges) **32**:83, 124
"Las Calles" (Borges) **22**:68; **32**:38, 80-1, 124
"Callie Ford" (Brooks) **7**:62, 69
Calligrammes (Apollinaire) **7**:3, 9-10, 12, 35-6, 42, 44, 46, 48-9
"A Calling" (Kumin) **15**:210
"Calling Cards" (Hughes) **53**:109
Calling Myself Home (Hogan) **35**:247, 248, 250, 252, 253, 257, 258
"The Calling of Names" (Angelou) **32**:13
"Calling on All Silent Minorities" (Jordan) **38**:137, 141
"Calling Out to Yeti" (Szymborska) **44**:285
Calling Out to Yeti (Szymborska)
See *Wołanie do Yeti*
"Calling To Minde Mine eie Long Went About" (Raleigh) **31**:201, 295-97, 312
"Callinge To Minde" (Raleigh)
See "Calling To Minde Mine eie Long Went About"
"Calliope" (H. D.) **5**:304
"Callow Captain" (Graves) **6**:133
"The Calls" (Owen) **19**:336
"The Calm" (Donne) **1**:122
"The Calm" (Gallagher) **9**:58
"Calming Kali" (Clifton) **17**:24
"Calmly We Walk Through This April's Day" (Schwartz) **8**:305-06
"Calverly's" (Robinson) **1**:466; **35**:362, 363
"Calypso" (Brathwaite) **56**:43, 96
"Calypso" (H. D.) **5**:306
"Calypso's Island" (MacLeish) **47**:196
"Cambios de nombre" (Parra) **39**:278, 294, 305, 307
"Cambridge" (Borges) **32**:43
"Cambridge, First Impressions" (Corso) **33**:35
"The Cambridge Ladies Who Live in Furnished Souls" (Cummings) **5**:94
"Cambridge, Spring 1937" (Schwartz) **8**:301
Camcar (Kabīr) **56**:342, 346
"Camden 1892" (Borges) **32**:100, 113
"The Camel" (Nash) **21**:278
"Camelia" (Tagore) **8**:417
"Camellia Sabina" (Moore) **49**:98, 119, 134
"El camello (auto de los Reyes Magos)" (Fuertes) **27**:8, 15, 31
"Camilo" (Guillén) **23**:128
"Caminata" (Borges) **32**:81, 125
"Camino blanco, viejo camino" (Castro) **41**:99
"Caminos" (Darío) **15**:82
"La camisa de fuerza" (Parra) **39**:271-72
La camisa de fuerza (Parra) **39**:279, 288
"Camouflaging the Chimera" (Komunyakaa) **51**:6
"Camp" (Fuertes) **27**:23
"Camp 1940" (Senghor) **25**:235
"Camp and Cloister" (Browning) **2**:26
"A Camp in the Prussian Forrest" (Jarrell) **41**:135-38, 173-74, 195-96
"Camp Notes" (Yamada) **44**:346
Camp Notes and Other Poems (Yamada) **44**:323, 325-26, 329-35, 337-46, 348-49
"Campau Bun" (Dafydd ap Gwilym) **56**:208
"Campeón Finlandés" (Mistral) **32**:188
"The Camperdown Elm" (Moore) **49**:150
"Camping at Split Rock" (Wright) **14**:366
"Campions" (Lawrence) **54**:227-31, 234-36
"El campo, la ciudad, el cielo" (Guillén) **35**:156
"Camps of Green" (Whitman) **3**:378
"campus theatre steps" (Birney) **52**:34
"Can Cranes Cogitate" (Stone) **53**:258
"Can Grande's Castle" (Lowell) **13**:60
Can Grande's Castle (Lowell) **13**:60, 62-3, 65-6, 72-4, 79-83, 93
"Can. Hist." (Birney) **52**:16
"Can I See Arcturus from Where I Stand?" (Warren) **37**:330, 333, 367, 378
"Can. Lit." (Birney) **52**:12, 17, 92-93
"Caña" (Guillén) **23**:98
"Canace and Machaire" (Gower) **59**:6
"Canada" (Birney) **52**:58
"canada" (Bissett) **14**:25, 34
"Canada: Case History" (Birney) **52**:8, 25, 42
"Canada Council" (Birney) **52**:31-32, 77
Canada Gees Mate for Life (Bissett) **14**:26
"The Canadian" (Bissett) **14**:10, 25
"Canadian Pacific" (Mahon) **60**:140, 213-15
"Canadians and Pottawatomies" (Sandburg) **41**:302
"Canal" (Tomlinson) **17**:313, 343
"Canal Bank Sonnets" (Kavanagh) **33**:145, 147
"Canal Bank Walk" (Kavanagh) **33**:95-6, 103, 115, 119, 138
"The Canal Garden" (Seifert) **47**:328
"The Canal's Drowning Black" (Hughes) **7**:148
"Cancarì" (Kabir)
See *Camcar*
"The Cancer Match" (Dickey) **40**:191, 199-200
"Cancer Winter" (Hacker) **47**:104, 107, 116-17
"Canción" (Parra) **39**:284
"Canción de la Muerte" (Mistral) **32**:179
"Canción de la mujer astuta" (Storni) **33**:299-300;
"Canción de otoño en primavera" (Darío) **15**:96, 107, 109-11
"Canción de taurus" (Mistral) **32**:181
"Canción de virgo" (Mistral) **32**:181
"La canción del bongo" (Guillén) **23**:106, 111-14, 132, 136, 139
"Canción otoñal" (Darío) **15**:82
"La canción que chua" (Mistral) **32**:180
"Canción tonta" (García Lorca) **3**:136
"Cancionero sin nombre" (Parra) **39**:292
Cancionero sin nombre (Parra) **39**:260, 266-67, 270, 272, 292, 295
Canciones (García Lorca) **3**:118-19, 148-49
"Canciones de cuna" (Mistral) **32**:161
Canciones rusas (Parra) **39**:271-72, 278, 285, 295
"Candelabro" (Guillén) **35**:201
"Candidate's Prayer before Master's Oral" (Birney) **52**:17
"candide" (Enzensberger) **28**:134, 136
"The Candle in the Cabin" (Lindsay) **23**:286
"Candle, Lamp, and Firefly" (Gallagher) **9**:59
"Candle Shuffle" (Alurista) **34**:24, 41
"Candle-Lightin' Time" (Dunbar) **5**:122
"Candles" (Cavafy) **36**:54, 57, 88
"Candles at 330" (McGuckian) **27**:91
Candles in Babylon (Levertov) **11**:198-201, 209
"The Candlestick" (Brodsky) **9**:3
"The Candlestick" (Guillén)
See "Candelabro"
"Cane" (Brathwaite) **56**:76
Cane (Toomer) **7**:309-11, 319, 323-24, 326, 330, 332-33, 335, 339-41
"la canería y el sol" (Alurista) **34**:5-6
"El cangrejo" (Guillén) **23**:124
"las canicas y mis callos" (Alurista) **34**:11, 36
"Canis Major" (Frost) **39**:233
"The Cannery" (Stryk) **27**:211
"Cannery Town in August" (Cervantes) **35**:116, 121
"canoe" (Bissett) **14**:23
The Canon Yeoman's Tale (Chaucer) **58**:266, 351
"The Canonization" (Amichai) **38**:43
"The Canonization" (Bridges) **28**:73
"The Canonization" (Donne) **1**:126, 130, 132-34
"Canon's Yeoman's Prologue" (Chaucer) **19**:26
"Canon's Yeoman's Tale" (Chaucer) **19**:13, 19
"Canso" (Merwin) **45**:24, 91
"Canst Thou Draw Out Leviathan With An Hook?" (Curnow) **48**:36
"Canta el sinsonte en el Turquino" (Guillén) **23**:124
"Cantares 1" (Castro) **41**:109
"Cantares 2" (Castro) **41**:109
"Cantares 3" (Castro) **41**:89, 109
"Cantares 4" (Castro) **41**:109
"Cantares 5" (Castro) **41**:90, 109
"Cantares 7" (Castro) **41**:109
"Cantares 8" (Castro)
See "Un arrogante gaitero"
"Cantares 9" (Castro) **41**:110
"Cantares 10" (Castro) **41**:109
"Cantares 11" (Castro) **41**:110
"Cantares 12" (Castro) **41**:109
"Cantares 13" (Castro) **41**:109-10
"Cantares 14" (Castro) **41**:109
"Cantares 16" (Castro) **41**:93, 110
"Cantares 17" (Castro) **41**:110
"Cantares 18" (Castro) **41**:109-10
"Cantares 19" (Castro) **41**:110
"Cantares 20" (Castro) **41**:110
"Cantares 21" (Castro) **41**:110
"Cantares 24" (Castro) **41**:109
"Cantares 26" (Castro) **41**:109
"Cantares 27" (Castro) **41**:110
"Cantares 28" (Castro) **41**:110
"Cantares 29" (Castro) **41**:110
"Cantares 30" (Castro) **41**:109
"Cantares 31" (Castro) **41**:109
"Cantares 32" (Castro) **41**:109
"Cantares 33" (Castro) **41**:110
"Cantares 37" (Castro) **41**:110
Cantares gallegos (Castro) **41**:79, 87-9, 93, 97, 106-9, 111, 115-16
Cantares Mexicanos I (Cardenal) **22**:127-28, 129, 132
Cantares Mexicanos II (Cardenal) **22**:127-28, 129, 132
"Cantares mexicanos (II)" (Cardenal) **22**:128, 130
"Cantares mexicanos(I)" (Cardenal) **22**:127, 130
"El cántaro roto" (Paz) **1**:361
"A Cantata" (Lanier) **50**:75
Canterburie-Tales (Chaucer)
See *Canterbury Tales*
Canterbury Tales (Chaucer) **19**:3, 6, 13, 16, 18, 20, 22, 24, 26-7, 34, 37, 43-50, 52-4, 60, 64; **58**:237, 277, 281, 283-86, 288, 299-300, 322, 325, 342, 352, 361, 363, 365, 367
"Canthara" (Williams) **7**:367
Canti (Leopardi) **37**:91-92, 118, 122-23, 125-32, 134, 141, 165, 169
"Canti Romani" (Ferlinghetti) **1**:183
"Canticle" (Berry) **28**:3-4
Canticle (Guillén)
See *Cántico*
"Canticles" (Sarton) **39**:357
Cántico (Guillén) **35**:139, 145, 152-153, 154, 155, 156, 157, 158, 159, 160, 169, 170, 174, 175, 179, 180, 181, 182, 183, 184, 185, 186, 187, 188, 189, 191, 192-93, 194-97, 200-2054, 207, 210, 211, 212, 213, 214-19, 225-32, 233, 235-40, 241
"Cantique des colonnes" (Valéry) **9**:366, 394
"Canto I" (Pound) **4**:334, 357
"Canto VIII" (Pound) **4**:353
"Canto XIV" (Pound) **4**:328, 358
"Canto XV" (Pound) **4**:358
"Canto XVI" (Pound) **4**:328
"Canto XXVI" (Pound) **4**:324
"Canto XXVII" (Pound) **4**:325, 345
"Canto XLI" (Pound) **4**:357
"Canto XLVII" (Pound) **4**:346-47, 349
"Canto L" (Pound) **4**:360, 362

"Canto LI" (Pound) **4**:326
"Canto LXXIV" (Pound) **4**:345-49, 352, 354
"Canto LXXV" (Pound) **4**:347, 349
"Canto LXXVI" (Pound) **4**:352-53
"Canto LXXVIII" (Pound) **4**:349
"Canto LXXIX" (Pound) **4**:349
"Canto LXXX" (Pound) **4**:345, 349
"Canto LXXXI" (Pound) **4**:349, 352
"Canto LXXXII" (Pound) **4**:349, 352
"Canto LXXXIII" (Pound) **4**:345, 348
"Canto LXXXIV" (Pound) **4**:345, 348
"Canto LXXXVI" (Pound) **4**:347
"Canto XCI" (Pound) **4**:354
"Canto C" (Pound) **4**:360-62
"Canto CI" (Pound) **4**:353
"Canto CIV" (Pound) **4**:357
"Canto CX" (Pound) **4**:353
"Canto CXIII" (Pound) **4**:353-54
"Canto CXV" (Pound) **4**:354
"Canto CXVI" (Pound) **4**:353-54
"Canto CXVIII" (Pound) **4**:353
"Canto CXX" (Pound) **4**:354
"Canto a Bolivar" (Neruda) **4**:279-80
"Canto à la Argentina" (Darío) **15**:82, 115
"Canto a las madres de los milicianos muertos" (Neruda) **4**:278
"Canto a Stalingrado" (Neruda) **4**:279
"Canto de la sangre" (Darío) **15**:91-2, 96, 105
"Canto di Apòllion" (Quasimodo) **47**:277
"Canto di marzo" (Carducci) **46**:55, 65
"Canto di Primavera" (Carducci) **46**:18
Canto general de Chile (Neruda) **4**:279-82, 291-96
"Canto nacional" (Cardenal) **22**:103
"Canto negro" (Guillén) **23**:134
"Canto notturno di un pastore errante dell'Asia" (Leopardi) **37**:83, 92, 102, 116, 121, 123-24, 126, 129, 131-32, 140-41, 165
"Canto notturno di un pastore errante nell'Asia" (Montale) **13**:109
"Canto of Signs Without Wonders" (Curnow) **48**:32-38
"Canto popolare" (Pasolini) **17**:294
"Canto primo" (Ungaretti) **57**:347
"Canto sobre unas ruinas" (Neruda) **4**:309
"Canto82" (Viereck) **27**:283
Cantos (Pound) **4**:332, 343-45, 350-54
Cantos de vida y esperanza (Darío) **15**:78, 80, 87, 89, 91-2, 96, 103-05, 107, 109, 115, 117, 120
Cantos para soldados y sones para turistas (Guillén) **23**:99, 101, 131, 133, 140
"Canvas" (Zagajewski) **27**:387-88, 393, 395
Canvas (Zagajewski) **27**:389, 393, 399
"CANVASS" (Niedecker) **42**:146-49
"Canyon de Chelly" (Ortiz) **17**:225
"Canzone" (Mandelstam) **14**:138
"Canzone" (Ungaretti) **57**:339, 374, 376
"La Canzone di Legnano" (Carducci) **46**:53
"Canzone on an Old Proverb" (Stryk) **27**:198
"Canzones" (Okigbo)
See "Four Canzones (1957-1961)"
Canzoni (Leopardi) **37**:123
Canzoni (Pound) **4**:317
Canzoniere (Petrarch) **8**:218, 220, 224-40, 242-45, 247-49, 251-65, 268-73, 276-78
"Cap" (Brathwaite) **56**:93
"The Cap and Bells" (Keats) **1**:279, 311
"Cape Breton" (Bishop) **3**:39, 58-9; **34**:104-105, 108
"Cape Cod" (Brodsky)
See "A Cape Cod Lullaby"
"A Cape Cod Lullaby" (Brodsky) **9**:7, 19
"Cape Dread" (Merwin) **45**:7
"Cape Hatteras" (Crane) **3**:86-7, 90, 96, 106-10
"Cape Mootch" (Pasternak) **6**:251
"Caperucita Roja" (Mistral) **32**:179
"Capital del invierno" (Guillén) **35**:154
Capital of Pain (Éluard)
See *Capitale de la douleur*
"Capital Punishment" (Alexie) **53**:21
Capitale de la douleur (Éluard) **38**:60, 64, 66, 68, 70, 76-7, 80, 99, 101-5, 107
"Capitol Air" (Ginsberg) **4**:62, 76, 83
"Cappadocian Song" (Carruth) **10**:89
"Capri" (Teasdale) **31**:322
"Caprice" (Cullen) **20**:55
"Caprice" (Wright) **36**:372
"Capricho" (Storni) **33**:275, 307;
"Capricorn Rising" (Mackey) **49**:6, 22
"Captain Carpenter" (Ransom) **61**:275, 311, 313, 320, 324-25
"Captain Cook" (Birney) **52**:21
"Captain Craig" (Robinson) **1**:460, 467, 483, 486
Captain Craig and Other Poems (Robinson) **1**:462-63, 470-72, 474, 490; **35**:362, 367
"Captain Haddock" (Szirtes) **51**:158
Captain Lavender (McGuckian) **27**:104-106
"A Captain of the Press Gang" (Carman) **34**:207
"The Captive" (Morris) **55**:344-45
The Captive of the Caucasus (Pushkin)
See *Kavkazsky plennik*
"A Captive of the Khan" (Tsvetaeva)
See "Khansky polon"
"Captivity" (Erdrich) **52**:174, 176, 195-97, 202
"Captivity" (Mueller) **33**:196
"The Captivity and Restoration of Mrs. Mary Rowlandson" (Howe) **54**:96
"Captivity of the Fly" (MacLeish) **47**:192
"Captured by the Khan" (Tsvetaeva)
See "Khansky polon"
"Car Journeys" (Abse) **41**:13-14
"Car Poem" (Shvarts) **50**:148
"Car Wreck" (Shapiro) **25**:205
"Cara a cara" (Guillén) **35**:157, 227
"Les carabosses" (Hacker) **47**:86
"Caracas" (Birney) **52**:41
"A Carafe That Is a Blind Glass" (Stein) **18**:318, 334
"Caravanserai" (Goodison) **36**:143
Carcari (Kabir)
See *Camcar*
"The Card Players" (Larkin) **21**:237
"A Card Skull in Atlantis" (Szirtes) **51**:159
"A Career" (Yevtushenko) **40**:343-44
"A Careful Passion" (Walcott) **46**:230, 273
"Careless Water" (Stein) **18**:334
"Caress" (Mistral)
See "Caricia"
"Caribbean Kingdoms" (Birney) **52**:16, 18, 103
"Caribbean Sunset" (Hughes) **1**:236
"Caribbean Wind" (Dylan) **37**:64-65
"Caribou" (Warren) **37**:367, 376
"Caribou Girl" (Cervantes) **35**:104, 107, 112, 117
"Caricia" (Mistral) **32**:179
"Caritas" (Cummings) **5**:94
"Carl Hamblin" (Masters) **36**:183
"Carlo Goldoni" (Carducci) **46**:52
"Carlos" (Ríos) **57**:312
"Carlos among the Candles" (Stevens) **6**:295
"Carmelites" (Erdrich) **52**:186
"Carmen" (Blok) **21**:26
Carmen (Horace)
See *Carmen Saeculare*
Carmen Saeculare (Horace) **46**:97, 99, 108, 211, 222
"Carnal Knowledge" (Gunn) **26**:182, 188, 199-200, 207, 210, 218
"Carnales el amor nos pertenece" (Alurista) **34**:23, 29
"el carnalismo nos une" (Alurista) **34**:31
"Carnaval" (Gautier) **18**:125
"La Carne de tus Labios" (Alurista) **34**:46
"Carnegie Hall: Rescued" (Moore) **4**:242; **49**:148
"The Carnegie Library" (Jarrell) **41**:165
"The Carnegie Library, Juvenile Division" (Jarrell) **41**:159, 167, 177, 194
"Carnegie, Oklahoma, 1919" (Momaday) **25**:221
"Carnevale" (Carducci) **46**:5, 51
"Carnevale di Gerti" (Montale) **13**:117
"Carnival" (Carducci)
See "Carnevale"
"Carol" (Merton) **10**:340
"Carol" (Nemerov) **24**:258
"A Carol for Children" (Nash) **21**:275
"Carolina Cabin" (Hughes) **53**:116
Carolina Said Song (Ammons) **16**:19
"Caroline Branson" (Masters) **36**:188
"Carousing Students" (Pushkin) **10**:407
"The Carpenter's Son" (Housman) **2**:192
"A Carpet Not Bought" (Merrill) **28**:253
"Le carreau" (Char) **56**:171, 173
"Carrefour" (Lowell) **13**:85
"A Carriage from Sweden" (Moore) **49**:100
"Carrick Revisited" (MacNeice) **61**:112-13
"Carrickfergus" (MacNeice) **61**:118, 120, 131, 137, 144
"Carrier" (Meredith) **28**:174, 186
The Carrier of Ladders (Merwin) **45**:10, 16, 18-19, 26-30, 32-3, 35, 37-8, 40-2, 45-7, 51, 57, 59, 66, 73-4, 77, 84, 90, 94-6, 98
The Carrier Pigeon (Seifert)
See *Poštovní holub*
"Carriers of the Dream Wheel" (Momaday) **25**:199, 217
"A Carrion" (Baudelaire)
See "Une charogne"
"Carrion Comfort" (Hopkins) **15**:144
"Carro del cielo" (Mistral) **32**:169
"Carrying Mission to the Frontier" (Wang Wei)
See "Arriving at the Frontier on a Mission"
"The Carrying Ring" (McGuckian) **27**:105
"Carta a Miguel Otero Silva, en Caracas, 1948" (Neruda) **4**:293
"Carta de creencia" (Paz) **1**:376; **48**:232
"Carta de la eme" (Fuertes) **27**:37
"Carta de la Habana" (Guillén) **23**:127
"Carta explicatoria de Gloria" (Fuertes) **27**:17, 48-9
"Carta lírca a una mujer" (Storni) **33**:254, 277-78;
"Carta lírica a otra mujer" (Storni) **33**:254, 277-78;
"Cartagena de Indias" (Birney) **52**:15, 21, 23, 34, 41, 44-45, 60-62, 80, 96-98
"Cartas a una desconocida" (Parra) **39**:285-86
"Cartas del poeta que duerme en una silla" (Parra) **39**:286
"Carte du 8 novembre" (Char) **56**:154
"Cartographies of Silence" (Rich) **5**:378-79, 394-95
"Cartoons of Coming Shows Unseen Before" (Schwartz) **8**:291
"The Cartridges" (Levine) **22**:213
"La cartuja" (Darío) **15**:102
"Caru Merch Fonheddig" (Dafydd ap Gwilym) **56**:245, 247
"Caru yn y Gaeaf" (Dafydd ap Gwilym) **56**:225, 227-33
"The Caruso Poem" (Bissett) **14**:4, 19
"Caryatid" (Benn) **35**:9
"La casa dei doganieri" (Montale) **13**:114
La casa dei doganieri (Montale) **13**:106, 138
"Casa Elena" (Borges) **22**:92
Casa Guidi Windows: A Poem (Browning) **6**:2, 6-9, 16, 36, 38, 41, 46
"Casa in costruzione" (Pavese) **13**:226
"Casa mia" (Ungaretti) **57**:346
"Casa sul mare" (Montale) **13**:137, 147, 164
"Casabianca" (Bishop) **3**:37, 56, 67; **34**:122, 149
"La casada infiel" (García Lorca) **3**:119, 132, 134
"Cascada en sequedal" (Mistral) **32**:161
Case d'armons (Apollinaire) **7**:21-2
"Case in Point" (Jordan) **38**:123, 126, 139
"A Case of Murder" (Hagiwara)
See "Satsujin jiken"
"Case-moth" (Wright) **14**:374
"Casi Juicio Final" (Borges) **32**:38

"Caspar Hauser Song" (Trakl) **20**:226, 259-60, 267, 269
"Cassandra" (Bogan) **12**:110
"Cassandra" (Jeffers) **17**:139
"Cassandra" (Robinson) **1**:487
"Cassinus and Peter, a Tragic Elegy" (Swift) **9**:262, 270, 274, 279, 286, 288, 298, 302-03
"The Cassis River" (Rimbaud)
See "La Rivière de Cassis"
"Cast rěci" (Brodsky) **9**:7, 19
Cast rěci (Brodsky) **9**:6-8, 13-15, 26-7, 29-31
"Castástrofe en Sewell" (Neruda) **4**:294
"The Castaway" (Cowper) **40**:44-6, 98, 126
"The Castaway" (Walcott) **46**:230, 274, 283-84, 290
The Castaway, and Other Poems (Walcott) **46**:229-31, 238, 259, 272, 274-75, 283-85, 322
"The Castaways" (McKay) **2**:221
"Castilian" (Wylie) **23**:310, 312
"Casting and Gathering" (Heaney) **18**:257
The Casting of Bells (Seifert)
See *Odlévání ní zvonů*
The Casting of the Bells (Seifert)
See *Odlévání ní zvonů*
Casting the Bells (Seifert)
See *Odlévání ní zvonů*
"The Castle" (Graves) **6**:131, 135, 142, 144
"The Castle" (Muir) **49**:232, 245, 248-49, 255-56
"The Castle" (Silverstein) **49**:343
"The Castle" (Tomlinson) **17**:308, 311
"Castles and Distances" (Wilbur) **51**:187-88, 207-9, 236
"Casual" (Hughes) **53**:115
"Casualty" (Heaney) **18**:198, 211, 240, 246
"The Casualty" (Hughes) **7**:114
"The Casualty" (MacNeice) **61**:126, 128, 141
"Cat" (Brathwaite) **56**:49
"The Cat" (Kinnell) **26**:286-7
"A Cat, a Kid, and a Mom" (Silverstein) **49**:342
"The Cat and I Dream Away the Days and Nights" (Shvarts)
See "My s koshkoi dremlem den' i noch"
"The Cat and the Moon" (Yeats) **20**:304
The Cat and the Moon (Yeats) **51**:108
"The Cat and the Saxophone" (Hughes) **1**:236; **53**:79
"Cat in an Empty Apartment" (Szymborska)
See "Kot w pustym mieszkaniu"
"cat walked in" (Alurista) **34**:32, 33
"Catalina Macaw" (Doty) **53**:69
"Catalina Parra" (Parra) **39**:285
"The Catalpa Tree" (Bogan) **12**:129, 131
"Catarina to Camoens" (Browning) **6**:16-17, 38
"Catastrophe at Sewell" (Neruda)
See "Castástrofe en Sewell"
"Cat-Boat" (Oppen) **35**:327
"the catch" (Bukowski) **18**:25
"Catch" (Francis) **34**:255
"The Catch" (Wilbur) **51**:335
"A Catch of Shy Fish" (Brooks) **7**:105
"Catching Frogs" (Kenyon) **57**:12
"Catchment" (Kumin) **15**:209, 211, 223
"Catedral" (Borges) **22**:92
"Categories" (Giovanni) **19**:110-12, 116
"Catering For The People" (Thumboo) **30**:301, 329, 333
Cathay (Pound) **4**:317, 364, 366
"The Cathedral Close" (Patmore) **59**:228
"Catherine of Alexandria" (Dove) **6**:107, 109
"Catherine of Siena" (Dove) **6**:107, 109
"Cato Braden" (Masters) **1**:33, 343
"Cats" (Hagiwara)
See "Neko"
"Cats and a Cock" (Rukeyser) **12**:209
Cats and Bats and Things with Wings (Aiken) **26**:24, 30
"Catterskill Falls" (Bryant) **20**:14-16, 43
"Cattle Gredo" (Milosz) **8**:207
"Cattle Show" (MacDiarmid) **9**:160, 176
"Catullus" (Nishiwaki) **15**:238
The Caucasian Captive (Pushkin)
See *Kavkazsky plennik*
"Cauchemar" (Gautier) **18**:142, 164
"Cauchemar" (Verlaine) **32**:387
"The Caucuses: A Romance" (Carver) **54**:28
"Caupolicán" (Darío) **15**:95
"Cause & Effect" (Swenson) **14**:264
"Causerie" (Baudelaire) **1**:45, 66
"Causerie" (Tate) **50**:230-31, 243, 250, 255, 316
"Causerie II" (Tate) **50**:316
"The Causes" (Borges) **32**:58, 66-7
Cautionary Tales for Children (Belloc) **24**:21, 26, 49
Cautionary Verses (Belloc) **24**:13-15, 17-18, 23, 27
"Le Cavalier poursuivi" (Gautier) **18**:142-43
"Cavalier Tunes" (Browning) **2**:26, 36
Cave Birds: An Alchemical Cave Drama (Hughes) **7**:153-58, 162-65, 171
"Cave Canem" (Millay) **6**:233
Cavender's House (Robinson) **1**:471-72, 475, 479, 483
"Caves" (Wakoski) **15**:363
"The Caves of Dahra" (Patmore) **59**:240
"Cawdor" (Jeffers) **17**:107-08, 110
Cawdor, and Other Poems (Jeffers) **17**:110,135
"Cayendo van los bravos combatientes" (Castro) **41**:116
"Ce n'est pas la poésie qui" (Éluard) **38**:69
"Ce que dit la bouche d'ombre" (Hugo) **17**:66, 83-84, 90
"Ce que dit l'homme de peine est toujours hors de propos" (Éluard) **38**:68
"Ce qui est à moi" (Césaire) **25**:43
Ce qui fut sans lumière (Bonnefoy) **58**:137, 139, 141, 150, 156-59, 165-66, 170
"Ce qu'on dit au poète à propos de fleurs" (Rimbaud) **57**:177, 202, 208, 210, 212, 214, 237, 247, 250, 255-56, 258, 261-62, 293
"Ce qu'on entend sur la montagne" (Hugo) **17**:91
"Ce siècle est grand et fort" (Hugo) **17**:94
"Cease, Cease, Aminta to Complain" (Behn) **13**:7
"The Cedars" (Wright) **14**:339, 346
"La ceinture" (Valéry) **9**:372, 374, 387, 396
"Celandine" (Thomas) **53**:318
"The Celebration" (Dickey) **40**:185
"A Celebration" (Williams) **7**:345
"Celebration: Birth of a Colt" (Hogan) **35**:258
A Celebration of Charis in Ten Lyric Pieces (Jonson) **17**:169-70, 180, 194-96, 207, 214
"Celebration of the trees and the hunter" (Char)
See "Fête des arbres et du chasseur"
"Celebrations" (Sarton) **39**:322, 356
"Celebrations of Hunger" (Rimbaud)
See "Fête de la faim"
Celebrations of Patience (Rimbaud)
See *Fête de la patience*
"Célébrer Giacometti" (Char) **56**:119
"Celestial Freedom" (Aleixandre) **15**:19
"Celestial Globe" (Nemerov) **24**:263, 274
Celestial Hoyden (Lowell) **3**:199
"Celestial Music" (Glück) **16**:158
"The Celestial Poets" (Neruda)
See "Los poetas celestes"
"Celestials at the Board of Projects" (Milosz) **8**:214
"Celia singing" (Carew) **29**:25
"Celia's Birthday Poem" (Zukofsky) **11**:342
"Celibacy at Twenty" (Olds) **22**:338
"Célibat, célibat, tout n'est que célibat" (Laforgue) **14**:76
"Cell Song" (Knight) **14**:40, 52-3
"The Cellar" (Soto) **28**:371
"Cellar Hole in Joppa" (Kumin) **15**:190
"The Cellar of Memory" (Akhmatova) **2**:20
"Celle de toujours, toute" (Éluard) **38**:77
"A Celle dont its rêvent" (Éluard) **38**:64
"Celle qui n'a pas la parole" (Éluard) **38**:70, 86
"Celle qui sort de l'onde" (Valéry) **9**:392
"Celles" (Hacker) **47**:87
"Cells" (Kipling) **3**:163
"The Celtic Fringe" (Smith) **12**:339
A Celtic Miscellany (Dafydd ap Gwilym) **56**:221
"Un cementerio que mira al mar" (Storni) **33**:246, 254;
"Cemetery, Stratford Connecticut" (Rose) **13**:239
"La cena triste" (Pavese) **13**:205, 208
"The Cenci" (Carducci) **46**:26
The Cenci (Shelley) **14**:165, 171-75, 182-83, 196, 202-03, 205, 208-10, 213
"La Cène" (Péret) **33**:210
Ceneri (Pasolini) **17**:294-95
"Le ceneri di Gramscí" (Pasolini) **17**:263, 265, 271, 284-85, 289-92, 294-95
Le ceneri di Gramscí (Pasolini) **17**:255, 263-67, 269-70, 272, 286-87, 293
"Census" (Szymborska) **44**:300
"The Census-Taker" (Frost) **1**:194; **39**:235
"The Centaur" (Swenson) **14**:248, 252, 255, 262-63, 281-82, 288
"The Centaur" (Thoreau) **30**:189
"Centennial Cantata" (Lanier) **50**:112
Centennial Cantata (Lanier) **50**:112-15, 118-19
The Centennial Edition of the Works of Sidney Lanier (Lanier) **50**:94, 97
"The Centennial Meditation of Columbia" (Lanier) **50**:74-75, 77, 112
"El centinela" (Borges) **22**:79; **32**:61, 89
"Centipede Sonnet" (Villa) **22**:351
"Central Europe" (Zagajewski) **27**:398
The Central Motion: Poems, 1968-1979 (Dickey) **40**:219, 222-23, 241
"Central Park" (Lowell) **3**:226
"Central Park at Dusk" (Teasdale) **31**:363
"Centre of Free Enterprise" (Birney) **52**:38
A Century of Roundels (Swinburne) **24**:313, 322-27
"The Century's Decline" (Szymborska) **44**:288, 295, 297
"Ceras eternas" (Mistral) **32**:176
"Cercanías" (Borges) **32**:81
Cerebro y corazón (Guillén) **23**:104, 133-34
"Ceremonies for Candlemasse Eve" (Herrick) **9**:99
"Ceremonies for Christmasse" (Herrick) **9**:99, 104
"Ceremony" (Wilbur) **51**:188, 192-93
Ceremony (Wilbur) **51**:236-37, 269, 291, 293, 296, 323, 330
"Ceremony after a Fire Raid" (Thomas) **2**:382, 388; **52**:258, 278, 290-91, 299-303
"A Ceremony for One of My Dead" (O'Hara) **45**:173
"Ceremony for the Banishment of the King of Swords" (Goodison) **36**:147-48, 151
A Certain Distance (Francis) **34**:251
"Certain Mercies" (Graves) **6**:152
"A Certain Morning Is" (Villa) **22**:350
"Certain Poets" (MacLeish) **47**:182
Certain Sonnets (Sidney)
See *Certaine Sonets*
Certaine Sonets (Sidney) **32**:235, 239-40, 244, 247, 249, 250, 273, 282, 286
"Certainty" (Paz)
See "Certeza"
"Certeza" (Paz) **1**:355; **48**:269
"A certi Censori" (Carducci) **46**:51
"César" (Valéry) **9**:391
"Cet amour à tous retiré" (Char) **56**:173-74
Cette fumée qui nous portait (Char) **56**:115
"Ceux qui luttent" (Smith) **12**:333
"Cezanne at Aix" (Tomlinson) **17**:304, 306, 335
"Chaadayevu" (Pushkin) **10**:408
"Chacun sa chimère" (Baudelaire) **1**:58
"Chad" (Brathwaite) **56**:6, 29
"Chahinkapa Zoo" (Erdrich) **52**:172, 192
"La chaine a mille anneaux" (Lamartine) **16**:284

"Chains" (Apollinaire)
See "Liens"
"A Chair" (Stein) **18**:319, 349
"Chair Gallows" (Komunyakaa) **51**:29
Chaitāli (Tagore) **8**:403, 409-10
"Le Chaitivel" (Marie de France) **22**:248-49, 255, 258, 260, 267-73, 295
"Chaka" (Senghor) **25**:241, 255
"Chalice" (Alurista) **34**:28, 41
"The Chalk Pit" (Thomas) **53**:286, 288, 291, 324
"Chalk White" (Szirtes) **51**:172
"Challenge" (Brown) **55**:110, 114, 118, 124-30
"The Challenge" (Graves) **6**:137
"The Challenge" (Longfellow) **30**:42
"The Chamber over the Gate" (Longfellow) **30**:42
"La chambre" (Bonnefoy) **58**:118
"La Chambre dans l'Espace" (Char) **56**:108
"La chambre double" (Baudelaire) **1**:54, 58
"Chameli-vitan" (Tagore) **8**:416
"Chamfort" (Sandburg) **41**:339
The Champion (Tsvetaeva)
See *Molodets*
Les Champs Magnétiques (Breton) **15**:58, 68, 73
"Chance" (H. D.) **5**:304
"Chance Meeting" (H. D.) **5**:304
"Chance Topic" (Tu Fu) **9**:324, 327
"The Chances" (Owen) **19**:334, 344, 347
"The Chances of Rhyme" (Tomlinson) **17**:333, 240
"Chanchal" (Tagore) **8**:415
"The Change" (Dickey) **40**:186
"The Change" (Finch) **21**:175
"The Change" (Hardy) **8**:93
"Change" (Kunitz) **19**:147
"Change" (Pasternak)
See "Peremena"
"Change" (Teasdale) **31**:347
"Change" (Wright) **14**:379
"Change and Fate" (Rossetti) **44**:254
"Change in Recurrence" (Meredith) **60**:299
"Change Is Not Always Progress" (Madhubuti) **5**:344
"The Change: Kyoto-Tokyo Express" (Ginsberg) **4**:50, 63, 81; **47**:17
"Change of Season" (Lorde) **12**:154, 157
A Change of World (Rich) **5**:352-53, 358, 360, 362, 369, 375, 387-88, 392
"Change upon Change" (Browning) **6**:32
"The Changed Woman" (Bogan) **12**:94, 103
"The Changeful World" (MacDiarmid) **9**:183
"The Changeling" (Curnow) **48**:12
"Changes" (Kenyon) **57**:19
"Changes; or, Reveries at a Window Overlooking a Country Road with Two Women Talking Blues in the Kitchen" (Komunyakaa) **51**:31-32
"Changing Diapers" (Snyder) **21**:300
The Changing Light at Sandover (Merrill) **28**:259-60, 262-63, 265-79, 281
"Changing Mind" (Aiken) **26**:14
"Changing the Children" (Kumin) **15**:215
Ch'ang-ku (Li Ho) **13**:44
"Channel 13" (Merrill) **28**:267
"Channel Firing" (Hardy) **8**:119-21
"A Channel Passage" (Brooke) **24**:53-4, 63, 83
"A Channel Passage" (Swinburne) **24**:313, 317-18
"Channels" (Silverstein) **49**:330
"Chanon's Yeoman's Tale" (Chaucer)
See "Canon's Yeoman's Tale"
"Chanson" (Hugo) **17**:80
Chanson complète (Éluard) **38**:79
"Chanson d'automne" (Verlaine) **32**:362, 368, 387
"Chanson de la plus haute tour" (Rimbaud) **57**:175, 251
"La chanson des ingénues" (Verlaine) **2**:431; **32**:353, 385, 388
"La chanson du mal-aimé" (Apollinaire) **7**:3, 7-9, 11, 15, 22, 44, 46-9
"Chanson du petit hypertrophique" (Laforgue) **14**:66, 93
"Chanson du Présomptif" (Perse) **23**:230
"Chanson du velours à côtes" (Char) **56**:157
"Chanson Juive" (Celan) **10**:127-28
"Chanson of a Lady in the Shade" (Celan) **10**:112
"Chanson un peu naïve" (Bogan) **12**:86, 90, 92, 101, 103
Chansons des rues et des bois (Hugo) **17**:55, 65, 67, 72
Chansons pour elle (Verlaine) **2**:417; **32**:407
"Chant d'amour" (Lamartine) **16**:291-92
"Chant d'automne" (Baudelaire) **1**:60, 62-3
"Chant de guerre parisien" (Rimbaud) **3**:255, 284; **57**:205
"Chant de l'horizon en champagne" (Apollinaire) **7**:22
"Chant de Printemps" (Senghor) **25**:258
"Le Chant de sauvegarde" (Bonnefoy) **58**:125
Le chant du sacre (Lamartine) **16**:279
"Chant for Dark Hours" (Parker) **28**:352, 360
"Chant for May Day" (Hughes) **53**:114
"A Chant for Young/Brothas and Sistuhs" (Sanchez) **9**:218, 225
"Chant to Be Used in Processions around a Site with Furnaces" (Merton) **10**:334, 337
"Chanteuse" (Doty) **53**:47, 52
Chanting at the Crystal Sea (Howe) **54**:107-8
"Chantre" (Apollinaire) **7**:48
Les chants de Crépuscule (Hugo) **17**:43, 45, 52, 63, 91-94
Chants de la Balandrane: Poèmes (Char) **56**:185-87, 189
Chants d'ombre (Senghor) **25**:224, 227, 230-33, 236, 238, 241, 243-44, 255
"Chants for Socialists" (Morris) **55**:329
Chants for Socialists (Morris) **55**:251, 340
"Les chants lyriques de Saül" (Lamartine) **16**:277, 290
Chants pour Naëtt (Senghor) **25**:225, 227, 232, 238-40
Chants pour signare (Senghor)
See *Chants pour Naëtt*
"Chaos" (Benn) **35**:33, 50, 58, 75, 77
"Chaos and Poetry" (Lawrence) **54**:215
"Chaos in Motion and Not in Motion" (Stevens) **6**:307-10, 313
"Chaos Poem" (Atwood) **8**:24
"Chaos Staggered" (Ammons) **16**:46
"The Chapel in Lyoness" (Morris) **55**:238, 299-300, 302, 348-49
"Chapelle Brancacci" (Bonnefoy) **58**:130
"The Chapel-Organist" (Hardy) **8**:100, 124
"Chaplinesque" (Crane) **3**:98-100
"A Character" (Montagu) **16**:338
"The Character of Holland" (Marvell) **10**:271
"The Character of the Happy Warrior" (Wordsworth) **4**:377
Characters of Women (Pope) **26**:239
"Charcutons charcutez" (Péret) **33**:203
"The Charge of the Light Brigade" (Tennyson) **6**:359
"The Chariot" (Dickinson)
See "Because I Could Not Stop for Death"
"Charioteer" (H. D.) **5**:268
"The Charioteer of Delphi" (Merrill) **28**:241
"La charite" (Ronsard) **11**:236, 243, 263-64
"Charity" (Cowper) **40**:49-50, 105, 116-17, 127, 139
"Charity Overcoming Envy" (Moore) **49**:145
"Charivari" (Atwood) **8**:38
"Charlemagne" (Brathwaite) **56**:93
"Charleroi" (Verlaine) **32**:361, 378, 411
"Charles Augustus Fortescue, Who always Did what was Right, and so accumulated an Immense Fortune" (Belloc) **24**:26
"Charles on Fire" (Merrill) **28**:253
"Charles Summer" (Longfellow) **30**:50
"Charleston in the 1860s" (Rich) **5**:383
"Charleston Plantations" (Sarton) **39**:321, 332
"Charlie Howard's Descent" (Doty) **53**:62
"Charlotte Corday" (Tomlinson) **17**:345-46, 350
"Charlotte's Delivery" (McGuckian) **27**:105
"A Charm" (Dickinson) **1**:112
Charmes; ou, Poèmes (Valéry) **9**:355, 358, 365-67, 371, 374, 386-88, 390-96
"Charms" (Snyder) **21**:294, 297
"The Charnel Rose" (Aiken) **26**:11, 15, 37
The Charnel Rose (Aiken) **26**:6, 22, 70, 72
"Une charogne" (Baudelaire) **1**:48
"Charon" (MacNeice) **61**:125, 176-77
"Chartres" (Oppen) **35**:321
"The Chase" (Merwin) **45**:48
"The Chase" (Toomer) **7**:338, 340
"Chasing the Paper-Shaman" (Rose) **13**:238
"Chasse à courre" (Péret) **33**:231
Chast' rechi (Brodsky)
See *Cast rěci*
"A Chastel" (Éluard) **38**:86
"Le chat" (Ronsard) **11**:280, 282
"chat bilingual" (Birney) **52**:32-33, 77
"Chateau de Muzot" (Tomlinson) **17**:315, 324
"Le Château du souvenir" (Gautier) **18**:125, 129, 157
"Le Châtiment de Tartufe" (Rimbaud) **57**:172, 289-90
"Le châtiment de Tartuff" (Rimbaud) **3**:283
Les Châtiments (Hugo) **17**:45, 53-54, 65, 74, 78-80, 91
"Les chats blancs" (Valéry) **9**:391
"Chatyrdah" (Mickiewicz) **38**:166
"Chaucer" (Longfellow) **30**:42
"Chaume des Vosges" (Char) **56**:150
"The Chaunty of the Nona" (Belloc) **24**:6, 31
"El Che en Praga en 1965" (Dalton) **36**:129
"Che fece ... il gran rifiuto" (Cavafy) **36**:57
"Che Guevara" (Guillén) **23**:127
Cheap (Stone) **53**:220, 228-29, 239, 258
"Checkers" (Brown) **55**:155
"Cheddar Pinks" (Bridges) **28**:80-1, 85
"The Cheek" (Hope) **56**:306
"The Cheer" (Meredith) **28**:205, 217
The Cheer (Meredith) **28**:177, 179-82, 197-200, 202, 205-09, 215
Cheerleader for the Funeral (Cassian) **17**:13
"Chekhov in Nice" (Stryk) **27**:187
"Chekhov on Sakhalin" (Heaney) **18**:214
"Chekhov's Story" (Kenyon) **57**:15
"Chelyuskintsy" (Tsvetaeva) **14**:328
"Chemin de fer" (Bishop) **34**:146, 160, 164
"Les chemins" (Bonnefoy) **58**:118, 167
"Le chêne" (Lamartine) **16**:293
"Chenille" (Dickey) **40**:191, 196
"Les chercheuses de poux" (Rimbaud) **3**:271, 276; **57**:191, 249
"Cherepki" (Akhmatova) **55**:52
"Les chères, mains qui furent miennes" (Verlaine) **2**:416
"Chérir Thouzon" (Char) **56**:156
"Cherish You Then the Hope I Shall Forget" (Millay) **6**:211
"Cherkesy" (Lermontov) **18**:278, 299
"Chernaia Paskha" (Shvarts) **50**:131-32, 139-41, 160
"Chernozem" (Mandelstam) **14**:150-51, 154
"Cherries" (Brathwaite) **56**:34, 51
"Cherry Blossoms" (Gallagher) **9**:65
"The Cherry Robbers" (Lawrence) **54**:166-67
"The Cherry Tree" (Gunn) **26**:205
"Cherrylog Road" (Dickey) **40**:161, 168-69, 189, 191-92
"The Chestnut Casts His Flambeaux" (Housman) **2**:199
Chetki (Akhmatova)
See *Chyotki*
"Un cheval de race" (Baudelaire) **1**:59
"The Cheval-Glass" (Hardy) **8**:100
Les chevaliers (Lamartine) **16**:269
"Chevaux de bois" (Verlaine) **32**:382
"La chevelure" (Baudelaire) **1**:45, 66-7, 69
"Chevelure" (Césaire) **25**:10, 17

"La Chevelure" (Char) **56**:197
"Chevrefoil" (Marie de France) **22**:248, 255, 257-58, 262-64, 266-67, 269, 272, 274, 301
"Chez Jane" (O'Hara) **45**:135
"Chhabi" (Tagore) **8**:414
"Chi vuol veder" (Petrarch) **8**:256
"Chiare fresche e dolci acque" (Petrarch) **8**:221, 230, 232-33, 235-36
"Chic Freedom's Reflection" (Walker) **30**:347, 359
"Chicago" (Sandburg) **2**:317, 322-23, 333, 335, 339; **41**:225, 229, 232-34, 237, 242, 248, 257, 261, 267, 271-74, 277, 279, 281, 295, 301, 304, 318, 326, 334, 336, 346, 356-58, 360-62, 364-65
"The Chicago Defender Sends a Man to Little Rock" (Brooks) **7**:62
"The Chicago Picasso" (Brooks) **7**:82
Chicago Poems (Sandburg) **2**:300-2, 307-8, 312, 314, 316-18, 321, 333, 335-36, 338-39; **41**:225-27, 229,233-34, 236-37, 239, 242-43, 246-48, 250, 252, 254-55, 257, 261, 269, 272-75, 277, 285, 287, 289, 293, 295-96, 298, 306, 308-10, 312-15, 318, 322, 325-29, 334, 339-41, 343, 347-52, 358-65, 367
"Chicago Poet" (Sandburg) **2**:339; **41**:244, 270, 278, 344
"The Chicago Train" (Glück) **16**:149, 153
"Chicano Heart" (Alurista) **34**:11, 46
"chicano infante" (Alurista) **34**:13, 38
"Chicken" (Stein) **18**:313
"Chicory and Daisies" (Williams) **7**:373, 407
Chief Joseph of the Nez Perce (Warren) **37**:325-27, 334, 342-45, 350, 358, 377, 381-82
"Chief Standing Water" (Tomlinson) **17**:309
"La chiesa di Polenta" (Carducci) **46**:54, 76, 81, 84, 88-89
"Chievrefueil" (Marie de France)
See "Chevrefoil"
"Chiffres et constellations amoureux d'une femme" (Breton) **15**:49
"Chilblain" (Wright) **36**:348
"The Child" (Carruth) **10**:71
"The Child" (Merwin) **45**:25
"Child" (Plath) **37**:202, 258
"Child" (Sandburg) **2**:329
"The Child" (Wright) **14**:352
"The Child Alone" (Mistral)
See "El niño solo"
"Child and Wattle Tree" (Wright) **14**:352
"Child, Child" (Teasdale) **31**:388
"The Child Dying" (Muir) **49**:299
"Child Harold" (Clare) **23**:25-6, 46
"A Child in the Ghetto Surrounded by Letters" (Shvarts)
See "Ditia v getto v okruzhenii bukv"
"Child Margaret" (Sandburg) **41**:296
"Child Moon" (Sandburg) **41**:334
"The Child Next Door" (Warren) **37**:297, 299
"Child of Europe" (Milosz) **8**:191-92
"Child of Our Time" (Boland) **58**:42
"Child of the Romans" (Sandburg) **41**:234, 272, 334
"Child of the Sixtieth Century" (Viereck) **27**:259, 280
"The Child on the Cliffs" (Thomas) **53**:271, 295
"Child Poems" (H. D.) **5**:305
"A Child To Be Born" (Alurista) **34**:24, 25, 39, 40
"The Child Who Is Silent" (Shapiro) **25**:303
"The Child Who Saw Midas" (Sitwell) **3**:308
"Child Wife" (Verlaine) **32**:396, 399, 411
"The Child World" (Riley)
See *A Child-World*
Childe Harold (Byron)
See *Childe Harold's Pilgrimage: A Romaunt*
Childe Harold's Pilgrimage: A Romaunt (Byron) **16**:69, 72-7, 81-90, 107, 111
"Childe Roland to the Dark" (Browning) **61**:88
"Childe Roland to the Dark Tower Came" (Browning) **2**:64, 85-6, 88
"Childe Rolandine" (Smith) **12**:302, 350, 354
"Childhood" (Muir) **49**:228, 238, 247, 270, 273, 287
"Childhood" (Trakl) **20**:226
"Childhood" (Walker) **20**:276-77
"Childhood among the Ferns" (Hardy) **8**:125-26
"The Childhood of Jesus" (Pinsky) **27**:157
"A Childish Prank" (Hughes) **7**:123, 143, 161
"Childless Father" (Wordsworth) **4**:374, 428
"Childlessness" (Merrill) **28**:221, 244, 249
"Children Coming Home from School" (Glück) **16**:159
"the children grow" (Alurista)
See "los niños crecen"
"Children of Darkness" (Graves) **6**:137
"Children of Darkness" (Wilbur) **51**:246, 284
"Children of Our Age" (Szymborska) **44**:275, 295
"Children of the Mississippi" (Brown) **55**:70-71, 83, 114, 151-52, 176
"Children of the Night" (Longfellow) **30**:63
"The Children of the Night" (Robinson) **1**:459, 467, 486
The Children of the Night (Robinson) **1**:459, 462-63, 466, 474
"The Children of the Poor" (Brooks) **7**:55, 62, 75, 78
"Children Selecting Books in a Library" (Jarrell) **41**:159, 179-80, 194
"Children's Children" (Brown) **55**:76, 83, 102, 152
"Children's Games" (MacNeice) **61**:177
"The Children's Hour" (Longfellow) **30**:37, 46-7
"Children's Rhymes" (Hughes) **53**:150
"The Children's Song" (Kipling) **3**:171
"A Child's Grave at Florence" (Browning) **6**:6
"The Child's Purchase" (Patmore) **59**:212, 223, 265
"Child's Talk in April" (Rossetti) **7**:274
"Child's Terror" (MacNeice) **61**:172
A Child-World (Riley) **48**:289, 300
"chile" (Bissett) **14**:24
"A Chile" (Guillén) **23**:127
"Chillianwallah" (Meredith) **60**:325
Chills and Fever (Ransom) **61**:267, 269, 280, 305-6, 322, 324
"Chilterns" (Brooke) **24**:56, 67
"Chimaera Sleeping" (Wylie) **23**:311, 314, 322
The Chimeras (Nerval)
See *Les Chimères*
"La Chimère" (Gautier) **18**:141-42
Les Chimères (Nerval) **13**:172, 174, 176, 179-80, 182, 184, 187, 191-92, 194-95
"Chimes for Yahya" (Merrill) **28**:260, 263
"The Chimney Sweeper" (Blake) **12**:7, 9, 34-5
China Poems (Brutus) **24**:117
"A Chinaman's Chance" (Chin) **40**:4
"Chinatown" (Song) **21**:349
"The Chinese Banyan" (Meredith) **28**:171, 175, 189
Chinese Dynasty Cantos (Pound) **4**:352
"The Chinese Nightingale" (Lindsay) **23**:269, 272-73, 275-76, 278, 281-82, 286-87, 291-94
The Chinese Nightingale, and Other Poems (Lindsay) **23**:292
"The Chinese Restaurant in Portrush" (Mahon) **60**:192-193
Chinesisch-deutsche Jahres-und Tageszeiten (Goethe) **5**:251
The Chipmunk (Ignatow) **34**:337
"Chiron" (Hölderlin) **4**:148, 166
Chistes parra desorientar a la policia (Parra) **39**:291-92, 313
"Chitateli gazet" (Tsvetaeva) **14**:315
Chitra (Tagore) **8**:408-09, 415, 418
Chō o yumemu (Hagiwara) **18**:176
"Choc Bay" (Walcott) **46**:272
"Chocorua to Its Neighbour" (Stevens) **6**:335
"The Choice" (Rossetti) **44**:219-20
A Choice of Kipling's Verse Made by T. S. Eliot with an Essay on Rudyard Kipling (Kipling) **3**:175
"A Choice of Weapons" (Kunitz) **19**:148
"Choices" (Sandburg) **41**:239, 350
"Choir" (Hongo) **23**:199
"The Choir" (Kinnell) **26**:261
"The Choir Invisible" (Eliot)
See "O May I Join the Choir Invisible"
Choix de poésies (Verlaine) **32**:359
"Choix entre deux pations" (Hugo) **17**:101
"Cholera" (Dove) **6**:108
"Choorka" (McGuckian) **27**:110
"Choose" (Sandburg) **41**:244, 348
"The Choosers" (Smith) **12**:327
"Chorai, Ninfas, os fados poderosas" (Camões) **31**:25
"Choral Symphony" (Lanier) **50**:77
"The Choral Union" (Sassoon) **12**:242
"Chorale" (Hope) **56**:269-70
"Chord" (Hughes) **53**:160
Chord of Light (Herbert)
See *Struna swiatła*
"Choriambics" (Brooke) **24**:62
"Choriambics II" (Brooke) **24**:57, 60
"Choros Sequence from Morpheus" (H. D.) **5**:304
"Chorus" (Lorde) **12**:159
"A Chorus of Ghosts" (Bryant) **20**:16
Chorus of the Newly Dead (Muir) **49**:238-39, 242, 244, 276
"Choruses from the Rock" (Eliot) **31**:121
Chosen Defects (Neruda)
See *Defectos escogidos: 2000*
Chosen Poems: Old and New (Lorde) **12**:142, 146, 148, 154, 157
"Choses Passagères à John Ashbery" (O'Hara) **45**:230-32, 235-36
"Le Chretien Mourant" (Lamartine) **16**:277
"Chrismus on the Plantation" (Dunbar) **5**:133-34
"Chrissie" (Ní Chuilleanáin) **34**:352
"Le Christ aux Oliviers" (Nerval) **13**:173, 177, 181, 198
"Christ for Sale" (Lowell) **3**:203
"Christ Has Arisen" (Pushkin)
See "Khristos Voskres"
"Christ in Alabama" (Hughes) **1**:264; **53**:110, 143, 148-50
"Christ in Flanders" (Lowell) **3**:203
Christ is Arisen (Bely)
See *Hristos voskres*
Christ is Risen (Bely)
See *Hristos voskres*
"Christ of Pershing Square" (Stryk) **27**:190, 203
"Christ Recrucified" (Cullen) **20**:72
Christabel (Coleridge) **11**:41-2, 51-3, 84-5, 90-1, 104, 110; **39**:120-22, 169, 176, 180, 182, 193, 224-25
"A Christian Country" (Hughes) **53**:110
"Christian Dallman" (Masters) **36**:230
"The Christian Statesman" (Masters) **1**:344
"Christiane R." (Goethe) **5**:246
"Le Christianisme" (Owen) **19**:336, 341
"Christina" (MacNeice) **61**:173
"The Christmas" (Muir) **49**:290
"Christmas at Black Rock" (Lowell) **3**:201
"A Christmas Ballad" (Brodsky) **9**:2, 4
"Christmas Bells" (Longfellow) **30**:47
"The Christmas Cactus" (Clampitt) **19**:87
"A Christmas Card" (Merton) **10**:340
"A Christmas Card of Halley's Comet" (Nemerov) **24**:289
"A Christmas Childhood" (Kavanagh) **33**:75, 81, 93, 102, 118, 133, 145-6, 151-3, 157
"A Christmas Colloquy" (Ransom) **61**:294
"Christmas Comes" (Birney) **52**:8
"Christmas Eve" (Ammons) **16**:58, 60, 65
"Christmas Eve" (Sexton) **2**:363

"Christmas Eve at St. Kavin's" (Carman) **34**:225
"Christmas Eve: Australia" (Shapiro) **25**:279, 286, 296, 300
"Christmas Eve Remembered" (Kavanagh) **33**:151, 161
"Christmas Eve under Hooker's Statue" (Lowell) **3**:200, 203
"Christmas Eve—Market Square" (Page) **12**:169
"A Christmas Greeting" (Wright) **36**:328-29, 341, 344, 399
"Christmas in India" (Kipling) **3**:186
"Christmas in Simla" (Kipling) **3**:182
"Christmas Light" (Sarton) **39**:360, 368
"The Christmas Mummers" (Kavanagh) **33**:62, 86, 118
"Christmas on the Hudson" (García Lorca)
See "Navidad en el Hudson"
"Christmas on the Plantation" (Dunbar)
See "Chrismus on the Plantation"
"Christmas Pines" (Mistral)
See "Pinos de Navidad"
"Christmas Poem, 1965" (Ondaatje) **28**:292
"Christmas Poem for Nancy" (Schwartz) **8**:316
"The Christmas Roses" (Jarrell) **41**:210, 214
"Christmas Shopping" (MacNeice) **61**:133-34, 138
"A Christmas Song for the Three Gaids" (Chesterton) **28**:125
"Christmas Star" (Mistral)
See "Estrella de Navidad"
"Christmas Tree" (Shapiro) **25**:269, 286
"Christmas Tree—Market Square" (Page) **12**:169
Christmas-Eve (Browning) **2**:31-2, 44, 70-1
Christmas-Eve and Easter Day (Browning) **2**:33, 36, 70, 95
"Christs Incarnation" (Herrick) **9**:119
"Christ's Twin" (Erdrich) **52**:191
Christus: A Mystery (Longfellow) **30**:21, 23, 39, 65-7
Chronophagia (Cassian) **17**:6, 13
"Chrysallis" (Montale) **13**:151
"Chrysanthemums" (Kenyon) **57**:11, 24, 35
"Chrysaor" (Longfellow) **30**:27
"Chtonian Revelation: A Myth" (Warren) **37**:326
"Chu Ming-How" (Stryk) **27**:198
"Chudishche" (Shvarts) **50**:135-36
"Chüeh-chü" (Tu Fu) **9**:323
"El Chulo" (Guillén) **23**:101
"Chumban" (Tagore) **8**:407
"The Church" (Herbert) **4**:103, 113
"The Church and the Hotel" (Masters) **1**:343
"Church Building" (Harper) **21**:198, 200, 213
"Church Fair" (Kenyon) **57**:40
"The Church Floore" (Herbert) **4**:109, 119
"Church Going" (Larkin) **21**:228, 230, 236-37, 247, 255, 259
"The Church Militant" (Herbert) **4**:100, 130
"Church Monuments" (Herbert) **4**:100, 119
"Church Music" (Herbert) **4**:100, 131
"The Church of Brou" (Arnold) **5**:6, 9, 12, 50
"The Church of Polenta" (Carducci)
See "La chiesa di Polenta"
"The Church Porch" (Herbert) **4**:100-01, 103, 107, 126
"The Church-Bell" (Wylie) **23**:328
"Church-Going" (Heaney) **18**:223
"Church-lock and Key" (Herbert) **4**:127
"Churchyard" (Gray)
See "Elegy Written in a Country Churchyard"
"Churning Day" (Heaney) **18**:186
"The Chute" (Olds) **22**:319-22
La chute d'un ange (Lamartine) **16**:263, 265, 269-70, 285-87, 293-94, 296-97
"Chuva Oblíqua" (Pessoa) **20**:151, 165
"Chuy" (Soto) **28**:372, 382
Chyotki (Akhmatova) **2**:3, 11, 14, 17
"Ciant da li ciampanis" (Pasolini) **17**:256, 265
"Ciants di muart" (Pasolini) **17**:256
"Cicadas" (Mueller) **33**:180
"Cicadas" (Wilbur) **51**:188
"The Cicadas" (Wright) **14**:346
"Cicadas" (Zagajewski) **27**:397
"El ciego" (Borges) **32**:90
"Ciel brouillé" (Baudelaire) **1**:61, 66
"Le ciel est, par-dessus le toit" (Verlaine) **32**:362-63, 379-80
"El cielo" (Storni) **33**:292, 294-95;
"Cielo de tercera" (Fuertes) **27**:31
"Los cielos" (Aleixandre) **15**:19-20
"Cierro los ojos" (Guillén) **35**:196, 198
"La cierva blanca" (Borges) **32**:90
"La cifra" (Borges) **32**:52, 56, 86
La cifra (Borges) **22**:95, 97, 99; **32**:91
"Un cigare allume que Fume" (Apollinaire)
See "Paysage"
"Cigarra en noche de luna" (Storni) **33**:293;
"Cigola la carrucola del pozzo" (Montale) **13**:164
"Cima de la delicia" (Guillén) **35**:153
"Le cimetière marin" (Bishop) **3**:46
"Le cimetière marin" (Valéry) **9**:348, 351-52, 355, 358, 361, 363-80, 382, 384, 387, 389-93, 395-96, 398
"Cincinnati" (Yamada) **44**:330-32, 342-43, 347, 351
"Cinderella" (Jarrell) **41**:171
"Cinema of a Man" (MacLeish) **47**:126, 128, 137, 156
"The cipher" (Borges)
See "La cifra"
The Cipher (Borges)
See *La cifra*
The Circassian (Lermontov)
See "Cherkesy"
The Circassian Boy (Lermontov)
See *Mtsyri*
"Circe" (Hope) **56**:298-99
"Circe's Power" (Glück) **16**:171
"Circle and Square" (Muir) **49**:300
The Circle Game (Atwood) **8**:3, 12, 15, 18, 26-8
"The Circle on the Grass" (Kenyon) **57**:19
"Circles in th Sun" (Bissett) **14**:8, 19, 33
Circles on the Water (Piercy) **29**:302, 307, 313
"Circonspection" (Verlaine) **32**:354
"The Circuit of Apollo" (Finch) **21**:162, 168
"Circuit total par la lune et par la couleur" (Tzara) **27**:224
"A Circular Play. A Play in Circles" (Stein) **18**:347
"The Circular Ruins" (Borges)
See "Las ruinas circulares"
"Circulation of the Song" (Duncan) **2**:127
"Círculos sin centro" (Storni) **33**:239, 269;
"Circumjack Cencrastus" (MacDiarmid) **9**:157
"Circumstance" (Lowell) **13**:94
"Circus Animals" (Szymborska) **44**:312
"The Circus Animals' Desertion" (Yeats) **20**:307, 311, 313, 327, 332, 336; **51**:111, 141
Circus On (Cage) **58**:200
"Cirque d'hiver" (Bishop) **3**:37; **34**:52, 70
"Les Ciseaux et leur père" (Éluard) **38**:90-91
"El cisne" (Darío) **15**:113
"Los cisnes" (Darío) **15**:115
"Los Cisnes" (Storni) **33**:272;
"Citadel" (Brathwaite) **56**:93
"The Cited" (García Lorca)
See "Romance del emplazado"
"Citeres" (Guillén) **35**:202
"Cities and Thrones and Powers" (Kipling) **3**:183
"Citizen Cain" (Baraka) **4**:17, 24
"Citizen Kane" (Alexie) **53**:14
"Citronia" (Heine) **25**:160, 171-80
"Città in campagna" (Pavese) **13**:227
"Una città lontana" (Quasimodo) **47**:283
"The City" (Blok) **21**:24
"The City" (Cavafy) **36**:3, 13-14, 59, 73, 78
"City" (Merwin) **45**:54
"The City" (Nash) **21**:272
"The City" (Pasternak)
See "Gorod"
"The City: A Cycle" (Stryk) **27**:216
"The City Asleep" (Wright) **14**:362
"A City Child's Day" (Corso) **33**:11
"A City Dead House" (Whitman) **3**:379
The City in Tears (Seifert)
See *Město v slzách*
"City in the Country" (Pavese)
See "Città in campagna"
"The City in the Sea" (Poe) **1**:426, 431, 434, 438, 443-45; **54**:278
"The City in Which I Love You" (Lee) **24**:241
The City in Which I Love You (Lee) **24**:240, 242-44
"The City Limits" (Ammons) **16**:11, 23, 37, 46
"City Midnight Junk Strains for Frank O'Hara" (Ginsberg) **4**:47
"The City of Evenings" (Wright) **36**:310
"City of Monuments" (Rukeyser) **12**:230
"City of Shadows" (Boland) **58**:62
"The City of the Dead" (Gibran) **9**:73
"City of the Wind" (Stryk) **27**:191
"The City Planners" (Atwood) **8**:13
"City Psalm" (Rukeyser) **12**:221
"City Trees" (Millay) **6**:207
"City Walk-Up, Winter 1969" (Forché) **10**:141, 144, 147, 157-58
"City Winter" (Mickiewicz)
See "Zima miejska"
A City Winter (O'Hara) **45**:116
"City without a Name" (Milosz) **8**:194-95
"City without Walls" (Auden) **1**:20
"The City-Mouse and the Country-Mouse" (Wyatt) **27**:331
"A City's Death by Fire" (Walcott) **46**:274
"The City's Love" (McKay) **2**:211
"Ciudad" (Borges) **22**:94
"Ciudad de los estíos" (Guillén) **35**:153
"Ciudad sin sueño" (García Lorca) **3**:139-40
"Ciudad viva, ciudad muerta" (Aleixandre) **15**:35
"Ciudades" (Cardenal)
See "Las ciudades perdidas"
"Las ciudades perdidas" (Cardenal) **22**:126-28, 132
"Civil Rights" (Lanier) **50**:92, 118-19
"Civil Rights Poem" (Baraka) **4**:11, 19
"Civilization and Its Discontents" (Ashbery) **26**:108, 113
"Clad All in Brown" (Swift) **9**:256-57
Clad in Light (Seifert)
See *Světlem oděná*
"The Claim" (Browning) **6**:14
"Clair de lune" (Apollinaire) **7**:45-6
"Clair de lune" (Verlaine) **2**:413, 420, 429; **32**:346, 348-51, 353, 364, 370-71, 390
Claire de terre (Breton) **15**:51-2
"El Clamor" (Storni) **33**:253;
Clamor (Guillén) **35**:140, 157, 170, 185, 187, 189, 195, 197, 202, 225, 228, 229, 234, 239, 241
"Clamped Almas" (Alurista) **34**:47
Clandestine Poems (Dalton) **36**:135-36
"Clara noticia" (Guillén) **35**:202
"Clarence" (Silverstein) **49**:333, 339
"Clarence Fawcett" (Masters) **36**:230
"Claribel" (Tennyson) **6**:358-60, 365
"Claribel A Melody" (McGuckian) **27**:83
"Clark Street Bridge" (Sandburg) **41**:273
"Clasping of Hands" (Herbert) **4**:130
"Class" (Tomlinson) **17**:320
"Class Struggle" (Baraka) **4**:30, 38
"Class Struggle in Music" (Baraka) **4**:40
"The Class Will Come to Order" (Kunitz) **19**:150
"Classic" (Herbert)
See "Klasyk"
"Classical Spring" (Carducci)
See "Primavera classica"

"Classicism and Romanticism" (Carducci)
See "Classicismo e romanticismo"
"Classicismo e romanticismo" (Carducci) **46**:78, 80
"Claud Antle" (Masters) **1**:334
"Claude Glass" (Ondaatje) **28**:314
"The Claude Glass" (Szirtes) **51**:158
"Claus von Stuffenberg 1944" (Gunn) **26**:197
"Clavering" (Robinson) **35**:367
"The Clavichord" (Sarton) **39**:318
"El clavicordio de la abuela" (Darío) **15**:80
"Claw-Foot" (Plath) **37**:188
"Clay" (Baraka) **4**:30
"clay and morning star" (Clifton) **17**:29
"Clean Gene" (Silverstein) **49**:347
"Cleaning Day" (Wright) **14**:356
"Cleaning the Candelabrum" (Sassoon) **12**:248, 259
"Clean,like,iodoform,between,the,tall" (Villa) **22**:356-57
"Cleanthus Trilling" (Masters) **36**:243
"Clear and gentle stream" (Bridges) **28**:83
"Clear Autumn" (Rexroth) **20**:209
"Clear, with Light Variable Winds" (Lowell) **13**:94
"Clearances" (Heaney) **18**:228-29, 232, 238
"Cleared" (Kipling) **3**:167
"The Clearing" (Baraka) **4**:5, 15
"The Clearing" (Berry) **28**:38
Clearing (Berry) **28**:7-9
"Clearing the Title" (Merrill) **28**:267, 269-70
"Clearness" (Wilbur) **51**:188-89, 193
"The Clearseeing" (Char)
See *Les Transparents*
Clear-seeing Ones (Char)
See *Les Transparents*
"The Cleaving" (Lee) **24**:241, 244, 248-49, 251-52
"Cleis" (Teasdale) **31**:380
"Cleon" (Browning) **2**:36, 82, 95
"Cleopomop y Heliodemo" (Darío) **15**:81
"La clepsidra" (Borges) **32**:90
"Clepsydra" (Ashbery) **26**:126, 157, 166
"The Clepsydras of the Unknown" (Elytis) **21**:119
"The Clerk's Journal" (Aiken) **26**:25
The Clerk's Journal: Being the Diary of a Queer Man (Aiken) **26**:46-8, 50
"Clerk's Tale" (Chaucer) **19**:13, 29, 54-60
The Clerk's Tale (Chaucer) **58**:265, 272, 286
"The Cliff" (Lermontov) **18**:297
"Cliff Klingenhagen" (Robinson) **1**:467, 486
"Clifford Ridell" (Masters) **1**:344-46; **36**:194
"Cliffs" (Thoreau) **30**:227, 233-34, 242
"The Cliffs and Springs" (Thoreau) **30**:182, 191, 192, 194, 228-29, 242
"The Cliff-Top" (Bridges) **28**:67
"The Climate of Thought" (Graves) **6**:139, 143
"Climb" (Kenyon) **57**:45
"Climbers" (Birney) **52**:34, 58
"Climbing a Mountain" (Hagiwara) **18**:177
"Climbing Alone" (Wagoner) **33**:352
"Climbing Alone All Day" (Rexroth) **20**:193
"Climbing Milestone Mountain" (Rexroth) **20**:203
"Climbing Pien-chüeh Temple" (Wang Wei) **18**:371
"Climbing T'ai-po's Peak" (Li Po) **29**:172
"Climbing the Streets of Worcester, Mass." (Harjo) **27**:66
"Climbing to the Monastery of Perception" (Wang Wei) **18**:384
"Clin d'oeil" (Péret) **33**:206-07, 214
"The Clinging Vine" (Robinson) **1**:468
"The Clipped Stater" (Graves) **6**:128, 137
"Clips" (Brathwaite) **56**:71
"A Cloak" (Levertov) **11**:176, 194
"La cloche fêlée" (Baudelaire) **1**:65
"Cloche fêlée" (Péret) **33**:207
Les cloches sur le coeur (Char) **56**:114, 120, 168
"The Clock" (Abse) **41**:3
"Clock" (Brathwaite) **56**:55
"A Clock in the Square" (Rich) **5**:352
"The Clock of Tomorrow" (Apollinaire)
See "L'lorloge de demain"
"The Clock Stopped" (Dickinson) **1**:108
"The Clod and the Pebble" (Blake) **12**:7
"Cloony the Clown" (Silverstein) **49**:334
"Clorinda and Damon" (Marvell) **10**:268, 271
"Close by Shelley's Grave" (Carducci)
See "Presso l'Urna di Percy Bysshe Shelley"
The Close Chaplet (Jackson) **44**:51, 61-2, 104
"Closed for Good" (Frost) **1**:213
"Close-Up" (Ammons) **16**:24
"The Closing Album" (MacNeice) **61**:118, 181
Clothed in Light (Seifert)
See *Světlem oděná*
"Clothes" (Sexton) **2**:367
"Clothes" (Szymborska) **44**:283
"The Clothes Pin" (Kenyon) **57**:42
"The clothesline post is set" (Niedecker) **42**:150, 169
"The Cloud" (Muir) **49**:218, 294-95
"The Cloud" (Shelley) **14**:167, 171, 196, 207, 212
"Cloud" (Toomer) **7**:338
"The Cloud" (Walcott) **46**:236, 240, 290
"Cloud and Wind" (Rossetti) **44**:169
Cloud, Stone, Sun, and Vine (Sarton) **39**:321, 326, 333-34, 338, 344
"Cloud-Catch" (Hongo) **23**:204
The Cloud-Messenger (Kālidāsa)
See *Meghadūta*
"Clouds" (Ashbery) **26**:124
"Clouds" (Brooke) **24**:57-8, 73, 85
"Clouds" (Erdrich) **52**:176
"Clouds" (Levine) **22**:214, 219, 222
"Clouds" (Tomlinson) **17**:312
The Clouds (Williams) **7**:370
"Clover" (Darío)
See "Trébol"
"Clover" (Lanier) **50**:54-55, 77
"The Clover" (Riley) **48**:328
"Clover-4" (Guillén) **35**:218
"Clover-7" (Guillén) **35**:218, 219
"Clover-8" (Guillén) **35**:218
"Clown" (Corso) **33**:25, 46-7
"The Clown Chastized" (Mallarmé)
See "Le pitre châtié"
Clown's Houses (Sitwell) **3**:290, 294, 301-02
"The Club" (Yamada) **44**:349-50
"Club 26" (Niedecker) **42**:182
The Club of Queer Trades (Chesterton) **28**:97
Cluster of Songs (Tagore)
See *Gitāli*
"A Clymene" (Verlaine) **32**:351, 384, 392
"Co mysli Pan Cogito o piekle" (Herbert) **50**:39
"Co robia nasi unmarli" (Herbert) **50**:6-7
"Coal" (Lorde) **12**:153
Coal (Lorde) **12**:142, 148
"The Coal Picker" (Lowell) **13**:84
"The Coast" (Hass) **16**:196
"The Coast Guard's Cottage" (Wylie) **23**:324
"Coast of Trees" (Ammons) **16**:45, 62
A Coast of Trees (Ammons) **16**:31, 45, 62
"The Coasts of Cerigo" (Hope) **56**:284, 288, 299
"The Coastwise Lights" (Kipling) **3**:162
"A Coat" (Yeats) **20**:320; **51**:81
A Coat for a Monkey (Matsuo Bashō)
See *Sarumino*
"The Coats" (Gallagher) **9**:60
"Coats" (Kenyon) **57**:8, 20
"The Cobbler of Hagenau" (Longfellow) **30**:43
"Cobwebs" (Rossetti) **7**:278
"Cocher ivre" (Rimbaud) **57**:253
"The Cock and the Fox" (Chaucer)
See "Nun's Priest's Tale"
"The Cocked Hat" (Masters) **1**:325-26, 328-29, 342; **36**:175
"Cockerel" (Hagiwara) **18**:173
"The Cockroach" (Alurista)
See "La Cucaracha"
"The Cocks" (Pasternak) **6**:253
"The Cocks" (Yevtushenko) **40**:343
"Cocks and Mares" (Stone) **53**:228, 254
"Coconut Palm" (Tagore)
See "Narikel"
"Cocotte" (Gozzano) **10**:178
"Coda" (Ekeloef) **23**:76, 86
"The Code" (Frost) **1**:195, 208, 226
"Code Book Lost" (Warren) **37**:312, 365
"A Code of Morals" (Kipling) **3**:190
"Codicil" (Stone) **53**:229
"Codicil" (Walcott) **46**:283
"Codziennosc duszy" (Herbert) **50**:39
"Coeur, couronne et miroir" (Apollinaire) **7**:32-6
"Le coeur du pître" (Rimbaud) **57**:253, 278
"Le coeur, l'eau non troublée" (Bonnefoy) **58**:118
Un coeur sous une soutane (Rimbaud) **57**:251
"La coeur volé" (Rimbaud) **3**:270
"Coffee and Sweet Rolls" (Stone) **53**:221
"Coffin" (Ignatow) **34**:293
"Cogióme sin prevención" (Juana Inés de la Cruz) **24**:234
"Cohorte" (Perse) **23**:254-57
"A Coin" (Sandburg) **41**:314
"The Coin" (Teasdale) **31**:350
"Coins" (Cavafy) **36**:39
Coins and Coffins (Wakoski) **15**:338, 344, 356, 369
"Cold" (Abse) **41**:29
"Cold" (Cassian) **17**:12, 15
"The Cold Before the Moonrise" (Merwin) **45**:20
"Cold Colloquy" (Warren) **37**:331, 333
"The Cold Divinities" (Wright) **36**:299, 360
"Cold in the Earth" (Brontë)
See "Remembrance"
"Cold Iron" (Kipling) **3**:171
"A Cold Spring" (Bishop) **34**:61, 120
A Cold Spring (Bishop) **34**:52, 174, 189
"Cold-Blooded Creatures" (Wylie) **23**:314
"The Colder the Air" (Bishop) **34**:54-55
"La colère de Samson" (Vigny) **26**:366, 368, 371, 380-81, 391, 401, 412, 416
"Coleridge" (McGuckian) **27**:101
"Colesberg" (Brutus) **24**:105
"Colin Clout" (Spenser)
See *Colin Clouts Come Home Againe*
Colin Clout (Skelton)
See *Collyn Cloute*
Colin Clouts Come Home Againe (Spenser) **8**:336, 367, 387, 396; **42**:248-49, 266
"The Coliseum" (Poe) **1**:439
The Coliseum (Poe) **54**:264
"Collage" (Stone) **53**:228
"The Collar" (Gunn) **26**:185
"The Collar" (Herbert) **4**:102-03, 112-13, 130-31
"The Collar" (Herrick) **9**:141
"A Colleague" (Hacker) **47**:120
Collected Earlier Poems (Williams) **7**:367-69, 374-75, 378, 382, 387-88, 392-94, 406-07, 409
Collected Early Poems (Pound) **4**:355
The Collected Greed, Parts 1-13 (Wakoski) **15**:356
Collected Later Poems (Williams) **7**:370, 375
The Collected Longer Poems of Kenneth Rexroth (Rexroth) **20**:197, 202, 204, 209-10, 214
Collected Lyrics (Millay) **6**:227
Collected Poem 1936-1976 (Francis) **34**:244-45, 247, 251-52, 258
Collected Poems (Aiken) **26**:21, 24, 43-5
The Collected Poems (Bishop) **34**:63-70, 86-87, 89-91
Collected Poems (Boland) **58**:66, 100
Collected Poems (Bridges) **28**:74, 77-8
Collected Poems (Camões) **31**:32

The Collected Poems (Chesterton) **28**:99, 109
Collected Poems (Cummings) **5**:82-4, 87, 107, 111
Collected Poems (Curnow) **48**:14
Collected Poems (Frost) **1**:203
Collected Poems (Graves) **6**:153, 165, 171
Collected Poems (Hardy) **8**:89, 95-6, 98, 101, 118, 124
Collected Poems (Jackson) **44**:5-12, 42, 44, 51-3, 57-8, 61-3, 65, 68-74, 77-9, 83, 87, 89-90, 96, 101-2, 107
Collected Poems (Jarrell) **41**:144, 148, 210
Collected Poems (Kavanagh) **33**:65, 68, 73, 77, 79, 82, 85, 87, 89, 98-9, 101-4, 113-122, 128-32, 136, 164-6, 169
Collected Poems (Larkin) **21**:256, 258
Collected Poems (Lawrence) **54**:162, 173, 179, 184, 186, 207, 228, 231-34, 239
Collected Poems (Lindsay) **23**:265, 280-82, 285-86, 288, 292, 294
Collected Poems (MacDiarmid) **9**:186
Collected Poems (MacNeice) **61**:106, 139, 141, 143-46, 166, 168-71, 173, 181, 185-86
Collected Poems (Mahon) **60**:231, 235
Collected Poems (Millay) **6**:227; **61**:223, 225, 242-45
Collected Poems (Milosz)
See *Czeslaw Milosz: The Collected Poems, 1931-1987*
Collected Poems (Moore) **4**:235-36, 238, 247, 254, 271; **49**:89, 113-14, 125, 136
Collected Poems (Muir) **49**:195, 206, 208, 211, 217, 226-27, 230-35, 237-44, 253-58, 262, 269-70, 276-80, 287
Collected Poems (Olson) **19**:316
Collected Poems (Oppen) **35**:285, 286, 287, 300, 304, 3311, 320, 321, 322-25, 332, 333, 335, 336, 337, 339, 340, 341, 354
Collected Poems (Patmore) **59**:271
Collected Poems (Pinsky) **27**:168
The Collected Poems (Plath) **1**:406; **37**:196, 209, 214, 216-20, 227, 237-41, 243, 247, 260-65
Collected Poems (Robinson) **1**:467, 469, 480
Collected Poems (Rossetti)
See *The Poetical Works of Christina Georgina Rossetti*
Collected Poems (Sandburg) **41**:354, 357
Collected Poems (Sitwell) **3**:299, 301, 303-05, 308, 318-21, 325
Collected Poems (Stevens) **6**:306
Collected Poems (Stryk) **27**:207, 209-10, 212-16
Collected Poems (Thomas) **52**:210, 217, 222, 226-27, 230-36, 239, 253, 256, 258, 263, 277, 303-4, 308, 310-11, 320, 330
Collected Poems (Thomas) **53**:282, 300-303, 305
Collected Poems (Tomlinson) **17**:342, 351, 355, 361
Collected Poems (Wagoner) **33**:334, 344, 347, 366, 369-72
Collected Poems (Wright) **36**:296, 301, 304-5, 308, 316-22, 346, 350, 366, 368, 371, 384-87
The Collected Poems (Yeats) **20**:307, 336-37; **51**:108, 119, 149
The Collected Poems (Yevtushenko) **40**:365, 368
Collected Poems 1934 (Williams) **7**:360, 372, 402
Collected Poems, 1938 (Graves) **6**:166
Collected Poems, 1955 (Graves) **6**:138, 140-43, 145
Collected Poems, 1909-1935 (Eliot) **5**:173, 176, 179, 211
Collected Poems, 1912-1944 (H. D.) **5**:297, 305
Collected Poems, 1917-1952 (MacLeish) **47**:164, 182-83, 192
Collected Poems, 1919-1976 (Tate) **50**:304-5, 307, 334
Collected Poems, 1923-1953 (Bogan) **12**:93, 95-6, 120, 125
Collected Poems, 1929-1933 (Day Lewis) **11**:123
Collected Poems, 1930-1970 (Hope) **56**:278-82, 301-4, 306-7
Collected Poems, 1930-1973 (Sarton) **39**:334, 344, 354, 359, 364-67
Collected Poems, 1940-1978 (Shapiro) **25**:313, 315
Collected Poems, 1947-1980 (Ginsberg) **4**:71-2, 76-9, 83-4, 86, 89; **47**:35
Collected Poems, 1948-1976 (Abse) **41**:18, 20-3, 25, 27, 31, 33
Collected Poems, 1948-1984 (Walcott) **46**:259
Collected Poems, 1950-1970 (Davie) **29**:101, 111, 122
Collected Poems, 1951-1971 (Ammons) **16**:10, 20, 27, 40, 46, 54, 61
The Collected Poems, 1952-1990 (Yevtushenko) **40**:370
Collected Poems: 1956-1976 (Wagoner) **33**:352, 354
Collected Poems, 1957-1982 (Berry) **28**:25-29, 32, 37-39, 43-4
The Collected Poems of A. E. Housman (Housman) **2**:175-76, 180
The Collected Poems of Archibald MacLeish (MacLeish) **47**:200-201, 203
The Collected Poems of Christopher Smart (Smart) **13**:347
The Collected Poems of C.P. Cavafy (Cavafy) **36**:117
The Collected Poems of Earle Birney (Birney) **52**:26-27, 44, 51, 58-59, 62, 78, 94-95
Collected Poems of Elinor Wylie (Wylie) **23**:304, 306, 312, 314, 330-31
The Collected Poems of Frank O'Hara (O'Hara) **45**:113, 119-20, 127, 132-34, 136-51, 153-57, 159-66, 171-73, 175-80, 184-85, 187, 189-93, 196, 198-202, 221-29, 231, 234, 237-39, 241-45
Collected Poems of H. D. (H. D.) **5**:268, 270, 276
The Collected Poems of Hart Crane (Crane) **3**:89-90
The Collected Poems of Henry Thoreau (Thoreau) **30**:182, 185, 187, 189-90, 232, 237, 256, 209-70, 272-76, 281
The Collected Poems of Howard Nemerov (Nemerov) **24**:298-99, 301
The Collected Poems of Jean Toomer (Toomer) **7**:340-41
The Collected Poems of Langston Hughes (Hughes) **53**:112, 115-16, 142, 158, 167-68, 182-83, 200, 202, 205-6
The Collected Poems of Muriel Rukeyser (Rukeyser) **12**:224, 226, 235
The Collected Poems of Octavio Paz, 1957-1987 (Paz) **1**:374-76; **48**:187, 191, 248-51
The Collected Poems of Robert Penn Warren (Warren) **37**:382-83
The Collected Poems of Rupert Brooke (Brooke) **24**:52, 54, 61, 71
The Collected Poems of Sara Teasdale (Teasdale) **31**:327, 339, 342, 362
The Collected Poems of Sterling A. Brown (Brown) **55**:79, 87, 89-90, 93-94, 101-5, 111-12, 140, 142-43, 157, 167
The Collected Poems of Stevie Smith (Smith) **12**:307, 309, 313-17, 320, 327, 346-47, 350, 352
The Collected Poems of Theodore Roethke (Roethke) **15**:281, 283-84, 288
The Collected Poems of Thomas Merton (Merton) **10**:336-337, 345, 348, 351
The Collected Poems of Wallace Stevens (Stevens) **6**:304
The Collected Poems of Wilfred Owen (Owen) **19**:351
Collected Poetry Notebook (Césaire) **25**:48-9
Collected Shorter Poems, 1927-1957 (Auden) **1**:30
Collected Shorter Poems, 1930-1950 (Auden) **1**:30
Collected Shorter Poems, 1946-1991 (Carruth) **10**:89, 91
The Collected Shorter Poems of Kenneth Rexroth (Rexroth) **20**:197-98, 202, 204-05
Collected Sonnets (Millay) **6**:227
Collected Works (Akhmatova) **2**:19
Collected Works (Rossetti) **44**:176, 214, 219, 221, 227
Collected Works (Rossetti)
See *The Poetical Works of Christina Georgina Rossetti*
The Collected Works of Billy the Kid: Left Handed Poems (Ondaatje) **28**:298, 304, 314-16, 327, 338-39
The Collected Works of Edgar Allan Poe (Poe) **54**:300, 305
The Collected Works of Shams (Rumi)
See *Divan-i Shams-i Tabrizi*
Collected Works of William Morris (Morris) **55**:306-7, 309, 325
"Collected Writings" (Borges) **32**:52
Collected Writings (Rossetti) **44**:255-56
Collection for a Myriad Ages (Yakamochi)
See *Man'yōshū*
Collection for Ten Thousand Ages (Yakamochi)
See *Man'yōshū*
A Collection of Celebrated Love Poems (Hagiwara)
See *Ren'aimeikashū*
Collection of Myriad Leaves (Yakamochi)
See *Man'yōshū*
Collection of One Thousand Leaves (Yakamochi)
See *Man'yōshū*
Collection of Short Songs on Innocent Love (Hagiwara)
See *Junjo shokyoku shu*
"Collective Dawns" (Ashbery) **26**:144, 153
"College Breakfast Party" (Eliot) **20**:125
"The College Garden" (Bridges) **28**:79-80
"The Collier's Wife" (Lawrence) **54**:187, 221
"Les collines" (Apollinaire) **7**:12
"Colloque sentimental" (Verlaine) **32**:350, 352, 371, 390, 393, 396
"Colloqui con gli alberi" (Carducci) **46**:51
"The Colloquies" (Gozzano) **10**:175, 180
The Colloquies (Gozzano)
See *I Colloqui*
"Colloquy" (Brown) **55**:114, 168-69
"Colloquy at Peniel" (Merwin) **45**:24
"Colloquy in Black Rock" (Lowell) **3**:201, 216-17, 227
"Colloquy of the Centaurs" (Darío)
See "Coloquio de los centauros"
"Collos. 3.3" (Herbert) **4**:130
Collyn Clout (Skelton)
See *Collyn Cloute*
Collyn Cloute (Skelton) **25**:329-30, 336, 337, 341-42, 348, 356, 374
"La colombe poisnardée et le jet d'eau" (Apollinaire) **7**:18, 20-2
"A Colombia" (Guillén) **23**:127
"Colombine" (Verlaine) **32**:351, 364, 390, 393
"The Colonel" (Forché) **10**:136, 138, 140, 145, 153, 167, 169
"Colonel Fantock" (Sitwell) **3**:293, 301, 325
"La Colonia a medianoche" (Storni) **33**:261, 295-96;
"Colonial Outlook" (Curnow) **48**:26
"The Colonists" (Boland) **58**:62
"Colony" (Boland) **58**:40, 50-51, 61-62
"A Colophon" (Carman) **34**:208
"Coloquio de los centauros" (Darío) **15**:88, 92, 96, 112, 114
Color (Cullen) **20**:52-54, 56-58, 62, 66-67, 72, 77, 79, 81-83, 85-86
"The Color Sergeant" (Johnson) **24**:142
"Colorado Blvd." (Cervantes) **35**:134

"The Colored Band" (Dunbar) **5**:134, 147
"The Colored Soldier" (Hughes) **53**:114
"The Colored Soldiers" (Dunbar) **5**:129-31, 133-34, 140
"Colors" (Cullen) **20**:65
"The Colors of Night" (Momaday) **25**:199, 202-203, 217-18
"Colossus" (Plath) **37**:177, 185-87, 214, 216-21, 243-44, 246
The Colossus, and Other Poems (Plath) **1**:380-81, 84, 388-89, 391, 394, 396, 404, 407, 410, 414; **37**:175-90, 196
"Colour" (Thumboo) **30**:300
"The Colour Shop" (McGuckian) **27**:106
"A Coloured Print by Shokei" (Lowell) **13**:61
"A Coltrane Poem" (Sanchez) **9**:225
"The Colubriad" (Cowper) **40**:125
"Columbia U Poesy Reading—1975" (Corso) **33**:44, 50
"Columbian Ode" (Dunbar) **5**:128
"Columbus, Ohio" (Stone) **53**:223
Colyn (Skelton)
See *Collyn Cloute*
Colyn Cloute (Skelton)
See *Collyn Cloute*
"The Combat" (Muir) **49**:212, 215, 224-26, 228, 234, 284-85
"Combat Cultural" (Moore) **4**:259; **49**:143
"Combat Pay for Jodie" (Komunyakaa) **51**:9
"Combat Pay for Jody" (Komunyakaa)
See "Combat Pay for Jodie"
"The Combe" (Thomas) **53**:278, 308, 332
"Come!" (Ignatow) **34**:323
"Come" (Smith) **12**:316
"Come Back" (Cavafy) **36**:74
"Come before His Countenance with a Joyful Leaping" (Wagoner) **33**:330
"Come Break with Time" (Bogan) **12**:87, 101, 105-06, 122
"Come, Come Now" (Aleixandre) **15**:15
"Come Dance with Kitty Stobling" (Kavanagh) **33**:76, 96, 104, 115
Come Dance with Kitty Stobling (Kavanagh) **33**:62-4, 68, 72-3, 79, 81, 95-6, 103, 146-7
"Come Death" (Smith) **12**:315
"Come Death (2)" (Smith) **12**:314, 317, 319
"come down my cheek raza roja" (Alurista) **34**:23, 24, 29
"Come Forth" (Wright) **36**:343
"Come Hither" (Mueller) **33**:180
"Come In" (Frost) **1**:197, 213, 230; **39**:234, 237, 239-40, 246, 253
"Come, Look Quietly" (Wright) **36**:378
"Come, O King of the Lacedaemonians" (Cavafy) **36**:4, 58
"Come on, Come back" (Smith) **12**:295
Come Out into the Sun (Francis) **34**:243, 245, 248
"Come Republic" (Masters) **1**:329, 343; **36**:177
"Come se Quando" (Bridges) **28**:76-9
"Come Thunder" (Okigbo) **7**:235
"Come to the Bower" (Heaney) **18**:197
"Come to the Stone . . ." (Jarrell) **41**:195, 198
"Come with Me" (Bly) **39**:42, 91
"Come, Words, Away" (Jackson) **44**:107
"The Comedian as the Letter C" (Stevens) **6**:293, 295-96, 304, 306, 310, 330, 335
"Comedian Body" (Francis) **34**:247
La comédie de la mort (Gautier) **18**:131-32, 134-35, 141, 143-6, 155, 159, 163
"Comédie de la soif" (Rimbaud) **57**:177, 245, 253
Comedy (Dante)
See *La divina commedia*
"Comedy of Thirst" (Rimbaud)
See "Comédie de la soif"
"Comes to Rest" (Cavafy) **36**:81, 109
"The Comet" (Aleixandre) **15**:5
"The Comet at Yell'ham" (Hardy) **8**:89
"Comfort" (Browning) **6**:21
"Comfort in Self-Despite" (Muir) **49**:245, 250-51
"The Comfort of Rooms" (Szirtes) **51**:167
"Coming" (Larkin) **21**:238, 244
"Coming and Going" (Paz) **48**:274
"Coming Awake" (Lawrence) **54**:169
"Coming Back to America" (Dickey) **40**:158, 254
"Coming Close" (Levine) **22**:220
"Coming Down" (Cruz) **37**:10
"Coming Down through Somerset" (Hughes) **7**:166
"The Coming Fall" (Levertov) **11**:185
The Coming Forth by Day of Osiris Jones (Aiken) **26**:8, 11, 57
"Coming Home" (Gallagher) **9**:36
"Coming Home from the Post Office" (Levine) **22**:221, 228
"Coming in for Supper" (Bly) **39**:44
"Coming of Age in Michigan" (Levine) **22**:220, 228
"The Coming of Arthur" (Tennyson) **6**:408
"The Coming of Kali" (Clifton) **17**:24
"The Coming of the End (Moments of Vision)" (Hardy) **8**:92
"The Coming of War" (MacNeice) **61**:138
"The Coming of Wisdom with Time" (Yeats) **20**:338
Coming through Slaughter (Ondaatje) **28**:298
"Commander Lowell 1887-1950" (Lowell) **3**:219, 235
"Commandments" (Lawrence) **54**:249
Comme deux gouttes d'eau (Éluard) **38**:62, 73
"Comme Dieu Dispense de Graces" (Stevens) **6**:294
"Comme on voit sur la branche" (Ronsard) **11**:218, 234, 236, 240
"Comme un beau pré despouillè de ses fleurs" (Ronsard) **11**:250
Commedia (Dante)
See *La divina commedia*
"The Commemoration" (Muir) **49**:297
"The Commemorative Mound of the Decorated Tree" (Ishikawa)
See "Nishikigizuka"
"Commendation" (Raleigh)
See "Walter Rawley of the Middle Temple, in Commendation of the Steele Glasse"
"Comment against the Lamp" (Hughes) **1**:266
"Comment on War" (Hughes) **53**:112
"Commentary" (Milosz) **8**:212-13
"Commiato" (Ungaretti) **57**:346
"A Commination" (Hope) **56**:266, 269
"Commodore Barry" (Davie) **29**:106, 109-10
"Common Beauty" (Kavanagh) **33**:140
"The Common Grave" (Dickey) **40**:196
"A Common Ground" (Levertov) **11**:169
"The common living dirt" (Piercy) **29**:315, 317-19
"The Commonweal" (Swinburne) **24**:312
"A Communal Feud" (Carducci)
See "Faida di Commune"
Communé présence (Char) **56**:111, 114-17, 128, 189
"Communication I" (Angelou) **32**:28
"Communication II" (Angelou) **32**:28
"Communication in White" (Madhubuti) **5**:340
"Communion" (Erdrich) **52**:191
"Communion" (Herbert) **4**:100
"Communion" (Ignatow) **34**:311
"Communique" (Komunyakaa) **51**:41
"Communism or capitalism" (Niedecker) **42**:149
"A Communist to Others" (Auden) **1**:15
"Community" (Piercy) **29**:308, 311
"The Commuted Sentence" (Smith) **12**:327
Cómo atar (Fuertes) **27**:27, 30
Cómo atar los bigotes al tigre (Fuertes) **27**:17-8, 25-7, 31, 49
"Como del cielo llovido" (Guillén) **23**:126
"Como en la noche mortal'" (Guillén) **34**:228
"Como les iba diciendo" (Parra) **39**:281
"Cómo llovía, suaviño" (Castro) **41**:110-11
"Como lo siento" (Cervantes) **35**:113
"Como quisimos" (Guillén) **23**:126
"The Compact: At Volterra" (Tomlinson) **17**:350
"La compagne du vannier" (Char) **56**:155, 188
Les compagnons dans le jardin (Char) **56**:107, 109, 120-22
"The Companion of a Mile" (Noyes) **27**:134
"Companionable Ills" (Plath) **37**:190
"The Companions" (Nemerov) **24**:263
"Company" (Dove) **6**:111, 119
"Company" (Smith) **12**:325
"The Company of Lovers" (Wright) **14**:336, 340, 351, 371
"A Comparative Peace" (Brutus) **24**:116
"Comparatives" (Momaday) **25**:191, 193-194
"The Comparison" (Donne)
See "Elegie VIII: The Comparison"
"Comparison" (Dunbar) **5**:125
"Compás de Expera'" (Guillén) **35**:228
"Compass" (Borges) **22**:74
The Compass Flower (Merwin) **45**:52, 55, 58-9, 63, 70-2, 81, 84, 86-8, 92, 95
"Compensation" (Dunbar) **5**:121
"Compensation" (Teasdale) **31**:359
"Complaint" (Wilbur) **51**:231, 247, 312
"The Complaint" (Wordsworth)
See "The Complaint of the Forsaken Indian Woman"
"Complaint of the Amorous Lizard" (Char)
See "Complainte du lézard amoureux"
"Complaint of the Dying Peasantry" (Muir) **49**:211, 299
"The Complaint of the Forsaken Indian Woman" (Wordsworth) **4**:347, 427-28
"Complaint of the Poor Knight Errant" (Laforgue)
See "Complainte du pauvre chevalier-errant"
"Complainte à Notre-Dame des soirs" (Laforgue) **14**:94
"Complainte de cette bonne lune" (Laforgue) **14**:93
Complainte de la bonne défunte (Laforgue) **14**:81, 98
"Complainte de la fin des journées" (Laforgue) **14**:98
"Complainte de la lune en province" (Laforgue) **14**:98
"Complainte de l'ange incurable" (Laforgue) **14**:85, 89-90, 98
"Complainte de l'automne monotone" (Laforgue) **14**:80
"Complainte de l'époux outragé" (Laforgue) **14**:81, 93
"Complainte de Lord Pierrot" (Laforgue) **14**:81, 93, 98
"Complainte de l'organiste de Nice" (Laforgue) **14**:93
"Complainte de l'orgue de barbarie" (Laforgue) **14**:95
"Complainte des blackboulés" (Laforgue) **14**:81, 96
"Complainte des complaintes" (Laforgue) **14**:95
"Complainte des consolations" (Laforgue) **14**:81
"Complainte des débats mélancoliques et littéraires" (Laforgue) **14**:64, 97
"Complainte des formalités nuptiales" (Laforgue) **14**:81, 96
"Complainte des grands pins dans une ville abandonée" (Laforgue) **14**:81, 96
"Complainte des pianos qu'on entend dans les quertiersaisés" (Laforgue) **14**:81, 93-5
"Complainte des printemps" (Laforgue) **14**:81, 98
"Complainte des voix sous le figuier bouddhique" (Laforgue) **14**:96
"Complainte du fœtus de Poète" (Laforgue) **14**:93, 96, 98
"Complainte du lézard amoureux" (Char) **56**:167, 182
"Complainte du pauvre chevalier-errant" (Laforgue) **14**:64, 98

"Complainte du pauvre corps humain" (Laforgue) **14**:81
"Complainte du pauvre jeune homme" (Laforgue) **14**:81, 93
"Complainte du Roi de Thulé" (Laforgue) **14**:81, 86, 89, 93, 98
"Complainte du sage de Paris" (Laforgue) **14**:95
"Complainte d'un certain dimanche" (Laforgue) **14**:96-8
"Complainte d'une convalescence en mai" (Laforgue) **14**:96, 98
"Complainte propitiatoire à l'inconscient" (Laforgue) **14**:66, 94-5
"Complainte sous le figuier boudhique" (Laforgue) **14**:81
"Complainte sur certains ennuis" (Laforgue) **14**:94, 97
"Complainte sur certains temps déplacés" (Laforgue) **14**:94
"Complainte-épitaphe" (Laforgue) **14**:95
"Complainte-Placet de Faust fils" (Laforgue) **14**:95, 98
Les complaintes (Laforgue) **14**:57, 64, 66, 68-9, 70-2, 80-1, 92, 94-5, 97-8
"Complaintes des pubertés difficiles" (Laforgue) **14**:80, 98
Complaints: Containing Sundrie Small Poemes of the Worlds Vanitie (Spenser) **8**:366
"The Complement" (Carew) **29**:32
The Complete Collected Poems of William Carlos Williams, 1906-1938 (Williams) **7**:348, 355
The Complete Poems (Dickinson) **1**:102
Complete Poems (Jarrell) **41**:164-70, 178, 180, 184-86, 189, 191, 194-97, 207
Complete Poems (Muir) **49**:291
Complete Poems (Sandburg) **2**:322-24, 328-29, 331, 333, 340; **41**:279, 282-83, 287, 300-01, 303-4, 306, 314, 322, 359
Complete Poems (Sidney) **32**:288
The Complete Poems (Thoreau) **30**:256
The Complete Poems, 1927-1979 (Bishop) **3**:50, 66; **34**:94, 123-27, 130-31, 137-40, 145-47, 159, 155, 158, 170, 174-76
The Complete Poems of C.P. Cavafy (Cavafy) **36**:117
The Complete Poems of D. H. Lawrence (Lawrence) **54**:204-8, 220-27, 239-40, 243-45, 249-50
The Complete Poems of Frances Ellen Watkins Harper (Harper) **21**:197
The Complete Poems of Marianne Moore (Moore) **4**:251, 254, 256, 270; **49**:122, 144, 149-50, 184-85, 188-85
The Complete Poem's of Paul Laurence Dunbar (Dunbar) **5**:120, 136
Complete Poems of Robert Frost (Frost) **39**:233
The Complete Poetical Works (Lowell) **13**:95
Complete Poetical Works of Samuel Taylor Coleridge (Coleridge) **11**:44, 71; **39**:215-16
Complete Verse (Belloc) **24**:23, 36, 39
Complete Works (Aleixandre)
See *Obras completas*
Complete Works (Borges)
See *Obras completas*
Complete Works (Jeffers) **17**:125
Complete Works (Mandelstam) **14**:106
Complete Works: From This Condensery (Niedecker)
See *From This Condensery: The Complete Writings of Lorine Niedecker*
The Complete Works of Edgar Allan Poe (Póe) **54**:302, 331, 337
"The Complete Works of Francois Villon" (Villon) **13**:413
The Complete Works of Geoffrey Chaucer (Chaucer) **58**:303
"Complete Works of Philip Sidney" (Sidney) **32**:235, 244-47, 249-50, 256, 257-58, 260, 268
"The Complex" (Ignatow) **34**:286
"Complicate" (Kunitz) **19**:156
"Complicity" (Gallagher) **9**:37
"Composed on Jade Maiden Spring in Ying Cheng, Anzhou" (Li Po) **29**:179, 182
"Composed on the Cold Food Day" (Wang Wei) **18**:362
"Composición escrita en un ejemplar de la gesta de Beowulf" (Borges) **32**:63, 94, 105-06, 133
"Composition as Process—I. Changes" (Cage) **58**:205
"Composition in Bhairavi" (Tagore)
See "Bhairavi gan"
"Composition in Retrospect" (Cage) **58**:200, 206, 208
"Comprehending" (Ortiz) **17**:246
"Comptine" (Césaire) **25**:31
"Compulsory Chapel" (Walker) **30**:347
"Comrades Four" (McKay) **2**:225
Comus: A Maske (Milton) **29**:200, 212, 221, 226, 228, 243, 252, 272
"Con la Carta de la Habana" (Guillén) **23**:126
"Conceit begotten by the eyes" (Raleigh) **31**:212, 214
"Conceit of Master Gysbrecht" (Browning) **2**:38
"Conceive a Man, Should He Have Anything" (Cummings) **5**:106
"Concerning Geoffray Teste Noire" (Morris) **55**:299, 301-2
"Concerning Some Recent Criticism of His Work" (Doty) **53**:61
"Concerning the Right to Life" (Graham) **59**:159
"The Concert" (Millay) **6**:215
"The Concert" (Yevtushenko) **40**:340
"Concert at the Railroad Station" (Mandelstam)
See "Koncert na vokzale"
"Concert in the garden" (Paz)
See "Concierto en el jardin"
"The Concert of Hyacinths" (Elytis) **21**:119
Concert on the Island (Seifert)
See *Koncert na ostrově*
"Concerto to a Runaway" (Bissett) **14**:9
"Conch" (Herbert)
See "Muszla"
"Conch-Shell" (Wright) **14**:364
"El concierto" (Guillén) **35**:185
"Concierto en el jardin" (Paz) **48**:207
Le concile féerique (Laforgue) **14**:72, 81, 96
"Conciliator, Who Had Never Believed" (Hölderlin) **4**:178
"Conclusion" (Sassoon) **12**:258
"Concord" (Swinburne) **24**:324, 326
"Concord Hymn" (Emerson) **18**:111
"Concord Ode" (Emerson) **18**:84, 88
"Concord River" (Rich) **5**:354
"The Condemned" (Page) **12**:174-75
"La condena" (Mistral) **32**:176
Condensery (Niedecker)
See *From This Condensery: The Complete Writings of Lorine Niedecker*
A Coney Island of the Mind (Ferlinghetti) **1**:164-65, 167-77, 184, 187
"A Confederate Veteran Tries to Explain the Event" (Warren) **37**:341
"A Conference of the Powers" (Kipling) **3**:160
Confessio Amantis (Gower) **59**:3-7, 9, 11-13, 15, 17, 20-22, 25-31, 39, 41-48, 54-59, 61-63, 65-70, 72, 76-80, 82-84, 87-89, 94-100, 103, 106-7, 109-11, 113-14, 116-19
"Confession" (Baudelaire) **1**:61
"confession" (Clifton) **17**:37
"Confession" (Glück) **16**:160
"Confession" (Heaney) **18**:243
"The Confession" (Lermontov)
See "Ispoved"
"A Confession" (Milosz) **8**:197
Confession Amantis (Gower)
See *Confessio Amantis*
"Confession to J. Edgar Hoover" (Wright) **36**:342
"The Confessional" (Browning) **2**:30; **61**:88
"Confessional" (Chesterton) **28**:95
"Confessions" (Browning) **6**:32
"Confessions of a Second-Rate, Sensitive Mind" (Tennyson) **6**:347
"The Confessions of Count Mowgli de Sade" (Nash) **21**:267
"Confessions of the Life Artist" (Gunn) **26**:207, 211, 226
"The Confidantes" (Kumin) **15**:215
"The Confidant's Alley" (Char) **56**:162
"Confidential Instructions" (Kunitz) **19**:148
"Configurations" (Ammons) **16**:23
Configurations (Paz) **1**:355
"Confinement" (McGuckian) **27**:101
"Confirmation" (Erdrich) **52**:191
"The Confirmation" (Muir) **49**:232, 289
"The Confirmation" (Shapiro) **25**:286, 300
"Confiteor" (Trakl) **20**:263-64, 269
"The Conflict" (Day Lewis) **11**:126, 150
"Confusion of the Senses" (Rexroth) **20**:221
"Congé au vent" (Char) **56**:150, 182
"Congedo" (Carducci) **46**:65, 74, 81
"Congo" (Lindsay) **23**:264, 266, 268, 270, 272-73, 275-76, 278, 282-84, 286-87, 289, 294, 297
The Congo and Other Poems (Lindsay) **23**:267-68, 295
"The Congo Love Song" (Johnson) **24**:151
"A Congratulatory Poem to Her Most Sacred Majesty on the Universal Hopes of All Loyal Persons for a Prince of Wales" (Behn) **13**:32
A Congratulatory Poem to . . . Queen Mary upon Her Arrival in England (Behn) **13**:9
"Conjectural Poem" (Borges)
See "Poema conjectural"
Los conjurados (Borges) **22**:95, 99; **32**:86, 91, 111
"Conjuration" (Wilbur) **51**:187-88, 193
"Conjuries That Endure" (Moore) **49**:161
"Conjuring in Heaven" (Hughes) **7**:159
Connecting the Dots (Kumin) **15**:224
"Connections" (Wright) **14**:376-77
"Conneries" (Rimbaud) **57**:252
"The Connoisseuse of Slugs" (Olds) **22**:312
"Connubii Flores, or the Well-Wishes at Weddings" (Herrick) **9**:86, 112
"The Conquererors" (Dunbar) **5**:131
"Conqueror" (Brathwaite) **56**:60
"The Conqueror Worm" (Poe) **1**:437, 443; **54**:272
"Conquête de l'aube" (Césaire) **25**:10
"Conquistador" (Hope) **56**:266, 276, 286, 293, 302
Conquistador (MacLeish) **47**:127-28, 130, 133, 137-40, 150, 152, 156, 158, 163, 188-90, 194-95, 197-204, 211, 213-14, 239, 253-54
"Conrad in Twilight" (Ransom) **61**:275
"Conrad Kain" (Birney) **52**:58
Conrad Wallenrod (Mickiewicz)
See *Konrad Wallenrod*
"A Conrado Benítez" (Guillén) **23**:128
"The Cons cientious Objector" (Shapiro) **25**:297
"Consalvo" (Leopardi) **37**:79
"Conscience" (Herbert) **4**:109, 129
"La Conscience" (Hugo) **17**:65, 85
"Conscience and Remorse" (Dunbar) **5**:115, 125
"Les consciences atténuantes" (Tzara) **27**:235
"Conscious" (Owen) **19**:347, 361-63
"Consciousness" (Milosz)
See "Świadomość"
"Conscript" (Larkin) **21**:225
"The Conscript" (MacNeice) **61**:141
"Conscription Camp" (Shapiro) **25**:313, 324-25
"Conscripts" (Sassoon) **12**:242, 280
"The Consecrating Mother" (Sexton) **2**:374
"The Consecration of Henry V" (Carducci)
See "La Sacra di Enrico Quinto"
"Conseil d'ami" (Valéry) **9**:391
"Conseil de la sentinelle" (Char) **56**:172
"Consequences" (Meredith) **28**:213

"Conservatism" (Moore)
See "Progress"
"Conserving the Magnitude of Uselessness" (Ammons) **16**:54
"Consider Me" (Hughes) **53**:122
"Considerations" (Sarton) **39**:321
"Considering the Snail" (Gunn) **26**:201, 207-208, 210, 213
"Consolation" (Ignatow) **34**:281-82
"Consolation" (McKay) **2**:225
"Consolations of Philosophy" (Mahon) **60**:134, 140
"Consorting with Angels" (Sexton) **2**:363
The Conspirators (Borges)
See *Los conjurados*
Constab Ballads (McKay) **2**:208, 210, 216, 221-22, 225-27
"Constance" (Gower) **59**:48, 68-70, 107-8
Constance (Kenyon) **57**:6, 11, 19-20, 23-24, 35, 37-38, 40, 45-46
"Constance Hately" (Masters) **36**:218
"Constancie" (Herbert) **4**:109
"The Constant" (Ammons) **16**:6
"Constant" (MacNeice) **61**:178
"Constantly Risking Absurdity" (Ferlinghetti) **1**:182
"Constellation" (Stryk) **27**:208, 212
Constellations (Breton) **15**:48-9, 55, 59-60, 62
"Construction" (Shapiro) **25**:295
"Constructions" (Loy) **16**:316
"Construyendo una Balsa" (Alurista) **34**:16, 24, 29, 47
"Consultorio sentimental" (Parra) **39**:277
"La consumación" (Mistral) **32**:191
"The Consumptive" (Hughes) **53**:115
"A Contact" (MacNeice) **61**:127
"Conte" (Rimbaud) **3**:261-63; **57**:174, 245, 247, 254, 271, 275
"Conte Colibri" (Césaire) **25**:44-5
"Contemplando Florencia" (Guillén) **35**:227
"Contemplation Basket" (Sandburg) **41**:323
"Contemplation of Beauty" (Carducci)
See "Contemplazione della bellezza'"
"Contemplations" (Bradstreet) **10**:7-8, 19-21, 27-30, 35, 42, 65
Les contemplations (Hugo) **17**:50, 53-54, 64, 66-67, 74, 78, 80-84, 86-87, 89-92, 95
"Contemplazione della bellezza'" (Carducci) **46**:75
"The Contender" (Hughes) **7**:155
"Content, to my dearest Lucasia" (Philips) **40**:297
"The Contention" (Sassoon) **12**:259
"Contest of the Bards" (Ginsberg) **4**:58-9
"The Continent" (Duncan) **2**:109-13
"The Continental Can Company at Six O'Clock" (Wright) **36**:391
"Continent's End" (Jeffers) **17**:131
"Contingency" (Ammons) **16**:6
Continuation des amours (Ronsard) **11**:220, 230
"Continuum" (Levertov) **11**:207-09
Continuum: New and Later Poems, 1972-1988 (Curnow) **48**:32-35, 37-40
"Contra mortem" (Carruth) **10**:83
Contra Mortem (Carruth) **10**:71
"A Contract" (Lermontov) **18**:303-4
"The Contract" (Patmore) **59**:207, 223, 259, 264, 267-68, 276
"Contralto" (Gautier) **18**:157
"The Contraption" (Swenson) **14**:250
"Contrapunto final" (Guillén) **35**:188
"The Contrariness of the Mad Farmer" (Berry) **28**:20
"The Contrary Poet" (Jarrell) **41**:139
"The Contrast" (Harper) **21**:207, 216
"Contravening" (Char)
See "Obéissez à vos porcs qui existent . . ."
"Contre les bûcherons de la forêt de Gastine" (Ronsard) **11**:236-37, 242
"Contre une maison sèche" (Char) **56**:154
"Le Contrediz de Franc Gontier" (Villon) **13**:415
"Contrevenir" (Char)
See "Obéissez à vos porcs qui existent . . ."
"The Contrite Heart" (Cowper) **40**:53-4
"Control" (Sarton) **39**:368
"Control Burn" (Snyder) **21**:292
"Contusion" (Plath) **1**:391, 394
"A Conundrum" (Carman) **34**:208
"The Conundrum of the Workshop" (Kipling) **3**:167
"The Convalescent" (Gozzano) **10**:177
"Convalescenza" (Quasimodo) **47**:271
"The Convent Threshold" (Rossetti) **7**:267, 281-2, 291, 295-6, 298
"Conventionality" (Kipling) **3**:190
"The Convergence of the Twain" (Hardy) **8**:116
"Convergences" (Warren) **37**:326, 336, 350
"Conversacíon" (Cardenal) **22**:117
"Conversación galante" (Parra) **39**:286
"Conversation" (Bishop) **34**:89
"Conversation" (Cowper) **40**:43, 45, 48, 50, 71
"Conversation" (Curnow) **48**:57, 61
"Conversation" (Giovanni) **19**:118
"The Conversation" (Masters) **1**:326
"Conversation" (Mickiewicz)
See "Rozmowa"
Conversation at Midnight (Millay) **6**:220, 223, 244
"Conversation in Moscow" (Levertov) **11**:197
"Conversation in the Park" (Hacker) **47**:86, 95
"The Conversation of Prayer" (Thomas) **2**:390; **52**:263
"Conversation with a Fireman from Brooklyn" (Gallagher) **9**:44, 60
"Conversation with a Stone" (Szymborska) **44**:299, 314
"Conversation with an American Writer" (Yevtushenko) **40**:343, 345
"Conversation with Calliope" (Hope) **56**:274, 294-95
"Conversation With Death" (Seifert) **47**:334
"Conversation With Landor" (Hope) **56**:292
"Conversation With My Friend Kwang Min Ah Loong Kwang of Outram Park" (Thumboo) **30**:333
"Conversation with my Inspiration" (Tsvetaeva)
See "Razgovor s geniem"
"Conversation with the Devil" (Jarrell) **41**:177, 195, 199
"Conversations with Jeanne" (Milosz) **8**:213
"Conversations with Trees" (Carducci)
See "Colloqui con gli alberi"
"Conversing with Paradise" (Nemerov) **24**:285
"Conversion" (Toomer) **7**:320, 334
"The Convert" (Shapiro) **25**:286, 296, 298
"Convict" (Brown) **55**:144, 155, 2110
"The Convict" (Wordsworth) **4**:373
"Convivio!" (Williams) **7**:361
Convivio (Dante) **21**:48-53, 66, 73-4, 83, 87-92
"Convoy" (MacNeice) **61**:140
"Cook County" (MacLeish) **47**:213
"Cooking" (Stein) **18**:322-326
"A Cooking Egg" (Eliot) **5**:184
"The Cookout" (Ignatow) **34**:318
"Cook's Mountains" (Page) **12**:183, 190
"A Cool Head in an Emergency" (Curnow) **48**:18
"Cool Park, 1929" (Yeats)
See "Coole Park, 1929"
"Cool Tombs" (Sandburg) **41**:235, 240, 245, 250, 253, 266-67, 272, 276-77, 297, 313, 339
"The Cool Web" (Graves) **6**:172
"Coole Park, 1929" (Yeats) **20**:322
Coon Dog Wess (Riley) **48**:306
"Coon Song" (Ammons) **16**:19, 41, 44, 46
"Cooney Potter" (Masters) **36**:170
"Coopérants du contingent" (Senghor) **25**:255
"Cootchie" (Bishop) **34**:69, 137-38, 189
"La copa" (Storni) **33**:254;
Copacetic (Komunyakaa) **51**:15, 30, 33-34, 36
"Copacetic Mingus" (Komunyakaa) **51**:15, 31, 33
"Coplas" (Mistral) **32**:153, 176, 178
"Coplas americans" (Guillén) **23**:126
"Cop-Out Session" (Knight) **14**:46, 52
"Copper Red and the Seven Dachsies" (Cassian) **17**:3
Copper Sun (Cullen) **20**:56-59, 61-62, 64-65, 75, 77, 85-86
"cops" (Baraka) **4**:12
"A Coquette Conquered" (Dunbar) **5**:122
"Coquetterie posthume" (Gautier) **18**:125, 157-60, 163
"Les coquillages" (Verlaine) **32**:349, 391
"Le cor" (Vigny) **26**:369, 402-403, 410
"Cor Mio" (Rossetti) **7**:278
"Cora of Pigeon Run" (Wagoner) **33**:367
"Corail" (Char) **56**:171
"Coral" (Char)
See "Corail"
El corazón amarillo (Neruda) **4**:287, 289
El corazón con que vivo (Guillén) **23**:133
"El corazón de Pedro de Valdivia" (Neruda) **4**:293
"Corazón Lapida" (Alurista) **34**:47
"El corazón magellanico" (Neruda) **4**:281
"Les Corbeaux" (Rimbaud) **57**:244, 253
"The Cord" (Stone) **53**:221, 254
"Cori descrittivi di stati d'animo di Didone" (Ungaretti) **57**:339
"Corinna, Pride of Drury-Lane" (Swift) **9**:283-84
"Corinna's Going a-Maying" (Herrick) **9**:99-101, 104-05, 116, 120, 122-23, 125, 132, 137, 142, 145
"Coriolanus and His Mother" (Schwartz) **8**:282-83, 290-91, 297-98, 301, 308-09, 312
Cork (Ní Chuilleanáin) **34**:381-82
"Corn" (Lanier) **50**:55, 61, 66, 69-71, 74, 85, 90-91, 98, 106-8
"The Corner of Night and Morning" (Lowell) **13**:64
"The Corner of the Eye" (Warren) **37**:326
"Corner seat" (MacNeice) **61**:160
"Cornet Solo" (Day Lewis) **11**:145
Cornhuskers (Sandburg) **2**:302, 304, 307, 309, 313-14, 316, 323, 338-39; **41**:239-40, 242-43, 244, 248, 250, 256, 266-67, 269-70, 274, 277, 282, 296-97, 313, 318, 325-29, 339, 351, 357
"Cornish Heroic Song for Valda Trevlyn" (MacDiarmid) **9**:180, 183
"Corno Inglese" (Montale) **13**:105
"A Corn-Song" (Dunbar) **5**:122
"Corona" (Hacker) **47**:107
La Corona (Donne) **1**:136-39, 145, 147
"A Coronal" (Williams) **7**:345, 362
"The Coronet" (Marvell) **10**:267, 271, 274, 277, 293, 313-14
"Corot" (Lawrence) **54**:228
"The Corporal" (Gunn) **26**:224
Corps perdu (Césaire) **25**:30-2, 35, 44
Corpse and Mirror (Yau) **61**:329
"The Corpse of a Cat" (Hagiwara)
See "Neko no shigai"
"Corpse Song" (Atwood) **8**:23, 25
"Correction: Eve Delved and Adam Span" (Nash) **21**:273
"Correspondances" (Baudelaire) **1**:55, 65, 69-70
"Correspondances" (Char) **56**:201
"Correspondences" (Rukeyser) **12**:226, 233
"La Corrida" (Hayden) **6**:194
"The Corridor" (Gunn) **26**:193
"El corro luminoso" (Mistral) **32**:175
"Cors de chasse" (Apollinaire) **7**:42
The Corsair (Byron) **16**:91-5, 109
The Corsair (Lermontov) **18**:299
"Corsica" (Cruz) **37**:15
"Corson's Inlet" (Ammons) **16**:21, 23, 29, 35-7, 54
Corson's Inlet (Ammons) **16**:4-5, 20, 28
"The Cortege" (Gibran) **9**:73

"Cortege" (Verlaine) **32**:349, 391
"Cortège for Rosenbloom" (Stevens) **6**:293
Cortege of Orpheus (Apollinaire)
See *Le bestiaire; ou, Cortège d'Orphée*
"Cory" (Robinson)
See "Richard Cory"
"Cosas" (Borges) **32**:89
"Cosmic Comics" (Nemerov) **24**:301
"The Cossack" (Pushkin) **10**:407
"Cossack Cradlesong" (Lermontov) **18**:268, 278, 281, 304
"The Cost of Pleasure" (Bryant) **20**:46
"Costa Magic" (Loy) **16**:313
"The Costa San Giorgio" (Loy) **16**:313, 318-20, 322, 327
"The Cottage Dweller" (Tagore)
See "Kutir-vasi"
"Cottage Street, 1953" (Wilbur) **51**:245-46, 250-51, 265, 281, 289-90
"The Cottar's Saturday Night" (Burns) **6**:50, 57, 74, 79, 96
Cotton Candy on a Rainy Day (Giovanni) **19**:114, 116-18, 123, 125, 128, 130, 134, 137, 142-43
"Cotton Song" (Toomer) **7**:319, 321
"Cottonmouth Country" (Glück) **16**:139
"Cougar Meat" (Gallagher) **9**:59, 62
"Could Man Be Drunk for Ever" (Housman) **2**:195
"Councell to a Bachelor" (Moore) **49**:109
"counsel at the highest level" (Enzensberger) **28**:143
"Count Gismond" (Browning) **61**:88
Count Nulin (Pushkin)
See *Graf Nulin*
"Counter Serenade" (Viereck) **27**:263
"Counter-Attack" (Sassoon) **12**:256-57, 264-65, 277-78
Counter-Attack and Other Poems (Sassoon) **12**:242, 250, 253, 257-58, 260, 263-64, 266-69, 272, 276-77
"A Counterpoint" (Aiken) **26**:4
"Counter-Walk, Reversals" (Viereck) **27**:277
The Countess Cathleen (Yeats) **20**:298, 302-3, 353; **51**:72, 75
The Countess from Minneapolis (Guest) **55**:217, 219-20
The Countess of Pembroke's Arcadia (Sidney) **32**:218-20, 225-31, 233-34, 236-37, 239-45, 248-49, 252-53, 255-56, 258-61, 264-69, 272-73, 277, 290, 320, 323-24
The Countesse of Mountgomeries Urania (Wroth) **38**:242-47, 249-51, 254-56, 258-59, 262-68, 272, 274-76, 278-82, 285-93, 296, 298, 304, 307, 309, 311, 314, 316-25, 328-29, 331, 333-34
Counting Backward (Cassian) **17**:6
"The Counting Houses" (Merwin) **45**:37
"Counting Small-Boned Bodies" (Bly) **39**:21, 50, 91, 94
"Counting the Beats" (Graves) **6**:136-37, 155
"Country and Western" (Hacker) **47**:87-88, 113
"Country & Western II" (Hacker) **47**:88
The Country between Us (Forché) **10**:136-38, 140, 143-46, 148, 150-53, 155, 157-59, 161, 165-66, 169
"A Country Burial" (Dickinson) **1**:79
"A Country Girl" (McKay) **2**:224
"A Country House" (Sarton) **39**:345
"A Country Life" (Jarrell) **41**:137, 139, 153-54, 168, 175
"Country Life" (Philips) **40**:269
"A Country Life: To His Brother, Master Thomas Herrick" (Herrick) **9**:86, 110-13, 115
"The Country Life, to the Honoured Master Endimion Porter, Groome of the Bed-Chamber to His Majesty" (Herrick) **9**:101, 139, 144
"Country Lover" (Angelou) **32**:15
The Country of a Thousand Years of Peace and Other Poems (Merrill) **28**:220, 225, 228-29, 231, 234, 238-42, 244, 246-47, 259
"Country of Marriage" (Berry) **28**:11-13, 44
The Country of Marriage (Berry) **28**:7, 13
"Country Places" (Hope) **56**:277
"Country School" (Curnow) **48**:29
Country Sentiment (Graves) **6**:127, 129, 132
"The Country Squire and the Mandrake" (Smart) **13**:348
"Country Stars" (Meredith) **28**:180, 192
"Country Town" (Wright) **14**:350
"The Country Was" (Jarrell) **41**:184
"The Country Whore" (Pavese)
See "La puttana contadina"
"The Countryman's Return" (Thomas) **52**:263
"The Countryside" (Pushkin)
See "Derevnya"
"The County Ball" (Patmore) **59**:230-31, 233, 260
"County Ward" (Soto) **28**:370, 376-77
"Le Coup de couteau du soleil dans le dos des villes surprises" (Césaire) **25**:30
Un coup de dés jamais n'abolira le hasard (Mallarmé) **4**:192, 199, 202-03, 208-09, 217-18
"Coup d'evential..." (Apollinaire) **7**:34-5
"The Couple" (Cassian) **17**:11
"Courage" (Akhmatova)
See "Muzhestvo"
"The Courage of Shutting Up" (Plath) **37**:255
"La courbe de tes yeux" (Éluard) **38**:71, 101, 104-7
"The Couriers" (Plath) **37**:258
"Courmayeur" (Carducci) **46**:49
Cours naturel (Éluard) **38**:68
"The Course of True Love" (Patmore) **59**:230, 233
Court Poems (Montagu) **16**:338
"A Courtesy" (Wylie) **23**:322
"Courtship" (Dove) **6**:112
The Courtship of Miles Standish (Longfellow) **30**:16, 21, 24-5, 35, 39, 44, 59, 61, 65, 74, 79-82, 84-8, 99
"A Courtyard Thaw" (Wilbur) **51**:187, 208, 220
"Courtyards in Delft" (Mahon) **60**:146, 148, 156, 161, 175-76, 190-92, 200-202, 211, 213, 219-20
Courtyards in Delft (Mahon) **60**:148, 161
"Cousin Kate" (Rossetti) **7**:270, 276, 280, 289, 291
"Cousin Sidney" (Abse) **41**:22
"Couteaux midi" (Césaire) **25**:37
"The Cove" (Clampitt) **19**:83
"The Covenant" (Muir) **49**:245-46, 249-50, 292
"Covered Bridge" (Warren) **37**:376
"Coversation" (Tagore)
See "Sambhashan"
"The Cow" (Nash) **21**:278
"The Cow in Apple-Time" (Frost) **1**:195, 197
The Cow Jumped over the Moon (Birney) **52**:97
"Cowley Rider" (Masters) **1**:334
"Cowper's Grave" (Browning) **6**:6, 21
"Cows: A Vision" (Gallagher) **9**:36
"The Cows at Night" (Carruth) **10**:85
"The Coy Mistress" (Marvell)
See "To His Coy Mistress"
"Crab" (Brathwaite) **56**:61
"Crab-Angel" (Loy) **16**:307
"The Crack" (Levertov) **11**:159
"The Cracked Bell" (Baudelaire)
See "La cloche fêlée"
"cracked walls" (Alurista)
See "grietas paredes"
"The Crack-up of American Optimism" (Viereck) **27**:284
"A Cradle Song" (Blake) **12**:7, 10, 33
"A Cradle Song" (Yeats) **20**:337
"Cradle Song for Eleanor" (MacNeice) **61**:139, 160
"Cradle Song for Miriam" (MacNeice) **61**:128
Craft (Tsvetaeva)
See *Remeslo*
"A Craftsman of Bowls" (Cavafy)
See "A Craftsman of Wine Bowls"
"A Craftsman of Wine Bowls" (Cavafy) **36**:34, 106
Craftsmanship (Tsvetaeva)
See *Remeslo*
"Crag Jack's Apostasy" (Hughes) **7**:147
"Craigvara House" (Mahon) **60**:193
"Cramped in That Funnelled Hole" (Owen) **19**:336
"Crash at Leithfield" (Curnow) **48**:29
"Crass Times" (Viereck) **27**:278, 281
"Crass Times Redeemed by Dignity of Souls" (Viereck) **27**:258-60, 273
"La cravate et la montre" (Apollinaire) **7**:32, 34-5
"Craving for Spring" (Lawrence) **54**:214
"Crazy Carlson's Meadow" (Bly) **39**:67, 100
"Crazy Dream" (Silverstein) **49**:342
"Crazy Horse names his daughter" (Clifton) **17**:25
"Crazy Jane" (Day Lewis) **11**:151
"Crazy Jane and Jack the Journeyman" (Yeats) **20**:328
"Crazy Jane Talks with the Bishop" (Yeats) **20**:327-28
"A Crazy Spiritual" (Ginsberg) **4**:79
"Crazy Weather" (Ashbery) **26**:153
"Creating the World" (Milosz) **8**:214
"creation" (Clifton) **17**:37
"The Creation" (Gibran) **9**:73
"The Creation" (Johnson) **24**:128-29, 133, 139, 143-44, 149, 152-53, 156, 164, 166-69
Creation (Noyes) **27**:138
"The Creation, according to Coyote" (Ortiz) **17**:231
"Creation Myth" (Berry) **28**:9
"Creation of Anguish" (Nemerov) **24**:261, 285
"Creation-Annihilation" (Wright) **14**:375
The Creative Writer (Birney) **52**:19, 47, 76, 78, 80, 82
"creative writing class" (Bukowski) **18**:19
"Creatures" (Kumin) **15**:182
"Creatures in the Dawn" (Aleixandre)
See "Criaturas de la Aurora"
"Crecen altas las flores" (Guillén) **23**:126
"Credat Judaeus" (Kipling) **3**:194
"Credences of Summer" (Ashbery) **26**:153
"Credences of Summer" (Stevens) **6**:306, 335, 338
"The Creditor" (MacNeice) **61**:132
"Credo" (Jeffers) **17**:117,129
"Credo" (Kumin) **15**:213, 215-16, 224
"Credo" (Mistral) **32**:174
"Credo" (Robinson) **1**:485-86
"Credo" (Stryk) **27**:198
"Credo Adoration" (Wagoner) **33**:372
"Credo in Intellectum Videntem" (Tate) **50**:256
"Credo in unam" (Rimbaud) **57**:255
"Creed" (Mistral)
See "Credo"
"Creeley" (Birney) **52**:29
"Cremation" (Thumboo) **30**:321-22
"The Cremona Violin" (Lowell) **13**:60, 77, 96
"Crêpe de Chine" (Doty) **53**:72
"Crepuscolo di sabbiatori" (Pavese) **13**:226
Crepúsculario (Neruda) **4**:276, 278
"Crépuscule" (Apollinaire) **7**:40
"Crépuscule" (Hugo) **17**:67, 81-82
"Le crépuscule du soir" (Baudelaire) **1**:58-9
"The Crescent Moon" (Yakamochi) **48**:105
"Crescent Moon like a Canoe" (Piercy) **29**:323
"Crest and Gulf" (Patmore) **59**:262
"The Crevasse" (Tsvetaeva)
See "Rasshchelina"
"Crevasses" (Césaire) **25**:33
"Crèvecoeur" (Niedecker) **42**:95, 100, 104, 109
"The Crew of the Chelyuskin" (Tsvetaeva)
See "Chelyuskintsy"
"Le cri de l'âme" (Lamartine) **16**:266

"Criaturas de la Aurora" (Aleixandre) **15**:6, 15, 38
"Crime" (Warren) **37**:284, 288-89, 323, 332-33
"Crime of Love" (Verlaine)
See *Crimen Amoris*
"Crimean Sonnets" (Mickiewicz) **38**:191
Crimean Sonnets (Mickiewicz)
See *Sonety Krymskie*
Crimen Amoris (Verlaine) **32**:369, 370-71, 396
The Criminal (Lermontov) **18**:299
"The Crimson Cyclamen" (Williams) **7**:350, 354
"Criollo You Lived Prohibition" (Alurista) **34**:28
"Cripple" (Sandburg) **41**:243
"Cripples and Other Stories" (Sexton) **2**:363, 365
"The Crisis" (Wagoner) **33**:369
"Crispus Attucks McKoy" (Brown) **55**:82-83, 120, 122
"Le Cristal automatique" (Césaire) **25**:20
"The Critic" (O'Hara) **45**:224
"The Critic and the Writer of Fables" (Finch) **21**:163
A Critical Fable (Lowell) **13**:65, 74-6
"Critical Observations" (MacLeish) **47**:145, 164
"Critics and Connoisseurs" (Moore) **4**:232, 257, 270; **49**:98, 112-13, 116, 127
"Critics on the Lawn" (MacLeish) **47**:197
"Critique de la poésie" (Éluard) **38**:68
"De Critters' Dance" (Dunbar) **5**:145
"La Crocifissione" (Pasolini) **17**:265
"Croesus" (Char) **56**:129
"Croesus in Autumn" (Warren) **37**:319, 331, 333
"Croft" (Smith) **12**:333
"A la croix" (Lamartine) **16**:284
Cronica tripertita (Gower) **59**:25-26, 32-33, 113
"The Crooked Stick" (Wylie) **23**:301
"Croon" (Hughes) **53**:161
"Croquis parisien" (Verlaine) **32**:375-76, 387-88
"Cross" (Hughes) **1**:235, 243, 263-64; **53**:85, 126, 143
"The Cross" (Tate) **50**:231, 243, 255, 257, 306
"The Cross of Snow" (Longfellow) **30**:21, 27, 51
"The Cross Spider" (Swenson) **14**:273
"The Crosse" (Donne) **1**:136
"The Crosse" (Herbert) **4**:111
"The Crossed Apple" (Bogan) **12**:101, 110-11
"Crossing" (Brown) **55**:176
"Crossing" (MacLeish) **47**:164, 214
"Crossing Aguadilla" (Tomlinson) **17**:361
"Crossing Brooklyn Ferry" (Sexton) **2**:361
"Crossing Brooklyn Ferry" (Tomlinson) **17**:337
"Crossing Brooklyn Ferry" (Whitman) **3**:377, 379, 391-93, 399-400, 410, 415
"The Crossing of the Removed" (Merwin) **45**:46
"Crossing Over" (Meredith) **28**:200
"Crossing the Atlantic" (Sexton) **2**:363
"Crossing the Bar" (Tennyson) **6**:359
"Crossing the Frontier" (Hope) **56**:278, 285-86
"Crossing the River" (Brathwaite) **56**:7, 85
"Crossing the Tuscan Maremma" (Carducci)
See "Traversando la Maremma Toscana"
Crossing the Water: Transitional Poems (Plath) **1**:391, 394, 396, 404; **37**:190-91
"Crossing the Yellow River to Ch'ing-ho" (Wang Wei) **18**:362, 366-68, 373
"Crossings" (Hogan) **35**:259, 277
"Crossroads" (Gunn) **26**:214
"The Cross-Roads" (Lowell) **13**:60, 76-7
"Crotchets" (Nemerov) **24**:290
"Crow" (Cervantes) **35**:105
"Crow Alights" (Hughes) **7**:130
"Crow and Mama" (Hughes) **7**:132
"Crow and the Birds" (Hughes) **7**:159
The Crow and the Heart (Carruth) **10**:70, 78, 89
"Crow and the Sea" (Hughes) **7**:144
"Crow Blacker Than Ever" (Hughes) **7**:138
"Crow Communes" (Hughes) **7**:143
Crow: From the Life and Songs of the Crow (Hughes) **7**:129-30, 133, 137-39, 141-43, 145, 152-53, 155-61, 163, 168-71
"Crow Frowns" (Hughes) **7**:159
"Crow Goes Hunting" (Hughes) **7**:142, 160-61
"Crow Hill" (Hughes) **7**:131, 150
"Crow Hill" (O'Hara) **45**:142
"Crow Jane in High Society" (Baraka) **4**:16
"Crow on a Withered Branch" (Matsuo Bashō) **3**:32
"Crow on the Beach" (Hughes) **7**:138, 144
"Crow Sickened" (Hughes) **7**:138
"Crow Song" (Atwood) **8**:25
"The Crowded Countries of the Bomb" (Oppen) **35**:293, 298
"The Crowded Street" (Bryant) **20**:5, 36
"A Crowded Trolley Car" (Wylie) **23**:309, 328, 332
"Crowdieknowe" (MacDiarmid) **9**:156
"Crowds" (Baudelaire)
See "Les foules"
"Crowing-Hen Blues" (Hughes) **1**:256
"The Crown of Bays" (Smith) **12**:319
"The Crown of Gold" (Smith) **12**:295, 315
"Crown of Thorns" (Celan)
See "Dornenkranz"
"Crowned Out" (Celan) **10**:113
Crowned with Dreams (Rilke) **2**:280
"Crowns and Garlands" (Hughes) **1**:252; **53**:115
"Crows" (Rimbaud)
See "Les Corbeaux"
"Crow's Account of St. George" (Hughes) **7**:161, 171
"Crow's Account of the Battle" (Hughes) **7**:133, 144, 152
"Crow's Battle Fury" (Hughes) **7**:143
"Crow's Elephant Totem Song" (Hughes) **7**:138, 144
"Crow's Last Stand" (Hughes) **7**:123, 144
"Crow's Nerve Fails" (Hughes) **7**:144
"Crow's Nests" (Wilbur) **51**:335
"Crows on the North Slope" (Merwin) **45**:20
"Crow's Playmates" (Hughes) **7**:144
"Crow's Theology" (Hughes) **7**:159, 161
"Crow's Undersong" (Hughes) **7**:167
"Crow's Vanity" (Hughes) **7**:144
"Crucibles of Love" (Graves) **6**:172
"Le crucifix" (Lamartine) **16**:278
Crucifix in a Deathhand: New Poems, 1963-1965 (Bukowski) **18**:21
"The Crucifix in the Filing Cabinet" (Shapiro) **25**:286, 290, 300
"The Crucifixion" (Akhmatova)
See "Raspiatie"
"Crucifixión" (García Lorca) **3**:140
"Crucifixion" (García Lorca)
See "Crucifixión"
"The Crucifixion" (Johnson) **24**:128, 144, 156, 165, 169
"Crucifixion on Thursday" (Wright) **36**:335, 337
"The Cruel Falcon" (Jeffers) **17**:117, 120
"The Cruell Maid" (Herrick) **9**:101
"Cruelty and Love" (Lawrence) **54**:236-37
"The Cruise" (Merrill) **28**:239, 241
"Cruising 99" (Hongo) **23**:196-98
"Crumbs or the Loaf" (Jeffers) **17**:130
"Crusade" (Warren) **37**:318
"Crusades of Silence" (Césaire) **25**:18
Crusoé (Perse) **23**:231
"Crusoe in England" (Bishop) **3**:48, 63-4, 66-7, 70; **34**:54, 74, 80, 82, 97, 104, 121, 146
"Crusoe's Island" (Walcott) **46**:231, 274, 280, 283-84
"Crusoe's Journal" (Walcott) **46**:231, 238, 274, 280, 283-84
"La cruz" (Parra) **39**:288
"The Cry" (Levertov) **11**:198
"The Cry" (Masters) **1**:326
"Cry Ararat!" (Page) **12**:168, 190, 198
Cry Ararat! (Page) **12**:167, 179, 184, 190, 197
"Cry Faugh" (Graves) **6**:135
"The Cry of Midnight" (Patmore) **59**:277
"The Cry of the Children" (Browning) **6**:6, 17, 21, 27, 30, 42
"The Cry of the Human" (Browning) **6**:7, 21
"Cry to Rome: From the Chrysler Building Tower" (García Lorca) **3**:141
"Crying" (Kinnell) **26**:260
"The Crystal" (Aiken) **26**:29-30, 45
"The Crystal" (Lanier) **50**:51
"The Crystal Cabinet" (Blake) **12**:36
"Crystal Gazer" (Plath) **37**:208
"The Crystal Gazer" (Teasdale) **31**:323, 371-72, 379, 389
"Crystals Like Blood" (MacDiarmid) **9**:187
Cuaderno San Martín (Borges) **22**:71, 73, 93-4; **32**:38, 84, 95, 109
"Cuadros y angulos" (Storni) **33**:247, 250, 275;
"a cualquier hora" (Alurista) **34**:33
"Cualquier tiempo pasado fue peor" (Guillén) **23**:126
"Cuando la cucaracha camine" (Alurista) **34**:24
"Las cuatro calles" (Guillén) **35**:157, 188
"Los cuatro ciclos" (Borges) **32**:65
"La Cucaracha" (Alurista) **34**:10, 46
"Cucarachas in paradise" (Birney) **52**:37
"Cuchualain" (Day Lewis) **11**:151
"Cuckoo" (Wagoner) **33**:356
"Cuckoo Song" (H. D.) **5**:267
"Cudjoe Fresh from de Lecture" (McKay) **2**:224, 226
La cueca larga (Parra) **39**:260, 270, 272, 277, 292, 300, 303
"La cuenta-mundo" (Mistral) **32**:161, 166
"Cuento de dos jardines" (Paz) **1**:361, 363; **48**:191, 207-8, 210, 264
"The Cuirassiers of the Frontier" (Graves) **6**:133
"The Culprit" (Housman) **2**:162, 164, 169, 179, 186
"The Cultivation of Philosophy" (Herbert)
See "Uprawa filozofii"
"Cultural Directives" (Szirtes) **51**:163
"Cultural Exchange" (Hughes) **1**:250, 252
"Cultural Exchange" (Kenyon) **57**:45
"Cultural Exchanges" (Hacker) **47**:113
"Culture and Anarchy" (Rich) **5**:386
"The Culture-Hug Blues" (Viereck) **27**:279
"cum cum cum cumly witchcraft i know you care" (Bissett) **14**:34
"Cum Ratione Insanire" (Cowper) **40**:102-3
"La cumbre" (Guillén) **35**:188
Cuna, rosas, balcón (Guillén) **35**:159
"The Cup" (Wright) **14**:347
Cup of Blizzards (Bely)
See *Kubok metelej: Chetviortiia simfoniia*
"The Cup of Paint" (Lindsay) **23**:286
The Cup of Snowstorms (Bely)
See *Kubok metelej: Chetviortiia simfoniia*
"Cupid and Psyche" (Elytis) **21**:135
"Cupid and Psyche" (Morris) **55**:306
"Cur secessisti?" (Char) **56**:151
"Curacao" (Birney) **52**:22
"Curatia Dionisia" (Herbert) **50**:9
"The Cure" (Graves) **6**:155
"A Cure at Porlock" (Clampitt) **19**:87
"A Cure of Souls" (Levertov) **11**:171
"Curettage" (Benn) **35**:4, 8
"A Curfew" (Clampitt) **19**:91
"Curfew" (Yamada) **44**:341
"A Curious Man's Dream" (Baudelaire)
See "Le rêve d'un curieux"
"Curl Up and Diet" (Nash) **21**:265
"The Current" (Berry) **28**:14-15
"The Current" (Merwin) **45**:34, 48, 86, 100
"Curriculum Vitae" (Mueller) **33**:195
"The Curse" (Millay) **6**:211
"A Curse against Elegies" (Sexton) **2**:351
"A Curse for a Nation" (Browning) **6**:27
"The Curse of Cromwell" (Yeats) **20**:326
"The Curse of the Wandering Foot" (Riley) **48**:303
"Curtain" (Dunbar) **5**:119

"The Curtain" (Wright) **14**:355
"Curtains" (Cisneros) **52**:157, 160
"Curtains" (Stone) **53**:230, 238, 251
"The Curve" (Levertov) **11**:176
"The curve of your eyes" (Éluard)
See "La courbe de tes yeux"
"Cushenden" (MacNeice) **61**:108
"Custer Speaks" (Alexie) **53**:4
"Custodian" (Kumin) **15**:223
"The Customs-Officer's House" (Montale)
See "La casa dei doganieri"
"Cut" (Plath) **1**:385, 392; **37**:232, 257
"A Cutlet" (Stein) **18**:349
"Cutting Down a Tree" (Wagoner) **33**:352
"The Cutting Edge" (Levine) **22**:215
"Cutting the Grapes Free" (Piercy) **29**:312
"Cuttings" (Roethke) **15**:291, 296-98, 312
"Cuttings (Later)" (Roethke) **15**:260, 297-98, 302, 312, 314
Cuttlefish Bones (Montale)
See *Ossi di seppia*
"Cutty Sark" (Crane) **3**:84, 90, 106
"Cutworm" (Wagoner) **33**:356
"Cybernetics" (Nemerov) **24**:261, 282-83, 301
"The Cycads" (Wright) **14**:346
"The Cyclads" (Aiken) **26**:36
"The Cyclamen" (Amichai) **38**:15
"The Cycle" (Jeffers) **17**:141
"The Cycle" (Roethke) **15**:265
"The Cyclical Night" (Borges)
See "La noche cíclica"
"Cyclops" (Shelley) **14**:227
"Le cygne" (Baudelaire) **1**:45, 66, 71
"Cyngor y Biogen" (Dafydd ap Gwilym) **56**:210
"Cynthia" (Shvarts) **50**:141, 160
Cynthia (Raleigh)
See *The Ocean to Cynthia*
"Cyparissus" (Duncan) **2**:103
"Cypress Avenue" (Davie) **29**:110
"Cypresses" (Francis) **34**:265
"Cyrano en España" (Darío) **15**:80
"Cyrano in Spain" (Darío)
See "Cyrano en España"
"Cyrchu Lleian" (Dafydd ap Gwilym) **56**:210-11
"Cystudd Cariad" (Dafydd ap Gwilym) **56**:247
"Cythere" (Verlaine) **32**:350
"Czaty" (Mickiewicz) **38**:212
"Czatyr Dagh" (Mickiewicz)
See "Czatyrdah"
"Czatyrdah" (Mickiewicz) **38**:221-23
Czeslaw Milosz: The Collected Poems, 1931-1987 (Milosz) **8**:190-91, 197-98, 202, 206-07, 213-15
"D. R." (Zukofsky) **11**:351, 396
"D. Scarlatti" (Corso) **33**:41
"Da, ia lezhu v zemle . . ." (Mandelstam) **14**:151
"Da terra" (Castro) **41**:88
"Da una torre" (Montale) **13**:113
"Daddy" (Plath) **1**:382-83, 386-87, 392-93, 395-97, 400-02, 406-07, 414; **37**:196-98, 200, 212, 216, 219-22, 227-29, 232-35, 243-44, 246-47, 255-56, 260, 268
"Daedalus" (Sikelianos) **29**:365-66, 368, 370-71
"The Daemon" (Bogan) **12**:100, 110
"The Daemon of the World" (Shelley) **14**:185
The Daffodil Murderer (Sassoon) **12**:252, 270, 274-77
"Daffodildo" (Swenson) **14**:277, 287
"Daffy Duck in Hollywood" (Ashbery) **26**:153
Dafydd ap Gwilym: Fifty Poems (Dafydd)
See *Fifty Poems*
"The dagger" (Borges)
See "El puñal"
"Dagrau Serch" (Dafydd ap Gwilym) **56**:245-46
"Daguerreotype Taken in Old Age" (Atwood) **8**:39
"Un dahlia" (Verlaine) **2**:431
"The Dahlia Gardens" (Clampitt) **19**:82, 90-1
"Dahomey" (Lorde) **12**:160
"The Daily Globe" (Nemerov) **24**:278
The Daily Holidays (Cassian) **17**:6
"Les daimons" (Ronsard) **11**:225, 279, 281-82
"The Dainty Monsters" (Ondaatje) **28**:292-93
The Dainty Monsters (Ondaatje) **28**:291-92, 294, 298-99, 318, 327, 331-32, 335
"Daisies" (Carman) **34**:207
"Daisies Are Broken" (Williams) **7**:406
"The Daisy" (Tennyson) **6**:357, 360
"Daisy Fraser" (Masters) **1**:334; **36**:182, 227
"Daisy-Cutter" (McGuckian) **27**:76, 103
"Daisy's Song" (Keats) **1**:311
"Dakar" (Borges) **32**:38
"Dakar Doldrums" (Ginsberg) **4**:72
"The Dale" (Lamartine)
See "Le vallon"
"Dalhousie Farm" (Meredith) **28**:181
"Dalla Sua Pace" (Hope) **56**:287
"Dalle rive del Balaton" (Quasimodo) **47**:289
"The Dalliance of the Eagles" (Whitman) **3**:397
"The Dam" (Rukeyser) **12**:210
Dam 'ah wabitisāmah (Gibran) **9**:73, 75, 77-8, 81
"Damastes (Also Known as Procrustes) Speaks" (Herbert)
See "Damastes z przydomkiem Prokustes mówi"
"Damastes z przydomkiem Prokustes mówi" (Herbert) **50**:16, 44
"Dämmerung" (Celan) **10**:124-25
"Dämmerung" (Stramm) **50**:174-75, 194, 199, 209
"The Damnation of Byron" (Hope) **56**:266, 268, 289, 301, 303
"Damnation of Vancouver" (Birney) **52**:21-22
The Damnation of Vancouver (Birney) **52**:43
Damned Album (Rimbaud)
See *Album zutique*
"Damned Women" (Baudelaire)
See "Femmes damnées"
"Damon Being Asked a Reason for Loveing" (Behn) **13**:18
"Damon the Mower" (Marvell) **10**:266, 293, 295-97, 315
"The Dampe" (Donne) **1**:130
"Dan y Bargod" (Dafydd ap Gwilym) **56**:225, 227-31, 233
"The Dance" (Baraka) **4**:16
"Dance" (Cassian) **17**:13
"The Dance" (Crane) **3**:84, 86, 88, 90
"The Dance" (Curnow) **48**:29
"The Dance" (Larkin) **21**:259
"The Dance" (Patmore) **59**:233
"Dance" (Pavese)
See "Balletto"
"The Dance" (Roethke) **15**:266-67, 269, 273, 279
"The Dance at the Phoenix" (Hardy) **8**:99
"Dance: Nicaragua" (Jordan) **38**:127
"The Dance of Death" (Blok)
See "Danse macabre"
"Dance of Death" (García Lorca)
See "Danza de la muerte"
The Dance of Death (Auden) **1**:8
"Dance of the Girls' Chemises" (Seifert) **47**:324
"Dance of the Hanged" (Rimbaud)
See "Bal des pendus"
"Dance of the Macabre Mice" (Stevens) **6**:296
"Dance the Orange" (Hayden) **6**:196
"The Dancer" (H. D.) **5**:305
"The Dancers of the Field" (Carman) **34**:209
"Dances of Death" (Blok)
See "Danse macabre"
"Dancin' in the Rain" (Silverstein) **49**:342
The Dancing Bears (Merwin) **45**:3, 5-6, 8-11, 21, 24, 29, 90-2
Dancing David (Shvarts)
See *Tantsuiushchii David*
"Dancing on the Grave of a Son of a Bitch" (Wakoski) **15**:346
Dancing on the Grave of a Son of a Bitch (Wakoski) **15**:336, 348, 365
"Dancing Pants" (Silverstein) **49**:347
"Danger" (Corso) **33**:26
"The Danger of Writing Defiant Verse" (Parker) **28**:350, 363
"A Dangerous Land" (Amichai) **38**:32-33
"Dangerous Thoughts" (Cavafy) **36**:79
"Dangers" (Cavafy) **36**:50
Dangers (McHugh) **61**:190, 196, 205
Dangling in the Tournefortia (Bukowski) **18**:15
"Daniel Bartoli" (Browning) **2**:84
"Daniel Grose" (Ní Chuilleanáin) **34**:369, 371
"Daniel Jazz" (Lindsay) **23**:264, 270, 286
"Die Dänin" (Benn) **35**:72
"A Danish Refuge" (Mahon) **60**:177
"Danny Deever" (Kipling) **3**:170-71, 179, 188-89, 191
"Dans la brume" (Éluard) **38**:71
"Dans la danse" (Éluard) **38**:70
"Dans la grotte" (Verlaine) **32**:349, 351, 391, 393
"Dans la marche" (Char) **56**:202
Dans la pluie giboyeuse (Char) **56**:138
"Dans le cylindre des tribulations" (Éluard) **38**:70
Dans le leurre du seuil (Bonnefoy) **58**:110, 113-14, 123, 137-40, 145, 150, 156-58, 161-62, 165-66, 168-70
"Dans le restaurant" (Eliot) **5**:185
"Dansa di Narcís" (Pasolini) **17**:281
"Danse Africaine" (Hughes) **53**:83, 143
"Danse macabre" (Blok) **21**:6, 14, 20
"Danse russe" (Williams) **7**:353, 367, 408
"Dante" (Carducci) **46**:52, 76
"Dante at Verona" (Rossetti) **44**:167, 202
Dante at Verona and Other Poems (Rossetti) **44**:184-86, 200
"Dante Études, Book Two" (Duncan) **2**:114-16, 127
Dante's Purgatory (Dante)
See *La divina commedia*
"Danza de la muerte" (García Lorca) **3**:121
"La danza del espiritu" (Cardenal) **22**:131
"Danza irregular" (Storni) **33**:283;
"danza leonina" (Alurista) **34**:46
"Danzón porteño" (Storni) **33**:262, 296;
"Daphnaida" (Spenser) **8**:365, 367
"Daphne" (Carman) **34**:208-09
"Daphne" (Meredith) **60**:244
"Daphne Heard with Horror the Addresses of the God" (Boland) **58**:14, 33-35, 58, 88
"Daphne with Her Thighs in Bark" (Boland) **58**:14, 19, 45
"Daphnis and Chloe" (Marvell) **10**:265, 271, 291-92, 301
Dare e avere (Quasimodo) **47**:289
"Dareios" (Cavafy)
See "Darius"
"Darest Thou Now O Soul" (Whitman) **3**:378
"Darien" (Graves) **6**:137, 144, 168
"Darius" (Cavafy) **36**:35, 43-49, 91, 93
"Darius" (Gower) **59**:58
"The Dark" (Stone) **53**:240-41, 255, 259
"The Dark and the Fair" (Kunitz) **19**:162, 169
"Dark August" (Walcott) **46**:236
"Dark Blood" (Walker) **20**:273, 282
"A Dark Christmas Song" (Shvarts) **50**:134
"The Dark Cup" (Teasdale) **31**:358, 360
"Dark Eye in September" (Celan) **10**:112
"The Dark Forest" (Thomas) **53**:297
"Dark Gift" (Wright) **14**:338, 353, 356
"Dark Girl's Rhyme" (Parker) **28**:356
"The Dark Hills" (Robinson) **1**:468
"Dark Ireland" (Kavanagh) **33**:100
"Dark Night of the Soul" (Warren) **37**:348, 350
"Dark of the Moon" (Brown) **55**:73, 159
Dark of the Moon (Teasdale) **31**:327, 330, 333, 335, 338, 341, 347, 349, 370-72, 379-80, 389
The Dark One (Tagore)
See *Shyamali*
"The Dark Ones" (Wright) **14**:373
"Dark Prophecy: I Sing of Shine" (Knight) **14**:39
"Dark Satanic Mills" (Lawrence) **54**:249

"Dark Song" (Ammons) **16**:4
"Dark Song" (Sitwell) **3**:291
Dark Summer (Bogan) **12**:87, 89, 105-06, 120-23
"Dark Waters of the Beginning" (Okigbo) **7**:231
"Dark Wild Honey" (Swenson) **14**:276
Dark World (Carruth) **10**:71, 91
"Dark Youth of the U.S.A." (Hughes) **53**:114
"Darkling Summer, Ominous Dusk, Rumorous Rain" (Schwartz) **8**:319
"The Darkling Thrush" (Hardy) **8**:98, 105-06, 121, 131
"Darkness" (Aleixandre) **15**:5
"Darkness" (Byron) **16**:86, 89
"Darkness Chex George Whitman" (Ferlinghetti) **1**:183
"Darkness of Death" (Pasternak) **6**:253
"Darling! Because My Blood Can Sing" (Cummings) **5**:108
"Darling Daughters" (Smith) **12**:326
"Darling, It's Frightening! When a Poet Loves ..." (Pasternak) **6**:251
"Darling Room" (Tennyson) **6**:353
"Darwin" (Niedecker) **42**:95, 100, 104, 109
"Darwin in 1881" (Schnackenberg) **45**:329-30, 336, 338
"Dary Tereka" (Lermontov) **18**:268, 281, 290, 295
"Dat Dirty Rum" (McKay) **2**:222
"Dat ol' Mare o' Mine" (Dunbar) **5**:134
"Date a volar" (Storni) **33**:251;
"Date Lilia" (Hugo) **17**:94
"Dates" (Ondaatje) **28**:327, 331
"Dates: Penkhull New Road" (Tomlinson) **17**:347, 352
"Dative Haruspices" (Rexroth) **20**:215
"Daughter" (Dickey) **40**:256
"A Daughter I" (Levertov) **11**:209
"A Daughter II" (Levertov) **11**:209
"Daughter Moon" (Wakoski) **15**:366
"The daughter of Menkera" (Cavafy) **36**:53
"The Daughter of the Forest" (Gibran)
See "Amām 'arsh al-jamāl"
Daughters, I Love You (Hogan) **35**:247, 252
"Daughters of Colony" (Boland) **58**:40, 62
Daughters of Dawn (Carman) **34**:205, 212
Daughters of Fire (Nerval)
See *Les filles du feu*
"Daughters with Curls" (Stevens) **6**:292
"Davanti ad una Cattedrale" (Carducci) **46**:23, 60
"Davanti al simulacro d'Illaria del Carretto" (Quasimodo) **47**:280
"Davanti il castel vecchio di Verona" (Carducci) **46**:52
"Davanti San Guido" (Carducci) **46**:50, 57-58, 65, 79-80
"David" (Birney) **52**:3-5, 7-8, 11, 21, 25, 27, 31, 34-35, 44-47, 58, 62, 65-66, 79, 102-3
"David" (Pasolini) **17**:252, 281
"David and Bathsheba in the Public Garden" (Lowell) **3**:205-06, 215
David and Other Poems (Birney) **52**:3-4, 6, 11, 26, 43, 45, 58
"David's Lamentation for Saul and Jonathan" (Bradstreet) **10**:6
"David's Night at Veliès" (Merrill) **28**:220
"Davis Matlock" (Masters) **36**:184
"Davy Jones' Door-Bell" (Lindsay) **23**:264
"Dawlish Fair" (Keats) **1**:311
"Dawn" (Borges)
See "Amanecer"
"Dawn" (Brathwaite) **56**:100
"Dawn" (Brooke) **24**:53, 64, 82
"Dawn" (Dunbar) **5**:125, 128
"Dawn" (García Lorca)
See "La aurora"
"Dawn" (Herbert)
See "Swit"
"Dawn" (Paz) **48**:180, 274
"Dawn" (Rimbaud)
See "Aube"
"Dawn" (Teasdale) **31**:331
"Dawn" (Thumboo) **30**:301
"Dawn Adventure" (Lowell) **13**:63
"Dawn after Storm" (Zukofsky) **11**:368
"Dawn Bombardment" (Graves) **6**:144
The Dawn Breakers: Les Matinaux (Char)
See *Les Matinaux*
"Dawn Chorus" (Mahon) **60**:148
"Dawn Eyed Cosmos" (Alurista) **34**:42
"Dawn near an Old Battlefield, in a Time of Peace" (Wright) **36**:378
"The Dawn of the Tired Man" (Guillén) **35**:217, 218
"The Dawn Wind" (Kipling) **3**:183
"Dawnbreaker" (Hayden) **6**:198
"The Dawning" (Herbert) **4**:102
Dawn's Eye (Alurista) **34**:15-16, 21-22, 26-29, 31
"Dawn's Rose" (Hughes) **7**:138, 144, 159
"Day" (Ammons) **16**:12
"The Day" (Muir) **49**:245-46, 248, 290
"The Day After" (Soto) **28**:302
Day after Day (Quasimodo)
See *Giorno dopo giorno*
"Day after Halloween" (Silverstein) **49**:334
"The Day after To-Morrow" (Patmore) **59**:208
"Day and Night" (Montale)
See "Giorno e notte"
"Day and Night" (Muir) **49**:217
"The Day before the Last Day" (Muir) **49**:257
"The Day Before the St. Petersburg Flood of 1824" (Mickiewicz)
See "The Day Preceding the St. Petersburg Flood of 1824"
"The Day Before the Trial" (Swinburne) **24**:355
Day by Day (Lowell) **3**:231-32
"The Day Dream" (Coleridge) **11**:91, 106
"The Day Is a Poem" (Jeffers) **17**:141
"The Day is Done" (Dunbar) **5**:126
"The Day is Done" (Longfellow) **30**:27, 46, 52, 103, 109
"The Day Is Gone" (Keats) **1**:279
"The Day Lady Died" (O'Hara) **45**:125, 131, 137, 154, 177, 184-86, 216, 243
"TH DAY MAY CUM" (Bissett) **14**:34
"Day My Dream" (Ignatow) **34**:278, 314-15
"The Day of Battle" (Housman) **2**:160
"The Day of Judgement" (Swift) **9**:259, 265, 281, 295
"Day of Kings" (Hugo) **17**:58
"Day of Renewal" (MacNeice) **61**:110
"A Day of Sunshine" (Longfellow) **30**:109
"Day of the Daughter of Hades" (Meredith) **60**:246-47, 250, 259, 284, 330-32
"The Day of the Eclipse" (Merrill) **28**:239, 243
"Day of the Refugios" (Ríos) **57**:319, 322
"A Day on the Big Branch" (Nemerov) **24**:257, 261
"Day or Night" (Rossetti) **7**:276
"The Day Preceding the St. Petersburg Flood of 1824" (Mickiewicz) **38**:168
"Day Six O'Hare Telephone" (Merton) **10**:336
"Day That I Have Loved" (Brooke) **24**:58, 62, 76
"The Day the First Snow Fell" (Brathwaite) **56**:65
"The Day the Mountains Move" (Yosano Akiko)
See "Yama no ugoku hi"
"The Day They Eulogized Mahalia" (Lorde) **12**:156
"Day Trip to Donegal" (Mahon) **60**:182, 184
"The day was five-headed" (Mandelstam)
See "Den' stoial na piati golovakh"
"A Day With Her" (McGuckian) **27**:76, 102
"The Day You Were Born" (Song) **21**:344
"Daybreak" (Borges)
See "Amanecer"
"Daybreak" (Hagiwara) **18**:178
"Daybreak" (Hughes) **1**:255
"Daybreak" (Kinnell) **26**:260-61
"Daybreak" (Longfellow) **30**:46-7
"Daybreak" (Merwin) **45**:9, 26
"Daybreak" (Soto) **28**:377-78
"Daybreak in Alabama" (Hughes) **53**:109, 150-53
"The Day-Dream" (Rossetti) **44**:172
"A Daydream in Summer" (Clare) **23**:25
"Daylight and Moonlight" (Longfellow) **30**:33, 41
"Daylight Savings" (Parker) **28**:362
"Days" (Emerson) **18**:76, 82, 84, 88-91, 96, 102
"Days" (Larkin) **21**:235, 246
Days and Nights (Brathwaite) **56**:88-89
"Day's Ending" (Teasdale) **31**:328, 333, 371, 380
"Days of '49" (Dylan) **37**:60
"Days of 1896" (Cavafy) **36**:75-6, 78
"Days of 1903" (Cavafy) **36**:74
"Days of 1908" (Cavafy) **36**:80
"Days of 1909, '10, and '11" (Cavafy) **36**:80, 86
"Days of 1935" (Merrill) **28**:235, 256
"Days of 1941 and '44" (Merrill) **28**:270
"Days of 1944: Three Friends" (Hacker) **47**:87
"Days of 1964" (Merrill) **28**:220-21, 250-51
"Days of 1971" (Merrill) **28**:230, 235, 258
"Days of 1992" (Hacker) **47**:107
"The Day's Ration" (Emerson) **18**:88
"Day's run" (Borges)
See "Singladura"
The Days Run Away Like Wild Horses over the Hills (Bukowski) **18**:14, 19
"Daystar" (Dove) **6**:111
"The Dazzling Victory of Sarrebrück" (Rimbaud)
See "L'Eclatante Victoire de Sarrebrück"
"Dionysus in Old Age" (Viereck) **27**:295
"Las de l'amer repos" (Mallarmé) **4**:203
"Dea Roma" (Lowell) **3**:199-200
"Deacon Taylor" (Masters) **1**:323
"The Dead" (Brooke) **24**:63, 74
"The Dead" (Day Lewis) **11**:147
"The Dead" (Herbert)
See "Umarli"
"The Dead" (Montale)
See "I morti"
The Dead and the Living (Olds) **22**:309-10, 314-16, 318-19, 321-22, 324, 326, 328, 338-39
"Dead Are My People" (Gibran) **9**:73
"The Dead at Quang Tri" (Komunyakaa) **51**:37
"The Dead Beat" (Owen) **19**:347
"Dead before Death" (Rossetti) **7**:288
"Dead Boy" (Ransom) **61**:269, 297, 310, 315-16
"The Dead by the Side of the Road" (Snyder) **21**:292-93
"The Dead Fox Hunter" (Graves) **6**:166
"Dead Hand" (Merwin) **45**:8
"Dead Horse in Field" (Warren) **37**:341
"The Dead in Melanesia" (Jarrell) **41**:174
"Dead is the roote" (Raleigh) **31**:283
"The Dead King" (Kipling) **3**:182
"Dead Language" (Patmore) **59**:222
The Dead Lecturer (Baraka) **4**:5-6, 16-17, 23, 31, 37
"Dead Men's Love" (Brooke) **24**:53, 56
"Dead Musicians" (Sassoon) **12**:267
"Dead of Night" (Mahon) **60**:211
"The Dead of Ninety-Two" (Rimbaud)
See "Morts de quatre-vingt-douze"
"The Dead Pan" (Browning) **6**:7, 19
The Dead Priestess Speaks (H. D.) **5**:305
"The Dead Princess and the Seven Heroes" (Pushkin)
See "Skazka o Mertvoy Tsarevne"
"The Dead Shall Be Raised Incorruptible" (Kinnell) **26**:245, 251, 254, 267
"Dead Tree" (Mistral)
See "Arbol muerto"
"The Dead II" (Brooke) **24**:59, 88
"The Dead Wingman" (Jarrell) **41**:171

"Deaf Donald" (Silverstein) **49**:327
"Deaf Poem" (Gallagher) **9**:62
"The Dean" (Patmore) **59**:229-30
"Dean Dixon, Welcome Home" (Stryk) **27**:204
"The Dean of St. Patrick's to Thomas Sheridan" (Swift) **9**:295
"The Dean to Himself on St. Cecilia's Day" (Swift) **9**:295
The Dean's Provocation for Writing the "Lady's Dressing Room" (Montagu) **16**:345
"The Dean's Reasons" (Swift) **9**:295
"Dear Child of God" (Smith) **12**:335
"Dear Female Heart" (Smith) **12**:295
"Dear Folks" (Kavanagh) **33**:64
"Dear John Wayne" (Erdrich) **52**:173
"Dear Judas" (Jeffers) **17**:109-10, 144
Dear Judas and Other Poems (Jeffers) **17**:109, 124, 135
"Dear Landlord" (Dylan) **37**:56
"Dear Little Sirmio" (Smith) **12**:331
Dear Lovely Death (Hughes) **53**:112, 115
"Dear Mr. President" (Hughes) **53**:115
"Dear Muse" (Smith) **12**:335
"Dear Patron of My Virgin Muse" (Burns) **6**:84
"Dear Paul: Four Versions" (Niedecker) **42**:95
"Dear Possible" (Jackson) **44**:29
"Dear Robert" (Ignatow) **34**:345
"Dear Strager Extant in Memory by the Blue Juaniata" (Kinnell) **26**:250, 267
"Dear Toni..." (Lorde) **12**:157
"Dear Villon, Dear Milarepa" (Corso) **33**:34
"Death" (Corso) **33**:35, 47
"Death" (Herbert) **4**:113
"Death" (Lermontov)
See "Smert"
"Death" (O'Hara) **45**:229
"Death" (Olds) **22**:325
"Death" (Shelley) **14**:166
"Death and Birth" (Swinburne) **24**:324
"Death and Co." (Plath) **1**:397; **37**:213, 230, 233, 258
"Death and Daphne" (Swift) **9**:260
"Death and Doctor Hornbook" (Burns) **6**:56, 88
"The Death and Dying Words of Poor Mailie" (Burns) **6**:52, 61, 63-4
"Death and Engines" (Ní Chuilleanáin) **34**:353, 361-62
"The Death and Last Confession of Wandering Peter" (Belloc) **24**:5
"Death and Love" (Browning) **6**:16
"Death and Morality" (Olds) **22**:323, 342
"Death and Murder" (Olds) **22**:326
"The Death and Resurrection of the Birds" (Wagoner) **33**:333
Death and Taxes (Parker) **28**:349-51, 363-65
"Death and the Compass" (Borges)
See "La muerte y la brújula"
"Death and the Maiden" (Nemerov) **24**:259, 268, 270-71
"Death and the Maiden" (Wylie) **23**:317
"Death and the Sun" (Mahon) **60**:176, 195, 210, 214
"Death As Death" (Jackson) **44**:8
"The Death Baby" (Sexton) **2**:373
"Death by Water" (Cavafy) **36**:8
"Death Carol" (Whitman) **3**:378
"Death Chant" (Hughes) **53**:119
"Death, corollary to Life" (Villa) **22**:354
"The Death Dance" (Madhubuti) **5**:339
"Death, from a Distance" (Wilbur) **51**:273
"Death Fugue" (Celan)
See "Todesfuge"
"Death, Great Smoothener" (Swenson) **14**:250, 286
"Death in Harlem" (Hughes) **53**:101, 114
"Death in Mexico" (Levertov) **11**:205-06, 209
"Death in Moonlight" (Kunitz) **19**:155
"A Death in the Desert" (Browning) **2**:36, 45, 72-73, 95
"A Death in the Desert" (Tolson) **17**:328
Death in This Garden (Bunuel)
See *La mort en ce jardin*
"Death in Yorkville" (Hughes) **53**:111
"Death Invited" (Swenson) **14**:266, 286
"Death Is a Woman" (Harjo) **27**:68, 70, 72-3
Death Mask and Clover (Storni)
See *Mascarilla y trébol*
Death meditated (Ungaretti)
See *La morte meditata*
The Death Notebooks (Sexton) **2**:360-61, 367-68, 370-72
"Death of a Cat" (MacNeice) **61**:128
"Death of a Ceiling" (McGuckian) **27**:90
"The Death of a Cranefly" (Wagoner) **33**:357
"Death of a Favorite Bird" (Merwin) **45**:9
"Death of a Favorite Cat" (Gray)
See "Ode on the Death of a Favourite Cat, Drowned in a Tub of Gold Fishes"
"Death of a Frog" (Hagiwara)
See "Kaeru no shi"
"The Death of A. G. A." (Brontë) **8**:65, 74
"Death of a Lawn Mower" (Ignatow) **34**:343
"Death of a Naturalist" (Heaney) **18**:200, 207, 247-48, 252
Death of a Naturalist (Heaney) **18**:186, 189-90, 192, 194, 199-201, 205-8, 215, 220, 238, 247, 255
"Death of a Student" (Shapiro) **25**:309, 316
"The Death of a Toad" (Wilbur) **51**:186, 214, 266, 297, 299
"Death of a Young Son by Drowning" (Atwood) **8**:38-9
"Death of an Actress" (MacNeice) **61**:139
"Death of an Alcoholic" (Hagiwara) **18**:167, 178
"Death of an Old Lady" (MacNeice) **61**:111
"Death of Antoñito the Camborio" (García Lorca)
See "Muerte de Antoñito el Camborio"
"The Death of Artists" (Baudelaire)
See "La mort des artistes"
"The Death of Aunt Alice" (Abse) **41**:10
"Death of Autumn" (Millay) **6**:236
The Death of Blanche the Duchess (Chaucer)
See *Book of the Duchess*
"The Death of Channing" (Bryant) **20**:46
"The Death of Crazy Horse" (Clifton) **17**:25
"Death of Deaths" (Stramm)
See "Urtod"
"Death of Emma Goldman" (Shapiro) **25**:311, 324
"The Death of Fred Clifton" (Clifton) **17**:25, 27
"The Death of God" (Montale)
See "La morte di Dio"
"Death of Little Boys" (Tate) **50**:228, 236, 246-48, 280, 296, 305, 311, 325
"The Death of Lovers" (Baudelaire)
See "La mort des amants"
"The Death of Marilyn Monroe" (Mahon) **60**:181
"The Death of Mr. Mounsel" (Smith) **12**:323
"The death of my poor father" (Niedecker) **42**:138
"The Death of Oenone" (Tennyson) **6**:360
"The Death of Potchikoo" (Erdrich) **52**:193
"The Death of Reason" (Boland) **58**:18, 60
"The Death of Richard Wagner" (Swinburne) **24**:323, 329
"The Death of Smet-Smet" (Brooke) **24**:56, 66
"Death of Socrates" (Lamartine)
See *La morte de Socrate*
"Death of the American Indian's God" (Corso) **33**:49
"The Death of the Ball Turret Gunner" (Jarrell) **41**:145, 168, 173, 178-79, 182, 187, 189, 203, 205, 218
"The Death of the Baron" (Lawrence) **54**:229-30
"The Death of the Beloved" (Rilke) **2**:272-73
"The Death of the Bird" (Hope) **56**:266, 272
"The death of the Emperor Tacitus" (Cavafy) **36**:53, 57
"The Death of the Fathers" (Sexton) **2**:356, 365-67
"The Death of the Firstborn" (Dunbar) **5**:140
"The Death of the Flowers" (Bryant) **20**:9, 12
"The Death of the Hired Man" (Frost) **1**:195, 197, 209, 216, 221, 226, 228-29; **39**:246, 253
"Death of the Hungarian hot pepper bush" (Piercy) **29**:315
"Death of the Lord Protector" (Marvell)
See "Poem upon the Death of O. C."
"The Death of the Other Children" (Atwood) **8**:39
"Death of the Poet" (Lermontov)
See "Smert' poeta"
"Death of the Poet" (Pasternak) **6**:268
"The Death of the Princess" (Senghor) **25**:232
"The Death of the Sheriff" (Lowell) **3**:200, 206
"The Death of the Wolf" (Vigny)
See "La mort du loup"
"A Death on Easter Day" (Swinburne) **24**:319
"Death Piece" (Roethke) **15**:272
"The Death Room" (Graves) **6**:142, 144
"Death Shall Have No Dominion" (Thomas)
See "And Death Shall Have No Dominion"
"Death Snips Proud Men" (Sandburg) **41**:313
"Death Song" (Wagoner) **33**:344
"A Death Song for Alfred Linnell" (Morris) **55**:340
"Death, That Struck when I Was Most Confiding" (Brontë) **8**:65
"Death the Barber" (Williams) **7**:388
"Death to Van Gogh's Ear!" (Ginsberg) **4**:63, 74-5
"A Death-Day Recalled" (Hardy) **8**:136
"Death-in-Love" (Rossetti) **44**:204
"Deaths" (Swenson) **14**:286
"Deaths and Entrances" (Thomas) **2**:380-82, 388, 390
Deaths and Entrances (Thomas) **52**:219, 239, 252, 286
"The Deaths of Uncles" (Kumin) **15**:202
"Debat du cuer et du corps de Villon" (Villon) **13**:394, 396
"The Debate" (Ignatow) **34**:282
"The Debate" (Lermontov) **18**:295, 297
"Debate with the Rabbi" (Nemerov) **24**:277
"Débauche" (Gautier) **18**:164
"Deborah as Scion" (Dickey) **40**:211-12, 238
"Deborah Burning a Doll Made of House-Wood" (Dickey) **40**:211-12, 236
"Deborah in Ancient Lingerie, in Think Oak Over Creek" (Dickey) **40**:237
"Deborah in Mountain Sound: Bell, Glacier, Rose" (Dickey) **40**:228
"Deborah, Moon, Mirror, Right Hand Rising" (Dickey) **40**:211-12, 236
"Dèbris" (Césaire) **25**:8-9
"The Debt" (Dunbar) **5**:120, 125
"A Debt" (Merwin) **45**:20
"Debt" (Oppen) **35**:315
"Debt" (Teasdale) **31**:325, 352
"Debtor" (Teasdale) **31**:360
Début et fin de la neige (Bonnefoy) **58**:150-51, 154
"A Decade" (Lowell) **13**:97
"Decalogue of the Artist" (Mistral) **32**:144
"Decay" (Herbert) **4**:102
"The Decay of Vanity" (Hughes) **7**:113
"December" (Belloc) **24**:29
"December 1" (Milosz) **8**:215
"December 4th" (Sexton) **2**:372
"December 9th" (Sexton) **2**:352-53
"December 10th" (Sexton) **2**:364
"December 12th" (Sexton) **2**:352-53
"December 14th" (Sexton) **2**:353
"December 16th" (Sexton) **2**:352-53
"December 18th" (Sexton) **2**:352
"December 24th, Paris—Notre Dame" (Cisneros) **52**:161
"December, 1903" (Cavafy) **36**:42, 107
"December 1920" (Seifert) **47**:331

"December Among the Vanished" (Merwin) **45**:20, 23
"December Night" (Lawrence) **54**:169
"December Night" (Merwin) **45**:20, 34
Decennalia (Carducci) **46**:4-5, 47
"Deceptions" (Larkin) **21**:237
"Deciduous Branch" (Kunitz) **19**:147
"The Deciduous Trees" (Meredith) **28**:190
"The deck that pouts" (Piercy) **29**:314
"Declaring One's Name" (Char)
See "Déclarer son nom"
Declaration (Wyatt) **27**:369
"Declaration of Independence" (Parra)
See "Acta de independecia"
"Declarations" (Hughes) **53**:101
"Déclarer son nom" (Char) **56**:111, 179
"Decline" (Trakl)
See "Untergang"
"De-Composition" (Birney) **52**:85
"The Deconstruction of Emily Dickinson" (Kinnell) **26**:294
"Decorum and Terror Homage to Goethe and Hart Crane" (Viereck) **27**:279
"Dedham, vu de Langham" (Bonnefoy) **58**:141
"Dedica" (Pasolini) **17**:281
"Dedication" (Akhmatova)
See "Posvyashchenie"
"Dedication" (Char) **56**:159-60, 162
"Dedication" (Curnow) **48**:27
"The Dedication" (Herbert) **4**:125
"A Dedication" (Merrill) **28**:240
"Dedication" (Milosz) **8**:193
"Dedication" (Wylie) **23**:303
Dedication (Ekeloef) **23**:75-6
"Dedication for a Plot of Ground" (Williams) **7**:362, 394
"Dedication in Time" (Schwartz)
See "Time's Dedication"
"A Dedication of Three Hats" (Gray) **6**:166
"Dedication to Hunger" (Glück) **16**:151, 154-55
"Dedication: To William Morris" (Swinburne) **24**:313
"Dedications" (Rich) **5**:401
Dedications and Other Darkhorses (Komunyakaa) **51**:6, 29, 33, 52
"Dedicatory Epistle" (Swinburne) **24**:351
"Dedicatory Ode" (Belloc) **24**:3, 6, 8, 11
"Dedicatory Poem" (Meredith) **28**:187
"Dedicatory Poem to Collected Poems, 1925-1948, To Hedli" (MacNeice) **61**:140, 146-47
"The Deeds of Jason" (Morris) **55**:305
"Deem as ye list upon good cause" (Wyatt) **27**:354
"Deep in the Night" (Teasdale) **31**:336
"The Deep Sea Cables" (Kipling) **3**:162
Deep Song (García Lorca)
See *Poema del cante jondo*
"Deep Woods" (Nemerov) **24**:288
"Deeper Than Love" (Lawrence) **54**:186
"Deeply Morbid" (Smith) **12**:329, 346
"Deep-sea Fishing" (MacDiarmid) **9**:167
"Deer among Cattle" (Dickey) **40**:158
"Deer Dancer" (Harjo) **27**:71
"Deer Enclosure" (Wang Wei)
See "Deer Park"
"Deer Park" (Wang Wei) **18**:383, 385-86, 391, 393
"Deer Season" (Kenyon) **57**:4, 39
"Deer Walled" (Wang Wei)
See "Deer Park"
"The Defeat" (Mistral)
See "La derrota"
"The Defeated" (Kavanagh) **33**:86, 103, 118, 121
"Defeated Saviour" (Wright) **36**:290-91
"A Defective Santa Claus" (Riley) **48**:301
Defectos escogidos: 2000 (Neruda) **4**:287
Defence (Wyatt) **27**:369-70
"The Defence of Guenevere" (Morris) **55**:238, 247, 257, 263-65, 267, 269, 300-302, 318-19, 348
The Defence of Guenevere, and Other Poems (Morris) **55**:239-40, 247, 251-52, 258, 266-67, 278-79, 284, 298-99, 301-2, 308-9, 322-23, 328-29, 344, 346, 348-49
"Defending My Tongue" (Clifton) **17**:28
Defenestration of Prague (Howe) **54**:39-42, 59, 61-65
"Defensa de Violeta Parra" (Parra) **39**:285
"Defensa del árbol" (Parra) **39**:304
"Defense of the Tree" (Parra)
See "Defensa del árbol"
Defensive Rapture (Guest) **55**:183, 204
"Deferred" (Hughes) **53**:123, 193
"definition for blk / children" (Sanchez) **9**:224, 232
"Definition in the Face of Unnamed Fury" (Dove) **6**:111
"Definition of Blue" (Ashbery) **26**:119, 123
"Definition of Creativity" (Pasternak) **6**:271
"The Definition of Love" (Marvell) **10**:264, 266, 271, 274, 277, 291, 294, 299-303, 312, 316, 319
"Definition of Love" (Sarton) **39**:322
"The Definition of Love" (Warren) **37**:288
"The Definition of Poetry" (Pasternak)
See "Opredelenyie poezii"
"The Definition of the Creative Power" (Pasternak) **6**:254
"Definitions of Old Age" (MacLeish) **47**:206
"Degas's Laundresses" (Boland) **58**:45
"Deher milan" (Tagore) **8**:407
"Dehorning" (Hughes) **7**:166
Dehors la nuit est gouvernée (Char) **56**:159, 162, 185-86, 189
"Deianira, Hercules, and Nessus" (Gower)
See "Tale of Deianira, Hercules, and Nessus"
"Dein Schimmer" (Celan) **10**:124-25
"Dejaneira" (Arnold) **5**:8
"Dejection" (Muir) **49**:205, 250
"Dejection" (Shelley) **14**:168
"Dejection: An Ode" (Coleridge) **11**:41, 52-3, 58, 69-73, 90-2, 105-09; **39**:162-63, 166-67, 176, 179-80
"Del infierno y del cielo" (Borges) **32**:85-6, 139
"Delfica" (Nerval) **13**:181, 194
"Delgusa Gardens" (Stryk) **27**:192
"Delicate Criss-Crossing Beetle Trails Left in the Sand" (Snyder) **21**:300
"Delicia" (Paz) **48**:184
"Deliciæ Sapientiæ de Amore" (Patmore) **59**:223, 276
"Delight" (Paz)
See "Delicia"
"Delight in Disorder" (Herrick) **9**:111-12, 115-16, 132, 135
"Delight in Disorder" (Patmore) **59**:232
"The Delight Song of Tsoai-talee" (Momaday) **25**:189, 196, 204, 213, 220
"The Delinquent" (Dunbar) **5**:119
"Délires" (Rimbaud) **57**:243, 249, 252, 254, 279
"Délires I" (Rimbaud) **57**:191, 199, 229
"Délires II" (Rimbaud) **57**:174, 191, 199
"Deliverance" (Graves) **6**:157
"The Deliverance" (Harper) **21**:192, 199-201, 211
"Deliverance From a Fit of Fainting" (Bradstreet) **10**:26, 61-2
"Della primavera trasportata al morale" (Williams) **7**:408
"Delphi" (H. D.) **5**:305
"The Delphic Oracle upon Plotinus" (Yeats) **20**:312, 329, 334
"Delphic Song" (Sikelianos) **29**:367
"Delphine et Hippolyte" (Baudelaire)
See "Femmes damnées"
"Delta" (Montale) **13**:134, 164
"Delta" (Walker) **20**:272-73, 275, 278, 281-83
"Le déluge" (Vigny) **26**:367, 380-81, 391, 398, 401-402, 411
"The Deluge" (Vigny)
See "Le déluge"
"Delusion?-No!" (Warren) **37**:379
"Dem aufgehenden Vollmonde" (Goethe) **5**:249
"Demain dès l'aube" (Hugo) **17**:64
"Démarrage" (Tzara) **27**:229-31
The Demesne of the Swans (Tsvetaeva)
See *Lebediny stan*
"Demetrius Soter" (Cavafy) **36**:20
"Demi-Exile. Howth" (Davie) **29**:107, 109, 119
"Demiurge" (Lawrence) **54**:199, 250
"The Demiurge's Laugh" (Frost) **1**:213; **39**:231
"Demobilization" (Shapiro) **25**:273, 296
"Democracy" (Hughes) **1**:241, 252, 258; **53**:153
"Democracy" (Rimbaud)
See "Démocratie"
"The Democratic Order" (Walker) **30**:350
"Démocratie" (Rimbaud) **57**:182-83, 199, 246
"Demolition" (Doty) **53**:45-46
"The Demon" (Pushkin) **10**:406, 412-13, 418
The Demon (Lermontov) **18**:271-72, 274, 279, 282-83, 297-98, 302
"Demon and Beast" (Yeats) **51**:76, 110
"The Demon Lover" (Rich) **5**:392
"Demon Time" (Muir) **49**:296
"Demonology" (Ronsard)
See "Les daimons"
"Demonstration" (Patmore) **59**:234
"Demos and Dionysus" (Robinson) **1**:470, 487; **35**:368
"An den Mond" (Goethe) **5**:246-47
"Den' stoial na piati golovakh" (Mandelstam) **14**:152
"Dend' aquí vexo un camiño" (Castro) **41**:92, 101
"Denial" (Herbert) **4**:114, 119-20
"Denouement" (Stone) **53**:228
"Denver Doldrum" (Ginsberg) **4**:74
"Deola Thinking" (Pavese) **13**:205
"Deola's Return" (Pavese)
See "Ritorno di Deola"
"Départ" (Gautier) **18**:155
"Départ" (Rimbaud) **57**:194, 224-25, 230, 236, 239, 248
Departmental Ditties (Kipling) **3**:155-56, 159, 165, 182, 190-91
"Departure" (Carducci)
See "Dipartita"
"Departure" (Forché) **10**:137, 144, 156, 169
"Departure" (Glück) **16**:142, 149-50, 172
"Departure" (Lawrence) **54**:197, 201
"Departure" (Millay) **6**:211
"The Departure" (Olds) **22**:310, 312, 321-22
"Departure" (Patmore) **59**:209, 222
"Departure" (Plath) **1**:388, 407-08; **37**:184
"Departure" (Rimbaud)
See "Départ"
"Departure" (Tomlinson) **17**:336, 346
"Departure" (Warren) **37**:312
"Departure in the Dark" (Day Lewis) **11**:145
"The Departure Song of the Divine Strings" (Li Ho) **13**:52
"Departure's Girl-Friend" (Merwin) **45**:8
Dependencies (Mueller) **33**:178-80
Depends: A Poet's Notebook (Montale)
See *Quaderno de quattro anni*
"Deposition from love" (Carew) **29**:3-4, 46
"Depressed by a Book of Bad Poetry, I Walk Toward an Unused Pasture and Invite the Insects to Join Me" (Wright) **36**:296, 326, 340-41, 350
"Depression" (Bly) **39**:7, 10, 79-80, 89-90
"Depression Before Spring" (Stevens) **6**:313
"Depression in Winter" (Kenyon) **57**:3, 43
"Depression Years" (Niedecker) **42**:104, 131
"Dept. of Philosophy" (Enzensberger) **28**:151
"Depth of Love" (Graves) **6**:172
"The Depths" (Apollinaire)
See "Loin du pigeonnier"
"DeQuincey At Grasmere" (Mahon) **60**:140, 181, 184, 215
"The Derelict" (Ignatow) **34**:292, 305

"The Derelict" (Kipling) **3**:183
"Derevnya" (Pushkin) **10**:421
"Derev'ya" (Tsvetaeva) **14**:317
Derivations: Selected Poems, 1950-1956 (Duncan) **2**:105-06
"Le dernier chant de pèlerinage de Childe Harold" (Lamartine) **16**:268, 279, 292
"Dernier jour du monde" (Hugo) **17**:87, 89
"Dernier malheur dernière chance" (Péret) **33**:231
Dernier Malheur, dernière chance (Péret) **33**:203
"Dernière Levée" (Breton) **15**:50
"Dernièrement" (Péret) **33**:231
Dernières Poésies (Gautier) **18**:143
"Derniers gestes" (Bonnefoy) **58**:172, 176
"Derniers vers" (Rimbaud) **3**:285
Derniers Vers (Rimbaud) **57**:175, 202, 208, 216, 250, 252, 260
Les derniers vers de Jules Laforgue (Laforgue) **14**:56-7, 59-62, 68-77, 80-3, 88, 93, 95-7
Les derniers vers de Pierre de Ronsard, gentilhomne vandomois (Ronsard) **11**:244, 269, 274
De derrière les fagots (Péret) **33**:202, 204, 220-21, 230
"La derrota" (Mistral) **32**:181, 191
"Derry Morning" (Mahon) **60**:146, 148, 150, 196, 232
"Des Beautés qui'il voudroit en s'amie" (Ronsard) **11**:247
"Des cris étouffés" (Péret) **33**:209, 213
"Des éventails brisés" (Éluard) **38**:91
"Des Faux" (Apollinaire) **7**:46
"Des imagistes" (Williams) **7**:345
"Desajuste en el desgaste" (Fuertes) **27**:27
"La desásída" (Mistral) **32**:189
"descarga en cueros" (Cruz) **37**:12
"Descartes" (Borges) **32**:58
"Descartes and the Stove" (Tomlinson) **17**:319
"Descending Figure" (Glück) **16**:151
Descending Figure (Glück) **16**:130-34, 144, 147, 150-51, 153-56, 159, 170
"The Descent" (Brooke) **24**:77
"The Descent" (Kinnell) **26**:236, 252, 280
"The Descent" (Williams) **7**:403
"The Descent from the Cross" (Rossetti) **7**:264, 285
"The Descent of Odin, an Ode" (Gray) **2**:146, 148-49, 152
The Descent of Winter (Williams) **7**:349, 352-53, 368, 400, 402
"A Descent through the Carpet" (Atwood) **8**:12, 19
"Description" (Doty) **53**:66
"Description" (Graham) **59**:130, 171-72
"Description" (Silverstein) **49**:340
"Description of a City Shower" (Swift) **9**:252, 265, 275-79
"Description of a Masque" (Ashbery) **26**:170
"The Description of Cooke-ham" (Lanyer) **60**:2, 9, 11, 15, 17, 20, 22, 33, 36, 40, 43-44, 48, 81, 88-90, 99, 101-3, 110-12, 114-15
"A Description of Some Confederate Dead" (Jarrell) **41**:127
"A Description of Some Confederate Soldiers" (Jarrell) **41**:183
"A Description of the Fifteenth of November: A Portrait of T. S. Eliot" (Stein) **18**:341
"A Description of the King" (Herbert) **50**:31-32
"Description of the Morning" (Swift) **9**:265
"Description without Place" (Stevens) **6**:338
Descriptive Sketches (Wordsworth) **4**:372
"Desde los cuatro puntos cardinales" (Castro) **41**:118
"El Desdichado" (Nerval) **13**:174-75, 178-80, 184-87, 195
"Desecration of the Gravestone of Rose P" (Pinsky) **27**:175
Le desert (Lamartine) **16**:276, 282, 284, 286
"The Desert Music" (Williams) **7**:374
The Desert Music, and Other Poems (Williams) **7**:371, 402-03
"Desert Places" (Frost) **1**:213, 229; **39**:233, 246, 253
"Desert Pools" (Teasdale) **31**:364
Desert Run (Yamada) **44**:323, 328-29, 344, 346, 348-49, 351
"Desert Storm" (Yamada) **44**:340, 346
"The Deserted House" (Reese) **29**:338, 345, 352
"The Deserted House" (Tennyson) **6**:358
"The Deserted Inn" (Carman) **34**:208
"The Deserted Plantation" (Dunbar) **5**:117, 123
"The Deserter" (Smith) **12**:300, 330-31, 333
"Desertion" (Brooke) **24**:57, 63
"Les déserts de l'amour" (Rimbaud) **57**:173-75, 177, 191, 243
"Deserts of Love" (Rimbaud)
See "Les Déserts de l'amour"
"Le Désespéranto" (Tzara) **27**:234
"Le désespoir" (Lamartine) **16**:279, 282-83, 290-91, 293
"Design" (Frost) **1**:227-28; **39**:253
"Désir" (Apollinaire) **7**:3
"Desir" (Lamartine) **16**:281
"Le Désir de la Gloire" (Hugo) **17**:88
"Desire" (Hughes) **1**:240
"Desire" (Toomer) **7**:338
Desire (Dylan) **37**:64
"Desk" (Tsvetaeva)
See "Stol"
"Desnudo" (Guillén) **35**:156
"A Desoignated National Park" (Ortiz) **17**:227
"Desolación" (Mistral) **32**:203-05
Desolación (Mistral) **32**:147, 149-59, 161, 164, 170, 173, 175, 178-81, 183, 187, 190-91, 194, 200, 203
Desolation (Mistral)
See *Desolación*
Desolation Is a Delicate Thing (Wylie) **23**:322
"Desolation Row" (Dylan) **37**:46-9, 51, 54-5, 60
"Despair" (Lamartine)
See "Le désespoir"
Despair (Mistral)
See *Desolación*
"Una despedida" (Borges) **22**:94; **32**:38
"Desperata" (Carducci) **46**:50
"A Desperate Vitality" (Pasolini)
See "Una Disperata Vitalita"
"Despite and Still" (Graves) **6**:154
"Despondency, an Ode" (Burns) **6**:71
Les Destinees (Vigny)
See *Les destinées: Poèmes philosophiques*
Les destinées: Poèmes philosophiques (Vigny) **26**:366-69, 371, 391-92, 394, 397, 401-404, 412-13
The Destinies: Philosophical Poems (Vigny)
See *Les destinées: Poèmes philosophiques*
"Destino de la carne" (Aleixandre) **15**:38
"Destino del poeta" (Paz) **1**:358
"Destiny" (Arnold) **5**:43, 50
"Destiny" (Corso) **33**:50
Destiny (Hagiwara)
See *Shukumei*
"The Destiny of Nations" (Coleridge) **11**:49, 63-4, 80; **39**:167
Deštník z Piccadilly (Seifert) **47**:317-21, 329, 336
"The Destroyer" (Graves) **6**:166
"Destroyers" (Kipling) **3**:183
La destrucción o el amor (Aleixandre) **15**:14-16, 18, 21-6, 31-4, 39-40, 42
"La destruction" (Baudelaire) **1**:63, 71
"The Destruction of Long Branch" (Pinsky) **27**:161, 163-5
Destruction or Love (Aleixandre)
See *La destrucción o el amor*
"Desvelada" (Mistral) **32**:152, 176
"Deszcz" (Herbert) **50**:8
"Detail" (Williams) **7**:369
"The Detective" (Plath) **37**:232
"Detente, sombra de mi bien esquivo" (Juana Inés de la Cruz) **24**:180, 184, 187, 238
"Detraction Execrated" (Suckling) **30**:130
"Detroit Conference of Unity and Art" (Giovanni) **19**:115
"Detskii sad cherez 30 let" (Shvarts) **50**:149-55, 160
"Deus Amanz" (Marie de France)
See "Les Dous Amanz"
"Deutsch Durch Freud" (Jarrell) **41**:158-59, 194-95
"Der Deutsche dankt" (Goethe) **5**:248
"Deutsches Requiem" (Borges) **32**:115
Deutschland: Ein Wintermärchen (Heine) **25**:132-38, 152, 179
"Deux Barques" (Bonnefoy) **58**:168
"Deux poèmes" (Char) **56**:120
Deuxième édition du cinquiesme livre des odes (Ronsard) **11**:246
"Devancier" (Char) **56**:118
Devastation (Mistral)
See *Tala*
"Developers at Crystal River" (Merrill) **28**:261
"Development" (Browning) **2**:96
"The Deviation" (Glück) **16**:135-36
The Devil and Billy Markham (Silverstein) **49**:314-16, 318
"The Devil and the Lady" (Tennyson) **6**:372, 408-09
"The Devil at Berry Pomery" (Graves) **6**:142, 144
"Devil on Ice" (Davie) **29**:114-15
"The Devils" (Pushkin)
See "Besy"
"The Devil's Advice to Story Tellers" (Graves) **6**:143
"The Devon Maid" (Keats) **1**:311
"A Devonshire Folk Song" (Noyes) **27**:136
"Dévotion" (Rimbaud) **57**:228, 230, 251, 271, 275, 282-84
"Devotion: That It Flow; That There Be Concentration" (Gallagher) **9**:45, 59
"Devotion to Duty" (Sassoon) **12**:257-58
The Devotional Poems of Mirabai (Mirabai) **48**:153-56
"Devotions" (Wright) **36**:337
"Devyatsat pyaty god" (Pasternak) **6**:265, 272
"Dew" (Teasdale) **31**:357
"Dezember" (Trakl) **20**:265
"Dharma prachar" (Tagore) **8**:407
"Diabetes" (Dickey) **40**:191, 199, 219
"A Diagram of Life" (Swenson) **14**:262
"Diagrams" (Gunn) **26**:195-196, 198
"The Dial Tone" (Nemerov) **24**:262
"Dialectic" (Cassian) **17**:13
"Dialogo" (Quasimodo) **47**:284, 289
Diálogos del conocimiento (Aleixandre) **15**:6-7, 12-13, 16-17, 39
"A Dialogu" (Swinburne) **24**:323
"A Dialogue" (Herbert) **4**:130
"A Dialogue" (Ignatow) **34**:207, 340
"Dialogue" (Muir) **49**:299
"Dialogue" (Sarton) **39**:325, 338
"Dialogue" (Wright) **14**:343
"Dialogue Between Ghost and Priest" (Plath) **37**:200
"A Dialogue between Old England and New" (Bradstreet) **10**:5, 17, 21, 33
"A Dialogue between the Resolved Soul, and Created Pleasure" (Marvell) **10**:265, 271, 274, 277, 290-91, 294, 314
"A Dialogue between the Soul and Body" (Marvell) **10**:265, 271, 274, 290, 313, 316
"A Dialogue between the Two Horses" (Marvell) **10**:276
"A Dialogue between Thyrsis and Dorinda" (Marvell) **10**:271, 314
"Dialogue of Island and Time" (Curnow) **48**:11, 29
"A Dialogue of Self and Soul" (Yeats) **20**:313, 315-16, 327, 333, 337; **51**:104, 111, 152
"A Dialogue of Watching" (Rexroth) **20**:218

"A Dialogue on Poverty" (Yakamochi)
See "Bingu mondo no uta"
"Dialogue on Women's Rights" (Harper) **21**:198
"Dialogue Over a Ouija Board: A Verse Dialogue" (Plath) **37**:209, 211-12, 236
"Dialogue with Four Rocks" (Curnow) **48**:20, 38-39, 65-67
"Dialogue—2 Dollmakers" (Corso) **33**:23
Dialogues of Knowledge (Aleixandre)
See *Diálogos del conocimiento*
"Dialogues of the Dogs" (Burns)
See "The Twa Dogs"
"Diamant du coeur" (Gautier) **18**:130, 157
"Diamantina" (Montale) **13**:138
The Diamond Cutters, and Other Poems (Rich) **5**:350, 352-54, 358, 362-63, 368-69, 388, 392
"The Diamond Merchant" (Wakoski) **15**:348
The Diamond Merchant (Wakoski) **15**:325
"Diaper" (Birney) **52**:21-22
"Diaries" (Cage) **58**:182-83
Diario del '71 (Montale) **13**:138, 144, 158
Diario del '71 e del '72 (Montale) **13**:138-39, 152, 160, 168
Diario del '72 (Montale) **13**:138, 144
El diario que a diario (Guillén) **23**:111, 133
Diaro de un poeta recien casado (Jiménez) **7**:197, 201-02, 208, 212, 214
Diary: How to Improve the World (You Will Only Make Matters Worse) Continued, Part 3 (Cage) **58**:195, 201-2
Diary of '71 and '72 (Montale)
See *Diario del '71 e del '72*
"Diary of a Change" (Rukeyser) **12**:218
"Diary of a Naturalist" (Milosz) **8**:206
Diary of a Newly-Wed Poet (Jiménez)
See *Diaro de un poeta recien casado*
"Diaspora" (Lorde) **12**:138, 140
"Il diaul cu la mari" (Pasolini) **17**:253
"Dibujos animados" (Storni) **33**:262, 294;
"Dice mía" (Darío) **15**:113
"Dices que no te acuerdas, Clori, y mientes" (Juana Inés de la Cruz) **24**:234
"La dicha" (Borges) **22**:95, 99
"Dichterberuf" (Hölderlin) **4**:169
"Dichtung" (Baraka) **4**:17
"Dichtung und Wahrheit" (Curnow) **48**:13, 16-17
Dichtungen (Char) **56**:111
"Dick, a Maggot" (Swift) **9**:296
"Dick Sapper" (Masters) **36**:211
"The Dictators" (Neruda) **4**:282
"The Dictatorship of the Proletariat" (Baraka) **4**:38-9
"Dictée en présence du glacier du Rhône" (Hugo) **17**:91
"The Dictionaries" (Soto) **28**:399
"Did you know that hair is flying around" (Ignatow) **34**:325
"Didactic Piece" (Bogan) **12**:122
"Dido" (O'Hara) **45**:155
"Dido's Farewell to Aeneas" (Smith) **12**:331
"An die Hofnung" (Hölderlin) **4**:148
"An die jungen Dichter" (Hölderlin) **4**:165
"An die Natur" (Hölderlin) **4**:142
"An die Verstummten" (Trakl) **20**:236
"An die Vertummten" (Trakl) **20**:232
"Died of Starvation" (Harper) **21**:191, 203, 210, 216
"Died of Wounds" (Sassoon) **12**:262
Dien cai dau (Komunyakaa) **51**:3, 6, 8-10, 15, 20, 33, 36-37, 39, 42, 52, 54, 56-57, 61, 63
"Un diente" (Storni) **33**:240, 262, 284
"Dies Irae" (Lawrence) **54**:249
"Dies irie sic" (Brathwaite) **56**:93
"Dieu" (Lamartine) **16**:265-66, 272, 274, 277, 285, 290-91
Dieu (Hugo) **17**:65-66, 73-74, 81, 84, 86, 91
"Difference" (Doty) **176**:19, 48
"The Differences" (Gunn) **26**:224
"The Difficult Land" (Muir) **49**:230, 280, 299
"Difficult Scene" (Sarton) **39**:321
"Diffugere Nives" (Noyes) **27**:136
"Dig and Be Dug" (Hughes) **53**:190-91
"Digging" (Heaney) **18**:200, 206-8, 216, 243
"Digging for China" (Wilbur) **51**:188, 198, 203, 267
"Digging I" (Thomas) **53**:295, 325-26, 328
"Dignity of Soul" (Viereck) **27**:281
"Digo que yo no soy un hombre puro" (Guillén) **23**:123-24
"A Digression" (Wilbur) **51**:334-35
The Digression (Mickiewicz) **38**:168-69
"Digression on Number 1, 1948" (O'Hara) **45**:241
Dikopis' poslednego vremeni (Shvarts) **50**:162-63
"Diktaren om dikten" (Ekeloef) **23**:90
"Dilemma" (Ignatow) **34**:275, 323
"The Dilemma" (Muir) **49**:229, 241
"Dilemma" (Parker) **28**:362
"Dili" (Pasolini) **17**:251
"Diligence Is to Magic As Progress Is to Flight" (Moore) **49**:113, 134, 161
"El dilitada guerra" (Neruda) **4**:295
"Dimanches" (Laforgue) **14**:72-3, 76, 78
"Dime" (Hughes) **53**:123
"Dime vencedor rapaz" (Juana Inés de la Cruz) **24**:234
"Dimensions" (Banks) **44**:44, 71, 78-9, 87
"Dimisión de Sancho" (Guillén) **35**:234, 239
"Dinanzi alle terme di Caracalla" (Carducci) **46**:39, 52, 82-83, 86-88
Dining (Nash) **21**:269
"Dining-Room Tea" (Brooke) **24**:77-8, 82, 88
"The Dinner" (Hope) **56**:304
"Dinner Guest: Me" (Hughes) **1**:252; **53**:115, 146
"Dinner Party" (Kenyon) **57**:6
"The Dinner Party" (Lowell) **13**:79
"Il Dio-Caprone" (Pavese) **13**:204, 207
"Diogenes" (Moore) **49**:116
"Dionysus" (Elytis) **21**:119
"Dionysus Encradled" (Sikelianos) **29**:368
"Dionysus' Escort" (Cavafy) **36**:46, 49
"Dionysus in Doubt" (Robinson) **1**:470
Dionysus in Doubt (Robinson) **1**:470
"Diorama" (Komunyakaa) **51**:63
Dios deseado y deseante: Animal de fondo con numerosos poemas iñeditos (Jiménez) **7**:197, 207
"Dios llama al fontanero" (Fuertes) **27**:28
"Dios lo quiere" (Mistral) **32**:151, 176
"Dios-fuerza" (Storni) **33**:262, 294-95;
"Dipartita" (Carducci) **46**:50
"Dipper" (Wagoner) **33**:356
"Diptych with Votive Tablet" (Paz)
See "Preparatory Exercise (Dyptych with Votive Tablet)"
"Directed by Desire" (Jordan) **38**:120-21
Directionscore: Selected and New Poems (Madhubuti) **5**:330, 336, 346
"Directive" (Frost) **1**:213, 227; **39**:253
"Director of Alienation" (Ferlinghetti) **1**:187
"Dirge" (Dylan) **37**:54-5
"Dirge" (Emerson) **18**:69, 102
"Dirge" (Smith) **12**:292, 344
"A Dirge" (Tennyson) **6**:359
"Dirge for a Righteous Kitten" (Lindsay) **23**:281
"Dirge for a Town in France" (Merton) **10**:350
"Dirge for the New Sunrise (August 6, 1945)" (Sitwell) **3**:327
"Dirge in the Woods" (Meredith) **60**:258, 289, 299, 327, 333-34
"A Dirge upon the Death of the Right Valiant Lord, Bernard Stuart" (Herrick) **9**:131
"Dirt and Not Copper" (Stein) **18**:319, 328
"Dirty Ears" (Corso) **33**:23
"The Dirty Word" (Shapiro) **25**:299
"Dis Aliter Visum" (Browning) **2**:68
"Disabled" (Owen) **19**:336, 354, 357
"Disappearing" (Carver) **54**:13
"The Disappearing Island" (Heaney) **18**:232
"Disappointed" (Enzensberger) **28**:167
"The Disappointment" (Behn) **13**:7, 10-11, 13-14, 16, 25-6, 28
"A Disaster" (Hughes) **7**:142, 160-61
"Disaster" (Valéry)
See "Sinistre"
"Disasters" (Oppen) **35**:300, 302
"The Discharge" (Herbert) **4**:109, 113, 120, 129
"Disciplina antica" (Pavese) **13**:226
"Discipline" (Herbert)
See "Throw Away Thy Rod"
"Discipline" (Lawrence) **54**:179
The Discipline of the Harp (Cassian) **17**:6
"Disclaimer of the Person" (Jackson) **44**:44, 71, 78-9, 87
"The Disclosure" (Levertov) **11**:169
"Discontents in Devon" (Herrick) **9**:108
"Discord" (Swinburne) **24**:324
"Discord in Childhood" (Lawrence) **54**:234-36
"La Discorde en ménage" (Éluard) **38**:91
Discorsi storici e letterari (Carducci) **46**:55
"Discotheque" (Merrill) **28**:254
Discours (Ronsard)
See *Discours des misères de ce temps*
"Discours à Pierre Lescot" (Ronsard) **11**:266
"Discours au Roy" (Ronsard) **11**:244, 284, 291
"Discours de misères de ce temps" (Ronsard) **11**:248
Discours des misères de ce temps (Ronsard) **11**:224, 250
"Discours en forme d'élégie" (Ronsard) **11**:248
"The Discourse of the Good Thief" (Parra) **39**:310
The Discourses of Rumi (Rumi)
See *Fihi ma fihi*
"The Discoverer of the North Cape" (Longfellow) **30**:40
"Discovering Michael as the King of Spain" (Wakoski) **15**:329
"Discovery" (Curnow) **48**:4
"The Discovery" (Hardy) **8**:101
"The Discovery of the Madeiras" (Frost) **1**:196, 206
"The Discovery of the Pacific" (Gunn) **26**:207-08
Discrepancies and Apparitions (Wakoski) **15**:323-24
"Discrete Series" (Oppen) **35**:327-28
Discrete Series (Oppen) **35**:282, 283, 288, 295-96, 300-01, 309, 319-20, 324-30, 332, 340-43, 345
"Discretions of Alcibiades" (Pinsky) **27**:162
"Discursos" (Parra) **39**:261, 273
Discusión (Borges) **32**:38
Discussions (Borges)
See *Discusión*
"Disdaine Returned" (Carew) **29**:32-34
"Disembarking at Quebec" (Atwood) **8**:36, 40
"Disenchantment a Tone Poem" (Aiken) **26**:7, 29
"Disillusionment" (Hughes) **1**:246
"The Disinherited" (Nerval)
See "El Desdichado"
"The Dismal Chimes of Bells" (Lermontov) **18**:302
"The Dismissal of Tyng" (Harper) **21**:190, 218
"The Disoblig'd Love" (Behn) **13**:20
"The Disorder" (Chin) **40**:27
"Disorder Overtakes Us All Day Long" (Schwartz) **8**:285
"Una Disperata Vitalita" (Pasolini) **17**:257-58, 286, 288-89
"Dispersal" (Sassoon) **12**:259
"Dispersiones, alianzas" (Paz) **48**:209
"Dispersions, alliances" (Paz)
See "Dispersiones, alianzas"
"Displaced People" (Pavese) **13**:218
"The Displeasure of the Seleucid" (Cavafy) **36**:3
"Disputation" (Heine) **25**:170
"Dispute" (Stramm)
See "Zwist"
"The Disquieted Muses" (Plath)
See "The Disquieting Muses"

"The Disquieting Muses" (Plath) **1**:388, 407; **37**:181-82, 185, 254
"Dissect This Silence" (Kunitz) **19**:148
"The Dissecting Table" (Szirtes) **51**:157
"Dissentient Voice" (Davie) **29**:93, 112-15
"The Dissolution" (Donne) **1**:154
"Distance" (Kumin) **15**:223-24
"Distance" (Milosz)
See "Odlegtose"
"Distance" (Parker) **28**:364
"The Distance Between: Picnic of Old Friends" (Warren) **37**:377
"The Distances" (Merwin) **45**:48
Distances (Okigbo) **7**:228, 234-35, 240-41, 243-47, 251, 253, 255
"Distancia" (Borges) **22**:92
Distant Byways (Matsuo Bashō)
See *Oku no hosomichi*
"The Distant Winter" (Levine) **22**:212, 216
"Distinctions" (Tomlinson) **17**:314, 328
"Distraction and Definition" (Curnow) **48**:58
"El distraído" (Guillén) **35**:187
"Distress Sale" (Carver) **54**:29
"The Distressed Damsel" (Smart) **13**:348
"The disturbance" (Piercy) **29**:314
"A Disused Shed in Co. Wexford" (Mahon) **60**:136-37, 140, 149, 151, 155-56, 158, 161, 169-71, 183, 202, 205, 211, 215, 220, 237
"Dit de la force d l'amour" (Éluard) **38**:78
"Dit d'errance" (Césaire) **25**:31, 38, 44
"Dithyrambes" (Ronsard) **11**:230-32
"Ditia v getto v okruzhenii bukv" (Shvarts) **50**:162-63
"Ditty" (Hardy) **8**:90
"Ditty" (Tate) **50**:231, 246, 283, 285
"Diuturna enfermedad de la Esperanza" (Juana Inés de la Cruz) **24**:225
"La Diva" (Gautier) **18**:135-140
"Divagación" (Darío) **15**:96, 103-05, 119-20
Divagations (Mallarmé) **4**:202, 210
Divan-i Shams-i Tabrizi (Rumi) **45**:274-76, 281-91, 313, 320-21, 323-24
"The Diver" (Hayden) **6**:187, 193, 198
"The Diverse Causes" (Ondaatje) **28**:292
Diversifications (Ammons) **16**:24, 61
"Divertidas estancias a don Juan" (Storni) **33**:280, 305;
"The Diverting History of John Gilpin" (Cowper) **40**:48
La divina commedia (Dante) **21**:48-57, 59, 63, 65-6, 69, 73-7, 80-5, 87-8, 90-3, 95, 97-9, 102, 104-05, 108-11
"Divina psiquis" (Darío) **15**:101
Divine Comedies: Poems (Merrill) **28**:220-21, 224-25, 227-32, 246, 260, 263, 272, 281
Divine Comedy (Dante)
See *La divina commedia*
The Divine Comedy: Hell, Purgatory, Heaven (Dante)
See *La divina commedia*
The Divine Comedy of Dante Aligheri: Purgatorio (Dante)
See *La divina commedia*
The Divine Comedy of Dante Alighieri (Dante)
See *La divina commedia*
"The Divine Image" (Blake) **12**:5, 7, 33
"A Divine Mistris" (Carew) **29**:9
The Divine Pilgrim (Aiken) **26**:10, 22, 47, 53
Divine Poems (Donne) **1**:158
"Divine Psyche" (Darío)
See "Divina psiquis"
The Divine Tragedy (Longfellow) **30**:23, 39, 59, 65, 67
"The Diviner" (Heaney) **18**:200
"Diving Board" (Silverstein) **49**:343
"Diving into the Wreck" (Rich) **5**:371, 374, 376, 394-95
Diving into the Wreck: Poems, 1971-1972 (Rich) **5**:360, 362, 365, 367-68, 370-72, 384, 388-90, 393
"Divinità in incognito" (Montale) **13**:133
"Divinitie" (Herbert) **4**:108, 130
"Divinity" (Kinnell) **26**:286
"Division" (Bogan) **12**:98, 106, 121
"The Division" (Hardy) **8**:93
"The Division of Parts" (Sexton) **2**:351, 359-60, 367
"Divorce" (Mueller) **33**:175
"A Divorce of Lovers" (Sarton) **39**:333, 338, 345, 354, 365
"The Divorce Papers" (Sexton) **2**:356, 367
"Divorce, Thy Name Is Woman" (Sexton) **2**:359
"Divorcing" (Levertov) **11**:197
Dīwān (Ekeloef)
See *Dīwān över fursten av Emigón*
Diwan (Rumi)
See *Divan-i Shams-i Tabrizi*
Dīwān över fursten av Emigón (Ekeloef) **23**:63-5, 67-71, 77-8, 85
Diwan-i shams-i tabrizi (Rumi)
See *Divan-i Shams-i Tabrizi*
"Les djinns" (Hugo) **17**:63, 70, 76
Dlatego żyjemy (Szymborska) **44**:268
"Do." (Cummings) **5**:106
"Do Apollina" (Herbert) **50**:7
"Do Ateny" (Herbert) **50**:7
"Do Jōzefa Sadzika" (Milosz) **8**:190
"Do Marka Aurelego" (Herbert) **50**:7
"Do not compare: the living are incomparable" (Mandelstam)
See "Ne sravnivai: zhivushchii nesravnim"
"Do Not Embrace Your Mind's New Negro Friend" (Meredith) **28**:187
"Do Not Go Gentle into That Good Night" (Thomas) **52**:218, 239, 276, 312-15, 325-29
"Do Not Touch" (Pasternak) **6**:260
"Do Not Touch the Exhibits" (Curnow) **48**:36, 51-52, 59-62
"Do przyjaciól Moskali" (Mickiewicz) **38**:169
"Do Take Muriel Out" (Smith) **12**:331, 337
"Do the Others Speak of Me Mockingly, Maliciously?" (Schwartz) **8**:306
"Do You Reckon?" (Hughes) **53**:115
"Doc Hill" (Masters) **1**:327; **36**:164, 172, 183, 202
"Dock Rats" (Moore) **4**:251; **49**:101
"Docker" (Heaney) **18**:200
"Dockery and Son" (Larkin) **21**:228-31, 233, 236-37, 241
"The doctor" (Abse) **41**:21
"The Doctor" (Smith) **12**:330
"The Doctor and the Devils" (Thomas) **52**:252
"Doctor Mohawk" (Lindsay) **23**:285, 287
"The Doctor of the Heart" (Sexton) **2**:365
Doctor Spock's Monologue (Yevtushenko) **40**:357
"A Document" (Wright) **14**:356, 362
"Dodger Point Lookout" (Snyder) **21**:300
"Dodwells Road" (Wilbur) **51**:215-16
"Does It Matter?" (Sassoon) **12**:267-68, 285
"Does the Road Wind Up-hill all the Way?" (Rossetti) **7**:293
"Dog" (Ferlinghetti) **1**:184
"Dog" (Ransom) **61**:314-15
"The Dog and the Water-Lily: No Fable" (Cowper) **40**:125, 127
"Dog Dreaming" (Merwin) **45**:23
"A Dog Named Ego, the Snowflakes as Kisses" (Schwartz) **8**:307, 314
"De Dog Rose" (McKay) **2**:223
"A Dog Sleeping on My Feet" (Dickey) **40**:178, 181-82, 231, 257
"Dog-Days" (Lowell) **13**:64
"Dogon Eclipse" (Mackey) **49**:5-6
"Dogovor" (Lermontov) **18**:303-4
"Dogs Are Shakespearean, Children Are Strangers" (Schwartz) **8**:306, 312
"A Dog's Best Friend Is His Illiteracy" (Nash) **21**:273
"A Dog's Life" (MacDiarmid) **9**:155
"Dog-Tired" (Lawrence) **54**:206
"A Doing Nothing Poem" (Bly) **39**:70
"Dolce Ossessione" (Viereck) **27**:259
"Le dolci rime d'amor ch'io solia" (Dante) **21**:88
"The Doll" (Lowell) **13**:84-5
"The Doll" (Wylie) **23**:321
"Doll Poem" (Corso) **33**:25, 41
"The Dolls" (Yeats) **20**:336, 340
"A Doll's 'Arabian Nights'" (Lindsay) **23**:264, 277
"The Dolls Museum in Dublin" (Boland) **58**:18-19, 61, 96-98
"Dolly's Mistake" (Clare) **23**:40
"Dolor" (Storni) **33**:246;
"Dolores" (Swinburne) **24**:308-09, 360, 362-63
"Dolorida" (Vigny) **26**:401, 411
The Dolphin (Lowell) **3**:224, 229-30, 232-33, 239-41
"The Dolphins and the Lovers" (Morris) **55**:306
A Dome of Many-Coloured Glass (Lowell) **13**:60, 69
"Dome of Sunday" (Shapiro) **25**:279-80, 283, 286, 295, 305, 308, 310, 315-17, 324-25
"La Domenica Uliva" (Pasolini) **17**:256
The Domesday Book (Masters) **1**:330-33, 335-36, 339; **36**:194-95
"A Domestic Faust" (Szirtes) **51**:169
"Domestic Interior" (Boland) **58**:45-46, 51-52, 54-56, 61
"Domestic Poem for a Summer Afternoon" (Page) **12**:181
"The Domestic Science of Sunday Dinner" (Goodison) **36**:158
"Domestic Song" (Ignatow) **34**:323
Domik v Kolomne (Pushkin) **10**:366, 381-86, 391, 400
"Domiki staroi Moskvy" (Tsvetaeva) **14**:318
"The Dominant Thought" (Leopardi)
See "Il Pensiero Dominante"
"Domination of Black" (Stevens) **6**:293-94
"Dominique aujourd'hui présente" (Éluard) **38**:78
"Le Dompteur de lions se souvient" (Tzara) **27**:224
"Don du poème" (Mallarmé) **4**:196
"Don José" (Quintana) **36**:255
"Don Juan" (Clare) **23**:26
Don Juan (Byron) **16**:77-88, 90-2, 95-102, 106-08, 110-13, 115-17, 120
"Don Juan aux enfers" (Baudelaire) **1**:47
"Don Juan gesellte sich zu uns" (Benn) **35**:48
"Don Juan in Hades" (Baudelaire)
See "Don Juan aux enfers"
"Don Julian II" (Quintana) **36**:275
"Donatello's Statue of Saint George" (Carducci)
See "San Giorgio di Donatello"
"La doncella y la muerte" (Parra) **39**:287
"Done Into Verse" (Belloc) **24**:43-4
"Donegal Triptych" (MacNeice) **61**:112, 119-20
"Dong, Sounds the Brass in the East" (Thoreau) **30**:182, 193, 202, 220
"The Donkey" (Chesterton) **28**:101
"The Donkey" (Smith) **12**:318
"Donna Clara" (Heine) **25**:145
"Donne che avete intelletto d'amore" (Dante) **21**:73, 86
"Donne perdute" (Pavese) **13**:225
Donner à voir (Éluard) **38**:100, 107
"Donner àvoir" (Éluard) **38**:102
"Donnerbach mühle" (Char) **56**:190-91, 193-95, 200
"Donneycarney" (Joyce)
See "XXXI"
"Don't Be Cross Amanda" (Nash) **21**:271
Don't Cry, Scream (Madhubuti) **5**:324-25, 328, 336, 338, 340-46
Don't Go Out of the Door (Li Ho) **13**:42
"Don't Grow Old" (Ginsberg) **4**:84
"Don't Laugh at my Prophetic Anguish" (Lermontov) **18**:281
"Don't Look Now But Mary Is Everbody" (Viereck) **27**:258, 274, 278
"Don't shoot the rail!" (Niedecker) **42**:150

"Don't Shoot the Warthog" (Corso) **33**:40, 43
"Don't Trust Yourself" (Lermontov) **18**:281
"Don't Wanna Be" (Sanchez) **9**:229
"Doom" (Darío)
See "Lo fatal"
"Doom Is the House without the Door" (Dickinson) **1**:111
"The Doom of King Acrisius" (Morris) **55**:242, 329
"Doomsday" (Borges) **32**:91
"Dooms-day" (Herbert) **4**:131
"A Door" (Merwin) **45**:72, 74-5, 77-9
The Door in the Wall (Tomlinson) **17**:360-61
Door into the Dark (Heaney) **18**:191, 194-95, 199-201, 203, 205-6, 209, 215, 220, 225-26, 238
"Door to the River" (Doty) **53**:61
"Doors" (Wagoner) **33**:335
"Doors, Doors, Doors" (Sexton) **2**:349
"Dopa una fuga" (Montale) **13**:134
"Dope" (Baraka) **4**:40
"Dopo Aspromonte" (Carducci) **46**:5, 51
"Doppel-Konzert" (Benn) **35**:26
"Dora" (Tennyson) **6**:360
"Dora Maar" (Guest) **55**:185
"Dora Markus" (Montale) **13**:106, 113-14, 119
"Dora Williams" (Masters) **1**:347
"Dormant Windows and Door onto the Roof" (Char) **56**:146
"Le dormeur du val" (Rimbaud) **57**:190-91, 203
"La dormeuse" (Valéry) **9**:365-66, 374, 387, 392-93, 396
Dormir, dormir dans les pierres (Péret) **33**:204, 224, 230-31
"Dormit Flumen" (Birney) **52**:27
"Dornenkranz" (Celan) **10**:128-30
"Dorothée" (Baudelaire)
See "La belle Dorothée"
"Las dos cartas" (Guillén) **23**:126
"Dos cuerpos" (Paz) **48**:199-200
"Dos niños" (Guillén) **23**:139
"Dos peras" (Guillén) **35**:204
"Dos versiones de 'Ritter, Tod und Teufel'" (Borges) **32**:89
"Dos vidas" (Aleixandre) **15**:7
"Dot de Maubergeonne" (Char) **56**:151
"Dot Leedle Boy" (Riley) **48**:334
"Dotage" (Herbert) **4**:130
"Dotterel" (Wright) **14**:348
"Les Douaniers" (Rimbaud) **57**:203, 205
"Double Absence" (Muir) **49**:299
The Double Axe and Other Poems (Jeffers) **17**:123-24, 130, 136, 146-47
"The Double Chamber" (Baudelaire)
See "La chambre double"
"The Double Dream of Spring" (Ashbery) **26**:115
The Double Dream of Spring (Ashbery) **26**:115, 118-119, 124-125, 128, 130, 138, 144, 148-149, 153-154, 169
"Double Feature" (Hayden) **6**:194-95
"The Double Image" (Sexton) **2**:350, 355-56, 359, 361-63, 372
"Double Image" (Wright) **14**:348
The Double Image (Levertov) **11**:163-64
"The Double Looking Glass" (Hope) **56**:284, 286-87, 306
"Double Monologue" (Rich) **5**:374
"Double Negative" (Nemerov) **24**:289
"Double Ode" (Rukeyser) **12**:225
Double Persephone (Atwood) **8**:21
"The Double Standard" (Harper) **21**:187, 191, 207
The Double Tree: Selected Poems, 1942-1976 (Wright) **14**:366
"The Double Voices" (Atwood) **8**:16, 32
"Doubled Mirrors" (Rexroth) **20**:217
"Doubleness in Time" (Warren) **37**:376-77
"Double-Nine Festival" (Li Po) **29**:183
"The Doubt of Truth" (Corso) **33**:36
"The Doubtful Passage" (Cardenal)
See "El estrecho dudoso"
"Doubts" (Brooke) **24**:57, 85
"Doubts" (Teasdale) **31**:356
"Les Dous Amanz" (Marie de France) **22**:258, 269, 271-73, 275
Douve (Bonnefoy)
See *Du mouvement et de l'immobilité de Douve*
"The Dove Breeder" (Hughes) **7**:116
"The Dove in Spring" (Stevens) **6**:313
"Dove la luce" (Ungaretti) **57**:349
The Dove of Popular Flight—Elegies (Guillén)
See *La paloma de vuelo popular: Elegiás*
"Dove or Swan" (Yeats) **51**:86-87
"Dover" (Auden) **1**:16
"Dover Beach" (Arnold) **5**:8, 13, 16-18, 35, 38, 47, 49, 53, 58, 64-5
"Dover Beach—A Note to That Poem" (MacLeish) **47**:157-58
"Dover: Believing in Kings" (Dickey) **40**:176, 178-79, 183
"Dov'era il tennis" (Montale) **13**:160
"The Doves of Mérida" (Wagoner) **33**:349
"Dow Kritt" (Masters) **36**:218
"Down" (Graves) **6**:142, 144
"Down and Out" (Hughes) **53**:113, 137
"Down at the bottom of things" (Piercy) **29**:314
"Down There" (Cisneros) **52**:146
"Down to the Capital" (Riley) **48**:288, 302, 352
"Down, Wanton, Down!" (Graves) **6**:151, 153, 165
"Down Where I Am" (Hughes) **53**:109
"The Downs" (Bridges) **28**:67, 83
"Downstream" (Carver) **54**:18
"The Dowser" (MacNeice) **61**:139
"Dowson and Company" (Mahon) **60**:133
"Dozing on the Lawn" (MacLeish) **47**:206
dq1In Seditionem Horrendam" (Cowper) **40**:101
"Dr. Swift to Mr. Pope while He Was Writing the Dunciad" (Swift) **9**:295
"The Draft Horse" (Frost) **1**:213; **39**:241
A Draft of Eleven New Cantos (XXXI-XLI) (Pound) **4**:321-22, 353, 357-58
"A Draft of Shadows" (Paz)
See *Pasado en claro*
A Draft of Shadows (Paz)
See *Pasado en claro*
Drafts and Fragments of Cantos CX to CXVII (Pound) **4**:352-54
"Dragon" (Ondaatje) **28**:298
"The Dragon and the Undying" (Sassoon) **12**:278
"The Dragon and the Unicorn" (Rexroth) **20**:204, 221
The Dragon and the Unicorn (Rexroth) **20**:181-82, 184, 192, 205, 208, 210, 212-14
"Dragon Music" (Hope) **56**:285
"Dragonfly" (Bogan) **12**:107-08
Dragon's Blood (Yau) **61**:348
Drake (Noyes) **27**:114-15, 119, 123, 125, 127, 134
"Drama for Winter Night (Fifth Avenue)" (Hughes) **53**:115
"A Drama of Exile" (Browning) **6**:6, 20-1, 26, 31, 34, 46
Dramatic Lyrics (Browning) **2**:26, 35, 66, 94; **61**:87
"Dramatic Poem: Voice of Silence" (Ishikawa)
See "Gekishi: Chimmoku no koe"
Dramatic Romances and Lyrics (Browning) **2**:94; **61**:87
Dramatis Personae (Browning) **2**:34, 45, 94-5; **61**:16, 57, 87
Dramatis Personae (Yeats) **20**:328
"The Draped Mirrors" (Borges) **32**:66
"Drawer" (Herbert) **50**:4
"Drawing" (Oppen) **35**:288, 294
"Drawing from the Past" (Kenyon) **57**:41
"Drawing Lessons" (Nemerov) **24**:302-03
Drawing-Room Verses (Parra)
See *Versos de salón*
"The Drawn-Out War" (Neruda)
See "El dilitada guerra"
"Dread Song" (Walcott) **46**:291
"The Dream" (Berry) **28**:38
"A Dream" (Blake) **12**:7, 33-4
"The Dream" (Bogan) **12**:111
"The Dream" (Borges) **32**:60
"The Dream" (Browning) **6**:19
"A Dream" (Bryant) **20**:15
"A Dream" (Burns) **6**:89
"The Dream" (Byron) **16**:73, 76
"Dream" (Heaney) **18**:201
"The Dream" (Hope) **56**:266, 268
"The Dream" (Ignatow) **34**:290, 317
"A Dream" (Jarrell) **41**:168
"Dream" (Juana Inés de la Cruz)
See "Primero sueño"
"The Dream" (Leopardi)
See "Il Sogno"
"The Dream" (Mickiewicz)
See "Sen"
"Dream" (Riley) **48**:315
"The Dream" (Roethke) **15**:288-89
"The Dream" (Sassoon) **12**:267
"A Dream" (Schnackenberg) **45**:329-30
"The Dream" (Stryk) **27**:204
"A Dream" (Swenson) **14**:288
"Dream" (Tagore)
See "Svapna"
"Dream" (Wright) **14**:367, 373
"The Dream, 1863" (Hayden) **6**:180, 188
"Dream and Madness" (Trakl)
See "Traum und Umnachtung"
"Dream Boogie" (Hughes) **1**:266; **53**:123, 159, 190, 197, 206
"Dream Boogie: Variation" (Hughes) **53**:92
"A Dream Deferred" (Hughes) **1**:266; **53**:150-51
"Dream Drumming" (Rukeyser) **12**:222
"The Dream Flood" (Dickey) **40**:180-81
"A Dream in Three Colors" (McGuckian) **27**:90
"The Dream Language of Fergus" (McGuckian) **27**:83, 88-90
"A Dream Lies Dead" (Parker) **28**:363
The Dream of a Common Language: Poems, 1974-1977 (Rich) **5**:373-76, 378, 384, 389
"The Dream of Angling the Dream of Cool Rain" (Wakoski) **15**:365
"Dream of Berlin" (O'Hara) **45**:163
"A Dream of Burial" (Wright) **36**:313
"A Dream of Comparison" (Smith) **12**:330, 332-33, 345, 352
"Dream of Constantine" (Schnackenberg) **45**:333
"A Dream of Fair Women" (Tennyson) **6**:353, 359-60
"The Dream of Knowledge" (Schwartz) **8**:297, 311
"Dream of Light in the Shade" (Stone) **53**:228
"A Dream of Nourishment" (Smith) **12**:326
"A Dream of Small Children" (Song) **21**:341, 343
"Dream of Summer" (Carducci)
See "Sogno d'estate"
"Dream of the Future" (Jeffers) **17**:141
"The Dream of the Unified Field" (Graham) **59**:137, 151, 159-61, 168, 185
The Dream of the Unified Field: Selected Poems 1974-1994 (Graham) **59**:146, 151, 160, 169, 181-83
"A Dream of What I Missing" (Bly) **39**:42
"A Dream of Whitman Paraphrased, Recognized, and Made More Vivid by Renoir" (Schwartz) **8**:318
"Dream of Wild Birds" (Stone) **53**:229
"Dream of Youth" (Tagore)
See "Yauvan-svapna"
"Dream; or Dream: Logic and 'The Magic Flute'" (Moore) **49**:130, 145
"A Dream or No" (Hardy) **8**:135
"A Dream Pang" (Frost) **39**:230-31, 237, 246
"A Dream (Real)" (Ekeloef) **23**:80
"Dream Variations" (Hughes) **1**:248; **53**:84

"A Dream within a Dream" (Poe) **1**:434
"Dream—August 1979" (Goodison) **36**:148
"Dreamdust" (Hughes) **1**:241
"The Dreame" (Donne) **1**:147, 152
"The Dreame" (Herrick) **9**:109
"Dreamed for Winter" (Rimbaud)
See "Rêve pour l'hiver"
"A Dreamed Realization" (Corso) **33**:48
"The Dreamer" (Pushkin) **10**:407
"The Dreamer" (Tennyson) **6**:372
"Dreamers" (Sassoon) **12**:284, 286
"The Dreamer's Song" (Ortiz) **17**:245
"The Dream-Follower" (Hardy) **8**:108
Dreaming of Butterflies (Hagiwara)
See *Chō o yumemu*
"Dreaming of Hair" (Lee) **24**:242, 247
"The Dreaming Saw" (Char)
See "La Scie rêveuse"
"Dream-Land" (Poe) **1**:433-34, 436, 438; **54**:308
"Dreamland" (Rossetti) **44**:259
"Dreams" (Giovanni) **19**:110
"Dreams" (Jarrell) **41**:168
"Dreams" (Poe) **1**:436
"Dreams about Clothes" (Merrill) **28**:254
"Dreams in War Time" (Lowell) **13**:84
"The Dreams of My Heart" (Teasdale) **31**:59
"Dreams of Suicide," (Meredith) **28**:199, 205
"Dreams Old and Nascent: Old" (Lawrence) **54**:175
"Dreamtigers" (Borges)
See "El hacedor"
Dreamtigers (Borges)
See *El hacedor*
"The Dreamt-Of Place" (Muir) **49**:231, 243, 265
"Drei alte Männer" (Benn) **35**:33, 34
Drei alte Männer (Benn) **35**:34
"Drei Blicke in einen Opal" (Trakl) **20**:261-62
Dresden Forefathers' Eve Wilno Forefathers' Eve (Mickiewicz)
See *Dziady III*
Dressed in Light (Seifert)
See *Světlem oděná*
"Dressing to Wait a Table" (McKay) **2**:205
"Drewniana kostka" (Herbert) **50**:4-7, 17
"Dried Marjoram" (Lowell) **13**:61
"The Drifter off Tarentum" (Kipling) **3**:183
"The Drifter's Escape" (Dylan) **37**:49
"Drifting" (Dickey) **40**:231
Drifting into War (Bissett) **14**:10, 33
"Driftwood" (Teasdale) **31**:359
"Driftwood" (Wilbur) **51**:187, 192, 229
"A Driftwood Altar" (Ashbery) **26**:163
"Driftword" (Brathwaite) **56**:70, 90, 97
"Drink, Eat, Sleep" (Kenyon) **57**:3
"Drink to Me Only with Thine Eyes" (Jonson)
See "Song to Celia"
"Drinker" (Char)
See "Buveuse"
"The Drinker" (Lowell) **3**:212
"Drinking Alone by Moonlight" (Li Po) **29**:188
"Drinking From a Helmet" (Dickey) **40**:155-56, 159-60, 190, 192, 208-9, 231
"The Drive Home" (Merwin) **45**:92
"The Driver" (Dickey) **40**:257-58
"Driving Gloves" (Wakoski) **15**:347
"Driving Home the Cows" (Reese) **29**:330
"Driving My Parents Home at Christmas" (Bly) **39**:86
"Driving through Ohio" (Bly) **39**:6
"Driving to Town Late to Mail a Letter" (Bly) **39**:23
"Driving toward the Lac Qui Parle River" (Bly) **39**:73, 83
"Droga nad przepascic w Czufut-Kale" (Mickiewicz) **38**:222-23
"Drohungen" (Benn) **35**:47
"Droll Husband" (Ignatow) **34**:202
"Dropping Eyelids Among the Aerial Ash" (Ammons) **16**:39
"Drought" (Alexie) **53**:4
"Drought" (Brathwaite) **56**:61
"Drought" (Wright) **14**:353
"Drought Year" (Wright) **14**:366
"The Drowned Child" (Glück) **16**:129-30, 150
"The Drowned Girl" (Szirtes) **51**:178
"The Drowning Poet" (Merrill) **28**:225
"Drowning With Others" (Dickey) **40**:179-80, 206
Drowning with Others (Dickey) **40**:158, 175-77, 180, 182, 190, 204, 206-7, 211-12, 225, 230-32, 257, 261-62
"Drozhzhi mira dorogie" (Mandelstam) **14**:153
"Drug Store" (Shapiro) **25**:268, 295, 319, 322
"Druidic Rimes" (Nemerov) **24**:301
"Drum" (Brathwaite) **56**:75
"A Drumlin Woodchuck" (Frost) **1**:213; **39**:233, 246-47
"Drummer Hodge" (Hardy) **8**:121
"Drumnotes" (Sandburg) **41**:241
"Drums" (Okigbo) **7**:234
Drum-Taps (Whitman) **3**:389, 414, 418
"Drunk Coachman" (Rimbaud)
See "Cocher ivre"
The Drunk in the Furnace (Merwin) **45**:3, 5, 7-9, 18, 24, 27-8, 31, 52, 70-1, 74
A Drunk Man Looks at the Thistle (MacDiarmid) **9**:151-52, 158, 167-70, 173, 175, 181, 186, 189-93
"The Drunkard" (Sitwell) **3**:299
"The Drunkards and the Tavern" (Rumi) **45**:278
"The Drunkard's Child" (Harper) **21**:191, 210, 216
"The Drunkard's Funeral" (Lindsay) **23**:269, 283-84
"The Drunkards in the Streetn" (Lindsay) **23**:284
"Drunken Americans" (Ashbery) **26**:167
The Drunken Boat (Rimbaud)
See *Le bateau ivre*
"The Drunken Fisherman" (Lowell) **3**:199-200, 202, 204, 212
"Dry Hill" (Mahon) **60**:142
"The Dry Salvages" (Eliot) **5**:164-65, 167-69, 180-81, 183, 186, 210
"The Dry Stone Mason" (Merwin) **45**:23
Dry Sun, Dry Wind (Wagoner) **33**:324-25, 364-70, 373
"Dryads" (Sassoon) **12**:240, 275
Du (Stramm) **50**:189-90, 195, 198, 200-202, 204, 206, 208, 214
"Du Bay" (Niedecker) **42**:98, 151
"Du coton dans les oreilles" (Apollinaire) **7**:22
"Du haut de la muraille de Paris" (Hugo) **17**:100
"Du liegst" (Celan) **10**:98
Du mouvement et de l'immobilité de Douve (Bonnefoy) **58**:108-9, 120, 123-24, 127, 130-35, 147, 150, 161, 171, 173, 176
"Du sei wei du" (Celan) **10**:100-01
"Dualidá en una despedida" (Borges) **32**:57, 83
"Dualities" (Abse) **41**:13
"Duality" (Abse) **41**:6, 9
"Duality on Saying Farewell" (Borges)
See "Dualidá en una despedida"
"Dublin" (MacNeice) **61**:109, 118
"Dublin Georgian" (Davie) **29**:110, 120-1
"Dublinesque" (Larkin) **21**:237, 244
"Dubrovnik October 14, 1980, 10:45 p. m." (Ginsberg) **4**:62
"The Duchess Potatoes" (Wakoski) **15**:330
"Duck Blind" (Hass) **16**:217
"A Duck for Dinner" (Stevens) **6**:322
"The Duckpond" (Stryk) **27**:188, 195-97, 202-03, 206
"Ducks" (Bly) **39**:71
Ducks (Bly) **39**:71
"Due donne in cima de la mente mia" (Dante) **21**:74
"Due nel crepuscolo" (Montale) **13**:107, 150
"Due sigarette" (Pavese) **13**:225-28
"Le due Torri" (Carducci) **46**:52
"Duel" (Hagiwara) **18**:167
"A Duel" (Morris) **55**:238
"Du-Gedichte" (Stramm) **50**:198
"The Dug-Out" (Sassoon) **12**:281, 283
Duineser Elegien (Rilke) **2**:268-69, 279-82, 285-87, 294-95
Duino Elegies (Rilke)
See *Duineser Elegien*
Duino Elegies/Elegies (Rilke)
See *Duineser Elegien*
Duke of Albany (Skelton) **25**:330
"Duke: Playing Piano at 70" (Brathwaite) **56**:55, 61
El dulce daño (Storni) **33**:235-36, 240-41, 246-48, 250, 274-77, 283, 287, 297, 307;
"Dulce Et Decorum Est" (Owen) **19**:347, 353, 357, 359-61, 364-65, 370-71
"Dulcia Linquimus Arva" (Borges) **22**:79; **32**:84
"Dull Water Spirit and Protean God" (Thoreau) **30**:216
"Dully Gumption's Addendum" (Hughes) **7**:120
"Dulnesse" (Herbert) **4**:112
"Dulzura" (Mistral) **32**:179
"La dulzura del ángelus" (Darío) **15**:81, 96
"Duma" (Lermontov) **18**:268-69, 279, 281, 283, 297, 304
"The Dump" (Shvarts)
See "Svalka"
"Duncan" (Gunn) **26**:228
"Duncan Gray" (Burns) **6**:57, 59, 100
The Dunciad (Pope) **26**:304-305, 314-17, 319, 321-22, 326-27, 334, 338-40, 357-61
Dunciad in Four Books (Pope) **26**:358-59
Dunciad Minimus (Hope)
See *Dunciad Minor: An Heroick Poem*
Dunciad Minor: An Heroick Poem (Hope) **56**:302
"Dunciad Variorum" (Pope) **26**:356-61
"Duncton Hill" (Belloc) **24**:10, 49
"Dunedin" (Curnow) **48**:12
"The Dungeon" (Wordsworth) **4**:373
"Dunkler Sommer" (Benn) **35**:67, 68
"Duns Scotus" (Lowell) **3**:201
"Duns Scotus's Oxford" (Hopkins) **15**:144
"Dünya Guzeli" (Cavafy) **36**:52
A Durable Fire (Sarton) **39**:340, 342-43
"Duranta asha" (Tagore) **8**:407
"Duration" (Paz) **1**:355
Durch die Stunde (Benn) **35**:6
"Durch jede Stunde" (Benn) **35**:9
"Durchs Erlenholz kam sie entlang gestrichen" (Benn) **35**:45, 50
"Durham in March" (Tomlinson) **17**:361
"During a Solar Eclipse" (Nemerov) **24**:288
"During a Transatlantic Call" (Lowell) **3**:241
"During Fever" (Lowell) **3**:206, 220, 243, 245
"During the Eichmann Trial" (Levertov) **11**:169, 193
"During the Passaic Strike of 1926" (Zukofsky) **11**:351, 396
"During Wind and Rain" (Hardy) **8**:88, 113
"Durwood Collins" (Hughes) **53**:115
"Dusha" (Pasternak) **6**:267, 285
"Dusha moja mrachna" (Lermontov) **18**:302
"Dusk in Winter" (Merwin) **45**:20, 23
"The Dusk of Horses" (Dickey) **40**:190
"Dusk on English Bay" (Birney) **52**:4, 39
"Dusk on the Bay" (Birney) **52**:5-6, 8, 24
"The Dust" (Brathwaite) **56**:69, 76, 84, 95, 100
"Dust" (Brooke) **24**:57
"Dust" (Dickey) **40**:160
"The Dust" (Reese) **29**:330, 333
"Dust" (Wright) **14**:379
"Dust Bowl" (Hughes) **1**:240
"Dust in the Eyes" (Frost) **1**:195
"Dust of Snow" (Frost) **1**:195, 218
"Dusting" (Dove) **6**:111, 113
"The Dustman" (Carman) **34**:200, 213
"Dusty Braces" (Snyder) **21**:293
"Dusza Pana Cogito" (Herbert) **50**:39, 41
"A Dutch Courtyard" (Wilbur) **51**:188, 192-93, 296, 325
"Dutch Graves in Bucks County" (Stevens) **6**:302

"Dutch Interiors" (Kenyon) **57**:26, 38-39, 46
"Dutch Painters" (Zagajewski) **27**:403
"A Dutch Picture" (Longfellow) **30**:71
"Dutiful Beast" (Moore) **49**:118
"Duty is my Lobster" (Smith) **12**:340
"Dva brata" (Lermontov) **18**:299
"Dva sokola" (Lermontov) **18**:288
Dvenadsat (Blok) **21**:8-12, 16-17, 21-2, 26-9, 31, 33-9, 41-3
"Dvukh stanov ne beots, a— esli gost sluchainyi" (Tsvetaeva) **14**:325
Dwarf Bamboo (Chin) **40**:3, 8, 27-8
"Dwie krople" (Herbert) **50**:8
"Dyâli" (Césaire) **25**:40
"Dyddgu" (Dafydd ap Gwilym) **56**:247
"A Dying Art" (Mahon) **60**:132
"Dying Away" (Meredith) **28**:200
"The Dying Bondman" (Harper) **21**:187, 207
"The Dying Christian" (Harper) **21**:208, 215-16
"The Dying Mother" (Harper) **21**:197
"The Dying Queen" (Harper) **21**:198
"The Dying Swan" (Tennyson) **6**:359, 389-91
"The Dykes" (Kipling) **3**:182
"Dynamik" (Benn) **35**:69
"Dynamiter" (Sandburg) **41**:234, 273, 347, 349, 351, 365
The Dynasts: A Drama of the Napoleonic Wars (Hardy) **8**:79-81, 85-7, 95-6, 104, 108, 111, 121-22
The Dynasty of Raghu (Kālidāsa)
See *Raghuvamśa*
"Dyne" (Char) **56**:155
"Dytiscus" (MacDiarmid) **9**:157, 183
"Dyvers Dothe Use" (Wyatt) **27**:316
"Dyvers Thy Death" (Surrey) **59**:327
"Dzhulio" (Lermontov) **18**:300
Dziady III (Mickiewicz) **38**:153-54, 157, 159, 161, 164-65, 167-69, 184, 190-92, 218-19, 229, 231
"D-Zug" (Benn) **35**:35, 46, 47, 54, 77
"E. C. Culbertson" (Masters) **36**:230, 232
"E. P. Ode Pour L'Election de son Sepulchre" (Pound) **4**:319
"E Questo il nido in che la mia Fenice?" (Hope) **56**:281
"Each and All" (Emerson) **18**:84, 94-96, 98-101, 107
"Each Bird Walking" (Gallagher) **9**:44
"Each Day of Summer" (Swenson) **14**:276
"Each of You" (Lorde) **12**:154
"Each One, Pull One" (Walker) **30**:344
"Each Stone" (Ignatow) **34**:325
"Eagle" (Kunitz) **19**:147
"The Eagle" (Tate) **50**:231, 256
"The Eagle and the Mole" (Wylie) **23**:301, 309, 322, 327, 334
"Eagle Confin'd in a College Court" (Smart) **13**:341
"Eagle Descending" (Warren) **37**:357
Eagle or Sun? (Paz)
See *iÁguila o sol?*
"Eagle Poem" (Harjo) **27**:67
"The Eagle That Is Forgotten" (Lindsay) **23**:277, 288, 294, 296
"The Eagle-Feather Fan" (Momaday) **25**:217
"Eagles" (Dickey) **40**:248
The Eagle's Mile (Dickey) **40**:230, 239, 259
"ΕΠΙΝΙΚΙΟΝ" (Cowper) **40**:103
"Ear Muff Tree Ripening" (Birney) **52**:28
"Earliest Memory" (Corso) **33**:44
"The Early Anthropologists" (Mahon) **60**:193
"Early Bright" (Hughes) **53**:191-92
"Early Chronology" (Sassoon) **12**:245
"Early Evening Quarrel" (Hughes) **1**:247; **53**:119
"Early January" (Merwin) **45**:20
"Early Losses: A Requiem" (Walker) **30**:354
"Early Lynching" (Sandburg) **2**:330
"Early March" (Sassoon) **12**:254, 259
"An Early Martyr" (Williams) **7**:353, 368
An Early Martyr, and Other Poems (Williams) **7**:350, 399, 402
"Early Mondrian" (O'Hara) **45**:125
"The Early Morning" (Belloc) **24**:5, 34
"Early Morning: Cape Cod" (Swenson) **14**:276
"The Early Morning Light" (Schwartz) **8**:294
"Early Morning Writings" (Corso) **33**:24
The Early Motion (Dickey) **40**:208-9
"Early Poems" (Noyes) **27**:138
Early Poems (Crane) **3**:90-1
Early Poems, 1935-1955 (Paz) **1**:373, 375; **48**:191, 198, 200, 251
"Early Recollections" (Ní Chuilleanáin) **34**:350, 352
"An Early Unconverted Saint" (Thoreau) **30**:202
Early Verse of Rudyard Kipling, 1877-99: Unpublished, Uncollected, and Rarely Collected Poems (Kipling) **3**:193
Early Writing: 1946-1950 (O'Hara) **45**:127, 130, 153, 155, 222, 224-25
"The Earrings" (Montale)
See "Gli orecchini"
"Ears in the Turrets Hear" (Thomas) **2**:379
"Earth" (Bryant) **20**:4, 17, 19, 35, 47
"The Earth" (Noyes) **27**:129
"The Earth" (Sexton) **2**:372, 374
"Earth" (Toomer) **7**:333
"Earth Again" (Milosz) **8**:209
"Earth and a Wedded Woman" (Meredith) **60**:249
"Earth and Fire" (Berry) **28**:11
"Earth and I Give You Turquoise" (Momaday) **25**:188, 193, 207
"Earth and Its Atmosphere" (Niedecker) **42**:94
"Earth and Man" (Meredith) **60**:256, 279, 290, 296-98, 331, 339
The Earth Compels (MacNeice) **61**:136-37, 181
Earth Deities (Carman) **34**:205, 212
"The Earth Drum" (Dickey) **40**:224, 227
"Earth, earth, you feed on people" (Shvarts) **50**:142
The Earth Gods (Gibran) **9**:71, 75, 80
"The Earth in Snow" (Blok) **21**:4-5
"The Earth is Called Juan" (Neruda)
See "La tierra se llama Juan"
"the Earth Lantern" (Bissett) **14**:7
"Earth Psalm" (Levertov) **11**:170
Earth Took from Earth (Graham) **59**:184
"Earth Triumphant" (Aiken) **26**:7
Earth Triumphant (Aiken) **26**:21, 50
"Earth Walk" (Meredith) **28**:214
Earth Walk: New and Selected Poems (Meredith) **28**:178, 180-81, 194-95, 207, 210, 213-15
"Earth Your Dancing Place" (Swenson) **14**:283
Earthlight (Breton) **15**:73-4
"Earthly Creatures" (Wylie) **23**:311
"Earthly Message" (Mistral)
See "Recado terrestre"
The Earthly Paradise (Morris) **55**:242, 245, 247-54, 257-60, 262, 268, 273-75, 277, 285-87, 289, 291-94, 296-97, 304-9, 311, 314-17, 323, 325, 328-32, 336, 340-41
The Earth-Owl and Other Moon-People (Hughes) **7**:120
"Earthquake" (Stone) **53**:247, 257-58
"Earth's Answer" (Blake) **12**:7, 35, 44
"Earth's Bubbles" (Blok) **21**:14, 24, 31
"Earth's Children Cleave to Earth" (Bryant) **20**:16
"Earth's Lyric" (Carman) **34**:207
"Earth-Song" (Emerson) **18**:79, 88
"Earthy Anecdote" (Stevens) **6**:294
"Earwigs" (Carver) **54**:14
"East Bronx" (Ignatow) **34**:306
"East Coker" (Eliot) **5**:164, 167-69, 171, 179-82, 198, 210
"East Coker" (Roethke) **15**:279
"East of Suez" (Kipling) **3**:179
"East of the Sun and West of the Moon" (Merwin) **45**:6, 29
"East of the Sun West of the Moon" (Wakoski) **15**:348
"East River" (Swenson) **14**:254
East Slope (Paz)
See *Ladera este*
"The East that is Now Pale, the East that is Now Silent" (Bely)
See "Vostok pobledneuskii, vostok onemesvshii"
"East, West, North, and South of a Man" (Lowell) **13**:87
East Wind (Lowell) **13**:76, 84-5
"Eastbourne" (Montale) **13**:106, 109, 120-21, 128-29, 148, 152
An East-End Coffee-Stall (Noyes) **27**:140
"An East-End Curate" (Hardy) **8**:101
"Easter" (Herbert) **4**:100, 120
"Easter" (Kinnell) **26**:238, 279
"Easter" (O'Hara) **45**:130, 135, 137, 148, 191, 242
"Easter" (Studwell)
See "Easter: Wahiawa, 1959"
"Easter, 1916" (Walcott) **46**:307
"Easter 1916" (Yeats) **20**:311, 313-14, 323, 325, 327, 349
"Easter, 1968" (Sarton) **39**:328
Easter Day (Browning) **2**:32, 45, 71-2, 75
"Easter Eve 1945" (Rukeyser) **12**:225
"Easter Greeting" (Niedecker) **42**:109
"Easter Hymn" (Hope) **56**:266, 285
"Easter Hymn" (Housman) **2**:184
"Easter Moon and Owl" (Wright) **14**:373, 375
"Easter Morning" (Ammons) **16**:30-2, 46, 63-4
"Easter Morning" (Sarton) **39**:342
"Easter of the Greeks" (Sikelianos) **29**:366-67
"Easter: Wahiawa, 1959" (Song) **21**:331, 335, 338, 340, 342-43, 350
"Easter Wings" (Herbert) **4**:114, 120, 130
Eastern Lyrics (Hugo)
See *Les orientales*
Eastern Slope (Paz)
See *Ladera este*
"Eastern War Time" (Rich) **5**:398
"Eastport to Block Island" (Rich) **5**:352
"Easy Comedy" (Meredith) **60**:292
"Eating Fire" (Atwood) **8**:27-8
"Eating the Cookies" (Kenyon) **57**:19, 38
"Eating the Dead" (Brathwaite) **56**:11-12, 74, 87, 100
Eating the Honey of Words: New and Selected Poems (Bly) **39**:115, 117
"Eaux-meres" (Char) **56**:184
"The Eavesdropper" (Carman) **34**:203-04, 210-11, 216
"Eavesdropper" (Plath) **37**:258
"Ebar phirao more" (Tagore) **8**:409
"Ébauche d'un serpent" (Valéry) **9**:352-53, 365-67, 371, 374, 384, 387, 390, 394-99
Ebb and Flow (Ishikawa) **10**:212-13, 215
"The Ebb Begins from Dream" (Birney) **52**:21, 36, 92
"éboulis" (Césaire) **25**:45
L'Ecarlate (Char) **56**:111, 115-16
"Ecce homo" (Corso) **33**:26, 41, 47
"Ecce Puer" (Joyce) **22**:140-41, 147-48, 151-52
"The Ecclesiast" (Ashbery) **26**:114
"Ecclesiastes" (Mahon) **60**:182, 216-17, 229
"Ecclesiastes 1:9" (Borges)
See "Eclesiastés 1,9"
Ecclesiastical Sketches (Wordsworth) **4**:399
Ecclesiastical Sonnets (Wordsworth)
See *Ecclesiastical Sketches*
"Echo" (Lorde) **12**:155
"Echo" (Rossetti) **7**:280-81
"Echo" (Tagore)
See "Pratidhyani"
"Echoes" (Carroll) **18**:46
"Echoes" (Jackson) **44**:7
"Echoes and Shadows" (Stone) **53**:244, 257, 259
Echoes from Vagabondia (Carman) **34**:205, 208, 228-29
"The Echoing Green" (Blake) **12**:7

"L'Eclairage du pénitencier" (Char) **56**:134, 151
"L'eclatante victoire de Saarebrück" (Rimbaud) **3**:283
"L'eclatante victorie de Sarrebruck" (Rimbaud) **3**:283
"Eclesiastés 1,9" (Borges) **32**:91
"El eclipse" (Jiménez) **7**:200
Eclipse (Hogan) **35**:247, 255
"Eclogue" (Oppen) **35**:308
"Eclogue" (Ronsard) **11**:262
"Eclogue" (Stevens) **6**:333
"Eclogue 4" (Vergil) **12**:363, 370, 372, 382-85, 392
"Eclogue 6" (Vergil) **12**:365, 371
"Eclogue 10" (Vergil) **12**:370-71
"Eclogue between the Motherless" (MacNeice) **61**:135, 137
"Eclogue by a Five-barred Gate" (MacNeice) **61**:127
"An Eclogue for Christmas" (MacNeice) **61**:124-25, 129
"Eclogue from Iceland" (MacNeice) **61**:107, 133
"Eclogue I: The Months" (Bridges) **28**:67, 84
"Eclogue II" (Bridges) **28**:87-8
"Eclogue IV: Winter" (Brodsky) **9**:22, 28-9
"Eclogue of the Liberal and the Poet" (Tate) **50**:252, 257
"An Eclogue, or Pastorall between Endymion Porter and Lycidas Herrick" (Herrick) **9**:86
"Eclogue V: Summer" (Brodsky) **9**:21, 28
"Eclogues" (Herrick) **9**:89
Eclogues (Petrarch) **8**:246
Eclogues (Vergil)
See *The Eclogues of Virgil*
The Eclogues of Virgil (Vergil) **12**:365, 370-72, 375, 383, 388
"Eclore en hiver" (Char) **56**:141, 156
"Ecologue" (Ginsberg) **4**:54, 82, 85, 89
"Economia de Tahuantinsuyo" (Cardenal) **22**:127-28, 132
"Economic Man" (Nemerov) **24**:289
"Economics and Exodus" (Walcott) **46**:279
"Economy" (Merwin) **45**:8
"The Economy of Tahuantinsuyo" (Cardenal)
See "Economia de Tahuantinsuyo"
Ecopoemas (Parra) **39**:312
Ecopoems (Parra)
See *Ecopoemas*
"Ecoutez la chanson bien douce" (Verlaine) **2**:416
"Écrit sur la Porte" (Perse) **23**:231
"Les Écrits s'en vont" (Breton) **15**:51
"The Ecstasy" (Carruth) **10**:71
"The Ecstasy" (Donne)
See "The Exstasie"
"Ecstatsy" (Mistral)
See "Extasis"
"Eddi's Service" (Kipling) **3**:183
"An Eddy" (Carew) **29**:10, 48
"Eden" (Dickey) **40**:225
"Eden" (Tomlinson) **17**:342, 354
"Eden" (Walcott) **46**:278
"Eden" (Wright) **14**:336, 341
"Eden Bower" (Rossetti) **44**:166-67
"Eden Retold" (Shapiro) **25**:290
"Eden Were Elysium" (Corso) **33**:49
"The Edge" (Char)
See "Seuil"
"The Edge" (Glück) **16**:125, 153
"Edge" (Plath) **1**:391, 393, 397; **37**:232, 258, 267-69
"The Edge" (Stryk) **27**:198, 203
"Edge of Love" (Aleixandre)
See "Filo del amor"
"The Edge of the World" (Silverstein) **49**:312
"Edgehill Fight" (Kipling) **3**:183
Edifico Sayonara (Yau) **61**:334, 348
"Edina, Scotia's Darling Seat!" (Burns) **6**:74
"Edinstvennye dni" (Pasternak) **6**:286
"Editor Whedon" (Masters) **36**:182, 230, 232, 240
"Editorial Impressions" (Sassoon) **12**:268
"Edmonton, thy cemetery . . ." (Smith) **12**:293, 300
"Education" (Madhubuti) **5**:338
"Education a Failure" (Williams) **7**:370
"Education and Government" (Gray)
See "Essay on the Alliance of Education and Government"
"Education by Poetry" (Frost) **39**:241, 253
"An Education in the Eighties" (Stone) **53**:248-49, 257
"Edward Gray" (Tennyson) **6**:358
"Edward III" (Blake)
See "King Edward the Third"
"Edward Munch" (Mahon) **60**:179, 201
"The Eel" (Montale)
See "L'anguilla"
"Eel" (Rukeyser) **12**:211
"The Eemis Stane" (MacDiarmid) **9**:158, 187
"eet me alive" (Bissett) **14**:34
"Efectos del bautismo" (Paz) **48**:210
"Effacement du Peuplier" (Char) **56**:183
"Effacing of the Poplar" (Char)
See "Effacement du Peuplier"
"Les effarés" (Rimbaud) **57**:184, 196, 202-3, 205, 244, 249, 253
"The Effect" (Sassoon) **12**:285
"The effects of baptism" (Paz)
See "Efectos del bautismo"
"The Effectual Marriage" (Loy) **16**:333
"Effet de nuit" (Verlaine) **32**:387
"Effie" (Brown) **55**:110
"Effigy of a Nun" (Teasdale) **31**:371, 389
"Effilage du sac de jute" (Char) **56**:147
"Effort at Speech" (Meredith) **28**:214
Effort at Speech (Meredith) **28**:216-17
"Efforts of Affection" (Moore) **49**:102, 126-27
Efterlämnade dikter (Ekeloef) **23**:78
"L'égalité des sexes" (Éluard) **38**:66
The Egerton Ms (Wyatt) **27**:360
"The Egg" (Glück) **16**:125, 138-39
"The Egg and the Machine" (Frost) **1**:203
"Egg-Head" (Hughes) **7**:116, 118, 135, 140, 161
"Eggs" (Hagiwara) **18**:168
"Eggs" (Olds) **22**:311, 338
"Eggs and Nestlings" (Wright) **14**:348
"Egle" (Carducci) **46**:49, 87
"Ego" (Shapiro) **25**:320
"Ego Tripping" (Giovanni) **19**:118, 123, 141
"The Egoist" (Neruda)
See "El egoísta"
"El egoísta" (Neruda) **4**:290
Egorushka (Tsvetaeva) **14**:326-27
Ego-Tripping and Other Poems for Young People (Giovanni) **19**:123, 136
"Egy ev" (Illyés) **16**:239
"Ehcu Fugaces" (Belloc) **24**:10
"ehre sei der sellerie" (Enzensberger) **28**:140
"The Eichmann Trial" (Levertov)
See "During the Eichmann Trial"
"Eidolon" (Warren) **37**:280, 282-84, 288, 331
"VIII" (Joyce) **22**:144-45, 153, 167, 170, 173
"8 Ahau" (Cardenal)
See "Katun 8 Ahau"
"Eight Balloons" (Silverstein) **49**:331
Eight Days (Seifert)
See *Osm dnů*
"Eight Drinking Immortals" (Tu Fu) **9**:330
"Eight Laments" (Tu Fu) **9**:333-38, 341-42
"Eight Little Dogs" (Mistral)
See "Ocho Perritos"
"Eight Observations on the Nature of Eternity" (Tomlinson) **17**:328
"Eight O'Clock" (Housman) **2**:162, 164, 169, 182
"Eight O'Clock" (Teasdale) **31**:359
"Eight Riddles from Symphosius" (Wilbur) **51**:273, 301
"824. Der Frauen Liebe und Leben" (Benn) **35**:46
"Eight Years After" (Davie) **29**:108
"Eight years after Viet Nam" (Quintana) **36**:257
"XVIII" (Joyce) **22**:145, 165, 167, 169
"1886" (Benn) **35**:71
"18 Nov 71" (Brutus) **24**:123
18 Poems (Thomas) **2**:378, 382, 384; **52**:245, 252, 271, 311
"Eighteen West Eleventh Street" (Merrill) **28**:222, 244, 258
"1887" (Housman) **2**:192, 194
"1805" (Graves) **6**:152
"Eighth Air Force" (Jarrell) **41**:138, 171, 173-74, 177, 189, 204-5
"The Eighth Crusade" (Masters) **1**:330
"Eighth Duino Elegy" (Rilke) **2**:291, 293
Eighth Isthmian (Pindar)
See *Isthmian 8*
Eighth Olympian (Pindar)
See *Olympian 8*
Eighth Pythian (Pindar)
See *Pythian 8*
80 Flowers (Zukofsky) **11**:392
Eighty-Five Poems (MacNeice) **61**:141
"84th Street, Edmonton" (Atwood) **8**:9
"Eikon Basilike" (Howe) **54**:134-35
"Einsamer nie—" (Benn) **35**:8, 20
Einstein (MacLeish) **47**:125, 127, 130, 136, 154, 183, 185-87, 191-92, 194-95, 215-17, 220-22, 239
"Einstein Freud & Jack" (Nemerov) **24**:302
"Einzelheiten" (Benn) **35**:8
"Der Einzige" (Hölderlin) **4**:150, 156, 166
"Eisenhower's Visit to Franco, 1959" (Wright) **36**:284, 358
"Ejercicios respiratorios" (Parra) **39**:272
Ejercicios respiratorios (Parra) **39**:278
"Ejercicios retóricos" (Parra) **39**:268
"Ekloga 4-aya: Zimnyaya" (Brodsky)
See "Eclogue IV: Winter"
"The Elderly Nun" (Shvarts)
See "Staritsa"
"Eldorado" (Poe) **1**:433, 439
Eleanor Rumming (Skelton)
See *The Tunnynge of Elynour Rummynge*
"Eleanore" (Tennyson) **6**:350
"Elected Silence" (Sassoon) **12**:258
"Electra en la niebla" (Mistral) **32**:208-10
"Electra on Azalea Path" (Plath) **1**:410-11; **37**:214-15, 217, 219-20, 243-44, 246, 248-50
"Electra-Orestes" (H. D.) **5**:305
"Electric Drills" (Yau) **61**:329, 337, 340-41, 343, 345
"Electric Elegy" (Zagajewski) **27**:389
"The Electric Tram" (Noyes) **27**:122
"Electrical Storm" (Hayden) **6**:186, 194-95
"Elegía" (Borges) **22**:95; **32**:58, 90
Elegía (Neruda) **4**:287
Elegía a Jacques Roumain (Guillén) **23**:133
"Elegía a Jesús Menéndez" (Guillén) **23**:100-101, 125
"Elegía a un joven muerto en el frente" (Paz) **1**:352; **48**:179
"Elegia del Monte Spluga" (Carducci) **46**:51, 89
"Elegía moderna del motivo cursi" (Guillén) **23**:109-10, 128
Elegia na odejscie (Herbert) **50**:36, 40-41
"Elegia podróżna" (Szymborska)
See "Rachunek Elegijny"
"Elegiac Calculation" (Szymborska)
See "Rachunek Elegijny"
"Elegiac Feelings American" (Corso) **33**:19, 36, 54
Elegiac Feelings American (Corso) **33**:18, 35-7, 44, 49, 50
"An Elegiac Fragment" (Duncan) **2**:101
"Elegiac Poem" (Yakamochi)
See "Bankashi"

"An Elegiac Poem on the Death of George Whitefield" (Wheatley) **3**:336, 340, 343, 348
"Elegiac Stanzas" (Wordsworth) **4**:406-07
"Elegiac Verse vi" (Longfellow) **30**:41
"Elegiac Verses" (Longfellow) **30**:41
"Elegiacs" (Tennyson) **6**:385
"Elegíade los portones" (Borges) **32**:84
"Élégie" (Gautier) **18**:135
"Elegie" (Goethe) **5**:248, 251
"Elegie IV: The Perfume" (Donne) **1**:130
"Elegie VIII: The Comparison" (Donne) **1**:124
"Elegie XI: The Bracelet" (Donne) **1**:122
"Elegie XII: His parting from her" (Donne) **1**:130
"Elegie XVI: On his mistris" (Donne) **1**:130
"Elegie à Cassandre" (Ronsard) **11**:246, 248
"L'Elégie à Guillaume des Autels sur le Tumulte d'Amboise" (Ronsard) **11**:248
"Elegie à Hélène" (Ronsard) **11**:229
"l'elegie à J. Hurault, sieur de la pitardière" (Ronsard) **11**:249
"Elegie á Janet, peintre du Roi" (Ronsard) **11**:243, 247
"L'elégie à Lovs de Masures" (Ronsard) **11**:248
"Elégie à Marie Stuart" (Ronsard) **11**:224, 237
"Elegie A M. A. De Muret" (Ronsard) **11**:246, 248
"Elegie à son livre" (Ronsard) **11**:248
"Elegie au Seigneur Baillon, trésorier de l'Epargne du Roi" (Ronsard) **11**:249
"Elegie au Seigneur L'Huillier" (Ronsard) **11**:242
"Elégie de minuit" (Senghor) **25**:255
"Elégie des circoncis" (Senghor) **25**:255
"Elégie des eaux" (Senghor) **25**:255, 258
"Elégie des Saudades" (Senghor) **25**:233
"Elegie du printemps" (Ronsard) **11**:242, 250
"Elegie du Verre à Jan Brinon" (Ronsard) **11**:247
"Elegie en forme d'épitaphe d'Antoine Chateignier" (Ronsard) **11**:246, 248
"An Elegie on the La: Pen: sent to my Mistresse out of France" (Carew) **29**:61-62, 71-73
"Elegie on the Lady Jane Pawlet, Marchion: of Winton" (Jonson) **17**:206
"Elégie pour Georges Pompidou" (Senghor) **25**:254-55, 257-59
"Elégie pour Jean-Marie" (Senghor) **25**:255-56, 259
"Elégie pour Martin Luther King" (Senghor) **25**:258
"An Elegie upon that Honourable and renowned Knight Sir Philip Sidney, who was untimely slaine at the Seige of Zutphon, Anno1586" (Bradstreet) **10**:31, 48, 54
"An Elegie upon the Death of the Deane of Pauls, Dr. John Donne" (Carew) **29**:17, 22, 63, 75
"Elegie upon the untimely death of the incomparable Prince Henry" (Donne) **1**:122
"Elegier I" (Ekeloef) **23**:76
"The Elegies" (Borges) **32**:94
Elegies (Donne) **1**:129-30, 147
Elegies (Jiménez)
See *Elejías*
Elegies (Ovid)
See *Tristia*
Elegies (Rilke) **2**:280-82, 285-87, 294
Elegies (Rukeyser) **12**:207, 211-13
"Elegies And Epistles" (Wylie) **23**:311
"Elegies for Paradise Valley" (Hayden) **6**:191-92, 194-95
Elégies majeures (Senghor) **25**:254-56, 258
Elegies of Gloom (Ovid)
See *Tristia*
The Elegies of Jutting Rock (Elytis)
See *Ta eleýa tis Oxópetras*
"Elegies on the Cardinal Points" (Shvarts) **50**:139
"Èlegiia na rentgenovskii snimok moego cherepa" (Shvarts) **50**:132, 140, 145, 147, 160
"Elegija" (Pushkin) **10**:413-14
"Elegy" (Angelou) **32**:28
"Elegy" (Berry) **28**:14-17, 19, 31
"Elegy" (Borges)
See "Elegía"
"Elegy" (Bridges) **28**:67, 87
"Elegy" (Ekeloef)
See *En Mölna-elegi*
"Elegy" (Hacker) **47**:79
"Elegy" (Heaney) **18**:241-43
"The Elegy" (Hope) **56**:304, 306
"Elegy" (Jonson) **17**:175
"Elegy" (Marvell)
See "Poem upon the Death of O. C."
"Elegy" (Pushkin)
See "Elegija"
"Elegy" (Roethke) **15**:267
"Elegy" (Tate) **50**:256, 319
"Elegy" (Thomas) **52**:277, 327
"Elegy" (Walcott) **46**:228-30, 273, 275-76, 285-86
"Elegy" (Walker) **20**:278-79
"Elegy" (Zagajewski) **27**:396
Elegy (Neruda)
See *Elegía*
"Elegy before Death: At Settignano" (Day Lewis) **11**:151
"Elegy fo Chloe Nguyen" (Chin) **40**:9
"Elegy for a Dead Soldier" (Shapiro) **25**:263, 269, 277, 279-80, 288-89, 295, 310, 316
"Elegy for a Firtree" (Wagoner) **33**:357
"Elegy for a friend killed in the civil war" (Paz)
See "Elegía a un joven muerto en el frente"
"Elegy for a Long-haired Student" (Stryk) **27**:203
"Elegy for a Nature Poet" (Nemerov) **24**:293
"Elegy for a Woman Who Remembered Everything" (Wagoner) **33**:348
"Elegy for a Youth Changed to a Swan" (Boland) **58**:37
"Elegy for Alto" (Okigbo) **7**:231, 235, 244
"An Elegy for D. H. Lawrence" (Williams) **7**:350, 354-55
An Elegy for Departure (Herbert)
See *Elegia na odejscie*
"Elegy for Eugenesis" (Tate) **50**:319
"Elegy for Father Stephen" (Merton) **10**:344
"An Elegy for Five Old Ladies" (Merton) **10**:333, 343
"Elegy for Georges Pompidon" (Senghor)
See "Elégie pour Georges Pompidou"
"Elegy for Jane" (Roethke) **15**:309
"Elegy for Jean-Marie" (Senghor)
See "Elégie pour Jean-Marie"
"Elegy for John Donne" (Brodsky)
See "The Great Elegy for John Donne"
"Elegy for Martin Luther King" (Senghor)
See "Elégie pour Martin Luther King"
"Elegy for Minor Poets" (MacNeice) **61**:115
"Elegy for N. N." (Milosz) **8**:186, 207
"Elegy: For Robert Lowell" (Brodsky) **9**:7, 8
"Elegy for Slit-Drum" (Okigbo) **7**:233, 235, 244
"Elegy for the Monastery Barn" (Merton) **10**:331, 342, 349
"An Elegy for the Poet Morgan Blum" (Wright) **36**:335, 341-42
"Elegy for Thelonious" (Komunyakaa) **51**:33
"Elegy for Y. Z." (Milosz) **8**:174, 198, 203
"Elegy in a Firelit Room" (Wright) **36**:279, 373
"Elegy in a Spider's Web" (Jackson) **44**:5, 103
Elegy in April and September (Owen) **19**:366
"Elegy: Jefferson Davis, 1818-1889" (Tate) **50**:306
"Elegy of Fortinbras" (Herbert)
See "Tren Fortynbrasa"
"Elegy of the Circumcised" (Senghor)
See "Elégie des circoncis"
"An Elegy of the Impossible Memory" (Borges) **32**:58
"Elegy of the Waters" (Senghor)
See "Elégie des eaux"
"Elegy of the Wind" (Okigbo) **7**:235
"Elegy: On a Lady Whom Grief for the Death of Her Betrothed Killed" (Bridges) **28**:87
"Elegy on an X-Ray of My Skull" (Shvarts)
See "Èlegiia na rentgenovskii snimok moego cherepa"
Elegy on Dead Fashion (Sitwell) **3**:295, 300, 304
"Elegy on my Father" (Curnow) **48**:4, 44-46, 51
"Elegy on Poor Mailie" (Burns)
See "The Death and Dying Words of Poor Mailie"
"Elegy on the Death of King James" (Finch) **21**:169
"Elegy on the Death of Robert Ruisseaux" (Burns) **6**:67
"Elegy on the Dust" (Gunn) **26**:190-191, 193, 203
"Elegy on the Ruins of Pickworth Rutlandshire Hastily composed and written with a Pencil on the Spot'" (Clare) **23**:12
"Elegy: The Summer-House on the Mound" (Bridges) **28**:80, 84
"Elegy to a young man killed on the front" (Paz)
See "Elegía a un joven muerto en el frente"
"Elegy to gates" (Borges)
See "Elegíade los portones"
"Elegy to Mount Spluga" (Carducci)
See "Elegia del Monte Spluga"
"Elegy to the Memory of an Unfortunate Lady" (Jonson) **17**:206
"Elegy to the Memory of an Unfortunate Lady" (Pope) **26**:314, 319, 324
"Elegy Written in a Country Churchyard" (Gray) **2**:134-37, 139-43, 145, 148, 151-52, 155
"Elegy Written in a Suburban Churchyard" (Wagoner) **33**:355
"Elegy Written on a Frontporch" (Shapiro) **25**:295
"Elegy XLII" (Jonson)
See *The Under-Wood XLII*
Elejías (Jiménez) **7**:184
"Element" (Page) **12**:168, 170
"Elemental Metamorphosis" (Kunitz) **19**:155
The Elemental Odes (Neruda)
See *Odas elementales*
Elementary Odes (Neruda)
See *Odas elementales*
"The Elementary Scene" (Jarrell) **41**:153, 169
"The Elements" (Bradstreet)
See "The Four Elements"
"The Elements" (Emerson) **18**:77
"The Elements" (Yau) **61**:335
"Elements And Angels" (Wylie) **23**:311
The Elements of San Joaquin (Soto) **28**:369, 371, 373, 376, 383-85
"The Elements of the Poem" (Char) **56**:144-45
"Eleonora Duse" (Lowell) **13**:91
"Elephant" (Goodison) **36**:155
"Elephants" (Moore) **4**:235, 260; **49**:94, 106, 108, 117, 119, 130
"Eleutheria" (Wright) **36**:289
"Elevated" (McHugh) **61**:191
"Elévation" (Baudelaire) **1**:46, 70
"Elevator Boy" (Hughes) **1**:263; **53**:181
"XI" (Joyce) **22**:136, 138, 145, 164, 169-70
"Eleven" (MacLeish) **47**:145, 164-65, 197, 212-13
"Eleven O'Clock at Night" (Bly) **39**:99
Eleven Poems on the Same Theme (Warren) **37**:286, 288, 322-24, 332, 380
"Eleven Times a Poem" (Corso) **33**:18, 24
"11/8" (Williams) **7**:368

"11Outlined Epitaphs" (Dylan) **37**:54, 68
"The 11th: and Last Booke of the Ocean to Scinthia" (Raleigh) **31**:228, 300-06
"Eleventh Century Doors" (Kumin) **15**:180
"11th Floor, West 4th Street" (Swenson) **14**:261
Eleventh Nemean (Pindar)
See *Nemean 11*
Eleventh Olympian (Pindar)
See *Olympian 11*
Eleventh Pythian (Pindar)
See *Pythian 11*
"El-Hajj Malik El-Shabazz" (Hayden) **6**:176, 180-81, 187, 196
"Eliduc" (Marie de France) **22**:239, 245, 248, 258, 265, 268-75, 278, 281-82, 294
"Elijah Browning" (Masters) **36**:191
Elinor Rumming (Skelton)
See *The Tunnynge of Elynour Rummynge*
"Élisabeth petite fille" (Char) **56**:120
"Elite Profession" (Yakamochi) **48**:100
"The Elixir" (Herbert) **4**:134
"Eliza Harris" (Harper) **21**:190, 192, 194, 201, 204-05, 215
"Elizabeth" (Ondaatje) **28**:292
"Elizabeth" (Poe) **1**:446
"Elizabeth Gone" (Sexton) **2**:359
Elk Heads on the Wall (Ríos) **57**:312
"The Elk Song" (Hogan) **35**:257
"Ella Mason and Her Eleven Cats" (Plath) **37**:253
"Ellen Hanging Clothes" (Reese) **29**:330, 348
"Elliott Hawkins" (Masters) **36**:230
"Ellsmereland" (Birney) **52**:79
"Elm" (Plath) **1**:390, 394
"Elm" (Stryk) **27**:212
"Elms" (Glück) **16**:152
"Eloa" (Vigny) **26**:391, 398, 411
Eloge d'une Soupçonnée (Char) **56**:163, 184-85, 189-90, 194
Éloges (Perse) **23**:209-11, 217, 222, 229-32, 234, 237, 241-43, 254
"Elogio de la seguidilla" (Darío) **15**:114
"Elogio de la sombra" (Borges) **32**:62, 140
Elogio de la sombra (Borges) **22**:71, 75-6; **32**:38, 41, 57, 59, 61, 66, 86, 88-9, 111, 116
"Elohim merakhem 'al yaldei hagan" (Amichai) **38**:5, 12, 14, 53
"Eloisa to Abelard" (Pope) **26**:318-19, 326, 339
Eloisa to Abelard (Pope) **26**:304
"Eloquence d'Orion" (Char) **56**:145
Elpenor (MacLeish) **47**:254
"Elsa Wertman" (Masters) **36**:171
"Elsewhere" (Sassoon) **12**:252
"A Elvire" (Lamartine) **16**:290
"Elvis Presley" (Gunn) **26**:219
Elynour Rummyng (Skelton)
See *The Tunnynge of Elynour Rummynge*
"Elysian Fields" (Hacker) **47**:103, 107
"Em quanto quis Fortuna que tivesse" (Camões) **31**:24
"The Emancipators" (Jarrell) **41**:143, 179
Emaux et camées (Gautier) **18**:127-28, 130, 138, 146, 154, 156, 158-59, 161, 164
"Embankment at Night, Before the War: Outcasts" (Lawrence) **54**:221-22
"Embarking on the Study of Anglo-Saxon Grammar" (Borges) **32**:94
Embassy Poetry Reading (Hacker) **47**:113
"Emblems" (Tate) **50**:230-31, 255
Emblems of a Season of Fury (Merton) **10**:334, 343, 349-51
"Emblems of Conduct" (Crane) **3**:82
"The Embrace" (Glück) **16**:156
"Emerald" (Doty) **53**:60-61
"The Emerald" (Merrill) **28**:222, 244, 257
Emerald Ice: Selected Poems 1962-1987 (Wakoski) **15**:370, 372
"Emergency Clinic" (Ignatow) **34**:286, 318
"Emergency Haying" (Carruth) **10**:91
"The Emergency Maker" (Wagoner) **33**:327
Emergency Poems (Parra) **39**:263, 270, 279, 287, 292, 306, 308-12
"TH EMERGENCY WARD" (Bissett) **14**:10-11, 17, 34
"Emerson" (Borges) **32**:45, 113-14, 116
"Emigrada judía" (Mistral) **32**:186
"L'emigrant de Landor Road" (Apollinaire) **7**:42, 47
"Emigranten" (Ekeloef) **23**:61
"The Emigrants" (Brathwaite) **56**:28, 99
"Emilie vor ihrem Brauttag" (Hölderlin) **4**:141
"Emily Before Her Wedding" (Hölderlin)
See "Emilie vor ihrem Brauttag"
"Emily Brontë" (Bridges) **28**:88
"Emily Brosseau" (Masters) **1**:333
"Emily Dickinson" (Tate) **50**:308
"Emily Hardcastle, Spinster" (Ransom) **61**:271, 274, 301, 303, 306
"Emily Sparks" (Masters) **1**:327, 347; **36**:169, 172, 183
"Emma and Eginhard" (Longfellow) **30**:63
"Empathy Again" (Stone) **53**:258
"Empedocles" (Meredith) **60**:250, 295
Empedocles (Hölderlin)
See *Empedokles*
"Empedocles on Etna" (Arnold) **5**:5, 9-10, 12, 23, 35-6, 42-3, 45, 50-1, 56-7
Empedocles on Etna, and Other Poems (Arnold) **5**:2, 25, 30, 35, 42, 50, 55, 57
Empedokles (Hölderlin) **4**:146
"Empeoro y mejoro" (Fuertes) **27**:15
"The Emperor of Ice-Cream" (Stevens) **6**:293, 296
"The Emperor's Dream" (Herbert) **50**:4, 31
"The Emperor's Entry into Rome" (Gower) **59**:58
"The Emperor's New Sonnet" (Villa) **22**:351
"Emperors of the Island" (Abse) **41**:6
"An Emphasis Falls on Reality" (Guest) **55**:196, 198
"Empire" (Graham) **59**:186
"Empire Builders" (MacLeish) **47**:146, 189
Empire Burlesque (Dylan) **37**:59
"Employment I" (Herbert) **4**:100, 111
"Employment II" (Herbert) **4**:111, 131
"Employments" (Herbert) **4**:100
"Emplumada" (Cervantes) **35**:104, 107, 113, 114, 115, 119, 121, 134
Emplumada (Cervantes) **35**:103, 104, 105, 106, 107, 108, 109, 110, 112, 113, 115, 119, 120, 121, 123, 127, 128, 129, 130, 132, 133, 134, 135
"Emporium" (Shapiro) **25**:295
Empty Chestnuts (Matsuo Bashō)
See *Minashi Guri*
"Empty Drawing Room" (Borges)
See "Sala vacía"
Empty Mirror (Ginsberg) **4**:48, 73, 80, 91; **47**:31, 46
"An Empty Place" (Bly) **39**:87
"The Empty Purse" (Meredith) **60**:254, 256, 259, 328, 335
"Empty talk" (Borges)
See "Vanilocuencia"
"An Empty Threat" (Frost) **39**:246
"Empty White Blotch on Map of Universe: A Possible View" (Warren) **37**:383
"Empty Words" (Cage) **58**:183
Empty Words: Writings, '73-'78 (Cage) **58**:183, 185-88, 191-92, 195-99, 203, 205, 207, 212, 220
"En avant" (Péret) **33**:230
"En bateau" (Verlaine) **2**:431; **32**:350, 389-91
"En dröm" (Ekeloef) **23**:57, 76
"En la Ausencia" (Fuertes) **27**:44
"En la plaza" (Aleixandre) **15**:6, 11-12, 17
"En las constelaciones" (Darío) **15**:99, 101
En las orillas del Sar (Castro) **41**:79-85, 87, 96-106, 111-14, 116, 118
En natt i Otocăc (Ekeloef) **23**:63, 69, 76
En natt på horisonten (Ekeloef) **23**:77
En natt vid horisonten (Ekeloef) **23**:62, 89
"En patinant" (Verlaine) **32**:349-50, 391
"En pocas palabras" (Fuertes) **27**:49
"En que describe racionalmente los efectos irracionales del amor" (Juana Inés de la Cruz) **24**:186
En självbiografi (Ekeloef) **23**:90
"En sourdine" (Verlaine) **32**:351, 354, 393
"En suma" (Guillén) **35**:229
En trente-trois morceaux (Char) **56**:142-43, 159
"En Trinacria" (Darío) **15**:107-09
"En último término" (Guillén) **35**:232
En un vasto dominio (Aleixandre) **15**:4, 7, 11-12, 17, 34, 41
"En una primavera" (Storni) **33**:278;
"En vano tu canto suena" (Juana Inés de la Cruz) **24**:225
"En värld är varje människa" (Ekeloef) **23**:57
"En verklighet" (Ekeloef) **23**:76
"En vertu de l'amour" (Éluard) **38**:78
Enamels and Cameos (Gautier)
See *Emaux et camées*
"El enamorado" (Borges) **22**:95; **32**:65-6
"The Enamoured Sage" (Meredith) **60**:328
"An Encampment at Morning" (Merwin) **45**:53
"Encargo a Blanca" (Mistral) **32**:184-85, 189
"The Enchanted Island" (Noyes) **27**:121-23
"The Enchanted knight" (Muir) **49**:204
"Enchanter's Handmaiden" (Wylie) **23**:324
"The Enchantment of the Flat Stone" (Castro)
See "O encanta da Pedra Chan"
"Enchantment through Fire" (Blok) **21**:20
"The Enclosure" (Dickey) **40**:175, 180, 189, 224
"Encore eux" (Char) **56**:189
"An Encounter" (Frost) **39**:232, 241
"The Encounter" (Glück) **16**:167
"Encounter" (Guillén) **35**:218
"Encounter" (Pavese) **13**:202
"Encounter" (Wright) **14**:374
"Encounter at a Greyhound bus station" (Abse) **41**:31
Encounter in April (Sarton) **39**:318, 320, 326, 329, 334, 345, 349-51, 353-56
"Encounter in August" (Kumin) **15**:209
"Encounter in the Cage Country" (Dickey) **40**:150, 152, 161, 168-69, 232
Encounters (Aleixandre) **15**:4
"Encoures au Lecteur" (Ronsard) **11**:249
"El encuentro" (Mistral) **32**:175
"End" (Hughes) **1**:240
"The End" (Merwin) **45**:42
"The End" (Owen) **19**:334
"The End" (Pasternak) **6**:268
"An End" (Rossetti) **7**:280
"The End" (Tomlinson) **17**:340
"The End and the Beginning" (Szymborska) **44**:305
The End and the Beginning (Szymborska) **44**:280, 286, 292, 298, 303-04, 306, 308
"An End in Spring" (Merwin) **45**:9, 22, 32
"The End of 1968" (Montale)
See "Fine del '68"
The End of a Fine Epoch (Brodsky)
See *Konets prekrasnoy epokhi*
"The End of a Journey" (Hope) **56**:278, 299, 303
"End of a Year" (Lowell) **3**:228
"End of Another Home Holiday" (Lawrence) **54**:187
"The End of Antony" (Cavafy) **36**:40
The End of Beauty (Graham) **59**:130-39, 142-43, 151-52, 154-59, 161, 168-69, 171, 173, 179, 184, 187-93, 195
"The End of March" (Bishop) **3**:48-9, 72; **34**:54, 131
"End of Play" (Graves) **6**:137
"The End of Science Fiction" (Mueller) **33**:176
"End of Season" (Warren) **37**:284, 287, 332
"End of Summer" (Amichai) **38**:34
"End of Summer" (Kunitz) **19**:186
"End of Summer ... 1969" (Stone) **53**:218
"The End of the 22 Boock, entreatings of Sorrow" (Raleigh) **31**:246

"The End of the Boockes, of the Ocean Love to Scinthia, and the Beginninge of the 22 Boock Entreating of Sorrow" (Raleigh) **31**:240, 258, 301
"The End of the Episode" (Hardy) **8**:91
"The End of the Owls" (Enzensberger) **28**:142, 147
"The End of the Rainbow" (Jarrell) **41**:155-58, 160, 163-64, 170-71, 215-16, 218
"The End of the Search" (Masters) **1**:344
"The End of the World" (Glück) **16**:152
"End of the World" (Jeffers) **17**:141
"The End of the World" (MacLeish) **47**:130, 143, 158, 164, 178, 185, 196, 213
"End of the World: Weekend, near Toronto" (Atwood) **8**:13
"End of the Year" (Tagore)
See "Varshashesh"
"End of the Year 1912" (Hardy) **8**:124
"The End of Your Life" (Levine) **22**:214
Endeavors of Infinite Man (Neruda)
See *Tentativa del hombre infinito*
"Endecasílabo" (Parra) **39**:272
"An Ending" (Kipling) **3**:194
"Endings" (Boland) **58**:53
"Endings" (Walcott) **46**:236, 240
The Endless Cueca Dance (Parra)
See *La cueca larga*
"Endless Life" (Ferlinghetti) **1**:180, 182-83, 185
Endless Life: Selected Poems (Ferlinghetti) **1**:180, 182, 184-85
"Endor" (Nemerov) **24**:261
"Ends" (Frost) **1**:213
"Endurance" (Forché) **10**:141-42, 144, 147, 156
"Endymion" (Longfellow) **30**:103
"Endymion" (Nemerov) **24**:259
Endymion (Keats)
See *Endymion: A Poetic Romance*
Endymion: A Poetic Romance (Keats) **1**:275-79, 282, 288, 290-91, 308-09, 311, 313-14
"The Enemies" (Cavafy) **36**:94, 95-97, 99
"Enemies" (Sassoon) **12**:242
Enemies: Poems 1934-36 (Curnow) **48**:24, 26
"Enemigo" (Guillén) **35**:228
"Energies" (Boland) **58**:53
"Enfance" (Rimbaud) **3**:262, 265; **57**:184, 236, 238-39, 243, 249-50, 278, 294
"Enfance I" (Rimbaud) **57**:283-84
"Enfance III" (Rimbaud) **57**:227
"Enfance V" (Rimbaud) **57**:281
"L'Enfant grect" (Hugo) **17**:75
"Les Enfants du quadrilatère" (Péret) **33**:201
"Enfermera de pulpos" (Fuertes) **27**:8, 26
"Engaged" (Paz)
See "Los novios"
"The Engagement" (Swenson) **14**:265
"Engführung" (Celan) **10**:96, 99, 117
"The Engine Drain" (Smith) **12**:327
"England" (Borges) **32**:58
"England" (Davie) **29**:98-99, 103
"England" (Moore) **4**:251; **49**:95, 97, 102
"England 1830" (Clare) **23**:37
"England: An Ode" (Swinburne) **24**:312
"England Before the Storm" (Meredith) **60**:250
"England in 1819" (Shelley) **14**:210
"Englisches Café" (Benn) **35**:46, 47, 67
"The English" (Hughes) **53**:115
An English Apocalypse (Szirtes) **51**:173, 175, 179
English as a Second Language (Mueller)
See *Second Language*
English Bards and Scotch Reviewers (Byron) **16**:77, 82
"The English Bull Dog, Dutch Mastiff, and Quail" (Smart) **13**:348
"English Cocker: Old and Blind" (Warren) **37**:341
"The English Flag" (Kipling) **3**:157, 161
"An English Garden in Austria" (Jarrell) **41**:154, 174, 196
"The English Graves" (Chesterton) **28**:99
"English Horn" (Montale)
See "Corno Inglese"
"English Idylls" (Tennyson) **6**:409
"English Lessons" (Pasternak) **6**:251
"English Poem" (Borges) **32**:58
"An English Revenant" (Davie) **29**:108
"English Thornton" (Masters) **36**:199
"An English Wood" (Graves) **6**:144, 166
"English Words" (Szirtes) **51**:169, 177
The English Works of George Herbert (Herbert) **4**:103
"The Englishman in Italy" (Browning) **2**:62
"The Englishman in Sorrento" (Browning) **2**:38
"An Enigma" (Poe) **1**:446
"Enigma for an Angel" (Brodsky) **9**:2
"Enivrez-vous" (Baudelaire) **1**:58
"The Enkindled Spring" (Lawrence) **54**:175
"Ennui" (Viereck) **27**:263
Enoch Arden (Tennyson) **6**:360, 365
"Enoch Dunlap" (Masters) **36**:182
"Enough" (Teasdale) **31**:322
"Enough" (Yamada) **44**:350, 351
"Enough: Jamestown, 1607-1957" (Moore) **4**:260; **49**:132-33, 141, 150
Enough Rope (Parker) **28**:345-48, 351, 353, 356-57, 359-61
"The Enquiry" (Philips) **40**:296
"Enriching the Earth" (Berry) **28**:11, 43
"Enryo" (Yamada) **44**:333-34, 346
"Enter No (Silence Is the Blood Whose Flesh)" (Cummings) **5**:111
"Entering the Kingdom of the Moray Eel" (Wright) **36**:358, 378
"Entering the Temple in Nîmes" (Wright) **36**:359
"L'enterrement" (Verlaine) **2**:431
"L'enthousiasme" (Lamartine) **16**:276, 290
The Enthusiastic Slinger (Neruda)
See *El hondero entusiasta, 1923-1924*
Enthussiasts' Highway (Yevtushenko) **40**:349
The Entire Son (Guillén)
See *El son entero*
"Entirely" (MacNeice) **61**:139
"Entrada a la madera" (Neruda) **4**:277, 306-07
"Entrance into Wood" (Neruda)
See "Entrada a la madera"
"Entre autres" (Éluard) **38**:70
"Entre autres Ombres" (Éluard) **38**:85
"Entre la piedra y la flor" (Paz) **48**:229
Entre la piedra y la flor (Paz) **1**:369; **48**:177, 185, 244
"Entre Lo Que Veo y Digo..." (Paz) **48**:189, 250-51, 273
Entries (Berry) **28**:30-1
"Entropy" (Mahon) **60**:134, 138
"Entry in an Album" (Lermontov) **18**:302
"Entwurf einer Hymne an die Madonna" (Hölderlin) **4**:150
"The Envelope" (Kumin) **15**:203, 207, 221-22
"Envoi" (Boland) **58**:4, 6, 29, 35, 48
"Envoi" (Ignatow) **34**:324
"Envoi" (Meredith) **28**:174, 187
"Envoi" (Ungaretti)
See "Commiato"
"Envoi" (Wilbur) **51**:273
"Envoûtement à La Renardière" (Char) **56**:150
"Envoy" (Johnson) **24**:145
"The Envoy of Mr. Cogito" (Herbert)
See "Przeslanie Pana Cogito"
"Envoy to Africa" (Hughes) **53**:115
Envoy to Bukton (Chaucer) **58**:231, 279, 369
"The Envoys" (Merrill) **28**:220
"Envy" (H. D.) **5**:305
"Envy" (Yevtushenko) **40**:344
"The Eolian Harp" (Coleridge)
See "The Aeolian Harp"
"Ephemera" (Lowell) **13**:74
"Ephemera" (Yeats) **20**:337
"Ephemerid" (Loy) **16**:316
"Ephemeron" (Carman) **34**:209
"Ephyphatha" (MacDiarmid) **9**:156
"L'épi de cristal égrène dans les herbes sa moisson transparente" (Char) **56**:156
"Epic" (Kavanagh) **33**:81, 100, 103, 142, 145-7
"Epidaurus" (Birney) **52**:78
"Epidermal Macabre" (Roethke) **15**:272
"Epigram" (Cowper) **40**:103
"Epigram I" (Rexroth) **20**:180
"Epigram CI" (Jonson) **17**:158, 167, 173, 175, 182, 189-90, 208
"Epigram CII" (Jonson) **17**:157, 197
"Epigram CIII" (Jonson) **17**:197-98, 202
"Epigram CIV" (Jonson) **17**:202
"Epigram CVII" (Jonson) **17**:166
"Epigram CVIII" (Jonson) **17**:166
"Epigram CXVI" (Jonson) **17**:164
"Epigram CXXIV" (Jonson) **17**:193
"Epigram CXXXIII" (Jonson) **17**:189
"Epigram IV" (Jonson) **17**:156
"Epigram LIX" (Jonson) **17**:164
"Epigram LXV" (Jonson) **17**:157, 197
"Epigram LXXVI" (Jonson) **17**:159, 174, 192, 198, 200, 205, 214
"Epigram on Lady Elizabeth" (Jonson)
See "Epigram CXXIV"
"Epigram: To a Friend, and Sonne" (Jonson)
See *The Under-Wood LXIX*
"Epigram X" (Jonson) **17**:157
"Epigram XCI" (Jonson) **17**:201
"Epigram XCIV" (Jonson) **17**:159, 202
"Epigram XIV" (Jonson) **17**:166, 174
"Epigram XLIII" (Jonson) **17**:199
"Epigram XLV" (Jonson) **17**:193
"Epigram XVIII" (Jonson) **17**:179
"Epigram XXIII" (Jonson) **17**:197
"Epigram XXXV" (Jonson) **17**:156
"Epigramas" (Guillén) **23**:121
Epigramas (Cardenal) **22**:104, 117, 124-25, 131
"Epigramas, II" (Guillén) **35**:229
Epigrammata (Martial) **10**:243
Epigrammaton libri (Martial)
See *Epigrammata*
Epigrams (Cardenal)
See *Epigramas*
Epigrams (Jonson) **17**:156-58, 169, 179, 196-97, 201-02, 206
Epigrams (Martial)
See *Epigrammata*
"Epilog" (Heine) **25**:162, 178
"Epilogue" (Akhmatova) **55**:4-6, 8, 10-11, 13, 15, 19, 43, 50, 54, 61
"Epilogue" (Brathwaite) **56**:67, 84
"Epilogue" (Browning) **61**:16
"Epilogue" (Carman) **34**:234
"Epilogue" (Cullen) **20**:57
"Epilogue" (Hughes) **53**:106
"The Epilogue" (Masters) **36**:195-96, 212, 220, 223, 243
"Epilogue" (Verlaine) **2**:432
"Epilogue (1)" (Akhmatova) **55**:27, 39, 57-58, 63
"Epilogue (2)" (Akhmatova) **55**:4, 28, 32, 39, 55-57, 60-61, 63-64
"Epilogue for FDR" (Ignatow) **34**:325
The Epilogue of the Man of Law's Tale (Chaucer) **58**:288
"Epilogue to the Drama Founded on 'St. Roman's Welle'" (Scott) **13**:293
Epilogue to the Satires (Pope) **26**:319-20, 340
"Epilogue to the Tragedy of Jane Shore" (Finch) **21**:154
"Epilogues" (Akhmatova) **55**:6
"Epimetheus; or, The Poet's Afterthought" (Longfellow) **30**:103
Epinicia (Pindar) **19**:378
Epipsychidion (Shelley) **14**:163, 171, 173-75, 178, 187, 189, 192-93, 196-97, 208, 233-37, 239-40
"Episode" (Herbert) **50**:4
"Episode" (Valéry) **9**:391
"Epistemology" (Wilbur) **51**:192, 211, 217
"Epistle" (Darío)
See "Epístola"

"An Epistle" (Hope) **56**:273
"Epistle" (Lee) **24**:242
"Epistle" (Tate) **50**:256
"An Epistle answering one that asked to be Sealed of the Tribe of Ben" (Jonson)
See *The Under-Wood XLVII*
"Epistle Containing the Strange Medical Experiences of Karshish the Arab Physician" (Browning) **2**:36
"An Epistle: Edward Sackville to Venetia Digby" (Hope) **56**:268-69, 280
"An Epistle from Ardelia to Mrs. Randolph in answer to her Poem upon Her Verses" (Finch) **21**:167
"An Epistle from Holofernes" (Hope) **56**:273, 296
"Epistle from Mrs. Yonge to Her Husband" (Montagu) **16**:346
Epistle III (Pope) **26**:325-26
"An Epistle, Inviting a Friend to Supper" (Jonson)
See "Epigram CI"
Epistle IV (Pope) **26**:325
"Epistle John Hamilton to Reynolds" (Keats) **1**:289, 305
"An Epistle Mendicant" (Jonson)
See *The Under-Wood LXXI*
Epistle, On the Art of Poetry (Horace)
See *Ars Poetica*
"Epistle to a Friend" (Jonson)
See *The Under-Wood XXXVII*
"Epistle to a Friend, to perswade him to the Warres" (Jonson)
See *The Under-Wood XV*
"An Epistle to a Lady, Who Desired the Author to Make Verses on Her, in the Heroick Style" (Swift) **9**:256, 259-60, 281
"Epistle to a Young Friend" (Burns) **6**:71, 96
Epistle to Arbuthnot (Pope)
See *An Epistle to Dr. Arbuthnot*
"Epistle to Augusta" (Byron) **16**:86
"Epistle to Augustus" (Pope) **26**:320-21
An Epistle to Bathurst (Pope) **26**:340
"Epistle To Be Left in the Earth" (MacLeish) **47**:127, 154-55, 188, 196
An Epistle to Burlington (Pope) **26**:353, 359
"Epistle to Dr. Arbuthnot" (Pope) **26**:318, 338, 361
An Epistle to Dr. Arbuthnot (Pope) **26**:311, 320, 339-46
"Epistle to Elizabeth Countesse of Rutland" (Jonson)
See *The Forest XII*
"Epistle to John Rankine, Enclosing Some Poems" (Burns) **6**:65, 83
"Epistle to J.R******" (Burns)
See "Epistle to John Rankine, Enclosing Some Poems"
"Epistle: To Katherine, Lady Aubigny" (Jonson)
See *The Forest XIII*
"Epistle to Léon-Paul Fargue" (MacLeish) **47**:190
"An Epistle to Master John Selden" (Jonson)
See *The Under-Wood XVI*
"Epistle to Sir Edward Sacvile, now Earl of Dorset" (Jonson)
See *The Under-Wood XIII*
"Epistle to the Olympians" (Nash) **21**:279-80
"Epistle to William Simpson of Ochiltree, May 1785" (Burns) **6**:69
"The Epistles" (Burns) **6**:49, 66-71, 79, 81
Epistles (Horace) **46**:97, 99-100, 102, 104, 114, 117-19, 131, 137, 140, 142, 145-46, 152-53, 163, 173, 191, 198, 203-6, 209, 211, 214, 222
Epistles (Ovid)
See *Heroides*
Epistles, Book I (Horace) **46**:95
Epistolæ Heroidum (Ovid)
See *Heroides*
"Epístola" (Darío) **15**:89-90
"Epistola a monsenor Casaldaliga" (Cardenal) **22**:103
"Epistre a ses amis" (Villon) **13**:395
"Epitáfio de B Dias" (Pessoa) **20**:155
"Epitafio para mi tumba" (Storni) **33**:236;
"Epitaph" (Coleridge) **39**:178
"Epitaph" (Merwin) **45**:19, 93
"Epitaph" (Muir) **49**:206
"Epitaph" (Parra) **39**:300
"Epitaph" (Tsvetaeva)
See "Nadgrobie"
"Epitaph" (Williams) **7**:345
"Epitaph" (Wylie) **23**:322-23
"Epitaph for a Darling Lady" (Parker) **28**:346
"Epitaph for a Lady's Man" (Wagoner) **33**:351
"Epitaph for a Poet" (Cullen) **20**:60
"Epitaph for an Old Woman" (Paz) **48**:189
"Epitaph for Anton Schmidt" (Gunn) **26**:203
"Epitaph for Flann O'Brien" (Mahon) **60**:134
"Epitaph for John McCutcheon" (MacLeish) **47**:197
"Epitaph for Liberal Poets" (MacNeice) **61**:141
"Epitaph for My Father" (Walker) **20**:289, 293
"Epitaph for Robert Flaherty" (Mahon) **60**:138
"Epitaph for the Race of Man" (Millay) **6**:217, 230
Epitaph for the Young: A Poem in XII Cantos (Walcott) **46**:277
"Epitaph: Hubert Hastings, Parry" (Bridges) **28**:77
"Epitaph of Antiochos, King of Commagene" (Cavafy)
See "Epitaph of Antiochos, King of Kommagini"
"Epitaph of Antiochos King of Kommagênê" (Cavafy)
See "Epitaph of Antiochos, King of Kommagini"
"Epitaph of Antiochos, King of Kommagini" (Cavafy) **36**:8, 40, 111
"Epitaph on an Army of Mercenaries" (Housman) **2**:177
"Epitaph on an Engraver" (Thoreau) **30**:227
"Epitaph on her Son H.P. at St. Syth's Church" (Philips) **40**:296
"Epitaph on Salathiel Pavy" (Jonson)
See "Epitaph on Salomon Pavy"
"Epitaph on Salomon Pavy" (Jonson) **17**:179
"Epitaph on the Lady S. Wife to Sir W.S." (Carew) **29**:62
"Epitaph on the Politician Himself" (Belloc) **24**:31, 40
"Epitaph on Thomas Clere" (Surrey) **59**:322-24
"Epitaph to Master Vincent Corbet" (Jonson) **17**:174
"An Epitaph upon a Child" (Herrick) **9**:129
"An Epitaph upon a Virgin" (Herrick) **9**:131
"Epitaphe Villon" (Villon) **13**:390, 394, 408, 410-11, 417-18
Epitaphium Damonis (Milton) **29**:241
"Epitaphs of the War" (Kipling) **3**:171, 192
"Epithalamie on Sir Clipseby Crew and His Lady" (Herrick)
See "A Nuptiall Song, or Epithalamie on Sir Clipseby Crew and His Lady"
"An Epithalamie to Sir Thomas Southwell and His Ladie" (Herrick) **9**:86
"Epithalamion" (Abse) **41**:14, 18
"Epithalamion" (Herrick)
See "A Nuptiall Song, or Epithalamie on Sir Clipseby Crew and His Lady"
"Epithalamion" (Hopkins) **15**:124
"Epithalamion" (Spenser) **8**:336, 389
"An Epithalamion, or mariage song on the Lady Elizabeth, and Count Palatine being married on St. Valentines day" (Donne) **1**:124
"The Epithalamium" (Housman) **2**:199
"Epithalamium" (Pessoa) **20**:165, 169
"An Epitome" (Sassoon) **12**:260
"Epitre a M. de Sainte-Beuve" (Lamartine) **16**:267
"Épître à Marie d'Orléans" (Villon) **13**:399, 413
"Epîtres à la Princesse" (Senghor) **25**:255
Epode (Jonson)
See *The Forest XI*
Epodes (Horace) **46**:99, 114, 137, 149, 155, 193, 197-98, 221-22
"Epte Wood" (Char)
See "Le Bois de l'Epte"
"Equal Opportunity" (Lorde) **12**:140
"The Equality of the Sexes" (Éluard)
See "L'égalité des sexes"
"Equilibrist" (Swenson) **14**:274, 283
"The Equilibrists" (Ransom) **61**:267-69, 272, 297, 299, 306, 308, 311
"Equinox" (Lorde) **12**:157
"Equitan" (Marie de France) **22**:239-41, 258, 265, 269, 271, 278, 296-98
"An Eqyptian Pulled Glass Bottle in the Shape of a Fish" (Moore) **49**:89, 101
"ER" (Banks) **44**:45
"Era la última noche" (Castro) **41**:84
"Era un aire suave" (Darío) **15**:79, 95, 107, 109, 118-19
"Eran, he ran" (Alurista) **34**:22, 29
Erasmus Wilson (Riley) **48**:358
Erato e Apòllion (Quasimodo) **47**:277, 279, 293, 300, 302
"Ere Sleep Comes Down to Soothe the Weary Eyes" (Dunbar) **5**:121, 124
"The Eremites" (Graves) **6**:140
"Erfüllung" (Stramm) **50**:168, 189, 195, 202
"Erhört" (Stramm) **50**:176, 191-93, 209
"Erige Cor Tuum ad Me in Coelum" (H. D.) **5**:307
"Erikönig" (Goethe) **5**:239, 254
Eril (Perse) **23**:246
"Erinna" (Eliot) **20**:137
"Erinna to Sappho" (Wright) **36**:335
"Erinnerung" (Stramm) **50**:172, 174, 189, 198
"Erinnerung an Frankreich" (Celan) **10**:121
"eriuuerung un die schrecken der jugend" (Enzensberger) **28**:136
Erklärung (Heine) **25**:162
"Erl-King" (Goethe)
See "Erikönig"
Erlkönig (Goethe) **5**:257
"A Ermes" (Quasimodo) **47**:297
"L'ermite" (Apollinaire) **7**:46-7
"Ermunterung" (Hölderlin) **4**:148
"Eroded Hills" (Wright) **14**:353, 378
Eroding Witness (Mackey) **49**:2-5, 7, 11, 15, 17-18, 21-22, 25-26, 30-33, 35, 42-43, 51-53, 58-59, 66, 71, 77
"Eroica" (Ginsberg) **4**:62
"L'eroismo" (Montale) **13**:156
"Eros" (Bridges) **28**:74-5, 86-7
"Eros" (Komunyakaa) **51**:64
"Eros" (Oppen) **35**:309, 310-11, 314
"A Eros" (Storni) **33**:242, 257, 284, 293-94;
"Eros and Psyche" (Patmore) **59**:212, 223, 265, 267
Eros and Psyche (Bridges) **28**:47, 59, 68, 86
"Eros at Temple Stream" (Levertov) **11**:169
"Éros suspendu" (Char) **56**:120
"Eros Turannos" (Robinson) **1**:468, 490, 493-94, 497
"Erosion" (Graham) **59**:148-49, 179
Erosion (Graham) **59**:132-33, 135, 139-40, 142-44, 146-47, 151, 154-58, 161, 168-69, 174, 176, 178-79, 184, 187
"Erosion: Transkei" (Brutus) **24**:113
Erotic Adventures (Ovid)
See *Amores*
The Errancy (Graham) **59**:163-64, 168-69, 175, 180, 182, 185-88
"Errand" (Carver) **54**:18
"The Errand Boy I" (Ignatow) **34**:271, 273, 278, 305, 316
"The Errand Boy II" (Ignatow) **34**:273
"Errol Flynn—On His Death" (Corso) **33**:37
"Error and Loss" (Morris) **55**:340

"Erwache, Friederike" (Goethe) **5**:246
"Erwiderung an Alexander Lernet-Holenia" (Benn) **35**:35
"Es así" (Neruda) **4**:311
"Es ist ein Garten" (Benn) **35**:71
"Es obligatorio" (Fuertes) **27**:12
"Es olvido" (Parra) **39**:270, 285, 296
"Es War Einmal" (Smith) **12**:312
"Escaparate" (Borges) **22**:92
"The Escape" (Dickey) **40**:196, 254
"The Escape" (Levine) **22**:233
"Escape" (MacLeish) **47**:182
"The Escape" (Muir) **49**:199, 232, 251, 289
"Escape" (Wylie) **23**:301, 309, 329
"Escaped from the Archipelago" (Char)
See "Evadé d'archipel"
"Eschatological Forebodings of Mr. Cogito" (Herbert)
See "Przeczucia eschatologiczne Pana Cogito"
"Esclava" (Storni) **33**:254, 278;
"Escolares" (Guillén) **23**:127
"Un escolio" (Borges) **32**:65
"Escrito" (Fuertes) **27**:48
"Escritura" (Paz) **48**:272
"Esequie della guida E.R." (Carducci) **46**:88, 90
"Eskimo and Others" (Schwerner) **42**:204
"Eso Basta" (Guillén) **35**:201
Esope (Marie de France)
See *The Fables*
Espacia (Jiménez) **7**:203, 213-14
"Espadas" (Borges) **32**:95
Espadas como labios (Aleixandre) **15**:6, 18, 21, 30-1, 39-41
España (Gautier) **18**:155
España en el corazón: himno a las glorias del pueblo en la guerra (1936-1937) (Neruda) **4**:278, 283, 287, 307-09, 311
"Espantapájaros" (Borges) **32**:125
"Especially When the October Wind" (Thomas) **2**:384; **52**:258, 260, 264, 268
"Espejo" (Paz) **48**:176
"Los espejos" (Borges) **32**:60, 66, 77, 133
"La espera" (Borges) **32**:66
"La espera inútil" (Mistral) **32**:161
"L'espoir luit comme un brin de paille dans l'étable" (Verlaine) **2**:416
The Espousals (Patmore) **59**:204, 220, 227, 239, 244
"L'Esprit Pur" (Vigny) **26**:371, 374, 392, 402-404, 413
"L'esprit saint" (Lamartine) **16**:264, 277
Espurgatoire (Marie de France)
See *L'Espurgatoire Saint Patrice*
L'Espurgatoire Saint Patrice (Marie de France) **22**:287-89, 291, 293, 300
"Essai de la débilité mentale" (Éluard) **38**:96
"Essai de la manie aiguë" (Éluard) **38**:96
"Essay Lamenting His Own Long Illness" (Yakamochi)
See "Jin'a jiiai bun"
An Essay on Criticism (Pope) **26**:300, 302-303, 314-15, 318, 320-22, 340
An Essay on Man (Pope) **26**:304, 307-308, 314, 318, 326, 328-33, 335, 338-40, 351-56, 359
"Essay on Mind" (Browning) **6**:27
An Essay on Mind, with other Poems (Browning) **6**:19-20, 26
"Essay on Poetics" (Ammons) **16**:10-11, 23, 28, 47-9
"Essay on Psychiatrists" (Pinsky) **27**:144-5, 160, 162, 173, 175-6
Essay on Rime (Shapiro) **25**:264-65, 267-68, 270, 274-79, 285, 288, 290-91, 296, 310, 319, 322-23
"Essay on Stone" (Carruth) **10**:83
"Essay on Style" (O'Hara) **45**:161
"Essay on the Alliance of Education and Government" (Gray) **2**:136
"An Essay on War" (Duncan) **2**:105
"An Essay on William Carlos Williams" (Cruz) **37**:20, 25
"Essays of a Song to the Muse" (Carducci)
See "Saggi di un canto alle Muse"
"Esse" (Milosz) **8**:182, 187
"Essential Beauty" (Larkin) **21**:229
The Essential Etheridge Knight (Knight) **14**:52-3
Essex Poems, 1963-1967 (Davie) **29**:113, 122-23
"Está bien" (Guillén) **23**:127
"Está el bisonte imperial" (Guillén) **23**:125
"Esta Noche" (Doty) **53**:46, 52
"Esta tarde, mi bien, cuando te hablaba" (Juana Inés de la Cruz) **24**:180
"Estación del Norte" (Guillén) **35**:157
La estación violenta (Paz) **1**:353, 359-60, 362; **48**:245
"Estar del cuerpo" (Aleixandre) **15**:35
"Estate di San Martino" (Pavese) **13**:244
"Estatua ecuestre" (Guillén) **35**:157, 174, 175, 176
"Una estatua en el silencio" (Neruda) **4**:289
"Estatura del vino" (Neruda) **4**:277, 301
"Este grave daño" (Storni) **33**:274;
"Este libro" (Fuertes) **27**:17, 38
"Este libro" (Storni) **33**:237, 251;
"Este que ves engaño colorido" (Juana Inés de la Cruz) **24**:225
Esthétique du Mal (Stevens) **6**:300, 302
"Estimable Mable" (Brooks) **7**:94
Estío (Jiménez) **7**:212
"Estival" (Darío) **15**:117
"El estrecho dudoso" (Cardenal) **22**:119-23, 125-27
"Estrella de Navidad" (Mistral) **32**:185
"Estuary" (Merwin) **45**:54
"Estudio preliminar" (Darío) **15**:80
"Et Le Sursaut Soudain" (Senghor) **25**:248
Et moi aussi je suis peintre (Apollinaire) **7**:34
"Et Resurrexit" (Curnow) **48**:24
Les états-généraux (Breton) **15**:50, 52, 62
"Etched Away" (Celan) **10**:97
"Été" (Valéry) **9**:351, 373, 392
"Été" (Verlaine) **32**:400-05
"Eternal Death" (Tagore)
See "Ananta maran"
"Eternal Life" (Tagore)
See "Ananta jivan"
"Eternal tripas" (Alurista) **34**:28, 29
Eternidades (Jiménez) **7**:187, 208, 212-13
"Eternite de la nature, brievete de l'homme" (Lamartine) **16**:283
"Eternity" (Crane) **3**:90
"An Eternity" (Williams) **7**:394
Eternity (Smart)
See *On the Eternity of the Supreme Being*
"The Eternity of Nature" (Clare) **23**:3-4, 26
"Eterno" (Ungaretti) **57**:342
Eterno femminino regale (Carducci) **46**:12, 55
"Ethelinda" (Smart)
See "To Ethelinda"
"Ether Either" (Howe) **54**:119-20
"Ethiopia" (Harper) **21**:189, 202, 208, 215, 217
Éthiopiques (Senghor) **25**:231-32, 238, 241, 255
"Ethnobotany" (Snyder) **21**:297
"Les etiquettes jaunes" (O'Hara) **45**:119
"L'Étoile" (Wilbur) **51**:188, 192, 324-26
"Les étoiles" (Lamartine) **16**:291
"Eton" (Gray)
See "Ode on a Distant Prospect of Eton College"
"Eton College Ode" (Gray)
See "Ode on a Distant Prospect of Eton College"
"Les étrennes des orphelins" (Rimbaud) **57**:196, 245, 249, 252, 299, 301
Etroits sont les vaisseaux (Perse) **23**:244-45
"Etude" (Stryk) **27**:183, 189
"Etude de mains" (Gautier) **18**:129, 158
"The Eucalypt and the National Character" (Wright) **14**:374
"L'eucalyptus" (Quasimodo) **47**:275, 301
"Euclid" (Millay) **6**:211
"Eugene Carman" (Masters) **1**:324; **36**:230
Eugene Onegin (Pushkin)
See *Yevgeny Onegin*
"Eulalie— A Song " (Poe) **1**:441
"Eulenspiegelei" (Smith) **12**:327, 342
"Eulogy for Slick" (Knight) **14**:49
"Eulogy on Vladimír Holan" (Seifert)
See "Pocta Vladimíru Holanovi"
"Las euménidas bonaerenses" (Storni) **33**:294-95;
"Eupheme" (Jonson) **17**:213
"Euphoria" (Ekeloef) **23**:76
"Euphrosyne" (Arnold) **5**:43
Eureka: A Prose Poem (Poe) **1**:422-24, 430-31, 437-38, 442-43, 450; **54**:276, 334, 336-37
"Europe" (Ashbery) **26**:113, 118, 138, 151
Europe: A Prophecy, 1794 (Blake) **12**:13, 26, 35, 57, 61
"Europe and America" (Ignatow) **34**:274
The Europe of Trusts: Selected Poems (Howe) **54**:79, 84, 99, 102, 123, 126-27, 129-30, 134, 137, 139-40
"European Nocturne" (Birney) **52**:3
"Eurydice" (H. D.) **5**:298, 304
"Euthanasia" (Tate) **50**:305
"Evacuation" (Yamada) **44**:339-42, 346-47
"Evadé d'archipel" (Char) **56**:145
"Evadne" (H. D.) **5**:267
"Evalena Fayner" (Masters) **36**:212
Evangeline: A Tale of Acadie (Longfellow) **30**:16, 20-1, 24, 30, 34-5, 38-40, 44, 52-56, 59-60, 64, 66, 71, 92, 99
"Evangelist" (Davie) **29**:93-94, 108, 111-12, 114-15
"The Evangelistic Beasts" (Lawrence) **54**:193-94, 224
"Evanston 4 June 72" (Brutus) **24**:123
"Eva's Farewell" (Harper) **21**:201, 208, 218
"Evasion" (Tzara) **27**:230-31
"Eve" (Rossetti) **7**:264, 291
"Eve" (Williams) **7**:350, 354, 394-95
"Eve in Heaven" (Wylie) **23**:326
"The Eve of All Souls" (Clampitt) **19**:87
"The Eve of Creecy" (Morris) **55**:238, 299-300
"The Eve of St. Agnes" (Keats) **1**:279, 282, 285-6, 288, 296, 298, 307-10
"The Eve of St. Agnes" (Morris) **55**:247
"The Eve of St. John" (Scott) **13**:269
"Eve of St. Mark" (Keats)
See "The Eve of St. Mark"
"The Eve of St. Mark" (Keats) **1**:279, 304
"Eve Scolds" (Wright) **14**:373, 375
"Eve Sings" (Wright) **14**:373
"Eve to her Daughter" (Wright) **14**:356
"Evelyn" (Stryk) **27**:208
"Evelyn Hope" (Browning) **2**:38
"Evelyn Ray" (Lowell) **13**:66, 91
"Even" (Burns) **6**:50
Even a Fist (Amichai)
See *Gam ha'egrof haya pa'am yad ptuba ve'etsba'ot*
"Even If All Desires Things Moments Be" (Cummings) **5**:95
"The Even Sea" (Swenson) **14**:249, 263
"Even Song" (Herbert) **4**:133
"Even such is Time" (Raleigh) **31**:215-16
Even the Fist Once Was an Open Hand and Fingers (Amichai)
See *Gam ha'egrof haya pa'am yad ptuba ve'etsba'ot*
"Evening" (Carver) **54**:28
"Evening" (Merton) **10**:340
"Evening" (Merwin) **45**:23
"Evening" (Trakl)
See "Der Abend"
"Evening" (Wheatley)
See "An Hymn to the Evening"
Evening (Akhmatova)
See *Vecher*

Evening Album (Tsvetaeva)
See *Vecherny albom*
"Evening at a Country Inn" (Kenyon) **57**:20, 39, 42
"The Evening Bell" (Ishikawa)
See "Yube no kane"
"Evening Dance of the Grey Flies" (Page) **12**:190
Evening Dance of the Grey Flies (Page) **12**:181, 198-99
"The evening darkens over" (Bridges) **28**:87
"Evening Fantasy" (Hölderlin) **4**:140
"Evening Hawk" (Warren) **37**:309, 331, 356, 360
"Evening Hour" (Warren) **37**:337
"Evening in Connecticut" (MacNeice) **61**:139
"Evening in France" (Sarton) **39**:332
"An Evening in Saint Peter's" (Carducci)
See "Un Sera in San Pietro"
"Evening in the Country" (Ashbery) **26**:124, 159
"Evening in the Sanitarium" (Bogan) **12**:92, 99-101, 107, 121
"The Evening Land" (Lawrence) **54**:196
"An Evening Light" (Curnow) **48**:51
"Evening Music" (Sarton) **39**:324
"The Evening of Ants" (Soto) **28**:378-79
"The Evening of the Holiday" (Leopardi)
See "La Sera del Dí di Festa"
"Evening of the Visitation" (Merton) **10**:339
"Evening on the Broads" (Swinburne) **24**:313, 322, 329, 343
"Evening Orison" (Rimbaud)
See "Oraison du soir"
"The Evening Primrose" (Parker) **28**:349, 351, 363
"Evening Ride" (Francis) **34**:251
"The Evening Sea" (Ishikawa)
See "Yūbe no umi"
"Evening Shadows" (Longfellow) **30**:109
"Evening Song" (Carducci)
See "Serenata"
"Evening Song" (Hughes) **53**:160
"Evening Song" (Lanier) **50**:77; **50**:56
"Evening Song" (Toomer) **7**:320
Evening Songs (Tagore)
See *Sandhya sangit*
"Evening Star" (Bogan) **12**:98, 100
"The Evening Star" (Longfellow) **30**:27
"Evening Star" (Poe) **1**:448
"Evening Sun" (Kenyon) **57**:29
"The Evening That Love Enticed You Down into the Ballroom" (Ronsard)
See "Le soir qu'amour vous fist en la salle descendre"
An Evening Thought: Salvation by Christ with Penetential Cries (Hammon) **16**:176-79, 183-87
"Evening Twilight" (Baudelaire)
See "Le crépuscule du soir"
"An Evening Under Newly Cleared Skies" (Wang Wei) **18**:369
"Evening Voluntary" (Wordsworth) **4**:408
"Evening with Lee Shore and Cliffs" (Merwin) **45**:7, 9
"The Evenings of Certain Lives" (Benn) **35**:9
"Evensong" (Aiken) **26**:5
"The Event" (Dove) **6**:110, 112, 114
"Event" (Plath) **37**:264
"An Event" (Wilbur) **51**:189, 216, 338
Events and Wisdoms: Poems, 1957-1963 (Davie) **29**:110-11, 123, 129
"Ever mine hap is slack" (Wyatt) **27**:357
"Everlasting Flowers for a Dead Mother" (Lawrence) **54**:245
"The Everlasting Gospel" (Blake) **12**:31
"The Everlasting Voices" (Yeats) **20**:309
"Everness" (Borges) **22**:89; **32**:60, 69, 88
"Every Blessed Day" (Levine) **22**:221
"Every Lovely Limb's a Desolation" (Smith) **12**:314
"Every Soul Is a Circus" (Lindsay) **23**:274, 280
"Every Traveler Has One Vermont Poem" (Lorde) **12**:138
Everyone Sang (Sassoon) **12**:280, 284, 289
"Everything and Nothing" (Borges) **32**:137
"Everything Came True" (Pasternak) **6**:266
"Everything Is Going to Be All Right" (Mahon) **60**:198, 238
"Eve's Apologie in defence of Women" (Lanyer) **60**:18, 20, 23, 34-35, 50, 53, 63, 67, 70, 72, 86, 96-98, 100
"eve's version" (Clifton) **17**:29, 36
Evgeni Onegin (Pushkin)
See *Yevgeny Onegin*
"Evidence" (Harjo) **27**:64
"The Evil" (Rimbaud)
See "Le mal"
"The Evil World-Soul" (Lawrence) **54**:198
"Eviradnus" (Hugo) **17**:59, 61
"Evolution" (Alexie) **53**:30-31
"Evolution" (Swenson) **14**:247, 251, 255, 275, 283-84, 286
"Evolution from the Fish" (Bly) **39**:13
"Evolutionary Poem No. 1" (Knight) **14**:42
"Evolutionary Poem No. 2" (Knight) **14**:42
"Evolution-Sustenance-Dissolution" (Tagore)
See "Srishti-sthiti-pralaya"
"The Evolver" (Baraka) **4**:24
"Evrion's Tomb" (Cavafy) **36**:112
"evry whun at 2 oclock" (Bissett) **14**:33
"Ewigkeit" (Borges) **32**:88
"Ex ponto" (Ekeloef) **23**:76
"Ex vermibus" (MacDiarmid) **9**:190
"Exactly what is unexact" (Villa) **22**:354
"Exageraciones divinas" (Fuertes) **27**:30
"The Exaggeration of Despair" (Alexie) **53**:34
"The Exam" (Olds) **22**:324
"Examination at the Womb-Door" (Hughes) **7**:159
"Examination of the Hero in a Time of War" (Stevens) **6**:318
"The Example" (Belloc) **24**:27
"Examples of Created Systems" (Meredith) **28**:200
"Excavation of Troy" (MacLeish) **47**:191
"The Excavator" (Yevtushenko) **40**:347
"Excellence" (Francis) **34**:254-55
"An Excellent Memory" (Curnow) **48**:46
"An Excellent New Ballad; or, The True English Dean to Be Hang'd for a Rape" (Swift) **9**:267
"Excelsior" (Longfellow) **30**:14, 21-3, 26-7, 34, 36, 45, 103, 107, 109-10
"Excerpt from a Letter" (Seifert)
See "Úryvek z dopisu"
"The Excesses of God" (Jeffers) **17**:132
"The Exchange" (Swenson) **14**:255, 288
"An Exchange of Gifts" (Sarton) **39**:326
"Exchanges" (Dickey) **40**:223
"Exchanging Hats" (Bishop) **3**:64; **34**:106
Exclamations: Music of the Soul (Nishiwaki) **15**:237
"Exclusive Blue" (Francis) **34**:244
"The Excrement Poem" (Kumin) **15**:207
"La excursión" (Fuertes) **27**:17
Excursion (Wordsworth)
See *The Excursion, Being a Portion of "The Recluse"*
The Excursion, Being a Portion of "The Recluse" (Wordsworth) **4**:377-78, 383, 392, 397-99, 402-03, 405-09
"Excuse" (Arnold)
See "Urania"
"The Excuse" (Raleigh) **31**:216, 313
"Excuse" (Walker) **30**:355
"Execration upon Vulcan" (Jonson)
See *The Under-Wood XLV*
"The Execution of Stenka Razin" (Yevtushenko) **40**:338, 347
"The Executive's Death" (Bly) **39**:49
Exegi monumentum (Horace) **46**:97
"Exercise" (Merwin) **45**:40, 83
"Exercise on a Sphere" (Hope) **56**:277
"Exeunt" (Wilbur) **51**:330
"Exhibitionist" (Boland) **58**:44-45, 98
"Exhortation" (Bogan) **12**:122
"Exhortation" (Hölderlin)
See "Ermunterung"
Exil (Perse) **23**:209, 211, 213-14, 216-18, 221-22, 231, 234, 240-42, 246, 248-50, 252, 254, 256
Exile and Other Poems (Perse)
See *Exil*
"Exiles" (Cavafy) **36**:40
Exile's Letter (Li Po) **29**:141
"Exile's Letter: After the Failed Revolution" (Chin) **40**:12, 15
"The Exile's Return" (Lowell) **3**:200, 202, 234
"Existence and Presence" (Graham) **59**:169
"The Exit" (Elytis) **21**:134
"Exit Molloy" (Mahon) **60**:133
"Exit, Pursued by a Bear" (Nash) **21**:271
"Exmoor" (Clampitt) **19**:81, 88
"Exodus" (Oppen) **35**:285
"The Exorcism" (Roethke) **15**:274, 278
"Exordium" (Noyes) **27**:127
"The Expatriate" (Forché) **10**:138, 141, 144, 156
"The Expatriates" (Sexton) **2**:359
"Expect Nothing" (Walker) **30**:339, 353
"Expecting the Barbarians" (Cavafy) **36**:7
"An Expedient-Leonardo da Vinci's-and a Query" (Moore) **4**:242; **49**:144-45
"Expendable" (Hughes) **53**:116
"Experience Is the Angled Road" (Dickinson) **1**:111
"L'Expiation" (Hugo) **17**:79-80
"The Expiration" (Donne) **1**:130
"Explaining a Few Things" (Neruda)
See "Explico algunas cosas"
"The Explanation" (Kipling) **3**:183
"Explanation" (Pasternak) **6**:266
"Explanation and Apology, Twenty Years After" (Carruth) **10**:78
An Explanation of America (Pinsky) **27**:143-46,153, 155-56, 162-63, 173, 176
"Explico algunas cosas" (Neruda) **4**:297, 310-11
"Exploit of the Steam Cylinder" (Char) **56**:162
"Explorations" (MacNeice) **61**:140
"The Explorers" (Atwood) **8**:13
"The Explorers" (Hope) **56**:266
"The Explorers" (Rich) **5**:362
"Explosion" (Harjo) **27**:56
"Una exposición" (Guillén) **35**:216
"Expostulation" (Cowper) **40**:50, 52, 106, 116, 127
"Expostulation and Reply" (Wordsworth) **4**:419
"An Expostulation with Inigo Jones" (Jonson) **17**:181-82
"Exposure" (Heaney) **18**:194, 205
"Exposure" (Owen) **19**:327, 332, 334
Exposure in the Fields (Matsuo Bashō)
See *Nozarashi kikō*
"La expresión" (Guillén) **35**:229, 230
"Express" (Sandburg) **2**:340
"Express Your Will" (Ignatow) **34**:323-24
"Expression" (Clare) **23**:44
"Expression" (Gunn) **26**:217
"Expressions of Sea Level" (Ammons) **16**:29, 42, 46; **108**:22
Expressions of Sea Level (Ammons) **16**:4-5, 20, 27, 53
"Express-Zug" (Benn) **35**:9
"The Exstasie" (Donne) **1**:126, 128, 130, 135, 147, 152
"L'Extase" (Éluard) **38**:75, 87
"Extase" (Hugo) **17**:91
"Extasis" (Mistral) **32**:152, 176
"Extempore Effusion upon the Death of James Hogg" (Wordsworth) **4**:402
"Exterior Possessions" (Char)
See "Possessions extérieures"
"An Extra Joyful Chorus for Those Who Have Read This Far" (Bly) **39**:27-8, 68

"Extracts from Addresses to the Academy of Fine Ideas" (Stevens) **6**:314
Extracts from an Opera (Keats) **1**:311
"Un extraño" (Gallagher) **9**:66
"Extraño accidente" (Fuertes) **27**:14, 27
"L'Extravagant" (Char) **56**:143, 153-54, 170
"The Extravagant One" (Char)
See "L'Extravagant"
Extravagario (Neruda) **4**:290
"Extreme Unction" (Erdrich) **52**:191
"Extremes and Moderations" (Ammons) **16**:10-11, 18, 23, 28, 47-9
Exultations (Pound) **4**:317
"Exvoto pour un naufrage" (Césaire) **25**:32
"Eyasion" (Tzara) **27**:230
"Eye" (Storni)
See "Ojo"
"The Eye" (Tate) **50**:275, 290-91, 293
"The Eye" (Wilbur) **51**:236, 278-80, 287, 314
"Eye and Tooth" (Lowell) **3**:215
"The Eye is More or Less Satisfied with Seeing" (Curnow) **48**:10, 24
"The Eye of the Storm" (Wagoner) **33**:370
"Eyeball Television" (Komunyakaa) **51**:41
"The Eye-Beaters" (Dickey) **40**:164, 166, 177-78, 181, 183, 188-90, 196, 199-200, 202-3, 220-21, 242-43, 248, 256-57
The Eye-Beaters, Blood, Victory, Madness, Buckhead, and Mercy (Dickey) **40**:165-66, 187-88, 194, 199-200, 202, 219-20, 229, 239, 242-48
"The Eyeglasses" (Williams) **7**:381-83
"The Eye-Mote" (Plath) **1**:389; **37**:177-78, 180, 182
"Eyes" (Amichai) **38**:36-7
"Eyes" (Corso) **33**:16, 50
"Eyes" (Seifert)
See "Ŏi"
"Eyes and Tears" (Marvell) **10**:270-71
Eyes at the Back of Our Heads (Levertov)
See *With Eyes at the Back of Our Heads*
"Eyes of Summer" (Merwin) **45**:33
"The Eyes of the Poor" (Baudelaire)
See "Les yeux des pauvres"
Eyeshot (McHugh) **61**:207
"Ezekiel Saw the Wheel" (Montale) **13**:109, 129, 165
"Ezerskij" (Pushkin) **10**:391, 394
"Ezra Pound" (Moore) **49**:130
"F O Matthiessen An Anniversary" (Shapiro) **25**:320, 322, 324
"Fable" (Cassian) **17**:13
"A Fable" (Cowper) **40**:124
"Fable" (Emerson) **18**:103-4
"A Fable" (Glück) **16**:161
"Fable" (Merwin) **45**:6, 9
"Fable" (Wylie) **23**:310, 316, 319
"Fable of the Cock and the Fox" (Chaucer)
See "Nun's Priest's Tale"
"The Fable of the Fragile Butterfly" (Wakoski) **15**:333
"Fable of two gardens" (Paz)
See "Cuento de dos jardines"
The Fables (Marie de France) **22**:287-88
Fables (Smart) **13**:341
"Fables about Error" (Meredith) **28**:175, 194, 213, 215
The Fables of La Fontaine (Moore) **49**:125, 136
"Fables of the Moscow Subway" (Nemerov) **24**:268
"Fabrications" (Wilbur) **51**:332
"The Fabulists, 1914-1918" (Kipling) **3**:172
"Fabulous Ballard" (Wylie) **23**:321
Façade (Sitwell) **3**:294, 303, 306, 319, 322, 325, 328
"The Face" (Jarrell) **41**:190, 200, 214
"The Face" (Levine) **22**:224
"A Face" (Moore) **49**:126-27, 129
"The Face" (Muir) **49**:296
"Face" (Toomer) **7**:310, 333
The Face against the Glass (Francis) **34**:245, 264
"Face and Image" (Tomlinson) **17**:348
"The Face and the Wind" (Paz) **48**:272-73
"Face behind the Pane (An Old Man's Gaze)" (Aleixandre)
See "Rostro tras el cristal (Mirada del viejo)"
"The Face in the Stream" (Carman) **34**:212
"Face Lift" (Plath) **1**:394; **37**:254
"The Face of War" (Hughes) **53**:111
"Face Your Fears Carnal" (Alurista) **34**:25, 42
"Face-Lift" (Mueller) **33**:191
"The Faces" (Stryk) **27**:202
"Faces" (Teasdale) **31**:360
"Faces" (Whitman) **3**:397
"Facile est bien" (Éluard) **38**:84
"La Facilité en personne" (Éluard) **38**:86
"Facing" (Swenson) **14**:284, 286
"Facing Africa" (Dickey) **40**:150, 176, 178
"Facing It" (Komunyakaa) **51**:9, 42, 54, 57
"Facing the Oxford" (Guillén)
See "Frente al Oxford"
Facing the Tree (Ignatow) **34**:306-10, 322-24
"Facing the Way" (Walker) **30**:354-55
"Facing Wine with Memories of Lord Ho; Introduction and Two Poems" (Li Po) **29**:146, 187
"Fackelzug" (Celan) **10**:127
"Fact" (Hughes) **53**:160
The Fact of a Doorframe: Poems Selected and New, 1950-1984 (Rich) **5**:388-89
"The Fact of their Two Bodies" (Ríos) **57**:325
"Facteur Cheval" (Breton) **15**:50
"Faction du muet" (Char) **56**:118, 141, 198
"Factory Windows Are Always Broken" (Lindsay) **23**:268, 273, 276
"Facts" (Levine) **22**:221
"Facts" (Snyder) **21**:295-97
"The Facts of Life" (Mahon) **60**:197
"Fadaises" (Verlaine) **32**:386
"Faded Leaves" (Arnold) **5**:13
Fadensonnen (Celan) **10**:96, 98
The Faerie Queene, Disposed into Twelve Bookes Fashioning XII Morall Vertues (Spenser) **8**:323-25, 327-28, 330, 332-34, 337, 339, 341-47, 349-50, 354, 360-61, 363, 365, 369, 371-72, 374-78, 380-82, 384-85, 388-93, 395-97; **42**:211-370
"Fafaia" (Brooke) **24**:62
"Fafnir and the Knights" (Smith) **12**:302, 329
"Le fagot harmonieux" (Éluard) **38**:91
"Faida di Commune" (Carducci) **46**:53
"The Failed Spirit" (Smith) **12**:333
"Failure" (Brooke) **24**:75
"A Failure" (Day Lewis) **11**:147
"The Failure of Buffalo to Levitate" (Hass) **16**:195
"Faim" (Rimbaud) **3**:271, 282
"Faim rouge" (Char) **56**:150
"Faina" (Blok) **21**:20
Faina (Blok) **21**:24
"Fair Choice" (Hughes) **7**:135
"Fair Daffodils" (Herrick)
See "To Daffadills"
"Fair Elenor" (Blake) **12**:31
"The Fair in the Woods" (Gunn) **26**:219
"Fair Margaret's Bridal Eve" (Meredith) **60**:251
"The Fair One in My Mind" (Tagore)
See "Manas-sundari"
Fair Realism (Guest) **55**:185, 189, 198
"Fair Recluse" (Smart) **13**:341
"The Fair Singer" (Marvell) **10**:270-71, 294, 300
"Fair Weather" (Parker) **28**:348
"Faire des pieds et des mains" (Péret) **33**:230
"Faire du chemin avec . . ." (Char) **56**:146, 199
"Faire Rocks, Goodly River" (Sidney) **32**:235
"Faire seeke not to be feared" (Sidney) **32**:235
"A Fairer Hope, A Brighter Morn" (Harper) **21**:190
"The Fairest One of All" (Kumin) **15**:201, 222
"The Fairie Temple: or, Oberons Chappell. Dedicated to Mr. John Merrifield, Counsellor at Law" (Herrick) **9**:86
Fairies and Fusiliers (Graves) **6**:165
"The Fairy" (Blake) **12**:34
"The Fairy Goldsmith" (Wylie) **23**:301, 318-21, 325-26, 329-30, 332
"Fairy Land" (Poe) **1**:440
"A Fairy Tale" (Lowell) **13**:96
"Fairy Tales" (Pushkin)
See "Skazki"
Fairy Tales (Pushkin)
See *Skazki*
"Fairytale" (Wright) **14**:338
"A Fairy-Tale for Children" (Lermontov)
See *Skazka dlya detey*
A Fairytale for Children (Lermontov)
See *Skazka dlya detey*
"Faith" (Herbert) **4**:100, 119
"Faith" (Lamartine)
See "La foi"
"The Faith" (Nemerov) **24**:287
"Faith and Doubt" (Suckling) **30**:156
"Faith Healer" (Komunyakaa) **51**:34
"Faith Healing" (Larkin) **21**:229-30, 258
Faith in Life (Guillén)
See *Cántico*
"A Faith on Trial" (Meredith) **60**:256, 258, 262, 284, 287, 289, 299, 327, 333-34
"Faith Upon the Waters" (Jackson) **44**:28, 61
Faithful for Ever (Patmore) **59**:221, 243-44
"The Faithful Friend" (Cowper) **40**:126
"Faithfully Tinyig at Twilight Voice" (Cummings) **5**:110
"Faithless" (Stramm)
See "Untreu"
"The Faithless Bride" (García Lorca)
See "La casada infiel"
"The Faithless Wife" (García Lorca)
See "La casada infiel"
"Fakes" (Apollinaire)
See "Des Faux"
"The Falcon" (Patmore) **59**:240
"The Falcon" (Wylie) **23**:328
"Falcon City" (Tsvetaeva)
See "Sokolinya slobodka"
"The Falcon of Ser Federigo" (Longfellow) **30**:62
"The Falcon Woman" (Graves) **6**:156, 172
"The Fall" (Ammons) **16**:42
"Fall" (Bly) **39**:7, 71
"Fall" (Darío)
See "Autumnal"
"Fall" (Keats)
See *The Fall of Hyperion: A Dream*
"The Fall" (Muir) **49**:240, 270, 278
"Fall" (Neruda)
See "Otoño"
"Fall" (Niedecker) **42**:100
"The Fall" (Sarton) **39**:342
The Fall (Keats)
See *The Fall of Hyperion: A Dream*
"Fall 1961" (Lowell) **3**:215
"Fall and Spring" (Soto) **28**:399, 403
"fall by Fury" (Birney) **52**:59
"Fall Comes in Back-Country Vermont" (Warren) **37**:345
"Fall Festival" (Hölderlin) **4**:141
"Fall in Connecticut" (Amichai) **38**:22
"Fall, Leaves, Fall" (Brontë) **8**:68-9
The Fall of America: Poems of These States 1965-1971 (Ginsberg) **4**:53-7, 59, 63-4, 66-7, 81
The Fall of an Angel (Lamartine)
See *La chute d'un ange*
"Fall of Europe" (Mistral)
See "Caída de Europa"
The Fall of Hyperion: A Dream (Keats) **1**:287
"The Fall of Night" (Merton) **10**:340
"The Fall of Rome" (Auden) **1**:23

The Fall of the City (MacLeish) **47**:139-40, 148, 151-52, 159, 161-63, 242, 247, 256
"The Fall of the Leaf" (Thoreau) **30**:215, 281-82, 287, 295
"The Fall of the Muse" (Mueller) **33**:182
"The Fall of Zalona" (Brontë) **8**:59
"Fall, Sierra Nevada" (Rexroth) **20**:205-06
"Fall Time" (Sandburg) **2**:316; **41**:313
"The Fallen" (Hogan) **35**:259
"The Fallen" (Wagoner) **33**:327
"The Fallen Angels" (Sexton) **2**:373
"Fallen Leaves" (Illyés) **16**:243
"Fallen Leaves" (Sandburg) **41**:360
"Fallen Majesty" (Yeats) **20**:330
"Fallen Moon" (Aleixandre) **15**:18, 20, 22
"The Fallen Tower of Siloam" (Graves) **6**:137, 143
"The Fallen Tree" (Bly) **39**:53
"Fallen Tree in a Churchyard" (Ní Chuilleanáin) **34**:350
"Fallen Women" (Pavese)
See "Donne perdute"
"Falling" (Dickey) **40**:152-54, 158, 160, 167-68, 176, 195, 199, 201, 208-9, 224, 232, 241, 256, 258, 263
"Falling Asleep by Firelight" (Meredith) **28**:171
"Falling Asleep over the 'Aeneid'" (Lowell) **3**:205
"Falling into Holes in Our Sentences" (Bly) **39**:41, 43
"Falling Leaves and Early Snow" (Rexroth) **20**:207
Falling, May Day Sermon, and Other Poems (Dickey) **40**:160, 192, 194, 197, 229, 232
"The Falling of the Leaves" (Yeats) **20**:344
The Falling Star's Path (Yosano Akiko) **11**:301
Falling Up (Silverstein) **49**:319, 340-43, 345-48
"The Fallow Deer at the Lonely House" (Hardy) **8**:124
"The Falls" (Kinnell) **26**:257
"Falls Country" (Wright) **14**:378
"The Falls of Love" (Moss) **28**:137, 140, 144
The False and True Green (Quasimodo)
See *Il falso e vero verde*
False Creek Mouth (Birney) **52**:67
"The False Heart" (Belloc) **24**:31
False Justice (Hagiwara)
See *Kyomō no seigi*
"False Nightmare" (Tate) **50**:253, 256, 274
"False Prophet" (Wylie) **23**:310, 324
"A False Spring" (Boland) **58**:56-57, 60
"A False Step" (Browning) **6**:23
"False Youth, Autumn, Clothes of the Age" (Dickey) **40**:223, 230, 232
"False Youth II" (Dickey) **40**:152
"False Youth: Two Seasons" (Dickey) **40**:260
"Falsetto" (Montale) **13**:115-16
"Falso Brilhante" (Mackey) **49**:5-6
Il falso e vero verde (Quasimodo) **47**:286-87
Fama y obras pósthumas (Juana Inés de la Cruz) **24**:227-29, 231
"Fame" (Borges) **32**:58-9
"Familiar Letter to Siegfried Sassoon" (Graves) **6**:131
"Families and Friends" (Mueller) **33**:193
"Family" (Brooks) **7**:93
"Family Affairs" (Angelou) **32**:7
"Family Album" (Szymborska)
See "Album"
"Family Group" (MacLeish) **47**:205, 215
"The Family in Spring" (Soto) **28**:400
"The Family Name" (Guillén)
See "El apellido"
"Family Of" (Walker) **30**:347
Family Pictures (Brooks) **7**:63-4, 66, 83, 91, 94-5
"Family Reunion" (Erdrich) **52**:176, 185
Family Reunion (Nash) **21**:267-68
"The Famine" (Longfellow) **30**:28
"The Famine Road" (Boland) **58**:37, 42
"Famous Poet" (Hughes) **7**:114, 139
The Famous Tragedy of the Queen of Cornwall (Hardy) **8**:95
"The Fan" (Montale)
See "Il ventaglio"
"Fan Poems" (Guest) **55**:213
"A Fancy" (Carew) **29**:70-72, 74-76
"Fancy Etchings" (Harper) **21**:193, 197
"Fanfara" (Montale) **13**:134
"Fanfare, Coda and Finale" (Walker) **20**:294
"Fanscombe Barn" (Finch) **21**:143
"Fantaisies d'hiver" (Gautier) **18**:129
"Fantasia" (Carducci) **46**:41-42, 64, 86-87
"Fantasia on 'The Nut-Brown Maid'" (Ashbery) **26**:134, 140, 156, 162
"A Fantasy" (Glück) **16**:158, 163
"Fantasy" (O'Hara) **45**:171, 173-74
"Fantasy in Purple" (Hughes) **53**:122
"Fantoches" (Verlaine) **2**:430; **32**:350, 390-91
"Un fantôme" (Baudelaire) **1**:64
"Fantômes" (Césaire) **25**:10
"Far Away" (Guillén)
See "Allá lejos"
"Far Away and Long Ago" (Stevens) **6**:293
"A Far Cry from Africa" (Walcott) **46**:234, 236, 285, 307, 312, 322
"The Far Field" (Roethke) **15**:280, 310, 317
The Far Field (Roethke) **15**:271, 282-83, 303, 309, 311
Far Horizons (Carman) **34**:205, 211
"Far in a Western Brookland" (Housman) **2**:180
"Far Known to Sea and Shore" (Housman) **2**:179
"Far Niente" (Gautier) **18**:172
"Far Off" (Jiménez)
See "A lo lejos"
"Far Rockaway" (Schwartz) **8**:291, 302-03, 305
"Far West" (Snyder) **21**:300
"Far West Once" (Warren) **37**:376
"La farandola dei fanciulli" (Montale) **13**:116
"Farewel Love and all thy lawes for ever" (Wyatt) **27**:304, 317-18, 340-41
"Farewell" (Amichai) **38**:12
"Farewell" (Carducci) **46**:7, 49
"The Farewell" (Hope) **56**:305
"Farewell" (Kinnell) **26**:287
"Farewell" (Kipling) **3**:189
"The Farewell" (Lamartine)
See "L'adieu"
"Farewell" (Lermontov) **18**:301
"A Farewell" (Owen) **19**:336
"Farewell" (Patmore) **59**:209
"Farewell" (Smith) **12**:301, 339
"Farewell" (Tagore)
See "Viday"
"Farewell" (Thoreau) **30**:181
"Farewell" (Wang Wei) **18**:387
"Farewell Angelina" (Dylan) **37**:58-59, 65
"Farewell Falce Love" (Raleigh)
See "Farewell to False Loue"
"Farewell in the Mountains" (Wang Wei) **18**:387
"Farewell Love, and all thy laws for ever!" (Wyatt)
See "Farewel Love and all thy lawes for ever"
"Farewell Rehearsed" (Tate) **50**:307
Farewell, Spring! (Seifert)
See *Jaro sbohem*
"The Farewell Stairway" (Guest) **55**:185, 188-90
"Farewell Sweet Dust" (Wylie) **23**:322
"A Farewell to Alexandria" (Brontë) **8**:73
"A Farewell to America" (Wheatley) **3**:341
"Farewell to Arcady" (Dunbar) **5**:140
"Farewell to Barn and Stack and Tree" (Housman) **2**:161
"A Farewell to Celadon, on His Going to Ireland" (Behn) **13**:8
"Farewell to False Loue" (Raleigh) **31**:201, 282-85, 295, 297, 304-05, 312-13
"A Farewell to False Love" (Raleigh)
See "Farewell to False Loue"
"Farewell to Florida" (Stevens) **6**:297, 305
"Farewell to Heaven" (Tagore)
See "Svarga ha'ite biday"
"Farewell to love" (Donne) **1**:147
"Farewell to Love" (Suckling) **30**:118, 125, 141, 145
"Farewell to Nancy" (Burns) **6**:58
"Farewell to Poetry" (Herrick) **9**:95, 102, 136
"Farewell to the Court" (Raleigh) **31**:211, 243, 249-51, 259, 266, 279, 313
"Farewell to the Vertuous Gentle-woman" (Jonson)
See "To the World. A Farwell for a Gentle-woman, Vertuous and Nobel"
"Farewell to Van Gogh" (Tomlinson) **17**:301, 314
La farfalla di Dinard (Montale) **13**:161
Le farfalle (Gozzano) **10**:177-78, 184
"The Faring" (Tomlinson) **17**:349
"The Faring" (Warren) **37**:302
"Farish Street" (Walker)
See *My Farish Street Green*
Färjesång (Ekeloef) **23**:57, 62, 76
"The Farm" (MacLeish) **47**:130, 145
"The Farm Child's Lullaby" (Dunbar) **5**:138
"Farmer" (Stryk) **27**:203, 210
"The Farmer" (Williams) **7**:384
"Farmer's Death" (MacDiarmid) **9**:187, 191
"The Farmer's Wife" (Sexton) **2**:350
"The Farmer's Wife" (Tomlinson) **17**:311, 349, 358
Farming: A Handbook (Berry) **28**:5-7, 11-12, 35-6, 43
Farm-Rhymes (Riley)
See *Riley Farm-Rhymes*
Farmstead of Time (Celan)
See *Zeitgehöft*
"Faro en la noche" (Storni) **33**:247, 268
"Farre off" (Ondaatje) **28**:336
"Farrelly's Half-barrel of Stout" (Kavanagh) **33**:91, 96
"Farwell Frost, or Welcome the Spring" (Herrick) **9**:109
Farys (Mickiewicz) **38**:158-167
"Fascist Festival" (Niedecker) **42**:95
"Fase d'oriente" (Ungaretti) **57**:342
"Fast-Anchor'd Eternal O Love!" (Whitman) **3**:396
Fasti (Ovid) **2**:238, 241, 243-45, 253-55, 260-61
De Fastis (Ovid)
See *Fasti*
"Fat" (Kenyon) **57**:12
"Fat Lip" (Guillén)
See "Negro bembón"
"The Fat Man in the Mirror" (Lowell) **3**:205
"Fat William and the Trains" (Sitwell) **3**:301
"Fata Morgana" (Longfellow) **30**:103
"Fata Morgana" (Rossetti) **7**:280
Fata Morgana (Breton) **15**:51-2, 55, 62
"Fatal Interview" (Wylie) **23**:305
Fatal Interview (Millay) **6**:213, 215-16, 218, 224, 230, 235, 239, 241, 243
"Fatal Sisters" (Gray) **2**:135
"Fate" (Olds) **22**:311, 322
"The Fate of the Jury" (Masters) **36**:194
The Fate of the Jury: An Epilogue to Domesday Book (Masters) **36**:195
"The Fates" (Owen) **19**:342
"Father" (Herbert)
See "Mój ojciec"
"Father" (Quintana) **36**:275, 275
The Father (Olds) **22**:319-21, 323-24, 326, 330, 332-34, 338, 340-42
"Father and Daughter" (Sanchez) **9**:220-21, 229
"Father and Daughter" (Song) **21**:337
"Father and Farther" (Alexie) **53**:15
"Father and Son" (Ignatow) **34**:323
"Father and Son" (Kenyon) **57**:5
"Father and Son" (Kunitz) **19**:152, 154, 165, 175, 177-79
"Father and Son" (Schwartz) **8**:301-03, 305, 314

"Father Ch., Many Years Later" (Milosz) **8**:181, 202, 205
"Father Explains" (Milosz) **8**:207
"Father Father Abraham" (Johnson) **24**:160
"A Father for a Fool" (Smith) **12**:333
"Father Mat" (Kavanagh) **33**:61, 74-5, 99, 127, 130-1, 138
"Father Missouri" (Brown) **55**:71
"The Father of My Country" (Wakoski) **15**:324, 345, 354, 358
The Father of the Predicaments (McHugh) **61**:202-3, 206
"Father, on His Unsonment" (Villa) **22**:349
"A Father out Walking on the Lawn" (Dove) **6**:109
"Fatherhood" (Pavese) **13**:203
"The Fathers" (Muir) **49**:233, 245, 248-49
"The Fathers" (Sassoon) **12**:168, 282
"Father's Bedroom" (Lowell) **3**:219-20
"Father's Song" (Kumin) **15**:201
"Fatigue" (Belloc) **24**:49
"Fatigue" (Lowell) **13**:60
A Faulx contente (Char) **56**:144, 187
"The Faun" (Carman) **34**:199
"The Faun" (Plath) **1**:388; **37**:182
"The Faun Sees" (Zukofsky) **11**:368
"Le Faune" (Verlaine) **32**:350, 391
"La fausse morte" (Valéry) **9**:393, 396
"Faust" (Ashbery) **26**:118
"Faustina; or, Rock Roses" (Bishop) **3**:60; **34**:87, 138, 189
"Faustus and Helen (II)" (Crane) **3**:79, 80, 96, 98, 100
"Faustus and I" (Sexton) **2**:367, 373
Faute de sommeil, l'écorce . . . (Char)
See *La Nuit talismanique*
"La Faux relevée" (Char) **56**:120, 144
"Favor of Alexander Balas" (Cavafy) **36**:75
"Favrile" (Doty) **53**:61
"The Fawn" (Millay) **6**:214
"Faynting I folowe" (Wyatt) **27**:343
"Fe Me Sal" (McKay) **2**:225
"The Fear" (Frost) **39**:247
"Fear" (Merwin) **45**:84
"Fear" (Silverstein) **49**:334
"Fear and Fame" (Levine) **22**:228
"Fear and Trembling" (Warren) **37**:326, 380
"Fear Is Hope" (Moore) **49**:113, 149
"Fear Is What Quickens Me" (Wright) **36**:332
"The Fear of Angels" (Sarton) **39**:342
"The Fear of Beasts" (Meredith) **28**:171
"The Fear of Bo-talee" (Momaday) **25**:189, 212-13
"Fear of Death Awakens Me" (Kenyon) **57**:35, 45
"The Fear of Death Disturbs Me" (Meredith) **28**:181
"The Fearful" (Plath) **37**:269
"Fearless" (Tagore)
See "Nirbhay"
"Fears" (Yevtushenko) **40**:350
"Fears and Scruples" (Browning) **2**:59
Fears in Solitude (Coleridge) **11**:100; **39**:177
"The Feast" (Wagoner) **33**:358, 370
The Feast of the Assumption 1676 (Juana Inés de la Cruz) **24**:177
"A Feather for Voltaire" (Graham) **59**:132, 175
"Feathers from the Hill" (Merwin) **45**:61
"A Feaver" (Donne) **1**:126, 130, 153
"Febrauray" (Teasdale) **31**:364
"February" (Hughes) **7**:147
"February" (Kumin) **15**:222
"February" (Merwin) **45**:33
"february 11, 1990" (Clifton) **17**:30
"February Afternoon" (Thomas) **53**:294, 321, 325
"February Evening in New York" (Levertov) **11**:167
February in Sydney (Komunyakaa) **51**:33-34
"February Seventeenth" (Hughes) **7**:162, 165
"February Twilight" (Teasdale) **31**:334
"The Fed" (Blok) **21**:11
"Feed Still Thyself Thou Fondling With Belief" (Raleigh)
See "Feede Still Thy Selfe, Thou Fondling With Belief!"
"feed th prisoners now baby" (Bissett) **14**:32
"Feede Still Thy Selfe, Thou Fondling With Belief!" (Raleigh) **31**:201, 212, 219
"The Feeders" (Davie) **29**:110
"Feeding Out Wintery Cattle at Twilight" (Hughes) **7**:166
"Feel Me" (Swenson) **14**:267, 270, 288
"Feeling and Form" (Hacker) **47**:104
"Feeling and Precision" (Moore) **4**:251
"Feeling Fucked Up" (Knight) **14**:43, 46
"The Feelings" (Olds) **22**:326
"Feelings on Getting Older" (Corso) **33**:43
Fekete feher (Illyés) **16**:232
"Feliciano me adora y le aborrezco" (Juana Inés de la Cruz) **24**:183
"Felix Randal" (Hopkins) **15**:170
Felling (Mistral)
See *Tala*
"The Felloe'd Year" (Graves) **6**:137
"A Fellow Being" (Curnow) **48**:19, 60, 62
"Fellow Citizens" (Sandburg) **41**:233, 239, 296, 365
"Fellow Creatures" (Nash) **21**:265
"Femenina" (Storni) **33**:306;
"Feminist Manifesto" (Loy) **16**:329, 332, 334
"Femme a la blonde aisselle coiffant sa chevelure a la lueur des etioles" (Breton) **15**:48
"La Femme adultere" (Vigny) **26**:381, 410-11
"Femme dans la nuit" (Breton) **15**:48
"Femme et chatte" (Verlaine) **2**:431
"Femme et oiseau" (Breton) **15**:48, 55-6, 58-60
"Femme noire" (Senghor) **25**:224, 239
"Femmes au bord d'un lac a la surface irisee par le passage d'un cygne" (Breton) **15**:49
"Femmes damnées" (Baudelaire) **1**:62
"Femmes sur la plage" (Breton) **15**:48
"Fenaison" (Char) **56**:152, 156
"The Fence" (Erdrich) **52**:187
"A Fence" (Sandburg) **41**:236, 239, 252, 316
"Fence Posts" (Snyder) **21**:307
"Fence Wire" (Dickey) **40**:191, 257
"Les fenêtres" (Apollinaire) **7**:18, 36, 44
"Les fenêtres" (Baudelaire) **1**:59
"Les fenêtres" (Mallarmé) **4**:208
Fenêtres dormantes et porte sur le toit (Char) **56**:146, 177, 185-89, 199
"Lo feo" (Mistral) **32**:145
"Feodosija" (Mandelstam) **14**:113
"Fergus and the Druid" (Yeats) **51**:72, 148
Ferishtah's Fancies (Browning) **2**:59
"A fermosura desta fresca serra" (Camões) **31**:25
"Fern" (Hughes) **7**:121
"Fern Beds in Hampshire County" (Wilbur) **51**:248
"Fern Hill" (Thomas) **2**:382, 385, 392, 396-99, 405; **52**:219, 247-48, 252, 256, 262, 270, 273-75, 277, 281, 283, 285-86, 314-15, 321-22, 330-31
"Fernão de Magalhães" (Pessoa) **20**:155
"Fern-Beds in Hampshire Country" (Wilbur)
See "Fern Beds in Hampshire County"
Ferrements (Césaire) **25**:13, 23, 32, 44
Ferrying Across (Tagore)
See *Kheya*
Fervor de Buenos Aires (Borges) **22**:68-9, 71-2, 79, 93-4; **32**:37-9, 52-3, 60, 80-3, 95, 102-03, 109, 120-22, 125, 127, 131, 133, 139
Fervor of Buenos Aires (Borges)
See *Fervor de Buenos Aires*
"Fessler's Bees" (Riley) **48**:288
"A Festival" (Moore) **49**:142
"Festival of Spring" (Tagore)
See "Vasanter Kusumer mela"
"Festividad" (Guillén) **35**:155, 157
Festus (Aiken) **26**:7, 29
"Fetchin' Water" (McKay) **2**:216, 223
"Fetching a Nun" (Dafydd)
See "Cyrchu Lleian"
"Fête de la faim" (Rimbaud) **57**:245
Fête de la patience (Rimbaud) **57**:252-53
"Fête des arbres et du chasseur" (Char) **56**:170, 173
"Fête d'hiver" (Rimbaud) **57**:236, 240, 273
"Fêtes de la faim" (Rimbaud) **3**:259
Fêtes galantes (Verlaine) **2**:413-15, 424-25, 430-32; **32**:342, 346-53, 359, 364, 366, 368, 370-71, 384, 389-90, 392-95, 399
Feu central (Péret) **33**:231
"Un feu va devant nous" (Bonnefoy) **58**:119
"Feuer-Nacht" (Bogan) **12**:94, 121
"Feuertaufe" (Stramm) **50**:170, 220-21
"Le Feuillage éclairé" (Bonnefoy) **58**:125
Les feuilles d'automne (Hugo) **17**:42-45, 52, 63, 66, 68, 90-93
Feuillets d'Hypnos (Char) **56**:106-7, 109-10, 112, 131-32, 160, 169, 175, 181, 185, 189-91, 196
"Fever" (Brathwaite) **56**:51
"A Fever" (Donne)
See "A Feaver"
"Fever" (Gunn) **26**:220
"A Fever" (Merrill) **28**:221
"Fever 103°" (Plath) **1**:382, 386, 393; **37**:232-33, 240, 256
"A Few Coins" (Soto) **28**:371
"A Few Figs from Thistles" (Millay) **6**:208, 211, 234
A Few Figs from Thistles (Millay) **6**:207, 211-12, 227, 230, 233-35, 237, 239
"Fiammetta Breaks Her Peace" (Dove) **6**:109
"Les fiançailles" (Apollinaire) **7**:43-4, 46, 48
"Fibrous Ruin" (Jordan) **38**:119
"Ficha Ingreso Hospital General" (Fuertes) **27**:3
"The Fiddle" (Riley) **48**:282
"Fiddler Jones" (Masters) **1**:333
"Fidelity" (Lawrence) **54**:185, 218
"Fidelity" (Wordsworth) **4**:383
"Field" (Abse) **41**:3
"Field" (Soto) **28**:375, 377-78, 384-85
"Field and Forest" (Jarrell) **41**:153-54
"Field Bath" (Mahon) **60**:141
Field Guide (Hass) **16**:194-95, 197, 199-201, 209, 212, 214, 216, 222, 228
"A Field Hospital" (Jarrell) **41**:147, 168
"A Field of Light" (Roethke) **15**:248, 254, 304, 307
"The Field of the Potter" (Muir) **49**:239
"The Field Pansy" (Clampitt) **19**:94, 96
"Field Report" (Corso) **33**:44
"Field Work" (Heaney) **18**:245
Field Work (Heaney) **18**:197-99, 211-12, 215, 238-40, 242, 245-47, 255-57
Fields of Wonder (Hughes) **1**:240-44, 247, 268; **53**:149
"The Fiend" (Dickey) **40**:151, 153, 158, 172, 189, 196, 213, 215-16, 226-27, 241, 256, 259, 263
"Fiend, Dragon, Mermaid" (Graves) **6**:142, 145
"Fierce Hope" (Tagore)
See "Duranta asha"
"Fiesole" (Carducci) **46**:49, 76, 81, 84, 88
"Fiesta" (Pasolini) **17**:253
"Fiesta" (Storni) **33**:281;
"Fiez-vous donc à moi . . ." (Rimbaud) **57**:248
Fifine at the Fair (Browning) **2**:42-4, 50, 72, 75, 80, 82, 96; **61**:32
"XV" (Joyce) **22**:138, 145, 170
"Fifteen to Eighteen" (Hacker) **47**:82
"Fifteen Years After" (Thumboo) **30**:300, 329, 332
"The Fifteenth Amendment" (Harper) **21**:197
"Fifteenth Farewell" (Bogan) **12**:86
Fifth Decad of Cantos (Pound) **4**:324
"Fifth Grade Autobiography" (Dove) **6**:120
Fifth Nemean (Pindar)
See *Nemean 5*
"Fifty Faggots" (Thomas) **53**:328, 346, 349-50
"Fifty for Richard Nonas" (Yau) **61**:337

"Fifty Males Sitting Together" (Bly) **39**:103
Fifty Poems (Cummings) **5**:84, 107-08
50 Poems (Cummings)
See *Fifty Poems*
Fifty Poems (Dafydd ap Gwilym) **56**:221
"52 Oswald Street" (Kinnell) **26**:258
"Fifty Years" (Johnson) **24**:127, 131, 143, 145-47, 154, 157-60
Fifty Years, and Other Poems (Johnson) **24**:127, 131, 141-49, 152-55, 157, 159, 162, 166
"50-50" (Hughes) **1**:247
55 Poems (Zukofsky) **11**:341
"Fight" (Bukowski) **18**:15
"Fight" (Sandburg) **41**:238
Fight Back: For the Sake of the People, for the Sake of the Land (Ortiz) **17**:222-223, 233, 239, 244
"Fight Him Fair Nigger" (Knight) **14**:49
"Fight to a Finish" (Sassoon) **12**:267
"Fighting South of the Ramparts" (Li Po) **29**:139
Fighting Terms: A Selection (Gunn) **26**:181, 183, 188, 197, 199-200, 205-206, 210-12, 215-19, 229
"La figlia che piange" (Eliot) **5**:153, 184; **31**:92
"La figue l'oeillet et la pipe a opium" (Apollinaire) **7**:32
"Figure for a Landscape" (Mueller) **33**:180
"Figure from Polities" (Meredith) **28**:187
"The Figure in the Scene" (Hardy) **8**:137
"Figure of Eight" (MacNeice) **61**:127
"FIGURE SKATER" (Birney) **52**:29, 76, 81-82
"The Figured Wheel" (Pinsky) **27**:163, 165, 173-6
The Figured Wheel (Pinsky) **27**:175
"The Figurehead" (Shapiro) **25**:316, 325
"Figures" (Hayden) **6**:196
The Figures of Human (Ignatow)
See *Figures of the Human*
"Figures of the Human" (Ignatow) **34**:277
Figures of the Human (Ignatow) **34**:274, 276-77, 281-82, 312
Figures of Thought: Speculations on the Meaning of Poetry and Other Essays (Nemerov) **24**:299, 303
"Figurine" (Hughes) **1**:245
Fihi ma fihi (Rumi) **45**:259, 261-62, 273-78, 320
"La fileuse" (Valéry) **9**:391
"Los filibusteros" (Cardenal) **22**:110
"La Fille de Jephte" (Vigny) **26**:401, 410
Les filles du feu (Nerval) **13**:176-78, 192, 195
"Filling Out a Blank" (Wagoner) **33**:327
"Filling Station" (Bishop) **34**:118, 149
"Filling the Boxes of Joseph Cornell" (Wakoski) **15**:324
"Film Script" (Mueller) **33**:193
"Filo del amor" (Aleixandre) **15**:19, 23
"La fin de la journée" (Baudelaire) **1**:54
La fin de Satan (Hugo) **17**:65, 74, 81, 84, 88, 91
Final (Guillén) **35**:185, 213-14, 225-26, 227, 229, 230, 232, 234
"Final Call" (Hughes) **1**:252
"Final Curve" (Hughes) **53**:125
"Final Face" (Aleixandre) **15**:4
"Final Fire" (Aleixandre) **15**:18-19
"Final Shadow" (Aleixandre) **15**:16
"The Final Slope" (Stryk) **27**:203
"the final solution" (Sanchez) **9**:224
"Finale" (Guillén) **35**:214
"Finale" (Longfellow) **30**:66
"Finale" (Wagoner) **33**:365
"Finally" (Merwin) **45**:24, 101
"A Finch Sitting Out a Windstorm" (Wright) **36**:393
"Finding" (Brooke) **24**:57-8
"Finding a Long Gray Hair" (Kenyon) **57**:23, 36-37, 43
"Finding a Teacher" (Merwin) **45**:92, 98
"Finding an Ant Mansion" (Bly)
See "Finding an Old Ant Mansion"
"Finding an Old Ant Mansion" (Bly) **39**:67, 99
"The Finding of Reasons" (Merwin) **45**:49
"The Finding of the Moon" (Wright) **14**:356
"Finding the Father" (Bly) **39**:44, 100
Finding the Islands (Merwin) **45**:72
"Finding the One Brief Note" (Kumin) **15**:215
"Finding the Right Direction" (Wagoner) **33**:352
Findings (Berry) **28**:5
"Fine Arts" (Birney) **52**:29
Fine Clothes to the Jew (Hughes) **1**:237-38, 244, 246, 254-55, 258, 260, 262-63, 268-71; **53**:79, 86, 106, 135-36, 138, 140, 164, 170, 181-83, 199
"Fine del '68" (Montale) **13**:134
"La fine dell'infanzia" (Montale) **13**:115-16
"Finis" (Montale) **13**:139
"Finis Poloniae" (Benn) **35**:66
"Finisterne" (Montale) **13**:156, 165-66
"Finisterre" (Warren) **37**:380
Finisterre (Montale) **13**:103, 106, 127-30
"Finnish Champion" (Mistral)
See "Campeón Finlandés"
"Fins" (Sandburg) **2**:307
"The Fire" (Atwood) **8**:39
"The Fire" (Belloc) **24**:32
"The Fire" (Brodsky) **9**:2
"The Fire" (Glück) **16**:127
"Fire" (Hughes) **53**:117, 119
"Fire" (Toomer) **7**:333
"Fire" (Zagajewski) **27**:380
"Fire and Earth" (Alurista) **34**:22
"Fire and Ice" (Frost) **1**:194, 197
"Fire and Sleet and Candlelight" (Wylie) **23**:301, 307
"Fire at Murdering Hut" (Wright) **14**:339
"Fire by the River" (Wagoner) **33**:333
"Fire Island" (Swenson) **14**:271, 285-86
"The Fire of Despair Has Been Our Saviour" (Bly) **39**:84
"The Fire of Drift-Wood" (Longfellow) **30**:36, 42
"Fire on the Hills" (Jeffers) **17**:117, 127
"Fire Poem" (Merrill) **28**:241-42
"Fire Practice" (McKay) **2**:225
The Fire Screen (Merrill) **28**:220-21, 228, 230-31, 258, 264, 281
"Fire Song" (Ekeloef) **23**:51
"Fire Station" (Bukowski) **18**:16
"'Fire Stop Thief Help Murder Save the World'" (Cummings) **5**:107
"Fire Storm" (Alexie) **53**:54
"A Fire Truck" (Wilbur) **51**:218, 301
"The Firebombers" (Sexton) **2**:365
"The Firebombing" (Dickey) **40**:151, 154-55, 157-58, 175, 184, 193-94, 209, 212-15, 231-32, 241, 246, 252-53, 255, 259
"The Fireborn Are at Home in Fire" (Sandburg) **41**:301
"Fired" (Hughes) **1**:247
"Fireflies" (Swenson) **14**:250
"Fireman's Lift" (Ní Chuilleanáin) **34**:361, 368-69
"The Firemen's Ball" (Lindsay) **23**:265, 268, 281
"Firenze" (Ferlinghetti) **1**:183
Fires: Essays, Poems, Stories, 1966-1982 (Carver) **54**:3, 7, 20, 31
"Firewarden on Kearsage" (Francis) **34**:244
"Fireworks" (Shapiro) **25**:269
Fir-Flower Tablets (Lowell) **13**:64, 74, 93
"The 1st" (Clifton) **17**:17
"First" (Kipling) **3**:160
"First, a poem must be magical" (Villa) **22**:352
First Alluvia (Char)
See *Premières alluvions*
"The First American" (Toomer) **7**:337
"The First and Last Night of Love" (Cassian) **17**:4, 6
The First and Second Anniversaries (Donne)
See *The Anniversaries*
The First Anniversarie. An Anatomie of the World. Wherein By Occasion of the untimely death of Mistris Elizabeth Drury, the frailtie and decay of this whole World is represented (Donne) **1**:122, 145-50, 152, 155-57
"The First Anniversary of the Government Under His Highness the Lord Protector" (Marvell)
See "The First Anniversary of the Government under O. C."
"The First Anniversary of the Government under O. C." (Marvell) **10**:270-71, 290, 294, 305, 312, 318
"The First Autumn" (Sarton) **39**:345
First Awakenings: The Early Poems of Laura Riding (Jackson) **44**:66, 68
First Book (Blok) **21**:2
The First Book of Urizen (Blake)
See *The Book of Urizen*
"First Calf" (Heaney) **18**:203
"First Carolina Said Song" (Ammons) **16**:5
"The First Celestial Adventure of M Antipyrine" (Tzara) **27**:249
The First Cities (Lorde) **12**:137
"First Communion" (Kinnell) **26**:239
"First Communions" (Rimbaud)
See "Les Premières Communions"
"First Dances" (O'Hara) **45**:114
"First Day of the Future" (Kinnell) **26**:277
"The First Days" (Wright) **36**:314, 378
"First Death in Nova Scotia" (Bishop) **34**:82
The First Decade: Selected Poems (Duncan) **2**:105-06
First Dream (Juana Inés de la Cruz) **24**:207
"First Early Mornings Together" (Pinsky) **27**:144
"The First Eight Days of the Beard" (Kenyon) **57**:46
"First Elegy" (Rilke) **2**:281, 286
"First Elegy" (Rukeyser) **12**:219
"First Encounter" (Quintana) **36**:272
The First Encounter (Bely)
See *Pervoe svidanie*
"First Epistle of the First Book of Horace" (Pope)
See *Satires and Epistles of Horace, Imitated*
"First Fig" (Millay) **6**:227
"First Fight. Then Fiddle" (Brooks) **7**:75
The First Four Books of Poetry (Merwin) **45**:52
"First Georgic" (Vergil) **12**:364
"The First Gloss" (Heaney) **18**:216
"First Goodbye" (Glück) **16**:165-67
The First Half of "A"-9 (Zukofsky) **11**:339, 396-97
"First Hymn to Lenin" (MacDiarmid) **9**:177-78, 182
First Hymn to Lenin, and Other Poems (MacDiarmid) **9**:158, 162, 171, 177, 196
"First Inclined to Take What It Is Told" (Brooks) **7**:74
First Indian on the Moon (Alexie) **53**:5-11, 30-31, 34, 40
"First Known When Lost" (Thomas) **53**:328
"The First Law of Motion" (Wagoner) **33**:334
"First Lesson about Man" (Merton) **10**:344-45
"First Letters from a Steamer" (McGuckian) **27**:82
First Light (Wagoner) **33**:359, 361-62, 364
"First Love" (Leopardi)
See "Il Primo Amore"
"The First Man" (Gunn) **26**:191
"First Meditation" (Roethke) **15**:272, 274, 279
The First Meetings (Bely)
See *Pervoe svidanie*
"First Memory" (Glück) **16**:157
First Mill (Char)
See *Moulin premier*
"First, Mills" (Hughes) **7**:149
"First Moment of Autumn Recognized" (Warren) **37**:379
The First Morning (Viereck) **27**:264-65
First Morning (Viereck) **27**:280-81, 283

First Nemean (Pindar)
See *Nemean 1*
"First News from Villafranca" (Browning) **6**:23-4
"First Night" (Olds) **22**:309
"The First Noni Daylight" (Harjo) **27**:64
"First Objectives" (MacDiarmid) **9**:154
"The First of All My Dreams Was of" (Cummings) **5**:109
"The First of January" (Lermontov) **18**:201
"The First of May" (Guest) **55**:218
First Olympian (Pindar)
See *Olympian 1*
"A First on TV" (Ignatow) **34**:310, 318
"First Page" (Stein) **18**:313
"The First Part" (Page) **12**:190
First Poems (Merrill) **28**:224, 228-9, 233-4, 238-40, 243-4, 262, 281
First Poems (Muir) **49**:211, 227-29, 235, 237-39, 270, 277, 286-88
First Poems, 1946-1954 (Kinnell) **26**:279
"First Praise" (Williams) **7**:405
First Pythian (Pindar)
See *Pythian 1*
"The First Rain" (Sikelianos) **29**:367, 373
First Satire of the Second Book of Horace Imitated (Pope)
See *Satires and Epistles of Horace, Imitated*
"The First, Second, Third and Fourth Circles" (Szirtes) **51**:172, 177
"First Snow" (Sarton) **39**:318-19
"The First Snow in Alsace" (Wilbur) **51**:187, 192, 266-67, 295, 315-19, 321
"First Snow in Lake County" (Mueller) **33**:180
"First Song" (Akhmatova)
See "Pervaya pesenka"
"First Song" (Kinnell) **26**:253, 257
First Song (Kinnell) **26**:236-38, 253, 262
"The First Step" (Cavafy) **36**:28, 100, 108
the first sufi line (Bissett) **14**:17
"The First Sunday in Lent" (Lowell) **3**:206
The First Symphony (Bely)
See *Severnaia simfoniia: Pervia geroicheskaia*
"The First Time" (Shapiro) **25**:283, 300, 302, 320
"The First Time" (Warren) **37**:367, 376
First Voronezh Notebook (Mandelstam) **14**:149, 152, 154
"The First Word" (Wagoner) **33**:370
"The First-Born" (Hope) **56**:277
Firstborn (Glück) **16**:124-25, 127, 130-32, 134, 138-40, 143-44, 147-49, 151, 153
"Der Fischer" (Goethe) **5**:239
"The Fish" (Bishop) **3**:37, 39, 42-3, 50-2, 54, 60, 66, 69, 75; **34**:53, 78, 90, 116, 187, 189
"The Fish" (Brooke) **24**:58, 63, 65, 87
"Fish" (Lawrence) **54**:189, 191, 224, 232-33
"The Fish" (Moore) **4**:236, 243, 252, 257; **49**:89-90, 98-99, 101, 155
"Fish" (Stryk) **27**:209
"Fish Crier" (Sandburg) **2**:332, 338; **41**:234, 239, 267, 269, 287, 320, 365
"Fish Monger" (Sandburg) **41**:267
Fish Monger (Sandburg)
See "Fish Crier"
"The Fish that Walked" (Sexton) **2**:370, 373
"Fisherman" (Kinnell) **26**:260
"The Fisherman" (Yeats) **20**:324-25
"The Fisherman and the Fish" (Pushkin)
See "Skazka o Rybake i Rybke"
The Fisherman's Art (Ovid)
See *Halieutica*
"The Fisherman's Wife" (Wagoner) **33**:348
"The Fisher's Son" (Thoreau) **30**:217, 233, 284, 293
"The Fisherwoman" (Ignatow) **34**:315-16
"Fishing" (Hogan) **35**:271
"Fishing at Dawn" (Hughes) **7**:120
"Fishing for Eel Totems" (Atwood) **8**:12
"Fishing the White Water" (Lorde) **12**:137
"Fishing with My Daughter in Miller's Meadow" (Stryk) **27**:204, 208, 214
"Fishnet" (Lowell) **3**:229
"Fission" (Graham) **59**:135, 143-45, 156
"Fist" (Levine) **22**:214, 223, 227
"The Fist" (Walcott) **46**:236, 279
The Fist Too Was Once the Palm of an Open Hand and Fingers (Amichai)
See *Gam ha'egrof haya pa'am yad ptuba ve'etsba'ot*
"A Fit against the Country" (Wright) **36**:336, 339, 343, 360
"Fit of Fainting" (Bradstreet)
See "Deliverance From a Fit of Fainting"
"A Fit of Rime Against Rime" (Jonson)
See *The Under-Wood XXXI*
"The Fitting" (Millay) **6**:230, 239
"The Fitting of the Mask" (Kunitz) **19**:154
"V" (Joyce) **22**:138, 162, 167
"Five Accounts of a Monogamous Man" (Meredith) **28**:171, 175, 193-94, 213
"Five Aspects of Fear" (Levertov) **11**:164
"The Five Day Rain" (Levertov) **11**:169
"Five Flights Up" (Bishop) **3**:48-9, 72; **34**:82, 149
Five Indiscretions (Ríos) **57**:323, 325
"5. Jahrhundert" (Benn)
See "V. Jahrhundert"
"5 Jan 72" (Brutus) **24**:124
"Five Men" (Herbert) **50**:4, 25, 33-35
The Five Nations (Kipling) **3**:192
"Five Poems about Poetry" (Oppen) **35**:299, 336
"Five Senses" (Wright) **14**:348, 363
Five Senses: Selected Poems (Wright) **14**:348, 354, 361, 371
"Five Songs" (Rilke) **2**:273
"Five Things" (Goethe) **5**:228
Five Variations on a Theme (Sitwell) **3**:304
"Five Vignettes" (Toomer) **7**:332
"Five Walks on the Edge" (Viereck) **27**:277
"Five-Finger Exercises" (Eliot) **5**:185
"Le flacon" (Baudelaire) **1**:45
Flagons and Apples (Jeffers) **17**:133, 138
"Le flambeau vivant" (Baudelaire) **1**:56, 61
"Les Flambeaux" (Bonnefoy) **58**:153
Flame and Shadow (Teasdale) **31**:322-25, 327, 330, 333, 338, 340, 347, 351, 355, 357-58, 360, 370-71, 379, 388
"The Flame Tree" (Wright) **14**:347
"Flame-Heart" (McKay) **2**:216, 228
"Flammonde" (Robinson) **1**:462, 468, 476; **35**:363
"The Flash" (Dickey) **40**:152, 160
"Flash" (Stone) **53**:220
"Flashes and Dedications" (Montale)
See "Flashes e dediche"
"Flashes e dediche" (Montale) **13**:106, 166-67
"Flat Lands" (Sandburg) **41**:328
"Flat-Foot Drill" (McKay) **2**:225
"Flatland" (Hope) **56**:275
"Flatted Fifth" (Hughes) **1**:267; **53**:92, 114, 191
"Flaubert in Egypt" (Warren) **37**:306, 340
"The Flaw" (Lowell) **3**:226-28
"The Flaw in Paganism" (Parker) **28**:351, 363
"A Flayed Crow in the Hall of Judgement" (Hughes) **7**:165
The Fle From Me (Wyatt)
See "They fle from me"
"The Flea" (Donne) **1**:134, 152
"Flèche D'or" (Merrill) **28**:254
"Fleckno" (Marvell) **10**:271, 294
"Flee on Your Donkey" (Sexton) **2**:351, 363-64
Fleeting Moments (Tagore)
See *Kshanikā*
Fleeting Thoughts (Tagore)
See *Kshanikā*
"Fleisch" (Benn) **35**:49, 50
Fleisch (Benn) **35**:3, 29, 30, 31, 50, 77
"Fleming Helphenstine" (Robinson) **1**:466
"Flemish Rain" (Szirtes) **51**:171
"Flesh" (Wright) **14**:347
"The Flesh and the Spirit" (Bradstreet) **10**:7-8, 13, 21, 29-30, 38
"Fletcher McGee" (Masters) **1**:345; **36**:190, 221
"Fletches" (Brathwaite) **56**:91
"La Fleur qui fait le printemps" (Gautier) **18**:128-29
"Fleurs" (Rimbaud) **57**:175, 234, 236, 250, 254, 284
Les fleurs du mal (Baudelaire) **1**:44-51, 53-8, 60, 62-5, 67-71
"Flexibilité de l'oubli" (Char) **56**:127
"Flexibility of Forgetfulness" (Char)
See "Flexibilité de l'oubli"
"Flies Enter through a Closed Mouth" (Neruda)
See "Por boca cerrada entran moscas"
"Flight" (Brooke) **24**:56
"Flight" (Hughes) **53**:198-99, 201, 206
"The Flight" (Mickiewicz)
See "Ucieczka"
"The Flight" (Mistral)
See "La fuga"
"The Flight" (Roethke) **15**:302
"Flight" (Sexton) **2**:347, 361
"The Flight" (Teasdale) **31**:322, 325
"Flight into Egypt" (Auden) **1**:38
"The Flight into Egypt" (Merton) **10**:330
A Flight of Cranes (Tagore)
See *Balākā*
A Flight of Swans (Tagore)
See *Balākā*
"Flight of the Heart" (MacNeice) **61**:139
"Flight to the City" (Williams) **7**:385, 387-88
"Flippancies" (Wilbur) **51**:301
"Flippancies 1: The Star System" (Wilbur) **51**:285
"Flippancies 2: What's Good for the Soul is Good for Sales" (Wilbur) **51**:285
"The Flitting" (McGuckian) **27**:78, 97
"Floating" (Rexroth) **20**:216
"Floating of the River of Han" (Wang Wei) **18**:362
"The Flood" (Bishop) **34**:94
"The Flood" (Erdrich) **52**:186
"The Flood" (Tomlinson) **17**:333
"The Flood" (Wright) **14**:337-38
The Flood (Tomlinson) **17**:332, 336, 349, 354
"The Flood of Years" (Bryant) **20**:10, 16-18
"Flooded Meadows" (Gunn) **26**:219
"Flooding" (Celan) **10**:105
La flor (Castro) **41**:93-4, 97, 103
"Flora" (Morris) **55**:323, 325
"The Floral Apron" (Chin) **40**:29
"Florence" (Lowell) **3**:213, 236
Floricanto en Aztlán (Alurista) **34**:3-5, 14-17, 21, 26, 31-36, 38-41, 45-48
"Florida" (Bishop) **3**:37; **34**:79, 116, 130
"La florida" (Guillén) **35**:153, 155, 156
"A Florida Sunday" (Lanier) **50**:56
Flow Chart (Ashbery) **26**:164
"Flow Gently Sweet Afton" (Burns)
See "Sweet Afton"
"The Flower" (Herbert) **4**:104, 109, 113, 118, 127, 131-32
"The Flower and the Rock" (Page) **12**:178
Flower, Fist, and Bestial Wail (Bukowski) **18**:3, 5
Flower Herding on Mount Monadnock (Kinnell) **26**:236, 257, 290
"Flower in the Crannied Wall" (Tennyson) **6**:358
"The Flower Master" (McGuckian) **27**:78
The Flower Master (McGuckian) **27**:77-80, 84-85, 95-97, 101, 104
"Flower of Five Blossoms" (Kinnell) **26**:286
"The Flower of Old Japan" (Noyes) **27**:116-17, 139
The Flower of Old Japan (Noyes) **27**:116, 139
"A Flower Passage" (Wright) **36**:364, 400
"Flower Poem" (Hope) **56**:285, 298-99
"Flowered Sitting Room" (McGuckian) **27**:105
"The Flower-Fed Buffaloes" (Lindsay) **23**:279

"The Flowering of the Rod" (H. D.) **5**:271-72, 274-75, 293, 296, 306, 309, 314-16
"Flowering Plum" (Glück) **16**:128, 154
"The Flowering Tree" (Bridges) **28**:77, 80
"Flowers" (Brathwaite) **56**:61
"The Flowers" (Kipling) **3**:161, 167
"Flowers" (Rimbaud)
See "Fleurs"
"Flowers and Men" (Lawrence) **54**:179
"flowers in the lake" (Alurista) **34**:34
The Flowers of Evil (Baudelaire)
See *Les fleurs du mal*
"Fluch" (Stramm) **50**:189
"The Flume" (Bogan) **12**:95, 121
"Flumen Tenebarum" (Wilbur) **51**:186
"La flûte" (Vigny) **26**:367, 392, 403, 413
"Flute Notes from a Reedy Pond" (Plath) **1**:389
"Flute of Spring" (Carman) **34**:208
"A Flute Overheard" (Rexroth) **20**:195
"Flute-Maker, with an Accompaniment" (Browning) **2**:88
"Flutender" (Celan) **10**:105
"Flux" (Sandburg) **41**:313
"FLux et reflux" (Hugo) **17**:100
"The Fly" (Blake) **12**:7, 34
"The Fly" (Brodsky) **9**:29
"The Fly" (Kinnell) **26**:255
"Fly" (Merwin) **45**:20
"The Fly" (Shapiro) **25**:269, 324, 326
"The Fly" (Wilbur) **51**:191
"A Fly that flew into my Mistress her Eye" (Carew) **29**:87
"Flying Above California" (Gunn) **26**:201, 219
"Flying Crooked" (Graves) **6**:149, 151
"The Flying Eagles of Troop" (Wright) **36**:363, 372, 392
"Flying Fish" (Sandburg) **41**:263
"Flying Home" (Kinnell) **26**:259, 261
"Flying Home from Utah" (Swenson) **14**:261
"The Flying Islands of the Night, a fantastic drama in verse" (Riley) **48**:289
"Flying out of It" (Ferlinghetti) **1**:175
"Flying to Byzantium" (Merrill) **28**:221
"Flying Underground" (Giovanni) **19**:143
"Foam" (Enzensberger) **28**:146-48, 156
"La Foce" (MacLeish) **47**:197
"Fog" (Cassian) **17**:6
"Fog" (Doty) **53**:46, 64, 71-74
"Fog" (Merwin) **45**:7
"Fog" (Sandburg) **2**:301, 303; **41**:228, 234, 239, 250, 276, 281, 298, 348, 358
"Fog" (Soto) **28**:377, 384
"Fog" (Thoreau) **30**:190, 194, 207, 216, 235, 257
"Fog" (Warren) **37**:303, 380
"Fog Argument" (Doty) **53**:51, 54
"Fog Envelops the Animals" (Dickey) **40**:176, 183-85, 189-90
"Fog Suite" (Doty) **53**:60
"The Foggy, Foggy Blue" (Schwartz) **8**:317
"Fog-Horn" (Merwin) **45**:7
"Fogs and Fires" (Sandburg) **41**:237
"La foi" (Lamartine) **16**:277, 291
"The Foilage Lit" (Bonnefoy)
See "Le Feuillage éclairé"
The Folding Cliffs (Merwin) **45**:102-9
"Folie de Minuit" (Lowell) **13**:90-1
"A Folk Singer of the Thirties" (Dickey) **40**:256
"Folk Song" (Parker) **28**:355
"Folk Tune" (Wilbur) **51**:217
"The Folk-Mote by the River" (Morris) **55**:340
"The Folks Inside" (Silverstein) **49**:341
"Folkways" (Brathwaite) **56**:75, 83, 99
Follas novas (Castro) **41**:79, 87-91, 93, 95-8, 100-2, 105-6, 111-16
"Follas novas IV" (Castro) **41**:89
"Follas novas VI" (Castro) **41**:91
"Follies" (Sandburg) **2**:303
"Follow that Stagecoach" (Wakoski) **15**:323
"Follower" (Heaney) **18**:200
"Following" (Ní Chuilleanáin) **34**:373
"Following the Recipe of Ancient Greco-Syrian Magicians" (Cavafy) **36**:63, 86, 112
"Folly" (MacDiarmid) **9**:153
"The Folly of Being Comforted" (Yeats) **20**:356
"Fonction du poète" (Hugo) **17**:77, 97
"Fond Memory" (Boland) **58**:3, 19
"Fontainebleau" (Teasdale) **31**:339
"Fontana di aga del me pais" (Pasolini) **17**:259
"Food" (Corso) **33**:47
"The Food Chain" (Kumin) **15**:208
"Food for Fire, Food for Thought" (Duncan) **2**:120-21
"A Fool, A Foul Thing, A Distressful Lunatic" (Moore) **49**:121
"The Fool by the Roadside" (Yeats) **51**:108
"Fool Errant" (Lowell) **13**:83
"Fool o' the Moon" (Lowell) **13**:67, 83, 86
Fool Youngens (Riley) **48**:292
"Fooling God" (Erdrich) **52**:186, 191
"Foolish About Windows" (Sandburg) **41**:287
"The Foolish Heart" (Cullen) **20**:59
"Foolish Men" (Juana Inés de la Cruz)
See "Hombres necios que acusáis"
"Foolish Pride" (Castro)
See "Sobrera"
"The Fools' Paradise" (Morris) **55**:306
"Foot of Pride" (Dylan) **37**:59
"Footnote to Howl" (Ginsberg) **4**:65, 68, 70; **47**:9-11, 34, 36-37, 44-45, 47, 61
Footprints (Levertov) **11**:189
"The footsteps" (Cavafy) **36**:57
"The Footsteps of Angels" (Longfellow) **30**:45, 96, 109
"The Foot-Washing" (Ammons) **16**:58
"For—" (Corso) **33**:49
"For" (Zukofsky) **11**:349
"For a better love/sex" (Dalton)
See "Para un mejor amor"
"For a Birthday" (Gunn) **26**:206
"For a Dead Citizen" (Tate) **50**:228, 306
"For a Dead Lady" (Robinson) **1**:461, 490, 492-93
"For a Dead Vole" (Smith) **12**:317
"For a Fatherless Son" (Plath) **1**:397; **37**:254, 260
"For a few Hopi Ancestors" (Rose) **13**:233
"For a Fiftieth Anniversary" (Hacker) **47**:107
"For a Friend" (Ignatow) **34**:313
"For a Good Dog" (Nash) **21**:268
"For a Grave at Komarovo" (Hope) **56**:282
"For a Lady Who Must Write Verse" (Parker) **28**:363
"For a Lovely Lady" (Cullen) **20**:52, 55
"For a Marriage" (Bogan) **12**:94
"For a Muse Meant" (Duncan) **2**:105
"For a Pastoral Family" (Wright) **14**:375, 378
"For a Photograph of My Mother at the Beach" (Stone) **53**:227
"For a Picture of St. Dorothea" (Hopkins) **15**:144, 159-62
"For a Poet" (Cullen) **20**:85
"For a Russian Poet" (Rich) **5**:383
"For a Sad Lady" (Parker) **28**:360
"For a Self-Possessed Friend" (Warren) **37**:331
"For a street in the West" (Borges)
See "Para una calle del Oeste"
"For a' that" (Scott) **13**:293
"For A' That and A' That" (Burns)
See "Is There for Honest Poverty"
"For a Woman Who Dreamed All the Horses were Dying" (Wagoner) **33**:349
"For a Woman Who Phoned Poetry Northwest Thinking It Was Poultry Northwest" (Wagoner) **33**:373
"For a Young Artist" (Hayden) **6**:187, 189-90, 196, 198
"For All Who Ever sent Lace Valentines" (Lindsay) **23**:265
"For All You Know" (Cervantes) **35**:113
"For Alva Benson and For Those Who Have Learned to Speak" (Harjo) **27**:55, 64
"For Ammonis, Who Died at 29, in A.D. 610" (Cavafy) **36**:8, 111
"For an Assyrian Frieze" (Viereck) **27**:260, 280
"For an Emigrant" (Jarrell) **41**:168, 184, 213
"For Andy Goodman—Michael Schwerner—and James Chaney (Three Civil Rights Workers Murdered in Mississippi on June 21, 1964)" (Walker) **20**:277-78, 287
"For Ann Scott-Moncrieff (1914-1943)" (Muir) **49**:232, 245
"For Anna Mae Pictou Aquash, Whose Spirit Is Present Here and in the Dappled Stars (For We Remember the Story and Tell It Again So that We May All Live)" (Harjo) **27**:71
"For Anne at Passover" (Kumin) **15**:180
"For Annie" (Poe) **1**:425, 434, 437, 444-45, 447
"For Black People" (Madhubuti) **5**:327, 345
"For Black Poets Who Think of Suicide" (Knight) **14**:42
"For C." (Wilbur) **51**:332, 335
"For Chekhov" (Hass) **16**:199, 214
"For Clarice" (Brooks) **7**:56
"For Danton" (Tomlinson) **17**:345-46, 350
"For Dave: 1976" (Jordan) **38**:122
"For Deliverance from a Fever" (Bradstreet) **10**:36, 60
"For Don Drummond" (Goodison) **36**:154
"For Each of You" (Lorde) **12**:157
"For Edward Long" (Cervantes) **35**:107, 113, 117
"For Eleanor and Bill Monahan" (Williams) **7**:392-93
"For Eleanor Boylan Talking with God" (Sexton) **2**:371
"For Eli Jacobsen" (Rexroth) **20**:181
"For Ellen" (Wilbur) **51**:223
"For Eric Dolphy" (Knight) **14**:39
For Farish Street (Walker)
See *My Farish Street Green*
"For Freckle-Faced Gerald" (Knight) **14**:41-2
"For George Lamming" (Birney) **52**:15, 102
"For George Santayana" (Lowell) **3**:219
"For God While Sleeping" (Sexton) **2**:351, 360-61, 371
"For Godsake hold your tongue, and let me love" (Donne)
See "The Canonization"
"For Guillaume Apollinaire" (Meredith) **28**:194, 208
"For Gwendolyn Brooks" (Giovanni) **19**:113
"For Helen" (Stryk) **27**:203
"For Hettie in Her Fifth Month" (Baraka) **4**:15
"For His Father" (Meredith) **28**:180, 191, 194
"For initiation of 7 = 4" (Yeats) **51**:77
"For Jane Myers" (Glück) **16**:128
"For John Clare" (Ashbery) **26**:125
"For John Keats" (Graham) **59**:179
"For John, Who Begs Me Not to Enquire Further" (Sexton) **2**:347, 350, 357
"For Johnny Pole on the Forgotten Beach" (Sexton) **2**:349-50, 353
"For Julia in Nebraska" (Rich) **5**:385
"For K. J., Leaving and Coming Back" (Hacker) **47**:87
"For Keats and Mozart" (Sarton) **39**:319, 354-56, 358
"For Koras and Balafong" (Senghor) **25**:231
"For Lil' Bit" (Jordan) **38**:127
For Lizzie and Harriet (Lowell) **3**:224, 226
"For M." (Zagajewski) **27**:396
"For Malcolm, a Year After" (Knight) **14**:38
"For Marianne Moore" (Ignatow) **34**:306
"For marilyn m" (Bukowski) **18**:22
"For Mark Rothko" (Graham) **59**:170, 177
"For Memory" (Rich) **5**:395
"For Miles" (Corso) **33**:14, 43
"For Miriam" (Tomlinson) **17**:336-37, 349
"For Monet" (Sarton) **39**:362

"For Mr. Death Who Stands with His Door Open" (Sexton) **2**:367, 372
"For My Brother" (Song) **21**:331, 341
"For My Brother Hanson" (Merwin) **45**:24, 85
"For My Brother Reported Missing in Action, 1943" (Merton) **10**:331-32, 342, 349
"For My Daughter" (Ignatow)
See "For My Daughter in Reply to a Question"
"For My Daughter in Reply to a Question" (Ignatow) **14**:348, 355, 362; **34**:293, 305
"For My Lady" (Sanchez) **9**:209, 225
"For My Lover, Returning to His Wife" (Sexton) **2**:353, 372
"For My Mother (May I Inherit Half Her Strength)" (Goodison) **36**:141, 154
"For My Mothers" (Glück) **16**:132, 138, 149; **160**:4-5, 45
"For My People" (Walker) **20**:272, 274, 280-81, 283, 285, 289, 294
For My People (Walker) **20**:274-76, 281-83, 285-86, 289, 292-93
"For My Sister Molly Who in the Fifties" (Walker) **30**:339, 365
"For My Son on the Highways of His Mind" (Kumin) **15**:192, 201
"For New England" (Wright) **14**:340, 362
"For Nobody Else" (Ignatow) **34**:327
"For Now" (Merwin) **45**:14, 24
"For One Moment" (Ignatow) **34**:272, 277
"For One Must Want / To Shut the Other's Gaze" (Graham) **59**:188
"For Patt, Whispering to a Burro" (Wagoner) **33**:348
"For Paul" (Niedecker) **42**:95, 99, 102, 123-24, 150, 172
"For Paul, Group Eight" (Niedecker) **42**:123-25
"For Peter Wee" (Thumboo) **30**:313-14, 329
"For Precision" (Wright) **14**:342-43, 347
"For Proserpine" (Kunitz) **19**:175
"For Proust" (Merrill) **28**:248
"For R. C. B." (Parker) **28**:362
"For Rhoda" (Schwartz) **8**:282
"For Robert Frost" (Kinnell) **26**:284
"For Rosa Parks" (Goodison) **36**:141, 154
"For Rose" (Ignatow) **34**:345
"For Sale" (Lowell) **3**:219-20
"For Sale" (Silverstein) **49**:339
"For Saundra" (Giovanni) **19**:114-15, 139
"For Semra, with Martial Vigor" (Carver) **54**:6
"For Shoshana-Pat Swinton" (Piercy) **29**:300, 303
"For Sidney Bechet" (Larkin) **21**:227
"For Signs" (Gunn) **26**:204, 214
"For Steve" (Birney) **52**:4, 8, 39-40
"For the Altarpiece of the Roseau Valley Church, Saint Lucia" (Walcott) **46**:238, 240, 278, 280
"For the Anniversary of My Death" (Merwin) **45**:26,31
"For the Asians Dying" (Merwin)
See "The Asians Dying"
"For the Bed at Kelmscott" (Morris) **55**:329
"For the Better" (Finch) **21**:181
"for the blind" (Clifton) **17**:26
"For the Boy Who Was Dodger Point Lookout Fifteen Years Ago" (Snyder) **21**:288
"For the Children" (Snyder) **21**:298
"For the Chinese New Year and for Bill Berkson" (O'Hara) **45**:133
"For the Commander of The Eliza" (Heaney) **18**:186-87, 200, 207
"For the Conjunction of Two Planets" (Rich) **5**:360
"For the Death of Lombardi" (Dickey) **40**:223, 229, 253
"For the Far-Out Experimental Writer" (Cruz) **37**:18-19
"For the Felling of a Tree in Harvard Yard" (Rich) **5**:359
"For the Furies" (Piercy) **29**:314
"For the Ghost of Robert Frost" (Francis) **34**:259, 265
For the Guitar (Borges)
See *Para las seis cuerdas*
"For the Heroes Are Dipped in Scarlet" (Lawrence) **54**:198-201
"For the Kent State Martyrs" (Brutus) **24**:119
"For the Last Wolverine" (Dickey) **40**:176, 197, 253, 257
"For the Marriage of Faustus and Helen" (Crane) **3**:81, 83, 90, 92, 95, 97
"For the New Railway Station in Rome" (Wilbur) **51**:219
"For the Nightly Ascent of the Hunter Orion Over a Forest Clearing" (Dickey) **40**:184-85
"For the One Who Would Not Take His Life in His Hands" (Schwartz) **8**:313
"For the One Who Would Not Take Man's Life In His Hands" (Schwartz) **8**:301, 313
"For the Prisoners in South Africa" (Brutus) **24**:111
"For the Proclamation of the Kingdon of Italy" (Carducci)
See "Per la Proclamazione del Regno d'Italia"
"For the Quaternary Age" (Wright) **14**:373
"For the Record" (Lorde) **12**:140
"For the Restoration of My Dear Husband from a Burning Ague" (Bradstreet) **10**:26, 62
"For the Revolutionary Outburst by Black People" (Baraka) **4**:39
"For the Shop" (Cavafy) **36**:105-106
For the six strings (Borges)
See *Para las seis cuerdas*
"For the Stranger" (Forché) **10**:144, 157, 168
"For the Student Strikers" (Wilbur) **51**:283, 301
For the Time Being (Auden) **1**:17, 23, 34, 36-7
"For the Union Dead" (Lowell) **3**:211-14, 223-24, 226, 232
For the Union Dead (Lowell) **3**:211-14, 223-24, 226, 232
"For the Warming of an Artist's Studio" (Wagoner) **33**:330
"For the Word is Flesh" (Kunitz) **19**:147, 152
"For the Year of the Insane" (Sexton) **2**:363
"For Those Sisters & Brothers in Gallup" (Ortiz) **17**:232
"For Though the Caves Were Rabitted" (Thoreau) **30**:182, 237
"For Tom Postell, Dead Black Poet" (Baraka) **4**:10-11, 19
"For Two Girls Setting Out in Life" (Viereck) **27**:262
"For Two Lovers in the Year 2075 in the Canadian Woods" (Meredith) **28**:199
"For Unborn Malcolms" (Sanchez) **9**:218-19, 224, 233
"For Virginia Chavez" (Cervantes) **35**:107, 108, 113, 120, 121, 134
"For Walter and Lilian Lowenfels" (Piercy) **29**:303
For You: Poems (Carruth) **10**:83
"For Your Fear" (Ignatow) **34**:320-21
"Forage Sestina" (Hacker) **47**:79
Forbidden Entries (Yau) **61**:334-36, 348, 357-58
"Force" (Walcott) **46**:240, 279
"Force clémente" (Char) **56**:155-56
"La Force de l'habitude" (Éluard) **38**:96
Force of Light (Celan)
See *Lichtzwang*
"The Force That through the Green Fuse Drives the Flower" (Thomas) **2**:384-84; **52**:227, 232, 256, 263, 267-68, 310, 314, 330-31, 336
"Forcing House" (Roethke) **15**:295
"Ford Madox Ford" (Lowell) **3**:219
"Ford Manor" (Mahon) **60**:139, 143
"Forebears" (Pavese)
See "Antenati"
"Foreboding" (Carver) **54**:18
"Foreclosure" (Brown) **55**:151-52
"Foreclosure" (Niedecker) **42**:101
Forefathers' Eve (Mickiewicz)
See *Dziady III*
"Foreign Flower" (Tagore)
See "Videshi phul"
"Foreigner" (Page) **12**:170
The Forerunner (Gibran) **9**:69, 71, 75, 79
"Forerunners" (Emerson) **18**:79, 84
"Foreshadowing" (Wagoner) **33**:367
"Forest" (Swenson) **14**:268
"The Forest" (Wright) **14**:348, 361
The Forest (Jonson) **17**:158-59, 169, 180, 194
"The Forest Hymn" (Bryant) **20**:3, 14, 18, 23, 29, 33
The Forest I (Jonson) **17**:180, 194
The Forest II (Jonson) **17**:158-9, 161, 163, 165, 169, 182, 189, 202-06, 209, 214
The Forest III (Jonson) **17**:158-59, 161, 163, 192, 210
Forest Leaves (Harper) **21**:185
Forest Moon (Paz)
See *Luna silvestre*
"The Forest of Wild Thyme" (Noyes) **27**:116
The Forest of Wild Thyme (Noyes) **27**:139
"Forest Path" (Ishikawa)
See "Mori no michi"
"The Forest Path" (Wright) **14**:339
The Forest VII (Jonson) **17**:176
The Forest XI (Jonson) **17**:159, 172
The Forest XII (Jonson) **17**:158, 160, 214, 217
The Forest XIII (Jonson) **17**:158, 160, 163, 192
The Forest XV (Jonson) **17**:162, 171-72
The Forests of Lithuania (Davie) **29**:95-96, 109
"Forêt dans la Hache" (Breton) **15**:52
"La foret merveilleuse ou je vis donne un bal" (Apollinaire) **7**:3
"Forever in My Dream & in My Morning Thought" (Thoreau) **30**:192
"The Forge" (Heaney) **18**:200, 221, 223
"The Forger" (Mahon) **60**:169, 199
"Le forgeron" (Rimbaud) **3**:277, 283, 285; **57**:184, 202, 244, 248, 251, 257, 290-91
"Forget" (Lawrence) **54**:250
"Forget not Yet" (Wyatt) **27**:315, 324, 357
"For-Get-Me-Not" (Stein) **18**:313
"The Forging" (Borges)
See "Forjadura"
"forgiving my father" (Clifton) **17**:18
"Forgotten Arietta" (Verlaine)
See "Ariettes oubliées"
"Forgotten Girlhood" (Jackson) **44**:106
"A Forgotten Miniature" (Hardy) **8**:137-38
"The Forgotten Pram" (Shvarts) **50**:143
"Forgotten Song" (Ashbery) **26**:162
"Forjadura" (Borges) **22**:72
"Forks with Points Up" (Ignatow) **34**:313
"The Forlorn Sea" (Smith) **12**:326
"Die Form" (Benn) **35**:63
"Form without Love" (Aleixandre) **15**:18-19, 22-3
"Forma en torno" (Guillén) **35**:228
Formal Division (Char)
See *Partage formel*
"Formal Feeling" (Boland) **58**:41
"The Formation of a Separatist, I" (Howe) **54**:59
Formations (Cage) **58**:221, 224
Formerly and Not So Long Ago (Verlaine)
See *Jadis et naguère*
"Forming Child" (Ortiz) **17**:225, 231
"Forms of Love" (Oppen) **35**:299, 304
"Forms of the Earth at Abiquiu" (Momaday) **25**:201-203
"Formula" (Hughes) **53**:169-71
"The Forsaken" (Lowell) **13**:62
"A Forsaken Garden" (Swinburne) **24**:324, 338, 344
"The Forsaken Merman" (Arnold) **5**:5-8, 12-13, 17-18, 34-5, 38-9, 42, 49
"The Forsaken One" (Mistral)
See "La desásída"

Forslin (Aiken) **26**:6-7, 27
"Forties Flick" (Ashbery) **26**:149
"The Fortress" (Sexton) **2**:362
The Fortunate Traveller (Walcott) **46**:247-48, 259, 322-23
"Fortunatus Nimium" (Bridges) **28**:73, 75, 89-90
"Fortune..." (Ferlinghetti) **1**:183
Fortune Hath Taken Thee Away My Love (Raleigh)
See "Fortune hathe taken away my love"
"Fortune hathe taken away my love" (Raleigh) **31**:245, 280, 304, 313
"Fortune, Nature, Love" (Sidney) **32**:235, 241
"The Fortunes of Gyges" (Morris) **55**:306
"Fortune-telling" (Herbert) **50**:19
"Fortune-Telling" (Tsvetaeva)
See "Gadan'e"
"45' for a Speaker" (Cage) **58**:201
"Forty Singing Seamen" (Noyes) **27**:133
Forty Singing Seamen and Other Poems (Noyes) **27**:133
45 Mercy Street (Sexton) **2**:356, 359, 367, 374
XLI Poems (Cummings) **5**:104
"Forward! Forward!" (Carducci)
See "Avanti! Avanti!"
"Forward Observers" (Stryk) **27**:203
"Fossile sanguinaire" (Char) **56**:154
"The Fostering of Aslaug" (Morris) **55**:307, 329
"Fosterling" (Heaney) **18**:259
"Les foules" (Baudelaire) **1**:59
"Found" (Rossetti) **44**:172
Found Objects (Zukofsky) **11**:346
"found paean to vancouver by rudyard kipling (1890)" (Birney) **52**:43
"The Foundation" (Yamada) **44**:326
"Founders Day. A Secular Ode on the Ninth Jubilee of Eton College" (Bridges) **28**:67, 71
"Founding Fathers, Nineteenth-Century Style, Southeast U.S.A." (Warren) **37**:340
"The Fountain" (Bryant) **20**:4, 43, 47
"The Fountain" (Wordsworth) **4**:374, 399
"A Fountain, a Bottle, a Donkey's Ear and Some Books" (Frost) **1**:194
"The Fountain of Ammannati" (Stryk) **27**:183-84, 192
"Fountain Piece" (Swenson) **14**:263-64
"The Fountains of Aix" (Swenson) **14**:250, 255, 285-86
"IV" (Joyce) **22**:145, 163, 166, 168, 173
"The Four" (Lawrence) **54**:250
"Four Ages" (Char) **56**:162
"The Four Ages" (Nemerov) **24**:293-24, 297
"The Four Ages of Man" (Bradstreet) **10**:4, 17, 30, 45
"Four Auguries" (Atwood) **8**:27-8
"The Four Brothers" (Sandburg) **2**:302; **41**:240, 270, 297
"Four Canzones (1957-1961)" (Okigbo) **7**:247-48
"The Four Cycles" (Borges)
See "Los cuatro ciclos"
"Four Dancers at an Irish Wedding" (Gallagher) **9**:37
"4 daughters" (Clifton) **17**:25
"Four Dheetziyama Poems" (Ortiz) **17**:225
"The Four Elements" (Bradstreet) **10**:11, 17, 41
"Four Evasions" (Atwood) **8**:24, 27-8
"Four Eyes" (Ondaatje) **28**:292, 329, 331
"Four feet between" (Birney) **52**:34, 37, 47, 79, 97
"Four for Sir John Davies" (Roethke) **15**:263, 273-74, 286
Four for Traine (Mackey) **49**:17
"The Four Gospels" (Goethe) **5**:229
"Four in a Family" (Rukeyser) **12**:223
"Four in the Morning" (Szymborska) **44**:289
"Four Kantian Lyrics" (Tomlinson) **17**:311, 342
"Four Little Elegies" (O'Hara) **45**:171-73
"Four Men" (Francis) **34**:245
The Four Men (Brooke) **24**:89
"The Four Monarchies" (Bradstreet) **10**:4-5, 17-18, 20-1, 27, 31, 33-4, 40, 46-7
"Four Notions of Love and Marriage" (Momaday) **25**:189
"Four O'Clock Summer Street" (McGuckian) **27**:82, 90
"4 Other Countries" (Zukofsky) **11**:348
"Four Poems" (Bishop) **34**:89
"Four Poems from New Zealand" (Wright) **14**:377
"Four Portraits of Fire" (Cervantes) **35**:104, 117
"Four Preludes on Playthings of the Wind" (Sandburg) **2**:316, 340; **41**:270-72, 274, 276, 298, 314
The Four Quartets (Eliot) **5**:162-65, 174, 178-80, 182, 186, 196, 198, 200, 205-06, 208, 210-11; **31**:117, 119, 124, 133, 138, 169
"The Four Seasons of the Year" (Bradstreet) **10**:17, 44
"Four Sides to a House" (Lowell) **13**:61
"Four Sonnets" (Nemerov) **24**:256
"The Four Sorrows" (Marie de France)
See "Le Chaitivel"
"4/25/89 late" (Clifton) **17**:30
"Four Villonesques on Desire" (Szirtes) **51**:172
"Four Walks in the Country near Saint Brieuc" (Mahon) **60**:133, 138
"Four Ways of Knowledge" (Bly) **39**:67
"Four Winds" (MacNeice) **61**:113
"Four Winds" (Teasdale) **31**:365
The Four Years' Notebook (Montale)
See *Quaderno de quattro anni*
The Four Zoas: The Torments of Love and Jealousy in the Death and Judgement of Albion the Ancient Man (Blake) **12**:13-21, 25-9, 32, 35-8, 41, 47, 49-50, 60-4, 73
"La Fourmi" (Péret) **33**:210
"Fourteen" (Hacker) **47**:80
"XIV" (Joyce) **22**:138, 145, 160, 163-66, 168-70
"14 de julio" (Cisneros) **52**:152
"14 Dec." (Ammons) **16**:22
Fourteenth Olympian (Pindar)
See *Olympian 14*
"Fourth Eclogues" (Sidney) **32**:301
"Fourth Georgic" (Vergil) **12**:365, 371
"Fourth Meditation" (Roethke) **15**:272, 278
"Fourth Mesostic" (Cage) **58**:214
"The Fourth Month of the Landscape Architect" (Rich) **5**:384
Fourth Nemean (Pindar)
See *Nemean 4*
"Fourth of July" (Hughes) **7**:119
"The Fourth of July" (Wilbur) **51**:234-36, 238, 281-82
"Fourth of July in Maine" (Lowell) **3**:226
"Fourth Poem from Niceragua Libre: Report from the Frontier" (Jordan) **38**:131
Fourth Pythian (Pindar)
See *Pythian 4*
Fourth Quarter and Other Poems (Wright) **14**:372-75
Fourth Satire of Donne (Pope)
See *Satires of Dr. Donne Versified*
The Fourth Symphony (Bely)
See *Kubok metelej: Chetviortiia simfoniia*
"Fourth Time Around" (Dylan) **37**:51
Fowre Hymnes (Spenser) **8**:332, 334, 337, 390
"The Fox" (Tomlinson) **17**:327
"Fox" (Wright) **14**:376
"Fox Trot" (Sitwell) **3**:297, 303
"Foxes' Moon" (Tomlinson) **17**:343
"Foxhunt" (Hughes) **7**:166
"Fra Lippo Lippi" (Browning) **2**:37, 88, 95; **61**:5, 92
Fra Rupert (Landor) **5**:95
"Frage" (Stramm) **50**:170, 188, 208-9
"Fragment" (Ashbery) **26**:118, 125, 135, 144, 156-157
"Fragment" (Borges)
See "Fragmento"
"A Fragment" (Bryant)
See "Inscription for the Entrance into a Wood"
"Fragment" (Finch) **21**:140, 172
"Fragment" (Johnson) **24**:142, 148
"Fragment: As Bronze may be much Beautified" (Owen) **19**:352
"Fragment from Correspondence" (Nemerov) **24**:298
"Fragment: I saw his Round Mouth's Crimson" (Owen) **19**:352
"Fragment of a Meditation" (Tate) **50**:231, 243, 249, 317
"Fragment of an 'Antigone'" (Arnold) **5**:48-9
"Fragment Thirty-Six" (H. D.) **5**:268, 270
Fragmenta Aurea (Suckling) **30**:117, 120, 125, 149, 155, 158
"Fragmente" (Benn) **35**:34, 36
"Fragmento" (Borges) **32**:87, 94-5
"Fragments" (Yeats) **51**:108
"Fragments du narcisse" (Valéry) **9**:348, 365-66, 372, 393, 395-96
"Fragments from a Parable (of the 1950's)" (Jordan) **38**:120-23, 144
"Fragments from a Poem to be entitled 'The Sentimental Exile'" (Brooke) **24**:68, 80, 89
"Fragments from an Apocryphal Gosepel" (Borges) **32**:140
"Fragments from the Deluge" (Okigbo) **7**:231, 246, 255
"Fragoletta" (Swinburne) **24**:361-62
"Frailty" (Herbert) **4**:135
"Le Fraisne" (Marie de France) **22**:241, 248, 258, 269, 271-72, 275, 277-78, 282
"Frame" (Rich) **5**:396
"Frame Structures" (Howe) **54**:108
Frame Structures: Early Poems, 1974-1979 (Howe) **54**:107-9, 124, 128, 130, 133-34, 140
"A Framed Photograph" (Curnow) **48**:42, 47-49
Frameless Windows, Squares of Light (Song) **21**:334, 344, 345-46
Framework (Parra)
See *Obra gruesa*
"Framing" (Graham) **59**:174
"Frammento" (Leopardi) **37**:81
"Frammento alla morte" (Pasolini) **17**:295
"France" (Sassoon) **12**:276, 278
"France 1870" (Meredith) **60**:250, 260
"France: An Ode" (Coleridge)
See "Ode to France"
"Francesco Petrarca" (Carducci) **46**:50
La Franciade (Ronsard)
See *Les quatre premiers livres de la Franciade*
"Francie's Fingers" (Wylie) **23**:324
"Francina" (Brathwaite) **56**:68, 76, 95
"Francine's Room" (Erdrich) **52**:178
"Francis Furini" (Browning) **2**:72, 75, 84-5
"Francisco, I'll Bring You Red Carnations" (Levine) **22**:225
"La frangia dei capelli" (Montale) **13**:111, 128
"Frank and Billy" (Colwin) **39**:270, 279, 292, 300, 302, 312
"Frankie and Johnny" (Brown) **55**:71, 74, 102-4, 154-55
The Franklin's Prologue (Chaucer) **58**:234
"Franklin's Tale" (Chaucer) **19**:11-13, 15, 17, 27, 33, 47, 53, 61
The Franklin's Tale (Chaucer) **58**:234, 249-50, 351
"Franz Schubert A Press Conference" (Zagajewski) **27**:382, 385, 401
"Frase" (Storni) **33**:268;
"Frases" (Parra) **39**:273
"Fraud" (Blok) **21**:37
"Fraulein Reads Instructive Rhymes" (Kumin) **15**:180
"Frayed" (Birney) **52**:16
"Fraying the Jute Sack" (Char)
See "Effilage du sac de jute"

"Freaks" (Alexie) **53**:31
"Frederick Douglass" (Dunbar) **5**:131, 134, 143
"Frederick Douglass" (Hayden) **6**:176, 183, 188, 196, 199
"Frederick Douglass: 1817-1895" (Hughes) **53**:150
"Fredericksted Dusk" (Walcott) **46**:278
"Frederiksted Nights" (Walcott) **46**:236, 278
"Free" (McKay) **2**:225
"The Free" (Merwin) **45**:42
"Free Fantasia: Tiger Flowers" (Hayden) **6**:194-95
"Free Flight" (Jordan) **38**:124
"Free Labor" (Harper) **21**:217-18
"Free Spirit" (Cruz) **37**:13
"Free Thoughts" (Blok) **21**:31
"The Freebooters" (Cardenal)
See "Los filibusteros"
"Freedman" (Heaney) **18**:205
"Freedom" (Hughes) **1**:252; **53**:153
"Freedom" (Kavanagh) **33**:115
"Freedom New Hampshire" (Kinnell) **26**:236, 238, 242, 284, 289
Freedom on Oath (Paz)
See *Libertad bajo palabra*
Freedom on Parole (Paz)
See *Libertad bajo palabra*
"Freedom Train" (Hughes) **1**:244; **53**:109, 193
Freedom under Parole (Paz)
See *Libertad bajo palabra*
Freedom under Word (Paz)
See *Libertad bajo palabra*
"Freedom's Plow" (Hughes) **1**:250, 258; **53**:116, 145
The Freeing of the Dust (Levertov) **11**:197-98, 213
"Freeing the Boat" (Tu Fu) **9**:320
"Freeway 280" (Cervantes) **35**:112, 113, 121, 131
"Freezing" (Meredith) **28**:177
"La frégate 'La Sérieuse'" (Vigny) **26**:411
"The French Child's Sunday" (Corso) **33**:25
"The French Master" (Abse) **41**:3, 9
"A French Poem" (Merton) **10**:337
"French Poems" (Ashbery) **26**:118
The French Revolution (Blake) **12**:13, 25, 63
"A French Rooster" (Stein) **18**:313
"Frente al Oxford" (Guillén) **23**:126
"Frenzy" (Sexton) **2**:368
"Fréquence" (Char) **56**:145, 153
Les Frères de mémoire (Char) **56**:115-16
Frescoes for Mr. Rockefeller's City (MacLeish) **47**:130, 134-35, 138-40, 143, 146-47, 151, 189-90, 240, 254-55
"Fresh Stain" (Gallagher) **9**:62, 64
"Freshness" (Yevtushenko) **40**:343
Fresko-Sonett (Heine) **25**:160
"Fresne" (Marie de France)
See "Le Fraisne"
"Freudenhaus" (Stramm) **50**:170-71, 175, 189, 198, 204, 209
The Friar's Prologue (Chaucer) **58**:291, 320
"Friar's Tale" (Chaucer) **19**:11, 13-14
"Friday the Thirteenth" (Ginsberg) **4**:75
"Friday: The Toilette: Lydia" (Montagu) **16**:338, 347-49
"A Friend" (Philips) **40**:274, 298
"The Friend" (Piercy) **29**:308-09
"The Friend" (Smith) **12**:318
"The Friend" (Thoreau) **30**:227
"The Friend of Grandmother Speranza" (Gozzano)
See "L'amica di nonna speranza"
"The Friend of the Fourth Decade" (Merrill) **28**:220-21, 269
"Friend Who Has Been Reading Jacques Lacan" (Hass) **16**:199
"The Friend Who Is Sleeping" (Pavese)
See "Adventures"
"Friends" (Ashbery) **26**:145
"The Friends" (Patmore) **59**:204, 230
"Friends" (Sexton) **2**:365
"Friends, When I loved" (Cavafy) **36**:52
"Friendship" (Cowper) **40**:44
"Friendship" (Stryk) **27**:204, 208
"Friendship" (Thoreau) **30**:273, 285, 293
"Friendship Between Ephelia and Ardelia" (Finch) **21**:164
"Friendship Heights" (Curnow) **48**:42
"Friendship in Embleme or the Seal To My Dearest Lucasia" (Philips) **40**:281, 296, 313, 320, 322-24
"Friendship's Mystery. To My Dearest Lucasia" (Philips) **40**:296, 298, 318
"Friendship's Steadfastness" (Thoreau) **30**:265
"The Frigate Pelican" (Moore) **49**:98-99, 134
"Fright" (Storni)
See "Miedo"
"The Frightened Man" (Bogan) **12**:86
The Frightening World (Blok) **21**:25
"Frilot Cove" (Brown) **55**:114
"Frimaire" (Lowell) **13**:97
"Fríos" (Storni) **33**:246;
"Friso" (Darío) **15**:112
"Frisson" (Gautier) **18**:164
"A Frivolous Conversation" (Milosz) **8**:194
"Frog Autumn" (Plath) **1**:388
"The Frog Prince" (Smith) **12**:305, 323, 341
"The Frog, That Naked Creature" (Sarton) **39**:325, 334
"Froid jaune" (Tzara) **27**:227
"A Frolick" (Herrick) **9**:103
"From a Daybook" (Swenson) **14**:273
"From a Dream" (Ignatow) **34**:291-92, 341
"From a Notebook" (Merrill) **28**:248
"From a Notebook, October '68—May '69" (Levertov) **11**:176, 180, 195
"From a Phrase of Simone Weil's and Some Words of Hegel's" (Oppen) **35**:335
"From a Suburban Window" (Abse) **41**:9
"From a Survivor" (Rich) **5**:360
"From a Tower" (Montale)
See "Da una torre"
"From a Train Window" (Millay) **6**:214
"From a Train-Window" (Sarton) **39**:320
"From All Our Journeys" (Sarton) **39**:332, 337
"From Amsterdam" (Alurista) **34**:21, 23
"From an Old House in America" (Rich) **5**:373-74, 394
"From Ancient Fangs" (Viereck) **27**:263
"From Another Sore Fit" (Bradstreet) **10**:61-2
"From Brecht's A Short Organum for the Theatre" (Graham) **59**:137-38
"From Dawn to Noon" (Rossetti) **44**:169
"From Disaster" (Oppen) **35**:290, 297
From Feathers to Iron (Day Lewis) **11**:123-24, 128-30, 135, 138-39, 142, 148-52
"From Grants to Gallup, New Mexico" (Ortiz) **17**:233
"From here I see a road" (Castro)
See "Dend' aquí vexo un camiño"
"From Here to There" (Wagoner) **33**:337, 340, 345, 363
"From House to Home" (Rossetti) **7**:260-1, 276, 282, 284, 290
"From love's first fever to her plague" (Thomas) **52**:247, 334-35
From Man (Amichai)
See *Me'adam*
"From Memory" (Forché) **10**:135
"From Memory" (Zagajewski) **27**:396
"From Monaghan to the Grand Canal" (Kavanagh) **33**:87, 95
"From Morpheus" (H. D.) **5**:270
"From My Diary, July, 1914" (Owen) **19**:338, 343, 346
"From My Notes for a Series of Lectures on Murder" (Smith) **12**:343
"From Mythology" (Herbert) **50**:34
"From Orient Point" (Hacker) **47**:87
"From Room to Room" (Kenyon) **57**:26
From Room to Room (Kenyon) **57**:2, 4, 6, 19, 22-23, 26, 36, 39, 45
From Sand Creek: Rising in This Heart Which Is Our America (Ortiz) **17**:222, 230, 234, 239-240
"From Sea to Shining Sea" (Jordan) **38**:123
From Snow and Rock, from Chaos: Poems, 1965-1972 (Carruth) **10**:71, 91
"From something, nothing" (Piercy) **29**:315
"From Superstition" (Pasternak) **6**:260
"From the Anthill" (Shvarts) **50**:159
"From the Book of Local Miracles, Largely Unrecorded" (Goodison) **36**:154
From the Book of Myths (Carman) **34**:205, 208, 222
From the Book of the Myths (Carman)
See *From the Book of Myths*
From the Book of the Valentines (Carman)
See *From the Book of Valentines*
From the Book of Valentines (Carman) **34**:205, 210, 226
From the Cables of Genocide: Poems on Love and Hunger (Cervantes) **35**:121, 132, 134, 135
"From the Cave" (Lorde) **12**:143
"From the Childhood of Jesus" (Pinsky) **27**:164, 175
"From the Coptic" (Smith) **12**:313-14
"From the Corpse Woodpiles, from the Ashes" (Hayden) **6**:194-95, 198
"From the Crest" (Berry) **28**:43
"From the Cupola" (Merrill) **28**:222-3, 226, 228, 234-5, 250, 257, 270
From the Cutting Room Floor (Merrill) **28**:269
"From the Dark Tower" (Cullen) **20**:57-58, 63, 70, 76
"From the Dressing Room" (McGuckian) **27**:98
"From the Eleventh Finger" (Wakoski) **15**:350
"From the End" (Herbert)
See "Od konca"
From the First Nine (Merrill) **28**:263
"From the First Underworld" (McGuckian) **27**:105
"From the Flats" (Lanier) **50**:56
"From the four points of the compass" (Castro)
See "Desde los cuatro puntos cardinales"
"From the Frontier of Writing" (Heaney) **18**:231-32
"From the Garden" (Sexton) **2**:351
From the Green Book of Bards (Carman) **34**:205, 209-10, 223
From the Green Book of the Bards (Carman)
See *From the Green Book of Bards*
"From the Hazel Bough" (Birney) **52**:8, 25, 85, 90-93
"From the Heart" (Castro)
See "¡Do íntimo!"
"From the House of Yemanjá" (Lorde) **12**:151
"From the Land" (Castro)
See "Da terra"
"From the Lives of Things" (Zagajewski) **27**:389
"From the Lookout Rock" (Wilbur) **51**:291-92
"From the Motorway" (Tomlinson) **17**:354-55
"From the New World" (Graham) **59**:135, 156, 160
"From the Painting Back from Marketby Chardin" (Boland) **58**:46
"From the Reformation Journal" (Graham) **59**:189
"From the Rising of the Sun" (Milosz)
See "From Where the Sun Rises"
From the Rising of the Sun (Milosz)
See *Gdziewschodzi stōnce i kedy zapada*
"From the Same" (Belloc) **24**:32
"From The School Anthology: Albert Frolov" (Brodsky) **9**:4
"From the Sea" (Teasdale) **31**:322, 379
"From the Seacoast" (Tsvetaeva)
See "S morya"
"From the Shore" (Sandburg) **41**:364
From the Sick-Bed (Tagore)
See *Rogsajyae*
"From 'The Snow Lamp'" (Hayden) **6**:194-95

"From the Surface" (Pinsky) **27**:145
"From the Top of the Stairs" (Herbert) **50**:14, 43
"From the Top of the Stairs" (Zagajewski) **27**:382
"From the Wave" (Gunn) **26**:196-197, 204, 215
"From the Wellington Museum" (Wright) **14**:377
"From the White Place" (Song) **21**:331, 340
"From the Woolworth Tower" (Teasdale) **31**:331, 335
"From This Condensery" (Niedecker) **42**:103
From This Condensery: The Complete Writings of Lorine Niedecker (Niedecker) **42**:96-7, 102-3, 110, 118-25, 127, 135-41, 143-44, 148-52, 155, 167
From Threshold to Threshold (Celan)
See *Von Schwelle zu Schwelle*
"From Time" (Dickey) **40**:236
"From Tuscan cam my ladies worthi race" (Surrey) **59**:315, 322
"From Virgil" (Oppen) **35**:314
"From Where the Sun Rises" (Milosz) **8**:203-05
From Where the Sun Rises to Where It Sets (Milosz)
See *Gdziewschodzi stōnce i kedy zapada*
"From Where We Sit: Corpus Christi" (Cervantes) **35**:113, 117
"Frondes Agrestes" (Tomlinson) **17**:315, 359
"A Front" (Jarrell) **41**:147, 149-50, 152, 173, 177, 189, 201
"Front de la rose" (Char) **56**:156
"Front Door Soliloquy" (Graves) **6**:143
"Front Lines" (Snyder) **21**:297, 319
"Front the Ages with a Smile" (Masters) **1**:335
"The Frontier" (Wright) **36**:398
"Frontispiece" (Komunyakaa) **51**:55
"Frontispiece" (Swenson) **14**:249, 253
"Die Frösche von Bikini" (Enzensberger) **28**:150
"Frost at Midnight" (Coleridge) **11**:51, 53, 57-8, 84, 89, 97, 100, 102-04; **39**:169, 221
Frost: Collected Poems, Prose, and Plays (Frost) **39**:256
"Frost Flowers" (Lawrence) **54**:185, 187
"The Frost of Death Was on the Pane" (Dickinson) **1**:104
"Frost-Bamboo Ranges" (Wang Wei) **18**:362
"Frostfeuer" (Stramm) **50**:202
"Frosty Night" (Graves) **6**:141
"The Frozen City" (Nemerov) **24**:255
"The Frozen Greenhouse" (Hardy) **8**:92
"The Frozen Sea" (Merwin) **45**:7
Das Frühwerk (Celan) **10**:121
"Fruit" (Francis) **34**:244
"Fruit" (Mistral)
See "Fruta"
"Fruit" (Zagajewski) **27**:394
"Fruit of the Flower" (Cullen) **20**:52-53, 86
"Fruit on a Straight-Sided Tray" (Boland) **58**:53, 58
"The Fruit Shop" (Lowell) **13**:78
"Fruitlands" (Toomer) **7**:323
"The Fruits of the Season" (Wright) **36**:311
"Frustration" (Parker) **28**:362
"Fruta" (Mistral) **32**:194-95
"fruto de bronce" (Alurista) **34**:37
"Fuerza blanca" (Storni) **33**:248;
"Fuerzas" (Storni) **33**:294, 301;
"La fuga" (Mistral) **32**:161, 181, 208, 210
"Fuga" (Pasolini) **17**:264
"La Fugitif" (Éluard) **38**:90-93
"The Fugitive" (Éluard)
See "La Fugitif"
"The Fugitive" (Lermontov) **18**:282
"The Fugitive" (Stryk) **27**:198
Fugitive (Tagore)
See *Palātakā*
"The Fugitive's Wife" (Harper) **21**:206
"El fugitivo" (Neruda) **4**:292
"A Fugue of Wings" (Sarton) **39**:342
"Fuite d'Enfance" (Smith) **12**:325, 344
"Fukú!" (Yevtushenko) **40**:357-58
Fukú (Yevtushenko) **40**:358
"Fulfilment" (Pasternak) **6**:267
"Full Circle" (Viereck) **27**:267-68
"Full Fathom Five" (Plath) **1**:388-89; **37**:179, 181-82, 214, 216-21, 241, 243-45, 254
"Full Moon" (Graves) **6**:136, 151
"Full Moon" (Hayden) **6**:187, 194-95
"Full Moon" (Wylie) **23**:322
"Full Moon and Little Frieda" (Hughes) **7**:137, 142, 168
"Full Moon New Guinea" (Shapiro) **25**:325
"Full Well Yt Maye be Sene" (Wyatt) **27**:316
"Fullness of Time" (Tomlinson) **17**:321
"Fumatori di carta" (Pavese) **13**:225, 227
"Fundamental Disagreement with Two Contemporaries" (Rexroth) **20**:196
"The Funeral" (Brooks) **7**:53, 87
"Funeral Address" (Parra) **39**:278
"The Funeral Bell" (Thoreau) **30**:193
"The Funeral of Bobo" (Brodsky) **9**:8
"The Funeral of Sarpedon" (Cavafy) **36**:53, 108
"The Funeral of Youth" (Brooke) **24**:53, 78
"Funeral Rites" (Heaney) **18**:203-4, 210-11
"A Funeral Toast" (Carducci)
See "Brindisi funebre"
"The Funerall" (Donne) **1**:130
"A Funerall Elegie" (Donne) **1**:146-47, 154-58; **24**:151, 184-85, 188
"The Funerall Rites of the Rose" (Herrick) **9**:126
"Funere mersit acerbo" (Carducci) **46**:38, 51, 76, 78
"Funes" (Borges)
See "Funes el memorioso"
"Funes el memorioso" (Borges) **32**:83
"Funes, His Memory" (Borges)
See "Funes el memorioso"
"Funes the Memorious" (Borges)
See "Funes el memorioso"
"Fünf Gesänge" (Rilke) **2**:265-69
"Funland" (Abse) **41**:10, 16-17, 19-20, 22-3, 26, 28, 30-2
Funland and Other Poems (Abse) **41**:10, 12, 15-16, 28
"Funnel" (Sexton) **2**:345, 350
"Funny Stanzas to Don Juan" (Storni)
See "Divertidas estancias a don Juan"
"Für die Mouche" (Heine) **25**:148
Fureur et mystère (Char) **56**:112, 115, 131-32, 134-35, 141, 143, 145, 149-57, 161, 167, 177, 185-86, 188, 190, 200
"Furi alla Certosa di Bologna" (Carducci) **46**:52, 59
Die Furie des Verschwindens (Enzensberger) **28**:150, 159, 161, 163
"The Furies" (Masters) **1**:329, 343; **36**:176
"The Furies" (Sarton) **39**:342
"The Furies" (Sexton) **2**:367
Furioso (Ariosto)
See *Orlando furioso di Ludovico Ariosto de Ferrara*
"Furious Versions" (Lee) **24**:240, 243, 248, 251
"The Furious Voyage" (Graves) **6**:130, 143
"The Furniture of a Woman's Mind" (Swift) **9**:295
Furor and Mystery (Char)
See *Fureur et Mystère*
"Fürstin" (Goethe) **5**:249
"Further Arrivals" (Atwood) **8**:36, 39
A Further Range (Frost) **1**:195-97, 202; **39**:232-33
"Fury Of Rain" (Harjo) **27**:66
"The Fury of Sundays" (Sexton) **2**:367, 373
"The Fury of the Cocks" (Sexton) **2**:371
"Fuscello teso" (Montale) **13**:134
"Les fusillés" (Hugo) **17**:101
"Futility" (Owen) **19**:330, 342, 347, 359, 365-68
"The Future" (Arnold) **5**:18, 43-5
"The Future" (Ignatow) **34**:306
"Future" (Szymborska) **44**:298
"Future and Past" (Browning) **6**:16
"Future Conditional" (Hacker) **47**:99
"The Future Life" (Bryant) **20**:4, 9
"Future Present" (Shapiro) **25**:324
"Future Religion" (Lawrence) **54**:197-98, 201, 203
"Futures" (Alexie) **53**:30
"Futuro" (Guillén) **23**:99
"Futuro" (Mistral) **32**:174
"Fuzzy-Wuzzy" (Kipling) **3**:156, 158, 167, 186-87
"Gadan'e" (Tsvetaeva) **14**:312-14
"Gaiety" (Sitwell) **3**:294
"Gairmscoile" (MacDiarmid) **9**:188-89, 193
"Gakusei" (Ishikawa) **10**:215
"Galatea Encore" (Brodsky) **9**:25, 27
"Galerías Preciadas" (Fuertes) **27**:13-4
Galician Songs (Castro)
See *Cantares gallegos*
"Galla Placidia" (Ekeloef) **23**:60
Gallant Festivals (Verlaine)
See *Fêtes galantes*
"The Gallery" (Marvell) **10**:271, 300
"The Galley" (Kipling) **3**:182
"The Galley-Slave" (Kipling) **3**:157
Gallician songs (Castro)
See *Cantares gallegos*
"Una gallina" (Storni) **33**:296;
"Gallo cedrone" (Montale) **13**:108, 111
"The Galloping Cat" (Smith) **12**:311
"Galloping Horses" (Bly) **39**:38, 42
"The Gallows" (Thomas) **53**:278, 295, 317
Galoots (Sandburg) **41**:251
"Galw ar Ddwynwen" (Dafydd ap Gwilym) **56**:211
Gam ha'egrof haya pa'am yad ptuba ve'etsba'ot (Amichai) **38**:32
"The Gambler: A Ballet with Words" (Kavanagh) **33**:79
"Gambling in Stateline, Nevada" (Wright) **36**:341, 366
"The Game" (Abse) **41**:7
"The Game" (Glück) **16**:124
"Game after Supper" (Atwood) **8**:3
"A Game at Salzburg" (Jarrell) **41**:139, 153, 173, 177, 185, 196, 208, 216
"The Game Between the Jews and the Indians Is Tied Going into the Bottom of the Ninth Inning" (Alexie) **53**:41
"Game Mistress" (Cassian) **17**:11
"A Game of Monopoly in Chavannes" (Kumin) **15**:211
"Gamecock" (Dickey) **40**:258
"Games Two" (Wilbur) **51**:282
"Gammes de l'accordeur" (Char) **56**:187
"Gangrene" (Levine) **22**:212
"Ganymed" (Goethe) **5**:247, 254
"Ganymede" (Hölderlin) **4**:148, 166
"The Gap" (Tomlinson) **17**:347
"A Garage in Co. Cork" (Mahon) **60**:146, 151, 189, 211
"Garage Sale" (Shapiro) **25**:322
"Garbo at the Gaumont" (McGuckian) **27**:107, 109-111
"The Garden" (Cowper) **40**:45, 48-52, 110, 123, 141-42
"The Garden" (Glück) **16**:130, 150-51, 168
"Garden" (Goodison)
See "Garden of the Women Once Fallen"
"Garden" (H. D.) **5**:275, 303
"The Garden" (Marvell) **10**:266, 268, 271-73, 277, 283-85, 287-92, 294, 297, 311, 313-14, 318
"The Garden" (Montale)
See "L'orto"
The Garden (Glück) **16**:129
"Garden Abstract" (Crane) **3**:81
"Garden by Moonlight" (Lowell) **13**:64, 98
"Garden Fancies" (Browning) **61**:88
"The Garden in September" (Bridges) **28**:67, 83

"The Garden of Boccaccio's" (Coleridge) **11**:104-09
"the garden of delight" (Clifton) **17**:36
"The Garden of Earthly Delights" (Milosz) **8**:181, 209
"The Garden of Epicurus" (Meredith) **60**:257
"The Garden of Gethsemane" (Pasternak) **6**:285
"Garden of Love" (Blake) **12**:7, 33
"Garden of Nightingales" (Blok)
See "The Nightingale Garden"
"The Garden of Proserpine" (Swinburne) **24**:345
The Garden of the Prophet (Gibran) **9**:75
"Garden of the Women Once Fallen" (Goodison) **36**:142, 154
"The Garden: On prospect of a fine day in early autumn" (Warren) **37**:283-84, 286, 288, 321-22, 331
"The Garden Party" (Belloc) **24**:27
"The Garden Party" (Davie) **29**:93
"The Garden Seat" (Hardy) **8**:100
"The Garden Sees" (Elytis) **21**:132
"The Garden Wall" (Levertov) **11**:169
"Garden Waters" (Warren) **37**:333
"Gardener" (Graves) **6**:151
"Gardener" (Silverstein) **49**:342, 347
Gardeners and Astronomers (Sitwell) **3**:321
"The Gardener's Daughter" (Tennyson) **6**:354
"Gare" (Tzara) **27**:223-24
"Gare au bord de la mer" (Laforgue) **14**:76
"Gareth and Lynette" (Tennyson) **6**:373, 376
"Gargoyle" (Sandburg) **41**:251, 270, 313
Garland (Skelton)
See *The Garlande of Laurell*
"Garland for You" (Warren) **37**:332
The Garland of Laurel (Skelton)
See *The Garlande of Laurell*
Garland of Laurell (Skelton)
See *The Garlande of Laurell*
Garland of Songs (Tagore)
See *Gitimālya*
Garlande (Skelton)
See *The Garlande of Laurell*
The Garlande of Laurell (Skelton) **25**:350-51, 353, 356, 369-75
Gasoline (Corso) **33**:5, 8, 13-15, 22, 35-6, 38-43, 45-48, 54
"Gaspar Becerra" (Longfellow) **30**:88
"The Gate" (Muir) **49**:197, 249
"The Gate at the Center" (Olson) **19**:283
"The Gate in His Head" (Ondaatje) **28**:294, 296, 322, 327, 334
"The Gates" (Rukeyser) **12**:224
The Gates (Rukeyser) **12**:220, 222, 225
The Gates of Paradise (Blake) **12**:46
"The Gates of the Arsenal" (Milosz) **8**:191
The Gates of Wrath: Rhymed Poems, 1948-1952 (Ginsberg) **4**:55-7, 63, 79, 91
"The Gateway" (Hope) **56**:279-80
"The Gateway" (Wright) **14**:338, 346
The Gateway (Wright) **14**:334, 336-38, 341, 345-46, 349, 354, 374
"Gather Ye Rosebuds while Ye May" (Herrick)
See "To the Virgins, to Make Much of Time"
"A Gathered Church" (Davie) **29**:101, 112-13
"Gathering Apricots" (Milosz) **8**:212, 215
"Gathering Leaves" (Frost) **1**:218
Gathering the Tribes (Forché) **10**:132-35, 137, 141-43, 145, 148, 152, 156, 158, 165-66, 168-69
"GATSBY'S THEORY OF AESTHETICS" (Baraka) **4**:19, 24
"Le Gaucher" (Char) **56**:151
Gaudete (Hughes) **7**:154-58, 161-65, 171
"Gauge" (Hughes) **53**:191
"Gaugin" (Walcott) **46**:242
"A gave in the West" (Davie) **29**:110
Gavriiliada (Pushkin) **10**:364, 410-12
The Gavriiliada (Pushkin)
See *Gavriiliada*
"Gay Chaps at the Bar" (Brooks) **7**:70, 73, 89
"Gazing Intently at the Peaches and Plums in My Spring Garden" (Yakamochi) **48**:106
"Gazing on the Great Peak" (Tu Fu) **9**:329
"Gazing on the Peak" (Tu Fu) **9**:328
"Gde, vysokaya, tvoy tsyganyonok" (Akhmatova) **2**:12
Gdziewschodzi stōnce i kedy zapada (Milosz) **8**:174-75, 178, 186, 188, 195-97, 206-07
"Le géant blanc lépreux du paysage" (Tzara) **27**:226-28
"geburtsanzeige" (Enzensberger) **28**:135
"Der Geburtstag" (Benn) **35**:8
"Geddondillo" (Nash) **21**:269
Gedichte (Trakl) **20**:245, 250
Gedichte, 1853 und 1854 (Heine) **25**:146, 161, 178
Gedichte 1938-1944 (Celan) **10**:121-24, 129
Gedichte: 1955-1970 (Enzensberger) **28**:159
"The Geese" (Graham) **59**:185
"The Geese" (Sarton) **39**:361
"Geese Gone Beyond" (Snyder) **21**:308
"Gefallen" (Stramm) **50**:202, 218
"gegen die lämmer" (Enzensberger) **28**:135
"Gegen-Strophen" (Rilke) **2**:295
"Gehazi" (Kipling) **3**:171, 182
Gehirne (Benn) **35**:3
"Gekishi: Chimmoku no koe" (Ishikawa) **10**:213
"Gemini" (Wilbur) **51**:301
"Gen. Rodimestev's story" (Niedecker) **42**:151
"The Genealogy of My Hero" (Pushkin)
See "Rodoslovnaya Moego Geroya"
"The General" (Sassoon) **12**:268
"General Bloodstock's Lament for England" (Graves) **6**:143
"The General Elliot" (Graves) **6**:150
"General Martínez" (Dalton) **36**:127
"General Prologue" (Chaucer) **19**:13, 15, 23-5, 34-6, 43-5, 50-2, 54, 60
The General Prologue to The Canterbury Tales (Chaucer) **58**:231-32, 242, 247, 264-65, 272, 288, 342
"General Quiroga Rides to His Death in a Carriage" (Borges)
See "El General Quiroga va en coche al muere"
"El General Quiroga va en coche al muere" (Borges) **32**:84
General Song (Neruda)
See *Canto general de Chile*
"General William Booth Enters into Heaven" (Lindsay) **23**:267, 276-78, 289, 294, 297
General William Booth Enters into Heaven, and Other Poems (Lindsay) **23**:264, 278, 282-83, 292
"The Generals" (Ferlinghetti) **1**:183
"Generals" (Silverstein) **49**:313, 347
"Generation" (Clifton) **17**:26
"Generation" (Page) **12**:177
"Generation III" (Lorde) **12**:143
Generations: A Memoir (Clifton) **17**:23, 25-27, 32
"The Generations of Men" (Frost) **1**:193
"Una generazione" (Pavese) **13**:213
"The Generous Enemy" (Borges) **32**:95
"Genesis" (Knight) **14**:52
"Genesis" (MacNeice) **61**:125
"Genesis" (Roethke) **15**:291-96
"Genesis" (Shapiro) **25**:284
Genesis: Book One (Schwartz) **8**:283-84, 301, 304, 308-10
"Genesis of After the Cries of the Birds" (Ferlinghetti) **1**:186
"Genetic Expedition" (Dove) **6**:122
"Geneva Restored" (Tomlinson) **17**:311, 359
"Genevieve" (Lorde) **12**:140
"Genevieve and Alexandra" (Robinson) **1**:470
"Genghis Chan: Private Eye I" (Yau) **61**:350
"Genghis Chan: Private Eye III" (Yau) **61**:353
"Genghis Chan: Private Eye IV" (Yau) **61**:351
"Genghis Chan: Private Eye VI" (Yau) **61**:352
"Genghis Chan: Private Eye VII" (Yau) **61**:353
"Genghis Chan: Private Eye VIII" (Yau) **61**:352-53
"Genghis Chan: Private Eye XIX" (Yau) **61**:354
"Genghis Chan: Private Eye XXII" (Yau) **61**:353
"Genghis Chan: Private Eye XXIV" (Yau) **61**:355
"Genghis Chan: Private Eye XXIX" (Yau) **61**:357
"Genghis Chan: Private Eye XXV" (Yau) **61**:336
"Genghis Chan: Private Eye XXX" (Yau) **61**:357
"Génie" (Rimbaud) **3**:261-62; **57**:171, 173-75, 194, 251, 265, 282
"Le génie dans l'obsurité" (Lamartine) **16**:290
"The Genie in the Bottle" (Wilbur) **51**:205
"Genie's Prayer under the Kitchen Sink" (Dove) **6**:123
"The Genius" (MacLeish) **47**:192
"Genius" (Rimbaud)
See "Génie"
"Gente che non capisce" (Pavese) **13**:218, 227
"Gentle Lady" (Joyce)
See "XXVIII"
"The Gentle Weight Lifter" (Ignatow) **34**:286, 316
The Gentle Weight Lifter (Ignatow) **34**:271, 274-76, 279-80, 311, 314, 325
"The Gentleman from Shallot" (Bishop)
See "The Gentleman of Shallot"
"The Gentleman of Shallot" (Bishop) **3**:37; **34**:52, 189
"Gentleman-Rankers" (Kipling) **3**:161
"A Gentleman's Bedroom" (Ní Chuilleanáin) **34**:349, 353
"Gentlemen, I Address You Publicly" (Rexroth) **20**:184
"The Gentlest Lady" (Parker) **28**:362
"Geographers" (Shapiro) **25**:270
"The Geographic Center" (Kumin) **15**:215-16
Geography III (Bishop) **3**:48-9, 63, 66, 69, 73, 75; **34**:54, 59, 94-97, 111, 139, 146, 158, 174, 176, 188, 193
The Geography of Lograire (Merton) **10**:334-35, 338, 348, 351
"Geography of the Trinity Corona" (Cruz) **37**:10
"Geometric Poem" (Corso) **33**:18, 24-5, 49
"Geometry" (Ransom) **61**:267, 293-94
"George Gray" (Masters) **36**:170
"George Jackson" (Dylan) **37**:62
"George Moore" (Moore) **49**:113-14
"George Trimble" (Masters) **36**:182
"George Washington and the Invention of Dynamite" (Wakoski) **15**:358
"George Washington and the Loss of His Teeth" (Wakoski) **15**:357
The George Washington Poems (Wakoski) **15**:324, 357-58
"George Washington: the Whole Man" (Wakoski) **15**:359
"Georgeline" (Rose) **13**:236
"Georges Braque" (Éluard) **38**:71
"Georgia Dusk" (Toomer) **7**:310, 319-20, 334
"Georgians" (Muir) **49**:228
"Geórgicas" (Guillén) **35**:229
Georgics (Vergil) **12**:358-61, 364-66, 370-71, 373-77, 383, 385-86, 391-92
"Georgie Grimes" (Brown) **55**:154
"Geraldine" (Brontë) **8**:67, 73-4
"Geraniums" (Hogan) **35**:257
"The German Girls! The German Girls!" (MacLeish) **47**:149, 190, 255
"Germanien" (Hölderlin) **4**:149
Germany: A Winter's Tale (Heine)
See *Deutschland: Ein Wintermärchen*
"Gerontion" (Day Lewis) **11**:151
"Gerontion" (Eliot) **5**:160-62, 165, 171, 173, 183-85, 189, 195-97, 204, 209
"Gerontion" (Tate) **50**:285
Gerontofagia pero (Dalton) **36**:129
"Gerry's Jazz" (Komunyakaa) **51**:34

"Gertha's Lovers" (Morris) **55**:331
Gesammelte Gedichte (Benn) **35**:8
Gesammelte Werke (Celan) **10**:100-01, 124
"Gesang der Geister über den Wassern" (Goethe) **5**:239
"Gesang des Abgeschiedenen" (Trakl) **20**:240-41
"Gesänge" (Benn) **35**:45, 47, 72
"Gesänge I" (Benn) **35**:26, 31
"Gesänge II" (Benn) **35**:31
"Gesta maximalista" (Borges) **22**:92
"Gestalt at Sixty" (Sarton) **39**:340
"The Gesture" (Oppen) **35**:299
"A Gesture by a Lady with an Assumed Name" (Wright) **36**:335
"Get hence foule Griefe, the canker of the minde" (Sidney) **32**:250
"Get the Gasworks" (Ignatow) **34**:341
"Gethsemane" (Kipling) **3**:171
"Gethsemani" (Lamartine) **16**:297
Gethsemani, Ky. (Cardenal) **22**:103, 125-26
"Gettin Down to Get Over" (Jordan) **38**:124
"Getting in the Wood" (Snyder) **21**:300, 302
"Getting There" (Plath) **1**:412; **37**:202, 241, 258
"Getting There" (Wagoner) **33**:352, 362-63
"Getting Throught" (Merrill) **28**:248
"Getting to the Poem" (Corso) **33**:35-6
"Getting Up Early" (Bly) **39**:76
"Gettysburg: July 1, 1863" (Kenyon) **57**:12, 20, 44
"Geue place ye louers" (Surrey) **59**:306-9, 330
"gewimmer und firmament" (Enzensberger) **28**:136
"Gewisse Lebensabende" (Benn) **35**:9
"Gewitter" (Stramm) **50**:172
"Das Gewitter" (Trakl) **20**:237-38, 251, 257
"The Geysers" (Gunn) **26**:198, 204, 208, 220
"Ghazal at Full Moon" (Jordan) **38**:145
"Ghede Poem" (Mackey) **49**:3
"Ghetto" (Borges)
See "Judería"
"A Ghost" (Baudelaire)
See "Un fantôme"
"Ghost" (Lowell) **3**:203
"The Ghost" (Teasdale) **31**:356
"A Ghost, A Real Ghost" (Jarrell) **41**:153, 158, 169
"Ghost Crabs" (Hughes) **7**:137, 158-59
"The Ghost Hammer" (Pinsky) **27**:158
"Ghost House" (Frost) **39**:246
"A Ghost May Come" (Ginsberg) **4**:74
"Ghost of a Chance" (Rich) **5**:363, 370
"Ghosts" (Sexton) **2**:350
"Ghosts, Angels, Unicorns" (Abse) **41**:22
"Ghosts as Cocoons" (Stevens) **6**:297
"The Ghost's Leave-taking" (Plath) **1**:381, 388; **37**:182
"Ghosts of 1619" (Hughes) **53**:152
"The Ghosts of James and Peirce in Harvard Yard" (Schwartz) **8**:302
"The Ghosts of the Buffaloes" (Lindsay) **23**:275, 279, 287
"The Ghost's Petition" (Rossetti) **7**:273
"Già la pioggia è con noi" (Quasimodo) **47**:281
"Giacometti" (Wilbur) **51**:186
Giambi ed epodi (Carducci) **46**:8, 13, 37, 47, 50, 73, 80, 89
"Giant Toad" (Bishop) **3**:65
"Giant Turtle" (Corso) **33**:48
"The Giant's Wife" (Carducci)
See "La Moglie del Gigante"
The Giaour: A Fragment of a Turkish Tale (Byron) **16**:91-2
"The Giaour and the Pacha" (Wilbur) **51**:186-88, 192, 327
"The Gibber" (Roethke) **15**:262
"Gibson" (Baraka) **4**:30
"Gic to Har" (Rexroth) **20**:193
"Gidget Agonistes" (Ashbery) **26**:137
"The Gift" (Bukowski) **18**:5
"The Gift" (Carver) **54**:23
"The Gift" (Glück) **16**:151
"The Gift" (H. D.) **5**:266, 270, 303
"The Gift" (Lee) **24**:240
"Gift" (Milosz) **8**:209
"Gift" (Tagore)
See "Upahar"
"The Gift" (Teasdale) **31**:344
"The Gift" (Williams) **7**:371
"Gift for a Believer" (Levine) **22**:223, 225
"The Gift of a Satin Brocade" (Tu Fu) **9**:318
"The Gift of Fire" (Mueller) **33**:174
"The Gift of God" (Robinson) **1**:462, 467-68
"The Gift of Harun Al-Rashid" (Yeats) **20**:319; **51**:72
"The Gift of the Sea" (Kipling) **3**:183
"The Gift Outright" (Frost) **1**:212-13, 224
"Gift Poem" (Rukeyser) **12**:231
Gifts at Meeting (Wylie) **23**:320
"Gifts of Rain" (Heaney) **18**:201, 210
"The Gifts of the Terek" (Lermontov)
See "Dary Tereka"
"Gigolo" (Plath) **37**:258
"Gigot Sleeves" (McGuckian) **27**:107-109
"A Gilded Lapse of Time" (Schnackenberg) **45**:331-33, 341
A Gilded Lapse of Time (Schnackenberg) **45**:331, 333-34, 339, 342-43, 345-50
"The Gilliflower of Gold" (Morris) **55**:299, 301
"Gin" (Levine) **22**:220
"La ginestra" (Leopardi) **37**:79-80, 92-93, 98, 102-3, 107, 109, 111-12, 118, 124-25, 132-33, 156-60
"Ginga no jo" (Matsuo Bashō) **3**:13
"Ginza Samba" (Pinsky) **27**:175
"Giorgio de Chirico" (Éluard) **38**:69-70, 103-5
Giorno dopo giorno (Quasimodo) **47**:266, 281-85
"Giorno e notte" (Montale) **13**:111
"Giovanni and the Indians" (Page) **12**:168
"Giovanni Franchi" (Loy) **16**:333
"Giovanni's Rape of the Sabine Women at Wildenstein's" (Oppen) **35**:311, 312
"The Gipsies" (Mahon) **60**:134, 209
Gipsies (Pushkin)
See *Tsygany*
"Gipsies Revisited" (Mahon) **60**:134
Gipsy Ballads (Lorca)
See *Primer romancero gitano*
"A Girl" (Wright) **36**:396
"A Girl and a Bird" (Dafydd)
See "Merch ac Aderyn"
"Girl Beatnik" (Yevtushenko) **40**:345
"Girl Drowned in a Well" (García Lorca) **3**:139
"A Girl in a Library" (Jarrell) **41**:140, 158-59, 171, 185, 189-91, 210-11, 216-17
"A Girl in a Window" (Wright) **36**:315, 336
A Girl in Winter (Larkin) **21**:225, 232
"The girl of live marble" (Gunn) **26**:212
"Girl Powdering Her Neck" (Song) **21**:347
"A Girl Sewing" (Szirtes) **51**:158
"The Girl the North Wind Brought" (Elytis) **21**:123
"A Girl Walking into a Shadow" (Wright) **36**:396
"The Girl Who Died No. 1" (Walker) **30**:339
"The Girl Who Died No. 2" (Walker) **30**:339, 365
"The Girl Who Loves to Shoot" (Smith) **12**:326
"Girls Bathing, Galway, 1965" (Heaney) **18**:224
"Girls in the Plural" (McGuckian) **27**:92-94
"Girls in their Season" (Mahon) **60**:138
"The Girls of Llanbadarn" (Dafydd)
See "Merched Llanbadarn"
"A Girl's Mood" (Reese) **29**:331
"Girls on the Bridge" (Mahon) **60**:148, 201-2
"The Girls on the Pier" (Mahon) **60**:200
"Girl's Song" (Bogan) **12**:90, 100
"Girls Working in Banks" (Shapiro) **25**:306, 322
"Git Dough" (Guillén)
See "Búscate plata"
Gitāli (Tagore) **8**:413, 427
Gitanjali (Tagore) **8**:402, 412-14, 416, 418
Gitimālya (Tagore) **8**:413
"Giuseppe Caponsacchi" (Browning) **2**:41
"La giustizia pia del lavoro" (Carducci) **46**:65
"Give All to Love" (Emerson) **18**:85, 88, 113
"Give and Take" (Meredith) **28**:199
"Give Way, Ye Gates" (Roethke) **15**:252, 261, 298-99, 301-02
Give Your Heart to the Hawks and Other Poems (Jeffers) **17**:135, 142-43, 147
"A Given Grace" (Tomlinson) **17**:309, 316, 335
"Given to Li Po" (Tu Fu) **9**:330
"The Giver" (Teasdale) **31**:388
The Giving Tree (Silverstein) **49**:305, 320-21, 346, 348-49
The Giving Tree and Other Shel Silverstein Songs (Silverstein) **49**:319
"Givings" (Ammons) **16**:63
Gladiolus (McGuckian) **27**:96
"Gladly Still" (Borges)
See "Jactancia de quietud"
"The Gladness of Nature" (Bryant) **20**:40
"Gladstone Street" (Tomlinson) **17**:319
"The Glance" (Herbert) **4**:132
"A Glance from the Bridge" (Wilbur) **51**:209
"Glanmore Sonnets" (Heaney) **18**:198
"Glanmore Sonnets IV" (Heaney) **18**:238
"Glass" (Francis) **34**:248
"The Glass" (Mistral)
See "El vaso"
"The Glass" (Olds) **22**:323, 332
"Glass" (Wakoski) **15**:325
"The Glass Air" (Page) **12**:178
The Glass Air (Page) **12**:189-90
"Glass Falling" (MacNeice) **61**:133
"A Glass House" (Ní Chuilleanáin) **34**:382
"The Glass King" (Boland) **58**:7
"A Glass of Water" (Sarton) **39**:339
"Glazed Glitter" (Stein) **18**:322
"The Gleaners" (Merwin) **45**:8
"Gleaning" (Jarrell) **41**:180, 210
"Gleneden's Dream" (Brontë) **8**:67
"Glengormley" (Mahon) **60**:132, 165, 181, 185, 191-92, 234
"Glimpse" (Hughes) **7**:153
"The Glimpse of the Coming Day" (Morris) **55**:339
"Glimpse of the Ice" (Merwin) **45**:20, 28
"The Global Lobal Blues" (Viereck) **27**:279
"Global Village" (Mahon) **60**:229
"The Globe in North Carolina" (Mahon) **60**:147-48, 151, 156, 172-74, 190, 194, 196-97, 215
"Globe of Gneiss" (Warren) **37**:314-15, 317
"Le gloire" (Lamartine) **16**:276, 298
"Gloire de Dijon" (Lawrence) **54**:189, 191
"Gloria" (Francis) **34**:244
"The Glory" (Thomas) **53**:275, 281-82
"The Glory Is fallen Out of" (Cummings) **5**:105
"The Glory of Ptolemies" (Cavafy) **36**:73, 75
"The Glory of the Day Was in Her Face" (Johnson) **24**:154
The Glory of the Nightingales (Robinson) **1**:472-73, 475, 479, 483
"Glory of Women" (Sassoon) **12**:267
"Glossary" (Brathwaite) **56**:86
Glossolalia Poéma o zvuke (Bely) **11**:9, 11
"Glove" (Abse) **41**:9
"The Glove" (Browning) **2**:29, 38
"Glück der Entfernung" (Goethe) **5**:246
"The Glutton" (Graves) **6**:150
"Gnat-Psalm" (Hughes) **7**:136-37, 159
"The Gnome, the Gnat, and the Gnu" (Silverstein) **49**:342
Gnomes and Occasions (Nemerov) **24**:284-86, 288
"Gnothi Seauton" (Emerson) **18**:97
"Go and Look for Bread" (Guillén)
See "Búscate plata"
"Go burning sighs" (Wyatt)
See "Goo burnyng sighes"

"Go Down Death" (Johnson) **24**:128-29, 139, 144, 156, 164-65, 167, 169
"Go, Fetch to Me a Pint o' Wine" (Burns) **6**:76
"Go Get Money" (Guillén)
See "Búscate plata"
"Go Home, The Act Is Over" (Abse) **41**:4
"Go it, Granny - Go it, Hog!" (Warren) **37**:346
"Go Slow" (Hughes) **53**:151-52
"Go-and-Get-the-Enemy-Blues" (Hughes) **53**:145
"Goat Ode in Mid-Dive" (Viereck) **27**:295
"The Goat of Slieve Donard" (Kavanagh) **33**:99, 103
"Goats and Monkeys" (Walcott) **46**:229-30, 283
"Goat's Leaf" (Marie de France)
See "Chevrefoil"
"Gobernador" (Guillén) **23**:127
The Goblet of Blizzards (Bely)
See *Kubok metelej: Chetviortiia simfoniia*
"The Goblet of Life" (Longfellow) **30**:13, 26, 37, 103
"Goblin Market" (Rossetti) **7**:259, 261, 266, 268, 272-3, 279-80, 282, 288-94, 298-304
Goblin Market, and Other Poems (Rossetti) **7**:259, 261, 279, 296-7
"Goblin Revel" (Sassoon) **12**:240
"God" (Swenson) **14**:281, 281, 286
The God (H. D.) **5**:303
"The God Abandons Antony" (Cavafy) **36**:7, 8, 20, 28, 40, 74, 76
"God and Devil" (Smith) **12**:331
God Desired and Desiring (Jiménez)
See *Dios deseado y deseante: Animal de fondo con numerosos poemas iñeditos*
"The God Forsakes Anthony" (Cavafy)
See "The God Abandons Antony"
"God Forsakes Antony" (Cavafy)
See "The God Abandons Antony"
"God Has Mercy on Kindergarten Children" (Amichai)
See "Elohim merakhem 'al yaldei hagan"
"God Has Pity on the Kindergarten Children" (Amichai)
See "Elohim merakhem 'al yaldei hagan"
"God in Woman" (Kavanagh) **33**:63, 137
"God Is a Distant, Stately Lover" (Dickinson) **1**:93
"The God of Broken Things" (Komunyakaa) **51**:65
"The God of Flowers" (Levertov) **11**:198
"The God of the Poor" (Morris) **55**:340
"The God of Youth" (Hölderlin)
See "Der Gott der Jugend"
"God Pities the Kindergarten Children" (Amichai)
See "Elohim merakhem 'al yaldei hagan"
"God Said" (Ignatow) **34**:274
"God? She's Black" (Corso) **33**:49
"God slain by Troops" (Niedecker) **42**:149
"God Speaks" (Smith) **12**:335
"God the Drinker" (Smith) **12**:326-27
"God the Eater" (Smith) **12**:326, 333
"God to Hungry Child" (Hughes) **53**:116
"God Wills It" (Mistral)
See "Dios lo quiere"
"God Works in a Mysterious Way" (Brooks) **7**:74
Godbey (Masters) **1**:339
"God-closed Age" (Corso) **33**:49
"The Goddess" (Levertov) **11**:159, 168
"Goddess in the Wood" (Brooke) **24**:57
Godel's Proof, New Poems 1965 (Rexroth) **20**:196
"God-Forgotten" (Hardy) **8**:104, 121
"The Godhead as Lynx" (Sarton) **39**:342, 365, 367
"GoDo" (Birney) **52**:83
"Godolphin Horne Who Was Cursed with the Sin of Pride and Became a Boot-Black" (Belloc) **24**:26
"Gods" (Cullen) **20**:53
"The Gods" (Merwin) **45**:21-2, 28, 49
"Gods" (Sexton) **2**:373
"God's Acre" (Longfellow) **30**:64
"The Gods Are Here" (Toomer) **7**:336
"Gods Can Die" (Thumboo) **30**:300, 301, 322, 323, 329
Gods Can Die (Thumboo) **30**:299, 300, 303, 322, 328
"Gods Change, Prayers Are Here to Stay" (Amichai) **38**:48-51, 55-56
"God's Education" (Hardy) **8**:121
"God's Funeral" (Hardy) **8**:131
"God's Providence" (Herrick) **9**:91
"God's Spies" (Howe) **54**:129
God's Trombones: Seven Negro Sermons in Verse (Johnson) **24**:128-29, 132-33, 141, 143-44, 149, 152-56, 159, 161, 164-70
"God's Wheel" (Silverstein) **49**:328
"God's World" (Millay) **6**:205, 215; **61**:213, 222
"God's World" (Pasternak) **6**:268-69
"Goe, and catche a falling starre" (Donne)
See "Song. 'Goe, and catche a falling starre'"
Goethe's Roman Elegies (Goethe)
See *Römische Elegien*
Goethe's Works (Goethe) **5**:223
"Gofyn Cymod" (Dafydd ap Gwilym) **56**:246
"Gog" (Hughes) **7**:126, 139
"The Go-goat" (Pavese)
See "Il Dio-Caprone"
"Goin' to Acapulco" (Dylan) **37**:59
"The Going" (Hardy) **8**:91, 113, 118, 133-35
"Going" (Larkin) **21**:227, 242
"Going Away" (Hagiwara)
See "Ryojō"
"Going Away" (Kenyon) **57**:15
"Going Away from the River" (Hacker) **47**:88
"Going Back to Oxford" (Ní Chuilleanáin) **34**:349, 351
"Going Back to the River" (Hacker) **47**:88
"Going Down" (Ignatow) **34**:342
Going for the Rain (Ortiz) **17**:222, 226-227, 231-232, 238, 244
"Going for Water" (Frost) **39**:230
"Going from the Capital to Feng-hsien, Singing My Feelings" (Tu Fu) **9**:332
"Going, Going, Gone" (Dylan) **37**:63-5
"Going Home" (Dickey) **40**:200
"Going Home" (Mahon) **60**:140, 184, 231-32
"Going Out to Check the Ewes" (Bly) **39**:42-43
"Going To and Fro" (Lowell) **3**:215
"Going to Church" (Patmore) **59**:233
"Going to Horse Flats" (Jeffers) **17**:141
"Going to Pieces" (Wagoner) **33**:333
"Going to School" (Shapiro) **25**:291, 320, 326
"Going to the Bakery" (Bishop) **34**:116, 139, 141
Going to War with All My Relations: New and Selected Poems (Rose) **13**:242
"going uptown to visit miriam" (Cruz) **37**:22
"Gold and Black" (Ondaatje) **28**:328
The Gold Cell (Olds) **22**:314-16, 318-21, 324, 326, 328
"Gold Coast Customs" (Sitwell) **3**:300, 305-06, 308-09, 314, 316, 319-20, 325-26
"Gold Hair" (Browning) **2**:95
"The Gold Hesperidee" (Frost) **39**:235
Gold in Azure (Bely)
See *Zoloto v lazuri*
"The Gold Key" (Sexton) **2**:364
"The Gold Lily" (Glück) **16**:170
"The Gold of the Tigers" (Borges) **32**:66, 140
The Gold of the Tigers: Selected Later Poems (Borges)
See *El oro de los tigres*
"Gold on Oak Leaves" (Oppen) **35**:301
"A Gold Ring from the Tomb of Isopata" (Hope) **56**:292
"The Golden Age" (Behn) **13**:8, 22, 26, 32-4, 39
"Golden Age" (Rimbaud)
See "Age d'or"
"The Golden Boat" (Tagore)
See "Sonar tari"
"The Golden Bough" (Mahon) **60**:151, 169, 195
"Golden Bough" (Wylie) **23**:314
"Golden Brown Blues" (Hughes) **53**:136
"The Golden Cockerel" (Reisman)
See "Skazka o Zolotom Petushke"
"TH GOLDEN DAWN" (Bissett) **14**:24, 32
"The Golden Echo" (Hopkins) **15**:125, 152
"The golden gates of sleep unbar" (Shelley) **14**:177
"Golden Hair" (Owen) **19**:338
The Golden Hynde and Other Poems (Noyes) **27**:117
The Golden Legend (Longfellow) **30**:16-18, 23-5, 35, 38-9, 56, 65, 73, 75
"Golden Milestone" (Longfellow) **30**:27, 42
"The Golden Net" (Blake) **12**:36
"Golden Silences" (Rossetti) **7**:271
"The Golden Stool" (Brathwaite) **56**:86
"The Golden Supper" (Tennyson) **6**:374
"The Golden Tortoise" (Darío)
See "La tortuga de oro..."
The Golden Treasury of Magazine Verse (Braithwaite) **52**:106-7
"Golden Venetian Light" (Olson) **19**:305
"The Golden Whales of California" (Lindsay) **23**:264, 269, 274, 288
"Golden Wings" (Morris) **55**:238, 267, 279, 282, 300-302
The Golden Year (Riley) **48**:327
"Goldfish" (Bukowski) **18**:5
"Goldilocks and Goldilocks" (Morris) **55**:340
"goldner schnittmusterbogen zur poetischen wiederaufrüstung" (Enzensberger) **28**:136-37, 141
"The Goldsmith" (Sassoon) **12**:257
"The Golem" (Borges) **32**:60, 63
"Le golfe de Baïa" (Lamartine) **16**:277, 290, 302
"Le golfe de Genes" (Lamartine) **16**:266
"Golgotha" (Sassoon) **12**:261-62
"Goliath of Gath. 1 Sam. Chap. XVII" (Wheatley) **3**:354-55, 357-61
"Golos proshlogo" (Bely) **11**:24
"El golpe" (Neruda) **4**:288
"Gone" (Heaney) **18**:201
"Gone" (Sandburg) **2**:303, 316; **41**:242, 312, 318, 336
"Gone, Gone Again" (Thomas)
See "Blenheim Oranges"
"Gone, Gone, Gone" (Bly) **39**:72-72
"Gone the Last Danger on Earth" (Corso) **33**:49
"Goner's Boner" (McHugh) **61**:208
"The Gong-gong" (Brathwaite) **56**:6
"Goo burnyng sighes" (Wyatt) **27**:352
"Good Advice" (Stone) **53**:256-57
"Good Frend" (H. D.) **5**:297, 302
"Good Friday" (Clampitt) **19**:81, 88
"Good Friday" (Donne)
See "Goodfriday 1613: Riding Westward"
"Good Friday" (Herbert) **4**:120
"Good Friday" (Rossetti) **7**:268, 283
"Good Friday and Easter Morning" (Ammons) **16**:63
"Good Friday on the Bus" (Stone) **53**:223
"Good Friday: Rex Tragicus, or Christ Going to His Crosse" (Herrick) **9**:109, 121
"Good Friday, Riding Westward" (Ní Chuilleanáin) **34**:363
Good Intentions (Nash) **21**:266
A Good Journey (Ortiz) **17**:224-27, 229-30, 232-33, 240, 244
"A Good Knight in Prison" (Morris) **55**:299, 301-2
"Good ladies, you that have your pleasure in exyle" (Surrey) **59**:297, 306-7, 310, 352
"The Good Life" (Hughes) **7**:119
"A Good Man" (Riley) **48**:301
"A Good Man in a Bad Time" (MacLeish) **47**:206
"The Good Man in Hell" (Muir) **49**:197, 202

"A Good Memory" (Komunyakaa) **51**:36
"Good Morning" (Hughes) **53**:193
"Good Morning, America" (Sandburg) **2**:330; **41**:288-89, 339, 341, 346
Good Morning, America (Sandburg) **2**:318-19, 321, 323; **41**:271, 274-75, 277, 284, 302, 319, 325, 330
"Good Morning Revolution" (Hughes) **1**:268; **53**:144
Good Morning, Revolution: Uncollected Social Protest Writings (Hughes) **53**:110-13
Good News About the Earth (Clifton) **17**:16, 22-24, 26, 35
"Good Night" (Williams) **7**:348
"The Good, Old-Fashioned People" (Riley) **48**:300, 353
"The Good Part" (Longfellow) **30**:48
"The Good Servant" (Wilbur) **51**:188
"Good Ships" (Ransom) **61**:301, 309, 311
The Good Song (Verlaine)
See *La bonne chanson*
A Good Time Was Had by All (Smith) **12**:292, 314-15, 317, 325
Good Times: Poems (Clifton) **17**:16-17, 20-21, 23-24, 26, 31, 35
"The Good Town" (Muir) **49**:197, 205, 229, 256, 258, 265, 277, 282-83, 299
Good Woman: Poems and a Memoir, 1969-1980 (Clifton) **17**:25-26, 38
"Good-By, Jim" (Riley) **48**:290
"Goodbye!" (Baraka) **4**:11
"Good-bye" (Emerson) **18**:74
"Goodbye" (Kinnell) **26**:292
"Goodbye Christ" (Hughes) **1**:268; **53**:144
Goodbye Spring (Seifert)
See *Jaro sbohem*
"Goodbye to Great Spruce Head Island" (O'Hara) **45**:163
"Goodbye to London" (MacNeice) **61**:177
"Goodbye to Serpents" (Dickey) **40**:192
"Good-bye to the Mezzogiorno" (Auden) **1**:17
"Goodbye to the Poetry of Calcium" (Wright) **36**:304, 340, 371
"Goodbye, Unwashed Russia" (Lermontov) **18**:281
"Goodfriday 1613: Riding Westward" (Donne) **1**:139, 158-59
"Goo-dmore-ning(en" (Cummings) **5**:107
"The Good-Morrow" (Amichai) **38**:43
"The good-morrow" (Donne) **1**:125, 130-34, 147, 152-54
"Goodnight" (Lee) **24**:241
"The Goodnight" (Ondaatje) **28**:318
"Goodnight Laides, Goodnight Sweet Ladies" (Walcott) **46**:230
Goodnight Willie Lee, I'll See You in the Morning (Walker) **30**:346, 348-50, 353-55
"Goody Blake and Harry Gill" (Wordsworth) **4**:381, 414
"Gook Nigger" (Quintana) **36**:275
"Gooks" (Quintana) **36**:272
"The Goose" (Stryk) **27**:203
"Goose Fair" (Lawrence) **54**:240
"The Goose Fish" (Nemerov) **24**:261, 289-90
"Goose Pond" (Kunitz) **19**:178
"The Goose Shed" (Dafydd)
See "Y Cwt Gwyddau"
"Gooseberry Fool" (Clampitt) **19**:86
"Góra Kikineis" (Mickiewicz) **38**:222-23
"Gorbunov and Gorchakov" (Brodsky) **9**:4-6, 10-12, 26-7
"The Gorge" (Stryk) **27**:189, 203
"Gorilla" (Silverstein) **49**:305
"Gorod" (Pasternak) **6**:264
"Gorodok" (Pushkin) **10**:410
"Gospel" (Dove) **6**:117
"The Gossamers" (Tomlinson) **17**:310, 312
"Gost" (Lermontov) **18**:288
"Got To Be on Time" (Alurista) **34**:31, 42
"Gothic Letter on a Hot Night" (Atwood) **8**:24
"Der Gott der Jugend" (Hölderlin) **4**:142
"Gott im Mittelalter" (Rilke) **2**:275
"Die Götter Griechenlands" (Heine) **25**:145
Götterdämmerung (Heine) **25**:145
"Das Göttliche" (Goethe) **5**:239
"The Gourd Dancer" (Momaday) **25**:198-99, 214-16, 221
The Gourd Dancer (Momaday) **25**:193-97, 200-202, 205, 212, 216, 219-20
"Le goût du néant" (Baudelaire) **1**:68
"Government" (Sandburg) **41**:348
"Gow's Watch" (Kipling) **3**:181
"Gra Pana Cogito" (Herbert) **50**:25, 38, 41
"Grabaciones" (Cardenal) **22**:131-32
"Grace" (Emerson) **18**:98
"Grace" (Herbert) **4**:111, 129
"Grace" (Jackson) **44**:5
"Grace" (Mistral)
See "La gracia"
"Grace" (Ransom) **61**:294
"Grace" (Wilbur) **51**:187, 193, 209
"Grace Abounding" (Ammons) **16**:63
"Grace before Sleep" (Teasdale) **31**:341
Grace Notes (Dove) **6**:120-22
"The Grace of Time" (Guillén) **35**:218
"Graceland" (Sandburg) **41**:226, 239
"Grace's House" (Merton) **10**:340-41, 350, 353
"La gracia" (Mistral) **32**:181
Gracias Haus (Merton) **10**:341
"Grackles, Goodbye" (Warren) **37**:346
Graf Nulin (Pushkin) **10**:366, 386, 390, 400-01
"Graffiti from the Gare Saint-Manqué" (Hacker) **47**:81
"Grafo-mundo" (Cruz) **37**:31, 35-36
A Grain of Mustard Seed (Sarton) **39**:328-29, 339-40, 342, 365-66
"La Graine" (Perse) **23**:228
"Grainne's Sleep Song" (McGuckian) **27**:82
Grains et issues (Tzara) **27**:241-42, 251-52
"Grammar and Goodness" (Hughes) **53**:97
"The Grammarian's Funeral" (Browning) **2**:37, 51
"La gran aventura" (Guillén) **35**:202
"Gran silencio" (Guillén) **35**:155
El gran zoo (Guillén) **23**:100
"Granaten" (Stramm) **50**:188, 205, 222
"Granatfeuer" (Stramm) **50**:222
"The Grand Canyon" (Merrill) **28**:247, 272
"Grand complainte de la ville de Paris" (Laforgue) **14**:97
"Grand Galop" (Ashbery) **26**:126, 143
Le grand jeu (Péret) **33**:201-03, 207, 212, 215-18, 220, 223-24, 230
"Le grand jour" (Éluard) **38**:71
"Grand Marshal Kao's Dapple" (Tu Fu) **9**:330
"Le Grand Midi" (Césaire) **25**:29-30
"The Grand Question Debated" (Swift) **9**:260
"Grand River Marshes" (Masters) **1**:330, 333
Le Grand Testament (Villon)
See *Le Testament*
"The Grand View" (Abse) **41**:3, 14, 25
"Une grande dame" (Verlaine) **2**:430-31
"La grande maison inhabitable" (Éluard) **38**:69, 84
"La grande neige" (Bonnefoy) **58**:153
"Grandes conspiraces" (Éluard) **38**:71
"The Grandfather" (Guillén)
See "El abuelo"
"Grandfather" (Mahon) **60**:132
"Grandfather Arthur Winslow" (Lowell) **3**:200
"Grandfather in the Old Men's Home" (Merwin) **45**:18
"Grandma We Are Poets" (Clifton) **17**:29-30
"Grandmother Dying" (Merwin) **45**:8
"Grandmother in the Garden" (Glück) **16**:124
"Grandmother Speranza's Friend" (Gozzano)
See "L'amica di nonna speranza"
"Grandmother Watching at Her Window" (Merwin) **45**:8
"Grandmother's Clavichord" (Darío)
See "El clavicordio de la abuela"
"Grandmother's Father" (Quintana) **36**:275
"Grandparents" (Lowell) **3**:217-20
"Grand-Pré" (Carman)
See "Low Tide on Grand Pré"
"Granite and Steel" (Moore) **4**:259, 261; **49**:144
The Granite Pail: The Selected Poems of Lorine Niedecker (Niedecker) **42**:103-7, 109-10, 155, 165, 170, 173-74, 176, 178
"Granny" (Riley) **48**:340
"Granted This World" (Sarton) **39**:320, 322
Granth (Kabir)
See *The Adi Granth*
"Grant's Tomb Revisited" (Shapiro) **25**:322
"Granville Calhoun" (Masters) **36**:229
"Grape Sherbet" (Dove) **6**:106, 109
"Graph for Action" (Williams) **7**:369
"Grappa in September" (Pavese) **13**:218
"Grappling in the Central Blue" (Kumin) **15**:209-10
"Grass" (Bly) **39**:69
"Grass" (Sandburg) **41**:240, 266-67, 270, 288, 297, 328
"Grasse: The Olive Trees" (Wilbur) **51**:206-7, 293
"Grasses" (Gunn) **26**:219
"A Grasshopper" (Wilbur) **51**:190, 301
"Gratitude" (Lermontov) **18**:281
"Gratitude" (Smart) **13**:361
"The Grauballe Man" (Heaney) **18**:210-11
"A Grave" (Moore) **4**:243, 251; **49**:89, 94, 98, 101, 150-51, 153-55
"A Grave Illness" (Page) **12**:199
"The Grave of the Countess Potocka" (Mickiewicz)
See "Grób Potockiej"
"The Gravedigger" (Carman) **34**:213
"Gravelly Run" (Ammons) **16**:29
"Graves" (Sandburg) **2**:303; **41**:338
"Graves Are Made to Waltz On" (Viereck) **27**:258
"Graves of the Harem" (Mickiewicz)
See "Mogiły haremu"
"The Grave-Tree" (Carman) **34**:211, 220-21
"A Graveyard" (Moore) **49**:150, 152
"Graveyard at Bolinas" (Hass) **16**:196, 209
"The Graveyard by the Sea" (Valéry)
See "Le cimetière marin"
"A Graveyard in the Middle of the Sea" (Moore) **49**:150-51
"Gravy" (Carver) **54**:17, 19
"Gray" (Cavafy) **36**:74
"Gray" (Walker) **30**:343
"Gray Dogs" (Ríos) **57**:328
"Gray Eyes" (Gallagher) **9**:51
"Gray Fox in a Roadside Zoo" (Wagoner) **33**:374
"the gray woods exploding" (Birney) **52**:34-36
"Grażyna" (Mickiewicz) **38**:164, 166, 219
"The Great Adventure of Max Breuck" (Lowell) **13**:60, 96
"Great American Waterfront Poem" (Ferlinghetti) **1**:188
"Great Canzon" (Rexroth) **20**:190
"The Great Carbuncle" (Plath) **37**:237-38, 241
"The Great Chinese Dragon" (Ferlinghetti) **1**:176
"The Great Elegy for John Donne" (Brodsky) **9**:2, 4, 10, 26
"The Great Explosion" (Jeffers) **17**:130
"The Great Figure" (Williams) **7**:399, 401, 410
"The Great Fillmore Street Buffalo Drive" (Momaday) **25**:221
"Great Friend" (Thoreau) **30**:192
"The Great Homecoming" (Sikelianos) **29**:373
"Great House" (Walcott)
See "Ruins of a Great House"
"The Great Hunger" (Kavanagh) **33**:61, 65-7, 71, 84, 92, 95-7, 124, 134-36, 140-4, 163-6
The Great Hunger (Kavanagh) **33**:58-9, 64, 70-2, 74-5, 77-81, 84-5, 87, 98, 100-105, 113-5, 117, 123-4, 126-131, 141, 146-7, 149, 154-6, 158-9, 161-2, 167, 169-71
"The Great Hunt" (Sandburg) **2**:300, 316; **41**:225

"The Great Lament of My Obscurity One" (Tzara) **27**:249
"The Great Lover" (Brooke) **24**:53, 56-7, 59, 65, 78, 87-8
"The great Macedon" (Surrey) **59**:303
"Great Measures" (Hogan) **35**:277-78
"The Great Mother" (Snyder) **21**:297
"The Great Nebula of Andromeda" (Rexroth) **20**:190
"The Great Palace of Versailles" (Dove) **6**:111
"Great Performances" (Mueller) **33**:192
"The Great Plain of India Seen from the Air" (Sarton) **39**:327, 340
"A Great Procession of Priests and Laymen" (Cavafy) **36**:36, 63
"Great Snoring and Norwich" (Sitwell) **3**:301
"The Great Society" (Bly) **39**:9
"The Great Society, Mark X" (Nemerov) **24**:280
"The Great Sunset" (Jeffers) **17**:130
"Great Things" (Hardy) **8**:112
Great Tranquillity: Questions and Answers (Amichai)
See *Shalvah gedolah: She'elot utshuvot*
"The Great Transparencies" (Sarton) **39**:340
"Great Unaffected Vampires and the Moon" (Smith) **12**:330-31
The Great Valley (Masters) **1**:329, 332, 342-43; **36**:176, 183
"Great Weaver" (Carman) **34**:212
The Great Whirl of Exile (Quintana) **36**:275-76
"Greater Love" (Owen) **19**:327, 332, 335, 337, 344, 347, 353-54, 358-59
Greater Testament (Villon)
See *Le Testament*
"The Greater Whiteness" (Swenson) **14**:264
"El Greco: Espolio" (Birney) **52**:11, 41, 44
"Greece" (Corso) **33**:6, 36, 49
"Greece" (Thoreau) **30**:251
"Greed" (Wakoski) **15**:325, 331, 351-52
Greed (Wakoski) **15**:325, 355-56, 372
Greed, Parts 1 & 2 (Wakoski) **15**:324
Greed, Parts 8, 9, 11 (Wakoski) **15**:345-46
Greed, Parts 5-7 (Wakoski) **15**:347
"The Greed to Be Fulfilled" (Wakoski) **15**:357
"Greek Anthology" (MacLeish) **47**:196
"The Greek Revolution" (Carducci)
See "Per la Rivoluzione di Grecia"
"The Greek Women" (Merton) **10**:349
"The Greeks Are Coming!" (Lawrence) **54**:197-98, 201, 203, 227
"Green" (Lawrence) **54**:178
"Green" (Verlaine) **2**:415; **32**:399
"Green Apples" (Stone) **53**:228
The Green Book of the Bards (Carman)
See *From the Green Book of Bards*
"Green Flows the River of Lethe-O" (Sitwell) **3**:309
"Green Grow the Rashes O" (Burns) **6**:67, 74
The Green Helmet (Yeats) **20**:328; **51**:71
"Green Lantern's Solo" (Baraka) **4**:16
"Green Linnaeus" (Zagajewski) **27**:394
"The Green Man" (Olson) **19**:283
"The Green Man: For the Boston Strangler" (Atwood) **8**:7
"Green Memory" (Hughes) **1**:267
"The Green Menagerie" (Viereck) **27**:296
"The Green Parrakeet" (Lowell) **13**:88
"Green Red Brown and White" (Swenson) **14**:261
"Green River" (Bryant) **20**:14, 16, 19, 34, 42
"Green Roads" (Thomas) **53**:297, 329
"Green Song" (Sarton) **39**:324
"Green Song" (Sitwell) **3**:312, 317
Green Song (Sitwell) **3**:308, 320
"Green Stream" (Wang Wei) **18**:378
The Green Wall (Wright) **36**:278, 291-94, 296, 299, 301-3, 314-15, 318, 335-38, 340, 343, 348-49, 35 7, 359, 361-62, 371, 373, 387, 389-90, 395, 398-99
The Green Wave (Rukeyser) **12**:204-05, 209, 213
"Green Ways" (Kunitz) **19**:162
"The Green Well" (Kumin) **15**:215
Green with Beasts (Merwin) **45**:3, 5-7, 9-11, 18, 21, 23-4, 28-9, 32, 53
"Green Wood" (Pavese) **13**:218
"The Greenest Continent" (Stevens) **6**:317-19
"The Greenhouse" (Merrill) **28**:243-44
"Greenwich Village Suicide" (Corso) **33**:46
"The Greeting" (Tomlinson) **17**:354
"A greeting to L. F." (Paz)
See "Saludo a León Felipe"
"Greetings for His Own Birthday" (Ungaretti)
See "Auguri per Proprio Compleanno"
"Greetings to the Eagle" (Darío)
See "Salutación al águila"
"Greetings to the Optimist" (Darío)
See "Salutación del optimista"
"Grège" (Char) **56**:155
"Gregorias" (Walcott) **46**:322
"Les grenades" (Valéry) **9**:387-90, 394, 396
"Grenades Are Not Free" (Sanchez) **9**:235
"Die Grenadiere" (Heine) **25**:140
"Grenouille" (Guillén) **23**:111
"Grenzen der Menschheit" (Goethe) **5**:239
"Los Grernios en el frente" (Neruda) **4**:309
"Gretel in Darkness" (Glück) **16**:125, 140, 143-44, 149
"The Grey Heron" (Kinnell) **26**:259
"The Grey Monk" (Blake) **12**:35-7, 70
"The Grey Ones" (MacNeice) **61**:178
"Grey Sparrow" (Levertov) **11**:160
"Greyday" (Angelou) **32**:30
"Greyness is All" (MacNeice) **61**:178
The Grid of Language (Celan)
See *Sprachgitter*
Un grido e paesaggi (Ungaretti) **57**:339
"Grief" (Browning) **6**:41
Grief (Ungaretti)
See *Il Dolore*
"A Grief Ago" (Thomas) **2**:405; **52**:226, 262, 335
"Grief for Dead Soldiers" (Hughes) **7**:114-15
"The Grief of Men" (Bly) **39**:100-01
"Grief Thief of Time" (Thomas) **2**:405; **52**:321
"grietas paredes" (Alurista) **34**:33
"Grifel' naja oda" (Mandelstam) **14**:121-22, 129, 148
"Griffey the Cooper" (Masters) **36**:183, 221
"Griffin of the Night" (Ondaatje) **28**:329
"Griggby's Station" (Riley) **48**:292, 315
"La Grille" (Char)
See "Je ne suis pas seul . . ."
"The Grindstone" (Frost) **1**:197; **39**:235
"Grób Potockiej" (Mickiewicz) **38**:149, 222
"The grocer Hudson Kearley, he" (Belloc) **24**:41
"Grodek" (Trakl) **20**:226, 229, 236-38, 244, 250-51, 253, 255-58, 260
"The Groom's Still Waiting at the Altar" (Dylan) **37**:65
"Grosse Fuge" (Doty) **53**:54
"La Grosse Margot" (Villon)
See "Ballade de la Grosse Margot"
"Grosses Geburtstagsblaublau mit Reimzeug und Assonanz" (Celan) **10**:124
"Grotesques" (Graves) **6**:142, 144
"Grotesques" (Lowell) **13**:77
"Grotesques" (Verlaine) **32**:387
"The Ground Mist" (Levertov) **11**:160
Ground Work: Before the War (Duncan) **2**:114-17, 119, 125
Ground Work II: In the Dark (Duncan) **2**:119, 127
"The Grove" (Muir) **49**:231
"Groves of Academe" (Hacker) **47**:103
"Growing in Spirit" (Cavafy) **36**:94, 99-100
"Growing Old" (Arnold) **5**:13, 19, 23
"Grown-up" (Millay) **6**:234-5
"Growth" (Jackson) **44**:96
"Growth" (Levine) **22**:220, 228
"The Growth of 'Lorraine'" (Robinson) **1**:461; **35**:368
The Growth of Love (Bridges) **28**:49, 68, 71, 86-8
"Grub First, Then Ethics" (Auden) **1**:24
"Guadeloupe, W.I." (Guillén) **23**:99
"Guadelupe" (Birney) **52**:18
"Guardia roja" (Borges) **32**:122
"The Guardian Angel" (Browning) **2**:73
"The Guardian Angel of the Little Utopia" (Graham) **59**:166-67, 182
"The Guardian Angel of the Swarm" (Graham) **59**:167
The Guardian of the Flock (Pessoa) **20**:167-68
"The Guardians" (Merwin) **45**:53, 84
"The Guard's advice" (Char)
See "Conseil de la sentinelle"
"The Guelder Roses" (Lawrence) **54**:227-31, 234, 236
"Guendolen" (Morris) **55**:238
"Guenevere" (Teasdale) **31**:329, 344, 349
"A Guerilla Handbook" (Baraka) **4**:16
"Guerre" (Breton) **15**:62
"Guerre" (Rimbaud) **3**:264; **57**:249
"The Guess" (Muir) **49**:195, 289
"A Guest Arrives" (Tu Fu) **9**:323
"Guest Room" (Oppen) **35**:312, 342
"Guía comercial" (Fuertes) **27**:12
"El guía de la abadía" (Fuertes) **27**:30
"A guichard" (Lamartine) **16**:286
"Guide" (Ammons) **16**:20, 34, 57
"A Guide to Dungeness Spit" (Wagoner) **33**:327-28, 344
Guide to Kulchur (Pound) **4**:354, 359
"A Guide to the Field" (Wagoner) **33**:364
Guide to the Ruins (Nemerov) **24**:255, 260, 264
Guide to the Underworld (Ekeloef) **23**:85
"A Guided Tour through the Zoo" (Ignatow) **34**:305
"Guigemar" (Marie de France)
See "Lay of Guigemar"
"Guildeluec and Gualadun" (Marie de France)
See "Eliduc"
Guillén Man-making Words (Guillén) **23**:102, 104, 120
"The Guilty Man" (Kunitz) **19**:160
"Guilty on Both Counts" (Yamada) **44**:346
"Guinea Woman" (Goodison) **36**:141, 154
"Guinness" (Hughes) **7**:123
"A Guiseppe Garibaldi" (Carducci) **46**:52
"Guiseppe Mazzini" (Carducci) **46**:72
"Guitar or Moon" (Aleixandre)
See "Guitarra o luna"
"Guitare" (Laforgue) **14**:80
"Guitarra o luna" (Aleixandre) **15**:20
"The Gulf" (Levertov) **11**:194
"The Gulf" (Walcott) **46**:230, 322
The Gulf, and Other Poems (Walcott) **46**:229-30, 233-39, 248, 259, 275, 285-87, 321-23
"Gulf of Georgia" (Birney) **52**:4, 8
"Gulls" (Hayden) **6**:185, 193-94
"Gulls" (Williams) **7**:378
"Gum" (Toomer) **7**:333
"Gumber" (Belloc) **24**:10
"Gum-Trees Stripping" (Wright) **14**:341-42, 347
"The Gun" (Shapiro) **25**:269, 295, 297, 312
"Gunga Din" (Kipling) **3**:157-58, 179, 187-89, 191
"The Gunman and the Debutante" (Parker) **28**:354
"Gunnar Thorgilsson" (Borges) **32**:63, 65
"Gunnar's Howe Above the House at Lithend" (Morris) **55**:340
"Guns as Keys: And the Great Gate Swings" (Lowell) **13**:60, 64, 72, 81-2
Guru Granth (Kabir)
See *The Adi Granth*
"The Guttural Muse" (Heaney) **18**:198, 217
"Guy" (Emerson) **18**:111
"Guyana" (Walcott) **46**:237, 325
"Guyana Lovesong" (Goodison) **36**:154
Gwaith Dafydd ap Gwilym (Dafydd ap Gwilym) **56**:207-12, 241, 245-47, 249, 254-55
"Gwin, King of Norway" (Blake) **12**:60

"The Gymnosophist" (Ekeloef) **23**:63, 86
"Gypsies" (Clare) **23**:15
The Gypsies (Pushkin)
See *Tsygany*
"The Gypsy" (Thomas) **53**:300
Gypsy Balladeer (García Lorca)
See *Primer romancero gitano*
Gypsy Ballads (García Lorca)
See *Primer romancero gitano*
"Gypsy Man" (Hughes) **1**:270
"The Gypsy Nun" (García Lorca)
See "La monja gitana"
"Gypsy Verses" (Shvarts)
See "Tsyganskie stikhi"
"The Gyres" (Yeats) **20**:314, 333; **51**:112
"Gyrtt in my giltlesse gowne" (Surrey) **59**:315
"H" (Rimbaud) **3**:261; **57**:254, 271, 282
"H. O." (Borges) **22**:80-1, 95
"Los H. P. (Hijos Pródigos)" (Dalton) **36**:128-29, 131-33
"Ha chi je na I Am Coming" (Forché) **10**:134
"Ha'ani lo ma'amin sheli" (Amichai) **38**:9
"Habit" (Stone) **53**:229, 238
"The Habit of Perfection" (Hopkins) **15**:136
"A Habitable Grief" (Boland) **58**:62
El habitante y su esperenza (Neruda) **4**:276, 281
"Habitat" (Stone) **53**:228
"Habits" (Giovanni) **19**:118
"L'habitude" (Éluard) **38**:69
"Habla un busto de Jano" (Borges) **32**:90
"Hablando al Padre" (Mistral) **32**:155
"Hace frio" (Parra) **39**:272
"El hacedor" (Borges) **22**:76, 95; **32**:58
El hacedor (Borges) **22**:71; **32**:46, 59-62, 66, 86, 91, 94, 111, 132-33, 139
"Hacia el nombre" (Guillén) **35**:210-11
"Hacia el poema" (Guillén) **35**:195, 196, 197, 198, 211, 229
Hacia el sueño (Guillén) **35**:156
"Hacia la esclava Quisqueya" (Guillén) **23**:125
"Hacia la poesía" (Guillén) **35**:229
"The Hacked Priest" (Shvarts)
See "Zarublennyi sviashchennik"
"Had I not this life decreed" (Villa) **22**:354
"Hafen" (Celan) **10**:105
"Haffār al-qubūr" (Gibran) **9**:79
"The Hag Is Astride" (Herrick) **9**:86
"Hagia Sophia" (Merton) **10**:334
"Hago versos, señores" (Fuertes) **27**:49
"Haidekampf" (Stramm) **50**:175, 188
"Haiku" (Sanchez) **9**:230
"Haiku for a Young Waitress" (Birney) **52**:22
"Hail in Kharkov" (Yevtushenko) **40**:345
"Hailstones" (Heaney) **18**:237
Haine du peu d'amour (Char) **56**:115
"Hair" (Bly) **39**:16, 18, 28, 68
"Hair" (Corso) **33**:15, 34, 43, 47
"The Hair" (Herbert) **50**:4
"Hair" (Ní Chuilleanáin) **34**:364
"hair lightener" (Niedecker) **42**:127
"Haircut" (Shapiro) **25**:288, 318, 322
"Hairy" (Swenson) **14**:253
"Halahal" (Tagore) **8**:405
"Halcyon" (H. D.) **5**:304
"Half and Hour" (Cavafy) **36**:39, 41, 42, 107
"Half Measure" (Yevtushenko) **40**:366
"The Half of Life Gone" (Morris) **55**:338, 340
Half Sun Half Sleep (Swenson) **14**:260, 285
The Halfbreed Chronicles and Other Poems (Rose) **13**:235-36, 239-40
"Half-Caste Girl" (Wright) **14**:351
"Half-Deity" (Moore) **49**:99, 101
"Half-dream" (Wright) **14**:373
"The Half-moon Westers Low, My Love" (Housman) **2**:183
"Hälfte des Lebens" (Hölderlin) **4**:143, 148, 167
"Halfway" (Ammons) **16**:6
Halfway (Kumin) **15**:179, 192, 198
Halfway to Silence (Sarton) **39**:347, 360-62, 367-68
Halieticon/On Fishing (Ovid)
See *Halieutica*
Halieutica (Ovid) **2**:232, 242, 253
"The Hall and the Wood" (Morris) **55**:340
"Hallelujah:A Sestina" (Francis) **34**:255
Halleyova kometa (Seifert)
See *Halleyová kometa*
Halleyová kometa (Seifert) **47**:317, 327-28, 335
Halley's Comet (Seifert)
See *Halleyová kometa*
"Hallowe'en" (Aiken) **26**:30, 41, 45, 53
"Hallowe'en" (Burns) **6**:50, 55, 57, 77, 91
"Halls" (Abse) **41**:28
"Halsted Street Car" (Sandburg) **41**:239, 273, 287, 337, 340, 349
"A Halt in the Desert" (Brodsky)
See "Ostanovka v pustyne"
"Hamatreya" (Emerson) **18**:79, 102-4, 111
"The Hambone and the Heart" (Sitwell) **3**:295
"The Ham-Bone of a Saint" (Shapiro) **25**:300
"El hambre" (Guillén) **23**:116
"Hame" (MacDiarmid) **9**:192
"Hamilton Greene" (Masters) **36**:171
"Hamlen Brook" (Wilbur) **51**:249-50, 311
The Hamlet of A. MacLeish (MacLeish) **47**:125, 128-29, 136-37, 140, 143-44, 147, 150, 153, 158, 178, 187-88, 190-91, 197, 213, 222-27, 253
The Hammer with No Master (Char)
See *Le Marteau sans maître*
"The Hammers" (Lowell) **13**:60, 78
"Hammock" (Silverstein) **49**:334
"Han venido" (Storni) **33**:245, 278;
"Ha'nacker Mill" (Belloc) **24**:8, 22
"HAND" (Bissett) **14**:32
"The Hand at Callow Hill Farm" (Tomlinson) **17**:311
"Hand Crocheted Rug" (Niedecker) **42**:119-20, 123
"Hand Games" (Piercy) **29**:311
"The Hand of God in the World" (Amichai)
See "Yad elohim ba'olam"
"A Hand of Snapshots" (MacNeice) **61**:111, 120-21
"The Hand That Signed the Paper" (Thomas) **2**:388; **52**:263
"A Handbook of Surfing" (Guest) **55**:219
"Handed Down" (Clampitt) **19**:102
A Handful of Lavender (Reese) **29**:330, 332, 335-3336, 339, 345-346, 351
A Handful of Sand (Ishikawa)
See *Ichiaku no suna*
"Handfuls" (Sandburg) **41**:227, 236, 269-70, 296
"The Handicapped at Risen Hotel" (Wakoski) **15**:369
"The Handing Down" (Berry) **28**:38
"Handprints" (Rose) **13**:238
"Handrolled Cigarettes" (Yevtushenko) **40**:369
"Hands" (Birney) **52**:5-6, 8, 37, 39, 46, 66
"Hands" (Levertov) **11**:159
The Hands of Day (Neruda)
See *Las manos del día*
"The Hands of God" (Lawrence) **54**:193, 197, 250
"The Hands of the Betrothed" (Lawrence) **54**:189
The Hands of Venus (Seifert)
See *Ruce Venušiny*
"Hands, on a Trip to Wisconsin" (Meredith) **28**:175
Handshakes (Illyés)
See *Kezfogasok*
"A Handy Bait In Pellet Form" (Curnow)
See "A Balanced Bait in Handy Pellet Form"
"Hanging in Heaven" (Hagiwara)
See "Tenjō Ishi"
"The Hanging Man" (Plath) **37**:208
"Hanging of the Crane" (Longfellow) **30**:30, 49, 103
"Hanging Pictures in Granny's Room" (Kenyon) **57**:23
"The Hangman at Home" (Sandburg) **41**:254, 277
"Hangman's Oak" (Millay) **6**:217
"Hangover Square" (Mahon) **60**:236
"Hannibal and Napoleon" (Bishop) **34**:87
"Hanoi Hannah" (Komunyakaa) **51**:8, 28, 33, 40, 60-61, 64
"Hansel and Gretel" (Sexton) **2**:364, 368
"Hapax" (Rexroth) **20**:217, 220
"Happier Dead" (Baudelaire)
See "Le mort joyeux"
"The Happiest Day..." (Poe) **1**:432
"Happiness" (Borges)
See "La dicha"
"Happiness" (Glück) **16**:131, 144, 151
"Happiness" (Kenyon) **57**:18, 20, 25, 43, 46
"Happiness" (Owen) **19**:355
"Happiness" (Philips) **40**:271
"Happiness" (Rimbaud)
See "Bonr"
"Happiness" (Sandburg) **2**:308, 332, 334; **41**:296, 365
"Happiness in Herat" (Paz) **1**:361
Happy Birthday (Corso)
See *The Happy Birthday of Death*
The Happy Birthday of Death (Corso) **33**:8, 15, 34-7, 43, 45-8
"The Happy Journalist" (Belloc) **24**:29
"The Happy Marriage" (MacLeish) **47**:183, 190, 209-10
The Happy Marriage, and Other Poems (MacLeish) **47**:125, 127, 131-32, 150, 183, 207, 222
"Happy New Year" (Niedecker) **42**:96
"Happy Warrior" (Wordsworth) **4**:391
"Harbor" (Celan) **10**:105
"The Harbor" (Sandburg) **41**:239, 267, 327, 329, 336-37, 349-50, 364
"The Harbor at Seattle" (Hass) **16**:217, 226
"Harbor Dawn" (Crane) **3**:88-9
"The Harbour" (Belloc) **24**:29
"Harbour" (Brathwaite) **56**:61, 89
"The Harbour" (Walcott) **46**:272, 274
"Hard Daddy" (Hughes) **1**:270; **53**:82, 140
"A Hard Death" (Sarton) **39**:328-29
Hard Facts: Excerpts (Baraka) **4**:29, 36-9
"Hard Fist" (Ammons) **16**:44
Hard Labor (Pavese)
See *Lavorare stanca*
A Hard Land (Illyés)
See *Nehez fold*
"Hard Lard" (Ammons) **16**:43
"Hard Lines" (Zukofsky) **11**:351
Hard Lines (Nash) **21**:263
Hard Loving (Piercy) **29**:308-09, 311
"Hard Luck" (Hughes) **1**:255, 269
"Hard Roads in Shu" (Li Po) **29**:144
"Hard Rock Returns to Prison" (Knight) **14**:42, 52
"Hard Time Blues" (Hughes) **53**:81
"Hard Times" (Ashbery) **26**:154
"Hard Times" (McKay) **2**:209
"The Hard Times in Elfland" (Lanier) **50**:107-8
"Hard Times Redeemed by Soft Discarded Values" (Viereck) **27**:258-59
"Hard Weather" (Meredith) **60**:298
"Hardcastle Crags" (Hughes) **7**:149
"Hardcastle Crags" (Plath) **1**:388; **37**:180, 182-83, 208
"Hardships of Travel" (Li Po) **29**:141
"Hare Drummer" (Masters) **36**:183
"The Harem at Erechtheion" (Ekeloef) **23**:66
"Harem Trousers" (McGuckian) **27**:90
"Harem's Graves" (Mickiewicz)
See "Mogiły haremu"
"Harlem" (Hughes) **53**:173
"Harlem Dance Hall" (Hughes) **1**:247
"The Harlem Dancer" (McKay) **2**:213-14
"Harlem Hopscotch" (Angelou) **32**:29
"Harlem Night Club" (Hughes) **53**:82

"Harlem Shadows" (McKay) **2**:213
Harlem Shadows (McKay) **2**:213-14, 227
"Harlem Sweeties" (Hughes) **1**:247
"Harlem Wine" (Cullen) **20**:63
"The Harlequin of Dreams" (Lanier) **50**:56
"The Harm of Living" (Montale)
See "Il male di vivere"
"Harmonie du soir" (Baudelaire) **1**:46, 68-9, 71
Les harmonies (Lamartine) **16**:262-67
Harmonies poétiques et religieuses (Lamartine) **16**:279-82, 285-86, 292-93
Harmonies religieuses (Lamartine) **16**:257-62
"Harmonium" (Sandburg) **41**:271
Harmonium (Stevens) **6**:292, 294-95, 297-98, 300-01, 305, 309-11, 313-15, 329-30, 332-33, 336-37
"Harmony at the Fair Grounds" (Yamada) **44**:341, 347
Harold the Dauntles (Scott) **13**:269, 281, 312
Harold's Leap (Smith) **12**:335
"Harom oreg" (Illyés) **16**:239
"The Harp and the King" (Wright) **14**:343, 347
"The Harp Song of the Dane Women" (Kipling) **3**:171, 183
Harps and Violins (Blok) **21**:25-6
"Harpsichord & Salt Fish" (Niedecker) **42**:94, 97, 102
Harpsichord & Salt Fish (Niedecker) **42**:100
"The Harp-Weaver" (Millay)
See "The Ballad of the Harp-Weaver"
The Harp-Weaver, and Other Poems (Millay) **6**:211, 214-15, 224-25, 228, 230-31, 242
"Harriet Beecher Stowe" (Dunbar) **5**:128
"Harriet Tubman" (Walker) **20**:289
"Harriet's Donkey" (Lowell) **3**:241
"Harrison Street Court" (Sandburg) **41**:336
"The Harrowing of Hell" (Rilke) **2**:275
"Harry Carey Goodhue" (Masters) **36**:218, 228-29
"Harry Gill" (Wordsworth)
See "Goody Blake and Harry Gill"
"Harry Ploughman" (Hopkins) **15**:134, 160
"Harry Semen" (MacDiarmid) **9**:180, 196-97
"Harry Wilmans" (Masters) **36**:182
"Hart-Leap Well" (Wordsworth)
See "Hartleap Well"
"Hartleap Well" (Wordsworth) **4**:404, 414, 427-28
"Harvest" (Levine) **22**:218
"Harvest" (McGuckian) **27**:100
"Harvest" (Sitwell) **3**:311
"Harvest" (Soto) **28**:377
"The Harvest" (Walcott) **46**:236
"The Harvest Bow" (Heaney) **18**:243
"Harvest Festival" (Tomlinson) **17**:328
"The Harvest Knot" (Heaney)
See "The Harvest Bow"
"The Harvest Moon" (Longfellow) **30**:42
"Harvest Song" (Toomer) **7**:311, 317, 320, 333, 335
"Harzreise im Winter" (Goethe) **5**:247
"Has She Forgotten?" (Riley) **48**:323
"Has Your Soul Sipped" (Owen) **19**:346, 352
"The Has-Been" (Sandburg) **41**:314
"Hassan's Journey into the World" (Thomas) **2**:402
"Hat" (Silverstein) **49**:311
"Hate Blows a Bubble of Despair into" (Cummings) **5**:107
"Hate whome ye list" (Wyatt) **27**:325
"Hate-bridled Fishermen" (Walcott) **46**:272
"Hatem—, i.e. Goethe" (Goethe) **5**:228
"Hatred" (O'Hara) **45**:223
"Hatred" (Szymborska) **44**:295
"Hatred of Men with Black Hair" (Bly) **39**:12, 50
"Haunted" (Sassoon) **12**:240
"The Haunted Chamber" (Longfellow) **30**:103
"Haunted Country" (Jeffers) **17**:117
"Haunted House" (Graves) **6**:142
"A Haunted House" (Swenson) **14**:248
"Haunted Houses" (Longfellow) **30**:27
"Haunted in Old Japan" (Noyes) **27**:127
"The Haunted Oak" (Dunbar) **5**:131
"The Haunted Palace" (Poe) **1**:424, 437-38, 443
"The Haunter" (Hardy) **8**:93, 118, 135, 138
"Hauntings" (Brooke) **24**:57, 85
"Haunts" (Sandburg) **41**:241, 270
"Havana Dreams" (Hughes) **53**:122
"Havana Rose" (Crane) **3**:90
Have Come, Am Here (Villa) **22**:346-47, 351
"Have Fun" (Silverstein) **49**:335
"Have Me" (Sandburg) **41**:313
"Have Mercy upon Me My Soul" (Gibran) **9**:73
"Have You Ever Eaten Stars?" (Warren) **37**:383
"Having a Coke with You" (O'Hara) **45**:118, 132
"Having Been Asked 'What Is a Man?' I Answer" (Levine) **22**:220
"Having Confessed" (Kavanagh) **33**:88, 119
"Having It Out With Melancholy" (Kenyon) **57**:11, 14-15, 19, 24, 27-28, 36, 40, 46
"Having Kittens About Having Babies" (Hacker) **47**:84, 100
"Having Lost My Sons, I Confront the Wreckage of the Moon: Christmas, 1960" (Wright) **36**:287, 340
"Having No Ear" (Davie) **29**:114-15
"The Haw Lantern" (Heaney) **18**:230, 233
The Haw Lantern (Heaney) **18**:226-28, 230, 232-33, 237
"Hawk" (Walcott) **46**:286
"The Hawk in the Rain" (Hughes) **7**:117-18, 121, 129, 165
The Hawk in the Rain (Hughes) **7**:112-13, 115-20, 123, 131, 135-36, 139-41, 150, 162-63, 165-66
"Hawk Roosting" (Hughes) **7**:113, 125, 140-41, 151, 164, 169
"The Hawks" (Montale) **13**:149
"Hawks" (Tomlinson) **17**:347
"The Hawk's Cry in Autumn" (Brodsky) **9**:27
"Hawkshead and Dachau in a Christmas Glass" (Davie) **29**:108
"The Hawthorn Hedge" (Wright) **14**:336, 340
"Hawthorn Tide" (Swinburne) **24**:313, 317-18
"The Hawthorn Tree" (Glück) **16**:171
"Hawthorne" (Lowell) **3**:212, 216
"Hay" (Tomlinson) **17**:347, 354
"Hay cortesías que merecen palos" (Parra) **39**:273
"Hay Fever" (Hope) **56**:277-78
"Hay un día feliz" (Parra) **39**:299, 303
"Hayāt al-hubb" (Gibran) **9**:78
"Haymaking" (Thomas) **53**:267, 325, 327-29, 349
"The Haystack in the Floods" (Morris) **55**:238, 248, 252, 258, 301, 303
"The Hayswater Boat" (Arnold) **5**:50
Hazard, the Painter (Meredith) **28**:179, 195-99, 206-07, 214, 216
"Hazard's Optimism" (Meredith) **28**:202, 215
"Haze" (Thoreau) **30**:190, 294
"The Hazel Grove" (Pasternak) **6**:252
"The Hazel Leaf" (Warren) **37**:330
Ha-Zeman (Amichai) **38**:2, 18-19, 23
Hazman (Amichai) **38**:31
"He" (Borges) **32**:60
"He" (Ferlinghetti) **1**:174-76
"He Abjures Love" (Hardy) **8**:90
"He Acts" (Zagajewski) **27**:385
"He and I" (Rossetti) **44**:204, 253-56, 259
"He Asked about the Quality" (Cavafy) **36**:68, 74, 81
"He Came to Read" (Cavafy) **36**:76, 77-78
"He Cracked a Word" (Curnow) **48**:13
"He 'Digesteth Harde Yron'" (Moore) **49**:161
"He Doesn't Know It" (Aleixandre) **15**:4
"He Has a Good Time There" (Duncan) **2**:101
"He hath put all things under his feet" (Bryant) **20**:7
"He Heard the Newsboy Shouting 'Europe! Europe!'" (Schwartz) **8**:293
"He Held Radical Light" (Ammons) **16**:34
"He Himself" (Cavafy) **36**:49
"He Is Last Seen" (Atwood) **8**:10
"He is not ded" (Wyatt)
See "He is not ded that sometyme hath a fall"
"He is not ded that sometyme hath a fall" (Wyatt) **27**:337-338, 340, 343
"He lived . . ." (Niedecker) **42**:141
"He Revisits His First School" (Hardy) **8**:102
"He Said Come" (Walker) **30**:339
"He Sees Through Stone" (Knight) **14**:43
"He Swears" (Cavafy) **36**:73
"He that loves a rosy cheek" (Carew)
See "Disdaine Returned"
"He Was a Man" (Brown) **55**:120
"He who finds a horseshoe" (Mandelstam)
See "Nashedshij podkovu"
"He who found a Horseshoe" (Mandelstam)
See "Nashedshij podkovu"
"He Will Not Leave a Note" (Ríos) **57**:326
"The Head above the Fog" (Hardy) **8**:97
"Head against White" (Atwood) **8**:27
"Head and Bottle" (Thomas) **53**:300
Head and Heart (Guillén)
See *Cerebro y corazón*
"Head of a Woman" (McGuckian) **27**:101
"Head of Hair" (Paz)
See "Cabellera"
"The Head-Aim" (Dickey) **40**:158
"The Headless Moon" (Shvarts)
See "Luna bez golovy"
"Headphone Harold" (Silverstein) **49**:340, 347
"Headwaters" (Momaday) **25**:197
"Healing Animal" (Harjo) **27**:70
Healing Earthquakes (Baca) **41**:74-7
"The Health-Food Diner" (Angelou) **32**:27, 29
"Hear Me" (Levine) **22**:223
"Hearing Inside Out" (Cruz) **37**:35
"Hearn in Matsue" (Stryk) **27**:187, 208
"Hearsay" (Komunyakaa) **51**:65
Hearse (Hughes) **53**:115
"The Heart" (Trakl)
See "Das Herz"
"Heart and Mind" (Sitwell) **3**:312, 323
"The Heart and the Lyre" (Bogan) **12**:126
A Heart Beneath a Cassock (Rimbaud)
See *Un coeur sous une soutane*
"Heart, Crown and Mirror" (Apollinaire)
See "Coeur, couronne et miroir"
"The Heart of a Constab" (McKay) **2**:216, 225-26
"Heart of Autumn" (Warren) **37**:313, 334, 338, 349, 358-60, 366
"The Heart of Harlem" (Hughes) **53**:116
"The Heart of Pedro de Valdivia" (Neruda)
See "El corazón de Pedro de Valdivia"
"Heart Stirrings" (McKay) **2**:223
"Heartbeat" (Harjo) **27**:56
"Heartease" (Goodison) **36**:140
Heartease (Goodison) **36**:140-41, 143, 147-48, 151, 153, 158
"Heartease I" (Goodison) **36**:151, 154
"Heartease II" (Goodison) **36**:154
"Heartease III" (Goodison) **36**:152, 154
"Heartease New England 1987" (Goodison) **36**:153
"Heartland" (Hogan) **35**:256
"Heartless Rhoda" (McKay) **2**:221
"The Hearts" (Pinsky) **27**:157-8, 161, 164-5, 170
"Hearts' and Flowers'" (MacLeish) **47**:185
The Heart's Garden/The Garden's Heart (Rexroth) **20**:204, 209-10, 213-14
"The Heart's Graveyard Shift" (Komunyakaa) **51**:36
The Heart's Journey (Sassoon) **12**:258, 271, 289
"Heat" (H. D.)
See "Garden"
"Heat" (Reese) **29**:336
"HEAt MAkes TH HEARt's wINDOw" (Bissett) **14**:32

"The Heated Minutes" (MacNeice) **61**:137
"Heatwave" (Hughes) **7**:120
"L'héautontimorouménos" (Baudelaire) **1**:63
"L'Héautontimorouménos" (Char) **56**:197-98
"Heaven" (Brooke) **24**:56, 64, 73, 78
"Heaven" (Herbert) **4**:102, 114, 130
"Heaven" (Tagore)
See "Svarga"
"Heaven Alive" (García Lorca) **3**:141
Heaven and Earth (Byron) **16**:88-9, 102-06, 109
"Heaven Is but the Hour" (Masters) **1**:344
"The Heaven of Animals" (Dickey) **40**:161, 163, 168, 183, 190, 207, 230
"Heavenly City, Earthly City" (Duncan) **2**:105
Heavenly City, Earthly City (Duncan) **2**:100, 126
"The Heavenly Feast" (Schnackenberg) **45**:337
"Heavensgate" (Okigbo) **7**:250-51
Heavensgate (Okigbo) **7**:221-25, 228, 231-32, 236, 240, 242, 245, 247-48
"The Heaviness of Clay" (Seifert) **47**:328
"The Heavy Bear That Goes with Me" (Schwartz) **8**:290-91, 297, 306-09, 311, 313-14
"die hebammen" (Enzensberger) **28**:140
"Heber" (Smith) **12**:327, 354
"Hebräische Melodien" (Heine) **25**:170, 175
"Hebrew Melodies" (Heine)
See "Hebräische Melodien"
"The Hebrides" (MacNeice) **61**:122, 134, 137
"Hector in the Garden" (Browning) **6**:16
"Hector Kane" (Robinson) **1**:476
"Hedge Island, a Retrospect and a Prophecy" (Lowell) **13**:72, 82
"A Hedge of Rubber Trees" (Clampitt) **19**:98
"The Hedgehog" (Clare) **23**:7
"Hedgerows" (Tomlinson) **17**:354
"He-goat God" (Pavese)
See "Il Dio-Caprone"
"Heidenröslein" (Goethe) **5**:254
"Height" (Ammons) **16**:6
The Heights of Macchu Picchu (Neruda)
See *Alturas de Macchu Picchu*
"Heil Heilige Nacht!" (Nash) **21**:266
"The Heiligenstadt Testament" (Shapiro) **25**:307
"Heimkehr" (Heine) **25**:130-37, 139, 141-42, 144-45, 158, 161, 163-64
Die Heimkehr (Heine) **25**:161
"Die Heimkehr No 20" (Heine) **25**:144
"Die Heimkehr No 25" (Heine) **25**:144
"Heimkunft" (Hölderlin) **4**:141, 146
"Heimlichkeit" (Stramm) **50**:189, 191, 201
"Heine La Salle" (Masters) **1**:334
"Heine's Grave" (Arnold) **5**:34, 52, 63-4
Heinrich Heine's Book of Songs (Heine)
See *Buch der Lieder*
"Heinrich Mann zum sechzigsten Geburtstag" (Benn) **35**:34
"The Heirs of Stalin" (Yevtushenko)
See "Stalin's Heirs"
Hélé ena (Vigny) **26**:367
"Helen" (Elytis) **21**:131
"Helen" (H. D.) **5**:268, 300
"Helen" (Parker) **28**:362
Helen in Egypt (H. D.) **5**:276-84, 292-93, 297-301
"Helen of Troy" (Masters) **1**:325, 328, 342; **36**:175
"Helen of Troy" (Teasdale) **31**:345
Helen of Troy, and Other Poems (Teasdale) **31**:321, 324, 329, 331, 340, 345, 362, 370, 378-79
"Hélène" (Valéry) **9**:380
"Hélène, la reine triste" (Valéry) **9**:380, 391
"Helen's Rape" (Gunn) **26**:182-183
"Helian" (Trakl) **20**:239-40, 253, 259
"Helicon" (Heaney) **18**:207
"Heliodora" (H. D.) **5**:270
Heliodora, and Other Poems (H. D.) **5**:267-68, 304-05
"Helios and Athene" (H. D.) **5**:290-92, 305
"Hell" (Graves) **6**:151
Hell (Dante)
See *Inferno*
"The Hell Cantos" (Pound) **4**:328, 357, 360
"Hell Gate" (Housman) **2**:162, 165, 167, 199
Hellas (Shelley) **14**:171, 175, 188-9, 195, 197, 241
"Hellenistics" (Jeffers) **17**:117
"Hello" (Corso) **33**:6
"Hello, drug addict" (Ignatow) **34**:323, 325, 341
"Hello Mudda, Hello Fadda" (Silverstein) **49**:346
"The Helmet" (Levine) **22**:223
Helmet of Clay (Seifert)
See *Přilba hlíny*
A Helmetful of Earth (Seifert)
See *Přilba hlíny*
Helmets (Dickey) **40**:158, 160, 187, 190-92, 208, 212, 231-32, 257, 261-62
"Helpstone" (Clare) **23**:11, 39
"Helter Skelter; or, The Hue and Cry after the Attorneys Going to Ride the Circuit" (Swift) **9**:271
"The Hemingway Hero" (Yevtushenko) **40**:345
"Hemmed-in Males" (Williams) **7**:369
"Hen" (Herbert) **50**:4
"The Hen Flower" (Kinnell) **26**:243, 249-50, 252, 266, 274
"Henceforth, from the Mind" (Bogan) **12**:105, 113
"Hendecasyllabics" (Swinburne) **24**:320
"Hendecasyllable" (Parra)
See "Endecasílabo"
"Hengist Cyning" (Borges) **32**:48, 94
"Hengist quiere hombres (449 A.D.)" (Borges) **32**:89-90
"Henri Matisse: 'Asphodèles'" (Benn) **35**:67
"Henri Rousseau and Friends" (Ondaatje) **28**:298
"Henry and Mary" (Graves) **6**:141
"Henry C. Calhoun" (Masters) **36**:229
"The Henry Manley Blues" (Kumin) **15**:208
"Henry Manley Living Alone Keeps Time" (Kumin) **15**:208
"Henry Phipps" (Masters) **36**:230-31
"Henry Purcell" (Hopkins) **15**:144, 168
"Henry Tripp" (Masters) **36**:190
"Her Becoming" (Roethke) **15**:269, 272-74
"Her Dead Brother" (Lowell) **3**:205-06
"Her Death and After" (Hardy) **8**:99
"Her Early Work" (Swenson) **14**:276-77
"Her Eyes" (Robinson) **1**:459
"Her Final Show" (Doty) **53**:72
"Her/Flesh" (Cummings) **5**:95
"Her Garden" (Belloc) **24**:38-9
"Her Hair" (Riley) **48**:323
"Her Immortality" (Hardy) **8**:131
"Her Kind" (Sexton) **2**:359
"Her Lips Are Copper Wire" (Toomer) **7**:320, 332, 340
"Her Management" (Swenson) **14**:248
"Her Music" (Belloc) **24**:29
"Her Second Weight" (Ríos) **57**:325
"Her Triumph" (Jonson) **17**:180
"Her, Whom I Must Stil Honour in the Dust" (Raleigh) **31**:238
"Hera of Samos" (Clampitt) **19**:87
"Heraclitus on Rivers" (Mahon) **60**:144, 172, 195, 204, 214, 217-18, 224-25
Herald of the Autochthonic Spirit (Corso) **33**:35-7, 44, 50
"Heraldic: Deborah and Horse in Morning Forest" (Dickey) **40**:211
"Heraldos" (Darío) **15**:96
"Herbseele" (Trakl) **20**:265
"Herbst" (Benn) **35**:69
Hercule Chrestien (Ronsard) **11**:273
"Hercules and Antaeus" (Heaney) **18**:203, 207-210
"The Herd of Does" (MacDiarmid) **9**:156
"The Herds" (Merwin) **45**:35, 86
"Here" (Abse) **41**:10
"Here" (Kenyon) **57**:2, 26
"Here" (Larkin) **21**:238-39, 253-55
"Here" (Niedecker) **42**:140
"Here" (Paz)
See "Aqui"
"Here" (Yamada) **44**:324, 346
"Here and Now" (Stryk) **27**:211
Here and Now (Levertov) **11**:159, 163, 188
"Here Come the Saints" (Gunn) **26**:206-207
"Here Is" (Char)
See "Voici"
"Here Lies a Lady" (Ransom) **61**:269, 273, 301, 306-7, 311
"Here, Rattler, Here" (Brown) **55**:149
"Here she lies, a pretty bud" (Herrick)
See "Upon a Child That Died"
"Here then, an aged shepherd dwelled" (Thoreau) **30**:202
"The Here-and Never" (MacNeice) **61**:120-22
"Heredity" (Hardy) **8**:129
"La herencia" (Guillén) **23**:118-19
"Here's to Opening and upward, to Leaf and to Sap" (Cummings) **5**:106
"Here's to the Mice" (Lindsay) **23**:269
Here's What is Happening to Me (Yevtushenko) **40**:356-57
"The Heretic's Tragedy" (Browning) **2**:37, 59, 88
"Heriot's Ford" (Kipling) **3**:181
"Heritage" (Cullen) **20**:52-54, 57, 64-65, 72, 82, 87
"Heritage" (Hogan) **35**:255
"Herman and Dorothea" (Goethe)
See *Hermann und Dorothea*
Hermann und Dorothea (Goethe) **5**:223, 225-26, 236, 239, 257-59, 261
"Hermaphroditus" (Swinburne) **24**:308-11, 317, 361-63
"Hermes" (H. D.) **5**:273
Hermes, Dog and Star (Herbert)
See *Hermes, pies i gwiazda*
"Hermes of The Ways" (H. D.) **5**:303
Hermes, pies i gwiazda (Herbert) **50**:4-7, 24-26
"Hermetic Definition" (H. D.) **5**:281, 283, 285, 289, 297, 299
"Hermetic Poem" (Kunitz) **19**:172
"The Hermit" (Apollinaire)
See "L'ermite"
"The Hermit" (Mahon) **60**:208
"The Hermit" (McKay) **2**:222
"The Hermit at Outermost House" (Plath) **1**:389; **37**:182, 188
"The Hermit Goes Up Attic" (Kumin) **15**:190
"Hernani" (Meredith) **60**:250
The Herne's Egg (Yeats) **20**:335
"The Hero" (Kavanagh) **33**:79, 121
"Hero" (Madhubuti) **5**:342
"The Hero" (Moore) **4**:265; **49**:92, 100-101, 161
"The Hero" (Sassoon) **12**:242, 263, 277, 280, 283, 285
"The Hero" (Thoreau) **30**:218
Hero and Leander (Marlowe) **57**:50-168
"The Hero Leaves His Ship" (Guest) **55**:212
"The Hero, the Girl and the Fool" (Yeats) **51**:108
"The Hero With One Face" (Wagoner) **33**:327, 369
"Herodes Atticus" (Cavafy) **36**:46
Hérodiade (Mallarmé) **4**:188, 190, 196-97, 199-203, 208, 213, 218-25
Herodias (Mallarmé)
See *Hérodiade*
"Heroes Are Gang Leaders" (Baraka) **4**:10
"Heroic" (Boland) **58**:41
Heroic and Elegiac Song for the Lost Second Lieutenant of the Alb nian Campaign (Elytis)
See *Ázma iroikó ke pénthimo yia ton haméno anthipolohaghó tis Alvanías*
"Heroic Bronze, Silver Stars" (Quintana) **36**:272

"Heroic Poem in Praise of Wine" (Belloc) **24**:13, 20, 22, 33, 39
"Heroic Sculpture" (O'Hara) **45**:200
"Heroic Simile" (Hass) **16**:198
"Heroic Stages" (Guest) **55**:185, 212
"Heroics" (Wylie) **23**:324
Heroides (Ovid) **2**:234, 238-9, 241, 243-46, 253-55
Heroines (Ovid)
See *Heroides*
"Heroique Stanzas to the Glorious Memory of Cromwell" (Dryden) **25**:101
"Heroism" (Cowper) **40**:74-6, 81
"Heroism" (Montale)
See "L'eroismo"
"Heron Rex" (Ondaatje) **28**:332, 334
"Herramientas" (Mistral) **32**:287
"Herrin" (Goethe) **5**:249
"Hers is the Noise, Also, of the Dogs Asleep and in Dreams" (Ríos) **57**:325
"Herself" (Cervantes) **35**:116
"Herself" (Jackson) **44**:94
"Hertha" (Swinburne) **24**:308, 312, 343
"Das Herz" (Trakl) **20**:235-36
"das herz von gröuland" (Enzensberger) **28**:138
"Her-zie" (Smith) **12**:339
"Hesperia" (Carducci) **46**:28
"Hesperia" (Swinburne) **24**:313, 316, 318, 323
"The Hesperides" (Tennyson) **6**:351
Hesperides: or, The Works Both Humane & Divine of Robert Herrick, Esq. (Herrick) **9**:85, 87, 89, 90, 92-6, 100, 102, 104-06, 108-10, 116-17, 122, 125, 127-29, 132-35, 138, 140, 143-46
"L'Heure de se taire" (Éluard) **38**:87, 91
"Hevyn and erth" (Wyatt) **27**:349-50
"He-Who-Came-Forth" (Levertov) **11**:177
"Hex" (Brathwaite) **56**:96
"Hey Yu" (Bissett) **14**:7
"Hey-Hey Blues" (Hughes) **1**:240
Hi no tori (Yosano Akiko) **11**:308
"Hiawatha" (Longfellow)
See *The Song of Hiawatha*
Hiawatha (Longfellow)
See *The Song of Hiawatha*
"Hiawatha's Photographing" (Carroll) **18**:46
"Hibernaculum" (Ammons) **16**:10, 12, 20, 23, 29, 47-9, 60
"Hibiscus on the Sleeping Shores" (Stevens) **6**:294-95, 305
"Les Hiboux" (Péret) **33**:210
"Hic Jacet" (Walcott) **46**:248, 286-87
"Hidden Door" (Ferlinghetti) **1**:166
"Hidden Ice" (MacNeice) **61**:137
"Hidden Things" (Cavafy) **36**:39, 41, 74-75, 101
"Hiding the Skeleton" (Meredith) **60**:312
Hiding the Universe: Poems by Wang Wei (Wang Wei) **18**:382, 390
"Hier ist kein Trost" (Benn) **35**:8
Hier régnant désert (Bonnefoy) **58**:109, 126, 150, 154-55, 167
"Hieroglyphic" (Harjo) **27**:66
"High Diver" (Francis) **34**:255
"The High Green Hill" (Bissett) **14**:20
The High Green Hill (Bissett) **14**:14, 16, 18-21
"High in the Mountains, I Fail to Find the Wise Man" (Li Po) **29**:176
"The High Malady" (Pasternak)
See "Vysokaya bolesn"
"High Noon" (Clampitt) **19**:97
"The High Oaks Barking Hall July 19th 1896" (Swinburne) **24**:318-20
"High Quality Information" (Snyder) **21**:326
"High Talk" (Yeats) **20**:336
"High to Low" (Hughes) **1**:258, 267
"High Windows" (Larkin) **21**:238, 259
High Windows (Larkin) **21**:250, 259
The Higher Mathamatics (Chesterton) **28**:99
"The Higher Patheism in a Nutshell" (Swinburne) **24**:320
"The Higher Unity" (Chesterton) **28**:94
"Highway 61 Revisited" (Dylan) **37**:48, 51
Highway 61 Revisited (Dylan) **37**:44, 46, 50-1, 60-1
The Highway Enthusiasts (Yevtushenko) **40**:341
"Highway: Michigan" (Roethke) **15**:246, 294
"Highway Patrol" (Ferlinghetti) **1**:187
"Highway Poems" (Mueller) **33**:189
"The Highwayman" (Noyes) **27**:133, 136
"El hijo" (Storni) **33**:261, 295, 301;
Hijo del Pueblo (Quintana) **36**:248-50, 260, 262, 264, 268
"Hiking on the Coast Range" (Rexroth) **20**:215
"Hilda" (Ransom) **61**:271
"The Hill" (Brooke) **24**:72, 77
"The Hill" (Masters) **1**:345; **36**:181, 190, 201-02, 220, 241
"The Hill" (Tomlinson) **17**:314, 316, 337
"The Hill and Grove at Bill-Borrow" (Marvell)
See "Upon the Hill and Grove at Billborow"
"Hill at Parramatta" (Shapiro) **25**:269
"Hill in Kikineis" (Mickiewicz)
See "Góra Kikineis"
"The Hill Wife" (Frost) **1**:195, 202, 229; **39**:L232, 253
The Hilliad (Smart) **13**:333
"Hill-Stone Was Content" (Hughes) **7**:149
"Himno al árbol" (Mistral) **32**:155
"Himno del mar" (Borges) **22**:92; **32**:37, 122
"Himno entre ruinas" (Paz) **1**:353, 360-61, 363
The Hind and the Panther (Dryden) **25**:81-2
"Hindola" (Kabīr) **56**:342, 346
Hinge and Sign: Poems, 1968-1993 (McHugh) **61**:201-2, 206-7
Hinge Picture (Howe) **54**:52-53, 71, 87, 107, 109
"Hinges" (Silverstein) **49**:323, 328
"L'hinne de Bacus" (Ronsard) **11**:230, 232-33
"The Hinterland" (Clampitt) **19**:90
"Hippocrene" (Clampitt) **19**:92
"Hippolytus" (H. D.) **5**:267
"The Hippopotamus" (Carroll) **18**:31
"The Hippopotamus" (Eliot) **5**:187
"The Hippopotamus" (Nash) **21**:280
"Hippo's Hope" (Silverstein) **49**:335
"Hippy Mo" (Smith) **12**:314, 327, 339
"Hir Face, Hir Tong, Hir Wit" (Raleigh) **31**:201
"The Hired Boy" (Kavanagh) **33**:156
"Hiroshima, Watts, My Lai" (Hayden) **6**:190
"His Age, Dedicated to His Peculiar Friend, M. John Wickes, under the Name Posthumus" (Herrick) **9**:103, 107, 114-15
"His Anthem, to Christ on the Crosse" (Herrick) **9**:121
"His Bargain" (Yeats) **20**:332
"His Bathrobe Pockets Stuffed with Notes" (Carver) **54**:18, 26
"His Blindness" (Browning) **6**:16
"His Carpets Flowered" (Niedecker) **42**:104
"His Confession" (Herrick) **9**:109, 117
"His Confidence" (Yeats) **20**:314, 332-33
"His Creed" (Herrick) **9**:104
"His Death" (Browning) **6**:16
"His Death" (Wright) **36**:396-97
"His Dream" (Wagoner) **33**:360
"His Embalming to Julia" (Herrick) **9**:127, 129
"His Est Locus Patriae" (Bonnefoy) **58**:130, 132-33, 174
"His farwell unto Poetrie" (Herrick)
See "Farewell to Poetry"
"His Grange, or Private Wealth" (Herrick) **9**:89
"His Lachrimae, or Mirth, Turn'd to Mourning" (Herrick) **9**:108
"His Majesty at His Passage into England" (Philips) **40**:268
"His Meditation upon Death" (Herrick) **9**:109
His Noble Numbers: or, His Pious Pieces, Wherein (amongst Other Things) He Sings the Birth of His Christ: and Sighes for His Saviours Suffering on the Crosse (Herrick) **9**:85, 87, 90-2, 94-5, 100-01, 104, 106, 109-10, 117-18, 122, 140-41
"His Own Epitaph" (Herrick) **9**:131
"His Phoenix" (Yeats) **20**:329
"His Poetry His Pillar" (Herrick) **9**:89, 106
"His Prayer for Absolution" (Herrick) **9**:94, 109, 117, 141
"His Prayer to Ben Jonson" (Herrick)
See "Prayer to Ben Jonson"
"His Returne to London" (Herrick) **9**:89, 98, 108
"His Shield" (Moore) **4**:247-48, 261; **49**:100, 119, 132, 134
"His Shining Helmet: Its Horsehair Crest" (Gallagher) **9**:62
"His Smell" (Olds) **22**:326
"His Smile" (Warren) **37**:363
"His Stillness" (Olds) **22**:321, 340
"His Story" (Cisneros) **52**:153, 160
"His Tears to Thamasis" (Herrick) **9**:108
"His Terror" (Olds) **22**:324
"His Tomb in Ohio" (Wright) **36**:396
"His Vigil" (Riley) **48**:303
"His Winding-Sheet" (Herrick) **9**:109
"His Words to Christ, Going to the Crosse" (Herrick) **9**:121
Hispanics (Quintana) **36**:254
"Hispaniola" (Clampitt) **19**:102
"Histoire du Régent" (Perse) **23**:230
Historia de Gloria (Fuertes) **27**:20-5, 34-42, 44-7
"Historia de la noche" (Borges) **32**:67
Historia de la noche (Borges) **22**:95-6; **32**:63-7, 86, 90, 112
Historia del corazón (Aleixandre) **15**:3-4, 7, 11, 15-16, 22, 41
"Historias de loca" (Mistral) **32**:181
Las historias prohibidas del pulgarcito (Dalton) **36**:128
"Historic Evening" (Rimbaud)
See "Soir historique"
Historical and Literary Lectures (Carducci)
See *Discorsi storici e letterari*
"L'Historienne" (Char) **56**:134
"Histories" (Jackson) **44**:7, 11
"Histories" (Tomlinson) **17**:326, 344, 350
"History" (Berry) **28**:8
"History" (Francis) **34**:243, 250
"History" (Graham) **59**:152
"History" (Hughes) **53**:150-51
"History" (Lawrence) **54**:169, 183
"History" (Ní Chuilleanáin) **34**:360
"History" (Soto) **28**:378
History (Lowell) **3**:224, 226, 228-29, 231-32
"History: 13" (Olds) **22**:319
"History among the Rocks" (Warren) **37**:275, 278, 284, 289, 319-21, 331
"History During Nocturnal Snowfall" (Warren) **37**:379
"History is the Memory of Time" (Olson) **19**:271
"History Lesson" (Kumin) **15**:194, 202
"History of a Literary Movement" (Nemerov) **24**:258
"The History of Fire" (Hogan) **35**:257
"The History of Karate" (Soto) **28**:400
"History of My Heart" (Pinsky) **27**:176
History of My Heart (Pinsky) **27**:163-4, 173, 176
History of Peter I (Pushkin)
See *The History of Peter the Great*
The History of Peter the Great (Pushkin) **10**:394
"The History of Red" (Hogan) **35**:278
The History of the Heart (Aleixandre)
See *Historia del corazón*
"A History of the Night" (Borges)
See "Historia de la noche"
A History of the Night (Borges)
See *Historia de la noche*
"History of the Poet as a Whore" (Madhubuti) **5**:329
"The History of the Twentieth Century" (Brodsky) **9**:19
"The History of the World: A T.V. Docu-Drama" (Ferlinghetti) **1**:184

"History on Wheels" (Baraka) **4**:29
"Hitchhiker" (Baca) **41**:47
"Hitherto Uncollected" (Moore) **4**:259; **49**:149
"The Hitlerian Spring" (Montale)
See "La primavera Hitleriana"
"Hitler's First Photograph" (Szymborska) **44**:284, 298
"Hitoyo enishi" (Hagiwara) **18**:168-69
"Hits and Runs" (Sandburg) **2**:316
"Hiver" (Verlaine) **32**:400-02, 405-06
"L'Hiver qui vient" (Laforgue) **14**:72-4, 78, 90
"L'hiver sur la prairie" (Éluard) **38**:71
"Hochbeglückt in deiner Liebe" (Goethe) **5**:247
"The Hock-Cart, or Harvest Home" (Herrick) **9**:141-42
"Hod Putt" (Masters) **1**:345; **36**:179, 181, 190, 244
"Hoeing" (Soto) **28**:378
"Hohensalzburg: Fantastic Variations on a Theme of Romantic Character" (Jarrell) **41**:163, 169, 179, 186, 192-93, 196, 208
Hojas de Parra (Parra) **39**:292-93, 301, 303
"Hold, Hard, These Ancient Minutes in the Cuckoo's Mouth" (Thomas) **52**:284
"Hold Me" (Levine) **22**:217
"Hölderlin" (Schwartz) **8**:316
"Holderlin's Journey" (Muir) **49**:207, 243, 270, 288
"The Holdfast" (Herbert) **4**:123
"Holding On" (Levine) **22**:214
"Holding Out" (Rich) **5**:357
"Holding the Mirror up to Nature" (Nemerov) **24**:291
"Hold-Up" (MacNeice) **61**:125
"A Hole in the Floor" (Wilbur) **51**:209-10, 301
Holes in the Sky (MacNeice) **61**:157-58
"Holiday" (Sitwell) **3**:311-12, 326
"Holiday Inn Blues" (Ferlinghetti) **1**:187
"The Hollow Men" (Eliot) **31**:111, 117, 133, 138, 156
The Hollow Men (Eliot) **5**:163, 171, 174, 180, 185, 191, 193, 198, 206, 209
"The Hollow Wood" (Thomas) **53**:274, 277-78, 289, 291
"Holly Berry and Mistletoe" (Braithwaite) **52**:106
"Hollywood" (Shapiro) **25**:295
"Holy Baptisme I" (Herbert) **4**:120
"The Holy Child's Song" (Merton) **10**:330, 340
"Holy City of Song" (Noyes) **27**:127
"Holy Cross Day" (Browning) **2**:38, 63
"The Holy Fair" (Burns) **6**:49, 53, 57, 83-4, 86-8, 91, 94
"The Holy Grail" (Tennyson) **6**:407
"holy night" (Clifton) **17**:18, 24, 38
"Holy Orders" (Erdrich) **52**:191
"The Holy Places" (Yeats) **51**:86
"Holy Saturday" (Carducci)
See "Sabato Santo"
"Holy Satyr" (H. D.) **5**:268
"Holy Scriptures I" (Herbert) **4**:126
"Holy Scriptures 2" (Herbert) **4**:133
"Holy Sonnet XIV: Batter my heart, three-person'd God" (Donne) **1**:138
Holy Sonnets (Donne) **1**:128, 136, 138-40
"Holy Spring" (Thomas) **2**:382, 390
"Holy Thursday" (Blake) **12**:5, 7, 23-4, 34-5
Holy Virgin (Mickiewicz)
See *Panno święta*
"Holy Willie's Prayer" (Burns) **6**:53, 65, 83, 85-6, 88-9, 96
"Homage" (Viereck) **27**:284
Homage and Desecrations (Paz)
See "Homenaje y profanaciones"
"Homage and Valediction" (Tomlinson) **17**:338
Homage: Joining of Lives (Guillén)
See *Homenaje: Reunión de vidas*
"Homage to Clichés" (MacNeice) **61**:135-37
Homage to Clio (Auden) **1**:17
"Homage to Diana Toy" (Chin) **40**:9
"Homage to Emerson, on Night Flight to New York" (Warren) **37**:367, 374
"Homage to Flanders" (Sarton) **39**:334, 336, 345
"A Homage to John Keats" (Clampitt) **19**:91
"Homage to Literature" (Rukeyser) **12**:211
"Homage to Malcolm Lowry" (Mahon) **60**:215-16
"homage to mine" (Clifton) **17**:24
"Homage to Paul Mellon, I.M. Pei, Their Gallery, and Washington City" (Meredith) **28**:198
"Homage to Paul Robeson" (Hayden) **6**:192, 195
"Homage to R.F." (Wilbur) **51**:288
"Homage to Rimbaud" (Montale)
See "Omaggio a Rimbaud"
"Homage to Sextus Propertius" (Pound) **4**:317-18, 333, 363-66
"Homage to Sextus Propertius" (Ungaretti) **57**:359
"Homage to the Empress of the Blues" (Hayden) **6**:188, 196
"Homage to the Tree" (Tagore)
See "Vriksha-vandana"
"Homage to Theodore Dreiser" (Warren) **37**:305, 340, 366
"Homage to William Cowper" (Davie) **29**:104
"Homage to Yalta" (Brodsky) **9**:7
"El hombre" (Storni) **33**:283;
"Hombre Ciego" (Alurista) **34**:10
"El Hombre de la esquina rosada" (Borges) **32**:87
"El hombre imaginario" (Parra) **39**:294-95
"Hombre pequeñito" (Storni) **33**:237, 241, 251-52, 275-76, 298, 305, 309, 318, 320;
"El hombre sereno" (Storni) **33**:251, 307;
Hombres (Verlaine) **32**:370
"Hombres de las orillas" (Borges)
See "El Hombre de la esquina rosada"
"Hombres necios que acusáis" (Juana Inés de la Cruz) **24**:220
"Home" (Brooke) **24**:57
"Home" (Herbert) **4**:102, 130-31; **50**:18
"Home" (Lorde) **12**:138-39
"Home" (Sandburg) **41**:336
"Home" (Thomas) **53**:279, 281-82, 331-32
"Home after Three Months Away" (Lowell) **3**:206, 209, 216, 221
"Home After Three Months Away" (Sexton) **2**:350
"Home at Grasmere" (Wordsworth) **4**:414
"Home Burial" (Frost) **1**:193, 195, 229; **39**:246-47, 253
Home Course in Religion (Soto) **28**:394; 396, 398-400, 403
"Home for Old Ladies" (Wagoner) **33**:364, 367
"Home for Thanksgiving" (Merwin) **45**:8
"Home for the Holidays" (Nemerov) **24**:295
"The Home Front" (Mahon) **60**:141
"Home Home Home" (Ferlinghetti) **1**:180
"Home Is So Sad" (Larkin) **21**:242
"Home Is Where the Music Is" (Cruz) **37**:31
"Home, James" (Viereck) **27**:264
"Home Sweet Home" (Castro)
See "Miña casiña"
"Home Thoughts" (Sandburg) **2**:309
"Home Town" (Ní Chuilleanáin) **34**:369
"The Home Voyage" (Riley) **48**:326
Homeage to the American Indians (Cardenal)
See *Homenaje a los indios americanos*
"Homecoming" (Brathwaite) **56**:10, 31, 68
"Homecoming" (Goodison) **36**:143
"The Homecoming" (Hardy) **8**:99
"Homecoming" (Mahon) **60**:132
"Homecoming" (Merwin) **45**:24
"Homecoming" (Sanchez) **9**:207, 209, 223
"Homecoming" (Shapiro) **25**:273
"Homecoming" (Viereck) **27**:265, 280
"Homecoming" (Yamada) **44**:325, 334
Homecoming (Heine)
See *Die Heimkehr*
Homecoming (Sanchez) **9**:204, 206-07, 210-13, 215-16, 218-19, 222, 224, 229, 231-34, 237-38, 242
"Homecoming: Anse La Raye" (Walcott) **46**:286
"Homecoming, from Tillie Olsen" (Yamada) **44**:353
"Homecomings" (Heaney) **18**:244
"Home-Folks" (Riley) **48**:352
Homegirls and Hand Grenades (Sanchez) **9**:228, 230-31, 234-36, 238, 244
"Homeland" (Bely)
See "Rodine"
"Homeland" (Clampitt) **19**:100, 102
"Homeland" (Merwin) **45**:46
"The Homeless" (Merwin) **45**:46
Homenaje (Guillén) **35**:140, 189, 195, 198, 200-205, 227, 228, 229, 234, 239, 241
Homenaje a los indios americanos (Cardenal) **22**:103, 124-26, 128, 131-32
Homenaje a Pablo Neruda de los poetas espanoles: Tres cantos materiales (Neruda) **4**:277, 306
Homenaje: Reunión de vidas (Guillén) **35**:189
"Homenaje y profanaciones" (Paz) **1**:356-57
"Homeric Simile" (Meredith) **28**:174, 182, 187
"Homesick" (Kenyon) **57**:40
"The Homestead" (Lanier) **50**:91
The Homestead Called Damascus (Rexroth) **20**:182, 209-12, 214
"Home-Thoughts" (McKay) **2**:228
"Hometown Piece for Messers Alston and Reese" (Moore) **4**:256, 259; **49**:132, 141, 147
"Hometown Piece for Messrs. Alston and Reese" (Moore)
See "Hometown Piece for Messers Alston and Reese"
"The Homework Machine" (Silverstein) **49**:328
"Homily" (Tate) **50**:293
"Homily" (Viereck) **27**:280
"Homily on the Piety of All Herd Animals (A Mammoth Idyll)" (Viereck) **27**:280
"L'homme" (Lamartine) **16**:275, 285, 290-91, 297-98
L'Homme approximatif (Tzara) **27**:234, 237-38, 240-42, 249
"Homo Will Not Inherit" (Doty) **53**:54-55, 63
"Homosexuality" (O'Hara) **45**:156, 224
"Homuneulue Artifex" (Merrill) **28**:248
El hondero entusiasta, 1923-1924 (Neruda) **4**:276
"Honest Lover Whosoever" (Suckling) **30**:140
"Honey" (Wright) **36**:393
"Honey" (Yevtushenko) **40**:345
Honey and Salt (Sandburg) **2**:336, 339; **41**:303-6, 308-11, 319, 321
"Honey Bud" (Tagore)
See "Madhumanjari"
"Honey Mah Love" (Brown) **55**:115
"Honeymoon" (Seifert) **47**:324
"The Honeysuckle" (Marie de France)
See "Chevrefoil"
"Honky Tonk in Cleveland, Ohio" (Sandburg) **41**:297
"Honoria" (Patmore) **59**:229
"Hook" (Wright) **36**:314, 378, 383-84, 401-3
"The Hooks of a Corset" (Milosz) **8**:182, 197, 210
"Hop o' My Thumb" (Ashbery) **26**:127, 160
"Hope" (Clare) **23**:44
"Hope" (Cowper) **40**:47, 51
"Hope" (Hughes) **53**:101
"The Hope" (Ignatow) **34**:277, 293
"Hope" (Jarrell) **41**:168, 195
"Hope" (Milosz) **8**:187-88, 192
"Hope" (Mueller) **33**:174
"Hope Atherton's Wanderings" (Howe) **54**:47, 60, 62, 64, 66, 93-94, 113
"Hope Dieth: Love Liveth" (Morris) **55**:340
"Hope Is a Subtle Glutton" (Dickinson) **1**:111
Hopelessly (Storni)
See *Irremediablemente*

Hopes and Impediments: Selected Essays (Achebe) **6**:1015
"Hope's Despari" (Tagore)
See "Ashar nairashya"
"The Hop-Garden" (Smart) **13**:330-31, 333, 342
"Hopi Overlay" (Rose) **13**:233
"La hora 19" (Storni) **33**:239, 271;
"La hora cero" (Cardenal)
See "La hora O"
"La hora O" (Cardenal) **22**:111
la hora 0 (Cardenal) **22**:103-4, 124-25, 131
Horace (Smart)
See *The Works of Horace, Translated into Verse*
"Horace, Lib. 2 Sat. 6. Part of It Imitated" (Swift) **9**:297
"Horace to Leuconoë" (Robinson) **1**:459
"A Horacio Quiroga" (Storni) **33**:235, 261;
"Horae Canonicae" (Auden) **1**:17
"Horatian Epode to the Duchess of Malfi" (Tate) **50**:229, 246, 258, 319
"An Horatian Ode upon Cromwell's Return from Ireland" (Marvell) **10**:259, 261-62, 264, 267-71, 275, 277, 289, 292, 294-95, 305-09, 311, 317-18
"Horatio Alger Uses Scag" (Baraka) **4**:30
"Horizon" (Graham) **59**:175
"Horizons and Rains" (Ortiz) **17**:227
"Horizons Home" (Ortiz) **17**:226
"Horizonte" (Pessoa) **20**:155
"Horizontes en círculo" (Guillén) **35**:154
"The Horn" (Vigny)
See "Le cor"
"The Horn of Egremont Castle" (Wordsworth) **4**:377
"Horned Purple" (Williams) **7**:368
"The Horned Rampion" (Clampitt) **19**:102
"Hornpipe" (Sitwell) **3**:297, 303
"L'horreur sympathique" (Baudelaire) **1**:55
"A Horrible Religious Error" (Hughes) **7**:144
"Horror Eroticus" (Shvarts) **50**:142, 145-46
"Hors des jours étrangers" (Césaire) **25**:31
"Horse" (Glück) **16**:164
"Horse" (Hughes) **7**:143
"Horse" (Hugo) **17**:67
"The Horse" (Wright) **36**:278-79, 335-36
"Horse and Swan Feeding" (Swenson) **14**:246, 262, 277
"The Horse Show" (Williams) **7**:391, 394
"The Horse That Died of Shame" (Momaday) **25**:189, 213
"Horse Weebles" (Brathwaite) **56**:96
"Horseman in Rain" (Neruda) **4**:282
"Horses" (Alexie) **53**:3, 24
"Horses" (Berry) **28**:9
"Horses" (Hughes) **7**:118
"Horses" (Merwin) **45**:48
"Horses" (Muir) **49**:227-28, 238, 258, 274, 287, 290-91, 293, 298
"Horses" (Sandburg) **2**:324
"Horses" (Walker)
See *Horses Make a Landscape Look More Beautiful*
"The Horses" (Wilbur) **51**:273
Horses (Harjo)
See *She Had Some Horses*
"Horses and Men in Rain" (Sandburg) **41**:297
"Horses and Prisoners" (Dickey) **40**:257
Horses Don't Bet on People and Neither Do I (Bukowski) **18**:15
Horses Make a Landscape Look More Beautiful (Walker) **30**:343-44, 346, 349, 370
"The horses of Achilles" (Cavafy) **36**:53
"The Horses of Achilles" (Sikelianos) **29**:368-69
"The Horsewoman" (Kumin) **15**:194
"Hortus" (Marvell) **10**:284, 286, 288
"Horus" (Nerval) **13**:180-81, 187-91
"Hosea" (Walker) **20**:278-79
"Hospes Comesque Corporis" (Wylie) **23**:310
"The Hospital" (Kavanagh) **33**:62, 67, 72, 79, 88, 103, 120, 147
"The Hospital" (Lermontov) **18**:284-85
"Hospital Barge at Cérisy" (Owen) **19**:342
"A Hospital named 'Hotel Universe'" (Viereck) **27**:263
"Hospital / poem (for etheridge 9/26/69)" (Sanchez) **9**:225
"The Hospital Window" (Dickey) **40**:161, 176, 179, 181, 185, 211, 262
"The Hostage" (Smith) **12**:329-30, 333
"Hostel" (McGuckian) **27**:76, 100
Hosties noires (Senghor) **25**:231, 233, 235, 238, 248, 254-55
"The Hosting of the Sidhe" (Yeats) **20**:344, 346
"Hot" (Bukowski) **18**:24
"Hot Springs" (Birney) **52**:28, 98
"Hôtel" (Apollinaire) **7**:48
"Hotel" (McGuckian)
See "Hostel"
"Hotel Bed" (Graves) **6**:143-44
"Hotel Breakfast" (MacLeish) **47**:214
"Hotel de l'Univers et Portugal" (Merrill) **28**:234
"Hotel Genève" (Song) **21**:335-36, 338-41
Hotel Lautreamont (Ashbery) **26**:161-164, 166
"Hotel nights" (Abse) **41**:31
"The Hotel Normandie Pool" (Walcott) **46**:247-48
"The Hotel of Lost Light" (Kinnell) **26**:273
"Hotel of Two Worlds" (Guillén) **335**:221
"Hotel Steinplatz" (Olson) **19**:305
"The Hour and the Ghost" (Rossetti) **7**:280
"The Hour of Cowdust" (Ondaatje) **28**:337
"The Hour of Fate" (Lindsay) **23**:281
"Hour of Proof" (Sarton) **39**:342
"The hourglass" (Borges)
See "La clepsidra"
Hours of Idleness (Byron) **16**:86
Hous of Fame (Chaucer)
See *House of Fame*
"House" (Browning) **2**:59, 66
"The House" (Hogan) **35**:257
"The House" (Jordan) **38**:121
"The House" (McHugh) **61**:190
"The House" (Merrill) **28**:273
"The House" (Sexton) **2**:361-62
"House and Land" (Curnow) **48**:5, 20, 28
"House and Man" (Thomas) **53**:329
"The House and the Vineyard" (Lamartine)
See "La vigne et la maison"
House, Bridge, Fountain, Gate (Kumin) **15**:192, 194, 202, 208
"House by the Sea" (Montale)
See "Casa sul mare"
"A House Divided" (Ondaatje) **28**:293
"House (fires)" (Alexie) **53**:30
"The House Fly" (Merrill) **28**:282-83, 285-87
"House Guest" (Bishop) **3**:56; **34**:139
"The House in Main St." (Lowell) **13**:84
"A House in Taos" (Hughes) **53**:94
"The House in the Wood" (Jarrell) **41**:194
"House in This World" (Hughes) **53**:180
"The House in Winter" (Sarton) **39**:345
"House of Dreams" (Teasdale) **31**:356
The House of Dust (Aiken) **26**:4, 6, 8, 13, 22, 27, 31, 36, 50, 72
The House of Falling Leaves (Braithwaite) **52**:106
House of Fame (Chaucer) **19**:5, 10, 14, 17-18, 20-3, 73
"The House of God" (Hope) **56**:266
"The House of Idiedaily" (Carman)
See "In the House of Idiedaily"
"The House of Life" (Rossetti) **44**:166-67, 169, 173, 185, 198, 202-6, 214, 220-21, 223-24, 227, 230, 238, 250, 253-57, 259, 261, 263
"A House of Mercy" (Smith) **12**:326, 334-35
"The House of Over-Dew" (Smith) **12**:330, 332-33
House of the Customs Men (Montale)
See *La casa dei doganieri*
"The House of the Dead" (Apollinaire)
See "La maison des mortes"
"The House of the Heart" (Wakoski) **15**:348, 354
"The House on Bishop Street" (Dove) **6**:113
The House on Marshland (Glück) **16**:125-30, 132-33, 136, 139-44, 147-49, 151, 153-54, 157
"House on the Cliff" (MacNeice) **61**:111
House on the Corner (Dove)
See *The Yellow House on the Corner*
"The House on the Hill" (Robinson) **1**:459
"House Party to Celebrate the Destruction of the Roman Catholic Church in Ireland" (Kavanagh) **33**:63, 79, 81
"The House, The Environment: The Emperor" (Piercy) **29**:325
"House Under Construction" (Pavese)
See "Casa in costruzione"
"A house where every / jigger" (Niedecker) **42**:150
Houseboat Days (Ashbery) **26**:140, 144-145, 153, 155, 162, 172
"Housecleaning" (Giovanni) **19**:140
"Household Poems" (Thomas) **53**:305
"The Householder" (Browning) **2**:59
"The Housekeeper" (Frost) **1**:193
"Houseman" (Brown) **55**:164
"The Houses of Old Moscow" (Tsvetaeva)
See "Domiki staroi Moskvy"
"Housewife" (Sexton) **2**:346, 370
"Houston 6 PM" (Zagajewski) **27**:402
"The Hovel of the Historian" (Char)
See "Le Bouge de l'historien"
"How" (Atwood) **8**:24
"The How and the Why" (Tennyson) **6**:347
"How Annandale Went Out" (Robinson) **1**:461
"How Aunt Maud Took to Being a Woman" (Stone) **53**:234, 237, 245
"How can one teach 'Spring and Fall: To a Young Child' in the Hawaiian Islands?" (Mueller) **33**:191
"How Come?" (Ignatow) **34**:275, 277, 287
"How Cruel is the Story of Eve" (Smith) **12**:309
"How Do You See?" (Smith) **12**:325, 332-33, 352
"How Do You Tell a Story?" (Wakoski) **15**:372
"How Everything Happens (Based on a Study of the Wave)" (Swenson) **14**:271
"How Faltering You Are, My Speech" (Yevtushenko) **40**:348
"How Few, of All the Hearts That Loved" (Brontë) **8**:50, 74
"How gently it rained" (Castro)
See "Cómo llovía, suaviño"
"How Happy I Used to Be" (Corso) **33**:48
"How I Came to Be a Graduate Student" (Rose) **13**:232
"How I Got That Name: An Essay on Assimilation" (Chin) **40**:8-9, 19, 21, 24, 31-2, 34
"How I See Things" (Komunyakaa) **51**:53
"How it feels to be touching you" (Piercy) **29**:301
"How It Goes On" (Kumin) **15**:207
"How It Is" (Kumin) **15**:204, 218-20
"How It Strikes a Contemporary" (Browning) **2**:80
"How John Quit the Farm" (Riley) **48**:319
"How Josette Takes Care of It" (Erdrich) **52**:193
"How 'Kaddish' Happened" (Ginsberg) **47**:27, 62-63
"How Like the Sound" (Kenyon) **57**:47
"How Lilies Came White" (Herrick) **9**:143
"How Lisa Loved the King" (Eliot) **20**:124
"How Love Looked for Hell" (Lanier) **50**:56
"How Lucy Backslid" (Dunbar) **5**:122, 146
"How Many Bards" (Keats) **1**:313
"How Many Heavens" (Sitwell) **3**:312
"How Many Nights" (Kinnell) **26**:257
"How Marigolds Came Yellow" (Herrick) **9**:102
"How Moss..." (Wagoner) **33**:348

"How Much Can It Hurt" (Levine) **22**:215
"How Much Earth" (Levine) **22**:219
"How My Fever Left" (Wright) **36**:340
"How Naked, How without a Wall" (Millay) **6**:238
"How Not to Have to Dry the Dishes" (Silverstein) **49**:311, 328
"How Piaf Departed" (Yevtushenko) **40**:347
"How Poems Are Made/ A Discredited View" (Walker) **30**:347
"How Potchikoo Got Old" (Erdrich) **52**:193
"How Raven Stole Light" (Wagoner) **33**:353
"How Roses Came Red" (Herrick) **9**:143
"How Roses Get Black" (O'Hara) **45**:164
"How Samson Bore Away the Gates of Gaza" (Lindsay) **23**:276
"How Shall I Woo Thee" (Dunbar) **5**:126
"How Shall My Animal" (Thomas) **52**:237, 316
"How Sigurd awoke Brynhild upon Hindfell" (Morris) **55**:333
"How Sleep the Brave" (Thoreau) **30**:203
"How Stone Held His Breath" (Wagoner) **33**:348, 353-54
"How Stump Dreamed of Earthmaker" (Wagoner) **33**:348, 353
"How Sweet I roam'd" (Blake) **12**:32, 36
"How the Ant Takes Part" (Bly) **39**:44
"How the Wallflower Came First" (Herrick) **9**:102
"How They Don't Let Potchikoo into Heaven" (Erdrich) **52**:193
"How They Got Her to Quiet Down" (Stone) **53**:245-46, 249, 257
"How to Be Old" (Swenson) **14**:250, 288
"How to Die" (Sassoon) **12**:267, 285
"How to Enter a Big City" (Merton) **10**:337, 344
"How to Get There" (O'Hara) **45**:125
"How to Make a Good Chili Stew" (Ortiz) **17**:228, 233
"How to Pass, Kick, Fall, and Run" (Cage) **58**:202
"How to Write the Great American Indian Novel" (Alexie) **53**:34
"How Very Often at a Fashionable Ball" (Lermontov) **18**:297
"How We Are Spared" (Merwin) **45**:21
"how we avoid prayr" (Bissett) **14**:32
"How We Danced" (Sexton) **2**:366
"How Yesterday Looked" (Sandburg) **2**:305
"How You Feel" (Cruz) **37**:5
"Howard Lamson" (Masters) **1**:338
"Howarth Churchyard" (Arnold) **5**:33-4, 52
"Howl" (Ginsberg) **4**:44-9, 51, 57-61, 63-5, 67-70, 73-5, 79; **47**:1-76
Howl, and Other Poems (Ginsberg) **4**:73, 87; **47**:3-5, 7-12, 30-37
Howl: Original Draft Facsimile (Ginsberg) **47**:49, 54-55, 57-60
Howling at the Moon (Hagiwara)
See *Tsuki ni hoeru*
"The Howling of Wolves" (Hughes) **7**:137, 142, 159
"Hříšné město" (Seifert) **47**:331
Hristos voskres (Bely) **11**:7, 24, 28, 31, 33
"Hsiang Consort" (Li Ho) **13**:51-2
"Hsin-i Village" (Wang Wei) **18**:362
"Huckleberry Woman" (Merwin) **45**:46
The Hudson Letter (Mahon) **60**:229-30, 235-36
"The Hudsonian Curlew" (Snyder) **21**:292, 297, 308
"Hue, carcan!" (Laforgue) **14**:93
"La huella" (Mistral) **32**:186
"Los huesos de los muertos" (Mistral) **32**:175-76
"Hug o' War" (Silverstein) **49**:313
Hugh Selwyn Mauberley (Pound) **4**:318-21, 330, 338-39, 341-42, 348
"Hughie At The Inn" (Wylie) **23**:311
"Hugo at Théophile Gautier's Grave" (Lowell) **3**:224
"Huhediblu" (Celan) **10**:124
"L'Huillier, si nous perdons ceste belle Princess" (Ronsard) **11**:250
"8e vision" (Lamartine) **16**:265
"The Human Abstract" (Blake) **12**:10, 34
"Human Affection" (Smith) **12**:310
"Human Applause" (Hölderlin)
See "Menschenbeifall"
"Human Balloon" (Silverstein) **49**:342
"Human Burning" (Aleixandre) **15**:19, 21
"Human Condition" (Gunn) **26**:185
"Human Cylinders" (Loy) **16**:322
"The Human Fold" (Muir) **49**:228
"Human Grief" (Trakl)
See "Menschliche Trauer"
"The Human Heart" (Riley) **48**:302
Human Shows, Far Phantasies, Songs, and Trifles (Hardy) **8**:89
"Human Ties" (Storni)
See "Ligadura humana"
Human Wishes (Hass) **16**:215-17, 221-22
"A Humane Materialist . . ." (Smith) **12**:331
"L'humanitè" (Lamartine) **16**:266, 281, 293
"The Humanities Building" (Shapiro) **25**:322
"Humanity I Love You" (Cummings) **5**:90
"Humanity Outfitted the Vast Child Progress" (Rimbaud)
See "L'Humanité chaussait le vaste enfant Progrès"
"Humanly Speaking" (Davie) **29**:110
"Humble Jar" (Song) **21**:344-48
"The Humble Petition of Frances Harris" (Swift) **9**:251, 296
"The humble Petition of poore Ben: To . . . King Charles" (Jonson)
See *The Under-Wood LXXVI*
"The Humble-Bee" (Emerson) **18**:79, 84-85, 93, 99
"Humildad" (Storni) **33**:279;
"Humiliation" (Blok) **21**:5, 15
"Humility" (Storni)
See "Humildad"
"The Humming-Bird" (Dickinson) **1**:79
"Hummingbirds" (Stone) **53**:241
"Humor" (Yevtushenko) **40**:343-44
"The Humours" (Bradstreet)
See "Of the Four Humours in Man's Constitution"
"Humpty-Dumpty" (Sarton) **39**:332
"Hunchback Girl: She Thinks of Heaven" (Brooks) **7**:53, 69, 80
"The Hunchback in the Park" (Thomas) **2**:394; **52**:281
"A Hundred Collars" (Frost) **1**:215
"Hunger" (Cullen) **20**:63, 76
"Hunger" (Rich) **5**:374
Hunger (Hogan)
See *The Book of Medicines*
Hunger and the Book of Medicines (Hogan)
See *The Book of Medicines*
"Hunger in the South" (Neruda) **4**:282
"Hungerfield" (Jeffers) **17**:129, 136
Hungerfield and Other Poems (Jeffers) **17**:123, 136
"Hungry and Laughing Men" (Sandburg) **41**:313
"Hung-Up Age" (Corso) **33**:36, 38
"The Hunt By Night" (Mahon) **60**:146, 148, 150, 174, 202, 213
The Hunt by Night (Mahon) **60**:145-50, 154-56, 172-74, 186, 189-92, 194, 196-97, 201
"A Hunt in the Black Forest" (Jarrell) **41**:179, 192
"Hunt the Thimble" (Abse) **41**:14, 28-30
"The Hunter" (O'Hara) **45**:164
"The Hunter" (Williams) **7**:360
"The Hunter of the Prairies" (Bryant) **20**:23
"Hunters" (Erdrich) **52**:172, 189, 191
"The Hunter's Serenade" (Bryant) **20**:15
"Hunting Civil War Relics at Nimblewill Creek" (Dickey) **40**:155-57, 176, 226
Hunting herbs (Char)
See *Aromates chasseurs*
The Hunting of the Snark: An Agony in Eight Fits (Carroll) **18**:30-33, 40-49
"Hunting Pheasants in a Cornfield" (Bly) **39**:79-80, 82
"Hunting Watch" (Wang Wei) **18**:389
"Huntress" (H. D.) **5**:269
"The Huntress and Her Dogs" (MacDiarmid) **9**:191
Huntsman, What Quarry? (Millay) **6**:230-31, 233-34, 242; **61**:240
"Hurk" (Silverstein) **49**:329
"Hurrah for Karamazov!" (Viereck) **27**:279
"Hurrah for Positive Science" (Whitman) **3**:384
"Hurrah for Thunder" (Okigbo) **7**:235, 247
"The Hurricane" (Bryant) **20**:15
"The Hurricane" (Finch)
See "A Pindarick Poem upon the Hurricane"
Hurricane Poem (Brathwaite)
See *Shar*
"Hurry Up Please It's Time" (Sexton) **2**:367-68
"Hurrying Away from the Earth" (Bly) **39**:13
"Hurt Hawks" (Jeffers) **17**:117, 129
"Hurt Hawks II" (Jeffers) **17**:110
"Hurucan" (Walcott) **46**:247
"Husband and Wife" (Patmore) **59**:231, 234
"Husband in the grave, son in prison" (Akhmatova)
See "Muzh v mogile, syn v tiur'me"
"Hush'd Be the Camps To-day" (Whitman) **3**:418
"The Huxter" (Thomas) **53**:300-301, 303
"The Hyacinth Symphony" (Elytis) **21**:131
Hybrids of Plants and of Ghosts (Graham) **59**:131-32, 145, 168-70, 174-76, 183, 185
"Hydra" (Erdrich) **52**:189
"The Hydra" (Merwin) **45**:9, 25
"Hydrangeas" (Sandburg) **41**:234
"L'hydre Univers tordant son corps écaillé d'astres" (Hugo) **17**:90
"Hylas" (Carman) **34**:208-09
"L'hylas" (Ronsard) **11**:235
"A Hymb of Faith" (Riley) **48**:333, 335
"Hyme" (Donne)
See "Hymne to God my God, in my sicknesse"
Hymen (H. D.) **5**:266-70
"Hymme to God My God, in My Sicknesse" (Donne)
See "Hymne to God my God, in my sicknesse"
"Hymmnnl" (Ginsberg) **47**:71
"Hymn" (Ammons) **16**:27, 40, 57-8, 60, 63-5
"Hymn" (Boland) **58**:45, 53
"Hymn" (Dunbar) **5**:137
"Hymn" (Poe) **1**:446
"Hymn" (Walker) **30**:340
"Hymn among the Ruins" (Paz)
See "Himno entre ruinas"
"Hymn before Sunrise in the Vale of Chamouni" (Coleridge) **11**:48-9, 53, 55-8, 92; **39**:156-57
"Hymn for My Brother's Ordination" (Longfellow) **30**:46
"A Hymn for the Ascension of the Holy Virgin" (Mickiewicz) **38**:162
"Hymn from a Watermelon Pavilion" (Stevens) **6**:292
"Hymn IV" (Ammons) **16**:22
Hymn No. IV (Evans) **40**:56
Hymn No. V (Evans) **40**:56
Hymn No. VIII (Cowper)
See "O Lord, I Will Praise Thee"
Hymn No. IX (Cowper)
See "The Contrite Heart"
Hymn No. 11 (Cowper)
See "Jehovah Our Righteousness"
Hymn No. 14 (Evans) **40**:56
Hymn No. 114 (Evans) **40**:56
Hymn No. 119 (Evans) **40**:56
Hymn No. III8 (Evans) **40**:56
Hymn No. IV1 (Evans) **40**:56

Hymn No. V8 (Cowper)
See "The New Convert"
Hymn No. VI7 (Cowper)
See "I will praise the Lord at all times"
"Hymn of Apollo" (Shelley) **14**:167, 170
"Hymn of Death" (Lamartine)
See "Hymne de la mort"
"Hymn of Not Much Praise for New York City" (Merton) **10**:344
"Hymn of Pan" (Shelley) **14**:167, 177
"Hymn of the Great Return" (Sikelianos)
See "The Great Homecoming"
"Hymn of the Morning" (Lamartine)
See "L'hymne du matin"
"A Hymn of the Sea" (Bryant) **20**:3, 13
"Hymn of the Waldenses" (Bryant) **20**:5
Hymn on the Morning of Christ's Nativity (Milton) **29**:220-21
"Hymn to Adversity" (Gray)
See "Ode to Adversity"
"Hymn to Aphrodite" (Sappho)
See "Ode to Aphrodite"
"Hymn to Artemis Orthia" (Sikelianos) **29**:372
"Hymn to Beauty" (Baudelaire)
See "Hymne à la beauté"
"Hymn to Beauty" (Spenser)
See "An Hymne in Honour of Beautie"
"Hymn to Colour" (Meredith) **60**:246, 278-81, 284, 299, 330
"Hymn to Death" (Bryant) **20**:4, 10, 13, 16, 18
"Hymn to death" (Ungaretti)
See "Inno alla morte"
"An Hymn to Diana" (Jonson) **17**:171,182, 207
"Hymn to Earth" (Wylie) **23**:304-306, 308, 311, 323
"An Hymn to God the Father" (Jonson) **17**:172
"An Hymn to Humanity" (Wheatley) **3**:338, 340-41, 348, 361, 363
"Hymn to Ignorance" (Gray) **2**:143, 155
"Hymn to Intellectual Beauty" (Shelley) **14**:166, 169, 177-8, 187, 217, 234, 237-8
"Hymn to Lanie Poo" (Baraka) **4**:15
"Hymn to Physical Pain" (Kipling) **3**:192
"Hymn to Priapus" (Lawrence) **54**:167, 169, 176, 241, 244
"Hymn to Proserpine" (Swinburne) **24**:316, 320, 338, 345-48
Hymn to Satan (Carducci)
See *Inno a Satana*
"An Hymn to the Evening" (Wheatley) **3**:361, 363
"An Hymn to the Morning" (Wheatley) **3**:361
"Hymn to the Night" (Longfellow) **30**:26, 45
"Hymn to the Seal" (Smith) **12**:295
"Hymn to the Supreme Being, on Recovery from a Dangerous Fit of Illness" (Smart) **13**:346
"Hymn to the Virgin" (Bishop) **34**:94
"Hymn to Venus" (Morris) **55**:329
"Hymne" (Baudelaire) **1**:63
"Eine Hymne" (Benn) **35**:26
"Hymne à la beauté" (Baudelaire) **1**:71
"Hymne au Christ" (Lamartine) **16**:280, 293
"L'hymne au soleil" (Lamartine) **16**:277
"Hymne de Calaïs et de Zetes" (Ronsard) **11**:287
"Hymne de la mort" (Lamartine) **16**:283
"Hymne de la Mort" (Ronsard) **11**:226-27, 244, 269, 272-74
"L'hymne de la nuit" (Lamartine) **16**:262, 266, 292
"Hymne de l'ange de la terre apres la destruction de globe" (Lamartine) **16**:265, 281, 287
"Hymne de l'autonne" (Ronsard) **11**:230, 232-34, 267, 279
"L'Hymne de l'hiver" (Ronsard) **11**:266
"Hymne de Pollux et de Castor" (Ronsard) **11**:284, 287
"L'hymne du matin" (Lamartine) **16**:267, 279, 292
"Hymne du printemps" (Ronsard) **11**:242
"An Hymne in Honour of Beautie" (Spenser) **8**:331, 337
"An Hymne in Honour of Love" (Spenser) **8**:337
"Hymne of Beauty" (Spenser)
See "An Hymne in Honour of Beautie"
"An Hymne of Heavenly Beautie" (Spenser) **8**:332, 336-37, 345
"An Hymne of Heavenly Love" (Spenser) **8**:329, 332, 336-37, 345
"Hymne of Love" (Spenser)
See "An Hymne in Honour of Love"
"A Hymne to Christ, at the authors last going into Germany" (Donne) **1**:139
"Hymne to God my God, in my sicknesse" (Donne) **1**:140, 158
"A Hymne to God the Father" (Donne) **1**:138-39
"Hymnes" (Spenser) **8**:331
Hymnes (Ronsard) **11**:248
Hymnes (Spenser)
See *Fowre Hymnes*
"Hymnes in Honor of Love and Beauty" (Spenser) **8**:331
Hymns (Ronsard)
See *Hymnes*
Hymns and Spiritual Songs for the Fasts and Festivals of the Church of England (Smart) **13**:332, 340-42, 368
Hymns for Children (Smart)
See *Hymns for the Amusement of Children*
Hymns for the Amusement of Children (Smart) **13**:340, 349, 361
Hymns for the Fasts and Festivals (Smart)
See *Hymns and Spiritual Songs for the Fasts and Festivals of the Church of England*
"Hymns to Death" (Ginsberg) **4**:58
"Hymns to the Sun, Moon, and the Elements" (Coleridge) **39**:131
"Hyōhakusha no uta" (Hagiwara) **18**:183
Hyōtō (Hagiwara) **18**:176, 181, 183-84
Hyperion (Keats) **1**:278-79, 281-82, 284, 287-91, 305, 309
Hyperions Schiksalslied (Hölderlin) **4**:151
"Hypocrite Auteur" (MacLeish) **47**:192
"Hypocrite lecteur" (Baudelaire)
See "Au lecteur"
"Hypocrite Swift" (Bogan) **12**:95, 101, 125
"I" (Borges)
See "Yo"
I. 3 (Pindar)
See *Isthmian 3*
I. 4 (Pindar)
See *Isthmian 4*
"I abide and abide" (Wyatt) **27**:302
"i accuse us" (Birney) **52**:42
"I am" (Borges)
See "Soy"
"I Am" (Clare) **23**:22
"I Am" (Smith) **12**:314
"I Am a Beggar Always" (Cummings) **5**:100
"I Am a Lonesome Hobo" (Dylan) **37**:70
"I Am a Parcel of Vain Strivings Tied" (Thoreau) **30**:181, 188, 193, 199, 240, 245, 252, 254, 258, 293
"I Am a Sioux Brave, He Said in Minneapolis" (Wright) **36**:319, 403
"I Am a Victim of Telephone" (Ginsberg) **4**:85
"I Am an Old Town Square" (Viereck) **27**:280
"I Am as I Am" (Wyatt) **27**:317
"I Am Becoming My Mother" (Goodison) **36**:142, 144-45, 148, 154
I Am Becoming My Mother (Goodison) **36**:141, 143-44, 147, 149, 158
"'I Am Cherry Alive,' the Little Girl Sang" (Schwartz) **8**:318
"I Am Dreaming of a White Christmas: The Natural History of a Vision" (Warren) **37**:301, 304-5, 307, 333
"I Am Guided in the Darkest Night" (Thoreau) **30**:258, 271
I Am in the Unstable Hour (Paz)
See *Vrindaban*
"I am Ireland" (Boland)
See "Mise Eire"
"I am Marilyn Mei Ling Chin" (Chin) **40**:31
"I Am Mortal" (Guillén) **35**:217, 220, 221
"I Am Not Even Dust" (Borges)
See "Ni siquiera soy polvo"
"I Am Not Yours" (Teasdale) **31**:379
"I Am of Ireland" (Yeats) **20**:328
"I am Raftery" (Mahon) **60**:134, 196
"I Am She" (Giovanni) **19**:143
"I Am Sick and Tired of My Separateness" (Shvarts)
See "Mne moia otdel'nost' nadoela"
"I Am the Autumnal Sun" (Thoreau) **30**:180, 240, 254, 258, 265
"I am the Individual" (Parra) **39**:277
"I Am the Little Irish Boy" (Thoreau) **30**:182, 236, 258
"I Am the People, the Mob" (Sandburg) **41**:274, 315-16, 329, 332, 348, 364-65, 367
"I Am to My Own Heart Merely a Serf" (Schwartz) **8**:306
"I am too close" (Szymborska) **44**:286
"I Am Untrue Yet I" (Jordan) **38**:120
"I Am Useless" (Storni)
See "Inútil soy"
"I am writing to you" (Lermontov) **18**:303
"I and Not I" (Muir) **49**:242
"I and Your Eyes" (Knight) **14**:39-40, 46
"I Apologize" (Komunyakaa)
See *I Apologize for the Eyes in My Head*
I Apologize for the Eyes in My Head (Komunyakaa) **51**:6, 15, 18-20, 30, 33, 52-54, 56, 62
"I Ask My Mother to Sing" (Lee) **24**:245
"I at creation" (Clifton) **17**:35
"i belong with th wind" (Bissett) **14**:34
"I Brought to Art" (Cavafy) **36**:75, 77, 91, 107
"I Built Myself a House of Glass" (Thomas) **53**:287-88
"I Came out of the Mother Naked" (Bly) **39**:16, 18, 22, 28, 55, 70, 94, 101, 103
"I Can Be Seen" (Ignatow) **34**:282
"I Cannot Forget the High Spell" (Bryant) **20**:29
"I Cannot Stand Tears" (Bukowski) **18**:4
"I Can't" (Alurista) **34**:9, 46
"I climb the mossy bank of the glade" (Bridges) **28**:86
"I Climbed into the Tousled Hayloft" (Mandelstam) **14**:118, 122
I Colloqui (Gozzano) **10**:173, 176-81, 183-86
"I come and go" (Brutus) **24**:116
"i come from halifax" (Bissett) **14**:31
"I Come to Speak for Your Dead Mouths" (Wright) **36**:319
"I confess" (Chin) **40**:4
"I Congratulate You, Mamma" (Yevtushenko) **40**:341
"I Could Believe" (Levine) **22**:234
"I Cry, Love! Love!" (Roethke) **15**:248, 284, 298-301
"I Did Not Know the Spoils of Joy" (Schwartz) **8**:299
"I Do Confess Thou Art Sae Fair" (Burns) **6**:81
"I Do Not Fear" (Thoreau) **30**:192
"I don't believe in the peaceful way" (Parra) **39**:311
"I Don't Know Why You Think" (Guillén)
See "No sé por qué piensas tú"
"I don't love you" (Baraka) **4**:19
"I don't understand" (Yevtushenko) **40**:345
"I Dream" (Ignatow) **34**:324
"I Dream a World" (Hughes) **1**:259
"I Dreamed I Saw St. Augustine" (Dylan) **37**:61-2
"I Dreamed My Genesis" (Thomas) **52**:237, 256
"I due Titani" (Carducci) **46**:54
"I dut chaoy i dhi i gody" (Blok) **21**:17
"I Dwell in Possibility" (Dickinson) **1**:102

"I Dwelled in Hell on Earth to Write This Rhyme" (Ginsberg) **4**:79
"I Explain a Few Things" (Neruda)
See "Explico algunas cosas"
"I Fellowed Sleep" (Thomas) **52**:245
"I Felt" (Ignatow) **34**:313, 317
"I find no peace, and all my war is done" (Wyatt)
See "I fynde no peace"
"I Foretell the Days of Yore" (Amichai) **38**:48
"I Found Her Out There" (Hardy) **8**:134
"I Found the Words to Every Thought" (Dickinson) **1**:102
"i found the world outside of me" (Alurista) **34**:38
"I from my window where the meuse is wide" (Belloc) **24**:11
"I fynde no peace" (Wyatt) **27**:342, 358
"I Give You Back" (Harjo) **27**:57, 61
"I Go Back to May 1937" (Olds) **22**:318
"I Had a Dream . . ." (Smith) **12**:295, 305-06, 318, 345
"I Had a Future" (Kavanagh) **33**:59-60, 62, 76
"I Had No Human Fears" (Wordsworth) **4**:420
"I Hate America" (Ginsberg) **4**:74
"I Have" (Guillén)
See "Tengo"
I Have (Guillén)
See *Tengo*
I Have a Name (Ignatow) **34**:344-45
"I Have Been Taught" (Muir) **49**:226, 299
"I Have Believed That I Prefer to Live" (Wylie) **23**:314
"i have evn herd uv thee" (Bissett) **14**:33
"I Have Forgotten the Word I Wanted to Say" (Mandelstam) **14**:116, 155
"I Have Found my Flesh" (Alurista) **34**:23, 29, 47
"I Have Had to Learn to Live With My Face" (Wakoski) **15**:326, 330
"I Have Lived in England" (Bukowski) **18**:5
"I Have Longed to Move Away" (Thomas) **2**:379, 389; **52**:236
"I Have Outlived My Desires" (Pushkin)
See "Ia Perezhil Svoi Zhelan'ia"
"I Have Seen the Spring" (Teasdale) **31**:336
"I Have Three Daughters" (Stone) **53**:228
"I Have Written You Off" (Ignatow) **34**:345
"I Hear an Army" (Joyce)
See "XXXVI"
"I Heard" (Niedecker) **42**:147
"I Heard Immanuel Singing" (Lindsay) **23**:284, 288
"I Heard Wild Geese" (Ekeloef) **23**:87
"i herd ya laffin in th water" (Bissett) **14**:33
"I Hoed and Trenched and Weeded" (Housman) **2**:192
"I, in My Intricate Image" (Thomas) **52**:226, 237, 241, 245
"I Jehova Decree" (Parra)
See "Yo Jehová decreto"
I kalosíni stis likoporiés (Elytis) **21**:128
"I Keep repeating the first line" (Tsvetaeva)
See "Vse Povtoryayv pervyi stikh"
"I knew a clean man" (Niedecker) **42**:183
"I Knew a Man by Sight" (Thoreau) **30**:181
"I Knew a Woman" (Roethke) **15**:275, 286, 289
"I Knew I'd Sing" (McHugh) **61**:196-97, 205
"I Knew Not 'Twas So Dire a Crime" (Brontë) **8**:72
"I Know" (Bely)
See "Znayu"
"I Know All This When Gipsy Fiddles Cry" (Lindsay) **23**:275, 280, 287
"I Know I Am but Summer" (Millay) **6**:225
"I Know This Vicious Minute's Hour" (Thomas) **2**:405
I, Laminarian (Césaire)
See *moi, Laminaire*
"I Lay Next to You All Night Trying Awake to Understand the Watering Places of the Moon" (Wakoski) **15**:364
"I Learned to Sew" (Yamada) **44**:346
"I like to Sleep" (Alurista) **34**:23, 29, 42
"I live in a proper kitchen garden" (Mandelstam)
See "Ia zhivu na vazhnykh ogorodakh"
"I Live in Subtraction" (Jordan) **38**:118
"I Live Up Here" (Merwin) **45**:22
"I Look at My Hand" (Swenson) **14**:281
"I Look at the Future With Fear" (Lermontov) **18**:281
"I Look into My Glass" (Hardy) **8**:90
"I love all beauteous things" (Bridges) **28**:84
"I love frosty breath . . . and reality is reality" (Mandelstam)
See "Liubliu moroznoe dykhan'e"
"I Love to Fly" (Ignatow) **34**:323
"I Lovve Loyyd" (Wyatt) **27**:371
"I Make This in a Warring Absence" (Thomas) **52**:263, 316
"I Make Ye An Offer" (Thoreau) **30**:193, 216
"I married" (Niedecker) **42**:100, 137, 183-84
"I, Maximus of Glouster, to You" (Olson) **19**:276, 280-81
"I May, I Might, I Must" (Moore) **4**:256; **49**:140
"I May Reap" (Kavanagh) **33**:99
"I Meet Them" (Stone) **53**:258
"I Met This Guy Who Died" (Corso) **33**:44
"I Might Have Seen It" (Ashbery) **26**:133
"I Miss My Dear Cats" (Corso) **33**:41
"I must live, though I've already died twice" (Mandelstam)
See "Ia dolzhen zhit', khotia ia dvazhdy umer"
"I Need, I Need" (Roethke) **15**:252, 272-73, 277, 298
"I Never Hear That One Is Dead" (Dickinson) **1**:94
"I Never Saw a Moor" (Dickinson) **1**:101
"I Never Saw That Land Before" (Thomas) **53**:307, 309, 317, 319
"I nuovi credenti" (Leopardi) **37**:92-93
"I Only Am Escaped Alone to Tell Thee" (Nemerov) **24**:261
"I Plant in Your Favor This Tree of Cybele" (Ronsard)
See "Je plante en la faveur cest arbre de Cybelle"
"I Poeti di Parte Bianca" (Carducci) **46**:52
"I Pressed My Hands Together..." (Akhmatova) **2**:11
"I Pursue a Form" (Darío)
See "Yo persigo una forma"
"I re magi" (Leopardi) **37**:165, 169
"I Reckon—When I Count at All—/First—Poets" (Dickinson) **1**:96
"I Remember" (Boland) **58**:47
"I Remember" (Smith) **12**:314, 320
"I Remember, I Remember" (Larkin) **21**:228, 231, 246
"I Rode with My Darling" (Smith) **12**:327
"I rose from marsh mud" (Niedecker) **42**:136, 169
"I Said" (H. D.) **5**:305
"I Said It" (Baraka) **4**:13
"I Said to Poetry" (Walker) **30**:344
"I Sailed Up a River with a Pleasant Wind" (Thoreau) **30**:192, 195
"I Save Your Coat, but You Lose It Later" (Gallagher) **9**:44, 60
"I Saw a Delicate Flower" (Thoreau) **30**:236
"I Saw Eternity" (Bogan) **12**:89, 100, 121
"I Saw in Louisiana a Live-Oak Growing" (Whitman) **3**:402
"I Saw Thee on Thy Bridal Day" (Poe)
See "Song"
"I See a Truck" (Ignatow) **34**:305
"I See around Me Tombstones Grey" (Brontë) **8**:74
"I See the Boys of Summer" (Thomas) **2**:384; **52**:232, 322
"I Seek the Present Time" (Thoreau) **30**:227
"I Seek the Word" (Szymborska) **44**:292
"I Shall Be Free" (Dylan) **37**:60
"I Shall Be Released" (Dylan) **37**:55
"I Shall Never See You Again" (Masters) **1**:333, 338
I Shall Not Be Moved (Angelou) **32**:25, 30
"I Shall Not Care" (Teasdale) **31**:345, 379, 387-88
"I Showed Him My Wound" (Ignatow) **34**:306, 350
"i shun like the owl" (othersAlurista) **34**:32
"I Sing of Olaf Glad and Big" (Cummings) **5**:88
"I Sing the Body Electric" (Whitman) **3**:385, 396
"I Sing to the Sea" (Parra)
See "Se canta al mar"
"I sing when my throat is moist . . ." (Mandelstam)
See "Poiu kngda gortan' syra . . ."
"I Sit by the Window" (Brodsky) **9**:8, 13
"I Sit in My Room" (Toomer) **7**:337
"I sonetti del ritorno" (Gozzano) **10**:188
"I Speak of the City" (Paz) **48**:188-89
"I Stood on Tiptoe" (Keats)
See "I Stood Tip-Toe"
"I Stood Tip-Toe" (Keats) **1**:291, 313
"I Stop Writing the Poem" (Gallagher) **9**:65
"I Struck a Diminished Seventh" (Ammons) **16**:39
"I Swore to Stab the Sonnet" (Shapiro) **25**:322
"I Take Back Everything I've Said" (Parra)
See "Me retracto de todo lo dicho"
"I Take Care of You: A Lantern Dashes by in the Glass" (Gallagher) **9**:50
"I Taste a Liquor Never Brewed" (Dickinson) **1**:80
"I Taste the Ashes of Your Death" (Bukowski) **18**:7
"I Tell You for Several Years of My Madness I Heard the Voice of Lilith Singing in the Trees of Chicago" (Carruth) **10**:85
"I the Woman" (Cisneros) **52**:160
"I think, yes, a leopard in Duty blue would" (Villa) **22**:355
"I Thirst" (Harper) **21**:198
"I Thought of You" (Teasdale) **31**:360
"I to My Perils" (Housman) **2**:180
"I Told Susan Reyna" (Cisneros) **52**:159, 164
"I, Too" (Hughes) **53**:94, 106, 109
I Too Am a Painter (Apollinaire)
See *Et moi aussi je suis peintre*
"I, Too, Sing America" (Hughes) **1**:241, 258-59
"I Travel as a Phantom Now" (Hardy) **8**:89
"I Uncork Another Bottle" (Parra) **39**:263
"I Vecchi" (Pound) **4**:317
"I visit the grave" (Niedecker) **42**:99
"I' vo pensando" (Petrarch) **8**:227
"I Wahodd Dyddgu" (Dafydd ap Gwilym) **56**:207, 238, 247
"I Wake Up at Dawan" (Parra) **39**:262-63
"I Wandered Lonely as a Cloud" (Wordsworth) **4**:388, 400
"I Want" (Ignatow) **34**:305
"I Want, I Want" (Plath) **37**:182
"I Want New York" (Nash) **21**:263
"I Want You" (Dylan) **37**:51
"I Wanted to be There When My Father Died" (Olds) **22**:325-26, 341-42
"I wanted to stay in September" (Cassian) **17**:5
"I Was a Poet in the House of Frankenstein" (Yau) **61**:337, 358
"I Was Afraid of Dying" (Wright) **36**:332
"I Was Angry" (Ignatow) **34**:282, 345
"I Was Born in Lucerne" (Levine) **22**:226
"I was Born Upon Thy Bank River" (Thoreau) **30**:216
"I was born with an unlined palm" (Shvarts) **50**:142, 144, 146
"i was just cummin" (Bissett) **14**:34
"I Was Made Erect and Lone" (Thoreau) **30**:245
"I was not born to hate" (Castro)
See "Yo no he nacido para odiar"

"I was not young long; I met the soul early" (Villa) **22**:351
"I Was Reading a Scientific Article" (Atwood) **8**:13
"I Was Taught Three" (Graham) **59**:131, 183
"I Was Washing Outside in the Darkness" (Mandelstam) **14**:122
"I Wasn't One of the Six Million" (Amichai) **38**:47-49
"I Watched a Snake" (Graham) **59**:132, 148, 151, 174
"I Went" (Cavafy) **36**:74, 108
"I Went into the Maverick Bar" (Snyder) **21**:293, 296-97
"I wept for my youth" (Kunitz) **19**:175
"I Where I Stand" (Corso) **33**:37
"I Will Be" (Cummings) **5**:93
"I will break God's seamless skull" (Villa) **22**:352
"I Will Lie Down" (Swenson) **14**:286
"I will praise the Lord at all times" (Cowper) **40**:55
"I Will Put Chaos into Fourteen Lines" (Millay) **6**:243, 246
"I Will Sing You One-O" (Frost) **1**:195
"I Will Wade Out" (Cummings) **5**:91
"I Wish I Had Great Knowledge or Great Art" (Schwartz) **8**:294
"I Wish I My Never Hear of the United States Again" (Wright) **36**:358
"I wonder by my troth" (Donne)
See "The good-morrow"
"I Would Have Been a Trumpet Player If I Hadn't Gone to College" (Baraka) **4**:36
"I Would I Were a Careless Child" (Byron) **16**:73, 86-8
"I Would Live in Your Love" (Teasdale) **31**:388
"I would not be thought less than a man" (Brutus) **24**:116
"I Would Not Paint—a Picture" (Dickinson) **1**:102
"I Would Return South" (Neruda)
See "Quiero volver a sur"
"I Would Steal Horses" (Alexie) **53**:41
I Would Steal Horses (Alexie) **53**:3
I Wouldn't Have Missed It: Selected Poems of Ogden Nash (Nash) **21**:277
"Ia dolzhen zhit', khotia ia dvazhdy umer" (Mandelstam) **14**:151
"Ia Perezhil Svoi Zhelan'ia" (Pushkin) **10**:412
"Ia zhivu na vazhnykh ogorodakh" (Mandelstam) **14**:152
iÁguila o sol? (Paz) **1**:354, 359; **48**:229-30, 244
Iambics and Epodes (Carducci)
See *Giambi ed epodi*
"Ibadan Lagos Kano London 5 Jan 72" (Brutus) **24**:123
Ibis (Ovid) **2**:238, 242, 244
IBM (Bissett) **14**:15
"Ibo" (Hugo) **17**:83, 89
"Ibsen" (Muir) **49**:243
"Icarian Bird" (Thoreau) **30**:216
"Icarian Wings" (Cullen) **20**:67
"Icarium Mare" (Wilbur) **51**:249, 309
Ice Cod Bell or Stone (Birney) **52**:11-14, 17, 44-46, 67, 74, 94
"Ice Cream at Blaunberg" (Tomlinson) **17**:353
"The Ice Eagle" (Wakoski) **15**:324, 363
"Ice Handler" (Sandburg) **41**:261, 365
The Ice Land (Hagiwara)
See *Hyōtō*
"Ice Storm" (Hayden) **6**:193-4
"Ice Storm" (Kenyon) **57**:4, 43
"The Iceberg" (Merwin) **45**:7
"The Ice-Cream Wars" (Ashbery) **26**:136
"Iceland First Seen" (Morris) **55**:340
"The Ice-Storm" (Pinsky) **27**:174
"Ich" (Stramm) **50**:175
"Ich-Gefühl" (Benn) **35**:50
Ichiaku no suna (Ishikawa) **10**:193, 200-02, 204-05, 210-11, 216
"Ichigatsu" (Nishiwaki) **15**:231-32
"Ich-Zerfall" (Benn) **35**:50
"Icicles" (Pinsky) **27**:158
Ici-haut. Pamyati Maksimilian Voloshin (Tsvetaeva) **14**:324
Iconographs (Swenson) **14**:268-72, 274, 281, 285-86
"The Icosasphere" (Moore) **49**:101, 126
"Ida Chicken" (Masters) **36**:230, 244
"Idaho" (Ashbery) **26**:137
"The Idea of Ancestry" (Knight) **14**:39, 41, 43-4, 52-3
"The Idea of Order at Key West" (Stevens) **6**:305, 307, 325, 327
"The Idea of Order at the József Attila Estate" (Szirtes) **51**:178
"The Idea of Trust" (Gunn) **26**:207, 220
"The Ideal Father" (Olds) **22**:322
"Ideal Landscape" (Rich) **5**:393
"Ideal Love" (Amichai) **38**:19
"Ideas" (Merrill) **28**:267
Ideas of Order (Stevens) **6**:296-97, 318-19, 330-32, 335, 337
"L'idee de Dieu" (Lamartine) **16**:265-66, 293
"L'Idée du devenir" (Éluard) **38**:96-97
"Lo idéntico" (Paz) **48**:207
"Identity" (Ammons) **16**:27, 29
"Identity: A Poem" (Stein) **18**:334
"Identity and Argument for Prayer" (Warren) **37**:313
"The Ides of March" (Cavafy) **36**:28
"Idillio di Maggio" (Carducci) **46**:49-50
"Idillio maremmano" (Carducci) **46**:11, 36-37, 50, 56-58, 62-66, 79-80
"The Idiocy of Human Aspiration" (Mahon) **60**:237
"Idiot" (Tate) **50**:228, 280, 311-13
"The Idiot Boy" (Wordsworth) **4**:372, 374, 381, 416-18, 426-27
"Idiot Wind" (Dylan) **37**:56
"Idoto" (Okigbo) **7**:223, 225
Idut belye snegi (Yevtushenko) **40**:359, 363
"Idyl" (Parker) **28**:355
"An Idyl of the King" (Riley) **48**:312, 340
"Idyll" (Roethke) **15**:246
"Idyll of the Maremma" (Carducci)
See "Idillio maremmano"
"Idylls in Colour Film" (Curnow) **48**:45
Idylls of the Bible (Harper) **21**:185
Idylls of the Hearth (Tennyson) **6**:360
Idylls of the King (Tennyson) **6**:358, 360, 369, 374, 376, 379, 406-08
"If" (Kipling) **3**:176, 183-84, 188
"If" (Thomas) **53**:296
"If Actually Dead" (Cavafy) **36**:112
"If Anyone Had Told Me" (Aleixandre)
See "If Someone Could Have Told Me"
"If Anything Will Level with You Water Will" (Ammons) **16**:54
"If Blood Were Not as Powerful as It Is" (Gallagher) **9**:59
"If Cynthia be a Queen, a Princes, and Supreme" (Raleigh)
See "If Synthia be a Queene, a princes, and supreame"
"If Dead Indeed" (Cavafy) **36**:20, 38
"If Death is Kind" (Teasdale) **31**:334
"If Ever You Go to Dublin Town" (Kavanagh) **33**:63, 81, 89, 147
"If Fun Is Fun Isn't That Enough?" (Nash) **21**:274
"If I Am Too Brown or Too White for You" (Rose) **13**:241
"If I Had Children" (Swenson) **14**:279
"if i have made, my lady, intricate" (Cummings) **5**:87
"If I Knew What Poets Know" (Riley) **48**:325
"If I Leave You" (Ríos) **57**:329
"If I Think About You Again It Will Be the Fifty-Third Monday of Next Year" (Harjo) **27**:70
"If I Were Dead" (Patmore) **59**:209
"If I Were Four-and-Twenty" (Yeats) **51**:147
"If I were Paris" (Johnson) **24**:144
"If I Were President of Chile" (Parra)
See "Si yo fuera presidente de Chile"
"If I Were Tickled by the Rub of Love" (Thomas) **2**:384, 386, 401; **52**:227
"If I Were to Own" (Thomas) **53**:328
"If in Beginning Twilight of Winter Will Stand" (Cummings) **5**:109-10
"If It All Went Up In Smoke" (Oppen) **35**:304
"If It Chance Your Eye Offend You" (Housman) **2**:184
"If It Were You" (Page) **12**:179
"If mine eyes can speake" (Sidney) **32**:235
"If, My Darling" (Larkin) **21**:236, 248
"If My Head Hurt a Hair's Foot" (Thomas) **2**:386, 407; **52**:262
"If Only" (Rossetti) **7**:280
"If perchance, my Fabio" (Juana Inés de la Cruz)
See "Si acaso, Fabio mío"
"If Snakes Were Blue" (Warren) **37**:378
"If Someone Could Have Told Me" (Aleixandre) **15**:4
"If Synthia be a Queene, a princes, and supreame" (Raleigh) **31**:218, 239, 304
"If the Pope Doesn't Break with the U.S.A." (Parra)
See "Si el Papa no rompe con el USA"
"If There are Any Heavens My Mother Will (All by Herself) Have" (Cummings) **5**:88
"If They Come in the Night" (Piercy) **29**:311
"If This Is the Way It Is" (Warren) **37**:326, 341
"If waker care if sudden pale colour" (Wyatt) **27**:368
"If We Must Die" (McKay) **2**:206-07, 211, 217, 220, 229
"If We Take All Gold" (Bogan) **12**:122
"If, When Don Cupid's Dart" (Suckling) **30**:138
"If yet I have not all thy love" (Donne)
See "Lovers infinitenesse"
If You Call This Cry a Song (Carruth) **10**:77
"If You Only Knew..." (Guillén)
See "Ay negra, si tu supiera"
"If You Saw a Negro Lady" (Jordan) **38**:126
"If You See Her, Say Hello" (Dylan) **37**:54
"If You See Me in L.A. It's Because I'm Looking for the Airport" (Cruz) **37**:30
"IFF" (Nemerov) **24**:289
"If-ing" (Hughes) **53**:115
Igitur (Mallarmé) **4**:199, 201-03, 208
"Ignis Fatuus" (Tate) **50**:229, 286, 318
"Ignorance" (Larkin) **21**:227, 246
"I,it,was,that,saw" (Villa) **22**:355
"Ikarus" (Benn) **35**:47, 48, 49, 68, 77
"Ike" (Dove) **6**:109
"Ike Walton's Prayer" (Riley) **48**:302
"Ikey (Goldberg)'s Worth I'm" (Cummings) **5**:82
"Il bove" (Carducci) **46**:11, 49, 75
"Il canto dell' amore" (Carducci) **46**:6, 11, 53, 55, 73, 89
"Il comune rustico" (Carducci) **46**:53, 76, 81, 84, 88
"Œil de sourd" (Éluard) **38**:69
Il dolore (Ungaretti) **57**:338-39, 360, 377
"Il Liuto e la Lira" (Carducci) **46**:52
"Il mio paese è l'Italia" (Quasimodo) **47**:284
"Il nini muart" (Pasolini) **17**:251, 256, 281, 284
"Il n'y a rien d'incompréhensible" (Éluard) **38**:96
"Il Passero Solitario" (Leopardi) **37**:81-82, 124, 139
"Il penseroso" (Gray) **2**:141
"Il Penseroso" (Milton) **19**:193, 201-02, 226, 229-33, 249, 255; **29**:232, 240-41
"Il Pensiero Dominante" (Leopardi) **37**:92, 103, 110, 123-24
"Il piccolo Rifiuto" (MacNeice) **61**:166
"Il plebiscito" (Carducci) **46**:56
"Il pleure dans mon coeur" (Verlaine) **32**:362-63
"Il pleut" (Apollinaire) **7**:20, 34
"Il poeta" (Carducci) **46**:81

"Il Ponte Vecchio Di Firenze" (Longfellow) **30**:51
Il Porto Sepolto (Ungaretti) **57**:338, 375
"Il Primo Amore" (Leopardi) **37**:78, 81, 84, 111, 123
"Il reduce" (Gozzano) **10**:184-85, 190
"Il Risorgimento" (Leopardi) **37**:109, 142, 145
"Il sabato del villaggio" (Leopardi) **37**:102, 115, 120
"Il Sogno" (Leopardi) **37**:82, 102, 123
"Il Sonetto" (Carducci) **46**:75
Il Taccuino del Vecchio (Ungaretti) **57**:339
"Il tramonto della luna" (Leopardi) **37**:102, 124, 126, 133, 138
"Il y a" (Apollinaire) **7**:22
Iliad (Homer) **23**:149, 151-53, 155-57, 159-63, 165-72, 175-89, 191
Iliads (Homer)
See *Iliad*
Ilias (Homer)
See *Iliad*
Ílios o prótos (Elytis) **21**:119-20, 124, 127
"I'll Be Your Baby Tonight" (Dylan) **37**:49
"I'll Come Back" (Ignatow) **34**:277
"I'll never forget it" (Castro)
See "Jamás lo olvidare!"
"I'll Run Wild in the Dark Streets Gypsy Camp" (Mandelstam) **14**:119
"I'll tell thee now (dear love) what thou shalt doe" (Donne)
See "A Valediction: of the booke"
"Illic Jacet" (Housman) **2**:184
"Illileo" (Riley) **48**:322
"Illinois Farmer" (Sandburg) **2**:316
"The Illiterate" (Meredith) **28**:188
"The Illumination" (Kunitz) **19**:174-75, 178
"Illuminations" (Glück) **16**:151
Illuminations (Rimbaud)
See *Les illuminations*
Les illuminations (Rimbaud) **3**:249, 254, 259-65, 279; **57**:191, 197, 214, 224-25, 227-30, 234-36, 238-41, 243-44, 246-47, 251, 253-54, 260, 266, 269, 271-74, 276-77, 280-82, 284-87, 293-94, 296, 300
The Illustrated Wilfred Funk (Ferlinghetti) **1**:186
"Illustration" (Ashbery) **26**:123, 137
"The Illustration" (Levertov) **11**:168
"Ilu, the Talking Drum" (Knight) **14**:39, 41, 44-6
"I'm a mosquito" (Niedecker) **42**:150
I'm a Stranger Here Myself (Nash) **21**:264
"Im Feuer" (Stramm) **50**:171, 188
Im Geschweige der Liebe (Stramm) **50**:176
"I'm Guided in the Darkest Night" (Thoreau) **30**:227, 268
"Im Hafen" (Heine) **25**:157-58, 160, 163-64
"I'm Here" (Ignatow) **34**:310
"I'm Here" (Roethke) **15**:270, 272, 279
"Im Osten" (Trakl) **20**:225-26, 250, 255-56
"I'm Still Not Patriarch" (Mandelstam) **14**:122
"I'm Sure of It" (Baca) **41**:37
"I'm Thankful that My Life doth not Deceive" (Thoreau) **30**:193
"I'm Unwilling" (Ammons) **16**:44
"I'm Wife....I'm Woman Now" (Dickinson) **1**:93
"I'm Working on the World" (Szymborska) **44**:299
"The Image" (Day Lewis) **11**:146
"The Image" (Ignatow) **34**:328
The Image and the Law (Nemerov) **24**:255, 260, 264, 285, 288-89, 298
"An Image from a Past Life" (Yeats) **20**:328
"An Image from Beckett" (Mahon) **60**:134, 144, 192, 195, 198
The Image Marker (Merrill) **28**:270
"The Image of God" (Browning) **6**:20
"An Image of Leda" (O'Hara) **45**:117, 201, 206-7
"Image of the Engine" (Oppen) **35**:297, 308, 338
"Imagen" (Storni) **33**:239;
"The Images" (Rich) **5**:385, 396
Images à Crusoé (Perse) **23**:210, 217, 228, 230, 234-35, 247, 254, 256-57
"Images d'un sou" (Verlaine) **32**:378
"Images for Godard" (Rich) **5**:366, 391
"Images in place of logging" (Birney) **52**:37
"Images of Angels" (Page) **12**:168-69, 177, 190
"Images of Perfection" (Tomlinson) **17**:349
"The Imaginary Iceberg" (Bishop) **34**:79, 188-89
"The Imaginary Man" (Parra)
See "El hombre imaginario"
"Imaginary Prisons" (Schnackenberg) **45**:330, 336, 342, 346-47, 349
"Imaginary Translation" (Hacker) **47**:80
"Imagination" (Wheatley)
See "On Imagination"
"Imago" (Boland) **58**:38, 40
"Imago" (Clampitt) **19**:82
"Imbécile habitant" (Éluard) **38**:85
"Imenos" (Cavafy) **36**:110, 111
L'imitation de Notre-Dame la lune (Laforgue) **14**:57, 61, 70-1, 80, 97
"Imitation from the Armenian" (Akhmatova) **55**:7
"Imitation of Boileau" (Shvarts) **50**:138
"Imitation of Byron" (Lermontov) **18**:302
Imitation of Horace, Epistle I, i (Pope)
See *Satires and Epistles of Horace, Imitated*
Imitation of Horace, Epistle II, i (Pope)
See *Satires and Epistles of Horace, Imitated*
Imitation of Horace, Satire II, i (Pope)
See *Satires and Epistles of Horace, Imitated*
"An Imitation of Spenser" (Blake) **12**:31
Imitation of the Second Epistle of the Second Book of Horace (Pope)
See *Satires and Epistles of Horace, Imitated*
Imitations (Lowell) **3**:213, 223, 228, 232
Imitations (Pope)
See *Satires and Epistles of Horace, Imitated*
"Imitations of Drowning" (Sexton) **2**:363
"Imitations of Horace" (Swift) **9**:265
Imitations of Horace (Pope)
See *Satires and Epistles of Horace, Imitated*
Imitations of Horace, The First Epistle of the Second Book (Pope)
See *Satires and Epistles of Horace, Imitated*
L'immaculée conception (Éluard) **38**:91, 96-7
"Immanence" (Warren) **37**:326
"Immature Pebbles" (Zukofsky) **11**:355
"The Immigrants" (Atwood) **8**:38
Immigrants in our Own Land (Baca) **41**:37-8, 55, 70
"The Immigration Department" (Cassian) **17**:5-6
"Immobilism" (Graham) **59**:175-76
"Immortal Autumn" (MacLeish) **47**:126-27, 188, 213, 253
"Immortal Helix" (MacLeish) **47**:130, 156, 197, 213
The Immortal Husband (Merrill) **28**:227
"The Immortal Part" (Housman) **2**:179, 192
"L'immortalité" (Lamartine) **16**:275, 279, 291, 300, 302
"Immortality" (Lamartine)
See "L'immortalité"
"Immortality" (Reese) **29**:333
"Immortality Ode" (Wordsworth)
See "Ode: Intimations of Immortality from Recollections of Early Childhood"
"Immortality over the Dakotas" (Warren) **37**:366, 377
"The Immortals" (Parker) **28**:360
"Immortelle" (Carman) **34**:202
Immortelle maladie (Péret) **33**:220, 223-24, 230-31
"Immutable Moods" (Corso) **33**:49
"The Impalpabilities" (Tomlinson) **17**:327, 357
"Impasse" (Hughes) **1**:260
"Impasse" (Sandburg) **41**:310
"L'Impatient" (Éluard) **38**:69, 87
"L'impenitent" (Verlaine) **2**:417
"The Impercipient" (Hardy) **8**:107-08, 112
Imperfect Thirst (Kinnell) **26**:288, 290, 293-94
"Imperia" (Gautier) **18**:125
"Imperial Adam" (Hope) **56**:270, 286, 288
"The Imperial Bison is" (Guillén)
See "Está el bisonte imperial"
"Imperialism" (Graham) **59**:131, 134, 152, 157-58
"Importnt" (Silverstein) **49**:328
"The Impossible Indispensibility of the Ars Poetica" (Carruth) **10**:86
"Impossible to Tell" (Pinsky) **27**:174-6
"The Impossible Woman/Ideal" (Jiménez)
See "Quimérica"
"The Imprefect Lover" (Sassoon) **12**:258
"Impressionism" (Mandelstam) **14**:118
"Impressionist Picture of a Garden" (Lowell) **13**:95
"Imprint for Rio Grande" (Toomer) **7**:337
"Impromptu" (Benn) **35**:26
"Impromptu In a Low Key" (Curnow) **48**:19, 42-43, 45
"Impromptu on Lord Holland's House" (Gray)
See "On Lord Holland's Seat near Margate, Kent"
"Improprieties" (Jackson) **44**:68
"An Improvisation" (Ignatow) **34**:300
"An Improvisation for the Stately Dwelling" (Ammons) **16**:32, 63
"Improvisations: Lights and Snow" (Aiken) **26**:50
"The Improvisatore" (Coleridge) **11**:105
"In a Back Alley" (Sandburg) **41**:314
"In a Bad Light" (Boland) **58**:25, 60, 96-97
"In a Bird Sanctuary" (Wilbur) **51**:188
"In a Boat" (Belloc) **24**:5
"In a Buggy at Dusk" (Milosz) **8**:205
"In a Burying Ground" (Teasdale) **31**:356
"In a Caledonian Forest" (MacDiarmid) **9**:176
"In a Castle" (Lowell) **13**:70
"In a Cemetery" (Aleixandre) **15**:18
"In a Churchyard" (Wilbur) **51**:259
"In a Clearing" (Merwin) **45**:15
"In a Copy of Browning" (Carman) **34**:203
"In a Cuban Garden" (Teasdale) **31**:360
"In a Dark Time" (Roethke) **15**:268, 276, 278, 281, 306, 313
"In a Darkening Garden" (Teasdale) **31**:339, 373
"In a District of Asia Minor" (Cavafy) **36**:33
"In a Dry Land" (Sarton) **39**:323
"In a Garden" (Carman) **34**:219
"In a Glass-Window for Inconstancy" (Niedecker) **42**:168
"In a Gondola" (Browning) **2**:26
"In a Gothic Cathedral" (Carducci)
See "In una Chiesa Gotica"
"In a Gothic Church" (Carducci)
See "In una Chiesa Gotica"
"In A Grand Pré Garden" (Carman) **34**:225
"In a Green Night" (Walcott) **46**:229-33, 238, 247, 270-74, 276, 285, 322-25
"In a Hospital" (Teasdale) **31**:358
In a Marine Light (Carver)
See *Ultramarine*
"In A Poem" (Frost) **39**:357
"In a redneck bar down the street" (Cisneros) **52**:147, 153, 160
"In a Rosary" (Swinburne) **24**:322, 324
"In a Ship Recently Raised from the Sea" (Page) **12**:168, 184
"In a Spanish Garden" (Stryk) **27**:187
"In a Station of the Metro" (Pound) **4**:355
"In a Strange House" (Kunitz) **19**:148

"In a Subway Station" (Teasdale) **31**:331
"In a Time of Dearth" (Lowell) **13**:83
"In a Time of Revolution for Instance" (Ferlinghetti) **1**:188
In a Time of Violence (Boland) **58**:17-21, 47-50, 68, 85, 92, 96-98, 100
"In a Township of Asia Minor" (Cavafy) **36**:40
"In a Train" (Bly) **39**:79
"In a Troubled Key" (Hughes) **1**:254-55
In a Vast Dominion (Aleixandre)
See *En un vasto dominio*
"In a Waiting-Room" (Hardy) **8**:107
"In a Whispering Gallery" (Hardy) **8**:108
"In Absence" (Lanier) **50**:71
"In Absentia" (Ignatow) **34**:202
"In an Artist's Studio" (Rossetti) **7**:284-85
"In an Iridescent Time" (Stone) **53**:227
In an Iridescent Time (Stone) **53**:215-18, 220, 227-28, 230, 239, 242
"In an Old Book" (Cavafy) **36**:75, 76
"In an Open Palm" (Ignatow) **34**:323
"In Another Fashion" (Ondaatje) **28**:298, 318
"In Answer of an Elegiacal Letter, upon the Death of the King of Sweden, from Aurelian Townsend, inviting me to write on that subject" (Carew) **29**:13, 50, 74
"In Arden" (Tomlinson) **17**:326, 343, 346-48, 353
"In Arthur's House" (Morris) **55**:261, 306
"In August" (Soto) **28**:380
"In Autumn" (Merwin) **45**:20-1
In Autumn (Ekeloef) **23**:71
"In Belfast" (Mahon) **60**:171, 182
"In Blood's Domaine" (Duncan) **2**:120
"In Broad Daylight" (Szymborska) **44**:297
In Broken Country (Wagoner) **33**:349, 352, 362
"In Broken Images" (Graves) **6**:134-35, 137, 151, 153
"In Buque-Escuela" (Storni) **33**:305;
"In Carrowdore Churchyard" (Mahon) **60**:157, 190, 193, 215, 220, 223
"In casa del sopravissuto" (Gozzano) **10**:180, 183, 185, 189
"In Celebration of My Uterus" (Sexton) **2**:352-53
"In Chopin's Garden" (Davie) **29**:110
"In Church" (Cavafy) **36**:38
"In City Gardens Grow No Roses as We Know Them" (Goodison) **36**:154
In Cold Hell, in Thicket (Olson) **19**:284
"In Country Heaven" (Thomas) **2**:395; **52**:283, 313
In Country Heaven (Thomas) **52**:274-76, 316-17, 324
"In Country Sleep" (Thomas) **2**:395; **52**:274-76, 281, 303, 315-18, 320-22, 324
"In court to serve" (Wyatt) **27**:367
"In Danger from the Outer World" (Bly) **39**:48, 51
"In Death, Cannot Reach What Is Most Near" (Ginsberg) **47**:38
"In Defense of Metaphysics" (Tomlinson) **17**:315
In Defense of the Earth (Rexroth) **20**:181, 186, 188, 190, 192, 194, 209
"In der Fremde" (Bridges) **28**:77, 81
"In deserto" (Gautier) **18**:156
"In 'Designing a Cloak'" (Moore) **49**:115, 117
"In Despair" (Cavafy) **36**:75, 77
"In Distrust of Merits" (Moore) **4**:236, 238, 240, 249, 261, 267-69; **49**:93, 101, 126, 134, 144
"In Dock" (Guest) **55**:195
In Dreams Begin Responsibilities, and Other Stories (Schwartz) **8**:281-82, 291, 294, 300-01, 305-07, 319
"In England" (Brodsky) **9**:8
"In Eternum I was ons Determed" (Wyatt) **27**:318, 324
"In Europe they grow a new bean while here" (Niedecker) **42**:151
"In Evening Air" (Roethke) **15**:275, 281
"In Examination" (Brooke) **24**:57
"In Excelsis" (Lowell) **13**:91, 97
"In Exchange for Haiku" (Niedecker) **42**:96, 102
In Exchange for Haiku (Niedecker) **42**:137-38
"In Exile" (Boland) **58**:88
"In Explanation of Our Times" (Hughes) **1**:258
"In Extremis: Poems about My Father" (Berry) **28**:30
"In Fear of Harvests" (Wright) **36**:340
"In Florida" (Swenson) **14**:272
"In Freiburg Station" (Brooke) **24**:62, 66
"In Gallarus Oratory" (Heaney) **18**:201, 223
"In Galleries" (Jarrell) **41**:185
In Gemäldegalerien (Heine) **25**:131
"In Gold Lacquer" (Carman) **34**:211
"In Golden Gate Park That Day" (Ferlinghetti) **1**:183
"In Gratitude to Beethoven" (Wakoski) **15**:345
"In Guernsey" (Swinburne) **24**:325-26
"In Harmony with Nature" (Arnold) **5**:31, 38, 49
"In Haste" (Guillén) **35**:218
"In Her Own Image" (Boland) **58**:13
In Her Own Image (Boland) **58**:5-6, 12, 29-30, 33, 37, 41, 44-45, 51, 72-73, 77, 91, 98
"In Her Praise" (Graves) **6**:171-72
"In Honor of David Anderson Brooks, My Father" (Brooks) **7**:62
"In Honour of Du Bartas" (Bradstreet) **10**:2, 6, 52
"In Honour of that High and Mighty Princess, Queen Elizabeth, of Happy Memory" (Bradstreet) **10**:37, 56
"In Hospital" (Pasternak)
See "V bol'nitse"
"In Imitation of Boileau" (Shvarts) **50**:135
"In Italy" (Brodsky) **9**:23
"In January" (Brooke) **24**:61, 82
"In Just-" (Cummings) **5**:88, 104
"In Kashmir" (Sarton) **39**:345-6
"In Laughter" (Hughes) **7**:159
"In Lieu" (MacNeice) **61**:176
"In Lieu of the Lyre" (Moore) **4**:259; **49**:145, 149
"In Limbo" (Wilbur) **51**:236-38, 247, 280, 335-36
"In limine" (Montale) **13**:114-15, 165
"In Llandough Hospital" (Abse) **41**:14, 19
"In Love for Long" (Muir) **49**:232, 245, 250-51, 298
"In Love Made Visible" (Swenson) **14**:274, 284
"In Loving Memory of the Late Author of Dream Songs" (Meredith) **28**:180, 199, 202, 205, 216-17
"In Lyric Season" (Carman) **34**:210
In Mad Love and War (Harjo) **27**:66-7
"In Meath in May" (Davie) **29**:120
"In Memoriam" (Brodsky) **9**:23
"In Memoriam" (Bryant) **20**:45
"In Memoriam" (Carruth) **10**:85
"In memoriam" (Mistral) **32**:154
"In Memoriam" (Reese) **29**:349
"In Memoriam" (Roethke) **15**:279
"In Memoriam" (Sarton) **39**:358
"In Memoriam" (Ungaretti) **57**:365
In Memoriam (Tennyson) **6**:354, 359-60, 362-64, 367-71, 379, 388, 392-94, 398-99, 403, 405-08, 412, 416
"In Memoriam (Easter, 1915)" (Thomas) **53**:325
"In Memoriam: Gertrud Kolmar, 1943" (Hope) **56**:277
In Memoriam James Joyce (MacDiarmid) **9**:163-66, 173, 180, 182-84, 186
"In Memoriam Mae Noblitt" (Ammons) **16**:62
"In Memoriam N. K. M. (1889-1947)" (Meredith) **28**:190
"In Memoriam PW Jr 1921-1980" (Kumin) **15**:221
"In Memoriam, R. L. M. G." (Curnow) **48**:5, 9
"In Memoriam Stratton Christensen" (Meredith) **28**:185, 209
"In Memoriam: Wallace Stevens" (Duncan) **2**:114
"In Memory: After a Friend's Sudden Death" (Levertov) **11**:206
"In Memory of A. I. Odoevsky" (Lermontov) **18**:268, 298
"In Memory of a Spanish Poet" (Wright) **36**:319, 338
"In Memory of Ann Jones" (Thomas)
See "After the Funeral: In Memory of Anne Jones"
"In Memory of Arthur Winslow" (Lowell) **3**:218
"In Memory of Charles Coffin" (Wright) **36**:377
"In Memory of Dylan Thomas" (Curnow) **48**:12
"In Memory of Elena" (Forché)
See "The Memory of Elena"
"In Memory of Eva Gore-Booth and Con Markiewicz" (Yeats) **20**:349
"In Memory of Jack" (Kenyon) **57**:35
"In Memory of Leopardi" (Wright) **36**:320
"In Memory of Major Robert Gregory" (Tomlinson) **17**:307
"In Memory of Major Robert Gregory" (Yeats) **20**:321, 327; **51**:98
"In Memory of My Dear Grandchild Elizabeth Bradstreet" (Bradstreet) **10**:27, 45
"In Memory of My Feelings" (O'Hara) **45**:120, 128, 130, 141-43, 147, 154, 168, 192, 225
"In Memory of My Mother" (Kavanagh) **33**:63, 73, 81, 96, 143, 147-8
"In Memory of Radio" (Baraka) **4**:14
"In Memory of Robert Frost" (Meredith) **28**:195, 202, 216
"In Memory of the Ottomans" (Wright) **36**:378
"In Memory of Vachel Lindsay" (Teasdale) **31**:346
"In Memory of W. B. Yeats" (Auden) **1**:14
"In Memory of Walter Savage Landor" (Swinburne) **24**:335
"In Michigan" (Masters) **1**:329; **36**:175-76
"In Mind" (Levertov) **11**:211-13
"In Montgomery" (Brooks) **7**:82
"In Monument Valley" (Merrill) **28**:255
"In morte del realismo" (Pasolini) **17**:259
"In Morte di G. B. Niccolini" (Carducci) **46**:51
"In Morte di Giovanni Cairoli" (Carducci) **46**:51
"In Mr. Minnit's House" (Ransom) **61**:274
"In My Craft or Sullen Art" (Thomas) **2**:383
"In My Day We Used to Call It Pussy-Whipped" (Bukowski) **18**:15
"In My Dreams" (Smith) **12**:343
In My Honor (Rilke) **2**:280
"In My Land" (Baca) **41**:37
"In My Life, On My Life" (Amichai) **38**:48
"In My Solitary Hours" (Bradstreet) **10**:62-3
"In Nature There Is Neither Right Nor Left Nor Wrong" (Jarrell) **41**:217
"In Neglect" (Frost) **1**:192
"In Nine Sleep Valley" (Merrill) **28**:223
"In Nineteen Twenty-Seven" (Jackson) **44**:6, 8, 10, 59-62
"in nova scotia th peopul" (Bissett) **14**:32
"In Ohio" (Wright) **36**:340
In Other Words (Swenson) **14**:272-74, 277, 279-80, 283, 287
In Our Terribleness (Some Elements and Meaning in Black Style) (Baraka) **4**:19-21
"In Our Time" (Rukeyser) **12**:216
In Parallel (Verlaine)
See *Parallèlement*
"In Paris in a Loud Dark Winter" (Ferlinghetti) **1**:165
"In Passing" (Mueller) **33**:197
"In Place of an Introduction" (Akhmatova) **55**:4
"In Place of Love" (Ignatow) **34**:305
"In Plaster" (Plath) **37**:201, 254
"In Plaster, with a Bronze Wash" (Meredith)
See "Thoughts on One's Head"
"In Praise of Cities" (Gunn) **26**:186, 231
"In Praise of Darkness" (Borges)
See "Elogio de la sombra"

In Praise of Darkness (Borges)
See *Elogio de la sombra*
"In Praise of Dreams" (Szymborska) **44**:298, 320
"In Praise of Johnny Appleseed" (Lindsay) **23**:280, 288
In Praise of Krishna (Levertov) **11**:181
"In Praise of Limestone" (Auden) **1**:17, 20
"In Praise of Marriages" (Wright) **14**:342, 365
"In Praise of My Lady" (Morris) **55**:302
"In Praise of My Sister" (Szymborska) **44**:290
"In Praise of Peace" (Gower) **59**:20, 25-33
"In Praise of Self-Deprecation" (Szymborska) **44**:290
"In Praise of Surfaces" (Mueller) **33**:181
"In Praise of the Fool" (Olson) **19**:283
"In Prison" (Bishop) **34**:66, 68
"In Process of a Noble Alliance" (Ransom) **61**:271
"In Procession" (Graves) **6**:138
"In Quest of the Tao in An-Ling, I Met Kai Huan Who Fashioned for Me a Register of the Realized Ones; (This Poem) Left Behind As a Present When About to Depart" (Li Po) **29**:169
"In Rain" (Berry) **28**:16
In Reckless Ecstasy (Sandburg) **2**:334; **41**:273, 293, 360-1
"In reference to her children" (Bradstreet) **10**:13, 26-7, 34-5, 43, 59
"In Reply When Lesser Officials of Chung-tu Brought a Pot of Wine and Two Fish to My Inn as Gifts" (Li Po) **29**:146
"In Response to a Manifesto Circulated by the Union of Concerned Scientists" (Jackson) **44**:38
"In Response to a Rumor that the Oldest Whorehouse in Wheeling, West Virginia, Has Been Condemned" (Wright) **36**:296, 319, 329, 341, 354-55, 358, 375
"In Response to 'Tongtang Tune' by Censor Lu" (Li Po) **29**:179-80, 182
"In Rome" (Ní Chuilleanáin) **34**:356, 380
"In Santa Maria del Popolo" (Gunn) **26**:186, 201, 219
"In Shadow" (Crane) **3**:98-9
"In Shame and Humiliation" (Wright) **36**:372, 374
"In Sickness" (Swift) **9**:295
"In Silence" (Merton) **10**:347, 349
"In Silence We Sat Across the Table" (Ignatow) **34**:309
"In Sleep" (Montale)
See "Nel sonno"
"In Sligo and Mayo" (MacNeice) **61**:108
"In Society" (Ginsberg) **4**:71
"In Sparta" (Cavafy) **36**:58
"In Spring, Santa Barbara" (Teasdale) **31**:359
"In Strange Cities" (Zagajewski) **27**:394
"In Strasbourg in 1349" (Ammons) **16**:39
"In Suffolk" (Sarton) **39**:367
"In Summer" (Dunbar) **5**:139
"In Tall Grass" (Sandburg) **2**:324; **41**:260, 297
"In Tenebris (I)" (Hardy) **8**:94, 110
"In Terror of Hospital Bills" (Wright) **36**:314, 341-42, 365-66
"In Texas" (Sarton) **39**:336, 357
"In Thankful Remembrance for My Dear Husband's Safe Arrival" (Bradstreet) **10**:60-1, 64
"In That Deep Wood" (Sarton) **39**:321
"In That Time when It Was Not the Fashion" (Gallagher) **9**:60
"In the Aran Islands" (Mahon) **60**:142
"In the Arboretum" (Stone) **53**:230, 244, 257-58
"In the Badlands" (Wagoner) **33**:344
"In the Baggage Room at Greyhound" (Ginsberg) **47**:5, 37
"In the Bahamas" (Hass) **16**:217
"In the Balance" (Tomlinson) **17**:346
"In the Bamboo Hut" (Kinnell) **26**:260
"In the Beach House" (Sexton) **2**:363
"In the Beauty Created by Others" (Zagajewski) **27**:381, 383
"In the Beginning" (Sanchez) **9**:228-29
"In the Beginning" (Thomas) **2**:403; **52**:232, 290, 293, 295
"In the Bodies of Words" (Swenson) **14**:287
"In the Bomly Village" (Cavafy) **36**:78
"In the cathedral" (Castro)
See "N'a catredal"
"In the Cemetery" (Parra) **39**:278
"In the Cities" (Lawrence) **54**:198
In the Clearing (Frost) **1**:212-13, 224; **39**:239-40
"In the Cold House" (Wright) **36**:340
"In the Constellations" (Darío)
See "En las constelaciones"
"In the Courtroom" (Sanchez) **9**:225
"In the Dark" (Lawrence) **54**:187
"In the Dark and Cloudy Day" (Housman) **2**:193
"In the Days of Prismatic Color" (Moore) **4**:251-52, 257-58; **49**:96, 101, 107, 121
"In the Deep Museum" (Sexton) **2**:346, 348, 351, 360-61
"In the desert soul are many, many" (Shvarts) **50**:134
"In The Duomo" (Curnow) **48**:16-18, 36, 50
"In the Ear of Christ" (Mistral)
See "Al oído de Cristo"
"In the Early Morning" (Corso) **33**:46
"In the East" (Trakl)
See "Im Osten"
"In the Elegy Season" (Wilbur) **51**:188, 278
"In the End" (Teasdale) **31**:360
"In the Face of Hatred" (Wright) **36**:340
"In the Field" (Wilbur) **51**:235, 305, 312
"In the Fleeting Hand of Time" (Corso) **33**:9, 40, 43, 47
"In the Forest" (Pasternak)
See "V lesu"
"In the friendly dark" (Brutus) **24**:122
"In the Fullness of Time" (Tomlinson) **17**:312, 321, 341
"In the Garden" (Boland) **58**:13-14
"In the Glass of Fashion" (Nemerov) **24**:289, 291
"In the great snowfall before the bomb" (Niedecker) **42**:106-7, 137
"In the Greenhouse" (Montale)
See "Nella serra"
"In the Hall of Mirrors" (Merrill) **28**:242, 244
"In the Hands of a Blindman" (Gallagher) **9**:60
"In the Heart of Contemplation" (Day Lewis) **11**:144
"In the Heart of the Hills" (Carman) **34**:211, 220
"In the Hills" (Bely) **11**:5
"In the Hills" (Niedecker) **42**:101-2
"In the Hotel" (Graham) **59**:138, 177
"In the Hotel of Lost Light" (Kinnell) **26**:251, 267
"In the House of Idiedaily" (Carman) **34**:201, 207, 219
In the Illusion of the Threshhold (Bonnefoy)
See *Dans le leurre du seuil*
"In the Land of..." (Silverstein) **49**:343
"In the Lobby of the Hotel del Mayo" (Carver) **54**:22
"In the Lupanar at Pompeii" (Dickey) **40**:181
In the Lure of the Threshold (Bonnefoy)
See *Dans le leurre du seuil*
"In the M5 Restaurant" (Hughes) **7**:162
"In the Marble Quarry" (Dickey) **40**:261
"In the Market-Place" (Nemerov) **24**:291
"In the Marshes of the Blood River" (Piercy) **29**:314
"In the Mecca" (Brooks) **7**:78, 81-2, 88-91
In the Mecca (Brooks) **7**:62-3, 66, 81-3, 88, 90-1, 94, 105, 107
"In the Middle of the Easel" (Guest) **55**:212
"In the Month of Athyr" (Cavafy) **36**:3, 4, 75, 89-90, 91-92, 105
"In the Month of March" (Viereck) **27**:278
"In the Moonlight" (Hardy) **8**:124
"In the Mountain Tent" (Dickey) **40**:186, 207, 212, 258
"In the mountains" (Wang Wei) **18**:376, 380, 383
"In the Mountains of Jerusalem" (Amichai) **38**:25
"In the Movies" (O'Hara) **45**:166
"In the Murhaka" (Amichai) **38**:24-25
"In the Naked Bed, in Plato's Cave" (Schwartz) **8**:291, 297, 301-02, 308-09, 311, 316
"In the Neolithic Age" (Kipling) **3**:167
"In the Night" (Smith) **12**:345
"In the Night Fields" (Merwin) **45**:18
"In the Nursing Home" (Kenyon) **57**:19-20, 47
"In the Open Season" (Wagoner) **33**:335
"In the Outhouse" (Yamada) **44**:342
"In the Park" (Kumin) **15**:209-11
"In the Park" (Montale) **13**:151
"In the Park" (Smith) **12**:345, 352-54
"In the Past" (Zagajewski) **27**:383
"In the Pasture" (Graham) **59**:163-64, 168
"In the Pink" (Sassoon) **12**:242, 262
"In The Plaza" (Aleixandre)
See "En la plaza"
"In the Pocket" (Dickey) **40**:229, 254
In the Presence of the Sun: A Gathering of Shields (Momaday) **25**:220-22
"In the Public Garden" (Moore) **4**:259; **49**:142
In the Quarried Rain (Char)
See *Dans la Pluie giboyeuse*
"In the Rain" (H. D.) **5**:304
"In the Restaurant" (Blok) **21**:3
"In the Restaurant" (Hardy) **8**:124
"In the Ruins of New York City" (Merton) **10**:344, 349
"In the Same Boat" (Kipling) **3**:183
"In the Sconset Bus" (Williams) **7**:409
"In the Secret Room" (Wakoski) **15**:348
"In the Shelter" (Day Lewis) **11**:151
"In the Smoking Car" (Wilbur) **51**:301
"In the Square" (Aleixandre)
See "En la plaza"
"In the Stopping Train" (Davie) **29**:115, 124, 126, 129
"In the Street" (Cavafy) **36**:74, 76, 78
"In the Summertime" (Dylan) **37**:66
"In the Survivor's Home" (Gozzano)
See "In casa del sopravissuto"
"In the Tank" (Gunn) **26**:203
"In the Tavernas" (Cavafy) **36**:75, 108
"In the Tents of Akbar" (Dunbar) **5**:138
"In the Theatre: A True Incident" (Abse) **41**:11, 14, 25, 32
"In the Time of the Blossoms" (Merwin) **45**:16, 26
"In the Tradition" (Baraka) **4**:40
"In the Tree House at Night" (Dickey) **40**:155, 164, 175-76, 226, 256
"In the Tunnel Bone of Cambridge" (Corso) **33**:14
"In the Turpitude of Time: N.D." (Warren) **37**:381
"In the Underworld" (Rukeyser) **12**:220
"In the Waiting Room" (Bishop) **3**:59, 69-70; **34**:56, 58, 61, 68, 73-74, 77-78, 82, 84, 86-87, 97, 101-02, 109, 120, 139-41, 144-46, 151, 170
"In the Ward: The Sacred Wood" (Jarrell) **41**:171, 173, 175, 177, 185
"In the Waxworks" (Shapiro) **25**:273
"In the White Giant's Thigh" (Thomas) **2**:395, 404; **52**:255-56, 274-76, 311, 313, 316-17
"In the Wilderness" (Graves) **6**:128-29
"In the winter in Paris" (Guillén) **23**:103
"In the Winter of My Thirty-Eighth Year" (Merwin) **45**:9, 21, 24-5
"In the Wood" (Pasternak) **6**:252-53, 259
"In the Woods" (Meredith) **60**:286-91
"In These Days" (Walker) **30**:344, 349

"In These Dissenting Times" (Walker) **30**:338, 367
In Thirty-three Pieces (Char)
See *En trente-trois morceaux*
"In This Age of Hard Trying, Nonchalance Is Good and ..." (Moore) **4**:229, 270; **49**:229, 270
"In Those Days" (Jarrell) **41**:146
"In those days you were like a moter to me" (Tsvetaeva)
See "V ony dni, ty mne byla kak mat'"
"in ths forest" (Bissett) **14**:27
"In Time Like Air" (Sarton) **39**:326, 333, 365, 369
In Time Like Air (Sarton) **39**:321, 324, 326, 329, 337-38, 340, 342-43
"In Time of Mourning" (Swinburne) **24**:319
"In Time of Plague" (Gunn) **26**:231
"In Time of 'The Breaking of Nations'" (Hardy) **8**:115, 121
"In Time of War" (Auden) **1**:18
"In una Chiesa Gotica" (Carducci) **46**:24, 30, 54
"In Vain I See the Morning Rise" (Thoreau) **30**:254
"In vain with eye a with a nail" (Tsvetaeva)
See "Naprasno glazom kak gvozdem"
"In Valleys Green and Still" (Housman) **2**:180
"In Warm Rooms Before a Blue Light" (Kumin) **15**:211
"In Warsaw" (Milosz) **8**:192
"In Weather" (Hass) **16**:196, 200, 202-03
In What Hour (Rexroth) **20**:177, 183, 192-93, 198, 214-15, 217
"In What Manner the Body Is United with the Soule" (Graham) **59**:147, 178
"In what torne ship" (Donne)
See "A Hymne to Christ, at the authors last going into Germany"
"In Which I Write My Feelings to be Sent to My Cousin Li Zhao of Binzhou" (Li Po) **29**:179, 183
"In Which the Ancient History I Learn is Not My Own" (Boland) **58**:19, 22
"In Yüeh Viewing the Past" (Li Po) **29**:145
"Inam" (Brathwaite) **56**:71
Inaugual Odes (Horace) **46**:117, 122
"Inaugural Rose" (Jordan) **38**:127
"Inauguration Day: January 1953" (Lowell) **3**:214, 218, 222
"Incantation" (Milosz) **8**:202
"Incantation" (Pinsky) **27**:166
"Incantation at Assisi" (Viereck) **27**:267
"Incantesimo" (Montale) **13**:110
"Incarnate Devil" (Thomas) **52**:227
"The Incarnate One" (Muir) **49**:290, 294-95
"Incarnation" (Rexroth) **20**:206, 216
"Incarnations" (Jackson) **44**:11
Incarnations: Poems, 1966-1968 (Warren) **37**:299, 301, 303-4, 307, 328, 347, 353, 355, 358, 361, 367, 371, 380
"Incense of the Lucky Virgin" (Hayden) **6**:195
"Incespicare" (Montale) **13**:134
"Incident" (Cullen) **20**:61
"Incident on a Journey" (Gunn) **26**:218
Incidental Numbers (Wylie) **23**:311, 321, 325-26, 331
Incidentals (Sandburg) **41**:293-94
"Inclusions" (Browning) **6**:5-6, 15
"Incompatibilities" (Hughes) **7**:113
"An Incomplete List of People I Wish Were Indian" (Alexie) **53**:23
"Incontro" (Montale) **13**:165
"Incontro" (Pavese) **13**:217
"Incorporeal Voluptuousness" (Shvarts) **50**:132
"The Incorrigible Dirigible" (Carruth) **10**:88
An Incorrigible Music (Curnow) **48**:13-16, 18-19, 23, 47-48, 50, 52
"Incredible Buys In" (Stone) **53**:257-58
"Indentured" (Wylie) **23**:305
"Independence" (Cavafy) **36**:55
"Independence" (Thoreau) **30**:216, 219, 281-82, 295
"Independence Day" (Bukowski) **18**:15
"The Independent Man" (Brooks) **7**:53
"An Indian at the Burial-Ground of His Father" (Bryant) **20**:36
"Indian Boarding School: The Runaways" (Erdrich) **52**:181-82
"Indian Boy Love Song (#4)" (Alexie) **53**:39
"Indian Boy Love Song (#3)" (Alexie) **53**:39
"Indian Bread" (Kinnell) **26**:238
"Indian Dances" (Sarton) **39**:321
"Indian Education" (Alexie) **53**:3
"The Indian Girl's Lament" (Bryant) **20**:10, 17
Indian Journals, March 1962-May 1963 (Ginsberg) **4**:53, 56, 60
"Indian Noël" (Mistral)
See "Noël indio"
"Indian Procession" (Mistral)
See "Procesión India"
"Indian Serenade" (Montale)
See "Serenata indiana"
"Indian Summer" (Parker) **28**:347
"Indian Summer" (Pavese)
See "Estate di San Martino"
"The Indian to His Love" (Yeats) **20**:343
"Indiana" (Crane) **3**:88, 106-07
"TH INDIANS WERE WELCOMED AS BRIDGEBUILDERS" (Bissett) **14**:33
L'Indicateur des chemins de coeur (Tzara) **27**:229, 231, 234
"Indictment of Senior Officers" (Olds) **22**:307
"Indifference" (Arnold)
See "Euphrosyne"
"The Indifferent" (Donne) **1**:125
"Indignation Jones" (Masters) **36**:182
"The Indigo Glass in the Grass" (Stevens) **6**:324
"Indigone" (Brathwaite) **56**:91
"Indisciplina" (Pavese) **13**:214, 226
"Indispensability of Eyes" (Olds) **22**:307
"The Individual Man" (Duncan) **2**:118
"Individuality" (Lanier) **50**:54, 56, 105
"The Indivisible Incompatibles" (Swenson) **14**:284
"Indolence" (Bridges) **28**:48, 83
"Indolence" (Keats)
See "Ode on Indolence"
"Indolence in Early Winter" (Kenyon) **57**:45
"The Indolent Monk" (Baudelaire)
See "Le mauvais moine"
"Les indolents" (Verlaine) **32**:351, 390, 393
"Indulgence" (Li Po) **29**:177
"The Indweller" (Tagore)
See "Antaryami"
"Infant" (Smith) **12**:310, 326
"Infant Boy at Mid-Century" (Warren) **37**:300
"Infant Joy" (Blake) **12**:7, 9, 33-4
"Infant Sorrow" (Blake) **12**:7, 31, 34
"Infanta Marina" (Stevens) **6**:311
"El infante" (Guillén) **35**:174
"An Inference of Mexico" (Hayden) **6**:194, 198
Inferno (Dante) **21**:53, 56, 59-67, 69-72, 75-7, 81-5, 89, 95-6, 98-9, 101, 103-08
Infidels (Dylan) **37**:60, 65
"Infiltration of the Universe" (MacLeish) **47**:192
"L'infini dans les cieux" (Lamartine) **16**:266, 280, 284-85
"The Infinite" (Leopardi)
See "L'Infinito"
"The Infinite Reason" (MacLeish) **47**:192
"L'Infinito" (Leopardi) **37**:82, 84, 102, 105, 109-11, 123-30, 134, 139-40, 143
"Inflation Blues" (Walker) **20**:294
"The Influence Coming into Play: The Seven of Pentacles" (Piercy) **29**:325
"The Influence Passing: The Knight of Swords" (Piercy) **29**:324
"The Informant" (Ní Chuilleanáin) **34**:360, 362
"El ingenuo" (Borges) **22**:97, 99; **32**:90
"Les ingénus" (Verlaine) **32**:349, 391, 393
"Ingoldsby Legends" (Browning) **2**:36
"Ingrateful Beauty Threatened" (Carew) **29**:3, 9, 18, 32, 34, 71
The Inhabitant and His Hope (Neruda)
See *El habitante y su esperenza*
"The Inheritance" (Lawrence) **54**:240
"Inheritances" (Hacker) **47**:80
"Inheritor" (Wright)
See "Eroded Hills"
"Inhuman World" (Aleixandre) **15**:20
"The Inhumanist" (Jeffers) **17**:136
"The Iniquity of the Fathers upon the Children" (Rossetti) **7**:289-90
"Initial, Daemonic, and Celestial Love" (Emerson) **18**:93
"The Initiate" (Merwin) **45**:35
"Initiations" (Okigbo) **7**:224-25, 232, 237
"Injudicious Gardening" (Moore) **4**:266; **49**:91, 114
"Injuria Anicitiae" (Philips) **40**:296
"The Injury" (Williams) **7**:360
"The Inlet" (Glück) **16**:125
"Lo inmenso del mar" (Guillén) **35**:229
The Inn Album (Browning) **2**:68, 96
"The Inn of Earth" (Teasdale) **31**:364
"The Inner Kingdom" (Darío)
See "El reino interior"
Inner Landscape (Sarton) **39**:309-12, 334-35, 341, 344, 348, 353-54, 356-57, 364
The Inner Room (Merrill) **28**:281
"Inner Voice" (Herbert) **50**:20-21
"Innisfree" (Yeats) **51**:103
"The Inniskeen Hellions" (Kavanagh) **33**:91
"Inniskeen Road: July Evening" (Kavanagh) **33**:74, 92, 97, 99-100, 102, 142, 150
"Inno a Nettuno" (Leopardi) **37**:165-66, 168, 170-71
Inno a Satana (Carducci) **46**:5, 16, 21, 23, 28, 37, 47, 56-57, 69, 76, 81, 84, 88
"Inno ai patriarchi" (Leopardi) **37**:171
"Inno alla morte" (Ungaretti) **57**:348
"Innocence" (Gunn) **26**:197, 201
"Innocence" (Kavanagh) **33**:74, 81, 100, 118, 128, 145
"Innocence" (Levine) **22**:228
"The Innocent" (Stone) **53**:229
"Innocent Landscape" (Wylie) **23**:305-306, 333-34
"The Innocents" (Wylie) **23**:302-303, 310
"¡No hay salida?" (Paz) **48**:232
"Inochi no fune" (Ishikawa) **10**:213, 215
"L'inoffensif" (Char) **56**:120, 134, 154
"The Inoffensive One" (Char)
See "L'Inoffensif"
La inquietud del rosal (Storni) **33**:234, 236, 241, 244, 267, 272-74, 297, 310-11;
"ins lesebuch für die oberstufe" (Enzensberger) **28**:135
"Insane Buildings" (Alurista) **34**:48
Inscription (Herbert)
See *Napis*
"Inscription Facing Western Sea" (Merwin) **45**:44
"Inscription for the Entrance into a Wood" (Bryant) **20**:4, 17, 19, 35, 40, 47
"Inscription for the Tank" (Wright) **36**:182, 317, 341-42, 366, 375
"Inscriptions" (Boland) **58**:25, 61
"Insensibility" (Owen) **19**:327, 337, 340, 347-48, 355, 357, 369-70
"Inside a mountain idles an idol" (Mandelstam)
See "Vnutri gory bezdeistvuet kumir"
"Inside and Outside" (Tate) **50**:256
"The Inside Dance" (Piercy) **29**:311
"Inside News" (Yamada) **44**:339
Inside the Blood Factory (Wakoski) **15**:324-25, 341, 348, 350-51, 362-63, 365
"Inside the River" (Dickey) **40**:156, 262
"The Insidious Dr. Fu Man Chu" (Baraka) **4**:15
"L'insinuant" (Valéry) **9**:395
"Insipidities" (Verlaine) **32**:386
"Insomnia" (Bishop) **34**:66, 146

"Insomnia" (Borges)
See "Insomnio"
"Insomnia" (MacLeish) **47**:164
"Insomnia" (Paz)
See "Insomnio"
Insomnia (Tsvetaeva) **14**:299, 301
"Insomnia at the Solstice" (Kenyon) **57**:15
"Insomnia. Homer. Tautly Swelling Sails. . ." (Mandelstam) **14**:141
"Insomniac" (Plath) **1**:399
"Insomnio" (Borges) **22**:92; **32**:39, 58, 85
"Insomnio" (Paz) **48**:176
"Insonnia" (Quasimodo) **47**:270
"Inspection" (Owen) **19**:335, 354, 356
"Inspiration" (Lowell) **3**:245
"Inspiration" (Thoreau) **30**:180, 190, 192, 223, 239-40, 254, 268, 281-82, 284, 295
"Inspiration for a Burned Bridge" (Merwin) **45**:8
"Installation of the Duke of Grafton as Chancellor of Cambridge" (Gray) **2**:143
"The Instant" (Levertov) **11**:166, 168
"Instead of a Foreword" (Akhmatova) **55**:8, 57, 63-64
"Instead of a Preface" (Akhmatova) **55**:36, 57-58, 63
"Instead of Camargue" (Swenson) **14**:249
"Instinct" (Pavese)
See "L'istinto"
"The Instruction Manual" (Ashbery) **26**:111, 129, 159, 164
Instructions to his Son and to Posterity (Raleigh) **31**:273
"Instructions to the Double" (Gallagher) **9**:58, 60
Instructions to the Double (Gallagher) **9**:35-7, 43, 53-4, 58
"Instructions to the Orphic Adept" (Graves) **6**:133
"Insufficiency" (Browning) **6**:15
"Insularum Ocelle" (Swinburne) **24**:326
"An Insult" (Kavanagh) **33**:101
"The Insulted and Injured" (Viereck) **27**:279
Intact Wind (Paz)
See *Viento entero*
"The Intangible" (Kavanagh) **33**:91
Integer uitae (Horace) **46**:94, 98
Intellectual Things (Kunitz) **19**:147-48, 153, 155, 159-61, 163, 185
"The Intellectuals" (Shapiro) **25**:270, 312
"Inter & Outer Rhyme" (Corso) **33**:50
Inter mezzo (Heine) **25**:131
"The Intercepter" (Muir) **49**:284
"Intercettazione telefonica" (Montale) **13**:133
"Interdeterminancy" (Cage) **58**:195
"Interface" (Wright) **14**:373
"Interference" (Ammons) **16**:6
"Intérieur" (Éluard) **38**:69
"Intérieur" (Valéry) **9**:365, 396
"Interim" (Levertov) **11**:176, 195-96
"Interim" (Millay) **6**:205-07, 214 **61**:212, 225, 254
"Interior" (Guillén) **35**:157
"Interior" (Sandburg) **41**:240
"Interior (with Jane)" (O'Hara) **45**:201
"Interjection Number" (Warren) **37**:378
"Interjection Number 7" (Warren) **37**:306
"Interjection Number Four: Bad Year, Bad War: A New Year's Card, 1969" (Warren) **37**:306
"Interjection Number Three: I Know a Place Where All Is Real" (Warren) **37**:305
"Interjection Number Two: Caveat" (Warren) **37**:304, 380
"Interlude" (Longfellow) **30**:62, 65-6
"The Interlude" (Shapiro) **25**:303, 326
"Intermezzo" (Carducci) **46**:23, 27
"Intermezzo" (Montale) **13**:106
"Intermezzo" (Schnackenberg) **45**:345
"Intermezzo No 1" (Heine) **25**:141
"Intermission 3" (Brooks) **7**:58, 62, 91, 104
"Interplay" (Wright) **14**:348
"Interregnum" (Muir) **49**:240
"Interrogaciones" (Darío) **15**:100
"Interrogaciones" (Mistral) **32**:161, 176
"Interrogate the Stones" (MacLeish) **47**:186
"The Interrogation" (Muir) **49**:199, 213, 229, 256, 264, 282-83
"The Interrogation of the Man of Many Hearts" (Sexton) **2**:352
Interrogations (Quintana) **36**:257, 260-61, 263, 265-67, 270-72, 275
"Interruption" (Cavafy) **36**:46, 53, 86
"Interruption" (Graves) **6**:137, 143-44
"Interruptions From the West" (Paz) **48**:256
"Interval" (Paz) **48**:273
"Interview" (Ekeloef) **23**:86-7
"Interview" (Parker) **28**:361
"Interview with a Spirit Healer" (Abse) **41**:19
"Interview with a Tourist" (Atwood) **8**:14
"Intifada" (Jordan) **38**:127
"Intima" (Mistral) **32**:151, 176-77
"Intimacy of Tone" (Guest) **55**:201
"Intimate Parnassus" (Kavanagh) **33**:63, 72, 88, 100, 103, 115, 119
"Intimates" (Lawrence) **54**:185
"Intimation" (Mistral)
See "Intima"
"Intimation of Immortality" (Smith) **12**:313
"The Intimations Ode" (Wordsworth)
See "Ode: Intimations of Immortality from Recollections of Early Childhood"
"Intimations of Immorality" (Sappho) **5**:418
"Intimations of Immortality" (Thomas) **2**:392
"Intimations of Immortality" (Wordsworth)
See "Ode: Intimations of Immortality from Recollections of Early Childhood"
Intimité marine (Césaire) **25**:22
"Into Her Lying Down Head" (Thomas) **52**:316, 333, 335
"Into My Heart and Air That Kills" (Housman) **2**:192
"Into My Own" (Frost) **1**:213; **39**:237, 240-41, 246
"Into the ark" (Szymborska) **44**:296
"Into the Golden Vessel of Great Song" (Millay) **6**:211
"Into the Matter" (Paz) **48**:274
"Into the Shandy Westerness" (Rexroth) **20**:196
"Into the Stone" (Dickey) **40**:180, 225
Into the Stone and Other Poems (Dickey) **40**:154, 166, 175-76, 179, 181, 184-85, 187, 189, 195, 204, 212, 229-30, 240, 261-62
"Into the Tree" (Milosz) **8**:198
"Into the Twilight" (Yeats) **20**:346
"Into Thirty Centuries Born" (Muir) **49**:297
"Introduction" (Akhmatova)
See "Vstuplenie"
"Introduction" (Blake) **12**:7, 32, 34-5, 43-7
"The Introduction" (Finch) **21**:155-57, 159, 161, 181
"Introduction" (Lawrence) **54**:207
"The Introduction" (MacNeice) **61**:178
"Introduction to Native American Literature" (Alexie) **53**:8
"Introitus" (Longfellow) **30**:65
"Introvert" (Birney) **52**:8
"Intruding" (Piercy) **29**:311
"The Intrusion" (Graves) **6**:156
"Inútil soy" (Storni) **33**:280;
"Les Invalides" (Kinnell) **26**:260
"Invasion Spring" (Birney) **52**:4
"Invasions" (Kunitz) **19**:148
"Invective Against Swans" (Stevens) **6**:294
Invectives (Verlaine) **2**:419
"Les Inventeurs" (Char) **56**:154
"L'invention" (Éluard) **38**:69
"Invention of the Cross" (Gower) **59**:31
"Inventory" (Carver) **54**:29
"Invernal" (Darío) **15**:117
"Invictus" (Parker) **28**:355
"De invierno" (Darío) **15**:107-08, 110
"INVISIBLE" (Villa) **22**:356
"The Invisible Hunter" (Shvarts) **50**:131, 144-45
"invisible presence" (Ekeloef)
See "osynlig närvaro"
Invisible Reality (Jiménez)
See *La realidad invisible*
"The Invitation" (Clare) **23**:23
"L'invitation au voyage" (Baudelaire) **1**:69
"L'Invitation au voyage" (Char) **56**:197
"The Invitation to Daphnis" (Finch) **21**:139, 153-54, 161
"Invitation to Dyddgu" (Dafydd)
See "I Wahodd Dyddgu"
"Invitation to Miss Marianne Moore" (Bishop) **3**:44; **34**:146
"Invitation to Miss Moore" (Bishop)
See "Invitation to Miss Marianne Moore"
"Invitation to the Country" (Bridges) **28**:66, 69
"Invite to Eternity" (Clare) **23**:22-4, 26
"Invocation" (Hacker) **47**:117
"Invocation" (Hope) **56**:268, 272
"L'invocation" (Lamartine) **16**:277, 279, 290
"Invocation" (Lamartine)
See "L'invocation"
"Invocation" (Levertov) **11**:177
"Invocation" (Sitwell) **3**:312
"The Invocation" (Suckling) **30**:130
"Invocation to Kali" (Sarton) **39**:320, 328, 339-40, 342, 344, 366
"An Invocation to Sleep" (Finch) **21**:143, 146, 179-80
"Invocation to the Social Muse" (MacLeish) **47**:164, 166, 190, 197, 240-41, 254
"The Inward Morning" (Thoreau) **30**:181, 191, 193, 198-99, 203, 213, 222, 241, 267
"Io poeta delle Ceneri" (Pasolini) **17**:292
"Iola, Kansas" (Clampitt) **19**:95-6
"Ione" (Dunbar) **5**:125
"Ionic" (Cavafy) **36**:73, 86, 112
"Iork" (Brodsky)
See "York: In Memoriam W. H. Auden"
"Irapuato" (Birney) **52**:77, 98
"An Irate Host" (Surrey) **59**:286, 353
"The Ireland of the Bombers" (Davie)
See "1969, Ireland of the Bombers"
"Iride" (Montale) **13**:109, 111, 121-22, 130-31, 152, 166
"Iris" (Montale)
See "Iride"
"Irises" (Lee) **24**:240
"An Irish Airman Foresees His Death" (Yeats) **20**:304
"An Irish Childhood in England" (Boland) **58**:3
"The Irish Cliffs of Moher" (Stevens) **6**:304
"Irish Stew" (Kavanagh) **33**:86
"The Irish Tradition" (Kavanagh) **33**:132
"An Irishman in London" (Mahon) **60**:182, 185
"Iron" (Sandburg) **41**:269
"Iron" (Zagajewski) **27**:381, 387
"Iron Age Burial" (Szirtes) **51**:161
"the Iron Characters" (Nemerov) **24**:262, 279
The iron coin (Borges)
See *La moneda de hierro*
"Iron Hans" (Sexton) **2**:365-68
"The Iron Horse" (Riley) **48**:283
"Iron Landscapes" (Gunn) **26**:197-198, 206, 214
"Iron Thunder" (Quintana) **36**:272
"Iron Train" (Zagajewski) **27**:402
"Ironing Grandmother's Tablecloth" (Kenyon) **57**:12
"Irregular Dance" (Storni)
See "Danza irregular"
"L'irrémédiable" (Baudelaire) **1**:55
"L'Irrémédiable" (Char) **56**:197
Irremediablemente (Storni) **33**:236-37, 244, 247, 251-52, 275-77, 297, 307, 311, 318;
"L'Irréparable" (Baudelaire) **1**:68
"Is" (Kavanagh) **33**:63, 96, 119-20
is 5 (Cummings) **5**:77, 92, 95, 104
"Is it possible?" (Wyatt) **27**:353
"Is It True?" (Sexton) **2**:368, 374

"Is It Wise" (Smith) **12**:343
"Is My Team Ploughing" (Housman) **2**:180, 193, 196
I's (Pronounced Eyes) (Zukofsky) **11**:357
"Is That What You Are" (Merwin) **45**:25
"Is There for Honest Poverty" (Burns) **6**:58, 83
"Is There No Way Out?" (Paz)
See "¿No hay salida?"
"Is Your Town Nineveh?" (Moore) **49**:116-17
"Isaac and Abraham" (Brodsky)
See "Isaak i Avraam"
"Isaac and Archibald" (Robinson) **1**:467, 486-87, 496
"Isaak i Avraam" (Brodsky) **9**:4, 6
"Isabel" (Tennyson) **6**:387
"Isabella" (Keats) **1**:279, 282, 288-89, 296
"Isabella" (Morris) **55**:247
"Isabella; or, The Pot of Basil" (Keats)
See "Isabella"
"Isaiah" (Walker) **20**:278
"Isaiah LXII: 1-8" (Wheatley) **3**:357
"Isaiah Beethoven" (Masters) **36**:183, 190-91
"Isba Song" (McGuckian) **27**:103
"Ischia" (Lamartine) **16**:287, 291
"Ishtar" (Wright) **14**:363
"La isla" (Guillén) **35**:181
Isla ignorada (Fuertes) **27**:10, 19, 21
"Isla ignorado" (Fuertes) **27**:43
"The Islam" (Borges) **32**:58
"The Island" (Dickey) **40**:160
"The Island" (Forché) **10**:138, 152, 161, 166
"Island" (Hughes) **1**:244, 248; **53**:119, 129
"The Island" (Jarrell) **41**:146
"The Island" (Muir) **49**:196, 200, 205, 298-99
"An Island" (Robinson) **1**:465, 467
The Island (Allard) **24**:116
The Island (Byron) **16**:86, 88, 90, 109
Island and Time (Curnow) **48**:3, 11, 23-29
"The Island Hawk" (Noyes) **27**:122
"Island in the Works" (Merrill) **28**:268, 270-71
"Island of Night" (Kinnell) **26**:257
"The Island of Statues" (Yeats) **20**:343, 346, 353
"Island of Summer" (Warren) **37**:301
"The Islanders" (Kipling) **3**:179, 192
"Islands" (Brathwaite) **56**:14
"The Islands" (H. D.) **5**:268
"The Islands" (Hayden) **6**:191, 193, 200
"Islands" (Merwin) **45**:87
"Islands" (Walcott) **46**:238
Islands (Brathwaite) **56**:8-11, 14-15, 17-18, 22, 24, 26, 31, 33-34, 49, 53, 59, 64-68, 70-71, 73-75, 77, 86-88, 94-95, 98, 100
"Islands and Exiles" (Brathwaite) **56**:39, 83
"Islands and Towers" (Zagajewski) **27**:389
"Islands of the Blest" (Yeats) **51**:103
"Ismaïl Bey" (Lermontov) **18**:278, 300
"Isola" (Quasimodo) **47**:302
"Isola di Ulisse" (Quasimodo) **47**:302-3
"Isola mattutina" (Quasimodo) **47**:301
"Isolation: To Marguerite" (Arnold) **5**:13, 18
"Isolationist" (Page) **12**:170
"L'isolement" (Lamartine) **16**:265, 274-77, 290, 298-301
"Ispoved" (Lermontov) **18**:300
"Israel" (Borges) **32**:58
"Israel" (Shapiro) **25**:283, 285, 297-98, 307, 320, 325
"Israeli Travel" (Amichai) **38**:48-49
"Israfel" (Poe) **1**:438, 447-48
"L'issue" (Char) **56**:120
"The Issues" (Olds) **22**:313
"Ister Bank Song" (Sidney) **32**:237, 243
Isthm. VII (Pindar)
See *Isthmian 7*
Isthmian 3 (Pindar) **19**:426
Isthmian 4 (Pindar) **19**:426
Isthmian 6 (Pindar) **19**:398, 414, 421-22
Isthmian 7 (Pindar) **19**:425
Isthmian 8 (Pindar) **19**:398, 424
"L'istinto" (Pavese) **13**:205, 213
"Isto" (Pessoa) **20**:172
"It breaks" (Piercy) **29**:314
It Catches My Heart in Its Hands: New and Selected Poems, 1955-1963 (Bukowski) **18**:5, 21
"It Could Well Be..." (Storni)
See "Bien pudiera ser"
"It Is" (Alurista) **34**:45, 47
"It Is a Living Coral" (Williams) **7**:369
"It Is a Spring Afternoon" (Sexton) **2**:352
"It Is Everywhere" (Toomer) **7**:337, 340
"It Is March" (Merwin) **45**:19-20
"It Is Much" (Sandburg) **41**:336
"It Is My Thoughts That Color My Soul" (Wylie) **23**:322
"It Is No Dream of Mine" (Thoreau) **30**:216
"It Is No Longer Possible" (Aleixandre) **15**:20
"It Is Not Always May" (Longfellow) **30**:26
"It Is Not Dead" (Warren) **37**:380
"It is over" (Guillén)
See "Se acabó"
"It Is Said" (Alurista) **34**:43
"It Is So" (Neruda)
See "Es así"
"It Is the First Mild Day of March" (Wordsworth)
See "Lines on the First Mild Day of March"
"It Is Too Late" (Curnow) **48**:11
"It Is Well" (Brooke) **24**:71-2
"It may be good, like it who list" (Wyatt) **27**:316, 329, 341
"It Must Be Sophisticated" (Ashbery) **26**:161
"It Must Be the Milk" (Nash) **21**:278-79
"It Must Give Pleasure" (Stevens) **6**:329
"It Nods and Curtseys and Recovers" (Housman) **2**:192-93
"It Rains" (Thomas) **53**:286
"It Was a Face Which Darkness Could Kill" (Ferlinghetti) **1**:183
"It Was a' for Our Rightfu' King" (Burns) **6**:99
"It Was a Funky Deal" (Knight) **14**:46
"It Was a Gentle Breeze" (Darío)
See "Era un aire suave"
"It Was a Soft Air" (Darío)
See "Era un aire suave"
"It Was All Very Tidy" (Graves) **6**:142, 144
"It Was Black Black Took" (Stein) **18**:328
"It Was That Indian" (Ortiz) **17**:234
"It Was Upon" (Thomas) **53**:266
It Was When (Snyder) **21**:289
"It Was Winter" (Milosz) **8**:194
"It weeps away" (Piercy) **29**:315
"It Will Not Change" (Teasdale) **31**:332, 359
"It will unveil you" (Ungaretti)
See "Ti svelerà"
"L'Italia" (Pasolini) **17**:270, 272
"Italia mia" (Petrarch) **8**:267, 270
"Italian Extravaganza" (Corso) **33**:6, 14, 41, 43
"Italian Garden" (Sarton) **39**:332
"The Italian Kitchen" (Ní Chuilleanáin) **34**:350
"Italian Morning" (Bogan) **12**:106
"An Italian Visit" (Day Lewis) **11**:150
"Italy and France" (Browning) **2**:26
"Itching Heels" (Dunbar) **5**:146
"Ite, missa est" (Darío) **15**:113
"Ithaca" (Cavafy) **36**:3, 28, 41, 50, 51, 73, 74, 76, 78, 86, 108
"Ithaca" (Glück) **16**:172
"Ithaka" (Cavafy)
See "Ithaca"
"Itinerary" (Kumin) **15**:220
"Itinerary of an Obession" (Kumin) **15**:220
"It's a New Day" (Sanchez) **9**:229
It's a New Day: Poems for Young Brothas and Sistuhs (Sanchez) **9**:207, 211-12, 215, 229, 237
"It's a Woman's World" (Boland) **58**:4, 12, 15, 45
"It's both boring and sad" (Lermontov) **18**:268-69
"It's Cold" (Parra)
See "Hace frio"
"Its Course" (Carver) **54**:13
"It's Dull and Dreary" (Lermontov) **18**:281
"Its Everlasting Possibility" (Pinsky) **27**:153
"Its Great Emptiness" (Pinsky) **27**:153-4
"It's Half an Hour Later Before" (Ammons) **16**:25
"Its Many Fragments" (Pinsky) **27**:153
"It's Miller Time" (Cruz) **37**:30
"It's Nation Time" (Baraka) **4**:19, 26, 40
It's Nation Time (Baraka) **4**:19, 20, 26
"It's Not Going to Happen Again" (Brooke) **24**:84-5, 93
"It's Oblivion" (Parra)
See "Es olvido"
"It's over a (See Just" (Cummings) **5**:108
"It's Raining" (Apollinaire)
See "Il pleut"
"It's Time, My Friend, It's Time" (Pushkin)
See "Pora, Moi Drug, Pora"
"It's Unbecoming" (Pasternak) **6**:265
Iustum et tenacem (Horace) **46**:104
I've Been a Woman (Sanchez) **9**:207, 211-12, 215-16, 218-22, 227, 229, 232, 238, 242
"I've Been Asleep" (Levine) **22**:218
"I've Been Thinking" (Moore)
See "Occasionem Cognosce"
"I've Looked So Much" (Cavafy) **36**:74, 107
"I've Nothing to Offer" (Ignatow) **34**:344-45
I-VI (Cage) **58**:212, 214
"The Ivory Statuette" (Wylie) **23**:321
Iz shesti knig (Akhmatova) **2**:18
Izbrannyye proizvedeniya (Yevtushenko) **40**:359, 363
Izya Kramer, Inspector of Lights (Yevtushenko) **40**:357
J. B. (MacLeish) **47**:167-70, 174, 177, 179-80, 197, 208, 212, 215, 228-30, 232, 234, 261-62
"Ja k vam pishu" (Lermontov) **18**:303
"Jabberers" (Sandburg) **41**:270
"Jabberwocky" (Carroll) **18**:36, 38-40, 48-50, 52, 59-60
Jablko z klína (Seifert) **47**:316, 325, 333
Jack Kelso: A Dramatic Poem (Masters) **1**:339
"Jack Straw's Castle" (Gunn) **26**:205
"Jacklight" (Erdrich) **52**:176, 189, 192
Jacklight (Erdrich) **52**:170-80, 182, 184-87, 189-91, 193
"Jack's Final Wire" (Yau) **61**:333
"Jack's Straw Castle" (Gunn) **26**:213, 228
Jack's Straw Castle, and Other Poems (Gunn) **26**:194-197, 204-206, 208, 210, 213, 219-220, 229
"Jackson, Mississippi" (Walker) **20**:283
"The Jacob's Ladder" (Glück) **16**:171
The Jacob's Ladder (Levertov) **11**:168, 193, 206
"The Jacquerie" (Lanier) **50**:90, 107-8
"Jactancia de quietud" (Borges) **22**:72; **32**:38, 123, 139
Jadis et naguère (Verlaine) **2**:416; **32**:355, 369, 375, 377-78, 385-86, 400-01
"Jadis, si je me souviens bien . . ." (Rimbaud) **57**:246, 251
"The Jaguar" (Hughes) **7**:118, 151, 163
"Jah" (Brathwaite) **56**:53-54, 75, 86, 100
"Jah Music" (Goodison) **36**:143, 154
Jah Music (Brathwaite) **56**:45, 51, 71
"J'ai Mal à Nos Dents" (Ní Chuilleanáin) **34**:360, 362, 364
"J'ai plus de souvenirs" (Baudelaire) **1**:67
"The Jailer" (Plath) **37**:230, 232-34
"The Jain Bird Hospital in Delhi" (Meredith) **28**:215
"Jam Session" (Hughes) **1**:245; **53**:192
"The Jam Trap" (Tomlinson) **17**:314
"Jamaica 1980" (Goodison) **36**:153-54
"Jamāl al-mawt" (Gibran) **9**:78
"Jamás lo olvidare!" (Castro) **41**:116
"James Wetherell" (Robinson) **1**:467
"Jamestown" (Jarrell) **41**:146, 169
"jamming naked" (Cruz)
See "descarga en cueros"

"jamming with drums" (Cruz)
See "descarga en cueros"
"The Jam-Pot" (Kipling) **3**:190
"Jan Kubelik" (Sandburg) **41**:318, 321, 365
"Jan, the Son of Thomas" (Sandburg) **41**:302
"Janet Waking" (Ransom) **61**:271, 301, 313, 323
"January" (Belloc) **24**:29
"January" (Hass) **16**:216
"January" (Nishiwaki)
See "Ichigatsu"
"January" (Song) **21**:341
"January 10, 1973" (Walker) **30**:354
"January 1904" (Cavafy) **36**:109
"January 1918" (Pasternak) **6**:261
"January 1919" (Pasternak) **6**:252
"January and May" (Chaucer)
See "Miller's Tale"
"A January Night" (Hardy) **8**:110
"A Japanese Elegy" (Yakamochi)
See "Nihon no Banka"
"Japanese Lament" (Yakamochi)
See "Nihon no Banka"
"Japanese Papers" (Sarton) **39**:349, 351
"Japanese Prints" (Sarton) **39**:339, 345
"El jardin botánico" (Borges) **32**:60
"Jardín de invierno" (Neruda) **4**:287, 289-90
"El jardín triste se pierde" (Jiménez) **7**:199
"Jardín zoológico de nubes" (Storni) **33**:295;
Jardines lejanos (Jiménez) **7**:209
Jaro sbohem (Seifert) **47**:323, 325, 333-34
"Jarrama" (Ekeloef) **23**:76
"La Jarre" (Éluard) **38**:67-68
"Jasmine Arbour" (Tagore)
See "Chameli-vitan"
"Jason" (MacLeish) **47**:182
"Jaufré Rudel" (Carducci) **46**:52
"Jaws" (Sandburg) **2**:330; **41**:269
"Jaybird" (Dunbar) **5**:144
"Jazbo" (Sandburg) **41**:270
"Jazz Band in a Parisian Cabaret" (Hughes) **53**:82
"Jazz Fantazia" (Sandburg) **41**:297
"Jazzonia" (Hughes) **1**:246, 261; **53**:80, 82, 86, 91, 117
Je ne mange pas de ce pain-là (Péret) **33**:220, 230
"Je ne suis pas seul . . ." (Char) **56**:120
"Je plaings le temps de ma jeunesse" (Villon) **13**:388-89
"Je plante en la faveur cest arbre de Cybelle" (Ronsard) **11**:277
Je sublime (Péret) **33**:202, 204, 206-07, 214-15, 220, 225, 231
"Je suis bruslé, Le Gast, d'une double chaleur" (Ronsard) **11**:250
"Je suis l'empire à la fin de la décadence" (Verlaine) **2**:416
"Je suis venu, calme orphelin" (Verlaine) **32**:379
"Je te dirais" (Péret) **33**:208
"The Jealous Man" (Graves) **6**:142, 144
"Jealousy" (Brooke) **24**:56
"Jealousy—A Confessional" (Wakoski) **15**:356
"Jean de Nivelle" (Verlaine) **32**:378
"Jeanne d'Arc" (Glück) **16**:140
"Jean's TV" (Carver) **54**:12, 14
"jed bi kor benkst trik" (Bissett) **14**:34
"Jedwab duszy" (Herbert) **50**:5
"Jefferson" (Shapiro) **25**:270
"Jefferson Howard" (Masters) **36**:230, 232
"Jehova" (Lamartine) **16**:280, 293
"Jehovah Our Righteousness" (Cowper) **40**:54
"Jehuda ben Halevy" (Heine) **25**:149
"A Jellyfish" (Moore) **49**:104, 140, 184-85
"Jemez" (Tomlinson) **17**:355
"Jen jedno jsem spatřil..." (Seifert) **47**:335
"Jener" (Benn) **35**:69
"Jenny" (Rossetti) **44**:165, 167, 175-77, 180, 191, 201-3, 237, 239-42, 252
"Jephthah's Daughter" (Vigny)
See "La Fille de Jephte"
"The Jerboa" (Moore) **4**:233, 236, 243; **49**:94, 97-98, 100, 119, 129, 142, 144, 149, 155
"Jeremiah" (Walker) **20**:278
"Jerome" (Jarrell) **41**:208
"Jeronimo's House" (Bishop) **3**:37, 47; **34**:130
"Jerusalem" (Blake) **12**:37
"Jerusalem" (Rich) **5**:383
"Jerusalem 1967" (Amichai) **38**:8, 54
"Jerusalem, Jerusalem, Why Jerusalem" (Amichai) **38**:47, 49
Jerusalem: The Emanation of the Giant Albion (Blake) **12**:13, 20, 27, 29-32, 34-40, 43-4, 51-9, 61-75, 80
"Jessie Cameron" (Rossetti) **7**:280
"Jessie Mitchell's Mother" (Brooks) **7**:58, 62, 68, 96, 99-100, 102
"Jestem za blisko" (Szymborska) **44**:269
"The Jester" (Gower) **59**:58
"The Jester" (Hughes) **1**:235; **53**:85
"The Jester, A Ballad" (Bely)
See "Shut, Bellada"
"Jester above It" (Bely)
See "Shut Nad ney"
"Jesu" (Herbert) **4**:100
"The Jesus" (Hughes) **53**:115
"Jesus and Isolt" (Pinsky) **27**:157, 175
"The Jesus Papers" (Sexton) **2**:360
"Jesus Walking" (Sexton) **2**:360-61, 373
"Le jet d'eau" (Baudelaire) **1**:61
"Le jeu de construction" (Éluard) **38**:79
"Jeu sublime" (Péret) **33**:215
"Jeune ménage" (Rimbaud) **57**:183, 219, 253
La jeune parque (Valéry) **9**:346-48, 351-58, 361, 363-67, 369-74, 379-85, 387, 390-96, 401-03
"La jeune prêtre" (Valéry) **9**:391
"Jeunesse" (Rimbaud) **3**:261, 263; **57**:239, 246, 250, 269, 271, 275
"Jew" (Abse) **41**:3, 8
"Jew" (Shapiro) **25**:296-97
"The Jew at Christmas Eve" (Shapiro) **25**:283, 286, 300
"The Jewel" (Wright) **36**:305, 313, 340, 355, 357, 374, 398-99
"The Jeweled Stairs' Grievance" (Li Po) **29**:144
"Jewelled Bindings" (Wylie) **23**:320
"Jewels" (Teasdale) **31**:356
"The Jewish Cemetery at Newport" (Longfellow) **30**:36
"Jewish Emigrant" (Mistral)
See "Emigrada judía"
"The Jewish Problem" (Shapiro) **25**:323
"The Jewish Time Bomb" (Amichai) **38**:51
"Jewish Travel" (Amichai) **38**:50
"J'habite une douleur" (Char) **56**:157
The Jig of Forslin (Aiken) **26**:5-7, 35
The Jig of Forslin: A Symphony (Aiken) **26**:16, 21-2
Jill (Larkin) **21**:225, 232
"Jillain the box" (Piercy) **29**:314
"Jim and Arabel's Sister" (Masters) **1**:328; **36**:175
"Jim at Sixteen" (McKay) **2**:223
"Jim Brown on the Screen" (Baraka) **4**:19
Jim Crow's Last Stand (Hughes) **1**:250, 253; **53**:145, 153
"jimi hendrix" (Alurista) **34**:39
"Jimmy" (Baca) **41**:68
"Jimmy Jet and His TV Set" (Silverstein) **49**:308, 311
"Jin'a jiiai bun" (Yakamochi) **48**:136, 139
Th Jinx Ship nd Othr Trips (Bissett) **14**:14
"Jitterbugs" (Baraka) **4**:12, 18
"Jivan devata" (Tagore) **8**:408
"Jivan madhyahna" (Tagore) **8**:407
"Jiving" (Dove) **6**:114, 117
"The Joachim Quartet" (Bridges) **28**:88
"Joal" (Senghor) **25**:241, 243-44, 246
"Joan and Darby" (Graves) **6**:156
"Joan Miró" (Éluard) **38**:71
"Joan of Arc" (Coleridge) **11**:80, 83, 97
"Joasaph and Fatumeh" (Ekeloef) **23**:67
"Job" (Blake) **12**:38
"A Job for Poetry: Notes on an Impulse" (Curnow) **48**:26
"Job Work" (Riley) **48**:299
"Job's Answer" (Wagoner) **33**:334
Jocelyn: Épisode; Journal trouvé chez un curé de village (Lamartine) **16**:257-61, 263-64, 269-70, 273-74, 286-87, 293, 297
"Jochanan Hakkadosh" (Browning) **2**:75
"Joe Harris" (Birney) **52**:8, 35-37, 39-40
"Joel" (Walker) **20**:278-79
"Joe's Jacket" (O'Hara) **45**:133, 145-47, 154, 193
"Joggin' Erlong" (Dunbar) **5**:145
"Johann" (Walker) **30**:340, 352, 357, 365
"A Johannes Brahms" (Borges) **22**:96
"Johannesburg Mines" (Hughes) **53**:111, 169-70
"John" (Thumboo) **30**:333
"John and Anne" (Meredith) **28**:199, 205
"John Anderson, My Jo" (Burns) **6**:78, 98
"John Barleycorn" (Burns) **6**:52
"John Brown" (Hayden) **6**:192, 195
"John Brown" (Lindsay) **23**:264-65, 275, 279, 286
"John Brown" (Robinson) **1**:468
"John Burke" (Olson) **19**:305
"John Cabanis" (Masters) **36**:230, 233
"John Chapman" (Wilbur) **51**:246, 283-84
"John Coltrane Arrived with An Egyptian Lady" (Mackey) **49**:4
"John Cowper Powys" (Masters) **1**:343
John Deth: A Metaphysical Legend (Aiken) **26**:12, 53
"John Donne in California" (Clampitt) **19**:92
"John Dryden" (Carruth) **10**:74
John Endicott (Longfellow) **30**:73
"John Gilpin" (Cowper)
See "The Diverting History of John Gilpin"
John Gilpin (Cowper)
See "The Diverting History of John Gilpin"
"John Gorham" (Robinson) **1**:462, 468, 478
"John Hancock Otis" (Masters) **36**:171
"John I:4" (Borges)
See "Juan I, 4"
"John I, 4" (Borges)
See "Juan I, 4"
"John L. Sullivan, the Strong Boy of Boston" (Lindsay) **23**:265, 270, 273, 276
"John Maydew; or, The Allotment" (Tomlinson) **17**:326, 341
"John McLean (1879-1923)" (MacDiarmid) **9**:179
John Wesley Harding (Dylan) **37**:49, 61-2
"Johnny Appleseed" (Masters) **1**:330
"Johnny Spain's White Heifer" (Carruth) **10**:74
"Johnny Thomas" (Brown) **55**:73, 156
"Johnson's Cabinet Watched by Ants" (Bly) **39**:9
"Joilet" (Sandburg) **2**:324
"Joke" (Bely)
See "Shutka"
"A Joker" (Baudelaire)
See "Un plaisant"
Jokes to Mislead the Police (Parra)
See *Chistes parra desorientar a la policia*
"La jolie rousse" (Apollinaire) **7**:3, 9, 49
"Jollie Gleeman" (Viereck) **27**:282
"The Jolly Beggars" (Burns) **6**:55-6, 58, 78, 90-6
"The Jolly Company" (Brooke) **24**:58
"Jonah" (Jarrell) **41**:174
"Jonah" (Sarton) **39**:342
"Jonas Keene" (Masters) **36**:171, 182
"Jonathan Edwards" (Lowell) **3**:212
"Jonathan Edwards in Western Massachusettes" (Lowell) **3**:216
"Jonathan Swift Somers" (Masters) **36**:222
"Jones' Private Argument" (Lanier)
See "Jones's Private Argyment"
"Jones's Private Argyment" (Lanier) **50**:107
"Jordan" (Herbert) **4**:102, 107, 113
"Jordan I" (Herbert) **4**:114, 129

"Jordan II" (Herbert) **4**:100, 114
Jorge Luis Borges: Selected Poems 1923-1969 (Borges) **22**:71
Joseffy: An Appreciation (Sandburg) **41**:341
"Joseph" (Forché) **10**:144, 156-57
"Josepha" (Meredith) **60**:308
"Joseph's Coat" (Herbert) **4**:130
"Joshua Tree" (Ammons) **16**:5
"Joue et dors" (Char) **56**:151
"Le joujou du pauvre" (Baudelaire) **1**:58
"Le jour au fond du jour sauvera-t-il . . ." (Bonnefoy) **58**:118
"Jour et nuit" (Césaire) **25**:30
"Journal Night Thoughts" (Ginsberg) **4**:52, 69
"Journal of an Airman" (Auden) **1**:5
Journalism (Mahon) **60**:220
"The Journalist Reader and Writer" (Lermontov) **18**:268-69, 281
Journals: Early Fifties, Early Sixties (Ginsberg) **4**:60, 69
The Journals of Susanna Moodie (Atwood) **8**:10-12, 15, 21, 29, 31, 33, 35-6, 40
"The Journey" (Boland) **58**:6-7, 30-32, 35, 47-48, 51, 68, 70
"The Journey" (Kumin) **15**:198, 203
"Journey" (Millay) **6**:206 **61**:212
"Journey" (Olds) **22**:322
"The Journey" (Wright) **36**:348, 360, 366, 378, 400
The Journey (Boland) **58**:3, 5-7, 11, 15-16, 47-48, 66-67, 80, 87, 96
"The Journey Back" (Heaney) **18**:256
"The Journey Back" (Muir) **49**:198, 200, 221, 296
"Journey for Love" (Dafydd)
See "Taith i Garu"
"Journey Home" (MacLeish) **47**:164
"Journey Home" (Page) **12**:178
"Journey North" (Tu Fu) **9**:332
"The Journey of Life" (Bryant) **20**:10
"Journey of the Magi" (Eliot) **5**:171, 177, 194, 197, 203, 205, 209
Journey to a Known Place (Carruth) **10**:70
"Journey to an Unknown Destination" (Tagore)
See "Niruddesh yatra"
A Journey to Kashima (Matsuo Bashō)
See *Kashima kikō*
Journey to Love (Williams) **7**:371, 403
A Journey to Sarashina (Matsuo Bashō)
See *Sarashina kikō*
"The Journey to the Interior" (Atwood) **8**:36
"Journey to the Interior" (Roethke) **15**:279, 310, 314
"Journey toward Poetry" (Sarton) **39**:323
"Journeys" (Brathwaite) **56**:5, 49
"Journeys and Faces" (Abse) **41**:3
Journeys and Places (Muir) **49**:228-29, 242-43, 246, 270, 278, 288-89
"Jouvence des Névons" (Char) **56**:126
"Jouvert" (Brathwaite) **56**:68, 74-75, 88
"La joven noche" (Borges) **32**:91
"Jóvenes" (Parra) **39**:309
"Joy" (Enzensberger) **28**:142
"Joy" (Jeffers) **17**:106
"Joy" (Levertov) **11**:192
"Joy" (Mueller) **33**:191, 193
"Joy" (Sandburg) **41**:243, 267, 338
"Joy" (Teasdale) **31**:321, 388
"The Joy and Agony of Improvisation" (Carruth) **10**:73
"Joy in Russia" (Bely) **11**:6
The Joy of Shipwrecks (Ungaretti)
See *Allegria di Naufragi*
"The Joy of Writing" (Szymborska) **44**:295, 314-15
"Joy sweetest lifeborn joy" (Bridges) **28**:89
"Joyce Carol Oates Plays the Saturn Piano" (Wakoski) **15**:368
"The Joycentenary Ode" (Mahon) **60**:171
"Joyeuse Garde" (Swinburne) **24**:355
"The Joyful Black Demon of Sister Clara Flies through the Midnight Woods on Her Snowmobile" (Wakoski) **15**:332
"Joys Faces Friends" (Cummings) **5**:110
"The Joys of the Road" (Carman) **34**:201, 206
"Juan Diego" (Alurista) **34**:41
"Juan Figueroa, Casa del Yodo 'Maria Elena,' Antofagasta" (Neruda) **4**:294
"Juan Figueroa, Iodine Factory 'Maria Elena,' Antofagasta" (Neruda)
See "Juan Figueroa, Casa del Yodo 'Maria Elena,' Antofagasta"
"Juan I, 4" (Borges) **22**:75, 96; **32**:58, 92
"Juan's Song" (Bogan) **12**:90, 92, 100
"Jubal" (Eliot) **20**:101, 117, 119-20, 124, 134-37, 144
"Jubilate Agno" (Smart) **13**:339-40, 342-44, 346-48, 350-52, 355, 357-58, 360-69
Jubilation (Tomlinson) **17**:361
"Jubilo" (Tate) **50**:252, 256
"Judas Iscariot" (Cullen) **20**:55-56, 67, 86
"Judas Kiss" (Kinnell) **26**:286-87
"Judería" (Borges) **32**:80
"Judge Somers" (Masters) **36**:230
Judgement Day (Johnson) **24**:128-29, 164-65, 169
"The Judgement of Paris" (Merwin) **45**:19, 26
Judges (Vigny) **26**:368
"Judging Logs" (Wagoner) **33**:352
"The Judgment" (Akhmatova) **2**:15
"Judgment" (Herbert) **4**:129
"Judgment of God" (Morris) **55**:238, 267, 302
"The Judgment of Midas" (Smart) **13**:348
"Judith of Bethulia" (Ransom) **61**:296
"Le Jugement d'Octobre" (Char) **56**:153, 182
"Le Jugement originel" (Éluard) **38**:96
"Juggler" (Wilbur) **51**:208, 219, 242
"Juggling Jerry" (Meredith) **60**:262, 293-94, 328
"Juice Joint: Northern City" (Hughes) **1**:243
"Juke Box Love Song" (Hughes) **53**:124-25
"Julia" (Wordsworth) **4**:399
"Julian and Maddalo" (Shelley) **14**:173, 175, 182, 240
"Julian and the Citizens of Antioch" (Cavafy) **36**:33, 39
"Julian at Nicodemia" (Cavafy) **36**:33
"Julian at the Mysteries" (Cavafy) **36**:39, 54, 58
"Julian M. and A. G. Rochelle" (Brontë) **8**:52
"Julian seeing Negligence" (Cavafy) **36**:33
"Julia's Petticoat" (Herrick) **9**:143
"Julio" (Lermontov)
See "Dzhulio"
"Julius and Ethel" (Dylan) **37**:65
"July" (Belloc) **24**:29
"July 8, 1656" (Bradstreet) **10**:60
"July, 1773" (Berry) **28**:38
"July 1914" (Akhmatova) **55**:36
"July, 1964" (Davie) **29**:124
"July 1968" (Levertov) **11**:194
"July, Against Hunger" (Kumin) **15**:207
"July in Vallombrosa" (Loy) **16**:313
"July in Washington" (Lowell) **3**:214
"July Midnight" (Lowell) **13**:64
"A July Night" (Ekeloef) **23**:58
"Jump to Glory Jane" (Meredith) **60**:262, 293
Jumping Out of Bed (Bly) **39**:70
"Jumping Rope" (Silverstein) **49**:347
"June" (Bryant) **20**:9, 14, 16, 18
"June" (Riley) **48**:315
"June" (Sandburg) **41**:348
"June, 1968" (Borges)
See "Junio, 1968"
"June Dreams in January" (Lanier) **50**:68
"June: Dutch Harbor" (Meredith) **28**:170, 172, 185, 187
"June Light" (Wilbur) **51**:188, 335
"June Night" (Teasdale) **31**:360
"June Thunder" (MacNeice) **61**:115, 117, 119, 137
"Der junge Hebbel" (Benn) **35**:48
"Junge Leiden" (Heine) **25**:139
"The Jungle" (Kavanagh) **33**:95, 118
"The Jungle and the Sea" (Aleixandre) **15**:3, 14
The Jungle Books (Kipling) **3**:162, 185, 188-89
"Jungle Knot" (Ammons) **16**:4
"Jungle Surrender" (Komunyakaa) **51**:28, 41-42
"Das jüngste Gericht" (Rilke) **2**:277
"Junín" (Borges) **32**:61
"Junio, 1968" (Borges) **32**:88
Junjo shokyoku shu (Hagiwara) **18**:176, 182
"Junk" (Wilbur) **51**:198, 202, 204, 209, 217, 222, 268, 273
"The Junk Man" (Sandburg) **41**:338
"Junkie Monkey Reel" (Angelou) **32**:28
"Junkman's Obbligato" (Ferlinghetti) **1**:165-66, 173
"Junta" (Walcott) **46**:286
"Just Don't Never Give Up on Love" (Sanchez) **9**:234, 238, 244
"Just For Starters" (Ashbery) **26**:165
Just Give me a Cool Drink of Water 'fore I Diiie (Angelou) **32**:3, 10-11, 26-7, 29
"Just Like a Woman" (Dylan) **37**:55
"Just like Tom Thumb's Blues" (Dylan) **37**:42-4, 46-9, 54-6
"Just Lost, When I Was Saved!" (Dickinson) **1**:97
"The Just Made Perfect" (Thoreau) **30**:254, 268
"The Just Man And" (Moore) **49**:113, 116
"The Just Remained Upright . . ." (Rimbaud)
See "Le Juste restait droit . . ."
"Just Whistle a Bit" (Dunbar) **5**:137
"Le Juste restait droit . . ." (Rimbaud) **57**:244, 246
"Justice" (Herbert) **4**:102
"Justice" (Hughes) **1**:252; **53**:150
"Justice II" (Herbert) **4**:131
"Justice Denied in Massachusetts" (Millay) **6**:223
"Justice Is Reason Enough" (Wakoski) **15**:336
"The Justice of the Peace" (Belloc) **24**:28
"La justicia por la mano" (Castro) **41**:116
"Juvat ire jugis" (Arnold) **5**:36
"Juveniles" (Stone) **53**:217
Juvenilia (Carducci) **46**:4, 8, 18, 36, 48, 50-52, 64, 69
"Juventudes" (Storni) **33**:262, 294-96;
"K Liciniju" (Pushkin) **10**:408
"K Likomedu, na Skiros" (Brodsky) **9**:5
"K moriu" (Pushkin) **10**:413
"K Muze" (Blok) **21**:6, 40
"K*** Ne dumaj chtob ja byl dostoin sozhalen'ja" (Lermontov) **18**:301, 304
"K pustoi zemle nevol'no pripadaia" (Mandelstam) **14**:155-56
"K smerti" (Akhmatova) **55**:29
K Uranii (Brodsky)
See *To Urania: Selected Poems 1965-1985*
"Ka 'Ba" (Baraka) **4**:18
"Kabekona Lake" (Bly) **39**:45, 60
"Kabi kahini" (Tagore) **8**:405
The Kabir Book (Kabīr) **56**:323
Kabir-granthavalì (Kabīr) **56**:344-46
Kabìr's Sayings (Kabir)
See *Sayings of Kabir*
Kabìr's Words (Kabīr) **56**:342
Kabìr-vanis (Kabir)
See *Sayings of Kabir*
Kabìr-yanìs (Kabir)
See *Sayings of Kabir*
"Lo kabrosh" (Amichai) **38**:51
"Kaddish" (Ginsberg) **4**:49-50, 53, 59, 61, 64-5, 72, 74, 81, 83-6, 91; **47**:16-19, 21-27, 33, 46-47, 49-54, 61-73
Kaddish, and Other Poems (Ginsberg) **4**:47
"Kaeru no shi" (Hagiwara) **18**:168, 179
"Kaeru yo" (Hagiwara) **18**:180
"Kafka and His Precursors" (Borges)
See "Los precursores de Kafka"
"Kafka y sus precursores" (Borges)
See "Los precursores de Kafka"
"Kahara" (Kabīr) **56**:342
Kahini (Tagore) **8**:410
Kai oi (Matsuo Bashō) **3**:24

"Kai, Today" (Snyder) **21**:289
"Kaisarion" (Cavafy) **36**:42, 109-10
"Kak svetoteni muchenik Rembrandt" (Mandelstam) **14**:154
"Kalaloch" (Forché) **10**:133-35, 168
"Kalamzoo" (Lindsay) **23**:270
"Kaleidoscope" (Verlaine) **32**:369
"Kaleidoscopes: Baroque" (Atwood) **8**:11
"Kali" (Clifton) **17**:23
"Kalimpong" (Tagore) **8**:426
"Kally" (Lermontov) **18**:300
"The Kallyope Yell" (Lindsay) **23**:266, 272, 274-76, 280, 284, 289, 296
Kalpana (Tagore) **8**:410-11, 415
Kamen' (Mandelstam) **14**:106, 108, 112-15, 117-18, 122, 135, 142
Kamennyi gost' (Pushkin) **10**:394
Kammený most (Seifert) **47**:335
"Kampfflur" (Stramm) **50**:173, 202
"Kamyk" (Herbert) **50**:4-6
"Kanashi Tsukio" (Hagiwara) **18**:168
Kanashiki gangu (Ishikawa) **10**:195-97, 200-01, 205, 210-11, 217
"Kansas" (Lindsay) **23**:273, 286
"Kansas City" (Harjo) **27**:55, 65, 72
"Kansas City to St. Louis" (Ginsberg) **4**:54, 57
"Kantian Lyrics I" (Tomlinson) **17**:346
"Kanun Blagoveshchen'ia" (Tsvetaeva) **14**:319-20, 322
"Das kapital" (Baraka) **4**:30, 38
"Das Kapitäl" (Rilke) **2**:275
"Kaplan" (Herbert) **50**:7
"Kapuzinerberg (Saltzberg)" (Bogan) **12**:100
"Karamojans" (Walker) **30**:346
Kari o komal (Tagore) **8**:406-7, 415
Kartofa (Mickiewicz)
See "Kartofel"
"Kartofel" (Mickiewicz) **38**:162
Kartofla (Mickiewicz)
See "Kartofel"
"Karyatide" (Benn) **35**:20, 45, 46, 47, 48, 49, 50, 54, 67, 77
Kashima kikō (Matsuo Bashō) **3**:27
Katha (Tagore) **8**:410
"Katharinal" (Heine) **25**:135
"Käthe Kollwitz" (Rukeyser) **12**:228-30
"Die Kathedrale" (Rilke) **2**:275
"Katherine's Dream" (Lowell) **3**:201
"Katun 8 Ahau" (Cardenal) **22**:129, 131
"Katun 11 Ahau" (Cardenal) **22**:128-29
Kavanagh's Weekly (Kavanagh) **33**:95
Kavkazsky plennik (Pushkin) **10**:357-58, 364-65, 371, 386-88, 395, 415-21
"Kay Rutledge" (Masters) **1**:334
"Kayanerenhkowa" (Cardenal) **22**:128-29, 131
"Kazach'ja kolybel'naja pesnja" (Lermontov) **18**:304
"Kazan University" (Yevtushenko) **40**:369
"Keats House" (Stryk) **27**:203
"Kednaminsha" (Kavanagh) **33**:150, 154, 157
"Keen" (Millay) **6**:225
"Keep a Pluggin' Away" (Dunbar) **5**:119
"Keep in a Cool Place" (Curnow) **48**:10-11
"keep on th grass" (Bissett) **14**:33
"Keeper of the Flocks" (Pessoa)
See "O Guardador de Rebanhos"
"The Keepers" (Wagoner) **33**:336
"Keeping Informed in D.C." (Nemerov) **24**:262
"Keeping Their World Large" (Moore) **4**:236, 268; **49**:93
"Kelche" (Benn) **35**:66
"Keller Gegen Dom" (Williams) **7**:378
"Kellyburn Braes" (Burns) **6**:78
"A Kensington Notebook" (Mahon) **60**:196, 199, 214
"Kent and Christendome" (Wyatt) **27**:331
"Kentucky Blues" (Brown) **55**:76, 154
"Kentucky Mountain Farm" (Warren) **37**:275, 286, 288, 319, 329, 331, 333, 354, 376, 378, 380-81
"Kenyon Review, After the Sandstorm" (Bukowski) **18**:15
"Kept" (Bogan) **12**:105, 122
"Kéramos" (Longfellow) **30**:37, 49, 71
"Kerr's Ass" (Kavanagh) **33**:73, 81, 100, 102-3, 119, 147
"The Key of Water" (Paz) **48**:192
"The Key to Everything" (Swenson) **14**:247
"Key West" (Bishop) **34**:123
"Key West: An Island Sheaf" (Crane) **3**:90
Kezfogasok (Illyés) **16**:231, 235
"Khadji Abrek" (Lermontov) **18**:285, 300
"Khalil al-kāfir" (Gibran) **9**:78
"Khansky polon" (Tsvetaeva) **14**:314-15
Khas Granth (Kabīr) **56**:341
Kheya (Tagore) **8**:412-13, 415
"Khristos Voskres" (Pushkin) **10**:411-12
"The Kid" (Aiken) **26**:16, 41-2
"Kid" (Hayden) **6**:196
The Kid (Aiken) **26**:24, 30, 45
"Kid Sleepy" (Hughes) **53**:100
"Kidnapped!" (Silverstein) **49**:313, 334, 344
"The Kids in School with Me" (Hughes) **53**:115
"The Kids Who Die" (Hughes) **1**:243
"Kierkegaard on Hegel" (Zagajewski) **27**:383, 385
"A Kike is the Most Dangerous" (Cummings) **5**:82, 84
"Killala" (Davie) **29**:110
"Killauea" (Kinnell) **26**:286
"Killed at the Ford" (Longfellow) **30**:47
"The Killer and the Dove" (Viereck) **27**:282
"KILLER WHALE" (Bissett) **14**:10-11, 17-18, 34
"Killers" (Sandburg) **41**:235, 238, 269
"Killiecrankie" (Burns) **6**:78
"Killing the Plants" (Kenyon) **57**:45
"Killing the Spring" (Sexton) **2**:365
"Killingworth" (Longfellow) **30**:72
"Kilroy" (Viereck) **27**:263
"Kilroy's Carnival" (Schwartz) **8**:311
Kimako's Story (Jordan) **38**:112
"Kimi Shinitamô koto nakare" (Yosano Akiko) **11**:320-26, 328-29
"Kimon Learchou, Aged 22, Student of Greek Letters (at Cyrene)" (Cavafy)
See "Kimon, Son of Learchos, 22, Student of Greek Literature in Kyrene"
"Kimon, Son of Learchos, 22, Student of Greek Literature in Kyrene" (Cavafy) **36**:89, 109
"Kin" (Sandburg) **41**:228
"Kin to Sorrow" (Millay) **6**:205; **61**:213
"The Kind Ghosts" (Owen) **19**:343
"The Kind Master and Dutiful Servant" (Hammon) **16**:177-78, 180-82, 190
"Kind of an Ode to Duty" (Nash) **21**:272
"A Kind of Ethics" (Gunn) **26**:206
"A Kind of People" (Mahon) **60**:141, 189
The Kind of Poetry I Want (MacDiarmid) **9**:180, 182, 184, 185-86
"Kind Sir: These Woods" (Sexton) **2**:358
Kindai no Guwa (Nishiwaki) **15**:231
"Kindergarten After Thirty Years" (Shvarts)
See "Detskii sad cherez 30 let"
"Kindliness" (Brooke) **24**:56, 77
"Kindness" (Plath) **1**:391, 393
Kindness in the Wolfpasses (Elytis)
See *I kalosíni stis likoporiés*
"Kinds of Wind" (Sarton) **39**:324
"The King" (Kipling) **3**:161, 166
"The King and His Steward's Wife" (Gower) **59**:5, 109
"King Arthur's Men Have Come Again" (Lindsay) **23**:283
"King Arthur's Tomb" (Morris) **55**:238, 240, 257, 264-65, 299-302, 348-49
"King Arthur's Tomb" (Swinburne) **24**:355
"King Ban" (Swinburne) **24**:355
King Bolo (Eliot) **5**:174
"King Claudius" (Cavafy) **36**:39, 40, 53, 54
"King Crow" (Corso) **33**:3
"King Demetrios" (Cavafy)
See "King Demetrius"
"King Demetrius" (Cavafy) **36**:7, 29
"King Edward the Third" (Blake) **12**:11, 61
"King Hamlet's Ghost" (Smith) **12**:311, 353
"King Harald's Trance" (Meredith) **60**:251, 263
"A King in Funeral Procession" (Smith) **12**:315
King Jasper (Robinson) **1**:479, 483; **35**:368
"King Kong Meets Wallace Stevens" (Ondaatje) **28**:327, 333
The King Maiden (Tsvetaeva)
See *Tsar-devitsa*
"King of Carrion" (Hughes) **7**:153
"The King of Denmark's Sons" (Morris) **55**:340
"The King of Harlem" (García Lorca) **3**:139
"The King of Owls" (Erdrich) **52**:192
"King of Swords" (Goodison)
See "Ceremony for the Banishment of the King of Swords"
"The King of the Ditchbacks" (Heaney) **18**:213
The King of the Great Clock Tower (Yeats) **20**:348
"King of the River" (Kunitz) **19**:157-59, 163, 168, 172-73, 175, 180
"The King of Yellow Butterflies" (Lindsay) **23**:281
"King Robert of Sicily" (Longfellow) **30**:25, 62
"King Solomon and the Queen of Sheba" (Lindsay) **23**:264, 280
"King Witlaf's Drinking-Horn" (Longfellow) **30**:27
"The Kingdom" (MacNeice) **61**:133, 141
"The Kingdom of Poetry" (Schwartz) **8**:289, 308-09
"The Kingfisher" (Clampitt) **19**:82, 84
"King-fisher" (Montale) **13**:139
The Kingfisher (Clampitt) **19**:82-3, 85-91, 93
"The Kingfishers" (Olson) **19**:286, 308
"The Kings" (Hope) **56**:266
"The Kings are Gone" (Bukowski) **18**:5
The King's Daughter (Bely) **11**:32
"King's Ransom" (Wylie) **23**:320
"The King's Task" (Kipling) **3**:183
"The King's Treasure-House" (Morris) **55**:306
"Kinsale" (Mahon) **60**:210
"Kinsey Keene" (Masters) **36**:218, 230, 232
"Kinship" (Heaney) **18**:195-96, 204, 210
"Kinship" (Wright) **14**:379
Kiosk (Enzensberger) **28**:166
"The Kirk's Alarm" (Burns) **6**:78
"The Kiss" (Patmore) **59**:269, 271
"The Kiss" (Rossetti) **44**:203-4
"The Kiss" (Sassoon) **12**:262
"The Kiss" (Sexton) **2**:353
"The Kiss" (Tagore)
See "Chumban"
"The Kiss" (Teasdale) **31**:363, 379
"The kiss at Bayreuth" (Gunn) **26**:212
"Kissee Lee" (Walker) **20**:286
"Kisses" (Cassian) **17**:12-13
"Kisses in the Train" (Lawrence) **54**:168
"The Kissing Place" (Szirtes) **51**:159
A Kist of Whistles: New Poems (MacDiarmid) **9**:182
"Kita no umi" (Ishikawa) **10**:213
"The Kitchen" (Carver) **54**:18
"Kitchenette Building" (Brooks) **7**:79
"The Kite" (Elytis) **21**:131
"Kite Flying" (McKay) **2**:223
"The Kites" (Patmore) **59**:204, 231
"Kitty Hawk" (Frost) **1**:213
"Kitty Stobling" (Kavanagh)
See "Come Dance with Kitty Stobling"
Kitty Stobling (Kavanagh)
See *Come Dance with Kitty Stobling*
"Kiwis" (Birney) **52**:79
"KKK" (Guillén) **23**:121
"Klage" (Trakl) **20**:229, 236-37, 244, 250, 255-56, 258
"Klage II" (Trakl) **20**:250-51, 253
"Klarisu yunosha lyubil" (Lermontov) **18**:288
"Klasyk" (Herbert) **50**:5
"Kleenex" (Shapiro) **25**:324
"Kleine Aster" (Benn) **35**:30, 36, 53, 67, 68

"Eine Kleine Nachtmusik" (Jarrell) **41**:169
"Eine Kleine Snailmusik" (Sarton) **39**:345
"Kleiner herbst dämon" (Enzensberger) **28**:140
"Kleitos Illness" (Cavafy)
See "The Sickness of Kleitos"
"Knee-Deep in June" (Riley) **48**:292, 334, 340
"Kneeling Down to Look into a Culvert" (Bly) **39**:100
"The Kneeling One" (Gallagher) **9**:57
"The Knight" (Hughes) **7**:126
"The Knight" (Rich) **5**:370
"The Knight, Death, and the Devil" (Jarrell) **41**:139, 171, 178, 181, 189, 196, 208
"The Knight Fallen on Evil Days" (Wylie) **23**:326
"Knight of the Swan" (Guest) **55**:221
"Knight's" (Chaucer)
See "Knight's Tale"
"Knights of the White Camelia & Deacons of Defense" (Komunyakaa) **51**:32
"Knight's Tale" (Chaucer) **19**:13, 56, 60, 70, 75
"The Knight's to the Mountain" (Scott) **13**:305
"A Knocker" (Herbert)
See "Kolatka"
"The Knocker" (Herbert)
See "Kolatka"
"Knockin' On Heaven's Door" (Dylan) **37**:59, 64
"Knocking Around" (Ashbery) **26**:133
"Knocking Donkey Fleas off a Poet from the Southside of Chi" (Madhubuti) **5**:323, 344
"The Knot" (Kumin) **15**:202
"The Knot" (Kunitz) **19**:176
"Knotted Letter" (Gallagher) **9**:63
"Know Deeply, Know Thyself More Deeply" (Lawrence) **54**:185-87
"The Knowing Heart" (Roethke) **15**:293
"Knowing Rubén Darío" (Aleixandre) **15**:6
"Knowledge" (Bogan) **12**:101, 103, 120
Knowledge, Acquaintance, Resort, Favour with Grace (Skelton) **25**:344-45
"Knox" (Parker) **28**:362
"Knoxville, Tennessee" (Giovanni) **19**:139-41
"Knucks" (Sandburg) **2**:308, 324; **41**:240
"Knut Hamsun in Old Age" (Mahon) **60**:148-49, 180
"Kodachromes of the Island" (Hayden) **6**:183, 193, 196, 198
"Kôgao no shi" (Yosano Akiko) **11**:324-26, 328
"Kogda b v pokornosti neznan'ja" (Lermontov) **18**:302
Kogda razglyaetsya (Pasternak) **6**:266-69, 284-85
"Kogda v mrachneyshey iz stolits" (Akhmatova) **2**:12
"The Koh-i-Noor" (Patmore) **59**:232, 259
"Koi wo koi suru hito" (Hagiwara) **18**:168, 180
"Koide shidō" (Hagiwara) **18**:183
Koigoromo (Yosano Akiko) **11**:306-07
"Kokain" (Benn) **35**:49, 50
"Koker" (Brathwaite) **56**:61
"Kolatka" (Herbert) **50**:8, 38
"Kolbel'naya treskovogo mysa" (Brodsky)
See "A Cape Cod Lullaby"
"Koliaska, zabytaia u magazina" (Shvarts) **50**:153-54
"Komboloi" (Merrill) **28**:256
"Komedyjki" (Szymborska) **44**:308-9
Koncert na ostrově (Seifert) **47**:327-28, 335
"Koncert na vokzale" (Mandelstam) **14**:115, 129
Konec prekrasnoj èpox (Brodsky)
See *Konets prekrasnoy epokhi*
Konets prekrasnoy epokhi (Brodsky) **9**:7
Koniec i poczatek (Szymborska) **44**:302
"the konkreet pome is on its hed" (Bissett) **14**:32
"konkreet vizual" (Bissett) **14**:33-4
Konrad Wallenrod (Mickiewicz) **38**:149, 158, 166-67, 172-77, 184, 191, 194-95
"Kootenay Still Life" (Birney) **52**:27, 58
Köp den blindes sång (Ekeloef) **23**:76
Kora in Hell: Improvisations (Williams) **7**:344, 349, 374-75, 377, 379-81, 383-84, 394, 400, 405, 410
"Kora wo omou uta" (Yakamochi) **48**:101, 131, 133-34, 139
"Kore" (Merwin) **45**:52, 54-5, 87-8
"A Korean Woman Seated by a Wall" (Meredith) **28**:177-78, 190
Körper des Sommers (Elytis) **21**:116
"Korsar" (Lermontov) **18**:299
"Kostroma—Dionysus" (Shvarts) **50**:143
"Kot w pustym mieszkaniu" (Szymborska) **44**:283-94, 306, 308
"Koumfort" (Brathwaite) **56**:70, 97
"The Kraken" (Tennyson) **6**:360, 389, 391, 406-10
"Kral Majales" (Ginsberg) **4**:82, 85
"Krasnopresnenskaya Station" (Momaday) **25**:202
"Krasnyi bychok" (Tsvetaeva) **14**:325
"Krebsbarack" (Benn) **35**:30, 35, 36
"Kreisler" (Sandburg) **41**:321
"Kremlin of Smoke" (Schnackenberg) **45**:335, 346
"Kretische Vase" (Benn) **35**:8, 46, 47
"Krieg" (Stramm) **50**:175, 207, 219
"Krieggrab" (Stramm) **50**:170, 188, 218, 223
"Kronos; To Coachman Kronos" (Goethe)
See "An Schwager Kronos"
"Kropka" (Herbert) **50**:7
Krug (Shvarts) **50**:131
"Krysolov" (Tsvetaeva) **14**:325-26
Kshanikā (Tagore) **8**:411
Księgi narodu polskiego i pielgrzymastwa polskiego (Mickiewicz) **38**:169-70, 180, 186, 194-95
"Kubla Khan" (Coleridge) **11**:41-7, 51, 59, 73, 75-9, 84-8, 90, 104, 107, 110; **39**:118-227
Kubok metelej: Chetviortiia simfoniia (Bely) **11**:3, 6-7, 14-17, 22
"Kubota" (Hongo) **23**:197
"küchenzettel" (Enzensberger) **28**:135, 140
"Kuda mne det'sia v etom Ianvare?" (Mandelstam) **14**:154
"Kudzu" (Dickey) **40**:171-72, 259
Kumārasambhava (Kālidāsa) **22**:178, 180, 182, 185, 188, 191-93, 196-206
"Kung Canto" (Pound) **4**:325
"Kure no kane" (Ishikawa) **10**:214
"Kurkonzert" (Benn) **35**:46
"Kuroi fūkin" (Hagiwara) **18**:178, 182-83
"The Kursaal at Interlaken" (Rich) **5**:359
"Kutir-vasi" (Tagore) **8**:416
"Kutoa Umoja" (Baraka) **4**:26
"Kwa Mamu Zetu Waliotuzaa (for our mothers who gave us birth)" (Sanchez) **9**:215-16, 221, 227, 229, 243
"Kyoko" (Ishikawa) **10**:213
Kyomō no seigi (Hagiwara) **18**:176, 182
Le La (Breton) **15**:54
"A la Ausencia" (Fuertes) **27**:44
"A la Colonne de la Place Vendôme" (Hugo) **17**:88-89
"À la désespérade" (Char) **56**:171
"A la flamme des fouets" (Éluard) **38**:71, 85
"A la luna" (Castro) **41**:81, 84
"A la muerte" (Fuertes) **27**:39, 45
"A la musique" (Rimbaud) **3**:258, 276, 283; **57**:191, 194, 202, 205-6, 210, 241, 245, 289, 294
A la orilla del mundo (Paz) **48**:184, 244
"La: Pen" (Carew)
See "An Elegie on the La: Pen: sent to my Mistresse out of France"
"A la Petra Camara" (Gautier) **18**:125
"A la recherche de l'innocense" (Éluard) **38**:91
"A la recíproca'" (Guillén) **35**:229
A la santé du serpent (Char) **56**:112, 132
"A la sombra te sientas de las desnudas rocas" (Castro) **41**:115
"L.A. to Wichita" (Ginsberg) **4**:54
"A la Virgen de la colina" (Mistral) **32**:174
"L'Abeille, la couleur" (Bonnefoy) **58**:167-68
Laberinto (Jiménez) **7**:200-01, 211
"Labor and Management" (Baraka) **4**:13
"The Laboratory" (Browning) **2**:60; **61**:88
"Laboratory Poem" (Merrill) **28**:241, 243
"The Laboring Skeleton" (Baudelaire)
See "Le squelette laboureur"
"The Labours of Hercules" (Moore) **49**:93
"The Labyrinth" (Muir) **49**:195, 200, 223-4, 228-9, 233-4, 256, 265, 272, 284, 289
Labyrinth (Jiménez)
See *Laberinto*
The Labyrinth (Muir) **49**:198, 213, 224-25, 229, 233, 235, 249, 256, 270, 273, 276-78, 282, 284, 289
"The Labyrinth of Life" (Walker) **20**:294
Labyrinths, with Path of Thunder (Okigbo) **7**:231, 233-35, 241-43, 248-49, 251-52, 254-56
"Le lac" (Lamartine) **16**:265, 268, 271, 276-77, 283, 290, 298, 301-02
"Lace" (Boland) **58**:96-97
"Lachin Y Gair" (Byron) **16**:86
"Lachrymae Christi" (Crane) **3**:82, 96-7, 102
"Lack of Discipline" (Pavese)
See "Indisciplina"
"Lack of Faith" (Pushkin)
See "Bezverie"
"Lackawanna" (Kinnell) **26**:294
"Lackawanna" (Merwin) **45**:45
"Laconic" (Elytis) **21**:116
"Lacrime" (Pasolini) **17**:265
"Ladder of St. Augustine" (Longfellow) **30**:27
Ladera este (Paz) **1**:354, 346, 361-63, 374, 376; **48**:191, 206-7, 211, 214, 264
"The Ladies" (Kipling) **3**:164, 166, 174
Ladies and Gentlemen (Belloc) **24**:27
"Ladies First" (Silverstein) **49**:311, 333
"Ladies' Praise" (Patmore) **59**:219, 240
"The Lads in Their Hundreds" (Housman) **2**:192
"The Lads of the Village" (Smith) **12**:330, 333
"Lady" (Carruth) **10**:74
"Lady Acheson Weary of the Dean" (Swift) **9**:295-96
"The Lady and the Unicorn" (Sarton) **39**:322, 333, 364-65
"Lady Bank Dick" (Wakoski) **15**:363
"Lady Bates" (Jarrell) **41**:139, 154, 171, 177, 191
"Lady Geraldine's Courtship" (Browning) **6**:10, 17-18, 26, 38-9, 42
"Lady Hsi" (Wang Wei) **18**:388-89
"Lady in the Leopard Coat" (Niedecker) **42**:122
"The Lady in the Pink Mustang" (Erdrich) **52**:172, 175
"The Lady in the Shingle" (Glück) **16**:139
"Lady Lazarus" (Plath) **1**:382, 386, 391, 395-97, 400-01, 406-07, 410, 413-14; **37**:196-98, 232-34, 241, 243, 257, 260-61, 268
"Lady Lost" (Ransom) **61**:274, 307, 322
"Lady Luncheon Club" (Angelou) **32**:3
"Lady of Cowrie Palace" (Li Ho) **13**:51-4
Lady of Miracles (Cassian) **17**:13
"The Lady of Shalott" (Swinburne) **24**:357
"The Lady of Shalott" (Tennyson) **6**:350, 358-59, 378, 380, 395, 409-10
"The Lady of the Highest Prime" (Li Po) **29**:164
The Lady of the Lake (Scott) **13**:257-58, 261, 267-68, 270-71, 273, 276-79, 281, 283, 285, 289, 291, 293, 304, 310-11, 319-20
"The Lady of the Land" (Morris) **55**:249, 268, 310
"The Lady of the Well-Spring" (Smith) **12**:304, 306, 329, 341
"Lady reservd by the heav'ns to do pastors company honnor" (Sidney) **32**:235, 247
"A Lady Thinks She Is Thirty" (Nash) **21**:274
"Lady Wentworth" (Longfellow) **30**:62
"The Lady Who Drove Me to the Airport" (Wakoski) **15**:369
"Lady Wife" (Lawrence) **54**:182
"Lady with a Falcon" (Sarton) **39**:325

"Lady's Boogie" (Hughes) **1**:266
"The Lady's Dressing Room" (Swift) **9**:257, 262, 268, 270, 273, 279, 281, 286-89, 291-92, 295, 298-99, 302-03
"A Ladys Lament for her Lover Overseas" (Surrey) **59**:286
"The Lady's Tower" (Ní Chuilleanáin) **34**:349
"Laes Gertrude Hoffman Girls" (Éluard) **38**:71
"Laeti et Errabundi" (Verlaine) **2**:417
"A l'Afrique" (Césaire) **25**:5, 30, 32
"The Lag" (Rich) **5**:363
Lagar (Mistral) **32**:164-66, 170, 176, 179, 182, 185, 187-91
"Il lago di Annecy" (Montale) **13**:138
"Una lágrima" (Storni) **33**:240, 262-63;
"Lai des Deuz Amanz" (Marie de France)
See "Les Dous Amanz"
"Laid in my quyett bedd" (Surrey) **59**:314-15
"Lair" (Pinsky) **27**:153
"Lais" (H. D.) **5**:268
Lais (Marie de France) **22**:246, 254-55, 260-62, 264-65, 268-75, 278, 281, 283-84, 287-88, 300 -303
Les Lais (Villon) **13**:374-75, 377, 387, 396-99, 402, 404-05, 408-10, 412-13
"The Lake" (Lamartine)
See "Le lac"
"The Lake" (Merwin) **45**:45
"The Lake" (Wright) **14**:348, 379
"Lake Boats" (Masters) **1**:330, 333
Lake Effect Country (Ammons) **16**:63
"The Lake Isle of Innisfree" (Yeats) **20**:310
"Lake Mapourika" (Curnow) **48**:29
"The Lake of Gaube" (Swinburne) **24**:312-20, 322, 341, 348
"A Lake Scene" (Swenson) **14**:262
"Lake Superior" (Niedecker) **42**:94, 96-7, 102, 106
"Lake Yi" (Wang Wei) **18**:379
L'Allegria di Naufragi (Ungaretti) **57**:335, 338-39, 342-43, 347, 373, 375, 377
"Lamarck" (Mandelstam) **14**:129
"Lamarck Elaborated" (Wilbur) **51**:188, 237
"The Lamb" (Blake) **12**:7, 9, 32, 62
"Lambert Hutchins" (Masters) **36**:230
"Lambkin: A Fable" (Hope) **56**:266
"The Lambs of Grasmere" (Rossetti) **7**:266
"The Lambs on the Boulder" (Wright) **36**:311
"The Lame Boy and the Fairy" (Lindsay) **23**:281
"The Lament" (Burns) **6**:53
"Lament" (Ginsberg) **47**:71
"Lament" (Hardy) **8**:135
"Lament" (Millay) **6**:211
"Lament" (Plath) **1**:410
"Lament" (Sexton) **2**:350
"Lament" (Thomas) **52**:233, 276, 311, 313, 326-28
"Lament" (Trakl)
See "Klage"
"Lament for Damon" (Milton) **19**:212
"Lament For Glasgerion" (Wylie) **23**:310
Lament for Ignacio Sánchez Mejías (García Lorca)
See *Llanto por Ignacio Sánchez Mejías*
"Lament for My Brother on a Hayrake" (Wright) **36**:335-36, 373
"Lament for Pasiphaé" (Graves) **6**:144
Lament for the Death of a Bullfighter (García Lorca)
See *Llanto por Ignacio Sánchez Mejías*
"Lament for the Makers" (Pinsky) **27**:164
"A Lament for the Martyrs" (Wright) **36**:310
"Lament for the Poles of Buffalo" (Hass) **16**:195, 197
"Lament for Weldon Kees" (Stryk) **27**:204
"Lament for Yin Yao" (Wang Wei) **18**:379
"Lament of a lovesick lizard" (Char)
See "Complainte du lézard amoureux"
"The Lament of Fortinbras" (Herbert)
See "Tren Fortynbrasa"
"Lament of Mary Queen of Scots" (Burns) **6**:78
The Lament of Tasso (Byron) **16**:76
"Lament of the Belle Heaulmiere" (Villon)
See "Les Regrets de la belle Heaulmière"
"Lament of the Drums" (Okigbo) **7**:224, 229-30, 244, 247, 254
"Lament of the Lavender Mist" (Okigbo) **7**:229, 248
"The Lament of the Masks: For W. B. Yeats: 1865-1939" (Okigbo) **7**:230, 245
"Lament of the Silent Sisters" (Okigbo)
See "Silences: Lament of the Silent Sisters"
"Lament over Love" (Hughes) **53**:124
"Lamentationen" (Heine) **25**:131
"Lamentations" (Glück) **16**:151, 154
"Lamentations" (Sassoon) **12**:267, 286
Lamentations (Glück) **16**:129
Lamentations (Jeremiah) **44**:109-61
"The Lamentations of Jeremy, for the most part according to Tremelius" (Donne) **1**:139
"Lamenting the Terms of Modern Praise" (Jackson) **44**:38-9, 55
Lamia, Isabella, The Eve of St. Agnes, and Other Poems (Keats) **1**:276, 279, 281, 296, 307-09, 311
"Lamium" (Glück) **16**:132, 171
"The Lamp" (Teasdale) **31**:335
"The Lamp and the Jar" (Hope) **56**:268, 301
"La lampe du temple" (Lamartine) **16**:292
"Lampfall" (Walcott) **46**:272
The Lamplit Answer (Schnackenberg) **45**:329-31, 335, 339, 342-43, 345-46
"The Lamp's Shrine" (Rossetti) **44**:204
"Lana Turner has Collapsed!" (O'Hara) **45**:145, 162, 243
"Lancelot" (Swinburne) **24**:355
Lancelot (Robinson) **1**:465, 468-70, 489, 491; **35**:362
"Lancer" (Housman) **2**:162
"Land" (Heaney) **18**:201
"The Land" (Kipling) **3**:171
"Land" (Ungaretti)
See "Terra"
"The Land Behind the Wind" (Wagoner) **33**:359
"The Land Betrayed" (Neruda)
See "La arena traicionada"
"Land East of the Sun and West of the Moon" (Morris) **55**:250, 285, 292, 308
"The Land of Dreams" (Blake) **12**:35
"The land of four o'clocks is here" (Niedecker) **42**:140
"The Land of Happy" (Silverstein) **49**:347
"The Land of Silence" (Sarton) **39**:323, 332
The Land of Silence and Other Poems (Sarton) **39**:321, 331, 337, 341-42, 347
Land of the Free—U.S.A. (MacLeish) **47**:148-49, 152, 191, 243, 257
Land of Unlikeness (Graham)
See *Region of Unlikeness*
Land of Unlikeness (Lowell) **3**:199, 202, 213, 216-17, 232
"The Land Where All Is Gained" (Tagore)
See "Sab-peyechhir desh"
"Landcrab II" (Atwood) **8**:43
Landesprcahe (Enzensberger) **28**:133-35, 141, 143, 165
"Landfall" (Wagoner) **33**:356-57
Landfall (Wagoner) **33**:354, 356, 359, 361-62
"Landfall in Unknown Seas" (Curnow) **48**:4, 11, 23
"The Landing" (Tomlinson) **17**:353
"Landing on the Moon" (Swenson) **14**:257
"Landlady, Count the Lawin" (Burns) **6**:81
"The Landlord's Wife" (Chin) **40**:3
"The Landmark" (Rossetti) **44**:173
Landor's Poetry (Pinsky) **27**:153
"Land's End" (MacLeish) **47**:126, 130, 143, 196
"The Landscape" (Masters) **1**:333, 344
"Landscape" (Merton) **10**:349
"Landscape" (Parker) **28**:362
"Landscape" (Parra)
See "Paisaje"
"Landscape" (Sarton) **39**:320
"Landscape after a Battle" (Neruda)
See "Paisaje después de una batalla"
"Landscape as a Nude" (MacLeish) **47**:189, 254
"Landscape for the Disappeared" (Komunyakaa) **51**:34
"Landscape I" (Pavese)
See "Paesaggio I"
"Landscape in Spring" (Soto) **28**:382
"Landscape of a Dead Love" (Storni)
See "Paisaje del amor muerto"
"Landscape of Patagonia" (Mistral)
See "Paisajes de la Patagonia"
"Landscape of the Heart" (Jiménez)
See "Paisaje del corozon"
"Landscape of the Star" (Rich) **5**:362
"Landscape of the Urinating Multitudes (Battery Place Nocturne)" (García Lorca)
See "Paisaje de la multitud que orina"
"Landscape of the Vomiting Multitudes (Coney Island Dusk)" (García Lorca)
See "Paisaje de la multitud que vomita"
"Landscape VI" (Pavese)
See "Paesaggio VI"
"Landscape VII" (Pavese)
See "Paesaggio VII"
Landscape West of Eden (Aiken) **26**:24, 29-30
"Landscape with Figures" (Ammons) **16**:6
"Landscape with Serifs" (Page) **12**:183
"Landscapes" (Eliot) **5**:166, 183
"Landscapes" (Wright) **14**:339, 342-43
Landscapes of Living and Dying (Ferlinghetti) **1**:180-81, 187
"The Lane" (Thomas) **53**:348
"The Lane of the Sky-Blue Waters" (Meredith) **28**:196
"The Lang Coortin" (Carroll) **18**:46
"Le langage des saints" (Péret) **33**:230
"L'Angelot maudit" (Rimbaud) **57**:253
Langour (Storni)
See *Languidez*
"Language" (Ortiz) **17**:231
Language Lattice (Celan)
See *Sprachgitter*
"The Language of Love and Tea with Roasted Almonds" (Amichai) **38**:47
"A Language of New York" (Oppen) **35**:312, 322, 340, 343
"The Language of the Brag" (Olds) **22**:328
language of the land (Enzensberger)
See *Landesprcahe*
"The Language of the Present Moment" (Wright) **36**:311
"Language-Mesh" (Celan)
See "Sprachgitter"
Languidez (Storni) **33**:236-37, 241, 244, 247-48, 252-53, 277-79, 282-83, 297-98, 307;
"L'anguilla" (Montale) **13**:111
"The Lantern" (Merwin) **45**:35
"The Lantern Out of Doors" (Hopkins) **15**:145, 156
L'Anti-Platon (Bonnefoy) **58**:119, 150
"Lanval" (Marie de France) **22**:241-45, 250-51, 254-55, 258, 260, 267-69, 271-72, 275, 282, 294, 29 7, 300-303
"Laocoön Dream Recorded in Diary Dated 1943" (Swenson) **14**:288
"Laodamia" (Wordsworth) **4**:394, 399, 406-07
Laon and Cythna, or the Revolution in the Golden City (Shelley) **14**:162, 169-73, 177, 181, 186-87, 189, 191-93, 213, 216-17, 233-38
"Laostic" (Marie de France)
See "Laüstic"
"Lápida filial" (Mistral) **32**:161
"Lapis Lazuli" (Yeats) **20**:314, 333; **51**:112, 142
"A lápiz" (Guillén) **35**:211
"Un lápiz" (Storni) **33**:240, 262, 295

"Lapraik II" (Burns)
See "Second Epistle to John Lapraik"
"Lapse" (Dunbar) **5**:126
Lara (Byron) **16**:92, 109
"L'Arbre, la lampe" (Bonnefoy) **58**:118, 167-68
"La larga busca" (Borges) **22**:95
"Large Bad Picture" (Bishop) **3**:37, 70-1; **34**:192
"Large Jigsaw Puzzle" (Mueller) **33**:192
"A Large Number" (Szymborska) **44**:269, 271-3, 294, 300, 317
"The Large Starfish" (Bly) **39**:23
Large Testament (Villon)
See *Le Testament*
"The Lark" (Merwin) **45**:95
"The Lark Ascending" (Meredith) **60**:252, 254, 296-97, 332-33
"Larks" (Bridges) **28**:85
"Larme" (Rimbaud) **3**:271; **57**:177
"Lasalle" (Davie) **29**:96
"Lassitude" (Verlaine) **32**:386-87
"Last" (Kipling) **3**:160
"Last Acts" (Olds) **22**:318, 323, 326, 337
Last and Lost Poems of Delmore Schwartz (Schwartz) **8**:311, 319
"The Last Battle" (Parra) **39**:310-11
"Last Before America" (MacNeice) **61**:110
"Last Canto of Childe Harold" (Lamartine)
See "Le dernier chant de pèlerinage de Childe Harold"
"The Last Chantey" (Kipling) **3**:161
"A Last Confession" (Rossetti) **44**:164, 166-67, 176, 202, 246, 261-63
"The Last Contention" (Meredith) **60**:254
"The Last Covenant" (Jackson) **44**:8, 69, 79
"The Last Dane" (Mahon) **60**:132
"The Last Day" (Olds) **22**:33-37
"Last Day in Viet Nam" (Quintana) **36**:272
"The Last Days of Alice" (Tate) **50**:230, 234-35, 242, 257, 280, 289, 301, 306
The Last Ditch (MacNeice) **61**:138, 141
"The Last Drunk" (Wright) **36**:308
"The Last Duchess" (Browning) **2**:30
The Last Epiphany (Aleixandre)
See *Nacimiento último*
Last Foray in Lithuania (Mickiewicz)
See *Pan Tadeusz; czyli, Ostatni zajazd na Litwie*
"The Last Gangster" (Corso) **33**:41
"Last Harmony" (Lawrence) **54**:235
The Last Harvest (Tagore)
See *Chaitāli*
"The Last Hiding Places of Snow" (Kinnell) **26**:259, 271-72
"Last Hill in a Vista" (Bogan) **12**:104
"The Last Instructions to a Painter" (Marvell) **10**:275
"The Last Invocation" (Whitman) **3**:378
"Last Kiss" (Olds) **22**:321
"The Last Laugh" (Owen) **19**:366
"The Last Laugh" (Warren) **37**:340
"Last Letter" (Glück) **16**:164-65
"Last Lines" (Brontë) **8**:59
"Last Load" (Hughes) **7**:166
"Last Looks at the Lilacs" (Stevens) **6**:292
The Last Lunar Baedeker (Loy) **16**:330, 333
"The Last Man" (Gunn) **26**:203
"The Last Meeting" (Sassoon) **12**:262
"The Last Metaphor" (Warren) **37**:319, 331
"The Last Mowing" (Frost) **1**:206
"The Last Mummer" (Heaney) **18**:201
"Last Night I Drove a Car" (Corso) **33**:6, 43
The Last Night of the Earth Poems (Bukowski) **18**:16, 19
"Last Night Train" (Book-Senninger) **37**:379
Last Octave (Tagore)
See *Shesh saptak*
"The Last of Saturdays" (Elytis) **21**:135
"The Last of the Fire Kings" (Mahon) **60**:135, 139, 152, 183-84, 193-94, 210-11, 214, 235
"The Last of the Flock" (Wordsworth) **4**:373, 415, 418
"The Last One" (Merwin) **45**:9, 21-2, 42, 45, 49, 64-66
"The Last Oracle" (Swinburne) **24**:320, 347
"The Last People" (Merwin) **45**:37-8
"Last Poems" (Tagore)
See "Śesh lekhā"
"Last Poems" (Yeats) **51**:152
Last Poems (Browning) **6**:23-4, 38, 40
Last Poems (Celan) **10**:120
Last Poems (Housman) **2**:161-67, 173-76, 180-81, 186, 191, 196, 199-201
Last Poems (Lawrence) **54**:171, 173, 195, 197-203, 214, 218, 226-27, 232, 249-50
Last Poems (Yeats) **20**:307, 311, 314, 332
"Last Poems: XX— The Night Is Freezing Fast" (Housman) **2**:196
The Last Poems of Elinor Wylie (Wylie) **23**:321
"Last Prelude" (Teasdale) **31**:380
"The Last Quatrain of the Ballad of Emmett Till" (Brooks) **7**:62
"The Last Question" (Parker) **28**:362
The Last Remains of Sir John Suckling (Suckling) **30**:125-26
The Last Remains Remains (Suckling)
See *The Last Remains of Sir John Suckling*
"The Last Rhyme of True Thomas" (Kipling) **3**:181-82
"The Last Ride of Wild Bill" (Brown) **55**:80, 113, 118, 120, 122
The Last Ride of Wild Bill and Eleven Narrative Poems (Brown) **55**:111, 114, 116-17, 121, 157
"The Last Ride Together" (Browning) **2**:75
"The Last River" (Kinnell) **26**:255, 257, 262, 290, 293
The Last Septet (Tagore)
See *Shesh saptak*
"The Last Signal" (Hardy) **8**:131
Last Song (Harjo) **27**:59, 64
"The Last Song of Lucifer" (Lindsay) **23**:284
Last Songs From Vagabondia (Carman) **34**:205, 218, 220-21
Last Songs of Vagabondia (Carman)
See *Last Songs From Vagabondia*
"Last Stop" (Cavafy) **36**:111
"Last Supper" (Wylie) **23**:303, 308, 310
"The Last Suttee" (Kipling) **3**:183
"The Last Tournament" (Tennyson) **6**:376
"Last Tree" (Mistral)
See "Ultimo árbol"
"The Last Turn of the Screw" (Smith) **12**:295
Last Volume (Swift) **9**:255
The Last Voyage (Noyes) **27**:133
"Last Walk of Season" (Warren) **37**:367, 378
"The Last War" (Muir) **49**:257-58, 284, 300
"The Last Warmth of Arnold" (Corso) **33**:25, 39-40
"The Last Will" (Herbert) **50**:24
"The Last Word" (Tagore)
See "Shesh katha"
"Last Words" (Olds) **22**:324
"Last Words" (Plath) **1**:396, 407
"Last Words of the Dying Recruit" (McKay) **2**:226
"Last Words of the Human Fly" (Wagoner) **33**:334
"Last Words to Miriam" (Lawrence) **54**:175
"Lastness" (Kinnell) **26**:252, 274-75
"Late" (Bogan) **12**:122
"Late" (Olds) **22**:318
"Late a Night During a Visit of Friends" (Bly) **39**:7
"Late Abed" (MacLeish) **47**:197, 207
"Late Afternoon in Manzanilla" (Birney) **52**:22, 99
Late Arrival on Earth (Ekeloef) **23**:66, 85, 88-90
"A Late Aubade" (Wilbur) **51**:215
"Late August" (Atwood) **8**:28-9, 42
"Late August Letter" (Hacker) **47**:88
"Late Beethoven" (Zagajewski) **27**:384-85
"Late Echo" (Ashbery) **26**:140
"Late Feast" (Zagajewski) **27**:395
"Late Fragment" (Carver) **54**:19, 24
"Late Hours" (Mueller) **33**:193
"Late Last Night" (Hughes) **1**:243
Late Lyrics and Earlier with Many Other Verses (Hardy) **8**:89, 123
"Late Moon" (Bly) **39**:87
"Late Movies With Skyler" (Ondaatje) **28**:338
"Late November in a Field" (Wright) **36**:345, 357
"Late Poem to My Father" (Olds) **22**:324
Late Settings (Merrill) **28**:266-68, 281
"The Late Snow & Lumber Strike of the Summer of Fifty-four" (Snyder) **21**:322
"Late Spring" (Hass) **16**:216, 222
"Late Spring Evening" (Bridges) **28**:85
"Late Subterfuge" (Warren) **37**:331
"Lately, Alas, I Knew A Gentle Boy" (Thoreau) **30**:203, 216, 251, 270
"Lately, at Night" (Kumin) **15**:200
"A Later Alexandrian" (Meredith) **60**:252
"Later Life" (Rossetti) **7**:278
Later Poems (Bridges) **28**:65
Later Poems (Carman) **34**:230
The Later Poems of John Clare 1837-1864 (Clare) **23**:46
"Latest Face" (Larkin) **21**:236
"The Latest Hotel Guest Walks over Particles That Revolve in Seven Other Dimensions Controlling Latticed Space" (Stone) **53**:235-36
"Latin America" (Dalton) **36**:125
"latin and soul" (Cruz) **37**:11
"The Latin Lesson" (Boland) **58**:47
"Lauda" (Milosz) **8**:201
"Lauda" (Paz) **1**:361
"The Laugh" (Graves) **6**:156
"The Laughers" (Francis) **34**:244
"Laughers" (Hughes)
See "My People"
"Laughing Corn" (Sandburg) **2**:316; **41**:241, 286, 326
"Laughing Gas" (Ginsberg) **4**:74, 81; **47**:22
Laughing Lost in the Mountains: Poems of Wang Wei (Wang Wei) **18**:391
"The Laughing Song" (Blake) **12**:4, 7, 23
"Laughing with One Eye" (Schnackenberg) **45**:329
"Laughter in the Senate" (Lanier) **50**:107-8
"Launcelot and Elaine" (Masters)
See "The Ballad of Launcelot and Elaine"
"Laundromat" (Niedecker) **42**:109
"Laura and Francisca" (Jackson) **44**:7, 11
"The Laureate" (Graves) **6**:142, 144
"Laus Veneris" (Swinburne) **24**:308, 360-61
Laus Veneris, and Other Poems and Ballads (Swinburne)
See *Poems and Ballads*
"Lausanne" (Mickiewicz) **38**:215
"Laüstic" (Marie de France) **22**:237, 258, 260, 264-66, 269-72, 301
"Lava" (Kinnell) **26**:260
"Lava" (Zagajewski) **27**:387
"Lava Cameo" (Boland) **58**:100
"Laval, Pomeret, Petain" (Niedecker) **42**:140
"The Lavender Woman-A Market Song" (Reese) **29**:329
"Laventille" (Walcott) **46**:284-85
"Lavorare stanca" (Pavese) **13**:203, 213, 225-27
Lavorare stanca (Pavese) **13**:201-02, 204-05, 210-14, 216-19, 222, 224-26, 228
"Law" (Lowell) **3**:214
"The Law for George" (Brown) **55**:164
"The Law I Love Is Major Mover" (Duncan) **2**:124
"Lawn Design" (Wagoner) **33**:365, 367
"A lawnmower's one of the babies" (Niedecker) **42**:151
"The Laws of God, the Laws of Man" (Housman) **2**:162, 179
The Lawyers Know Too Much (Sandburg) **41**:277

"Lay Down Your Weary Tune" (Dylan) **37**:65-6
"Lay le Freyne" (Marie de France)
See "Le Fraisne"
"Lay of Guigemar" (Marie de France) **22**:239-45, 258, 263-66, 268-76, 278, 293-94, 301
The Lay of the Last Minstrel (Scott) **13**:246, 248-51, 256, 258, 266, 269, 271, 273, 274-76, 279-83, 285, 303, 311-12, 315, 317-18
"The Layers" (Kunitz) **19**:180-81
Laying Down the Tower (Piercy) **29**:323, 327
"Laying the Dust" (Levertov) **11**:165
Lays (Marie de France)
See *Lais*
Lays of Twilight (Hugo) **17**:44
"Lazarillo and the Beggar" (Aleixandre) **15**:4, 6
"Lazarus" (Robinson) **1**:468
"Lazarus" (Sarton) **39**:341
"Lazarus's place" (Guillén) **35**:221-22
"Lead Soldiers" (Lowell) **13**:78
"The Leaden Echo and the Golden Echo" (Hopkins) **15**:130-31, 143-44, 161
"The Leaden-Eyed" (Lindsay) **23**:268, 276, 281, 296
"The Leader" (Belloc) **24**:11
"The Leaders" (Brooks) **7**:63, 90
"The Leaders of the Crowd" (Yeats) **51**:75
"A Leaf" (Curnow) **48**:9-10
"The Leaf" (Warren) **37**:353-55, 360, 362
"The Leaf-House" (Dafydd)
See "Y Deildy"
"A Leaf Treader" (Frost) **39**:232
"Leaflets" (Rich) **5**:396
Leaflets: Poems, 1965-1968 (Rich) **5**:357, 365, 370-72, 383, 388-89, 396, 399
"A Lean and Hungry Look" (Nemerov) **24**:291
"The Leap" (Dickey) **40**:158, 226, 258
"Leaping Falls" (Kinnell) **26**:238
"Lear Is Gay" (Hayden) **6**:187
"The Lea-Rig" (Burns) **6**:82
"The Learned Men" (MacLeish) **47**:197
"Learning a Dead Language" (Merwin) **45**:4, 1, 13-14, 24
"Learning About Water" (Sarton) **39**:328, 339
"Learning By Doing" (Nemerov) **24**:270
"Learning the Trees" (Nemerov) **24**:285
"Learning to Read" (Harper) **21**:192, 198, 200, 213
"Learning to Write" (Lorde) **12**:136
"The Least of Love" (Carman) **34**:226
"Leather Jacket" (Page) **12**:172
"Leather Leggings" (Sandburg) **2**:302; **41**:240, 270
"Leave" (Jarrell) **41**:155
"Leave me, O Love, which reaches but to dust" (Sidney) **32**:239
"Leaves" (Mahon) **60**:140, 167, 211-12
"Leaves before the Wind" (Sarton) **39**:324
"Leaves Compared with Flowers" (Frost) **39**:233
"Leaves of a Magazine" (Moore) **49**:109
Leaves of Grass (Whitman) **3**:370, 378-79, 382, 384, 386-87, 389, 397-99, 401, 404-08, 410-14, 416-17
Leaves of Hypnos (Char)
See *Feuillets d'Hypnos*
The Leaves of the Tree (Sarton) **39**:335, 337
"Leave-taking Near Shoku" (Pound) **4**:331
"Leave to the Wind" (Char)
See "Congé au vent"
"Leaving" (Song) **21**:333, 335, 342-43
"Leaving" (Wilbur) **51**:249-50, 274
"Leaving Barbados" (Kenyon) **57**:40, 45
"Leaving Barra" (MacNeice) **61**:135, 137
"Leaving Early" (Plath) **37**:254
"Leaving L'Atelier-Aix-en-Provence" (Rexroth) **20**:196
"Leaving Modernity" (Guest) **55**:196, 199
"Leaving New York with Harry" (Stone) **53**:224
"Leaving the Atocha Station" (Ashbery) **26**:113
"Leaving the Door Open" (Ignatow) **34**:334
Leaving the Door Open (Ignatow) **34**:324-25, 327, 332
"Leaving the Temple at Nimes" (Wright) **36**:387
"Leaving Town" (Kenyon) **57**:39
"LEBANON VOICES" (Bissett) **14**:32
lebanon voices (Bissett) **14**:2
Lebediny stan (Tsvetaeva) **14**:313-14
"lebenslanf" (Enzensberger) **28**:135
"Lebenslauf" (Hölderlin) **4**:147
"L'Eclair" (Rimbaud) **57**:191, 195, 243
"L'Eclatante victoire de Sarrebruck" (Rimbaud) **57**:203, 205, 253
"Lectura" (Guillén) **35**:175
"Lecture" (Milosz) **8**:200
"Lecture I" (Milosz) **8**:202
"Lecture IV" (Milosz) **8**:203
"Lecture VI" (Milosz) **8**:199
"Lecture VII" (Milosz) **8**:202
"Lecture on Commitment" (Cage) **58**:205
"Lecture on Mystery" (Zagajewski) **27**:400
"Lecture on Nothing" (Cage) **58**:219
"Lecture on the Weather" (Cage) **58**:188, 212-13, 215
"A Lecture upon the Shadow" (Donne) **1**:135, 145, 147
"Leda and the Swan" (Montale) **13**:150
"Leda and the Swan" (Yeats) **20**:315, 319; **51**:74
Lee: A Dramatic Poem (Masters) **1**:339
"Leech Gatherer" (Wordsworth) **4**:390, 394
"Leffingwell" (Robinson) **1**:466
"Left Behind" (Lowell) **13**:97
"The Leg" (Shapiro) **25**:268, 288, 297, 300-301
"Legacies" (Browning) **6**:16
"Legacies" (Giovanni) **19**:111
"Legacies" (Mahon) **60**:133
"Legacy" (Harjo) **27**:71
"A Legacy" (Quintana) **36**:257
"The Legal System" (Hogan) **35**:257
"Legend" (Crane) **3**:101
"Legend" (Wright) **14**:338
Legend (Chaucer)
See *Legend of Good Women*
Legend (Longfellow)
See *The Golden Legend*
"The Legend Beautiful" (Longfellow) **30**:62
Legend of Good Women (Chaucer) **19**:7, 10, 21, 23-4, 34, 60, 64, 74; **58**:295
The Legend of Jubal, and Other Poems (Eliot) **20**:116, 123, 125, 131-32
"A Legend of Porcelain" (Lowell) **13**:61, 65
The Legend of the Centuries (Hugo)
See *La légende des siècles*
"Legende" (Celan) **10**:126
"Lègende" (Laforgue) **14**:74
La légende des siècles (Hugo) **17**:49, 54-57, 60-61, 65, 68, 78, 80, 83-86, 89, 91
Legende of Good Women (Chaucer)
See *Legend of Good Women*
"Légende théologique" (Gautier) **18**:162
"Legender" (Ekeloef) **23**:69, 71
Legends (Lowell) **13**:60-3, 65, 74, 83, 93
"Legends and Dirges" (Ekeloef) **23**:69
"La Leggenda di Teodorico" (Carducci) **46**:52
"The Legion Club" (Swift) **9**:281
"The Legions of Caesar" (Wright) **36**:310
"The Legs" (Graves) **6**:151
"Leisure" (Teasdale) **31**:328, 371
"The Leisure of the Theory Class" (Howe) **54**:150
"Lemonade" (Carver) **54**:18, 28
"The Lemons" (Montale) **13**:149
"Lemons" (Walcott) **46**:289
"Lemuel's Blessing" (Merwin) **45**:33-4, 72-3, 82, 85
"Lengas dai frus di sera" (Pasolini) **17**:256
"Lenore" (Poe) **1**:434, 438, 445; **54**:260, 311
"Lenox Avenue: Midnight" (Hughes) **1**:265; **53**:101
"Lent" (Herbert) **4**:100
"The Lent Lily" (Housman) **2**:184, 192
"L'Entaile" (Bonnefoy) **58**:136
"Lenteur de l'avenir" (Char) **56**:137
"L'Envoi" (Morris) **55**:253
"Leon" (Cardenal) **22**:110
"Leonainie" (Riley) **48**:283, 287
"A Leone Traverso" (Montale) **13**:139
"Léonides" (Char) **56**:149
"Leonine Elegiacs" (Tennyson) **6**:385-86
"The Leopard" (Brathwaite) **56**:64
"Lepanto" (Chesterton) **28**:94, 99-100, 108, 125, 128-30
"L'Epars, l'indivisible" (Bonnefoy) **58**:168
"L'epaule" (Bonnefoy) **58**:118-19
"The Leper" (Swinburne) **24**:307, 337
"Lepidopterist" (Goodison) **36**:143
"Lerici" (Gunn) **26**:218
"leroy" (Baraka) **4**:19, 23
The Lesbians (Baudelaire)
See *Les fleurs du mal*
Les Lesbiennes (Baudelaire)
See *Les fleurs du mal*
"Lesbos" (Plath) **1**:394; **37**:256, 269
"L'Esprit" (Rimbaud) **57**:246
"The Less Deceived" (Larkin) **21**:222
The Less Deceived (Larkin) **21**:224, 226-27, 230, 233, 235, 251-52, 255, 256, 259
Lesser Testament (Villon)
See *Les Lais*
"The Lesson" (Levertov) **11**:167
"The Lesson" (Lowell) **3**:211
"A Lesson in Geography" (Rexroth) **20**:215
"Lessons" (Teasdale) **31**:355
"Lestnitsa" (Tsvetaeva)
See "Poèma lestnitsy"
"Lestrygonians" (Boland) **58**:20
"Let Evening Come" (Kenyon) **57**:31-33, 37
Let Evening Come (Kenyon) **57**:5-6, 11, 19, 23, 36, 38, 40-41, 45
"Let It Be Forgotten" (Teasdale) **31**:323, 335, 357
"Let Koras and Balafong Accompany Me" (Senghor)
See "Que m'accompagnent Kôras et Balafong"
"Let Me Begin Again" (Levine) **22**:219, 225
"Let Me Enjoy" (Hardy) **8**:98
"Let me go, Voronezh . . ." (Mandelstam)
See "Pusti menia, Voronezh . . ."
"Let Me Live with Marriage" (Jordan) **38**:119, 122
"let me tell yu a story of how they met" (Bissett) **14**:17
"Let My People Go" (Johnson) **24**:128-29, 139, 144, 166, 169
"Let No Charitable Hope" (Wylie) **23**:314, 323-24, 333-34
"Let not Love go to" (Noyes) **27**:134
"Let Pure Hate Still Underprop" (Thoreau) **30**:180, 192, 203, 247, 265, 273, 293
"Let Something Good Be Said" (Riley) **48**:304
"Let the Light Enter! The Dying Words of Goethe" (Harper) **21**:210
"Let There be Light" (Lawrence) **54**:249
Let Us Be Great (Yevtushenko) **40**:344
"Let us gather at the river" (Piercy) **29**:303, 315
"Let Us Prepare" (Swenson) **14**:268
"Let Yourself Be Sidetracked by Your Güiro" (Alurista) **34**:23
"Letanía de los montes de la vida" (Fuertes) **27**:39
"Letanía de nuestro Señor Don Quijote" (Darío) **15**:96
"Letanías de la tierra muerts" (Storni) **33**:254;
"Leter 20: not a pastoral letter" (Olson) **19**:274
"L'Eternité" (Rimbaud) **57**:250
"Léthé" (Baudelaire) **1**:72
"Le lethe" (Baudelaire)
See "Léthé"
"Lethe" (H. D.) **5**:287, 304
"Lethe" (Yamada) **44**:351
"L'Étoile a pleuré rose" (Rimbaud) **57**:174
"Let's Beat Down the Poor" (Baudelaire)
See "Assommons les pauvres"
"Let's, from Some Loud Unworld's Most Rightful Wrong" (Cummings) **5**:109

"A Letter" (Berry) **28**:6
"A Letter" (Bogan) **12**:95, 127
"Letter" (Hass) **16**:196
"The Letter" (Kenyon) **57**:6, 42
"Letter" (Montale)
See "Lettera"
"The Letter" (Owen) **19**:347, 363-65
"Letter 2" (Olson) **19**:277, 281-82
"Letter 3" (Olson) **19**:273, 280, 282, 284
Letter 3 (Brutus) **24**:106, 115
"Letter 4" (Olson) **19**:283
"Letter 5" (Brutus) **24**:101, 106
"Letter 5" (Olson) **19**:266, 271, 282-83
"Letter 6" (Olson) **19**:280, 282-83
Letter 6 (Brutus) **24**:115
Letter 7 (Brutus) **24**:115
"Letter 8" (Olson) **19**:280, 283
"Letter 9" (Olson) **19**:267, 281, 283-84
Letter 9 (Brutus) **24**:115
"Letter 10" (Brutus) **24**:115
"Letter 10" (Olson) **19**:267, 281, 283-84
"Letter 11" (Olson) **19**:296
Letter 13 (Brutus) **24**:99, 106, 115
"Letter 14" (Brutus) **24**:100
"Letter 14" (Olson) **19**:273
"Letter 15" (Olson) **19**:277
"Letter 16" (Brutus) **24**:101
Letter 17 (Brutus) **24**:106, 115
"Letter for Jan" (Lorde) **12**:152
"Letter for Melville" (Olson) **19**:297
"Letter from a Coward to a Hero" (Warren) **37**:277, 284, 289, 321, 332
"Letter from Chicago for Virginia Woolf" (Sarton) **39**:329
"Letter from Costa Brava" (Tomlinson) **17**:315
"A Letter from Gussie" (Merwin) **45**:24
"A Letter from Li Po" (Aiken) **26**:45, 56-7
A Letter from Li Po, and Other Poems (Aiken) **26**:24, 29-30
"Letter from New York" (Mahon) **60**:218
"Letter from Our Man in Blossomtime" (Glück) **16**:124
"A Letter from Phillis Wheatley" (Hayden) **6**:189, 192, 195
"Letter from Prague, 1968-78" (Forché) **10**:144, 156, 168-69
"A Letter from Rome" (Hope) **56**:278, 302-3
"Letter from the End of the World" (Mueller) **33**:198
"Letter from the Line" (Hope) **56**:295-96
"Letter from the North" (Bukowski) **18**:4
"A Letter Home" (Sassoon) **12**:262
"Letter I" (Olson) **19**:282, 284
"A Letter in a Bottle" (Brodsky) **9**:3, 4
"Letter, May 2, 1959" (Olson) **19**:306
"Letter Number Forty-One" (Olson) **19**:306
"Letter of a Mother" (Warren) **37**:320, 331
"Letter of Advice to a Young Poet" (Swift) **9**:272
"Letter of Recommendation" (Amichai) **38**:46
"Letter of Testimony" (Paz) **48**:273, 275
"Letter of the Seer" (Rimbaud)
See "Lettre du voyant"
"Letter on August 15" (Hacker) **47**:86
"Letter Perfect Is Not Perfect" (Moore) **49**:134
"Letter Sycorax" (Brathwaite) **56**:61
"Letter to a Bourgeois Friend Whom Once I Loved (and Maybe Still Do If Love Is Valid)" (Giovanni) **19**:115
"A Letter to a Brother of the Pen in Tribulation" (Behn) **13**:7, 30
"Letter to a Conceivable Great-Grandson" (Birney) **52**:28
"Letter to a Cuzco Priest" (Birney) **52**:41-42, 99
"Letter to a Friend" (Warren) **37**:288
"Letter to a Friend" (Wright) **14**:336, 338
"Letter to a Psychiatrist" (Sarton) **39**:340
"Letter to a Wound" (Auden) **1**:22
"Letter to a Wound" (Hacker) **47**:107
"A Letter to Alex Comfort" (Abse) **41**:11, 16, 18
"A Letter to An Aspiring Junkie" (Angelou) **32**:28
"Letter to an Indian Friend" (Sarton) **39**:322-23, 332
"Letter to Ann Landers" (Ondaatje) **28**:328
"A Letter to Basil" (Brutus) **24**:106, 108
"Letter to Bob Kaufman" (Komunyakaa) **51**:34
"Letter to California" (Mueller) **33**:191
"A Letter to Dafnis April: 2nd 1685" (Finch) **21**:165
"A Letter to Dr. Martin Luther King" (Sanchez) **9**:244
"A Letter to Franz Wright" (Wright) **36**:311-12, 366
"Letter to G.N. from Wrest" (Carew) **29**:7-8, 11, 41-43, 46-48
"Letter to Graham and Anna" (MacNeice) **61**:124, 135
"Letter to Her" (Bly) **39**:103
"A Letter to Her Husband, Absent upon Public Employment" (Bradstreet) **10**:8, 28, 30, 34, 40, 65
"Letter to Hona" (Cisneros) **52**:161
"A Letter to James Stephens" (Sarton) **39**:320-21, 335, 348
"Letter to Jean-Paul Baudot, at Christmas" (Stryk) **27**:182, 196, 200, 202, 204-5, 215, 218
"Letter to John Franco—Venice" (Cisneros) **52**:154, 161
"Letter to León Felipe" (Paz) **48**:273
"Letter to Lord Byron" (MacNeice) **61**:123
Letter to Lord Byron (Auden) **1**:22, 34
A Letter to Lucian and Other Poems (Noyes) **27**:135
"A Letter to Lucian the Sceptic Dated from the Island of Cos in the year AD 165" (Noyes) **27**:136
"Letter to Maxine Sullivan" (Carruth) **10**:87
"Letter to Miguel Otero Silva, in Caracas, 1948" (Neruda)
See "Carta a Miguel Otero Silva, en Caracas, 1948"
"A Letter to my Aunt Discussing the Correct Approach to Modern Poetry" (Thomas) **52**:263
"Letter to My Father from 40,000 Feet" (Olds) **22**:324-25
"A Letter to My Friends" (Merton) **10**:346-47
"Letter to No One" (Cervantes) **35**:135
"A Letter to Sara Hutchinson" (Coleridge) **11**:69-72, 91
"Letter to the Academy" (Hughes) **53**:110, 115
"Letter to the Countesse of Huntingdon" (Donne) **1**:130
"Letter to the Front" (Rukeyser) **12**:228, 231-34
"Letter to the Local Police" (Jordan) **38**:117
"A Letter to the Same Person" (Finch) **21**:160, 164
"Letter to V-" (Wylie) **23**:324
"Letter to Vincent Van Gogh" (Goodison) **36**:158
"A Letter to William Carlos Williams" (Rexroth) **20**:193
"Letter Written during a January Northeaster" (Sexton) **2**:351
"Letter Written on a Ferry Crossing Long Island Sound" (Sexton) **2**:351, 361
"Lettera" (Montale) **13**:161
"Lettera" (Quasimodo) **47**:285
"Lettera amorosa" (Char) **56**:110, 115-16, 169
"Letters" (Cassian) **17**:5
Letters (Duncan) **2**:106
Letters (Ovid)
See *Heroides*
Letters (Riley) **48**:343
"Letters and Other Worlds" (Ondaatje) **28**:315-16, 327, 329, 331
"Letters for the Dead" (Levine) **22**:220, 223
"Letters from a Land of Sinners" (Rich) **5**:354
Letters from a Traveller's Pannier (Matsuo Bashō)
See *Oi no obumi*
Letters from Iceland (Auden) **1**:9, 13
Letters from Iceland (MacNeice) **61**:181
"Letters from Maine" (Sarton) **39**:361, 369
Letters from Maine (Sarton) **39**:361-62, 368-69
"Letters from the Island" (Cruz) **37**:31
"Letters from the Ming Dynasty" (Brodsky) **9**:29
"Letters from the Poet Who Sleeps in a Chair" (Parra) **39**:308-10
The Letters of Carl Sandburg (Sandburg) **41**:351
"Letters of the Dead" (Szymborska) **44**:279
Letters of the Heroines (Ovid)
See *Heroides*
"Letters to a Cuzco Priest" (Birney) **52**:16
"Letters to Dead Imagists" (Sandburg) **41**:360
Letters to Martha and Other Poems from a South African Prison (Brutus) **24**:99-100, 102, 104-09, 112, 114-15, 118-20
Letters to Martha II (Brutus) **24**:100
"Letters to the Egyptian" (Goodison) **36**:143
"Lettre" (Verlaine) **32**:351, 390, 392, 394
"Lettre à une femme" (Hugo) **17**:100
"Lettre du voyant" (Rimbaud) **57**:211-13, 216, 283-85
Lettre du voyant (Rimbaud) **57**:232
"Lettre-Océan" (Apollinaire) **7**:18, 25-9, 32, 34-7
"Lettres de l'Hivernage" (Senghor) **25**:232-33, 235, 247-51
"lettrs (for a passing comet)" (Bissett) **14**:20
Letzte Gedichte und Gedanken (Heine) **25**:172
"Letzter Abend" (Rilke) **2**:267
"Letzter Frühling" (Benn) **35**:71
Leurs yeux toujours purs (Éluard) **38**:71
"Levántate y Rie" (Alurista) **34**:46
"Levedad" (Jiménez) **7**:201
"The Levee: Letter to No One" (Cervantes) **35**:133, 134
"The Level at Which Sky Began" (Soto) **28**:370, 378
"Le Lever du soleil" (Breton) **15**:48
Levia gravia (Carducci) **46**:4, 8, 11, 13, 37, 47, 49-51
"Leviathan" (Curnow) **48**:17, 36-37
"Leviathan" (Merwin) **45**:6-7, 9
"Leviathan" (Neruda) **4**:282
"Leviathan" (Oppen) **35**:333
"Leviathan" (Shvarts) **50**:142
"Levkoienwelle" (Benn) **35**:46, 70
"Lews estoilles envoyées à Monsieur de Pibrac en Polonne" (Ronsard) **11**:236-37, 239
"L'Homme juste" (Rimbaud) **57**:174, 205, 290, 296
"L'Humanité chaussait le vaste enfant Progrès" (Rimbaud) **57**:253
"Li occi dolenti" (Dante) **21**:73
"The Liar" (Baraka) **4**:17
"The Liars (March, 1919)" (Sandburg) **2**:304; **41**:298, 329
"Libation" (Ammons) **16**:4
"Libation" (Brathwaite) **56**:84
"Libation" (Levertov) **11**:197
Liber Spectaculorum (Martial) **10**:230
"Libera II" (Char) **56**:147
liberating skies (Bissett) **14**:7-8, 16
"Liberation" (Glück) **16**:156
"Liberation" (Stone) **53**:219
"Liberation Poem" (Sanchez) **9**:209
"The Liberators" (Neruda)
See "Los libertadores"
Libertad bajo palabra (Paz) **1**:353; **48**:183, 244, 258, 267
"Libertad sin Lágrimas" (Alurista) **34**:10, 46
"Los libertadores" (Neruda) **4**:292
"La liberte, ou une nuit a Rome" (Lamartine) **16**:278, 291
"The Liberties" (Howe) **54**:126, 129-30, 134
The Liberties (Howe) **54**:42-43, 52, 57, 59, 90
"The Libertine" (Behn) **13**:4

"The Libertine" (MacNeice) **61**:141
"Liberty" (Pushkin)
See "Vol'nost': Oda"
"Liberty" (Thomas) **53**:296, 317-18
"Liberty. An Ode" (Pushkin)
See "Vol'nost': Oda"
"Liberty and Peace" (Wheatley) **3**:337, 341, 363
Liberty behind the Words (Paz)
See *Libertad bajo palabra*
Liberty under parole (Paz)
See *Libertad bajo palabra*
"Liberty without Tears" (Alurista)
See "Libertad sin Lágrimas"
"Liberty's Twilight" (Mandelstam)
See "The Twilight of Freedom"
"Libido" (Brooke) **24**:53
"The Librarian" (Olson) **19**:280
"The Library Is on Fire" (Char) **56**:146
"A Library of Law" (MacLeish) **47**:182
"El libro" (Darío) **15**:99, 101-02
Libro de las preguntas (Neruda) **4**:287, 290
Libro de poemas (García Lorca) **3**:117-18, 147-49
Un libro levemente odioso (Dalton) **36**:128
Un libro rojo para Lenin (Dalton) **36**:131-32
Libros inéditos de poesía (Jiménez) **7**:201
The Lice (Merwin) **45**:5, 9-10, 15, 18-21, 23-7, 30-2, 34-5, 38, 41-4, 49, 52, 54, 57, 59, 61, 63, 70-1, 75, 81, 83-8, 90, 93, 100
"Licentiousness" (Cassian) **17**:5
Lichee Nuts (Masters) **1**:338
"Les Lichens" (Char) **56**:151
Lichtzwang (Celan) **10**:96, 98, 121
"Liddy's Orange" (Olds) **22**:315
"Lidice" (Day Lewis) **11**:146
"The Lie" (Raleigh) **31**:202, 212-13, 219, 234, 259, 277-78, 281, 285, 304
"Liebe" (Benn) **35**:8
"Liebesgedichte" (Stramm) **50**:189
"Liebeskampf" (Stramm) **50**:168, 193-95, 208-9
"(Liebeslied.)" (Celan) **10**:123-24
"Liebeslied" (Stone) **53**:230
"Liebestod" (Parker) **28**:362
"Liebhaber in allen Gestalten" (Goethe) **5**:246, 251
"Lieder" (Pasolini) **17**:256
Lieder (Heine) **25**:155
"Liens" (Apollinaire) **7**:28, 49
"Lieu de la salamandre" (Bonnefoy) **58**:134, 147, 174
"Lieu du combat" (Bonnefoy) **58**:123
Lieutenant Schmidt (Pasternak) **6**:265, 272
"Life" (Aleixandre) **15**:25-6
"Life" (Bryant) **20**:16
"Life" (Dunbar) **5**:121, 124-26, 130
"Life" (Herbert) **4**:100, 113
"The Life" (Wright) **36**:328, 345, 397
"Life and Death at Sunrise" (Hardy) **8**:124
The Life and Death of Jason (Morris) **55**:240-42, 248-49, 251-52, 254, 259, 274, 305, 328-30
"The Life and Genuine Character of Dr. Swift" (Swift) **9**:280, 295
"Life and Letters" (Rich) **5**:352
"Life and Song" (Lanier) **50**:54, 67, 98
"Life at War" (Levertov) **11**:176, 194
"The Life Beyond" (Brooke) **24**:57
"Life Cycle of Common Man" (Nemerov) **24**:283
"A Life History: in Harmonies and Discords" (Lawrence) **54**:235-36
"Life in a Love" (Browning) **61**:88
Life in the Forest (Levertov) **11**:205, 207-10
"Life Is a Summer's Day" (Thoreau) **30**:187, 189
"Life is More True than Reason Will Decieve" (Cummings) **5**:108
"Life Is Motion" (Stevens) **6**:333
"A Life Lesson" (Riley) **48**:309
"Life, Love, and Death" (Rossetti) **44**:255
Life of a Man (Ungaretti)
See *Vita d' un uomo*
"The life of Borodin" (Bukowski) **18**:22
"Life of Life" (Patmore) **59**:201
"Life of Life" (Shelley) **14**:181
"The Life of Lincoln West" (Brooks) **7**:85, 91-2
"The Life of My Friend" (Blok) **21**:6, 20
"The Life of the Dead" (Jackson) **44**:7, 11, 44-5, 102
"Life on Earth" (O'Hara) **45**:156
Life Sentence (Cassian) **17**:10-13
Life Studies (Lowell) **3**:205-09, 211-14, 216-19, 221, 223, 227, 230, 232-33, 242-43
Life Studies: Secular Love (Ondaatje) **28**:316
"The Life That Is" (Bryant) **20**:8
"The Life They Lead" (Ignatow) **34**:324
"Lifeboat" (Silverstein) **49**:349
"The Lifeguard" (Dickey) **40**:150, 166, 175, 180, 257
"Life-in Love" (Rossetti) **44**:204
"Life's Noonday" (Tagore)
See "Jivan madhyahna"
"Life's Rendezvous" (Cullen) **20**:77
"Life's Work" (Kumin) **15**:202
"Life-Size is Too Large" (Jackson) **44**:89
"A Lifetime" (Bryant) **20**:8, 12, 46
"A Lifetime Later" (Ferlinghetti) **1**:183
"Lift Every Voice and Sing" (Johnson) **24**:136, 130-31, 143-44, 146, 154, 159-60, 166, 170
"The Lifting" (Olds) **22**:318, 325, 334-36, 340
"Lifting Belly" (Stein) **18**:327, 341-42
"th lifting hands" (Bissett) **14**:34
"Lifting Illegal Nets By Flashlist" (Wright) **36**:322, 351
"Lifting my forehead and lowering my eyes" (Tsvetaeva)
See "Zakinuv golovu i opustiv glaza"
"Lifting Stone" (Sarton) **39**:324
"Ligadura humana" (Storni) **33**:278
"The Light" (Ferlinghetti) **1**:183
"Light" (Ondaatje) **28**:339-40
"Light" (Wakoski) **15**:369
"Light against Darkness" (Williams) **7**:385
"The Light and Glory of the Word" (Cowper) **40**:84
Light and Serious Verse (Carducci)
See *Levia gravia*
The Light around the Body (Bly) **39**:8-15, 17, 22, 27, 37, 42, 47-50, 52, 63, 66, 71, 83-4, 90-1, 94, 100-01
"Light Baggage" (Walker) **30**:354
"Light Becomes Darkness" (Williams) **7**:384, 388
"Light Becomes Where No Sun Shines" (Thomas)
See "Light Breaks Where No Sun Shines"
Light Beyond the Darkness (Harper) **21**:189
"Light Breaks Where No Sun Shines" (Thomas) **2**:304; **52**:245, 256, 262, 271
"A Light Breather" (Roethke) **15**:268, 309
Light Compulsion (Celan)
See *Lichtzwang*
"Light in Darkness" (Harper) **21**:197
"A Light in the Attic" (Silverstein) **49**:323
A Light in the Attic: Poems and Drawings (Silverstein) **49**:305-6, 309-13, 322-24, 327-29, 331, 333-36, 338-41, 343-44, 346-48
"The Light in the Hallway" (Wright) **36**:342
"Light is Speech" (Moore) **49**:134
"Light Love" (Rossetti) **7**:289
"Light Music" (Mahon) **60**:143, 195
"The Light of Day" (Parra)
See "La Luz del día"
"Light of My Eyes" (Walcott) **46**:262
"The Light of Stars" (Longfellow) **30**:22, 26, 36, 96, 103, 108-09
"The Light of the World" (Walcott) **46**:266
"The Light on the Pewter Dish" (Rexroth) **20**:196
"Light on the Subject" (Komunyakaa) **51**:29
"Light Sleeping" (Gunn) **26**:218
"A Light Snow-Fall after Frost" (Hardy) **8**:124
"The Light Tree" (Elytis) **21**:123
The Light Tree and the Fourteenth Beauty (Elytis) **21**:123, 133
"Light Verse on a Rock" (Wang Wei) **18**:358-59
The Light Years (Sarton) **39**:325
"A Lighted Cigar That Is Smoking" (Apollinaire)
See "Paysage"
"The Lighted House" (Day Lewis) **11**:145-46
"The Lighted Window" (Teasdale) **31**:335, 351
"Lightenings" (Heaney) **18**:259
"The Lighthouse" (Longfellow) **30**:42
"A Lighthouse in Maine" (Mahon) **60**:146, 170, 198, 214
"Lighthouse with Dead Leaves" (McGuckian) **27**:104
"Lighting a Candle" (Shvarts)
See "Zazhigaia svechu"
"Lighting a Candle for W. H. Auden" (Wright) **36**:359
"Lighting of the Penitentiary" (Char)
See "L'Eclairage du pénitencier"
"Lightness" (Jiménez)
See "Levedad"
"Lightness" (Wilbur) **51**:193, 281, 292
"Lightnin' Blues" (Dove) **6**:117
"Lightning" (Lawrence) **54**:174-75, 206-7
"Lightning" (Rimbaud)
See "L'Eclair"
"The Lightning" (Swenson) **14**:285
"Lightning Bugs Asleep in the Afternoon" (Wright) **36**:370, 378
"The Lightning Speed of the Past" (Carver) **54**:11
"Lightning Storm on Fuji" (Nemerov) **24**:295
"Lights" (Boland) **58**:45
"Lights of my Eyes" (Guest) **55**:194
"Lights Out" (Thomas) **53**:271, 275, 293, 297-98, 309, 317, 349
"Light-Winged Smoke, Icarian Bird" (Thoreau) **30**:192, 205, 208-09, 211, 216, 221, 235, 257, 267, 294
"Like a Bulwark" (Moore) **49**:112, 129, 136
Like a Bulwark (Moore) **4**:257; **49**:125, 133, 136
"Like a Rolling Stone" (Dylan) **37**:50, 56, 62-3, 65, 70
"Like a Sitting Breeze" (Viereck) **27**:267-68, 283
"Like an Eddy" (Birney) **52**:46, 76, 82
"Like Ankle-rings" (Ekeloef) **23**:87
"Like Decorations in a Nigger Cemetery" (Stevens) **6**:308, 318
"Like Ghosts of Eagles" (Francis) **34**:244, 247, 249
Like Ghosts of Eagles (Francis) **34**:244-45
"Like Rembrandt, martyr of chiaroscuro" (Mandelstam)
See "Kak svetoteni muchenik Rembrandt"
"Like Snow" (Graves) **6**:144, 172
"Like the Inner Wall of a House" (Amichai) **38**:42
"Like the Thistledown" (Aleixandre) **15**:15
"Like the Touch of Rain" (Thomas) **53**:338
"Like, This Is What I Meant" (Baraka) **4**:38
"Like This Together" (Rich) **5**:364, 382
"Like Three Fair Branches from One Root Deriv'd" (Hass) **16**:199
"Like to a Hermite Poore in Place Obscure" (Raleigh) **31**:201, 216, 266, 269-71
"Like Truthles Dreames" (Raleigh) **31**:201, 219, 266, 268, 271, 297
"Likewise" (Hughes) **53**:193
"Lilacs" (Lowell) **13**:64, 67, 84-5, 98-9
"Lilacs in New York City" (Doty) **53**:61
"Lilian" (Patmore) **59**:218-19, 239-40
"Lilian" (Tennyson) **6**:359
"The Lilies" (Mickiewicz)
See "Lilje"
"Lilis Park" (Goethe) **5**:246
"Lilje" (Mickiewicz) **38**:151

"The Lilly" (Blake) **12**:34-5
"The Lilly in a Christal" (Herrick) **9**:112-13, 115, 137-38, 144
"Lily, Rosemary, and the Jack of Hearts" (Dylan) **37**:54, 56-57
"Limbes" (Verlaine) **32**:356
Les Limbes (Baudelaire)
See *Les fleurs du mal*
"Limbo" (Brathwaite) **56**:23, 86
"Limbo" (Coleridge) **11**:52, 85
"Limbo" (Graves) **6**:166
The Lime Orchard Woman (Ríos) **57**:323, 325-26
"Lime Trees in Winter Retouched" (McGuckian) **27**:102-104
"The Limit" (Aleixandre) **15**:6
"Limitation of Perfection" (Tagore)
See "Purner abhav"
"Limitations" (Sassoon) **12**:245
"Limited" (Sandburg) **2**:312; **41**:236, 239, 254, 314, 321
"Limites" (Borges) **32**:58
"Límites y espejo" (Aleixandre) **15**:42-3
"Limits" (Borges)
See "Limites"
"Limits" (Brathwaite) **56**:7, 29, 85
"Limits" (Okigbo) **7**:241-42
Limits (Okigbo) **7**:223-28, 233-34, 246-48, 250-51
"Limits and mirror" (Aleixandre)
See "Límites y espejo"
"I limoni" (Montale) **13**:114, 119, 122
"Limosna" (Storni) **33**:242, 313;
"L'Impossible" (Rimbaud) **57**:191, 195, 243, 249, 251
"The Lincoln Relics" (Kunitz) **19**:175, 178-80
"Lindau" (Montale) **13**:146
"The Linden Branch" (MacLeish) **47**:192-93
"Lineage" (Hughes) **7**:159
"Lineage" (Walker) **20**:281
"Linen Town" (Heaney) **18**:202
"Liner Notes For the Poetically Unhep" (Hughes) **53**:115
"The Liner She's a Lady" (Kipling) **3**:161
"Lines" (Cowper)
See "Lines Written during a Period of Insanity"
"Lines" (Harper) **21**:190, 218
"Lines" (Williams) **7**:351-52
"Lines about the Unknown Soldier" (Mandelstam)
See "Stikhi o neizvestnom soldate"
"Lines Above Tintern Abbey" (Wordsworth)
See "Lines Composed a Few Miles Above Tintern Abbey"
"Lines & Circularities" (Nemerov) **24**:288, 301
"Lines Composed a Few Miles Above Tintern Abbey" (Wordsworth) **4**:373, 387, 391, 409-12, 418-19, 425-26, 428
"Lines Composed While Climbing the Left Ascent of Drockley Coomb, Somersetshire, May 1795" (Coleridge) **11**:82
"Lines for a Book" (Gunn) **26**:185, 189
"Lines for a Picture of St. Dorothea" (Hopkins) **15**:144
"Lines for a Prologue" (MacLeish) **47**:156, 164, 167
"Lines for Akhmatova" (Kenyon) **57**:15
"Lines for an Album" (Montale)
See "Per album"
"Lines for an Internment" (MacLeish) **47**:145, 190
"Lines for an Ode-Threnody on England" (Brooke) **24**:89
"Lines for an Old Man" (Eliot) **5**:170
"Lines in a Country Churchyard" (Shelley) **14**:166
"Lines in New England" (Walcott) **46**:322
"Lines Left upon a Seat in a Yew-Tree, Which Stands near the Lake of Esthwaite, on a Desolate Part of the Shore, Commanding a Beautiful Prospect" (Wordsworth) **4**:373, 418
"Lines on a Young Lady's Photograph Album" (Larkin) **21**:236
"Lines on an Autumnal Evening" (Coleridge) **11**:106
"Lines on Revisiting the Country" (Bryant) **20**:37-8
"Lines on the First Mild Day of March" (Wordsworth) **4**:418
"Lines on the Loss of the Royal George" (Cowper) **40**:44
"Lines to a Don" (Belloc) **24**:11, 29, 38
"Lines to a Movement in Mozart's E-Flat Symphony" (Hardy) **8**:114
"Lines to Miles O'Reilly" (Harper) **21**:197
"Lines to Mr. Henry Vaughan, Silurist, on His Poems" (Philips) **40**:270
"Lines to Myself" (Heaney) **18**:191
"Lines to Sour-Faced Gila" (Juana Inés de la Cruz) **24**:176
"Lines written a few miles above Tintern Abbey" (Wordsworth)
See "Lines Composed a Few Miles Above Tintern Abbey"
"Lines Written after Detecting in Myself a Yearning toward the Large, Wise, Calm, Richly Resigned, Benignant Act Put on by a Great Many People after Having Passed the Age of Thirty Five" (Bogan) **12**:115
"Lines Written among the Euganean Hills" (Shelley) **14**:171, 177, 235
"Lines Written at a Small Distance from My House, and Sent by My Little Boy to the Person to Whom They Are Addressed" (Wordsworth) **4**:418
"Lines Written during a Period of Insanity" (Cowper) **40**:46
"Lines Written in an Asylum" (Carruth) **10**:84, 89
"Lines Written in Anticipation of a London Paper Attaining a Guaranteed Circulation of Ten Million Daily" (Sassoon) **12**:251-52
"Lines Written in Early Spring" (Wordsworth) **4**:418
"Lines Written in Kensington Gardens" (Arnold) **5**:19, 35, 49
"Lines Written in the Library of Congress after the Cleanth Brooks Lecture" (Kumin) **15**:222
"Lines Written Nov. 22, 23—1963—In Discord" (Corso) **33**:49
"Lines Written on a Seat on the Grand Canal, Dublin" (Kavanagh) **33**:63, 96, 103, 120
"Lines Written on My Nineteenth Birthday" (Owen) **19**:371
"A l'infini" (Éluard) **38**:84
"The Lingam and the Yoni" (Hope) **56**:287, 304
"Lingard and the Stars" (Robinson) **1**:464
"Lingua" (Pasolini) **17**:272
"Links" (Apollinaire)
See "Liens"
"The Linnet in the Rocky Dells" (Brontë) **8**:68-9
"Linoleum" (Gallagher) **9**:44, 56, 60
"The Lion" (Belloc) **24**:24
"Lion" (Wright) **14**:346
"Lion & Honeycomb" (Nemerov) **24**:262
"The Lion and the Lamb" (Wylie) **23**:309, 324
"The Lion and the Rose" (Sarton) **39**:321, 323-24, 340
The Lion and the Rose (Sarton) **39**:318, 321-22, 331, 335-37, 339-40, 342-43, 353, 356-59
"The Lion in Love" (Moore) **4**:261
"Lions" (Borges) **32**:66
"The Lions" (Hayden) **6**:194, 197
The Lion's Tail and Eyes: Poems Written Out of Laziness and Silence (Bly) **39**:13, 73-4
"Liquid Metal Fast Breeder Reactor" (Snyder) **21**:293
Lirici greci (Quasimodo) **47**:293, 295-98
"Lis" (Cummings) **5**:100
"Lisa" (Eliot) **20**:102
"Lisa May" (Dunbar) **5**:137
"Lisbon Revisited, 1923" (Pessoa) **20**:158, 169
"Listen" (Nash) **21**:274
"Listen Carefully" (Levine) **22**:234
"listen children" (Clifton) **17**:26
"Listen Here Blues" (Hughes) **1**:270
"Listen, Lord" (Johnson) **24**:144, 164
"Listen. This Is the Noise of Myth" (Boland) **58**:20, 48
"Listen to the Mustn'ts" (Silverstein) **49**:339
"Listenen to Big Black at S.F. State" (Sanchez) **9**:225
"Listening" (Lawrence) **54**:244
"Listening to a Cricket in the Wainscoting" (Bly) **39**:53, 69
"Listening to Bach" (Bly) **39**:43, 71
"Listening to Foxhounds" (Dickey) **40**:175, 182, 185
"Listening to Music of Arsenio Rodríquez is Moving Closer to Knowledge" (Cruz) **37**:12
"Listening to Presiden Kennedy Lie about the Cuban Invasion" (Bly) **39**:12
"Listening to the Mourners" (Wright) **36**:400
Le lit la table (Éluard) **38**:74
"The Litanie" (Donne) **1**:136-39, 147, 150
"Les litanies de satan" (Baudelaire) **1**:45, 71
"The Litanies of Satan" (Baudelaire)
See "Les litanies de satan"
"Litany" (Ashbery) **26**:131-135, 140-143, 145, 156, 169-170, 172
"Litany" (Sandburg)
See "The Long Shadow of Lincoln: A Litany"
"The Litany for Survival" (Lorde) **12**:137
"The Litany of the Dark People" (Cullen) **20**:57, 75
"The Litany of the Heroes" (Lindsay) **23**:266, 272, 285, 295
"Literary Adventures" (Kavanagh) **33**:96
"Literary Statement On Struggle!" (Baraka) **4**:30
"The Literate Farmer and the Planet Venus" (Frost) **1**:210; **39**:233
"The Lithuanian" (Lermontov)
See "Litvinka"
"Lithuanian Dance Band" (Ashbery) **26**:145
"Lithuanian Nocturne" (Brodsky) **9**:22-4, 27
"Litovskii noktyurn" (Brodsky)
See "Lithuanian Nocturne"
"Little Abigail and the Beautiful Pony" (Silverstein) **49**:312, 332
"Little Aster" (Benn) **35**:54
"The Little Beauty That I Was Allowed" (Wylie) **23**:314
"A Little Bit of a Tumbler" (Stein) **18**:321, 334, 353
"The Little Black Boy" (Blake) **12**:7-8
"The Little Blue Engine" (Silverstein) **49**:312
A Little Book on the Human Shadow (Bly) **39**:85
"The Little Box of Olinalá" (Mistral)
See "La cajita de Olinalá"
"Little Boy and Lost Shoe" (Warren) **37**:306
"The Little Boy and the Old Man" (Silverstein) **49**:308, 313, 325-26
"The Little Boy Found" (Blake) **12**:7
"A Little Boy Lost" (Blake) **12**:7, 23, 33-5
"Little Boy Lost" (Smith) **12**:321, 325, 332
"Little Boy Sick" (Smith) **12**:318
"Little Boy Stanton" (García Lorca) **3**:143
"Little Breeches" (Riley) **48**:299
"Little Brown Baby" (Dunbar) **5**:142
"A Little Called Pauline" (Stein) **18**:331
"A Little Child Shall Lead Them" (Harper) **21**:187
The Little Children of the Snow (Bryant)
See "The Little People of the Snow"
"Little Clown, My Heart" (Cisneros) **52**:147
"The Little Coat" (Riley) **48**:340

"A Little Dawn Song for My Companion" (Guillén) **35**:217
"A little demon in wet fur crept in" (Mandelstam)
See "Vlez besenok v mokroi sherstke"
"The Little Dog's Day" (Brooke) **24**:59
"Little Elegy" (O'Hara) **45**:172
"Little Elegy" (Wylie) **23**:314-15
"Little Exercise" (Bishop) **3**:49; **34**:52-53, 130
"Little Fanfare for Felix MacGowan" (Merrill) **28**:253
"The Little Friend" (Browning) **6**:14
Little Friend, Little Friend (Jarrell) **41**:137, 139, 146, 178-80, 218
"Little Fugue" (Plath) **1**:390; **37**:214, 218-21, 246, 249
"The Little General" (Muir) **49**:289
"The Little Ghost" (Millay) **6**:206; **61**:212
"Little Gidding" (Eliot) **5**:165-67, 169-70, 181-83, 185, 193, 204-05, 208, 210-11; **31**:169
"Little Gidding" (Wilbur) **51**:209
"The Little Girl Found" (Blake) **12**:7, 33-4, 61
"The Little Girl Lost" (Blake)
See "A Little Girl Lost"
"A Little Girl Lost" (Blake) **12**:7, 33-4, 61
"Little Girl, My String Bean, My Lovely Woman" (Sexton) **2**:363
"Little Girl Wakes Early" (Warren) **37**:367, 375
"Little Girls" (Page) **12**:176-77
"Little Green Sea" (Elytis) **21**:123
"Little Green Tree" (Hughes) **1**:243
Little Henrietta (Reese) **29**:337, 339, 348, 353
"The Little Hill" (Millay) **6**:214, 233
"Little Horse" (Merwin) **45**:98
The Little House of Kolomna (Pushkin)
See *Domik v Kolomne*
"Little Jim" (McKay) **2**:216, 222
"The Little June Book" (Stevens) **6**:332-33
"The Little Larousse" (Zagajewski) **27**:401
"Little Lion Face" (Swenson) **14**:280
"Little Lobeila's Song" (Bogan) **12**:100-01, 111
"A Little Love of Life" (Stein) **18**:313
"Little Lyric" (Hughes) **1**:240; **53**:102
"Little Man" (Storni)
See "Hombre pequeñito"
"Little Mandy's Christmas-Tree" (Riley) **48**:302
The Little Mariner (Elytis) **21**:134-35
"Little Marvel Stove" (Bishop) **34**:91
"Little Mattie" (Browning) **6**:24
"Little Miss Muffet Sat on a Prophet" (Nash) **21**:265
"Little Old Letter" (Hughes) **1**:243
"The Little Old Women" (Baudelaire)
See "Les petites vielles"
"The Little Ones" (Soto) **28**:371
"Little Orphant Annie" (Riley) **48**:309, 340
"The Little Peasant" (Sexton) **2**:364, 368
"The Little People of the Snow" (Bryant) **20**:15-16
"De Little Pikaninny's Gone to Sleep" (Johnson) **24**:162
Little Poems in Prose (Baudelaire)
See *Petits poèmes en prose: Le spleen de Paris*
"The Little Rapids" (Swenson) **14**:262
"Little Red Riding Hood" (Mistral)
See "Caperucita Roja"
"The Little Robber Girl Gets on in the Wide World" (Hacker) **47**:82
The Little Sailor (Elytis)
See *The Little Mariner*
"A Little Scraping" (Jeffers) **17**:117
The Little Seafarer (Elytis)
See *The Little Mariner*
"The Little Serving Maid" (Belloc) **24**:5
"Little Sleep's-Head Sprouting Hair in the Moonlight" (Kinnell) **26**:251, 283, 291
"Little Songs for Gaia" (Snyder) **21**:301
"Little Sonnet" (Wylie) **23**:332
"The Little Straw" (Mistral)
See "La pajita"
"Little T. C." (Marvell)
See "The Picture of Little T. C. in a Prospect of Flowers"
"A Little Testament" (Montale)
See "Piccolo testamento"
"The Little Tower" (Morris) **55**:299, 302
"The Little Town o' Tailholt" (Riley) **48**:329, 332, 334
"Little Tree" (Cummings) **5**:93
"A Little Uncomplicated Hymn" (Sexton) **2**:363
"The Little Utopia" (Graham) **59**:166
"The Little Vagabond" (Blake) **12**:7
"A Little While" (Teasdale) **31**:340, 359
"The Little White Rose" (MacDiarmid) **9**:154, 176, 186
"Little Word, Little White Bird" (Sandburg) **41**:309
"Little Words" (Parker) **28**:363
"Little Worker" (Mistral)
See "Obrerito"
"Littleblood" (Hughes) **7**:153, 168-69
"Littoral" (Brathwaite) **56**:69, 74
Liturgies intimes (Verlaine) **2**:417-18
"Litvinka" (Lermontov) **18**:300
"Liubliu moroznoe dykhan'e" (Mandelstam) **14**:154
"Live" (Sexton) **2**:351, 364
"Live Niggers—Stop Bullshitting" (Baraka) **4**:18
Live or Die (Sexton) **2**:349, 351, 356, 362-65
"The lively sparks that issue from those eyes" (Wyatt) **27**:357
"Lives" (Mahon) **60**:139, 150, 155, 178, 193, 195
"Lives" (Rimbaud)
See "Vies"
"Lives" (Rukeyser) **12**:207, 217, 228
Lives (Mahon) **60**:132-34, 138, 140-41, 144, 154, 183, 200-201, 203
"Living" (Guillén) **35**:221
"Living" (Levertov) **11**:186
"Living by the Red River" (Wright) **36**:355
"Living Earth" (Toomer) **7**:336-37
"Living in Sin" (Rich) **5**:351, 369
"Living in the City" (Ignatow) **34**:305
"Living in the Country" (Kavanagh) **33**:87
"Living in the Country: I" (Kavanagh) **33**:102
"Living in the Country: II" (Kavanagh) **33**:120
"Living in the Moment" (Hacker) **47**:104
"Living in the Mountain on an Autumn Night" (Wang Wei) **18**:391
"Living in the Open" (Piercy) **29**:310
Living in the Open (Piercy) **29**:304, 310-11
"Living Near the Water" (Song) **21**:345-46
"Living Off the Land" (Wagoner) **33**:352
"A Living Pearl" (Rexroth) **20**:186-87, 216, 218
"Living Room" (Jordan) **38**:127
Living Room (Jordan) **38**:123, 127
"LIVING WITH TH VISHYUN" (Bissett) **14**:34
living with th vishyun (Bissett) **14**:16-17
"Livingshayes" (Davie) **29**:115
Le Livre de l'Espurgatorie (Marie de France)
See *L'Espurgatoire Saint Patrice*
Le livre ouvert, 1938-1940 (Éluard) **38**:63, 74
"Le livre, pour vieillir" (Bonnefoy) **58**:118-19, 167-68
"Lix" (Brathwaite) **56**:51
"LIX" (Carman) **34**:224-25
"A Liz Town Humorist" (Riley) **48**:288
"Lladrata Merch" (Dafydd ap Gwilym) **56**:232
Llanto por Ignacio Sánchez Mejías (García Lorca) **3**:121-22, 124, 126, 128
"Llegada" (Guillén) **23**:99, 105-106
"Llewellyn and the Tree" (Robinson) **1**:462, 468
"Llovizna" (Storni) **33**:239, 261;
"La lluvia lenta" (Mistral) **32**:144, 179
"Llychwino Pryd y Ferch" (Dafydd ap Gwilym) **56**:232
"Lo! A Child Is Born" (MacDiarmid) **9**:178-79
"Lo fatal" (Darío) **15**:96
"Lo lo lógico" (Fuertes) **27**:22
"El lo sabe" (Fuertes) **27**:15
"The Load of Sugar-Cane" (Stevens) **6**:293
"Loam" (Sandburg) **41**:242, 297, 339
"Loan Exhibit (Francis) **34**:250
"Lob" (Thomas) **53**:267, 301-4, 332, 349
"Localities" (Sandburg) **41**:240
"Locas letanías" (Mistral) **32**:159, 161, 181
The Location of Things (Guest) **55**:183, 196, 207-8, 210, 225
"Loch Torridon" (Swinburne) **24**:313
"lock lied" (Enzensberger) **28**:138-39
"Lockerbie Fair" (Riley) **48**:326
"Lockerbie Street" (Riley) **48**:292, 326
"The Lockless Door" (Frost) **1**:218
"Locks" (Bukowski) **18**:15
"Locksley Hall" (Tennyson) **6**:354, 357, 359-60, 363
"Locus" (Hayden) **6**:189, 194, 196
"The Locust Tree in Flower" (Williams) **7**:363
"The Locusts" (Merrill) **28**:231, 243
"Locutions des Pierrots, I" (Laforgue) **14**:81
"Locutions des Pierrots XIV" (Laforgue) **14**:89
"The Lode" (Dickey) **40**:228, 236
"The Lodger" (Carman) **34**:212
"Lofty in the Palais de Danse" (Gunn) **26**:220
"A Lofty Sky" (Thomas) **53**:287
"Log" (Merrill) **28**:221-2, 256
"Logging 2" (Larkin) **21**:322
"Logic and 'The Magic Flute'" (Moore) **49**:126, 130-31, 134, 139, 161
"Logos" (Hughes) **7**:120, 159
"Logos" (Muir) **49**:237-38
"Lohengrin" (Cavafy) **36**:53
"Loi de formation du progrès" (Hugo) **17**:100
"Loin Cloth" (Sandburg) **2**:329
Loin de nos cendres (Char) **56**:189
"Loin des oiseaux" (Rimbaud) **3**:274
"Loin du pigeonnier" (Apollinaire) **7**:18, 21, 23
"Loisaida" (Cruz) **37**:31
"Loitering with a Vacant Eye" (Housman) **2**:193
"Lollocks" (Graves) **6**:137, 142, 144
"London" (Blake) **12**:7, 25, 34
"London" (Jarrell) **41**:127
"London" (Pinsky) **27**:150
"London Bridge" (Robinson) **1**:466, 468
"London hast thow accused me" (Surrey) **59**:306-10
"London Rain" (MacNeice) **61**:138
"London Snow" (Bridges) **28**:51, 61, 70, 83
Loneliness (Paz)
See *Soledad*
"Lonely" (Wright) **36**:395-96
"A Lonely Character" (Hagiwara)
See "Sabishii jinkaku"
"Lonely Particular" (Walker) **30**:339
"The Lonely Street" (Williams) **7**:362
"Lonesome" (Dunbar) **5**:119
"Lonesome Valley" (Brown) **55**:143-44
"Long Afternoons" (Zagajewski) **27**:395
"Long Ages Past" (Owen) **19**:351
"Long Ago" (Cavafy) **36**:75
Long Ago and A Short While Ago (Verlaine)
See *Jadis et naguère*
Long Ago and Not So Long Ago (Verlaine)
See *Jadis et naguère*
"The Long Alley" (Roethke) **15**:248, 254
Long and Short Poems (Shvarts)
See *Stikhotvoreniia i poemy*
The Long Approach (Kumin) **15**:214, 221
"The Long Death" (Piercy) **29**:311
Long Division: A Tribal History (Rose) **13**:232
"A Long Dress" (Stein) **18**:349
"The Long Garden" (Kavanagh) **33**:81, 152, 154, 160-1
"Long Gone" (Brown) **55**:89, 108, 110-11, 174
"The Long Hill" (Teasdale) **31**:323, 334, 336
"Long Hot Summer" (MacLeish) **47**:197
"The Long Hunter" (Berry) **28**:38
"Long John Brown & Little Mary Bell" (Blake) **12**:35
"Long John Nelson and Sweetie Pie" (Walker)

20:286
Long Live Man (Corso) **33**:15, 34-8, 44, 48-9
"Long Live the Cordillera of the Andes / Death to the Cordillera of the Coast!" (Parra)
See "Viva la cordillera de los Andes / Muera la cordillera de la Costa!"
"The long love" (Wyatt)
See "The longe love that in my thought doth harbour"
"Long Past Moncada" (Rukeyser) **12**:231-32
"Long Screams" (Hughes) **7**:150
"Long Shadow at Dulce" (Momaday) **25**:219
"The Long Shadow of Lincoln: A Litany" (Sandburg) **2**:334; **41**:301-2
"The Long Small Room" (Thomas) **53**:285-86, 329
"A Long Story" (Gray) **2**:143, 152-53
"A Long Time" (Guillén) **35**:218
"Long To'ds Night" (Dunbar) **5**:147
"Long Track Blues" (Brown) **55**:80, 95-96, 114, 177
"The Long Tunnel Ceiling" (Hughes) **7**:148
"Long walk" (Borges)
See "Caminata"
"The Long Waters" (Roethke) **15**:310, 316-17
"A Long Way" (Ungaretti) **57**:359
"The longe love" (Wyatt)
See "The longe love that in my thought doth harbour"
"The longe love that in my thought doth harbour" (Wyatt) **27**:340, 355, 358
"Longing" (Arnold) **5**:42-3
"Longing" (Brutus) **24**:114
"The Longing" (Roethke) **15**:272, 274, 310, 312-15
"Longing" (Teasdale) **31**:325
Longing (Ishikawa)
See *Akogare*
"Longing for Heaven" (Bradstreet) **10**:27, 30, 42
A Longing for the Light: Selected Poems of Vicente Aleixandre (Aleixandre) **15**:24
"Longing Is Like the Seed" (Dickinson) **1**:111
"Longings" (Cavafy) **36**:66, 73, 76
"Long-Legged Fly" (Yeats) **20**:315
Longshot Poems for Broke Players (Bukowski) **18**:3-4
Longshot Pomes for Brave Players (Bukowski) **18**:5
"the lonliness of literacy" (Bissett) **14**:34
"The Look" (Olds) **22**:342
"Look!" (Smith) **12**:342
"The Look" (Teasdale) **31**:332, 334, 337-38
"Look Back" (Snyder) **21**:300
"Look Down from the High Terrace Seeing Off Reminder Li" (Wang Wei) **18**:370
"Look for You Yesterday, Here You Come Today" (Baraka) **4**:14-15
"Look Hart That Horse You Ride Is Wood" (Viereck) **27**:284
"The Look of the Hedge" (Reese) **29**:334
"Look on This Picture and on This" (Rossetti) **7**:277
"Look, Stranger, on This Island Now" (Auden) **1**:7-8, 12, 22, 30
Look! We Have Come Through! (Lawrence) **54**:169-70, 175, 182-83, 186, 189, 197-98, 207, 212-13, 232, 237, 240, 244
"Look What You Did, Christopher!" (Nash) **21**:275
"Look You I'll Go Pray" (Lindsay) **23**:281
"Looking at a Map" (Abse) **41**:13
"Looking at a Picture on an Anniversary" (Hardy) **8**:137-38
"Looking at My Father" (Olds) **22**:321
"Looking at Pictures to be Put Away" (Snyder) **21**:287
"Looking at Some Flowers" (Bly) **39**:21
"Looking at Stars" (Kenyon) **57**:35
"Looking at the Fall" (Ní Chuilleanáin) **34**:350
"Looking Book" (Merwin) **45**:48
Looking for Luck (Kumin) **15**:213, 216, 221, 223-24
"Looking for Luck in Bangkok" (Kumin) **15**:214
"Looking for Mushrooms at Sunrise" (Merwin) **45**:21, 26, 87
"Looking for Nothing" (Snyder) **21**:310
"Looking for th Lammas" (Bissett) **14**:7
"Looking for the Buckhead Boys" (Dickey) **40**:166, 200, 220
"Looking for Work" (Carver) **54**:19
"Looking Forward" (Rossetti) **7**:277
"Looking from Oregon" (Birney) **52**:42
"Looking Glass" (Gunn) **26**:206, 218
"Looking in a Mirror" (Atwood) **8**:32, 38
"Looking into History" (Wilbur) **51**:227, 229, 266-67
"Looking Out" (Yamada) **44**:344-45
"Looking Up at the Top of a Blue Tree" (Hagiwara) **18**:177
"The Looking-Glass Dictionary" (Szirtes) **51**:173
"The Loom" (Masters) **1**:333
The Loon (Bly) **39**:45, 67, 69-71
"loon about to laugh" (Birney) **52**:33, 83
"The Loon's Cry" (Nemerov) **24**:257, 292-93, 295, 299-300
"Loons Mating" (Wagoner) **33**:361
"The Loop" (Masters) **1**:329; **36**:175-76
"Loop" (Ondaatje) **28**:331
The Loop in Lone Kauri Road: Poems: 1983-85 (Curnow) **48**:21, 32
"A Loose Gown" (Ignatow) **34**:328
"A Loose Mountain Telescopic" (Frost) **39**:233
Loose Woman (Cisneros) **52**:146-47, 151, 156
"Loot" (Kipling) **3**:160, 163, 174, 187
"The Lord in the Air" (Dickey) **40**:200
"Lord Lundy" (Belloc) **24**:18
"Lord of Elbë, on Elbë Hill" (Brontë) **8**:73
The Lord of the Isles (Scott) **13**:277, 281, 288, 294, 296, 304, 311-12, 318, 321
Lord Weary's Castle (Lowell) **3**:200, 202-03, 206-07, 211-12, 216-18, 224, 230-33
"Lord's Prayer" (Lawrence) **54**:250
"Lord's Prayer" (Parra)
See "Padre nuestro"
"Lorelei" (Plath) **1**:388-89; **37**:179-82, 238, 241
"L'Orgie parisienne" (Rimbaud) **57**:202, 205-6, 208, 210, 246
"L'lorloge de demain" (Apollinaire) **7**:32
"The Los Cities" (Cardenal)
See "Las ciudades perdidas"
"De los periódicos" (Fuertes) **27**:12
"The Loser" (Stryk) **27**:201
"Losing a Language" (Merwin) **45**:93
"Losing Track" (Levertov) **11**:160, 169
"Loss" (H. D.) **5**:303
"Loss" (Jarrell) **41**:139, 174
"Loss" (Stone) **53**:229
"Loss, of Perhaps Love, in Our World of Contingency" (Warren) **37**:309, 333
"The Loss of the Eurydice" (Hopkins) **15**:147, 162
"The Loss of The Nabara" (Day Lewis)
See "The Nabara"
"The Losse" (Finch) **21**:146, 179
"Losses" (Jarrell) **41**:144, 188, 195, 202, 218
"Losses" (Sandburg) **41**:313
Losses (Jarrell) **41**:136-39, 146, 178-79
"Lost" (Bukowski) **18**:24
"Lost" (Sandburg) **2**:303; **41**:225, 238, 244, 267, 285, 318, 350, 364
"Lost and Found" (Levine) **22**:224
"Lost and Found" (Mueller) **33**:192-93
"The Lost Angel" (Levine) **22**:213
lost angel mining company (Bissett) **14**:6-7, 9, 17, 19
Lost Body (Césaire)
See *Corps perdu*
"The Lost Bower" (Browning) **6**:7
"Lost Box" (Yau) **61**:330
"Lost Child" (Wright) **14**:349, 352
"The Lost Children" (Jarrell) **41**:186, 217-18
"Lost Commagene" (Elytis) **21**:135
Lost Copper (Rose) **13**:235, 237-38, 240
"The Lost Dancer" (Toomer) **7**:336
"Lost Days" (Rossetti) **44**:174
"The Lost Federation" (Walcott) **46**:234, 274
"The Lost Girls" (Hogan) **35**:256
"Lost Horizon" (Ashbery) **26**:127
"Lost in Heaven" (Frost) **39**:233
Lost in the Bonewheel Factory (Komunyakaa) **51**:29, 33, 35, 49
"Lost in Translation" (Merrill) **28**:227, 232, 242, 260, 269
"The Lost Ingredient" (Sexton) **2**:350, 359
"The Lost Kiss" (Riley) **48**:297
"The Lost Land" (Boland) **58**:38, 50
"The Lost Land" (Muir) **49**:287
The Lost Land (Boland) **58**:38, 40, 47-48, 50-51, 65
"The Lost Lilies" (Brooke) **24**:81
"Lost Love" (Graves) **6**:129
"The Lost Love" (Jarrell) **41**:168
"The Lost Man" (Wright) **14**:339, 346
"The Lost Mistress" (Browning) **2**:38
"The Lost Money" (Szirtes) **51**:178
"Lost My Voice? Of Course" (Walker) **30**:339, 341
"Lost Sheep" (Storni)
See "Oveja descarriada"
"Lost Sister" (Song) **21**:331-32, 343, 350
"The Lost Son" (Roethke) **15**:248, 250, 255, 262-63, 267-68, 270, 272, 275-76, 278, 284, 298-99, 301-02
The Lost Son, and Other Poems (Roethke) **15**:246-50, 260, 282-83, 290-91, 296-97, 304, 308-09
"The Lost Wine" (Valéry)
See "Le vin perdu"
"The Lost World" (Jarrell) **41**:169, 177, 189, 217-18
The Lost World (Jarrell) **41**:142, 156, 162, 181, 206, 211, 217
"Lot and His Daughters" (Hope) **56**:271, 285
"The Lotos-Eaters" (Tennyson) **6**:352, 358-60, 409-12
"Lots: I" (Cervantes) **35**:106
"Lots: II" (Cervantes) **35**:106
"Lots II: Herself" (Cervantes) **35**:123
"Lot's Wife" (Nemerov) **24**:255
"Lot's Wife 1988" (Clifton) **17**:29
Lotto-Poems (Cassian) **17**:6
"Lotus and Frost" (Lawrence) **54**:175
"The Lotus and the Rose" (Lindsay) **23**:292
"Louenge a la court" (Villon) **13**:394-95
"The louer lamentes the deth of his loue" (Wyatt) **27**:340
"Lough Derg" (Kavanagh) **33**:121
Lough derg (Kavanagh) **33**:158, 167, 169-71
"A Lough Neagh Sequence" (Heaney) **18**:201
"Louis Curel de la Sorgue" (Char) **56**:155, 157, 171
"Louise" (O'Hara) **45**:155
"Le loup criait" (Rimbaud) **57**:250
"Love" (Boland) **58**:19, 49
"Love" (Brooke) **24**:85
"Love" (Coleridge) **39**:180
"Love" (Hagiwara)
See "Airen"
"Love" (Herbert) **4**:100, 114
"Love" (Thoreau) **30**:258, 272-73
Love (Verlaine)
See *Amour*
"Love III" (Herbert) **4**:121
Love: A Building on Fire (Byrne) **46**:279
"Love Again" (Larkin) **21**:259
"Love among the Ruins" (Browning) **2**:88; **61**:88
"Love and Death" (Leopardi)
See "Amore e Morte"
"Love and Debt Alike Troublesome" (Suckling) **30**:127, 161
"Love & Fame & Death" (Bukowski) **18**:5

"Love and Friendship" (Brontë) **8**:51
"Love and Harmony Combine" (Blake) **12**:32
"Love and Honour" (Belloc) **24**:29
"Love and Money" (Stone) **53**:224
"Love and Music" (Guillén) **35**:219
"The Love and the Hate" (Jeffers) **17**:136
"Love and the Times" (Davie) **29**:110
Love and War, Art and God (Shapiro) **25**:318, 322
"Love Arm'd" (Behn) **13**:4, 7, 15, 23-5
Love as Love (Jackson) **44**:59
"Love at First Sight" (Szymborska) **44**:285
"Love Calls Us to the Things of This World" (Wilbur) **51**:188, 197, 210-11, 213-14, 217, 244, 248, 257-59, 261, 267-68, 272, 299, 302, 314, 323-24
"Love Came Back at Fall of Dew" (Reese) **29**:333
Love, Death, and the Changing of the Seasons (Hacker) **47**:83, 85-88, 90-92, 96-97, 100,108
"Love Despoiled" (Dunbar) **5**:125
Love Elegies (Donne)
See *Elegies*
"The Love for October" (Merwin) **45**:88
"Love Fossil" (Olds) **22**:310, 317
"Love from the North" (Rossetti) **7**:260, 278, 280, 289
"Love Fulfilled" (Morris) **55**:340
"Love in a Life" (Browning) **61**:88
"Love in a Meadow" (Kavanagh) **33**:104
"Love in America?" (Moore) **49**:149
"Love in Barrenness" (Graves) **6**:172
"Love in Blood Time" (Olds) **22**:316
"Love in Fantastic Triumph Sat" (Behn)
See "Love Arm'd"
"Love in Idleness" (Patmore) **59**:233
"Love in Its Separate Being" (Jarrell) **41**:127
"Love in Moonlight" (Glück) **16**:169
"Love in the Museum" (Rich) **5**:393
"Love in the Valley" (Meredith) **60**:243-44, 246, 250, 254-55, 259, 263, 293, 295, 328
"Love Is" (Swenson) **14**:283
"Love Is a Deep and a Dark and a Lonely" (Sandburg) **41**:303
Love Is a Dog From Hell (Bukowski) **18**:19
"Love Is a Piece of Paper Torn to Bits" (Bukowski) **18**:6
"Love is Enough" (Morris) **55**:259-60
Love Is Enough (Morris) **55**:273-74, 276-78, 329-33, 337-39, 343
"Love is More Thicker than Forget" (Cummings) **5**:108
"Love is the Only God" (Cummings) **5**:107
"Love Joy" (Herbert) **4**:122-23, 125
"Love Justified" (Patmore) **59**:228, 232
"A Love Letter" (Dunbar) **5**:147
"Love Letter" (Meredith) **28**:170-71, 185
"Love Letter" (Schnackenberg) **45**:337
Love Letter from an Impossible Land (Meredith) **28**:170, 172, 177, 182-87, 194, 209-10, 216
"Love Letter From an Impossible Lane" (Meredith) **28**:190
"Love Letter Postmarked Van Beethoven" (Wakoski) **15**:326, 331
"Love Lies Sleeping" (Bishop) **34**:119-20
"Love Me!" (Smith) **12**:346
"Love Me" (Teasdale) **31**:338
"Love Medicine" (Erdrich) **52**:176, 184
"The Love Nut" (Ferlinghetti) **1**:187
"The Love of Alcestis" (Morris) **55**:310
"The Love of Christ which Passeth Knowledge" (Rossetti) 7:268, 290
"A Love of Death" (Pinsky) **27**:154
"LOVE OF LIFE, the 49th parallel" (Bissett) **14**:7, 10, 18
"Love of the Puppets" (Wilbur) **51**:188, 289-90
"The Love of Two Seasons" (Corso) **33**:25
"The Love of Windows" (Szirtes) **51**:169
"Love on my hear from heaven fell" (Bridges) **28**:59
"Love on the Farm" (Lawrence) **54**:221, 236-37
"Love Passes Beyond the Incredible Hawk of Innocence" (Wakoski) **15**:351
"Love Poem" (Glück) **16**:150
"Love Poem" (Lorde) **12**:158
"Love Poem" (Page) **12**:177
"Love Poem" (Stryk) **27**:197, 203
"Love Poem For Real" (Giovanni) **19**:126
"Love Poem for the Forty-Second Street Library" (Ignatow) **34**:287, 335
Love Poems (Sanchez) **9**:207, 212, 216, 218-21, 227, 229, 234, 237, 242
Love Poems (Sexton) **2**:349, 351-53, 355, 364-65
Love Poems, and Others (Lawrence) **54**:161-62, 174, 236, 240
The Love Poems of Marichiko (Rexroth) **20**:203, 218
The Love Poems of May Swenson (Swenson) **14**:274-75, 280, 283-84
"Love, Reason, Hate" (Suckling) **30**:119-20
Love Respelt (Graves) **6**:154, 156
"Love Sex and Romance" (Wakoski) **15**:357
"Love Song" (Amichai) **38**:46
"Love Song" (Eliot)
See "The Love Song of J. Alfred Prufrock"
"Love Song" (Levertov) **11**:159, 171
"Love Song" (Sexton) **2**:363
"Love Song" (Williams) **7**:345, 406-07
"Love Song" (Wylie) **23**:314
"Love Song from the Gaelic" (Yeats) **20**:345-46
"A Love Song in the Modern Taste" (Swift) **9**:252, 268
"The Love Song of J. Alfred Prufrock" (Eliot) **5**:153-54, 157, 160, 206; **31**:91-198
"Love Song of Prufrock Junior" (Viereck) **27**:264
"Love Song to Eohippus" (Viereck) **27**:280
Love Songs (Loy) **16**:310, 314-15, 320-21, 323, 325-26, 328
Love Songs (Teasdale) **31**:322, 324, 330-31, 337, 339,-40, 347, 355, 369-70, 388
"Love Songs I" (Loy) **16**:306
"Love Songs in Age" (Larkin) **21**:229, 258
Love Songs to Joannes (Loy) **16**:316, 332
"Love Songs VI" (Loy) **16**:307
"Love Story" (Dalton) **36**:136
"A Love Story" (Graves) **6**:129, 133, 136-37, 144, 163, 172
"Love Thy Neighbour" (Lawrence) **54**:249
"The Love Tree" (Cullen) **20**:85
"Love Turn'd to Hatred" (Suckling) **30**:146
"Love Unknown" (Herbert) **4**:109, 112, 123, 129
"The love which is imprinted in my soule" (Sidney) **32**:250
"Love Winter When the Plant Says Nothing" (Merton) **10**:334
"Love without Hope" (Graves) **6**:141, 144, 149-50
"Love You Right Back" (Brooks) **7**:94
"The Love-Letters" (Patmore) **59**:230, 234, 258
"Loveliest of Trees" (Housman) **2**:184-85, 192, 194-95
"Lovely Chance" (Teasdale) **31**:358
"Lovely Flowers and White as Became Him Well" (Cavafy) **36**:81
"Lovely Ladies" (Tu Fu) **9**:330
"The Lovely Lady" (Tu Fu) **9**:322
"A Lovely Love" (Brooks) **7**:81, 96, 100-01
"Lovely White Flowers" (Cavafy) **36**:75, 76, 79, 80-81
Love-Poems (Ovid)
See *Amores*
"The Lover" (Borges)
See "El enamorado"
"The Lover" (Montagu) **16**:337
"The Lover hopeth of better chance" (Wyatt) **27**:338
"The lover lamentes the death of his love" (Wyatt)
See "The louer lamentes the deth of his loue"
"The Lover of Love" (Hagiwara)
See "Koi wo koi suru hito"
"The Lover Pleads with His Friend for Old Friends" (Yeats) **20**:330
"The Lover Seweth how He is Forsaken of Fortune who Sometime Favoured Him" (Wyatt) **27**:309
"A Lover since Childhood" (Graves) **6**:129
"The Lover Tells of the Rose in His Heart" (Morris) **55**:284
"The Lover Tells of the Rose in His Heart" (Yeats) **20**:338
"The Lovers" (Graham) **59**:132, 173
"The Lovers" (Merrill) **28**:239, 243
"Lovers' Death" (Baudelaire)
See "La mort des amants"
"Lovers infinitenesse" (Donne) **1**:130, 153
"The Lovers of Gudrun" (Morris) **55**:245, 250, 259-60, 262, 285, 307, 309, 329, 332
"Lovers of the Poor" (Brooks) **7**:86, 88, 96
"A Lover's Affliction" (Dafydd)
See "Cystudd Cariad"
"A Lovers' Quarrel" (Browning) **61**:88
"The Lover's Song" (Yeats) **20**:308
"The Lover's Tale" (Tennyson) **6**:358, 373-74, 379-80
The Lovers Watch (Behn)
See *La Montre; or, The Lover's Watch*
"Loves Alchymie" (Donne) **1**:147, 159
"Love's Apology" (Patmore) **59**:219, 240
"Love's Causes" (Browning) **6**:17
"Love's Clock" (Suckling) **30**:162
"Love's Diet" (Donne) **1**:127
"Love's Draft" (Dunbar) **5**:126
"Love's Expression" (Browning) **6**:17
"Love's Farewell" (Brontë) **8**:57
"Love's Gleaning Tide" (Morris) **55**:340
"Loves Growth" (Donne) **1**:153
"Loves Invalides" (Thoreau) **30**:245
"Love's Loneliness" (Yeats) **20**:333
"Love's New Creation" (Browning) **6**:17
"Love's Nocturn" (Rossetti) **44**:257-60
"Love's Nocturne" (Rossetti) **44**:257-60
"Love's Obstacles" (Browning) **6**:16
"The Loves of the Plants" (Noyes) **27**:129
"Love's Parable" (Warren) **37**:286, 288, 322, 332
"Love's Philosophy" (Shelley) **14**:167
"Love's Progress" (Roethke) **15**:289
"Love's Refuge" (Browning) **6**:17
"Love's Repetitions" (Browning) **6**:17
"Love's Reward" (Morris) **55**:340
"Loves Riddles" (Donne) **1**:153
"Love's Sacrifice" (Browning) **6**:17
"Loves Siege" (Suckling) **30**:145
"Love's Tears" (Dafydd)
See "Dagrau Serch"
"Love's Trappist" (Chesterton) **28**:95
"Love's World" (Suckling) **30**:118, 142
"(Lovesong.)" (Celan)
See "(Liebeslied.)"
"The Love-Song of a Leprechaun" (Noyes) **27**:136
"Love-Sweetness" (Rossetti) **44**:166
"Loving a Noble Girl" (Dafydd)
See "Caru Merch Fonheddig"
Loving a Woman in Two Worlds (Bly) **39**:74, 84, 98, 100-04
"Loving an Honest Man" (Piercy) **29**:309
"Loving and Beloved" (Suckling) **30**:140, 146
"Loving him secretly" (Char)
See "L'amoureuse en secret"
"The Loving Shepherdess" (Jeffers) **17**:110, 131
"Loving the Killer" (Sexton) **2**:352-53
"Low Barometer" (Bridges) **28**:77
"Low down" (Brown) **55**:150
"The Low Sky" (Jeffers) **17**:117

"Low Tide" (Carman)
See "Low Tide on Grand Pré"
"Low Tide" (Millay) **6**:236
"Low Tide at Grand Pré" (Carman)
See "Low Tide on Grand Pré"
"Low Tide at Schoodic" (Clampitt) **19**:86, 90
"Low Tide on Avon" (Carman) **34**:236
"Low Tide on Grand Pré" (Carman) **34**:203-05, 210, 214, 235-37
Low Tide on Grand Pré: A Book of Lyrics (Carman) **34**:198, 205, 208, 210, 212, 214-15, 217-18, 224, 235, 237-38
"Low to High" (Hughes) **1**:258, 267
"Low-anchored Cloud" (Thoreau) **30**:190, 194, 207, 216
"The Lower East Side of Manhattan" (Cruz) **37**:31
"Lower Field—Enniscorthy" (Olson) **19**:293
"The Lowest Place" (Rossetti) **7**:274, 291
"The Lowest Room" (Rossetti)
See "The Lowest Place"
"The Lowestoft Boat" (Kipling) **3**:183
Les Loyaux Adversaires (Char) **56**:186
"A Lu Mountain Song for the Palace Censor Empty-Boat Lu" (Li Po) **29**:156
"Lub O' Mine" (McKay) **2**:221
"Lucas XXIII" (Borges) **32**:48
"Lucasia" (Philips) **40**:295
"Lucca" (Ungaretti) **57**:347
"Lucien Létinois" (Verlaine) **2**:416
"Lucifer" (Lawrence) **54**:218
"Lucifer in Starlight" (Meredith) **60**:253, 262, 295, 326, 335-36, 338-40
"Lucifer in the Train" (Rich) **5**:354, 362, 393
"lucifer speaks in his own voice" (Clifton) **17**:37
"lucifer understanding at last" (Clifton) **17**:30
"Lucifer's Feast" (Noyes) **27**:122
"Lucina Schynning in Silence of the Nicht ..." (Ní Chuilleanáin) **34**:348
"Lucinda Matlock" (Masters) **36**:183, 185
"Luck" (Carver) **54**:31
"Lucks my fair falcon and your fellows all" (Wyatt) **27**:367
The Lucky Bag (MacDiarmid) **9**:158
"Lucrece" (Gower) **59**:55, 58, 60-61
"Lucrece and Nara" (Jackson) **44**:29, 62-3
"Lucretius" (Tennyson) **6**:358, 360, 378, 380
"lucy and her girls" (Clifton) **17**:13
"Lucy Gray" (Coleridge) **11**:73-4
"Lucy Gray" (Wordsworth) **4**:398, 404, 428
Lueurs des tirs (Apollinaire) **7**:22
"Lugar da Lázaro" (Guillén) **35**:215
"Luis Cernuda 1902-1963" (Paz) **48**:184
"Luke Havergal" (Robinson) **1**:467, 475, 490-94
"Lull" (Roethke) **15**:246-50, 282
"Lull" (Wagoner) **33**:367
"Lull (November, 1939)" (Roethke) **15**:250
"Lullaby" (Dunbar) **5**:122
"Lullaby" (Glück) **16**:170
"Lullaby" (Goodison)
See "A Lullaby for Jean Rhys"
"The Lullaby" (Jackson) **44**:5
"A Lullaby" (Jarrell) **41**:200
"Lullaby" (Sexton) **2**:359
"Lullaby" (Sitwell) **3**:309, 311, 326
"Lullaby" (Stone) **53**:221
"Lullaby" (Yeats) **20**:328
"Lullaby" (Zagajewski) **27**:389
"A Lullaby for Jean Rhys" (Goodison) **36**:143, 154
"Lullaby for Jumbo" (Sitwell) **3**:303
"The Lullaby of Broadway" (Szirtes) **51**:178
"The Lullaby of Charles V" (Carducci)
See "Nina Nanna di Carlo V"
Lullay Lullay like a Child (Skelton) **25**:345
"Lumber Yard Pools at Sunset" (Sandburg) **41**:322
"The Lumens" (Olds) **22**:340
"La lumière, changée" (Bonnefoy) **58**:118-19
"La Lumière du soir" (Bonnefoy) **58**:167-68
"Lumuba's Grave" (Hughes) **53**:111
"La luna" (Borges) **22**:100; **32**:42, 74, 132
"Luna bez golovy" (Shvarts) **50**:161
Luna de enfrente (Borges) **22**:71-2, 93-4; **32**:37-8, 57, 60, 83-4, 95, 124
"Luna de marzo sobre el mar" (Storni) **33**:239, 269, 271;
"Luna Habitabilis" (Gray) **2**:155
"Luna llena" (Alurista) **34**:28
Luna silvestre (Paz) **1**:367; **48**:176, 243
"Lunar Baedecker" (Loy) **16**:306-08, 321
Lunar Baedecker (Loy) **16**:306, 310, 316, 321-22, 330
Lunar Baedecker and Time-tables (Loy) **16**:306, 316
"The Lunar Cycle" (Piercy) **29**:311
The Lunar Cycle (Piercy) **29**:300, 303
"The Lunar Probe" (Kumin) **15**:180
"Lunch" (Stein) **18**:328
"The Lunch Hour FYI" (O'Hara) **45**:170
"Lunch in the Sun" (Mistral)
See "Almuerzo al sol"
Lunch Poems (O'Hara) **45**:116, 132, 135, 145, 214, 216, 218-19
"Lundi rue Christine" (Apollinaire) **7**:18, 36
"Lune de miel" (Eliot) **5**:185, 191
"La lune est sterile" (Laforgue) **14**:61
Lupercal (Hughes) **7**:115, 118-20, 123, 135-38, 140-41, 150, 158, 162-63, 165, 169
Lusiad (Camões)
See *Os Lusíadas*
Os Lusíadas (Camões) **31**:5-15, 17-21, 24, 26-29, 31-32, 34-40, 43-51, 53-54, 56-62, 64-70, 72-84,
The Lusiads (Camões)
See *Os Lusíadas*
"Lust" (Brooke) **24**:53, 56, 85
"Lustra" (Okigbo) **7**:221, 225, 232, 239, 250
Lustra (Pound) **4**:320, 365
"Lusts" (Verlaine)
See "Luxures"
"The Lute and the Lyre" (Carducci)
See "Il Liuto e la Lira"
"Luto" (Mistral) **32**:170
"Lux" (Hugo) **17**:54
"Luxures" (Verlaine) **2**:416
"La Luz del día" (Parra) **39**:294
"Luz natal" (Guillén) **35**:174, 229
"La luz sobre el monte" (Guillén) **35**:158
"LVIII" (Carman) **34**:228
"LXI" (Storni) **33**:287, 290;
"LXVII" (Carman) **34**:210
"LXVII" (Storni) **33**:287;
"LXVIII" (Carman) **34**:211
"LXXIX" (Carman) **34**:210
"LXXXIV" (Carman) **34**:211
"Lycambes Talks to John" (Tate) **50**:319
"Lyceia" (Graves) **6**:156
"Lycidas" (Arnold) **5**:7
"Lycidas" (Milton) **19**:193, 202, 211-13, 217, 219-26, 242, 250-53
"Lycidas" (Swinburne) **24**:320
Lycidas (Milton) **29**:212, 214, 241, 243, 272
"Lydia Is Gone This Many a Year" (Reese) **29**:333, 347
"Lyell's Hypothesis Again" (Rexroth) **20**:216, 218
"Lying" (Wilbur) **51**:249, 311, 315, 335
"Lying in a Hammock at William Duffy's Farm in Pine Island, Minnesota" (Wright) **36**:283, 285, 300, 309, 326, 339-40, 350, 352, 364, 374, 396
"Lying Spying" (Jackson) **44**:5
"Lynch I" (Césaire) **25**:30
"The Lynching" (McKay) **2**:205-06, 212, 217
"Lynching Song" (Hughes) **1**:241; **53**:114
"Lyonnesse" (Plath) **37**:208
"La Lyre" (Ronsard) **11**:266
"A Lyric" (Carman) **34**:202, 208
"The Lyric Beasts" (Dickey) **40**:228
"Lyric Intermezzo" (Heine)
See *Lyrisches Intermezzo*
"Lyric LIII" (Carman) **34**:227
"Lyric LIV" (Carman) **34**:211, 227, 233
"Lyric LXIII" (Carman) **34**:226
"Lyric V" (Carman) **34**:227
"Lyric VI" (Carman) **34**:227
"Lyric XXXIX" (Carman) **34**:228
"The Lyric Year" (Darío)
See "El año lírico"
Lyrical Ballads (Coleridge) **11**:37, 59-60, 68, 91; **39**:169, 182
Lyrical Ballads, with a Few Other Poems (Wordsworth) **4**:372-73, 375, 378, 380, 400, 412, 415-19, 425-29
"Lyrical Letter to Another Woman" (Storni)
See "Carta lírica a otra mujer"
"A Lyrick to Mirth" (Herrick) **9**:94, 103
Lyrics, 1962-1985 (Dylan) **37**:59-65
Lyrics of Life and Love (Braithwaite) **52**:106, 110, 122
Lyrics of Love and Laughter (Dunbar) **5**:119, 139
Lyrics of Lowly Life (Dunbar) **5**:117-18, 132, 136, 140
Lyrisches Intermezzo (Heine) **25**:130-31, 139, 141, 143, 161
"Lyrisches Intermezzo No 10" (Heine) **25**:142
"Lyrisches Intermezzo No 39" (Heine) **25**:144
"Lyrisches Intermezzo No.33" (Heine) **25**:142
"Lysergic Acid" (Ginsberg) **4**:74, 81
"Lyubil i ya v bylye gody" (Lermontov) **18**:293
"Lyubka" (Pasternak) **6**:253-54
"M AA l'anti-philosophe" (Tzara) **27**:235
"A M Alphonse de Lamartine" (Hugo) **17**:75, 90
"M Anti-psychologue" (Tzara) **27**:235
"M Antipyrine" (Tzara) **27**:235
"M Antitête" (Tzara) **27**:235
"A M de Chateaubriand" (Hugo) **17**:90
M: Writings, '67-'72 (Cage) **58**:195, 205-7, 217-19
"Ma bohème" (Rimbaud) **3**:271, 276, 283; **57**:173, 178, 191, 196, 202, 208-9, 253
"Ma Man" (Hughes) **1**:270
"Ma Rainey" (Brown) **55**:72, 76, 90, 94, 102, 113-14, 142, 145, 151-52, 154, 178-79
"Macarius and the Pony" (Merton) **10**:351
"Macaw" (Bogan) **12**:86
Macchu Picchu (Neruda)
See *Alturas de Macchu Picchu*
MacFlecknoe; or, A Satire upon the Trew-Blew-Protestant Poet, T. S. (Dryden) **25**:70, 114-16, 118, 120-23
"The Machine Gun" (Jarrell) **41**:213
"Macho" (Cervantes) **35**:134
"Machu Picchu" (Birney) **52**:15-16, 45, 57, 96, 98
"Mackinnon's Boat" (Tomlinson) **17**:344
"MacMoransbridge" (Ní Chuilleanáin) **34**:354
"Macpherson's Farewell" (Burns) **6**:55
"MacStatesman and Co." (MacDiarmid) **9**:176
"Mad As the Mist and the Snow" (Yeats) **20**:328-29
"The Mad Druggist" (Warren) **37**:350
"The Mad Farmer Manifesto: The First Amendment" (Berry) **28**:13
"Mad Judy" (Hardy) **8**:102
Mad Love (Harjo)
See *In Mad Love and War*
"The Mad Maid's Song" (Herrick) **9**:87
"The Mad Monk" (Coleridge) **11**:69
"The Mad Mother" (Wordsworth) **4**:374, 380
"A Mad Negro Soldier Confined at Munich" (Lowell) **3**:205, 218, 222
"The Mad Scene" (Merrill) **28**:254
"Mad Song" (Blake) **12**:31-2
"Mad Yak" (Corso) **33**:25, 40-1
"Madam and Her Might-Have Been" (Hughes) **1**:243
"Madam and the Army" (Hughes) **53**:115
"Madam and the Movies" (Hughes) **53**:115
"Madam and the Wrong Visitor" (Hughes) **1**:243
"Madame de Soubise" (Vigny) **26**:410-11

"Madame Decrepitude" (Cassian) **17**:13
"A Madame Sand" (Nerval) **13**:178
"Madame Withouten Many Wordes" (Wyatt) **27**:316, 328, 330
"Das Mädchen spricht" (Goethe) **5**:249
"Madeleine" (Apollinaire) **7**:32
"Mademoiselle Bistouri" (Baudelaire) **1**:58
"A Mademoiselle Louise B" (Hugo) **17**:93
"Mademoiselle Veronique" (Brodsky) **9**:10
"Madhouse Bells" (Browning) **2**:30
"Madhouse Cells" (Browning) **2**:26
"Madhumanjari" (Tagore) **8**:416
"The Madison Experience" (Jordan) **38**:126
"Madison in the Mid-Sixties" (Stone) **53**:243
The Madman, His Parables and Poems (Gibran) **9**:69, 71, 75, 77-80, 82
"Madman's Song" (Wylie) **23**:301, 309, 326, 328
"Madness" (Baraka) **4**:27
"Madness" (Dickey) **40**:176, 183-84, 199-200, 244, 246
"The Madness of King Goll" (Yeats) **20**:344, 354
"A Madona Poesía" (Storni) **33**:257, 262, 285, 294;
"The Madonna" (Tennyson) **6**:353
"Madonna of the Evening Flowers" (Lowell) **13**:60, 64, 67, 96
"La madre" (Carducci) **46**:32, 49, 64-65
"La madre granada" (Mistral) **32**:179-80
"Madre Sofia" (Ríos) **57**:312
"La madre triste" (Mistral) **32**:201
"Madre Tumba Soledad" (Alurista) **34**:28, 47
"Madrid 1937" (Neruda) **4**:310
"Madrigal" (Nemerov) **24**:256
"Madrigal triste" (Baudelaire) **1**:61
"Madrigali privati" (Montale) **13**:106, 167
"Madrugada" (Fuertes) **27**:7
"Madurai" (Paz) **1**:361
"The Madwoman's Miracle" (Wylie) **23**:321
"Maenad" (Plath) **37**:243
"La maestra rural" (Mistral) **32**:208
"Le maestrine" (Pavese) **13**:221
"Mag" (Sandburg) **41**:272-73, 334, 364
"Magadalena" (Gautier) **18**:163-64
"Magasins du Louvre" (Loy) **16**:312, 328
The Magdalene Sermon (Ní Chuilleanáin) **34**:350, 352, 354, 360-62, 373, 380, 382
The Magdalene Sermon and Earlier Poems (Ní Chuilleanáin) **34**:360
"The Magellanic Clouds" (Wakoski) **15**:325, 363
The Magellanic Clouds (Wakoski) **15**:350-51, 363, 365-66
"The Magellanic Heart" (Neruda)
See "El corazón magellanico"
"Les mages" (Hugo) **17**:83, 87
"Maggie, a Lady" (Rossetti) **7**:291
"Maggiolata" (Carducci)
See "Idillio di Maggio"
"The Magi" (Glück) **16**:125, 140, 149
"Magias parciales del Quijote" (Borges) **32**:60
"Magic" (Dove) **6**:113
"Magic" (Levertov) **11**:209
"Magic Carpet" (Silverstein) **49**:332
Magic City (Komunyakaa) **51**:21-22, 29, 31-34, 56, 58
"The Magic Flute" (Carman) **34**:208
"Magic Island" (Song) **21**:344
The Magic Lantern (Tsvetaeva)
See *Volshebny fonar*
"TH MAGIC LURE OF SEA SHELLS" (Bissett) **14**:34
"The Magic Morning" (Smith) **12**:331
"Magic Psalm" (Ginsberg) **47**:22
"Magician" (Shapiro) **25**:309
The Magician (Abse) **41**:3-4
The Magician's Feastletters (Wakoski) **15**:356
"The Magician's Retreat" (Moore) **49**:150, 161
Magique (Césaire) **25**:36
"Magna est Veritas" (Smith) **12**:333
"The Magnet" (Sarton) **39**:322
"The Magnet" (Stone) **53**:217
The Magnetic Fields (Breton)
See *Les Champs Magnétiques*
The Magnetic Mountain (Day Lewis) **11**:123-26, 128-30, 135, 138-39, 143-45, 148, 151-52
"Magnets" (Cullen) **20**:60
"Magnitudo parvi" (Hugo) **17**:89
"Magnolia Flower" (Hughes) **1**:237
"The Magnolia Shadow" (Montale)
See "L'ombra della magnolia"
"Magnolias" (Mueller) **33**:193
"Magnolias in Snow" (Hayden) **6**:194, 196
"The Magpie's Advice" (Dafydd)
See "Cyngor y Biogen"
"Magpie's Song" (Snyder) **21**:297
"Magpiety" (Milosz)
See "Śroczość"
"The Magus" (Dickey) **40**:176, 179
"Mahomets Gesang" (Goethe) **5**:247
Mahua (Tagore) **8**:415-16
"Mai Village" (Brathwaite) **56**:93
"The Maid Servant at the Inn" (Parker) **28**:353
"A Maiden" (Teasdale) **31**:363, 379
"The Maiden Marriage" (Swinburne) **24**:357
"Maiden May" (Rossetti) **7**:277
"Maiden Song" (Rossetti) **7**:264, 274-6, 289
"The Maiden without Hands" (Sexton) **2**:365
"Maidenhood" (Longfellow) **30**:13-14, 21, 45
"A Maiden's Pledge" (Hardy) **8**:98
"Maiden's Sorrow" (Bryant) **20**:15
"The Maiden's Virtues" (Dafydd)
See "Campau Bun"
"The Maid's Thought" (Jeffers) **17**:117
"Maifest" (Goethe) **5**:251
"The Mail" (Carver) **54**:12
"Mail Call" (Jarrell) **41**:189, 200
"Mail Order" (Quintana) **36**:275
"Mailied" (Goethe) **5**:245
"Mailie's Dying Words and Elegy" (Burns)
See "The Death and Dying Words of Poor Mailie"
"Maillol" (Tomlinson) **17**:311, 314, 335
"The Maimed Man" (Tate) **50**:268, 290-96, 329, 331-33
Mainland (Cruz) **37**:10, 12, 16, 25, 33-4
"Mairegen" (Stramm) **50**:175, 205
"Maisie" (Merrill) **28**:228, 254
"La maison des mortes" (Apollinaire) **7**:47
"Maison doyenne" (Char) **56**:150
"La maison du Berger" (Vigny) **26**:370, 377, 386-87, 391-94, 396, 402, 404, 406, 409, 413
"La Maison d'Yves" (Breton) **15**:63-7
"Maison flake" (Tzara) **27**:233
"Maithuna" (Paz) **1**:361, 368
"The Maja and the Old Woman" (Aleixandre) **15**:5-6
"A Majestic Love Song" (Amichai) **38**:46
"Le Majeur Ydow" (Smith) **12**:331
"Major Macroo" (Smith) **12**:309, 317
"A Major Work" (Meredith) **28**:201
Majors and Minors (Dunbar) **5**:115, 117-18, 128, 132, 135-36, 142
"Make Big Money at Home! Write Poems in Spare Time!!" (Nemerov) **24**:267
"The Maker" (Borges)
See "El hacedor"
"The Maker" (Illyés)
See "Teremteni"
The Maker (Borges)
See *El hacedor*
"The Makers" (Nemerov) **24**:289-90
"Making a Living" (Sexton) **2**:367
"Making a Sacher Torte" (Wakoski) **15**:355, 372
"Making, Camp" (Wagoner) **33**:359
"The Making of an Irish Goddess" (Boland) **58**:12, 14, 31-35, 48, 56-58, 88, 93
The Making of Personality (Carman) **34**:205
"the making of poems" (Clifton) **17**:27
"The Making of the Drum" (Brathwaite) **56**:50, 75, 84
"Making the Connection" (Kumin) **15**:208
"Making Up" (Boland) **58**:4, 29, 35, 44, 98
"Le mal" (Rimbaud) **3**:283; **57**:244
"Malabaress" (Baudelaire)
See "A une Malabaraise"
"Malachowski's Ravine" (Herbert)
See "Wawóz Malachowskiego"
"Malachy Deagan" (Masters) **1**:343
"Malade" (Lawrence) **54**:175
"Mal'akhei goral" (Amichai) **38**:7
"Malarz" (Herbert) **50**:5
"Malcolm" (Sanchez) **9**:224, 231
"Malcolm" (Walker) **20**:277
"Malcolm Spoke/Who listened? (This Poem Is for My Consciousness Too)" (Madhubuti) **5**:328, 341
"Il male di vivere" (Montale) **13**:105
"Male Gorillas" (Stone) **53**:247, 257
"La malédiction" (Éluard) **38**:70
"Malediction Upon Myself" (Wylie) **23**:303, 310
Les Malheurs des immortels (Éluard) **38**:88-89, 92-93
"Malinconia" (Ungaretti) **57**:346
"Le maline" (Rimbaud) **3**:283
"Malines" (Verlaine) **32**:395
"The Malingerer" (McKay) **2**:226
"'Mallorca,' un poema en el olvido" (Borges) **22**:92
"Malmaison" (Lowell) **13**:71, 78, 84
"Malourène" (Apollinaire) **7**:48
"Mama Don't Want U" (Alurista) **34**:27
"Maman" (Walcott) **46**:239
"Mamie" (Sandburg) **41**:234, 261, 273, 295, 318
Maminka (Seifert) **47**:326, 335
"Mammon" (Brathwaite) **56**:67, 76
"Mammorial Stunzas for Aimee Simple McFarcin" (Birney) **52**:11, 20, 26-27, 62, 79
"the mammoth corridors" (Birney) **52**:36, 38, 72
"Mammy Hums" (Sandburg) **2**:324; **41**:270
"Mammy Songs" (Hughes) **53**:101
"Man" (Brooke) **24**:71, 75
"Man" (Corso) **33**:35, 37-8, 44, 48-9
"Man" (Herbert) **4**:100-01, 103
"Man" (Lamartine)
See "L'homme"
"Man!" (MacLeish) **47**:127
"The Man" (Storni)
See "El hombre"
"The Man against the Sky" (Robinson) **1**:462, 471, 490, 492-94
The Man against the Sky (Robinson) **1**:462-63, 467-68, 474; **35**:368
"Man and Bat" (Lawrence) **54**:187, 236
"Man and Bird" (Mahon) **60**:163-64, 167, 169
"Man and Dog" (Sassoon) **12**:255
"Man and Dog" (Thomas) **53**:326
"The Man and the Echo" (Yeats) **20**:314, 335
"Man and Wife" (Lowell) **3**:206, 209, 221, 245
"Man and Wife" (Sexton) **2**:363
"Man and Woman Go through a Cancer Ward" (Benn)
See "Mann und Frau gehn durch die Krebsbaracke"
"The Man beneath the Tree" (Wright) **14**:343, 345, 347
"Man Bites Dog-Days" (Nash) **21**:265
"Man Born to Be King" (Morris) **55**:242, 259
The Man Born to be King (Morris) **55**:249
"The Man Born to Farming" (Berry) **28**:26
"Man Coming of Age" (Warren) **37**:284, 331
Man Does, Woman Is (Graves) **6**:154
"Man Doesn't Exist" (Aleixandre) **15**:20, 22
"Man Eating" (Kenyon) **57**:14, 38, 47
"The Man Has Lost His Shadow" (Alurista) **34**:10
"The Man He Killed" (Hardy) **8**:102-03

"A Man I Am" (Smith) **12**:295
"Man in Black" (Plath) **1**:389; **37**:179-80
"Man in Majesty" (Jarrell) **41**:170
"Man in Moonlight" (Warren) **37**:295
The Man in the Black Coat Turns (Bly) **39**:63, 65-6, 98-104
A Man in the Divided Sea (Merton) **10**:338, 346-47, 350
"The Man in the Street Is Fed" (Sandburg) **41**:332
"The Man in the Yellow Terry" (Walker) **30**:361
"Man into Men" (Hughes) **1**:241, 243
"Man is a Snow" (Birney) **52**:8, 39, 47, 51-52, 54
"Man is a Spirit" (Smith) **12**:297, 316
"A Man Meets a Woman on the Street" (Jarrell) **41**:169, 178, 180-81, 189
"Man of Lawe's Tale" (Chaucer)
See "Man of Law's Tale"
"Man of Law's Tale" (Chaucer) **19**:13, 15, 24, 26, 45, 54-6, 59-60, 62
"A Man of the Middle Class" (Brooks) **7**:62
"The Man of Tyre" (Lawrence) **54**:187, 197, 199-201, 250
"Man of Words" (Ashbery) **26**:126
"Man on a Tractor" (Birney) **52**:8, 36-37, 39-40
"The Man on His Death Bed" (Aleixandre) **15**:8
"The Man on the Dump" (Ashbery) **26**:153
"The Man on the Hotel Room Bed" (Kinnell) **26**:286
"Man on the Pink Corner" (Borges)
See "El Hombre de la esquina rosada"
"Man Ray" (Éluard) **38**:86
Man Root (Paz)
See *Raíz del hombre*
"the man say we making noise" (Alurista) **34**:35
"The Man Seeking Experience Enquires His Way of a Drop of Water" (Hughes) **7**:116, 118
"Man Sleeping" (Kenyon) **57**:47
"Man Splitting Wood in the Daybreak" (Kinnell) **26**:293
"Man Spricht Deutsch" (Enzensberger) **28**:142
"The Man that are Falling" (Stevens) **6**:310
"Man, the Man-Hunter" (Sandburg) **2**:308
"Man the Master" (Merton) **10**:345
"man thinks you just began it" (Alurista) **34**:39
"Man Waking" (Kenyon) **57**:20, 47
"A Man Walking and Singing" (Berry) **28**:3-4, 7, 18
"Man Was Made to Mourn" (Burns) **6**:68
"Man Watching a Woman" (Ní Chuilleanáin) **34**:367
"The Man Who Came to the Last Floor" (Cruz) **37**:10, 18
"The Man Who Died" (Lawrence) **54**:230, 234
The Man Who Died Twice (Robinson) **1**:469, 472, 475, 477, 483, 489-90
"The Man Who Dreamed of Fairyland" (Yeats) **20**:343, 354
"A Man Who Loves Love" (Hagiwara)
See "Koi wo koi suru hito"
"The Man Who Never Laughed Again" (Morris) **55**:305
The Man Who Shook Hands (Wakoski) **15**:366
"The Man Who Writes Ants" (Merwin) **45**:50
"The Man Whose Pharynx Was Bad" (Stevens) **6**:294
"The Man with a Past" (Hardy) **8**:93
Man with a Sling (Neruda)
See *El hondero entusiasta, 1923-1924*
The Man with Night Sweats (Gunn) **26**:224, 228, 230-231
"Man with One Small Hand" (Page) **12**:170
The Man with Seven Toes (Ondaatje) **28**:298-302, 318, 322, 326-27
"The Man with the Blue Guitar" (Stevens) **6**:298, 323-24, 326, 337, 339
The Man with the Blue Guitar, and Other Poems (Stevens) **6**:304
"Man Without Sense of Direction" (Ransom) **61**:275, 289
"A Man Writes to a Part of Himself" (Bly) **30**:7, 18, 79-80, 84, 94, 102-03
"A Man Young and Old" (Yeats) **20**:328
"The Manager" (Ignatow) **34**:273
"Una mañana de 1649" (Borges) **32**:116
"Mañana gris" (Storni) **33**:268;
"El manantial" (Guillén) **35**:155, 157, 232
"Manas-sundari" (Tagore) **8**:408
"La manca" (Mistral) **32**:180
"Manciple's Tale" (Chaucer) **19**:11, 13, 48
The Manciple!s Tale (Chaucer) **58**:336
"Mandalay" (Kipling) **3**:158, 160, 162, 167, 188-89, 192
"The Mandolin, the Carnation and the Bamboo" (Apollinaire)
See "La mandoline, l'oeillet et le bambou"
"Mandoline" (Verlaine) **32**:350-51, 370-71, 390-91
"La mandoline, l'oeillet et le bambou" (Apollinaire) **7**:18, 20-2, 34, 36
"Manfred" (Meredith) **60**:250
Manfred (Byron) **16**:68-72, 82-4, 86-90, 108, 111
"Mangham" (Dickey) **40**:200
Mango (Cervantes) **35**:132
"Mango Grove" (Tagore)
See "Amravan"
"Mango of Poetry" (Goodison) **36**:158
"The Mango on the Mango Tree" (Warren) **37**:331
"Manhattan: Grace Church" (Clampitt) **19**:100
"Manhattan: Luminism" (Doty) **53**:69
"Manhattan May Day Midnight" (Ginsberg) **4**:84
"Manhood" (Thoreau) **30**:180, 197
"Mania di solitudine" (Pavese) **13**:225
"Mania for solitude" (Pavese)
See "Mania di solitudine"
"Manicure" (Brooks) **7**:53
"Manie" (Éluard) **38**:69
"Manifest Destiny" (Graham) **59**:135, 138, 159, 177
"Manifesto" (Lawrence) **54**:185-86, 194-95, 211, 214, 232-33
"Manifesto" (Parra) **39**:275-76, 293, 295, 305-6, 309-10
"Manifesto" (Thomas)
See "Poetic Manifesto"
"Manitoba Childe Roland" (Sandburg) **41**:240
"Mankind" (Trakl)
See "Menschheit"
"The Man-Moth" (Bishop) **3**:37, 65; **34**:79, 82, 95, 97, 146, 160, 163-64, 189
"Mann und Frau gehn durch die Krebsbaracke" (Benn) **35**:4, 30
"The Manner of the World Nowadays" (Skelton) **25**:337
Mannerly Margery Milk and Ale (Skelton) **25**:345
"Manners" (Bishop) **34**:69, 95
"The Manor Farm" (Thomas) **53**:329; **53**:267, 274, 349
"The Manor Garden" (Plath) **1**:389; **37**:182-83
"Manos de obreros" (Mistral) **32**:187
Las manos del día (Neruda) **4**:288
"A Man's a Man for a' That" (Burns) **6**:60
"A Man's Last Word" (Carman) **34**:226
"Man's Medley" (Herbert) **4**:101, 127
"Manscape" (Tomlinson) **17**:351-52
"Mansion" (Ammons) **16**:16, 20
"Le Manteau de Pascal" (Graham) **59**:185-87
"Mantis" (Zukofsky) **11**:341, 347, 356, 392-99
"'Mantis,' an Interpretation" (Zukofsky) **11**:341, 356, 394
"Manual System" (Sandburg) **2**:304
"Manuel Comnenus" (Cavafy) **36**:3, 35
"Manuelzinho" (Bishop) **3**:59-60; **34**:139
"Manuscript Found in a Book of Joseph Conrad" (Borges)
See "Manuscrito hallado en un libro de Joseph Conrad"
"Manuscrito hallado en un libro de Joseph Conrad" (Borges) **32**:83
"Many Farms Notes" (Ortiz) **17**:231
"Many Handles" (Sandburg) **41**:302
"Many Have Fallen" (Corso) **33**:50
Many Inventions (Kipling) **3**:160
Many Long Years Ago (Nash) **21**:266
"Many Loves" (Ginsberg) **47**:54
"The Many Mansions" (Levertov) **11**:201
"Many of Our Waters: Variations on a Poem by a Black Child" (Wright) **36**:301, 309, 317, 320-21, 366, 371
"Many Swans" (Lowell) **13**:61, 64-5, 83
Manyo (Yakamochi)
See *Man'yōshū*
Manyo Anthology (Yakamochi)
See *Man'yōshū*
"Manyone Flying" (Swenson) **14**:283
Manyōshiu Kogi (Yakamochi) **48**:72
The Manyōshū (Yakamochi)
See *Man'yōshū*
Manyōshū (Yakamochi)
See *Man'yōshū*
Man'yôshû (Yakamochi)
See *Man'yōshū*
Manyoshu (Yakamochi)
See *Man'yōshū*
Man'yōshū (Yakamochi) **48**:72-146
The Manyoshu: One Thousand Poems Selected and Translated from the Japanese (Yakamochi)
See *Man'yōshū*
"Manzanita" (Snyder) **21**:297
"The Map" (Bishop) **3**:37, 50-2; **34**:54, 63, 67, 81, 115, 122, 146, 149, 161
"The Map" (Stryk) **27**:203
"Map for Despair" (Sarton) **39**:321
The Map of Love (Thomas) **2**:381, 390
"A Map of the Antilles" (Walcott) **46**:231, 272-73, 322
"A Map of the City" (Gunn) **26**:219
"Maple" (Frost) **39**:235
"Maple and Sumach" (Day Lewis) **11**:144
"Mappemounde" (Birney) **52**:9, 21-22, 44-47, 56-57, 79, 91
"Las máquinas" (Guillén) **35**:142
"El mar" (Borges) **22**:99
"El mar" (Paz) **48**:181
"Mar de pantalla" (Storni) **33**:262, 294, 296;
"Mar de Sangres" (Alurista) **34**:46, 46
"Mar Portuguese" (Pessoa) **20**:170
El mar y las campanas (Neruda) **4**:287-88
"Mar y noche" (Aleixandre) **15**:16
"Mara" (Jeffers) **17**:146
"Marathon" (Glück) **16**:152, 164, 166-67
"Marble" (Warren) **37**:336
"marbles and calluses" (Alurista)
See "las canicas y mis callos"
"Marburg" (Pasternak) **6**:270-71, 281
Marcel Duchamp, James Joyce, Erik Satie: An Alphabet (Cage) **58**:219
"March" (Bryant) **20**:12
"March" (Kavanagh) **33**:132
"March" (MacLeish) **47**:127
"March" (Thomas) **53**:328, 332
"March" (Wilbur) **51**:280
"March 1, 1847. By the First Post" (Boland) **58**:25, 60-61
"March 21 1987" (Brutus) **24**:110
"March is a Silversmith" (Kavanagh) **33**:140
"March Moon" (Hughes) **53**:85
The March of Coxey's Army (Wagoner) **33**:337
"The March of the Cameron Men" (Robinson) **1**:476
"March Twilight" (Bogan) **12**:111
Marcha triunfal (Darío) **15**:79-80, 85, 111
"Marchas pawnees" (Cardenal) **22**:131
"Marché aux Oiseaux" (Wilbur) **51**:298
"Marche de funèbre pour la mort de la terre" (Laforgue) **14**:95
"Marche Funèbre" (Seifert) **47**:328
"La marche impériale" (Valéry) **9**:391

"The Märchen" (Jarrell) **41**:157-60, 168, 185-86, 194
"Marchenbilder" (Ashbery) **26**:127, 150
"The Marching Morrows" (Carman) **34**:219
"Marching Song" (Wang Wei) **18**:389
"Marcia funebre" (Pasolini) **17**:264
Marconi's Cottage (McGuckian) **27**:84, 91-92, 94-95, 99, 104-105, 110
"Maremma Idyl" (Carducci)
See "Idillio maremmano"
"Margaret" (Sandburg) **2**:303; **41**:335
"Margaret" (Wordsworth) **4**:399
"Margaret Fuller Slack" (Masters) **36**:182, 222
"Margaret!s Bridal Eve" (Meredith) **60**:328
"Margarita" (Castro) **41**:80, 82, 99
"Margarita Debayle" (Darío) **15**:80, 95
"Marginal Employment" (Clampitt) **19**:81, 88
"Marginalia" (Wilbur) **51**:266, 281
"Margite, Marguerite and Margherita" (Stein) **18**:325, 334
"Margrave" (Jeffers) **17**:142
"I mari del sud" (Pavese) **13**:210, 212, 216, 220-26, 228
"Maria" (Gautier) **18**:126
Maria Neféli (Elytis) **21**:130-31
Maria Nephele (Elytis)
See *Maria Neféli*
"Maria Stuart" (Pasternak) **6**:267
"Maria Wentworth" (Carew) **29**:59
"Maria Who Made Faces and a Deplorable Marriage" (Belloc) **24**:24
"The Mariachis—A Glimpse" (Wakoski) **15**:332
"Le Mariage des feuilles" (Péret) **33**:212, 230
"Marian" (Meredith) **60**:308
"Marian Drury" (Carman) **34**:203-04
"Mariana" (Tennyson) **6**:359, 364, 387, 389, 391, 406-09, 411
"Mariana in the South" (Tennyson) **6**:350
A Marianne Moore Reader (Moore) **49**:92, 136
"Marianne, My Mother, and Me" (Kumin) **15**:210-12
"Marichika" (Tagore) **8**:407
"Marietta, Minnesota" (Bly) **39**:69
"Marijuana Notation" (Ginsberg) **4**:79
Marilyn Monroe and Other Poems (Cardenal)
See *Oracion por Marilyn Monroe y otros poemas*
"Marina" (Brooke) **24**:58
"Marina" (Eliot) **5**:164, 195, 205-06, 210
"Marine" (Rimbaud) **3**:261; **57**:239, 273-74, 284
"Marine" (Verlaine) **32**:387
Mariner (Coleridge)
See *The Rime of the Ancient Mariner: A Poet's Reverie*
"Marines USA" (Guillén) **23**:126
Marino Faliero: Doge of Venice (Byron) **16**:103
"Mariposa de obsidiana" (Paz) **1**:364
"Maritime Ode" (Pessoa)
See "Ode Marítima"
"The Mark" (Bogan) **12**:87-8, 98, 106, 121
"Market" (Hayden) **6**:194, 196
"Market at Turk" (Gunn) **26**:186, 219
"Market Day" (Hacker) **47**:87
"Market Street Woman" (Brown) **55**:150
"Mark's Sheep" (MacLeish) **47**:214
"The Marlon Brando Memorial Swimming Pool" (Alexie) **53**:4
Marmion (Scott) **13**:249-51, 256, 258, 261, 264, 266-68, 270-71, 273, 275-76, 279, 281-85, 287-90, 304, 311-12, 317-18
"The Marmozet" (Belloc) **24**:24
"Marrana Placa" (Alurista) **34**:47
"Marriage" (Corso) **33**:5-7, 15-6, 23, 25, 34-6, 42-44, 47, 52-4
"Marriage" (Ignatow) **34**:282, 286
"Marriage" (Moore) **4**:230-31, 233, 243, 249, 251-52, 254-55, 258, 260-61; **49**:91-92, 101, 103, 112, 131, 155
Marriage (Moore) **49**:88
"Le marriage d'André Salmon" (Apollinaire)
See "Poème lu au mariage d'André Salmon"
"The Marriage II" (Levertov) **11**:167
"A Marriage in the Sixties" (Rich) **5**:363
The Marriage of Heaven and Hell (Blake) **12**:12, 28, 36, 39-41, 47-51, 60-1, 64
"The Marriage of Hector and Andromache" (Sappho) **5**:414, 418
"The Marriage of Lord Fauconberg and Lady Mary Cromwell" (Marvell) **10**:270
"The Marriage Ring" (Blake) **12**:34
"Marriage Was a Foreign Country" (Yamada) **44**:334
"The Married Lover" (Patmore) **59**:250
"The Married Man" (Kipling) **3**:192
"The Marring of Malyn" (Carman) **34**:202, 213
"The Marrow" (Roethke) **15**:277, 281
"La Marseillaise" (Éluard) **38**:85
"Marsh Leaf" (Wagoner) **33**:324, 364-65
"Marsh Song at Sunset" (Lanier) **50**:55
"Marshall Washer" (Carruth) **10**:74
"The Marshes of Glynn" (Lanier) **50**:54, 56, 62, 79-81, 83-86, 92, 98-100
"Marsyas" (Masters) **1**:329; **36**:176
Le marteau sans maître (Char) **56**:112, 115, 127-30, 134, 158, 161, 184-85, 189
"The Marten" (Clare) **23**:7
"Martha" (Lorde) **12**:140, 157
"A Martial Law Carol" (Brodsky) **9**:26-7
"Martín" (Baca) **41**:39-40, 45, 65, 68, 70-1, 73
Martín and Meditations (Baca)
See *Martín and Meditations on the South Valley*
Martín and Meditations on the South Valley (Baca) **41**:39-40, 61, 63, 65-7, 70, 74
"Martín VIII" (Baca) **41**:42
"Martín V" (Baca) **41**:42
"Martín IV" (Baca) **41**:42
"Martín IX" (Baca) **41**:42
"Martín I" (Baca) **41**:41
"Martín VII" (Baca) **41**:42
"Martín VI" (Baca) **41**:42
"Martín II" (Baca) **41**:40-1
"Martino Lutero" (Carducci) **46**:52
"Martin!s Puzzle" (Meredith) **60**:262, 294
"Martirio de Santa Olalla" (García Lorca) **3**:132, 146
"The Martyr of Alabama" (Harper) **21**:190
The Martyr of Alabama, and Other Poems (Harper) **21**:189
"The Martyr Poets Did Not Tell" (Dickinson) **1**:96
"A Martyr: The Vigil of the Feast" (Rossetti) **7**:285
"The Martyrdom of Bishop Farrar" (Hughes) **7**:112
"Martyrdom of Saint Eulalia" (García Lorca)
See "Martirio de Santa Olalla"
"Une martyre" (Baudelaire) **1**:45, 48, 62
"Marvella, for Borrowing" (Ríos) **57**:325
The Marvelous Arithmetics of Distance (Lorde) **12**:153
"Mary" (Blake) **12**:35, 43
"Mary and Gabriel" (Brooke) **24**:59, 78, 84
"Mary and Mildred" (Patmore) **59**:228-29
"Mary and the Seasons" (Rexroth) **20**:209
"Mary at the Feet of Christ" (Harper) **21**:191
"Mary Bly" (Wright) **36**:340, 351
"Mary Desti's Ass" (O'Hara) **45**:133, 141
"The 'Mary Gloster'" (Kipling) **3**:161, 167, 181
"Mary Kroger" (Erdrich) **52**:186, 188
"Mary Morison" (Burns)
See "Ye Are Na Mary Morison"
"Mary, Pity Women" (Kipling) **3**:161, 192
"Mary Rowlandson" (Howe)
See "The Captivity and Restoration of Mrs. Mary Rowlandson"
"Mary Sheffield" (Dickey) **40**:226
"Mary Winslow" (Lowell) **3**:206, 217-18
"mary's dream" (Clifton) **17**:19
"Mary's Song" (Plath) **37**:230, 232-33
"Marz has Ruined Nature, for the Moment" (Stevens) **6**:297
"Más allá" (Guillén) **35**:186, 187, 191, 204, 227, 229, 230, 234
"Más esplendor" (Guillén) **35**:179, 181, 182, 183
"Más verdad" (Guillén) **35**:228
Mascarilla y trébol (Storni) **33**:239, 242, 255-59, 261-62, 269, 272, 284-85, 291-97, 305;
"Mascha riait aux anges" (Éluard) **38**:70
"The Mask" (Baudelaire)
See "Le masque"
"Mask" (Illyés) **16**:245, 250
Mask and Clover (Storni)
See *Mascarilla y trébol*
A Mask for Janus (Merwin) **45**:3, 10-11, 18-19, 24, 29, 52, 74, 89-90, 93, 99
The Mask of Anarchy (Shelley)
See *The Masque of Anarchy*
Mask of Comus (Milton)
See *Comus: A Maske*
"The Masked Face" (Hardy) **8**:119
"Masked Woman's Song" (Bogan) **12**:100-01
"The Mask-Maker" (Abse) **41**:4, 8
"Masks" (Brathwaite) **56**:7
"Masks" (Moore) **49**:114, 121
"Masks" (Stryk) **27**:191, 197
Masks (Brathwaite) **56**:3, 5-8, 11-12, 17-18, 21-23, 26, 29-30, 33-34, 49-50, 59, 65, 67, 70, 73-75, 77, 84-86, 88, 98
"Masks of Dawn" (Paz) **1**:359
"Masks of Woman" (Yamada) **44**:351
Masnavi (Rumi)
See *Mathnawi*
Masnavi-yi Ma'navi (Rumi) **45**:293-302
"Mas'ot Binyamin ha'aharon mitudela" (Amichai) **38**:5, 8-9, 13-14, 16, 19, 26
"Le masque" (Baudelaire) **1**:45, 65, 72
A Masque for Janus (Merwin)
See *A Mask for Janus*
"Masque funèbre" (Char) **56**:157
"Masque nègre" (Senghor) **25**:224
The Masque of Anarchy (Shelley) **14**:171, 175, 210
A Masque of Mercy (Frost) **1**:211
The Masque of Pandora (Longfellow) **30**:23, 51
"The Masque of Plenty" (Kipling) **3**:181
A Masque of Reason (Frost) **1**:203-04, 206, 217
The Masque of Snow (Blok)
See *Snezhnye maski*
"Masque of Tsars" (Viereck) **27**:280
"Masquerade in the Park" (Akhmatova) **2**:6
"Masqueraders" (Page) **12**:178
"Mass for the Day of St. Thomas Didymus" (Levertov) **11**:198, 200-01
"Mass Man" (Walcott) **46**:286
"The Mass of the Grove" (Dafydd)
See "Offeren Y Llwyn"
"Massacre of the Innocents" (Hope) **56**:270-71
"The Massage" (Kinnell) **26**:286
"Masses" (Sandburg) **41**:239, 269, 349
"Mastectomy" (Boland) **58**:37
"Master" (Abse) **41**:7-8
"The Master" (H. D.) **5**:306
"The Master" (Merwin) **45**:18
"The Master" (Robinson) **1**:461, 465, 467; **35**:362, 368
"Master and Man" (Brown) **55**:168
"Master and Mistress" (Kunitz) **19**:148
"Master Herrick's Farewell unto Poetry" (Herrick)
See "Farewell to Poetry"
"Master Hugues of Saxe-Gotha" (Browning) **2**:37, 61, 88
Master Thaddeus; or, The Last Foray in Lithuania (Mickiewicz)
See *Pan Tadeusz; czyli, Ostatni zajazd na Litwie*
"Masterpiece" (Corso) **33**:49
"The Masters of the Heart Touched the Unknown" (Schwartz) **8**:292
"Masters of War" (Dylan) **37**:71
"Mastery" (Teasdale) **31**:355

"Masts at Dawn" (Warren) **37**:299, 302, 307, 347-48, 362, 365, 375
"The Matachines" (Tomlinson) **17**:328-29
"The Match" (Marvell) **10**:271, 300
"Mateo XXV, 30" (Borges) **22**:73-5; **32**:38, 58, 60, 86, 93
"Materia humana" (Aleixandre) **15**:34
Materialism (Graham) **59**:137-38, 145, 150-53, 155, 157-59, 161, 163, 168-69, 175-78, 186
The Materials (Oppen) **35**:284, 292, 295, 297, 308, 310, 312, 314, 315, 320, 321, 322, 325, 326, 330, 331, 333, 338
"Materias" (Mistral) **32**:160
"Maternità" (Pavese) **13**:213
"Mathew VIII, 28ff" (Wilbur) **51**:215-16, 281
"Mathilde in Normady" (Rich) **5**:352, 359
Mathnavi (Rumi)
See *Mathnawi*
Mathnawi (Rumi) **45**:273-80, 294-96, 298-302, 305-10, 312-13, 320-22
"Un Matin" (Péret) **33**:231
"Matin" (Rimbaud) **57**:246
"Matinal and Nocturne" (Carducci)
See "Mattutino e notturno"
The Matinals (Char)
See *Les Matinaux*
Les matinaux (Char) **56**:126, 131, 134-38, 144, 146, 149-51, 154-55, 166, 170, 173-74, 176-78, 184-86, 188-89
"Matinée d'ivresse" (Rimbaud) **3**:261, 263, 271-73, 281-82; **57**:249-50, 265-66, 268-70, 275, 282-83
"Matinees" (Merrill) **28**:285-87
"Matins" (Glück) **16**:170-71
"Matins" (Levertov) **11**:166
"Matka" (Herbert) **50**:7, 9
"Matoaka" (Clampitt) **19**:101-02
"Matrimony" (Erdrich) **52**:191
"Matrix" (Clampitt) **19**:102
"Matros v Moskve" (Pasternak) **6**:283
"Mattens" (Herbert) **4**:119
"Mattens, or Morning Prayer" (Herrick) **9**:118
"Matthew V. 29-30" (Mahon) **60**:135, 186, 188
"Matthew VIII, 28ff" (Wilbur)
See "Mathew VIII, 28ff"
"Matthew XXV: 30" (Borges)
See "Mateo XXV, 30"
Matthias at the Door (Robinson) **1**:473-74, 479; **35**:368
"Mattinata" (Carducci) **46**:50
"Mattino" (Pavese) **13**:230
"Mattutino e notturno" (Carducci) **46**:42, 48
"Maturity" (Ginsberg) **4**:87
"Mauberley, 1920" (Pound)
See *Hugh Selwyn Mauberley*
Maud, and Other Poems (Tennyson) **6**:354, 356-57, 360, 363, 366, 373, 379-80, 383, 385, 387, 407
"Maude Clare" (Rossetti) **7**:260, 280, 291
"Maumee Ruth" (Brown) **55**:73, 75, 80
"Maundy Thursday" (Owen) **19**:352, 358
"Mausfallen-Sprüchlein" (Mörike) **1**:114
Mausoleum (Enzensberger) **28**:148-50, 154-55, 158, 165
"Le mauvais moine" (Baudelaire) **1**:59
"Mauvais sang" (Rimbaud) **57**:182-83, 189-91, 194-99, 244-46, 248-49, 251-53, 277-78
"Le mauvais vitrier" (Baudelaire) **1**:67
"Mawl i'r Haf" (Dafydd ap Gwilym) **56**:233
"Mawu" (Lorde) **12**:143
"Max Ernst" (Éluard) **38**:69, 71
Maximilian (Masters) **36**:189
"Maximus" (Lawrence) **54**:197, 199
"Maximus at the Harbor" (Olson) **19**:312-13
"Maximus From Dogtown—IV" (Olson) **19**:306
"Maximus of Gloucester" (Olson) **19**:294, 304
The Maximus Poems (Olson) **19**:266-67, 270-71, 273-75, 277, 279-83, 285-87, 294, 296-98, 304-7, 316
"Maximus, to Himself" (Olson) **19**:269
Maximus, Vol. II (Olson) **19**:306
Maximus, Vol. III (Olson) **19**:285, 287-88, 295, 305-7
"May" (Rossetti) **7**:265
"May 20, 1928" (Borges) **22**:76
"May 23" (Thomas) **53**:302, 304, 349
"May 24, 1980" (Brodsky) **9**:24
"May 1943" (H. D.) **5**:307
"May 1954" (Thumboo) **30**:332
"May 1968" (Olds) **22**:339
"may all thes blessings" (Bissett) **14**:30
"May and June" (Carman) **34**:208
"May Banners" (Rimbaud)
See "Bannières de mai"
"May Day" (Teasdale) **31**:331, 340
"May Day Sermon to the Women of Gilmer County, Georgia, by a Woman Precher Leaving the Baptist Church" (Dickey) **40**:158, 166, 183, 191-92, 195-96, 201, 208, 224, 232, 241-42, 248, 255
"May Festival" (Goethe)
See "Maifest"
"May It Be" (Pasternak) **6**:261
"The May Magnificat" (Hopkins) **15**:124-25, 165
"May Morning" (Thoreau) **30**:181, 233-34
"May Night" (Carducci)
See "Notte di Maggio"
The May Queen (Tennyson) **6**:359
"May Song" (Carducci)
See "Idillio di Maggio"
"Maya" (Muir) **49**:237
Maya Angelou: Poems (Angelou) **32**:25
"The Mayan Ground" (Oppen) **35**:316, 349
"Mayapán" (Cardenal) **22**:128, 131
"Mayavada" (Tagore) **8**:408
"Maybe this is a sign of madness" (Mandelstam) **14**:155
"Maybe this is the beginning of madness" (Mandelstam)
See "Mozhet byt' eto tochka bezumiia"
"May-Day" (Emerson) **18**:76, 88, 111
May-Day and Other Pieces (Emerson) **18**:75, 113
"Mayflies" (Wilbur) **51**:334
Mayflies (Wilbur) **51**:331-35
"Mayflower" (Aiken) **26**:41-2, 45
"Mayfly" (MacNeice) **61**:131, 170
"Mayo nuestro" (Guillén) **35**:182, 183
"The Mayo Tao" (Mahon) **60**:142-43, 167, 238
"The Mayor of Gary" (Sandburg) **2**:304, 308
"The Maypole Is Up" (Herrick) **9**:102, 145
"May's Love" (Browning) **6**:24
"A Maze of Sparks of Gold" (Rexroth) **20**:190
"Mazeppa" (Hugo) **17**:75
Mazeppa (Byron) **16**:83
"Mazurka" (McGuckian) **27**:101
"M.B." (Brodsky) **9**:10
"McAndrew's Hymn" (Kipling) **3**:161, 167, 170, 186, 192
"Mcyri" (Lermontov)
See *Mtsyri*
"Me Again" (Rexroth) **20**:218
Me Again: Uncollected Writings of Stevie Smith (Smith) **12**:314, 333-34, 340, 343-44, 346-47
"Me centuplant Persée" (Césaire) **25**:31
"Me crucé con un entierro" (Fuertes) **27**:11
"Me from Myself to Banish" (Dickinson) **1**:94
"Me retiro con mis Sueños" (Alurista) **34**:31, 46
"Me retracto de todo lo dicho" (Parra) **39**:264, 278, 306-7, 309-10
"Me tuviste" (Mistral) **32**:202
"Me Whoppin' Big-Tree Boy" (McKay) **2**:226
Me'adam (Amichai) **38**:22-23, 32-35
"The Meadow" (Carver) **54**:11
"Meadow Milk" (Bogan) **12**:110
Meadowlands (Glück) **16**:171-73
"Meadowlands 3" (Glück) **16**:171
"Meadowlarks" (Teasdale) **31**:340, 359
"Mean Old Yesterday" (Hughes) **53**:115
"Meaning" (Milosz) **8**:215
"The Meaning of Death" (Tate) **50**:243-45, 251
"The Meaning of Fall" (McHugh) **61**:190
"The Meaning of Life" (Tate) **50**:231, 243-45, 251, 259
"The Measure" (Stone) **53**:217
"The Measure of Poetry" (Nemerov) **24**:303
"Meat without Mirth" (Herrick) **9**:98
"Mechanism" (Ammons) **16**:40
"Meciendo" (Mistral) **32**:201-02
"Médaillon" (Char) **56**:156-57
"Le médaillon toujours ferme" (Apollinaire) **7**:22
The Medall. A Satire Against Sedition (Dryden) **25**:74
"Medallion" (Plath) **37**:182
The Medea, and Some Poems (Cullen) **20**:60-62, 66
Medea the Sorceress (Wakoski) **15**:372-73
Le médecin malgré lui (Williams) **7**:349
"La medianoche" (Mistral) **32**:181
Medicamina Faciei (Ovid) **2**:238-39, 243, 251, 253, 258
"Medicine" (Bissett) **14**:20
MEDICINE my mouths on fire (Bissett) **14**:16, 19, 27
Médieuses (Éluard) **38**:84
"A Medieval Miniature" (Szymborska) **44**:277
Medieval Scenes (Duncan) **2**:109
Medieval Welsh Lyrics (Dafydd ap Gwilym) **56**:221
"Médiocriteé" (Laforgue) **14**:88
"Mediocritie in love rejected" (Carew) **29**:25, 32
"Meditation" (Baudelaire)
See "Recueillement"
"A Meditation" (Ignatow)
See "A Meditation on Violence"
"Meditation" (Lermontov)
See "Duma"
"Meditation" (Tate) **50**:250
"Meditation at Lagunitas" (Hass) **16**:200, 209, 211, 219
"Meditation at Oyster River" (Roethke) **15**:265, 276, 310, 313, 316
"A Meditation for His Mistresse" (Herrick) **9**:101
"Meditation in Sunlight" (Sarton) **39**:321, 357
"Meditation in the Spring Rain" (Berry) **28**:6
"A Meditation in Time of War" (Yeats) **20**:314
"A Meditation in Tuscany" (Browning) **6**:16
"The Meditation of the Old Fisherman" (Yeats) **20**:337
"Meditation on a June Evening" (Aiken) **26**:7, 50
"A Meditation on John Constable" (Tomlinson) **17**:341-42
"A Meditation on Philosophy" (Bly) **39**:64
"Meditation on Saviors" (Jeffers) **17**:142, 144-45
"A Meditation on Violence" (Ignatow) **34**:279
"Meditation under Stars" (Meredith) **60**:261, 280, 327
"Meditations" (Baca)
See "Meditations on the South Valley"
"Meditations" (Schwerner) **42**:209
Les meditations (Lamartine) **16**:256-62, 265, 268-69
"Meditations in an Emergency" (O'Hara) **45**:158, 190, 228-29
Meditations in an Emergency (O'Hara) **45**:116, 132, 205
"Meditations in Time of Civil War" (Yeats) **20**:314, 342, 349; **51**:73, 102, 111
"Meditations of an Old Woman" (Roethke) **15**:262, 264-65, 273
"Meditations on the National Problem" (Herbert)
See "Meditations on the Problem of the Nation"
"Meditations on the Problem of the Nation" (Herbert) **50**:18

"Meditations on the South Valley" (Baca) **41**:39-40, 42, 65, 69, 72-3
"Meditations on the South Valley III" (Baca) **41**:42
"Meditations on the South Valley XXVIII" (Baca) **41**:43
"Meditations on the South Valley XXV" (Baca) **41**:67
"Meditations on the South Valley XXI" (Baca) **41**:42
"Meditations on the South Valley XXVII" (Baca) **41**:43
Méditations poétiques (Lamartine) **16**:270, 272-82, 284-85, 287, 289-93, 302
"Mediterranean" (Sarton) **39**:324, 343
"The Mediterranean" (Tate) **50**:250, 270, 272, 274, 279, 289, 295, 301, 320-21, 335
The Mediterranean (Tate) **50**:230-31
"Mediterranean Basin" (Warren) **37**:337
"Mediterraneo" (Montale) **13**:115
"Medium for Stasis" (Stone) **53**:224
Medny Vsadnik (Pushkin) **10**:367-68, 373-74, 385, 390-400, 414
"Medusa" (Bogan) **12**:85, 104-06, 111-12, 115, 117
"Medusa" (Cullen) **20**:69
"Medusa" (Dove) **6**:123
"Medusa" (Gower) **59**:88, 91-92
"Medusa" (Merrill) **28**:229
"Medusa" (Plath) **37**:255
"The Meehoo with an Exactlywatt" (Silverstein) **49**:335
"Meer- und Wandersagen" (Benn) **35**:49, 74
"The Meeting" (Abse) **41**:4
"Meeting" (Arnold) **5**:42
"The Meeting" (Hope) **56**:287, 299
"The Meeting" (Longfellow) **30**:103
"The Meeting" (Mistral)
See "El encuentro"
"Meeting" (Montale)
See "Incontro"
"A Meeting" (Pasternak)
See "Vstrecha"
"The Meeting" (Rukeyser) **12**:231
"Meeting a Bear" (Wagoner) **33**:336, 339, 373
"Meeting among the Mountains" (Lawrence) **54**:186
"Meeting in Winter" (Morris) **55**:340
"Meeting Mescalito at Oak Hill Cemetery" (Cervantes) **35**:106, 116, 117
"A Meeting of Minds" (Lorde) **12**:135
"Meeting of Strangers" (Birney) **52**:16, 23, 97
"Meeting of two Smiles" (Éluard) **38**:90-91
"Meeting Point" (MacNeice) **61**:138
"A Meeting with My Father" (Amichai) **38**:26, 28
"Meeting-House Hill" (Lowell) **13**:67
"Megalopolis" (Cruz) **37**:10
Meghadūta (Kālidāsa) **22**:177-78, 182, 185, 188-89, 192, 194-95, 204-05, 207-08
La meglio gioventù (Pasolini) **17**:250-51, 254, 262, 264-67, 275, 279, 281-83, 293
"A Mehinaku Girl in Seclusion" (Song) **21**:344
Me-horei Kol Zeh Mistater Osher Gadol (Amichai) **38**:16, 19, 43, 45-6, 51
"mehrere elstern" (Enzensberger) **28**:139
"Mein Karren knarrt nicht mehr" (Celan) **10**:124
"A Mei-p'i Lake Song" (Tu Fu) **9**:330-31, 333
"Melampus" (Meredith) **60**:330, 332
"Melancholia" (Gautier) **18**:135
"Melancholia" (Verlaine) **32**:386-87
"Melancholia en Orizba" (Neruda) **4**:281
"Melancholy" (Bely) **11**:6
"Melancholy" (Bridges) **28**:76
"Melancholy" (Thomas) **53**:285-86
"Melancholy" (Ungaretti)
See "Malinconia"
"Melancholy in Orizaba" (Neruda)
See "Melancholia en Orizba"
"A Melancholy Moon" (Baudelaire)
See "Les tristesses de la lune"
"Melancholy of Jason Cleander" (Cavafy)
See "Melancholy of Jason, son of Cleander, poet in Syria Commagene, A.D. 595"
"Melancholy of Jason Kleander, Poet in Kommagini, A.D. 595" (Cavafy)
See "Melancholy of Jason, son of Cleander, poet in Syria Commagene, A.D. 595"
"Melancholy of Jason, son of Cleander, poet in Syria Commagene, A.D. 595" (Cavafy) **36**:34, 46, 69, 111
Melancolía (Jiménez) **7**:211
"Melancthon" (Moore) **4**:251, 254; **49**:90, 100, 180, 185-87
"Mélange adultère de tout" (Eliot) **5**:185
"Melbourne" (Shapiro) **25**:269
"Melchior Vulpius" (Moore) **49**:142
"Melibea's Orchard" (Guillén) **35**:220
"Melibee" (Chaucer)
See "Tale of Melibee"
"Melinda on an Insipid Beauty in imitation of a fragment of Sapho's" (Finch) **21**:167
"Mellow" (Hughes) **53**:191
"Melodien" (Benn) **35**:20, 24, 25, 26, 27
"Melody" (Tomlinson) **17**:341
"The Melongene" (Wilbur) **51**:295
"Melpomene in Manhattan" (Ignatow) **34**:310, 343
"Melville's Marginalia" (Howe) **54**:105-6
"Meminisse Horret" (Carducci) **46**:29, 71
"Memo" (Jordan) **38**:127
"Memo: For the Race Orators" (Brown) **55**:82, 114
"Memo from the Cave" (Glück) **16**:147-48
"Memo to Non-White People" (Hughes) **53**:110, 116
"Memoir" (Pinsky) **27**:157
"Memoir of a Proud Boy" (Sandburg) **41**:240, 274
"Mémoire" (Rimbaud) **3**:262, 268; **57**:171, 175, 177, 216-18, 222, 245
"Memoirs" (Meredith) **28**:199
"The Memoirs of Glükel of Hameln" (Jarrell) **41**:171
"Memoirs of the World" (Gunn) **26**:203
"Memorabilia" (Masters) **1**:343
"Memoranda to Horace" (MacNeice) **61**:118, 143-44, 176, 178
"Memorandum Confided by a Yucca to a Passion-Vine" (Lowell) **13**:61, 64
"À Memória do President Rei Sidónio" (Pessoa) **20**:154
"Memorial" (Pinsky) **27**:153
"Memorial" (Sanchez) **9**:224
"Memorial II" (Lorde) **12**:140, 157
"Memorial Candle" (Shvarts)
See "Pominal'naia svecha"
"Memorial Day" (Niedecker) **42**:147
"Memorial Day, 1950" (O'Hara) **45**:127, 135, 181-82, 200, 223, 238
"Memorial for the City" (Auden) **1**:23
"Memorial Rain" (MacLeish) **47**:190, 197
"Memorial Tablet" (Sassoon) **12**:269
"Memorial Thresholds" (Rossetti) **44**:221
"Memories..." (Jiménez)
See "Recuerdos..."
"Memories of Mortalities" (Jackson) **44**:8, 11-12, 57, 63-4, 76
"Memories of My Father" (Kinnell) **26**:286
"Memories of the Forest" (Ishikawa)
See "Mori no omoide"
"Memories of West Street and Lepke" (Lowell) **3**:206, 208, 220, 223, 237
"Memories of Youth" (Parra) **39**:278
"Memory" (Bogan) **12**:101, 120, 122
"A Memory" (Brooke) **24**:85-6
"A Memory" (Pavese) **13**:203
"Memory" (Rimbaud)
See "Mémoire"
"Memory" (Roethke) **15**:275
"Memory" (Sassoon) **12**:269
"Memory" (Walker) **20**:283
"Memory" (Wright) **14**:376
"Memory I" (Rossetti) **7**:277
"Memory Green" (MacLeish) **47**:126, 165
"Memory of a Strange Refreshment" (Shvarts)
See "Vospominanie o strannom ugoshchenii"
"Memory of Africa" (Ungaretti) **57**:360
"Memory of Brother Michael" (Kavanagh) **33**:157
"The Memory of Elena" (Forché) **10**:136, 139, 152-53, 166, 169
"A Memory of Love,—Terms and Conditions" (Amichai) **38**:32
"memory of my crickets" (Alurista) **34**:34
"Memory of My Father" (Kavanagh) **33**:75, 93, 149
"Memory of Spring" (Merwin) **45**:16
"The Memory of Swans" (Sarton) **39**:321
"Memory of V. I. Ulianov" (Zukofsky) **11**:396
"A Memory Picture" (Arnold) **5**:49
"Memphis Blues" (Brown) **55**:73, 76, 82, 110, 153-54, 174, 177
"Men" (Angelou) **32**:28
"Men" (MacLeish) **47**:126, 130, 166
"Men" (Parker) **28**:347, 354
"Men" (Parra) **39**:289
"Men" (Toomer) **7**:336
Men (Verlaine)
See *Hombres*
Men and Women (Browning) **2**:66, 77, 94; **61**:57, 87
"Men Improve with the Years" (Yeats) **20**:314
"Men Loved Wholly beyond Wisdom" (Bogan) **12**:104, 126
"The Men of Sheepshead" (Oppen) **35**:308
"Men of the North" (Harper) **21**:190
Men, Women, and Ghosts (Lowell) **13**:63, 71, 73, 76, 79, 85, 93
"The Menace" (Gunn) **26**:228
"Menaces du témoin" (Bonnefoy) **58**:124
"The Mendicants" (Carman) **34**:199, 201, 207, 220
"El mendigo que entregaba un papel" (Fuertes) **27**:30
"Mending Wall" (Frost) **1**:225, 227, 229; **39**:230, 237, 240, 246, 253, 256
"Mendocino Rose" (Hongo) **23**:199
"Menelaus" (Walcott) **46**:266
"Menelaus and Helen" (Brooke) **24**:56, 65, 76, 79, 82
"Meng Tzu's Song" (Merwin) **45**:24
"Menons Klagen um Diotima" (Hölderlin) **4**:141-2
"Mens Creatrix" (Kunitz) **19**:159
Mensagem (Pessoa) **20**:154-57, 159-63, 165, 168, 170
"Mensaje" (Aleixandre) **15**:6, 10
"Menschenbeifall" (Hölderlin) **4**:165
"Die Menschheit" (Stramm) **50**:170-71, 173, 175-76, 201, 206, 214
"Menschheit" (Trakl) **20**:250, 253-55
"Menschliche Trauer" (Trakl) **20**:253
"Menschliches Elend" (Trakl) **20**:253
"Menses" (Boland) **58**:37
"Menses" (Millay) **6**:233
"Menstruation at Forty" (Sexton) **2**:363
"Mental Cases" (Owen) **19**:330, 336, 340-41, 343, 347, 353, 355, 359, 365, 368, 370-71
"The Mental Traveller" (Blake) **12**:36, 46, 48
"Menthol Sweets" (Amichai) **38**:46
"Merch ac Aderyn" (Dafydd ap Gwilym) **56**:247
"The Merchantmen" (Kipling) **3**:161
"Merchant's Tale" (Chaucer) **19**:13, 15, 28, 33, 62-3
The Merchant!s Tale (Chaucer) **58**:246, 248-49, 344, 351, 365
"Merched Llanbadarn" (Dafydd ap Gwilym) **56**:249
"Mercifully" (Moore) **49**:150
"Mercury and the Elephant" (Finch) **21**:159, 161
"Mercy" (Dickey) **40**:219-20, 242-43, 246
"Mercy on Broadway" (Doty) **53**:60-61, 63

"Merely Statement" (Lowell) **13**:86
"Mericano" (Ortiz) **17**:228
"Meridian" (Clampitt) **19**:83
"Meriggiare pallido e assorto" (Montale) **13**:105
"Merlin" (Emerson) **18**:81-82, 88, 99, 104, 106
"Merlin" (Muir) **49**:209, 247
Merlin: A Poem (Robinson) **1**:462-63, 465, 468-71, 482-83, 488-89, 491; **35**:362
"Merlin and the Gleam" (Tennyson) **6**:389, 407
"Merlin Enthralled" (Wilbur) **51**:189, 227
"The Mermaid's Children" (Lowell) **3**:241
"The Mermen" (Crane) **3**:90
Merope (Arnold) **5**:8, 12, 35, 37, 45, 47, 58-60, 62-3
"The Merry Guide" (Housman) **2**:180, 192
"Merry Margaret" (Skelton) **25**:336
"The Merry Muses" (Burns) **6**:96
"Merry-Go-Round" (Hughes) **53**:126-27
"The merry-go-round at night" (Abse) **41**:31
"Meru" (Yeats) **20**:326
"Merveilles de la guerre" (Apollinaire) **7**:3, 22
"Mes bouguins refemés" (Mallarmé) **4**:199
"Mes deux Filles" (Hugo) **17**:82
"De Mes Haras" (Césaire) **25**:10
"Mes petites amoureuses" (Rimbaud) **3**:262, 284; **57**:202-4, 209-10, 212, 214, 292, 295
"Mes Sources" (Péret) **33**:220
"Mesa Blanca" (Cruz) **37**:18
"Mesa Blanca/White Table" (Cruz) **37**:18
"Mescaline" (Ginsberg) **4**:74, 81
"Un mese fra i bambini" (Montale) **13**:134
"Meseta" (Guillén) **35**:156
Les meslanges (Ronsard) **11**:247, 266
"Mess Hall Discipline" (Yamada) **44**:341, 343
"Message" (Aleixandre)
See "Mensaje"
"Message" (Forché) **10**:139, 144, 154-55
"The Message" (Levertov) **11**:171
"The Message" (Sassoon) **12**:248
Message (Pessoa)
See *Mensagem*
"A Message All Blackpeople Can Dig (& A Few Negroes Too)" (Madhubuti) **5**:329, 341
"Message at Sunset for Bishop Berkeley" (McHugh) **61**:202
"Message for the Sinecurist" (Gallagher) **9**:62
"Message from Abroad" (Tate) **50**:248-50
"Message from the NAACP" (Baraka) **4**:11
"Message from Your Toes" (Stone) **53**:230, 255, 258
"A Message Hidden in an Empty Wine Bottle That I Threw into a Gulley of Maple Trees One Night at an Indecent Hour" (Wright) **36**:319, 340
"the message of crazy horse" (Clifton) **17**:25
"The Message of the March Wind" (Morris) **55**:329, 338
"Message to a Black Soldier" (Madhubuti) **5**:339
"Messages" (Dickey) **40**:200, 219
"Messages" (Senghor) **25**:255
"The Messenger" (Atwood) **8**:18
"The Messenger" (Gunn) **26**:219, 226
"Messenger" (Herbert) **50**:14
"The Messenger" (Merton) **10**:339
"The Messenger" (Sassoon) **12**:259
"A Messenger from the Horizon" (Merton) **10**:334
"Messengers" (Glück) **16**:127, 133, 142
"The Messiah" (Pope) **26**:314, 319, 322
"Messiah (Christmas Portions)" (Doty) **53**:61
"Messianic Eclogue" (Vergil)
See "Eclogue 4"
"Messias" (Shapiro) **25**:284, 317
Město v slzách (Seifert) **47**:315, 330-31
"The Metal and the Flower" (Page) **12**:168, 178
The Metal and the Flower (Page) **12**:167, 171, 193
Die Metamorphose der Pflanzen (Goethe) **5**:239-40
Metamorphoses (Ovid) **2**:233, 238-241, 244-45, 260
"Les métamorphoses du vampire" (Baudelaire) **1**:48, 71
"The Metamorphoses of the Vampire" (Baudelaire)
See "Les métamorphoses du vampire"
"Metamorphosis" (Glück) **16**:163
"Metamorphosis" (Sitwell) **3**:304
"Metamorphosis" (Stone) **53**:218, 221, 256
"Metamorphosis" (Walcott) **46**:286
Metamorphosis (Ovid)
See *Metamorphoses*
"Metaphors of a Magnifico" (Stevens) **6**:311-12
"Metaphors of the Arabian Nights" (Borges) **32**:66
"The Metaphysical Automobile" (Nemerov) **24**:284
"The Metaphysical Garden" (Sarton) **39**:325, 332
Metaphysical Ironies (Abse) **41**:3
"Metaphysical Poem" (O'Hara) **45**:119
"Metaphysics" (Ginsberg) **47**:38
"Meta-Rhetoric" (Jordan) **38**:121-22, 126
"Metempsicosis" (Darío) **15**:101
"Meteor of August 13" (Char)
See "Météore du 13 août"
"Météore du 13 août" (Char) **56**:132
"The Meteorite" (Jarrell) **41**:154
"Metho Drinker" (Wright) **14**:333, 341
"Metro" (Szirtes) **51**:160-61, 167, 171
Metro (Szirtes) **51**:160, 169
"Metro North" (Doty) **53**:61
"The Metropolis" (Clampitt) **19**:90
"Métropolitain" (Rimbaud) **3**:265; **57**:232, 238-39, 247, 282, 284-86
"The Metropolitan Tower" (Teasdale) **31**:331
"Mexican Child" (Mistral)
See "Niño mexicano"
"Mexican Divertimento" (Brodsky) **9**:12
"Mexican Divertissement" (Brodsky)
See "Mexican Divertimento"
"Mexican Impressions" (Corso) **33**:5, 24, 41, 43, 47
"Mexicans Begin Jogging" (Soto) **28**:387
"Mexico" (Birney) **52**:46
"Mexico" (Cervantes) **35**:118, 124, 126
"Mexico" (Dalton) **36**:127
"Mexico Is a Foreign Country: Five Studies in Naturalism" (Warren) **37**:287, 332
"Mezzo Cammin" (Longfellow) **30**:50, 64
"Mezzo Forte" (Williams) **7**:405
"Mezzogiorno alpino" (Carducci) **46**:48, 61, 88
"Mi Abuelo" (Ríos) **57**:311
"Mi chiquita" (Guillén) **23**:142
"Mi suerte" (Fuertes) **27**:14, 27
"Mi vida entera" (Borges) **22**:93; **32**:57-8, 83, 99
"Mi voz" (Aleixandre) **15**:40
"Mía" (Darío) **15**:107, 113
"La mia musa" (Montale) **13**:139
"Mia vita a te non chiedo lineamenti" (Montale) **13**:139
"Miami You Are About to be Surprised" (Merton) **10**:351
"Miość od pierwszego wejrzenia" (Szymborska) **44**:308
"MIA's (Missing in Action and Other Atlantas)" (Sanchez) **9**:230, 235, 244
"Micah" (Walker) **20**:278
"Micene" (Quasimodo) **47**:293
"Michael" (Wordsworth) **4**:380-81, 394, 399, 402, 412, 414, 425, 428
Michael Angelo (Longfellow) **30**:23, 43, 67, 72-3
"Michael Gallagher" (Masters) **36**:211
Michael Robartes and the Dancer (Yeats) **20**:310, 314
"Michel et Christine" (Rimbaud) **3**:264, 281; **57**:177, 203
"The Microbe" (Belloc) **24**:15, 25
"Mid/Life" (Brathwaite) **56**:97
"Midas Among Goldenrod" (Merrill) **28**:239
"Mid-August at Sourdough Mountain Lookout" (Snyder) **21**:286
"Midday in the Alps" (Carducci)
See "Mezzogiorno alpino"
"Middle Distance" (Graham) **59**:188
"Middle Flight" (Meredith) **28**:174, 186
"Middle of a Long Poem on 'These States'" (Ginsberg) **4**:47
"Middle of Life" (Hölderlin)
See "Hälfte des Lebens"
"The Middle of the World" (Lawrence) **54**:227
"Middle Passage" (Hayden) **6**:176-81, 183, 187-88, 194, 196-200
Middle Passages (Brathwaite) **56**:55-56, 61, 66, 71
"The Middle-Aged" (Rich) **5**:362-63, 367, 369
"The Middleness of the Road" (Frost) **39**:233
"Midnight" (Heaney) **18**:192
"Midnight" (Mistral)
See "La medianoche"
"Midnight" (Parker) **28**:351, 364
"Midnight" (Wright) **14**:337
"Midnight Chippie's Lament" (Hughes) **1**:255
"Midnight II <27" (Ignatow) **34**:342
"Midnight in Early Spring" (Merwin) **45**:96
"Midnight in Moscow" (Mandelstam) **14**:122
"A Midnight Interior" (Sassoon) **12**:246
"Midnight Mass for the Dying Year" (Longfellow) **30**:45
"Midnight Nan at Leroy's" (Hughes) **1**:246
"Midnight on the Great Western" (Hardy) **8**:107
"The Midnight Show" (Ríos) **57**:324
"Midnight Show" (Shapiro) **25**:295
"Midnight Snack" (Merrill) **28**:249
"Midnight Verses" (Akhmatova) **2**:16
Midnight Verses (Akhmatova) **55**:48
"A Midnight Woman to the Bobby" (McKay) **2**:224
"Midsummer" (Mahon) **60**:141, 199
Midsummer (Walcott) **46**:241-42, 244-45, 259, 322-23
The Midsummer Cushion (Clare) **23**:45
"Midsummer, England" (Walcott) **46**:237
"A Midsummer Holiday" (Swinburne) **24**:313, 329
"Mid-Term Break" (Heaney) **18**:189
"Midway" (Graves) **6**:143
"Midway Between the Dial and the Foot of a Garden Clock" (Moore) **49**:118
"Midwinter Blues" (Hughes) **53**:140
"Midwinter Notes" (Mueller) **33**:196
"A Midwinter Prayer" (Ní Chuilleanáin) **34**:348
"Midwinter, Presolstice" (Atwood) **8**:2
"The Midwives" (Enzensberger) **28**:142
"Miedo" (Storni) **33**:279;
"Miedo divino" (Storni) **33**:258;
"La miej zoventút" (Pasolini) **17**:281
"Mientras dura vida, sobra el tiempo" (Forché) **10**:135
"Mientras la Gracia me excita" (Juana Inés de la Cruz) **24**:188
"Might These be Thrushes Climbing through Almost (Do They" (Cummings) **5**:108
"The Mighty Flight" (Baraka) **4**:26
"Mignonne, allons voir si la rose" (Ronsard)
See "Ode à Cassandre: 'Mignonne, allon voir'"
"Migration" (Boland) **58**:42
"Migration" (Carver) **54**:13
"Migration, 1902" (Alexie) **53**:24
"Migratory" (Doty) **53**:66
"El milagro secreto" (Borges) **32**:50
"Mildred's Thoughts" (Stein) **18**:346
"Mildred's Umbrella" (Stein) **18**:334
"A Mild-Spoken Citizen Finally Writes to the White House" (Meredith) **28**:206
Mileposts I (Tsvetaeva)
See *Vyorsty I*
Mileposts II (Tsvetaeva)
See *Vyorsty II*

Miles Standish (Longfellow)
See *The Courtship of Miles Standish*
"Militant" (Hughes) **53**:110, 113
"Military Band" (O'Hara) **45**:130
"Military Cemetery" (O'Hara) **45**:224
"Military Review" (Mickiewicz) **38**:168
"Milk" (Stein) **18**:323, 330
"The Milk Factory" (Heaney) **18**:237
"A Milkweed" (Wilbur) **51**:289
"Milkweed" (Wright) **36**:326-27, 329-30, 369, 374
"Milk-Wort and Bog Cotton" (MacDiarmid) **9**:160, 176, 199
"The Mill" (Robinson) **1**:468, 475, 478; **35**:368
"The Mill" (Wilbur) **51**:312
"The Mill Field at Aetnaville, Ohio: 1960" (Wright) **36**:390
"Mill Mountain" (Brown) **55**:114
"Mill Song" (Ekeloef) **23**:54
"Mill-Doors" (Sandburg) **41**:239, 243, 349, 364
"Mille fois" (Péret) **33**:216, 231
"Miller's" (Chaucer)
See "Miller's Tale"
"The Miller's Daughter" (Tennyson) **6**:350
"Miller's Tale" (Chaucer) **19**:11, 13-14, 40, 44, 54, 61
The Miller!s Tale (Chaucer) **58**:248-49, 266, 346
"Millibars of the Storm" (Césaire) **25**:17
"Millibars of the Storn" (Césaire) **25**:17
"Millie's date" (Abse) **41**:31
"A Million Laughs, A Bright Hope" (Szymborska) **44**:277
"A Million Young Workmen, 1915" (Sandburg) **41**:297
"The Millionaire" (Bukowski) **18**:13
"Millpond Lost" (Warren) **37**:336
"The Mills" (Hughes) **53**:111
"The Mills of the Kavanaughs" (Lowell) **3**:204, 206-07, 215, 217, 224, 226, 231
The Mills of the Kavanaughs (Lowell) **3**:204, 206-07, 215, 217, 224, 226, 231
"The Mill-Water" (Thomas) **53**:328-29
"Milly; ou, La terre natale" (Lamartine) **16**:280, 286, 293
"Milonga de Calandria" (Borges) **32**:87
"Milonga del forastero" (Borges) **32**:66
"Milpa" (Cardenal) **22**:131
"Milton" (Muir) **49**:219
Milton (Blake) **12**:13, 27, 30, 36-8, 42, 44-5, 50, 62-5, 73, 75-80
"Milton: A Sonnet" (Warren) **37**:379
"Milun" (Marie de France) **22**:258, 264, 266, 268, 270-75, 295-96
"Mima: Elegía pagana" (Darío) **15**:110-11
"Miña casiña" (Castro) **41**:89
Minashi Guri (Matsuo Bashō) **3**:11
"Mind" (Graham) **59**:181
"Mind" (Wilbur) **51**:209, 304-5, 307, 311
"Mind Breaths" (Ginsberg) **47**:59, 73
Mind Breaths: Poems, 1972-1977 (Ginsberg) **4**:61, 82
"The Mind Hesitant" (Williams) **7**:390
"The Mind, Intractable Thing" (Moore) **4**:243; **49**:145, 157
"The Mind is an Enchanted Thing" (Moore)
See "The Mind Is an Enchanting Thing"
"The Mind Is an Enchanting Thing" (Moore) **4**:261; **49**:127, 130, 134, 144-45, 161
"The Mind of the Frontispiece to a Book" (Jonson)
See *The Under-Wood XXVI*
Mindfield (Corso) **33**:42-4, 53
"The Mind-Reader" (Wilbur) **51**:231-34, 260-61, 276, 278, 285, 303, 305, 308, 335
The Mind-Reader (Wilbur) **51**:234, 236, 238, 245, 247, 250, 260-61, 287, 289-90, 301
"The Mind's Own Place" (Oppen) **35**:336, 349, 357
Mindwheel (Pinsky) **27**:157, 171
"Mine and Thine" (Morris) **55**:325
"Mine Own John Poins" (Wyatt)
See "Myne owne John Poynts sins ye delight to know"
"Mine own John Poyntz" (Wyatt)
See "Myne owne John Poynts sins ye delight to know"
Mine the Harvest (Millay) **6**:226, 231-33, 237, 242
"The Mine: Yamaguchi" (Stryk) **27**:185-86, 191, 202, 214
"Mined Country" (Wilbur) **51**:192, 289-91, 315, 317-20
"Mineral" (Page) **12**:170
"Miners" (Owen) **19**:342-43, 346, 348, 365, 370
"Miners" (Wright) **36**:319, 340, 385-86, 390, 399
"The Miner's Revenge" (Parra)
See "La venganza del minero"
"Minesweepers" (Kipling) **3**:183
"Miniature" (Meredith) **28**:171
"Minicursi" (Fuertes) **27**:23
"Miniver Cheevy" (Robinson) **1**:462, 467, 478, 487, 496; **35**:362, 377
"The Minneapolis Poem" (Wright) **36**:319-20, 324, 328-29, 341, 345, 353-54, 360, 366, 384, 392
"Minneapolis Story" (Warren) **37**:326
"Minnesbilder" (Ekeloef) **23**:69
"Minnesota Recollection" (Warren) **37**:376
"Minnie and Mattie" (Rossetti) **7**:274
"Minnie Mooch" (Quintana) **36**:256
"A Minor Prophet" (Eliot) **20**:123, 140-41
"Minor Works of Camoens" (Camões) **31**:32
"Minotaur" (Wylie) **23**:302-303, 306, 323
"The Minstrel Man" (Hughes) **53**:85
Minstrels (Sitwell) **3**:290
"Minstrel's Song, on the Restoration of Lord Clifford the Shepherd" (Wordsworth) **4**:377
The Minstrelsy of the Scottish Border (Scott) **13**:249, 269, 278, 281, 306
"Minus 18 Street" (McGuckian) **27**:80
"The Minute" (Shapiro) **25**:306
"The Minute before Meeting" (Hardy) **8**:90
"Minutes from the Meeting" (Jordan) **38**:122
"La minutieuse" (Char) **56**:150
Mira Bai and Her Padas (Mirabai) **48**:164-69
"Mirabeau Bridge" (Apollinaire)
See "Le pont Mirabeau"
Mirabell: Books of Numbers (Merrill) **28**:233, 235-38, 240, 251, 260-64, 275-77, 279, 281
"Miracle" (Carver) **54**:15, 18, 28-29
"The Miracle" (Gunn) **26**:220
"The Miracle" (Stone) **53**:230
"Miracle Fair" (Szymborska) **44**:280
Miracle Fair (Szymborska) **44**:317, 320
"A Miracle for Breakfast" (Bishop) **3**:46, 57; **34**:78, 124-27, 137, 190-91
"A Miracle for Breakfast" (Curnow) **48**:44
"Miracles" (Abse) **41**:21
"Miracles" (Whitman) **3**:381
"Miraculous Weapons" (Césaire)
See "Les armes miraculeuses"
"una mirada" (Storni) **33**:271;
"Mirage" (Tagore)
See "Marichika"
"Mirage des Aiguilles" (Char) **56**:112, 135, 152
"Mirage of the Desert" (Masters) **1**:344
"Mirage of the Peaks" (Char)
See "Mirage des Aiguilles"
"The Mirages" (Hayden) **6**:193, 197
"Miramar" (Carducci) **46**:9, 26, 52, 85-86
"Miramar" (Walcott) **46**:238
"Miranda Dies in the Fog, 1816" (Neruda)
See "Miranda muere en la niebla, 1816"
"Miranda muere en la niebla, 1816" (Neruda) **4**:295
"Miranda's Supper" (Wylie) **23**:302, 307, 314-15, 321
"El mirasol" (Storni) **33**:294;
"Miriam Tazewell" (Ransom) **61**:274, 323
"Miriam's Song" (Harper) **21**:194-95
"Miró Celi una rosa que en el prado" (Juana Inés de la Cruz) **24**:225
"Le miroir d'un moment" (Éluard) **38**:71, 105
Mirour de l'Omme (Gower) **59**:20, 41-45, 113, 117-19
"The Mirror" (Borges) **32**:66
"Mirror" (Merrill) **28**:225, 242, 245-47
"Mirror" (Paz)
See "Espejo"
"The Mirror" (Rossetti) **44**:238, 255-56
"Mirror Image" (Glück) **16**:162-63
"The Mirror in the Roadway" (Tomlinson) **17**:334
"The Mirror in the Woods" (Rexroth) **20**:181
"The Mirror in Which Two Are Seen as One" (Rich) **5**:368
"The Mirror Of Madmen" (Chesterton) **28**:108
"Mirror Sermon" (Brutus) **24**:99
"Mirrors" (Borges)
See "Los espejos"
"The Mirrors" (Williams) **7**:370
"Mirrors & Windows" (Nemerov) **24**:292
Mirrors and Windows (Nemerov) **24**:256, 261, 264, 295-96
"The Mirth of Shipwrecks" (Ungaretti) **57**:358
"Mis libros" (Mistral) **32**:149-50
"Mis queridos difuntos" (Fuertes) **27**:12
"Misanthropos" (Gunn) **26**:188-190, 192-193, 214, 223, 225-226
Misanthropos (Gunn) **26**:203
Miscellaneous Poems (Harper)
See *Poems on Miscellaneous Subjects*
Miscellaneous Poems (Longfellow) **30**:26
Miscellaneous Poems (Marvell) **10**:257, 277, 311
Miscellanies (Swift) **9**:251, 253, 255, 275
"Miscellany" (Castro)
See "Varia"
Miscellany (Surrey)
See *Tottel's Miscellany*
A Miscellany of New Poems (Behn) **13**:7
Miscellany Poems on Several Occasions, Written by a Lady, 1713 (Finch) **21**:140, 148, 161, 163-64, 172-73
"Mise Eire" (Boland) **58**:4-5, 15, 37, 48-49, 66, 69, 87
"Mise en Scene" (Lowell) **13**:96
"Misericords" (Szirtes) **51**:157
"Miserie" (Herbert) **4**:108, 121
"Misery" (Hughes) **1**:328; **53**:113, 124
"The Misfit" (Day Lewis) **11**:147
"Misgiving" (Frost) **1**:195; **39**:232
"Misiricords" (Szirtes)
See "Misericords"
"Miss B—" (Clare) **23**:25
"Miss Book World" (Abse) **41**:10, 14-15
"Miss Drake Proceeds to Supper" (Plath) **1**:398-99
"Miss Gada-Nigi" (Seifert) **47**:333
"Miss Gee" (Auden) **1**:30
"Miss Own" (Brathwaite) **56**:96
"Miss Rosie" (Clifton) **17**:32-33
"Miss Universe" (Kavanagh) **33**:88, 136
"The Missing" (Gunn) **26**:224
"The Missing Knot" (Herbert) **50**:20-21
The Missing Piece Meets the Big O (Silverstein) **49**:305
"Missing the Mountains" (Goodison) **36**:154
"Missing the Trail" (Wagoner) **33**:337, 340
"The Mission" (Warren) **37**:313
"Mississippi Levee" (Hughes) **1**:256
"Mississippi Mother" (Brooks) **7**:96
"Mississippi Winter" (Walker) **30**:343
"Mississippi Winter III" (Walker) **30**:370
"Missus Dorra" (Niedecker) **42**:140
"the missyun" (Bissett) **14**:24, 34
"Mist in the Valley" (Noyes) **27**:134
"Míster no!" (Guillén) **23**:126
"Mister Samuel and Sam" (Brown) **55**:155
"Mr. Tambourine Man" (Dylan) **37**:45-9
"Mithridates" (Emerson) **18**:71

"Mito" (Pavese) **13**:210, 228-29
"Mitotera" (Quintana) **36**:273
"Mixed Feelings" (Ashbery) **26**:124, 127
"The Mixer" (MacNeice) **61**:141
"Mne moia otdel'nost' nadoela" (Shvarts) **50**:162
"Mnemonic" (Lee) **24**:243
"Może być bez tytuu" (Szymborska) **44**:304
"Może to wszystko" (Szymborska) **44**:308
"The Mob" (Brutus) **24**:108
Mock Beggar Hall (Graves) **6**:127-28
"Mock Confessional" (Ferlinghetti) **1**:187
"Mock Orange" (Glück) **16**:145, 164
"The Mocking Bird" (Lanier) **50**:56, 77
"The Mockingbird" (Jarrell) **41**:162
Mockingbird, Wish Me Luck (Bukowski) **18**:19
"Models" (Clampitt) **19**:99
"Models" (Nemerov) **24**:290
"Modern Elegy of the Motif of Affectation" (Guillén)
See "Elegía moderna del motivo cursi"
Modern Fable Poems (Nishiwaki)
See *Kindai no Guwa*
"Modern Love" (Keats) **1**:311
Modern Love (Meredith) **60**:246, 252, 258, 263-71, 274-76, 280, 286, 290-92, 294, 299-310, 312-13, 315, 317-26, 328, 341-42, 344-46
"The Modern Patriot" (Cowper) **40**:102-3
"Modern Poetry Is Prose (But It Is Saying Plenty)" (Ferlinghetti) **1**:182-83
"A Modern Sappho" (Arnold) **5**:12
"Modern Times" (Parra) **39**:11
The Modern Traveller (Belloc) **24**:25-7, 35
"Moderna" (Storni) **33**:251;
"A Modernist Ballade" (Belloc) **24**:39
"Modes of Being" (Levertov) **11**:197-98
"Modes of Pleasure" (Gunn) **26**:186, 219
"Modest Proposal" (Enzensberger) **28**:158, 161
"A Modest Proposal" (Hughes) **7**:118
"Modest Proposal" (Jordan) **38**:125
"Modlitwa Pana Cogito-Podróznika" (Herbert) **50**:40-41
"Modulations for a Solo Voice" (Levertov) **11**:209
A Moelna Elegy (Ekelöf)
See *En Mölna-elegi*
"Moesta et Errabunda" (Baudelaire) **1**:70
"Mogiły haremu" (Mickiewicz) **38**:222
"La Moglie del Gigante" (Carducci) **46**:52, 54
"Mogollon Morning" (Momaday) **25**:221
"Moharram" (Stryk) **27**:214
Mohn und Gedächtnes (Celan) **10**:95
moi, Laminaire (Césaire) **25**:33, 41, 45
"Moïse" (Vigny) **26**:369, 380-81, 384, 391, 398, 401, 410-11
"Mój ojciec" (Herbert) **50**:7
"Mole" (Stryk) **27**:199-200
"El Molino Rojo" (Ríos) **57**:312-13
"Molitva" (Tsvetaeva) **14**:312
"Molitvy" (Lermontov) **18**:303
"Molly Means" (Walker) **20**:291-92
En Mölna-elegi (Ekeloef) **23**:50-8, 62-3, 77-87
Molodets (Tsvetaeva) **14**:313, 325-26
Moly (Gunn) **26**:192, 196-197, 203-204, 206-207, 209, 212, 214-215, 219, 221, 226, 228-229
"The Moment" (Abse) **41**:13, 27-28
"Moment" (Nemerov) **24**:264
"Moment" (Zagajewski) **27**:381, 396
"The Moment Cleary" (Kursh) **15**:179
"Moment of Eternity" (MacDiarmid) **9**:193
"The Moment of Grace" (Amichai)
See "She'at ha-Hesed"
"Moment On the Canal" (Kavanagh) **33**:161
"Momento" (Storni) **33**:251;
"Momento epico" (Carducci) **46**:49, 77
"Moments of Glory" (Jeffers) **17**:141
"Moments of Minnie" (Ransom) **61**:271
Moments of the Italian Summer (Wright) **36**:308-09
"Momma and the Neutron Bomb" (Yevtushenko) **40**:358, 366, 370
"Momma Welfare Roll" (Angelou) **32**:3, 29
"Momus" (Sandburg) **41**:313
"Mon Allas, Mona Lisa" (Yau) **61**:335
"Mon Dieu m'a dit" (Verlaine) **2**:415; **32**:341
"Mon Enfance" (Hugo) **17**:75
"Mon héroïsme, quelle farce" (Césaire) **25**:56
"Mon petit mont blanc" (Éluard) **38**:91
"Mon rêve familier" (Verlaine) **32**:341, 386
"Monadnoc" (Emerson) **18**:71, 74, 102-3, 111
"The Monarch of the Id" (Birney) **52**:8
"Monarchs" (Olds) **22**:307
"Monax" (Pushkin) **10**:407
"Monday" (Dalton) **36**:136
"Monday: Roxana; or The Drawing-room" (Montagu) **16**:338, 348
"Mondblick" (Stramm) **50**:189, 202, 207
"Mondschein" (Stramm) **50**:171-72, 189
La moneda de hierro (Borges) **22**:96-7; **32**:64, 69, 86
"Monet Refuses the Operation" (Mueller) **33**:196
"Monet's 'Waterlilies'" (Hayden) **6**:183, 195
"Money" (Jarrell) **41**:135-36
"Money" (Nemerov) **24**:262, 281
"Money and Grass" (Ignatow) **34**:286
"Money Goes Upstream" (Snyder) **21**:300
"Money, Honey, Money" (Walker) **20**:294
"Money/Love" (Corso) **33**:37
"Mongo" (Lermontov) **18**:281
"Mongolian Idiot" (Shapiro) **25**:300, 325
"La monja gitana" (García Lorca) **3**:132
"La monja y el ruiseñor" (Darío) **15**:107-08
"The Monk" (Pushkin)
See "Monax"
"The Monkey" (Szymborska) **44**:312
"The Monkey Puzzle" (Moore) **49**:89, 97, 99-100
"The Monkeys" (Moore) **4**:270; **49**:93, 121, 161
The Monkey's Cloak (Matsuo Bashō)
See *Sarumino*
The Monkey's Raincoat (Matsuo Bashō)
See *Sarumino*
Monkey's Straw Raincoat (Matsuo Bashō)
See *Sarumino*
"The Monks of Casal-Maggiore" (Longfellow) **30**:43, 63
"Monk's Tale" (Chaucer) **19**:13, 42, 45, 56, 63
The Monk!s Tale (Chaucer) **58**:336
"The Monk's Walk" (Dunbar) **5**:121, 137-38, 141
"Monna Innominata" (Rossetti) **7**:271, 275, 280-1
"Le monocle de mon oncle" (Stevens) **6**:292, 295, 303, 327
"Monody" (Zukofsky) **11**:368
"Monody on a Century" (Birney) **52**:3, 39
"Monody on the Death of Chatterton" (Coleridge) **11**:49, 52
The Monogram (Elytis) **21**:123
"The Monoliths" (Momaday) **25**:219
"Monolog" (Benn) **35**:23, 24
"Monologue at Midnight" (Warren) **37**:284, 288, 322, 332, 377, 380
"Monologue of a Broadway Actress" (Yevtushenko) **40**:357
"Monologue of a Fox on an Alaskan Fur Farm" (Yevtushenko) **40**:357
"Monologue of a Mother" (Lawrence) **54**:175, 244
"Monologue of a Polar Fox on an Alaskan Fur Farm" (Yevtushenko)
See "Monologue of a Fox on an Alaskan Fur Farm"
"Monologue of a Silver Fox on a Fur Farm in Alaska" (Yevtushenko)
See "Monologue of a Fox on an Alaskan Fur Farm"
Monologue of a Spanish Guide (Yevtushenko) **40**:357
"Monologue of the Beatniks" (Yevtushenko) **40**:345
"Monotone" (Sandburg) **2**:303; **41**:261
"Monotony" (Boland) **58**:14, 53
"Monotony" (Cavafy) **36**:57
"Monsieur Prudhomme" (Verlaine) **32**:374, 376
"The Monster" (Shvarts)
See "Chudishche"
"The Monster of Mr. Cogito" (Herbert)
See "Potwór Pana Cogito"
"Le Monstre" (Verlaine) **32**:392
"Mont Blanc" (Brathwaite) **56**:93
"Mont Blanc" (Shelley) **14**:206, 211-12, 217, 241
"Le mont des Oliviers" (Vigny) **26**:367-68, 370, 380, 383, 385, 391, 401, 412
"Montage of a Dream Deferred" (Hughes) **53**:94
Montage of a Dream Deferred (Hughes) **1**:244-45, 247-48, 251, 253, 258, 261, 263, 265-68, 270; **53**:108, 114, 121, 123, 126, 129, 140, 145, 152, 156-64, 176-78, 183-85, 188-93, 197
"La montaña rusa" (Parra) **39**:251, 254, 260, 278, 305-6, 308
"Montcalm" (Davie) **29**:96
"Montevideo" (Borges) **32**:83
"A Month among Children" (Montale)
See "Un mese fra i bambini"
"The Months: A Pageant" (Rossetti) **7**:280
"Montparnasse" (Apollinaire) **7**:34
La Montre; or, The Lover's Watch (Behn) **13**:3
Une montre sentimentale (Nishiwaki) **15**:237
"The Monument" (Bishop) **3**:37, 41-3, 48-9, 72; **34**:66, 109, 136-37, 144-45, 189
"Monument" (Oppen) **35**:311, 312
"Monument" (Pushkin)
See "Pamjatnik"
"A Monument in Utopia" (Schnackenberg) **45**:334, 348, 350
"Monument Mountain" (Bryant) **20**:14, 29, 47
"Monument of Love" (Jiménez) **7**:184
"The Monument to Peter the Great" (Mickiewicz) **38**:168
"Mood" (Cullen) **20**:63, 75
"The Moon" (Borges)
See "La luna"
"The Moon" (Carruth) **10**:71
"The Moon" (Ignatow) **34**:279, 292, 319
"Moon" (Walcott) **46**:286
Moon across the Way (Borges)
See *Luna de enfrente*
"Moon and Insect Panorama: Love Poem" (García Lorca) **3**:141
"Moon and Oatgrass" (Chin) **40**:25, 27, 31, 33-5
"The Moon and the Yew Tree" (Plath) **1**:390, 409
"The Moon Being the Number 19" (Wakoski) **15**:364
"Moon Compasses" (Frost) **39**:246
Moon Crossing Bridge (Gallagher) **9**:62-5
"Moon Down Elphinstone" (Birney) **52**:40
"The Moon Explodes in Autumn as a Milkweed Pod" (Wakoski) **15**:364
"The Moon Has a Complicated Geography" (Wakoski) **15**:364
"Moon in Hydra" (Cisneros) **52**:153
"The Moon in Your Hands" (H. D.) **5**:275
"The Moon is Always Female" (Piercy) **29**:311
The Moon Is Always Female (Piercy) **29**:311, 323
"The Moon Is the Number Eighteen" (Olson) **19**:293-94, 321
"Moon Lines, after Jiminez" (Ondaatje) **28**:335
"The Moon Moves Up her Smooth and Sheeny Path" (Thoreau) **30**:192
"The Moon Now Rises to Her Absolute Rule" (Thoreau) **30**:266
"Moon over the Gasworks" (Seifert) **47**:324
"Moon Poems" (Lindsay) **23**:281
"Moon Tiger" (Levertov) **11**:177
"The Moondial" (Carman) **34**:212
"Moonlight" (Apollinaire)
See "Clair de lune"
"Moonlight" (Harjo) **27**:56

"Moonlight" (Ransom) **61**:293
"Moonlight" (Teasdale) **31**:360, 380, 388
"Moonlight" (Verlaine)
See "Clair de lune"
"Moonlight and Jellyfish" (Hagiwara) **18**:168
"Moonlight and Maggots" (Sandburg) **41**:322
"Moonlight Night" (Tu Fu) **9**:321
"Moonlight Night: Carmel" (Hughes) **1**:240
"Moonrise" (Lawrence) **54**:169
"Moonrise" (Plath) **1**:406; **37**:176, 184
"Moonrise" (Sappho) **5**:416
"The Moon's Funeral" (Belloc) **24**:49
"Moon's Revenge" (Carducci)
See "Vendette della luna"
"Moon-Set" (Carruth) **10**:85
"Moonset Glouster" (Olson) **19**:322-23
"Moon-Skin" (Wagoner) **33**:354
"Moonstruck" (MacDiarmid) **9**:160
The Moor of Peter the Great (Pushkin)
See *Arap Petra Velikogo*
"Moortown" (Hughes) **7**:162
Moortown (Hughes) **7**:157-58, 162-63, 165, 171
"The Moose" (Bishop) **3**:58-60, 73, 75; **34**:54, 56, 58, 62, 72, 78, 82, 100, 104, 107-13, 143, 146, 187, 193
"The Moose" (Bly) **39**:72
"Moose in the Morning" (Sarton) **39**:368
"The Moose Wallow" (Hayden) **6**:194-95
A Moral Alphabet (Belloc) **24**:16-18, 26
"Moral Clothing" (Lawrence) **54**:249
Moral Essays (Pope) **26**:320, 340
Moral Tales (Laforgue)
See *Moralités légendaires*
"Morale" (Gautier) **18**:158
"La moralité" (Mickiewicz) **38**:180
Moralités légendaires (Laforgue) **14**:70
"Morality" (Arnold) **5**:42
"The Morality of Poetry" (Wright) **36**:299, 315-16, 338, 340, 380-81
"Morality Play" (Oppen)
See "A Morality Play: Preface"
"A Morality Play: Preface" (Oppen) **35**:336, 337
"Un morceau en forme de poire" (Wakoski) **15**:372
Morceaux choisis (Tzara) **27**:223-4
"More" (Stein) **18**:319, 330
"A More Ancient Mariner" (Carman) **34**:201, 207
More Beasts—For Worse Children (Belloc) **24**:24-6, 35
"More Clues" (Rukeyser) **12**:225
"More Foreign Cities" (Tomlinson) **17**:318
More Pansies (Lawrence) **54**:184-85, 224, 249
More Peers (Belloc) **24**:26-7, 41, 43, 49
More Poems (Housman) **2**:167, 171-74, 176, 182-83, 188
More Poems, 1961 (Graves) **6**:154-56
More Poems to Solve (Swenson) **14**:276
More Songs From Vagabondia (Carman) **34**:200, 207, 218, 237-38
"More Sonnets at Christmas" (Tate) **50**:252-53, 255, 261
More Sonnets at Christmas (Tate) **50**:240, 251
"More Than a Fool's Song" (Cullen) **20**:57
"Morfudd a Dyddgu" (Dafydd ap Gwilym) **56**:245
"Morfudd and Dyddgu" (Dafydd)
See "Morfudd a Dyddgu"
"Morfudd Fel yr Haul" (Dafydd ap Gwilym) **56**:246
"Morfudd Like the Sun" (Dafydd)
See "Morfudd Fel yr Haul"
"Der Morgen" (Stramm) **50**:171-72, 175
"Morgue II" (Benn) **35**:50
Morgue und andere Gedichte (Benn) **35**:3, 7, 8, 22, 23, 24, 29, 30, 46, 47, 50, 53, 54, 83
"Mori no michi" (Ishikawa) **10**:213
"Mori no omoide" (Ishikawa) **10**:212-13
Morituri salutamus (Longfellow) **30**:49, 73, 103
"Moriturus" (Millay) **6**:236
"A Morning" (Dickey) **40**:189, 224, 227-28
"Morning" (Glück) **16**:152
"Morning" (Ransom) **61**:307
"Morning" (Rimbaud)
See "Matin"
"Morning" (Teasdale) **31**:325
"Morning" (Wheatley)
See "An Hymn to the Morning"
"Morning" (Williams) **7**:352
"Morning After" (Hughes) **1**:256; **53**:120
"Morning at the Window" (Eliot) **31**:159
"The Morning Baking" (Forché) **10**:142
"The Morning Bell" (Ishikawa)
See "Akatsuki no kane"
"The Morning Call" (Patmore) **59**:228-29
"The Morning Dream" (Cowper) **40**:105, 119
"Morning Exercises" (Cassian) **17**:11
"Morning Express" (Sassoon) **12**:275
The Morning Glory, Another Thing That Will Never Be My Friend (Bly) **39**:22, 24, 29, 37, 43, 69
"Morning Glory Pool" (Plath) **37**:257
"Morning Hymn to a Dark Girl" (Wright) **36**:315, 335-36, 375
"A Morning Imagination of Russia" (Williams) **7**:350
"Morning in the Square" (Szirtes) **51**:158
"The Morning Moon" (Walcott) **46**:236-37
"The Morning News" (Berry) **28**:11
"Morning, Noon, and Night" (Page) **12**:173
"Morning of Intoxication" (Rimbaud)
See "Matinée d'ivresse"
Morning Poems (Bly) **39**:116
Morning Poems (Yevtushenko) **40**:344
"Morning Radio" (Mahon) **60**:150
"A Morning Ride" (Kipling) **3**:194
"Morning Sea" (Cavafy) **36**:50
"Morning Song" (Carducci)
See "Mattinata"
"Morning Song" (Plath) **1**:390; **37**:256
"Morning Song" (Teasdale) **31**:360, 370
"The Morning Song of Lord Zero" (Aiken) **26**:15, 24
Morning Songs (Tagore)
See *Prabhat sangit*
"The Morning Star" (Pavese)
See "Lo steddazzu"
"Morning Sun" (MacNeice) **61**:123, 126
"Morning, the Horizon" (Ortiz) **17**:245
"The Morning They Shot Tony Lopez" (Soto) **28**:375
"A Morning Wake among Dead" (Kinnell) **26**:256-57
"Morning with Broken Window" (Hogan) **35**:257
"Morning-Land" (Sassoon) **12**:240
"Mornings in a New House" (Merrill) **28**:221
"Mornings in various years" (Piercy) **29**:315
"Moro Assassinato" (Curnow) **48**:12, 15-19, 43, 46, 49-51
Morový sloup (Seifert) **47**:317, 319-20, 328-29, 336
"Mors" (Carducci) **46**:6, 54
"Mors" (Hugo) **17**:83
"Morskaya tsarevna" (Lermontov) **18**:292
"La mort" (Leopardi) **37**:169-70
"Mort!" (Verlaine) **32**:396
"La mort dans la conversation" (Éluard) **38**:69
"La Mort dans la vie" (Gautier) **18**:131, 155
"La Mort de Narcisse" (Ronsard) **11**:251
"La mort des amants" (Baudelaire) **1**:54, 73
"La mort des artistes" (Baudelaire) **1**:45
"Mort du duc de Berry" (Hugo) **17**:75
"La mort du loup" (Vigny) **26**:367, 369-70, 380-81, 401-402, 412-15
"La Mort du Soldat est près des choses naturelles (5 Mars)" (Stevens) **6**:294
La mort en ce jardin (Bunuel) **15**:207, 218
"Le mort joyeux" (Baudelaire) **1**:45
"La Mort l'amour la vie" (Éluard) **38**:78
"La mort rose" (Breton) **15**:52
"Mortal" (Jackson) **44**:28
Mortal Acts, Mortal Words (Kinnell) **26**:257, 260-61, 271, 280, 292
"Mortal Enemy" (Parker) **28**:362
"The Mortal Face" (Bonnefoy)
See "Le visage mortel"
"Mortal Girl" (Rukeyser) **12**:231
"Mortal Limit" (Warren) **37**:364, 366, 376-77
"Le morte chitarre" (Quasimodo) **47**:286-88
"Morte d'Arthur" (Tennyson) **6**:354, 358-59, 409
La morte de Socrate (Lamartine) **16**:263, 266, 273, 278-79, 291
"La morte di Dio" (Montale) **13**:133
La morte meditata (Ungaretti) **57**:347
"Le Mortel Partenaire" (Char) **56**:155
"I morti" (Montale) **13**:105, 112
"Mortification" (Herbert) **4**:100-01, 120, 127, 133
"Mortmain" (Robinson) **1**:470
"Mortmain" (Warren) **37**:307, 360, 367
"Morts de quatre-vingt-douze" (Rimbaud) **57**:249
"Morts de quatre-vingt-douze et de quatre-vingt-treize" (Rimbaud) **3**:283
"A Mortul Prayer" (Riley) **48**:300
"Mosaic of the Nativity: Serbia, Winter 1993" (Kenyon) **57**:20, 46
"Moscow Freight Station" (Yevtushenko) **40**:342-43
Moscow Mansions (Guest) **55**:183-85, 214
Moscow Notebooks (Mandelstam) **14**:150
"Moses" (Muir) **49**:197, 298
"Moses" (Nemerov) **24**:295
"Moses" (Shapiro) **25**:296
Moses: A Story of the Nile (Harper) **21**:185, 187-89, 191-98, 201
"Mosquito" (Lawrence) **54**:187
"Mossbawn: Sunlight" (Heaney) **18**:197, 232
"The Most Humble Poem" (Seifert)
See "Básezn nejpokornější"
The Most Humble Poem (Seifert)
See *Město v slzách*
"Most Likely You'll Go Your Way and I'll Go Mine" (Dylan) **37**:51
"Most of a Dialogue in Cuzco" (Birney) **52**:16, 42, 96, 99
"The Most of It" (Frost) **1**:205-06, 230-31; **39**:238
"Most Things at Second Hand through Gloves We Touch" (Schwartz) **8**:293
"Most wretched heart" (Wyatt) **27**:353
"Mostly Hospital and Old Age" (Viereck) **27**:294
"Mostru o pavea" (Pasolini) **17**:253
"Mot" (Césaire) **25**:31
Mot (Césaire) **25**:38
"The Mote" (Carman) **34**:207
"The Motel" (Olds) **22**:341
"Motet" No. 1 (Montale) **13**:120-22
"Motet" No. 2 (Montale) **13**:120, 122
"Motet" No. 3 (Montale) **13**:118-20
"Motet" No. 4 (Montale) **13**:120
"Motet" No. 5 (Montale) **13**:118, 121-22, 125, 127
"Motet" No. 6 (Montale) **13**:121-22, 150
"Motet" No. 7 (Montale) **13**:119, 122
"Motet" No. 8 (Montale)
See "Mottetto" No. 8
"Motet" No. 9 (Montale) **13**:119, 122-24
"Motet" No. 10 (Montale) **13**:123
"Motet" No. 11 (Montale) **13**:124-25
"Motet" No. 12 (Montale) **13**:124
"Motet" No. 13 (Montale) **13**:124
"Motet" No. 14 (Montale) **13**:124
"Motet" No. 15 (Montale) **13**:125
"Motet" No. 17 (Montale) **13**:125-26
"Motet" No. 18 (Montale) **13**:125, 127
"Motet" No. 19 (Montale) **13**:126
"Motet" No. 20 (Montale) **13**:126
"Motet XX" (Montale) **13**:136
"The Mother" (Brooks) **7**:67
"Mother" (Hacker) **47**:80

"The Mother" (Olds) **22**:309
"Mother" (Shvarts)
See "Vospominanie o strannom ugoshchenii"
"Mother" (Smith) **12**:326
Mother (Seifert)
See *Maminka*
The Mother (Sitwell) **3**:299, 302, 319
"Mother, among the Dustbins" (Smith) **12**:352
"Mother and Child" (Ignatow) **34**:272
"Mother and Daughter" (Sexton) **2**:365
"Mother and Poet" (Browning) **6**:30-1
"Mother and Son" (Morris) **55**:338-39
"Mother and Son" (Tate) **50**:230-31, 255, 302
"Mother Dear" (McKay) **2**:222
"Mother Earth: Her Whales" (Snyder) **21**:293, 297
"Mother Farewell!" (Johnson) **24**:145
"Mother Goose" (Niedecker) **42**:95, 98, 141, 152
"Mother Goose" (Rexroth) **20**:195, 218
Mother Goose (Niedecker) **42**:149
"Mother Goose's Garland" (MacLeish) **47**:130
"Mother Hubberd's Tale" (Spenser)
See "Prosopopoia; or, Mother Hubberds Tale"
"mother i am mad" (Clifton) **17**:19
"Mother in Wartime" (Hughes) **1**:252
"Mother Marie Therese" (Lowell) **3**:205
"Mother Night" (Johnson) **24**:127, 137, 159, 166
"Mother of God" (Sikelianos) **29**:366
"Mother of God I Shall Pray in Humility" (Lermontov) **18**:296
Mother Poem (Brathwaite) **56**:34-35, 41-45, 50-51, 61-62, 70-71, 89-90, 96-98, 100
"Mother Pomegranae" (Mistral)
See "La madre granada"
"Mother Rosarine" (Kumin) **15**:191
"Mother Stone" (Stone) **53**:258
"Mother the Great Stones Got to Move" (Goodison) **36**:153
"Mother to Son" (Hughes) **1**:241, 248-49, 262; **53**:84, 125, 187
"The Mother Tongue" (Boland) **58**:38, 62
Mother, What is Man? (Smith) **12**:326
"The Mothering Blackness" (Angelou) **32**:29
"Motherland" (Lermontov)
See "Rodina"
"Mother-Right" (Rich) **5**:384
"Mothers" (Giovanni) **19**:140
"The Mother's Blessing" (Harper) **21**:197
"A Mother's Heroism" (Harper) **21**:194, 206, 217
"The Mother's Story" (Clifton) **17**:29
"Moths" (Boland) **58**:19, 49
"The Moths" (Merwin) **45**:22
"The Moth-Signal" (Hardy) **8**:99
"Motion and Rest" (Toomer) **7**:338
"Motion of Wish" (Kunitz) **19**:160
"The Motions" (Ammons) **16**:5
"The Motive for Metaphor" (Stevens) **6**:312-13, 340
Motivos de son (Guillén) **23**:97-98, 104-08, 110, 133, 141-45
"Motor Lights on a Hill Road" (Lowell) **13**:60
"A Motorbike" (Hughes) **7**:162
The Motorcycle Betrayal Poems (Wakoski) **15**:325-26, 331-32, 345, 350, 363, 366, 369-70
"Motoring" (Brooke) **24**:68
"Motteti" (Montale) **13**:105
"Mottetto" No. 8 (Montale) **13**:105, 113, 122, 127
"Motto" (Hughes) **1**:267; **53**:150-52, 159
"The Motto on the Sundial" (Rexroth) **20**:192
"Motto to the Songs of Innocence and of Experience" (Blake) **12**:10
"Moules à la Marinière" (Curnow) **48**:36, 38
Moulin premier (Char) **56**:121, 129-30, 142, 158-59, 185
"Moulin Rouge" (Mueller) **33**:193
"The Mound Builders" (Kunitz) **19**:158
"Mount Chungnan" (Wang Wei) **18**:362-63
"Mount Kikineis" (Mickiewicz)
See "Góra Kikineis"
"Mount Mary" (Wright) **14**:343
"The Mount of Olives" (Vigny)
See "Le mont des Oliviers"
"Mount Zion" (Hughes) **7**:147
"th mountain" (Bissett) **14**:20
"The Mountain" (Frost) **1**:226
"The Mountain" (Merwin) **45**:18, 29
"Mountain Blueberries" (Francis) **34**:261
"The Mountain Chapel" (Thomas) **53**:326
"A Mountain Gateway" (Carman) **34**:229
Mountain Interval (Frost) **1**:197, 202, 207, 215; **39**:232-33, 235
"Mountain Lion" (Hogan) **35**:276
"Mountain Plateau" (Warren) **37**:330
"The Mountain Spirit" (Wang Wei) **18**:382
Mountain Talk (Ammons) **16**:14
"The Mountain Village of Bastundzhi" (Lermontov)
See "Aul Bastundzi"
"The Mountaineers" (Abse) **41**:7
"The Mountaineer's Ballard" (Wylie) **23**:311
"Mountains" (Auden) **1**:17
"Mountains" (Hayden) **6**:194, 196
"Mountains" (Hughes) **7**:137
"The Mountains" (Muir) **49**:243, 297
Mountains and Rivers without End (Snyder) **21**:299
"The Mountains in the Horizon" (Thoreau) **30**:285-87, 293
"A Mounted Umbrella" (Stein) **18**:334, 349
Mourir de ne pas mourir (Éluard) **38**:60, 73, 103
"The Mourner" (Merwin) **45**:9, 49
"The Mourner's Bench" (Masters) **1**:339, 343; **36**:194
"Mournin' for Religion" (Masters) **1**:344; **36**:194
"Mourning" (Marvell) **10**:271, 301, 314
"Mourning Dove" (Niedecker) **42**:143-44, 147-48
"A Mourning Forbidding Valediction" (Ashbery) **26**:161
"Mourning Pablo Neruda" (Bly) **39**:64
"Mourning to Do" (Sarton) **39**:362
"The Mouse's Nest" (Clare) **23**:7
"The Mouth of the Hudson" (Lowell) **3**:215
"The Mouth of Truth" (Ferlinghetti) **1**:183
"Les moutons" (Éluard) **38**:91
"Mouvement" (Rimbaud) **57**:183, 234
"Mouvement" (Tzara) **27**:227
"Move the Meeting Be Adjourned" (Parra)
See "Pido que se levante la sesión"
"Move Un-noticed to be Noticed: A Nationhood Poem" (Madhubuti) **5**:345
"The Movement of Fish" (Dickey) **40**:182, 190
"Movement to Establish My Identity" (Wakoski) **15**:350
"Movements" (Tomlinson) **17**:327
"Movements II" (Tomlinson) **17**:343
"Movements IV" (Tomlinson) **17**:326, 341
"Movies" (Hughes) **1**:266; **53**:162, 190
"Moving" (Jarrell) **41**:174, 198, 200
"Moving Books to a New Study" (Bly) **39**:53
"The Moving Floor" (Szirtes) **51**:159
"Moving Fred's Outhouse/Geriatrics of Pine" (Ondaatje) **28**:335
"The Moving Image" (Wright) **14**:337, 362
The Moving Image (Wright) **14**:334-35, 338-41, 345-51, 353, 357, 368
"Moving into the Garden" (Wagoner) **33**:348
"Moving Right Along" (Stone) **53**:230
"Moving South" (Wright) **14**:373
The Moving Target (Merwin) **45**:3, 5, 8, 10, 14, 18-19, 24, 26-8, 30, 32-3, 50, 52, 58, 61, 63-4, 71-4, 78-9, 81-3, 85, 87-8, 90, 97
"The Moving to Griffin" (Ondaatje) **28**:291
Moving Towards Home (Jordan) **38**:140
"The Mower against gardens" (Marvell) **10**:266, 293, 297
"The Mower to the Glo-Worms" (Marvell) **10**:266, 296-97, 315
"The Mower's Song" (Marvell) **10**:266, 296-97
Moya Rodoslovnaya (Pushkin) **10**:391
"Mozart, 1935" (Stevens) **6**:296
Mozart in Prague (Seifert) **47**:320
"Mozhet byt' eto tochka bezumiia" (Mandelstam) **14**:152
"Mr. Bleaney" (Larkin) **21**:228-29, 241, 247-48
"Mr. Brodsky" (Tomlinson) **17**:311, 353
"Mr. Burnshaw and the Statue" (Stevens) **6**:297, 321
Mr. Cogito (Herbert)
See *Pan Cogito*
"Mr. Cogito About the Magic" (Herbert)
See "Pan Cogito o magii"
"Mr. Cogito and Longevity" (Herbert)
See "Pan Cogito a dlugoniecznosc"
"Mr. Cogito and Maria Rasputin-An Attempt at Contact" (Herbert)
See "Pan Cogito a pop"
"Mr. Cogito and Pop Music" (Herbert)
See "Pan Cogito a pop"
"Mr. Cogito and Pure Thought" (Herbert)
See "Pan Cogito a mysl czysta"
"Mr. Cogito and the Imagination" (Herbert) **50**:13, 24, 42
"Mr. Cogito and the Movement of Thoughts" (Herbert)
See "Pan Cogito a ruch mysli"
"Mr. Cogito and the Poet of Certain Age" (Herbert)
See "Pan Cogito a poeta w pewnym wieku"
"Mr. Cogito Bemoans the Pettiness of Dreams" (Herbert)
See "Pan Cogito biada nad maloscia snów"
"Mr. Cogito Considers the Difference between the Human Voice and the Voice of Nature" (Herbert)
See "Pan Cogito rozwaza róznice miedzy glosem ludzkim a glosem przyrody"
"Mr. Cogito Laments the Pettiness of Dreams" (Herbert)
See "Pan Cogito biada nad maloscia snów"
"Mr. Cogito looks at his own face in the mirror" (Herbert)
See "Pan Cogito obserwuje w lustrze swoja twarz"
"Mr. Cogito observes his dead friend" (Herbert)
See "Pan Cogito obserwuje zmarlego przjaciela"
"Mr. Cogito on the Need for Precision" (Herbert) **50**:13, 15
"Mr. Cogito on Upright Attitudes" (Herbert)
See "Pan Cogito o postawie wyprostowanej"
"Mr. Cogito on Virtue" (Herbert)
See "Pan Cogito o cnocie"
"Mr. Cogito Seeks Advice" (Herbert)
See "Pan Cogito szuka rady"
"Mr. Cogito Tells about the Temptation of Spinoza" (Herbert)
See "Pan Cogito oponiada o kuszeniu Spinozy"
"Mr. Cogito Thinks about Returning to his Native Town" (Herbert)
See "Pan Cogito mysli o powrocie . . ."
"Mr. Cogito's Adventures with Music" (Herbert)
See "Pana Cogito przygody z muzyka"
"Mr. Cogito's Game" (Herbert)
See "Gra Pana Cogito"
"Mr. Cogito's Precipice" (Herbert)
See "Przepasc Pana Cogito"
"Mr. Cogito's Reflections About Suffering" (Herbert)
See "Pan Cogito rozmysla o cierpieniu"
"Mr. Cogito's Soul" (Herbert)
See "Dusza Pana Cogito"

"Mr. Cogito-The Return" (Herbert)
See "Pan Cogito-Powrót"
"Mr. Edwards and the Spider" (Lowell) **3**:215
"Mr. Eliot's Sunday Morning Service" (Eliot) **5**:184
"Mr. Flood's Party" (Robinson) **1**:478; **35**:377
"Mr. Francis Finch" (Philips) **40**:296
"Mr. Longfellow and His Boy" (Sandburg) **41**:301
"Mr. Mammon I" (Ignatow) **34**:273
"Mr. Mammon II" (Ignatow) **34**:273
"Mr. Mine" (Sexton) **2**:352
"Mr. Nixon" (Pound) **4**:320
"Mr. Over" (Smith) **12**:297, 339
"Mr. Pope" (Tate) **50**:228, 246, 282-83, 304, 306, 309
Mr. Pope and Other Poems (Tate) **50**:229, 231, 282, 285, 309, 311, 318
"Mr. Seurat's Sunday Afternoon" (Schwartz)
See "Seurat's Sunday Afternoon along the Seine"
"Mr. Silberberg" (Riley) **48**:340
"Mr. Sludge, 'The Medium'" (Browning) **2**:72, 82
"Mr. Styrax" (Pound) **4**:317
"Mrs. Alfred Uruguay" (Stevens) **6**:304
"Mrs Arbuthnot" (Smith) **12**:314
"Mrs. Benjamin Pantier" (Masters) **1**:347; **36**:169, 182
"Mrs. Hempel and her Katz" (Stone) **53**:218
"Mrs. Kessler" (Masters) **36**:239
"Mrs. Mandrill" (Nemerov) **24**:259, 268
"Mrs. Purkapile" (Masters) **36**:182
"Mrs Simpkins" (Smith) **12**:344
"Mrs. Small" (Brooks) **7**:62, 69, 96-8
"Mrs. Throckmorton's Bulfinch" (Cowper)
See "On the Death of Mrs. Throckmorton's Bulfinch"
"Mrs. Walpurga" (Rukeyser) **12**:204
"Mrs. Williams" (Masters) **1**:347
"Mt. Gabriel" (Mahon) **60**:190
"Mtsiri" (Lermontov)
See *Mtsyri*
"Mtsyri" (Lermontov)
See *Mtsyri*
Mtsyri (Lermontov) **18**:279, 282-83, 298, 302
"mu" (Mackey) **49**:25, 30
"Muchacha recién crecida" (Guillén) **23**:126
"Muchas gracias, adiós" (Guillén) **35**:184
"Muckers" (Sandburg) **41**:273
"Mud" (Cassian) **17**:4
"Mud" (Kumin) **15**:182
"The Mud Turtle" (Nemerov) **24**:274
"The Mud Vision" (Heaney) **18**:227-28, 230, 237
"Muerte de Antoñito el Camborio" (García Lorca) **3**:131
"La muerte y la brújula" (Borges) **32**:69
"Muerto de amor" (Guillén) **35**:182
"El muerto huyente" (Storni) **33**:295;
"Los Muertos" (Fuertes) **27**:12
"Mugging" (Ginsberg) **4**:85
"Mugitusque Boum" (Hugo) **17**:83
"Muiopotmos; or, the Fate of the Butterflie" (Spenser) **8**:365, 367-68, 371
"Una mujer" (Mistral) **32**:184
"Una mujer de movimientos de rio" (Paz) **48**:251
"Mujer de prisionero" (Mistral) **32**:186
La mujer desnuda (1918-1923) (Jiménez) **7**:213-14
"La mujer fuerte" (Mistral) **32**:174
"Mujer nueva" (Guillén) **23**:105
"Mujeres" (Parra) **39**:286
"Mulata" (Guillén) **23**:110, 142
"The Mulatta and the Minotaur" (Goodison) **36**:143, 147
"The Mulatta as Penelope" (Goodison) **36**:143, 147, 152
"Mulatta Song" (Goodison) **36**:143, 154
"Mulatta Song II" (Goodison) **36**:154
"Mulatto" (Hughes) **1**:238, 263-64, 270
"The Mulch" (Kunitz) **19**:159
"Mulholland's Contract" (Kipling) **3**:161
Multitudes, Multitudes (Clampitt) **19**:87-8
"Mummia" (Brooke) **24**:77
Mundo a solas (Aleixandre) **15**:3, 18-24, 32-3
"Mundo continuo" (Guillén) **35**:196, 198
"El mundo de siete pozos" (Storni) **33**:235, 272;
"Mundo en claro" (Guillén) **35**:180, 181
"Mundus and Paulina" (Gower) **59**:68, 88, 108
"The Munich Mannequins" (Plath) **1**:384, 391; **37**:258, 269
"The Municipal Gallery Revisited" (Yeats) **20**:322, 324
Muoyce (Cage) **58**:204-05
"La muraglia" (Quasimodo) **47**:283
Muraka (Amichai) **38**:24
"Murano" (Doty) **53**:60
"The Murder" (Brooks) **7**:68
"The Murder" (Page) **12**:178
"Murder in the Cathedral" (Niedecker) **42**:105
"Murder Mystery" (Wagoner) **33**:333, 371
The Murder of Lidice (Millay) **6**:220
"The Murder of William Remington" (Nemerov) **24**:258, 280
"Murder Poem No. 74321" (Rexroth) **20**:187
"The Murdered Traveller" (Bryant) **20**:40
"The Murderer" (Ignatow) **34**:286
"The Murderess" (Glück) **16**:126
Mureau (Cage) **58**:183-85, 188, 192, 195, 205
A Muriel Rukeyser Reader (Rukeyser) **12**:234
"Murmurings in a Field Hospital" (Sandburg) **41**:239, 249, 351
"The Muse as Donkey" (Sarton) **39**:362-63, 369
"The Muse as Medusa" (Sarton) **39**:342, 365-6
"Muses No More But Mazes Be Your Names" (Raleigh) **31**:305
"Museum" (Szymborska) **44**:296-97, 299
Museum (Dove) **6**:104-07, 109, 115-16, 118, 121
"Museum Guards (London)" (Stryk) **27**:214
"Museum Piece" (Wilbur) **51**:192, 210, 326
"Museum Vase" (Francis) **34**:244
"The Mushroom Gatherers" (Davie) **29**:95
"Mushrooms" (Atwood) **8**:43
"Mushrooms" (Plath) **1**:389, 404, 406, 408
"Mushrooms" (Tomlinson) **17**:334, 347, 354
"A Music" (Berry) **28**:4
"Music" (Herbert) **4**:100
"Music" (O'Hara) **45**:127, 135-37, 139-40, 243
"Music" (Pasternak)
See "Muzyka"
"Music" (Stone) **53**:251
"Music" (Thoreau) **30**:182, 195, 227
"the music in my veins travels" (Alurista)
See "la musica en mis venas navega"
"The Music of Poetry" (Kinnell) **26**:288
"The Music of Time" (Larkin) **21**:227
"Music Swims Back to Me" (Sexton) **2**:359
"The Music That Hurts" (Komunyakaa) **51**:18-19
"la musica en mis venas navega" (Alurista) **34**:38
"Música, sólo música" (Guillén) **35**:185
"A Musical Comedy Thought" (Parker) **28**:354
"A Musical Instrument" (Browning) **6**:23
"Musical Moments" (Abse) **41**:32
"The Musical Voice" (Ishikawa)
See "Gakusei"
"Musician" (Bogan) **12**:124
"Musicks Empire" (Marvell) **10**:313
"La Musique" (Char) **56**:197-98
"Musketaquid" (Emerson) **18**:88, 91, 111
"Mussel Hunter at Rock Harbour" (Plath) **1**:388, 407; **37**:180, 182
"Muszla" (Herbert) **50**:5
"Mutabilitie Cantos" (Spenser)
See "Two Cantos of Mutabilitie"
"Mutability" (Brooke) **24**:56-7, 72, 85
"Mutability" (Shelley) **14**:166
"Mutation" (Bryant) **20**:34, 44
"Mutation of the Spirit" (Corso) **33**:24-6, 36, 49
"Mutations" (MacNeice) **61**:140
"Mute Phenomena" (Mahon) **60**:167, 178
"Muted Music" (Warren) **37**:365, 378
"Mutilateurs" (Char) **56**:155
"Mutilation" (Lawrence) **54**:187
"Mutra" (Paz) **1**:369; **48**:232, 264
"Mutterings over the Crib of a Deaf Child" (Wright) **36**:290, 335, 338
"Mutton" (Stein) **18**:323-24
"Mutual Trust" (Merrill) **28**:257
"Muza" (Akhmatova) **55**:14
"Muzh v mogile, syn v tiur'me" (Akhmatova) **55**:55
"Muzhestvo" (Akhmatova) **2**:19
"Muzyka" (Pasternak) **6**:288
"Mwilu/or Poem for the Living" (Madhubuti) **5**:346
"My Alba" (Ginsberg) **47**:52
My Alexandria (Doty) **53**:45-47, 49, 52-53, 61-63, 65, 72
"My Apish Cousins" (Moore) **49**:121
"My Autumn Walk" (Bryant) **20**:5, 46
"My Beard Rough as the Beginning" (Ignatow) **34**:308
My Best Poems (Aleixandre) **15**:18
"My boddy in the walls captived" (Raleigh) **31**:218, 239, 251, 301, 303-04
"My Bohemian Life" (Rimbaud)
See "Ma bohème"
"My Books" (Longfellow) **30**:51
"My Books I'd Fain Cast Off" (Thoreau) **30**:181, 192, 194, 203, 214-15, 225, 235, 240, 258
"My Books I'd Fain Cast Off, I Cannot Read" (Thoreau)
See "My Books I'd Fain Cast Off"
"My Boots" (Thoreau) **30**:182, 229, 287
"My Brothers the Silent" (Merwin) **45**:23
"My Cats" (Smith) **12**:339
"My Chili" (Ríos) **57**:329
"My City" (Johnson) **24**:144, 154
"My coat threadbare" (Niedecker) **42**:150-51
"My Comforter" (Burroughs) **8**:51
"My Corn-cob Pipe" (Dunbar) **5**:133
"My Country in Darkness" (Boland) **58**:61-62
"My Cousin in April" (Glück) **16**:154
"My Cousin Muriel" (Clampitt) **19**:97
"My Daughter Is Coming!" (Walker) **30**:370
"My Daughter the Junkie on a Train" (Lorde)
See "To My Daughter the Junkie on a Train"
"My Daughter's Aquarium" (Stryk) **27**:204
"My Day's Delight, My Springtime Joys Foredone" (Raleigh) **31**:217
"My Dear and Loving Husband" (Bradstreet)
See "To My Dear and Loving Husband His Goeing into England"
"My delight and thy delight" (Bridges) **28**:70
"My Dove, My Beautiful One" (Joyce)
See "XIV"
"My Doves" (Browning) **6**:21
"my dream about being white" (Clifton) **17**:36
"My Dreams Are a Field Afar" (Housman) **2**:182
"My Dreams, My Work, Must Wait till after Hell" (Brooks) **7**:74
"My Enemy" (Lawrence) **54**:249
"My Entire Life" (Borges)
See "Mi vida entera"
"My Erotic Double" (Ashbery) **26**:133
"My Fairy Godmother" (Hyde) **7**:147
My Farish Street Green (Walker) **20**:294
"My Father and My Childhood" (Jackson) **44**:8
"My Father Fought their War for Four Years" (Amichai) **38**:27-28
"My Father Laughing in the Chicago Theater" (Wagoner) **33**:374
"My Father Moved through Dooms of Feel" (Cummings)
See "My Father Moved through Dooms of Love"
"My Father Moved through Dooms of Love" (Cummings) **5**:81, 89

"My Father Paints the Summer" (Wilbur) **51**:188, 192-93, 269
"My Father Speaks to Me from the Dead" (Olds) **22**:323, 325, 338
"My Father's Breasts" (Olds) **22**:328
"My Fathers Came from Kentucky" (Lindsay) **23**:265
"My Father's Eyes" (Olds) **22**:332
"My Father's Funeral" (Shapiro) **25**:305
"My Father's Irish Setters" (Merrill) **28**:284
"My Father's Love Letters" (Komunyakaa) **51**:23
"My Father's Wedding" (Bly) **39**:65, 99-100
"My Fire" (Wagoner) **33**:355
"My first borne love unhappily conceived" (Raleigh) **31**:201
"My First Weeks" (Olds) **22**:338
"My Foe" (Riley) **48**:304
"My Friend" (Gibran) **9**:77
My Friend Tree (Niedecker) **42**:94, 102, 106, 134-35, 152, 183
"My Friends" (Merwin) **45**:5
"My Friends, Why Should We Live" (Thoreau) **30**:254-55
"My galley charged with forgetfulness" (Wyatt) **27**:323-324, 357-358
"My Garden" (Emerson) **18**:76, 88
"My Garden, My Daylight" (Graham) **59**:147-48
My Geneology (Pushkin)
See *Moya Rodoslovnaya*
"My Gentlest Song" (Viereck) **27**:263, 278, 281
"My Grandmother's Ghost" (Wright) **36**:338, 373
"My Grandmother's Gold Pin" (Mueller) **33**:178-79
"My Grandmother's Love Letters" (Crane) **3**:98
"My Granny's Hieland Hame" (Burns) **6**:98
"My Grave" (Levine) **22**:228
"My Ground is High" (Thoreau) **30**:195
My Hair Turning Gray among Strangers (Quintana) **36**:273-74
"My Hat" (Smith) **12**:331
"My Heart" (O'Hara) **45**:164
"My Heart and I" (Browning) **6**:23
"My Heart, Being Hungry" (Reese) **29**:332
"My Heart Goes Out" (Smith) **12**:318, 325
"My Heart is Heavy" (Teasdale) **31**:359
"My Heart Was Full" (Smith) **12**:333
"My Hermitage in the Bamboo Grove" (Wang Wei) **18**:358
"My Heroes Have Never Been Cowboys" (Alexie) **53**:7-9
"My Hero's Genealogy" (Pushkin)
See "Rodoslovnaya Moego Geroya"
"My home" (Ungaretti)
See "Casa mia"
"My Honey" (Guillén)
See "Mi chiquita"
"My House" (Giovanni) **19**:112-13, 116, 140, 142-43
My House (Giovanni) **19**:107, 110-14, 116, 118, 121-25, 136-37, 140-41, 144
"My 'I don't Believe" (Amichai)
See "Ha'ani lo ma'amin sheli"
"My Indigo" (Lee) **24**:240, 244
"My Issei Parents, Twice Pioneers, Now I Hear Them" (Yamada) **44**:346
"My Kate" (Browning) **6**:23
"My Lady of the Castle Grand" (Dunbar) **5**:134, 138
"My Lady's Lamentation and Complaint against the Dean" (Swift) **9**:295-96
"My Lady's Lips Are Like de Honey" (Johnson) **24**:141
"My Last Afternoon with Uncle Devereux Winslow" (Lowell) **3**:219, 222
"My Last Duchess" (Browning) **2**:37, 94; **61**:88
"My Last Poem" (Goodison) **36**:141
"My Life By Water" (Niedecker) **42**:107, 138-39, 165
"My Life with the Wave" (Paz) **1**:354
"My Light with Yours" (Masters) **1**:333
"My Little Lovers" (Rimbaud)
See "Mes petites amoureuses"
"My Lord" (Bishop) **34**:161
"My Lost Youth" (Longfellow) **30**:27, 34, 40, 46-7, 71
"My Love Must Be As Free" (Thoreau) **30**:192, 216
"My Loved Subject" (Jeffers) **17**:131
"My lute awake" (Wyatt) **27**:328, 339, 349, 357, 362
"My Luve Is Like a Red, Red Rose" (Burns) **6**:75, 77, 99
"My most. My most. O my lost!" (Villa) **22**:349
"My Mother" (McGuckian) **27**:96
"My Mother Remembers That She Was Beautiful" (Gallagher) **9**:58
"My Mother Would Be a Falconress" (Duncan) **2**:127
"My Mother's Life" (Meredith) **28**:182
"My Mother's Maids" (Wyatt)
See *My mothers maydes when they did sowe and spynne*
My mothers maydes when they did sowe and spynne (Wyatt) **27**:304, 371
"My Mother's Sea Chanty" (Goodison) **36**:158
"My Mountain Home" (McKay) **2**:222
"My Muse" (Montale)
See "La mia musa"
"My Muse" (Smith) **12**:312, 324, 336
"My Muse, what ailes this Ardoure?" (Sidney) **32**:235
"My Name It Is Sam Hall" (Jarrell)
See "O My Name It Is Sam Hall"
"My Native Land" (Ignatow) **34**:318
"My Native Land" (Lermontov)
See "Rodina"
"My Native Land, My Home" (McKay) **2**:216, 224
"My Neighbor" (Ignatow) **34**:314
"My New-Cut Ashlar" (Kipling) **3**:183
"My nocturnal torments" (Shvarts) **50**:134
"My Non-Credo" (Amichai)
See "Ha'ani lo ma'amin sheli"
"My Nose Garden" (Silverstein) **49**:347
"My Own" (Parker) **28**:350-51
"My Own Sweet Good" (Brooks) **7**:55
"My Parents' Lodging Place" (Amichai) **38**:50
"My pen take payn" (Wyatt) **27**:339, 341
"My People" (Hughes) **1**:270; **53**:93, 108-9
"My People" (Kavanagh) **33**:156
"My People" (Sandburg) **41**:330
"My Philosofy" (Riley) **48**:299, 334-35, 352
"My Physics Teacher" (Wagoner) **33**:361
"My Poem" (Giovanni) **19**:111
"My Poets" (Levine) **22**:212
"My Portrait" (Pushkin) **10**:407
"My Powers" (Kavanagh) **33**:120
"My President Weeps" (Ignatow) **34**:323, 325
"My Pretty Dan" (McKay) **2**:221
"My Pretty Rose Tree" (Blake) **12**:34
"My Ruthers" (Riley) **48**:302
"My s koshkoi dremlem den' i noch" (Shvarts) **50**:162
"My Sad Captains" (Gunn) **26**:186, 197
My Sad Captains, and Other Poems (Gunn) **26**:181, 186, 189, 194-195, 197, 201-202, 207, 209, 211, 216, 218-219, 221, 223, 225-226
"My Sadness Sits Around Me" (Jordan) **38**:118
"My Senses Do Not Deceive Me" (Moore) **49**:105
"My Shy Hand" (Owen) **19**:336
"My Silks in Fine Array" (Blake) **12**:31
My Sister, Life (Pasternak)
See *Sestra moia zhizn*
"My Sisters, O My Sisters" (Sarton) **39**:318, 322, 337, 342, 358-59, 364
"My Sister's Sleep" (Rossetti) **44**:174, 227
"My Soldier Lad" (McKay) **2**:223
"My Son Was Drafted" (Amichai) **38**:47-48, 55-56
"My Song" (Brooke) **24**:62, 72, 76
"My Songs" (Yosano Akiko)
See "Waga Uta"
"My Sort of Man" (Dunbar) **5**:131
"My Soul" (Bradstreet) **10**:60-1
"My Soul Accused Me" (Dickinson) **1**:94
"My soul is dark" (Lermontov) **18**:202
"My Spectre around Me" (Blake) **12**:13
"My spirit kisseth thine" (Bridges) **28**:85
"My Spirit Will Not Haunt the Mound" (Hardy) **8**:118
"My Star" (Browning) **2**:59
"My sweet Ann Foot, my bonny Ann" (Clare) **23**:25
"My Sweet Brown Gal" (Dunbar) **5**:119
"My Trip in a Dream to the Lady of Heaven Mountain" (Li Po)
See "My Trip in a Dream to the Lady of Heaven Mountain: A Farewell to Several Gentlemen of Eastern Lu"
"My Trip in a Dream to the Lady of Heaven Mountain: A Farewell to Several Gentlemen of Eastern Lu" (Li Po) **29**:153
"My true love hath my hart" (Sidney) **32**:260
"My Two Springs" (Lanier) **50**:56, 91
"My Vegetarian Friend" (Eliot) **20**:123
"My Vision of Summer" (Riley) **48**:293
"My Voice" (Aleixandre)
See "Mi voz"
"My Voice Not Being Proud" (Bogan) **12**:101, 120
"My Whole Life" (Borges)
See "Mi vida entera"
"My Wicked Uncle" (Mahon) **60**:132
My Wicked Wicked Ways (Cisneros) **52**:137, 144, 148, 151-52, 156-57, 160-62, 164
"My Wife" (Carver) **54**:15
"My Wife and My Mother-In-Law" (Merwin) **45**:74
"My Will" (Goodison) **36**:150
"Mycerinus" (Arnold) **5**:13, 33-4, 37, 39, 48
"Mye Love toke Skorne" (Wyatt) **27**:316
Mylo Jones (Riley) **48**:306
"Mylo Jones's Wife" (Riley) **48**:315, 318-19
"Myne owne Iohn poyntz" (Wyatt)
See "Myne owne John Poynts sins ye delight to know"
"Myne owne John Poynts sins ye delight to know" (Wyatt) **27**:333-337, 341
"Myne owne John Poyntz" (Wyatt)
See "Myne owne John Poynts sins ye delight to know"
"My-ness" (Milosz) **8**:179
"Myopia: A Night" (Lowell) **3**:215
"Myres: Alexandria, A.D. 340" (Cavafy) **36**:8, 41, 75, 79
The Myriad Leaves Collection (Yakamochi)
See *Man'yōshū*
"Le myrte" (Bonnefoy) **58**:118-19, 148
"Myrtho" (Nerval) **13**:180
"Myself I Sing" (Oppen) **35**:293
"Myself Was Formed—a Carpenter" (Dickinson) **1**:96
"Le mystère des trois cors" (Laforgue) **14**:73
"Mysteries" (Abse) **41**:10
"The Mysteries" (H. D.) **5**:305
"The Mystery" (Braithwaite) **52**:107
"Mystery" (Hughes) **53**:117
"The Mystery" (Teasdale) **31**:359
"'Mystery Boy' Looks for Kin in Nashville" (Hayden) **6**:196
"The Mystery of Gilgal" (Riley) **48**:299
"Mystic" (Lawrence) **54**:247
"The Mystic" (Muir) **49**:239
"The Mystic" (Noyes) **27**:138
"Mystic" (Plath) **37**:258, 260
Mysticism for Beginners (Zagajewski) **27**:396, 398-401
Mystics and Zen Masters (Merton) **10**:352
"Mystique" (Rimbaud) **3**:260; **57**:236, 246, 250, 272
"The Myth" (Muir) **49**:207, 210, 246-49, 298

"Myth" (Pavese)
See "Mito"
"Myth" (Rukeyser) **12**:228
"Myth" (Sarton) **39**:342
"Myth of Mountain Sunrise" (Warren) **37**:359-60, 380
Myth of the Blaze (Oppen) **35**:324
"Myth on Mediterranean Beach: Aphrodite as Logos" (Warren) **37**:301, 307
"The Mythical Journey" (Muir) **49**:215, 243, 270, 295
"Mythology" (Hacker) **47**:96
"A Mythology Reflects its Region" (Stevens) **6**:306
"Myths" (Erdrich) **52**:189, 191
Myths and Texts (Snyder) **21**:290-92, 297, 299, 322
N. 4 (Pindar)
See *Nemean 4*
N. 7 (Pindar)
See *Nemean 7*
N. 9 (Pindar)
See *Nemean 9*
"N'a catredal" (Castro) **41**:94, 105
"A na fruta" (Pasolini) **17**:274-77
"Na krasnom kone" (Tsvetaeva) **14**:315
"Na pokoj grecki w eomu księżnej Zeneidy Wǿkońskiej w Moskwie" (Mickiewicz) **38**:226-27, 229-31
Na rannikh poezdakh (Pasternak) **6**:282
Na vlnách T. S. F. (Seifert) **47**:316, 324, 332, 348
"The Nabara" (Day Lewis) **11**:127, 130-31, 144
"Nachlied" (Trakl) **20**:259
"Nacht" (Benn) **35**:50, 68, 75, 77
"Nachtcafé" (Benn) **35**:7, 23, 24, 25, 36, 46, 50, 53, 54
Nachtgesänge (Hölderlin) **4**:142, 146, 148, 166
"Nachtmusik" (Szirtes) **51**:169
"nachts wird kälter" (Enzensberger) **28**:140
"Nachwort" (Heine) **25**:172-75, 177, 179
"Nachzeichnung" (Benn) **35**:71
"Naci en una buhardilla" (Fuertes) **27**:49
"Nací para poeta o para muerto" (Fuertes) **27**:49
"Nacimiento de Cristo" (García Lorca) **3**:141
Nacimiento último (Aleixandre) **15**:9, 16
"Nada" (Jiménez) **7**:202
"Nadezhdoi Sladostnoi" (Pushkin) **10**:412
"Nadgrobie" (Tsvetaeva) **14**:325, 327
"Nadie" (Aleixandre) **15**:20, 22
"Nadie" (Guillén) **23**:125
"Nadie me estorba" (Guillén) **35**:229
"Nafsī muthqa ah bi athmāriha" (Gibran) **9**:82
"Nah, im Aortenbogen" (Celan) **10**:101
"Nähe des Todes" (Trakl) **20**:248
"La naîade" (Gautier) **18**:141
"The Nail" (Hughes) **7**:143
"The Nailhead" (Ignatow) **34**:277
"The Nails" (Merwin) **45**:18, 83
"Naissance du duc de Bordeaux" (Hugo) **17**:75
"The naïve person" (Borges)
See "El ingenuo"
"A Naive Poem" (Milosz)
See "The World"
Naivedya (Tagore) **8**:411-13
"Naked and Essential" (Montale) **13**:141
"Naked Girl and Mirror" (Wright) **14**:356, 362
Nakedness Lost (Char)
See *Le Nu perdu*
"Nam" (Brathwaite) **56**:93
"Nam Samiran" (Kabīr) **56**:333
"A Name for All" (Crane) **3**:90, 104
"The Name I Call You" (Piercy) **29**:311, 315
"The Name of Old Glory" (Riley) **48**:325-26
"The Nameless" (Abse) **41**:26
"Nameless" (Pasternak)
See "Bez nazvaniya"
"Nameless Flower" (Wright) **14**:347, 379
Nameless Songs (Parra)
See *Cancionero sin nombre*
"Nameless Thing" (Warren) **37**:341
"Names" (Guillén)
See "Los nombres"
"Names" (Hayden) **6**:194
"Names" (Stone) **53**:230, 244
"Names" (Walcott) **46**:275, 279-80, 290
The Names of the Lost (Levine) **22**:223-24
"Names Scarred at the Entrance to Chartres" (Wright) **36**:318
"Naming" (Brathwaite) **56**:87
Naming Our Destiny: New and Selected Poems (Jordan) **38**:126, 132, 137, 139, 144
"Naming the Animals" (Hogan) **35**:276, 277
"The Nana-Hex" (Sexton) **2**:365
"Nancy" (Wylie) **23**:301, 318-19, 324
"The Nancy's Pride" (Carman) **34**:213
"Nani" (Ríos) **57**:316, 324
"Nanny" (Goodison) **36**:141
"Nano-Knowledge" (McHugh) **61**:204
"The Nap Taker" (Silverstein) **49**:342
"The Nape of the Neck" (Graves) **6**:166
Napis (Herbert) **50**:5, 7, 9, 19-20, 25
"Napoléon" (Meredith) **60**:247
"Napoleon na El'be" (Pushkin) **10**:409, 421
"Napoleon on the Elba" (Pushkin)
See "Napoleon na El'be"
"Naprasno glazom kak gvozdem" (Tsvetaeva) **14**:325
"Naptha" (O'Hara) **45**:137
"När man kommit så långt" (Ekeloef) **23**:76
"Narcisse parle" (Valéry) **9**:350, 356, 363, 365, 385, 392, 395
"Narcissus" (Gower) **59**:88, 92-93, 95, 102
"Narcissus" (Lawrence) **54**:232-34
"Narcissus and the Women" (Kavanagh) **33**:73
"Narcissus Speaks" (Valéry)
See "Narcisse parle"
"Narikel" (Tagore) **8**:416
"Narita" (Curnow) **48**:53
Narraciones (García Lorca) **3**:148
"A Narrative" (Oppen) **35**:315, 317, 322, 340, 343, 350
"Narrative" (Stein) **18**:313
"A Narrow Escape" (Merrill) **28**:239, 243
"The Narrow Place" (Muir) **49**:255, 258
The Narrow Place (Muir) **49**:224, 228-29, 231, 245-46, 250, 254-56, 270, 272-73, 276-77, 279, 282-84, 289
The Narrow Pond (Matsuo Bashō)
See *Oku no hosomichi*
The Narrow Road to the Deep North (Matsuo Bashō)
See *Oku no hosomichi*
"The Narrow Valley" (Amichai) **38**:25
"The Narrow Way" (Cowper) **40**:42
"Nascita del canto" (Quasimodo) **47**:301-3
"I nascondigli" (Montale) **13**:138
"Nashedshij podkovu" (Mandelstam) **14**:121, 125, 130
Nashville Skyline (Dylan) **37**:60
"Nasse Zäune" (Benn) **35**:71
"Natal'ia Shishigina—instrument dlia proiavleniia dukhov, perchatka, i telefon" (Shvarts) **50**:153
"The Nation Is Like Ourselves" (Baraka) **4**:19
"National Security" (MacLeish) **47**:205, 261
"National Thoughts" (Amichai) **38**:45
"Nationality in Drinks" (Browning) **2**:59
Nationchild Plumaroja (Alurista) **34**:4, 15-16, 21, 23, 24, 26-29, 31, 39-43, 45, 47
"The Native American Broadcasting System" (Alexie) **53**:31
"The Native Born" (Kipling) **3**:161-62
"A Native Hill" (Berry) **28**:39
Native Land (Blok) **21**:16
Native Land (Rich)
See *Your Native Land, Your Life*
"Nativity" (Sarton) **39**:326, 334-35, 343
"A Nativity" (Yeats) **20**:319
"A Nativity (1914-18)" (Kipling) **3**:183, 189
"Nativity Ode" (Milton)
See "On the Morning of Christ's Nativity"
"Nativity Poem" (Glück) **16**:125, 141
"Nativity Scene" (Szirtes) **51**:156
"Natrabach i na cytrze" (Milosz) **8**:186, 214
"The Natural" (Oppen) **35**:304
"Natural History" (Plath) **37**:254
"Natural History" (Walcott) **46**:237
"Natural History II" (Walcott) **46**:279
"Natural Music" (Jeffers) **17**:134-35
Natural Numbers: New and Selected Poems (Rexroth) **20**:209
"Natural or Divine" (Guillén)
See "Naturaleza con altavoz"
"Natural Resources" (Rich) **5**:374, 380, 384-85
"Naturaleza con altavoz" (Guillén) **35**:185, 241
"Naturaleza viva" (Guillén) **35**:193, 228
"Naturally" (Gallagher) **9**:43
"Naturally the Foundation Will Bear Your Expenses" (Larkin) **21**:223
"Nature" (Longfellow) **30**:51
"Nature" (Masters) **1**:336
"Nature II" (Emerson) **18**:102
"Nature and Free Animals" (Smith) **12**:323
"Nature Doth Have Her Dawn" (Thoreau) **30**:191, 193, 268, 271, 293
"Nature morte" (Brodsky) **9**:4, 12
"Nature Morte" (MacNeice) **61**:139
"The Nature of a Mirror" (Warren) **37**:304
"The Nature of an Action" (Gunn) **26**:185
"The Nature of This Flower Is to Bloom" (Walker) **30**:341
"Nature Poem" (Tomlinson) **17**:345, 348
Nature: Poems Old and New (Swenson) **14**:283, 287-88
"Nature that gave the bee so feet a grace" (Wyatt) **27**:346-47
"Nature that washt her hands in milke" (Raleigh) **31**:201, 215, 235, 302
"Nature's Lineaments" (Graves) **6**:150-51
"Nature's Nation" (Wagoner) **33**:360
"Nature's Questioning" (Hardy) **8**:96
"Navidad en el Hudson" (García Lorca) **3**:141
"Navigator" (Sarton) **39**:322, 337
"The Navigators" (Curnow) **48**:4
"The Navigators" (Hacker) **47**:79
"Nayarit" (Birney) **52**:78
Ne forte credas (Horace) **46**:97
"Ne muchnistoi babochkoiu beloi" (Mandelstam) **14**:152, 156
"Ne plus partager" (Éluard) **38**:70
"Ne Plus Ultra" (Coleridge) **11**:52
"Ne s'entend pas" (Char) **56**:131, 157
"Ne sravnivai: zhivushchii nesravnim" (Mandelstam) **14**:154
"Neap-tide" (Swinburne) **24**:313, 341, 343
"Near a Monastery" (Carducci)
See "Presso Una Certosa"
"Near, as All That Is Lost" (Gallagher) **9**:64
"Near Avalon" (Morris) **55**:279, 282, 301-2
Near False Creek Mouth (Birney) **52**:15-16, 44, 46, 74, 79
"Near Keokuk" (Sandburg) **2**:332
Near Klamath (Carver) **54**:3
"Near Lanivet, 1872" (Hardy) **8**:97, 125-26
"Near Mullingar" (Davie)
See "1977, Near Mullingar"
"Near the Ocean" (Lowell) **3**:226-28, 233
Near the Ocean (Lowell) **3**:232
"Nearing Forty" (Walcott) **46**:237
"Nearing La Guarira" (Walcott) **46**:231, 273
"Nearly a Valediction" (Hacker) **47**:107
"Nearness of Death" (Trakl)
See "Nähe des Todes"
"Nebraska" (Shapiro) **25**:313
"Nebuchadnezzar's Punishment" (Gower) **59**:9
"Necessities" (Mueller) **33**:189
Necessities of Life: Poems, 1962-1965 (Rich) **5**:356, 363-64, 370-71, 382, 388-89, 397
"The Necessity for Belief" (Warren) **37**:380
"The Neckan" (Arnold) **5**:12
The Necklace (Tomlinson) **17**:299, 302-04, 317-18, 320-22, 327, 334-35, 341
"The Necktie and the Watch" (Apollinaire)
See "La cravate et la montre"

"Necrological" (Ransom) **61**:267, 299, 308
"Necropolis" (Shapiro) **25**:279, 297, 318
"Need: A Chorale for Black Women's Voices" (Lorde) **12**:144, 154, 156, 158
"The Need of Being Versed in Country Things" (Frost) **1**:229, 231
"The Need to Confide" (Jackson) **44**:90
The Need to Hold Still (Mueller) **33**:175-76, 178-79, 188
"A Needed Poem for My Salvation" (Sanchez) **9**:208-09
Needle's Eye (Oppen)
See *Seascape: Needle's Eye*
"Nefertiti" (Yevtushenko) **40**:343, 347, 352
"Negative" (Szymborska) **44**:319
"Negatives" (Walcott) **46**:234
"Negro" (Hughes) **53**:108, 122
"The Negro Artist and the Racial Mountain" (Hughes) **53**:94, 108
"Negro bembón" (Guillén) **23**:98, 142
"Un negro canta en Nueva York" (Guillén) **23**:127
"A Negro Cemetery Next to a White One" (Nemerov) **24**:281
"Negro Dancers" (Hughes) **1**:236; **53**:80, 82, 86, 117
"Negro Ghetto" (Hughes) **53**:115
"The Negro Hero" (Brooks) **7**:86
"A Negro Love Song" (Dunbar) **5**:132, 142
"Negro Mask" (Senghor) **25**:227-30
Negro Mask (Senghor)
See "Masque nègre"
"The Negro Mother" (Hughes) **53**:114, 119, 122, 125
The Negro Mother (Hughes) **53**:114
The Negro of Peter the Great (Pushkin)
See *Arap Petra Velikogo*
"Negro Servant" (Hughes) **1**:247
"Negro Song" (Guillén) **23**:131
"A Negro Speaks of Rivers" (Hughes) **1**:241-42, 248, 258-59, 263, 268; **53**:84, 89, 93-94, 105, 108-9, 118, 142
"Negro Spiritual" (McKay) **2**:214
"The Negro's Complaint" (Cowper) **40**:105, 119
"Negus" (Brathwaite) **56**:10, 74-75, 87-88
Nehez fold (Illyés) **16**:233, 238-39, 245
"La neige" (Vigny) **26**:401-402, 410-11
"Neige sur Paris" (Senghor) **25**:227, 239
"Neiges" (Perse) **23**:213, 216-18, 220-21, 232, 234, 250, 253, 256-57
"Neighbor" (Hughes) **53**:129
"Neighborhood Bully" (Dylan) **37**:70
Neighborly Poems and Dialect Sketches (Riley) **48**:327, 332
"Neighbors" (Sandburg) **41**:320
"Neither Brings Charges" (McHugh) **61**:203
"Neither Out Far nor in Deep" (Frost) **1**:197, 218, 227-28; **39**:248
"Neither Sweet Pity, nor Lamentable Weeping" (Ronsard)
See "Ny la douce pitie, ny le pleur lamentable"
"Neither Wanting More" (Swenson) **14**:284
"Neko" (Hagiwara) **18**:181
"Neko no shigai" (Hagiwara) **18**:182
"Nel giusto tempo umano" (Quasimodo) **47**:277
"Nel Mezzo del Commin di Nostra Vita" (Duncan) **2**:103
"Nel parco di Caserta" (Montale) **13**:127
"Nel sonno" (Montale) **13**:107, 128, 150
"Nele de Kantule" (Cardenal) **22**:127, 132
"Nell' annuale della fondazione di Roma" (Carducci) **46**:44, 52, 82, 84, 87
"Nella Piazza di San Petronio in una Sera d'Inverno" (Carducci) **46**:6, 54, 84, 87-89
"Nella serra" (Montale) **13**:110
"Nell'antica" (Quasimodo) **47**:276, 301
"Nelly Meyers" (Ammons) **16**:5, 19
Nem. IV (Pindar)
See *Nemean 4*
Nem. VIII (Pindar)
See *Nemean 8*
Nemean 1 (Pindar) **19**:398, 412
Nemean 2 (Pindar) **19**:425
Nemean 3 (Pindar) **19**:425
Nemean 4 (Pindar) **19**:387, 391
Nemean V (Pindar)
See *Nemean 5*
Nemean 5 (Pindar) **19**:388, 420, 424
Nemean 7 (Pindar) **19**:388, 413, 425
Nemean 8 (Pindar) **19**:388, 413, 420, 425
Nemean 9 (Pindar) **19**:405, 425
Nemean 10 (Pindar) **19**:398, 405, 412
Nemean 11 (Pindar) **19**:405
"Neon Signs" (Hughes) **53**:190-91
Neon Vernacular: New and Selected Poems (Komunyakaa) **51**:24, 29, 31-33, 35, 45, 52, 56-57, 62-63
"Les Néréides" (Gautier) **18**:129, 141
"The Nereids of Seriphos" (Clampitt) **19**:92
"Nero's Term" (Cavafy) **36**:32
"Neruda" (Wright) **36**:312
"Nerve Gas part II" (Bissett) **14**:7
The Nesting Ground (Wagoner) **33**:327, 329, 333, 347, 367, 369, 373
"Nestor's Bathtub" (Dove) **6**:109
"Nestus Gurley" (Jarrell) **41**:154, 165, 168-69, 181, 185, 188
"The Net" (Teasdale) **31**:359
"Net, eto ne ia" (Akhmatova) **55**:25
"Net Menders" (Plath) **37**:177
"Nether, Nether, Netherland" (Alurista) **34**:21
Nets to Catch the Wind (Wylie) **23**:300-301, 306, 309, 311, 324-34
Nettles (Lawrence) **54**:171, 173, 220, 224, 249
Netzahualcóyotl (Cardenal) **22**:128, 130-31
Neue Gedichte (Heine) **25**:129-132
Neue Gedichte (Rilke) **2**:266-8, 275, 280-1
Der neue Pausias und sein Blumenmädchen (Goethe) **5**:239-40
Neuer Frühling (Heine) **25**:129-31
"Neuf merci" (Char) **56**:120
"The Neurotic" (Day Lewis) **11**:147
"Neutral Tones" (Hardy) **8**:88, 126, 130
"Neutrality" (MacNeice) **61**:109, 141, 160-61, 181
"Never" (Silverstein) **49**:334
"Never" (Stone) **53**:258-59
"Never Again Would Birds' Song Be the Same" (Frost) **1**:231
"Never Offer Your Heart" (Walker) **30**:355
"Never Such Love" (Graves) **6**:137
"Never to Dream of Spiders" (Lorde) **12**:143
"Nevermore" (Verlaine) **32**:368, 386-89
"Nevertheless" (Moore) **49**:102, 130
Nevertheless (Moore) **49**:106, 126
"Nevicata" (Carducci) **46**:51
"The New Age" (Smith) **12**:313, 316
"The New America" (Blok) **21**:8, 26, 29
New and Collected Poems (Wilbur) **51**:247-50, 257, 261, 264, 266, 274, 276-85, 303, 309, 315-18, 322, 333
New and Collected Poems, 1917-1976 (MacLeish) **47**:193, 195, 197, 207
New and Selected (Viereck) **27**:275, 279, 280-82, 284
New & Selected Poems (Kenyon)
See *Otherwise*
New and Selected Poems (Meredith) **28**:210, 215
New and Selected Poems (Nemerov) **24**:258, 260, 262, 264, 266, 268, 284, 286
New and Selected Poems (Soto) **28**:404
New and Selected Poems: 1923-1985 (Warren) **37**:364-67
New and Selected Poems, 1940-1986 (Shapiro) **25**:318-22
New and Selected Things Taking Place (Swenson) **14**:274, 277, 280-81, 287
New Arcadia (Sidney) **32**:316, 322
"The New Believers" (Leopardi)
See "I nuovi credenti"
"New Birth" (Morris) **55**:338
"New Brunswick" (Birney) **52**:48-49, 51
New Cautionary Tales (Belloc) **24**:27
New Collected Poems (Graves) **6**:166
"The New Congo" (Brown) **55**:114, 164
"The New Convert" (Cowper) **40**:56
"New Dawn" (Warren) **37**:335, 377
"A New Day" (Levine) **22**:223-24
New Days: Poems of Exile and Return (Jordan) **38**:114, 120
New Desire (Hagiwara)
See *Atarashiki yokujō*
"A New Diary" (Abse) **41**:10, 15
"New England, 1967" (Borges) **32**:88
New England Tragedies (Longfellow) **30**:23, 39, 59, 65-6
New Found Land: Fourteen Poems (MacLeish) **47**:125, 127-28, 137, 188, 194, 253
"New Georgia" (Jarrell) **41**:174, 209
New Goose (Niedecker) **42**:94, 97, 102, 105, 134-35, 139, 148, 150-52, 167, 174
"New Granddaughter" (Abse) **41**:33
"New Grown Girl" (Guillén)
See "Muchacha recién crecida"
"New Hampshire" (Eliot) **5**:166, 169
"New Hampshire" (Frost) **39**:234-35, 243-44, 254
New Hampshire (Frost) **1**:215, 224; **39**:233-35, 243, 245, 254-55
"New Heaven and Earth" (Lawrence) **54**:170, 176, 213-14, 232-34
"New Heavens for Old" (Lowell) **13**:85, 88
"The New House" (Thomas) **53**:269, 286, 294
"New Jerusalem" (MacNeice) **61**:176-78
"New Koide Road" (Hagiwara)
See "Koide shidō"
New Leaves (Castro)
See *Follas novas*
"New leaves! I feel like laughing" (Castro)
See "¡Hojas nuevas! risa siento"
"New Legends" (Graves) **6**:149
New Life (Dante)
See *La vita nuova*
"The New Little Larousse" (Zagajewski) **27**:401
"The New Love" (Parker) **28**:356
"New Love and Old" (Teasdale) **31**:365, 379
A New Lovesong for Stalingrad (Neruda)
See *Nuevo canto de amor a Stalingrado*
"New Mexico Poems" (Quintana) **36**:248
"New Moon in November" (Merwin) **45**:20
"New Morality" (Coleridge) **11**:102-03
"New Mother" (Olds) **22**:312
"New Objectives, New Cadres" (Rexroth) **20**:215
"New Orleans" (Harjo) **27**:65
"New Orleans 30 Oct 71" (Brutus) **24**:124
"The New Pastoral" (Boland) **58**:45
A New Path to the Waterfall (Carver) **54**:15, 20-21, 26
"New Poems" (Wright) **36**:350
New Poems (Arnold) **5**:12, 43, 50
New Poems (Bridges) **28**:51, 67, 69
New Poems (Heine)
See *Neue Gedichte*
New Poems (Lawrence) **54**:207, 217, 225, 232, 239-40
New Poems (Montale) **13**:143-46
New Poems (Rexroth) **20**:197, 204
New Poems (Rilke)
See *Neue Gedichte*
New Poems, 1962 (Graves) **6**:154
"The New Proletarian" (Morris) **55**:338
"A New Psalm for the Chapel of Kilmarnock" (Burns) **6**:89
"A New Reality Is Better Than a New Movie!" (Baraka) **4**:30
"A New Record" (Duncan) **2**:103
New Rhymes (Carducci)
See *Rime nuove*
"The New Saddhus" (Pinsky) **27**:176
"New Season" (Levine) **22**:223

New Selected Poems (Levine) **22**:220-221, 223-24, 226, 228
"The New Sheriff" (Baraka) **4**:10, 15
"The New Ships" (Brathwaite) **56**:67
"The New Sirens" (Arnold) **5**:5, 39
"A New Song" (Heaney) **18**:202, 241
"A New Song" (Hughes) **53**:113, 115
A New Song (Hughes) **1**:242, 250, 253-54, 268; **53**:111-12
"The New Spirit" (Ashbery) **26**:108, 130, 169-170
The New Spoon River (Masters) **1**:333-34, 344-45; **36**:184, 190, 194, 209-12, 215, 220, 238, 243
"New St. Louis Blues" (Brown) **55**:74, 80, 110, 144, 150-51, 154, 160
"New Stanzas" (Montale)
See "Nuove stanze"
"New Stanzas to Augusta" (Brodsky)
See "Novye stansy k Avguste"
"New Steps" (Brown) **55**:174-75
"A New Story" (Ortiz) **17**:234
"New Territory" (Boland) **58**:42
New Territory (Boland) **58**:42-43, 91
"A New Theme" (Ignatow) **34**:305
"New Thoughts on Old Subjects" (Coleridge) **11**:105
"New Vows" (Erdrich) **52**:177
"The New Warden" (Baca) **41**:37
"New Weather" (Sandburg) **41**:310
"The New Woman" (Guillén)
See "Mujer nueva"
"New World" (Brathwaite) **56**:22, 86
"New World" (Momaday) **25**:199, 216
"New World" (Walcott) **46**:290
The New World (Masters) **1**:339
"New World A-Comin" (Brathwaite) **56**:4, 26, 38, 75, 99
"The New Year" (Thomas) **53**:322
The New Year (Mickiewicz) **38**:157
"New Year Letter" (Brathwaite) **56**:65
New Year Letter (Auden) **1**:16, 21, 23-24, 34
"New Year Resolve" (Sarton) **39**:369
"New Year Wishes" (Sarton) **39**:322, 343
"The New Yeares Gift, or Circumcision Song" (Herrick)
See "Another New-yeeres Gift; or song for the Circumcision"
"New Year's Dawn, 1947" (Jeffers) **17**:141
"New Year's Eve" (Hardy) **8**:104, 119
"New Year!s Eve" (Lawrence) **54**:169
"New Year's Eve 1959" (Kursh) **15**:224
"New Year's Gift" (Herrick)
See "A New-Yeares Gift Sent to Sir Simeon Steward"
"New Year's Greetings" (Tsvetaeva)
See "Novogodnee"
"New Year's Song" (Seifert) **47**:325
"New York" (Gunn) **26**:209, 220
"New York" (Moore) **49**:90-91, 94, 96, 128
"New York" (Senghor) **25**:255
"New York" (Viereck) **27**:274
"New York 1962: Fragment" (Lowell) **3**:215
"New York at Night" (Lowell) **13**:79
"New York City 1970" (Lorde) **12**:146, 158
The New York Head Shop and Museum (Lorde) **12**:146-47, 154
"New York in August" (Davie) **29**:97, 110
"New York: Office and Denunciation" (García Lorca)
See "Nueva York: Oficina y denuncia"
"The New York Times" (Kumin) **15**:200
"The New Yorkers" (Giovanni) **19**:142
"New Yorkers" (Hughes) **53**:161
"Los New Yorks" (Cruz) **37**:33-34
The New Youth (Pasolini)
See *La nuova gioventù*
"New Zealand City" (Curnow) **48**:26
"New Zealand Poems" (Wright) **14**:377
"Newborn Death" (Rossetti) **44**:254
"Newborn Girl-Child" (Guillén) **23**:132
"Newcomer" (Okigbo) **7**:233, 240
"Newport Beach 1979" (Komunyakaa) **51**:34
"Newport Jazz Festival" (Jordan) **38**:126
"News" (Niedecker) **42**:98
"The News" (Stone) **53**:222
"The News Carried To Macedonia" (Carver) **54**:28
"News for the Delphic Oracle" (Yeats) **20**:312-13, 316, 334-35
"News from Mount Amiata" (Montale)
See "Notizie dall'Amiata"
"News from the Cabin" (Swenson) **14**:253-54
"News Item" (Kavanagh) **33**:79
"News Item" (Parker) **28**:347, 359
"News of the Assassin" (Merwin) **45**:9, 22
News of the Universe (Bly) **39**:54, 58, 100
"News Photo" (Warren) **37**:304
"News Report" (Ignatow) **34**:273, 284, 308
"Newspaper Readers" (Tsvetaeva)
See "Chitateli gazet"
"The News-Reel" (MacNeice) **61**:142
"Newsreel: Man and Firing Squad" (Atwood) **8**:23
"A New-Yeares Gift Sent to Sir Simeon Steward" (Herrick) **9**:102, 145
"A New-yeares gift. To the King" (Carew) **29**:52
"Next!" (Nash) **21**:270
"Next Day" (Jarrell) **41**:185, 189, 191, 200
Next: New Poems (Clifton) **17**:24, 26-28, 35-36
"Next, Please" (Larkin) **21**:226-27, 230, 235, 242, 246
The Next Room of the Dream (Nemerov) **24**:259, 262, 264, 266, 289
"Next to of Course God America I" (Cummings) **5**:89
Next-to-Last Things: New Poems and Essays (Kunitz) **19**:186
"Nezabudka" (Lermontov) **18**:188-89
Nezhnost (Yevtushenko) **40**:344-46, 350
"Ni siquiera soy polvo" (Borges) **32**:66
Ni tiro (Fuertes) **27**:17
Ni tiro ni veneno (Fuertes) **27**:16
"Niagara" (Lindsay) **23**:275
"Nic Darowane" (Szymborska) **44**:308
"Nic ladnego" (Herbert) **50**:5
"Nicaraguan canto" (Cardenal)
See "Canto nacional"
"Niccolò" (Carducci) **46**:52
"A nice day" (Bukowski) **18**:23
"Nice Guy" (Ignatow) **34**:305
"A Nice Shady Home" (Stevens) **6**:292
"Nicholas Bindle" (Masters) **36**:170
"Nichóri" (Cavafy) **36**:52
"Nick and the Candlestick" (Plath) **1**:390; **37**:257
"Nicodemus" (Robinson) **1**:476, 485
"Nido en una estatua" (Storni) **33**:294;
"Niebla" (Guillén) **35**:154
"Niebo" (Szymborska) **44**:303, 309
"Niedzwiedzie" (Herbert) **50**:8
"Niektórzy lubia poezje" (Szymborska) **44**:305
Die Niemandsrose (Celan) **10**:95, 98-99, 113, 117, 121
"Nienawiść" (Szymborska) **44**:305
"Niespodziane spotkanie" (Szymborska) **44**:269
"La nieve" (Guillén) **35**:186-87, 188
"Nieve" (Guillén) **23**:109
"Nigerian Unity/or Little Niggers Killing Little Niggers" (Madhubuti) **5**:329, 341-42
"Nigger" (Sanchez) **9**:223, 232
"Nigger" (Sandburg) **41**:337, 365
"Nigger" (Shapiro) **25**:270
The Nigger of Peter the Great (Pushkin)
See *Arap Petra Velikogo*
"Nigger Song: An Odyssey" (Dove) **6**:105;
"Nigger's Leap: New England" (Wright) **14**:335-36, 338, 340, 349-50, 368, 374
"Niggy the Ho" (Baraka) **4**:29, 38
"Night" (Blake) **12**:7-8, 23, 33, 61
"Night" (Bogan) **12**:96, 104
"Night" (Celan) **10**:112
"Night" (Giovanni) **19**:141
"Night" (Jeffers) **17**:107, 131, 145
"Night" (Pasternak)
See "Noch'"
"Night" (Pavese)
See "La notte"
"Night" (Rilke) **2**:275
"Night, a street, a lamp, a chemist's" (Blok)
See "Noch' ulitsa fonar' apteka'"
"Night and Day" (Lanier) **50**:56
"Night and Day in 1952" (O'Hara) **45**:163, 189
"Night and Sleep" (Patmore) **59**:258
"Night and the Child" (Wright) **14**:352
"Night Bear Which Frightened Cattle" (Atwood) **8**:39
"The Night Before" (Robinson) **1**:460
"The Night before Goodbye" (Yamada) **44**:330-34, 343, 347
"The Night before Great Babylon" (Sitwell) **3**:310
"The Night before the Night before Christmas" (Jarrell) **41**:139, 163, 171-73, 180, 194, 216-17
"Night Café" (Benn)
See "Nachtcafé"
"Night City" (Bishop) **34**:160
Night Crossing (Mahon) **60**:132-34, 137-38, 154, 171, 181, 199
"The Night Dances" (Plath) **1**:388, 390
"Night, Death, Mississippi" (Hayden) **6**:194, 196
"The Night Dream" (MacLeish) **47**:190
"Night Feed" (Boland) **58**:13, 46, 52-53, 57
Night Feed (Boland) **58**:12, 14-15, 44-45, 47, 52, 66-67
"Night, Four Songs" (Hughes) **1**:240
"The Night Game" (Pinsky) **27**:159, 176
"Night Hours" (Blok) **21**:5
"Night in Arizona" (Teasdale) **31**:365, 379
"Night in Maine" (Lowell) **3**:226
"Night in the Forest" (Kinnell) **26**:240
"Night in the Old Home" (Hardy) **8**:105
"The Night Is Freezing Fast" (Housman)
See "Last Poems: XX— The Night Is Freezing Fast"
"Night is Personal" (Warren) **37**:302
"The Night Journey" (Brooke) **24**:60
"Night Journey" (Roethke) **15**:246
"Night Journey in the Cooking Pot" (Bly) **39**:25, 27-8, 84-5
"Night Journeys" (Ní Chuilleanáin) **34**:351, 353, 380
"Night Launch" (Kumin) **15**:209
"Night Letter" (Kunitz) **19**:154, 157, 161, 169
"The Night Life" (Ignatow) **34**:323
"The Night My Father Got Me" (Housman) **2**:191
"Night of Frost in May" (Meredith) **60**:248, 280, 284, 295
"Night of Hell" (Rimbaud)
See "Nuit de l'enfer"
"Night of Sine" (Senghor)
See "Nuit de Sine"
"Night of the Shirts" (Merwin) **45**:51
"Night Operations Coastal Command RAF" (Nemerov) **24**:287
"A Night Out" (Abse) **41**:9, 18-19, 25
"Night Out" (Harjo) **27**:55
"Night People" (Ignatow) **34**:273
"Night Piece" (Heaney) **18**:201, 217
"A Night Piece" (Smart) **13**:341, 347
"Night Pleasures" (Pavese)
See "Piaceri notturni"
"Night Practice" (Swenson) **14**:266
"Night Shift" (Plath) **1**:388; **37**:176
"Night Sky" (Erdrich) **52**:175, 178, 192
"Night Song" (Glück) **16**:145-47
"Night Song at Amalfi" (Teasdale) **31**:322, 379
"Night Song for Amalfi" (Teasdale) **31**:364
"Night Song of an Asiatic Wandering Shepherd" (Montale)
See "Canto notturno di un pastore errante nell'Asia"

"Night Storm" (Sarton) **39**:342
"Night Taxi" (Gunn) **26**:231
"Night Thoughts" (Smith) **12**:337
"Night Train" (Hagiwara)
See "Yogisha"
"Night Transfigured" (Tomlinson) **17**:319, 342
"Night Visits with the Family" (Swenson) **14**:281
"Night Watch in the City of Boston" (MacLeish) **47**:205, 211
"The Night-Blooming Cereus" (Hayden) **6**:194-95, 198
The Night-Blooming Cereus (Hayden) **6**:182, 184, 187, 190, 194
"Nightbreak" (Rich) **5**:358
"Nightfishing" (Schnackenberg) **45**:345
"Night-Flowering Cactus" (Merton) **10**:334
"The Nightingale" (Coleridge) **11**:85, 106
"The Nightingale" (Finch)
See "To the Nightingale"
"Nightingale" (Keats)
See "Ode to a Nightingale"
"The Nightingale" (Marie de France)
See "Laüstic"
"The Nightingale and Glow-worm" (Cowper) **40**:124
"The Nightingale Garden" (Blok) **21**:20
The Nightingale of the Catholic Church (Pasolini)
See *L'usignuolo della Chiesa Cattolica*
The Nightingale Sings Badly (Seifert)
See *Slavík zpívášpatně*
The Nightingale Sings out of Tune (Seifert)
See *Slavík zpívášpatně*
The Nightingale Sings Poorly (Seifert)
See *Slavík zpívášpatně*
"Nightingales" (Bridges) **28**:64, 66, 70, 75-6
"The Nightingales" (Williams) **7**:345
Nightingales (Robinson)
See *The Glory of the Nightingales*
"The Nightingales Nest" (Clare) **23**:4-5
"Nightmare" (Kumin) **15**:198
"Nightmare" (Lowell) **13**:78
"Nightmare" (Page) **12**:168
The Nightmare Factory (Kumin) **15**:190, 200, 208
"Nightmare of Peace" (Muir) **49**:257
"Night-Music" (Rukeyser) **12**:209, 211
"Night-Piece" (Kunitz) **19**:148, 153
"Night-Piece" (Sassoon) **12**:240
"The Night-Piece to Julia" (Herrick) **9**:94, 132
"Nights and Days" (Rich) **5**:375
Nights and Days (Merrill) **28**:220, 225-28, 230-32, 234, 240, 250, 252-54, 281
"Nights of 1962: The River Merchant's Wife" (Hacker) **47**:87, 105, 114
"Nights of 1964-1966: The Old Reliable" (Hacker) **47**:87-88, 105
"Nightsong: City" (Brutus) **24**:113
"Night-Time in the Cemetery" (Smith) **12**:316
"The Nihilist as Hero" (Lowell) **3**:229
"Nihon no Banka" (Yakamochi) **48**:99-100, 132-33, 137-39
"Nikki-Rosa" (Giovanni) **19**:139
"Nilamanilata" (Tagore) **8**:416
"Nimm fort die Amarylle" (Benn) **35**:69
"Nimmo" (Robinson) **1**:468
"Nimrod in September" (Sassoon) **12**:278
"Nina Nanna di Carlo V" (Carducci) **46**:52
"Nina Replies" (Rimbaud)
See "Les reparties de Nina"
"IX" (Joyce) **22**:160, 167
"Nine Charms against the Hunter" (Wagoner) **33**:333
"9 from 8" (Lanier) **50**:106-7
"Nine Lives" (Merrill) **28**:283
"Nine Nectarines" (Moore) **49**:94, 98, 146
"Nine Poems for the Unborn Child" (Rukeyser) **12**:228
"Nine Sleep Valley" (Merrill) **28**:254-55
"Nine Variations in a Chinese Winter Setting" (Tomlinson) **17**:299, 331
"Nine Verses of the Same Song" (Berry) **28**:5
"XIX" (Joyce) **22**:145, 169, 171
"1912-1952 Full Cycle" (Viereck) **27**:264
"MCMXIV" (Larkin) **21**:229, 234
"1914" (Owen) **19**:352
1914, and Other Poems (Brooke) **24**:61, 63, 80, 85, 87-8
1921-1925 (Mandelstam) **14**:151, 155
"1977, Near Mullingar" (Davie) **29**:105, 108
"1909" (Apollinaire) **7**:46-7
"1984" (Komunyakaa) **51**:62
"1954" (Kavanagh) **33**:59
"1959" (Corso) **33**:43, 49
"1953" (Corso) **33**:48
"1941" (Stone) **53**:243, 258
"1914" (Jarrell) **41**:169
"Nineteen Hadley Street" (Schnackenberg) **45**:329, 342, 345, 349
"Nineteen Hundred and Nineteen" (Yeats) **20**:314, 325, 350-51
"Nineteen Hundred Nineteen" (Walcott) **46**:307
"1977: Poem for Mrs. Fannie Lou Hamer" (Jordan) **38**:127
"1969" (Warren) **37**:306
"1930's" (Oppen) **35**:327
"1937" (Niedecker) **42**:140
"1933" (MacLeish) **47**:130, 150-51
"1964" (Borges) **32**:64
"1969, Ireland of the Bombers" (Davie) **29**:105-06, 108, 120
"1963" (Dove) **6**:106
"The Nineteenth Century and After" (Yeats) **20**:314
1933 (Levine) **22**:217-18, 223
"90 North" (Jarrell) **41**:127, 188, 191-92, 213-14
95 Poems (Cummings) **5**:109-10
"96 Tears" (Hongo) **23**:199
Ninfeas (Jiménez) **7**:197, 199
"Niño" (Guillén) **35**:157
"Niño mexicano" (Mistral) **32**:161
"El niño solo" (Mistral) **32**:174, 179
"los niños crecen" (Alurista) **34**:38
"Ninth Elegy" (Hope) **56**:275
"Ninth Elegy" (Rilke) **2**:281, 286-87
"Ninth Elegy: The Antagonists" (Rukeyser) **12**:223
Ninth Nemean (Pindar)
See *Nemean 9*
"Ninth Psalm" (Sexton) **2**:367
Ninth Pythian (Pindar)
See *Pythian 9*
"The Ninth Symphony of Beethoven Understood at Last as a Sexual Message" (Rich) **5**:360, 370
"Niobe in Distress for Her Children Slain by Apollo" (Wheatley) **3**:338, 355, 357-60
Niobjeta ziemia (Milosz) **8**:179, 211
"Nipping Pussy's Feet in Fun" (Smith) **12**:339
"Nirbhay" (Tagore) **8**:415
"Nirjharer svapnabhanga" (Tagore) **8**:406
"Niruddesh yatra" (Tagore) **8**:408
"Nirvâna" (Lanier) **50**:56, 67
"Nishikigizuka" (Ishikawa) **10**:213
"Nitrate" (Levine) **22**:224
"Niwatori" (Hagiwara) **18**:174, 180
"Nixon's the One" (Meredith) **28**:176, 206
"No" (Kenyon) **57**:20, 42
"No" (Stein) **18**:327
"No. 54, chicano infante" (Alurista)
See "chicano infante"
"No. 57, sacred robe" (Alurista) **34**:13
"No Answer" (Ignatow) **34**:274
"No Believers in the Resurrection" (Mandelstam) **14**:120
"No Better than 'a withered daffodil" (Moore) **49**:142
"No Boy Knows When He Goes to Sleep" (Riley) **48**:299
"No Buyers: A Street Scene" (Hardy) **8**:101
"No Coward Soul Is Mine" (Brontë) **8**:51, 60, 69-70
"No dejan escribir" (Fuertes) **27**:49
"No Difference" (Silverstein) **49**:313
"No Doubt What he Saw" (Corso) **33**:25
"No Grown-ups" (Silverstein) **49**:342
"¿No hay salida?" (Paz) **1**:364
"No Hearing (Discovering)" (Lowell) **3**:228
No Hiding Place (Brown) **55**:81, 89, 94, 111, 113-15, 117, 158, 164, 166-69, 172
"No Lamp Has Ever Shown Us Where to Look" (MacLeish) **47**:186
"No Loser, No Weeper" (Angelou) **32**:27
"No Man Believes" (Thomas) **52**:292-93, 298
"No Man's Land" (Heaney) **18**:202
"No Matter, Never Mind" (Snyder) **21**:297
"No more" (Milosz) **8**:190, 193
"No More Ghosts" (Graves) **6**:132
"No More Marching" (Madhubuti) **5**:339
"No More Mozart" (Abse) **41**:15
"No More Sacrifices" (Ortiz) **17**:223, 234
No Nature: New and Selected Poems (Snyder) **21**:324-25
"No Need" (Carver) **54**:15, 19
"No No No No" (Angelou) **32**:12
"No One Remembers" (Levine) **22**:223
"No One Sentence" (Stein) **18**:313
"No One So Much As You" (Thomas) **53**:271-72, 275-76
The No One's Rose (Celan)
See *Die Niemandsrose*
"No Possom, No Sop, No Taters" (Stevens) **6**:302
"No renunciation" (Char) **56**:131
"No Resurrection" (Jeffers) **17**:141
"No retiring" (Niedecker) **42**:149
"No Road" (Larkin) **21**:230, 235
"No Sanctuary" (Heaney) **18**:202
"No sé por qué piensas tú" (Guillén) **23**:140
"No Second Coming" (Curnow) **48**:28
"No Speech from the Scaffold" (Gunn) **26**:202
"No Steps" (Kenyon) **57**:45
"No Swan So Fine" (Moore) **49**:172, 176, 178
"No, Thank You, John!" (Rossetti) **7**:267, 281, 291
No Thanks (Cummings) **5**:106-07
"No, That Is Not I" (Akhmatova)
See "Net, eto ne ia"
"No Theory" (Ignatow) **34**:277, 309, 323, 325
"No Title Required" (Szymborska)
See "Może być bez tytuu"
"No Way of Knowing" (Ashbery) **26**:124, 144
"No Way of Knowing When This Song Began" (Mandelstam) **14**:118
"No, we didn't suffer together in vain" (Akhmatova) **55**:35
"No Word" (Corso) **33**:42
"No Word" (Kunitz) **19**:170, 186
"No Worst, There Is None" (Hopkins) **15**:175
Noah and the Waters (Day Lewis) **11**:127-28, 144, 152-53
"Noah Built the Ark" (Johnson) **24**:128-29, 144, 155, 164-65, 169
"Noah's Raven" (Merwin) **45**:8, 14, 32, 34
"The Nobel Prize" (Pasternak)
See "Nobelevskaya premiya"
"Nobelevskaya premiya" (Pasternak) **6**:268, 284
"The Noble Lady's Tale" (Hardy) **8**:99
"The Noble Lord" (Belloc) **24**:41
Noble Numbers, or Pious Pieces (Herrick)
See *His Noble Numbers: or, His Pious Pieces, Wherein (amongst Other Things) He Sings the Birth of His Christ: and Sighes for His Saviours Suffering on the Crosse*
"Noble Sisters" (Rossetti) **7**:272, 274, 276, 280
"The Nobleman Orsha" (Lermontov) **18**:300
"The Noblest Service" (Riley) **48**:301
Nobodaddy (MacLeish) **47**:175-76, 178, 183-87, 192, 253
"Nobody" (Aleixandre)
See "Nadie"
"Nobody" (Guillén)
See "Nadie"

"Nobody" (Silverstein) **49**:327
"Nobody Comes" (Hardy) **8**:101, 125
"Nobody Owns th Earth" (Bissett) **14**:10
Nobody Owns th Earth (Bissett) **14**:10-12, 18
"Nobody Riding the Roads Today" (Jordan) **38**:118
"Nobody's Lookin' but de Owl and de Moon" (Johnson) **24**:141
The Nobody's Rose (Celan)
See *Die Niemandsrose*
Les Noces d'Hérodiade (Mallarmé)
See *Hérodiade*
"Noch'" (Pasternak) **6**:285
"Noch' I" (Lermontov) **18**:302
"Noch' II" (Lermontov) **18**:302
"Noch' ulitsa fonar' apteka" (Blok) **21**:44
"De noche" (Guillén) **35**:157
"La noche cíclica" (Borges) **22**:73; **32**:39, 63, 85-6
"Noche de luna" (Guillén) **35**:153
"Noche de resurrecciones" (Paz) **48**:181
"Noche del Caballero" (Guillén) **35**:233, 234, 237, 238-39, 240
"Noche del gran estío" (Guillén) **35**:157
"Noche encendida" (Guillén) **35**:158
"La noche, la calle, los astros" (Guillén) **35**:156, 157
"Nocturnal Beacon" (Storni)
See "Faro en la noche"
"Nocturnal Pleasures" (Pavese)
See "Piaceri notturni"
"A Nocturnal Reverie" (Finch) **21**:140-41, 143, 146, 157, 160, 173-75
"Nocturnal Song of a Wandering Shepherd in Asia" (Leopardi)
See "Canto notturno di un pastore errante dell'Asia"
"A Nocturnal upon S. Lucies day, Being the shortest day" (Donne) **1**:130, 134, 149-50, 154
"A nocturnall upon S. Lucies day" (Donne)
See "A Nocturnal upon S. Lucies day, Being the shortest day"
"Nocturne" (Ignatow) **34**:315
"Nocturne" (MacLeish) **47**:156, 185
"Nocturne" (Mistral)
See "Nocturno"
"Nocturne" (Mueller) **33**:192
"Nocturne" (Pavese)
See "Notturno"
"Nocturne" (Paz)
See "Nocturno"
"Nocturne in a Deserted Brickyard" (Sandburg) **2**:301, 303; **41**:228, 234, 257, 259, 276, 298, 312, 322, 337
"Nocturne in Black and Gold" (Doty) **53**:51, 54
"Nocturne of a Wandering Shepherd in Asia" (Leopardi)
See "Canto notturno di un pastore errante dell'Asia"
Nocturne of Remembered Spring and Other Poems (Aiken) **26**:50, 72
"Nocturne of the Descent" (Mistral)
See "Nocturno del descendimiento"
"Nocturne of the Void" (García Lorca)
See "Nocturno del hueco"
"Nocturne Parisien" (Verlaine) **32**:375
"Nocturne vulgaire" (Rimbaud) **3**:264; **57**:239, 275
Nocturnes (Senghor) **25**:231-33, 238-40, 255
"Nocturnes of Consummation" (Mistral)
See "Nocturnos de la Consumacíón"
"Nocturno" (Mistral) **32**:155, 161, 174, 176, 183, 190-94
"Nocturno" (Paz) **48**:176
"Nocturno" (Storni) **33**:237, 307;
"Nocturno de San Ildefonso" (Paz) **1**:370-72, 375; **48**:191, 204, 233
"Nocturno del descendimiento" (Mistral) **32**:181
"Nocturno del hueco" (García Lorca) **3**:139
"Nocturno en los muelles" (Guillén) **23**:106
"Nocturnos de la Consumacíón" (Mistral) **32**:181
"Nodier raconte" (Pound) **4**:317
"Noel: Christmas Eve" (Bridges) **28**:77, 81
"Noël indio" (Mistral) **32**:185
"Noise Day" (Silverstein) **49**:341
"The Noise of Myth" (Boland)
See "Listen. This Is the Noise of Myth"
"A Noiseless Patient Spider" (Whitman) **3**:390
"Noli Me Tangere" (Lawrence) **54**:249
"Nollekans" (Jarrell) **41**:174
"Un nom" (Lamartine) **16**:287
"Nomad Exquisite" (Stevens) **6**:293
"Nomad Songs" (Merwin) **45**:48
No-man's Rose (Celan)
See *Die Niemandsrose*
"Los nombres" (Guillén) **35**:193, 210-11, 229-30
"Le non godute" (Gozzano) **10**:184
"Non Omnis Moriar" (Tate) **50**:319
Non Serviam (Ekeloef) **23**:51, 58-9, 63, 76
"The Nonconformist" (Davie) **29**:102
The Nonconformist's Memorial (Howe) **54**:82, 84-85, 87, 95, 97, 105-6, 125-27, 134-35, 137
"None with Him" (Rossetti) **7**:276, 284
Nones (Auden) **1**:23
"Nonne Preestes Tale" (Chaucer)
See "Nun's Priest's Tale"
"Nonsense Rhyme" (Wylie) **23**:305
"Nonsun Blob a" (Cummings) **5**:109
"Noom" (Brathwaite) **56**:54, 56
"Noon" (Levine) **22**:214, 219, 222
"Noon" (Thoreau) **30**:234
"Noon Hour" (Sandburg) **41**:335, 364
"Noon of the Sunbather" (Piercy) **29**:308
"Noon Walk on the Asylum Lawn" (Sexton) **2**:359
"Noonday Grace" (Ransom) **61**:292-93
"Noone' Autumnal This Great Lady's Gaze" (Cummings) **5**:107
"A Noon-Piece" (Smart) **13**:347
"Noons of Poppy" (Carman) **34**:213
"Nor We of Her to Him" (Smith) **12**:326, 330
"Nora" (Toomer) **7**:317
"Die Nordsee" (Heine) **25**:139, 145, 158, 160, 162, 163
"Norfolk Sprang Thee" (Surrey) **59**:327
"Noria" (Césaire) **25**:33
"Norma" (Sanchez) **9**:234
"Norma y paraíso de los negros" (García Lorca) **3**:150
"A Norse Child's Requiem" (Carman) **34**:220
"North" (Heaney) **18**:203
North (Heaney) **18**:194-95, 197-99, 203, 205, 208-11, 215, 230, 238-39, 241, 246, 255
"th north aint easy to grow food in" (Bissett) **14**:25, 33
"North American Sequence" (Roethke) **15**:309-10, 312
"North American Time" (Rich) **5**:395
"North and South" (McKay) **2**:207
North & South (Bishop) **3**:37, 39, 50; **34**:52, 67, 125, 127, 153, 161, 164, 174
"North Central" (Niedecker) **42**:107
North Central (Niedecker) **42**:90, 94, 100, 102, 106-7, 111
"The North Country" (Lawrence) **54**:222
"North Dakota North Light" (Momaday) **25**:219
"North Dublin" (Davie) **29**:95, 108, 120
"North Haven" (Bishop) **34**:113
"North Labrador" (Crane) **3**:83
North of Boston (Frost) **1**:193-95, 202, 207, 214, 217, 223-26
"North of Superior" (Birney) **52**:20, 38
"The North Sea" (Davie) **29**:113
"The North Sea Undertaker's Complaint" (Lowell) **3**:216
The North Ship (Larkin) **21**:224-26, 230, 232-33, 235, 241, 251, 257, 259
"North Star West" (Birney) **52**:21, 58
"North Wind" (Montale)
See "Tramontana"
"North Wind in October" (Bridges) **28**:67
"North Wind: Portrush" (Mahon) **60**:146, 152, 207, 232
"The North Wind To a Dutiful Beast..." (Moore) **49**:114
North Winter (Carruth) **10**:70-71
"A Norther—Key West" (Bishop) **34**:69
Northern Birds in Color (Bissett) **14**:25
"Northern Door" (Ortiz) **17**:234
"Northern Elegies" (Akhmatova) **2**:4, 18
"The Northern Farmer" (Tennyson) **6**:358, 360
"The Northern Farmer—Old Style" (Tennyson) **6**:406
Northern Heroic (Bely)
See *Severnaia simfoniia: Pervia geroicheskaia*
"A Northern Hoard" (Heaney) **18**:202-3
"Northern Liberal" (Hughes) **1**:252; **53**:115
"Northern Pike" (Wright) **36**:324, 360, 376
"Northern River" (Wright) **14**:340
"The Northern Sea" (Ishikawa)
See "Kita no umi"
Northern Symphony (Bely)
See *Severnaia simfoniia: Pervia geroicheskaia*
"A Northern Vigil" (Carman) **34**:203-04, 210-11, 216
Northfield Poems (Ammons) **16**:4-5, 28
"Northumberland House" (Smith) **12**:296
Northwest Ecolog (Ferlinghetti) **1**:187
"Northwood Path" (Glück) **16**:126
De nos oìseaux (Tzara) **27**:233
"The Nose" (Stone) **53**:228, 254
"Nossis" (H. D.) **5**:268
"Nostalgia" (Carducci) **46**:50
"Nostalgia" (Jiménez)
See "Nostaljia"
"Nostalgia" (Shapiro) **25**:269, 288, 325
"Nostalgia for India" (Sarton) **39**:327
"Nostalgias" (Mahon) **60**:141, 183
"Nostalgic Catalogue" (Hongo) **23**:198-99
"Nostalgies d'obélisques" (Gautier) **18**:158, 163
"Nostaljia" (Jiménez) **7**:201
"Not a fighter for two positions, but— if I'm a casual guest" (Tsvetaeva)
See "Dvukh stanov ne beots, a— esli gost sluchainyi"
"Not a Movie" (Hughes) **53**:162, 191
"Not a Prayer" (McHugh) **61**:202-3, 206-7
"Not a Suicide Poem" (Jordan) **38**:119
"Not Adlestrop" (Abse) **41**:19
"Not Both" (Meredith) **28**:208
"La not di maj" (Pasolini) **17**:252
"Not Every Day Fit for Verse" (Herrick) **9**:114
"Not Feeling" (Graham) **59**:166
Not for the Sake of Remembering (Amichai)
See *Ve-Lo al Menat Lizkor*
"Not Going to New York: A Letter" (Hass) **16**:198-99
"The Not Impossible Him" (Millay)
See "To the Not Impossible Him"
Not In Narrow Seas: Poems with Prose (Curnow) **48**:23-29
Not Just to Remember (Amichai)
See *Ve-Lo al Menat Lizkor*
"Not Leaving the House" (Snyder) **21**:289
"Not Like a Cypress" (Amichai)
See "Lo kabrosh"
"Not like a floury white butterfly" (Mandelstam)
See "Ne muchnistoi babochkoiu beloi"
"Not Like Dante" (Ferlinghetti) **1**:182
"Not Looking" (Jordan) **38**:119
"Not Marble Nor the Gilded Monuments" (MacLeish) **47**:165, 188, 196, 209
"Not Planning a Trip Back" (Ashbery) **26**:165
Not So Deep as a Well (Parker) **28**:365
"Not So Far as the Forest" (Millay) **6**:238
"Not So, Not So" (Sexton) **2**:373

"Not That From Life, and All Its Woes" (Bryant) **20**:16
"Not There" (Gallagher) **9**:59
Not This Pig (Levine) **22**:212-13, 215-17, 220, 223, 226
Not Wanting To Say Anything About Marcel (Cage) **58**:183
"Not Waving but Drowning" (Smith) **12**:293, 300, 307, 319-21, 324, 328, 331, 333, 337, 347, 349, 354
Not Waving but Drowning (Smith) **12**:292-93
"Not with libations, but with Shouts and Laughter" (Millay) **6**:211, 244-46
"Nota biográfica" (Fuertes) **27**:18, 48-9
"Notas de viaje" (Parra) **39**:283-84
"A Note" (Ní Chuilleanáin) **34**:361
"Note" (Thomas) **52**:222
"A Note Left in Jimmy Leonard's Shack" (Wright) **36**:281, 337
"A Note Left on the Mantelpiece" (Abse) **41**:12
"Note sibérienne" (Char) **56**:154, 173
"note to myself" (Clifton) **17**:30
"Note with the Gift of Bird's Nest" (Wagoner) **33**:356
"Notebook" (Levertov)
See "From a Notebook, October '68—May '69"
Notebook 1967-68 (Lowell) **3**:223-26, 231-32, 239-40
"The Notebook in the Gate-legged Table" (Lowell) **13**:84
"Notebook of a Return to the Native Land" (Césaire)
See *Cahier d'un retour au pays natal*
The Note-Book of William Blake (Blake) **12**:11, 34-5
"Noted in the New York Times" (Kumin) **15**:209
"Notes after Blacking Out" (Corso) **33**:43, 48
"Notes at Edge" (Wright) **14**:375, 377
Notes for a Guidbook (Stryk) **27**:181, 183, 191-94, 197, 210, 214, 216, 218
"Notes for a Guidebook" (Stryk) **27**:186, 195
"Notes for a Little Play" (Hughes) **7**:130, 152
"Notes for a Speech" (Baraka) **4**:5
"Notes for an Elegy" (Meredith) **28**:170, 173, 181, 184-85, 187, 210
"Notes for the Legend of Salad Woman" (Ondaatje) **28**:329
"Notes from a Nonesitent Hmalayan Expedition" (Szymborska) **44**:296, 318
"Notes from a Nonexistent Himalayan Expedition" (Szymborska) **44**:296, 318
"Notes from India" (Sarton) **39**:345
Notes from New York, and Other Poems (Tomlinson) **17**:333-34, 336, 353-54
"Notes From Robin Hill Cottage" (Carruth) **10**:85
"Notes From the Air" (Ashbery) **26**:163
"Notes from the Other Side" (Kenyon) **57**:12, 35
"Notes Made in the Piazzo San Marco" (Swenson) **14**:261
"Notes on a Conspiracy" (Rose) **13**:241
Notes on Literature (Guest) **55**:222
"Notes on the Reality of the Self" (Graham) **59**:138, 150, 152-53, 158-59, 176
"Notes toward a Poem That Can Never Be Written" (Atwood) **8**:18, 43
"Notes toward a Supreme Fiction" (Hope) **56**:286
Notes toward a Supreme Fiction (Stevens) **6**:310, 314, 324, 326-37, 329, 335, 337
"Notes Toward Home" (Jordan) **38**:127
"Nothin' to Say, My Daughter" (Riley) **48**:288-89, 292, 297, 314, 362
"Nothing" (Abse) **41**:19
"Nothing" (Szymborska) **44**:298
"Nothing and Something" (Harper) **21**:187, 191
Nothing but Love (Seifert)
See *Samá láska*
"Nothing Down" (Dove) **6**:110, 112
"Nothing Endures" (Cullen) **20**:59
Nothing for Tigers: Poems, 1959-1964 (Carruth) **10**:70
"Nothing Gold Can Stay" (Frost) **1**:194; **39**:239
"Nothing is Right" (Walker) **30**:365
"Nothing Makes Sense" (Giovanni) **19**:112
"Nothing Significant Was Really Said" (Larkin) **21**:259
"Nothing Special" (Herbert)
See "Nic ladnego"
"Nothing Stays Put" (Clampitt) **19**:94
"Nothing to Be Said" (Larkin) **21**:227
"Nothing Twice" (Szymborska) **44**:285, 293
"(Nothing Whichful About" (Cummings) **5**:108
"Nothing Will Cure the Sick Lion but to Eat an Ape" (Moore) **49**:134
"Nothing will yield" (Nemerov) **24**:262
"Notice" (Parra)
See "Aviso"
"Noticia de la lengua española" (Guillén) **35**:230
"Notizia di cronaca" (Quasimodo) **47**:289
"Notizie dall'Amiata" (Montale) **13**:106, 121, 127
"Notre Dame de Chartres" (Meredith) **28**:171, 188-89
"Notre Nuit meilleure que nos jours" (Éluard) **38**:83, 87
"Notre vie" (Éluard) **38**:78
"Notre-Dame" (Gautier) **18**:144-46
"La notte" (Pavese) **13**:230
"Notte di Maggio" (Carducci) **46**:23, 49
"Una notte di settembre" (Quasimodo) **47**:289
"Notturno" (Benn) **35**:26, 70
"Notturno" (Pavese) **13**:230
"Noubousse" (Apollinaire) **7**:48
"Noun" (Shapiro) **25**:276
"Nourish the Crops" (Ignatow) **34**:319-20
"Nous n'osons plus chanter les roses" (Cavafy) **36**:108
"Nous prenions par ces prés" (Bonnefoy) **58**:167
"Nous sommes" (Éluard) **38**:79
"Nous tombons" (Char) **56**:120
Nouveaux Poèmes (Éluard) **38**:70
"nouvelle bonte" (Césaire) **25**:45
Nouvelle confidences (Lamartine) **16**:293
Nouvelles méditations poétiques (Lamartine) **16**:266, 271, 273-74, 277-79, 287, 290-09
Nouvelles Odes (Hugo) **17**:88
"Nouvelles Variations sur le Point-du-Jour" (Verlaine) **32**:378
"Nova" (Jeffers) **17**:130
"A Novel" (Glück) **16**:158, 161
"Novel" (Rimbaud)
See "Roman"
"Novelettes" (MacNeice) **61**:138-39, 141
"November" (Belloc) **24**:34
"November" (Bryant) **20**:37, 44
"November" (Hughes) **7**:119, 132-33, 136
"November" (MacLeish) **47**:197
"November" (Merwin) **45**:53
"November" (Ransom) **61**:294
"November" (Teasdale) **31**:336
"November" (Thomas) **53**:325
"November 22, 1983" (Alexie) **53**:39
November and May (Szirtes) **51**:157
"November Cotton Flower" (Toomer) **7**:319, 333-34
"November Graveyard" (Plath) **37**:177, 184
"A November Night" (Teasdale) **31**:331
"November Sun" (Walcott) **46**:283
"November Surf" (Jeffers) **17**:117, 120, 132
"November Walk near False Creek Mouth" (Birney) **52**:17-19, 22, 36, 49, 57-58, 62, 71-74
The Novice (Lermontov)
See *Mtsyri*
"The Novices" (Levertov) **11**:169
"Novices" (Moore) **49**:93, 101
"Los novios" (Paz) **48**:198
"Novissima verba" (Lamartine) **16**:268, 280, 283, 292-93, 297
"Novogodnee" (Tsvetaeva) **14**:325
"Novye stansy k Avguste" (Brodsky) **9**:4
"Now" (Sexton) **2**:352
"Now" (Walker) **20**:276
"Now Air Is Air and Thing Is Thing: No Bliss" (Cummings) **5**:110
"Now and in Other Days" (Amichai) **38**:14
Now and in Other Times (Amichai)
See *'Akhshav 'vayamim ha'aherim*
Now and Then: Poems, 1976-1978 (Warren) **37**:310, 312, 317, 330, 334-35, 338, 341, 350, 355, 357-58, 365, 367, 380
"Now Close the Windows" (Frost) **1**:197
"Now Does Our World Descend" (Cummings) **5**:111
"Now He Knows All There Is to Know: Now He Is Acquainted with the Day and Night" (Schwartz) **8**:319
"Now Hollow Fires" (Housman) **2**:189
"Now I Become Myself" (Sarton) **39**:324, 345
"Now I Hear" (Ignatow) **34**:324
Now in Wintry Delights (Bridges) **28**:76-7
Now Is Time (Birney) **52**:4, 11, 37, 39, 45, 67
"Now It Is Clear" (Merwin) **45**:66
"Now It Is You I Praise, Banner" (Rilke) **2**:273
"Now Pine-Needles" (Smith) **12**:318
"Now Returned Home" (Jeffers) **17**:141
Now Sheba Sings the Song (Angelou) **32**:25
"Now that Holocaust and Crucifixion are Coffee-Table Books" (Viereck) **27**:293-94, 296
"Now That I Am Never Alone" (Gallagher) **9**:62
"Now that the shapes of mist" (MacNeice) **61**:160, 183-84
"Now That We Live" (Kenyon) **57**:29
"Now the Record Now Record" (Duncan) **2**:103
"Now This Cold Man" (Page) **12**:168, 170, 178, 184
"Now Voyager" (Sarton) **39**:322
"Now we have present made" (Raleigh) **31**:259, 299
"Nox" (Hugo) **17**:54
Nozarashi Diary (Matsuo Bashō) **3**:6
Nozarashi kikō (Matsuo Bashō) **3**:11, 28
"Nozze" (Carducci) **46**:21
"Le Nozze del Mare" (Carducci) **46**:5
Le Nu perdu (Char) **56**:113, 130, 134-35, 137-40, 144, 149-57, 185-89, 198
"NUCLEAR CICULAR" (Bissett) **14**:6, 24, 32
"Nude" (Cassian) **17**:4
"The Nude" (Guest) **55**:185
"Nude Interrogation" (Komunyakaa) **51**:55
"Nude Photograph" (Clifton) **17**:29
"Nude Pictures" (Komunyakaa) **51**:8
"The Nude Swim" (Sexton) **2**:352
"Nude Young Dancers" (Hughes) **1**:246; **53**:83, 143
"Nudite de la vérité" (Éluard) **38**:70, 103
"Nudity of Truth" (Éluard)
See "Nudite de la vérité"
"La Nue" (Gautier) **18**:125, 129
"Nue nue comme ma maîtresse" (Péret) **33**:216, 230
"Les Nuées" (Bonnefoy) **58**:168
"Nuestra Casa" (Alurista) **34**:40
"Nuestra Casa—Denver '69" (Alurista) **34**:24, 39-40
"Nueva York: Oficina y denuncia" (García Lorca) **3**:141, 151
Nuevo canto de amor a Stalingrado (Neruda) **4**:279-80
Nuevos sermones y prédicas del Cristo de Elqui (Parra) **39**:292
"The Nuisance" (Piercy) **29**:309
"La nuit blanche" (Kipling) **3**:172
"Nuit blanche" (Lowell) **13**:89-90
"La nuit d'Avril, 1915" (Apollinaire) **7**:3
"Nuit de l'enfer" (Rimbaud) **57**:190, 247-49, 252
"Nuit de Sine" (Senghor) **25**:224, 227, 255

"Nuit du Walpurgis classique" (Verlaine) **32**:388
La Nuit I (Char)
See *La Nuit talismanique*
La nuit talismanique (Char) **56**:120-24, 126, 134, 137-38, 140-41, 143-44, 161, 187-88, 196
La Nuit talismanique qui brillait dans son cercle (Char)
See *La Nuit talismanique*
"Nuits de juin" (Hugo) **17**:64
"Nuits partagées" (Éluard) **38**:67-8, 73
La Nuit II (Char)
See *La Nuit talismanique*
"Nul I" (Éluard) **38**:69
"Nul II" (Éluard) **38**:69
"Nullo" (Toomer) **7**:320, 330-31, 334
"Number" (Hughes) **53**:115
"number 18" (Baca) **41**:76
"Number 57" (Villa) **22**:346
"Number Man" (Sandburg) **2**:322
"Number 68" (Villa) **22**:347
"Number Three on the Docket" (Lowell) **13**:79, 84-5
"The Numbers" (Ammons) **16**:5
"Numbers" (Hughes) **1**:267; **53**:159
"Numbers" (Smith) **12**:317
"Numbers, Letters" (Baraka) **4**:19
"The Numerous Blood" (Guillén)
See "La sangre numerosa"
"Numpholeptos" (Browning) **2**:86, 88
"The Nun" (Wagoner) **33**:324
"Nun of Nidaros" (Longfellow) **30**:20
"Nunc dimittis" (Brodsky) **9**:5
"Nunca se sabe" (Fuertes) **27**:17
"Nuns at Lunch on the Bus" (Stone) **53**:223, 254
"A Nun's Complaint" (Rilke) **2**:270
"Nuns Fret Not" (Millay) **6**:242
"Nuns in the Wind" (Rukeyser) **12**:211
"Nun's Priest's Tale" (Chaucer) **19**:6, 13-15, 26, 31-2, 48, 52, 57, 75
La nuova gioventù (Pasolini) **17**:282-83, 287
"Nuova poesia in forma di rose" (Pasolini) **17**:274, 278
Nuove odi barbare (Carducci) **46**:8, 47
Nuove poesie (Carducci) **46**:13, 47
Nuove poesie (Quasimodo) **47**:279, 300, 302-4
Nuove Rime (Carducci)
See *Rime nuove*
"Nuove stanze" (Montale) **13**:106, 120-21
The Nuptial Countenance (Char)
See *Le Visage nuptial*
"Nuptial Sleep" (Rossetti) **44**:164, 166, 203-4, 206
"A Nuptiall Song, or Epithalamie on Sir Clipseby Crew and His Lady" (Herrick) **9**:86, 102, 139
"Nuptials" (Tate) **50**:319
"The Nuptials of Attila" (Meredith) **60**:247, 250, 263-64, 294, 328
"Nuremberg" (Longfellow) **30**:46
"Nürnberge Rede" (Enzensberger) **28**:164
"Nurse Whitman" (Olds) **22**:322, 328
"The Nurse-Mother" (Sandburg) **41**:267
"A Nursery Rhyme" (Brooke) **24**:66
"Nursery Rhyme" (Niedecker) **42**:140
"Nursery Rhyme" (Stone) **53**:254
"Nursery Rhyme for a Seventh Son" (Wright) **14**:338
"Nursery Rhymes for Little Anglo-Indians" (Kipling) **3**:190
Nursery Rhymes from Mother Stone (Stone) **53**:221
"Nurse's Song" (Blake) **12**:7, 21-2, 34
"Nurse's Song" (Glück) **16**:148
"Nurse's Songs" (Thomas) **52**:330
"Nursing Home" (Page) **12**:176
"Nurture" (Kumin) **15**:209, 211
Nurture (Kumin) **15**:209-14, 221, 223
"Nusch" (Éluard) **38**:68
Nux (Ovid) **2**:244
"Ny la douce pitie, ny le pleur lamentable" (Ronsard) **11**:278
Nye and Riley's Railway Guide (Riley) **48**:346
"The Nymph and the Faun" (Marvell)
See "The Nymph Complaining for the Death of Her Faun"
"The Nymph Complaining for the Death of Her Faun" (Marvell) **10**:260-62, 266-67, 271, 274, 277, 290, 294, 297, 301-02, 309-10, 315-16, 319, 325
"A Nympholept" (Swinburne) **24**:312-319, 322, 326, 341, 348
"Nymph's Reply to the Shepherd" (Raleigh) **31**:235, 269
"O" (Wilbur) **51**:295
O. 1 (Pindar)
See *Olympian 1*
O. 7 (Pindar)
See *Olympian 7*
O. 8 (Pindar)
See *Olympian 8*
O. 9 (Pindar)
See *Olympian 9*
O. 14 (Pindar)
See *Olympian 14*
"O Africans" (Goodison) **36**:154
"O Be a Fine Girl" (Hope) **56**:277
"O Black and Unknown Bards" (Johnson) **24**:127, 146, 152, 160, 166
"O Breath" (Bishop) **34**:84, 88-90, 105
"O Captain! My Captain!" (Whitman) **3**:404, 418, 422
"O Carib Isle!" (Crane) **3**:90
"O City, City" (Schwartz) **8**:302, 316
"O Daedalus, Fly Away Home" (Hayden) **6**:176, 179, 189
"O das Quinas" (Pessoa) **20**:155
"O Desejado" (Pessoa) **20**:156
"O Deus immense" (Gower) **59**:25
"O Didn't He Ramble" (Johnson) **24**:151, 170
"O dos Castelos" (Pessoa) **20**:155
"O Dreams O Destinations" (Brathwaite) **56**:28, 84
"O Dreams, O Destinations" (Day Lewis) **11**:145
"O encanta da Pedra Chan" (Castro) **41**:93
"O Florida, Venereal Soil" (Stevens) **6**:305, 339
O fons Bandusiae (Horace) **46**:107
"O Geist" (Benn) **35**:50
"O Glorious France" (Masters) **1**:342
"O Guardador de Rebanhos" (Pessoa) **20**:151-52
"O happie dames" (Surrey) **59**:297, 306, 307, 310, 315, 334
"O Happy Dogs of England" (Smith) **12**:318, 330
"O Hell" (Loy) **16**:316
"O Infante" (Pessoa) **20**:155
"O Krytykach i Recenzentach" (Mickiewicz) **38**:156, 167
"O Lady, when the Tipped Cup of the Moon Blessed You" (Hughes) **7**:113
"O Lay Thy Loof in Mine, Lass" (Burns) **6**:76
"O, Let Me in This Ae Night" (Burns) **6**:81
"O Lord, I Will Praise Thee" (Cowper) **40**:55
"O lothsome place" (Surrey) **59**:297, 353
"O Love, my muse" (Bridges) **28**:59
"O Love, Sweet Animal" (Schwartz) **8**:313
"O Love, the Interest Itself in Thoughtless Heaven..." (Auden) **1**:22
"O Lull Me, Lull Me" (Roethke) **15**:261, 273, 299, 302
"O May I Join the Choir Invisible" (Eliot) **20**:123, 131, 136, 139, 143
"O me donzel" (Pasolini) **17**:252
"O Mon Dieu, vous m'avez blessé d'amour" (Verlaine) **2**:416
"O Mostrengo" (Pessoa) **20**:155
"O muse contiens-toi! muse aux hymnes d'airain" (Hugo) **17**:97
"O my companions, O my sister Sleep" (Belloc) **24**:38
"O my joy" (Bridges) **28**:63
"O My Name It Is Sam Hall" (Jarrell) **41**:136
"O my thoughtes" (Sidney) **32**:235
"O my vague desires" (Bridges) **28**:59
"O Nacht" (Benn) **35**:50
"O Pastor Amoroso" (Pessoa) **20**:152
"O Pug!" (Smith) **12**:301
"O saisons, ô châteaux!" (Rimbaud) **3**:275; **57**:252-53
"O Saisons! O Châteaux!" (Sarton) **39**:322
"O Sion of my heart" (Kunitz) **19**:175
"O Southland!" (Johnson) **24**:137, 142, 147, 160
"O Sweet Spontaneous" (Cummings) **5**:105
"O sweete woodes" (Sidney) **32**:235
"O Taste and See" (Levertov) **11**:169
O Taste and See (Levertov) **11**:159, 169, 171, 211
"O, Tempora! O Mores!" (Poe) **1**:449
"O, Thou Opening, O" (Roethke) **15**:284, 300, 302-03
"O tlumaczeniu wierszy" (Herbert) **50**:5
"O to Be a Dragon" (Moore) **4**:249; **49**:107, 146, 161
O to Be a Dragon (Moore) **49**:136, 140, 184
"O Troi" (Herbert) **50**:7
"O Virtuous Light" (Wylie) **23**:311, 315
"O Wander Not So Far Away!" (Burroughs) **8**:73
"O Wha's Been Here afore Me, Lass" (MacDiarmid) **9**:155, 160
"O Word I Love to Sing" (McKay) **2**:217, 219
"O World of many Worlds" (Owen) **19**:352
"O Ye Tongues" (Sexton) **2**:367, 372-73
Oak and Ivy (Dunbar) **5**:128, 132
"The Oak and the Rose" (Silverstein) **49**:327
"Oak Hill Cemetery" (Cervantes) **35**:104
"The Oak Leaf" (Lermontov) **18**:281
"Oaks" (Castro)
See "Los robles"
"Oasis" (Stryk) **27**:187
"The Oath" (Tate) **50**:231, 235, 244, 251, 257, 260
"Oatmeal" (Kinnell) **26**:286
"Oaxaca, 1974" (Cervantes) **35**:108, 118, 130, 131, 133
"Obedience" (Herbert) **4**:119, 125-26
"Obéissez à vos porcs qui existent . . ." (Char) **56**:120, 145
"Obermann Once More" (Arnold) **5**:19, 63-4
"Oberon's Chappell" (Herrick)
See "The Fairie Temple: or, Oberons Chappell. Dedicated to Mr. John Merrifield, Counsellor at Law"
"Oberon's Feast" (Herrick) **9**:90
"Oberon's Palace" (Herrick) **9**:86, 90, 137
"Obit Dean, September 30, 1955" (O'Hara) **45**:172
"Obituary" (Tate) **50**:246
"Obituary for a Living Lady" (Brooks) **7**:66-7, 69
"The Objection to Being Stepped On" (Frost) **1**:215
"Objects" (Herbert)
See "Przedmioty"
"Objects" (Wilbur) **51**:186-88, 192-93, 220-21, 237
"Objects and Apparitions" (Paz) **48**:274
"Objet d'Art" (Stryk) **27**:204
"Oblique Prayers" (Levertov) **11**:198, 201
Oblique Prayers (Levertov) **11**:198, 200-02, 209
"Oblivion" (Smith) **12**:317, 354
"Oboe sommerso" (Quasimodo) **47**:301
Oboe sommerso (Quasimodo) **47**:268, 275, 278, 297, 300-303
"O-Bon: Dance for The Dead" (Hongo) **23**:199
"Oboroniaet son moiu donskuiu son" (Mandelstam) **14**:154
Obra gruesa (Parra) **39**:364, 370, 372, 392, 301-4, 311
Obra Poetica (Paz) **48**:258

Obra poetica, 1923-1964 (Borges) **32**:60, 81-6, 88, 90, 94, 112, 135
Obra poética 1923-1967 (Borges) **22**:72, 96
Obra poética: 1923-1976 (Borges) **22**:95; **32**:86-7
Obras (Castro) **41**:107, 110-19
Obras completas (Aleixandre) **15**:7, 18, 34
Obras completas (Borges) **32**:69, 102, 124, 126, 133
Obras completas (Juana Inés de la Cruz) **24**:202, 233
Obras de Luis de Camões (Camões) **31**:13
Obras incompletas (Fuertes) **27**:3-5, 19-21, 23-5, 33-47
"Obrerito" (Mistral) **32**:179
"El obrero" (Storni) **33**:279;
"Obsequies to the Lady Anne Hay" (Carew) **29**:6, 36, 38, 59-60, 66, 74
"Observation" (Larkin) **21**:259
"An Observation" (Sarton) **39**:329
"Observation Car" (Hope) **56**:268, 270, 276, 302
"Observation of Facts" (Tomlinson) **17**:299, 315, 335
Observations (Moore) **4**:229-30, 244, 249-52; **49**:88-90, 92, 95-96, 105, 113-14, 117, 134, 150, 152, 159, 180, 185-86
"Observations From the Outer Edge" (Wagoner) **33**:331
"The Observatory" (Noyes) **27**:128
"The Observer" (Rich) **5**:370
"La obsesión" (Mistral) **32**:161, 176
"Obsessed by Her Beauty" (Viereck) **27**:263
"Obsidian Butterfly" (Paz)
See "Mariposa de obsidiana"
"Obsolete" (Ignatow) **34**:323
Obus couleur de lune (Apollinaire) **7**:22
"Occasional Verses" (Hacker) **47**:80
"Occasioned by Sir William Temple's Late Illness and Recovery" (Swift) **9**:250
"Occasionem Cognosce" (Moore) **49**:133, 149
Le occasioni (Montale) **13**:103-05, 108-09, 113-14, 117-21, 126-28, 131-32, 136, 141 , 160, 165-66
The Occasions (Montale)
See *Le occasioni*
"L'occident" (Lamartine) **16**:266
"The Occultation of Orion" (Longfellow) **30**:82
"The Occupation" (Abse) **41**:3
"The Occurrences" (Oppen) **35**:286, 295, 312, 317, 335, 336, 343
The Ocean (Raleigh)
See *The Ocean to Cynthia*
The Ocean to Cynthia (Raleigh) **31**:201, 211-16, 218-22, 225-28, 230-32, 237-44, 246-47, 249, 251-60, 264, 278, 285-90, 292, 297, 313
"Ocean Waves" (Tagore)
See "Sindhu-taranga"
"Ocean-Letter" (Apollinaire)
See "Lettre-Océan"
"Oceano Nox" (Hugo) **17**:64
The Ocean's Love to Cynthia (Raleigh)
See *The Ocean to Cynthia*
"Ocean's Love to Ireland" (Heaney) **18**:196
Ocher (Storni)
See *Ocre*
"Ocho Perritos" (Mistral) **32**:184
"Ocho Rio" (Goodison) **36**:156
"Ocho Rios I" (Goodison) **36**:150
"Ocho Rios II" (Goodison) **36**:150, 155, 157
Ochre (Storni)
See *Ocre*
Ocre (Storni) **33**:236-37, 244-45, 256, 266, 277, 279-82, 290-92, 297, 299;
Octavie: L'illusion (Nerval) **13**:177
"The Octets" (Mandelstam) **14**:152
"October" (Frost) **1**:225
"October" (Hayden) **6**:193, 195
"October" (Kavanagh) **33**:81, 96, 120
"October" (Komunyakaa) **51**:64
"October" (Lorde) **12**:154
"October" (Mahon) **60**:143
"October" (Sassoon) **12**:240
"October" (Thomas) **53**:275,290
"October 26 1952 10:30 o'clock" (O'Hara) **45**:227
"October at Hellbrünn" (Muir) **49**:238, 287
October Blast (Yeats) **51**:92, 108
"October Dawn" (Hughes) **7**:115
"October Frost" (Bly) **39**:86
"October in Bloomsbury" (MacNeice) **61**:176-77
"October in Hyde Park" (Mahon) **60**:210, 215
"October Journey" (Walker) **20**:284, 289
October Journey (Walker) **20**:284, 287, 289
"October Judgment" (Char)
See "Le Jugement d'Octobre"
"October Maples, Portland" (Wilbur) **51**:209, 291-92
"October Thought" (Heaney) **18**:191
"October Trees" (Sassoon) **12**:248, 254
"The Octopus" (Merrill) **28**:239, 242
"An Octopus" (Moore) **4**:233, 252, 254-55, 264; **49**:94, 97, 102, 112, 128, 155
"Od konca" (Herbert) **50**:8
"Oda a España" (Paz) **48**:179-80
"Oda a Salvador Dali" (García Lorca) **3**:136, 138, 143
"Oda a Walt Whitman" (García Lorca) **3**:121, 127, 150
"Oda al edificio" (Neruda) **4**:285
"Oda al santísimo sacramento del altar: exposición y mundo" (García Lorca) **3**:136, 138, 143
"Oda al sueño" (Paz) **48**:179, 181-82
"Oda compuesta en 1960" (Borges) **32**:111
Oda do młodości (Mickiewicz) **38**:150, 154, 157
"Oda escrita en 1966" (Borges) **32**:111
"Oda inicial" (Guillén) **35**:146
"Oda k nuzhniku" (Lermontov) **18**:284-85
"Oda o Mlodości" (Mickiewicz) **38**:162, 189
"Oda solar al ejérito del pueblo" (Neruda) **4**:309
Odas elementales (Neruda) **4**:285, 287
Odas Mínimas (Guillén) **23**:100
"Odd" (Abse) **41**:6, 13
"Oddjob, a Bull Terrier" (Walcott) **46**:236, 240
"Ode" (Lamartine) **16**:291
"Ode" (MacNeice) **61**:145
"Ode" (Marvell)
See "An Horatian Ode upon Cromwell's Return from Ireland"
"Ode" (Tennyson) **6**:357
"Ode" (Wordsworth) **4**:377, 399, 403-04, 407
"Ode à Cassandre: 'Mignonne, allon voir'" (Ronsard) **11**:218-21, 234, 240
Ode à Charles Fourier (Breton) **15**:52, 61
"Ode á Joachim du Bellay" (Ronsard) **11**:280
"Ode à l'Amitié" (Hugo) **17**:87-88
"Ode à Michel de l'Hospital" (Ronsard) **11**:258, 287-91
"Ode à Victor Hugo" (Gautier) **18**:144
"Ode at the Grave of Jackson Pollock" (O'Hara) **45**:148, 143
"Ode de la Paix" (Ronsard) **11**:283, 286, 289-91
"An Ode (Dedicated to the Under-Secretary for India in expectation of his immediate promotion to Cabinet rank through the Postmaster-General)" (Belloc) **24**:41
"Ode for All Rebels" (MacDiarmid) **9**:171, 176
"An Ode for Him" (Herrick) **9**:86
"Ode for Music" (Gray) **2**:153, 155
"Ode for St. Cecilia's Day" (Pope) **26**:315
"Ode Inscribed to W. H. Channing" (Emerson) **18**:88, 111
"Ode: Intimations of Immortality from Recollections of Early Childhood" (Wordsworth) **4**:387-88, 390, 395, 401, 403, 411
"Ode Marítima" (Pessoa) **20**:166, 169
"Ode: My Twenty-Fourth Year" (Ginsberg) **4**:73
"Ode: O Bosky Brook" (Tennyson) **6**:388-89
"Ode on a Distant Prospect of Eton College" (Gray) **2**:133-34, 137, 149-50, 153
"Ode on a Drop of Dew" (Marvell) **10**:269, 271, 277, 296, 313-14
"Ode on a Grecian Urn" (Keats) **1**:281-82, 290-98, 300, 303-04, 307, 313-15
"Ode on Causality" (O'Hara) **45**:130, 148-49, 243-45
"Ode on Indolence" (Keats) **1**:302-04, 307-08, 314
"Ode on Lust" (O'Hara) **45**:147-48
"Ode on Melancholy" (Keats) **1**:298-300, 306-07, 309, 312
"Ode on Spring" (Gray) **2**:133, 135, 143, 145, 152
Ode on the Coronation of King Edward (Carman) **34**:205, 211
"Ode on the Death of a Favourite Cat, Drowned in a Tub of Gold Fishes" (Gray) **2**:133, 146, 148, 152
Ode on the Morning of Christ's Nativity (Milton) **29**:212, 214, 238-41, 272
"Ode on the Pleasure Arising from Vicissitude" (Gray) **2**:143, 152-53
"Ode on the Progress of Poesy" (Gray)
See "The Progress of Poesy"
"Ode on the Spring" (Gray)
See "Ode on Spring"
"Ode on Vicissitude" (Gray)
See "Ode on the Pleasure Arising from Vicissitude"
"Ode: Salute to the French Negro Poets" (O'Hara) **45**:165
"Ode secrète" (Valéry) **9**:394-96
"Ode sur la naissance du duc de Bordeaux" (Lamartine) **16**:291
"Ode: The Medusa Face" (Merwin) **45**:93
"Ode to a Beloved Woman" (Sappho)
See "Ode to Anactoria"
"The Ode to a Girl" (Sappho) **5**:408
"Ode to a Nightingale" (Keats) **1**:281-83, 295-98, 301, 303, 305, 307-09, 314-15
"Ode to Adversity" (Gray) **2**:133, 135, 138-39, 141, 152
"Ode to Anactoria" (Sappho) **5**:407, 411, 413
"Ode to Aphrodite" (Sappho) **5**:408, 411, 413, 431
"Ode to Apollo" (Keats) **1**:313
"Ode to Arnold Schoenberg" (Tomlinson) **17**:308, 317, 328, 337
"Ode to Atthis" (Sappho) **5**:416
"Ode to Autumn" (Keats) **1**:282-83, 298-302, 314-15
"Ode to Beauty" (Emerson) **18**:81
"Ode to Bill" (Ashbery) **26**:135, 159
"Ode to Coit Tower" (Corso) **33**:15, 36, 39, 46-8
"Ode to Dr. William Sancroft" (Swift) **9**:250
"Ode to dream" (Paz)
See "Oda al sueño"
"Ode to Duty" (Wordsworth) **4**:401, 406-07
"Ode to Ethiopia" (Dunbar) **5**:124, 129, 131-34, 143
"Ode to Fame" (Masters) **1**:332
"Ode to Fear" (Day Lewis) **11**:147
"Ode to Fear" (Tate) **50**:243-44
"Ode to France" (Coleridge) **11**:92, 94, 99-101; **39**:167
"ode to frank silvera" (Bissett) **14**:34
"Ode to Freedom" (Pushkin)
See "Vol'nost': Oda"
"Ode to General Draper" (Smart) **13**:342
"The Ode to Hesperus" (Sappho) **5**:418
"Ode to Himself" (Jonson) **17**:166, 174
"Ode (to Joseph LeSueur) on the Arrow That Flieth by Day" (O'Hara) **45**:134-35, 147-48
"Ode to Joy" (O'Hara) **45**:147-49
"Ode to Liberty" (Pushkin)
See "Vol'nost': Oda"
"Ode to Liberty" (Shelley) **14**:178
"An Ode to Love" (Behn) **13**:30

"Ode to Mæcenas" (Wheatley) **3**:333, 340-41, 344-45, 348, 354, 356-57, 361-62
"Ode to Memory" (Tennyson) **6**:347, 359-60
"Ode to Michael Goldberg's Birth and Other Births" (O'Hara) **45**:142-43, 164, 171
"Ode to Neptune" (Wheatley) **3**:354, 357, 361
"Ode to Our Young Pro-Consuls of the Air" (Tate) **50**:252-53, 322, 335
"Ode to Phœbus" (Carducci) **46**:4
"Ode to Plurality" (Zagajewski) **27**:381, 383, 385, 395-96
"Ode to Prized Koi and Baby Finches" (Chin) **40**:11
"Ode to Psyche" (Keats) **1**:295, 301, 305, 308-09, 314
"Ode to Rhyme" (Carducci)
See "Alla rima"
"Ode to Rome" (Carducci)
See "Roma"
"Ode to Salvador Dali" (García Lorca)
See "Oda a Salvador Dali"
"Ode to San Francisco" (Tomlinson) **17**:361
"An Ode to Sir Clipsebie Crew" (Herrick) **9**:103
"Ode: To Sir William Sydney, on his Birth-day" (Jonson) **17**:158-59
"Ode to Sir William Temple" (Swift) **9**:250
"Ode to Spain" (Paz)
See "Oda a España"
Ode to Stalin (Mandelstam) **14**:133, 148-49, 153-55
"Ode to Suburbia" (Boland) **58**:43
"Ode to Sura" (Corso) **33**:25, 44
"Ode to the Athenian Society" (Swift) **9**:250
"An Ode to the Birth of Our Saviour" (Herrick) **9**:119-20
"Ode to the Clitumnus" (Cardozo-Freeman) **46**:7
"Ode to the Comic Spirit" (Meredith) **60**:261
"Ode to the Confederate Dead" (Tate) **50**:228, 230-31, 243, 251-52, 262, 264, 271-74, 277, 280, 288, 295-96, 300, 304-7, 313-16, 318, 326, 335, 337-38, 340-41
"Ode to the Departing Year" (Coleridge) **11**:49, 54, 93-4; **39**:167
"Ode to the Latrine" (Lermontov)
See "Oda k nuzhniku"
"Ode to the Most Blessed Sacrament" (García Lorca)
See "Oda al santísimo sacramento del altar: exposición y mundo"
"Ode to the Most Holy Eucharist: Exposition and World" (García Lorca)
See "Oda al santísimo sacramento del altar: exposición y mundo"
"Ode to the Nightingale" (Keats)
See "Ode to a Nightingale"
"Ode to the Sacrament" (García Lorca)
See "Oda al santísimo sacramento del altar: exposición y mundo"
"Ode to the Sky Lark" (Shelley) **14**:167, 171, 175, 196, 198, 207, 212
"Ode to the Spirit of Earth in Autumn" (Meredith) **60**:296, 327
"Ode to the Spleen" (Finch) **21**:140-41, 145-46, 150, 152, 156-57, 159, 163, 165-66, 168, 172, 180-81
"Ode to the Spring" (Gray)
See "Ode on Spring"
"Ode to the Springs of Clitumnus" (Carducci)
See "Alle fonti del Clitumno"
"Ode to the West Wind" (Shelley) **14**:167-9, 171, 177, 196, 205-06, 208, 211-12, 234, 236-37, 239-40
"Ode to Venus" (Sappho)
See "Ode to Aphrodite"
"The Ode To Venus" (Sappho) **5**:408
"Ode to Walt Whitman" (García Lorca)
See "Oda a Walt Whitman"
"Ode to Willem de Kooning" (O'Hara) **45**:147
"Ode to Youth" (Mickiewicz)
See "Oda o Mlodości"
Ode to Youth (Mickiewicz)
See *Oda do młodości*
"Ode Triunfal" (Pessoa) **20**:169
Odes (Gray) **2**:135
Odes (Horace) **46**:95, 97-99, 102, 104-5, 108, 114, 117-18, 126, 128-32, 135, 138-40, 149-52, 155, 157-58, 160-63, 168-71, 173-74, 177-78, 181-85, 194, 204-5, 207, 211-14, 221-22
Odes (Hugo) **17**:55, 70, 87-90
Odes (O'Hara) **45**:147, 165
Odes (Pindar) **19**:380
Odes (Ronsard) **11**:230, 234, 280, 287, 289, 291-92
Odes (Valéry) **9**:365
Odes en son honneur (Verlaine) **32**:407
Odes et ballades (Hugo) **17**:45, 62, 74-75, 90-91
Odes et poésies diverses (Hugo) **17**:62
Odes in Contribution to the Song of French History (Meredith) **60**:259-60, 292, 335
The Odes of Horace (Horace)
See *Odes*
Odes to Simple Things (Neruda)
See *Odas elementales*
"Ode-Thnrenody on England" (Brooke) **24**:70
"Les Odeurs de l'amour" (Péret) **33**:218
Odi barbare (Carducci) **46**:4, 6-8, 11, 13, 16, 23, 26-27, 35, 37, 47, 50, 62, 64-65, 73
"Odious Scenery" (Hagiwara) **18**:177
"Odlegtose" (Milosz) **8**:189
Odlévání ní zvonů (Seifert) **47**:317, 328, 335
"The Odour" (Herbert) **4**:102, 134
Odysseis (Homer)
See *Odyssey*
Odysses (Homer)
See *Odyssey*
"Odysseus to Telemachus" (Brodsky) **9**:4
Odyssey (Homer) **23**:151-53, 155-58, 161, 165-66, 176-79, 186, 188-91
"Odyssey, Book Twenty-Three" (Borges) **32**:65
"Odyssey of Big Boy" (Brown) **55**:74, 80, 87-90, 101, 108, 110-11, 123, 125, 156, 160, 174
"Oeconomic divina" (Milosz) **8**:186-87
"Oedipus" (Muir) **49**:229, 233-35, 278-79
"Oedipus and the Riddle" (Borges) **32**:62
"Oedipus Crow" (Hughes) **7**:138
Oedipus Tyrannus; Or Swellfoot the Tyrant (Shelley) **14**:175, 202
"The Oedipus Within" (Wakoski) **15**:324
"Oenone" (Tennyson) **6**:359, 410-12
"Oeuvre" (Stryk) **27**:193, 195, 201
Oeuvres (Rimbaud) **57**:257, 282-83
Oeuvres (Ronsard) **11**:247, 254, 269, 272, 276
Oeuvres complètes (Césaire) **25**:33
Oeuvres complètes (Char) **56**:147, 149, 158-59, 161-62, 164, 184-90, 196-201
Oeuvres complètes (Mallarmé) **4**:198
Oeuvres completes (Perse) **23**:254
Oeuvres complètes (Rimbaud) **57**:243-54, 264
Oeuvres complètes (Tzara) **27**:232
Les Oeuvres de Francois Villon (Villon) **13**:373, 394
Oeuvres poétiques (Apollinaire) **7**:36
Oeuvres poétiques (Verlaine) **32**:409
Oeuvres poetiques completes (Lamartine) **16**:268
"Of Beginning Light" (Tomlinson) **17**:333
"Of Being" (Levertov) **11**:199, 202
"Of Being Numerous" (Oppen) **35**:287-88, 312, 322-23, 337, 341, 342, 343-45, 354-55, 357
Of Being Numerous (Oppen) **35**:287-88, 293, 294, 301-02, 307, 308, 310, 323, 324, 325, 333, 334, 337, 340, 343-45, 354
"Of De Witt Williams on His Way to Lincoln Cemetery" (Brooks) **7**:85
"Of Distress Being Humiliated by the Classical Chinese Poets" (Carruth) **10**:87-88
"Of Dying Beauty" (Zukofsky) **11**:368
"Of Forced Sightes and Trusty Ferefulness" (Graham) **59**:158
"Of Goats and Monkeys" (Walcott)
See "Goats and Monkeys"
"Of heaven and hell" (Borges)
See "Del infierno y del cielo"
"Of Heavens" (Sarton) **39**:328
"Of his love called Anna" (Wyatt) **27**:342
"Of Hours" (Oppen) **35**:324
"Of Itzig and His Dog" (Abse) **41**:25
"Of Liberation" (Giovanni) **19**:108
"Of Margaret" (Ransom) **61**:271, 306
"Of Modern Poetry" (Stevens) **6**:324
"Of Night" (Guillén)
See "De noche"
"Of others fained sorrow and the lovers fained mirth" (Wyatt) **27**:340
Of Pen and Ink and Paper Scraps (Stryk) **27**:214
"Of Rabbi Yose" (Abse) **41**:25
Of Reformation Touching Church-Discipline in England (Milton) **29**:238
"OF TH LAND DIVINE SERVICE" (Bissett) **14**:30
OF TH LAND DIVINE SERVICE (Bissett) **14**:2, 10
"Of the Contention betwixt the Queens" (Morris) **55**:334
"Of the Four Humours in Man's Constitution" (Bradstreet) **10**:17, 41
"Of the Jews A.D. 50" (Cavafy) **36**:31
"Of the Muse" (Sarton) **39**:369
Of the Progres of the Soule (Donne)
See *The Second Anniversarie. Of the Progres of the Soule. Wherein, By Occasion Of the Religious death of Mistris Elizabeth Drury, the incommodities of the Soule in this life, and her exaltation in the next, are Contemplated*
"Of the Vanity of All Worldly Creatures" (Bradstreet)
See "The Vanity of All Worldly Things"
Of the War (Duncan) **2**:104
"Of the West" (Jeffers) **17**:130
"Of Thee (kind boy)" (Suckling) **30**:146-47
"Off from swing shift" (Hongo) **23**:196-97, 203
"Off Point Lotus" (Kunitz) **19**:171
"Off Shore" (Swinburne) **24**:313
"Off The Campus: Wits" (Brutus) **24**:106, 114
"Off the Peg" (MacNeice) **61**:176
"Off the Turnpike" (Lowell) **13**:78, 85
"The Offending Eel" (Carver) **54**:18
"Offeren Y Llwyn" (Dafydd ap Gwilym) **56**:210
"Offering" (Tagore)
See "Utsarga"
"An Offering for Mr. Bluehart" (Wright) **36**:293-94, 306, 337
"Offering of Man to God" (Alurista) **34**:41
An Offering to the Lares (Rilke) **2**:280
"Offhand Compositions" (Wang Wei) **18**:370, 374
"An Officers' Prison Camp Seen from a Troop-Train" (Jarrell) **41**:178-79
"Offices" (Page) **12**:173
"Often I Am Permitted to Return to a Meadow" (Duncan) **2**:120, 127
"Often Rebuked, yet Always Back Returning" (Brontë) **8**:50
"Ogier the Dane" (Morris) **55**:250, 261, 286, 329
"The Ogre" (Williams) **7**:349, 378, 393
"Ogres and Pygmies" (Graves) **6**:139, 142, 144, 151
"Ogun" (Brathwaite) **56**:69, 74, 100
"Oh" (Sexton) **2**:365
"Oh Christianity, Christianity" (Smith) **12**:325, 352
"Oh, Dear! Oh Dear! A Sonnet" (Brooke) **24**:52
"Oh death shall find me" (Brooke) **24**:52, 72, 76
"Oh do not die" (Donne)
See "A Feaver"
"Oh Fair Enough Are Sky and Plain" (Housman) **2**:193

"Oh Fairest of the Rural Maids" (Bryant) **20**:35
"Oh general en tu Pentágono!" (Guillén) **23**:126
"Oh General in Your Pentagon!" (Guillén)
See "Oh general en tu Pentágono!"
"Oh Happy Day" (Parra)
See "Hay un día feliz"
Oh, Hell (Silverstein) **49**:314-17
"Oh Irene" (Ignatow) **34**:328
"Oh ivy green on ivy green" (Niedecker) **42**:96
"Oh, Look - I can Do It, Too" (Parker) **28**:354
Oh Mercy (Dylan) **37**:60
"Oh n'insultez jamais une femme qui tombe!" (Hugo) **17**:66
"Oh, oh, you will be sorry for that word!" (Millay) **61**:242
Oh Pray My Wings Are Gonna Fit Me Well (Angelou) **32**:3, 11, 26
"Oh seasons, oh castles" (Rimbaud)
See "Ô saisons, ô chateaux!"
"Oh, See How Thick the Gold Cup Flowers" (Housman) **2**:183, 185, 196
"Oh Think Not I Am Faithful to a Vow" (Millay) **6**:211
"Oh You Are Coming" (Teasdale) **31**:359, 388
"Oh You Sabbatarians!" (Masters) **1**:344
"Ohio Valley Swains" (Wright) **36**:309, 317, 348, 377
"Ohio Winter" (Walcott) **46**:240
"Ohioan Pastoral" (Wright) **36**:347
"Ohnedaruth's Day Begun" (Mackey) **49**:4
"Ŏi" (Seifert) **47**:349
Oi no kobumi (Matsuo Bashō) **3**:6
Oi no obumi (Matsuo Bashō) **3**:12
"Oil" (Hogan) **35**:254
"Oil Painting of the Artist as the Artist" (MacLeish) **47**:189
"Oil Refinery" (Birney) **52**:38
"Un oiseau a fienté sur mon veston salaud" (Péret) **33**:202
"L'oiseau spirituel" (Char) **56**:120
Oiseaux (Perse) **23**:239-41, 247-48, 253-54, 256-57
"Oitaru mi ni yamai wo kasane, toshi wo hete tashinami, kor wo omou ni itaru uta" (Yakamochi) **48**:131, 134, 139
"Ojo" (Storni) **33**:269, 282-83;
Oktyabr' (Yevtushenko) **40**:362-63
Oku no hosomichi (Matsuo Bashō) **3**:13, 27-30
Ol. IX (Pindar)
See *Olympian 9*
Ol. XI (Pindar)
See *Olympian 11*
"The Ol' Tunes" (Dunbar) **5**:122, 145
"The Old Adam" (Levertov) **11**:170
"Old Age Compensation" (Wright) **36**:328, 341, 345
"The Old Age of Queen Maeve" (Yeats) **51**:73
"Old Amusement Park'" (Moore) **49**:145
Old and Modern Poems (Vigny)
See *Poèmes antiques et modernes*
"Old and New Art" (Rossetti) **44**:227, 250
"The Old and the New Masters" (Jarrell) **41**:160-61, 163, 184
Old Arcadia (Sidney) **32**:235, 246, 281-82, 314-15
The Old Band (Riley) **48**:292
"Old Bill Pheasant" (Stone) **53**:219
"Old Boards" (Bly) **39**:85
"The Old Chartlist" (Meredith) **60**:262
"The Old Clock on the Stairs" (Longfellow) **30**:21, 46
"Old Communists and Guerillas" (Dalton) **36**:130
"Old Countryside" (Bogan) **12**:87, 94, 113
"An Old Cracked Tune" (Kunitz) **19**:158
"The Old Cumberland Beggar" (Wordsworth) **4**:411-12, 428
"Old Dog Dead" (Warren) **37**:377
"Old Dogs" (Smith) **12**:331-32
"Old Dominion" (Hass) **16**:198
"Old Dwarf Heart" (Sexton) **2**:361
"Old England" (McKay) **2**:225
"An Old Field Mowed for Appearances' Sake" (Meredith) **28**:194
"Old Flag" (Merwin) **45**:49, 86
"The Old Flagman" (Sandburg) **41**:330
"Old Flame" (Lowell) **3**:212, 215
"Old Flame" (Warren) **37**:337
"Old Florist" (Roethke) **15**:295
"Old Folks Home" (Stryk) **27**:210
"Old Folk's Home, Jerusalem" (Dove) **6**:123
"The Old Front Gate" (Dunbar) **5**:122
"Old Furniture" (Hardy) **8**:105
"The Old Gods" (Muir) **49**:210
"The Old Gray Couple" (MacLeish) **47**:197, 207
"The Old Gray Couple II" (MacLeish) **47**:207
"The Old Gray Wall" (Carman) **34**:229
"Old Hills" (Ortiz) **17**:231
The Old Home Folks (Riley) **48**:349
"The Old Horsefly" (Shapiro) **25**:324
The Old Horsefly (Shapiro) **25**:323
"Old House" (Wright) **14**:348-49, 353
The Old House in the Country (Reese) **29**:337-339, 348, 352
"The Old Huntsman" (Sassoon) **12**:240, 242, 250, 252-53, 275-76
The Old Huntsman and Other Poems (Sassoon) **12**:249, 252, 256-57, 260, 263-64, 269, 272, 277
"The Old Italians Dying" (Ferlinghetti) **1**:182
"Old King Cole" (Robinson) **1**:468; **35**:362
"Old King Cotton" (Brown) **55**:110
"The Old King's New Jester" (Robinson) **1**:487
"An Old Lady's Winter Words" (Roethke) **15**:272, 278
"Old Laughter" (Brooks) **7**:61
"Old Lem" (Brown) **55**:80-81, 83, 94, 113-14, 140, 152-53, 168
"The Old Life" (Kinnell) **26**:277
"Old Lines" (Montale)
See "Vecchi versi"
"The Old Lovers" (Aleixandre)
See "Los amantes viejos"
"The Old Maid" (Teasdale) **31**:388
"An Old Man" (Cavafy) **36**:95
"Old Man" (Thomas) **53**:276-77, 280, 291-92, 296-97, 300-301, 309-10, 332, 347-48
"The Old Man and Jim" (Riley) **48**:297, 325, 327
"Old Man at the Beach" (Wagoner) **33**:324
"Old Man Feeding Hens" (Francis) **34**:252
"The Old Man Is Like Moses" (Aleixandre) **15**:4, 24
"Old Man, Old Man" (Wagoner) **33**:334
"Old Man Playing with Children" (Ransom) **61**:305, 311-12
"Old Man Potchikoo" (Erdrich) **52**:174, 178, 193
Old Man Rubbing His Eyes (Bly) **39**:85
"The Old Man to the Lizard" (MacLeish) **47**:165
"The Old Man Travelling" (Wordsworth) **4**:374, 416
Old Man Whiskery-Whee-Kum-Wheeze (Riley) **48**:292
"Old Man who seined" (Niedecker) **42**:169
"The Old Man's Counsel" (Bryant) **20**:35, 41
"The Old Man's Funeral" (Bryant) **20**:10
"An Old Man's Winter Night" (Frost) **39**:246
"Old Mansion" (Ransom) **61**:268, 275, 311
"The Old Marlborough Road" (Thoreau) **30**:233, 236, 242
"Old Marrieds" (Brooks) **7**:53, 69, 79
"Old Mary" (Brooks) **7**:106
"The Old Masters" (Herbert) **50**:31
"Old Medium" (Enzensberger) **28**:167
"An Old Memory" (Dunbar) **5**:140
"Old Men" (Nash) **21**:263, 274
"Old Mother turns blue and from us" (Niedecker) **42**:140, 182
"The Old Neighbour and the New" (Hardy) **8**:104
"Old Nigger on One-Mule Cart Encountered Late at Night When Driving Home from Party in the Back Country" (Warren) **37**:330, 380
"Old Oak of Summer Chace" (Tennyson) **6**:356
"Old, Old, Old Andrew Jackson" (Lindsay) **23**:280, 288
"Old Osawatomie" (Sandburg) **41**:297
"Old Paint, Old Partner" (Kumin) **15**:220
"Old Park" (Jiménez) **7**:183
"The old people" (Paz)
See "Los viejos"
"The Old Peppermint Ladies" (Francis) **34**:258
"An old Photograph" (Nemerov) **24**:255
"An Old Photograph of strangers" (Meredith) **28**:193
"Old Photograph of the Future" (Warren) **37**:366, 376
"Old Pictures in Florence" (Browning) **2**:37
"Old Pictures in Florence" (Rossetti) **44**:250
"Old poet" (Bukowski) **18**:22
"The Old Poet" (Shapiro) **25**:304
"The Old Poet Moves to a New Apartment 14 Times" (Zukofsky) **11**:353
"The Old Pond" (Matsuo Bashō) **3**:32
Old Possum's Book of Practical Cats (Eliot) **6**:174
"The Old Prison" (Wright) **14**:359
"The Old Prometheus" (Herbert)
See "Stary Prometeusz"
"The Old Reliable" (Hacker)
See "Nights of 1964-1966: The Old Reliable"
"Old Revolution" (Enzensberger) **28**:166
"The Old Sceptic" (Noyes) **27**:139
The Old sceptic (Noyes) **27**:139
Old Shirts & New Skins (Alexie) **53**:3-5, 8, 11-15, 24, 26, 29-31, 39-40
"The Old Soldier's Story" (Riley) **48**:331, 350
"Old Song" (Crane) **3**:90
"An Old Song" (Jarrell) **41**:169
"An Old Song" (Thomas) **53**:227
"An Old Song Ended" (Rossetti) **44**:202
"An Old Steel Engraving" (Boland) **58**:58, 85
"The Old Stoic" (Brontë) **8**:60
"An Old Story" (Robinson) **1**:459; **35**:368
"An Old Sweetheart of Mine" (Riley) **48**:308, 323-24, 336, 350
"The Old Swimmin' Hole" (Riley) **48**:284, 312, 329, 332, 340
The Old Swimmin' Hole, and 'Leven More Poems (Riley) **48**:282, 284, 328, 339, 342, 347, 356
"Old Timers" (Sandburg) **2**:302; **41**:240, 270
"Old Trails" (Robinson) **1**:462
"The Old Trundle Bed" (Riley) **48**:324
"The Old Vicarage, Grantchester" (Brooke) **24**:54, 58, 63-5, 68, 78, 86, 93
"Old Walt" (Hughes) **1**:257; **53**:104
"The Old Warrior Terror" (Walker) **30**:339, 365
"Old Weavers" (Mistral)
See "Tejedores viejos"
"Old West Vancouver Ferry" (Birney) **52**:58
"Old Woman" (Pinsky) **27**:160-1
"Old Woman" (Sandburg) **41**:323
"An Old Woman" (Sitwell) **3**:312, 326
"The Old Woman and the Statue" (Stevens) **6**:297
"An Old Woman Remembers" (Brown) **55**:81, 114, 166
"Old Woman's Old Man" (Rimbaud)
See "Vieux de la vieille"
"Old Words" (Sanchez) **9**:221
"An Old World Thicket" (Rossetti) **7**:277
"The Old WPA Swimming Pool in Martin's Ferry, Ohio" (Wright) **36**:304, 358, 363, 377, 392, 396, 398
The Oldest Killed Lake in North America (Carruth) **10**:91
"Old-Fashioned Roses" (Riley) **48**:290, 315, 317, 319, 327, 356
"Olena's Feet" (Yevtushenko) **40**:347

"Oleszkiewicz" (Mickiewicz) **38**:169
"Olfactory Pursuits" (Abse) **41**:25, 28
"Olive Branch" (Meredith) **60**:245
"Olive Grove" (Merrill) **28**:228
The Olive Grove (Sarton) **39**:324, 340
"The Olive in Its Orchard" (Housman) **2**:189-90
"The Olive Wood Fire" (Kinnell) **26**:278
Olney Hymns (Cowper) **40**:42, 53
"Olson as Oracle" (Curnow) **48**:56-57
"The Olympian" (Dickey) **40**:230
Olympian 1 (Pindar) **19**:380-81, 388-89, 396, 398, 400, 402, 407, 413-17, 420, 422
Olympian 2 (Pindar) **19**:381, 423
Olympian 3 (Pindar) **19**:425
Olympian 6 (Pindar) **19**:381, 389-90, 398, 414, 420
Olympian VII (Pindar)
See *Olympian 7*
Olympian 7 (Pindar) **19**:396, 401, 406, 414
Olympian 8 (Pindar) **19**:422-23
Olympian 9 (Pindar) **19**:390
Olympian 10 (Pindar) **19**:387-88
Olympian 11 (Pindar) **19**:389, 412
Olympian 13 (Pindar) **19**:387, 391, 398
Olympian 14 (Pindar) **19**:421-23
Olympian Odes 1 (Pindar)
See *Olympian 1*
"A Olympio" (Hugo) **17**:76
Om hösten (Ekeloef) **23**:76
"Omaggio a Rimbaud" (Montale) **13**:111, 157
El Ombligo de Aztlán (Alurista) **34**:31, 34
"Ombra" (Ungaretti) **57**:347
"L'ombra della magnolia" (Montale) **13**:109-10, 118, 126
"Ombra mai fu" (Wilbur) **51**:282
"L'ombre aux soupirs" (Éluard) **38**:69
"Ombre Chinoise" (Lowell) **13**:94
"Omero" (Carducci) **46**:52
Omeros (Walcott) **46**:249, 254, 257-63, 265-69, 287, 292, 294-98, 300, 304-16, 324-26
Ommateum with Doxology (Ammons) **16**:4-5, 20, 24, 27, 39-44, 52-3
"Omnibus" (Birney) **52**:44
"Omnibus" (Tsvetaeva)
See "Avtobus"
Omniscience (Smart)
See *On the Omniscience of the Supreme Being*
"Omoide" (Ishikawa) **10**:213
"On a Bust" (Masters) **1**:342
"On a Certain Engagement South of Seoul" (Carruth) **10**:84, 89
"On a Child's Death" (Blok) **21**:15
"On a Clean Book" (Dunbar) **5**:125
"On a Conventicle" (Behn) **13**:7
"On a Copy of Verses Made in a Dream, and Sent to Me in a Morning before I Was Awake" (Behn) **13**:31
"On a Discovered Curl of Hair" (Hardy) **8**:137
"On a Distant Prospect of Eton College" (Gray)
See "Ode on a Distant Prospect of Eton College"
"On a Drawing by Flavio" (Levine) **22**:223
"On a Drop of Dew" (Marvell)
See "Ode on a Drop of Dew"
"On a Fine Morning" (Hardy) **8**:108
"On a Goldfinch Starved to Death in His Cage" (Cowper) **40**:126
"On a Heath" (Hardy) **8**:93
"On a Juniper Tree, Cut Down to Make Busks" (Behn) **13**:7, 27-8
"On a March Day" (Teasdale) **31**:341
"On a Month's Reading of the English Newspapers" (Corso) **33**:26
"On a Mountainside" (Wagoner) **33**:373
"On a New Year's Eve" (Jordan) **38**:122-23
"On a night without ornament" (Char)
See "Sur une nuit sans ornement"
"On a Phrase from Southern Ohio" (Wright) **36**:313, 322, 404
"On a Pietà of Tintoretto" (Bonnefoy) **58**:147
"On a Political Prisoner" (Yeats) **20**:314, 349
"On a Presentation of Two Birds to My Son" (Wright) **36**:335, 337
"On a Raised Beach" (MacDiarmid) **9**:157, 172, 176, 180
"On a Red Steed" (Tsvetaeva)
See "Na krasnom kone"
"On a Rocky Spur of Peoria" (Mandelstam) **14**:117
"On a Sentence by Pascal" (Schwartz) **8**:285, 292
"On a September Day" (Baca) **41**:37
"On a Side Street" (Zagajewski) **27**:389
"On a Singing Girl" (Wylie) **23**:324
"On a Sledge, Overlaid with Straw" (Mandelstam) **14**:119
"On a Sleeping Friend" (Belloc) **24**:9
"On a Solemn Music" (Milton) **19**:211, 253
"On a Starry Night" (Dunbar) **5**:125-27
"On a Theme by Frost" (Francis) **34**:244
"On a Tree Fallen Across the Road" (Frost) **1**:213
"On a Winter Night" (Sarton) **39**:332
"On a winter's night long time ago" (Belloc) **24**:34
"On acquiring an encyclopedia" (Borges)
See "Al adquirir una Enciclopedia"
"On Acrocorinth" (Sikelianos) **29**:372
"On Affliction" (Finch) **21**:144, 146
"On an Anthology of Chinese Poems" (Jeffers) **17**:140
"On an Early Photograph of My Mother" (Hope) **56**:277
"On an Engraving by Casserius" (Hope) **56**:281
"On an Old Photograph of My Son" (Carver) **54**:18, 29
"On an Old Roundel" (Swinburne) **24**:324-25, 328-29
"On Anactoria" (Sappho)
See "Ode to Anactoria"
"On Angels" (Milosz) **8**:201
"On Annunciation Day" (Tsvetaeva)
See "V den' Blagoveshchen'ia"
"On Another Politician" (Belloc) **24**:36-7
"On Another's Sorrow" (Blake) **12**:7, 33
On Ballycastle Beach (McGuckian) **27**:80, 83-85, 90, 92-95, 99-102, 104
"On Barbara's Shore" (Wakoski) **15**:333
"On Becoming a Mermaid" (Goodison) **36**:143, 145-46
"On Becoming a Tiger" (Goodison) **36**:154
"On Beginning the Study of Anglo-Saxon Grammar" (Borges)
See "Al iniciar el estudio de la gramática anglosajona"
"On Being Asked to Write a Poem Against the War in Vietnam" (Carruth) **10**:77
"On Being Brought from Africa to America" (Wheatley) **3**:338, 340, 346, 349, 353, 362-63
"On Being Given Time" (Sarton) **39**:325
"On Being Yanked from a Favorite Anthology" (Shapiro) **25**:323
"On Blake's Victory over the Spaniards" (Marvell)
See "On the Victory Obtained by Blake over the Spaniards"
"On byl v krayu svyatom" (Lermontov) **18**:289
"On Cartagena de Indias, His Native City" (Birney) **52**:15
"On Cheating the Fiddler" (Parker) **28**:362
"On Childhood" (Bradstreet) **10**:38
"On Christmas Eve" (Lowell) **13**:85
"On Court-worme" (Jonson) **17**:197
"On Death" (Clare) **23**:44
"On Desire. A Pindarick" (Behn) **13**:8, 10, 14
"On Diverse Deviations" (Angelou) **32**:17
"On Don Surly" (Jonson) **17**:197
"On Duelling" (Graves) **6**:144
"On Each Journey" (Merwin) **45**:48, 101
On Early Trains (Pasternak)
See *Na rannikh poezdakh*
"On Elgin Marbles" (Keats) **1**:279
"On Falling Asleep by Firelight" (Meredith) **28**:189-90, 213
"On Falling Asleep to Bird Song" (Meredith) **28**:192, 213
"On Fields O'er Which the Reaper's Hand has Passed" (Thoreau) **30**:207
"On Finding the Slide of John in the Garden" (Cervantes) **35**:134
"On Flower Wreath Hill" (Rexroth) **20**:220-21
"On Food" (Belloc) **24**:17
"On Freedom" (Ignatow) **34**:342
"On Freedom's Ground" (Wilbur) **51**:250, 302
"On Friendship" (Wheatley) **3**:363
"On Going Back to the Street after Viewing and Art Show" (Bukowski) **18**:5
"On Going to the Wars" (Birney) **52**:38
"On Going Unnoticed" (Frost) **1**:205; **39**:241
"On Gut" (Jonson) **17**:174
"On Handling Some Small Shells from the Windward Islands" (Swenson) **14**:287
"On Having Mis-identified a Wild Flower" (Wilbur) **51**:301
"On Hearing of Love" (Cavafy) **36**:41
"On Himselfe" (Herrick) **9**:87, 89, 131
"On his being arrived at the age of twenty-three" (Milton)
See "Sonnet 7"
"On His Blindness" (Borges) **32**:89
"On His Books" (Belloc) **24**:31
"On His Having Arrived at the Age of Twenty-Three" (Milton)
See "Sonnet 7"
"On His Mistris" (Donne)
See "Elegie XVI: On his mistris"
"On Huntingdon's 'Miranda'" (Lanier) **50**:69
"On Imagination" (Wheatley) **3**:336, 338, 353-55
"On Installing an American Kitchen in Lower Austria" (Auden) **1**:24
"On Jenkins' Hill" (Meredith) **28**:206
"On Julia's Clothes" (Herrick)
See "Upon Julia's Clothes"
"On Leaving Some Friends" (Keats) **1**:313; **73**:311
"On Lieutenant Shift" (Jonson) **17**:197
"On Looking at a Copy of Alice Meynell's Poems Given to Me Years Ago by a Friend" (Lowell) **13**:85, 89-90, 99-100
"On Looking into E. V. Rieu's Homer" (Kavanagh) **33**:100, 118
"On Looking Up by Chance at the Constellations" (Frost) **39**:233
"On Lookout Mountain" (Hayden) **6**:180, 194
"On Lord Holland's Seat near Margate, Kent" (Gray) **2**:143
"On Lucy Countesse of Bedford" (Jonson)
See "Epigram LXXVI"
"On Madison" (Tomlinson) **17**:353
"On Major General Lee" (Wheatley)
See "Thoughts on His Excellency Major General Lee"
"On Making Certain Anything Has Happened" (Frost) **39**:233
"On Minding One's Own Business" (Wright) **36**:288
"On Moral Leadership as a Political Dilemma" (Jordan) **38**:127
"On Mount Marius" (Carducci)
See "Su Monte Mario"
"On Mr. J. H. in a Fit of Sickness" (Behn) **13**:8
"On My First Daughter" (Jonson) **17**:172, 197
"On My First Son" (Jonson) **17**:172, 177, 197
"On My Own" (Levine) **22**:226
"On My Picture Left in Scotland" (Jonson)
See *The Under-Wood II*
"On My Son's Return out of England" (Bradstreet) **10**:36, 60
"On My Way Out I Passed over You and the Verrazano Bridge" (Lorde) **12**:138-39
"On Myselfe" (Finch) **21**:146, 155, 165
"On Neal's Ashes" (Ginsberg) **4**:74

"On no work of words" (Thomas) **52**:304
"On Not Being Listened To" (McGuckian) **27**:90
"On Obedience" (Duncan) **2**:114
"On Observing Some Names of Little Note in the Biographia Britannica" (Cowper) **40**:124
"On Open Form" (Merwin) **45**:39
"On Palatine" (Corso) **33**:37
"On Parting with My Wife, Jamina" (Milosz) **8**:211
"On Passing the New Menin Gate" (Sassoon) **12**:246
"On Patmos" (Sarton) **39**:341
On Poetry (Char)
See *Sur la poésie*
"On Poetry: A Rhapsody" (Swift) **9**:249
"On Police Brutality" (Walker) **20**:294
"On Ponkawtasset, Since We Took Our Way" (Thoreau) **30**:181, 202, 266
"On Ponkawtasset, since, with such delay" (Thoreau)
See "On Ponkawtasset, Since We Took Our Way"
"On Portents" (Graves) **6**:149, 172-73
"On Prime Ministers" (Belloc) **24**:37
"On Rachmaninoff's Birthday #158" (O'Hara) **45**:226
On Radio Waves (Seifert)
See *Na vlnách T. S. F.*
"On Reaching Forty" (Angelou) **32**:27
"On Reading a Book of Common Wild Flowers" (Kavanagh) **33**:100, 119, 121
"On Reading an Anthology of Postwar German Poetry" (Mueller) **33**:175, 197
"On Reading an Old Baedeker in Schloss Leopoldskron" (Kumin) **15**:209, 212
"On Reading Christopher Marlowe" (Carducci) **46**:26
"On Reading John Cage" (Paz) **1**:355, 363, 374
"On Reading Omar Khayyam" (Lindsay) **23**:283
"On Reading William Blake's 'The Sick Rose'" (Ginsberg) **4**:55
"On Recollection" (Wheatley) **3**:332, 340, 361
"On Restless River" (Brown) **55**:112
"On Returning to Detroit" (Forché) **10**:144, 156
"On Righteous Indignation" (Chesterton) **28**:114
"On San Gabriel Ridges" (Snyder) **21**:291
"On Sark" (Sarton) **39**:362
"On Scratchbury Camp" (Sassoon) **12**:259
"On Seeing an X-Ray of my Head" (Wagoner) **33**:328
"On Seeing Diana go Maddddddddd" (Madhubuti) **5**:344
"On Seeing Two Lovers in the Street" (Muir) **49**:245
"On Sir Voluptuous Beast" (Jonson) **17**:174, 212
"On Spies" (Jonson)
See "Epigram LIX"
"On Squaw Peak" (Hass) **16**:217
"On Stripping the Bark from Myself" (Walker) **30**:349
"On Swimming" (Zagajewski) **27**:396
"On That Day" (Lawrence) **54**:239, 243
"On the Aisle" (Kenyon) **57**:23, 40
"On the Alliance of Education and Government" (Gray)
See "Essay on the Alliance of Education and Government"
"On the Anniversary of the Founding of Rome" (Carducci)
See "Nell' annuale della fondazione di Roma"
On the Art of Poetry (Horace)
See *Ars Poetica*
"On the Author of . . . The Way to Health . . ." (Behn) **13**:8
"On the Balcony" (Lawrence) **54**:206-7
"On the Banks o' Deer Crick" (Riley) **48**:334
On the Banks of the River Sar (Castro)
See *En las orillas del Sar*
"On the Battle of Kulikovo Field" (Blok) **21**:8, 26, 29
"On the Beach" (Birney) **52**:15-16, 22, 28, 78
"On the Beach at Fontana" (Joyce) **22**:136
"On the Beach at Night" (Whitman) **3**:401
"On the Beach at Ostia" (Ferlinghetti) **1**:184
"On the Benefit Received by His Majesty from Sea-Bathing in the Year 1789" (Cowper) **40**:98, 120
"On the Birth of a Black/Baby/Boy" (Knight) **14**:43
On the Boiler (Yeats) **20**:311
"On the Building of Springfield" (Lindsay) **23**:277, 281, 296
"On the Burning of Lord Mansfield's Library" (Cowper) **40**:101
"On the Cliffs" (Swinburne) **24**:313, 315, 317, 319-20, 343
"On the Coming Victory" (Brutus) **24**:117
"On the Cosawattee" (Dickey) **40**:191, 258
"On the Death of G. B. Niccolini" (Carducci)
See "In Morte di G. B. Niccolini"
"On the Death of Giovanni Cairoli" (Carducci)
See "In Morte di Giovanni Cairoli"
"On the Death of Little Mahala Ashcraft" (Riley) **48**:334-35
"On the Death of Mr. Grinhill, the Famous Painter" (Behn) **13**:8
"On the Death of Mrs. Throckmorton's Bulfinch" (Cowper) **40**:123, 126-27
On the Death of Pushkin (Lermontov)
See "Smert' poeta"
"On the Death of Sir W. Russell" (Cowper) **40**:46
"On the Death of the Late Earl of Rochester" (Behn) **13**:8
"On the Death of the Lucky Gent" (Corso) **33**:25, 41
"On the Death of the Noble Prince King Edward the Fourth" (Skelton) **25**:339
"On the Death of the Queen" (Finch) **21**:171-72
"On the Death of the Rev. Mr. George Whitefield" (Wheatley)
See "An Elegiac Poem on the Death of George Whitefield"
"On the Death of the Reverend Dr. Sewall" (Wheatley) **3**:342
"On the Decline of Oracles" (Plath) **37**:238, 243
"On The Dedication of Dorothy Hall" (Dunbar) **5**:131, 134
"On the Departure Platform" (Hardy) **8**:90
"On the Difficulty of Conjuring Up a Dryad" (Plath) **37**:237, 254
"On the Double Ninth Remembering My Brothers" (Wang Wei) **18**:365, 386
"On the Downs" (Chesterton) **28**:98
"On the Duke of Buckingham" (Carew) **29**:61
"On the Dunes" (Teasdale) **31**:325, 334
"On the Eastern Front" (Trakl)
See "Im Osten"
"On the Edge" (Levine) **22**:212
"On the Edge" (Lorde) **12**:137
On the Edge (Levine) **22**:211-12, 216
"On the Escalator" (Zagajewski) **27**:381
On the Eternity of God (Smart)
See *On the Eternity of the Supreme Being*
On the Eternity of the Supreme Being (Smart) **13**:328, 343
"On the Extinction of the Venetian Republic" (Wordsworth) **4**:377
"On the Eyes of an SS Officer" (Wilbur) **51**:250, 317
"On the Fair Weather Just at the Coronation" (Philips) **40**:268, 271, 295, 318
"On the Famous Voyage" (Jonson)
See "Epigram CXXXIII"
"On the Ferry across Chesapeake Bay" (Bly) **39**:7
"On the Field of Kulikovo" (Blok)
See "On the Battle of Kulikovo Field"
"On the Fields of Marengo" (Carducci)
See "Sui Campi di Marengo"
"On the First Discovery of Falseness in Amintas. By Mrs. B." (Behn) **13**:20-1
"On the First of January 1657" (Philips) **40**:317
"On the Foreclosure of a Mortgage in the Suburbs" (Wright) **36**:390-91
On the Goodness of the Supreme Being (Smart) **13**:340, 359-60
"On the Grecian Room in Princess Zeneida Volkonskaia's House i n Moscow" (Mickiewicz)
See "Na pokoj grecki w eomu księżnej Zeneidy Wøkońskiej w Moskwie"
"On the Hall at Stowey" (Tomlinson) **17**:341, 344
"On the Happ Life" (Martial)
See "Vitam quae faciunt beatiorem"
"On the Highest Pillar" (Montale)
See "Sulla colonna più alta"
"On the Hill and Grove at Billborow" (Marvell)
See "Upon the Hill and Grove at Billborow"
"On the Honourable Sir Francis Fane . . ." (Behn) **13**:8
"On the Idle Hill of Summer" (Housman) **2**:185
On the Immensity of the Supreme Being (Smart) **13**:343
"On the Island" (Brutus) **24**:115
"On the Lake" (Goethe)
See "Auf dem See"
"On the Last Performance of" (Hongo) **23**:197
"On the Liberation of Woman" (Wright) **36**:377
"On the Loss of the Royal George" (Cowper)
See "Lines on the Loss of the Royal George"
"On the Mantelpiece" (Lowell) **13**:83
"On the Monument of Dante to be erected in Florence" (Leopardi)
See "Sopra il monumento di Dante"
"On the Morning of Christ's Nativity" (Milton) **19**:209, 251-54; **29**:229, 232
On the Motion and Immobility of Douve (Bonnefoy)
See *Du mouvement et de l'immobilité de Douve*
"On the Mountain" (Amichai) **38**:28
"On the Mountain" (Merwin) **45**:100
"On The Move" (Abse) **41**:4
"On the Move" (Gunn) **26**:184-5, 188-9, 196, 200, 202, 206-9
"On the Murder of Lieutenant José Del Castillo by the Falangist Bravo Martinez, July 12, 1936" (Levine) **22**:223, 225
"On the Night Shift" (Hope) **56**:292
"On the Ninth" (Li Po) **29**:185
"On the numerous accesse of the English to waite upong the King in Holland" (Philips) **40**:318
"On the Occasion of National Mourning" (Nemerov) **24**:289
"On the Ocean Floor" (MacDiarmid) **9**:191
On the Omniscience of the Supreme Being (Smart) **13**:344
"On the Outskirts of Antioch" (Cavafy) **36**:33, 52, 63
"On the Pechora" (Yevtushenko) **40**:347
"On the Platform" (Nemerov) **24**:262
"On the Plethora of Dryads" (Plath) **37**:237
"On The Portrait of a Beautiful Woman" (Leopardi) **37**:124
On the Power of the Supreme Being (Smart) **13**:344
"On the Promotion of Edward Thurlow, Esq. to the Lord High Chancellorship of England" (Cowper) **40**:100
"On the Pulse of Morning" (Angelou) **32**:23-4, 30-2
"On the Queen's Visit to London" (Cowper) **40**:98, 120

On the Radio Waves (Seifert)
See *Na vlnách T. S. F.*
"On the Republic" (Elytis) **21**:123
"On the Rhine" (Arnold) **5**:19, 43
"On the River" (Levine) **22**:228
"On the River Adda" (Carducci)
See "Su l'Adda"
"On the River Encountering Waters Like the Sea, I Wrote a Short Poem on the Spot" (Tu Fu) **9**:326
"On the Road" (Heaney) **18**:214
"On the Road" (McKay) **2**:205, 220
"On the Road Again" (Dylan) **37**:51
"On the Road Home" (Stevens) **6**:311-12
"On the Road to Delphi" (Herbert)
See "W drodze do Delf"
"On the Road to Woodlawn" (Roethke) **15**:291, 293-95
"On the Same" (Cowper) **40**:101
On the Scale of One to One (Cassian) **17**:6, 9
"On the Ship" (Cavafy) **36**:75
On the Sick-Bed (Tagore)
See *Rogsajyae*
"On the Skeleton of a Hound" (Wright) **36**:279, 335-36, 371, 373
"On the South Coast" (Swinburne) **24**:313, 329
"On the Spring" (Gray)
See "Ode on Spring"
"On the Spur of the Moment" (Tu Fu) **9**:323
"On the Stage of Ghosts a Pale Gleaming" (Mandelstam) **14**:120
"On the Stairs" (Cavafy) **36**:41, 42, 74, 76, 81
"On the Street" (Stone) **53**:257
"On the Subject of Poetry" (Merwin) **45**:92
"On the Subway" (Olds) **22**:314
"On the Sussex Downs" (Teasdale) **31**:333, 379
"On the Tennis Court at Night" (Kinnell) **26**:260
"On the Threshold" (Gozzano) **10**:174
"On the Threshold of His Greatness, the Poet Comes Down with a Sore Throat" (Nemerov) **24**:267
"On the Verge of the Path" (Guest) **55**:183
"On the Victory Gained by Sir George Rodney" (Cowper) **40**:103
"On the Victory Obtained by Blake over the Spaniards" (Marvell) **10**:270-71
On the Waves of the Wireless (Seiler)
See *Na vlnách T. S. F.*
On the Waves of Wireless Telegraphy (Seifert)
See *Na vlnách T. S. F.*
"On the Way" (Robinson) **1**:468; **35**:368
"On the Way" (Sandburg) **41**:341, 364
"On the Way to Lycomedes of Scyrus" (Brodsky)
See "K Likomedu, na Skiros"
"On the Way to School" (Aleixandre) **15**:24
"On the Wide Heath" (Millay) **6**:215, 232, 238
"On the windshield of a new Fiat for James Klosty (who had not made up his mind where to go) and Carolyn Brown" (Cage) **58**:218
"On the Works of Providence" (Wheatley)
See "Thoughts on the Works of Providence"
On the World's Shore (Paz)
See *A la orilla del mundo*
On These I Stand: An Anthology of the Best Poems of Countee Cullen (Cullen) **20**:75-76, 79, 82-83
"On These Islands" (MacNeice) **61**:137
On This Island (Auden)
See "Look, Stranger, on This Island Now"
"On Those That Hated 'The Playboy of the Western World'" (Yeats) **20**:320
"On Torture, a Public Singer" (Belloc) **24**:34
"On Translating Poetry" (Herbert)
See "O tlumaczeniu wierszy"
"On Troy" (Herbert) **50**:18
"On Two Ministers of State" (Belloc) **24**:33, 41
"On Universalism" (Knight) **14**:37-8
"On Virtue" (Wheatley) **3**:361
"On Visiting the Tomb of Burns" (Keats) **1**:314
"On Walking into a Dark Alley" (Ignatow) **34**:274
"On Walking Slowly After an Accident" (Smith) **12**:314, 316
"On Warsaw Critics and Reviewers" (Mickiewicz)
See "O Krytykach i Recenzentach"
"On Watching a World Series Game" (Sanchez) **9**:210, 225
"On Wenlock Edge" (Housman) **2**:180
"On Working White Liberals" (Angelou) **32**:28
"Once" (Celan) **10**:97
Once (Walker) **30**:337, 340, 342, 344-47, 349-50, 352-59, 362, 365
Once Again (Tagore)
See *Punascha*
"Once again the metaphor" (Borges)
See "Otra vez la metáfora"
"Once and Again" (Carruth) **10**:91
"the once and future dead" (Clifton) **17**:19
"Once by the Pacific" (Frost) **1**:221
"Once I Wrote Now and in Other Days" (Amichai) **38**:49
"Once in May" (Levine) **22**:217-18
"Once it was the colour of saying" (Thomas) **52**:264
"Once More At Chartres" (Sarton) **39**:339
"Once More, the Round" (Roethke) **15**:302
"Once upanza time" (Quintana) **36**:267
"The Once-in-Passing" (MacNeice) **61**:121-22
"L'Ondine et le pêcheur" (Gautier) **18**:141
"Une" (Éluard) **38**:71, 84
"I" (Joyce) **22**:138, 144, 158, 162, 164, 166, 168
"The One" (Kavanagh) **33**:64, 120, 138, 162
"One and the same" (Paz)
See "Lo idéntico"
"One Art" (Bishop) **3**:62-3, 66-8; **34**:59, 74-75, 82, 102, 109, 134, 141, 146, 148, 161, 185, 187, 193
"One at One with his Desire" (Ammons) **16**:50
"One by One" (Levine) **22**:218
"One Day" (Brooke) **24**:86
"One Day in Spring" (Sitwell) **3**:311
"One Day We Play a Game" (Cullen) **20**:67
"One Ear to the Ground" (Wagoner) **33**:334
"187" (Quintana) **36**:275
"One Foot in Eden" (Muir) **49**:196, 261-62, 280
One Foot in Eden (Muir) **49**:208, 215, 225, 233, 235, 250, 253, 270, 273, 277, 280, 290, 295
One for the Rose (Levine) **22**:220, 226
"The One Girl at the Boys Party" (Niedecker) **42**:163
"The One Girl at the Boys' Party" (Olds) **22**:311
"One grief of thine" (Bridges) **28**:86
One Handful of Sand (Ishikawa)
See *Ichiaku no suna*
"The 151st Psalm" (Shapiro) **25**:285
One Hundred Poems from the Chinese (Rexroth) **20**:188, 204
100 Selected Poems (Cummings) **5**:86
"164 East 72nd Street" (Merrill) **28**:285
"125th Street" (Hughes) **53**:162
"125th Street and Abomey" (Lorde) **12**:155, 160
"1 Jan." (Ammons) **16**:21
"1 January 1924" (Mandelstam) **14**:121, 134
"One Last Look at the Adige: Verona in the Rain" (Wright) **36**:312
"One Last Look at the Adige: Vienna in the Rain" (Wright) **36**:320
"One Leaf" (Ignatow) **34**:329
"One: Many" (Ammons) **16**:6
"One More" (Carver) **54**:18
"One More Brevity" (Frost) **1**:213
"One More Car Poem for Julie" (Hacker) **47**:107
"One More Round" (Angelou) **32**:2
"One More 'S' in the U.S.A." (Hughes) **53**:115
"One Morning in New Hampshire" (Swenson) **14**:249, 275
"One ne peut me connaître" (Éluard) **38**:73
"One Need Not Be a Chamber to Be Haunted" (Dickinson) **1**:94
"One Night" (Cavafy) **36**:74, 108
"One Night in a Familiar Room" (Ríos) **57**:325
"One Night Stand" (Baraka) **4**:6
"One Night's Bond" (Hagiwara) **18**:168-69
"One O'Clock at Night" (Loy) **16**:312, 327
"One of Many" (Smith) **12**:314, 331, 333
"One of the Rooming Houses" (Doty)
See "One of the Rooming Houses of Heaven"
"One of the Rooming Houses of Heaven" (Doty) **53**:61
"One of Their Gods" (Cavafy) **36**:32, 50, 73, 112
"One of These Nights" (Mahon) **60**:150, 178, 207
"One of Those Springs" (Seifert) **47**:328
"One of Us Must Know (Sooner or Later)" (Dylan) **37**:51
"1.1.87" (Heaney) **18**:258
"One or Two I've Finished" (Stein) **18**:342
"One Perfect Rose" (Parker) **28**:361
"One Person" (Wylie) **23**:304-305, 311, 314, 317-18, 321-24
"One Ralph Blossom Soliloquizes" (Hardy) **8**:124
"The One Remains" (Owen) **19**:368
"One self" (Jackson) **44**:97
"One Should Not Talk to a Skilled Hunter about What is Forbidden by the Buddha" (Snyder) **21**:292
"One Sided Shoot-Out" (Madhubuti) **5**:321, 345
"One Soldier" (Rukeyser) **12**:231
"One Spring Day" (Abse) **41**:3, 5, 8
"One Spring Morning" (Niedecker) **42**:164
"One Springtime" (Storni)
See "En una primavera"
"One Stick Song" (Alexie) **53**:20
One Stick Song (Alexie) **53**:23-24
"One Tennis Shoe" (Silverstein) **49**:349
"The One Thing That Can Save America" (Ashbery) **26**:127, 148
"One Thousand Fearful Words for Fidel Castro" (Ferlinghetti) **1**:187
1x1 (Cummings) **5**:83, 107-08
"One Viceroy Resigns" (Kipling) **3**:181, 186
"One View of the Question" (Kipling) **3**:184
"One Volume Missing" (Dove) **6**:114
One Way Ticket (Hughes) **1**:241, 243, 247, 252, 260-61, 268; **53**:114, 153, 185
"One We Knew" (Hardy) **8**:99, 132
"One Who Used To Beat His Way" (Kinnell) **26**:240
"The One Who Was" (Aleixandre) **15**:4
"One Woman to All Women" (Lawrence) **54**:183
"One Word" (Benn)
See "Ein Wort"
"One Word More" (Browning) **2**:66, 71, 95
"One World" (Tomlinson) **17**:333
"One year" (Illyés)
See "Egy ev"
"One Year" (Olds) **22**:341
"The One-Armed" (Mistral)
See "La manca"
"One-Eye" (Merwin) **45**:28
"One-Eye, Two-Eyes, Three-Eyes" (Sexton) **2**:365
"The One-Eyed King" (Levine) **22**:213
Onegin's Journey (Pushkin) **10**:400-01
"One-Legged Man" (Sassoon) **12**:242, 263
One-Legged on Ice (Abse) **41**:31
"The One-Legged stool" (Komunyakaa) **51**:41
"One's-Self I Sing" (Whitman)
See "Song of Myself"
"The Onion" (Szymborska) **44**:320
"Onion Days" (Sandburg) **41**:226, 234, 239, 274, 349, 351, 365
"Onion Fields" (Francis) **34**:244
"Onirocritique" (Apollinaire) **7**:12

"Only a Curl" (Browning) **6**:24, 30
"Only a Few Left" (Madhubuti) **5**:340
"Only a Little Sleep, a Little Slumber" (Hughes) **7**:154
"Only Child" (Page) **12**:170, 175-76
Only Love (Seifert)
See *Samá láska*
"Only Once I Caught a Glimpse..." (Seifert)
See "Jen jedno jsem spatřil..."
"The Only One" (Hölderlin)
See "Der Einzige"
"Ons As Me Thought" (Wyatt) **27**:316
"The Onset" (Frost) **1**:222; **39**:233
"Ontological Episode of the Asylum" (Carruth) **10**:89
"The Oon Olympian" (MacDiarmid) **9**:197
"Oonts" (Kipling) **3**:158
"The Open Boat" (Levine) **22**:223
"Open Books" (Alexie) **53**:24
Open Closed Open (Amichai) **38**:47-51, 54-56
Open Eye, Open Heart (Ferlinghetti) **1**:186-88
"Open House" (Roethke) **15**:291, 293, 302
Open House (Roethke) **15**:245-46, 248, 250, 256, 259, 282, 287, 290-91, 293-95, 298, 304
"Open It, Write" (Ekeloef) **23**:62, 64
"An Open Letter to George Bush" (Quintana) **36**:272
"Open Rose" (McGuckian) **27**:105
"The Open Sea" (Meredith) **28**:182, 190, 212
"Open Sea" (Neruda) **4**:282
The Open Sea (Masters) **1**:333, 335
The Open Sea (Meredith) **28**:171, 174-75, 177, 181, 187-92, 194, 200-01, 210-11, 213, 215
"Open the Door to Me, O" (Burns) **6**:75
"Open the Gates" (Kunitz) **19**:155, 162, 173-74, 176-77, 186
"Open Windows" (Hacker) **47**:81
The Opening of the Field (Duncan) **2**:103-04, 106, 113-14, 120, 122, 124-25, 127-28
Opening the Hand (Merwin) **45**:97
Openings (Berry) **28**:5, 15-16
"L'Opera di Dante" (Carducci) **46**:55
"An Opera House" (Lowell) **13**:79
"The Operation" (Sexton) **2**:348, 350, 353, 361, 365
"The Operation" (Tomlinson) **17**:360
"Ophélie" (Rimbaud) **3**:283; **57**:255, 283
"Opiário" (Pessoa) **20**:166
Opposites (Wilbur) **51**:243
"Opposition" (Lanier) **50**:56
"Oppositions" (Wright) **14**:379
"Oppositions debate with Mallarmé" (Tomlinson) **17**:338-39
"Oppression" (Hughes) **53**:149
"oppressive chains" (Alurista)
See "Cadenas rotas"
"An Oppressive Climate, a Populous Neighbourhood" (Curnow) **48**:45-46
"Opredelenyie poezii" (Pasternak) **6**:272, 285
"The Optimist's Salutation" (Darío)
See "Salutación del optimista"
"Opulence" (Graham) **59**:150, 177, 182-83
Opus incertum (Ekeloef) **23**:63, 76
Opus incertum II (Ekeloef) **23**:77
Opus Posthumous (Stevens) **6**:306, 339
"Opyt análiza chetyryokhstópnogo yàmba" (Bely) **11**:18
"... Or a Wind" (Birney) **52**:39
Or Else: Poem/Poems, 1968-1974 (Warren) **37**:308, 329, 333, 335, 347, 356, 366, 378, 380
"Or, Solitude" (Davie) **29**:122-24
"Or When Your Sister Sleeps Around for Money" (Knight)
See "The Violent Space (or when your sister sleeps around for money)"
"Oración" (Fuertes) **27**:5, 11, 30
"Oracion" (Neruda) **4**:278
"La oración de la maestra" (Mistral) **32**:208
"Oración para altas horas de la madrugada" (Fuertes) **27**:39
Oracion por Marilyn Monroe y otros poemas (Cardenal) **22**:125
"Oracle" (Heaney) **18**:201, 203
"The Oracle" (Merton) **10**:339
"Oracle over Managua" (Cardenal)
See "Oráculo sobre Managua"
"The Oracles" (Housman) **2**:164
"Les oracles" (Vigny) **26**:369, 403, 405
"Oráculo sobre Managua" (Cardenal) **22**:103-06
"Oraculos" (Cardenal) **22**:131
"Oraison du soir" (Rimbaud) **57**:174, 209-10, 245, 253, 295, 299
"The Oral Tradition" (Boland) **58**:48, 92, 95
Oral Tradition (Sikelianos)
See "Agraphon"
"Orange In" (Stein) **18**:318, 328
"Orange of Midsummer" (Lowell) **13**:97
"The Orange Picker" (Ignatow) **34**:273, 284
"Orange Poem Praising Brown" (Stone) **53**:229
"The Orange Tree" (Levertov) **11**:169
"Orangerie" (Bonnefoy) **58**:130
"Oranges" (Cervantes) **35**:119
"Oranges" (O'Hara) **45**:116, 130, 156, 177, 224
"Oranges: 12 Pastorals" (O'Hara)
See "Oranges"
"Orange-Tree" (Wright) **14**:341
"Oration on Death" (Bryant) **20**:13
The Orators (Auden) **1**:4-5, 8-11, 16, 22, 25, 30-1, 37
"The Orb Weaver" (Francis) **34**:242, 250, 257, 261-62
The Orb Weaver (Francis) **34**:243, 245, 248, 265
"Orbits" (Cassian) **17**:11
"Orchard" (H. D.)
See "Priapus"
"Orchard" (Stone) **53**:216-17
"The Orchard of the Dreaming Pigs" (Wagoner) **33**:350
"The Orchard Pit" (Rossetti) **44**:237
"The Orchid House" (McGuckian) **27**:97
The Order of Nature (Bryant) **20**:5
"Order to View" (MacNeice) **61**:139
"Orders" (Duncan) **2**:125
"The Ordinariness of the Soul" (Herbert)
See "Codziennosc duszy"
"The Ordinary" (Stryk) **27**:208, 214
"An Ordinary Evening in New Haven" (Stevens) **6**:338
"An Ordinary Girl" (Sirkis) **8**:417
"An Ordinary Morning" (Levine) **22**:224
An Ordinary Woman (Clifton) **17**:21, 23-24, 26, 34, 37
"Ordinary Women" (Stevens) **6**:295
Ordinary Words (Stone) **53**:239, 243-49, 252, 255, 259
"The Ordination" (Burns) **6**:83, 88
L'Ordre des Oiseaux (Perse) **23**:254, 256
"Oread" (H. D.) **5**:268, 275, 304
"Gli orecchini" (Montale) **13**:108, 128
"Una oreja" (Storni)
See "La oreja"
"La oreja" (Storni) **33**:240, 259, 262;
"Orestes at Tauris" (Jarrell) **41**:135
"Orestes-Theme" (H. D.) **5**:305
"Organelle" (Swenson) **14**:247
"Organic Bloom" (Kunitz) **19**:148
"Organo ad Libitum" (Curnow) **48**:12, 19, 52-53
"Organs" (Swenson) **14**:276
"L'orgie Parisienne; ou, Paris se Repeuple" (Rimbaud) **3**:281
"Oriana" (Tennyson) **6**:359
"The Orient" (Borges) **32**:58
"Orient and Immortal Wheat" (Walcott) **46**:247
"The Orient Express" (Jarrell) **41**:139, 153, 177, 196, 208
"The Oriental Ballerina" (Dove) **6**:113
Les orientales (Hugo) **17**:45, 50-52, 55, 62-63, 70, 74-76, 87, 90-91
"Oriental phase" (Ungaretti)
See "Fase d'oriente"
Orientations (Elytis)
See *Prosanatolizmí*
"Origin" (Harjo) **27**:64
Origin (Niedecker) **42**:105
An Origin Like Water: Collected Poems 1967-1987 (Boland) **58**:42, 48, 91-92, 98-99
"The Origin of Cities" (Hass) **16**:199
"Original Child Bomb" (Merton) **10**:337
"Original Memory" (Harjo) **27**:68
"The Original Place" (Muir) **49**:265
"Original Sin" (Cisneros) **52**:141
"Original Sin" (Jeffers) **17**:132
"Original Sin" (O'Hara) **45**:162
"Original Sin: A Short Story" (Warren) **37**:285, 287-88, 313, 322-23, 332-33
"The Originators" (Merton) **10**:345
"Origins" (Ignatow) **34**:204
"Origins and History of Consciousness" (Rich) **5**:374
Orillas (Castro)
See *En las orillas del Sar*
Orillas del Sar (Castro)
See *En las orillas del Sar*
"Orinda to Lucasia" (Philips) **40**:312, 325
"Orinda Upon Little Hector Philips" (Philips) **40**:293, 296
"Orion" (Elytis) **21**:118
Orlando furioso di Ludovico Ariosto de Ferrara (Ariosto) **42**:3-4, 7, 8, 9-15, 17-22, 24-5, 27, 29-43, 45, 47-58, 60-4, 73-5, 81, 85-7
"Orlovu" (Pushkin) **10**:409
"Ornières" (Rimbaud) **3**:264; **57**:232, 238, 241, 247, 282, 284
El oro de los tigres (Borges) **22**:79-81, 93, 95; **32**:52, 56, 61, 63, 65-6, 86, 89-91
"Orophernes" (Cavafy) **36**:73, 75
"Orozco's Christ" (Erdrich) **52**:190
The Orphan Angel (Wylie) **23**:329
"The Orphan Reformed" (Smith) **12**:326
"Orphans' New Year's Gifts" (Rimbaud)
See "Les Etrennes des orphelins"
"L'Orphée" (Ronsard) **11**:251
"Orphée" (Valéry) **9**:351
"L'orphelin" (Mallarmé) **4**:202
"Orpheus" (Hope) **56**:292
"Orpheus" (Meredith) **28**:191-92
Orpheus (Hope) **56**:290-92
Orpheus (Rukeyser) **12**:207, 213-14, 220
"Orpheus and Eurydice" (Graham) **59**:173
"Orpheus and Eurydice" (Noyes) **27**:118, 134
"Orpheus and Eurydice" (Shvarts) **50**:142
"Orpheus' Dream" (Muir) **49**:280
"Orpheus. Eurydike. Hermes" (Rilke) **2**:295
"Orphic Scenario" (Nemerov) **24**:257, 294-97
"Orphische Zellen" (Benn) **35**:70
"L'orto" (Montale) **13**:109-10, 113, 121-22, 133, 151
"Osgar" (Pushkin) **10**:407
"Osiris and Set" (Duncan) **2**:103
"Osiris, Come to Iris" (Thomas) **2**:402
Osiris Jones (Aiken) **26**:12, 29
Osm dnů (Seifert) **47**:325, 334
"Osobny zeszyt" (Milosz) **8**:186-87, 199, 204
Osorio (Coleridge)
See *Remorse*
Ossi di seppia (Montale) **13**:103, 105-07, 109, 112-17, 119, 122, 126-27, 131, 133-34, 139, 141, 143, 160, 162-66
"Ossian's Grave" (Jeffers) **17**:117
"Ostanovka v pustyne" (Brodsky) **9**:3, 5, 7
"Osterinsel" (Benn) **35**:8, 33, 35, 36, 49, 50, 73, 74, 75, 76, 77
"L'ostessa di Gaby" (Carducci) **46**:88
"Ostriches & Grandmothers" (Baraka) **4**:15
"osynlig närvaro" (Ekeloef) **23**:88-92
"The Other" (Borges)
See "El otro, el mismo"
"The Other" (Dickey) **40**:175, 184, 204-6, 210
"The Other" (Sexton) **2**:365
"Other" (Stone) **53**:222-23

"The Other" (Thomas) **53**:269, 297, 305, 308-9, 322, 329, 337
"The Other" (Wagoner) **33**:357
"Other Countries" (Cisneros) **52**:153, 161
"Other Days (1900-1910)" (Sandburg) **41**:227
Other Exiles (Brathwaite) **56**:34, 36, 49, 65, 88
"The Other Friend" (Storni)
See "La otra amiga"
The Other Half (Wright) **14**:349, 355-56, 362, 366
"The other, himself" (Borges)
See "El otro, el mismo"
"The Other Noah" (Elytis) **21**:123
"The Other Oedipus" (Muir) **49**:235, 278
"The Other One" (Borges)
See "El otro, el mismo"
"The Other One" (Mistral)
See "La otra"
"The Other Side" (Heaney) **18**:205
The other, the same (Borges)
See *El otro, el mismo*
"The Other Tiger" (Borges)
See "El otro tigre"
"Other Times Have Come" (Yevtushenko) **40**:347
"Other Travellers to the River" (Merwin) **45**:45
"The Other Whitman" (Borges)
See "El otro Whitman"
"Others" (Guest) **55**:200-201
"Others I Am Not the First" (Housman) **2**:179, 195
"Otherwise" (Kenyon) **57**:12, 18, 34, 38, 40-41
"Otherwise" (Stone) **53**:252
Otherwise (Kenyon) **57**:12-13, 15-16, 18-19, 21, 25-26, 28, 34, 38, 41, 44-46
Otho the Great (Keats) **1**:279
Otkuda vy? (Yevtushenko) **40**:364
"Otoño" (Neruda) **4**:290
"Otoño" (Paz) **48**:176
El otoño (Guillén) **35**:231
"El otoño: isla" (Guillén) **35**:153, 156, 157, 182
"La otra" (Mistral) **32**:183
"La otra amiga" (Storni) **33**:245
"Otra vez la metáfora" (Borges) **32**:125
"El otro" (Borges)
See "El otro, el mismo"
"El otro, el mismo" (Borges) **22**:74
El otro, el mismo (Borges) **22**:71, 73-4, 95-6, 98, 100; **32**:38-40, 56, 58, 64-6, 69, 93, 95, 111, 117, 139
"Otro poema de los dones" (Borges) **32**:38
"El otro tigre" (Borges) **22**:73, 96-7; **32**:43, 66, 139
"El otro Whitman" (Borges) **32**:100
"Otrok" (Tsvetaeva) **14**:315-16
"Otros poemas" (Parra) **39**:272
Otros poemas (Parra) **39**:279, 286-87
"Otryvok-A Fragment" (Lermontov) **18**:302
"The Otter" (Heaney) **18**:217, 239, 245
"An Otter" (Hughes) **7**:136, 140
"Où es-tu" (Péret) **33**:207-08, 215
"Là où retombe la flèche" (Bonnefoy) **58**:150
"L'Ouest derrière soi perdu" (Char) **56**:155
"Ou'est-ce pour nous, mon coeur . . ." (Rimbaud) **57**:250
"Ougadougou" (Brathwaite) **56**:29, 85
"Ouija" (Plath) **37**:208-10, 213, 236
"Our Bodies" (Levertov) **11**:169
"Our Bog Is Dood" (Smith) **12**:331, 333
"our bread" (Alurista)
See "el pan nuestro"
"Our Cabal" (Behn) **13**:7, 20
"Our Country" (Thoreau) **30**:287
Our Dead Behind Us (Lorde) **12**:137-39, 141-43, 148, 154-55, 157-58
"Our English Friends" (Harper) **21**:198
"Our Father" (Parra)
See "Padre nuestro"
"Our Forefathers Literary" (Birney) **52**:28
"Our Forward Shadows" (Swenson) **14**:276
"Our Friends in Jail" (Bissett) **14**:7
"Our Grandmothers" (Angelou) **32**:28
Our Ground Time Here Will Be Brief (Kumin) **15**:214, 217, 221
"Our Kind of a Man" (Riley) **48**:301
"Our Lady of the Rocks" (Rossetti) **44**:172, 214
"Our Lady of the Sackcloth" (Kipling) **3**:183
"Our Lady of Youghal" (Ní Chuilleanáin) **34**:383
"Our Land" (Hughes) **53**:84
"Our Long Sweet Sommers Day" (Raleigh) **31**:238-39
"Our Lord and Our Lady" (Belloc) **24**:5
"Our Mother Pocahontas" (Lindsay) **23**:288
"Our Mothers" (Rossetti) **7**:286
"Our Mothers Depart" (Yevtushenko) **40**:343
"Our Names" (Ortiz) **17**:245
"Our Need" (Walker) **20**:283
"Our Prayer of Thanks" (Sandburg) **2**:316; **41**:334
"Our Storm" (Pasternak) **6**:271
"Our Whole Life" (Rich) **5**:391
"Ourselves or Nothing" (Forché) **10**:137, 143-44, 148, 154, 158-59, 161, 168
"Ourselves We Do Inter with Sweet Derision" (Dickinson) **1**:102
"Out" (Hughes) **7**:123, 149
"Out in the Dark" (Thomas) **53**:271-72, 274, 309, 349
"Out Is Out" (Nash) **21**:268
"Out of Debt" (McKay) **2**:222
"Out of My Head" (Swenson) **14**:255, 266, 282
"Out of Superstition" (Pasternak)
See "From Superstition"
"Out of the Aegean" (Elytis) **21**:118
"Out of the Cradle Endlessly Rocking" (Whitman) **3**:378, 382, 391-92, 397, 401
"Out of the Rainbow End" (Sandburg) **41**:303
"Out of the Sea, Early" (Swenson) **14**:264
"Out of the Sighs" (Thomas) **52**:228
"Out of the Watercolored Window, When You Look" (Schwartz) **8**:301
"Out of Three of four in a Room" (Amichai) **38**:42
"Out of Work" (Hughes) **53**:139-40
"Out on the Lawn I Lie in Bed..." (Auden) **1**:22
"OUT ON THE TOWN JOY RIDIN" (Bissett) **14**:31
"Out, Out—" (Frost) **1**:227
"Out Picking Up Corn" (Bly) **39**:87
"Out the Alley Our Soul Awaits Us" (Alurista) **34**:40
"Out to Old Aunt Mary's" (Riley) **48**:328, 336
"Out to the Hard Road" (Lorde) **12**:138
"Out Upon It" (Suckling) **30**:137, 156
"Out Walking" (Zagajewski) **27**:396
"Outbound" (Carman) **34**:213
"Outcast" (McKay) **2**:213, 217, 221
The Outcasts (Sitwell) **3**:321
"The Outcome of Mr. Buck's Superstition" (Nash) **21**:267
"The Outcome of the Matter: The Sun" (Piercy) **29**:326
"The Outdoor Concert" (Gunn) **26**:195, 208
Outdoor Show (Cassian) **17**:6
"Outer and Inner" (Meredith) **60**:298
"The Outer Banks" (Rukeyser) **12**:224
"Outer Egypt" (Mackey) **49**:4
Outlantish (Mackey) **49**:17
"The Outlaw" (Heaney) **18**:200
"Outlines" (Lorde) **12**:137
"Outside a Gate" (Lowell) **13**:94
"Outside Eden" (Muir) **49**:264
"Outside Fargo, North Dakota" (Wright) **36**:300, 344
"Outside History" (Boland) **58**:8, 17, 48, 51, 55-56, 59, 61, 82, 85, 87
Outside History: Selected Poems, 1980-90 (Boland) **58**:8, 12-21, 26, 29-30, 33, 47-49, 51, 67, 84-85, 87-89, 91-92, 96, 98
"Outside my window" (Viereck) **27**:278
"Outside or Underneath?" (Silverstein) **49**:332
"outside, over there" (Alurista)
See "allá ajüera"
"Outside the Crowd" (Meredith) **60**:263
"Outside the Diner" (Gunn) **26**:214
"Outside the Gates" (Goodison) **36**:154
"Outside the House" (Cavafy) **36**:74
"Outside the Monastery of Bologna" (Carducci)
See "Furi alla Certosa di Bologna"
"Outside the Operating Room of the Sex-Change Doctor" (Olds) **22**:316
"The Outskirts of the Capital" (Mickiewicz) **38**:168
"Ouvriers" (Rimbaud) **57**:241, 243, 275
"Oveja descarriada" (Storni) **33**:274;
"The Oven Bird" (Frost) **1**:222; **39**:253
"Ovenstone" (Guillén) **23**:102
"Over 2,000 Illustrations" (Bishop)
See "Over 2,000 Illustrations and a Complete Concordance"
"Over 2,000 Illustrations and a Complete Concordance" (Bishop) **3**:67; **34**:54, 78, 97, 108, 113, 187
Over All the Obscene Boundaries: European Poems & Transitions (Ferlinghetti) **1**:183-85
"Over Brooklyn Bridge" (Tomlinson) **17**:359
"Over Cities" (Milosz) **8**:186
"Over Denver Again" (Ginsberg) **4**:57
"Over Sir John's Hill" (Thomas) **2**:395, 404; **52**:224, 259, 266-67, 270, 274-76, 316-17
"Over St. John's Hill" (Thomas)
See "Over Sir John's Hill"
"Over these brookes" (Sidney) **32**:266
"Over Troubled Water" (Sarton) **39**:363
"Over Us If (as what Was Dusk Becomes" (Cummings) **5**:109
"Overcrowding" (Baca) **41**:38
"Overdues" (Silverstein) **49**:333
"The Overgrown Pasture" (Lowell) **13**:60, 78, 85
"Overheard" (Kipling) **3**:193
"Overheard" (Levertov) **11**:160
"Overland to the Islands" (Levertov) **11**:188, 192, 196
Overland to the Islands (Levertov) **11**:166, 188, 202
"Overlooking the River Stour" (Hardy) **8**:116-17
"Overnights" (Walker) **30**:343
"Overpopulation" (Ferlinghetti) **1**:167, 175, 187
"Overture to a Dance of Locomotives" (Williams) **7**:345, 410
"Overtures to Death" (Day Lewis) **11**:144
Overtures to Death and Other Poems (Day Lewis) **11**:127-30, 144
"Ovid in Exile" (Graves) **6**:164
"Ovid in Tomis" (Mahon) **60**:146, 151, 178, 188, 196-97
"Ovid, Old Buddy, I Would Discourse with You a While" (Carruth) **10**:88
Ovnis' (Cardenal)
See *Los ovnis de oro*
Los ovnis de oro (Cardenal) **22**:126, 132
"Owatari Bridge" (Hagiwara)
See "Ōwatari-bashi"
"Ōwatari-bashi" (Hagiwara) **18**:183
"Owen Ahern and His Dancers" (Yeats) **20**:328
"The Owl" (Thomas) **53**:295, 317, 320
"The Owl in the Sarcophagus" (Stevens) **6**:304
"The Owl King" (Dickey) **40**:149-50, 155-56, 163-64, 166, 176-77, 180-81, 183, 185, 190, 201, 230
"Owl Song" (Atwood) **8**:25
Owl's Clover (Stevens) **6**:297-98, 317-20
"Owl's Song" (Hughes) **7**:160-61
"Ownership" (Reese) **29**:336, 344
"The Ox" (Carducci)
See "Il bove"
"The Ox Tamer" (Whitman) **3**:377
"The Oxen" (Hardy) **8**:112, 121

"Oxen: Ploughing at Fiesole" (Tomlinson) **17**:311
"Oxford" (Auden) **1**:30
"Oysters" (Heaney) **18**:217, 239, 241
"Oysters" (Sexton) **2**:365
"Oysters" (Snyder) **21**:292
"Ozone" (Dove) **6**:121-23
P. 1 (Pindar)
See *Pythian 1*
P. 2 (Pindar)
See *Pythian 2*
P. 3 (Pindar)
See *Pythian 3*
P. 4 (Pindar)
See *Pythian 4*
P. 5 (Pindar)
See *Pythian 5*
P. 6 (Pindar)
See *Pythian 6*
P. 8 (Pindar)
See *Pythian 8*
"P. N. in the heart" (Paz)
See "Pablo Neruda en el corazón"
"Pablo Casals" (MacLeish) **47**:197
"Pablo Neruda en el corazón" (Paz) **48**:183
"A Pablo Picasso" (Éluard) **38**:71, 86
Pacchiarotto (Browning) **2**:71
"Pachuchan Miners" (Birney) **52**:22, 99
"The Pachuco's Wedding" (Quintana) **36**:254
"Pacific Door" (Birney) **52**:35, 92
"Pacific Gazer" (Warren) **37**:331
"Pacific Letter" (Ondaatje) **28**:316
"A Pacific State" (Milosz) **8**:205
"A Packet of Letters" (Bogan) **12**:94
"The Paddiad" (Kavanagh) **33**:62, 74, 79, 95-6, 102, 111, 118
"The Paddiad or The Devil as a Patron of Irish Letters" (Kavanagh) **33**:86
"Padre nuestro" (Parra) **39**:272, 301
Paean 8 (Pindar) **19**:396
"Paean to Place" (Niedecker) **42**:96, 99, 104-5, 132, 137
"Paesaggio I" (Pavese) **13**:204, 212, 220, 225-26
"Paesaggio II" (Pavese) **13**:212
"Paesaggio III" (Pavese) **13**:212
"Paesaggio V" (Pavese) **13**:212
"Paesaggio VI" (Pavese) **13**:228
"Paesaggio VII" (Pavese) **13**:204, 212
"Paesaggio VIII" (Pavese) **13**:212, 230
"Paestum" (Dickey) **40**:254
"The Pagan Isms" (McKay) **2**:219-20
"Pagan Prayer" (Cullen) **20**:65, 72
"Page d'ascendants pour l'an 1964" (Char) **56**:196, 199
"Page of Gaspé" (Birney) **52**:21
A Pageant, and Other Poems (Rossetti) **7**:270
The Pageant of Seasons (Anonymous)
See *Rtusamhāra*
Pages from Parra (Parra)
See *Hojas de Parra*
"Pagett, M. P." (Kipling) **3**:190
"La página blanca" (Darío) **15**:103-04
"Página musical" (Storni) **33**:294;
"Página para recordaral coronel Suárez, vencedor en Junín" (Borges) **32**:107
Paginas (Jiménez) **7**:208, 212
"The Pahty" (Dunbar) **5**:116, 119, 122-23, 146
Paid on Both Sides (Auden) **1**:5, 8, 20, 30, 34
"The Pail" (Bly) **39**:29
"Pain and Time Strive Not" (Morris) **55**:340
"Pain for a Daughter" (Sexton) **2**:363
"Pain Tells You Want to Wear" (McGuckian) **27**:103
"The Pains of Sleep" (Coleridge) **11**:41, 44; **39**:164, 170, 176, 179, 224-25
"The Painted Cup" (Bryant) **20**:23
"Painted Head" (Ransom) **61**:301-3
Painted Lace and Other Pieces (1914-1937) (Stein) **18**:341
"Painted Steps" (Gallagher) **9**:45
"The Painter" (Ashbery) **26**:112, 167
"Painter" (Herbert)
See "Malarz"
"The Painter Dreaming in the Scholar's House" (Nemerov) **24**:285, 300
The Painter Went Poor into the World (Seifert)
See *Šel malíř chudě do světa*
"The Painters" (Kenyon) **57**:45
"The Painting" (Williams) **7**:394
"Painting the North San Juan School" (Snyder) **21**:300
"A Pair of Blue Eyes" (Moore) **49**:122
"Pairing Time Anticipated" (Cowper) **40**:124
"Paisaje" (Parra) **39**:276
"Paisaje de la multitud que orina" (García Lorca) **3**:140
"Paisaje de la multitud que vomita" (García Lorca) **3**:140
"Paisaje del amor muerto" (Storni) **33**:239;
"Paisaje del corozon" (Jiménez) **7**:199
"Paisaje después de una batalla" (Neruda) **4**:309
"Paisajes de la Patagonia" (Mistral) **32**:174
"La Paix à la campagne" (Éluard) **38**:91
"Los Pájaros Anidan" (Fuertes) **27**:51
"Pajaros sin descenso" (Aleixandre) **15**:19-21
"La pajita" (Mistral) **32**:180
"Palabras" (Aleixandre) **15**:39
"Las palabras" (Paz) **1**:358
"Las palabras del poeta" (Aleixandre) **15**:41
"Palabras en el trópico" (Guillén) **23**:106
"Palabras manidas a la luna" (Storni) **33**:295;
"Palabras serenas" (Mistral) **32**:159, 174
"Palace" (Apollinaire)
See "Palais"
"The Palace" (Ondaatje) **28**:337
"The Palace of Art" (Tennyson) **6**:353, 359-60, 370, 375, 378-80, 382, 409, 412
"The Palace of Pan" (Swinburne) **24**:313
"The Palace of the Babies" (Stevens) **6**:293
"Palais" (Apollinaire) **7**:45-6, 48
"Palais des Arts" (Glück) **16**:130, 150
"Palamon and Arcite" (Chaucer)
See "Knight's Tale"
Palātakā (Tagore) **8**:415
"Palau" (Benn) **35**:8, 33, 35-6, 49-50, 73-7
"A Pale Arrangement of Hands" (Song) **21**:334, 341-42
"Pale Horse" (Hagiwara) **18**:176-77
"Pale, Intent Noontide" (Montale)
See "Meriggiare pallido e assorto"
"The Pale Panther" (MacNeice) **61**:175
"Palimpsest" (Komunyakaa) **51**:63
"Pâline" (Apollinaire) **7**:48
"Palinodia al marchese Gino Capponi" (Leopardi) **37**:92-93, 103, 105
"Palladium" (Arnold) **5**:8
"Pallas Athene" (Masters) **1**:344
"Palm" (Valéry)
See "Palme"
"Palm and Pine" (Kipling) **3**:179
"Palme" (Valéry) **9**:363, 365, 367, 393-94
"Palo Alto: The Marshes" (Hass) **16**:218
"Una paloma" (Storni) **33**:239;
La paloma de vuelo popular: Elegiás (Guillén) **23**:100, 124, 128, 133
"Pals" (Sandburg) **2**:303
"Paltry Nude" (Stevens) **6**:295
"The Paltry Nude Starts on a Spring Voyage" (Stevens) **6**:295
"Pamiatnik" (Pushkin)
See "Pamjatnik"
"Pamjatnik" (Pushkin) **10**:408, 412, 415
Pamphilia to Amphilanthus (Wroth) **38**:242-47, 249-51, 254-56, 258-59, 262, 264, 268, 275, 296-300, 304-5, 307-11, 313-19, 324, 328, 332
"Pan" (Hugo) **17**:91
"Pan" (Mistral) **32**:160
"Pan" (Riley) **48**:328
"Pan" (Sikelianos) **29**:369
"Pan and Luna" (Browning) **2**:88-9
"Pan and Thalassius" (Swinburne) **24**:315
Pan Cogito (Herbert) **50**:5, 7, 9, 19-20, 22, 25, 36-37, 39-40, 42
"Pan Cogito a dlugoniecznosc" (Herbert) **50**:36
"Pan Cogito a mysl czysta" (Herbert) **50**:37-38
"Pan Cogito a poeta w pewnym wieku" (Herbert) **50**:41
"Pan Cogito a pop" (Herbert) **50**:39
"Pan Cogito a ruch mysli" (Herbert) **50**:38-39
"Pan Cogito biada nad maloscia snów" (Herbert) **50**:38
"Pan Cogito mysli o powrocie . . ." (Herbert) **50**:37
"Pan Cogito o cnocie" (Herbert) **50**:23, 39
"Pan Cogito o magii" (Herbert) **50**:39
"Pan Cogito o postawie wyprostowanej" (Herbert) **50**:14, 21, 38-39
"Pan Cogito o potrzebie scislosci" (Herbert) **50**:40
"Pan Cogito obserwuje w lustrze swoja twarz" (Herbert) **50**:37
"Pan Cogito obserwuje zmarlego przjaciela" (Herbert) **50**:39
"Pan Cogito oponiada o kuszeniu Spinozy" (Herbert) **50**:41, 45
"Pan Cogito rozmysla o cierpieniu" (Herbert) **50**:37
"Pan Cogito rozwaza róznice miedzy glosem ludzkim a glosem przyrody" (Herbert) **50**:9
"Pan Cogito szuka rady" (Herbert) **50**:41
"Pan Cogito z Maria Rasputin-Próba Kontaktu" (Herbert) **50**:41
"Pan Cogito-Powrót" (Herbert) **50**:40
"el pan nuestro" (Alurista) **34**:35
Pan Tadeusz; czyli, Ostatni zajazd na Litwie (Mickiewicz) **38**:149, 160-61, 169-71, 180-82, 185-88, 192, 194-203, 205-7, 210, 212-16, 218-20, 231, 233, 237
"Pan with Us" (Frost) **39**:231, 246
"Pana Cogito przygody z muzyka" (Herbert) **50**:40
"Pana/Ramas" (Cruz) **37**:17
"Panamá" (Guillén) **23**:126
"Panchishe vaisakh" (Tagore) **8**:415
"A Panegerick to Sir Lewis Pemberton" (Herrick) **9**:102
"A Panegyrick on the Dean in the Person of a Lady in the North" (Swift) **9**:262, 274, 295
"Panegyrique de la Renommée" (Ronsard) **11**:243
"Pangloss's Song" (Wilbur) **51**:191, 301
"The Pangolin" (Moore) **4**:235; **49**:99, 155, 160
Panic: A Play in Verse (MacLeish) **47**:134, 139-40, 150-51, 241-42, 255
"Panicz i dziewczyna" (Mickiewicz) **38**:153
Panno święta (Mickiewicz) **38**:197
"Panorama" (Éluard) **38**:84
"Panorama" (Guillén) **35**:154
"Panorama ceigo de Nueva York" (García Lorca) **3**:141
"Panoramas" (Cruz) **37**:30-1
Pansies (Lawrence) **54**:171, 173, 175, 185-86, 220, 224, 231, 248-49
"La pantera" (Borges) **32**:90
"The panther" (Borges)
See "La pantera"
"Panther" (Hughes) **53**:148
The Panther and the Lash: Poems of Our Times (Hughes) **1**:251-52, 257-58, 260, 262, 268; **53**:94, 110-11, 117, 147-53
"Pantomime" (Verlaine) **2**:430; **32**:348-51, 353, 364, 390
"Paolo e Virginia" (Pavese) **13**:221
"The Papa and Mama Dance" (Sexton) **2**:349, 352-53
"Papà beve sempre" (Pavese) **13**:214
"Papa Love Baby" (Smith) **12**:315, 322, 325-26, 343
"El papagayo" (Mistral) **32**:180
"Paper and Sticks" (Thomas) **52**:239-40
"Paper Cities" (Schnackenberg) **45**:337-38

"The Paper Cutter" (Ignatow) **34**:273
"The Paper Nautilus" (Moore) **4**:255
"The Paper on the Floor" (Bukowski) **18**:3
"The Paper Wind Mill" (Lowell) **13**:78
"The Paperweight" (Schnackenberg) **45**:342
"Le papillon" (Lamartine) **16**:278
Papo Got His Gun (Cruz) **37**:16, 25, 29
"Pappel" (Benn) **35**:49
"Par la bouche de l'engoulevent" (Char) **56**:134
Para las seis cuerdas (Borges) **22**:71; **32**:86-7
"Para un mejor amor" (Dalton) **36**:131
"Para una calle del Oeste" (Borges) **32**:39
"Parable" (Wilbur) **51**:188, 192
"Parable of Cervantes and Don Quixote" (Borges) **32**:66
"Parable of the Hostages" (Glück) **16**:171
"The Parable of the Old Man and the Young" (Owen) **19**:335, 354, 356, 359, 370
"The Parabolic Ballad" (Yevtushenko) **40**:343
Paracelsus (Browning) **2**:26-31, 34, 42-3, 48, 65-6, 73, 82, 91-3, 96
"Parachutes, My Love, Could Carry Us Higher" (Guest) **55**:211, 232
"Parade" (Hughes) **53**:190
"Parade" (Rimbaud) **57**:241, 247, 275, 278, 296
"Parade of Painters" (Swenson) **14**:253
"Parades Parades" (Walcott) **46**:234, 274
"The Paradigm" (Tate) **50**:243
"Paradis Perdu" (Nishiwaki) **15**:237
"Paradise" (Gallagher) **9**:64
"Paradise" (Glück) **16**:161
"Paradise" (Herbert) **4**:114, 130
"Paradise" (Mistral)
See "Paraíso"
Paradise Lost (Milton) **19**:193-200, 203-12, 219, 224, 234-36, 238, 240-49, 252, 254, 258; **29**:194-292
"Paradise of Tears" (Bryant) **20**:10
"The Paradise of the Theologians" (Herbert)
See "Raj teologów"
"Paradise on the Roofs" (Pavese) **13**:204
Paradise Regain'd (Milton)
See *Paradise Regained*
Paradise Regained (Milton) **19**:204-06, 208, 214-16, 219; **29**:212, 218, 244, 261, 266-68
"Paradise Saved" (Hope) **56**:284
'Paradise': Selected Poems (Shvarts) **50**:140, 146-47
Paradiso (Dante) **21**:49-50, 53-5, 57-8, 67, 69, 72, 75-7, 81-2, 92, 94, 96, 103-06, 109-11
"Paradox" (Francis) **34**:258
"Paradox" (Lowell) **13**:85
The Paradox (Noyes) **27**:138
"Paradox of Time" (Warren) **37**:326
"Les Parages d'Alsace" (Char) **56**:118
"The Paragon" (Patmore) **59**:228
"Paragraphs" (Carruth) **10**:74-5, 83, 85
"Paragraphs from a Daybook" (Hacker) **47**:117
"Paraíso" (Mistral) **32**:181
"Parajaya sangīt" (Tagore) **8**:405
"Paralipomeni della Batracomiomachia" (Leopardi) **37**:103
Paralipomeni della Batracomiomachia (Leopardi) **37**:91-97, 122
Parallel Destinies (Cassian) **17**:6
Parallèlement (Verlaine) **2**:414, 416-17, 419, 425-26; **32**:359, 366, 378, 385-86
"Paralysis" (Brooke) **24**:56, 77
"Paralytic" (Plath) **1**:391; **37**:232, 258
"Paranoia in Crete" (Corso) **33**:6, 35
"Paranoid" (Page) **12**:175
"Paraphrase" (Crane) **3**:102
Paraphrases (Surrey) **59**:297
"The Parasceve, or Preparation" (Herrick) **9**:117, 119
"Paratile of a Certain Virgin" (Parker) **28**:348
"The Parcel" (Boland) **58**:49
"Parchiarotto" (Browning) **2**:63, 71, 75
"Pardners" (Brown) **55**:110
"Pardon" (Éluard) **38**:85-86
"The Pardon" (Wilbur) **51**:188, 223, 266
"Pardon Keeps the Sun" (Ignatow) **34**:286, 313
"Pardoner's Prologue" (Chaucer) **19**:26, 46
The Pardoner!s Prologue (Chaucer) **58**:365, 368
"Pardoner's Tale" (Chaucer) **19**:13, 30, 46, 49, 51-2, 68
"Paréntesis pasional" (Borges) **22**:92
"Parents" (Meredith) **28**:180, 208
"The Parents: People Like Our Marriage, Maxie and Andrew" (Brooks) **7**:80
"Parfum exotique" (Baudelaire) **1**:45
"Parfum exotique" (Char) **56**:197
"Paring the Apple" (Tomlinson) **17**:331
"Paris" (Corso) **33**:41
"Paris" (Ondaatje) **28**:298-99
"Paris" (Stryk) **27**:214
"Paris" (Vigny) **26**:402, 411-12
"Paris, 7 a.m." (Bishop) **34**:78-79
"París, 1856" (Borges) **32**:114
"Paris and Helen" (Schwartz) **8**:311
"Paris at Nightfall" (Baudelaire)
See "Le crépuscule du soir"
"Paris in the Snow" (Senghor) **25**:241
Paris Spleen (Baudelaire)
See *Petits poèmes en prose: Le spleen de Paris*
"A Parisian Dream" (Baudelaire)
See "Rêve parisien"
"Parisian Orgy or Paris Repopulated" (Rimbaud) **57**:246
The Parisian Prowler (Baudelaire)
See *Petits poèmes en prose: Le spleen de Paris*
"Parisien, mon frère" (Verlaine) **32**:375
"Parisina" (Byron) **16**:109
"The Park" (Stryk) **27**:211
"Park Bench" (Hughes) **1**:242
"The Parklands" (Smith) **12**:317
Parlement (Chaucer)
See *Parlement of Foules*
Parlement of Foules (Chaucer) **19**:10, 12, 20-3, 38, 74
"Parle-moi" (Péret) **33**:231
"Parleying with Charles Avison" (Browning) **2**:83
"Parleying with Gerard de Lairesse" (Browning) **2**:81, 83, 86
Parleyings with Certain People of Importance in Their Day (Browning) **2**:64, 85, 95-6
"Parlez-vous français" (Schwartz) **8**:302-03
"Parliament Hill Fields" (Plath) **1**:391
Parliament of Fowls (Chaucer)
See *Parlement of Foules*
"Parlour-Piece" (Hughes) **7**:140
"Parnell's Funeral" (Yeats) **20**:326, 348
"Parodos" (Glück) **16**:159-62
"Parola" (Quasimodo) **47**:297, 301-2
"La Parole" (Éluard) **38**:69, 83-84
"Le parole" (Montale) **13**:134
"La Parole aux Oricous" (Césaire) **25**:12
La parole en archipel (Char) **56**:113-15, 120, 138, 149-52, 154, 156, 161, 167, 176, 184, 202
"Paroles sur la dune" (Hugo) **17**:64
"A Parrot" (Sarton) **39**:345
"A Parrot at Sea" (Shvarts) **50**:141
"Parrots" (Wright) **14**:348
"The Parrots at Karekare" (Curnow) **48**:14
"The Parrott" (Mistral)
See "El papagayo"
"Parsifal" (Verlaine) **32**:341
"Parsley" (Dove) **6**:105, 110
"The Parson's Daughter and the Seminarist" (Bely) **11**:3
The Parson!s Prologue (Chaucer) **58**:368
"Parson's Tale" (Chaucer) **19**:37, 45, 47
The Parson!s Tale (Chaucer) **58**:235, 246, 266-67
A Part (Berry) **28**:4, 9-10
"Part of a Bird" (Cassian) **17**:4, 12-13
"Part of a Letter" (Wilbur) **51**:187
"Part of a True Story" (Hacker) **47**:82, 87
"A Part of Speech" (Brodsky)
See "Cast rěci"
A Part of Speech (Brodsky)
See *Cast rěci*
"Part of the Doctrine" (Baraka) **4**:18
"Part of the Seventh Epistle of the First Book of Horace Imitated and Addressed to the Earl of Oxford" (Swift) **9**:296
"Part of the Vigil" (Merrill) **28**:221, 224
"Part Song" (Wagoner) **33**:326, 370, 372
Partage formel (Char) **56**:112, 121, 132, 164
"Parted" (Dunbar) **5**:125, 140
"Párthen" (Cavafy) **36**:39, 40, 86
"Partial Accounts" (Meredith) **28**:205, 215
Partial Accounts: New and Selected Poems (Meredith) **28**:211-16
"Partial Comfort" (Parker) **28**:362
"Partial Enchantments of the Quixote" (Borges)
See "Magias parciales del Quijote"
"Partial Magic in the Quixote" (Borges)
See "Magias parciales del Quijote"
"Partida" (Storni) **33**:246;
"Parting" (Ammons) **16**:63
"Parting" (Arnold) **5**:43, 55
"The Parting" (Harper) **21**:194
"The Parting" (Li Po) **29**:140
"Parting at Dawn" (Ransom) **61**:301, 307, 309
"Parting Gift" (Wylie) **23**:321
"Parting, Without a Sequel" (Ransom) **61**:288, 307
Partitur (Ekeloef) **23**:68-9, 78
"Partly from the Greek" (Belloc) **24**:32
"The Partner" (Roethke) **15**:256
"The Partner's Desk" (McGuckian) **27**:105
Parts of a World (Stevens) **6**:299, 311, 318
"A Part-Sequence for Change" (Duncan) **2**:103
"Parturition" (Loy) **16**:313-14, 318, 320, 325, 329, 333
"The Party" (Dunbar)
See "The Pahty"
"Party on Shipboard" (Oppen) **35**:342
"The Party Wall" (Ní Chuilleanáin) **34**:361
"Les pas" (Valéry) **9**:366, 374, 396
Pasado en claro (Paz) **1**:369, 371-72, 374; **48**:174, 188, 245, 258, 273
"Pascuas sangrientas de 1956" (Guillén) **23**:128
"El Paseo de Julio" (Borges) **32**:60
"Pasión" (Storni) **33**:239, 269, 283;
Pasión de la tierra (Aleixandre) **15**:3, 10, 18, 29-32, 34, 40
"Pasiphae" (Hope) **56**:298-99
"Paso a la aurora" (Guillén) **35**:228, 234
"Pass on by" (Guillén)
See "Sigue"
Pass th Food Release th Spirit Book (Bissett) **14**:15-16, 24
"Passage" (Ammons) **16**:6
"Passage" (Crane) **3**:82
"Passage" (Levertov) **11**:202
"Passage" (Okigbo) **7**:223-24, 231, 236-39, 248-49, 251, 255
"Passage de l'oiseau divin" (Breton) **15**:49
"Passage to India" (Whitman) **3**:378, 394-98
Le Passager du transatlantique (Péret) **33**:223, 230
"Passagers de seconde classe et leurs cheveux" (Péret) **33**:230
"Passages 13" (Duncan) **2**:116
"Passages 21" (Duncan) **2**:116
"Passages 25" (Duncan) **2**:25
"Passages 26" (Duncan) **2**:116
"Passages 27" (Duncan) **2**:116
"Passages 29" (Duncan) **2**:116
"Passages 31" (Duncan) **2**:117
"Passages 35 (Tribunals)" (Duncan) **2**:116, 118
"Passages 36" (Duncan) **2**:115-17
The Passages of Joy (Gunn) **26**:208-209, 211-212, 214, 216-217, 220, 230-231
"Le Passe" (Hugo) **17**:64
"La Passe de Lyon" (Char) **56**:151
"Passe forth my wonted cryes" (Wyatt) **27**:362

"Passer mortuus est" (Millay) **6**:228
"A Passer-By" (Bridges) **28**:67, 70
"Passers-By" (Sandburg) **41**:340
"Passers-By on a Snowy Night" (Warren) **37**:380
"Passing by San Guido" (Carducci)
See "Davanti San Guido"
"Passing Chao-ling Again" (Tu Fu) **9**:322
"The Passing Cloud" (Smith) **12**:339
"Passing Losses On" (Frost) **1**:200
"The Passing of Arthur" (Tennyson)
See "Morte d'Arthur"
"The Passing of the Hawthorn" (Swinburne) **24**:313, 317
"Passing Over in Silence" (Ní Chuilleanáin) **34**:367, 373, 383-84
"Passing Things to John Ashbery" (O'Hara)
See "Choses Passagères à John Ashbery"
"Passing Through" (Cavafy) **36**:74, 108
"Passing Through" (Kunitz) **19**:187
"Passing Through Little Rock" (Ortiz) **17**:227
Passing Through: The Later Poems New and Selected (Kunitz) **19**:186
"Passing Visit to Helen" (Lawrence) **54**:168
"Passion" (Trakl) **20**:269
"A Passion For Travel" (Curnow) **48**:20, 51
Passion: New Poems, 1977-1980 (Jordan) **38**:112, 117-19, 122-23, 127, 131
The Passion of Claude McKay: Selected Poetry and Prose, 1912-1948 (McKay) **2**:218
Passion of the Earth (Aleixandre)
See *Pasión de la tierra*
"The Passionate Man's Pilgrimage..." (Raleigh) **31**:210, 217, 236
"La passione" (Pasolini) **17**:288
Passione e ideologia (Pasolini) **17**:250, 252, 263-64, 291, 295
"The Passions" (Coleridge) **39**:213
"Passions" (Komunyakaa) **51**:35
Passport to the War (Kunitz) **19**:148, 154, 160-62
"The Past" (Bryant) **20**:9
"The Past" (Emerson) **18**:76
"Past" (Sanchez) **9**:219
The Past (Kinnell) **26**:277-78, 292-93
"Past and Future" (Browning) **6**:16, 41
"Past and Present" (Masters) **1**:343
The past clarified/copied out (Paz)
See *Pasado en claro*
"Past Days" (Swinburne) **24**:327, 329
"The Past Is the Present" (Moore) **4**:237; **49**:92, 115, 117, 122
"The Past Reordered" (Ignatow) **34**:283
"Past Tense" (Francis) **34**:251
"Pastor hacia el puerto" (Aleixandre) **15**:35
"Pastoral" (Dove) **6**:120-21
"The Pastoral" (Soto) **28**:370
"Pastoral" (Tate) **50**:231
"Pastoral" (Viereck) **27**:271
"Pastoral" (Williams) **7**:367, 378
Pastoral (Williams) **7**:349
"Pastoral Dialogue" (Swift) **9**:261
"A Pastoral Fetish" (Corso) **33**:46
"Pastoral II" (Meredith) **60**:287
"A Pastoral Pindaric . . ." (Behn) **13**:8
Pastoral Poesy (Clare) **23**:4
"A Pastoral to Mr. Stafford" (Behn) **13**:8, 32
"Pastoral VI" (Meredith) **60**:287
"Pastorale" (Crane) **3**:98-9
Pastorales (Jiménez) **7**:184
"A Pastorall Song to the King" (Herrick) **9**:86
Pastorals (Pope) **26**:319, 321
Pastorals (Vergil)
See *Georgics*
"Pastorela di Narcis" (Pasolini) **17**:253, 282
"The Pasture" (Frost) **1**:197, 212, 225; **39**:236, 256-57
Pastures and Other Poems (Reese) **29**:336-337, 339, 348
"Patagonian Lullaby" (Mistral)
See "Arrullo patagón"
"Patch and Mend" (Hope) **56**:276
"Patchwork" (Boland) **58**:45, 53, 59
"Patent Leather" (Brooks) **7**:58, 68, 79
"Pater Filio" (Bridges) **28**:89
"Paternità" (Pavese) **13**:213, 229
"Paternity" (Pavese)
See "Paternità"
"Paterson" (Ginsberg) **4**:73-5
Paterson (Williams) **7**:350, 354-60, 362, 364-65, 370-75, 377, 379, 392-95, 402-03, 408-10
Paterson I (Williams) **7**:354, 357-58, 360, 365
Paterson II (Williams) **7**:363, 391-92
Paterson IV (Williams) **7**:363, 392
Paterson V (Williams) **7**:364-65, 370-71, 393
"Paterson: Episode 17" (Williams) **7**:360
"The Path" (Dunbar) **5**:125
"The Path" (Thomas) **53**:328, 348
"The Path Among the Stones" (Kinnell) **26**:252, 269, 273, 275-76
"Path of the Chameleon" (Wylie) **23**:330
"Path of Thunder" (Okigbo) **7**:228, 246-47, 255
Path of Thunder (Okigbo)
See *Labyrinths, with Path of Thunder*
"Pathfinders" (Brathwaite) **56**:6, 29, 85
"Pathology of Colours" (Abse) **41**:11, 25, 28
The Paths and the Roads of Poetry (Éluard)
See *Les sentiers et les routes de la poésie*
"Paths and Thingscape" (Atwood) **8**:36
"Patience" (Éluard) **38**:63
"Patience" (Graves) **6**:154
"Patience" (Lowell) **13**:60
"Patience" (Stone) **53**:244, 257
"La patience, Le ciel" (Bonnefoy) **58**:118, 167
"Un patio" (Borges) **32**:53, 81
"Patmos" (Hölderlin) **4**:148, 150-51, 153, 155-57, 159, 166, 172
Patria o muerte! The Great Zoo, and Other Poems by Nicolás Guillén (Guillén)
See *El gran zoo*
"Patricia's Poem" (Jordan) **38**:126
"The Patriot Engineer" (Meredith) **60**:250
"Patriotic Poem" (Wakoski) **15**:358
"The Patroit" (Browning) **2**:60
"Patrouille" (Stramm) **50**:172, 175, 209, 220
"Patterns" (Lowell) **13**:60, 71, 76-7, 84-5, 89, 96
"Patterns" (Wright) **14**:376
"Paul" (Niedecker) **42**:169
"Paul" (Wright) **36**:359, 363
"Paul and Virginia" (Gozzano) **10**:176, 178, 180-84
Paul Celan: Poems (Celan) **10**:95-6, 107-08, 114
"Paul Klee" (Éluard) **38**:71
"Paul Revere's Ride" (Longfellow) **30**:25, 44, 48, 61-2
"Paul Robeson" (Brooks) **7**:92-3
"Paul Valéry Stood on the Cliff and Confronted the Furious Energies of Nature" (Warren) **37**:353
"Paula Becker To Clara Westhoff" (Rich) **5**:379
Pauline: A Fragment of a Confession (Browning) **2**:25-6, 42-3, 48, 66, 90-2, 94
"Pauline Barrett" (Masters) **36**:183
"Paul's Wife" (Frost) **1**:194; **39**:235
"Paumanok" (Clampitt) **19**:102
"Pause au château cloaque" (Char) **56**:137-38
"A Pause for Thought" (Rossetti) **7**:280, 297
"Pauvre Lélian" (Verlaine) **2**:416
"Les pauvres à l'église" (Rimbaud) **3**:255; **57**:203, 205, 250
"Les pauvres gens" (Hugo) **17**:61
"Pavitra prem" (Tagore) **8**:407
"The Paw" (Merwin) **45**:29
"The Pawnbroker" (Kumin) **15**:180, 192, 200
"Pax" (Darío) **15**:82, 115
"Pax" (Lawrence) **54**:250
"Pay Day" (Hughes) **1**:255
"Pay Day" (McKay) **2**:226
"Paying a Debt" (Dafydd)
See "Talu Dyled"
"Paying Calls" (Hardy) **8**:105
"Pays Natal" (Walcott) **46**:272
"Paysage" (Apollinaire) **7**:32, 34-5
"Paysage" (Verlaine) **32**:378
"Paysage Moralisé" (Auden) **1**:23
"Le Paysage nu" (Éluard) **38**:87
"Paysages belges" (Verlaine) **2**:415
"Paz" (Storni) **33**:251;
"Peace" (Brooke) **24**:59, 74, 79-80, 87-9
"Peace" (Clare) **23**:44
"Peace" (Darío)
See "Pax"
"Peace" (Herbert) **4**:101, 134
"Peace" (Hopkins) **15**:127
"Peace" (Kavanagh) **33**:73, 81, 100
"Peace" (Levine) **22**:219
"Peace" (Yeats) **20**:329
"The Peace of Cities" (Wilbur) **51**:187
"The Peace-Offering" (Hardy) **8**:93
"Peach" (Lawrence) **54**:187, 225-27
"Peach Blossom Spring" (Wang Wei) **18**:374
"The Peaches" (Thomas) **52**:284
"Peachstone" (Abse) **41**:10, 14
"Peacock" (Merrill) **28**:234
"The Peacock Room" (Hayden) **6**:193-95, 198
"The Peal of Bells" (Thoreau)
See "The Peal of the Bells"
"The Peal of the Bells" (Thoreau) **30**:193, 254
"The Pear" (Kenyon) **57**:23, 40, 43
"The Pear" (Stone) **53**:227
"Pear Tree" (H. D.) **5**:275
"The Pearl" (Herbert) **4**:100, 128
"The Pearl" (Patmore) **59**:232
"The Pearl Diver" (Wylie) **23**:321
"Pearl Fog" (Sandburg) **41**:364
"Pearl Harbor" (Howe) **54**:37
"Pearl Horizons" (Sandburg) **2**:307
"Peasant" (Kavanagh) **33**:156
"Peasant: His Prayer to the Powers of the World" (Merwin) **45**:23
"The Peasant Whore" (Pavese)
See "La puttana contadina"
"The Peasant's Confession" (Hardy) **8**:124
"Pebble" (Herbert)
See "Kamyk"
"Pebbles" (Brathwaite) **56**:68
"Pedantic Literalist" (Moore) **4**:229; **49**:114, 116-17, 120, 155
"Pedestrian" (Oppen) **35**:284
"Pedro as el cuando..." (Neruda) **4**:288
"Peekaboo, I Almost See You" (Nash) **21**:269-70
"Peele Castle" (Wordsworth)
See "Stanzas on Peele Castle"
"Peers" (Toomer) **7**:336-37
Peers (Belloc) **24**:49
"Pegasus" (Kavanagh) **33**:62, 75, 77, 85, 93-4, 96
"Pegasus in Pound" (Longfellow) **30**:88
"A pelear" (Alurista) **34**:27
"The Pelican" (Wilbur) **51**:190
"Pelleas and Ettarre" (Tennyson) **6**:376
"Pelota en el agua" (Storni) **33**:293-96;
"The Pen" (Carver) **54**:14
"The Pen" (Kinnell) **26**:293
"Penance" (Erdrich) **52**:191
"A Pencil" (Hass) **16**:196
"Pencils" (Sandburg) **41**:302
"Penelope" (Boland) **58**:20
"Penelope" (Parker) **28**:362
"Penelope at Her Loom" (Graham)
See "Self-Portrait as Hurry and Delay"
"Penelope's Song" (Glück) **16**:172
"Penetra" (Alurista) **34**:27
"The Peninsula" (Heaney) **18**:200, 222-23
"The Penitent" (Millay) **6**:211
"Penmanship" (Graham) **59**:170, 175
Penniless Painter Goes Out into the World (Seifert)
See *Šel malíř chudě do světa*

"A Penniless Painter Went Out into the World" (Seifert)
See *Šel malíř chudě do světa*
"Penniwit, the Artist" (Masters) **36**:182
Penny Wheep (MacDiarmid) **9**:151, 158, 166, 179, 188
"The Penny Whistle" (Thomas) **53**:300
"The Pennycandystore beyond the El" (Ferlinghetti) **1**:187
"Penobscot" (Oppen) **35**:314
"Pénombre" (Char) **56**:155
"The Pens" (Merwin) **45**:77
"El Pensador de Rodin" (Mistral) **32**:154
"Pensar, dudar" (Hugo) **17**:92, 96-97
"Pensées des morts" (Lamartine) **16**:280
"Penshurst Place" (Mahon) **60**:142
"Pensieri di Deola" (Pavese) **13**:214
"The Pensioners" (Carman) **34**:203, 210, 217
"Pente" (Tzara) **27**:229-31
"La pente de la rêverie" (Hugo) **17**:48, 91, 93
"Penthesilea" (Noyes) **27**:115
"Penúltima canción de Don Simón" (Fuertes) **27**:40
"Penumbra" (Lowell) **13**:64
"People" (Toomer) **7**:336-37
"The People" (Yeats) **20**:328
"People Are Sick of Pretending That They Love the Boss" (Wright) **36**:390-91
"People Asking Me" (Alurista) **34**:21-22
"THE PEOPLE BURNING" (Baraka) **4**:12
"People Getting Divorced" (Ferlinghetti) **1**:183
"People of the Eaves, I Wish You Good Morning" (Sandburg) **41**:287
"People of Unrest" (Walker) **20**:282
"The People on a Bridge" (Szymborska) **44**:313, 315
People on a Bridge (Szymborska) **44**:274, 279, 293
"The People on the Bridge" (Szymborska) **44**:313, 315
"The People People" (Oppen) **35**:316
"People Were Laughing Behind A Wall" (Yevtushenko) **40**:347
"People Who Don't Understand" (Pavese)
See "Gente che non capisce"
"People Who Have No Children" (Brooks) **7**:75
"People Who've Been There" (Pavese) **13**:218
"The People Will Live On" (Sandburg) **41**:332
"The People, Yes" (Sandburg) **41**:279, 330, 332-33, 346
The People, Yes (Sandburg) **2**:317-18, 320-23, 325-26, 328, 330, 333, 335-39, 341; **41**:279, 330, 332-33, 346
A Peopled Landscape (Tomlinson) **17**:305, 309, 317-18, 327, 333, 335, 337, 341
"People's Surroundings" (Moore) **49**:93-94, 112
Pepel' (Bely) **11**:3-4, 6-7, 24, 30-2
Pequeña antología de Gabriela Mistral (Mistral) **32**:166
"La Pequeña oda a un negro boxeador cubano" (Guillén) **23**:98-99, 103, 105-107
"El pequeño burgués" (Parra) **39**:277
"Per album" (Montale) **13**:130
"Per Eduardo Corrazzini" (Carducci) **46**:51
"Per Giuseppe Monti e Gaetano Tognetti" (Carducci) **46**:51
"Per il Santo Natale" (Leopardi) **37**:169
"Per il Trasporto delle Relique di Ugo Foscolo in Santa Croce" (Carducci) **46**:51
"Per la Morte di Eugenio Napoleone" (Carducci) **46**:52, 84
"Per la Proclamazione del Regno d'Italia" (Carducci) **46**:51
"Per la Rivoluzione di Grecia" (Carducci) **46**:5, 51
"Per quella via che la bellezza corre" (Dante) **21**:74
"Per un ritorna al paese" (Pasolini) **17**:266
"The Perch" (Kinnell) **26**:287
"Lo perdido" (Borges) **22**:80
"Perdition" (Césaire) **25**:29
"Perdón si por mis ojos..." (Neruda) **4**:288
"Peregrinaciones" (Darío) **15**:82
"Peregrinations" (Darío)
See "Peregrinaciones"
"Peregrine" (Wylie) **23**:307, 310, 324
"El peregrino" (Parra) **39**:283-84
"Perekop" (Tsvetaeva) **14**:326-27
"Peremena" (Pasternak) **6**:285
"The Perennial Answer" (Rich) **5**:351-52
"Perennials" (Levine) **22**:228
Pereulochki (Tsvetaeva) **14**:325-26
"Perfección del círculo" (Guillén) **35**:154, 211
"Perfect" (MacDiarmid) **9**:177
"The Perfect Husband" (Nash) **21**:278
"The Perfect Sky" (Gallagher) **9**:59
"Perfection" (Walker) **30**:339
"Perfection of the Cirlce" (Guillén)
See "Perfección del círculo"
"Perforation, Concerning Genius" (Pinsky) **27**:144
"The Performance" (Dickey) **40**:159, 166-67, 175, 181, 183, 189, 192, 258
"The Performers" (Hayden) **6**:195
"Perhaps Because I Love You" (Alurista)
See "Tal vez porque te quiero"
"Perhaps No Poem But All I Can Say and I Cannot Be Silent" (Levertov) **11**:198
"Perhaps the Best Time" (Meredith) **28**:174
"Perjury Excused" (Suckling) **30**:127
"The Permanent Hell" (Ignatow) **34**:283
"Permanent invisible" (Char) **56**:152
"The Permanent Tourists" (Page) **12**:178, 181-89
"The perpetual migration" (Piercy) **29**:303
"Perpetuum Mobile: The City" (Williams) **7**:350
"Le Perroquet" (Perse) **23**:228, 254-56
"Persée et Andromède" (Laforgue) **14**:93
"Persephone" (Smith) **12**:331-32
"Perseus" (Plath) **37**:254
"The Persian" (Smith) **12**:330
"A Persian Suite" (Stryk) **27**:186-87
"The Persian Version" (Graves) **6**:143, 152
Persimmon (Viereck) **27**:282, 284
The Persimmon Tree (Viereck) **27**:271
"Persimmons" (Lee) **24**:243, 246
"Persistent Explorer" (Ransom) **61**:289
Person, Place, and Thing (Shapiro) **25**:261-64, 267-69, 276, 285, 288, 295, 308, 318-19, 322, 324
Personae (Pound) **4**:317
"Personae Separatae" (Montale) **13**:106, 126
"Personal" (Hughes) **1**:241, 259
A Personal Anthology (Borges)
See *Antologia personal*
Personal Anthology (Borges)
See *Antologia personal*
"Personal Helicon" (Heaney) **18**:200, 217
"Personal Landscape" (Page) **12**:178, 190
"Personal Letter No. 2" (Sanchez) **9**:224, 232-33
"Personal Letter No. 3" (Sanchez) **9**:225
A Personal Library (Borges)
See *Antologia personal*
"Personal Poem" (O'Hara) **45**:145, 184, 189, 227-28, 243
"A Personal Problem" (Kavanagh) **33**:74, 81, 89
"Personism" (Mahon) **60**:229
"Persons Half Known" (Sandburg) **41**:241
"Perspectives" (MacNeice) **61**:176
"Persuasions to Love" (Carew)
See "To A.L. Perswasions to Love"
"Perswasions to Enjoy" (Carew) **29**:36
"La perte de l'anio" (Lamartine) **16**:292
Pervaja simfonija (Bely) **11**:17
"Pervaya pesenka" (Akhmatova) **2**:9
"Perversity" (Dickey) **40**:201
Pervoe svidanie (Bely) **11**:3, 7-11, 17-21, 28-9, 31-3
"La Pesadilla" (Borges) **32**:77
"Pesnia poslednei vstrechi" (Akhmatova) **2**:11; **55**:48
Pesnja pro kuptsa Kalashinikova (Lermontov)
See *Pesnya pro tsarya Ivana Vasilievicha, molodogo oprichnika i undalogo kuptsa Kalashnikova*
Pesnya pro tsarya Ivana Vasilievicha, molodogo oprichnika i undalogo kuptsa Kalashnikova (Lermontov) **18**:278, 281-82, 304
"Peso ancestral" (Storni) **33**:243, 252;
"Pet Shop" (MacNeice) **61**:178
"Peter" (Moore) **4**:257; **49**:99-100, 180, 185-88
"Peter" (Ondaatje) **28**:292-93, 298-99, 318, 321
"Peter" (Wilbur) **51**:281
"Peter and John" (Wylie) **23**:324
Peter Bell (Wordsworth) **4**:399, 420
Peter Bell the Third (Shelley) **14**:175
"Peter Goole" (Belloc) **24**:18
"Peter Lorre Dreams He Is the Third Reincarnation of a Geisha" (Yau) **61**:358
"Peter Lorre Improvises Mr. Moto's Monologue" (Yau) **61**:336, 358
"Peter Lorre Records His Favorite Walt Whitman Poem for Posterity" (Yau) **61**:346, 358
"Peter Lorre Speaks to the Spirit of Edgar Allan Poe During a Séance" (Yau) **61**:358
"Peter Quince at the Clavier" (Stevens) **6**:293, 295, 300-01
"Peterhot Holiday" (Lermontov) **18**:285
"Petersburg" (Mickiewicz) **38**:168
"Petersburg Tale" (Akhmatova) **55**:3, 24
"The Petit Bourgeois" (Parra)
See "El pequeño burgués"
"Petit Paul" (Hugo) **17**:56
"Petit Poème en Prose" (O'Hara) **45**:178
"Le Petit Roi de Galicie" (Hugo) **17**:61
Le Petit Testament (Villon)
See *Les Lais*
"Petit, the Poet" (Masters) **36**:167, 199, 211
"La petite Enfance de Dominique" (Éluard) **38**:84, 86
Petite prière sans prétentions (Laforgue) **14**:63
"Petite Ville" (Tzara) **27**:223
"Petite Ville en Sibérie" (Tzara) **27**:223
"Les petites vielles" (Baudelaire) **1**:45, 64
"Pétition" (Laforgue) **14**:73
"Petition" (Raleigh)
See "Petition to Queen Anne"
"The Petition for an Absolute Retreat" (Finch) **21**:142-43, 145-48, 156-57, 164, 170, 172, 175
"Petition to Queen Anne" (Raleigh) **31**:201, 210, 217, 221
"Petition to the Queen" (Raleigh)
See "Petition to Queen Anne"
Petits poèmes en prose: Le spleen de Paris (Baudelaire) **1**:48-9, 58-9
"Petrarca" (Carducci) **46**:52
"Petrificada petrificante" (Paz) **1**:367
"Petrou his name was sorrow" (Niedecker) **42**:140
"Pettichap's Nest" (Clare) **23**:5
"A Petticoat" (Stein) **18**:330, 341
"Pevitsa" (Tsvetaeva) **14**:325, 327
"Phaedra" (H. D.) **5**:267
"Phaestos is a Village with 25 Families" (Corso) **33**:11
"Phaeton" (Meredith) **60**:260
"Phaius Orchid" (Wright) **14**:346, 361
"Phallus" (Hope) **56**:301, 306
"Phantasia for Elvira Shatayev" (Rich) **5**:377
"Phantasmagoria" (Komunyakaa) **51**:55
Phantasmagoria (Carroll) **18**:46, 48
"Phantasy" (Meredith) **60**:262
Phantom Dwelling (Wright) **14**:374-75, 379
"The Phantom Horsewoman" (Hardy) **8**:91, 136
"The Phantom Light of All Our Day" (Mackey) **49**:5-6
"Phantom or Fact" (Coleridge) **39**:170
"Pharaoh" (Kenyon) **57**:12, 15, 24
"Les Phares" (Char) **56**:199

"The Phase after History" (Graham) **59**:136, 152, 156, 180, 184-85
"The Phases of the Moon" (Yeats) **51**:151
"Ph.D." (Hughes) **53**:115, 171
"Phèdre" (Smith) **12**:331-32
"Phénix" (Bonnefoy) **58**:174
Le phénix (Éluard) **38**:78
"Phenomenal Survivals of Death in Nantucket" (Glück) **16**:131, 135, 139
"Phenomenal Woman" (Angelou) **32**:27
Phenomenal Woman (Angelou) **32**:23, 25, 28
"The Phenomenology of Anger" (Rich) **5**:371-72, 384, 394
"The Phenomenon" (Carver) **54**:22
"Philai Te Kou Philai" (Oppen) **35**:314, 340
"Philemon and Baucis" (Gunn) **26**:214
"Philhellene" (Cavafy) **36**:40, 46, 49
Philip Sparow (Skelton)
See *Boke of Phyllyp Sparowe*
Philip Sparrow (Skelton)
See *Boke of Phyllyp Sparowe*
Phillip Sparrow (Skelton)
See *Boke of Phyllyp Sparowe*
"Phillis; or, The Progress of Love, 1716" (Swift) **9**:253
"Philomela" (Arnold) **5**:37-8, 41, 46-7
"Philomela" (Ransom) **61**:274, 319
"The Philosopher and His Mistress" (Bridges) **28**:87
"The Philosopher to His Mistress" (Bridges) **28**:87
"The Philosophers" (Merton) **10**:337
"Philosophy" (Dunbar) **5**:144
"Philosophy" (Parker) **28**:361
"Philosophy in Warm Weather" (Kenyon) **57**:16, 43
"The Philosophy of Composition" (Poe) **54**:263-64, 268-71, 278-79, 282, 284, 292, 294-99, 307-9, 311-17, 320-24, 326, 334-35, 341-42
"Phoebus with Admetus" (Meredith) **60**:259, 330-31
"Phoenix" (Lawrence) **54**:197, 203, 218, 251
"The Phoenix" (Sarton) **39**:326, 332, 342
The Phoenix (Éluard)
See *Le phénix*
"The Phoenix Again" (Sarton) **39**:362
"The Phoenix and the Tortoise" (Rexroth) **20**:178
The Phoenix and the Tortoise (Rexroth) **20**:180, 182-84, 192-94, 198-202, 210, 212-13, 217
"The Phoenix Gone, The Terrace Empty" (Chin) **40**:11, 13, 16, 19, 21-3, 31-5
The Phoenix Gone, The Terrace Empty (Chin) **40**:8-9, 11-13, 27-9, 34
"Phone Call from Mexico" (Page) **12**:198
"The Photograph" (Cavafy) **36**:41, 76
"The Photograph" (Smith) **12**:308, 346
"Photograph of My Father in His 22nd Year" (Carver) **54**:6
"Photograph of My Room" (Forché) **10**:144, 156
"Photograph of the Girl" (Olds) **22**:313
"The Photograph of the Unmade Bed" (Rich) **5**:366
"The Photograph on My Father!s Desk" (Boland) **58**:12, 58
"The Photographer in Winter" (Szirtes) **51**:171
"Photographs Courtesy of the Fall River Historical Society" (Olds) **22**:307
"Photomontage of the Urban Parks" (Viereck) **27**:280
"Photos of a Salt Mine" (Page) **12**:167-68, 189
"Phrases" (Rimbaud) **3**:263; **57**:234-35, 253, 285
"P.H.T." (Thomas) **53**:305, 307-8
Phyllyp Sparowe (Skelton)
See *Boke of Phyllyp Sparowe*
Phyllyp Sparrow (Skelton)
See *Boke of Phyllyp Sparowe*
"Physcial Union" (Tagore)
See "Deher milan"
"Physical Love" (Ignatow) **34**:282
"Physician's Tale" (Chaucer) **19**:15, 62
The Physician!s Tale (Chaucer) **58**:291
"A Physics of Sudden Light" (Ríos) **57**:329
"Piaceri notturni" (Pavese) **13**:205, 226
"Piano" (Lawrence) **54**:167-68, 176
"Piano" (Shapiro) **25**:269
"A Piano" (Stein) **18**:318, 350
"Piano after War" (Brooks) **7**:73
"Le piano que baise une main frê" (Verlaine) **32**:360-63
"Piano Solo" (Parra)
See "Solo de piano"
"The Piano Tuner's Wife" (Shapiro) **25**:303
"Pianto antico" (Carducci) **46**:51, 56, 76, 78
"Piazza di Spagna, Early Morning" (Wilbur) **51**:189, 209
"Piazza Piece" (Ransom) **61**:271, 301, 306-7
"Piazzas" (Guest) **55**:185, 212
"La pica" (Fuertes) **27**:30
"Picasso" (Pasolini) **17**:295
Piccadilly (Seifert)
See *Deštník z Piccadilly*
"Piccola commedia" (Wilbur) **51**:279, 285
"Piccolini" (Wright) **36**:311
"Piccolo testamento" (Montale) **13**:104, 113, 165-66, 168
Pickering MS (Blake) **12**:35-7, 43
"Picking and Choosing" (Moore) **49**:96
"Picking Piñons" (Baca) **41**:47
"Pickthorn Manor" (Lowell) **13**:60, 77, 84
"Picnic Boat" (Sandburg) **41**:321, 365
"Picnic Remembered" (Warren) **37**:284, 286, 288, 307, 322, 331-32, 377
"Pictor Ignatus" (Browning) **2**:30
"The Picture" (Coleridge) **39**:223
"A Picture" (Nemerov) **24**:281
"The Picture" (Tagore)
See "Chhabi"
"Picture Bride" (Song) **21**:334-36, 347-48, 350
Picture Bride (Song) **21**:331-38, 340-41, 343-44, 346-50
"Picture Galleries" (MacNeice) **61**:139
"Picture of a 23-Year-Old Painted by his Friend of the Same Age, an Amateur" (Cavafy) **36**:75, 76
"Picture of a Black Child with a White Doll" (Merton) **10**:341, 345
"The Picture of J. T. in a Prospect of Stone" (Tomlinson) **17**:326
"A Picture of Lee Ying" (Merton) **10**:341
"The Picture of Little J A" (Ashbery) **26**:172
"The Picture of Little T. C. in a Prospect of Flowers" (Marvell) **10**:271, 274, 277, 289, 294, 303-04
"Picture Puzzle Piece" (Silverstein) **49**:334-35
Picture Show (Sassoon) **12**:257-58, 269
"Pictures By Vuillard" (Rich) **5**:350
Pictures from Brueghel, and Other Poems (Williams) **7**:371-72, 374, 377, 392-93, 403, 408
"Pictures in the Smoke" (Parker) **28**:361
Pictures of the Floating World (Lowell) **13**:73-4, 93-4, 96
Pictures of the Gone World (Ferlinghetti) **1**:167-69, 171-75, 186
"Pido que se levante la sesión" (Parra) **39**:271
"Pie de árbol" (Storni) **33**:257-58, 305;
"A Piece of Coffee" (Stein) **18**:333, 349
"Pied Beauty" (Hopkins) **15**:133, 158
"The Pied Piper" (Tsvetaeva)
See "Krysolov"
"Pied Piper of Hamelin" (Browning) **2**:36, 63
"Piedmont" (Carducci)
See "Piemonte"
"Piedra" (Soto) **28**:378, 383
"Piedra de sol" (Paz) **1**:353
Piedra de sol (Paz) **1**:355-56, 358-59, 368-69, 371, 373, 375-77; **48**:180, 191, 193, 212, 229, 231, 233, 235, 244-45, 272, 274-75
"Piedra Miserable" (Storni) **33**:251;
"Piedra roca niebla" (Alurista) **34**:28
"Pielgrzym" (Mickiewicz) **38**:160
"Piemonte" (Carducci) **46**:26, 52, 56
"The Pier" (Hongo) **23**:201
"The Pier" (Merrill) **28**:267
"Pierce Street" (Gunn) **26**:231
Pierce-Arrow (Howe) **54**:118-22, 149-54
"The Pier-Glass" (Graves) **6**:137, 142, 172
The Pier-Glass (Graves) **6**:128, 147, 150
"Une Pierre" (Bonnefoy) **58**:168
Pierre écrite (Bonnefoy) **58**:109, 118, 123, 156, 165-68, 170
"Pierre Menard, Author of the Quixote" (Borges)
See "Pierre Menard, autor del Quixote"
"Pierre Menard, autor del Quijote" (Borges)
See "Pierre Menard, autor del Quixote"
"Pierre Menard, autor del Quixote" (Borges) **32**:107
"Pierrot" (Teasdale) **31**:332, 336
"Pierrot" (Verlaine) **32**:365
Pierrot fumiste (Laforgue) **14**:81
"Pietà" (Glück) **16**:130
"La pietà" (Ungaretti) **57**:376
"Pig Cupid" (Loy) **16**:314-15, 326
"Pig Game" (Stone) **53**:228
"Pig Glass, 1973-1978" (Ondaatje) **28**:327, 335, 337, 339-40
"The Pig-boy" (Ní Chuilleanáin) **34**:351
"Le pigeon" (Hugo) **17**:100
"Pigeon Woman" (Swenson) **14**:265
"Pigeons" (Moore) **49**:120, 129
"Pigeons, Sussex Avenue" (Ondaatje) **28**:292
"Piggy to Joey" (Smith) **12**:321
"Pig's Eye View of Literature" (Parker) **28**:348, 353, 362
"Pike" (Hughes) **7**:136, 158
"The Pike" (Lowell) **13**:69
"The Pilgrim" (Boland) **58**:42
"A Pilgrim" (Bradstreet)
See "As Weary Pilgrim"
"Pilgrim" (Mickiewicz)
See "Pielgrzym"
"A Pilgrim Dreaming" (Levertov) **11**:209
"Pilgrim Fish Heads" (Bly) **39**:73
"The Pilgrimage" (Herbert) **4**:109
"Pilgrimage" (Olds) **22**:309
"Pilgrimage" (Pinsky) **27**:158
The Pilgrimage of Festus (Aiken) **26**:13, 22
The Pilgrims of Hope (Morris) **55**:326, 329, 332, 338-39, 343
"A Pilgrim's Progress Through Iniskeen in the Thirties" (Kavanagh) **33**:143
Pili's Wall (Levine) **22**:226
"The Pillar of Fame" (Herrick) **9**:106
"Pillar of Salt" (Mueller) **33**:196-97
"The pillar perished is" (Wyatt)
See "The piller pearisht is whearto I Lent"
"Pillars" (Paz) **48**:273
"The piller pearisht is whearto I Lent" (Wyatt) **27**:357-58
"Pillow" (Hogan) **35**:257
"A Pilot from the Carrier" (Jarrell) **41**:202
"Pilots, Man Your Planes" (Jarrell) **41**:136, 148, 185, 202
"Le pin" (Ronsard) **11**:277
A Pindaric on the Death of Our Late Sovereign (Behn) **13**:8
A Pindaric Poem on the Happy Coronation of . . . James II (Behn) **13**:8
"Pindaric Poem to the Reverend Doctor Burnet" (Behn) **13**:32
"A Pindaric to Mr. P. Who Sings Finely" (Behn) **13**:8
"A Pindarick Poem upon the Hurricane" (Finch) **21**:163, 180
"Pine" (Dickey) **40**:241-42, 244-46
"The Pine" (Ronsard)
See "Le pin"
The Pine Apple and the Bee (Cowper) **40**:70
"The Pine Planters (Marty South's Reverie)" (Hardy) **8**:101
"The Pine Trees and the Sky" (Brooke) **24**:76

"The Pine with Pine Cones" (Mistral)
See "El piño de piñas"
The Pink Church (Williams) **7**:370
"The Pink Corner Man" (Borges)
See "El Hombre de la esquina rosada"
"Pink Dog" (Bishop) **3**:65; **34**:105, 119
"The Pink Dress" (Wakoski) **15**:345, 374-75
"Pink Hands" (Soto) **28**:398-99
"Pink Melon Joy" (Stein) **18**:346
"The pinks along my garden walks" (Bridges) **28**:85
"El piño de piñas" (Mistral) **32**:179-80
"Piñones" (Quintana) **36**:256-57
"Pinos de Navidad" (Mistral) **32**:185
"Pinoy at The Coming World" (Hongo) **23**:198
"Pioggia d'agosto" (Gozzano) **10**:184-85
"Pioneers" (Niedecker) **42**:94, 151
"The Piper" (Blake) **12**:9
Pipes O' Pan at Zekesbury (Riley) **48**:290
"The Pipes of Pan" (Carman) **34**:208, 222
The Pipes of Pan (Carman) **34**:205, 208, 210, 214, 221, 224
Pippa Passes (Browning) **2**:28, 30, 35, 37, 67
"Il Pirla" (Montale) **13**:138
The Pisan Cantos (Pound) **4**:320, 337, 344-48, 352, 357-58, 360
"Píseň o lásce" (Seifert) **47**:334
Píseň o Viktorce (Seifert) **47**:321, 323, 326-27, 335
"The Pit" (Roethke) **15**:302
"The Pit" (Stryk) **27**:195, 202
The Pit and Other Poems (Stryk) **27**:181, 183, 190, 193-94, 198, 214, 216
"Pit Viper" (Momaday) **25**:188, 193-94, 199
"Pitcher" (Francis) **34**:242, 244, 246, 253, 255
"The Pitchfork" (Heaney) **18**:256
La Pitié suprême (Hugo) **17**:65
"Le pitre châtié" (Mallarmé) **4**:202
"Pity for Poor Africans" (Cowper) **40**:105, 119-20
"Pity Me" (Wylie) **23**:321, 324
"Pity Me Not" (Millay) **6**:225
"Pity the Deep in Love" (Cullen) **20**:57
"Pity 'Tis, 'Tis True" (Lowell) **13**:84
"A Pity. We Were Such a Good Invention" (Amichai) **38**:43, 53
Placard pour un chemin des écoliers (Char) **56**:159-62, 169
Placard pour un chemin des écoliers suivi de Dehors la nuit est gouvernée (Char)
See *Dehors la nuit est gouvernée*
"The Place" (Warren) **37**:366, 378
"Place; & Names" (Olson) **19**:296
"Place and Time" (Mueller) **33**:196
"Place for a Third" (Frost) **1**:194, 221
"A Place for Lazarus" (Guillén)
See "Lazarus's place"
"Place of a Skull" (MacNeice) **61**:144
"Place of combat" (Bonnefoy)
See "Lieu du combat"
"The Place of Light and Darkness" (Muir) **49**:269, 288-89
The Place of Love (Shapiro) **25**:267, 269, 309, 311, 315
"Place of the Salamander" (Bonnefoy)
See "Lieu de la salamandre"
"The Place of Value" (Nemerov) **24**:255
"Place Pigalle" (Wilbur) **51**:317, 320
"The Place That Is Feared I Inhabit" (Forché) **10**:143
"A Place to Stand" (Wagoner) **33**:370-71
A Place to Stand (Wagoner) **33**:325-27, 333, 347, 366, 368-70, 372-73
"Place We Have Been" (Ortiz) **17**:228
"A Place Where Nothing Is" (Warren) **37**:302
"The Placeless Heaven: Another Look at Kavanaugh" (Heaney) **18**:233
"Places" (Hardy) **8**:91, 104, 135-36
"Places" (Teasdale) **31**:323, 357, 359
"Places, Loved Ones" (Larkin) **21**:246
The Plague Column (Seifert)
See *Morový sloup*
The Plague Monument (Seifert)
See *Morový sloup*
"A Plague of Starlings" (Hayden) **6**:185, 195
"The Plaid Dress" (Millay) **6**:234
"A Plain Song for Comadre" (Wilbur) **51**:220, 268
The Plaint of a Rose (Sandburg) **41**:293
"Plainte d'automne" (Mallarmé) **4**:187
"Plainview: 1" (Momaday) **25**:195, 203, 207, 213
"Plainview: 2" (Momaday) **25**:189, 195-96, 200, 213
"Plainview: 3" (Momaday) **25**:196, 213-14
"Plainview: 4" (Momaday) **25**:196, 213-14
"Un plaisant" (Baudelaire) **1**:59
"Das Plakat" (Benn) **35**:45, 50
"The Plan" (Stone) **53**:232
Plan (Alurista)
See *El Plan Espiritual de Aztlán*
El Plan Espiritual de Aztlán (Alurista) **34**:17
"Plan for the Young English King" (Pound) **4**:364
"Plan of Future Works" (Pasolini) **17**:257
"The Planctus" (Hope) **56**:289
"Planes" (Merwin) **45**:18
Planet News: 1961-1967 (Ginsberg) **4**:51-2, 65-6; **47**:50
Planet Waves (Dylan) **37**:63
"Planetarium" (Rich) **5**:366, 370
"Planh for the Young English King" (Pound) **4**:364
"Planning the Garden" (Lowell) **13**:64
"Planning the Perfect Evening" (Dove) **6**:106
"Planos de un crepúsculo" (Storni) **33**:294-95;
Plant and Phantom (MacNeice) **61**:139
Plant Dreaming Deep (Sarton) **39**:333
Plantain (Akhmatova)
See *Podorozhnik*
"The Plantation" (Heaney) **18**:201, 225
"A Plantation Bacchanal" (Johnson) **24**:153
"A Plantation Portrait" (Dunbar) **5**:147
"The Planted Skull" (Viereck) **27**:265
"The Planters" (Atwood) **8**:36
"Planting a Cedar" (Hogan) **35**:256
"Planting Trees" (Berry) **28**:37
"The Plaster" (Merwin) **45**:25
Platero and I (Jiménez)
See *Platero y Yo*
Platero and I: An Andalusion Elegy (Jiménez)
See *Platero y Yo*
Platero y Yo (Jiménez) **7**:185-89, 191, 199-201, 203
"Plato Elaborated" (Brodsky) **9**:19, 20
"Platonic Lassitude" (Warren) **37**:378
"Platypus" (Wright) **14**:372
"Play Again" (Ignatow) **34**:318
"THe Play Way" (Heaney) **18**:187
"The Player Piano" (Jarrell) **41**:180-81, 188
The Player Queen (Yeats) **20**:353
"Playing Cards" (Atwood) **8**:5, 7
"Playing the Inventions" (Nemerov) **24**:285-87
"Playing the Machine" (Nemerov) **24**:301
"Plaza en invierno" (Storni) **33**:239, 246;
"Plea for a Captive" (Merwin) **45**:8
"Pleading" (McKay) **2**:223
"Please" (Komunyakaa) **51**:24, 64
"Please, Master" (Ginsberg) **4**:54, 90; **47**:41
"pleases Davie no end" (Niedecker) **42**:130
"Pleasure Bay" (Pinsky) **27**:157-58, 161, 164-65, 169, 174, 176
Pleasure Dome: New and Collected Poems (Komunyakaa) **51**:50, 57
"The Pleasure of Princes" (Hope) **56**:268-69, 286, 288
"Pleasures" (Levertov) **11**:159, 164, 189
"Pleasure's Lament" (Tagore)
See "Sukher vilap"
"Pleasures of Spring" (Clare) **23**:14
"Plebiscitum" (Carducci)
See "Il plebiscito"
"Pledge" (Merrill) **28**:284
"Plegaria" (Jiménez) **7**:198
"Plegaria de la traición" (Storni) **33**:306;
"Plegaria por el nido" (Mistral) **32**:155
"Pleiades from the Cables of Genocide" (Cervantes) **35**:134
"Plein Ciel" (Hugo) **17**:62, 87
"Pleine Mer" (Hugo) **17**:62, 89
"Plennyi rytsar" (Lermontov) **18**:291
"Pleno amor" (Guillén) **35**:180, 183
"Plessy vs. Ferguson: Theme and Variations" (Merton) **10**:345
"Pleurs dans la nuit" (Hugo) **17**:89
"Plighted to Shame" (Jackson) **44**:69
"Ploja fòur di dut" (Pasolini) **17**:287
"Ploja tai cunfins" (Pasolini) **17**:250-52, 265, 287
The plotters (Borges)
See *Los conjurados*
"Plough Horses" (Kavanagh) **33**:77
"Ploughing" (Pasternak) **6**:267
"Ploughing on Sunday" (Stevens) **6**:297, 333
"Ploughman" (Kavanagh) **33**:65, 68-9, 77, 113, 155
Ploughman and Other Poems (Kavanagh) **33**:60, 68-71, 82, 92, 113, 117, 167
"Plowboy" (Sandburg) **41**:321
Plowman (Kavanagh)
See *Ploughman and Other Poems*
"Plugging In" (Silverstein) **49**:340
Pluies (Perse) **23**:211, 213-14, 221, 232, 233-34, 247, 249-51, 253
"Plumbing" (Stone) **53**:253
"The Plumet Basilisk" (Moore) **4**:243; **49**:94, 98, 107-8, 144, 160-61
"The Plum's Heart" (Soto) **28**:381
"Plurality" (MacNeice) **61**:139
"Plus Intra" (Swinburne) **24**:324
Le plus jeune (Éluard) **38**:71
"Plus près de nous" (Éluard) **38**:69
"Plus Ultra" (Swinburne) **24**:324
Plusieurs sonnets (Mallarmé) **4**:214-15
"Pluto Incognito" (Viereck) **27**:296
"Plutonian Ode" (Ginsberg) **4**:61-2
Plutonian Ode: Poems, 1977-1980 (Ginsberg) **4**:61-2
"Pnomes, Jukollages, and Other Stunzas" (Birney) **52**:31, 46, 78, 82, 102
"Po' Boy Blues" (Hughes) **1**:254, 270; **53**:82
Po Pechore (Yevtushenko) **40**:364
"Počitadlo" (Seifert) **47**:332, 348
"Pocomania" (Walcott) **46**:273
"Pocta Vladimíru Holanovi" (Seifert) **47**:336
"Pod jedną gwiazdką " (Szymborska) **44**:273, 286, 296, 300
"Poderoso Quienseas" (Fuertes) **27**:38
"Podolie" (Apollinaire) **7**:48
Podorozhnik (Akhmatova) **2**:3, 13, 18
"Podrazhanije Bajronu" (Lermontov) **18**:302
"Poem" (Alexie) **53**:30
"The Poem" (Amichai) **38**:35
"Poem" (Bishop) **3**:54-5, 70; **34**:54, 75, 155, 158, 185
"Poem" (Enzensberger) **28**:151
"Poem" (Glück) **16**:142
"Poem" (Hughes) **53**:84
"The Poem" (Kinnell) **26**:240-41
"Poem" (Kunitz) **19**:147
"The Poem" (Lowell) **13**:83
"Poem" (Meredith) **28**:199
"Poem" (Merton) **10**:349
"The Poem" (Merwin) **45**:3
"Poem" (Rukeyser) **12**:233
"Poem" (Sanchez) **9**:232
"A Poem" (Stein) **18**:313
"Poem" (Tomlinson) **17**:315, 323, 328, 332, 339, 342, 345
"The Poem" (Williams) **7**:399
"Poem #1" (Akhmatova) **55**:27, 29-30, 37, 42-44, 57-58, 61
"Poem 1" (Ferlinghetti) **1**:167
"Poem #2" (Akhmatova) **55**:29-30, 37, 42-44, 59, 61
"Poem 2" (Ferlinghetti) **1**:173

"Poem #3" (Akhmatova) **55**:28-30, 38, 61
"Poem 3" (Ferlinghetti) **1**:174
"Poem #4" (Akhmatova) **55**:27-30, 38, 42-43, 50-52, 55-56, 58, 61
"Poem IV" (Auden) **1**:10
"Poem 4" (Ferlinghetti) **1**:174
"Poem #5" (Akhmatova) **55**:27-28, 30, 38, 52, 57, 60-61
"Poem 5" (Ferlinghetti) **1**:168, 172
"Poem V" (Rich) **5**:378
"Poem #6" (Akhmatova) **55**:27, 29-30, 38, 52, 61
"Poem 6" (Ferlinghetti) **1**:168, 173-74
"Poem #7" (Akhmatova) **55**:28-30, 38, 42, 61
"Poem 7" (Ferlinghetti) **1**:187
"Poem VII" (Rich) **5**:378-79
"Poem #8" (Akhmatova) **55**:27-31, 38, 42-44, 55, 61
"Poem 8" (Ferlinghetti) **1**:174
"Poem #9" (Akhmatova) **55**:27-30, 32, 38, 42, 61-62
"Poem IX" (Auden) **1**:10
"Poem #10" (Akhmatova) **55**:29, 38, 43-44, 51, 61
"Poem 10" (Ferlinghetti) **1**:172-73
"Poem 11" (Ferlinghetti) **1**:174-75
"Poem 13" (Ferlinghetti) **1**:169, 174
"Poem XIII" (Rich) **5**:379
"Poem 14" (Ferlinghetti) **1**:168, 170
"Poem 15" (Ferlinghetti) **1**:175
"Poem 16" (Ferlinghetti) **1**:175
"Poem 17" (Ferlinghetti) **1**:176
"Poem 18" (Ferlinghetti) **1**:174
"Poem 19" (Ferlinghetti) **1**:173, 175
"Poem 20" (Ferlinghetti) **1**:174, 176
"Poem XX" (Rich) **5**:379
"Poem 21" (Ferlinghetti) **1**:175
"Poem 22" (Ferlinghetti) **1**:169, 176
"Poem 23" (Ferlinghetti) **1**:172, 174
"Poem 24" (Ferlinghetti) **1**:168, 171, 175
"Poem XXV" (Auden) **1**:10
"Poem 25" (Ferlinghetti) **1**:169, 174-75
"Poem 26" (Ferlinghetti) **1**:174-75
"Poem 27" (Ferlinghetti) **1**:174
"Poem 143: The Festival Aspect" (Olson) **19**:306
"Poem: A View of the Mountain" (Ignatow) **34**:308
"A Poem about George Doty in the Death House" (Wright) **36**:315, 335, 337, 399
"Poem about Morning" (Meredith) **28**:214
"Poem About My Rights" (Jordan) **38**:116-18, 123-26, 128-29, 131-32, 145
"Poem about People" (Pinsky) **27**:161-2, 173-4, 176
"Poem About Police Violence" (Jordan) **38**:117
"Poem about the Future" (Enzensberger) **28**:142
"Poem about the Imperial Family" (Tsvetaeva) See "Poema o tsarskoi sem'e"
"Poem Against the Rich" (Bly) **39**:90
"Poem (All the Mirrors in the World)" (O'Hara) **45**:120
"The Poem as Mask: Orpheus" (Rukeyser) **12**:228
"Poem (At night Chinamen jump)" (O'Hara) **45**:163, 226
"Poem at Thirty" (Sanchez) **9**:224, 232-33, 240
"poem beginning in no and ending in yes" (Clifton) **17**:30
"Poem Beginning 'The'" (Zukofsky) **11**:366-69, 373-74, 381, 383-86, 390, 395
"Poem Beginning with a Line by Cavafy" (Mahon) **60**:196
"A Poem Beginning with a Line by Pindar" (Duncan) **2**:121-22, 127
"A Poem Boldly Expressing My Own Feelings" (Yakamochi) **48**:101
"Poem by the Sub-Official Otomo no Sukune Minaka When Hasetsukabe no Tatsumaro, Clerk with the Office of Land Allotment in the Province of Settsu, Strangled Himself in the First Year of the Tempyo Era" (Yakamochi) **48**:132
"Poem Catching Up with an Idea" (Carruth) **10**:88
"A Poem, composed when the Tenno ascended Kagu Hill to behold the country" (Yakamochi) **48**:99
"Poem Dedicatory" (MacLeish) **47**:126
"Poem en Forme de Saw" (O'Hara) **45**:218
"A Poem entreating of Sorrow" (Raleigh) **31**:261
"A Poem for 3rd World Brothers" (Knight) **14**:42
"Poem for a Birthday" (Plath) **1**:381, 390
"Poem for a Decorative Panel" (Hughes) **53**:84
"A Poem for a Poet" (Madhubuti) **5**:327, 344
"A Poem for Anna Russ and Fanny Jones" (Baraka) **4**:39
"Poem for Aretha" (Giovanni) **19**:110
"A Poem for Black Hearts" (Baraka) **4**:18-19
"A Poem for Black Relocation Centers" (Knight) **14**:39, 52
"Poem (For BMC No. 2)" (Giovanni) **19**:139
"A Poem for Children, with Thoughts on Death" (Hammon) **16**:177-78, 180, 183, 187-89
"Poem (for DCS 8th Graders—1966-67)" (Sanchez) **9**:224
"Poem for Don Cherry" (Mackey) **49**:4
"Poem for Etheridge" (Sanchez) **9**:225, 242
A Poem for Farish Street (Walker) See *My Farish Street Green*
"A Poem for Max 'Nordau" (Robinson) **1**:459
"Poem for Maya" (Forché) **10**:142, 157
"Poem for My Birthday" (Mueller) **33**:192
"A Poem for My Father" (Sanchez) **9**:220, 225, 240
"Poem for My Son" (Kumin) **15**:199, 201
"A Poem for Myself" (Knight) **14**:39
"A Poem for Negro Intellectuals (If There Bes Such a Thing)" (Madhubuti) **5**:329
"Poem (For No Name No. 2)" (Giovanni) **19**:108
"Poem for Personnel Managers" (Bukowski) **18**:4, 6
"Poem for South African Women" (Jordan) **38**:128
"A Poem for Sterling Brown" (Sanchez) **9**:229
"A Poem for the Birth-day of the Right HonBLE the Lady Catherine Tufton" (Finch) **21**:164
"A Poem for the End of the Century" (Milosz) **8**:213
"POEM For the portrait of an African boy after the manner of Gauguin" (Hughes) **53**:83
"Poem for the Young White Man Who Asked Me How I, an Intelligent, Well-Read Person Could Believe in the War Between Races" (Cervantes) **35**:104, 110, 113, 117, 131
"A Poem for Willie Best" (Baraka) **4**:10-11
"Poem From Taped Testimony in the Tradition of Bernhard Goetz" (Jordan) **38**:124
"Poem (Hate is only one of many responses)" (O'Hara) **45**:223
A Poem Humbly Dedicated to the Great Pattern of Piety and Virtue Catherine Queen Dowager (Behn) **13**:8
"poem I" (Storni) **33**:287, 289;
"Poem (I lived in the first century of world wars. . . .)" (Rukeyser) **12**:222
"poem II" (Storni) **33**:287;
"Poem in C" (Toomer) **7**:333
"Poem in Lieu of a Preface" (Alurista) **34**:17
"Poem in October" (Thomas) **2**:382, 392, 404; **52**:218, 247, 258-59, 271, 281-83, 314-15, 324
"poem in praise of menstruation" (Clifton) **17**:29-30, 36
"Poem in Prose" (Bogan) **12**:100, 107, 112
"Poem in Prose" (MacLeish) **47**:209
"Poem in Three Parts" (Bly) **39**:7, 11, 79-80
"Poem in Which I Refuse Contemplation" (Dove) **6**:120
"Poem Instead of a Columbus Day Parade" (Jordan) **38**:127
"poem IV" (Storni) **33**:286;
"Poem Jottings in the Early Morn" (Corso) **33**:50
"Poem (Khrushchev Is Coming on the Right Day!)" (O'Hara) **45**:141, 219
"poem L" (Storni) **33**:287;
"poem LIV" (Storni) **33**:289;
"Poem LIX" (Storni) **33**:287;
"A Poem Looking for a Reader" (Madhubuti) **5**:323
"poem LX" (Storni) **33**:288;
"poem LXIV" (Storni) **33**:287;
"poem LXV" (Storni) **33**:290;
"Poem No. 2" (Sanchez) **9**:220
"Poem No. 8" (Sanchez) **9**:242
"Poem No. 13" (Sanchez) **9**:213
"Poem (Now it is light, now it is the calm)" (O'Hara) **45**:225
"Poem #19 in the Old Manner" (Li Po) **29**:146
"Poem of Apparitions in Boston in the 73rd Year of These States" (Whitman) **3**:386
"Poem of Autumn" (Darío) See "Poema de otoño"
Poem of Autumn, and Other Poems (Darío) See *Poema del otoño y otros poemas*
"The Poem of Flight" (Levine) **22**:225
"A Poem of 'Good Departure, Good Return'" (Yakamochi) **48**:99
"Poem of Lament for the Transience of the Mundane World" (Yakamochi) See "Zokudo no, kari ni ai sunawachi hanare, sariyasuku todomarigataki koto wo kanashiburu shi"
"Poem of Memory" (Akhmatova) **2**:16
"A Poem of Praise" (Sanchez) **9**:242
"Poem of the Air" (Tsvetaeva) See "Poema vozdukha"
"Poem of the Body" (Whitman) **3**:385
Poem of the Cante Jondo (García Lorca) See *Poema del cante jondo*
"Poem of the Daily Work of the Workmen and Workwomen of These States" (Whitman) **3**:385
The Poem of the Deep Song (García Lorca) See *Poema del cante jondo*
"Poem of the End" (Tsvetaeva) See "Poèma kontsa"
"Poem of the Fourth Element" (Borges) See "Poema del cuarto elemento"
"Poem of the Gifts" (Borges) See "Poema de los dones"
"Poem of the Hill" (Tsvetaeva) See "Poèma gory"
"Poem of the Mountain" (Tsvetaeva) See "Poèma gory"
"Poem of the Poet" (Whitman) **3**:386
"Poem of the Singers and of the Works of Poems" (Whitman) **3**:386
Poem of the Son (Mistral) See "Poema del hijo"
"Poem of the Staircase" (Tsvetaeva) See "Poèma lestnitsy"
"Poem of These States" (Ginsberg) **4**:66
"A Poem of Towers" (Wright) **36**:306
"A Poem of Walt Whitman, an American" (Whitman) **3**:384, 414
"A Poem Off Center" (Giovanni) **19**:116
"Poem on a Japanese Paulownia Zither" (Yakamochi) **48**:102
"Poem on His Birthday" (Thomas) **2**:391; **52**:237-38, 276-77, 301, 303-5, 322, 332
"Poem on the Road" (Jordan) **38**:126
"Poem on Thinking of His Children" (Yakamochi) See "Kora wo omou uta"
"A Poem Once Significant Now Happily Not" (Cullen) **20**:85

"Poem, or Beauty Hurts Mr. Vinal" (Cummings) **5**:96
"Poem out of Childhood" (Rukeyser) **12**:231, 235
"Poem Read at Joan Mitchell's" (O'Hara) **45**:178-79, 226
"A Poem Some People Will Have to Understand" (Baraka) **4**:16
"A Poem to Complement Other Poems" (Madhubuti) **5**:329, 342
"A Poem to Galway Kinnell" (Knight) **14**:38
"A Poem to My Daughter" (Pinsky) **27**:153
"Poem to My Husband from My Father's Daughter" (Olds) **22**:322
"A Poem to Peanut" (Brooks) **7**:90
"Poem to Set a Confused Heart Straight" (Yakamochi) **48**:100, 129
"Poem Toward the Bottom Line" (Jordan) **38**:123
"Poem (Twin spheres full of fur and noise)" (O'Hara) **45**:150
"A Poem Upon the Death of His Late Highness the Lord Protector" (Marvell)
See "Poem upon the Death of O. C."
"Poem upon the Death of O. C." (Marvell) **10**:270-71, 305, 312
"Poem V (F) W" (O'Hara) **45**:222
"poem VI" (Storni) **33**:287;
"A Poem with Children" (Guillén)
See "Poema con niños"
"A Poem with No Ending" (Levine) **22**:221, 224
"Poem With Refrains" (Pinsky) **27**:175
"Poem Without a Hero" (Akhmatova) **55**:64
Poem without a Hero (Akhmatova)
See *Poema bez geroia*
Poem without a Hero: Triptych (Akhmatova)
See *Poema bez geroya: Triptykh*
"Poem Written in a Copy of Beowulf" (Borges)
See "Composición escrita en un ejemplar de la gesta de Beowulf"
"Poem Written on One of my Yearly Visits Home form California" (Quintana) **36**:274
"poem XI" (Storni) **33**:287-88;
"poem XL" (Storni) **33**:289;
"Poem XLIX" (Storni) **33**:288-90
"poem XLVI" (Storni) **33**:289;
"poem XV" (Storni) **33**:287;
"Poem XVII" (Storni) **33**:287-88;
"poem XX" (Storni) **33**:287;
"Poem XXII" (Storni) **33**:287-88
"poem XXIII" (Storni) **33**:287;
"Poem XXIV" (Storni) **33**:288;
"poem XXIX" (Storni) **33**:290;
"Poem XXV" (Storni) **33**:288;
"poem XXVI" (Storni) **33**:288;
"poem XXXIII" (Storni) **33**:290;
"poem XXXVIII" (Storni) **33**:289;
"Poema" (Mistral) **32**:166-67, 169-70
"Poema a la eñe" (Fuertes) **27**:37
Poema bez geroia (Akhmatova) **55**:3, 5, 13, 24, 38, 48-49
Poema bez geroya (Akhmatova)
See *Poema bez geroia*
Poema bez geroya: Triptykh (Akhmatova) **2**:4, 6-8, 16, 18-21
"Poema Chicano" (Cruz) **37**:31
"Poema con niños" (Guillén) **23**:139
"Poema conjectural" (Borges) **32**:49, 61, 85-6, 115-17
"Poema conjetural" (Borges)
See "Poema conjectural"
"Poema de amor" (Dalton) **36**:132
"Poema de Chile" (Mistral) **32**:165-66, 170
"Poema de los dones" (Borges) **32**:42, 131
"Poema de otoño" (Darío) **15**:81-2, 91, 96
Poema del cante jondo (García Lorca) **3**:118, 123, 127, 129, 135, 137
"Poema del cuarto elemento" (Borges) **22**:74; **32**:85
"Poema del hijo" (Mistral) **32**:153, 164-65, 176
Poema del otoño y otros poemas (Darío) **15**:86
"Poema en ón" (Fuertes) **27**:37
"Poèma gory" (Tsvetaeva) **14**:325
"Poema komnaty" (Tsvetaeva) **14**:325
"Poèma kontsa" (Tsvetaeva) **14**:301-02, 306, 316, 325
"Poèma lestnitsy" (Tsvetaeva) **14**:325
"Poema o tsarskoi sem'e" (Tsvetaeva) **14**:326-27
"Poèma para los Californios Muertos" (Cervantes) **35**:131, 135
"Poema vozdukha" (Tsvetaeva) **14**:325
Poemas (1935-1975) (Paz) **48**:175-77, 179-84, 229, 232-33
Poemas de amor (Guillén) **23**:100, 133
Poemas de la consumación (Aleixandre) **15**:4, 6-7, 12, 16-17, 25, 39, 41-4
"Poemas de las madres" (Mistral) **32**:208
Poemas de transición (Guillén) **23**:108
Poemas y antipoemas (Parra) **39**:260, 263, 266-67, 269-72, 276, 279, 282-82, 285, 287-88, 292, 295, 297, 300-2, 304, 306-9
"Poème" (Rimbaud) **57**:174
Poeme à l'étrangèr (Perse) **23**:211-13, 217, 232, 234, 250, 256-57
"Poème de la femme" (Gautier) **18**:125, 129-30, 139, 157
"Le poème de la mer" (Rimbaud) **3**:272
"Poème liminaire" (Senghor) **25**:247
"Poème lu au mariage d'André Salmon" (Apollinaire) **7**:48
"Poème pour M Valery Larbaud" (Perse) **23**:223-24
Le poême pulverisé (Char) **56**:114, 170, 173, 189-90
Poémes (Breton) **15**:53
Poèmes (Éluard) **38**:69
Poèmes (Ronsard) **11**:249
Poèmes (Senghor) **25**:232
Poëmes (Vigny) **26**:401, 410
Poèmes antiques et modernes (Vigny) **26**:367, 372, 374, 398-99, 401-402, 404, 410-12
Poemes bibliques et modernes (Vigny) **26**:391
Poèmes des deux années (Char) **56**:108
Poèmes et prose choisis (Char) **56**:113, 115
Poèmes militants (Char) **56**:129, 158, 186
Poemes Philosophiques (Vigny) **26**:368, 372, 412
Les Poèmes saturniens (Verlaine) **2**:413-15, 430-32; **32**:340, 346, 361, 368, 375-77, 384-87, 389, 393, 399, 407
Poèmes variés (Villon)
See *Poésies diverses*
Poèmes: Yves Bonnefoy (Bonnefoy) **58**:148
"Poemo" (Fuertes) **27**:49
"Poem-Painting" (Guest) **55**:223
"Poems" (Cooke) **6**:348, 394, 416
"Poems" (Shapiro) **25**:294, 320
"Poems" (Stein) **18**:313
Poems (Arnold) **5**:12, 43, 50
Poems (Auden) **1**:4, 8, 10
Poems (Berry) **28**:14-15
Poems (Bishop) **34**:167
Poems (Brooke) **24**:55, 83
Poems (Browning) **6**:14, 16-17, 19, 21, 25-7, 32, 36-8, 41-2
Poems (Clare)
See *The Poems of John Clare*
Poems (Coleridge)
See *The Poems of Samuel Taylor Coleridge*
Poems (Emerson) **18**:82, 84, 100
Poems (García Lorca)
See *Libro de poemas*
Poems (Guest) **55**:212, 214, 217-18, 227
Poems (Harper) **21**:185, 189, 193, 196-97, 209
Poems (Hope) **56**:265, 269, 271
Poems (Ignatow) **34**:271, 274, 279-80, 286, 311
Poems (Longfellow) **30**:38, 45-6, 50, 53, 62-5, 67-8
Poems (MacNeice) **61**:181
Poems (Mandelstam) **14**:106, 135
Poems (Meredith) **60**:250, 292, 308, 328
Poems (Milton) **19**:221, 249-50
Poems (Moore) **4**:228, 239, 250-51, 264; **49**:88, 96, 111
Poems (Owen) **19**:325
Poems (Pasolini)
See *Poesi*
Poems (Poe) **1**:428, 437, 441
Poems (Rimbaud)
See *Poésies*
Poems (Ronsard)
See *Poèmes*
Poems (Rossetti) **7**:265
Poems (Rossetti) **44**:165, 201-6; 257-8
Poems (Tate) **50**:293
Poems (Thomas) **53**:264
Poems (Williams) **7**:367, 374, 395, 398
Poems (Wordsworth) **4**:375, 401, 415
Poems (Wroth) **38**:305-7, 309-15
Poems (Yeats) **20**:347
Poems 1911 (Brooke) **24**:52-4, 61, 80
Poems, 1953 (Graves) **6**:154-55
Poems, 1914-1926 (Graves) **6**:132
Poems: 1922-1931 (Tate) **50**:256
Poems, 1922-1947 (Tate) **50**:241, 255, 337
Poems, 1923-1954 (Cummings) **5**:85, 89
Poems, 1924-1933 (MacLeish) **47**:128, 131, 142-44, 147-48, 153, 165, 184, 190, 213, 222
Poems, 1926-1930 (Graves) **6**:132
Poems 1928-1931 (Tate) **50**:230, 242
Poems, 1934-1969 (Ignatow) **34**:295, 301, 307, 310-11, 313, 319, 322-23, 329, 335
Poems, 1938-1945 (Graves) **6**:129
Poems, 1940-1953 (Shapiro) **25**:285, 297, 313, 317
Poems, 1943-1947 (Day Lewis) **11**:147
Poems, 1943-1956 (Wilbur) **51**:186, 191
Poems: 1948-1962 (Amichai) **38**:27-28, 44
Poems, 1949-1957 (Curnow) **48**:3, 6, 12, 24
Poems, 1957-1967 (Dickey) **40**:150, 154, 180-82, 185, 192, 195, 197, 226, 239, 241, 259
Poems, 1962-1978 (Mahon) **60**:138-39, 145, 154, 157, 165, 170-72, 175, 181-84, 186-97, 199-200, 203, 205
Poems, 1965-1975 (Heaney) **18**:206, 211
"Poems 1978-1980" (Wright) **14**:377-78
The Poems: A New Edition (Yeats) **51**:108, 110
Poems About Abroad (Yevtushenko) **40**:344
Poems about God (Ransom) **61**:267, 273, 291-92, 294, 305-6, 312-15
"Poems about Having Disease Added to His Aged Body, Suffering through the Years, and Coming to Long for His Children" (Yakamochi) **48**:131, 134, 139
Poems about Moscow (Tsvetaeva) **14**:299
"Poems about St. Petersburg, II" (Akhmatova) **2**:12
Poems and Antipoems (Parra)
See *Poemas y antipoemas*
Poems and Ballads (Swinburne) **24**:309, 314, 321, 324, 334, 337, 345, 347, 358, 362-63
Poems and Ballads, second series (Swinburne) **24**:319
Poems and Drawings (Bukowski) **18**:5
Poems and Fragments (Hölderlin) **4**:171
The Poems and Letters of Andrew Marvell (Marvell) **10**:277
Poems and Lyrics of the Joy of Life (Meredith) **60**:329
Poems and Lyrics of the Joy of the Earth (Meredith) **60**:289-90, 292, 294, 295, 298, 328, 333, 336, 339
Poems and New Poems (Bogan) **12**:89, 91, 107, 120, 124-26
Poems and Poem Outlines (Lanier) **50**:118
Poems and Satires (Graves) **6**:135
Poems Barbarous (Nishiwaki) **15**:237
Poems before Congress (Browning) **6**:6, 23, 27, 36
Poems by Currer, Ellis, and Acton Bell (Brontë) **8**:46
Poems by George Meredith (Meredith) **60**:287

Poems. By the Incomparable Mrs. K.P. (Philips) **40**:272, 280, 295-99, 312, 318, 328
Poems by the Way (Morris) **55**:325, 329, 338, 340
Poems by Thomas Carew, Esquire (Carew) **29**:64, 87
Poems by Two Brothers (Tennyson) **6**:358
Poems by William Cowper, of the Inner Temple, Esq. (Cowper) **40**:70,111
Poems, Chiefly in the Scottish Dialect (Burns) **6**:49
Poems, Chiefly Lyrical (Tennyson) **6**:347, 385, 406-09
"Poems Continual" (Jackson) **44**:7, 11
Poems Descriptive of Rural Life and Scenery (Clare) **23**:38-44
"Poems Done on a Late Night Car" (Sandburg) **41**:321, 336
"Poems for a Woman" (Amichai) **38**:54
Poems for People Who Don't Read Poems (Enzensberger) **28**:141, 143-44, 156
Poems for the Times (Heine)
See *Zeitgedichte*
"Poems from a Cycle Called 'Patriotic Songs'" (Amichai) **38**:44-5
Poems from Algiers (Brutus) **24**:112, 115, 117
Poems from Prison (Knight) **14**:38, 41, 46, 48, 52-3
"Poems from the Margins of Thom Gunn's 'Moly'" (Duncan) **2**:127
"Poems from the Plum Blossom Banquet" (Yakamochi) **48**:103, 106
Poems from the Portuguese of Luis De Camõens (Camões) **31**:24-25, 28-32, 49-53
Poems, Golders Green (Abse) **41**:2-4, 6, 9-10, 16, 22, 25
Poems Here at Home (Riley) **48**:286, 290
"The Poems I Have Lost" (Ortiz) **17**:227
"Poems in Classical Prosody" (Bridges) **28**:65
"Poems in Imitation of the Fugue" (Schwartz) **8**:289, 305
"Poems in Praise of Wine" (Yakamochi) **48**:100
Poems in Prose from Charles Baudelaire (Baudelaire)
See *Petits poèmes en prose: Le spleen de Paris*
Poems in the Shape of a Rose (Pasolini)
See *Poesia in forma di rosa*
Poems in Wartime (Day Lewis) **11**:145
Poems New and Collected 1957-1997 (Szymborska) **44**:317
"Poems of 1912-13" (Hardy) **8**:91-4, 132, 137-8
Poems of a Jew (Shapiro) **25**:282, 285, 287, 290, 297-302, 320
Poems of Akhmatova (Akhmatova) **2**:16
Poems of André Breton: A Bilingual Anthology (Breton) **15**:54
Poems of Consummation (Aleixandre)
See *Poemas de la consumación*
The Poems of Coventry Patmore (Patmore) **59**:218, 225, 237, 239-45
Poems of Ferdinand Pessoa (Pessoa) **20**:168
"Poems of Final Occasion" (Jackson) **44**:7, 10
The Poems of Francois Villon (Villon) **13**:412
Poems of Gerard Manley Hopkins (Hopkins) **15**:129, 133
"Poems of Immediate Occasion" (Jackson) **44**:7, 10
The Poems of John Clare (Clare) **23**:3, 9, 11-14
The Poems of Laura Riding (Jackson)
See *Collected Poems*
The Poems of Laura Riding: A New Edition of the 1938 Collection (Jackson) **44**:45, 83, 86-7, 89-90
"Poems of Longing for the Boy Called Furuhi" (Yakamochi) **48**:131-33, 136, 139
"Poems of Mythical Occasion" (Jackson) **44**:7, 10
Poems of Nature (Thoreau) **30**:197, 281
"Poems of Night" (Kinnell) **26**:257
"The Poems of Our Climate" (Stevens) **6**:299
Poems of Paul Celan (Celan)
See *Paul Celan: Poems*
The Poems of Samuel Taylor Coleridge (Coleridge) **11**:70, 81, 83, 104
Poems of Shadow (Jiménez) **7**:183
The Poems of Sir Walter Ralegh (Raleigh) **31**:228, 245, 249, 258
The Poems of Stanley Kunitz, 1928-1978 (Kunitz) **19**:175-76, 186
Poems of the Past and Present (Hardy) **8**:121, 123, 125
Poems of Tragic Life (Meredith) **60**:298
Poems of Various Years (Yevtushenko)
See *Stikhi raznykh let*
Poems on Affairs of State (Marvell) **10**:311
Poems on Miscellaneous Subjects (Harper) **21**:184-6, 188, 193, 196-7, 203, 206, 208-9, 215, 217-8
"poems on my fortieth birthday" (Clifton) **17**:18
Poems on Slavery (Longfellow) **30**:80-1
Poems on Various Subjects, Religious and Moral, by Phillis Wheatley, Negro Servant to Mr. John Wheatley of Boston, in New England, 1773 (Wheatley) **3**:332-34, 336, 338, 345, 349-52, 356
Poems Retrieved: 1950-1966 (O'Hara) **45**:127, 130, 153, 155, 157-58
Poems Selected and New (Page) **12**:180
Poems: Selected and New, 1950-1974 (Rich) **5**:384, 387
"Poems Speaking of Buddha" (Lindsay) **23**:283
Poems: The Empty Purse (Meredith) **60**:292, 294
Poems: The Location of Things, Archaics, the Open Skies (Guest) **55**:211, 225
"Poems to a Brown Cricket" (Wright) **36**:301, 329-30, 355
Poems to Akhmatova (Tsvetaeva)
See "Stikhi K Akhmatovoi"
Poems to Blok (Tsvetaeva)
See *Stikhi K Blok*
"Poems to Bohemia" (Tsvetaeva)
See "Stikhi k Chekhii"
"Poems to my Son" (Tsvetaeva)
See "Stikhi k synu"
"Poems to Pushkin" (Tsvetaeva)
See "Stikhi k Pushkinu"
Poems to Solve (Swenson) **14**:276
Poems upon Several Occasions, with a Voyage to the Island of Love (Behn) **13**:3, 7-8, 16, 18
Poems written before jumping out of an 8 story window (Bukowski) **18**:13
"Poemsicle" (Silverstein) **49**:335
"poem XXXII" (Storni) **33**:290;
Poesi (Pasolini) **17**:278
"Poesi i sak" (Ekeloef) **23**:77
"La Poesía" (Borges) **32**:74
"Poesía" (Jiménez) **7**:183
"La poesía" (Paz) **1**:353; **48**:182, 184
Poesía (Jiménez) **7**:202
"La poesía castellana" (Darío) **15**:95
"Poesia in forma di rosa" (Pasolini) **17**:274, 276-77
Poesia in forma di rosa (Pasolini) **17**:249, 273-74, 276, 286
La poesía juvenil (Borges) **22**:92-3
Poesía, moral, público (Aleixandre) **15**:9
Poesia política (Parra) **39**:292, 301, 304
Poesía superrealista (Aleixandre) **15**:3, 22, 24
Poesías completas (Darío) **15**:93, 107
Poesías últimas escojidas (1918-1958) (Jiménez) **7**:214
"Poésie" (Valéry) **9**:366, 394
Poesie (Carducci) **46**:4, 47
Poesie (Pavese) **13**:207, 210, 215, 220-21, 223-30
Poesie (Quasimodo) **47**:293
Poesie (Ungaretti) **57**:343-45, 347-49, 352
"Poesie a Casarsa" (Pasolini) **17**:281
Poesie a Casarsa (Pasolini) **17**:252, 254, 257, 262, 264-67, 279-82
Poesie e prose (Gozzano) **10**:184-85
Poesie edite e inedite (Pavese) **13**:208, 219, 230
"Poesie incivili" (Pasolini) **17**:273
"Poésie ininterrompue" (Éluard) **38**:64
"Poésie; ou, Le paysage dans le Gòlfe de Glafenes" (Lamartine) **16**:262
"Poesie, ou Paysage dans le Golfe de Genes" (Lamartine) **16**:292
"Poésie sacrée" (Lamartine) **16**:274, 290
Poèsies (Gautier) **18**:126
Poésies (Rimbaud) **57**:205, 237, 244-45, 249, 252-54, 289
Poésies (Valéry) **9**:399
Poésies complètes (Gautier) **18**:147
Poésies complètes (Laforgue) **14**:72
Poésies complétes (Mallarmé) **4**:206
Poésies diverses (Villon) **13**:394-95, 397, 402-03, 407, 411
"A Poet" (Akhmatova) **55**:48
"The Poet" (Aleixandre)
See "El poeta"
"The Poet" (Bryant) **20**:11, 33
"The Poet" (Carducci)
See "Il poeta"
"The Poet" (Carruth) **10**:84
"The Poet" (Cullen) **20**:85
"The Poet" (Darío)
See "El poeta"
"The Poet" (Day Lewis) **11**:146
"The Poet" (Dunbar) **5**:121, 136
"The Poet" (Emerson) **18**:88-89
"The Poet" (H. D.) **5**:306
"A Poet" (Hardy) **8**:90
"Poet" (Kavanagh) **33**:161
"The Poet" (Lermontov) **18**:281, 298
"Poet" (MacLeish) **47**:197
"The Poet" (Muir) **49**:217
"The Poet" (Rilke) **2**:280
"Poet" (Shapiro) **25**:283, 286, 311
"The Poet" (Tennyson) **6**:369
"Poet" (Viereck) **27**:259, 263, 272, 282
"Poet: A Lying Word" (Jackson) **44**:44, 71, 77-8
"The Poet acquires speech from afar. . ." (Tsvetaeva)
See "Poèt—izdaleka zovodit rech'. . ."
"The Poet and His Book" (Millay) **6**:220
"The Poet and His Song" (Dunbar) **5**:118, 121, 134
"The Poet and the Grey Friar" (Dafydd)
See "Y Bardd a'r Brawd Llwyd"
"The Poet and the Muse" (Cavafy) **36**:52
"The Poet at Forty" (Nemerov) **24**:267
"Poet at Seventy" (Milosz) **8**:180, 197, 209
Poet in New York (García Lorca)
See *Poeta en Nueva York*
Poet in Our Time (Montale) **13**:146
"The Poet in Residence" (Mahon) **60**:193
"Poet in Residence" (Sarton) **39**:335-6
"The Poet in the Machine Age" (Viereck) **27**:284
"The Poet in the World" (Levertov) **11**:172-74
"The Poet Is a Hospital Clerk" (Ignatow) **34**:281, 286
"The Poet Laments the Coming of Old Age" (Sitwell) **3**:317
"The Poet of Ignorance" (Sexton) **2**:368
"A Poet of the Thirteenth Century" (Borges)
See "Un poeta del siglo XIII"
"A Poet Recognizing the Echo of the Voice" (Wakoski) **15**:350
"The Poet Reflects on Her Solitary Fate" (Cisneros) **52**:148
"The Poet, the Oyster and Sensitive Plant" (Cowper) **40**:124
"A Poet to His Baby Son" (Johnson) **24**:144
"The Poet, to His Book" (Merton) **10**:337
"Poet to Tiger" (Swenson) **14**:280
"El poeta" (Aleixandre) **15**:3, 15, 38, 40
"El poeta" (Darío) **15**:99

Poeta de guardia (Fuertes) **27**:13, 15-8, 21, 25, 27-31, 50
"Un poeta del siglo XIII" (Borges) **32**:106
Poeta en Nueva York (García Lorca) **3**:120-21, 125, 136-38, 140, 143, 148-51
"El poeta pregunta por Stella" (Darío) **15**:113
"Los poetas celestes" (Neruda) **4**:293
"Le Poète" (Hugo) **17**:91
"La poéte Mourant" (Lamartine) **16**:271, 273-74, 278
"Les poètes de sept ans" (Rimbaud) **3**:258; **57**:173-77, 184, 216, 234, 246, 249-50, 253
Les poètes maudites (Verlaine) **32**:355
"The Poetess" (Guest) **55**:185-86, 188
The Poetic Art (Horace)
See *Ars Poetica*
Poetic Contemplations (Lamartine)
See *Les recueillements poétiques*
"Poetic Manifesto" (Thomas) **52**:297
"The Poetic Principle" (Poe) **54**:265, 268, 275-76, 331, 342-43
Poetic works (Borges)
See *Obra poética: 1923-1976*
The Poetic Year for 1916: A Critical Anthology (Braithwaite) **52**:106, 109
"Poetica" (Pavese) **13**:228
The Poetical Meditations of M. Alphonse de La Martine (Lamartine)
See *Méditations poétiques*
Poetical Sketches (Blake) **12**:31-2, 36, 43, 60-1
Poetical Works (Montagu) **16**:338, 341
The Poetical Works of Christina Georgina Rossetti (Rossetti) **7**:282-83
The Poetical Works of Rupert Brooke (Brooke) **24**:61, 75-6, 80-1, 89
The Poetical Works of S. T. Coleridge (Coleridge) **11**:75; **39**:169-70, 222
"Poetics" (Ammons) **16**:21-2, 28
"Poetics" (Pavese)
See "Poetica"
"The Poetics of the Physical World" (Kinnell) **26**:289
"Poeticus Eficacciae" (Dalton) **36**:127
"Poetik" (Ekeloef) **23**:77
"Poèt—izdaleka zovodit rech'. . ." (Tsvetaeva) **14**:323
"Poetry" (Arnold) **5**:41
"Poetry" (Goethe) **5**:227
"Poetry" (Moore) **4**:232, 235, 249, 251, 254, 270-71; **49**:95-96, 161
"Poetry" (O'Hara) **45**:170, 183-84, 227
"Poetry" (Pasternak) **6**:252, 262, 272, 279, 282
"Poetry" (Paz)
See "La poesía"
"Poetry" (Yevtushenko) **40**:338, 346
Poetry (Pavese)
See *Poesie*
Poetry (Szymborska)
See *Poezje*
"Poetry and Happiness" (Wilbur) **51**:254
"Poetry and Landscape" (Wilbur) **51**:255
"Poetry and Pleasure" (Pinsky) **27**:165
"Poetry and Politics" (Oppen) **35**:340
"Poetry and Religion" (Corso) **33**:35
"Poetry and the Landscape" (Wilbur)
See "Poetry and Landscape"
"Poetry and the World" (Pinsky) **27**:158
Poetry and the World (Pinsky) **27**:156-58, 160-61, 176
"Poetry = Anger x Imagination" (Alexie) **53**:3, 15
"Poetry Days" (Yevtushenko) **40**:350
"Poetry dusint have to be" (Bissett) **14**:13, 27
"Poetry Festival" (Enzensberger) **28**:162
"Poetry Finished Me Off" (Parra) **39**:264
"Poetry for the Advanced" (Baraka) **4**:31, 39
Poetry Is (Hughes) **7**:158
"Poetry is Not a Luxury" (Lorde) **12**:143
"Poetry is the Smallest" (Ammons) **16**:43
"Poetry of Departures" (Larkin) **21**:229
The Poetry of Life (Carman) **34**:205-06, 230-31
"The Poetry of Milton" (Meredith) **60**:336
"Poetry of the Present" (Lawrence) **54**:184
"Poetry Perpetuates the Poet" (Herrick) **9**:146
"Poetry the True Fiction" (Guest) **55**:196
"The Poets" (Boland) **58**:42
"Poets" (Herrick) **9**:91, 106
"Poets and Painters: Rivals or Partners" (Birney) **52**:76
"The Poets are Silent" (Smith) **12**:354
The Poet's Calendar (Longfellow) **30**:99
"The Poet's Death" (Lermontov)
See "Smert' poeta"
"The Poet's Death Is His Life" (Gibran) **9**:73
"The Poet's Delay" (Thoreau) **30**:193, 203, 226, 240, 251, 276
"Poet's Epitaph" (Paz) **48**:250
"Poets Hitchhiking on the Highway" (Corso) **33**:5, 23, 31-2, 43, 48
"The Poets Lament for His Lost Boyhood" (Surrey) **59**:352
"The Poets of Seven Years" (Rimbaud)
See "Les poètes de sept ans"
"The Poets of the Nineties" (Mahon) **60**:156
"The Poets of the White Faction of Dante's Florence" (Carducci)
See "I Poeti di Parte Bianca"
"The Poet's Story" (Tagore)
See "Kabi kahini"
"The Poet's Vow" (Browning) **6**:38-9
"The poet's words" (Aleixandre)
See "Las palabras del poeta"
"Poet's Work" (Niedecker) **42**:106, 136, 181
"Poet-Tree 1" (Birney) **52**:31, 82
Poezje (Herbert) **50**:17, 19, 21-22, 25
Poezje (Szymborska) **44**:269
"The Point" (Hayden) **6**:193
"The Point" (Soto) **28**:371
"Le Point du Jour" (Verlaine)
See "Point du Jour de Paris"
"Point du Jour de Paris" (Verlaine) **32**:378
"Point Joe" (Jeffers) **17**:130, 136
"A Point of Origin" (McHugh) **61**:200
Point Reyes Poems (Bly) **39**:22-3
"Point Shirley" (Plath) **1**:389; **37**:177, 181-82
"Point-of-View" (Graham) **59**:166
"Le poison" (Baudelaire) **1**:45, 61
"Poison" (Tagore)
See "Halahal"
"A Poison Tree" (Blake) **12**:7
"The Poisoned Man" (Dickey) **40**:192
Poisson soluble (Breton) **15**:48, 63, 68, 70
"Poiu kngda gortan' syra . . ." (Mandelstam) **14**:150, 154
"Pokeberries" (Stone) **53**:230
Polar Bear Hunt (Bissett) **14**:16-17, 19
"Polder" (Heaney) **18**:245
"Pole Star" (MacLeish) **47**:179, 190, 255
"Polémica" (Dalton) **36**:129
"Police" (Corso) **33**:15, 25, 47-8
"A Police Manual" (Wagoner) **33**:334
"Policía" (Guillén) **23**:101
"A Polish Dictionary" (Zagajewski) **27**:381
"Polish Pilgrims" (Mickiewicz)
See "Pielgrzym"
Politica Poetry (Parra)
See *Poesia política*
"A Political Cartoon" (Ignatow) **34**:318
"Political Poem" (Baraka) **4**:10
"A Political Poem" (Oppen) **35**:300, 302
"Political Relations" (Lorde) **12**:141
"Politics" (Meredith) **28**:206, 214
"Pollock and Canvas" (Graham) **59**:133, 150, 173, 189-90, 194
"Polonius Passing Through a Stage" (Nemerov) **24**:294-95
Poltava (Pushkin) **10**:366-69, 371, 373, 390-91, 394, 409, 411
"Pomade" (Dove) **6**:111, 113
"The Pomegranate" (Boland) **58**:19, 48
"Pomegranate" (Glück) **16**:126, 140-41
"Pomegranates" (Valéry)
See "Les grenades"
Pomes for Yoshi (Bissett) **14**:11, 17-18
"Pominal'naia svecha" (Shvarts) **50**:163
"Les Pommes" (Bonnefoy) **58**:152
"Pomona" (Morris) **55**:323, 325-27
"Pompilia" (Browning) **2**:41
"The Pond" (Glück) **16**:134
"The Pond" (Nemerov) **24**:261
"The Pond at Dusk" (Kenyon) **57**:15, 26, 37
"Pondy Woods" (Warren) **37**:287
"Le pont Mirabeau" (Apollinaire) **7**:11, 21
"Ponte Veneziano" (Tomlinson) **17**:342, 347, 349
"Les ponts" (Rimbaud) **3**:264; **57**:232, 236, 239, 254, 274
"Pony Hill" (MacLeish) **47**:213
"The Poodler" (Merrill) **28**:234, 242
"The Pool and the Star" (Wright) **14**:346
"The pool that swims in us" (Piercy) **29**:316, 318
"Poor" (Brooke) **24**:59
"Poor Art" (Montale)
See "L'arte povera"
"The Poor at Church" (Rimbaud)
See "Les Pauvres à l'église"
"The Poor Child's Toy" (Baudelaire)
See "Le joujou du pauvre"
"A Poor Christian Looks at the Ghetto" (Milosz) **8**:191-92, 214
"Poor Clare" (Erdrich) **52**:186, 188
"Poor Girl" (Angelou) **32**:27
"The Poor House" (Teasdale) **31**:321
"The Poor in Church" (Rimbaud)
See "Les pauvres à l'église"
"Poor Mailie's Elegy" (Burns)
See "The Death and Dying Words of Poor Mailie"
"A Poor Man's Wealth" (Riley) **48**:302
"The Poor of London" (Belloc) **24**:28
"The Poor Old Deaf Woman" (Castro)
See "¡A probiña qu' esta xorda . . . !"
"Poor Pierrot" (Masters) **1**:330, 333
"Poor Poll" (Bridges) **28**:77-9
"Poor Susan" (Wordsworth) **4**:374
"The Poor Washed Up by Chicago Winter" (Wright) **36**:319, 366, 391
"Poor Woman in a City Church" (Heaney) **18**:200
"A Poor Young Shepherd" (Verlaine) **32**:399
"The Pope" (Browning) **2**:41, 72
"Pope to Bolingbroke" (Montagu) **16**:342
"The Pope's Penis" (Olds) **22**:316
"Poplar Memory" (Kavanagh) **33**:149
"Poplar, Sycamore" (Wilbur) **51**:187, 204
"Poplars" (Sandburg) **41**:324
"Poppa Chicken" (Walker) **20**:273, 276, 286
"Poppies" (Sandburg) **2**:303
"Poppies in July" (Plath) **1**:381, 388
"Poppies in October" (Plath) **1**:384; **37**:257
"A Poppy" (Bridges) **28**:67
Poppy and Memory (Celan)
See *Mohn und Gedächtnes*
"Poppy Flower" (Hughes) **1**:240
"Poppycock" (Francis) **34**:248
"Popular Demand" (Merrill) **28**:284-85
"Popular Songs" (Ashbery) **26**:162
"Population Drifts" (Sandburg) **41**:239, 243, 325-27, 329, 364
"Populist" (Oppen) **35**:301
"Populist Manifesto" (Ferlinghetti) **1**:176, 182, 188
"Popytka komnaty" (Tsvetaeva) **14**:308, 325
"Popytka revnosti" (Tsvetaeva) **14**:306, 308
"Por boca cerrada entran moscas" (Neruda) **4**:290
"Por de pronto" (Guillén) **35**:221
"Pora, Moi Drug, Pora" (Pushkin) **10**:410
"Porcelain Bowl" (Glück) **16**:150
"Porch Swing" (Kumin) **15**:215
"The Porcupine" (Kinnell) **26**:240-42, 244, 257, 262, 291
"the pores of my skin" (Alurista) **34**:32
"Pornographer" (Hass) **16**:195
"Porphyria's Lover" (Browning) **61**:88

"The Port" (Merwin) **45**:37-9
"Port of Call" (Abse) **41**:3
"Port of Embarcation" (Jarrell) **41**:144
"Portail" (Gautier) **18**:143-45, 155-56
"Porte ouverte" (Éluard) **38**:69
"Porter" (Hughes) **1**:242
"Pórtico" (Darío) **15**:113
"A Portion of History" (Kenyon) **57**:12, 45
"Portland, 1968" (Glück) **16**:129, 150, 154
"The 'Portland' Going Out" (Merwin) **45**:7
"Portovenere" (Montale) **13**:151
"Portrait" (Bogan) **12**:87, 101, 103
"A Portrait" (Browning) **2**:59
"Portrait" (Éluard) **38**:87
"The Portrait" (Graves) **6**:144
"The Portrait" (Kunitz) **19**:176-77, 179
"A Portrait" (Parker) **28**:360
"The Portrait" (Rossetti) **44**:174, 176, 195, 238-39, 244-45, 250-52
"A Portrait" (Rossetti) **7**:296-7
"Portrait" (Wright) **14**:356, 362
"Portrait by a Neighbor" (Millay) **6**:233
"Portrait de Paul Éluard" (Péret) **33**:230
"A Portrait in Greys" (Williams) **7**:409
"Portrait of a Girl" (Aiken) **26**:24, 72
"Portrait of a Lady" (Eliot) **5**:153, 161, 183, 185-86; **31**:131, 134, 137, 140, 162, 166, 190
"A Portrait of a Modern Lady" (Swift) **9**:259
"Portrait of a Women in Bed" (Williams) **7**:348, 367
"Portrait of an Artist" (Kavanagh) **33**:76, 98-9
"Portrait of an Old Woman on the College Tavern Wall" (Sexton) **2**:358
"Portrait of García Lorca" (Storni)
See "Retrato de García Lorca"
"Portrait of Georgia" (Toomer) **7**:310, 320, 334
"Portrait of Marina" (Page) **12**:168, 176, 189-90
"Portrait of Mrs Spaxton" (Tomlinson) **17**:311
"Portrait of My Father in an English Landscape" (Szirtes) **51**:173, 178
Portrait of My Father in an English Landscape (Szirtes) **51**:172
"A Portrait of the Artist" (Mahon) **60**:179, 199
"Portrait of the Artist" (Parker) **28**:351, 361
"Portrait of the Artist" (Sarton) **39**:319
"Portrait of the Artist" (Tomlinson) **17**:320
"Portrait of the Artist as a Middle-aged Man" (Abse) **41**:19
"Portrait of the Artist as a Prematurely Old Man" (Nash) **21**:279
"Portrait of the Artist as a Young Chicana" (Cisneros) **52**:148
"Portrait of the Author" (Pavese) **13**:205
"Portrait of the Author as a Young Anarchist" (Rexroth) **20**:187
"A Portrait of the Self as Nation, 1990-1991" (Chin) **40**:9, 19-20, 23-4
"Portrait of Three Conspirators" (Nemerov) **24**:292
"Portraits" (Cummings) **5**:94
Portraits and Elegies (Schnackenberg) **45**:329, 336, 338-39, 342-43, 345
Portraits with a Name (Aleixandre)
See *Retratos con nombre*
"Portret blokady cherez zhanr, natiurmort, i peizazh" (Shvarts) **50**:162
"The Portuguese Sea" (Pessoa)
See "Mar Portuguese"
"Die posaunenstelle" (Celan) **10**:98, 111
"Pose After the painting Mrs. Badhamby Ingres" (Boland) **58**:45
"Poseidonians" (Cavafy) **36**:40
"Posesión del ayer" (Borges) **22**:95
"The Posie" (Burns) **6**:76
Positives (Gunn) **26**:202, 208, 219, 226
"Positives: For Sterling Plumpp" (Madhubuti) **5**:346
"Posle grozy" (Pasternak) **6**:267-68, 285
Posle razluki (Bely) **11**:3, 25, 32-3
Posle Rossii (Tsvetaeva) **14**:298, 306, 310-11, 315, 317, 324-25, 327
"Possessing Eden" (Kavanagh) **33**:142
"Possession" (Brathwaite) **56**:23-24, 88
"Possessions" (Crane) **3**:83
"Possessions extérieures" (Char) **56**:138
"Possessive Case" (Stein) **18**:327
"Possibilities" (Szymborska) **44**:300
"Possom Trot" (Dunbar) **5**:133
"Possum Song" (Johnson) **24**:163
"Post aetatem nostram" (Brodsky) **9**:4
"Post mortem" (Jeffers) **17**:117, 141
"POST RESSURECTION CITY BLUES" (Bissett) **14**:31-2
"Post the Lake Poets Ballad" (O'Hara) **45**:186
"A Postcard from Berlin" (Mahon) **60**:148, 150, 198
"Postcard from Cornwall" (Abse) **41**:3
"Postcard from Picadilly Street" (Ondaatje) **28**:329
"A Postcard from the Volcano" (Stevens) **6**:297
"Postcard to the Lace Man—The Old Market, Antibes" (Cisneros) **52**:161
"Postcards for Bert Meyers" (Hongo) **23**:197
"Post-Graduate" (Parker) **28**:362
"A Post-Impressionist Susurration for the First of November, 1983" (Carruth) **10**:88
"Postlude" (Williams) **7**:345
"Postlude Home" (Brathwaite) **56**:5, 28
"Postman Cheval" (Breton)
See "Facteur Cheval"
"Postmark" (Abse) **41**:3
"Postmeridian" (Cassian) **17**:12
"A Post-Mortem" (Sassoon) **12**:248
Poštovní holub (Seifert) **47**:324-25, 332
"Postponement of Self" (Jackson) **44**:29
"Postscript" (Kunitz) **19**:147
Postscripts (Tagore)
See *Punascha*
"Posvyashchenie" (Akhmatova) **55**:4-5, 8-9, 13, 15-19, 27-30, 36, 41, 43-44, 49, 57-60, 63
"The Posy" (Herbert) **4**:129
"The Pot of Earth" (MacLeish) **47**:125, 127, 129, 132, 136-37, 140, 150, 156, 164, 175, 177, 183-85, 187, 191-92, 222
"The Pot of Flowers" (Williams) **7**:388
"Potato" (Kenyon) **57**:12
"The Potato" (Mickiewicz)
See "Kartofel"
"Potato" (Viereck) **27**:279
"Potato" (Wilbur) **51**:187, 193, 266-67, 295
"Potato Blossom Songs and Jigs" (Sandburg) **2**:316; **41**:240, 270
"The Potatoes' Dance" (Lindsay) **23**:281
"Potchikoo Greets Josette" (Erdrich) **52**:193
"Potchikoo Marries" (Erdrich) **52**:193
"Potchikoo Restored" (Erdrich) **52**:193
"Potchikoo's Detour" (Erdrich) **52**:193
"Potchikoo's Life after Death" (Erdrich) **52**:188, 193
"Potchikoo's Mean Twin" (Erdrich) **52**:193
"Potega smaku" (Herbert) **50**:13, 22, 24, 40
"Potluck at the Wilmot Flat Baptist Church" (Kenyon) **57**:39, 43
"Potter" (Ondaatje) **28**:318
"Potwór Pana Cogito" (Herbert) **50**:19, 32-33, 38, 40, 46
"Un Pouacre" (Verlaine) **32**:378
"Poui" (Goodison) **36**:142-43, 149-50
"Pouir fêter des oiseaux" (Perse) **23**:254
Pour feter une enfance (3) (Perse) **23**:217, 221, 257
"Pour le livre d'amour" (Laforgue) **14**:80
"Pour Prende Congé" (Parker) **28**:362
"Pour saluer le tiers monde" (Césaire) **25**:13
"Pour se prendre au piège" (Éluard) **38**:69-70
"Pour un anniversaire" (Éluard) **38**:75
"Pouring the Milk Away" (Rukeyser) **12**:224
"Pourquoi mon âme est-elle triste?" (Lamartine) **16**:280
"Poussin" (MacNeice) **61**:124
Poverkh barierov (Pasternak) **6**:263, 268-69
"Poverty" (Ammons) **16**:32
"Poverty" (Thoreau) **30**:181
"P.O.W" (Yamada) **44**:334
"Powder Monkey" (Carver) **54**:11
"Power" (Corso) **33**:6, 9, 15, 25, 36, 44-5, 47-8
"Power" (Lorde) **12**:155
"Power" (Rich) **5**:377
"Power" (Rukeyser) **12**:210
"Power" (Wright) **14**:362
"Power and Light" (Dickey) **40**:151-52, 154, 161, 168-70, 175, 255, 258, 260
"The Power and the Glory" (Sassoon) **12**:246
"The Power of God" (Ransom) **61**:294
"The Power of Perez" (Guillén) **35**:241
"The Power of Taste" (Herbert)
See "Potega smaku"
"Power of the Many" (Curnow) **48**:24
Power Politics (Atwood) **8**:9, 12, 14-16, 21-4, 26, 31, 44
"Power to the People" (Walker) **20**:294
"Powers" (Milosz) **8**:202, 211
"Powhatan's Daughter" (Crane) **3**:86, 88, 105
"Powrót prokonsula" (Herbert) **50**:32, 36
"Powroty" (Szymborska) **44**:269, 277
"Powwow Love Songs" (Alexie) **53**:25
"Powwow Polaroid" (Alexie) **53**:11
Prabhat sangit (Tagore) **8**:405-6
"Practical People" (Jeffers) **17**:117
"A Practical Program for Monks" (Merton) **10**:334
"Praeteritio" (Ní Chuilleanáin) **34**:358
Praeteritio (Ní Chuilleanáin) **34**:373
Prague (Seifert)
See *Praha*
"Prague in a Dream" (Seifert)
See "Praha ve snu"
Praha (Seifert) **47**:335
"Praha ve snu" (Seifert) **47**:341
"The Prairie" (Clampitt) **19**:93, 96-7
"Prairie" (Sandburg) **2**:303, 304, 307, 314, 316, 339; **41**:242, 260-1, 270, 274, 296-7, 327
"Prairie Waters" (Sandburg) **41**:270
"Prairie Waters by Night" (Sandburg) **2**:316
"The Prairies" (Bryant) **20**:14, 19, 23-4, 29, 34, 40-1, 47
Praise (Hass) **16**:197-201, 210, 212, 215-16, 222, 226
"Praise II" (Herbert) **4**:121
"Praise III" (Herbert) **4**:125
"Praise Be" (Kumin) **15**:214
"Praise for an Urn" (Crane) **3**:90, 100
"Praise for Sick Women" (Snyder) **21**:325
"Praise for the fountain open'd" (Cowper) **40**:55
"Praise Him" (Walcott) **46**:262
"Praise in Summer" (Wilbur) **51**:188, 193, 267, 283
"Praise to the End!" (Roethke) **15**:254, 272, 274, 284, 298-99, 301-02, 304, 307
Praise to the End! (Roethke) **15**:248-51, 256, 282-84, 298-99, 301-03, 309
"Praised be Dianas faire and harmles light" (Raleigh) **31**:202, 219, 238, 248-50, 253, 259
Prāntik (Tagore) **8**:422-24
"Pratidhyani" (Tagore) **8**:406
"Pravahini" (Tagore) **8**:415
"Pray to What Earth Does This Sweet Cold Belong" (Thoreau) **30**:267
"Prayer" (Boland) **58**:34
"The Prayer" (Browning) **6**:19
"Prayer" (Cavafy) **36**:53, 79
"The Prayer" (Herbert) **4**:102, 130
"Prayer" (Hughes) **1**:240
"Prayer" (Jiménez)
See "Plegaria"
"A Prayer" (Lermontov) **18**:303
"The Prayer" (Mistral)
See "El ruego"
"Prayer" (Olds) **22**:316, 328
"Prayer" (Ransom) **61**:294
"Prayer" (Roethke) **15**:260
"A Prayer" (Teasdale) **31**:322
"Prayer" (Toomer) **7**:320-22, 334-35

"A Prayer" (Tsvetaeva)
See "Molitva"
"Prayer" (Wright) **14**:356, 366
"Prayer I" (Herbert) **4**:115
"Prayer at Sunrise" (Johnson) **24**:145, 153
"Prayer before Birth" (MacNeice) **61**:126, 142
The Prayer Before the Poem (Yevtushenko) **40**:356
"Prayer Before Work" (Sarton) **39**:320, 341, 344, 356
"Prayer for a Prayer" (Parker) **28**:351, 364
"Prayer for a Second Flood" (MacDiarmid) **9**:155-56, 197-98
"Prayer for Change" (Yamada) **44**:346
"A Prayer for Faith" (Kavanagh) **33**:162
A Prayer for Marilyn Monroe and other poems (Cardenal)
See *Oracion por Marilyn Monroe y otros poemas*
"A Prayer for my Daughter" (Tomlinson) **17**:307
"A Prayer for My Daughter" (Yeats) **20**:320, 328, 336, 338-39, 342; **51**:98, 134, 142
"A Prayer for My Son" (Yeats) **20**:336, 339-40; **51**:84
"A Prayer for Old Age" (Yeats) **51**:137
"Prayer for Peace" (Senghor)
See "Prière de paix"
"Prayer for the Great Family" (Snyder) **21**:297
"Prayer in Mid-Passage" (MacNeice) **61**:142
"A Prayer of Columbus" (Whitman) **3**:379, 384, 395
"Prayer of Descending Order" (Stone) **53**:259
"Prayer of Mr. Cogito—Traveler" (Herbert)
See "Modlitwa Pana Cogito-Podróznika"
"The Prayer of Nature" (Byron) **16**:87
"Prayer to Ben Jonson" (Herrick) **9**:86, 96
"A Prayer to Escape from the Market Place" (Wright) **36**:326-27, 332, 350
"A Prayer to Go to Paradise with the Donkeys" (Wilbur) **51**:190
"Prayer to Masks" (Senghor)
See "Prière aux Masques"
"Prayer to My Mother" (Pasolini) **17**:289
"Prayer to the Father of Heaven" (Skelton) **25**:337, 339
"Prayer to the Good Poet" (Wright) **36**:335, 377, 391, 393
"A Prayer to the Lord Ramakhrishna" (Wright) **36**:341-42, 355
"Prayers of Steel" (Sandburg) **2**:302, 311; **41**:240, 262, 270, 329
"Praying on a 707" (Sexton) **2**:373
"Prayrs for th One Habitation" (Bissett) **14**:20
"Praze" (Seifert) **47**:316
"The Preacher: Ruminates behind the Sermon" (Brooks) **7**:53, 87, 94
"A Preaching from a Spanish Young Princess" (Meredith) **60**:263-64
"Preamble" (Rukeyser) **12**:209
"Prece" (Pessoa) **20**:155-56
"Precedent" (Dunbar) **5**:133
"Precession of the Equinoxes" (Rexroth) **20**:193, 196
"The Precinct. Rochester" (Lowell) **13**:83
"Preciosa and the Wind" (García Lorca)
See "Preciosa y el aire"
"Preciosa y el aire" (García Lorca) **3**:146
"Precious Angel" (Dylan) **37**:59
"Precious Guilt" (Warren) **37**:376
"Precious Moments" (Sandburg) **2**:331
"Precious Yeast of the World" (Mandelstam)
See "Drozhzhi mira dorogie"
"The Precipice" (Wright) **14**:354
"A Precise Woman" (Amichai) **38**:54
"Los precursores de Kafka" (Borges) **32**:47
"Preface" (Cisneros) **52**:148
"Préface" (Gautier) **18**:154, 156
"La préface" (Olson) **19**:318-21, 323
"Preface of the Galaxy" (Matsuo Bashō)
See "Ginga no jo"
"Preface to a Love Poem" (Mahon) **60**:163, 165-67, 190, 193
Preface to a Twenty Volume Suicide Note (Baraka) **4**:5-6, 14-17, 27, 31, 37
"Preface to an Excursion to the Matsura River" (Yakamochi) **48**:102-3
"The Preferred Voice" (Baudelaire)
See "La Voix"
"Preguntas Frente al lago" (Cardenal) **22**:111
Preguntas y respuestas (Parra) **39**:297
"Prehistoric" (Silverstein) **49**:334
"Prelenstnitse" (Lermontov) **18**:303
"Prelude" (Brathwaite) **56**:26, 49, 67, 75, 82, 98
"Prélude" (Hugo) **17**:91-93
"Prelude" (Kavanagh) **33**:63, 86, 95, 121-2, 148-9
"Prelude" (Longfellow) **30**:19, 26, 44, 62
"Prelude" (Swinburne) **24**:313, 355, 357
"A Prelude" (Tomlinson) **17**:327, 333
"Prelude" (Tomlinson) **17**:328
"Prelude" (Walcott) **46**:272-73, 279, 322
The Prelude (Wordsworth)
See *The Prelude; or, Growth of a Poets Mind: Autobiographical Poem*
The Prelude; or, Growth of a Poets Mind: Autobiographical Poem (Wordsworth) **4**:397, 402-09, 412, 414, 421-27
"Prelude: The Troops" (Sassoon) **12**:264
"Prelude to a Fairy Tale" (Sitwell) **3**:295, 300, 304
"Prelude to an Evening" (Ransom) **61**:276-77, 298
"Prelude to Our Age: A Negro History Poem" (Hughes) **53**:115
"Preludes" (Eliot) **5**:153; 31; 131, 133-34, 159
"Les préludes" (Lamartine) **16**:278
Preludes (Aiken) **26**:23, 29-30
"Préludes autobiographiques" (Laforgue) **14**:66, 95
Preludes for Memnon; or, Preludes to Attitude (Aiken) **26**:23, 29-30, 33, 38, 52-3, 57-69, 72
Preludes to Attitude (Aiken) **26**:38-39
Preludes to Definition (Aiken) **26**:38-9
"Le Premier Jour" (Péret) **33**:231
Premier livre des amours (Ronsard) **11**:246
Le premier livre des poemes (Ronsard) **11**:280
"Le premier regret" (Lamartine) **16**:293
"Premier sourire du printemps" (Gautier) **18**:128
La Première Aventure céleste de Mr Antipyrine (Tzara) **27**:227
"Première du monde" (Éluard) **38**:71, 76-7
"Première soirèe" (Rimbaud) **3**:258, 283; **57**:202, 236
Premières alluvions (Char) **56**:129
"Les premières communions" (Rimbaud) **3**:260; **57**:184, 202-3, 205, 250, 253, 294
"Les Premiers Instants" (Char) **56**:156
"Premonition" (Carman) **34**:207
"The Premonition" (Roethke) **15**:293
"Prendimiento de Antoñito el Camborio" (García Lorca) **3**:131
"PREPAID CATASTROPHE COVERAGE" (Birney) **52**:79
"Preparatory Exercise (Dyptych with Votive Tablet)" (Paz) **1**:374; **48**:192
"Prepare Thy Self" (Roethke) **15**:293
"The Prepositions" (Olds) **22**:320
"Pres Spoke in a Language" (Baraka) **4**:39
"Presagios" (Guillén) **35**:155, 156
"Prescription of Painful Ends" (Jeffers) **17**:141-144-45
"The Prescriptive Stalls As" (Ammons) **16**:25, 44
Présence (Char)
See *Communé présence*
"The Presence" (Graves) **6**:137
"The Presence" (Kumin) **15**:181
"Presence" (Zagajewski) **27**:389, 393
"Presencia del aire" (Guillén) **35**:157
"Présense" (Césaire) **25**:10
"The Presense" (Elytis) **21**:130
"Present" (Cage) **58**:218
"Present" (O'Hara) **45**:150
"Present" (Sanchez) **9**:219
"Present, Afterwards" (Aleixandre)
See "Presente, después"
"The Present Age" (Harper) **21**:190
"A Present for the Queen of France" (Cowper) **40**:103
Presentation Piece (Hacker) **47**:79-80, 88, 90, 115
"Presente, después" (Aleixandre) **15**:6
Presented to Ch'en Shang (Li Ho) **13**:44
"Presented to Wang Lun" (Li Po) **29**:146
"Presented to Wei Pa, Gentleman in Retirement" (Tu Fu) **9**:322
"Preseul, ovile regis" (Gower) **59**:25
"The President About to Address the Nation in the Eighth Year of the Vietnam War" (Bly) **39**:51
"President Harding's Tomb in Ohio" (Wright) **36**:396
"President Lincoln's Proclamation of Freedom" (Harper) **21**:197
"Prèsomptif" (Perse) **23**:230
"Press Release" (Merriman) **28**:284-85
"Presso l'Urna di Percy Bysshe Shelley" (Carducci) **46**:9, 16, 26, 54, 87
"Presso Una Certosa" (Carducci) **46**:31
"Pressure to Grow" (Baraka) **4**:30
"Pressures" (Wright) **14**:375
"Preston North End" (Szirtes) **51**:179
"Prestupnik" (Lermontov) **18**:289
"Pretiolae" (Moore) **49**:126
"Pretty" (Smith) **12**:301, 318, 321, 328
"The Pretty Bar-Keeper of the Mitre" (Smart) **13**:341, 347
"The Pretty Barmaid" (Smart)
See "The Pretty Bar-Keeper of the Mitre"
"The Pretty Redhead" (Apollinaire)
See "La jolie rousse"
"The Pretty Redhead, from the French of Apollinaire" (Wright) **36**:308-9
"A Pretty Woman" (Browning) **61**:90
"Pretty Words" (Wylie) **23**:314, 324
"Prevalent at One Time" (Moore) **49**:150
"Priapus" (H. D.) **5**:275, 303
Priapus and the Pool and Other Poems (Aiken) **26**:46
"Pricing" (Ignatow) **34**:305
"La prière" (Lamartine) **16**:276-77, 291, 299-301
"Prière aux Masques" (Senghor) **25**:224, 227, 229-30, 241
"Prière de paix" (Senghor) **25**:231,254
"Prière du matin" (Verlaine) **2**:416
"La prière pour tous" (Hugo) **17**:45
"The Priest" (H. D.) **5**:306
"Priest" (Herbert) **50**:18, 25
"The Priest and the Matador" (Bukowski) **18**:4
"Priest of the Temple of Serapis" (Cavafy) **36**:32
"Prigovor" (Akhmatova) **2**:8-9; **55**:5, 10, 25-26, 28, 42, 58, 60, 62
Přilba hlíny (Seifert) **47**:316, 326, 335
"Prima del viaggio" (Montale) **13**:134
"Primal Death" (Stramm)
See "Urtod"
"Primal Vision" (Benn) **35**:8
Primal Vision (Benn) **35**:7, 8, 9
"Primäre Tage" (Benn) **35**:67
"Primary Colors" (Song) **21**:333-34, 343, 350
"A Primary Ground" (Rich) **5**:361
"La primavera" (Jiménez) **7**:193-94
"Primavera classica" (Carducci) **46**:48, 77-78, 80
"Primavera delgada" (Guillén) **35**:186, 188
"La primavera Hitleriana" (Montale) **13**:104, 109, 145, 148, 165-66
"Primaveral" (Darío) **15**:117
"Primavere Dorica" (Carducci) **46**:40, 42, 86

"Primavere elleniche" (Carducci) **46**:23, 37, 43, 54, 58, 64, 78, 86
"Prime" (Hughes) **53**:150
"Prime" (Lowell) **13**:64, 67
Primer for Blacks (Brooks) **7**:83, 86
"A Primer of the Daily Round" (Nemerov) **24**:257, 283
Primer romancero gitano (García Lorca) **3**:119-21, 127, 130, 133-34, 136-38, 145-49
Primeras poesias (Jiménez) **7**:209
"Primero sueño" (Juana Inés de la Cruz) **24**:182-83, 189, 191-94, 198, 209, 211, 217, 220
"Primeros Sonidos" (Cruz) **37**:31
"The Primitive" (Madhubuti) **5**:322
"Primitive" (Olds) **22**:307
"Primitive" (Oppen) **35**:300-01
"The Primitive" (Swenson) **14**:264
Primitive (Oppen) **35**:300-01, 302, 303, 304, 324, 325, 335, 338
"A Primitive Like an Orb" (Stevens) **6**:314, 335
"'Primitivism' Exhibit" (Kumin) **15**:209
"Primo vere" (Carducci) **46**:87
"The Primrose" (Donne) **1**:126, 130
"Primrose" (Herrick) **9**:125
"Primrose" (Kavanagh) **33**:97, 118, 162
"Primrose" (Williams) **7**:345
The Primrose Path (Nash) **21**:263
"The Prince" (Wald) **46**:230
"Prince Athanase" (Shelley) **14**:189, 192, 202, 234-35
Prince Hohenstiel-Schwangau (Browning) **2**:43, 47, 82, 95
"Prince Meow" (Cassian) **17**:3
"The Prince of Darkness Passing through this House" (Wakoski) **15**:363
"Prince Tank" (Viereck) **27**:260, 280
"The Prince's Progress" (Rossetti) **7**:262-4, 279-80, 287, 289, 293-4, 296-8
The Prince's Progress, and Other Poems (Rossetti) **7**:261, 263, 266, 296
The Princess: A Medley (Tennyson) **6**:354, 360, 364-65, 371, 409
The Princess and the Knights (Bely) **11**:24
"Principalities of June" (Doty) **53**:69
De principiis (Gray)
See *De principiis cogitandi*
De principiis cogitandi (Gray) **2**:154
"Prinkin' Leddie" (Wylie) **23**:301
"Printemps" (Tzara) **27**:223
"Printemps" (Verlaine) **32**:400-05
"Prioress's Tale" (Chaucer) **19**:13, 15, 54-6
"The Priory of St. Saviour, Glendalough" (Davie) **29**:108-09
"La Prison" (Vigny) **26**:380, 401-403, 410
"The Prisoner" (Brontë)
See "Julian M. and A. G. Rochelle"
"The Prisoner" (Browning) **6**:26
"The Prisoner" (Paz)
See "El prisonero"
"The Prisoner" (Tagore)
See "Bandi"
The Prisoner of Chillon, and Other Poems (Byron) **16**:87
"The Prisoner of the Caucasus" (Lermontov) **18**:278
The Prisoner of the Caucasus (Pushkin)
See *Kavkazsky plennik*
"The Prisoner of Zenda" (Wilbur) **51**:285
"El prisonero" (Paz) **1**:364-65
"Prisoners" (Boland) **58**:44
"The Prisoners" (Hayden) **6**:194-95
"Prisoners" (Komunyakaa) **51**:61
"The Prisoner's Complaint" (Scott) **13**:292
"The Prisoner's Dream" (Montale)
See "Il Sogno del prigioniero"
"The Prisoner's Woman" (Mistral)
See "Mujer de prisionero"
"Privacy" (Rexroth) **20**:221
"A Private" (Thomas) **53**:326
"A private bestiary" (Piercy) **29**:314
The Private Dining Room (Nash) **21**:270-71
"The Private Life" (Graham) **59**:166
"The Private Life" (Mueller) **33**:180
The Private Life (Mueller) **33**:175-76, 178-80, 186
"Private Madrigals" (Montale)
See "Madrigali privati"
"Private Means is Dead" (Smith) **12**:309, 333
A Private Mythology (Sarton) **39**:321, 326-28, 333, 338-43, 345
"The Private Place" (Muir) **49**:242
The Privilege (Kumin) **15**:180-81, 200, 208
"The Prize" (Muir) **49**:232
"Prize Fighter" (Hughes) **53**:181
"A Prize Poem submitted by Mr. Lambkin of Burford to the Examiners of the University of Oxford on the Prescribed Poetic Theme Set by Them in 1893, 'The Benefits of the Electric Light'" (Belloc) **24**:4
"Pro Nobis" (Oppen) **35**:307
"The Probationer" (Page) **12**:176
"Probity" (Graham) **59**:186, 190
"A Problem" (Borges) **32**:46
"The Problem" (Emerson) **18**:74, 79, 84, 100-2
"A Problem from Milton" (Wilbur) **51**:193
"A Problem in Spatial Composition" (Warren) **37**:331, 356, 366, 380
"Problemas del subdesarrollo" (Guillén) **23**:121
"Problems of Knowledge" (Warren) **37**:381
"Problems of Underdevelopment" (Guillén)
See "Problemas del subdesarrollo"
"Problems With Hurricanes" (Cruz) **37**:23
"Procedure" (Stone) **53**:253
"Procedures for Underground" (Atwood) **8**:13, 19
Procedures for Underground (Atwood) **8**:2-3, 12, 15-16, 21
"Le Procès à la Révolution" (Hugo) **17**:102
"Procesión India" (Mistral) **32**:185
"A Process" (Tomlinson) **17**:323, 331, 339
"A Process in the Weather of the Heart" (Thomas) **52**:310, 322
"Processe of tyme worketh suche wounder" (Wyatt) **27**:317, 320
"Processes" (Tomlinson) **17**:322,327, 337-40
"Procession" (Tate) **50**:256
"A Procession at Candlemas" (Clampitt) **19**:82-3, 89, 98
"Procession Poem" (Wakoski) **15**:324
"Processionals, II" (Duncan) **2**:101
"Proda di Versilia" (Montale) **13**:112, 148
"The Prodigal Son" (Bishop) **34**:82, 97
"The Prodigal Son" (Bly) **39**:63-4, 100
"The Prodigal Son" (Johnson) **24**:128-29, 133, 156, 164, 169
"The Prodigal Son" (Merwin) **45**:11-12, 14-15, 24
"The Prodigal's Return" (Harper) **21**:208
"The Produce District" (Gunn) **26**:203, 231
"Product" (Oppen) **35**:284, 293
"Proem" (Hughes) **53**:84
"Proem" (Patmore) **59**:261, 275
"Proem: To Brooklyn Bridge" (Crane) **3**:85, 88, 90, 107, 109
Profane Proses (Darío)
See *Prosas profanas, y otros poemas*
"Profer'd Love Rejected" (Suckling) **30**:126
"The Professional" (Ignatow) **34**:273
"Professor of Middle English Confronts Monster" (Birney) **52**:15
"Profezie" (Pasolini) **17**:277
"Proffitt and Batten" (Smith) **12**:339
"Profile" (Hope) **56**:278
"Profit Is a Dead Weight" (Moore) **49**:146
"Les profondeurs" (Apollinaire) **7**:32, 34
The profound rose (Borges)
See *La rosa profunda*
"De profundis" (Browning) **6**:5, 23
"De profundis" (MacDiarmid) **9**:153
"De Profundis" (Trakl) **20**:261-62
"Profusion du soir" (Valéry) **9**:391
"Prognosis" (Kenyon) **57**:15
"Prognosis" (MacNeice) **61**:138
"Progress" (Kumin) **15**:214
"Progress" (Moore) **49**:110, 123, 126
"The Progress of Beauty, 1720" (Swift) **9**:253, 257, 298-99
The Progress of Error (Cowper) **40**:51, 70-1
"The Progress of Faust" (Shapiro) **25**:296
"The Progress of Poesy" (Gray) **2**:133, 135, 137, 139, 143-44, 146, 148-49, 151-55
"The Progress of Poetry" (Gray)
See "The Progress of Poesy"
"The Progress of Poetry" (Hope) **56**:292
"The Progress of Poetry" (Swift) **9**:249
"Progress Report" (Ammons) **16**:45
"Progress Report" (Kumin) **15**:204, 208, 219
"Progression" (Niedecker) **42**:145
"Progression" (Smith) **12**:316
"Progressive Insanities of a Pioneer" (Atwood) **8**:4
"Prohibido para mayores" (Dalton) **36**:128
"The Prohibition" (Donne) **1**:130
"Projected Slide of an Unknown Soldier" (Atwood) **8**:7
"Projection" (Hughes) **53**:123, 191
"Projection" (Nemerov) **24**:268
A Prolegomenon to a Theodicy (Rexroth) **20**:179, 183, 210-11
"Prolija memoria" (Juana Inés de la Cruz) **24**:180
"Prolog" (Benn) **35**:72
"Prolog" (Heine) **25**:131
"Prolog" (Herbert) **50**:12, 19
"Prólogo" (Borges) **22**:95
"Prólogo" (Guillén) **23**:127
"El prólogo" (Guillén) **35**:153, 193
"Prologue" (Akhmatova) **55**:36, 55-56, 58, 60, 63
"The Prologue" (Bradstreet) **10**:2, 6, 11, 52
"Prologue" (Chaucer)
See "General Prologue"
"Prologue" (Herbert)
See "Prolog"
"Prologue" (Hughes) **7**:154
"Prologue" (Hugo) **17**:97
"Prologue" (Ignatow) **34**:282, 286
"Prologue" (Lorde) **12**:156
"Prologue" (MacLeish) **47**:185, 189, 201
"Prologue" (Marie de France) **22**:246-48, 260, 264-66, 283-85, 293, 298
"Prologue" (Noyes) **27**:119, 128
"Prologue" (Thomas)
See "Author's Prologue"
"Prologue" (Verlaine) **2**:432
"Prologue" (Yevtushenko) **40**:338-39, 342
"Prologue: An Interim" (Levertov)
See "Interim"
"Prologue at Sixty" (Auden) **1**:20
"Prologue in Six Parts" (Schwerner) **42**:196
"Prologue to a Saga" (Parker) **28**:363-64
"Prologue to King John" (Blake) **12**:31
"Prologue to the Wife of Bath's Tale" (Chaucer) **19**:26
"Prologue"(Vox Clamantis) (Gower)
See *Vox Clamantis*
Prolusion (Milton) **29**:228
"Promenade" (Ignatow) **34**:275
"Promenade on Any Street" (Kunitz) **19**:147-48
"Proměny" (Seifert) **47**:334
"Promethean Aspiration: To Be a Pythagorean and a Woman" (Howe) **54**:37
"Prometheus" (Carducci) **46**:26
"Prometheus" (Dunbar) **5**:146
"Prometheus" (Goethe) **5**:247, 254
"Prometheus" (Graves) **6**:137
"Prometheus" (Longfellow) **30**:103
"Prometheus" (Tomlinson) **17**:315, 319, 322, 325-27, 341
Prometheus Bound, and Miscellaneous Poems (Browning) **6**:16, 18
"Prometheus in Straits" (Ransom) **61**:275
Prometheus on His Crag (Hughes) **7**:155-56
"Prometheus Unbound" (Yeats) **20**:333, 336

Prometheus Unbound (Shelley) **14**:166-67, 171-75, 177, 183, 186-91, 193, 196-97, 202, 206, 212-13, 215-16, 218-21, 224-28, 232, 240-41
"The Promise" (Toomer) **7**:338
Promise (Yevtushenko) **40**:341
"Promise and Fulfillment" (Dunbar) **5**:121
"Promise Me" (Kunitz) **19**:147
"Promise of a Brilliant Funeral" (Niedecker) **42**:145
"The Promise of the Hawthorn" (Swinburne) **24**:313, 317
The Promised Land (Ungaretti) **57**:339
"The Promised One" (Wright) **14**:337
"The Promisers" (Owen) **19**:336, 343
"Promises" (Warren) **37**:307
Promises: Poems, 1954-1956 (Warren) **37**:296-97, 299-300, 307, 310, 328-30, 332, 347, 349, 354, 361, 370, 373, 380
"La promisión en alta mar" (Borges) **32**:38, 57
"Promontoire" (Rimbaud) **3**:264; **57**:234, 236, 239, 241, 254, 276, 280-81
"Promontory" (Rimbaud)
See "Promontoire"
"Prooimion" (Viereck) **27**:259
"Property" (Shapiro) **25**:295
"Property is poverty" (Niedecker) **42**:138
"Prophecy" (Wylie) **23**:310, 323
"Prophecy on Lethe" (Kunitz) **19**:162, 173-75
"The Prophet" (Lermontov) **18**:281
"The Prophet" (Pushkin)
See "Prorok"
The Prophet (Gibran) **9**:69-75, 80-2
"The Prophet Lost in the Hills at Evening" (Belloc) **24**:30
"Prophetic Soul" (Parker) **28**:357, 360
"Prophetie" (Césaire) **25**:9, 19, 30
"The Prophets" (Amichai) **38**:35
"Prophets for a New Day" (Walker) **20**:278, 288
Prophets for a New Day (Walker) **20**:275, 278-79, 283, 287-89, 292
"Prophets Who Cannot Sing" (Patmore) **59**:222
"Propogation House" (Roethke) **15**:296
"A propos d'Horace" (Hugo) **17**:64
"Proposal" (Carver) **54**:17, 19
"Propriety" (Moore) **49**:130
"Prorok" (Pushkin) **10**:409, 414
Prosanatolizmí (Elytis) **21**:118-19, 124, 127, 134
Prosas profanas, y otros poemas (Darío) **15**:78, 80, 82-4, 87-9, 91-2, 94-5, 97, 103-05, 109, 112-14, 117-20
Prosas profanos, and Other Poems (Darío)
See *Prosas profanas, y otros poemas*
"Prose Poem" (Tomlinson) **17**:338, 340
Prose Poems (Baudelaire)
See *Petits poèmes en prose: Le spleen de Paris*
"Prosopopoia; or, Mother Hubberds Tale" (Spenser) **8**:335, 365, 368-71, 390
"Prospective Immigrants Please Note" (Rich) **5**:370
"Prospectors of the Future" (Yevtushenko) **40**:341
Prospectus to the Excursion (Wordsworth)
See *The Excursion, Being a Portion of "The Recluse"*
"Prosperity in Poza Rica" (Birney) **52**:37, 98
"Prospice" (Browning) **2**:51, 66
"Protection of Moveable Cultural Heritage" (Komunyakaa) **51**:34
"Protest" (Cullen) **20**:57
Protest Against Apartheid (Brutus) **24**:100
"Protestant Easter" (Sexton) **2**:363
"Proteus" (Sarton) **39**:342
"Prothalamion" (Kumin) **15**:180
"Prothalamion" (Schwartz) **8**:290-91, 299, 301-02, 304-05
Prothalamion; or, A Spousall Verse (Spenser) **8**:336, 390
"Protocols" (Jarrell) **41**:198, 218
"The Proud Farmer" (Lindsay) **23**:287
"Proud King" (Morris) **55**:308
"A Proud Lady" (Wylie) **23**:309, 321, 332
"Proud Maisie" (Scott) **13**:272, 278, 280
"A Proud Poem" (O'Hara) **45**:160
"Provence" (MacNeice) **61**:139
"La Provence Point Oméga" (Char) **56**:136
"Proverbs of Hell" (Blake) **12**:36, 49-50
"Provide, Provide" (Frost) **1**:227-28, 231
"Providence" (Herbert) **4**:102, 134
"La providence à l'homme" (Lamartine) **16**:276, 283, 291, 293
Provinces (Milosz) **8**:212, 214-15
"Provincia deserta" (Pound) **4**:366
"Provision" (Merwin) **45**:21, 24
"Provisional Conclusions" (Montale) **13**:131
Provisional Conclusions (Montale) **13**:135
"Provisions for the Return" (Char) **56**:162
"Provoda" (Tsvetaeva) **14**:309, 311, 315
"Proximity" (Corso) **33**:44, 50
"prozession" (Enzensberger) **28**:135-36
"Prufrock" (Boland) **58**:12
"Prufrock" (Eliot)
See "The Love Song of J. Alfred Prufrock"
Prufrock and Other Observations (Eliot) **5**:152, 173, 184-85, 195, 204, 206; **31**:101, 120-21,
"Przeczucia eschatologiczne Pana Cogito" (Herbert) **50**:35, 39
"Przedmioty" (Herbert) **50**:4-5
"Przepasc Pana Cogito" (Herbert) **50**:37
"Przeslanie Pana Cogito" (Herbert) **50**:12, 15, 22-24, 33, 38-39
"Przylot" (Szymborska) **44**:294, 299
"The Psalm" (Bridges) **28**:80
"Psalm" (Celan) **10**:98, 101, 118, 120
"A Psalm" (Merton) **10**:332
"Psalm" (Oppen) **35**:298, 323
"Psalm II" (Ginsberg) **4**:81
"Psalm 2" (Smart) **13**:330
"Psalm 94" (Smart) **13**:362
"Psalm 104" (Smart) **13**:332
"Psalm 105" (Smart) **13**:362
"Psalm 120" (Smart) **13**:363
"Psalm Concerning the Castle" (Levertov) **11**:177
"Psalm of Death" (Longfellow) **30**:21, 45
"A Psalm of Life" (Longfellow) **30**:21-2, 26-7, 34, 36-9, 45, 47, 95-8, 103, 105-11
"Psalm of the West" (Lanier) **50**:54-56, 75, 77, 80, 106
"Psalm of Those Who Go Forth before Daylight" (Sandburg) **41**:259, 270, 321
"Psalm: Our Fathers" (Merwin) **45**:16-17, 27
"Psalm Praising the Hair of Man's Body" (Levertov) **11**:171
"Psalms" (Smart)
See *A Translation of the Psalms of David, Attempted in the Spirit of Christianity, and Adapted to the Divine Service*
Psalms (Sidney) **32**:225, 247-50, 293-96
Psalms of David (Smart)
See *A Translation of the Psalms of David, Attempted in the Spirit of Christianity, and Adapted to the Divine Service*
"Pseudodoxia Epidemica" (Hope) **56**:289
"Psyche's Discontent" (Patmore) **59**:207, 267
"Der Psychiater" (Benn) **35**:50, 68
"The Psychiatrist's Song" (Bogan) **12**:101, 115
"Der Ptolemäer" (Benn) **35**:33, 34
"Public Bar TV" (Hughes) **7**:120, 122
"Public Garden" (Lowell) **3**:199-200, 215
The Public Rose (Éluard)
See *La rose publique*
Public Speech: Poems (MacLeish) **47**:139-40, 148-49, 151, 190, 241, 255
Published and Unpublished Poems (Pavese)
See *Poesie edite e inedite*
"Puck of Pook's Hill" (Kipling) **3**:192
"Puck's Song" (Kipling) **3**:183, 192
"La Pudeur bien en vue" (Éluard) **38**:91
"Pueblo Pot" (Millay) **6**:215
"Puedes?" (Guillén) **23**:116, 124, 127
Puella (Dickey) **40**:205, 210-12, 228, 235, 237-40, 259
"Puella Mea" (Cummings) **5**:104
"Puerta Rica" (Cruz) **37**:22
"Puesto del Rastro" (Fuertes) **27**:22, 45-6
"the pull" (Bissett) **14**:22
"The Pulley" (Herbert) **4**:102
"The Pulling" (Olds) **22**:318, 323, 326, 340
"Pulse-Beats and Pen-Strokes" (Sandburg) **41**:293
The pulverised poem (Char)
See *Le Poème pulvérisé*
"Pulvis et umbra" (Carman) **34**:202, 211, 215
"Puma in Chapultepec Zoo" (Corso) **33**:39, 43, 47
"El puñal" (Borges) **32**:87
Punascha (Tagore) **8**:417
Punch: The Immortal Liar (Aiken) **26**:22
"Puncture" (Ransom) **61**:311
"Punishment" (Heaney) **18**:196, 204, 210-11, 238
"The Puppets" (Page) **12**:184
Purabi (Tagore) **8**:415
"Purdah" (Plath) **37**:241
"Pure Death" (Graves) **6**:137, 151
"The Pure Fury" (Roethke) **15**:258, 272, 277, 290
"Pure Love" (Tagore)
See "Pavitra prem"
"The Pure Ones" (Hass) **16**:198
"Purely" (Villa) **22**:353
"Purely Local" (Rich) **5**:352
Purgatorio (Dante) **21**:49, 52-4, 58, 62-3, 69-82, 84-6, 91, 95-6, 104-05, 107-09
"Purgatory" (Lowell) **3**:241
"A Purgatory" (Merwin) **45**:49
Purgatory (Dante)
See *Purgatorio*
Purgatory (Marie de France)
See *L'Espurgatoire Saint Patrice*
The Purgatory of St. Patrick (Marie de France)
See *L'Espurgatoire Saint Patrice*
"The Puritan" (Shapiro) **25**:270, 286
"A Puritan Lady" (Reese) **29**:331
"The Puritan's Ballard" (Wylie) **23**:310
"Purner abhav" (Tagore) **8**:414
"Puro Mejicano" (Quintana) **36**:252
"Purple Grackles" (Lowell) **13**:64, 67, 87, 98-9
"The Purpose of Altar Boys" (Ríos) **57**:324
"Les Pur-Sang" (Césaire) **25**:8-9, 18
"The Purse of Aholibah" (Huneker) **27**:165
"The Purse Seine" (Jeffers) **17**:117
"Pursuit" (H. D.) **5**:287-88
"Pursuit" (Plath) **37**:236, 241, 260
"Pursuit" (Warren) **37**:284, 287, 289, 323, 332
"Pursuit from Under" (Dickey) **40**:183, 196, 258
"Pushkin Pass" (Yevtushenko) **40**:350
"Pushkinskomu domu" (Blok) **21**:44
"Puss in Boots" (Moore) **49**:161
"Pusti menia, Voronezh . . ." (Mandelstam) **14**:152
"Put Off the Wedding Five Times and Nobody Comes to It" (Sandburg) **41**:298
Put Out the Lights (Seifert)
See *Zhasněte světla*
"Put Something In" (Silverstein) **49**:330
Putem vseia zemli (Akhmatova) **55**:53
"La puttana contadina" (Pavese) **13**:210, 219
"Puttin' on Dog" (Brown) **55**:114
"Putting to Sea" (Bogan) **12**:123
"Puzzle" (Parra)
See "Rompecabezas"
"Pygmalion" (H. D.) **5**:270, 304
"Pygmalion" (Hope) **56**:268, 270-71, 286-87, 306
"Pygmalion's Image" (Ní Chuilleanáin) **34**:354, 373
"Pygmies Are Pygmies Still, Though Percht on Alps" (Brooks) **7**:55
"The Pyramids" (Brooke) **24**:66, 80

"Pyramis; or, The House of Ascent" (Hope) **56**:268, 272, 275
"Pyrotechnics" (Bogan) **12**:117
"Pyrotechnics" (Lowell) **13**:83
Pytania zadawane sobie (Szymborska) **44**:268, 281
Pyth. III (Pindar)
See *Pythian 3*
Pyth. X (Pindar)
See *Pythian 10*
Pyth XI (Pindar)
See *Pythian 11*
"Pythagorean Lines" (Mahon) **60**:178-79
Pythagorean Silence (Howe) **54**:37-40, 45, 68, 99-100, 102, 141, 151
Pythian 1 (Pindar) **19**:381, 389, 392-93, 400, 411-12, 424-25
Pythian 2 (Pindar) **19**:402, 410, 420
Pythian 3 (Pindar) **19**:390, 398, 402, 410, 412
Pythian 4 (Pindar) **19**:381, 390, 396, 398-99, 405, 413, 420, 425
Pythian 5 (Pindar) **19**:396, 408-11, 422-23, 425
Pythian 6 (Pindar) **19**:400, 406
Pythian 7 (Pindar) **19**:412
Pythian 8 (Pindar) **19**:381, 391, 400, 406-07, 413, 426
Pythian 9 (Pindar) **19**:391, 398, 400, 412-13
Pythian 10 (Pindar) **19**:411-12, 425-26
Pythian 11 (Pindar) **19**:413
Pythian Odes 10 (Pindar)
See *Pythian 10*
"La pythie" (Valéry) **9**:353, 365-66, 369, 373, 379, 393
"The QPP" (Walker) **30**:339
Quaderno de quattro anni (Montale) **13**:128, 153, 156, 160, 168
"The Quadroon Girl" (Longfellow) **30**:48
"Quaerendo Invenietis" (Nemerov) **24**:288
"Quai d'Orléans" (Bishop) **3**:37; **34**:63-66
"The Quail" (Wright) **36**:280, 362
"The Quake" (Stryk) **27**:203, 211
"Quake Theory" (Olds) **22**:309
"The Quaker Graveyard at Nantucket (for Warren Winslow, Dead at Sea)" (Lowell) **3**:200-02, 204, 212, 217, 223, 233, 235-38
"Quaker Hill" (Crane) **3**:86, 90, 106
"Quality Time" (Silverstein) **49**:342
"Qualm" (Ashbery) **26**:152
"Quand vous serez bien vieille" (Ronsard) **11**:218-21
Quando caddreo gli alberi e le mura (Quasimodo) **47**:287
"Quando de minhas magoasa comprida" (Camões) **31**:24
"Quando il soave mio fido conforto" (Petrarch) **8**:235
"Quarant' Ore" (Ní Chuilleanáin) **34**:360
"The Quarrel" (Aiken) **26**:24
"The Quarrel" (Kunitz) **19**:175
"Quarrel" (Stramm)
See "Zwist"
"Quarrel in Old Age" (Yeats) **20**:328-31
"The Quarry" (Clampitt) **19**:82, 89
"Quarry Pigeon Cove" (Kumin) **15**:181
Quarry West (Cervantes) **35**:132
"Le quart d'une vie" (Péret) **33**:229-30
"Quartär" (Benn) **35**:4, 8, 67
"Quartets" (Eliot) **31**:99
"Quashie to Buccra" (McKay) **2**:215, 223
"Quasi un madrigale" (Quasimodo) **47**:284-86
"Quasi-Slum" (Curnow) **48**:26
"Quatrains" (Emerson) **18**:77
"Quatre à quatre" (Péret) **33**:220-22, 230
Quatre de P. de Ronsard aux injures et calomnies (Ronsard) **11**:291
"Quatre Dols" (Marie de France)
See "Le Chaitivel"
Les quatre premiers livres de la Franciade (Ronsard) **11**:226, 234, 246, 271, 283, 286-87, 290
Les quatre vents de l'esprit (Hugo) **17**:65
"4e epoque" (Lamartine) **16**:264
"Los que a través de sus lágrimas" (Castro) **41**:103
"La que comprende" (Storni) **33**:246, 307-08;
"Lo que el difunto dijo de sí mismo" (Parra) **39**:285
Que estás en la tierra (Fuertes) **27**:44
"Que font les olives" (Péret) **33**:202
"Que m'accompagnent Kôras et Balafong" (Senghor) **25**:255
"Los que no danzan" (Mistral) **32**:175
"Que no me quiera Fabio, al verse amado" (Juana Inés de la Cruz) **24**:183
"Que nous avons le doute en nous" (Hugo) **17**:92-93
Que van a dar a la mar (Guillén) **35**:214-16
"quebec bombers" (Bissett) **14**:21-2
"Quechua Song" (Mistral)
See "La canción que chua"
"The Queen and the Young Princess" (Smith) **12**:326, 352
"Queen Anne's Lace" (Jordan) **38**:122
"Queen Jane Approximately" (Dylan) **37**:55
Queen Mab (Shelley) **14**:170, 173, 178, 185-86, 212-17, 219, 222
"Queen of Bubbles" (Lindsay) **23**:277
"The Queen of Hearts" (Rossetti) **7**:272, 274
"The Queen of pentacles" (Piercy) **29**:323
"The Queen of the Night Walks Her Thin Dog" (Wakoski) **15**:363
"The Queen of the North" (Morris) **55**:306
"Queen Worship" (Browning) **2**:26
"Queen Yseult" (Swinburne) **24**:355
"Queen-Anne's Lace" (Williams) **7**:374
"The Queen's Bearing" (Char) **56**:162
"The Queen's Room" (Patmore) **59**:230
"Queja" (Storni) **33**:253;
"Quelque bonté" (Éluard) **38**:68
"Quelques Complaintes de la vie" (Laforgue) **14**:95
"Qu'en dis-tu, voyageur" (Verlaine) **32**:375
"Querent's Attitude as It Bears Upon the Matter: The Three of Cups" (Piercy) **29**:325
"The Quest" (Noyes) **27**:130
"The Quest" (Wright) **36**:346
"The Quest of the Purple-Fringed" (Frost) **1**:218
"Qu'est-ce pour nous mon coeur" (Rimbaud) **57**:182-84, 302, 304-6
"A Question" (Arnold) **5**:38
"The Question" (Muir) **49**:245, 251
"The Question" (Rukeyser) **12**:225
"Question" (Swenson) **14**:250, 252, 282, 286
"Question and Answer" (Browning) **6**:5
"Question and Answer" (Warren) **37**:322, 332
"Question at Cliff-Thrust" (Warren) **37**:366-67, 380
"Question au clerc du quichet" (Villon) **13**:394
"A Question of Climate" (Lorde) **12**:136
"A Question of Essence" (Lorde) **12**:140
"The Question of Loyalty" (Yamada) **44**:339
"Question to Life" (Kavanagh) **33**:103, 120
"The Question Whither" (Meredith) **60**:290, 299
Questions and Answers (Parra)
See *Preguntas y respuestas*
"Questions Beside the Lake" (Cardenal)
See "Preguntas Frente al lago"
"Questions of Travel" (Bishop) **3**:55, 67; **34**:106, 158
Questions of Travel (Bishop) **3**:48, 53, 59; **34**:58, 61, 66-67, 91, 94, 155, 160, 174, 189-90
Questions Put to Myself (Szymborska) **44**:318
"A questo punto" (Montale) **13**:158
"A qui la faute?" (Hugo) **17**:101
"Qui regna amore" (Carducci) **46**:77
"Qui sait—" (Benn) **35**:75
"Qui S'Excuse, S'Accuse" (Moore) **49**:105, 109, 121, 134
Quia pawper amavi (Pound) **4**:317
"Quick I the Death of Thing" (Cummings) **5**:108
"Quick Trip" (Silverstein) **49**:324
"A Quickening: A Song for the Visitation" (Merton) **10**:339
"The Quickening of St. John Baptist" (Merton) **10**:339
"Quickly Delia" (Finch) **21**:178
"The Quids" (Jackson) **44**:5
"A quien leyere" (Borges) **22**:94
"¿Quién seré?" (Guillén) **35**:229
"Quiero saber" (Aleixandre) **15**:31
"Quiero volver a sur" (Neruda) **4**:281
"Quiet!" (Castro)
See "¡Silencio!"
"The Quiet After the Storm" (Leopardi)
See "La quiete dopo la tempesta"
"Quiet Evening" (Glück) **16**:172
A Quiet Road (Reese) **29**:329-330, 335-336, 339, 345-346
"The Quiet Thing" (Francis) **34**:251
"Quiet Work" (Arnold) **5**:12, 36, 38, 49
"La quiete dopo la tempesta" (Leopardi) **37**:102, 120, 124
"Quietness" (Williams) **7**:382
"Qu'il vive" (Char) **56**:184
Quill, Solitary, APPARITION (Guest) **55**:196, 199
"A Quilt Pattern" (Jarrell) **41**:158, 173, 176-77, 186, 194
"Quilted Spreads" (Ammons) **16**:44
Quilting: Poems 1987-1990 (Clifton) **17**:28-29, 36
"Quimérica" (Jiménez) **7**:197
"Quinnapoxet" (Kunitz) **19**:175, 178-79
"The Quip" (Herbert) **4**:100, 102, 108, 119, 130
Quitter (Char) **56**:117
"R. A. F." (H. D.) **5**:307
"The Rabbi" (Hayden) **6**:195, 198
"Rabbi Ben Ezra" (Browning) **2**:51, 75, 95
"The Rabbi's Song" (Kipling) **3**:183
"The Rabbit" (Millay) **6**:238
"The Rabbit Catcher" (Plath) **37**:232, 264
"Räber-Schiller" (Benn) **35**:48
"Race" (Darío)
See "Raza"
"The Race" (Olds) **22**:319, 323, 326
"The Racer's Widow" (Glück) **16**:139
"Rachunek Elegijny" (Szymborska) **44**:220, 306, 308
"Rack" (Ammons) **16**:39
Radiant Silhouette: New and Selected Work 1974-88 (Yau) **61**:334, 340, 348
"Radical" (Moore) **49**:100, 113, 185-86
"Radio" (Benn) **35**:70
"A radio made of seawater" (Villa) **22**:356-57
"Radiometer" (Merrill) **28**:267
"Raft" (Ammons) **16**:20, 27
"The Raft" (Lindsay) **23**:273
Rag and Bone Shop (Birney) **52**:72, 75, 83
The Rag and Bone Shop of the Heart: Poems for Men (Bly) **39**:98
"Rag & Bone" (Birney) **52**:32
"The Rag Man" (Hayden) **6**:195
"Raga Malkos" (Ekeloef) **23**:87
"Rage for Order" (Mahon) **60**:168, 172, 187, 194, 200, 233, 235
"The Rage for the Lost Penny" (Jarrell) **41**:179, 183, 213
"Rages de césars" (Rimbaud) **3**:283
"Ragged ending" (Piercy) **29**:313
"Ragged Point" (Brathwaite) **56**:65
"The Ragged Schools of London" (Browning)
See "A Song for the Ragged Schools of London"
"The Ragged Stocking" (Harper) **21**:191
"The Raggedy Man" (Riley) **48**:292, 306, 340
Raghuvamśa (Kālidāsa) **22**:180, 182, 185, 188-90, 198, 204-07
"The Railing" (Yevtushenko) **40**:345
"Railing Rimes Returned upon the Author by Mistress Mary Wrothe" (Wroth) **38**:258
"Railroad Avenue" (Hughes) **1**:237

The Railway Timetable of the Heart (Tzara) **27**:250
"Rain" (Borges) **32**:140
"Rain" (Brown) **55**:74
"Rain" (Giovanni) **19**:109
"The Rain" (Herbert)
See "Deszcz"
"Rain" (Hogan) **35**:257
"The Rain" (Levertov) **11**:176
"Rain" (Ransom) **61**:309
"Rain" (Soto) **28**:370, 377
"Rain" (Stryk) **27**:201
"Rain" (Thomas) **53**:278, 285-86, 288-89, 295, 317, 328
"Rain" (Williams) **7**:349
"Rain" (Wright) **36**:391
"Rain at Bellagio" (Clampitt) **19**:87
"Rain at Night" (Merwin) **45**:93
"Rain Charm for the Duchy, a Blessed, Devout Drench for the Christening of a Prince Harry" (Hughes) **7**:171
"Rain Downriver" (Levine) **22**:224-25
"Rain Festival" (Tagore)
See "Varsha-mangal"
"The Rain Guitar" (Dickey) **40**:223, 232, 256
"Rain in January" (Kenyon) **57**:3, 13, 19, 43
The Rain in the Trees (Merwin) **45**:89, 93-4, 97-8
"The Rain, It Streams on Stone and Hillock" (Housman) **2**:162
"Rain on a Grave" (Hardy) **8**:134
"Rain on the Borders" (Pasolini) **17**:287
"Rain or Hail" (Cummings) **5**:88
"Rain Outside of Everything" (Pasolini) **17**:287
"Rain Towards Morning" (Bishop) **34**:89
"The Rainbow" (Kinnell) **26**:259-60
"rainbow music" (Bissett) **14**:24
"La Rainette" (Char) **56**:152
"Rainforest" (Wright) **14**:375, 377
"The Rainmaker" (Cassian) **17**:4
"Rain-Song" (Dunbar) **5**:125
"The Rainy Day" (Longfellow) **30**:45, 64
"Rainy Mountain Cemetery" (Momaday) **25**:190, 197
"The Rainy Season" (Meredith) **28**:187
"Rainy Season: Sub-Tropics" (Bishop) **34**:116
"Raise a Song" (Brown) **55**:114
"raise the shade / will youse dearie" (Cummings) **5**:89
"Raison de plus" (Éluard) **38**:69
Raíz del hombre (Paz) **48**:179, 243
"Raj teologów" (Herbert) **50**:5
"Raleigh" (Cardenal) **22**:107, 110
"Raleigh Was Right" (Williams) **7**:360
Ralentir Travaux (Char) **56**:168
"Ralph Rhodes" (Masters) **36**:231
"Rama del otoño" (Guillén) **35**:153, 154
"La rameur" (Valéry) **9**:367, 395-96
"El ramo azul" (Paz) **48**:230
"Rampart of Twigs" (Char)
See "Le Rempart de Brindilles"
"The Range in the Desert" (Jarrell) **41**:171
"Rank and File" (Noyes) **27**:122
"Rano Raraku" (Breton) **15**:53-4
"Ransom" (Ní Chuilleanáin) **34**:349, 351
"Ransom" (Warren) **37**:284, 287-88, 321, 331-32
"A Rant" (O'Hara) **45**:164
"Rap of a Fan..." (Apollinaire)
See "Coup d'evential..."
"Rape" (Rich) **5**:361
"Rape is Not a Poem" (Jordan) **38**:123, 126, 128
"The Rape of Aurora" (Meredith) **60**:244, 294
"Rape of the Leaf" (Kunitz) **19**:147
The Rape of the Lock (Pope) **26**:303, 307-309, 314-19, 322-23, 326-27, 340, 346-51
"The Raper from Passenack" (Williams) **7**:353, 368, 399
"Rapids" (Ammons) **16**:63
"Rapids by the Luan Trees" (Wang Wei) **18**:370
"Raport z oblezonego miasta" (Herbert) **50**:11, 14, 22, 41
Raport z oblezonego miasta (Herbert) **50**:11-12, 15, 17, 20, 22-24, 36, 39-41
"A Rapture" (Carew) **29**:10, 18, 27-28, 32, 34, 36-38, 48, 71-72, 75-76, 87-88
"Rapunzel" (Morris) **55**:238, 267-68, 272, 282, 300, 302
"Rapunzel" (Sexton) **2**:368
"Rapunzel, Rapunzel" (Smith) **12**:341
"Raree Show" (MacLeish) **47**:186
"Raspiatie" (Akhmatova) **2**:15; **55**:10, 27, 31-32, 38, 51-52, 57
"Rasshchelina" (Tsvetaeva) **14**:306-08
Rat Jelly (Ondaatje) **28**:294, 327-35
"Ratbert" (Hugo) **17**:59
"The Ratcatcher" (Tsvetaeva)
See "Krysolov"
"Rathlin Island" (Mahon) **60**:146, 192, 194, 220, 232
"Rational Man" (Rukeyser) **12**:220, 230
The Rationale of Verse (Poe) **54**:264
"Rationality" (Oppen) **35**:315
"The Rats" (Levine) **22**:213
"ratschlag auf höchster ebene" (Enzensberger) **28**:136
"The Rattle Bag" (Dafydd)
See "Y Rhugl Groen"
"rattle poem" (Bissett) **14**:21
"Rattlesnake Country" (Warren) **37**:305, 308, 340
"The Ravaged Face" (Plath) **37**:206
"Ravel and Unravel" (Graham) **59**:191-93
"The Raven" (Poe) **1**:419-20, 424, 427, 429-34, 436, 439-40, 443-44, 447, 452-53; **54**:256, 258, 260, 263-66, 268-82, 284-312, 314-16, 320-27, 330-32, 334-37, 339, 341-43
"The Raven: A Christmas Tale" (Coleridge) **11**:109-17
The Raven, and Other Poems (Poe) **1**:437, 449; **54**:293, 305, 330
"Ravenna" (MacNeice) **61**:178
"The Ravine" (Carruth) **10**:85, 90
"Raving Mad" (Césaire) **25**:15
"Rawhead and Bloody Bones" (Hope) **56**:285
"Ray-Flowers" (Dickey) **40**:211-12, 237
Les rayons et les ombres (Hugo) **17**:45, 50-53, 63-64, 67, 76-77, 87, 91-92, 97
"Raza" (Darío) **15**:115
"Razgovor s geniem" (Tsvetaeva) **14**:325
Rbaiyyat (Khayyam)
See *Rubáiyát*
Re:Creation (Giovanni) **19**:108-11, 114, 118, 122, 128, 136-37, 140-41
"Reaching Out" (Stone) **53**:228
"The reaching out of warmth is never done" (Viereck) **27**:278
"Reaching Out with the Hands of the Sun" (Wakoski) **15**:363
"Re-Act for Action" (Madhubuti) **5**:338
"The Reader over My Shoulder" (Graves) **6**:143, 151
"Reading" (Stone) **53**:257
"Reading Aloud" (Gallagher) **9**:60
"Reading Aloud to My Father" (Kenyon) **57**:12, 27, 47-48
"Reading Apollinaire by the Rouge River" (Ferlinghetti) **1**:181, 187
"Reading Holderlin on the Patio with the Aid of a Dictionary" (Dove) **6**:109
"Reading in the Fall Rain" (Bly) **39**:86
"Reading in Wartime" (Muir) **49**:195, 232, 252
"Reading Late of the Death of Keats" (Kenyon) **57**:4
"Reading my poems from World War II" (Meredith) **28**:180, 195
"Reading Myself" (Lowell) **3**:229
A Reading of Earth (Meredith) **60**:257, 289-90, 298, 333
A Reading of Life (Meredith) **60**:287, 289-90, 292, 294
"The Reading of the Psalm" (Francis) **34**:244
"Reading Plato" (Graham) **59**:133, 152
"Reading the Brothers Grimm to Jenny" (Mueller) **33**:175
"Reading the Headlines" (Ignatow) **34**:310
"Reading the Japanese Poet Issa" (Milosz) **8**:189
"Reading the Landscape" (Wagoner) **33**:352
"Reading the Sky" (Wagoner) **33**:358
"Reading the Will" (Kipling) **3**:190
"Reading Time: 1 Minute 26 Seconds" (Rukeyser) **12**:206
"Readings of History" (Rich) **5**:355
"Ready for Goodbye" (Cassian) **17**:3
"Ready to Kill" (Sandburg) **41**:347
"Reah habenzin 'oleh be'api" (Amichai) **38**:6, 33-5
"The Real Estate Agents Tale" (Lowell) **13**:84
"Real Life" (Baraka) **4**:30
"Real Life" (Enzensberger) **28**:159
Real Live (Dylan) **37**:59
"Real Mammy Song" (Brown) **55**:164
"The Real Revolution Is Love" (Harjo) **27**:70
"The Real Southwest by Greyhound" (Stone) **53**:223
"The Real Thing" (Ní Chuilleanáin) **34**:361, 371
"A Real Toad in a Real Garden" (Mueller) **33**:189
"The Real Work" (Snyder) **21**:324-25
The Real World (Snyder) **21**:291
La realidad invisible (Jiménez) **7**:207
"Realities" (MacLeish) **47**:182
"Reality" (Pasolini) **17**:258
"Reality Demands" (Szymborska) **44**:300
Reality Sandwiches (Ginsberg) **4**:67, 81; **47**:16
"A Reaper and the Flowers" (Longfellow) **30**:21, 26, 45
"Reapers" (Toomer) **7**:319, 333-34
"Reaping" (Lowell) **13**:60
"Reaping in Heat" (Heaney) **18**:191
"The Rear-Guard" (Sassoon) **12**:266
"Rearmament" (Jeffers) **17**:117, 121-22
"Reason and Imagination" (Smart) **13**:341, 347
The Reason of Church Government (Milton) **29**:272
"Reason tell me thy mind" (Sidney) **32**:235
"Reasons for Attendance" (Larkin) **21**:223, 229, 244, 247
"Reasons for Music" (MacLeish) **47**:192
"Reawakening" (Pavese)
See "Risveglio"
"The Rebel" (Belloc) **24**:12, 30, 38
"Le rebelle" (Baudelaire) **1**:55
"Rebellion" (Brathwaite) **56**:23-24, 31, 87
"Rebellion" (Lowell) **3**:318
"The Rebels" (Ferlinghetti) **1**:184
"Rebirth" (Pushkin) **10**:408
"Rebuke of the Rocks" (Warren) **37**:319, 380
"A Rebus by I. B." (Wheatley) **3**:338
"Recado de Chile" (Mistral) **32**:165
"Recado sobre Chile" (Mistral)
See "Recado de Chile"
"Recado terrestre" (Mistral) **32**:188
"Recall to Earth" (Curnow) **48**:26
"Recalling War" (Graves) **6**:137, 142, 144, 165
"The Recantation: An Ode. By S. T. Coleridge" (Coleridge) **11**:94, 99
"Recapitulations" (Shapiro) **25**:272-73, 285, 296-97, 319-20, 324
"Receive Thy Sight" (Bryant) **20**:6
"The Recent Past" (Ashbery) **26**:143
"Recent Poems" (Davie) **29**:99
Recent Poems (Curnow) **48**:24
"The Reception" (Jordan) **38**:125
"Réception d'Orion" (Char) **56**:137, 145
"Recessional" (Masters) **1**:333
"Rechauffe" (MacNeice) **61**:178
Recherche de la base et du sommet (Char) **56**:108-9, 112, 114, 120, 128, 132, 134, 136, 139-40, 148, 191, 195
"Recipe for Happiness in Khaboronsky" (Ferlinghetti) **1**:183

"The Recital" (Ashbery) **26**:130, 149
"Rècitation à l 'Éloge d'une Reine" (Perse) **23**:230
"Recitative" (Crane) **3**:81, 83
"Recitativo di Palinuro" (Ungaretti) **57**:339
Recklings (Hughes) **7**:120, 122-23
"The Recluse" (Smith) **12**:299, 331, 333
The Recluse; or Views on Man, Nature, and on Human Life (Wordsworth) **4**:406-07, 409
"The Recognition" (Wagoner) **33**:370, 372
"La Recoleta" (Borges) **32**:59
"Recollection" (Wheatley)
See "On Recollection"
"Recollection in Upper Ontario, from Long Before" (Warren) **37**:336
"A Recollection of School Days" (Carducci)
See "Rimembranze di Scuola"
"The Recollections" (Leopardi)
See "Le ricordanze"
"Recollections" (Swinburne) **24**:329
"Recollections of Bellagio" (Meredith) **28**:198, 215
"Recollections of Solitude" (Bridges) **28**:60
"Recollections of the Arabian Nights" (Tennyson) **6**:347, 359, 389, 406, 408-09
Recollections of Tsarskoe-Selo (Pushkin)
See "Vospominanie v Tsarskom Sele"
"The Recompense" (Tomlinson) **17**:349
"Reconciliation" (Day Lewis) **11**:147
"Reconciliation" (Milosz) **8**:213
"Reconciliation" (Sassoon) **12**:289
"Reconciliation" (Whitman) **3**:378
"The Record" (Berry) **28**:30
Record of a Journey to Sarashina (Matsuo Bashō)
See *Sarashina kikō*
"Records" (Tate) **50**:255-56
The Records of a Travel-worn Satchel (Matsuo Bashō)
See *Oi no kobumi*
Records of a Weather Exposed Skeleton (Matsuo Bashō)
See *Nozarashi kikō*
"Recours au ruisseau" (Char) **56**:137, 157, 171
"Recourse to the river" (Char)
See "Recours au ruisseau"
"Recovered from the Storm" (Graham) **59**:153-55, 158-59, 161
"Recovering" (Rukeyser) **12**:225
"Recovery" (Ammons) **16**:6
"The Recovery" (Pushkin) **10**:408
Recovery (Tagore)
See *Ārogya*
"Recreaciones arqueológicas" (Darío) **15**:96
"Re-creating the Scene" (Komunyakaa) **51**:38
"The Recruit" (Housman) **2**:196
"A Recruit on the Corpy" (McKay) **2**:226
"Recruiting Team" (Yamada) **44**:339
"Reçu" (Péret) **33**:231
"Recueillement" (Baudelaire) **1**:65
Les recueillements poétiques (Lamartine) **16**:263, 268, 284-85
"Recuerdo" (Millay) **6**:215
"El Recuerdo" (Storni) **33**:306;
"Recuerdos..." (Jiménez) **7**:199
"Recuerdos de juventud" (Parra) **39**:283, 286
"The Recurrence" (Muir) **49**:196
"Red Armchair" (McGuckian) **27**:105
"The Red Balloon" (Abse) **41**:6-7
Red Beans (Cruz) **37**:15-16, 20, 25, 31
"Red Blues" (Alexie) **53**:12-13
"A Red Carpet for Shelley" (Wylie) **23**:322, 333
"Red Clay" (Hogan) **35**:258
Red Clay (Hogan) **35**:257, 263, 264
"Red Clay Blues" (Hughes) **53**:116, 200
Red Dirt (Cervantes) **35**:132
Red Dust (Levine) **22**:211, 213-15, 217-18, 222-23, 227-28
"A Red Flower" (Moore) **49**:105, 110
"Red Geranium and Godly Mignonette" (Lawrence) **54**:199, 227
"Red Guard" (Borges)
See "Guardia roja"
"The Red Knight" (Lowell) **13**:84
"The Red Lacquer Music Stand" (Lowell) **13**:78
"Red Maple Leaves" (Rexroth) **20**:221
"Red Maples" (Teasdale) **31**:360
"The Red Mullet" (Warren) **37**:299, 302, 362
"Red Poppy" (Gallagher) **9**:64
"A Red, Red Rose" (Burns)
See "My Luve Is Like a Red, Red Rose"
"Red Riding Hood" (Sexton) **2**:354, 364
"Red Rising" (Brathwaite) **56**:51
"Red Roses" (Hughes) **53**:115
Red Roses for Bronze (H. D.) **5**:270-71, 304
"Red Silk Stockings" (Hughes) **1**:269
"The Red Sleep of Beasts" (Erdrich) **52**:192
"Red Slippers" (Lowell) **13**:79
"Red Son" (Sandburg) **41**:227
"The Red Steer" (Tsvetaeva)
See "Krasnyi bychok"
"The Red Wheelbarrow" (Williams) **7**:378, 401-02, 409-10
"Red, White and Blue" (Quintana) **36**:272
"The Red Wolf" (Carman) **34**:213
"Redbirds" (Teasdale) **31**:359
"The Redbreast and the Butterfly" (Wordsworth) **4**:376
"Redcap" (Brown) **55**:164
"Red-Cotton Nightcap Country" (Browning) **2**:46, 96
"A Redeemer" (Jeffers) **17**:131, 141
"The Redeemer" (Sassoon) **12**:242, 249-51, 261-62, 276, 278, 287
"Redemption" (Herbert) **4**:119, 130
"Redeployment" (Nemerov) **24**:287, 290
"Red-Headed Restaurant Cashier" (Sandburg) **41**:286, 318
"Rediscovering America" (Alexie) **53**:9
"Redness of the Dawn Breakers" (Char)
See "Rougeur des Matinaux"
"Redonnez-leur . . ." (Char) **56**:134
"Red-Tail Hawk and Pyre of Youth" (Warren) **37**:310-12, 336, 355, 357, 360, 370
"Redwing" (Gallagher) **9**:62
"Redwing Blackbirds" (Warren) **37**:326
"Redwings" (Wright) **36**:311
"The Reed" (Lermontov) **18**:304
"A Reed Boat" (Komunyakaa) **51**:55
"The Reedbeds of the Hackensack" (Clampitt) **19**:87
"The Reefy Coast" (Ishikawa)
See "Ariso"
"Reeve's Tale" (Chaucer) **19**:10, 13-14, 61
The Reeve!s Tale (Chaucer) **58**:265, 363
"Reference Back" (Larkin) **21**:228
"The Refiner's Gold" (Harper) **21**:189
"The Refinery" (Pinsky) **27**:158, 171-2, 176
"The Reflection: A Song" (Behn) **13**:18, 20-1
"Reflection in a Forest" (Auden) **1**:17
"Reflection in a Green Arena" (Corso) **33**:49
"Reflection in an Ironworks" (MacDiarmid) **9**:155
"Reflection on Ice-Breaking" (Nash) **21**:279
"Reflections" (MacNeice) **61**:125
"Reflections" (Tomlinson) **17**:316, 324
"Reflections at Lake Louise" (Ginsberg) **4**:84
"Reflections by a Mailbox" (Kunitz) **19**:154
"Reflections in a Double Mirror" (Sarton) **39**:325
"Reflections in an Old House" (Tate) **50**:284-86
"Reflections on a Scottish Slum" (MacDiarmid) **9**:181
"Reflections on Having Left a Place of Retirement" (Coleridge) **11**:81
"Reflective" (Ammons) **16**:6
"Reflexion" (Lamartine) **16**:266, 285
"Reformation" (Finch) **21**:166
"Refrain" (Dove) **6**:117
"Refuge" (Teasdale) **31**:322
"Refugee in America" (Hughes) **53**:94, 149-50
"Refugee Ship" (Cervantes) **35**:108, 118, 130, 131
"The Refugees" (Jarrell) **41**:169
"Refugees" (MacNeice) **61**:139
"The Refugees" (Muir) **49**:251, 256, 273, 277, 282-83, 296, 299
"Refugees" (Zagajewski) **27**:402
"The Refusal" (Wright) **36**:337
"Refusal Song" (Char) **56**:131
"A Refusal to Mourn" (Mahon) **60**:132, 134, 193
"A Refusal to Mourn" (Thomas)
See "A Refusal to Mourn the Death, by Fire, of a Child in London"
"A Refusal to Mourn the Death, by Fire, of a Child in London" (Thomas) **2**:382-83, 386, 388, 390, 398, 400; **52**:218, 264-65, 268, 278, 280-81, 313, 322, 335-36
"The Refuse Man" (Ignatow) **34**:310
"Regarding Wave" (Snyder) **21**:297, 304-06
Regarding Wave (Snyder) **21**:285, 288-92, 300, 304-08, 310, 317, 322
"The Regatta" (Wilbur) **51**:255-58, 261
"Regent's Park Sonnets" (Hacker) **47**:81
Regina Cœli (Patmore) **59**:223
Region of Unlikeness (Graham) **59**:131, 133-39, 143-45, 155-59, 161, 163, 168-69, 175-76, 178, 184
"Règle" (Tzara) **27**:230-31
"Régles de l'Ode" (Hugo) **17**:90
"Regreso a la cordura" (Storni) **33**:257-58, 295;
"Regreso a mis pájaros" (Storni) **33**:257, 259, 294;
"Regreso en sueños" (Storni) **33**:268, 284
"Regressiv" (Benn) **35**:68
"Regret Not Me" (Thomas) **52**:283
"Les Regrets de la belle Heaulmière" (Villon) **13**:389-90
"Rehabilitation & Treatment in the Prisons of America" (Knight) **14**:53
"The Rehearsal" (Smith) **12**:330
"Reincarnation I" (Dickey) **40**:155, 176, 197, 248
"Reincarnation II" (Dickey) **40**:158, 166, 197, 202, 248, 255, 259
"El reino interior" (Darío) **15**:79-80, 92, 96, 114
"Re-interment: Recollection of a Grandfather" (Warren) **37**:376
"Reise" (Benn) **35**:49, 74
"Reisen" (Benn) **35**:70
"The Rejected Lover" (Dafydd)
See "Y Cariad a Wrthodwyd"
"Rejoice in the Lamb" (Smart)
See "Jubilate Agno"
"Rejoice, Liars" (Jackson) **44**:101
Rekviem: Tsikl stikhotvorenii (Akhmatova) **2**:4, 7, 9, 15-16, 19-20
Relations and Contraries (Tomlinson) **17**:317, 342
"Relatives" (Stone) **53**:240-41, 248
"Relearning the Alphabet" (Levertov) **11**:195-98
Relearning the Alphabet (Levertov) **11**:176-78, 180, 193-94
"Release" (Lawrence) **54**:168
"The Release" (MacLeish) **47**:190
"A Reliable Service" (Curnow) **48**:19-20
"Relief" (Curnow) **48**:25
"Religio" (Hugo) **17**:66
Religio Laici; or, A Layman's Faith (Dryden) **25**:79-82, 97, 101
"Religion" (Dunbar) **5**:125
"The Religion of My Time" (Pasolini) **17**:257-59
The Religion of My Time (Pasolini) **17**:285
La religione del mio tempo (Pasolini) **17**:264-66, 270, 272-73, 295
"Religious Isolation" (Arnold) **5**:42
"A Religious Man" (Smith) **12**:352
"Religious Musings" (Coleridge) **11**:49-51, 53, 80-2, 93-6; **39**:128, 152, 155-56, 163, 167, 179-81
"Religious Propaganda" (Tagore)
See "Dharma prachar"

Le Reliquare (Rimbaud) **57**:298
"The Relique" (Donne) **1**:126, 130
"Relocation" (Ortiz) **17**:231
"El reloj de arena" (Borges) **62**:60
"Reluctance" (Frost) **39**:246
Remains of Elmet (Hughes) **7**:146, 149, 162
"Rémanence" (Char) **56**:157
"Rembrandt to Rembrandt" (Robinson) **1**:487
"Remember" (Harjo) **27**:59
"Remember" (Rossetti) **7**:269, 280
"Remember?" (Walker) **30**:348
"Remember my little granite pail" (Niedecker) **42**:98, 106-7, 140, 176-77
"Rememberance" (Hölderlin)
See "Andenken"
"Remembering a Strange Treat" (Shvarts) **50**:142, 144, 146
"Remembering in Osolo the Old Picture of the Magna Carta" (Bly) **39**:79
"Remembering Nat Turner" (Brown) **55**:114, 166
"Remembering Pearl Harbor at the Tutankhamen Exhibit" (Kumin) **15**:196, 206, 208
"Remembering Robert Lowell" (Meredith) **28**:177, 180
"Remembering the Thirties" (Davie) **29**:98
"Remembering Watching Romy Schneider" (Ríos) **57**:325
"Remembrance" (Angelou) **32**:16
"Remembrance" (Brontë) **8**:52, 56, 60, 65, 68, 74-5
"A Remembrance" (Carman) **34**:229
"Remembrance" (Muir) **49**:287
"Remembrance Has a Rear and Front" (Dickinson) **1**:94
"Remembrance in Tsarskoe Selo" (Pushkin)
See "Vospominanie v Tsarskom Sele"
Remembrance of Crimes Past (Abse) **41**:32
"Remembrances" (Leopardi)
See "Le ricordanze"
Remeslo (Tsvetaeva) **14**:315, 318, 324-25
"Remind Me of Apples" (Francis) **34**:249, 253-54
"Reminiscence" (Ishikawa)
See "Omoide"
"Réminiscence" (Mallarmé)
See "L'orphelin"
"Reminiscences at Tsarskoe Selo" (Pushkin)
See "Vospominanie v Tsarskom Sele"
"Reminiscences of Childhood" (MacNeice) **61**:169
"Reminiscene" (Niedecker) **42**:43
"Reminiscent of a Wave at the Curl" (Moore) **49**:150
"Remittance Man" (Wright) **14**:340, 348, 368
"Remonstrance" (Lanier) **50**:55
"Remordimiento" (Borges)
See "Remordimiento por cualquier defunción"
"Remordimiento por cualquier defunción" (Borges) **32**:64
"Remords posthume" (Baudelaire) **1**:45
"Remorse" (Sassoon) **12**:282
Remorse (Coleridge) **11**:58
"Remorse for Intemperate Speech" (Yeats) **20**:328, 333
"Remorse Is Memory Awake" (Dickinson) **1**:111
"Remote-a-Dad" (Silverstein) **49**:319, 340
"The Removal" (Merwin) **45**:45-6
"Removing the Plate of the Pump on the Hydraulic System of the Backhoe" (Snyder) **21**:307
"Le Rempart de Brindilles" (Char) **56**:108
Ren'aimeikashū (Hagiwara) **18**:170, 172
"Renaissance" (Lawrence) **54**:235-36
"Renaming the Kings" (Levine) **22**:215
"Renascence" (Lawrence) **54**:235
"Renascence" (Millay) **6**:204-05, 207-08, 211, 214-15, 217, 221, 224, 226-27, 242
Renascence (Millay) **61**:209-58
Renascence, and Other Poems (Millay) **6**:204-06, 225, 240; **61**:211, 222
"Rencontre de deux sourires" (Éluard) **38**:90-91, 93
"Rendezvous" (Kumin) **15**:213, 224
"The Renewal" (Roethke) **15**:275
"Renewal" (Thumboo) **30**:313
"Renewal of Strength" (Harper) **21**:189
Renga (Paz) **48**:221-26
"Renka" (Nishiwaki) **15**:238
"Rent Day Blues" (Brown) **55**:178
"Renunciation" (Curnow) **48**:24-25
"Renunciation" (Parker) **28**:360
"Reparation" (Reese) **29**:335
"Les reparties de Nina" (Rimbaud) **3**:271; **57**:191, 202, 204, 241, 244-45, 249, 252
"El reparto" (Mistral) **32**:184-85
"Repas" (Valéry) **9**:391
"Repent" (Kumin) **15**:209, 211
"Repentance" (Herbert) **4**:120
Répétitions (Éluard) **38**:88, 101-2, 105-6
"The Repetitive Heart" (Schwartz) **8**:292-93, 302
"Repining" (Rossetti) **7**:287
"Reply" (Bridges) **28**:66, 69
"Reply to Censure" (Roethke) **15**:291
"A Reply to Matthew Arnold" (Wright) **36**:369
"Reply to Mr. Wordsworth" (MacLeish) **47**:192
"Reply to the Warsaw Critics" (Mickiewicz)
See "O Krytykach i Recenzentach"
"A Replycacion" (Skelton) **25**:374, 385
"Reponse aux adieux de Sir Walter Scott" (Lamartine) **16**:283
"Report" (Harper) **21**:207, 216
"Report" (Illyés) **16**:243
"Report from Paradise" (Herbert) **50**:34
"Report from the Besieged City" (Herbert)
See "Raport z oblezonego miasta"
Report from the Besieged City (Herbert)
See *Raport z oblezonego miasta*
"Report from the Skull's Diorama" (Komunyakaa) **51**:28, 41
"Report to the Mother" (Knight) **14**:52
"Repos d'été" (Éluard) **38**:75
"Repose of Rivers" (Crane) **3**:83, 90, 96
"Repression of War Experience" (Sassoon) **12**:264, 267, 288
"The Reprimand" (Bishop) **34**:160-61
"The Reproach" (Glück) **16**:152, 156, 164
"Reproach" (Graves) **6**:140, 144
"Reproach to Dead Poets" (MacLeish) **47**:126, 167
"A Reproof of Gluttony" (Belloc) **24**:17
"The Republic" (Ondaatje) **28**:298
"Republican Living Rooms" (Olds) **22**:307
"Repulse Bay" (Chin) **40**:4
"Request" (Sarton) **39**:319, 347
"Request for Blanca" (Mistral)
See "Encargo a Blanca"
"Request for Requiems" (Hughes) **1**:243
"Request of Blanca" (Mistral)
See "Encargo a Blanca"
"Request to a Year" (Wright) **14**:375
"A Request to the Graces" (Herrick) **9**:88
"Requeste à Monseigneur de Bourbon" (Villon)
See "Requête à Monseigneur de Bourbon"
"Requête à Monseigneur de Bourbon" (Villon) **13**:413
"Requiem" (Berry) **28**:16-17
"Requiem" (Ignatow) **34**:324, 344
"Requiem" (Nash) **21**:273
Requiem (Akhmatova) **55**:3-67
Requiem (Rilke) **2**:267, 279
Requiem: A Cycle of Poems (Akhmatova)
See *Rekviem: Tsikl stikhotvorenii*
"Requiem for 'Bird' Parker, Musician" (Corso) **33**:46
"Requiem for the Death of a Boy" (Rilke) **2**:279
"Requiem for the Spanish Dead" (Rexroth) **20**:192
"Requiescat" (Arnold) **5**:12
"Le Requin et al mouette" (Char) **56**:156
Rerum vulgarium fragmenta (Petrarch)
See *Canzoniere*
"Rescue Poem" (Wakoski) **15**:324, 361
"Rescue the Dead" (Ignatow) **34**:286-87, 294, 298, 309, 313, 320, 324, 341
Rescue the Dead (Ignatow) **34**:277, 279, 281, 289-93, 318-19, 321, 323-24, 344
"Rescue with Yul Brynner" (Moore) **4**:242, 256, 259; **49**:147
"Reservation Drive-In" (Alexie) **53**:8
"Reservation Mathematics" (Alexie) **53**:10
"A Reservation Table of Elements" (Alexie) **53**:6
Residence on Earth (Neruda)
See *Residencia en la tierra*
Residence on Earth and Other Poems (Neruda)
See *Residencia en la tierra*
Residencia en la tierra (Neruda) **4**:277, 2809, 282-83, 285, 293, 295, 300-01, 304, 306
Residencia en la tierra, Vol. 1, 1925-31 (Neruda)
See *Residencia en la tierra*
Residencia en la tierra, Vol. 2, 1931-35 (Neruda)
See *Residencia en la tierra*
Residencia I (Neruda)
See *Residencia en la tierra*
Residencia II (Neruda)
See *Residencia en la tierra*
Residencia III (Neruda)
See *Residencia en la tierra*
"Resignation" (Arnold) **5**:6, 18, 32, 34, 37-41, 43, 47, 49-51, 54
"Resignation" (Dunbar) **5**:133
"Resignation" (Longfellow) **30**:21, 49
"Resolution" (Warren) **37**:289
"Resolution and Independence" (Wordsworth) **4**:399, 404, 406, 411-12, 426
"The Resolve" (Levertov) **11**:170
"Resolve" (Plath) **1**:406; **37**:184
"Respectability" (Browning) **2**:95
"The Respectable Burgher on 'The Higher Criticism'" (Hardy) **8**:124
"The Respectable Folks-/Where Dwell They?" (Thoreau) **30**:201
Responce aux injures (Ronsard) **11**:234
"Responde tú" (Guillén) **23**:117, 127
"Respondez!" (Whitman) **3**:405
"Response" (Dunbar) **5**:139
"Résponse à une acte d'accusation" (Hugo) **17**:64, 82
Responsibilities, and Other Poems (Yeats) **20**:311, 320, 323, 342; **51**:81
"Responsibilities of the Poet" (Pinsky) **27**:160, 170
"Responso a Verlaine" (Darío) **15**:98
"A Responsory, 1948" (Merton) **10**:333
"Respuesta a un cónsul" (Paz) **48**:184
"Restore To Them . . ." (Char)
See "Redonnez-leur . . ."
"Ressouvenir du lac Leman" (Lamartine) **16**:286
"Ressurection, Imperfect" (Donne) **1**:147
"Rest" (Rossetti) **7**:277, 280
"The Rest I Will Tell to Those Down in Hades" (Cavafy) **36**:39, 41
"Restless" (Tagore)
See "Chanchal"
"Restless Night" (Tu Fu) **9**:319, 323
"Restraint" (Curnow) **48**:25-26
"Restricted Area" (Birney) **52**:8
"Résumé" (Parker) **28**:347, 363
"Resumen" (Guillén) **35**:202
"Resumption" (Carducci)
See "Ripresa"
"Resurgam" (Carman) **34**:203, 229
"Resurgam" (Tate) **50**:228
"Resurgir" (Storni) **33**:241, 306;
"Resurrection" (Atwood) **8**:40
"Resurrection" (Jeffers) **17**:141
"The Resurrection" (Ransom) **61**:294

"The Resurrection" (Schnackenberg) **45**:333, 337
"The Resurrection of Jesus" (Harper) **21**:189
"Resurrection of the Right Side" (Rukeyser) **12**:225
"Le Rétablissement de la Statue de Henri IV" (Hugo) **17**:88
Retaliation (Blok)
See *Vozmezdie*
"A Retir'd Friendship To Ardelia" (Philips) **40**:295
"Retired Ballerina, Central Park West" (Ferlinghetti) **1**:183
"The Retired Colonel" (Hughes) **7**:140
"Retirement" (Cowper) **40**:44-5, 49, 111-12, 130
"Retirement" (Philips) **40**:269
"Retort" (Dunbar) **5**:125, 127
"Retort to Jesus" (Lawrence) **54**:249
"Le retour" (Lamartine) **16**:286
Retour amont (Char) **56**:110-13, 115, 117-19
Retour au pays natal (Césaire)
See *Cahier d'un retour au pays natal*
"Retraction" (Chaucer) **58**:284
"Retractions" (Chaucer)
See "Retraction"
"Retrato de García Lorca" (Storni) **33**:240, 269;
"Retrato de un muchacho que se llama Sigfrido" (Storni) **33**:240;
Retratos con nombre (Aleixandre) **15**:4, 12, 16
"Retribution" (Blok) **21**:31
"Retribution" (Harper) **21**:190
Retribution (Blok)
See *Vozmezdie*
The Retrieval System (Kumin) **15**:203-09, 217, 221
"Retrievers in Translation" (Doty) **53**:60
"Retroduction to American History" (Tate) **50**:228-29, 243, 246, 248, 274, 316
"Retrospect" (Brooke) **24**:62, 64, 86
"Return" (Alurista) **34**:29
"The Return" (Brathwaite) **56**:7, 20, 62, 83, 85
"The Return" (Brooke) **24**:61
"Return" (Brown) **55**:110
"Return" (Corso) **33**:50
"Return" (Forché) **10**:136-41, 144-45, 152, 154-56, 162, 167
"The Return" (Hayden) **6**:194
"Return" (Heaney) **18**:201
"Return" (Jeffers) **17**:117, 119, 131, 141, 147
"Return" (Lawrence) **54**:168
"Return" (MacLeish) **47**:126, 188
"The Return" (MacNeice) **61**:139
"The Return" (Mahon) **60**:140, 142, 152, 184-85, 192-93
"The Return" (Muir) **49**:202, 206, 260-61, 289, 297
"The Return" (Oppen) **35**:310, 333
"Return" (Paz)
See "Vuelta"
"The Return" (Pound) **4**:355-56, 365
"The Return" (Roethke) **15**:274
"The Return" (Sikelianos)
See "The Great Homecoming"
"The Return" (Teasdale) **31**:334
"Return" (Wright) **14**:342
Return (Alurista) **34**:45-48
The Return (Bely)
See *Vozvrat: Tretiia simfoniia*
Return (Paz)
See *Vuelta*
The Return (Sarton) **39**:325
"The Return: an Elegy" (Warren) **37**:276, 279, 286, 288, 320, 329, 331-33, 376
"Return from Greece" (Cavafy)
See "Returning Home from Greece"
"Return from the Freudian Isles" (Hope) **56**:286
"Return in Dreams" (Storni)
See "Regreso en sueños"
"Return in Hinton" (Tomlinson) **17**:311, 327-28
"The Return of Aphrodite" (Sarton) **39**:343
"The Return of Helen" (McGuckian) **27**:77, 100
"The Return of Icarus" (Wagoner) **33**:348
"The Return of Odysseus" (Muir) **49**:252, 264, 279, 289
"The Return of Persephone" (Hope) **56**:268, 273, 278, 281
"The Return of Robinson Jeffers" (Hass) **16**:195, 203, 228
"The Return of the Birds" (Bryant) **20**:46
"The Return of the Goddess" (Graves) **6**:137, 144
"The Return of the Greeks" (Muir) **49**:245, 251-52, 297
"The Return of the Muses" (Guest) **55**:219
"The Return of the Proconsul" (Herbert)
See "Powrót prokonsula"
"Return of the Sun" (Brathwaite) **56**:91
"Return to a Country House" (Teasdale) **31**:335, 341
"Return to Cardiff" (Abse) **41**:3, 5
"Return to Chartres" (Sarton) **39**:343, 345
"Return to DeKalb" (Stryk) **27**:214
"Return to D'Ennery, Rain" (Walcott) **46**:234, 272
"Return to Hiroshima" (Stryk) **27**:187, 202, 216
"Return to Kraków in 1880" (Milosz) **8**:204
"A Return to Me" (Neruda)
See "Se vuelve a yo"
Return to My Native Land (Césaire)
See *Cahier d'un retour au pays natal*
"Return to Oneself" (Neruda)
See "Se vuelve a yo"
"Return to Solitude" (Bly) **39**:7, 11
"Return to the River" (Wagoner) **33**:352
"Return to the Swamp" (Wagoner) **33**:356
"Return to Wang River" (Wang Wei) **18**:392
"The Return to Work" (Williams) **7**:369
"The Return Trip" (Ekeloef) **23**:54
"Returning" (Lowell) **3**:226
"Returning" (Quintana) **36**:273
"Returning a Lost Child" (Glück) **16**:124
"Returning Birds" (Szymborska)
See "Przylot"
"Returning Home from Greece" (Cavafy) **36**:40, 74, 76
"Returning North of Vortex" (Ginsberg) **4**:76
"Returning to Mount Sung" (Wang Wei) **18**:371
"Returning to the Rhetoric of an Early Mode" (Duncan) **2**:109, 113
"Returns" (Szymborska)
See "Powroty"
"Reuben Bright" (Robinson) **1**:467, 496
"Reuben Pantier" (Masters) **1**:347; **36**:169
"Reunion" (Forché) **10**:137, 142-44, 147, 157, 168
"The Reunion" (Harper) **21**:200, 214
"A Reunion" (Szirtes) **51**:157
"The Rev. Abner Peet" (Masters) **36**:230
"Le rêve d'un curieux" (Baudelaire) **1**:54
"Rêve Expérimental" (Tzara) **27**:242
"Rêve parisien" (Baudelaire) **1**:47, 54
"Rêve pour l'hiver" (Rimbaud) **57**:196, 245
"The Revealer" (Robinson) **35**:368
"Reveillé" (Housman) **2**:164
"Reveille" (Hughes) **7**:123, 159
"The Reveillon" (Belloc) **24**:11
"Revelation" (Amichai) **38**:8
"Revelation" (Warren) **37**:284, 287, 289, 322, 332-33, 376
"The Revelation" (Wright) **36**:288
"Revelations" (Brown) **55**:110, 174, 178
"The Revenant" (Meredith) **28**:181
The Revenant (MacNeice) **61**:141
"Revenge Fable" (Hughes) **7**:132, 143
"The Revenge of Hamish" (Lanier) **50**:56
"Revenir dans une ville" (Éluard) **38**:71
"Reverdure" (Berry) **28**:8-9
"Reverie" (Browning) **2**:96
"Reverie" (Muir) **49**:287
"Reveries" (Castro)
See "Vaguedás"
"Reversibilité" (Baudelaire) **1**:56, 67
"Reversionary" (Smith) **12**:314
"A Revery" (Philips) **40**:271
Revised Arcadia (Sidney) **32**:314-15
"Revisiting the MacDowell Colony" (Kumin) **15**:222
"The Revolt" (Carducci) **46**:26
The Revolt of Islam (Shelley)
See *Laon and Cythna, or the Revolution in the Golden City*
"Revolution" (Hughes) **53**:110
"The Revolution at Market Hill" (Swift) **9**:260
"Revolution in the Revolution in the Revolution" (Snyder) **21**:306
"The Revolutionary" (Stryk) **27**:208
"Revolutionary Dreams" (Giovanni) **19**:111
"Revolutionary Music" (Giovanni) **19**:110
"Revolutionary Petunias" (Walker) **30**:339, 363-65
Revolutionary Petunias (Walker) **30**:337, 340, 342, 343, 346-47, 349-53, 355-56, 363, 365
"Revolutions" (Arnold) **5**:51
"Les revolutions" (Lamartine) **16**:280-81, 293
Le revolver á cheveux blancs (Breton) **15**:50-2
"Revolving Meditation" (Kunitz) **19**:174, 178
"Revulsion" (Hardy) **8**:91
"The Revulsion" (Patmore) **59**:228, 234
Rewards and Fairies (Kipling) **3**:184
"Reyerta" (García Lorca) **3**:131
"Rhapsody" (O'Hara) **45**:137, 218, 243
Rhapsody in Plain Yellow (Chin) **40**:36
"The Rhapsody of Life's Progress" (Browning) **6**:6
"Rhapsody on a Windy Night" (Eliot) **5**:153, 155, 171; **31**:131, 133,-34, 140
"A Rhapsody on Irish Themes" (Jarrell) **41**:158, 160
"A Rhapsody on Poetry" (Swift) **9**:281
"Der Rhein" (Hölderlin) **4**:143, 148, 153, 155, 173-4
"Rhénane d'automne" (Apollinaire) **7**:42
"Rhetorical Exercises" (Parra)
See "Ejercicios retóricos"
"Rhododendrons" (Gallagher) **9**:60
"The Rhodora" (Emerson) **18**:74, 82, 94, 96, 98-100, 102
"A Rhyme about an Electrical Advertising Sign" (Lindsay) **23**:296
"A Rhyme for All Zionists" (Lindsay) **23**:283
"The Rhyme of Reb Nachman" (Pinsky) **27**:175
"The Rhyme of the Duchess May" (Browning) **6**:28
"The Rhyme of the Three Captains" (Kipling) **3**:181-82
"The Rhyme of the Three Sealers" (Kipling) **3**:182
"Rhymed Address to All Renegade Campbellites Exhorting Them to Return" (Lindsay) **23**:265
Rhymed Ruminations (Sassoon) **12**:252
Rhymes (Jiménez)
See *Rimas*
Rhymes and Rhythms (Carducci)
See *Rime e ritmi*
Rhymes of Childhood (Riley) **48**:290, 346-47, 357
"Rhyming Poems" (Lawrence) **54**:207, 232
"Rhythm & Blues 1" (Baraka) **4**:16
"Rhythm, Content & Flavor: New & Selected Poems" (Cruz) **37**:16, 25, 31
"Rhythm, etc." (Cage) **58**:219
"Rhythm of Autumn" (García Lorca)
See "Ritmo de otoño"
"The Rib" (Dickey) **40**:185, 225
Rib of Earth (Thumboo) **30**:299
"La ricchezza" (Pasolini) **17**:270, 273, 295
"Richard Bone" (Masters) **1**:324
"Richard Cory" (Robinson) **1**:467, 475, 486; **35**:361-78
"Richard Hunt's 'Arachne'" (Hayden) **6**:186
"Richard Roe and John Doe" (Graves) **6**:141
"Riche de larmes" (Char) **56**:163, 165, 190, 194-95
"Riches" (Teasdale) **31**:357

"A Richland County Lyric for Elizabeth Asleep" (Jordan) **38**:144
"Le ricordanze" (Carducci) **46**:63
"Le ricordanze" (Leopardi) **37**:102, 109-11, 123-25, 127, 141, 143, 165
"The Riddle" (Auden) **1**:34
"The Riddle" (Heaney) **18**:229, 232, 237
"A Riddle" (Wilbur) **51**:301
"Riddle in the Garden" (Warren) **37**:301, 307, 362
"Riddles" (Guillén) **23**:131
"Riddles" (Parra)
See "Rompecabezas"
"The Ride" (Smith) **12**:315
"The Ride" (Wilbur) **51**:249, 302, 309-10, 335
"The Ride of Paul Revere" (Longfellow)
See "Paul Revere's Ride"
"A Ride on the Swan-Boats" (Bishop) **34**:96
"Ride to Aix" (Browning) **2**:35
"The Rider Victory" (Muir) **49**:232
"The Ridge Farm" (Ammons) **16**:46-7, 50-1
"Riding in cars" (MacNeice) **61**:137
"Riding the Elevator into the Sky" (Sexton) **2**:373
"Riding Together" (Morris) **55**:238, 248, 252, 302, 344-47
"Rien d'autre" (Éluard) **38**:85
"Rigamarole" (Williams) **7**:383, 389
"Right in the Trail" (Snyder) **21**:327
"The Right of Way" (Williams) **7**:387, 409, 411
"The Right Thing Happens to the Happy Man" (Roethke) **15**:270
"The Right to Grief" (Sandburg) **41**:234, 262, 334, 338, 364
"Right Wing Opinions" (Davie) **29**:97
"The Righteous" (Francis) **34**:246
"The Righteous Ones" (Borges) **32**:58
"The Rightful One" (Ignatow) **34**:213, 282, 313, 317
Rights of Passage (Brathwaite) **56**:3-8, 17-18, 20, 22-23, 26, 29-30, 33-34, 37-41, 43, 49, 59, 62, 64-68, 73, 75, 77, 79, 82-84, 88, 95-96, 98-99
"Right's Security" (Dunbar) **5**:127
"Rigor" (Guillén) **35**:146
"Rigorists" (Moore) **49**:91, 143
Riley Farm-Rhymes (Riley) **48**:315, 318
Riley Love Lyrics (Riley) **48**:323
"Rillons, Rillettes" (Wilbur) **51**:285
Rimas (Jiménez) **7**:197, 199
"The Rime" (Coleridge)
See *The Rime of the Ancient Mariner: A Poet's Reverie*
Rime (Carducci) **46**:13, 16, 35, 46
Rime (Petrarch)
See *Canzoniere*
Rime e ritmi (Carducci) **46**:26, 48, 54, 76, 81
Rime nuove (Carducci) **46**:8, 35, 37, 47, 50, 56, 64-65, 69, 73-75, 81, 88
"The Rime of the Ancient Mariner" (Coleridge)
See *The Rime of the Ancient Mariner: A Poet's Reverie*
The Rime of the Ancient Mariner: A Poet's Reverie (Coleridge) **11**:37-42, 44, 51, 53, 55, 58-69, 81, 84, 88-9, 92-7, 104, 106, 110, 117; **39**:123, 131, 135, 140, 153, 156-57, 160, 169, 171, 175-76, 178-81, 185, 187, 203, 215
The Rime of the Ancyent Marinere (Coleridge)
See *The Rime of the Ancient Mariner: A Poet's Reverie*
Rime sparse (Petrarch)
See *Canzoniere*
"Rimembranze di Scuola" (Carducci) **46**:23, 34, 37
"Un rimorso" (Gozzano) **10**:188
The Ring and the Book (Browning) **2**:39-40, 42-4, 46-7, 53, 56, 63, 66-7, 73, 76-7, 82-3, 85, 88, 95; **61**:1-103
"The Ring and the Castle" (Lowell) **13**:60-1
"The Ring Cycle" (Merrill) **28**:285-87
"The Ring Given to Venus" (Morris) **55**:249, 323
"The Ring of the Unicorn" (Char)
See "L'anneau de la licorne"
"Ring out your belles" (Sidney) **32**:250-51
"Ringing the Bells" (Sexton) **2**:350, 353
"Ringless" (Wakoski) **15**:324
The Rings of Saturn (Wakoski) **15**:368-69
"Río de la Plata en celeste nebliplateado" (Storni) **33**:294;
"Río de la Plata en gris áureo" (Storni) **33**:294-95;
"Rio De La Plata En Lluvia" (Storni) **33**:260;
"Río de la Plata en lluvia" (Storni) **33**:295;
"Río de la Plata en negro y ocre" (Storni) **33**:294;
"Los ríos del canto" (Neruda) **4**:293
"Riot" (Brooks) **7**:82, 88-9, 91
Riot (Brooks) **7**:63-4, 66, 82, 88, 91, 94
"Rip" (Wright) **36**:320
"Riposo dell'erba" (Quasimodo) **47**:301-2
Ripostes (Pound) **4**:317, 355
"The Ripple" (Levertov) **11**:171
"A Ripple Song" (Kipling) **3**:183
"Riprap" (Snyder) **21**:284, 299, 302
Riprap (Snyder) **21**:286-87, 290-91, 297, 300, 322
"Ripresa" (Carducci) **46**:50
"Rise" (Alexie) **53**:25
"The Risen Lord" (Lawrence) **54**:249
"The Risen One" (Rilke) **2**:271
"Rising" (Berry) **28**:16, 18-19
"The Rising of the Sun" (Milosz)
See "From Where the Sun Rises"
"The Rising Out" (McGuckian) **27**:102-104
"The Rising Sun" (Jarrell) **41**:155
"Risks and Possibilities" (Ammons) **16**:3, 29, 40
"Risveglio" (Pavese) **13**:229
"Rite of Passage" (Olds) **22**:312
"Rites" (Brathwaite) **56**:69, 76, 87
"The Rites for Cousin Vit" (Brooks) **7**:66, 78, 81
"Rites for the Extrusion of a Leper" (Merton) **10**:345
"Rites of Passage" (Gunn) **26**:204
"Rites of Passage" (Stryk) **27**:204, 210
"Ritmo de otoño" (García Lorca) **3**:125
"Ritorno di Deola" (Pavese) **13**:229
"Ritratto" (Pound) **4**:317
"Ritratto d'autore" (Pavese) **13**:213
"Ritter" (Rilke) **2**:266-67
"The Ritual" (Erdrich) **52**:186, 188
"Ritual" (Ignatow) **34**:291-92, 313, 321
"Ritual" (Stone) **53**:223
"Ritual Two" (Ignatow) **34**:298
"Ritual Three" (Ignatow) **34**:287
"The Ritual of Memories" (Gallagher) **9**:60
"Rituals" (Ignatow) **34**:308
"The Rival" (Plath) **1**:390
"The Rivals" (Dunbar) **5**:122
"The Rivals" (Johnson) **24**:141
"The River" (Arnold) **5**:19, 43
"The River" (Carver) **54**:14, 26
"The River" (Crane) **3**:84-6, 88-90, 95
"The River" (Emerson) **18**:97
"The River" (Muir) **49**:197, 272-73, 282
"The River" (Patmore) **59**:218, 239-40, 257
"The River" (Tagore)
See "Pravahini"
"River" (Viereck) **27**:277
The River (Hughes) **7**:163, 171
"The River, By Night" (Bryant) **20**:17
"The River Down Home" (Wright) **36**:319, 329, 366
"The River God" (Smith) **12**:331, 337
"River in Spate" (MacNeice) **61**:125, 129, 132
"The River Merchant's Wife" (Hacker)
See "Nights of 1962: The River Merchant's Wife"
"The River Merchant's Wife: A Letter" (Amichai) **38**:43
"The River of Bees" (Merwin) **45**:20-1, 23, 25, 35
The River of Heaven (Hongo) **23**:198-99, 201, 204
"River Roads" (Sandburg) **2**:316; **41**:241, 270
"River Sound Remembered" (Merwin) **45**:7
"River Stop" (Tu Fu) **9**:319
"The River Swelleth More and More" (Thoreau) **30**:180, 195, 198, 241
"River Village" (Tu Fu) **9**:319
"River, with Boats" (Ní Chuilleanáin) **34**:350, 366
"Riverbank Blues" (Brown) **55**:110, 154
Riverbed (Wagoner) **33**:333-34, 347-48
"The Riverman" (Bishop) **34**:84, 91, 116
"The River-Merchant's Wife: A Letter" (Li Po) **29**:144, 176
Rivers and Mountains (Ashbery) **26**:107-108, 113-114, 116, 129, 142-143, 148, 154-155, 167, 173-174
"The Rivers of Song" (Neruda)
See "Los ríos del canto"
"The River's Story" (Tagore)
See "Tatinir katha"
Rivers to the Sea (Teasdale) **31**:321, 324-25, 330-31, 337, 345, 347, 351, 354-55, 359, 370, 379
The Riverside Chaucer (Chaucer) **58**:302, 363
"La rivière" (Éluard) **38**:69, 105-7
"Riviere" (Montale) **13**:162
"La Rivière de Cassis" (Rimbaud) **57**:244, 250
"The Rivulet" (Bryant) **20**:12, 14-15
"Rizpah" (Tennyson) **6**:372-73, 377, 379, 381, 411
"Rizpah, the Daughter of Ai" (Harper) **21**:191, 209, 218
"The Road" (Aiken) **26**:24, 46
"The Road" (Muir) **49**:229-30, 243, 273, 289
"The Road" (Pinsky) **27**:168
"The Road" (Sassoon) **12**:242
"Road along the Precipice in Czufut-Kale" (Mickiewicz)
See "Droga nad przepascic w Czufut-Kale"
"The Road and the End" (Sandburg) **2**:300; **41**:225, 242
"The Road Between Here and There" (Kinnell) **26**:292
"The Road from Delphi" (Stryk) **27**:214
"The Road Not Taken" (Frost) **1**:202, 205, 213, 221, 230; **39**:230, 232, 254
"The Road of the Dread" (Goodison) **36**:140-41, 153
"The Road to Hate" (Kavanagh) **33**:118
"Road to Mandalay" (Kipling) **3**:179
"The Road to Nijmegen" (Birney) **52**:22, 37, 44-45, 47, 60
The Road to Ruin (Sassoon) **12**:252, 270
"The Road to Russia" (Mickiewicz) **38**:168
"The Road to Shelter" (Gozzano) **10**:177
The Road to Shelter (Gozzano)
See *La via del refugio*
"Road Up" (Smith) **12**:317
"Roads" (Darío)
See "Caminos"
"Roads" (Thomas) **53**:271, 296, 317, 327, 330
"The Roads Also" (Owen) **19**:343
"Roan Stallion" (Jeffers) **17**:107, 111, 113, 116, 127, 130, 135, 146
Roan Stallion, Tamar, and Other Poems (Jeffers) **17**:106, 122, 132, 135-37
Roaratorio (Cage) **58**:219
"Roarers in a Ring" (Hughes) **7**:123
"Roast Opossum" (Dove) **6**:111
"Roastbeef" (Stein) **18**:327
"The Roasted Englishman in Moscow" (Shvarts)
See "Zharenyi anglichanin v Moskve"
"Robben Island" (Brutus) **24**:120
"The Robber" (MacDiarmid) **9**:155
"The Robber Bridegroom" (Tate) **50**:256
The Robber Brothers (Pushkin)
See *Bratya Razboiniki*

"Robbery" (Shapiro) **25**:312
"Robe of Love" (Yosano Akiko)
See *Koigoromo*
"Robert Carpenter" (Masters) **36**:210
"Robert Frost at Bread Loaf His Hand against a Tree" (Swenson) **14**:247, 253
"Robert Fulton Tanner" (Masters) **36**:222
"Robert G. Ingersoll" (Masters) **1**:343
"Robert Gould Shaw" (Dunbar) **5**:121
"Robert Louis Stevenson" (Reese) **29**:346
"Robert Lowell" (Shapiro) **25**:323
"Robert Schumann, Or: Musical Genius Begins with Affliction" (Dove) **6**:108
"Robert Sitting in My Hands" (Wright) **36**:396
"Roberta Lee" (Brown) **55**:164
"Robin Hood's Heart" (Wylie) **23**:311
"Robin Song" (Hughes) **7**:134
"Los robles" (Castro) **41**:84, 117
"A Robyn" (Wyatt)
See "A Robyn Joly Robyn"
"A Robyn Joly Robyn" (Wyatt) **27**:315
"Rocaille" (Gautier) **18**:141
"The Rock" (Merwin) **45**:54
"The Rock" (Stevens) **6**:303, 313
Rock and Hawk (Jeffers) **17**:137
"The Rock Below" (Graves) **6**:128-29
"Rock Music" (Mahon) **60**:147, 172, 174, 179, 205, 211
"Rock 'N' Roll Band" (Silverstein) **49**:334
"The Rock of Rubies and the Quarry of Pearls" (Herrick) **9**:146
"Rockabye" (Silverstein) **49**:325-26
"Rockefeller is yo vice president, & yo mamma don't wear no drawers" (Baraka) **4**:30
"Rockets and Carts" (Yevtushenko) **40**:343-44
"Rockpool" (Wright) **14**:376
Rocks on a Platter: Notes on Literature (Guest) **55**:200-202, 204-5, 215, 221-22, 231
"Rocky Acres" (Graves) **6**:151
"Rodina" (Lermontov) **18**:281, 297
"Rodine" (Bely) **11**:24
"Rodoslovnaya Moego Geroya" (Pushkin) **10**:391, 394
"Rodrigo" (Heine) **25**:159, 161
"Rodrigo de Barro" (Cisneros) **52**:163
"Rodrigo Poems" (Cisneros) **52**:156, 163
"Rodriguez Street" (Ríos) **57**:312
"The Roe Deer" (Tomlinson) **17**:335, 343
"Roger Bernard" (Char) **56**:191
"Roger Clay's Proposal" (Merrill) **28**:234, 250
"Roger Heston" (Masters) **36**:182
Rogsajyae (Tagore) **8**:424-26
Rokeby (Scott) **13**:265, 267-68, 277-78, 281, 285, 304, 307, 311, 318
"Roland Hayes Beaten" (Hughes) **1**:241, 243, 252
"The Roll of the Ages" (Noyes) **27**:136
"Roller Coaster" (Parra)
See "La montaña rusa"
"Rolling in at Twilight" (Snyder) **21**:288
"Rolling, Rolling" (Toomer) **7**:337
"Roma" (Carducci) **46**:52
Roma 1950 diario (Pasolini) **17**:260
"Roma o morte" (Carducci) **46**:51
"Roman" (Rimbaud) **3**:271, 276; **57**:174, 234, 244
Roman Bartholow (Robinson) **1**:479, 483, 489; **35**:368
"Roman Cadences" (Viereck) **27**:278
The Roman Calendar (Ovid)
See *Fasti*
Roman Elegies (Goethe)
See *Römische Elegien*
Roman Elegies II (Brodsky) **9**:21
"Roman Fountain" (Bogan) **12**:99
"The Roman Road" (Smith) **12**:346
"Romance" (Cassian) **17**:4
"Romance" (Reese) **29**:335
"Romance" (Robinson) **1**:495
"Romance" (Stone) **53**:258
Romance 48 (Juana Inés de la Cruz) **24**:215, 217-18
"Romance de la Guardia Civil Española" (García Lorca) **3**:131, 148
"Romance de la luna, luna" (García Lorca) **3**:133
"Romance de la pena negra" (García Lorca) **3**:133
"Romance del emplazado" (García Lorca) **3**:133
"Romance moderne" (Williams) **7**:345
"A Romance of the Age" (Browning)
See "Lady Geraldine's Courtship"
"Romance of the Spanish Civil Guard" (García Lorca)
See "Romance de la Guardia Civil Española"
"The Romance of the Swan's Nest" (Browning) **6**:32
"Romance sonámbulo" (García Lorca) **3**:131, 133, 147
Romancero (Heine)
See *Romanzero*
Romancero (Pasolini) **17**:253-54, 279, 281
Romancero gitano (García Lorca)
See *Primer romancero gitano*
Romances sans paroles (Verlaine) **2**:414-15, 418-19, 424, 431-32; **32**:340, 342, 359, 361, 378, 382, 385, 394-96, 399-402, 407, 409-12
Romanees and Ballads (Mickiewicz)
See *Ballady i Romanse*
"Romans Angry about the Inner World" (Bly) **39**:13
"The Romantic" (Bogan) **12**:87, 100-01, 103
Romanticism (Mickiewicz)
See *Romantycznoś*
Romantycznoś (Mickiewicz) **38**:156-57
"Romantyczność" (Mickiewicz) **38**:162-64
"The Romany Girl" (Emerson) **18**:77
Romanzen (Heine) **25**:131, 158-59
Romanzero (Heine) **25**:167
"The Romaunt of Margret" (Browning) **6**:32
"The Romaunt of the Page" (Browning) **6**:30, 37-8, 42-3, 45
Rome 1950 A Diary (Pasolini) **17**:260-61
"Rome-Sickness" (Arnold) **5**:19
Römische Elegien (Goethe) **5**:239-40, 249, 255, 257
"Römische Sarkophage" (Rilke) **2**:278
"Rompecabezas" (Parra) **39**:292, 307
"Ronda de la ceiba equatoriana" (Mistral) **32**:175, 180
"Rondalla" (Gautier) **18**:125
"Roofers" (Hass) **16**:248
"The Roofwalker" (Rich) **5**:363, 392-93, 395
"The Room" (Aiken) **26**:24
"The Room" (Ignatow) **34**:291-92, 321
"The Room" (Merwin) **45**:20
"The Room" (Reese) **29**:330
"The Room of Mirrors" (Masters) **1**:344
"The Room of My Life" (Sexton) **2**:373
"Room Tone" (Graham) **59**:130, 139, 171
"A Room with a View" (Wagoner) **33**:330, 333
"The Room with the Tapestry Rug" (Giovanni) **19**:143
"Rooming-house, Winter" (Atwood) **8**:14
"Rooms" (Stryk) **27**:215, 218
"The Rooms of Other Women Poets" (Boland) **58**:18, 30, 92, 94-95
"Roosevelt" (Lindsay) **23**:288
"Rooster" (Hagiwara)
See "Niwatori"
"The Roosters" (Bishop) **3**:37, 46-8, 56-7, 60, 66; **34**:52, 68, 78, 137, 139, 146, 165, 170, 189, 192
"Root Cellar" (Roethke) **15**:260, 295
"The Root of All Evil" (Lawrence) **54**:249
Root of Man (Paz)
See *Raíz del hombre*
"Root-Light; or, The Lawyer's Daughter" (Dickey) **40**:210, 222
"Roots" (Heaney) **18**:202
"Roots" (Hongo) **23**:198
"Roots" (Meredith) **28**:171, 175, 192, 194
"Roots" (Walcott) **46**:270, 272, 323, 325
"Roots and Branches" (Duncan) **2**:103, 110
Roots and Branches (Duncan) **2**:102, 105-06, 109, 113-14, 119, 125
"The Ropewalk" (Longfellow) **30**:43, 71
"Rory" (Mahon) **60**:141
"La rosa" (Guillén) **35**:157
"Rosa divina que en gentil cultura" (Juana Inés de la Cruz) **24**:225
"Rosa Mystica" (Hopkins) **15**:148, 159, 165
La rosa profunda (Borges) **22**:97; **32**:63, 86, 90, 95, 108
La rosa separada: obra póstuma (Neruda) **4**:287
"Una rosa y Milton" (Borges) **32**:114, 117
Rosalind and Helen (Shelley) **14**:173, 175, 192, 234
"Rosania's private marriage" (Philips) **40**:298
The Rosary (Akhmatova)
See *Chyotki*
"A Rosary of Your Names" (Goodison) **36**:147, 151, 153
"A Rosary of Your Names II" (Goodison) **36**:147, 153
"Rosary Songs" (Trakl)
See "Rosenkranzlieder"
"Rosas" (Borges) **32**:80
"Rosas de elegía" (Guillén) **23**:100
"Roscoe Purkapile" (Masters) **36**:182, 199
"Le Rose" (Gautier) **18**:125
"The Rose" (Roethke) **15**:310-11
"The Rose" (Williams) **7**:386, 410
"The Rose" (Yeats) **20**:310
Rose (Lee) **24**:239-44
The Rose (Yeats) **20**:326, 328, 343, 347
"The Rose and the Cross" (Blok) **21**:31
"The Rose and the Eagle" (Piercy) **29**:300
"La rose de l'infant" (Hugo) **17**:60-61, 65
"La rose des vents" (Wilbur) **51**:193, 217-18
"Rose in fiamme" (Ungaretti) **57**:347
"The Rose Marble Table" (Guest) **55**:185
"The Rose of the World" (Patmore) **59**:205
"The Rose of the World" (Yeats) **20**:329
"Rose on the Heath" (Goethe)
See "Heidenröslein"
La rose publique (Éluard) **38**:62, 68, 73
"Rose, Rose" (Bukowski) **18**:5
"rose th night nd th green flowr" (Bissett) **14**:28, 33
"The Rose Trellis" (McGuckian) **27**:94
"Roseamond" (Apollinaire)
See "Rosemonde"
"Rosebud" (Alexie) **53**:14
The Rose-Geranium (Ní Chuilleanáin) **34**:360-61, 380
"Rosemary" (Moore) **49**:126, 128, 138
"Rosemonde" (Apollinaire) **7**:45, 47-8
"Rosen" (Benn) **35**:71
"Rosenkranzlieder" (Trakl) **20**:233, 248
"Rosenschimmer" (Celan) **10**:122
"Roses" (Dove) **6**:109
"Roses" (Guest) **55**:185
"Roses" (Sandburg) **2**:324
"Roses in flames" (Ungaretti)
See "Rose in fiamme"
"Roses Only" (Moore) **49**:89, 91-92, 94, 114
"Le rossignol" (Lamartine) **16**:293
"Le Rossignol" (Verlaine) **32**:387
"Röster under jorden" (Ekeloef) **23**:76
"Rostro tras el cristal (Mirada del viejo)" (Aleixandre) **15**:43
"Rosy" (Glück) **16**:138
"The Rosy Bosom'd Hours" (Patmore) **59**:267
"Rosy Ear" (Herbert) **50**:4
"Rosy-Checked Death" (Yosano Akiko)
See "Kôgao no shi"
"Rot" (Benn) **35**:70, 73
"Rotten Sample" (Stone) **53**:225
"Rotting Clam" (Hagiwara) **18**:167, 177

"A Rotting Corpse" (Baudelaire)
See "Une charogne"
"Rougeur des Matinaux" (Char) **56**:121, 174, 185
The Rough Rider, and Other Poems (Carman) **34**:205, 211, 228
"Rough times" (Piercy) **29**:303, 305
"A Round & A Canon" (Olson) **19**:281
"Round Dance Somewhere Around Oklahoma City/November Night" (Harjo) **27**:69
"The Round of Grief" (Jordan) **38**:120
"The Round of the Ecuadorian Ceiba Tree" (Mistral)
See "Ronda de la ceiba equatoriana"
"Round the Corner" (MacNeice) **61**:177-78
"Round the Turning" (Pasternak) **6**:267
"Round Time" (McHugh) **61**:204
"Round Trip" (Page) **12**:163
"The Roundel" (Swinburne) **24**:319, 322-23
A Roundhead's Rallying Song (Noyes) **27**:138
"Route" (Oppen) **35**:289, 293, 337, 340, 341, 346, 357
"De Route March" (McKay) **2**:225
"Route Marchin'" (Kipling) **3**:160
"A Route of Evanescence" (Dickinson) **1**:104
"Route Six" (Kunitz) **19**:175
"Rover" (Kunitz) **19**:175
"A Rover's Song" (Carman) **34**:207
"Rowing" (McGuckian) **27**:104
"Rowing" (Sexton) **2**:373
"The Rowing Endeth" (Sexton) **2**:371
"A Roxbury Garden" (Lowell) **13**:77-8, 96
"The Royal Palms" (Walcott) **46**:271
"A Royal Princess" (Rossetti) **7**:272, 291
"Royauté" (Rimbaud) **3**:261-63
"Rozhdenie ulybki" (Mandelstam) **14**:152-53
"Rozmowa" (Mickiewicz) **38**:196
"Rozmyslania o ojcu" (Herbert) **50**:37
"R.T.S.L." (Walcott) **46**:247
Rtusamhāra (Kālidāsa) **22**:177, 182, 184-85, 208
Ruba'iyat (Khayyam)
See *Rubáiyát*
Rubáiyát (Khayyam) **8**:143-45, 151-53, 157-70
"Rubáiyát of Doc Sifers" (Riley) **48**:304, 351
"Ruben's Women" (Szymborska) **44**:313
"Rubies" (Emerson) **18**:77
"Ruby Brown" (Hughes) **1**:249
Ruce Venušiny (Seifert) **47**:316, 325-26, 333
"Rückenfigur" (Howe) **54**:151-54
"Rückfall" (Benn) **35**:50
"Rue de Belleyme" (Hacker) **47**:118
La rueda dentada (Guillén) **23**:109, 127, 133
"Rueful Associations" (Surrey) **59**:357-58
"El ruego" (Mistral) **32**:153, 155, 164, 175-76
"Rugaroo" (Erdrich) **52**:177
"Rugby Chapel" (Arnold) **5**:33
"Rugby Football Excursion" (MacNeice) **61**:137
"Ruin" (García Lorca)
See "Ruina"
"The Ruin" (Tomlinson) **17**:325-26, 335
"Ruina" (García Lorca) **3**:139
"Las ruinas circulares" (Borges) **32**:60
"The Ruined Cottage" (Muir) **49**:299
"The Ruined Cottage" (Wordsworth) **4**:416, 418
"The Ruined Temple" (Tagore)
See "Bhagna mandir"
"The Ruines of Time" (Spenser) **8**:366-67, 371
"Ruins of a Great House" (Walcott) **46**:271, 275, 285, 313, 325
"Ruit hora" (Carducci) **46**:50, 86
Ruka a plamen (Seifert) **47**:335
"Ruminants" (Joyce) **22**:149
"Rumor at Twilight" (Warren) **37**:376
Rumor Verified: Poems, 1979-1980 (Warren) **37**:325-36, 335, 340-42, 345, 350, 358, 367, 380
"Rumors from an Aeolian Harp" (Thoreau) **30**:180, 192-93, 202-03, 227, 259
"Rumour" (Tomlinson) **17**:317
"Rumpelstiltskin" (Sexton) **2**:364
"run tonight" (Bissett) **14**:16-17
Run with the Hunted (Bukowski) **18**:4-5
"Runagate, Runagate" (Hayden) **6**:176, 178-80, 183, 185, 188, 194, 197-98
"The Runaway" (Frost) **1**:194
The Runaway, and Other Stories (Tagore)
See *Palātakā*
"Runaway Colors" (Sandburg) **41**:311
"The Runaway Slave at Pilgrim's Point" (Browning) **6**:30, 37-8, 42-3, 45
"Runaways" (Erdrich) **52**:172, 189
"Runaways Café I" (Hacker) **47**:85
"Runaways Café II" (Hacker) **47**:86
"Rune of the Finland Woman" (Hacker) **47**:119
"Runes" (Nemerov) **24**:262, 265, 268, 291
"Runes on Weland's Island" (Kipling) **3**:171
"Running on the Shore" (Swenson) **14**:288
"Running Water Music" (Snyder) **21**:306
"Rupture" (Pasternak) **6**:260
The Rural Muse (Clare) **23**:44
"Rural Objects" (Ashbery) **26**:124
"Rus in Urbe" (Meredith) **28**:171, 190
"Rusalka" (Lermontov) **18**:289-90, 292
Rush/What Fuckan Theory (Bissett) **14**:13
"Rusia en 1931" (Hass) **16**:224
Ruslan and Lyudmila (Pushkin)
See *Ruslan i Lyudmila*
Ruslan i Lyudmila (Pushkin) **10**:357-58, 363-64, 375, 381-82, 386-88, 398, 404-09
"Russell Kincaid" (Masters) **36**:191
"Russia" (Borges) **32**:121
"Russia" (Williams) **7**:370
"Russia comes into Poland" (Zagajewski) **27**:389, 394
Russian Songs (Parra)
See *Canciones rusas*
"Russian Sonia" (Masters) **1**:327; **36**:168, 182
"A Russian Tale" (Herbert) **50**:31
"Russian Tanks in Prague" (Yevtushenko) **40**:369-70
"The Rustic Commune" (Carducci)
See "Il comune rustico"
Rustic Elegies (Sitwell) **3**:294-95, 319
Rustic moon (Paz)
See *Luna silvestre*
"Rusty Crimson (Christmas Day, 1917)" (Sandburg) **2**:331
"Ruth" (Wordsworth) **4**:380, 402
"Ruth and Naomi" (Harper) **21**:191, 194, 209, 218
"Ruts" (Rimbaud)
See "Ornières"
"Ru'ya'" (Gibran) **9**:79
"Ryght True It is" (Wyatt) **27**:318
"Ryojō" (Hagiwara) **18**:178
"Rzeczywistość wymaga" (Szymborska) **44**:305
"S morya" (Tsvetaeva) **14**:325
s th story i to (Bissett) **14**:3, 5, 7-8
"Saadi" (Emerson) **18**:81, 87-88, 98, 104, 107
"Sábado" (Borges) **32**:102
"Sábado" (Storni) **33**:274;
"Sábado de gloria" (Guillén) **35**:176
"Sábados" (Borges) **22**:93; **32**:82, 102-03
"Sabala" (Tagore) **8**:415
"Sabás" (Guillén) **23**:103
"Sabato Santo" (Carducci) **46**:51
"A Sabbath Morning at Sea" (Browning) **6**:14
"Sabbath Park" (McGuckian) **27**:101
Sabbaths (Berry) **28**:34, 39, 43-4
Sabbaths: 1987-1990 (Berry) **28**:38, 43
"Sabishii jinkaku" (Hagiwara) **18**:177, 181
Sabotage (Baraka) **4**:38
"Sab-peyechhir desh" (Tagore) **8**:412
"El sacamuelas" (Fuertes) **27**:35
"La Sacra di Enrico Quinto" (Carducci) **46**:52
"Sacrament" (Cullen) **20**:85
"The Sacraments" (Erdrich) **52**:191
"The Sacré-Coeur CAfé" (Corso) **33**:37
"Sacred Chant for the Return of Black Spirit and Power" (Baraka) **4**:27
"The sacred disease" (Abse) **41**:31
"The Sacred Order" (Sarton) **39**:365
"sacred robe" (Alurista)
See "No. 57, sacred robe"
"The Sacred Way" (Hope) **56**:277
"The Sacred Way" (Sikelianos) **29**:366, 368, 370-71, 373
"The Sacred Wood" (Sarton) **39**:323
"The Sacrifice" (Herbert) **4**:107, 117, 120
"A Sacrifice in the Orchard" (Bly) **39**:67
"The Sacrifice of Er-Heb" (Kipling) **3**:181
"The Sacrilege" (Hardy) **8**:99
Sad Airs (Jiménez)
See *Arias tristes*
"A Sad Distant View" (Hagiwara) **18**:176
The sad field-hand (Illyés)
See *Szomoru beres*
"The Sad Garden Dissolves" (Jiménez)
See "El jardín triste se pierde"
"Sad Moments" (Gallagher) **9**:64
"Sad Moonlit Night" (Hagiwara)
See "Kanashi Tsukio"
"The sad ones" (Castro)
See "Los tristes, IV"
"The Sad Shepherd" (Yeats) **20**:354
"Sad Song" (Kunitz) **19**:147, 155
"Sad Steps" (Larkin) **21**:229-30
"Sad Strains of a Gay Waltz" (Stevens) **6**:296-97
"The Sad Supper" (Pavese)
See "La cena triste"
Sad Toys (Ishikawa)
See *Kanashiki gangu*
"The Sad Voice of the Hubble" (Stone) **53**:224
"Sad Wine" (Pavese)
See "Il vino triste"
"Sadako" (Soto) **28**:385
"Sad-Eyed Lady of the Lowlands" (Dylan) **37**:56, 60
"Sadie and Maude" (Brooks) **7**:67, 69
Sadness and Happiness: Poems (Pinsky) **27**:143-44, 153, 156, 160-62, 173, 175-76
"The Sadness of Brothers" (Kinnell) **26**:260
"The Sadness of Lemons" (Levine) **22**:211
"Saethu'r Ferch" (Dafydd ap Gwilym) **56**:247
"Safe Flights" (Guest) **55**:209-11
"Safe Subjects" (Komunyakaa) **51**:35
"Safety" (Brooke) **24**:59, 80, 88
"Safety" (Wright) **36**:396
"Saffron" (Smith) **12**:295
"Saga" (Viereck) **27**:265
Saga Diary (Matsuo Bashō)
See *Saga nikki*
Saga nikki (Matsuo Bashō) **3**:29
"The Saga of King Olaf" (Longfellow) **30**:19, 25, 61-2
Sagan om Fatumeh (Ekeloef) **23**:60, 65-6, 68-71, 77-8, 85
"The Sage Enamoured and the Honest Lady" (Meredith) **60**:261, 335
"Sagesse" (H. D.) **5**:275
"Sagesse" (Hugo) **17**:77-78, 97
Sagesse (H. D.) **5**:282, 285
Sagesse (Verlaine) **2**:413, 415-19, 425-26, 430; **32**:343, 359, 361, 363, 369, 374-75, 379, 382, 386, 402
"Saggi di un canto alle Muse" (Carducci) **46**:47
"Sahara" (Patmore) **59**:231
"Said Song" (Ammons) **16**:19
"Said the Poet to the Analyst" (Sexton) **2**:358-59
"The Sail" (Lermontov) **18**:297
"The Sail of Ulysses" (Stevens) **6**:326, 328
"Sailboat, Your Secret" (Francis) **34**:255
"Sailing after Lunch" (Stevens) **6**:297, 338
"Sailing Home from Rapallo" (Lowell) **3**:205, 220, 245
"Sailing of the Swallow" (Swinburne) **24**:356-57
"The Sailing of the Swan" (Swinburne) **24**:313, 349, 357
"The Sailing of the Sword" (Morris) **55**:279, 302
"Sailing or Drowning" (Curnow) **48**:4

Sailing or Drowning (Curnow) **48**:3, 11-12, 23
"Sailing to Byzantium" (Yeats) **20**:308, 310, 316, 329, 333, 335, 346, 349; **51**:67-153
"Sailor Ashore" (Merwin) **45**:7, 31
"A Sailor in Africa" (Dove) **6**:110
"Sailor in Moscow" (Pasternak)
See "Matros v Moskve"
"The Sailor's Mother" (Wordsworth) **4**:398, 402
"Saint" (Graves) **6**:141, 144, 151
"Saint" (Merrill) **28**:240-41
"The Saint" (Shapiro) **25**:268, 286
"A Saint about to Fall" (Thomas) **2**:408-09
"Saint Anthony and the Rose of Life" (Smith) **12**:308
"St. Augustine-by-the-Sea" (Swenson) **14**:288
"Saint Clare" (Erdrich) **52**:186, 188
"Saint Escolastica" (Castro)
See "Santa Escolástica"
"Saint Francis and Lady Clare" (Masters) **1**:325, 333; **36**:175
"Saint Francis and the Sow" (Kinnell) **26**:259-60, 292
"Saint Judas" (Wright) **36**:295-96, 302-4, 306, 315-16, 324, 344, 360-62, 379, 387, 399
Saint Judas (Wright) **36**:281-82, 292-94, 296, 299, 314-17, 337-38, 341, 349, 353, 358, 360, 373-74, 380, 385-87, 390, 396
"Saint Nicholas" (Moore) **49**:119-20, 143, 146
"Saint Nightingale" (Longfellow) **30**:46
"The Saint of the Uplands" (Merwin) **45**:33
"Saint Valentine's Day" (Patmore) **59**:224
"Sainte" (Mallarmé) **4**:201
"Une Sainte enson auréole" (Verlaine) **32**:393
"Sainte Lucie" (Walcott) **46**:233, 237, 240-41, 262, 290
"Sainte-Nitouche" (Robinson) **1**:460
"Saints" (Brown) **55**:80
"Saints" (Corso) **33**:3
"Saints and Singing" (Stein) **18**:346
La Saisiaz (Browning) **2**:66, 68, 71-2, 74
"La Saison des amours" (Éluard) **38**:87
"Une Saison en enfer" (Rimbaud) **57**:299-300
Une saison en enfer (Rimbaud) **3**:249, 252-53, 260-66, 268, 270, 279, 286; **57**:174, 177-78, 183-85, 188-91, 193-95, 197, 199, 224, 227, 229, 235-36, 243, 246-51, 254, 260, 273, 276-77, 279-80, 299, 301
"Sais-tu" (Péret) **33**:216
"Un sajón" (Borges) **22**:98; **32**:96
"Sakyamuni Coming Out from the Mountain" (Ginsberg) **4**:49
"Sal" (Mistral) **32**:161
"Sal" (Tagore) **8**:416
"Sala vacía" (Borges) **32**:82
"La Salade" (Ronsard) **11**:240
The Salamander (Paz)
See *Salamandra*
"Salamandra" (Paz) **48**:235-40
Salamandra (Paz) **1**:353, 357, 360-62, 369
"Salamater" (Paz)
See "Salamandra"
"Sale" (Rimbaud)
See "Solde"
"Sale of a Historian's Library" (Shvarts) **50**:140-41, 143
"The Salesman" (Ignatow) **34**:273
"Saleswoman of Ties" (Yevtushenko) **40**:345
"La salida" (Guillén) **35**:160
"Saliences" (Ammons) **16**:6, 23
Salisbury Plain (Wordsworth) **4**:429
"Sallie Chisum/Last Words on Billy the Kid. 4 a.m." (Ondaatje) **28**:338-39
"The Sallow Bird" (Smith) **12**:326
"El salmo de la pluma" (Darío) **15**:93
"Salmon" (Graham) **59**:152, 184
"The Salmon Fisher to the Salmon" (Heaney) **18**:225
"The Salmon Leap" (MacDiarmid) **9**:153
"Salmon-Fishing" (Jeffers) **17**:131
Salmos (Cardenal) **22**:103, 117-19, 125, 129-31
Salmos Psalms of Struggle and Liberation (Cardenal) **22**:118
"Salome" (Cavafy) **36**:103
"Salomé" (Laforgue) **14**:69, 72
"Salome's Dancing-lesson" (Parker) **28**:351, 363
"Salon des indépendents" (Szirtes) **51**:156
"Salsa Con Crackers" (Alurista) **34**:23
"Salt" (Stone) **53**:215-16
Salt (Szymborska)
See *Sól*
"The Salt Garden" (Nemerov) **24**:261
The Salt Garden (Nemerov) **24**:260-61, 264, 288-89
"Salt Lick" (Sarton) **39**:349, 369
"The Salt Marsh" (Dickey) **40**:156, 257
"The Salt Pond" (Merwin) **45**:97
"Saltfish and Akee" (Birney) **52**:16
"Saltimbanque Elegie" (Rilke)
See "Saltimbanques"
"Saltimbanques" (Rilke) **2**:278, 295
"Les Saltimbanques" (Tzara) **27**:224
"Salts and Oils" (Levine) **22**:224
"Saludo a León Felipe" (Paz) **48**:181
"Saludo al hombre" (Storni) **33**:280, 305;
"Salutación al águila" (Darío) **15**:77, 90, 107, 115
"Salutación del optimista" (Darío) **15**:81, 115
"Salutamus" (Brown) **55**:70-71, 110
"Salutation to the Eagle" (Darío)
See "Salutación al águila"
"Salute" (MacLeish) **47**:188
"Salute to Guinea" (Césaire) **25**:32
"Salute to Our Allies" (Brutus) **24**:119
Salutes and Censures (Brutus) **24**:118-20
"Saluto d'autunno" (Carducci) **46**:87
"Saluto Italico" (Carducci) **46**:52
"Salvación de la primavera" (Guillén) **35**:180, 181, 182, 183
"Salvador Díaz Mirón" (Darío) **15**:118
"Salvage" (Sandburg) **41**:226, 360
"Salvation of Springtime" (Guillén) **35**:219
Salve Deus Rex Judæorum (Lanyer) **60**:2, 4, 9, 15-16, 18, 20, 22, 24, 26, 29, 31, 33, 39-40, 44-45, 47-48, 52-54, 58-60, 62-65, 67, 69-70, 76-81, 88-90, 92-93, 95-99, 101, 103, 105-14, 118-22, 124-26
Salz. Gedichte (Szymborska) **44**:268
"Sam Hookey" (Masters) **36**:170
"Sam Smiley" (Brown) **55**:71, 73, 140, 150
"Sam Yancey" (Brown) **55**:1120
Samá láska (Seifert) **47**:315, 331-33
"Sambhashan" (Tagore) **8**:417
"The Same Again" (Kavanagh) **33**:73, 76, 96
"Same in Blues" (Hughes) **53**:120, 123, 158
"Sammy Lou of Rue" (Walker) **30**:352
"Samos" (Merrill) **28**:233
"Samothrake" (Ekeloef) **23**:76
"Samoubiistvennoe more" (Shvarts) **50**:163
"A Sampler" (MacLeish) **47**:182
"Samson" (Blake) **12**:31
"Samson" (Péret) **33**:201, 217
Samson Agonistes (Milton) **29**:212, 227, 232, 244
Samson's Anger (Vigny)
See "La colère de Samson"
Sämtliche Werke (Heine) **25**:172
"The Samuel Pie" (Belloc) **24**:42
"San Diego Poem" (Ortiz) **17**:226, 233
"San Fernando Road" (Soto) **28**:369, 377, 384-85
"A San Francesco le soir" (Bonnefoy) **58**:155, 158
"San Francisco Poems" (Oppen) **35**:295
"San Fruttuoso: The Divers" (Tomlinson) **17**:349
"San Giorgio di Donatello" (Carducci) **46**:52
"San Ildefonso Nocturne" (Paz)
See "Nocturno de San Ildefonso"
"A San Juan de la Cruz" (Fuertes) **27**:14
San Martín Copybook (Borges)
See *Cuaderno San Martín*
San Martin Notebook (Borges)
See *Cuaderno San Martín*
"San Martino" (Carducci) **46**:48, 56, 58, 78
"San Onofre, California" (Forché) **10**:141, 152-53, 155, 158
"San Sepolcro" (Graham) **59**:139, 146, 149, 152, 178
"Sanctuary" (Reese) **29**:335
"The Sanctuary" (Teasdale) **31**:360, 370
"Sanctuary" (Wright) **14**:343
"Sanctuary" (Wylie) **23**:323, 329
Sanctuary (Carman) **34**:205, 210-11
"Sand" (Guest) **55**:212
"The Sand Altar" (Lowell) **13**:95
Der Sand aus den Urnen (Celan) **10**:95, 121
"Sand Draift" (Teasdale) **31**:334
"Sand Dunes" (Frost) **1**:203, 218
Sand from the Urns (Celan)
See *Der Sand aus den Urnen*
"Sand Martin" (Clare) **23**:5
"The Sand Roses" (Hogan) **35**:252, 272
"Sandalphon" (Longfellow) **30**:27
"The Sand-Diggrers' Twilight" (Pavese)
See "Crepuscolo di sabbiatori"
Sandhya sangit (Tagore) **8**:405-6
"Sandpiper" (Bishop) **3**:53-4
"Sands" (Cassian) **17**:11
"The Sandy Hole" (Kenyon) **57**:17
"Sandy Star" (Braithwaite) **52**:107
"Le Sang, la note si" (Bonnefoy) **58**:167-68
Le sanglot de la terre (Laforgue) **14**:57, 64, 68-71, 74, 80-1, 95
"Sanglot perdu" (Laforgue) **14**:86, 88
Sangre (Quintana) **36**:249, 252-58, 260-66, 266-71
"La sangre numerosa" (Guillén) **23**:128-29
Sangschaw (MacDiarmid) **9**:151, 158, 166, 187, 190-91, 196
"Sans âge" (Éluard) **38**:63
"Sans chercher à savoir" (Char) **56**:185
"Sans musique" (Éluard) **38**:69
"Sans rancune" (Éluard) **38**:70
"Sans toi" (Éluard) **38**:74
"Sans tomates pas d'artichauts" (Péret) **33**:202
Sant Kabīr (Kabīr) **56**:344
"Santa" (Sexton) **2**:365
"Santa Barbara Road" (Hass) **16**:217
"Santa Claus" (Nemerov) **24**:267
"Santa Cruz Propositions" (Duncan) **2**:116
"Santa Escolástica" (Castro) **41**:104
"Santa Fe" (Harjo) **27**:66, 70
"The Santa Fé Trail" (Lindsay) **23**:264, 268, 273, 278, 286-87, 294
"Santa Filomena" (Longfellow) **30**:27, 46
"Santa Lucia" (Hass) **16**:211
"Santa Maria a Monte" (Carducci) **46**:4
"Santa Maria degli Angeli" (Carducci) **46**:49, 76
"Santarém" (Bishop) **3**:64-5; **34**:79, 99, 191, 193
"Santorini: Stopping the Leak" (Merrill) **28**:267-69
"Santos" (Bishop) **34**:52
Saōgi (Yosano Akiko) **11**:310
"The Sap is Gone Out of the Trees" (Ammons) **16**:39
"Sapho" (Lamartine) **16**:277
"Sapo y mar" (Storni) **33**:246;
"Sapobsidiana" (Alurista) **34**:42
"Sapphics" (Swinburne) **24**:320
"Sappho" (Teasdale) **31**:379
"Sappho" (Wright) **36**:299, 335-36
Sappho: One Hundred Lyrics (Carman) **34**:205, 210-12, 214, 226, 231-35
The Sar (Castro)
See *En las orillas del Sar*
"Sara" (Nishiwaki) **15**:241
"Sara Cynthia Sylvia Stout Would Not Take the Garbage Out" (Silverstein) **49**:313, 344
"Sara in Her Father's Arms" (Oppen) **35**:308, 310
"Sarah and Tobias" (Gower) **59**:72
"Sarajevo" (Nemerov) **24**:291

"el sarape de mi personalidad" (Alurista) **34**:12, 36
"sarape of my personality" (Alurista)
See "el sarape de mi personalidad"
Sarashina kikō (Matsuo Bashō) **3**:26
"Sarcophagi I" (Montale) **13**:116
Sardanapalus (Byron) **16**:91, 103, 109-10
"Sardegna" (Quasimodo) **47**:302
"Sarmiento" (Borges) **32**:60
"Sarum Plain" (Patmore) **59**:228-29
Sarumino (Matsuo Bashō) **3**:3, 4, 29
"Sarvaneshe" (Tagore) **8**:414
"Sashes and bearskins in the afternoon" (Davie) **29**:107
"Sashka" (Lermontov)
See *Sashka*
Sashka (Lermontov) **18**:278
"Satan Says" (Olds) **22**:319
Satan Says (Olds) **22**:307, 310, 312, 315, 317, 319-20, 322, 327-28
"A Satana" (Carducci)
See *Inno a Satana*
"Satanic Form" (Swenson) **14**:252
Satin-Legs Smith (Brooks)
See "The Sundays of Satin-Legs Smith"
"Satire" (Surrey) **59**:297
Satire II, i (Pope)
See *Satires and Epistles of Horace, Imitated*
"Satire III" (Wyatt) **27**:342
Satires (Donne)
See *Satyres*
Satires (Horace) **46**:97, 99-100, 102, 104, 114, 117-19, 126, 140, 145-46, 170-71, 190-95, 197-98, 212-14, 220-22
Satires and Epistles of Horace, Imitated (Pope) **26**:321
"Satires of Circumstance" (Hardy) **8**:124
Satires of Circumstance (Hardy) **8**:91, 97
Satires of Dr. Donne Versified (Pope) **26**:324-25
Satires of Horace (Pope) **26**:359
"A Satirical Elegy on the Death of a Late Famous General" (Swift) **9**:256, 294, 307
Satirical Poems (Sassoon) **12**:258
"The Satirist" (MacNeice) **61**:141, 185
"The Satisfactions of the Mad Farmer" (Berry) **28**:43
"The Satrapy" (Cavafy) **36**:52, 57, 84
"Satsujin jiken" (Hagiwara) **18**:177, 180
"Satturday: The Small Pox: Flavia" (Montagu) **16**:349
Satura (Montale) **13**:131-34, 138, 143, 148, 152, 161, 167
"A Saturday" (Borges)
See "Sábado"
"Saturday" (Storni)
See "Sábado"
"Saturdays" (Borges)
See "Sábados"
Saturnine Poems (Verlaine)
See *Les Poèmes saturniens*
"Saturn's Rings" (Wakoski) **15**:369
"A Satyr" (Montagu) **16**:338
"The Satyr in the Periwig" (Sitwell) **3**:294
"Le satyre" (Hugo) **17**:62, 65, 85, 87, 89
"Satyre II" (Donne) **1**:144
"Satyre III" (Donne) **1**:125, 143, 147
Satyres (Donne) **1**:140-42, 145
"Saudade" (Dalton) **36**:129
"Saul" (Browning) **2**:36, 67-8, 72, 75
"Sausages" (Stein) **18**:353
"La sauvage" (Vigny) **26**:368-70, 372, 382, 402, 412
"Saved" (Dylan) **37**:72
"Saved by Faith" (Harper) **21**:189, 208
"The Saving" (Pinsky) **27**:159
Savings (Hogan) **35**:256, 257
"A Saxon" (Borges)
See "Un sajón"
"Say Goodbye to Big Daddy" (Jarrell) **41**:185
"Say, Lad, Have You Things to Do" (Housman) **2**:179, 192
"Say Pardon" (Ignatow) **34**:317-18, 327
Say Pardon (Ignatow) **34**:270-72, 275-76, 281, 283, 285, 311, 313, 316-17, 324
"Saying Dante Aloud" (Wright) **36**:311
"Saying It to Keep It from Happening" (Ashbery) **26**:136
Sayings of Kabir (Kabīr) **56**:341-42, 346
"Scale" (Silverstein) **49**:340
"A Scale in May" (Merwin) **45**:15-16, 20, 27, 34, 61, 83-4
"The Scales of the Eyes" (Nemerov) **24**:261-62
"The Scanning" (Graham) **59**:183
"Scapegoats and Rabies" (Hughes) **7**:137
"The Scar" (Boland) **58**:62
"Scar" (Lorde) **12**:139
"Scarab" (Brutus) **24**:111
"Scarecrow" (Borges)
See "Espantapájaros"
"Scarecrow" (Stryk) **27**:197
"The Scarred Girl" (Dickey) **40**:226
"Scars on Paper" (Hacker) **47**:117
"The Scattered Term" (Char)
See "Le Terme épars"
"Scattering As Behavior Toward Risk" (Howe) **54**:52, 57
A Scattering of Salts (Merrill) **28**:281-82, 284-87
"Scenario for a Little Black Movie" (Hughes) **53**:114
"Scenarios" (Mueller) **33**:193
"The Scene" (Curnow) **48**:11, 28
"A Scene on the Banks of the Hudson" (Bryant) **20**:14, 46
"Scènes" (Rimbaud) **57**:175, 177
"Scenes from the Fall of Troy" (Morris) **55**:258
"Scenes of Childhood" (Merrill) **28**:248
"Schädelstätten" (Benn) **35**:75, 76
"Ein Schatten an der Mauer" (Benn) **35**:68
"Schattenbild" (Enzensberger) **28**:139
"schaum" (Enzensberger) **28**:136
"Scheherazade" (Ashbery) **26**:127, 150
"Scheherezade Is Mailed and Nailed in Five Days" (Stone) **53**:225
"Der Scheidende" (Heine) **25**:178-80
"Die Schildkröte" (Enzensberger) **28**:165
"Schizophrene" (MacNeice) **61**:141
"Schlacht" (Stramm) **50**:178, 208-9
"Schlachtfeld" (Stramm) **50**:173, 198, 216-17
"schläferung" (Enzensberger) **28**:139
"Schneebett" (Celan) **10**:114
Schneepart (Celan) **10**:96, 98
"The Scholar" (Baraka) **4**:23
"The Scholar Gypsy" (Arnold)
See "The Scholar-Gipsy"
"The Scholar-Gipsy" (Arnold) **5**:7, 13, 18-24, 33-5, 37, 47, 51, 53, 53, 59
"A Scholium" (Borges)
See "Un escolio"
"Schön" (Stramm) **50**:189
"Schöne Jugend" (Benn) **35**:30
"The School Children" (Glück) **16**:128, 132, 149
"School Days" (Ashbery) **26**:137
School Figures (Song) **21**:341, 347
"School Lesson Based on Word of Tragic Death of Entire Gillum Family" (Warren) **37**:296
"School Nights" (Soto) **28**:399
"The School of Babylon" (Sarton) **39**:344
"The School of Desire" (Swenson) **14**:276, 284
"The School of Night" (Hope) **56**:288, 305
"A School of Prayer" (Baraka) **4**:10, 18
School of Udhra (Mackey) **49**:15, 17, 25, 29-33, 35-36, 39-40, 42, 51-53, 57, 59-60, 64-66, 68, 72, 75-78
"The School-Boy" (Blake) **12**:7, 34
Schoolboy Lyrics (Kipling) **3**:190, 193
"Schoolgirl's Company" (Char) **56**:162
"Schoolmaster" (Larkin) **21**:234, 241
"The Schoolmistresses" (Pavese)
See "Le maestrine"
"Schooner" (Brathwaite) **56**:65
"The Schooner Flight" (Walcott) **46**:260, 312, 322-23
"Schopenhauer's Crying" (Zagajewski) **27**:384
"Schöpfung" (Benn) **35**:34
"Schrapnell" (Stramm) **50**:170, 202, 222
"Schrei" (Stramm) **50**:175, 188
"Schutt" (Benn) **35**:33, 50, 73, 75, 76, 77
Schutt (Benn) **35**:8
"An Schwager Kronos" (Goethe) **5**:245, 247, 251
"Schwermut" (Stramm) **50**:176, 195
"La Scie rêveuse" (Char) **56**:138
"Science" (Jeffers) **17**:113
"Science has looked" (Owen) **19**:371
"The Science of the Night" (Kunitz) **19**:153, 170, 182
"Scilla" (Glück) **16**:169
"Scirocco" (Graham) **59**:146, 176, 179
"Scirocco" (Montale) **13**:105, 125
"The Scissors and their father" (Éluard) **38**:90-91
"Scoglio di Quarto" (Carducci) **46**:52
"Scorpion" (Smith) **12**:301, 319, 333
Scorpion and Other Poems (Smith) **12**:299, 315
"Scotland, 1941" (Muir) **49**:212, 214, 254-55, 299
"Scotland's Winter" (Muir) **49**:253-54, 299
Scots Unbound (MacDiarmid) **9**:158, 175-76, 196
"Scots Wha Hae wi' Wallace Bled" (Burns) **6**:78
"Scottsboro" (Hughes) **53**:148
Scottsboro Limited: Four Poems and a Play in Verse (Hughes) **53**:111, 148, 181
"Scotty Has His Say" (Brown) **55**:155
"Scouting" (Levine) **22**:220-21, 228, 231-32
"Screaming Tarn" (Bridges) **28**:68
"The Screen of Distance" (Guest) **55**:185
"A Screened Porch in the Country" (Dickey) **40**:155, 182, 185, 212
"Screvo meu livro à beira-mágoa" (Pessoa) **20**:155-56
"Screw: A Technical Love Poem" (Wakoski) **15**:332
"Screw Guns" (Kipling) **3**:158
"Scripts for the Pageant" (Merrill) **28**:233-38, 243, 260-64, 276-78, 281
Scritti e interventi (Ungaretti) **57**:333
"Scroll" (Noyes) **27**:130
"Scrub" (Millay) **6**:235
"The Sculptor" (Plath) **1**:388-89; **37**:188-89
"Sculptor from Tyaneia" (Cavafy)
See "Sculptor of Tyana"
"Sculptor of Tyana" (Cavafy) **36**:46, 73
"Sculpture Musicale" (Cage) **58**:219
"Scurry" (Swenson) **14**:254
"Scuttle up the workshop" (Niedecker) **42**:150
"Scyros" (Shapiro) **25**:268, 279
"Scythe Lifted Again" (Char)
See "La Faux relevée"
The Scythians (Blok)
See *Skify*
"Se acabó" (Guillén) **23**:117, 125
"Se canta al mar" (Parra) **39**:299
"Se me ocurren ideas luminosas" (Parra) **39**:286
"Se réchauffer l'ardeur" (Char) **56**:148
"Se rencontrer paysage avec Joseph Sima" (Char) **56**:146
"A se stesso" (Leopardi) **37**:92, 102, 121, 123-24, 134, 142-43
"Se vuelve a yo" (Neruda) **4**:287
"The Sea" (Borges)
See "El mar"
"The Sea" (Parker) **28**:351
"The Sea" (Swenson) **14**:288
"The Sea" (Williams) **7**:385, 387
"Sea and land are but his neighbors" (Thoreau) **30**:203
"Sea and Night" (Aleixandre)
See "Mar y noche"
The Sea and the Bells (Neruda)
See *El mar y las campanas*

The Sea and the Honeycomb (Bly) **39**:68-69
"The Sea and the Mirror: A Commentary on Shakespeare's Tempest" (Auden) **1**:22, 34
"The Sea Battle" (Cavafy) **36**:84
"Sea Calm" (Hughes) **1**:236; **53**:85
"Sea Canes" (Walcott) **46**:236, 279
"Sea Change" (Tomlinson) **17**:321
"Sea Change" (Wagoner) **33**:359
"Sea Changes" (O'Hara) **45**:130
"Sea Chanty" (Corso) **33**:43
"A Sea Child" (Carman) **34**:210, 216
"Sea Children" (Carman) **34**:225
"Sea Dirge" (Carroll) **18**:46
"Sea Dreams" (Tennyson) **6**:360
Sea Garden (H. D.) **5**:266-67, 288-90, 303
"Sea Grapes" (Walcott) **46**:272, 279
Sea Grapes (Walcott) **46**:233, 236-37, 240, 248, 259, 274-75, 278-79, 289-91, 323-24
"The Sea Horse" (Graves) **6**:154
"Sea hymn" (Borges)
See "Himno del mar"
"The Sea in Winter" (Mahon) **60**:142-43, 147, 155, 171, 179, 186-88, 192, 196, 198, 200, 203, 205-9, 215, 220, 233
"Sea Iris" (H. D.) **5**:289
"Sea Lily" (H. D.) **5**:288
"Sea Lullaby" (Wylie) **23**:332
"Sea Monster" (Merwin) **45**:7
"Sea of Forgetfulness" (Guillén) **35**:218
"The Sea of Suicide" (Shvarts)
See "Samoubiistvennoe more"
"Sea Poppies" (H. D.) **5**:288
"Sea Surface Full of Clouds" (Stevens) **6**:304, 332
"Sea Unicorns and Land Unicorns" (Moore) **4**:233; **49**:94, 161
"The Sea Urchins of Pégomas" (Char) **56**:162
"Sea Violet" (H. D.) **5**:289
"The Sea Was Asleep" (Zagajewski) **27**:394
"Sea-Blue and Blood-Red" (Lowell) **13**:60, 64, 66, 72, 81, 83
"A Sea-Chantey" (Walcott) **46**:231, 248, 259, 272-73
"A Sea-Drift" (Carman) **34**:216
"The Sea-Elephant" (Williams) **7**:360
"The Sea-Fairies" (Tennyson) **6**:348, 359
"Seafarer" (MacLeish) **47**:155, 165
"The Seafarer" (Pound) **4**:317, 331, 364
"A Seamark, a Threnody for Robert Louis Stevenson" (Carman) **34**:220
Seamarks (Perse)
See *Amers*
"The Seamless Garment" (MacDiarmid) **9**:177
"The Seamstress" (Song) **21**:331, 333-34, 336, 341, 350
"Séance" (Szymborska) **44**:269
"Seans" (Szymborska) **44**:308
"Sea-Nymph's Prayer to Okeanos" (Zukofsky) **11**:368
"The Search" (Abse) **41**:3
"The Search" (Herbert) **4**:101
"The Search" (Masters) **1**:343-44
"The Search" (Merwin) **45**:48
"Search" (Silverstein) **49**:324
Search for the Base and the Summit (Char)
See *Recherche de la base et du sommet*
"Searching for the Canto Fermo" (Wakoski) **15**:362
"Searching, Not Searching" (Rukeyser) **12**:224
"Searchlight Practice" (Wright) **14**:354
"Sea-Reverie" (Sandburg) **41**:360
"Sea-Rose" (H. D.) **5**:288, 303
"Seascape" (Bishop) **3**:37; **34**:116
Seascape: Needle's Eye (Oppen) **35**:293, 294, 324, 331, 332, 334, 336 338, 340
"Sea-Serpent" (MacDiarmid) **9**:193
The Seashell Game (Matsuo Bashō)
See *Kai oi*
"The Seashore" (Emerson) **18**:76, 80, 89, 91
"Seaside" (Brooke) **24**:58, 76, 84, 86, 88
The Seaside and the Fireside (Longfellow) **30**:27
"A Sea-Side Meditation" (Browning) **6**:20
"Seaside Postcard" (Szirtes) **51**:169
"The Season" (Stone) **53**:216
A Season in Hell (Rimbaud)
See *Une saison en enfer*
"The Season of Phantasmal Peace" (Walcott) **46**:247
The Season of Violence (Paz)
See *La estación violenta*
Season Songs (Hughes) **7**:157, 162, 171
"Seasonal" (Ashbery) **26**:166
"The Seasonless" (Wright) **36**:303, 336
"Seasons" (Bradstreet)
See "The Four Seasons of the Year"
"Seasons" (Tomlinson) **17**:326
The Seasons (Kālidāsa)
See *Rtusamhāra*
"The Seasons of the Soul" (Tate) **50**:245, 252-54, 256-57, 259, 266-67, 276-77, 280, 290-95
"Seaspin" (Corso) **33**:48
"Seat Belt Fastened?" (Stone) **53**:219
"Seated Figure" (Glück) **16**:153
Seaton Prize Odes (Smart) **13**:329
"Seattle 7 May 72" (Brutus) **24**:123
"Seattle, 1987" (Alexie) **53**:14
"A Sea-Voyage from Tenby to Bristol" (Philips) **40**:298
"Seaweed" (Longfellow) **30**:27, 31
"Sea-Wind" (Mallarmé) **4**:187
Sebastian im Traum (Trakl) **20**:236, 241, 244, 250
"Sebastian in Traum" (Trakl) **20**:228, 230-31
"Sécheresse" (Perse) **23**:255, 257
"Second Air Force" (Jarrell) **41**:154, 160, 173-74, 201
"The Second Angel" (Levine) **22**:213
The Second Anniversarie. Of the Progres of the Soule. Wherein, By Occasion Of the Religious death of Mistris Elizabeth Drury, the incommodities of the Soule in this life, and her exaltation in the next, are Contemplated (Donne) **1**:122, 145-51, 155-57
"Second April" (Millay) **6**:206
Second April (Millay) **6**:211-12, 214-15, 233, 242-44; **61**:243
"Second Avenue" (O'Hara) **45**:130, 135, 148, 160, 175-76, 191, 219, 224, 242
"The Second Best" (Arnold) **5**:42
"Second Best" (Brooke) **24**:59, 60, 76, 84
"Second Best Bed" (Shapiro) **25**:316
The Second Birth (Pasternak) **6**:253-54, 268, 281
A Second Book (Mandelstam)
See *Vtoraya kniga*
"The Second Chambermaid's Song" (Yeats) **20**:332
"Second Chance" (Wakoski) **15**:347
"The Second Coming" (Abse) **41**:9, 19
"The Second Coming" (Yeats) **20**:308, 312-13, 319-20, 349; **51**:107
"Second Diptych" (Yau) **61**:332
"Second Elegy" (Rilke)
See "Second Song"
"Second Epistle to John Lapraik" (Burns) **6**:68-70, 78
"Second Fig" (Millay) **6**:227
"Second Generation: New York" (Hughes) **53**:116
"Second Georgic" (Vergil) **12**:359, 365
"Second Glance at a Jaguar" (Hughes) **7**:136-37
"Second Hymn to Lenin" (MacDiarmid) **9**:158, 177, 180-81, 197
Second Hymn to Lenin, and Other Poems (MacDiarmid) **9**:156, 179, 196
The Second Jungle Book (Kipling) **3**:162, 185, 188-89
"Second Language" (Gallagher) **9**:60
Second Language (Mueller) **33**:176, 189-91
Second livre des poemes (Ronsard) **11**:282
"A Second Meeting with my Father" (Amichai) **38**:27
"Second Night in N.Y.C. After Three Years" (Corso) **33**:11, 25
"Second Nun's Tale" (Chaucer) **19**:13, 15
"Second Oldest Story" (Parker) **28**:362
Second Olympian (Pindar)
See *Olympian 2*
"Second Populist Manifesto" (Ferlinghetti)
See "Adieu á Charlot"
"A Second Psalm of Life" (Longfellow)
See "The Light of Stars"
Second Pythian (Pindar)
See *Pythian 2*
"The Second Rapture" (Carew) **29**:10
"The Second Sermon on the Warpland" (Brooks) **7**:63
"Second Song" (Bogan) **12**:90, 129
"Second Song" (Rilke) **2**:273-4, 286
"Second Song for the Worship of the Goddess at Yü Mountain: 'Bidding the Godeess Farewell'" (Wang Wei) **18**:369
"The Second Spring" (Sarton) **39**:337, 365
The Second Symphony (Bely)
See *Vtoraia simfoniia: Dramaticheskaia*
"Second Thoughts on the Abstract Gardens of Japan" (Sarton) **39**:339
Second Voronezh Notebook (Mandelstam) **14**:133-34, 149, 152-53
"The Second Voyage" (Ní Chuilleanáin) **34**:360
The Second Voyage (Ní Chuilleanáin) **34**:349-50, 359, 361
Second Year of Chang-ho (Li Ho) **13**:42
"The Second-Best Bed" (Nemerov) **24**:291
"Second-Class Constable Alston" (McKay) **2**:205
Second-Hand Coat (Stone) **53**:220, 226, 229-39, 242-46, 251-55, 258
"The Secret" (Kenyon) **57**:45
"The Secret" (Merton) **10**:348
"The Secret" (Ní Chuilleanáin) **34**:384
"A Secret" (Plath) **37**:255
"Secret Festival; September Moon" (Levertov) **11**:177
"A Secret Gratitude" (Wright) **36**:368
"Secret History of the Dividing Line" (Howe) **54**:124, 126, 130, 134
Secret History of the Dividing Line (Howe) **54**:36-37, 40, 65, 107, 109, 140-47
"Le secret humain" (MacLeish) **47**:129, 156, 186
The Secret Meaning of Things (Ferlinghetti) **1**:173-74, 176, 186-87
"The Secret Miracle" (Borges)
See "El milagro secreto"
"Secret Music" (Sassoon) **12**:247
"The Secret of Light" (Wright) **36**:311, 356, 370, 376
"The Secret of Machu Pichhu" (Cardenal)
See "El Secreto de Machu-Picchu"
"The Secret of the Sea" (Longfellow) **30**:27
"Secret Treasure" (Teasdale) **31**:380
"Secretary" (Hughes) **7**:140
"El Secreto de Machu-Picchu" (Cardenal) **22**:132
Secrets from the Center of the World (Harjo) **27**:65, 68
The Secrets of the Heart (Gibran) **9**:72
"Secrets of the Trade" (Akhmatova) **2**:5
Section: Rock-Drill, 85-95 de los cantares (Pound) **4**:352, 357
Secular Hymn (Horace) **46**:122
Secular Love (Ondaatje) **28**:314-17, 340
"Sed de Correr" (Clampitt) **19**:100
"Sediment" (Ignatow) **34**:320-21
"Seduction" (Giovanni) **19**:111, 113, 117
"Seed and Bran" (Tzara) **27**:242
"The Seed Cutters" (Heaney) **18**:203
"Seed Journey" (Corso) **33**:49
"Seed Leaves" (Wilbur) **51**:270, 287-88, 305, 310, 312
"The Seed Picture" (McGuckian) **27**:79, 97

"Seed Pods" (Snyder) **21**:305
Seeds and Bran (Tzara)
See *Grains et issues*
Seeds for a Hymn (Paz)
See *Semillas para un himno*
Seeds for an Anthem (Paz)
See *Semillas para un himno*
"Seed-Time" (Meredith) **60**:298, 327
"Seeing a Friend Off" (Li Po) **29**:146
"Seeing in the Dark" (Komunyakaa) **51**:41
Seeing Is Believing (Tomlinson) **17**:302, 306, 317-18, 321, 323-24, 332-33, 335, 338, 341-42, 346, 352, 359
"Seeing the Bones" (Kumin) **15**:207, 209
"Seeing the Wind" (Wagoner) **33**:360
"Seeing Things" (Nemerov) **24**:302
Seeing Things (Heaney) **18**:254-61
Seeing through the Sun (Hogan) **35**:244, 245, 247, 255, 256, 259
"Seeking Religion" (Brown) **55**:156
"The Seekonk Woods" (Kinnell) **26**:278, 293
"Seele im Raum" (Jarrell) **41**:139, 171, 177, 182, 189, 194-95, 208, 211
"Seen by the Waits" (Hardy) **8**:130
"Segments of a Bamboo Screen" (Chin) **40**:3
Segund antolojía poética (Jiménez) **7**:178, 201
"Sehnen" (Stramm) **50**:168, 170, 208
"Le Seigneur habite en toi" (Gautier) **18**:144
"Les Seigneurs de Maussane" (Char) **56**:154
"Seizure" (Sappho)
See "Ode to Anactoria"
A Seizure of Limericks (Aiken) **26**:24
Šel malíř chudě do světa (Seifert) **47**:323, 326, 335
"Ein Selbstmörder" (Benn) **35**:48
"Seldom yet Now" (Graves) **6**:156
Selected Failings (Neruda)
See *Defectos escogidos: 2000*
Selected letters (Williams) **7**:374
"Selected Poems" (Ignatow) **34**:309
Selected Poems (Abse) **41**:9, 11, 13-14, 16-17
Selected Poems (Amichai) **38**:32, 44
Selected Poems (Ashbery) **26**:158
Selected Poems (Bly) **39**:72, 82-5, 87, 98, 100-02, 104
Selected Poems (Breton) **15**:57
Selected Poems (Brooks) **7**:81, 102
Selected Poems (Corso) **33**:38, 53
Selected Poems (Davie) **29**:127
The Selected Poems (Dickey) **40**:262
Selected Poems (Duncan) **2**:102
Selected Poems (Frost) **1**:195
Selected Poems (Goodison) **36**:154
Selected Poems (Guest) **55**:185, 187, 196, 206, 209-11, 213, 221, 224, 227
Selected Poems (H. D.) **5**:274
Selected Poems (Hayden) **6**:176, 178-79
Selected Poems (Herbert)
See *Wybór wierszy*
Selected Poems (Hope) **56**:289
Selected Poems (Jackson) **44**:7, 9, 84, 96-7
Selected Poems (Jordan) **38**:126
Selected Poems (Kinnell) **26**:261-62, 288
Selected Poems (Levine) **22**:220
Selected Poems (Lowell) **3**:226-27
Selected Poems (MacNeice) **61**:173-74
Selected Poems (Mahon) **60**:175, 184, 187, 191, 195, 198, 204-5, 220
Selected Poems (McKay) **2**:207, 228
Selected Poems (Meredith) **28**:207
Selected Poems (Milosz) **8**:174
Selected Poems (Montale) **13**:135
Selected Poems (Moore) **4**:240, 242, 253; **49**:88, 96, 98, 113-14, 159, 161
Selected Poems (Muir) **49**:286
Selected Poems (Niedecker) **42**:102
Selected Poems (Pasolini) **17**:289
Selected Poems (Philips) **40**:300
Selected Poems (Ransom) **61**:267, 271-72, 274-76, 279, 288, 304-5, 308, 320, 323
Selected Poems (Rukeyser) **12**:210
Selected Poems (Senghor) **25**:238, 241, 245
Selected Poems (Sexton) **2**:347-48
Selected Poems (Shapiro) **25**:315
Selected Poems (Sitwell) **3**:320
Selected Poems (Smith) **12**:293, 309, 350
Selected Poems (Stryk) **27**:185, 187-89, 191, 197-98, 201-3
Selected Poems (Tate) **50**:230, 246, 337
Selected Poems (Tomlinson) **17**:327, 345
Selected Poems (Walcott) **46**:238, 247-48
Selected Poems, 1923-1943 (Warren) **37**:286, 300, 308, 318, 324-25, 330-31, 335, 339, 350, 354, 356, 359-60, 363-64, 372, 382
Selected Poems, 1923-1967 (Borges) **32**:93-5, 99, 135-36, 138
Selected Poems, 1928-1958 (Kunitz) **19**:148, 155, 157, 159, 161-63, 168-70, 173-76
Selected Poems (1938-1958): Summer Knowledge (Schwartz)
See *Summer Knowledge: New and Selected Poems, 1938-1958*
Selected Poems, 1940-1966 (Birney) **52**:6, 20, 22-24, 37, 47, 51, 55, 80
Selected Poems, 1940-1989 (Curnow) **48**:43, 53, 59, 62-63
Selected Poems, 1950-1975 (Gunn) **26**:206
Selected Poems, 1951-1974 (Tomlinson) **17**:325
Selected Poems, 1957-1967 (Hughes) **7**:163
Selected Poems 1965-1975 (Atwood) **8**:23
Selected Poems: 1965-1990 (Hacker) **47**:104, 115, 119
Selected Poems: 1976-1996 (Szirtes) **51**:171
Selected Poems and New (Villa) **22**:349, 351, 353-54
Selected Poems and Prose of John Clare (Clare) **23**:3-8, 11, 13-14
Selected Poems: Beyond Even Faithful Legends (Bissett) **14**:27-30, 34-5
Selected Poems: German-English Bilingual Edition (Enzensberger) **28**:166
Selected Poems: in five sets (Jackson) **44**:52
Selected Poems, Joseph Brodsky (Brodsky) **9**:8
The Selected Poems of David Ignatow (Ignatow) **34**:303-05, 307-10, 323
The Selected Poems of Frank O'Hara (O'Hara) **45**:127, 205, 221
The Selected Poems of Langston Hughes (Hughes) **1**:248, 258; **53**:94, 108-9, 111, 113, 116-19, 138, 144, 146-50, 153, 158, 182
The selected poems of Lizette Woodworth Reese (Reese) **29**:334-335, 339, 347, 352
Selected Poems, Revised and Enlarged (Ransom) **61**:267
Selected Poetry (Amichai) **38**:26, 33, 35, 42, 45
Selected Poetry of Amiri Baraka/LeRoi Jones (Baraka) **4**:31
The Selected Poetry of Hayden Carruth (Carruth) **10**:84
The Selected Poetry of Robinson Jeffers (Jeffers) **17**:111, 123, 130, 133, 136-37, 141
The Selected Poetry of Yehuda Amichai (Amichai) **38**:53
Selected Shorter Poems (Schwerner) **42**:204
Selected Translations, 1948-1968 (Merwin) **45**:21, 30-1
Selected Writings (Olson) **19**:268, 276-77, 305, 316-17
Selected Writings of Juan Ramon Jimenez (Jiménez)
See *Antolojía poética (1898-1953)*
Selection of the Poems of Laura Riding (Jackson) **44**:101, 103, 106
"Selective Service" (Forché) **10**:137, 144, 146, 157, 165
"Selene Afterwards" (MacLeish) **47**:167, 185
"Self" (Hacker) **47**:88
"Self and Life" (Eliot) **20**:136
"The Self and The Other" (Borges)
See "El otro, el mismo"
The Self and the Other (Borges)
See *El otro, el mismo*
"Self in 1958" (Sexton) **2**:351
"Self Portrait" (Wylie) **23**:321
Self Portrait (Dylan) **37**:60, 63
"The Self Unsatisfied Runs Everywhere" (Schwartz) **8**:285
"The Self-Abuser and the Suicide" (Viereck) **27**:279
"The Self-Betrayal Which Is Nothing New" (Schwartz) **8**:294
"Self-Criticism and Answer" (Day Lewis) **11**:128, 144
"Self-Criticism in February" (Jeffers) **17**:123, 132
"Self-Dependence" (Arnold) **5**:19, 42-3, 49
"Self-Employed" (Ignatow) **34**:326
"The Self-Hatred of Don L. Lee" (Madhubuti) **5**:337
"The Selfish One" (Neruda)
See "El egoísta"
"Self-Knowledge" (Graham) **59**:166
"Self-Portrait" (Cassian) **17**:7
"Self-Portrait" (Cervantes) **35**:117
"Self-portrait" (Parra)
See "Autoretrato"
"Self-Portrait as Apollo and Daphne" (Graham) **59**:133, 157
"Self-Portrait as Demeter and Persephone" (Graham) **59**:158, 173
"Self-Portrait as Hurry and Delay" (Graham) **59**:157-58
"Self-Portrait as the Gesture between Them" (Graham) **59**:152, 157-58, 184
"A Self-Portrait: David" (Tomlinson) **17**:346, 348
"Self-Portrait in a Convex Mirror" (Ashbery) **26**:109, 119-21, 123-24, 126, 134, 140, 142-43, 147-50, 159, 171-72, 174
Self-Portrait in a Convex Mirror (Ashbery) **26**:115-16, 118, 124, 126-27, 130, 145, 148-50, 160, 169, 171, 174
"Self-Portrait in Tyvek (tm) Windbreaker" (Merrill) **28**:287
"The Self-Portrait of Ivan Generalić" (Schnackenberg) **45**:337
"Self-Portrait on a Summer Evening" (Boland) **58**:6
"Self-Portrait with Max Beckmann" (Yau) **61**:358
"Self-Portraits" (Graham) **59**:138, 157-58, 171, 174
"Self-Praise" (Graves) **6**:139
"Self's Despite" (Muir) **49**:206
"The Self-slaved" (Kavanagh) **33**:63
"The Self-Unseeing" (Hardy) **8**:88, 129
"Selige Sehnsucht" (Goethe) **5**:248
"Selina, Countess of Huntingdon" (Davie) **29**:115-16
"Selinda and Cloris" (Behn) **13**:30
"Sella" (Bryant) **20**:15
"A Seltzer Bottle" (Stein) **18**:334
"Selva austral" (Mistral) **32**:166
"Selva Oscura" (MacNeice) **61**:186
"Selvas de mi ciudad" (Storni) **33**:239, 246;
"The Selves" (Page) **12**:198
"La semaine pâle" (Péret) **33**:202
"La semaine Sainte" (Lamartine) **16**:277, 299
"The Semblables" (Williams) **7**:360
"A Semblance" (Ignatow) **34**:313
"Seme" (Quasimodo) **47**:302
Semillas para un himno (Paz) **1**:353, 366; **48**:244
"Semper eadem" (Baudelaire) **1**:61, 72
"Semper eadem" (Verlaine) **32**:385
"Semplicità" (Pavese) **13**:229
"Sen" (Mickiewicz) **38**:196-97
"Senaida" (Quintana) **36**:274
"The Sence of a Letter Sent Me, Made into Verse; to a New Tune" (Behn) **13**:31
"Sence You Went Away" (Johnson) **24**:132, 141, 151, 154, 162
"Send No Money" (Larkin) **21**:234, 242, 248
"Sending to the War" (Morris) **55**:338

"The Send-Off" (Owen) **19**:347
Senlin: A Biography (Aiken) **26**:4, 6, 12, 22, 29, 70-2
"Señor Diego Valverde" (Juana Inés de la Cruz) **24**:186
"Señor, para responderos" (Juana Inés de la Cruz) **24**:187
"Señora doña Ros" (Juana Inés de la Cruz) **24**:211
"Sensation" (Rimbaud) **3**:275, 283; **57**:191, 234, 241, 244, 248, 252, 255, 284
"Sensation Time at the Home" (Merton)
See "A Song: Sensation Time at the Home"
"Sensational Disclosures! (Kavanagh Tells All)" (Kavanagh) **33**:76, 87, 96
"Sense and Conscience" (Tennyson) **6**:372-73
"The Sense of an Ending" (Graham) **59**:132, 149, 155-56, 179
The Sense of Movement (Gunn) **26**:181, 184-185, 188-189, 200-201, 206-207, 210, 212, 218-220, 230
A Sense of Time (Ungaretti)
See *Sentimento del tempo*
"Sensemayá" (Guillén) **23**:131-32, 134
"Sensibility! O La!" (Roethke) **15**:257, 278, 299, 301
The Sensitive Plant (Shelley) **14**:167, 171, 175, 193, 196, 198
"The Sensualists" (Roethke) **15**:275
sent på jorden (Ekeloef) **23**:62, 75, 77, 88
"Sent to My Two Little Children in the East of Lu" (Li Po) **29**:146
"The Sentence" (Akhmatova)
See "Prigovor"
"The Sentence" (Graves) **6**:157
"A Sentence for Tyranny" (Hass) **16**:248
"Sentences" (Milosz) **8**:189
"Sentences" (Parra)
See "Frases"
Sentences (Nemerov) **24**:288
"The Sententious Man" (Roethke) **15**:272, 278
Les sentiers et les routes de la poésie (Éluard) **38**:78
"Le Sentiment de la nature" (Éluard) **38**:96
Sentiment of Time (Ungaretti)
See *Sentimento del tempo*
"Sentimental Colloquy" (Verlaine)
See "Colloque sentimental"
"The Sentimental Surgeon" (Page) **12**:176
"The Sentimentalist" (Moore) **49**:104, 109
Sentimento del tempo (Ungaretti) **57**:334, 338-39, 347, 358, 360, 375-76
"Sentiments for a Dedication" (MacLeish) **47**:165
"The Sentry" (Borges)
See "El centinela"
"Separate Lives" (Hacker) **47**:87
"The Separate Notebooks" (Milosz)
See "Osobny zeszyt"
The Separate Notebooks (Milosz) **8**:182, 195-97
The Separate Rose (Neruda)
See *La rosa separada: obra póstuma*
"Separation" (Merwin) **45**:8
Separations (Hacker) **47**:80, 104
"Les sept epées" (Apollinaire) **7**:46
"Les Sept poémes d'amour en guerre" (Éluard) **38**:79
"Les sept vieillards" (Baudelaire) **1**:45, 65, 70
"September" (Belloc) **24**:29
"September" (Benn) **35**:9, 34, 66
"September" (Hughes) **7**:113, 118
"September" (Zagajewski) **27**:396
"September 1, 1939" (Auden) **1**:14, 25
"September 17" (Herbert) **50**:12-13
"September 22nd" (Kumin) **15**:190
"September, 1903" (Cavafy) **36**:41, 42
"September 1913" (Yeats) **20**:324-25
"September Afternoon in the Abandoned Barracks" (Zagajewski) **27**:391
"September Garden Party" (Kenyon) **57**:40
"September in Great Yarmouth" (Mahon) **60**:134
"September on Jessore Road" (Ginsberg) **4**:59
"September Shooting" (Nemerov) **24**:288
"September Twilight" (Glück) **16**:170
"Septet for the End of Time" (Mackey) **49**:2, 77
Septet for the End of Time (Mackey) **49**:4-6, 17, 22
"Le Septiesme livre des poemes" (Ronsard) **11**:246
Septimi Gadis (Horace) **46**:94
"Sepulchre" (Herbert) **4**:120
Sequel to Drum-Taps (Whitman) **3**:418, 422
"Sequence" (Wylie) **23**:310, 315, 322
A Sequence for Francis Parkman (Davie) **29**:96, 98, 109
"Sequence, Sometimes Metaphysical" (Roethke) **15**:311
Sequences (Sassoon) **12**:247-48, 255, 257-60, 271
"Sequoia" (Herbert) **50**:15
"La Sera del Dí di Festa" (Leopardi) **37**:83, 102, 111, 124, 126-27, 130-31, 142
"Un Sera in San Pietro" (Carducci) **46**:49
"Sera nella valle del Màsino" (Quasimodo) **47**:279, 303
"The Seraphim" (Browning) **6**:6, 20, 22, 26-7
The Seraphim, and Other Poems (Browning) **6**:14-15, 19, 26, 29, 31-2
"Serata romana" (Pasolini) **17**:265
"Serenade" (Carducci)
See "Serenata"
"Sérénade" (Verlaine) **32**:388
"Serenade" (Viereck) **27**:263
"Serenade: Any Man to Any Woman" (Sitwell) **3**:309, 311, 314
"Serenata" (Carducci) **46**:50
"Serenata indiana" (Montale) **13**:107, 128
"Serene Words" (Mistral)
See "Palabras serenas"
"The Serepta Scold" (Masters)
See "Serepta the Scold"
"Serepta the Scold" (Masters) **36**:177, 181
"The Sergeant's Weddin'" (Kipling) **3**:164, 192
"A Serious Step Lightly Taken" (Frost) **1**:203
"Seriously Comma" (Cage) **58**:207
"Sermon for Our Maturity" (Baraka) **4**:19
"A Sermon on the Warpland" (Brooks) **7**:63
Sermones (Horace) **46**:114
Sermones y prédicas del Cristo de Elqui (Parra) **39**:289-90, 292, 298-99, 303, 313
Sermons and Homilies of the Christ of Elqui (Parra)
See *Sermones y prédicas del Cristo de Elqui*
"Le serpent" (Valéry)
See "Ébauche d'un serpent"
"Le serpent qui danse" (Baudelaire) **1**:62
"Le Serpent qui danse" (Char) **56**:197
The Serrated Wheel (Guillén)
See *La rueda dentada*
"A Servant to Servants" (Frost) **1**:193, 228
"La servante au grand coeur" (Baudelaire) **1**:67-68
"Ses purs ongles très haut dèdiant leur onyx" (Mallarmé)
See "Sonnet en -yx"
"Sesenheimer Lyrik" (Goethe) **5**:245
"Śesh lekhā" (Tagore) **8**:424, 426-27
"A Session of the Poets" (Suckling) **30**:118, 121, 134, 144, 149, 155
"A Sessions of the Poets" (Suckling)
See "A Session of the Poets"
"Sestina" (Bishop) **34**:58-59, 61, 76, 91, 120, 160, 165, 190, 192
"Sestina" (Curnow) **48**:29
Sestina (Rukeyser) **12**:232
"Sestina: Altaforte" (Pound) **4**:356
"Sestina for the Ladies of Tehuántepec" (Birney) **52**:41, 79, 98
"Sestina from the Home Gardener" (Wakoski) **15**:360
"Sestina of the Tramp Royal" (Kipling) **3**:160
Sestra moia zhizn (Pasternak) **6**:250-51, 254-55, 260, 263-65, 268-69, 271-72, 278-80, 282, 285
"Set by Mr. H. Lawes / A Dialogue between Lucasia and Orinda" (Philips) **40**:318
"Set of Country Songs" (Hardy) **8**:127
"A Set of Romantic Hymns" (Duncan) **2**:103
"Setting a Snare" (Wagoner) **33**:352
"The Setting of the Moon" (Leopardi)
See "Il tramonto della luna"
"The Setting Sun" (Clare) **23**:40
"The Settle Bed" (Heaney) **18**:259
"The Settlers" (Atwood) **8**:12
"Seuil" (Char) **56**:106, 137-38, 141, 155, 190-91, 193-95, 200
"Un seul corps" (Éluard) **38**:61
"Le seul savant, c'est encore Moïse" (Verlaine) **2**:416
"Le seul témoin" (Bonnefoy) **58**:133, 173, 175
"Seule" (Éluard) **38**:75
"La seule, rose" (Bonnefoy) **58**:154
Seuls demeurent (Char) **56**:112, 131, 184-89
"Seurat's Sunday Afternoon along the Seine" (Schwartz) **8**:289-99, 317-18
"VII" (Joyce) **22**:136, 144, 167
"The Seven Ages" (Auden) **1**:39
"Seven Days for Eternity" (Elytis) **21**:123
"7.IV.64" (Snyder) **21**:287
"Seven Laments for the Fallen in the War" (Amichai) **38**:43
"Seven Laments for the War-Dead" (Amichai)
See "Seven Laments for the Fallen in the War"
"Les 7 500 000 oui (Publie en Mai 1870)" (Hugo) **17**:98
"Seven Moments of Love" (Hughes) **53**:99
"Seven Moments of Love: An Un-Sonnet Sequence in Blues" (Hughes) **53**:99, 101
"The Seven Old Men" (Baudelaire)
See "Les sept vieillards"
Seven Poems and a Fragment (Yeats) **51**:108
"Seven Poems for Marthe, My Wife" (Rexroth) **20**:181
"Seven Seals" (Lawrence) **54**:168
The Seven Seas (Kipling) **3**:159-62, 164, 167, 192-93
"Seven Songs for a Journey" (Wright) **14**:369
"Seven Songs Written during the Ch'ien-yüan Era while Staying at T'ung-ku-hsien" (Tu Fu) **9**:322
"Seven Strophes" (Brodsky) **9**:22
"The Seven Swords" (Apollinaire)
See "Les sept epées"
"Seven Things" (Carman) **34**:210
"Seven Years from Somewhere" (Levine) **22**:219
Seven Years from Somewhere (Levine) **22**:218-19, 234
"Seven-year-old Poets" (Rimbaud)
See "Les Poètes de sept ans"
The Seven-League Crutches (Jarrell) **41**:139, 194, 216-17
"XVII" (Joyce) **22**:136, 144, 164, 167
"Seventeen" (Zagajewski) **27**:389
"A Seventeen Morning" (Ammons) **16**:44
"1777" (Lowell) **13**:78, 84
"Seventeen Years" (Berry) **28**:9
"A Seventeenth Century Suite" (Duncan) **2**:115-16, 127
"The Seventh Angel" (Herbert) **50**:3, 34
"Seventh Birthday of the First Child" (Olds) **22**:318
"Seventh Elegy" (Rilke) **2**:281, 286
Seventh Isthmian (Pindar)
See *Isthmian 7*
Seventh Nemean (Pindar)
See *Nemean 7*
"Seventh Psalm" (Sexton) **2**:367
"The Seventh Summer" (Levine) **22**:220
73 Poems (Cummings) **5**:109-11

Several Poems Compiled with Great Variety of Wit and Learning, Full of Delight (Bradstreet) **10**:43-5, 51
"Several Voices Out of a Cloud" (Bogan) **12**:100, 107, 124
Severnaia simfoniia: Pervia geroicheskaia (Bely) **11**:3, 12-15, 21
"A Sewerplant Grows in Harlem or I'm a Stranger Here Myself When Does the Next Swan Leave?" (Lorde) **12**:158
"Sewing a dress" (Niedecker) **42**:100, 121
"Sex without Love" (Olds) **22**:328-29, 339
"El sexo" (Aleixandre) **15**:34
"Sexsmith the Dentist" (Masters) **36**:233
"Sext" (Auden) **1**:23
"Sextet" (Brodsky) **9**:19, 22
"Sexual Water" (Neruda)
See "Agua sexual"
"Sh, This Poem Wants to Say Something" (Ignatow) **34**:306
"Shack Dye" (Masters) **36**:183
Shackles (Césaire)
See *Ferrements*
"The Shad-Blow Tree" (Glück) **16**:126-27, 142
"Shade of Fonvizin" (Pushkin) **10**:408
Shades (McHugh) **61**:201
"The Shadow" (Lowell) **13**:60-1, 83
"Shadow" (Stryk) **27**:201
"Shadow: 1970" (Wright) **14**:371
"Shadow and Shade" (Tate) **50**:231, 280
The Shadow of Cain (Sitwell) **3**:320, 327
"The Shadow of Death" (Lawrence) **54**:244
"The Shadow of Fire" (Wright) **14**:376
Shadow of Paradise (Aleixandre)
See *Sombra del paraíso*
"A Shadow Play for Guilt" (Piercy) **29**:309
"Shadow Suite" (Brathwaite) **56**:64
Shadow Train: Fifty Lyrics (Ashbery) **26**:151-152, 154, 166-167
"Shadow Wash" (Silverstein) **49**:347
"Shadow-Maker" (Swenson) **14**:261
"Shadows" (Lawrence) **54**:203, 251
"Shadows of Taste" (Clare) **23**:14
"Shadows on the Wall" (Blok) **21**:14
The Shadowy Waters (Yeats) **20**:303, 353
"Shad-Time" (Wilbur) **51**:249, 310, 331
"The Shaft" (Tomlinson) **17**:342
The Shaft (Tomlinson) **17**:325-27, 334-36, 338, 342-43, 347, 350, 353-54
Shaker, Why Don't You Sing? (Angelou) **32**:26-7
"Shakespeare" (Arnold) **5**:49
"Shakespeare" (Pasternak) **6**:252
"Shakespeare in Harlem" (Hughes) **1**:239, 242, 246-47, 254-56, 268, 270; **53**:99-100, 171-73
Shakespeare in Harlem (Hughes) **53**:94, 98-100, 119, 137, 139, 173
"Shakespeare Say" (Dove) **6**:109
"A Shakespearean Sonnet: To a Woman Liberationist" (Knight) **14**:46
"Shaking" (Silverstein) **49**:333
Shall We Gather at the River (Wright) **36**:294, 296, 299-300, 302, 304-6, 314, 317, 319, 325, 327, 329-30, 341, 342, 344-47, 350-51, 353-55, 358, 360, 363, 365-66, 368, 375, 391-92, 396, 399-400, 403
"The Shallot" (Wilbur) **51**:246, 282
"Shalom" (Levertov) **11**:170
Shalvah gedolah: She'elot utshuvot (Amichai) **38**:10, 19, 25-8, 36
"Shaman Mountain is High" (Li Ho) **13**:51
"Shame" (Mistral)
See "Desvelada"
"Shame" (Wilbur) **51**:266
"Shame Mi Lady" (Goodison) **36**:142, 150
"Shame on You" (Hughes) **53**:162
"The Shampoo" (Bishop) **34**:105, 146
"Shancoduff" (Kavanagh) **33**:70, 73, 77, 81, 83, 91, 99, 102, 147, 150
"Shango" (Brathwaite) **56**:61
"Shanna in the Sauna" (Silverstein) **49**:342
"Shantung" (Lindsay) **23**:265
"Shantung Or the Empire of China Is Crumbling Down" (Lindsay) **23**:280
"Shape and Tonal Equilibrium" (Komunyakaa) **51**:62
"Shape of Boeotia" (Elytis) **21**:116
"The Shape of Death" (Swenson) **14**:286
"The Shape of the Fire" (Roethke) **15**:248, 254, 272, 274, 277, 282, 284-85, 287, 298
"The shapers: Vancouver" (Birney) **52**:36
Shar (Brathwaite) **56**:43, 46, 71
"Sharecroppers" (Brown) **55**:167-69
"Shared Nights" (Éluard)
See "Nuits partagées"
"Sharing Eve's Apple" (Keats) **1**:311
"Shark Meat" (Snyder) **21**:292, 308
"The Shark: Parents and Children" (Wakoski) **15**:356
"The Shark's Parlor" (Dickey) **40**:183, 186, 213, 216, 221, 241, 254
"The Sharp Ridge" (Graves) **6**:156
"Sharpeville" (Brutus) **24**:117
Sharps and Flats (Tagore)
See *Kari o komal*
"Shatabdir surya" (Tagore) **8**:412
"Shatter Me, Music" (Rilke) **2**:275
"A Shawl" (Stein) **18**:328, 348
"She" (Roethke) **15**:275
"She" (Wilbur) **51**:235, 312
"She Being Brand-New" (Cummings) **5**:95
"She Belongs to Me" (Dylan) **37**:54
"She Bitches about Boys" (Hacker) **47**:79
"SHE CALLS ME ADONIS" (Bissett) **14**:32
"She Carries a 'Fat Gold Watch'" (Ondaatje) **28**:292
"She Had Some Horses" (Harjo) **27**:64-65
She Had Some Horses (Harjo) **27**:56-8, 60, 64-5
"She had tumult of the brain" (Niedecker) **42**:151
"She Hid in the Trees from the Nurses" (Wright) **36**:279, 335
"She Looks Back" (Lawrence) **54**:186
"She of All Time, All" (Éluard)
See "Celle de toujours, toute"
"She of the Dancing Feet Sings" (Cullen) **20**:63
"She Remembers the Future" (Harjo) **27**:56
"She Said . . ." (Smith) **12**:326
"She Said as Well to Me" (Lawrence) **54**:185-87, 239
"She Shall Be Called Woman" (Sarton) **39**:318-19, 325, 335, 337, 342, 354-56, 358
She Steals My Heart (Li Ho) **13**:44
"She Tells Her Love while Half Asleep" (Graves) **6**:144
"She Thinks of Him" (Li Po) **29**:176
"She, to Him" (Hardy) **8**:90
"She Weeps over Rahoon" (Joyce) **22**:137
"She Wept, She Railed" (Kunitz) **19**:151
"she won't ever forgive me" (Clifton) **17**:25
"A Sheaf for Chicago" (Stryk) **27**:187, 195, 210, 214
"She'at ha-Hesed" (Amichai) **38**:19, 23-24
"The Sheaves" (Robinson) **1**:478
"Sheep" (Francis) **34**:255-56
"Sheep" (Sandburg) **41**:249
"The Sheep Child" (Dickey) **40**:153, 171-72, 176, 183, 221, 232, 248, 259
"A Sheep Fair" (Hardy) **8**:101
"Sheep in a Fog" (Plath) **1**:408-09; **37**:258, 260
"Sheep in the Rain" (Wright) **36**:378
"The Sheep Went On Being Dead" (Hughes) **7**:149
Sheepfold Hill: Fifteen Poems (Aiken) **26**:24
"Shell" (Sarton) **39**:368
"Shell" (Zagajewski) **27**:403
"Shells" (Nemerov) **24**:299
"Shelter" (Erdrich) **52**:178
"Shelter" (Niedecker) **42**:138
"Shelter from the Storm" (Dylan) **37**:55
"Sheltered Garden" (H. D.) **5**:269, 303
"Shem el Nessim" (Cavafy) **36**:53
"Shemselnihar" (Meredith) **60**:309
"Shenandoah" (Sandburg) **41**:270
"Shenendoah" (Shapiro) **25**:284-85
The Shepheardes Calender: Conteyning Twelve Æglogues Proportionable to the Twelve Monethes (Spenser) **8**:326-28, 335, 385-87; **42**:266
"The Shepherd" (Blake) **12**:7, 32
"Shepherd" (Brathwaite) **56**:74-75, 86
"The Shepherd" (H. D.) **5**:305
"The Shepherd" (Soto) **28**:371
"Shepherd and Goatherd" (Yeats) **51**:110
"Shepherd Bound for Mountain Pass" (Aleixandre) **15**:12, 18
"A Shepherd in Lesbos" (Carman) **34**:208-09
"The Shepherd's Brow, Fronting Forked Lightning" (Hopkins) **15**:168
The Shepherd's Calendar, with Village Stories, and Other Poems (Clare) **23**:10, 16-21, 37-8, 40, 44
Shepherd's Home (Vigny) **26**:371
"The Shepherd's Praise of Diana" (Raleigh) **31**:260
Sherwood (Noyes) **27**:123
"She's Awake" (Wright) **36**:304
"She's Free" (Harper) **21**:204
"She's Your Lover Now" (Dylan) **37**:66
"Shesh katha" (Tagore) **8**:407
Shesh saptak (Tagore) **8**:417
"Shiberia no uta" (Ishikawa) **10**:213
"The Shield of Achilles" (Auden) **1**:23
"Shiftless" (Carver) **54**:32
"The Shih-men Monastery in the Lan-t'ien Mountains" (Wang Wei) **18**:378
"Shillin' a Day" (Kipling) **3**:191
"The Shimmer of Evil" (Roethke) **15**:278
"Shine" (Knight) **14**:49
"Shine, Perishing Republic" (Jeffers) **17**:107, 117-19, 132
"Ship" (Merwin) **45**:48
"The Ship of Death" (Lawrence) **54**:172-73, 176, 178, 181, 187, 197-99, 201-3, 218, 226-27, 234, 250
"Ship of Fools" (MacLeish) **47**:246
"Shipbuilding Office" (Page) **12**:173, 176
"Shipman's" (Chaucer)
See "Shipman's Tale"
"Shipman's Tale" (Chaucer) **19**:13, 26
The Shipman!s Tale (Chaucer) **58**:352
Shipovnik tsevetyot (Akhmatova) **2**:9
Ships and Other Figures (Meredith) **28**:171, 173, 186-87, 189, 210, 217
"The Ships of Yule" (Carman) **34**:208
"Ships That Pass in the Night" (Dunbar) **5**:121
"The Shipwreck of Idomeneus" (Meredith) **60**:245, 293
"Shiraha no toribune" (Ishikawa) **10**:214
The Shires (Davie) **29**:116
Shirim: 1948-1962 (Amichai) **38**:23, 26-28, 32-33, 35-36
"The Shirt" (Kenyon) **57**:12, 46
"The Shirt" (Pinsky) **27**:158, 164-65, 176
"Shitsurakuen" (Nishiwaki) **15**:237, 239
"Shiv and the Grasshopper" (Kipling) **3**:183
"Shizumeru kane" (Ishikawa) **10**:214
"The Shoes of Wandering" (Kinnell) **26**:243, 249, 266, 272-73
"Shoot It Jimmy" (Williams) **7**:383
"Shoot the Buffalo" (Momaday) **25**:214
"A Shooting Incident" (Smith) **12**:318, 346
"Shooting the Girl" (Dafydd)
See "Saethu'r Ferch"
"Shooting Script" (Rich) **5**:366-67, 378, 383, 396-97
"Shootings of the Third of May" (Heaney) **18**:205
"Shop" (Browning) **2**:59
"The Shore" (Clampitt) **19**:90
"Shoreline" (Heaney) **18**:201, 203
"Shoreline Horses" (Ríos) **57**:323
"Shores" (Montale)
See "Riviere"
"The Shorewatchers' House" (Montale) **13**:150

"A Short History of Bill Berkson" (O'Hara) **45**:142
"A Short Note to My Very Critical and Well-Beloved Friends and Comrades" (Jordan) **38**:117
"Short Poem" (Sanchez) **9**:212, 223
Short Prose Poems (Baudelaire)
See *Petits poèmes en prose: Le spleen de Paris*
"A Short Recess" (Milosz) **8**:183, 186
Short Songs of Pure Feelings (Hagiwara)
See *Junjo shokyoku shu*
"Short Summary" (Bogan) **12**:101
"Short Thoughts for Long Nights" (Warren) **37**:380
Short Wave (Szirtes) **51**:158-59
Shorter Poems (Bridges) **28**:52-3, 67, 69, 82-3
Shorter Poems (Schwerner)
See *Selected Shorter Poems*
"The Shot" (Graves) **6**:143-44
"The Shot" (Pushkin)
See "Vystrel"
Shot of Love (Dylan) **37**:65
"Should lanterns shine" (Thomas) **52**:237
"Should We Legalize Abortion" (O'Hara) **45**:226
"The Shovel Man" (Sandburg) **2**:332; **41**:226, 296, 321, 365
"The Show" (Owen) **19**:327, 336-37, 341, 343-44, 347, 353, 355, 359
"The Shower" (Riley) **48**:293
"Shower" (Swift)
See "Description of a City Shower"
"The Shower of Secret Things: 3" (Mackey) **49**:3
"Showing How to Make the Right Kind of a Man Out of the Right Kind of a Boy" (Riley) **48**:304
"The Showings; Lady Julian of Norwich, 1342-1416" (Levertov) **11**:210
"The Shrike" (Thoreau) **30**:184
"The Shrine" (H. D.) **5**:270
A Shropshire Lad (Housman) **2**:159-67, 171-78, 180-81, 183-84, 186-88, 191-95, 197, 199-200
"The Shroud" (Millay) **6**:205
"The Shroud of Color" (Cullen) **20**:52, 54-55, 57, 62, 64, 67, 69, 73, 84
"Shūchō" (Ishikawa) **10**:212
Shukumei (Hagiwara) **18**:176
Shundeishū (Yosano Akiko) **11**:305
"Shun'ya" (Hagiwara) **18**:181
"Shut, Bellada" (Bely) **11**:24
"Shut Nad ney" (Bely) **11**:24
"Shut Out" (Rossetti) **7**:280
"Shut: Plamen" (Bely) **11**:24
"Shutka" (Bely) **11**:24
"Shuttles" (Swenson) **14**:273
Shyamali (Tagore) **8**:417
"Shylock" (Shapiro) **25**:283
"Si acaso, Fabio mío" (Juana Inés de la Cruz) **24**:180, 184, 187
"Si daros los buenos años" (Juana Inés de la Cruz) **24**:180
"Si el desamor o el enojo" (Juana Inés de la Cruz) **24**:186, 234
"Si el Papa no rompe con el USA" (Parra) **39**:275, 311
"Si es amor causa productiva" (Juana Inés de la Cruz) **24**:189
"Si los riesgos del mar cpmsoderara" (Juana Inés de la Cruz) **24**:225
"Si tu aimes" (Éluard) **38**:74
"Si tú supiera" (Guillén)
See "Ay negra, si tu supiera"
"Si yo fuera presidente de Chile" (Parra) **39**:272
"Siberian note" (Char)
See "Note sibérienne"
"Siberian Wooing" (Yevtushenko) **40**:366
"Sibir" (Tsvetaeva) **14**:326
"Sibling Mysteries" (Rich) **5**:373, 384
"Sibrandus Schafnaburgensis" (Browning) **2**:59
"A Sibyl" (Atwood) **8**:25
Sibylline Leaves (Coleridge) **11**:57, 60, 97, 115
"Sic Transit" (Lowell) **3**:213
"Sic Vita" (Thoreau) **30**:188-89, 258, 275, 293
"Sicilia e la Rivoluzione" (Carducci) **46**:5, 51, 56
"Sicilian Cyclamens" (Lawrence) **54**:187
"The Sick" (Page) **12**:176
"Sick" (Silverstein) **49**:310
"Sick at Summer's End" (Kenyon) **57**:29, 34
"A Sick Bed" (Bryant) **20**:17, 46
"The Sick Child" (Glück) **16**:132, 136, 138
"A Sick Child" (Jarrell) **41**:171, 174
"The Sick King in Bokhara" (Arnold) **5**:6, 39, 49
"Sick Leave" (Sassoon) **12**:267, 288
"Sick Love" (Graves) **6**:136-37, 142, 144, 151, 169
"The Sick Rose" (Blake) **12**:7
"The Sick Wife" (Kenyon) **57**:21, 25-26, 44, 48
"Sickly Face at the Bottom of the Ground" (Hagiwara) **18**:175
"Sickness" (Ransom) **61**:294
"Sickness and Schooling" (Jackson) **44**:63
"The Sickness of Kleitos" (Cavafy) **36**:34, 75, 79, 109
"The Sickness unto Death" (Sexton) **2**:372
"Sideboard" (Rimbaud)
See "Le Buffet"
"Side by Side" (Brown) **55**:168
Sidestreets (Tsvetaeva)
See *Pereulochki*
"Sie erlischt" (Heine) **25**:178
"Sie haben wegen der Trunkenheit" (Heine) **25**:162
"Siede" (Stramm) **50**:168, 176, 194, 202
"Siegfried" (Jarrell) **41**:169, 178, 203, 218
"Siegmund Freud" (Parra) **39**:274-75, 287
"Siempre aguarda mi sangre" (Guillén) **35**:229
"Siena mi fe'; disfecemi Maremma" (Pound) **4**:319
"Sierra" (Guillén) **35**:231
"Sierra" (Storni) **33**:270;
"Sierra Nevada" (Cardenal) **22**:125, 131
"Siesta" (Storni) **33**:254-55;
"Siesta: Barbados" (Kenyon) **57**:45
Siete poemas (Borges) **32**:61-2
"A Sigh" (Finch) **21**:141
"The Sigh" (Hardy) **8**:104
"Sigh" (Mallarmé)
See "Soupir"
"Sigh No More" (Lawrence) **54**:184
"The Sigh That Heaves the Grasses" (Housman) **2**:183, 191
"Sighs and Groans" (Herbert)
See "Sighs and Grones"
"Sighs and Grones" (Herbert) **4**:120, 133-34,
"Sighs are my food, drink are my tears" (Wyatt) **27**:369
"Sight" (Parker) **28**:365
"Sight of the Hills from the Kozłlowa Steppes" (Mickiewicz)
See "Widok gór ze stepów Kozłlowa"
"Sightseeing on a Winter Day" (Wang Wei) **18**:373
"Sign" (Apollinaire)
See "Signe"
"The Sign" (Masters) **1**:333, 337
"The Sign of Saturn" (Olds) **22**:324
"The Sign of the Golden Shoe" (Noyes) **27**:124
Sign towards the long way round (Char)
See *Placard pour un chemin des écoliers*
"The Signal" (MacLeish) **47**:197
"Signal" (Silverstein) **49**:334
"Signal" (Stramm) **50**:176
"Signal" (Tzara) **27**:229-31
"The Signal from the House" (Kunitz) **19**:172-73
"The Signature" (Jackson) **44**:74
"Signature for Tempo" (MacLeish) **47**:127, 156, 185, 197
"The Signature of All Things" (Rexroth) **20**:196, 217
The Signature of All Things: Poems, Songs, Elegies, Translations, and Epigrams (Rexroth) **20**:181, 183-84, 192-94, 203
"Signe" (Apollinaire) **7**:44, 48
"The Significance of Veteran's Day" (Ortiz) **17**:226, 232
"The Signifying Monkey" (Knight) **14**:49
"Signing the Pledge" (Harper) **21**:191
"A Signiture. A Herold. A Span" (Brooks) **7**:90
"La Signorina Felicita" (Gozzano) **10**:176-77, 180-83
"Signpost" (Jeffers) **17**:129, 131, 145
"The Sign-Post" (Thomas) **53**:270, 332
"Signs" (Merwin) **45**:16
"Signs and Tokens" (Hardy) **8**:111
"Signs of Winter" (Clare) **23**:28
"Sigue" (Guillén) **23**:142
"Sigurd rideth with the Niblungs, and wooeth Brynhild for King Gunnar" (Morris) **55**:334
Sigurd the Volsung (Morris) **55**:260, 262, 273, 277, 324, 328-30, 332-35, 337-41, 262261
"Silas Dement" (Masters) **36**:231
"Die silbe schmerz" (Celan) **10**:102, 105
"The Silence" (Berry) **28**:5, 7, 43
"Silence" (Eliot) **5**:217
"Silence" (Lawrence) **54**:167, 250
"Silence" (Masters) **1**:325, 333, 342
"Silence" (Moore) **49**:100
"The Silence" (Sarton) **39**:328, 369
"Silence" (Szymborska) **44**:298
"Silence" (Wright) **14**:342
"Silence and Tears" (Smith) **12**:341
"The Silence Answered Him Accusingly" (Schwartz) **8**:293
"Silence de l'Evangile" (Éluard) **38**:70
Silence in the Snowy Fields (Bly) **39**:3, 5-6, 8-15, 17, 19, 22, 24, 37, 42, 48-9, 52-3, 64, 67, 69-71, 73-6, 78-87, 89-91, 94, 98-100, 102-03, 115
"The Silence Now" (Sarton) **39**:369
The Silence Now (Sarton) **39**:347-50, 360, 362-63, 368-69
"The Silence of Plants" (Szymborska) **44**:320
The Silence of the Sea (Mickiewicz) **38**:158
"The Silence of Tudor Evans" (Ackerley) **41**:19, 25
A Silence Opens (Clampitt) **19**:100-01
Silence: Selected Lectures and Writings (Cage) **58**:193-95, 198, 203-4, 221, 224
"Silence Wager Stories" (Howe) **54**:87-88, 106-7
"Silences: Lament of the Silent Sisters" (Okigbo) **7**:225, 228, 234, 244-47, 251
"The Silent Angel" (Wright) **36**:311, 369
"The Silent Battle" (Teasdale) **31**:360
"Silent Faces at Crossroads" (Okigbo) **7**:255
"Silent in America" (Levine) **22**:212, 222
"Silent Love" (Mistral)
See "El amor que calla"
"Silent Noon" (Rossetti) **44**:174
"Silent Poem" (Francis) **34**:244, 249, 252
"Silent Service" (Sassoon) **12**:252
"Silent Sisters" (Okigbo)
See "Silences: Lament of the Silent Sisters"
"The Silent Slain" (MacLeish) **47**:186, 197
"Silhouette of a Serpent" (Valéry)
See "Ébauche d'un serpent"
"Silk of a Soul" (Herbert)
See "Jedwab duszy"
"The Silken Tent" (Frost) **1**:196, 214
"Silly Song" (García Lorca)
See "Canción tonta"
"Silos" (Dove) **6**:120
"Silver" (Ammons) **16**:5
"Silver Filigree" (Wylie) **23**:314, 322, 332
"The Silver Lily" (Glück) **16**:170
"The Silver Swan" (Rexroth) **20**:221
"The Silver Tassie" (Burns) **6**:97
"A Silvia" (Carducci) **46**:63

"A Silvia" (Leopardi) **37**:102, 109, 120-21, 123-24, 141
"Simaetha" (H. D.) **5**:266
"Simeon" (Cavafy) **36**:40, 104
Simfonija (1-aga) (Bely)
See *Severnaia simfoniia: Pervia geroicheskaia*
Simfonija (2-aja) (Bely)
See *Vtoraia simfoniia: Dramaticheskaia*
"A Simile for Her Smile" (Wilbur) **51**:188, 193, 209
"Simon" (Wright) **36**:313
"Simon Lee" (Wordsworth) **4**:374, 416-17, 425-26, 428
"Simon Legree" (Lindsay) **23**:264, 269, 273, 287
"Simon Surnamed Peter" (Masters) **1**:325, 342
"Simon the Cyrenian Speaks" (Cullen) **20**:56, 65
"Simple agonie" (Laforgue) **14**:73
"Simple Autumnal" (Bogan) **12**:87-8, 106, 121
"Simple Frescoes" (Verlaine)
See "Simples Fresques"
A Simple Lust: Selected Poems Including Sirens, Knuckles, Boots; Letters to Martha; Poems from Algiers, Thoughts Abroad (Brutus) **24**:113-16, 118
"A Simple Recipe" (Riley) **48**:304
"Simple Sonatina" (Gallagher) **9**:60
The Simple Truth (Levine) **22**:228, 232-33
"Simple Twist of Fate" (Dylan) **37**:56
"Simples Fresques" (Verlaine) **32**:402
"Simple-Song" (Piercy) **29**:309
"Simplicity" (Pavese)
See "Semplicità"
"Simplicity" (Stone) **53**:224
Simplicity (Stone) **53**:220-21, 223-25, 243, 251-54, 256, 258
"Simposio" (Parra) **39**:272
"Sin" (Herbert) **4**:100
"Sin I" (Herbert) **4**:130
"Sin lamento" (Guillén) **35**:174
"Sin nido" (Castro) **41**:113, 116
"Sinaloa" (Birney) **52**:36-37, 44, 46, 97
"Since 1619" (Walker) **20**:275, 283
"Since Death Brushed Past Me" (Teasdale) **31**:372
"Since I am comming" (Donne)
See "Hymne to God my God, in my sicknesse"
"Since Nine O'Clock" (Cavafy) **36**:109
"Since There is no Escape" (Teasdale) **31**:360
"Since we loved" (Bridges) **28**:86
"Since ye delight to know" (Wyatt) **27**:353
"Since You've Come" (Baca) **41**:47
"Sindhu-taranga" (Tagore) **8**:407
"Sinew" (Carver) **54**:14
"Sinfonía en gris mayor" (Darío) **15**:93, 96
"Sinful City" (Seifert)
See "Hříšné město"
"The Singer" (Guillén) **35**:158
"The Singer" (Levertov) **11**:183
"The Singer" (Tsvetaeva)
See "Pevitsa"
"A Singer Asleep" (Hardy) **8**:125
"Singers" (Hughes) **7**:123
"The Singers" (Longfellow) **30**:103
"Singers of Provence" (Ignatow) **34**:314, 323
"Singing Nigger" (Sandburg) **2**:316
"Singing School" (Heaney) **18**:205
"Singladura" (Borges) **32**:125
"Single Sonnet" (Bogan) **12**:90, 107
"Single Vision" (Kunitz) **19**:154
"Singling & Doubling Together" (Ammons) **16**:63-4
Sing-Song: A Nursery Rhyme-Book (Rossetti) **7**:291
Singularities (Howe) **54**:79, 81-82, 84, 88, 92-93, 95, 97, 100, 110-14, 124-28, 130-31, 133-34, 136-37
"Sinistre" (Valéry) **9**:359, 381, 399-401
The Sinking of the Titanic (Enzensberger)
See "Der Untergand der Titanic"
"The Sinking Ship" (Rimbaud)
See "L'eclatante victoire de Saarebrück"
"Sinners" (Lawrence) **54**:187
"Sinners in the Hands of an Angry God" (Lowell) **3**:203
"The Sins of Kalamazoo" (Sandburg) **2**:308; **41**:246, 254, 298, 314
"Sin's Round" (Herbert) **4**:114
"Sion" (Herbert) **4**:100
"Siostra" (Herbert) **50**:37
"Sir Federigo's Falcon" (Longfellow)
See "The Falcon of Ser Federigo"
"Sir Galahad" (Masters) **1**:330, 333
"Sir Galahad" (Tennyson) **6**:359
"Sir Galahad: A Christmas Mystery" (Morris) **55**:238, 240, 300, 302, 348-51
"Sir Hubert" (Patmore) **59**:218, 243
"Sir James South Side" (Cisneros) **52**:157
"Sir John Herschel Remembers" (Noyes) **27**:129
"Sir Peter Harpdon's End" (Morris) **55**:238, 258, 301
"Sir Thopas" (Chaucer) **19**:25, 33-4, 37, 47, 50-1
"Sir William Herschel's Long Year" (Hope) **56**:291
"Sire" (Merwin) **45**:8, 24
"Siren" (Birney) **52**:83
"Siren Limits" (Okigbo) **7**:240-46
"Siren Song" (Atwood) **8**:23, 25-6, 41
"La sirena" (Storni) **33**:294
"Sirens, Knuckles, Boots" (Brutus) **24**:98-9, 112-13, 119
"The Sirens' Welcome to Cronos" (Graves) **6**:144, 146
"Sirmione" (Carducci) **46**:52
"Sirocco" (Montale)
See "Scirocco"
"Sister Helen" (Rossetti) **44**:167, 202
"Sister Lou" (Brown) **55**:108, 115, 153, 176
"Sister Maude" (Rossetti) **7**:260, 270, 272-3, 276, 280
"Sister Water" (Warren) **37**:313
"The Sisters" (Lowell) **13**:67
The Sisters: A Tragedy (Swinburne) **24**:348-50, 352
"Sisters in Arms" (Lorde) **12**:141, 151-53
"Sisters of Charity" (Rimbaud)
See "Les Soeurs de charité"
"Sitcom on the Greyhound in Rutland, Vermont" (Stone) **53**:258
"Site of Ambush" (Ní Chuilleanáin) **34**:360, 381
Site of Ambush (Ní Chuilleanáin) **34**:350, 359, 381
"Sit-Ins" (Walker) **20**:276
"The Sitter" (Silverstein) **49**:333
"The Sitting" (Day Lewis) **11**:147
"The Sitting" (McGuckian) **27**:101
"Sitting Alone on an Autumn Night" (Wang Wei) **18**:388
"The Situation in the West Followed by a Holy Proposal" (Ferlinghetti) **1**:172
The Situation of Poetry: Contemporary Poetry and Its Traditions (Pinsky) **27**:143, 153, 160, 162, 173
"S.I.W." (Owen) **19**:354, 357, 369, 371
"VI" (Joyce) **22**:136, 138, 145, 160, 167, 173
Six and One Remorses for the Sky (Elytis) **21**:118, 122, 124, 133
"Six Brothers" (Cisneros) **52**:160
"Six Casually Written Poems" (Wang Wei) **18**:388
Six Epistles to Eva Hesse (Davie) **29**:99-100, 102, 104, 109
"Six Lectures in Verse" (Milosz) **8**:199-200, 202-03, 211
Six Moral Tales from Jules Laforgue (Laforgue)
See *Moralités légendaires*
"Six O'Clock in Princes Street" (Owen) **19**:342
Six Odes (Auden) **1**:8
Six Plays (MacLeish) **47**:208, 211
Six Poems (Muir) **49**:239-40
"Six Poems Matching Poems Expressing Kumagori's Feelings" (Yakamochi)
See "Tsutsushimite Kumagori no tame ni sono kokorozashi wo noburu uta ni kotauru rokushu"
"Six Poems to Tamar" (Amichai) **38**:14-15
Six Quatrains Composed in Jest (Tu Fu) **9**:327
"Six Religious Lyrics" (Shapiro) **25**:320
"Six Songs for Chloe" (Hope) **56**:302, 305
"Six Variations" (Levertov) **11**:183
"Six Winter Privacy Poems" (Bly) **39**:27, 71-2
"Six Years Later" (Brodsky) **9**:7, 8, 19, 26
"Six Years Later" (Wilbur) **51**:249
"Six Young Men" (Hughes) **7**:113
"Six-Bit Blues" (Hughes) **1**:256
"Six-Sided Square: Actopan" (Birney) **52**:28, 36, 79, 95-96
"XVI" (Joyce) **22**:145, 162, 170
"Sixteen Months" (Sandburg) **41**:296
"16.ix.65" (Merrill) **28**:220
"The Sixteenth Floor" (Lowell) **13**:97
"Sixth Elegy" (Rilke) **2**:273
"Sixth Elegy. River Elegy" (Rukeyser) **12**:231-32
Sixth Isthmian (Pindar)
See *Isthmian 6*
Sixth Olympian (Pindar)
See *Olympian 6*
Sixth Pythian (Pindar)
See *Pythian 6*
65 Poems (Celan) **10**:120
Sixty-Two Mesostics re: Merce Cunningham (Cage) **58**:182-83, 218
"The Size" (Herbert) **4**:100, 108
"Size and Tears" (Carroll) **18**:46
"Skateboard" (Gunn) **26**:215
"The Skaters" (Ashbery) **26**:107, 114, 129, 143, 151, 154-156
"The Skaters" (Jarrell) **41**:127, 158
Skazka dlya detey (Lermontov) **18**:282, 303
"Skazka o Mertvoy Tsarevne" (Pushkin) **10**:382
"Skazka o Pope i o Rabotnike Yego Balde" (Pushkin) **10**:382
"Skazka o Rybake i Rybke" (Pushkin) **10**:382
"Skazka o Tsare Sultane" (Pushkin) **10**:381-83
"Skazka o Zolotom Petushke" (Pushkin) **10**:382-83
"Skazki" (Pushkin) **10**:408
Skazki (Pushkin) **10**:381-86
Skeeters Kirby (Masters) **36**:188
"Skeleton Crow" (Szirtes) **51**:158
"The Skeleton in Armor" (Longfellow) **30**:12, 21, 26, 48, 99, 103
"The Skeleton of the Future" (MacDiarmid) **9**:176, 179
"The Skeleton of the Great Moa in the Canterbury Museum, Christchurch" (Curnow) **48**:27
"Skeptic" (Frost) **39**:233
"Sketch" (Sandburg) **2**:303, 335; **41**:238, 259, 364
"A Sketch" (Wilbur) **51**:237, 281
"Sketch for a Landscape" (Swenson) **14**:246, 262
"A Sketch in the Manner of Hogarth" (Patmore) **59**:240
"Sketches for a Portrait" (Day Lewis) **11**:148
Sketches of Southern Life (Harper) **21**:185, 187, 189, 191-93, 197-98, 200-01, 211, 213-14
"Skier" (Francis) **34**:243, 255
"Skiers" (Warren) **37**:299
"The Skies" (Aleixandre)
See "Los cielos"
Skify (Blok) **21**:9, 17, 21-2, 26, 28-9, 31, 35, 41
"The Skilled Man" (Sarton) **39**:348
"Skin" (Larkin) **21**:229
"Skin Canoe" (Forché) **10**:134
"Skin Dreaming" (Hogan) **35**:277, 278

"the skinny voice" (Cummings) **5**:99
"Skizze zu einem Sankt Georg" (Rilke) **2**:267
"Skullshapes" (Tomlinson) **17**:340, 357
"The Skunk" (Heaney) **18**:244
"Skunk Hour" (Lowell) **3**:209-11, 213-14, 221, 223, 227, 235, 243-46
"Skunk Hour" (Sexton) **2**:350
"Sky" (Szymborska) **44**:284, 304, 308-9
"The Sky Falling" (Soto) **28**:370
"The Sky Is Blue" (Ignatow) **34**:273, 291, 312, 327-28
"The Sky Lark" (Clare) **23**:6
"Sky-House" (McGuckian) **27**:78
"Skylarks" (Hughes) **7**:121-22, 136-37
"The Skylarks of Mykonos" (Clampitt) **19**:87
Skylight One: Fifteen Poems (Aiken) **26**:24
"Skylights" (Gallagher) **9**:45
"Skyscraper" (Sandburg) **41**:226, 295
"The Skyscraper Loves Night" (Sandburg) **41**:327
"Slabs of the Sunburnt West" (Sandburg) **2**:306, 308, 310-11, 314, 323, 330; **41**:346
Slabs of the Sunburnt West (Sandburg) **2**:306, 308, 311, 314, 323; **41**:249-52, 255, 260-61, 263, 271, 274, 277, 314, 319, 325, 329-30
"The Slacker Apologizes" (Viereck) **27**:273
"The Slacker Need Not Apologize" (Viereck) **27**:263
"Slam, Dunk, & Hook" (Komunyakaa) **51**:23
The Slant Door (Szirtes) **51**:156
"The Slanting Rain" (Pessoa)
See "Chuva Oblíqua"
"Slapstick" (Szymborska)
See "Komedyjki"
"The Slate Ode" (Mandelstam)
See "Grifel' naja oda"
"Slave" (Storni)
See "Esclava"
"The Slave Auction" (Harper) **21**:190, 194, 205-06, 216-17
"slave cabin sotterly plantation maryland 1989" (Clifton) **17**:30
"The Slave Mother" (Harper) **21**:192, 194, 197, 203-04, 216
"The Slave Mother, A Tale of Ohio" (Harper) **21**:197, 204-05, 210, 218
"Slave Quarters" (Dickey) **40**:151, 154, 158, 178, 197, 209, 212, 214-16, 259
Slavík zpíváśpatně (Seifert) **47**:316, 324, 332-33
"The Sleep" (Browning) **6**:21
"Sleep" (Hope) **56**:268
"Sleep" (Hughes) **1**:240
"Sleep" (Johnson) **24**:145, 159
"Sleep" (Mickiewicz)
See "Sen"
"Sleep" (Pushkin) **10**:407
"Sleep and Poetry" (Keats) **1**:280, 289, 291-92, 313
"Sleep at Sea" (Rossetti) **7**:293, 296-7
"Sleep Brings No Joy to Me" (Brontë) **8**:74
"Sleep defends my Don drowsiness" (Mandelstam)
See "Oboroniaet son moiu donskuiu son"
"Sleep Is a Suspension Midway" (Sandburg) **41**:332
"Sleep of the Valiant" (Elytis) **21**:123
"The Sleep of the Valiant (Variation)" (Elytis) **21**:116
"The Sleep Worker" (Hardy) **8**:129
"The Sleeper" (Bly) **30**:43, 44
"The Sleeper" (Poe) **1**:434, 443-44; **54**:270
"The Sleepers" (Carman) **34**:213
"The Sleepers" (Whitman) **3**:391, 396-97, 401
"Sleepers in Jaipur" (Kenyon) **57**:20, 44
"Sleepers Joining Hands" (Bly) **39**:22, 26, 71, 79, 95, 103
Sleepers Joining Hands (Bly) **39**:15, 18, 22, 24-5, 27-8, 37, 43, 45, 52, 55, 64, 67, 70-1, 84, 90, 92, 94-5, 102-03
"Sleeping at Last" (Rossetti) **7**:287
"Sleeping Beauty" (Clifton) **17**:29
"The Sleeping Beauty" (Owen) **19**:358
"Sleeping Beauty" (Wylie) **23**:321
The Sleeping Beauty (Carruth) **10**:75-8, 83-4, 86, 91
The Sleeping Beauty (Sitwell) **3**:292-94, 298, 300-01, 303, 307-08, 310, 316-17, 320, 324-25
"Sleeping Beauty IV" (Stone) **53**:223
"The Sleeping Beauty: Variation of the Prince" (Jarrell) **41**:173, 177, 186, 196
"The Sleeping Fury" (Bogan) **12**:100, 104
The Sleeping Fury (Bogan) **12**:88-90, 105, 109, 111, 120, 122-25, 131
"The Sleeping God" (Sarton) **39**:327, 341
"Sleeping in the Woods" (Wagoner) **33**:347-48
Sleeping in the Woods (Wagoner) **33**:334, 344, 348, 353
Sleeping on Fists (Ríos) **57**:312
"Sleeping on Stones" (Wagoner) **33**:356-57, 361
"Sleeping on the Ceiling" (Bishop) **3**:37; **34**:120, 123, 156
"Sleeping Out at Easter" (Dickey) **40**:154, 189, 212, 240, 258
"Sleeping Out Full Moon" (Brooke) **24**:57
"The Sleeping Rocks" (Mackey) **49**:4, 6
"Sleeping Standing Up" (Bishop) **34**:66, 79, 86, 123, 156
Sleeping windows and door on the roof (Char)
See *Fenêtres dormantes et porte sur le toit*
"Sleeping with Animals" (Kumin) **15**:209, 211, 215, 223
"Sleepless at Crown Point" (Wilbur) **51**:246, 279
"A Sleepless Night" (Levine) **22**:214
"Sleepless Night" (Paz) **48**:273
The Sleepless Night of Eugene Delacroix (Yau) **61**:328, 340
"Sleepwalker Ballad" (García Lorca)
See "Romance sonámbulo"
"Sleet Storm on the Merritt Parkway" (Bly) **39**:89
"The slender wire above the sea of oats" (Tsvetaeva)
See "U tonkoi pnovoloki nad volnoi ovsov"
"Slim Greer" (Brown) **55**:71-73, 75, 110, 120, 156
"Slim Hears 'The Call'" (Brown) **55**:112, 121, 156
"Slim in Atlanta" (Brown) **55**:120-21, 140, 156
"Slim in Hell" (Brown) **55**:112, 115-16, 121, 156
"Slim Lands a Job?" (Brown) **55**:110, 112, 120, 156
"Slipped Quadrant" (Mackey) **49**:20-21, 25, 62, 68
"The Slippers of the Goddess of Beauty" (Lowell) **13**:67
"Slips" (McGuckian) **27**:97
"Slip-Shoe Lovey" (Masters) **1**:333, 336; **36**:176
"Sliver" (Alurista) **34**:27
"Slow Coon" (Brown) **55**:110
Slow down men at work (Char)
See *Ralentir Travaux*
"The Slow Rain" (Mistral)
See "La lluvia lenta"
"The Slow Sounding and Eventual Emergence Of" (Graham) **59**:175
"The Slow Sting of Her Company" (Erdrich) **52**:178
"Slow through the Dark" (Dunbar) **5**:131
Slow Under Construction (Char)
See *Ralentir Travaux*
"Slowness of the Future" (Char) **56**:137-38
"Slug" (Roethke) **15**:274
"Slug in Woods" (Birney) **52**:6, 8, 33, 64-65, 85
"The Sluggish Smoke Curls Up from Some Deep Dell" (Thoreau) **30**:181, 216, 227, 235, 257
"Sluicegates of Thought" (Tzara) **27**:235
"A Slumber Did My Spirit Steal" (Wordsworth) **4**:420
"Small Action Poem" (Tomlinson) **17**:325
"The Small Blue Heron" (Wright) **36**:341-42, 345
"Small Comment" (Sanchez) **9**:224
A Small Desperation (Abse) **41**:9-10, 15, 28, 30
"Small Frogs Killed on a Highway" (Wright) **36**:366
"Small Garden near a Field" (Gallagher) **9**:62
"A Small Grove" (Wright) **36**:311
"The Small Hours" (Parker) **28**:359
"Small Hours" (Plath) **1**:391
Small Hours of the Night: Selected Poems of Roque Dalton (Dalton) **36**:135-37
"The Small Lady" (Smith) **12**:295
"A Small Light" (Song) **21**:344
"Small Moment" (Nemerov) **24**:293
"Small Ode to a Black Cuban Boxer" (Guillén)
See "La Pequeña oda a un negro boxeador cubano"
"A Small Peice of Wood" (McGuckian) **27**:107, 110-111
"Small Perfect Manhattan" (Viereck) **27**:263, 278
"Small Poems for the Winter Solstice" (Atwood) **8**:44
"small port in the outer Fijis" (Birney) **52**:36, 38
"A Small Room with Large Windows" (Curnow) **48**:7-8, 10, 61
A Small Room with Large Windows (Curnow) **48**:3
"Small Song for Crossing a Big River" (Césaire) **25**:32
Small Testament (Villon)
See *Les Lais*
"Small White House" (Warren) **37**:305
"A Small Will" (Montale)
See "Piccolo testamento"
"Small Woman on Swallow Street" (Merwin) **45**:8
The Smallest Muscle in the Human Body (Ríos) **57**:327, 329
"Smalltown Dance" (Wright) **14**:378-79
"The Smell of Gasoline Ascends in My Nose" (Amichai)
See "Reah habenzin 'oleh be'api"
"Smelt Fishing" (Hayden) **6**:196
"Smert" (Lermontov) **18**:302
"Smert' poeta" (Lermontov) **18**:277, 281, 285
"The Smile" (Blake) **12**:35, 43
"The Smile" (Merrill) **28**:248
"Smile" (Silverstein) **49**:349
"Smile, Smile, Smile" (Owen) **19**:354, 357, 359
"The Smile Was" (Abse) **41**:11, 22, 30
"The Smitten Purist" (Riley) **48**:340
"Smoke" (Mahon) **60**:236
"Smoke" (McGuckian) **27**:97
"Smoke" (Reese) **29**:340
"Smoke" (Thoreau) **30**:168, 126, 190, 204, 294
"Smoke and Earth" (Aleixandre) **15**:18-19
"Smoke and Steel" (Sandburg) **2**:304, 316
Smoke and Steel (Sandburg) **41**:243-44, 248, 250, 254-56, 260-62, 267, 270, 274, 277, 284, 286, 297-98, 302, 313-14, 318, 325, 327, 329-30
"The Smokers" (Shapiro) **25**:323
"Smokers of Cheap Cigarettes" (Pavese)
See "Fumatori di carta"
"Smokey the Bear Sutra" (Snyder) **21**:291
"Smooth Gnarled Crape Myrtle" (Moore) **49**:128
"Smothered by the World" (Bly) **39**:12
"Smudging" (Wakoski) **15**:331, 364
Smudging (Wakoski) **15**:332, 345, 364
"Snail" (Hughes) **1**:241; **53**:122
"The Snail's Road" (Wright) **36**:313, 355
"The Snake" (Abse) **41**:25
"The Snake" (Berry) **28**:25
"Snake" (Hughes) **1**:241
"Snake" (Lawrence) **54**:176-77, 179, 181, 187, 189, 223-24, 236
"Snake" (Roethke) **15**:272

"Snake Hunt" (Wagoner) **33**:336
"Snake Hymn" (Hughes) **7**:159
"Snake River" (McKay) **2**:216
"Snakebite" (Dickey) **40**:152, 158, 160, 188, 192
"Snakecharmer" (Plath) **1**:388-89; **37**:188, 207, 238
"Snakes, Mongooses, Snake-Charmers, and the Like" (Moore) **49**:97, 161
"Snakeskin on a Gate" (Wright) **14**:356
"Snap-Dragon" (Lawrence) **54**:163-64, 221
"Snapping the Fringe" (Alexie) **53**:11
Snaps (Cruz) **37**:3, 5, 10-14, 17, 25, 30
"Snaps of Immigration" (Cruz) **37**:35
"Snapshots for Boris Pasternak" (O'Hara) **45**:156
"Snapshots of a Daughter-in-Law" (Rich) **5**:370-72, 396
Snapshots of a Daughter-in-Law: Poems, 1954-1962 (Rich) **5**:354, 358, 363, 369-72, 374, 382, 388, 392
"Snarley-Yow" (Kipling) **3**:158
"Snatch of Sliphorn Jazz" (Sandburg) **41**:287
Snezhnye maski (Blok) **21**:20, 24
"The Snob" (Shapiro) **25**:295
"Snorri Sturluson, (1179-1241)" (Borges) **32**:95
"Snow" (Frost) **1**:195, 215
"Snow" (Hayden) **6**:193, 196
"Snow" (Hughes) **7**:155
"Snow" (Levine) **22**:225
"Snow" (MacNeice) **61**:115, 130, 137, 146, 160
"Snow" (Mueller) **33**:174
"Snow" (Rich) **5**:366
"Snow" (Stone) **53**:228
"Snow" (Thomas) **53**:274
"Snow. Christine sick" (Niedecker) **42**:121
"snow cummin" (Bissett) **14**:20
"The Snow Fairy" (McKay) **2**:228
"The Snow Fences" (Tomlinson) **17**:341
"Snow in Tokyo: A Japanese Poem" (Yevtushenko) **40**:370
"Snow Jobs" (Merrill) **28**:284-85
"The Snow King" (Dove) **6**:108
"Snow King Chair Lift" (Merrill) **28**:222, 257
"The Snow Lamp" (Hayden) **6**:189, 192
"The Snow Leopard" (Jarrell) **41**:174
"The Snow lies sprinkled on the beach" (Bridges) **28**:89
"Snow Maiden" (Blok) **21**:9
The Snow Mask (Blok)
See *Snezhnye maski*
"Snow Melting" (Schnackenberg) **45**:338
"Snow on a Southern State" (Dickey) **40**:182
"The Snow Party" (Mahon) **60**:135, 139, 155, 184, 211
The Snow Party (Mahon) **60**:132, 134, 136, 138-41, 144, 154, 158, 183-84, 198-202, 205-11
The Snow Poems (Ammons) **16**:23-6, 42-7, 49-51, 54, 61-2, 65
"The Snow Queen" (Hacker) **47**:81-82
"Snow) Says! Says" (Cummings) **5**:106
"Snow Shower" (Bryant) **20**:15-16
"Snow Signs" (Tomlinson) **17**:342, 345
"Snow, snow" (Piercy) **29**:315
"The Snow Storm" (Emerson) **18**:79-80, 88, 98, 107
"Snow Upon Paris" (Senghor)
See "Neige sur Paris"
"Snow White" (Sexton) **2**:368
"Snowbanks North of the House" (Bly) **39**:65
"Snowbed" (Celan)
See "Schneebett"
"Snowdrop" (Hughes) **7**:169
"Snowed In" (Austin) **39**:43-44
"Snowfall" (Carducci)
See "Nevicata"
"Snowfall" (Gunn) **26**:203
"Snowfall" (Teasdale) **31**:334
"Snowfall" (Vigny)
See "La neige"
"Snowfall" (Warren) **37**:377-78
"Snowfall in the Afternoon" (Bly) **39**:76, 78, 85
"Snowflakes as Kisses" (Schwarzweller) **8**:314
"The Snowman" (Page) **12**:167-68, 183
"Snows" (Perse)
See "Neiges"
"Snows" (Stryk) **27**:202-3
"So Be It" (Stone) **53**:239-40, 252
"So crewell prison" (Surrey) **59**:316, 327, 330, 338, 352-58
"So Far As the Future Is Concerned" (Moore)
See "The Past Is the Present"
"So Frost Astounds" (Warren) **37**:331
"So I Said I Am Ezra" (Ammons) **16**:39
"So Intricately Is This World Resolved" (Kunitz) **19**:170
"So Long!" (O'Hara) **45**:192
"So Long Charlie Parker" (Brathwaite) **56**:45
"So Many Things Terrify, So Many" (Cisneros)
See "Tantas Cosas Asustan, Tantas"
"So Mexicans Are Taking Jobs from Americans" (Baca) **41**:37
"So Much Depends" (Williams) **7**:362
"So Old" (Snyder) **21**:307
"So Slight" (Jackson) **44**:29
"So, so breake off this last lamenting kisse" (Donne)
See "The Expiration"
"So sweet love seemed that April morn" (Bridges) **28**:86
"So To Fatness Come" (Smith) **12**:326
"So trust me . . ." (Rimbaud)
See "Fiez-vous donc à moi . . ."
"So We Grew Together" (Masters) **1**:326-26, 328; **36**:175
"So What" (Stone) **53**:258
"So What's Wrong" (Stone) **53**:256
"the So-and-So's" (Cisneros) **52**:163
"Soap Suds" (MacNeice) **61**:176-77
Sobranie sochinenij (Mandelstam) **14**:113, 117, 123
"Sobrera" (Castro) **41**:89
Sochineniia (Akhmatova) **55**:25
Social Credit, An Impact (Pound) **4**:328
Social Ironies (Abse) **41**:3
"The Social Muse" (MacLeish) **47**:134, 151
"Social Revolution in England" (Abse) **41**:7
"Sociedad de amigos y protectores" (Fuertes) **27**:16
"Socrates' Ghost Must Haunt Me Now" (Schwartz) **8**:302, 315
"Les soeurs de charité" (Rimbaud) **57**:174, 177, 245, 251
"The Sofa" (Cowper) **40**:45, 51, 58, 127, 130
"The Sofa" (McGuckian) **27**:98
"Soft Wood" (Lowell) **3**:211
"Softer-Mother's Tale" (Wordsworth) **4**:373
"Il Sogno del prigioniero" (Montale) **13**:104
"Sogno d'estate" (Carducci) **46**:50, 63, 65-66
"Sograzhdanam" (Akhmatova) **55**:16
Söhne (Benn) **35**:29, 30, 45, 46
"Soho Cinema" (Lorde) **12**:140
"Soho: Saturday Night" (Abse) **41**:3
"Sohrab and Rustum" (Arnold) **5**:9, 12-13, 33, 35, 37, 45, 52, 62
"Soil" (Szirtes) **51**:172
"Soiled Dove" (Sandburg) **41**:336
"The Soil-Map" (McGuckian) **27**:97
"Un soir" (Apollinaire) **7**:46
"Le Soir" (Bonnefoy) **58**:167-68
"Le soir" (Lamartine) **16**:275-76, 298-99, 302
"Soir de carnaval" (Laforgue) **14**:92
"Soir historique" (Rimbaud) **57**:239-40, 247, 283
"Le soir qu'amour vous fist en la salle descendre" (Ronsard) **11**:264-66
"Le Soir Tombe" (Borges) **32**:103
"Une soirée perdue" (Gautier) **18**:136-37
"Sojourn in a Whale" (Moore) **49**:100-101, 112, 116, 122, 161
"Sokolinya slobodka" (Tsvetaeva) **14**:326
"El sol" (Aleixandre) **15**:25
Sól (Szymborska) **44**:268
"Sol e amore" (Carducci) **46**:48
"Sol en la boda" (Guillén) **35**:182, 188
"El sol victorioso" (Aleixandre) **15**:19
"Sola con esperanza" (Fuertes) **27**:8, 29
Sola en la sala (Fuertes) **27**:17-8, 21, 38
"SOLACE IN WORDS" (Bissett) **14**:33
"Solar" (Larkin) **21**:250-51
"Solar Ode to the People's Army" (Neruda)
See "Oda solar al ejérito del pueblo"
"Un soldado de Lee" (Borges) **32**:87
"Soldati" (Ungaretti) **57**:359
"Solde" (Rimbaud) **3**:261, 264; **57**:194, 228, 248, 271
"The Soldier" (Brooke) **24**:54, 59, 63-4, 71, 74, 80, 86-7, 89
"Soldier" (Herbert)
See "Zolnierz"
"The Soldier" (Hopkins) **15**:144
"The Soldier" (Jarrell) **41**:179
The Soldier (Aiken) **26**:24
"Soldier Asleep at the Tomb" (Schnackenberg) **45**:334
"Soldier, Soldier" (Kipling) **3**:163, 188-89
"A Soldier under Lee" (Borges)
See "Un soldado de Lee"
"The Soldier Walks under the Trees of the University" (Jarrell) **41**:180
"The Soldiers" (Duncan) **2**:104
"Soldiers" (Ungaretti)
See "Soldati"
"Soldier's Dream" (Owen) **19**:341, 356
"Soldier's Farm" (Wright) **14**:340
"A Soldier's Son" (Boland) **58**:42
"Soldier's Song" (Burns) **6**:78
"De Sole" (Tomlinson) **17**:336
"Soledad" (Hayden) **6**:194, 196
"Soledad" (Storni) **33**:235, 239, 271;
Soledad (Paz) **1**:366
"Soledades of the Sun and Moon" (Hope) **56**:268, 273, 307
Soleil Cou-Coupé (Césaire) **25**:15, 23, 30-2, 35, 44
Le soleil des eaux (Char) **56**:181
"Soleil et chair" (Rimbaud) **3**:251, 280, 283, 285; **57**:174, 202, 208, 244-46, 248, 250-51, 284
"Soleil était encore chaud . . ." (Rimbaud) **57**:243-45, 248, 253
"Soleil route usée" (Péret) **33**:230
"Soleils couchants" (Verlaine) **32**:362-63, 382, 387
"Soliloquio del individuo" (Parra) **39**:261, 288
"Soliloquy" (Jeffers) **17**:132
"Soliloquy" (Muir) **49**:224, 227, 229, 233
"Soliloquy for Cassandra" (Szymborska) **44**:300
"Soliloquy of a Misanthrope" (Hughes) **7**:116
"Soliloquy of the Spanish Cloister" (Browning) **2**:37
"Le solitaire" (Lamartine) **16**:281
"The Solitary" (Teasdale) **31**:323, 333, 371, 380, 389
"The Solitary Life" (Leopardi)
See "La vita solitaria"
"The Solitary Place" (Muir) **49**:242, 288
"The Solitary Reaper" (Wordsworth) **4**:399, 404
"The Solitary Sparrow" (Leopardi)
See "Il Passero Solitario"
"Solitude" (Ishikawa)
See "Kyoko"
"La solitude" (Lamartine) **16**:277
"A Solitude" (Swinburne) **24**:327
"Solitude Late at Night in the Woods" (Bly) **39**:82
"Solitudes at Sixty" (Sassoon) **12**:259
"Solo de lune" (Laforgue) **14**:74-6
"Solo de piano" (Parra) **39**:264, 299
Solo na raskalennoi trube (Shvarts) **50**:162
Solo on a White-Hot Trumpet (Shvarts)
See *Solo na raskalennoi trube*
"Sólo por juego, nunca" (Guillén) **35**:198-99

"Solominka, The Straw" (Mandelstam) **14**:111-12, 124
"Solomon and the Witch" (Yeats) **51**:151
"Solonique" (Apollinaire) **7**:48
"Solstice" (Jeffers) **17**:111, 127, 141
"Solstice" (Lorde) **12**:153
Solstice and Other Poems (Jeffers) **17**:111, 125, 135
Solstices (MacNeice) **61**:125, 176, 182
"Solution" (Oppen) **35**:331
"The Solution" (Stone) **53**:221
"Som de escalina" (Eliot) **5**:201
Sombra del paraíso (Aleixandre) **15**:6, 8, 10-11, 15-16, 18, 21, 22-5, 33-4, 37-8, 40-1
"Sombre Figuration" (Stevens) **6**:298, 318, 320
Some (Ashbery) **26**:167, 172
"Some Answers Are Cold Comfort to the Dead" (Schwartz) **8**:293
"Some Are Born" (Smith) **12**:316
"Some Brilliant Sky" (Wakoski) **15**:336
some changes (Jordan) **38**:114, 118-20, 122
"Some Contemporary Poets of the Negro Race" (Braithwaite) **52**:118
"Some Dreams They Forgot" (Bishop) **34**:190
"Some Extensions on the Sovereignty of Science" (Ríos) **57**:327
"Some Eyes Condemn" (Thomas) **53**:271
"Some Foreign Letters" (Sexton) **2**:350, 361, 363
"Some Foreign Wife" (Sexton) **2**:359
"Some Friends from Pascagoula" (Stevens) **6**:337
"Some Greek Writings" (Corso) **33**:33-34, 38, 44
"Some Last Questions" (Merwin) **45**:9, 21-2, 42
"Some Like Poetry" (Szymborska)
See "Some People Like Poetry"
"Some Lines" (Viereck) **27**:280
"Some Lines in Three Parts" (Viereck) **27**:263, 278, 280, 282
"Some Negatives: X at the Chateu" (Merrill) **28**:242
"Some Notes on Organic Form" (Levertov) **11**:160-62
"Some People" (Jordan) **38**:127, 145
"Some People Like Poetry" (Szymborska) **44**:292
"Some Quadrangles" (Swenson) **14**:273
"Some San Francisco Poems" (Oppen) **35**:285, 335, 337, 340, 342
"Some Things You'll Need to Know Before You Join the Union" (Stone) **53**:220, 229, 243, 253
Some Time (Zukofsky) **11**:343
"Some Trees" (Ashbery) **26**:118
Some Trees (Ashbery) **26**:111, 113, 118, 129, 135, 137, 143, 162, 164
"Some Verses Upon the Burning of Our House, July 10th, 1666" (Bradstreet) **10**:8, 19, 21, 27, 29-30, 34, 36-7, 42
"Some Years" (Ríos) **57**:325
"Somebody" (Borges) **32**:58
"Somebody's Song" (Parker) **28**:351
"Somehow It Doesn't Write Itself" (Ignatow) **34**:310
"Someone Is Harshly Coughing as Before" (Schwartz) **8**:301
"Someone Talking to Himself" (Wilbur) **51**:208, 223, 232, 308
"Somersault" (Sarton) **39**:325, 332
"Something A Direction" (Tomlinson) **17**:312
"Something Borrowed" (Piercy) **29**:302
"Something for Hope" (Frost) **1**:200
"Something Like a Sonnet for Phillis Miracle Wheatley" (Jordan) **38**:125
"Something Missing" (Silverstein) **49**:324
"Something There Is" (Corso) **33**:38, 44
"Something to Wear" (Levertov) **11**:165-66, 168
"Something Was Happening" (Hughes) **7**:154
Sometimes (Yau) **61**:333
"Sometimes Even Now" (Brooke) **24**:62
"Sometimes I Am Very Happy and Desperate" (Amichai) **38**:46
"Sometimes I fled the fire that me brent" (Wyatt) **27**:368
"Somewhat Delayed Spring Song" (Parker) **28**:355
"Somewhere" (Abse) **41**:31
"Somewhere" (Nemerov) **24**:262
"Somewhere East o' Suez" (Kipling) **3**:189
"Somewhere I Have Never Travelled, Gladly Beyond" (Cummings) **5**:88
"Somewhere in Africa" (Sexton) **2**:364, 371
"Sommarnatten" (Ekeloef) **23**:76
"Sommation" (Hugo) **17**:98, 100
"Sommeil aux Lupercales" (Char) **56**:123, 157
"Le Sommet de la tour" (Gautier) **18**:143, 146
"Somnambulent Ballad" (García Lorca)
See "Romance sonámbulo"
"Somnambulist Ballad" (García Lorca)
See "Romance sonámbulo"
"Son" (Brathwaite) **56**:51
"Son and Mother" (Blok) **21**:14
"Son del bloqueo" (Guillén) **23**:126
El son entero (Guillén) **23**:100, 108, 131, 139, 142
"Son más en una mazorca" (Guillén) **23**:125
Son Motifs (Guillén)
See *Motivos de son*
"Son numero 6" (Guillén) **23**:127, 130, 132, 139
"The Son of Croesus" (Morris) **55**:305
"Son of Judas" (Wright) **36**:377
Son of the People (Quintana)
See *Hijo del Pueblo*
"Soñador que camina" (Guillén) **35**:230
"Soñar" (Storni) **33**:319;
"Sonar tari" (Tagore) **8**:408
Sonar tari (Tagore) **8**:409, 418, 427
"Sonata" (Schnackenberg) **45**:330, 337
"Sonata for Methylated Prose" (Ekeloef) **23**:85
"sonatform denaturerad prosa" (Ekeloef) **23**:75
"Sonatina" (Darío) **15**:79-80, 95, 107-08, 110, 119-20
"Los soñetos de la muerte" (Mistral) **32**:143, 149-50, 152, 154, 161, 165, 176
Soñetos de la muerte (Mistral) **32**:164, 200
"Sonetos de la poda" (Mistral) **32**:188-89
Sonetos espirituales (Jiménez) **7**:191-92, 194-96, 202, 211
Sonette (Goethe) **5**:248, 250
Sonette an Orpheus (Rilke) **2**:267-68, 277, 280-81, 283, 290, 293, 295
Die Sonette an Orpheus/Sonnets to Orpheus (Rilke)
See *Sonette an Orpheus*
Sonety Krymskie (Mickiewicz) **38**:158, 166, 191, 194, 215, 221, 223-25
"Song" (Abse) **41**:6
"Song" (Behn)
See "Love Arm'd"
"Song" (Berry) **28**:7-8
"Song" (Blake) **12**:6
"Song" (Bogan) **12**:86, 90, 103
"Song" (Brontë) **8**:62
"Song" (Cage) **58**:220
"A Song" (Carew) **29**:19
"Song" (Cummings) **5**:109
"Song" (H. D.) **5**:304
"The Song" (Ignatow) **34**:312
"Song" (Kenyon) **57**:14, 36
"Song" (Mackey) **49**:66, 68, 78
"song" (MacNeice) **61**:171
"Song" (Meredith) **60**:245
"Song" (Muir) **49**:205, 226, 245, 250
"Song" (Nemerov) **24**:256
"Song" (O'Hara) **45**:158, 219
"Song" (Poe) **1**:432
"The Song" (Roethke) **15**:269
"Song" (Rossetti) **7**:273, 276, 289
"Song" (Sarton) **39**:325
"Song" (Sitwell) **3**:313
"Song" (Suckling) **30**:127, 130, 139, 158
"Song" (Williams) **7**:408
"Song" (Wright) **14**:338, 342, 347
"A Song about Girls" (Seifert) **47**:340
"Song About Love" (Seifert)
See "Píseň o lásce"
"The Song and Dance of" (Olson) **19**:273
Song and Sonnets (Longfellow) **30**:27
"Song: Aske me no more" (Carew) **29**:73
"Song at Capri" (Teasdale) **31**:340
"Song at Fifty" (Kavanagh) **33**:81
"Song at the End of Winter" (Wagoner) **33**:370-71
"Song Before Drinking" (Li Po) **29**:142
"The Song before Sailing" (Carman) **34**:213
Song Books (Cage) **58**:218
"Song Coming toward Us" (Forché) **10**:132
"Song for a Banjo Dance" (Hughes) **53**:91-92
"Song for a Dark Girl" (Hughes) **1**:238, 243
"Song for a Hypothetical Age" (Muir) **49**:280
"Song for a Lady" (Sexton) **2**:352
"Song for a Lyre" (Bogan) **12**:90, 92
"Song for a Phallus" (Hughes) **7**:132, 159, 171
"Song for a Red Night Gown" (Sexton) **2**:352-53
"Song for a Slight Voice" (Bogan) **12**:90, 92
"Song for a Viola d'Amore" (Lowell) **13**:88, 97
"Song for Billie Holiday" (Hughes) **53**:114
"The Song for Colin" (Teasdale) **31**:330, 332, 338
"A Song for J. H." (Behn) **13**:19
"A Song for New-Ark" (Giovanni) **19**:143
"Song for Nobody" (Merton) **10**:349
"A Song for Occupations" (Whitman) **3**:385, 401-02
"SONG FOR OOLJAH" (Bissett) **14**:33
"A Song for Rosemarie" (Villa) **22**:354
"A Song for Simeon" (Eliot) **5**:194, 196-97, 203, 205, 209
"A Song for Soweto" (Jordan) **38**:130-31
Song for St Cecilia's Day (Dryden) **25**:75-8
"Song for Sunsets" (Birney) **52**:74
"Song for the Death of Averroës" (Merton) **10**:343
"Song for the Last Act" (Bogan) **12**:124
"A Song for the Middle of the Night" (Wright) **36**:335, 373
"Song for the Mothers of Dead Militiamen" (Neruda)
See "Canto a las madres de los milicianos muertos"
"Song for the Next River" (Gallagher) **9**:35
"Song for the Pockets" (Soto) **28**:375
"A Song for the Ragged Schools of London" (Browning) **6**:7, 23
"Song for the Rainy Season" (Bishop) **3**:67; **34**:91, 105
"Song for the Renewal of Power" (Wagoner) **33**:353
"Song for the Saddest Ides" (Nash) **21**:263
"Song for the Squeeze Box" (Roethke) **15**:256
"A Song for the Year's End" (Zukofsky) **11**:349
"Song from the Highest Tower" (Rimbaud)
See "Chanson de la plus haute tour"
"Song from the Second Floor" (Wagoner) **33**:357, 367
"A Song from the Structures of Rime Ringing as the Poet Paul Celan Sings" (Duncan) **2**:117
"Song. 'Goe, and catche a falling starre'" (Donne) **1**:125
"Song I" (Rilke) **2**:273
"Song in a Wine-Bar" (Wright) **14**:333
"Song in a year of Catastrophe" (Berry) **28**:43
"A Song in the Front Yard" (Brooks) **7**:69
"Song in the Songless" (Meredith) **60**:327
"Song: Lift-Boy" (Graves) **6**:142, 144
"The Song Maker" (Teasdale) **31**:321
"Song Making" (Teasdale) **31**:351, 359-60, 379
"Song: Not There" (Jarrell) **41**:174
"Song of a camera" (Gunn) **26**:212
"Song of a Dream Visit to T'ien-mu: Farewell to Those I Leave Behind" (Li Po) **29**:147

"Song of a Hebrew" (Abse) **41**:6
"Song of a Man Who Has Come Through" (Lawrence) **54**:182-83, 216-17
"Song of a Man Who Is Loved" (Lawrence) **54**:183
"Song of a Man Who Is Not Loved" (Lawrence) **54**:183
"The Song of a Rat" (Hughes) **7**:142, 155-56, 159
"The Song of Absinthe Granny" (Stone) **53**:228-29, 237-38, 258
"Song of Another Tribe" (Rukeyser) **12**:217
"Song of Autumn in Spring" (Darío)
See "Canción de otoño en primavera"
"Song of Color" (Walker) **30**:352
"The Song of Courtesy" (Meredith) **60**:294, 308
"Song of Days" (Meredith) **60**:331
"Song of Death" (Mistral)
See "Canción de la Muerte"
"Song of Defeat" (Tagore)
See "Parajaya sangīt"
"Song of Despair" (Carducci)
See "Desperata"
"Song of Despair" (Neruda) **4**:301
"The Song of Diego Valdez" (Kipling) **3**:182
"The Song of God's Child" (Li Ho) **13**:52
The Song of Hiawatha (Longfellow) **30**:16, 20-2, 25, 28-30, 34-5, 38-40, 44, 55-57, 59-61, 65, 73-4, 77-80, 82-4, 87-8
"Song of Invisible Boundaries" (Glück) **16**:166
"A Song of Joys" (Whitman) **3**:402
"Song of Li Ling" (Wang Wei) **18**:389
"A Song of Liberty" (Blake) **12**:33
"The Song of Love" (Carducci)
See "Il canto dell' amore"
"Song of Love" (Lamartine)
See "Chant d'amour"
"A Song of my heart" (Bridges) **28**:69
"Song of Myself" (Whitman) **3**:370, 394, 396-97, 399, 401-03, 405, 411-12, 414-17
"The Song of Nature" (Emerson) **18**:88
"Song of Opposites" (Keats) **1**:312
"Song of P'eng-ya" (Tu Fu) **9**:321, 332
"Song of Praise" (Cullen) **20**:52, 63
"A Song of Praise" (Sanchez) **9**:243
"The Song of Safe Conduct" (Bonnefoy)
See "Le Chant de sauvegarde"
"A Song of Sherwood" (Noyes) **27**:136-137
"Song of Siberia" (Ishikawa)
See "Shiberia no uta"
"A Song of Sojourner Truth" (Jordan) **38**:125
"Song of Spain" (Hughes) **53**:115
"Song of Taurus" (Mistral)
See "Canción de taurus"
"Song of the Andoumboulou: 1" (Mackey) **49**:37
"Song of the Andoumboulou: 3" (Mackey) **49**:31, 37-38, 43
"Song of the Andoumboulou: 4" (Mackey) **49**:6
"Song of the Andoumboulou: 5" (Mackey) **49**:3, 39, 71, 74
"Song of the Andoumboulou: 6" (Mackey) **49**:4, 31, 42-44
"Song of the Andoumboulou: 7" (Mackey) **49**:4, 37, 42
"Song of the Andoumboulou: 10" (Mackey) **49**:39
"Song of the Andoumboulou: 11" (Mackey) **49**:71
"Song of the Andoumboulou: 14" (Mackey) **49**:39
"Song of the Andoumboulou: 15" (Mackey) **49**:30, 40, 70
"Song of the Andoumboulou: 16" (Mackey) **49**:42, 54-55, 61, 64, 68, 70
"Song of the Andoumboulou: 1-7" (Mackey) **49**:30, 55-7
"Song of the Andoumboulou: 18" (Mackey) **49**:57, 63, 77-79
"Song of the Andoumboulou: 19" (Mackey) **49**:68
"Song of the Andoumboulou: 20" (Mackey) **49**:57
"Song of the Andoumboulou: 23" (Mackey) **49**:42, 74
"Song of the Andoumboulou: 24" (Mackey) **49**:42
"Song of the Andoumboulou: 26" (Mackey) **49**:57, 67
"Song of the Andoumboulou: 27" (Mackey) **49**:58
"Song of the Andoumboulou: 30" (Mackey) **49**:80
"Song of the Andoumboulou: 31" (Mackey) **49**:58
"Song of the Andoumboulou: 34" (Mackey) **49**:68, 76
"Song of the Andoumboulou: 35" (Mackey) **49**:58, 64, 80
"Song of the Andoumboulou: 8-15" (Mackey) **49**:30
Song of the Andoumboulou: 18-20 (Mackey) **49**:2-3, 17, 25, 29, 31-36, 38-42, 45, 47, 51-53, 56, 58-59, 61-62, 65-68, 71-72, 74-75, 77-78
"Song of the Answerer" (Whitman) **3**:386, 390
"Song of the Banjo" (Kipling) **3**:160-61
"Song of the Beasts" (Brooke) **24**:59, 82
"Song of the Beautiful Ladies" (Tu Fu) **9**:320
"Song of the Bird" (Tagore)
See "Vihanger gan"
"Song of the Blind Artificer" (Schwerner)
See "Tablet XXVI"
"The Song of the Bongo" (Guillén)
See "La canción del bongo"
"The Song of the Bower" (Rossetti) **44**:165
"The Song of the Chattahoochee" (Lanier) **50**:77-78, 98-99; **50**:56, 92
"The Song of the Children" (Chesterton) **28**:100
"Song of the Children in Heaven" (Brooke) **24**:76
"The Song of the Cities" (Kipling) **3**:162
The Song of the Cold (Sitwell) **3**:320, 326
"Song of the Columns" (Valéry)
See "Cantique des colonnes"
"Song of the Crows roosting at night" (Li Po) **29**:143
"Song of the Dead" (Kipling) **3**:160, 162
"A Song of the Dust" (Sitwell) **3**:327
"A Song of the English" (Kipling) **3**:160-62, 164
"The Song of the Exiles" (Kipling) **3**:194
"The Song of the Final Meeting/Song of the Last Meeting" (Akhmatova)
See "Pesnia poslednei vstrechi"
"The Song of the Galley Slaves" (Kipling) **3**:170
"The Song of the Happy Shepherd" (Yeats) **20**:354; **51**:149
"Song of the Heavenly Horse" (Li Po) **29**:159, 161
"Song of the Highest Tower" (Rimbaud) **3**:259
"The Song of the Ill-beloved" (Apollinaire)
See "La chanson du mal-aimé"
"Song of the Little Square" (García Lorca)
See "Ballada de la Placeta"
The Song of the Merchant Kaláshnikov (Lermontov)
See *Pesnya pro tsarya Ivana Vasilievicha, molodogo oprichnika i undalogo kuptsa Kalashnikova*
"Song of the Native Land" (Seifert) **47**:326
Song of the Night (Leopardi)
See "Canto notturno di un pastore errante dell'Asia"
"Song of the Open Road" (Whitman) **3**:387
"Song of the Peach Fountainhead" (Wang Wei) **18**:389
"The Song of the Pilgrims" (Brooke) **24**:76
"The Song of the Poorly Beloved" (Apollinaire)
See "La chanson du mal-aimé"
"The Song of the Red War-Boat" (Kipling) **3**:183
"A Song of the Rosy Cros" (Yeats) **51**:103
"Song of the Son" (Toomer) **7**:310, 317, 319, 334
"The Song of the Sons" (Kipling) **3**:162
"A Song of the Soul of Central" (Hughes) **1**:268
"Song of the Sower" (Bryant) **20**:14
"Song of the Stars" (Bryant) **20**:4
"Song of the Taste" (Snyder) **21**:297
Song of the Tsar Ivan Vasilievich, the young oprichnik and the bold Merchant Kalashnikov (Lermontov)
See *Pesnya pro tsarya Ivana Vasilievicha, molodogo oprichnika i undalogo kuptsa Kalashnikova*
"Song of the Worms" (Atwood) **8**:19, 25
"Song of Theodolinda" (Meredith) **60**:250
The Song of Tzar Ivan Vasiljevich, His Young Life-Guardsman, and the Valiant Merchant Kaláshnikov (Lermontov)
See *Pesnya pro tsarya Ivana Vasilievicha, molodogo oprichnika i undalogo kuptsa Kalashnikova*
The Song of Viktorka (Seifert)
See *Píseň o Viktorce*
"Song of Virgo" (Mistral)
See "Canción de virgo"
"Song of Women" (Masters) **1**:330, 333
Song Offerings (Tagore)
See *Gitanjali*
"A Song on Gazing at Chung-nan Mountain For Hsü of the Secretariat" (Wang Wei) **18**:369
"A Song on Greife" (Finch) **21**:150, 152, 179
"Song over Some Ruins" (Neruda)
See "Canto sobre unas ruinas"
"A Song: Sensation Time at the Home" (Merton) **10**:345
"A Song Sparrow Singing in the Fall" (Berry) **28**:7
"Song. 'Sweetest love, I do not goe'" (Donne) **1**:130
"Song: The Rev. MuBngwu Dickenson Ruminates behind the Sermon" (Brooks) **7**:94
"A Song to a Negro Wash-woman" (Hughes) **53**:169-70
"A Song to a Scotish Tune (Come My Phillis Let Us Improve)" (Behn) **13**:18
"Song to a Scotish Tune (When Jemmy First Began to Love)" (Behn) **13**:4, 7, 18, 32
"Song to Alfred Hitchcock and Wilkinson" (Ondaatje) **28**:291
"Song to Awaken a Little Black Child" (Guillén) **23**:132
"Song to Celia" (Jonson) **17**:170, 180
A Song to David (Smart) **13**:328-34, 336-46, 352-54, 358, 360-65, 367-69
"Song to Ishtar" (Levertov) **11**:169
"A Song to No Music" (Brodsky) **9**:4, 9, 12
"Song to Woody" (Dylan) **37**:67
"A Song Untitled" (Hagiwara) **18**:173
"Song Winds of Downhill" (Oppen) **35**:340
"Song without Music" (Brodsky)
See "A Song to No Music"
"Songe D'Athalie" (Smith) **12**:331
"Songin Black Armor" (Wylie) **23**:308, 310, 332
"Songless" (Walker) **30**:348
Sóngoro cosongo: Poemas mulatos (Guillén) **23**:98-100, 105-106, 111, 114, 131, 139, 142-44
"Songs" (Benn) **35**:54
"Songs" (Hughes) **1**:241; **53**:134
"Songs" (Lawrence) **54**:183
"Songs" (Mistral)
See "Coplas"
Songs (García Lorca)
See *Canciones*
"Songs:65o N" (Larkin) **21**:226

Songs and Satires (Masters) **1**:328, 335, 342; **36**:174, 176, 183
Songs and Sonets (Donne) **1**:130, 139, 145
Songs and Sonnets (Donne)
See *Songs and Sonets*
Songs and Sonnets (Masters) **36**:221
Songs and Sonnets (Surrey) **59**:290, 310
Songs and Sonnets, second series (Masters) **1**:321, 325, 332
Songs before Sunrise (Swinburne) **24**:312
"Songs for a Colored Singer" (Bishop) **3**:37, 46-7; **34**:69, 78, 137-38, 160, 188, 190
Songs for a Summer Day (MacLeish) **47**:182
Songs for Eve (MacLeish) **47**:175-80, 192, 197, 208, 214
"Songs for My Father" (Komunyakaa) **51**:36
"Songs For My Son" (Goodison) **36**:148
"Songs for Myself" (Teasdale) **31**:333, 358, 360, 370, 379
Songs for Naëtt (Senghor)
See *Chants pour Naëtt*
Songs for Soldiers and Tunes for Tourists (Guillén)
See *Cantos para soldados y sones para turistas*
"Songs for the Dream Catchers" (Wagoner) **33**:348
"Songs for the People" (Harper) **21**:189
Songs for the Republic (Cassian) **17**:6
Songs from a Northern Garden (Carman) **34**:205, 210, 225
"Songs from Cyprus" (H. D.) **5**:304
Songs from Vagabondia (Carman) **34**:198, 200, 205-08, 214, 218-20, 229, 231, 237-38
"Songs in a Cornfield" (Rossetti) **7**:275
Songs of Bhanusigh Thakur (Tagore)
See *Bhanusingh Thakurer padavali*
Songs of Crow (Hughes) **7**:140
"Songs of Education" (Chesterton) **28**:99
Songs of Experience (Blake) **12**:9-10, 23-5, 31, 33-5, 42-7, 61-2
Songs of Innocence (Blake) **12**:8-9, 19, 21-4, 32-4, 42, 61
Songs of Innocence and of Experience: Shewing the Two Contrary States of the Human Soul (Blake) **12**:8-11, 33-4, 42-3, 51
Songs of Jamaica (McKay) **2**:208, 210, 216, 221, 223-27
Songs of Kabir (Kabīr) **56**:316
Songs of Life and Hope (Darío)
See *Cantos de vida y esperanza*
"The Songs of Maximus" (Olson) **19**:282-83
"Songs of Release" (Goodison) **36**:152
"Songs of the Hen's Head" (Atwood) **8**:41
"Songs of the Ingenues" (Verlaine)
See "La chanson des ingénues"
"songs of the old frogs" (Alurista) **34**:32
"Songs of the Pixies" (Coleridge) **39**:212
"Songs of the Runaway Bride" (Gallagher) **9**:37
Songs of the Sea Children (Carman) **34**:205, 209-11, 224-26
"Songs of the Shade" (Senghor)
See *Chants d'ombre*
Songs of the Springtides (Swinburne) **24**:322
"Songs of the Transformed" (Atwood) **8**:23, 25-6
Songs of Victory (Pindar)
See *Victory Odes*
"Songs out of Sorrow" (Teasdale) **31**:322, 355-56
"Songs to Survive the Summer" (Hass) **16**:199, 201, 210-16
Songs without Words (Verlaine)
See *Romances sans paroles*
"sonik prayr" (Bissett) **14**:27
"The Sonne" (Herbert) **4**:109
"The Sonne hath twyse" (Surrey) **59**:312
"Sonnet" (Bishop) **34**:55, 63, 69, 90-91
"Sonnet" (Bogan) **12**:98, 110
"A Sonnet" (Raleigh) **31**:297
"Sonnet" (Rimbaud) **57**:271-72
"Sonnet" (Wilbur) **51**:300
"Sonnet II" (Thomas) **2**:388
"Sonnet III" (Thomas) **2**:388
"Sonnet 7" (Milton) **19**:214, 256
"Sonnet VIII" (Thomas) **2**:388
"Sonnet X" (Thomas) **2**:388
"Sonnet XVI" (Browning) **6**:17
"Sonnet 16 (On his blindness)" (Milton) **19**:214
"Sonnet at Christmas" (Tate) **50**:234
"Sonnet boiteux" (Verlaine) **32**:375, 401, 406
"Le Sonnet des voyelles" (Rimbaud) **57**:226
"Sonnet du trou du cul" (Rimbaud) **57**:203
"Sonnet en -yx" (Mallarmé) **4**:214-15, 218
"Sonnet Entitled How to Run the World)" (Cummings) **5**:106
"Sonnet for the Seventh of August" (Belloc) **24**:43-4
"A Sonnet from the Stony Brook" (Jordan) **38**:125
"Sonnet héroïque" (Verlaine) **2**:416
"Sonnet I" (Meredith) **60**:310, 313, 315, 317-18, 320
"Sonnet I" (Patmore) **59**:257
"Sonnet II" (Meredith) **60**:265, 272, 310, 313, 315, 319-20
"Sonnet II" (Suckling) **30**:129
"Sonnet III" (Meredith) **60**:266, 310-11, 315, 319-20
"Sonnet III" (Suckling) **30**:140
"Sonnet IL" (Meredith) **60**:314-15
"Sonnet in Polka Dots" (Villa) **22**:351
"Sonnet in time of Revolt" (Brooke) **24**:62, 82
"Sonnet IV" (Meredith) **60**:264-65, 274, 311, 313-15, 319-2
"Sonnet IX" (Meredith) **60**:265, 271-72, 274, 311, 313, 315, 317, 320-21, 323, 342-43
"Sonnet L" (Meredith) **60**:275-76, 305, 313, 315, 317, 345
"Sonnet No. 1" (Surrey) **59**:285
"Sonnet No. 4" (Surrey) **59**:285
"Sonnet No. 6" (Surrey) **59**:285
"Sonnet No. 8" (Surrey) **59**:285
"Sonnet No. 9" (Surrey) **59**:285
"Sonnet No. 11" (Surrey) **59**:285
"Sonnet No. 12" (Surrey) **59**:285
"Sonnet No. 13" (Surrey) **59**:285
"Sonnet No. 14" (Surrey) **59**:285
"Sonnet No. 16" (Surrey) **59**:285
"Sonnet No. 18" (Surrey) **59**:285
"Sonnet No. 19" (Surrey) **59**:285
"Sonnet No. 20" (Surrey) **59**:285
"Sonnet No. 21" (Surrey) **59**:285
"Sonnet No. 40" (Surrey) **59**:285
"Sonnet No. 44" (Surrey) **59**:285
"Sonnet No. 45" (Surrey) **59**:285
"Sonnet No. 47" (Surrey) **59**:285
"Sonnet No. 91" (Surrey) **59**:286
"Sonnet of the Blood" (Tate) **50**:245, 255
"Sonnet of the Vowels" (Rimbaud)
See "Le Sonnet des voyelles"
"Sonnet on an Alpine Night" (Parker) **28**:351
"Sonnet on Beauty" (Tate) **50**:228-29
"Sonnet on Rare Animals" (Meredith) **28**:172, 188
"Sonnet On Seeing a Piece of Our Artillery Brought Into Action" (Owen) **19**:336
"Sonnet Reversed" (Brooke) **24**:56, 64
"Sonnet (Suggested by some of the Proceedings of the Society for Physical Research)" (Brooke) **24**:58, 73
"Sonnet: To a Child" (Owen) **19**:343
"Sonnet to an Ox" (Carducci)
See "Il bove"
"Sonnet— to My Mother" (Poe) **1**:439, 445-46
"Sonnet to Satan" (Plath) **37**:207-8
"Sonnet 2" (Suckling)
See "Sonnet II"
"Sonnet V" (Meredith) **60**:272, 311, 315, 319-20, 342
"Sonnet V" (Wylie) **23**:304
"Sonnet VI" (Meredith) **60**:265, 271, 309, 311, 315, 318-20, 342
"Sonnet VII" (Meredith) **60**:265, 272, 274-75, 310-11, 342
"Sonnet VIII" (Meredith) **60**:310-11, 314, 320-21, 323, 342
"Sonnet with the Compliments of the Season" (Chesterton) **28**:114
"Sonnet X" (Meredith) **60**:311, 320-21
"Sonnet XI" (Meredith) **60**:313, 321, 344
"Sonnet XII" (Meredith) **60**:313, 323
"Sonnet XIII" (Meredith) **60**:271, 301, 344
"Sonnet XIV" (Meredith) **60**:273, 312, 322
"Sonnet XIX" (Meredith) **60**:271, 312, 314, 321-22
"Sonnet XL" (Meredith) **60**:267, 312, 314, 322, 324
"Sonnet XLI" (Meredith) **60**:275, 312, 314
"Sonnet XLII" (Meredith) **60**:267, 275, 312, 343
"Sonnet XLIII" (Meredith) **60**:267, 270, 276, 303-4, 312, 314, 324, 343-44
"Sonnet XLIV" (Meredith) **60**:272, 276, 280, 313-14, 323
"Sonnet XLIX" (Meredith) **60**:268, 273, 303-5, 313, 317, 320
"Sonnet XLV" (Meredith) **60**:267, 310, 314
"Sonnet XLVI" (Meredith) **60**:267, 314, 344
"Sonnet XLVII" (Meredith) **60**:276, 303-5, 313-14, 324, 344
"Sonnet XLVIII" (Meredith) **60**:268, 272, 304-5, 310, 313-14, 323, 344
"Sonnet XV" (Meredith) **60**:266, 271, 312, 342
"Sonnet XVI" (Meredith) **60**:266, 313, 321, 323
"Sonnet XVII" (Meredith) **60**:300, 306, 312-13, 321
"Sonnet XVL" (Meredith) **60**:323
"Sonnet XX" (Meredith) **60**:265, 312
"Sonnet XXI" (Meredith) **60**:313, 321
"Sonnet XXII" (Meredith) **60**:311, 313, 342
"Sonnet XXIII" (Meredith) **60**:267, 311, 313-14, 317, 321, 323-24, 343
"Sonnet XXIV" (Meredith) **60**:267, 311, 313, 341, 344
"Sonnet XXIX" (Meredith) **60**:273, 312-14, 345
"Sonnet XXV" (Meredith) **60**:266, 271, 312-13, 322
"Sonnet XXVI" (Meredith) **60**:275, 310
"Sonnet XXVII" (Meredith) **60**:266, 273, 310, 312-13, 321-22
"Sonnet XXVIII" (Meredith) **60**:266, 269, 310, 312-14, 345
"Sonnet XXX" (Meredith) **60**:273, 313-14, 344-45
"Sonnet XXXI" (Meredith) **60**:272-73, 311, 314, 324
"Sonnet XXXII" (Meredith) **60**:273, 313, 344-45
"Sonnet XXXIII" (Meredith) **60**:266, 273, 275, 310, 313-14, 324
"Sonnet XXXIV" (Meredith) **60**:267, 310, 312, 322, 343
"Sonnet XXXIX" (Meredith) **60**:267, 273-74, 314, 321, 343
"Sonnet XXXV" (Meredith) **60**:267, 312
"Sonnet XXXVI" (Meredith) **60**:273
"Sonnet XXXVII" (Meredith) **60**:312
"Sonnet XXXVIII" (Meredith) **60**:267, 271, 312, 314
"Sonnets" (Suckling) **30**:118
Sonnets (Carruth) **10**:91
Sonnets (Mickiewicz)
See *Sonety Krymskie*
Sonnets (Rilke) **2**:280-82
Sonnets and Verse (Belloc) **24**:11, 31-3, 36, 38, 40
"Sonnets at Christmas" (Tate) **50**:252, 255-56
Sonnets at Christmas (Tate) **50**:231, 251
Sonnets et madrigals pour astrée (Ronsard) **11**:250
Sonnets for Hélène (Ronsard)
See *Sonnets pour Hélène*
"Sonnets from an Ungrafted Tree" (Millay) **6**:224-25, 228, 230-32, 235, 239

Sonnets from the Crimea (Mickiewicz)
See *Sonety Krymskie*
Sonnets from the Portuguese (Browning) **6**:4-6, 15-8, 22, 32, 36-9, 41-2, 46
"Sonnets of Death" (Mistral)
See "Los soñetos de la muerte"
Sonnets of Death (Mistral)
See *Soñetos de la muerte*
"Sonnets of Pruning" (Mistral)
See "Sonetos de la poda"
"Sonnets of the Blood" (Tate) **50**:230, 244, 255, 275, 293
"Sonnets of the Twelve Months" (Belloc) **24**:29
"Sonnets on Death" (Mistral)
See "Los soñetos de la muerte"
Sonnets pour Hélène (Ronsard) **11**:218, 220-22, 239, 242, 250, 254, 275-76, 278, 283
"Sonnets That Please" (Stein) **18**:341
"Sonnets to Baudelaire" (Hope) **56**:281, 289, 298, 300, 304
"Sonnets to Duse" (Teasdale) **31**:340
Sonnets to Duse, and Other Poems (Teasdale) **31**:321, 324, 329, 335, 337, 344, 346, 378
"Sono pronto ripeto, ma pronto a che?" (Montale) **13**:139
"sonora desert poem" (Clifton) **17**:27
"The Son's Sorrow: From the Icelandic" (Morris) **55**:340
"Soon to be a National Geographic Special" (Alexie) **53**:24
"Soonest Mended" (Ashbery) **26**:125-126, 134, 138, 141, 149
"The soote season" (Surrey) **59**:285, 297, 311-12, 319-20
"Sophist Leaving Syria" (Cavafy) **36**:76, 80, 104, 106
"Sopra il monumento di Dante" (Leopardi) **37**:79, 98-100, 150
"Sorapis, 40 anni fa" (Montale) **13**:138
Sordello (Browning) **2**:26-30, 34, 42, 50, 65-6, 73-6, 82, 92-6
"Sore Fit" (Bradstreet)
See "From Another Sore Fit"
Sorgen och stjärnan (Ekeloef) **23**:76
"La Sorgue" (Char) **56**:173
"The Sorgue: a song for Yvonne" (Char)
See "La Sorgue"
"Sorrow" (Millay) **61**:213
"Sorrow" (Muir) **49**:205, 245-46, 249-50
The Sorrow Dance (Levertov) **11**:175-77, 191-94
"Sorrow Home" (Walker) **20**:281-83
"Sorrowful Moonlit Night" (Hagiwara)
See "Kanashi Tsukio"
"Sort of an Apocalypse" (Amichai) **38**:35-37
"Sortes Vergilianae" (Ashbery) **26**:149
"Sorting It Out" (Stone) **53**:257
"SOS" (Baraka) **4**:20
"Sosedka" (Lermontov) **18**:291
"Sotto la pioggia" (Montale) **13**:122
"Sought by the World, and Hath the World Disdain'd" (Raleigh) **31**:201
"The Soul" (Pasternak)
See "Dusha"
"Soul, Be Calm" (Ishikawa)
See "Tama yo shizume"
"A Soul for Sale" (Kavanagh) **33**:86
A Soul for Sale (Kavanagh) **33**:61-2, 71-5, 77, 81, 85, 93-5, 97, 102, 146
"A Soul, Geologically" (Atwood) **8**:3, 8, 19
"The Soul Has Bandaged Moments" (Dickinson) **1**:94
"Soul in Space" (Rilke) **2**:275
"The Soul of the World" (Rumi) **45**:251
"The Soul on Weekdays" (Herbert)
See "Codziennosc duszy"
"Soul Says" (Graham) **59**:136, 157
"Soul's Adventure" (Kunitz) **19**:148
"Soul's Beauty" (Rossetti) **44**:255
"Soul's Desire" (Masters) **1**:342
"The Soul's Expression" (Browning) **6**:20, 26, 30
"The Souls of Old Men" (Cavafy) **36**:95
"The Souls of the Slain" (Hardy) **8**:120-21
Souls of Violet (Jiménez)
See *Almas de violeta*
"The Soul's Season" (Thoreau) **30**:281, 282, 295
"A Soul's Tragedy" (Browning) **2**:30, 37
The Sound I Listened For (Francis) **34**:245, 259
"The Sound of the Sea" (Longfellow) **30**:31
"The Sound of the Trees" (Frost) **1**:197, 202; **39**:232, 237, 239, 246-47
"Sound of War" (Aleixandre) **15**:4-6
"Sound Poem I" (Toomer) **7**:333
"Sound Poem II" (Toomer) **7**:333
"Sound Sleep" (Rossetti) **7**:267, 280
"Sounds" (Browning) **6**:20
"The sounds begin again" (Brutus) **24**:114, 116
Sounds, Feelings, Thoughts (Szymborska) **44**:274, 295
"Sounds of Rain" (Heaney) **18**:260
"Sounds of the River Naranjana" (Schwerner) **42**:196, 202, 204
Sounds of the River Naranjana and The Tablets I-XXIV (Schwerner) **42**:202-4
"Sounds Out of Sorrow" (Masters) **1**:333
"Soup" (Sandburg) **41**:252
"Soup of the evening beautiful Soup" (Carroll) **18**:49
"Soupir" (Mallarmé) **4**:187
Sour Grapes (Williams) **7**:344, 349, 367, 377, 381, 399-400, 409-10
"Source" (Doty) **53**:70
"The Source" (Olds) **22**:338
"Source" (Péret) **33**:231
"The Source" (Wagoner) **33**:360
Source (Doty) **53**:69
"La source dans les bois" (Lamartine) **16**:292
"Sources" (Levine) **22**:224
Sources (Rich) **5**:389-90, 397
"La sourd et l'aveugle" (Éluard) **38**:70
"Sous la menace rouge" (Éluard) **38**:71, 84
"Sous le feuillage" (Char) **56**:155
"South" (Brathwaite) **56**:64, 83
"The South" (Hughes) **53**:85
"South" (Stryk) **27**:181, 200
"South Cottage" (Wang Wei) **18**:367
"The South Country" (Belloc) **24**:8, 10, 30
"South of My Days" (Wright) **14**:340, 349, 351, 360, 378
"South Sangamon" (Cisneros) **52**:160
"South Sea Island" (Benn) **35**:49
"The South Wind" (Bridges) **28**:66
"Southeast Corner" (Brooks) **7**:58, 69, 80
"Southern Mammy Sings" (Hughes) **53**:120
"A Southern Night" (Arnold) **5**:8
"Southern Pacific" (Sandburg) **2**:302; **41**:240, 316
"Southern Road" (Brown) **55**:73-75, 80, 110, 113, 149, 158, 160-61, 174
Southern Road (Brown) **55**:73-77, 80-81, 86-87, 89, 93-94, 96, 98, 100-101, 109-17, 120-21, 124-26, 128-29, 131, 134-35, 143, 148, 154, 156-59, 164, 166-67, 175, 178
"Southern Song" (Walker) **20**:272, 281-83
"The Southerner" (Shapiro) **25**:283, 296, 313
"Southpaw" (Mueller) **33**:191
"South-West Wind in the Woodland" (Meredith) **60**:287, 294-95
"The South-Wester" (Meredith) **60**:278, 280, 283
"Le Souvenir" (Bonnefoy) **58**:156, 158
"Souvenir de Monsieur Poop" (Smith) **12**:313
"Le souvenir d'enfance; ou, La vie cachée" (Lamartine) **16**:276, 300, 302
"Souvent sur la montagne" (Lamartine) **16**:302
"Sovente una riviera" (Quasimodo) **47**:303
The Sovereign Sun: Selected Poems (Elytis) **21**:118-19
"Sovereign Thought" (Leopardi)
See "Il Pensiero Dominante"
"Soviet Union" (Guillén)
See "Unión Soviética"
"Sow" (Plath) **1**:388, 404; **37**:254
Soweto (Brathwaite) **56**:42, 90
"The Sowing" (Teasdale) **31**:323
"Sowing" (Thomas) **53**:328
"The Sowing of Meaning" (Merton) **10**:332
"Soy" (Borges) **32**:58, 76, 90
"Soy como un árbol florido" (Guillén) **23**:125
"Soy Sauce" (Snyder) **21**:300
"Soy sólo una mujer" (Fuertes) **27**:7
Soyti na tikhoy stantsiy Zima, Otkuda vy? (Yevtushenko) **40**:363
Space (Aleixandre)
See *Ambito*
Space (Jiménez)
See *Espacia*
space travl (Bissett) **14**:34
"The Space We Live" (Levine) **22**:215
"Spaces We Leave Empty" (Song) **21**:343
"Spade" (Brathwaite) **56**:99
"The Spades" (Brathwaite) **56**:82
Spain (Auden) **1**:22
Spain (Gautier)
See *España*
Spain at Heart (Neruda)
See *España en el corazón: himno a las glorias del pueblo en la guerra (1936-1937)*
Spain in My Heart (Neruda)
See *España en el corazón: himno a las glorias del pueblo en la guerra (1936-1937)*
Spain in the Heart (Neruda)
See *España en el corazón: himno a las glorias del pueblo en la guerra (1936-1937)*
Spaltung (Benn) **35**:8, 33
The Spanish Gypsy (Eliot) **20**:90-100, 104-6, 111-15, 122-23, 126, 128-31, 137-39, 141-48
"Spanish Harlem" (Dylan) **37**:54
"The Spanish Needle" (McKay) **2**:228
"Spanish School" (Smith) **12**:316
The Spanish Student (Longfellow) **30**:23, 25, 34-5, 52, 63-4, 68
"Spare Us from Loveliness" (H. D.) **5**:273
"spark" (Bukowski) **18**:20
"The Spark" (Cullen) **20**:58
"A Spark in the Tinder of Knowing" (Rexroth) **20**:221
"A Sparkler" (Ashbery) **26**:137
"Sparrow Hills" (Pasternak) **6**:258
"Sparrow Nights" (Carver) **54**:18
"A Sparrow Sheltering Under a Column of the British Museum" (Merwin) **45**:6
"Sparrow Song" (Li Po) **29**:140
"The Sparrow's Fall" (Harper) **21**:189
The Sparrow's Fall and Other Poems (Harper) **21**:187, 189
"Spasskoye" (Pasternak) **6**:252, 259
"Spät" (Benn) **35**:36
"Spät II" (Benn) **35**:72
"Spät, V" (Benn) **35**:67
"Das späte Ich" (Benn) **35**:8, 75
"Spätherbst in Venedig" (Rilke) **2**:267, 277, 282, 288-90
"Spätlese" (Hope) **56**:278
"Speak" (Wright) **36**:305-6, 317, 344, 350
Speak, Parrot (Skelton)
See *Speke, Parot*
"Speak, You Also" (Celan) **10**:99
"La Speakerine de Putney" (Smith) **12**:354
Speaking for Scotland (MacDiarmid) **9**:159
"Speaking of Love (of" (Cummings) **5**:105
"speaking speaking" (Bissett) **14**:31
"Specchio" (Quasimodo) **47**:301
"Special Pleading" (Lanier) **50**:55
"Special Starlight" (Sandburg) **2**:331
"Specimen of an Induction to a Poem" (Keats) **1**:313
Spectacula (Martial)
See *Liber Spectaculorum*
"Spectacular Blossom" (Curnow) **48**:6-7
Spectaculorum Liber (Martial)
See *Liber Spectaculorum*

"Spectral Lovers" (Ransom) **61**:267, 272, 306, 311
Spectrum (Nishiwaki) **15**:228, 237
Speculum Meditantis (Gower) **59**:113
"The Speech at Soli" (Oppen) **35**:294
"Speech for the Repeal of the McCarran Act" (Wilbur) **51**:226, 228
"Speech to a Crowd" (MacLeish) **47**:147, 190, 242
"Speech to Scholars" (MacLeish) **47**:147, 256
"Speech to the Detractors" (MacLeish) **47**:190
"Speech to the Young. Speech to the Progress-Toward" (Brooks) **7**:91, 94
"Speech to those who say Comrade" (MacLeish) **47**:145, 147, 190, 242
Speeches (Parra)
See "Discursos"
"Speeches at the Barriers" (Howe) **54**:63
"Speeches for Doctor Frankenstein" (Atwood) **8**:11
"Speech-Grille" (Celan)
See "Sprachgitter"
Speech-Grille, and Selected Poems (Celan)
See *Sprachgitter*
The Speed of Darkness (Rukeyser) **12**:216, 222, 228, 230
Speke, Parot (Skelton) **25**:329-31, 336, 341, 348, 351-52, 360, 374, 377-78, 380-85
Speke Parott (Skelton)
See *Speke, Parot*
Speke, Parrot (Skelton)
See *Speke, Parot*
Spektorsky (Pasternak) **6**:253, 265, 283, 285
"Spel Against Demons" (Snyder) **21**:291-92, 297
"Speleology" (Warren) **37**:337
"The Spell" (Kumin) **15**:192
"Spell" (Montale)
See "Incantesimo"
"The Spell of the Rose" (Hardy) **8**:93, 136
"Spell-Bound" (Morris) **55**:238, 279-80, 282
"Spelling" (Duncan) **2**:104
"Spelling Bee" (Silverstein) **49**:324
"Spelt from Sibyl's Leaves" (Hopkins) **15**:128, 132-33, 138, 144
"A Spending Hand" (Wyatt)
See "A spending hand that alway poureth out"
"A spending hand that alway poureth out" (Wyatt) **27**:371
"Spenser's Ireland" (Moore) **4**:258; **49**:100, 128, 161
"Sperm" (Kumin) **15**:202
"The Sperm and Egg" (Stone) **53**:254
"Sphere" (Ammons) **16**:31, 53
Sphere: The Form of a Motion (Ammons) **16**:23, 25, 27-30, 33, 46-7, 54, 60-1
"The Sphinx" (Emerson) **18**:71, 84, 88, 93, 102, 110
"Le Sphinx" (Gautier) **18**:141
"The Sphinx" (Hayden) **6**:186
Sphinx: A Poem Ascrib'd to Certain Anonymous Authors: By the Revd. S—t (Swift)
See "Ode to the Athenian Society"
"Le Sphynx vertébral" (Breton) **15**:51
"The Spice Tree" (Lindsay) **23**:268
"Spicewood" (Reese) **29**:330
Spicewood (Reese) **29**:335, 339, 347-348, 351
"Spider Blues" (Ondaatje) **28**:320, 327, 333
"Spiders" (Cervantes) **35**:104, 117
"Spider's Song" (Zagajewski) **27**:389
"Spiel" (Stramm) **50**:189-91, 201, 209
"Spight hathe no Powre" (Wyatt) **27**:315
Spik in glyph? (Alurista) **34**:15, 23, 26, 31, 43
"Spilt Milk" (Yeats) **20**:314
Spin a Soft Black Song: Poems for Children (Giovanni) **19**:136
"Spindrift" (Kinnell) **26**:257
"The Spinner" (Valéry)
See "La fileuse"
"Spinning Tops" (Reese) **29**:330
"Spinoza" (Borges) **32**:60, 68, 71
"Spinoza's Bed" (Herbert) **50**:45
"Spinster" (Plath) **1**:388
"Spirals" (Niedecker) **42**:145-48
"The Spire Cranes" (Thomas) **2**:408
"Spirit" (Corso) **33**:50
"Spirit" (Soto) **28**:370
Spirit (Corso) **33**:50
"The Spirit Medium" (Yeats) **20**:314
"The Spirit of Earth in Autumn" (Meredith) **60**:298
"Spirit of History" (Milosz) **8**:204
"The Spirit of Lake Switzez" (Mickiewicz)
See "Switezianka"
"The Spirit of Place" (Rich) **5**:386
"The Spirit of Poetry" (Longfellow) **30**:33
The Spirit of Romance (Pound) **4**:352
Spirit Reach (Baraka) **4**:19-20, 26
"The Spirit's Epochs" (Patmore) **59**:205
"Spirit's House" (Teasdale) **31**:355
"Spirit's Song" (Bogan) **12**:90, 92, 100, 124
"Spirits Summoned West" (Lawrence) **54**:245
"A Spiritual" (Dunbar) **5**:123
"Spiritual" (Pasolini) **17**:253
"Spiritual Diary" (Cowper) **40**:48, 51
"Spiritual Laws" (Emerson) **18**:94
Spiritual Sonnets (Jiménez)
See *Sonetos espirituales*
"Spirituals" (Hughes) **53**:91, 109, 118
"Spite" (Bukowski) **18**:5
"Spleen" (Baudelaire)
See "Le spleen"
"Le spleen" (Baudelaire) **1**:55
"Spleen" (Eliot) **31**:100, 138
"The Spleen" (Finch)
See "Ode to the Spleen"
"Spleen" (Laforgue) **14**:84-5, 89
"Spleen" (O'Hara) **45**:223
"Spleen" (Verlaine) **2**:415
Le spleen de Paris (Baudelaire)
See *Petits poèmes en prose: Le spleen de Paris*
"Splendour of the Sun and Moon" (Hope) **56**:302
"Split, Conjugate, Whatever" (Stone) **53**:254
"Splitting Wood at Six Above" (Kumin) **15**:206, 219
"The Spoiler's Return" (Walcott) **46**:247, 322
"Spoke Joe to Jack" (Cummings) **5**:88
"Sponsa Dei" (Patmore) **59**:210, 223, 265, 268
"Spontaneous Combustion" (Hogan) **35**:256
"Spontaneous Me" (Whitman) **3**:387
"Spontaneous Requiem for the American Indian" (Corso) **33**:44, 49
The Spoon River Anthology (Masters) **1**:321-42, 344-49; **36**:161-245
"The Spooniad" (Masters) **1**:327; **36**:169, 172, 182, 195-96, 212, 220, 223, 228
The Spooniad (Masters) **36**:243
"Spor" (Lermontov) **18**:291
"Sport" (Hughes) **1**:270
"Sporting Beasley" (Brown) **55**:72, 75, 155
"Sports Field" (Wright) **14**:362
"Sports Page" (MacNeice) **61**:177
"Spot in Space and Time" (McHugh) **61**:200
"Sprachgitter" (Celan) **10**:112, 115, 129-30
Sprachgitter (Celan) **10**:95-6, 121
"Sprawozdanie z raju" (Herbert) **50**:9
"Spraying the Potatoes" (Kavanagh) **33**:62, 81, 94, 99, 118, 145-6, 152, 154, 157, 162
"Sprich zu dir selbst, dann sprichst du zu den Dingen" (Benn) **35**:70
"A Sprig of Rosemary" (Lowell) **13**:64
"Spring" (Baca) **41**:47
"Spring" (Blake) **12**:7, 32
"The Spring" (Carew) **29**:8-9, 19
"Spring" (Darío)
See "Primaveral"
"Spring" (Gray)
See "Ode on Spring"
"Spring" (Hass) **16**:209
"Spring" (Hopkins) **15**:152
"Spring" (McGuckian) **27**:96
"Spring" (Millay) **6**:236
"Spring" (Pasternak) **6**:251
"Spring" (Rexroth) **20**:209
"Spring" (Sitwell) **3**:311
"Spring" (Teasdale) **31**:321
"Spring" (Williams) **7**:345, 399
"Spring 1942" (Curnow) **48**:12
Spring and All (Williams) **7**:349, 351, 353, 355, 373-78, 381-83, 387-88, 400-02, 405-06, 409-11
"Spring and Fall" (Hopkins) **15**:144
"The Spring and the Fall" (Millay) **6**:225
"Spring Blades" (Brathwaite) **56**:34
"Spring Cleaning" (MacNeice) **61**:176
"Spring Comes to Murray Hill" (Nash) **21**:266
"Spring Day" (Ashbery) **26**:124
"Spring Day" (Lowell) **13**:79
"Spring Day" (Sarton) **39**:325
"Spring Drawing" (Hass) **16**:215, 221
"Spring Drawing 2" (Hass) **16**:216
"Spring Ecstasy" (Reese) **29**:331
"Spring Evening" (Kenyon) **57**:18, 28
"Spring Flood" (Pasternak) **6**:266
"Spring goeth all in white" (Bridges) **28**:66-7
"Spring Images" (Wright) **36**:316, 359, 374, 398
"Spring in Belfast" (Mahon) **60**:235
"Spring in Hellas" (Carducci)
See "Primavere elleniche"
"Spring in New Hampshire" (McKay) **2**:228
Spring in New Hampshire, and Other Poems (McKay) **2**:213, 228
"Spring in the Garden" (Millay) **6**:215
"Spring in These Hills" (MacLeish) **47**:197
"Spring Lake" (Masters) **1**:343
"Spring Lament" (Surrey) **59**:291
"Spring Magic" (Carman) **34**:223
"Spring Night" (Hagiwara)
See "Shun'ya"
"Spring Night" (Teasdale) **31**:378
"Spring Night in Lo-yang-Hearing a Flute" (Li Po) **29**:145
"Spring Oak" (Kinnell) **26**:237-38, 257
"Spring Ode I" (Bridges) **28**:84
"Spring Ode II" (Bridges) **28**:84
"Spring Offensive" (Owen) **19**:334, 337, 341-42, 344, 347, 353-55
"Spring Pastoral" (Wylie) **23**:321-22
"Spring Poem" (Atwood) **8**:24
"Spring Pools" (Frost) **1**:206; **39**:239
"Spring Prospect" (Tu Fu) **9**:322
"Spring Rain" (Hass) **16**:221-22
"Spring Rain" (Pasternak) **6**:251
"Spring Rains" (Teasdale) **31**:356
"Spring Season of Muddy Roads" (Brodsky) **9**:2
"Spring Snow" (Kenyon) **57**:45
"Spring Song" (Amichai) **38**:25
"Spring Song" (Baraka) **4**:39
"Spring Song" (Clifton) **17**:16
"Spring Street in '58" (Walcott) **46**:237
"Spring Sunshine" (MacNeice) **61**:129, 134
Spring Thaw (Yosano Akiko)
See *Shundeishū*
"Spring Thunder" (Rich) **5**:383
"Spring Torrents" (Teasdale) **31**:360
"Spring Uncovered" (Swenson) **14**:247, 250, 268
"The Spring Vacation" (Mahon) **60**:153, 171, 182-85, 190, 193
"Spring Warning" (Larkin) **21**:259
"A Spring Wooing" (Dunbar) **5**:145
"The Springboard" (MacNeice) **61**:160
Springboard (MacNeice) **61**:140, 142
"Springer Mountain" (Dickey) **40**:163-64, 166
"Springfield Magical" (Lindsay) **23**:284
Spring's Bedfellow (Morris) **55**:325
"The Springs of the Clitumnus" (Carducci)
See "Alle fonti del Clitumno"
"Spring's Saraband" (Carman) **34**:208
"The Sprinter at Forty" (Dickey) **40**:229

"The Sprinter's Sleep" (Dickey) **40**:175
"Spruce Woods" (Ammons) **16**:45
"Sprüche" (Goethe) **5**:248
"Spuk" (Benn) **35**:72
"Spur" (Yeats) **51**:120
"The Spur of Love" (MacDiarmid) **9**:189-90
"The Spy" (Francis) **34**:264-65
"Squares and Angles" (Storni)
See "Cuadros y angulos"
"Squares and Courtyards" (Hacker) **47**:118-19
Squares and Courtyards (Hacker) **47**:117, 120
"Squarings" (Heaney) **18**:254, 257-58
"Squash in Blossom" (Francis) **34**:242
"Le squelette laboureur" (Baudelaire) **1**:45
"Squieres Tale" (Chaucer)
See "Squire's Tale"
"Squince" (Mahon) **60**:174
"Squire Hawkins's Story" (Riley) **48**:288
"Squire's Tale" (Chaucer) **19**:13
"The Squirrel" (Stryk) **27**:189, 203
"Squishy Touch" (Silverstein) **49**:336
"Srishti-sthiti-pralaya" (Tagore) **8**:406
"Śroczość" (Milosz) **8**:187
"St. Barthomomew's On the Hill" (Carman) **34**:225
"St. Brandan" (Arnold) **5**:12
"St Eustace" (Mahon) **60**:202
"St. John" (Lawrence) **54**:194
"St. Launce's Revisited" (Hardy) **8**:136
"St. Louis Blues" (Hughes) **53**:81
"St. Louis woman" (Niedecker) **42**:125-27
"St. Lucies Day" (Donne)
See "A Nocturnal upon S. Lucies day, Being the shortest day"
"St. Luke the Painter" (Rossetti) **44**:227-28, 232, 250
"St. Lukes, Service for Thomas" (Corso) **33**:46
"St. Mark" (Lawrence) **54**:170
"St. Mary Magdalene Preaching at Marseilles" (Ní Chuilleanáin) **34**:350, 360
"St. Matthew" (Lawrence) **54**:224
St. Patrick's Purgatory (Marie de France)
See *L'Espurgatoire Saint Patrice*
"St. Paul and All That" (O'Hara) **45**:151, 216, 218-19
"St. Peter Relates an Incident of the Resurrection Day" (Johnson) **24**:133, 141, 144, 153, 161, 170
St. Peter Relates an Incident: Selected Poems (Johnson) **24**:130, 159, 162
"St. Praxed's Church" (Browning) **2**:30
"St. Simeon Stylites" (Tennyson) **6**:411
"St. Thomas's Ruins" (Curnow) **48**:29
"St Valentine Is Past" (Birney) **52**:22
"St. Valentine's Day" (Patmore) **59**:208-9
"St. Vincent's" (Merwin) **45**:63-4
"The Staff of Aesculapius" (Moore) **49**:126, 136, 138
"Stage-directions" (Niedecker) **42**:101, 148
"Stages" (Ignatow) **34**:326
"Stages" (Meredith) **28**:180
"Stages of a Journey Westward" (Wright) **36**:288, 340
"Stagirius" (Arnold) **5**:38
"Staircase" (Tsvetaeva)
See "Poèma lestnitsy"
Staische Gedichte (Benn) **35**:4, 5, 6, 8, 42
"Stalin" (Lowell) **3**:223
"Stalin Epigram" (Mandelstam) **14**:149, 153
"Stalin's Heirs" (Yevtushenko) **40**:343, 346, 350, 352, 368, 370
Stalin's Heirs (Yevtushenko) **40**:365
"The Stalker" (Momaday) **25**:212-13
"Stan" (Tagore) **8**:407
"Stances" (Gautier) **18**:163
"Stances de la fontaine de'Helene" (Ronsard) **11**:241
"Stand who so list upon the slipper top" (Wyatt) **27**:331, 362, 367
Stand with Me Here (Francis) **34**:241, 244
"La Standard Oil Co." (Neruda) **4**:296
"The Standard Oil Co." (Neruda)
See "La Standard Oil Co."
"Standardization" (Hope) **56**:266, 284, 306
"Standards and Paradise of the Blacks" (García Lorca)
See "Norma y paraíso de los negros"
"A Standing Ground" (Berry) **28**:43
"Standing in the Middle of a Desert" (Wagoner) **33**:352
"Standing Is Stupid" (Silverstein) **49**:330
Standing Still and Walking in New York (O'Hara) **45**:154, 163
"Standomi un giorno solo a la fenestra" (Petrarch) **8**:253-57
"The standstillness of unthought" (Villa) **22**:354
"The Stand-To" (Day Lewis) **11**:146
"Stand-to: Good Friday Morning" (Sassoon) **12**:241, 251, 262, 280
"Stanley Kunitz" (Ignatow) **34**:345
Stantsiya Zima (Yevtushenko) **40**:359, 363-65
"Stanza" (Bogan) **12**:103
"Stanzas" (Brodsky) **9**:4
"Stanzas" (Mandelstam) **14**:151
"Stanzas from the Grande Chartreuse" (Arnold) **5**:18, 24, 33, 35, 52-3, 58
Stanzas in Love with Life and August Again Again (Viereck) **27**:265
"Stanzas in Meditation" (Stein) **18**:309-316, 335-37, 339-41, 343, 345-48
Stanzas in Meditation (Stein) **18**:309-316, 335-37, 339-41, 343, 345-48
"Stanzas in Memory of Edward Quillinan" (Arnold) **5**:52
"Stanzas in Memory of the Author of 'Obermann'" (Arnold) **5**:42, 50, 52
"Stanzas on Peele Castle" (Wordsworth) **4**:394, 410-11
"Stanzas to Bettine" (Browning) **6**:15
"Stanzas to Tolstoi" (Pushkin) **10**:409
"Stanzas Written at Night in Radio City" (Ginsberg) **4**:55
"Stanzas Written on Battersea Bridge during a South-Westerly Gale" (Belloc) **24**:30-1, 36
"Star" (Bedier) **46**:236
"A Star" (Kavanagh) **33**:117, 120
"The Star" (Masters) **1**:326, 333, 337, 342
The Star (Bely)
See *Zvezda*
"A Star in a Stone-Boat" (Frost) **1**:194, 221; **39**:233, 235
"Star Suite" (Goodison) **36**:152
"Star Woman Falling" (Wagoner) **33**:354
The Star-Apple Kingdom (Walcott) **46**:259, 322-23, 325
stardust (Bissett) **14**:30
"The Stare of the Man from the Provinces" (Nemerov) **24**:268
"Star-Fall" (Warren) **37**:312, 337
"Starfish" (Cervantes) **35**:104, 114, 117
"Star-Gazer" (MacNeice) **61**:177
"Staring at the Sea on the Day of the Death of Another" (Swenson) **14**:288
"Staritsa" (Shvarts) **50**:137, 143
"Starlight" (Meredith) **28**:171
"Starlight like Intuition Pierced the Twelve" (Schwartz) **8**:290-91
"The Starlight Night" (Hopkins) **15**:144, 152, 160, 162
"Starlight Scope Myopia" (Komunyakaa) **51**:26-27, 30, 37-38
"The Starling" (Lowell) **13**:61
"The Starling" (Smith) **12**:326
"The Starling" (Soto) **28**:375
"The Starred Coverlet" (Graves) **6**:156
"The Starry Night" (Sexton) **2**:350, 371-72
"Starry Night" (Sexton) **2**:350, 371-72
"Stars" (Hayden) **6**:184-85, 190, 194, 196
"Stars, Songs, Faces" (Sandburg) **41**:313
"The Star-Song: A Carroll to the King; Sung at White Hall" (Herrick) **9**:118, 119
"The Star-Splitter" (Frost) **1**:194; **39**:233, 235
"Start Again Somewhere" (Gallagher) **9**:58
"Star-Talk" (Graves) **6**:166
"Starting from San Francisco" (Ferlinghetti) **1**:187
Starting from San Francisco (Ferlinghetti) **1**:166, 172-76, 187
Starting Point (Day Lewis) **11**:129
"Starting Therapy" (Kenyon) **57**:46
"Starvation" (Brathwaite) **56**:34
"Starvation Camp Near Jaslo" (Szymborska) **44**:299
"Starved Lovers" (MacLeish) **47**:192
Starved Rock (Masters) **1**:332, 335, 338, 342-44
"Stary Prometeusz" (Herbert) **50**:39
"Stasis" (Stone) **53**:228
"The State" (Jarrell) **41**:172, 195, 198
"The State of Age" (Meredith) **60**:255
"State of Siege" (Guillén) **35**:218
"The State of World Affairs from a Third Floor Window" (Bukowski) **18**:3
"Statement" (Curnow) **48**:44
"Statement" (Francis) **34**:251
"Statement" (Hughes) **53**:101-2
"Statement of the Times" (Ignatow) **34**:323
"Statement on Poetics" (Hayden) **6**:198
Statements After an Arrest Under the Immorality Act (Brutus) **24**:119
"The Staten Island Ferry" (Clampitt) **19**:100
"The State's Claim" (Ortiz) **17**:233
"Static Landscape" (Sarton) **39**:320
Static Poems (Benn)
See *Staische Gedichte*
"The Station" (Merwin) **45**:18
"Station" (Olds) **22**:307, 328
"Station Island" (Heaney) **18**:220, 240
Station Island (Heaney) **18**:211-12, 214-16, 218, 226, 228, 232, 237
Station Zima (Yevtushenko)
See "Zima Station"
"The Stationary Journey" (Muir) **49**:239, 289, 297
"Stations" (Hughes) **7**:137
"Stations" (Lorde) **12**:140
"Statische Gedichte" (Benn) **35**:33
"Statistics" (Sandburg) **41**:235, 269
"The Statue" (Belloc) **24**:9
"La Statue" (Hugo) **17**:64
"Statue and Birds" (Bogan) **12**:94, 101, 127
"The Statue and the Bust" (Browning) **61**:96
"The Statue at the World's End" (Stevens)
See "Mr. Burnshaw and the Statue"
"Statue at Tsarskoye Selo" (Akhmatova) **2**:12
The Statue Guest (Pushkin)
See *Kamennyi gost'*
"The Statue in Stocks-Market" (Marvell) **10**:276
"The Statue in the Garden" (Lowell) **13**:61
"A Statue in the Silence" (Neruda)
See "Una estatua en el silencio"
"The Statue of Liberty" (Hardy) **8**:99
"The Statues" (Yeats) **20**:324, 334
"Status Quo," (Birney) **52**:39
"Status Quo" (Curnow) **48**:25
"A Statute of Wine" (Neruda)
See "Estatura del vino"
"A Stave of Roving Tim" (Meredith) **60**:262, 294-95
"Stay With Me" (Hongo) **23**:203
"Staying Alive" (Levertov) **11**:178-79, 195-96
"Staying Alive" (Wagoner) **33**:333, 348, 359
Staying Alive (Wagoner) **33**:329, 332-33, 352, 359, 373
"Staying at Grandma's" (Kenyon) **57**:40-41
"Steak" (Snyder) **21**:292-93
"Steal Away to Jesus" (Johnson) **24**:170
"Stealing Trout on a May Morning" (Hughes) **7**:120, 170
"The Stealthy School of Criticism" (Rossetti) **44**:206
"Steam Shovel Cut" (Masters) **1**:343
"The Steamboat Whistle" (MacLeish) **47**:197
"Lo steddazzu" (Pavese) **13**:229
"Steele" (Quintana) **36**:272

"Steelhead" (Jeffers) **17**:141
"Steely Silence" (Wakoski) **15**:332
Steeple Bush (Frost) **1**:200, 205-06, 217; **39**:233
"The Steeple-Jack" (Bishop) **34**:106
"The Steeple-Jack" (Moore) **4**:256; **49**:100-101, 108
"Steering Wheel" (Graham) **59**:152, 177
"Stella's Birthday, March 13, 1718-19" (Swift) **9**:255, 297
"Stella!s Portrait" (Howe) **54**:130
"Stellenbosch" (Kipling) **3**:176
"The Stenographers" (Page) **12**:163, 173
"A Step Away from Them" (O'Hara) **45**:115, 127, 141, 145, 147, 170, 178, 184, 216, 243
"Stepchild" (Hongo) **23**:197
"Stephen A. Douglas" (Masters) **1**:334
"The Steppes of Akkerman" (Mickiewicz)
See "Stepy Akermańskie"
"Stepping Backward" (Rich) **5**:352
"Stepping Outside" (Gallagher) **9**:35
Stepping Outside (Gallagher) **9**:35
"Stepping Westward" (Wordsworth) **4**:395
"Steps for Three" (Ignatow) **34**:321
"The Steps of the Commander" (Blok) **21**:6
"Stepy Akermańskie" (Mickiewicz) **38**:158
"Sterling, Colorado" (Quintana) **36**:249, 270
"The Stethoscope" (Abse) **41**:22, 25, 29-30
Stevie Smith: A Selection (Smith) **12**:331, 348
"Stifled cries" (Péret)
See "Des cris étouffés"
Stikhi (Shvarts) **50**:134, 142, 145
"Stikhi K Akhmatovoi" (Tsvetaeva) **14**:321
Stikhi K Blok (Tsvetaeva) **14**:299, 311-12
"Stikhi k Chekhii" (Tsvetaeva) **14**:325, 327
"Stikhi k Pushkinu" (Tsvetaeva) **14**:324-25
"Stikhi k synu" (Tsvetaeva) **14**:328
"Stikhi o neizvestnom soldate" (Mandelstam) **14**:145, 148-49, 152, 155
Stikhi o prekrasnoi dame (Blok) **21**:13, 18, 24, 30
Stikhi raznykh let (Yevtushenko) **40**:341
Stikhotvoreniia i poemy (Akhmatova) **55**:26
Stikhotvoreniia i poemy (Shvarts) **50**:162
Stikhotvoreniya (Bely) **11**:29
"still" (Birney) **52**:83
"Still at Annecy" (Montale)
See "Ancora ad Annecy"
"Still, Citizen Sparrow" (Wilbur) **51**:187, 221
"Still Do I Keep My Look, My Identity" (Brooks) **7**:71
"Still Falls the Rain" (Sitwell) **3**:310, 323, 326
"Still Here" (Hughes) **53**:150-51
"Still Life" (Glück) **16**:128, 136, 139, 142
"Still Life" (Graham) **59**:175
"Still Life" (Hughes) **7**:121, 137
"Still Life" (Sandburg) **41**:297
"Still Life in Snowstorm" (Sarton) **39**:328
"Still Life with Window and Fish" (Graham) **59**:179
"Still Night" (Smith) **12**:317
"Still Night Thoughts" (Li Po) **29**:145
"Still on Water" (Rexroth) **20**:206, 216
"The Still Time" (Kinnell) **26**:260, 281
"Still Will I Strive to Be" (Thoreau) **30**:128
"Stillborn" (Plath) **1**:391, 405
"Stillborn Love" (Rossetti) **44**:169
"Stilleben" (Benn) **35**:69
"Stillness" (Pasternak)
See "Tishina"
"Stimme des Heilegen Landes" (Sachs) **18**:147, 156
"Stimme des Volks" (Hölderlin) **4**:166
"Die Stimme hinter dem Vorhang" (Benn) **35**:32, 34
"Stinging" (Cummings)
See "Sunset"
"Stings" (Plath) **1**:394, 410, 412-14; **37**:239, 241, 262
"The Stirrup-Cup" (Lanier) **50**:56, 77
"Stixi na smert T. S. Èliota" (Brodsky) **9**:2, 4
Sto pociech (Szymborska) **44**:268
"Stokely Malcolm Me" (Hughes) **53**:111, 151
"Stol" (Tsvetaeva) **14**:318
Stolen Apples (Yevtushenko) **40**:365
"The Stolen Child" (Yeats) **20**:337, 346
"Stolen Trees" (Hogan) **35**:250
"Stone" (Brathwaite) **56**:43
"The Stone" (Carruth) **10**:71
"The Stone" (Soto)
See "Piedra"
Stone (Mandelstam)
See *Kamen'*
"A Stone Age Figure Far Below" (Mahon) **60**:214
The Stone Bridge (Seifert)
See *Kammený most*
"A Stone Church Damaged by a Bomb" (Larkin) **21**:259
"The Stone from the Sea" (Celan) **10**:112
"The Stone Garden" (Sarton) **39**:327, 339
The Stone Guest (Pushkin)
See *Kamennyi gost'*
"Stone, paper, knife" (Piercy) **29**:315-16, 318-19, 321-22
Stone, Paper, Knife (Piercy) **29**:312-13, 316-17, 321
"The Stone Sermon" (Brathwaite) **56**:76, 100
"The Stone Verdict" (Heaney) **18**:229, 233
"The Stonecarver's Poem" (Levertov) **11**:169
"Stone-Head" (Plath) **37**:188
"The Stones" (Plath) **1**:389-90; **37**:190-91
"Stones" (Zagajewski) **27**:389
"Stony, Fifteen Years in the Joint" (Baca) **41**:37
"Stony Grey Soil" (Kavanagh) **33**:62, 75, 86, 93, 102, 127, 129, 150, 154-7
"Stony Limits" (MacDiarmid) **9**:156, 176
Stony Limits (MacDiarmid) **9**:156, 158, 172-73, 175-76, 179-80, 182-84, 196, 200
"Stony Lonesome" (Hughes) **53**:119
"Stool" (Herbert) **50**:4
"Stopped Dead" (Plath) **37**:256
"Stopping by Woods on a Snowy Evening" (Frost) **1**:194, 197, 208, 213-14, 221, 225; **39**:230-57
"Stop-Short" (Belloc) **24**:39
"La storia" (Montale) **13**:134
"Stories of Snow" (Page) **12**:164, 167-69, 172, 190, 197
Stories of the Sioux (Chief Standing Bear) **10**:333, 341-42
"Stork Story" (Silverstein) **49**:341
"The Storm" (Bly) **39**:115
"The Storm" (Mickiewicz)
See "Burza"
"The Storm" (Montale)
See "La bufera"
"Storm" (Owen) **19**:353-54
"Storm" (Stryk) **27**:195, 212
"Storm" (Wright) **14**:342
The Storm and Other Things (Montale)
See *La bufera e altro*
"The Storm Came" (Kipling) **3**:171, 183
"Storm Ending" (Toomer) **7**:317, 330-32
"Storm Fear" (Frost) **39**:244, 246-47
"A Storm in April" (Wilbur) **51**:278
"The storm is over" (Bridges) **28**:83
"Storm of Love" (Aleixandre) **15**:19
"Storm Warnings" (Rich) **5**:392, 396
"Storm Windows" (Nemerov) **24**:264-67, 270-71
"Story" (Boland) **58**:24
"Story" (Ignatow) **34**:270
"A Story" (Jarrell) **41**:127, 168, 213
"The Story" (Mueller) **33**:179
"Story" (Wakoski) **15**:365
"Story Between Two Notes" (McGuckian) **27**:91
"The Story of a Citizen" (Gallagher) **9**:60, 62
"A Story of a Cock and a Bull" (Smart) **13**:348
"Story of a Love" (Dalton) **36**:122
"The Story of a Well-Made Shield" (Momaday) **25**:189, 213
"The Story of Adrastus" (Morris) **55**:305
"The Story of Aristomenes" (Morris) **55**:306-7, 309
"A Story of Courage" (Ortiz) **17**:246
"The Story of Cupid and Psyche" (Morris) **55**:242, 249
"The Story of Dorothea" (Morris) **55**:305-6
"A Story of How a Wall Stands" (Ortiz) **17**:225
"The Story of Orpheus and Eurydice" (Morris) **55**:306-7
"The Story of Rhodope" (Morris) **55**:308
"The Story of Richard Maxfield" (Wakoski) **15**:346, 355, 361
"The Story of Solomon and the Hoopoe" (Rumi) **45**:312
"The Story of the Churn" (Stone) **53**:217
The Story of the Great War (Braithwaite) **52**:106
The Story of the Heart (Aleixandre)
See *Historia del corazón*
"The Story of Tommy" (Kipling) **3**:194
"Story of Two Gardens" (Paz)
See "Cuento de dos jardines"
"The Story's Ending" (Morris) **55**:339
"Stotras to Kali Destroyer of Illusions" (Ginsberg) **47**:21, 39
"Stra" (Mackey) **49**:25, 53, 57
"La strada" (Pasolini) **17**:253
"Strada di Agrigentum" (Quasimodo) **47**:279, 288
"Stradivarius" (Eliot) **20**:123, 125
"Straight from Your Prejudice" (Amichai) **38**:19
"Straight Talk" (Giovanni) **19**:112
"Straight-Creek—Great Burn" (Snyder) **21**:297
The Straightening (Celan)
See *Sprachgitter*
Strains (Brutus) **24**:121-22, 124
"The Strait" (Ammons) **16**:4
The Strait of Anian (Birney) **52**:11, 39, 45, 49, 52, 67, 92
"The Straitening" (Celan)
See "Engführung"
The Straitjacket (Parra) **39**:310
"Strand" (Benn) **35**:49, 75
"The Strand" (MacNeice) **61**:110, 128, 186
"Strands" (Stone) **53**:249, 257
"The Strange and True Story of My Life with Billy the Kid" (Momaday) **25**:221
"The Strange Case" (Ondaatje) **28**:329
"Strange Fits of Passion Have I Known" (Wordsworth) **4**:420
"Strange Fruit" (Harjo) **27**:71
"Strange Fruit" (Heaney) **18**:196
The Strange Islands (Merton) **10**:331, 342, 347, 349, 351
"Strange Legacies" (Brown) **55**:71, 76, 79-80, 95
"Strange Meeting" (Owen) **19**:325-27, 329, 332, 335-37, 341-45, 347, 353, 355, 359, 370-71
"Strange People" (Erdrich) **52**:192
"A Strange Song" (Wylie) **23**:324
"A Strange Story" (Wylie) **23**:307, 310
"Strange Victory" (Teasdale) **31**:372
Strange Victory (Teasdale) **31**:326, 330, 333, 339, 341-42, 346, 349, 364, 370, 372-73, 380, 389-90
"Strangeness of Heart" (Sassoon) **12**:254
"The Stranger" (Blok) **21**:4, 24
"Stranger" (Merton) **10**:349
"The Stranger" (Rich) **5**:384
"The Strangers" (Berry) **28**:7
"Strategy" (Gallagher) **9**:59
"Stratford on Avon" (Davie) **29**:102
"Strato in Plaster" (Merrill) **28**:258
"Stratton Water" (Rossetti) **44**:202-3
"Straw Hat" (Dove) **6**:110, 114
"Strawberries" (Merwin) **45**:97
"Strawberry Hill" (Hughes) **7**:119, 148
"Strawberrying" (Swenson) **14**:273
"Stray Animals" (Song) **21**:332
"The Strayed Reveller" (Arnold) **5**:5, 12, 39, 50

The Strayed Reveller, and Other Poems (Arnold) **5**:8, 31, 38-9, 42, 48
"Stream and Sun at Glendalough" (Yeats) **20**:328
"The Stream of the Golden Honey was Pouring So Slow . . ." (Mandelstam) **14**:141
"The Stream's Secret" (Rossetti) **44**:164, 194-95, 203, 210-11, 259-60
"Street" (Ní Chuilleanáin) **34**:352, 382-84
"The Street" (Paz)
See "La calle"
"The Street" (Soto) **28**:378, 383, 386
"Street" (Storni)
See "Calle"
"Street Car Gang" (Brown) **55**:114
"Street Entertainment" (Szirtes) **51**:169, 171-72
"The Street Has Changed" (Jarrell) **41**:169
A Street in Bronzeville (Brooks) **7**:52-4, 56-8, 60-1, 67, 70, 75, 79-80, 85-7, 95, 102, 105
"Street Scene" (MacNeice) **61**:115
"Street Scenes" (Hacker) **47**:107
"Street Song" (Hughes) **53**:162
"Street Song" (Sitwell) **3**:311
Street Songs (Sitwell) **3**:308, 320
"Street Window" (Sandburg) **2**:309
"Street with a pink store" (Borges)
See "Calle con almacén rosado"
"Streetcorner Man" (Borges)
See "El Hombre de la esquina rosada"
"Streets" (Borges)
See "Las Calles"
"Streets" (Verlaine) **2**:415; **32**:371
"The Streets Grow Young" (Wright) **36**:307
Streets in the Moon (MacLeish) **47**:126-27, 165, 183, 185-86, 188, 190, 192, 212, 215, 222
"The Streets of Laredo" (MacNeice) **61**:140, 157-61
"The Strength of Fields" (Dickey) **40**:222, 258
The Strength of Fields (Dickey) **40**:219, 222, 229, 232
"Strengthening the Spirit" (Cavafy) **36**:39, 41, 74, 107
"Strephon and Chloe" (Swift) **9**:257-58, 262, 270, 274, 286, 288, 294, 298, 301
"Strephon's Song" (Belloc) **24**:6
"Stretcher Case" (Sassoon) **12**:242, 262
"Strick" (Mackey) **49**:25, 53
Strick: Song of the Andoumboulou: 16-25 (Mackey) **49**:17, 25, 33, 41-42
Strike (Viereck) **27**:280-82, 284
Strike Through the Mask! (Viereck) **27**:262-63, 278
"Strine Authors Meet" (Birney) **52**:63
"The String" (Dickey) **40**:175, 179, 192
"Stripping the vista to its depth" (Tomlinson) **17**:342
"Striptease-Tänzerinnen" (Enzensberger) **28**:165
"Strive Not With Love" (Surrey) **59**:353
"The Stroke" (Dove) **6**:111
"The Stroke" (Smith) **12**:314
"Stroll" (Borges)
See "Caminata"
"The Stroller" (Kenyon) **57**:11, 13, 44
"Strong Men" (Brown) **55**:70-71, 77, 82, 95-96, 110, 113-14, 152, 178
"Strong Men, Riding Horses" (Brooks) **7**:106
"A Strong New Voice Pointing the Way" (Madhubuti) **5**:346
"The Strong Woman" (Mistral)
See "La mujer fuerte"
Strountes (Ekeloef) **23**:59-61, 63, 76-8
"The Structure of Rime" (Duncan) **2**:116, 124-25, 126
The Structure of Rime (Duncan) **2**:126
"The Structure of Rime II" (Duncan) **2**:125
"The Structure of Rime XXVIII" (Duncan) **2**:114
"The Structure of the Plane" (Rukeyser) **12**:202
"Struggle" (Hughes) **7**:165-66
"The Struggle between the Statistical Mentality and Eros" (Ignatow) **34**:304-05
"The Struggle Staggers Us" (Walker) **20**:289, 294
"Struggling Sea" (Guillén) **35**:221
"Strumpet Song" (Plath) **1**:388
Struna swiatła (Herbert) **50**:4, 7, 18-19, 24
"Stubborn Hope" (Brutus) **24**:112
Stubborn Hope: New Poems and Selections from "China Poems" and "Strains" (Brutus) **24**:112, 116, 118, 122
"Stuck Inside of Mobile with the Memphis Blues Again" (Dylan) **37**:52, 54-56
"The Student" (Moore) **4**:260; **49**:100, 119
Studi letterari (Carducci) **46**:55
"Studies in Secrecy" (Graham) **59**:164
Studies in Song (Swinburne) **24**:322
"The Studies of Narcissus" (Schwartz) **8**:311
"The Studio" (Mahon) **60**:178, 188, 190-91, 201-2
Studium przedmiotu (Herbert) **50**:4-5, 7, 18, 20, 25
"A Study" (Masters) **1**:342
"The Study of History" (Rich) **5**:365
Study of the Object (Herbert)
See *Studium przedmiotu*
"Study to Deserve Death" (Smith) **12**:318
"Studying the Language" (Ní Chuilleanáin) **34**:356, 384-85
"Stumbling" (Montale)
See "Incespicare"
"Stump" (Heaney) **18**:202
Stunden-Buch (Rilke) **2**:277, 282, 288-90
Stundenbuch/Das Stundenbuch/A Book for the Hours of Prayer (Rilke)
See *Stunden-Buch*
"Stupid" (Carver) **54**:12
"The Stupid Pencil Maker" (Silverstein) **49**:347
"Stupid Piety" (Goethe) **5**:229
"Stupra" (Rimbaud) **57**:203
Les Stupra (Rimbaud) **57**:252
"The Sturgeon" (Carver) **54**:18
"Sturmangriff" (Stramm) **50**:218-19
"Stutgard" (Hölderlin) **4**:147
"Style" (Baraka) **4**:9
"Style" (Moore) **4**:259; **49**:126, 133, 139
"Style" (Sandburg) **41**:234, 359, 361
"Styx" (Duncan) **2**:119
"Su l'Adda" (Carducci) **46**:27, 42, 54, 84
"Su Monte Mario" (Carducci) **46**:9, 54, 87
"Su persona" (Guillén) **35**:188
"La suave agonie" (Valéry) **9**:391-92
"Suavidades" (Mistral) **32**:201
"Sub Contra" (Bogan) **12**:120
Sub Specie Aeternitatis (Hayden) **6**:194
"Sub Terra" (Williams) **7**:377
"A Subaltern" (Sassoon) **12**:242
"The Subalterns" (Hardy) **8**:111, 119
"Sub-entries" (Niedecker) **42**:148, 150
"Submission" (Philips) **40**:271
"The Substance" (Herbert) **50**:19
"A Substance In A Cushion" (Stein) **18**:321, 328, 349
"Subterranean Homesick Blues" (Dylan) **37**:54, 59, 71
"Suburb" (Borges)
See "Arrabal"
"Suburb" (Smith) **12**:317
"Suburb. Evening. Autumn" (Abse) **41**:8
"Suburb in which the country lies heavily" (Borges)
See "Arrabal en que pesa el campo"
"Suburban Dream" (Muir) **49**:245
"Suburban Woman" (Boland) **58**:13, 43-44
"Suburban Woman: A Detail" (Boland) **58**:15, 47-48
"Suburbia Mad Song" (Corso) **33**:25, 49
"The Subverted Flower" (Frost) **1**:198; **39**:246
"The Subway" (Tate) **50**:231, 246, 280, 288, 309, 312-14
"Subway No Way" (Alurista) **34**:22
"Subway Rush Hour" (Hughes) **53**:193
"Success" (Brooke) **24**:56-7
"Succory" (Reese) **29**:336
"The Succubus" (Graves) **6**:163
Such Counsels You Gave to Me and Other Poems (Jeffers) **17**:135
"Suche Happe as I ame Happed in" (Wyatt) **27**:317, 352
"Sudden Death" (Alexie) **53**:39
"Sudden Frost" (Wagoner) **33**:324, 367
"Sudden Journey" (Gallagher) **9**:50
"Sudden Light" (Rossetti) **44**:173
"The Sudder Bazaar" (Kipling) **3**:190, 194
"El sueño" (Storni) **33**:262, 296, 313;
El Sueño (Juana Inés de la Cruz) **24**:212-15, 224-27, 235
"Suenos" (Parra) **39**:261
"Suffer the Children" (Lorde) **12**:157
"Suffering" (Page) **12**:190
Suffering (Ungaretti)
See *Il dolore*
"The Sufficient Place" (Muir) **49**:230, 242, 265
Suffised not, Madam (Wyatt) **27**:317
"Suffryng in sorow in hope to attayn" (Wyatt) **27**:310
"Sugar" (Stein) **18**:320, 322-23, 328, 334
"Sugar Loaf" (Hughes) **7**:121
"Sugar Town" (Alexie) **53**:24
"Sugestión de un sauce" (Storni) **33**:262, 296;
"Sugestión de una cuna vacía" (Storni) **33**:261;
"Suggestion from a Friend" (Kenyon) **57**:28
"Suggestiones de un canto de pájaro" (Storni) **33**:295;
"Sui Campi di Marengo" (Carducci) **46**:11, 53
"El suicida" (Borges) **32**:90, 140
"The suicide" (Borges)
See "El suicida"
"Suicide" (Bukowski) **18**:5
"Suicide" (Hughes) **1**:255
"The Suicide" (Millay) **6**:206; **61**:212, 225, 245
"Suicide Blues" (Rukeyser) **12**:228
"The Suicide in the Copse" (Graves) **6**:142, 144
"Suicide in the Trenches" (Sassoon) **12**:267, 285
"Suicide in Two Voices" (Ignatow)
See "Two Voices"
"Suicide off Egg Rock" (Plath) **1**:389
"Suicide's Note" (Hughes) **1**:236; **53**:85
"Suis-je" (Laforgue) **14**:85
"The Suit" (Levine) **22**:225
"A Suite for Augustus" (Dove) **6**:106
"A Suite for Marriage" (Ignatow) **34**:320
"Suite furlana" (Pasolini) **17**:281-82
Suite furlana (Pasolini) **17**:252, 256, 279, 281
"Suite I" (Éluard) **38**:69
"Suite ii" (Éluard) **38**:69
"The Suitor" (Kenyon) **57**:19, 43
"Sukher vilap" (Tagore) **8**:405
"Sulla colonna più alta" (Montale) **13**:109, 111
"Sulla Greve" (Montale) **13**:152
"Sulle rive del Lambro" (Quasimodo) **47**:279, 303
"Sultry" (Lowell) **13**:95-6
"Sultry Rain" (Pasternak) **6**:257
"The Sumac in Ohio" (Wright) **36**:393, 400
Summa poética 1929-1946 (Guillén) **23**:104
"Summary" (Sanchez) **9**:224, 232
"Summary" (Sarton) **39**:335
"Summer" (Ashbery) **26**:124-125
"Summer" (Bryant) **20**:12
"Summer" (Darío)
See "Estival"
"Summer" (Glück) **16**:156, 166
"Summer" (Rossetti) **7**:280
"Summer" (Stryk) **27**:196, 208
"The Summer" (Trakl) **20**:226
"Summer" (Wright) **14**:377, 379
"Summer 1961" (Levertov) **11**:165
"Summer 1969" (Heaney) **18**:205
"Summer between Terms I" (Lowell) **3**:241
"Summer Dawn" (Morris) **55**:238, 258
"A Summer Day" (Riley) **48**:333

"Summer Day in the Mountains" (Li Po) **29**:145
"Summer Fog" (Carver) **54**:19
"Summer Holiday" (Jeffers) **17**:132
"Summer Home" (Heaney) **18**:203
"'Summer Is Over" (Cummings) **5**:108-09
"Summer Knowledge" (Schwartz) **8**:297-98, 312-19
Summer Knowledge: New and Selected Poems, 1938-1958 (Schwartz) **8**:289-91, 296, 301-02, 305, 309, 311
"Summer Landscape" (Doty) **53**:69
"A Summer Morning Walk" (Kavanagh) **33**:87
"Summer Music" (Sarton) **39**:323, 332
"A Summer Night" (Arnold) **5**:36, 42, 49, 50
"Summer Night" (Hughes) **53**:201
"A Summer Night" (Jarrell) **41**:169
"Summer Night Piece" (Lowell) **13**:64, 67
The Summer of Black Widows (Alexie) **53**:15, 25, 34
"The Summer People" (Merrill) **28**:224-25, 230-31, 235
"Summer Place" (Ammons) **16**:23, 47
"Summer Poem" (Enzensberger) **28**:141, 147-48
"A Summer Ramble" (Bryant) **20**:37, 39
"Summer Resort" (Page) **12**:173
"Summer Session" (Ammons) **16**:50
"Summer Sonatina" (Chin) **40**:36
"Summer time T. V. (is witer than ever)" (Sanchez) **9**:210-11, 213, 225
"The Summer Tree" (Sarton) **39**:367
"The Summer We Almost Split" (Piercy) **29**:311
"Summer Wind" (Bryant) **20**:40
"Summer Wish" (Bogan) **12**:94-5, 98, 100, 106, 121-22
"Summer Words of a Sistuh Addict" (Sanchez) **9**:225
"Summer-end in the Sharon" (Amichai) **38**:33-34
"A Summer's Dream" (Bishop) **3**:47; **34**:160
"Summer's Elegy" (Nemerov) **24**:291
"Summertime and the Living..." (Hayden) **6**:194, 196
"Summing It Up" (Stone) **53**:258
"Summit Beach, 1921" (Dove) **6**:121
"Summoner's Tale" (Chaucer) **19**:13
"The Summons" (Auden) **1**:38
"The Summons" (Dickey) **40**:150, 184-85, 228
"A Summons to Town" (Suckling) **30**:148-49, 150
Summonses of the Times (Bely)
See *Zovy vremen*
"Sumptuous Destitution" (Wilbur) **51**:293
"Sun" (Corso) **33**:40, 47
"Sun" (Dickey) **40**:158, 160, 181
"The Sun" (Milosz) **8**:192, 207
"Sun" (Moore) **4**:243; **49**:113-14, 122, 136, 149
"The Sun" (Nishiwaki)
See "Taiyo"
"The Sun" (Noyes) **27**:129
"The Sun" (Piercy) **29**:305
"The Sun" (Sexton) **2**:351, 372
"The Sun" (Trakl) **20**:226
"Sun and Flesh" (Rimbaud)
See "Soleil et chair"
"Sun and Love" (Carducci)
See "Sol e amore"
"Sun and Moon" (Kenyon) **57**:43
"Sun and Rain" (Merwin) **45**:97
"The Sun Burns" (Thomas) **52**:290, 293-95
"The Sun Does Not Move" (Bissett) **14**:5
"Sun Dog" (Wagoner) **33**:353-54
"The Sun Is near Meridan Height" (Brontë) **8**:73
"The Sun of the Waters" (Char)
See *Le Soleil des eaux*
"The Sun on the Letter" (Hardy) **8**:97
Sun Poem (Brathwaite) **56**:34-35, 41, 43-44, 51, 60-62, 71, 90-92, 100
"The Sun Rising" (Donne)
See "The Sunne Rising"
"The Sun Says His Prayers" (Lindsay) **23**:281
"Sun Stone" (Paz)
See "Piedra de sol"
Sun Stone (Paz)
See *Piedra de sol*
"Sun the First" (Elytis) **21**:131
Sun the First (Elytis)
See *Ílios o prótos*
The Sun Was Still Warm . . ." (Rimbaud)
See "Soleil était encore chaud . . ."
"Sun, Wind" (Wagoner) **33**:365-66, 368
"Sunbathing on a Rooftop in Berkeley" (Kumin) **15**:203
"Sunday" (Herbert) **4**:100
"Sunday" (Hughes) **1**:255
"Sunday" (Nemerov) **24**:277
"A Sunday" (Soto) **28**:397-98, 400
"Sunday" (Stone) **53**:230, 235
"Sunday" (Williams) **7**:351
"Sunday, 4 a.m." (Bishop) **34**:116
"Sunday at Key West" (Bishop) **34**:65, 123
"Sunday Evening" (Abse) **41**:26
"Sunday in the Country" (Swenson) **14**:247, 250, 264
"Sunday Lemons" (Walcott) **46**:240, 278
"Sunday Morning" (MacNeice) **61**:130-34
"Sunday Morning" (Stevens) **6**:292, 301, 304, 306, 327, 336
"Sunday Morning" (Whitman) **3**:391
"Sunday Morning" (Wilbur) **51**:237
"Sunday Morning Apples" (Crane) **3**:83, 90, 100
"Sunday Morning Prophecy" (Hughes) **53**:117
"A Sunday Morning Tragedy" (Hardy) **8**:99
"Sunday New Guinea" (Shapiro) **25**:269, 286, 295
"Sunday Night" (Hacker) **47**:98
"A Sunday with Shepherds and Herdboys" (Clare) **23**:13
sunday work(?) (Bissett) **14**:5, 16
"Sundays before noon" (Bukowski) **18**:23
"Sundays Kill More Men than Bombs" (Bukowski) **18**:4
"The Sundays of Satin-Legs Smith" (Brooks) **7**:69, 79-80, 85
"Sundays, Too" (Alexie) **53**:26, 31
"Sunderland" (Nemerov) **24**:295
"Sundew" (Atwood) **8**:13
Sundry Phansies (Kipling) **3**:193
"Sunflower" (Breton)
See "Tournesol"
"The Sunflower" (Montale) **13**:138, 141, 149
"Sunflower Possessed" (Goodison) **36**:142
"Sunflower Sonnets" (Jordan) **38**:122
"Sunflower Sutra" (Ginsberg) **4**:48, 50, 92; **47**:5, 37-38
"Sung beneath the Alps" (Hölderlin) **4**:142
Sung into the Rotary Press (Seifert) **47**:325
"The Sunken Bell" (Ishikawa)
See "Shizumeru kane"
"Sun-King" (Hope) **56**:307
"Sunlight" (Gunn) **26**:204, 214, 219
"Sunlight" (Heaney) **18**:203
"Sunlight and Flesh" (Rimbaud)
See "Soleil et chair"
"Sunlight Is Imagination" (Wilbur) **51**:235, 266
"The Sunlight on the Garden" (MacNeice) **61**:117, 119, 131-32, 137, 139, 147
"The Sunne Rising" (Donne) **1**:125, 134, 145, 147, 152, 154
"Sunny Prestatyn" (Larkin) **21**:229
"Sunrise" (Corso) **33**:44, 50
"Sunrise" (Lanier) **50**:54-56, 62, 82-84, 86, 93, 98, 100-101
"Sunrise" (Reese) **29**:330
"Sunset" (Corso) **33**:44
"Sunset" (Cummings) **5**:70, 94
"Sunset" (Dunbar) **5**:138-39
"Sunset" (Glück) **16**:170
"Sunset" (Ransom) **61**:291
"Sunset from Omaha Hotel Window" (Sandburg) **41**:297
Sunset Gun (Parker) **28**:347-48, 351, 353, 362-63
"Sunset of the Century" (Tagore)
See "Shatabdir surya"
"A Sunset of the City" (Brooks) **7**:68-9, 96
"Sunset on the Spire" (Wylie) **23**:324, 328
"Sunset Over Villa Ortuzar" (Borges)
See "Ultimo sol en Villa Ortúzar"
"The Sunset Piece" (MacLeish) **47**:158
"Sunset Piece: After Reaching Rémy De Gourmont" (Cummings) **5**:71
"Sunset Walk in Thaw-Time in Vermont" (Warren) **37**:305, 379
"Sunsets" (Abse) **41**:25
Sunstone (Paz)
See *Piedra de sol*
"Sunsum" (Brathwaite) **56**:7-8, 11, 30
"Sunthin' in the Pastoral Line" (Riley) **48**:298
"Superfluous Advice" (Parker) **28**:362
"Superiorities" (Wilbur) **51**:266-67
"A Supermarket in California" (Ginsberg) **47**:4, 38
"Supernatural Love" (Schnackenberg) **45**:330, 334, 338, 341, 346-47
Supernatural Love Poems (Schnackenberg) **45**:341, 343, 348
"A Superscription" (Rossetti) **44**:255-56
"Suplication" (Sidney) **32**:247
"The Supper after the Last" (Kinnell) **26**:238, 257, 279
"Supper Time" (Hughes) **1**:255; **53**:99-100
"A Supplication for Love" (Browning) **6**:31
"Supplication to Venus" (Gower) **59**:20
"Supposed Confessions of a Second-Rate Sensitive Mind not in unity with itself" (Tennyson) **6**:406, 409
"Supreme Fiction" (Ammons) **16**:23
"Supreme Surrender" (Rossetti) **44**:169
"Supuesto, discurso mío" (Juana Inés de la Cruz) **24**:180, 184
Sur la poésie (Char) **56**:126, 129, 137, 142-44
"Sur l'eau" (Valéry) **9**:391-92
"Sur les lagunes" (Gautier) **18**:125
"Sur l'herbe" (Verlaine) **2**:430; **32**:348, 350, 385, 390-91
"Sur une nuit sans ornement" (Char) **56**:120, 179
"Sura" (Corso) **33**:25, 49
"The Surface" (Graham) **59**:177
"The Surface" (Swenson) **14**:261, 282
"The Surface as Object" (Guest) **55**:185
"Surf-Casting" (Merwin) **45**:45
"The Surfer" (Wright) **14**:345
"The Surgeons" (Kunitz) **19**:151
"The Surname" (Guillén)
See "El apellido"
"La Surprise" (Éluard) **38**:96-97
"Surprise" (Parker) **28**:362
"Surprise" (Silverstein) **49**:326
"Surprise, Surprise!" (Abse) **41**:3, 6
"Surprises" (Kumin) **15**:210, 223
Surrealist Poetry (Aleixandre)
See *Poesía superrealista*
"Surrey Poems" (Mahon) **60**:141, 192, 199
"The Surround" (Dickey) **40**:211, 236, 238
"Surrounded by Wild Turkeys" (Snyder) **21**:326
"Survey of Literature" (Ransom) **61**:300, 308
"Survival as Tao, Beginning at 5:00 a.m." (Carruth) **10**:88
"Survival: Infantry" (Oppen) **35**:284
"Survival of the Fittest" (Gozzano) **10**:183
"Survivor" (Goodison) **36**:145
"The Survivor" (Graves) **6**:137, 142, 144
"A Survivor" (Merwin) **45**:46
"The Survivor" (Wagoner) **33**:335
"Survivors" (Sassoon) **12**:267-68, 285
"Susan Tichy, a Poet from Colorado" (Amichai) **38**:22
"Suspenders" (Carver) **54**:15, 18, 28
"Suspension" (Lorde) **12**:158
"The suspicion" (Cavafy) **36**:53

"Suspicor Speculum: To Sisyphus" (Merwin) **45**:19
"Sussex" (Kipling) **3**:167, 192
"Sustainment" (Dickey) **40**:158
"Svalka" (Shvarts) **50**:146, 160
"Svapna" (Tagore) **8**:410-11
"Svarga" (Tagore) **8**:414
"Svarga ha'ite biday" (Tagore) **8**:409
Světlem oděná (Seifert) **47**:316, 335
"Svoe muchenie nochnoe" (Shvarts) **50**:134
"Swamp Plant" (Wright) **14**:374
"The Swan" (Baudelaire)
See "Le cygne"
"The Swan" (Roethke) **15**:275, 288
"Swan, Elemental" (Lawrence) **54**:187
"The Swans" (Darío)
See "Los cisnes"
"The Swans" (Lowell) **13**:86
"The Swans" (Sarton) **39**:323
"Swans" (Stone) **53**:218, 228
"The Swans" (Storni)
See "Los Cisnes"
"Swans" (Teasdale) **31**:322
The Swans' Encampment (Tsvetaeva)
See *Lebediny stan*
"The Swarm" (Graham) **59**:166
"The Swarm" (Plath) **1**:410, 412
Swarm (Graham) **59**:184-90
"Swathed round in mist" (Meredith) **60**:287
"Swaziland" (Giovanni) **19**:141
"Swedes" (Thomas) **53**:329
"Sweeney among the Nightingales" (Eliot) **5**:184; **31**:121
Sweeney Astray: A Version from the Irish (Heaney) **18**:215-18, 235
"Sweeney Redivivus" (Heaney) **18**:215, 228, 233
"The Sweeper of Ways" (Nemerov) **24**:282
"Sweet Afton" (Burns) **6**:77
"Sweet Ar the Thoughtes" (Raleigh)
See "Sweete Are the Thoughtes Wher Hope Persvadeth Happe"
"Sweet Boy, Give me Yr Ass" (Ginsberg) **4**:90
"A Sweet Flying Dream" (Ferlinghetti) **1**:183, 188
The Sweet Harm (Storni)
See *El dulce daño*
"Sweet Hopes" (Pushkin)
See "Nadezhdoi Sladostnoi"
"Sweet like a Crow" (Ondaatje) **28**:338
Sweet Machine (Doty) **53**:60-61, 63
"Sweet Mary Dove" (Clare) **23**:25
"Sweet Meat Has Sower Sauce or, the Slave-Trader in the Dumps" (Cowper) **40**:119
"Sweet Michel" (Browning) **2**:30
"The Sweet o' the Year" (Noyes) **27**:114
"The Sweet Primroses" (Hardy) **8**:130
"Sweet Susan" (Clare) **23**:25
"Sweet Things" (Gunn) **26**:209, 211
"Sweet Violets" (Parker) **28**:351
Sweet Will (Levine) **22**:221, 224, 226
"Sweete Are the Thoughtes Wher Hope Persvadeth Happe" (Raleigh) **31**:284, 294-95, 309, 312
"Sweetened Change" (Ammons) **16**:63
"Sweetest love, I do not goe" (Donne)
See "Song. 'Sweetest love, I do not goe'"
"Sweetness" (Mistral)
See "Dulzura"
Swellfoot (Shelley)
See *Oedipus Tyrannus; Or Swellfoot the Tyrant*
Swellfoot the Tyrant (Shelley)
See *Oedipus Tyrannus; Or Swellfoot the Tyrant*
"Swells" (Ammons) **16**:32, 63
"Swete were the sauce" (Raleigh) **31**:294
"Świadomość" (Milosz) **8**:209
"The Swift" (Char) **56**:131
"Swiftly walk over the western wave" (Shelley) **14**:177
"Swimmer" (Francis) **34**:243, 250
"The Swimmer" (Olds) **22**:323, 325
"Swimmers" (Swenson) **14**:265, 276, 287
"The Swimmers" (Tate) **50**:268, 281, 290-96, 307, 325, 329, 331-34, 336
"A Swimmer's Dream" (Swinburne) **24**:313, 325
"Swimming Chenango Lake" (Tomlinson) **17**:316, 319, 321, 328
"The Swimming Race" (Noyes) **27**:116
"Swineherd" (Ní Chuilleanáin) **34**:351-52
"Swit" (Herbert) **50**:5
"Switchback" (Parra)
See "La montaña rusa"
"Switchboard Girl" (Niedecker) **42**:102, 123
"Switezianka" (Mickiewicz) **38**:153
"Switzerland" (Arnold) **5**:12-13
Sword Blades and Poppy Seed (Lowell) **13**:69-70, 76, 93
"A Sword in a Cloud of Light" (Rexroth) **20**:190
"Swords" (Borges)
See "Espadas"
Swords Like Lips (Aleixandre)
See *Espadas como labios*
"The Sycamore" (Berry) **28**:25
"The Sycamore" (Moore) **49**:126, 135, 138
"Sydney Bridge" (Shapiro) **25**:269
"Sygil" (H. D.) **5**:306
"The Syllable Pain" (Celan) **10**:102
"Le sylphe" (Valéry) **9**:387, 391, 393
"Les Sylphides" (MacNeice) **61**:138
Sylvae (Dryden) **25**:80
Sylvan Moon (Paz)
See *Luna silvestre*
"Sylvia's Death" (Sexton) **2**:364, 370
Symbiosis (Guest) **55**:211, 221-23
"Symbolism in Painting" (Yeats) **20**:299
"The Symbolism of Poetry" (Yeats) **51**:147
The Symbolism of Poetry (Yeats) **20**:336
"Symbols" (Yeats) **51**:148
"Symmetrical Companion" (Swenson) **14**:274, 284
"Sympathetic Portrait of a Child" (Williams) **7**:349
"Sympathy" (Dunbar) **5**:134
"Sympathy" (Thoreau) **30**:168, 278-81, 293
"Symphonie en blanc majeur" (Gautier) **18**:124-27, 129-30
"The Symphony" (Lanier) **50**:55-56, 61-62, 72-74, 84, 90, 98, 106-8
"Symposium" (Boland) **58**:15
"Symposium" (Parra)
See "Simposio"
"Symptoms of Love" (Graves) **6**:155
"The Synagogue" (Shapiro) **25**:263, 269, 283, 296, 299-300
"Synamism" (Niedecker) **42**:148
"Synthese" (Benn) **35**:50
"Syrinx" (Merrill) **28**:223, 256
"The Syrophenician Woman" (Harper) **21**:208, 215-16
"The System" (Ashbery) **26**:108, 130
"The System" (Stone) **53**:223
"The Szechwan Road" (Li Po) **29**:140
Szomoru beres (Illyés) **16**:238, 247
T. V. Baby Poems (Ginsberg) **4**:47
"Ta bouche au lèvres d'or" (Éluard) **38**:71
"Ta chevelure d'oranges" (Éluard) **38**:71
Ta eleýa tis Oxópetras (Elytis) **21**:134-35
"Ta foi" (Éluard) **38**:70
"Ta Lettre sur le Drap" (Senghor) **25**:233-34, 249
"Tabacaria" (Pessoa) **20**:166, 169
Taberna otros lugares (Dalton) **36**:120, 129
"Tabibito" (Nishiwaki) **15**:229
Tabibito Kaerazu (Nishiwaki) **15**:229-36
"Las tablas" (Parra) **39**:284-85
"A Table" (Stein) **18**:320-22, 324, 328, 330, 350
"Table I" (Milosz) **8**:210
"Table II" (Milosz) **8**:210
"Table Talk" (Mahon) **60**:146, 148, 178-79
Table Talk (Cowper) **40**:101
"Tableau" (Cullen) **20**:64
"Tables of Longevity" (Char) **56**:138
"The Tables of the Law" (Yeats) **51**:76, 101-3, 106-7
"Tablet XVIII" (Schwerner) **42**:202-3
"Tablet XV" (Schwerner) **42**:201-2
"Tablet V" (Schwerner) **42**:202
"Tablet IV" (Schwerner) **42**:188, 192
"Tablet IX" (Schwerner) **42**:203
"Tablet I" (Schwerner) **42**:192, 202-3
"Tablet VII" (Schwerner) **42**:192, 204
"Tablet XVII" (Schwerner) **42**:203
"Tablet VI" (Schwerner) **42**:190, 202
"Tablet XVI" (Schwerner) **42**:202
"Tablet XIII" (Schwerner) **42**:204
"Tablet III" (Schwerner) **42**:192, 203
"Tablet XII" (Schwerner) **42**:190
"Tablet XXVII" (Schwerner) **42**:193, 196, 205, 208
"Tablet XXVI" (Schwerner) **42**:192-93, 196
"Tablet II" (Schwerner) **42**:192, 203
"Table-Talk" (Cowper) **40**:47-50, 56-7, 71, 104, 116, 142
The Tablets (Schwerner) **42**:187-96, 198, 200-209
"Tablets Journals" (Schwerner) **42**:194, 202, 205
"Tachycardia at the Foot of the Fifth Green" (Wagoner) **33**:335
"Tag" (Hughes) **53**:192
"Tag och skriv" (Ekeloef) **23**:51, 76, 78
"Tagore's Last Poems" (Tagore)
See "Śesh lekhā"
"Tahirassawichi en Washington" (Cardenal) **22**:131
"Taipei Girl" (Quintana) **36**:266, 271
"Taith i Garu" (Dafydd ap Gwilym) **56**:241
"Taiyo" (Nishiwaki) **15**:240-41
"Take" (Hagiwara) **18**:179
"Take a whole holiday in honour of this" (Day Lewis) **11**:130
"Take Anguish for Companion" (Sarton) **39**:324
"Take from My Palms" (Mandelstam) **14**:117
"Take heed of loving mee" (Donne)
See "The Prohibition"
"Take Them Out!" (Jordan) **38**:127
"Take This Hammer" (Brown) **55**:159
"Take Wine" (Li Po) **29**:161
"take you down" (Alurista) **34**:39
"Taken Aback" (McKay) **2**:221
"Taking" (Ondaatje) **28**:327, 332
"Taking In Wash" (Dove) **6**:111
"Taking justice into one's own hands" (Castro)
See "La justicia por la mano"
"Taking Leave of Zenka" (Hacker) **47**:118
"Taking Notice" (Hacker) **47**:105
Taking Notice (Hacker) **47**:81, 104
"Taking Off My Clothes" (Forché) **10**:133, 135
"Taking the Forest" (Howe) **54**:64, 69, 113-14
"Taking the Hands" (Bly) **39**:69
"Taking the Lambs to Market" (Kumin) **15**:216
"Takkakaw Falls" (Birney) **52**:22, 35, 58
"Tal vez porque te quiero" (Alurista) **34**:25, 40-41
Tala (Mistral) **32**:147, 149-50, 159-62, 164, 166, 168-71, 173, 179-83, 185, 208, 210
"Talbot Road" (Gunn) **26**:220, 229
"A Tale" (Bogan) **12**:85, 111, 127
"A Tale" (Coleridge) **11**:101
"A Tale" (Finch) **21**:166
"Tale" (Rimbaud)
See "Conte"
"Tale of Apollonius" (Gower) **59**:76-78, 80, 84
The Tale of Balen (Swinburne) **24**:348, 350-54, 357
"A Tale of Bananas" (Cruz) **37**:18
"Tale of Ceix and Alceone" (Gower) **59**:107
"The Tale of Custard the Dragon" (Nash) **21**:265
"Tale of Deianira, Hercules, and Nessus" (Gower) **59**:14, 41, 98-99

"Tale of Diogenes" (Gower) **59**:4
The Tale of Fatumeh (Ekeloef)
See *Sagan om Fatumeh*
"Tale of Florent" (Gower) **59**:108
"Tale of Hercules and Faunus" (Gower) **59**:102
"Tale of Iphis and Ianthe" (Gower) **59**:98, 100, 102, 108
"The Tale of Me" (Ní Chuilleanáin) **34**:385
"Tale of Melibee" (Chaucer) **19**:26, 33, 47
"Tale of Nectanabus" (Gower) **59**:15
"Tale of Orestes" (Gower) **59**:109
"Tale of Rosiphelee" (Gower) **59**:106
The Tale of Sir Thopas (Chaucer) **58**:368
"A Tale of Starvation" (Lowell) **13**:60, 84
The Tale of Sunlight (Soto) **28**:371, 384, 386
"Tale of Tereus, Progne, and Philomene" (Gower) **59**:5, 109
"A Tale of the Airly Days" (Riley) **48**:284, 315, 319
"The Tale of the Dead Princess and the Seven Heroes" (Pushkin)
See "Skazka o Mertvoy Tsarevne"
"Tale of the False Bachelor" (Gower) **59**:15
"The Tale of the Female Vagrant" (Wordsworth) **4**:373, 419
"The Tale of the Fisherman and the Fish" (Pushkin)
See "Skazka o Rybake i Rybke"
The Tale of the Golden Cockerel (Pushkin)
See "Skazka o Zolotom Petushke"
"The Tale of the Parson and His Man Balda" (Pushkin)
See "Skazka o Pope i o Rabotnike Yego Balde"
"A Tale of the Thirteenth Floor" (Nash) **21**:270-71
"The Tale of the Tsar Sultan" (Pushkin)
See "Skazka o Tsare Sultane"
"Tale of Time" (Warren) **37**:307, 380
A Tale of Time: New Poems, 1960-1966 (Warren) **37**:355
"Tale of Tobias and Sara" (Gower) **59**:110
"Tale of Two Cities" (Kavanagh) **33**:86
"A Tale of Two Gardens" (Paz)
See "Cuento de dos jardines"
A Tale of Two Gardens: Poems from India, 1952-1995 (Paz) **48**:264
"Tale of Ulysses and Telegonus" (Gower) **59**:15
Tales (Chaucer)
See *Canterbury Tales*
"Tales of a Wayside Inn" (Noyes) **27**:129
Tales of a Wayside Inn (Longfellow) **30**:18-19, 24-5, 36, 40-1, 43, 47-8, 61, 63, 65, 68, 75, 99, 107
Tales of Canterbury (Chaucer)
See *Canterbury Tales*
"Tales of Shatz" (Abse) **41**:19
"Tales of the Islands" (Walcott) **46**:272
"Tales of the Madwoman" (Mistral)
See "Historias de loca"
Tales of the Mermaid Tavern (Noyes) **27**:123-4, 126, 129, 134, 137
Talifer (Robinson) **1**:475, 477, 479, 483
"A Talisman" (Moore) **4**:232; **49**:89, 108
"Talismanes" (Borges) **32**:58, 90
"Talismans" (Borges)
See "Talismanes"
Talismatic Night (Char)
See *La Nuit Talismanique*
"Talk 1" (Cage) **58**:205
"A Talk with Friedrich Nietzsche" (Zagajewski) **27**:389, 392
"The Talking Back of Miss Valentine Jones" (Jordan) **38**:125, 127, 138-39
"Talking Back (to W. H. Auden)" (Meredith) **28**:216
"Talking Dirty to the Gods" (Komunyakaa) **51**:61
Talking Dirty to the Gods (Komunyakaa) **51**:50, 57, 60, 64-65
"Talking in the Woods with Karl Amorelli" (Knight) **14**:43
"Talking Late with the Governor about the Budget" (Snyder) **21**:300, 326
"Talking Oak" (Tennyson) **6**:356
"Talking to Myself" (Ignatow) **34**:309
"Talking to the Dead" (Stone) **53**:223-24
"Tall Ambrosia" (Thoreau) **30**:182, 232-36
"The Tall Girl" (Ransom) **61**:271, 307
"A Tall Man" (Sandburg) **41**:321
"Tall Nettles" (Thomas) **53**:280, 317, 329
"The Tall Sailing Ship" (Quasimodo)
See "L'alto veliero"
"Talu Dyled" (Dafydd ap Gwilym) **56**:247
"Tam Glen" (Burns) **6**:59
"Tam o' Shanter" (Burns) **6**:55-8, 73-4, 76, 78, 81, 89, 96
"Tama yo shizume" (Ishikawa) **10**:213
"Tamar" (Jeffers) **17**:106-07, 111, 116, 130-32, 135, 138, 141, 146
Tamar and Other Poems (Jeffers) **17**:122, 124, 128, 135, 138, 146
"Tamara" (Lermontov) **18**:291-92, 298
Tamarind Season (Goodison) **36**:140-43, 150, 158
"Tamarisk" (Herbert) **50**:3
"Tamarlane" (Poe) **1**:428, 436-38, 442, 444-45, 448
Tamarlane, and Other Poems, By a Bostonian (Poe) **1**:428, 432, 437, 449
"Tambourines" (Hughes) **53**:91
The Tambov Treasurer's Wife (Lermontov)
See *Tambovskaya kaznacheysha*
Tambovskaya kaznacheysha (Lermontov) **18**:278, 282
"Tamer and Hawk" (Gunn) **26**:200, 221
"Tamerton Church-Tower" (Patmore) **59**:237, 239-40, 244, 257
Tamerton Church-Tower (Patmore) **59**:205, 218-19, 239-40
"Tampa Robins" (Lanier) **50**:62, 77
"T' My Birth & Life: S:" (Howe) **54**:103
T& G: The Collected Poems (Niedecker) **42**:94, 96, 101-2, 106, 133, 135
"Tanghi-Garu Pass" (Paz) **1**:361
"Tangible Disaster" (Césaire) **25**:18
"Tangled Up in Blue" (Dylan) **37**:56-9
"Tango" (Glück) **16**:151, 154
"Tankas" (Borges) **22**:78
"Tano" (Brathwaite) **56**:8, 75, 100
"Tantas Cosas Asustan, Tantas" (Cisneros) **52**:152
"Tanto e Amara" (Olson) **19**:320
"Tantsuiushchii David" (Shvarts) **50**:137
Tantsuiushchii David (Shvarts) **50**:134-36, 141-45, 147, 159
"Tanu" (Tagore) **8**:407
"Tanz" (Stramm) **50**:171, 201, 206
"Die Tänzerin (D.H.)" (Sachs) **18**:162
"The Tao and the Art of Leavetaking" (Chin) **40**:27
"Tape for the Turn of the Year" (Ammons) **16**:31
Tape for the Turn of the Year (Ammons) **16**:3-4, 6, 21-4, 28, 35, 42-3, 47-50, 59-61, 64-5
"The Tapestry" (Bridges) **28**:79
"Tapestry" (Cassian) **17**:5
The Tapestry (Bridges) **28**:76, 80-1
"Tapestry and Sail" (Dickey) **40**:236
"Taproot" (Forché) **10**:142
Taproot (Stryk) **27**:191, 197-98, 215, 218
"Taps" (Quintana) **36**:253
"Tarakar atmahatya" (Tagore) **8**:405
"Tarantella" (Belloc) **24**:7, 22, 31
"Tarde" (Mistral) **32**:203-05
"Tarde fresca" (Storni) **33**:251;
"Tarde mayor" (Guillén) **35**:233, 234
"The Tarentinians carouse" (Cavafy) **36**:55
Target Study (Baraka) **4**:38
"Tarkington Thou Should'st Be Living in This Hour" (Nash) **21**:273
"th tarot match covr uv th lovrs" (Bissett) **14**:33
"Tarquin, Aruns, and Lucrece" (Gower) **59**:7, 58, 60, 61, 63
"Tarquins" (Gower) **59**:60-61, 63
"Tarrant Moss" (Kipling) **3**:183
"Tarsier" (Szymborska) **44**:312
"Tartuffe's Punishment" (Rimbaud)
See "Le châtiment de Tartuff"
"tarzan collage" (Bissett) **14**:31
"A Task" (Milosz) **8**:206
The Task (Cowper) **40**:39, 42-43, 45, 50, 56-60, 64-68, 70, 72-74, 76-77, 79, 81-93, 96, 99, 101, 104-7, 109-11, 113-14, 116-20, 122-23, 125, 127, 129-31, 133-35, 137, 139-43
The Tasking (Sassoon) **12**:271
"The Taste" (Oppen) **35**:285, 331
"Tata Juan" (Alurista) **34**:25
"Tatinir katha" (Tagore) **8**:406
"The Tattooed Man" (Hayden) **6**:195
"Tattooing Ruth" (Silverstein) **49**:342
"Tavern" (Dalton) **36**:121, 136
"Tavern" (Millay) **6**:205
The Tavern and Other Places (Dalton)
See *Taberna otros lugares*
The Tavern and Other Poems (Dalton)
See *Taberna otros lugares*
"Tavern by the Hellespont" (Birney) **52**:22
"The Taxi" (Lowell) **13**:93
"The Taxis" (MacNeice) **61**:177, 184-85
"Taylor Street" (Gunn) **26**:213, 231
"T-Bar" (Page) **12**:177, 183, 188
"TCB" (Sanchez) **9**:225
"Tea at My Shetland Aunt's" (Birney) **52**:79
"Tea at the Palaz of Hoon" (Stevens) **6**:304
"The Tea Party" (MacLeish) **47**:187
"Teacher" (Kenyon) **57**:45
"Teacher" (Walker) **20**:273, 286
"Teaching a Dumb Calf" (Hughes) **7**:166
"Teaching in Belfast" (Mahon) **60**:140, 143, 182-83
"The Teamster" (Pavese) **13**:218
"A Teamster's Farewell" (Sandburg) **41**:234, 273
"Teamsters Union" (Shapiro) **25**:316
"Tear" (Hogan) **35**:259
"The Tear" (Pushkin) **10**:407
A Tear and a Smile (Gibran)
See *Dam 'ah wabitisāmah*
"A Tear for Cressid" (Wylie) **23**:314
"Tear Gas" (Rich) **5**:393, 396
"Tears" (Reese) **29**:330, 332-333, 335, 346-347, 352-353
"Tears" (Sitwell) **3**:326
"Tears" (Thomas) **53**:290
"Tears" (Whitman) **3**:379
"Tears and Laughter" (Gibran)
See *Dam 'ah wabitisāmah*
"Tears of an Excavator" (Pasolini) **17**:258, 289
The Tears of the Blind Lions (Merton) **10**:339
"The tears of the sisters of Phäethon" (Cavafy) **36**:53
"Teasing the Nuns" (Shapiro) **25**:286, 300
"Teatro Bambino" (Lowell) **13**:94
"Techiman" (Brathwaite) **56**:29, 85
"The Technique of Perfection" (Graves) **6**:128
"Technologies" (Oppen) **35**:308, 348-53
"Teddungal" (Senghor) **25**:255
"Teddy Bears" (Swenson) **14**:273
"Tedio Invernale" (Carducci) **46**:23, 50, 78
"The Teeth-Mother Naked at Last" (Bly) **39**:12-16, 18, 22, 24-5, 37, 92-4
"Tegnér's Drapa" (Longfellow) **30**:49, 91-5
"Tehran 3 May 68" (Brutus) **24**:123
"Tejedores viejos" (Mistral) **32**:181, 191
"Telegramas de urgencia escribo" (Fuertes) **27**:16
"Telemachus Remembers" (Muir) **49**:220, 279-80
"The Telephone" (Angelou) **32**:27
"The Telephone Call" (Yau) **61**:337, 340, 342-44
"Telephoning God" (Soto) **28**:375
"Telescopic" (Frost)
See "A Loose Mountain Telescopic"

"Television Is a Baby Crawling Toward That Death Chamber" (Ginsberg) **4**:51, 76
"Television Poem" (Sanchez) **9**:210
"Tell Me" (Hughes) **1**:244; **53**:123, 191
"Tell Me" (Silverstein) **49**:342
"Tell Me" (Toomer) **7**:335
"Tell Me a Story" (Warren) **37**:380
Tell Me Again How the White Heron Rises and Flies Across the Nacreous River at Twilight Toward the Distant Islands (Carruth) **10**:86-7
"Tell Me Some Way" (Reese) **29**:333
"Tell Me, Tell Me" (Moore) **49**:148
Tell Me, Tell Me: Granite, Steel, and Other Topics (Moore) **4**:242, 259; **49**:113, 144, 146-47, 149
"tell me what attackd yu" (Bissett) **14**:32
"Telling the Bees" (Reese) **29**:333
"Temas candentes Agricultura" (Fuertes) **27**:28
"The Temper" (Herbert) **4**:100, 118
"The Temper I" (Herbert) **4**:101, 111
The Tempers (Williams) **7**:344, 348, 367, 378, 395, 398, 405
"Tempest and Music" (Viereck) **27**:278, 280
"Tempid: Bellosguardo" (Montale) **13**:126
"The Temple" (Brown) **55**:82, 114
"The Temple" (Herrick)
See "The Fairie Temple: or, Oberons Chappell. Dedicated to Mr. John Merrifield, Counsellor at Law"
"Le temple" (Lamartine) **16**:277
"The Temple of Fame" (Pope) **26**:318-19, 331
The Temple: Sacred Poems and Private Ejaculations (Herbert) **4**:99-102, 106, 110, 114-18, 120-21, 123, 126, 129, 132-33
"Il tempo passa" (Pavese) **13**:209, 226
"Le Temps" (Char) **56**:146
Le temps déborde (Éluard) **38**:75, 78
"Le Temps et les Cités" (Hugo) **17**:88
"Temps Perdu" (Parker) **28**:365
"Temptation" (Cassian) **17**:4
"Temptation in Harvest" (Kavanagh) **33**:71, 94, 102, 117, 121, 127, 131, 137
"The Temptation of St. Joseph" (Auden) **1**:38-39
"Tempyo gannen tsuchinoto mi, Settsu no kuni no handen no shisho Hasetsukabe no Tatsumaro mizukara wanaki mimakarishi toki, hangan Otomo no Sukune Minaka no tsukuru uta" (Yakamochi) **48**:132
Temy i variatsi (Pasternak) **6**:252, 255, 261, 264-65, 269, 271, 275, 277-81, 283
Temy i var'iatsii (Pasternak)
See *Temy i variatsi*
"X" (Joyce) **22**:136, 138, 145, 153, 160, 162, 168
"10 April 67" (Brutus) **24**:122
Ten Burnt Offerings (MacNeice) **61**:181
The Ten Thousand Leaves (Yakamochi)
See *Man'yōshū*
"A Tenancy" (Merrill) **28**:249-50, 268
"The Tenant" (Brodsky) **9**:2
Tenants of the House (Abse) **41**:2-4, 7, 9-11, 13, 15-16, 19, 27
"Ten-Day Leave" (Meredith) **28**:180, 186
Tender Buttons: Objects, Food, Rooms (Stein) **18**:316-34, 336, 341-42, 344, 349-54
Tender only To One (Smith) **12**:292, 326, 340, 343, 349
"Tenderness" (Ignatow) **34**:270
Tenderness (Mistral)
See *Ternura*
Tenderness (Yevtushenko)
See *Nezhnost*
"Tenderness toward Existence" (Kinnell) **26**:251
"Tenebrae" (Celan) **10**:101-02, 118
"Tenebrae" (Levertov) **11**:176
"Tengo" (Guillén) **23**:106, 115
Tengo (Guillén) **23**:124-25, 127, 130-31, 133
"Tengo que deciros" (Fuertes) **27**:4
"Tenjō Ishi" (Hagiwara) **18**:178-79
"Tenki" (Nishiwaki) **15**:228
"The Tennessee Hero" (Harper) **21**:206, 218
"Tennessee June" (Graham) **59**:150, 181
"Tennis" (Pinsky) **27**:144, 162
"The Tennis Court Oath" (Ashbery) **26**:113
The Tennis Court Oath (Ashbery) **26**:108, 112-113, 118, 129, 137-138, 143, 163
"Tenor" (Guillén) **23**:122, 124
Tentativa del hombre infinito (Neruda) **4**:276
"Tentative Description of a Dinner to Promote the Impeachment of President Eisenhower" (Ferlinghetti) **1**:167
"Tentative Gardening" (Hacker) **47**:118
"Tenth Elegy" (Rilke) **2**:273, 286-87
"Tenth Muse" (Lowell) **3**:213
The Tenth Muse Lately sprung up in America (Bradstreet) **10**:2-3, 6-8, 12, 18, 20-1, 25-7, 29-31, 34, 37, 40-1, 43, 46, 51-2, 59
Tenth Nemean (Pindar)
See *Nemean 10*
Tenth Olympian (Pindar)
See *Olympian 10*
"Tenth Psalm" (Sexton) **2**:372
Tenth Pythian (Pindar)
See *Pythian 10*
"Tenuous and Precarious" (Smith) **12**:312, 337
"Teodoro Luna's Two Kisses" (Ríos) **57**:316
Teodoro Luna's Two Kisses (Ríos) **57**:325
Tercera residencia, 1935-1945 (Neruda) **4**:291, 306
"Tercero antolojía poética" (Jiménez) **7**:195
"Teremteni" (Illyés) **16**:235, 249
"Terence, This Is Stupid Stuff" (Housman) **2**:193
"Teresa" (Wilbur) **51**:284
"A Term" (Aleixandre) **15**:4
"Le Terme épars" (Char) **56**:137
"Terminal" (Shapiro) **25**:324
"The Terminal Bar" (Mahon) **60**:172
"Terminal Day at Beverly Farms" (Lowell) **3**:219
"Terminal Resemblance" (Glück) **16**:158
"Terminus" (Emerson) **18**:75-77, 113
"Terminus" (Heaney) **18**:227
Ternura (Mistral) **32**:147, 149, 164, 171, 179-80, 183, 208
"Terorysta, on patrzy" (Szymborska) **44**:270, 283
"Terra" (Quasimodo) **47**:272, 302
"Terra" (Ungaretti) **57**:342
La terra impareggiabile (Quasimodo) **47**:287, 289, 304
La terra promessa (Ungaretti) **57**:339-40, 376-77
"The Terrace" (Wilbur) **51**:188
"The Terrace at Berne" (Arnold) **5**:12, 19, 49
"The Terraced Valley" (Graves) **6**:135, 139, 143-44, 172
"La Terre" (Bonnefoy) **58**:168-69
"A Terre" (Owen) **19**:327, 331, 336, 339-40, 357, 359, 368
"Terre bianche" (Quasimodo) **47**:278
"The Terrestrial Paradise" (Morris) **55**:306
"Territory" (Kumin) **15**:207
"Terror" (Levertov) **11**:169
"Terror" (Warren) **37**:284, 287, 289, 323-24, 332, 380
"Terror and Decorum" (Viereck) **27**:267, 271
Terror and Decorum (Viereck) **27**:258-63, 277-84
"The Terror of Existing" (Montale)
See "Il terrore di esistere"
"Il terrore di esistere" (Montale) **13**:139
"The Terrorist, He Watches" (Szymborska)
See "Terorysta, on patrzy"
Terze Odi Barbare (Carducci) **46**:8
"Tess's Lament" (Hardy) **8**:85
"The Test" (Emerson) **18**:77
"Test" (Parra) **39**:271, 277, 302, 307, 310
"Test of Atlanta 1979" (Jordan) **38**:144
"The Test of Manhood" (Meredith) **60**:262
"A Testament" (Lermontov) **18**:278
"Testament" (Sandburg) **41**:256, 270
"Testament" (Stryk) **27**:215
The Testament (Villon)
See *Le Testament*
Le Testament (Villon) **13**:374-75, 377, 379, 387-90, 393-418
"Testament Coran" (Pasolini) **17**:262, 279
The Testament of Beauty (Bridges) **28**:48-50, 54-6, 59, 62, 65, 70-3, 76-8, 81
"The Testament of Love" (Bridges) **28**:65
Testament of Love (Chaucer)
See *Legend of Good Women*
"Testament of the Thief" (Kinnell) **26**:240
Testimonies (Dalton) **36**:120
"Testimony" (Komunyakaa) **51**:55, 63
"Testimony of a Canadian Educational Leader" (Birney) **52**:17
"The Testing Tree" (Kunitz) **19**:175, 178, 180, 183
The Testing-Tree (Kunitz) **19**:157, 161, 163, 168, 172-74, 176, 185-86
"Tête de faune" (Rimbaud) **3**:271; **57**:175, 191, 236
"Têtes du serail" (Hugo) **17**:75
"Tetrameter Ode" (Kenyon) **57**:46
"Teurer Freund" (Heine) **25**:161
"Texas" (Lowell) **13**:86
"The Text" (Riley) **48**:300
"Le Texte interdit" (Éluard) **38**:83, 87
"Th' Ambrosia of the God's A Weed On Earth" (Thoreau) **30**:226
"Thalamus" (MacDiarmid) **9**:168, 176-77
"Thalassa" (MacNeice) **61**:113, 166
"Thalerò" (Sikelianos) **29**:373
"Thamár y Amnón" (García Lorca) **3**:120, 131-32, 134, 146
"Thammuz" (Mahon) **60**:135
"Thanatopsis" (Bryant) **20**:10, 12, 14, 16-19, 21-3, 26-30, 32, 34, 41, 43, 47
"Thank God for Little Children" (Harper) **21**:197
"Thank You, Fog" (Auden) **1**:31
"Thank You, Thank You" (Kavanagh) **33**:96, 138
"Thanking My Mother for Piano Lessons" (Wakoski) **15**:325, 347
"A Thanksgiving" (Auden) **1**:31
"Thanksgiving" (Glück) **16**:124, 129, 150
"Thanksgiving for a Habitat" (Auden) **1**:24
"Thanksgiving Ode" (Wordsworth) **4**:399
"Thanksgiving's Over" (Lowell) **3**:206
"A Thank-You Note" (Szymborska) **44**:319
"Thar's More in the Man Than Thar Is in the Land" (Lanier) **50**:91
"Th'Assyryans king" (Surrey) **59**:303
"That April night's menu" (Enzensberger) **28**:155
"That Blessed Hope" (Harper) **21**:189, 208, 217
"That Bright Chimeric Beast" (Cullen) **20**:67
"That Day" (Sexton) **2**:353
"That Day" (Stone) **53**:256
"That Day That Was That Day" (Lowell) **12**:85
"That Force" (Zagajewski) **27**:385
"That is sufficient" (Guillén)
See "Eso Basta"
"That Kind of Thing" (Gallagher) **9**:61
"That Moment" (Hardy) **8**:94
"That Moment" (Wagoner) **33**:364
"That None Beguiled Be" (Suckling) **30**:143
"That Pheaton of Our Day" (Thoreau) **30**:268
"That Swan's Way" (Aleixandre) **15**:5
"That the Night Come" (Yeats) **20**:351
"That the Science of Cartography Is Limited" (Boland) **58**:18, 25, 59-60
"That Which is Now Behind, Previous Condition: The Eight of Swords" (Piercy) **29**:324
"That which is one they shear and make it twain" (Belloc) **24**:37-8
"That Which is White" (Storni)
See "Lo blanco"
"That Which Opposes the Overthrowing of the Tower: The Nine of Cups" (Piercy) **29**:324

"That Winter" (Stone) **53**:252
"That Woman There" (Stryk) **27**:203
"That women are but men's shadows" (Jonson)
See *The Forest VII*
"That Year" (Olds) **22**:308, 320, 322
"That-Air Young 'Un" (Riley) **48**:340, 362
"The Thatcher" (Heaney) **18**:200
"That's the Man" (Cavafy) **36**:106
"That's the Place Indians Talk About" (Ortiz) **17**:228, 230-31, 234
That's What We Live For (Szymborska) **44**:281, 318
That's Why We Are Alive (Szymborska)
See *That's What We Live For*
"Thaw" (Thomas) **53**:328
"The Thaw" (Thoreau) **30**:192, 194, 234, 241, 245
"The" (Zukofsky)
See "Poem Beginning 'The'"
"Theater Impressions" (Szymborska) **44**:278
"The Theatre" (Abse) **41**:32
"Théâtre" (Bonnefoy) **58**:130, 132, 134
"Theatre of Sidon A.D. 400" (Cavafy) **36**:66, 76
"Thébaide" (Gautier) **18**:146
Theban Dithyramb (Pindar) **19**:423
"The,bright,Centipede" (Villa) **22**:350
"The,caprice,of,canteloupe,is,to,be" (Villa) **22**:356-57
Thee (Aiken) **26**:24, 29
"Their Beginning" (Cavafy) **36**:69, 76, 78, 81, 91
"Their Behaviour" (Brutus) **24**:99
"Their Camp" (Wagoner) **33**:359
"Their Frailty" (Sassoon) **12**:267
"Their Mouths Full" (Ignatow) **34**:310
"Their Poem" (Cruz) **37**:5
"Their Shelter" (Wagoner) **33**:359
"Their Week" (Merwin) **45**:34
"Thekla's Answer" (Arnold) **5**:50
"thel" (Clifton) **17**:30
"Thelassius" (Swinburne) **24**:312-315
"Them, Crying" (Dickey) **40**:196, 215
"Theme and Variation" (Hayden) **6**:186, 197
"Theme and Variations" (Pasternak) **6**:251
"Theme for English B" (Hughes) **53**:94, 126, 128, 163, 192-93
Themes and Variations (Pasternak)
See *Temy i variatsi*
Themes & Variations (Cage) **58**:200-201, 205-6
"Then" (Hacker) **47**:88
"Then" (Muir) **49**:231, 249
"Then" (Stone) **53**:240, 258
"Then" (Wilbur) **51**:223
"Then Follows" (Jackson) **44**:13
"Then I Saw What the Calling Was" (Rukeyser) **12**:223
"Then It Is a Prison" (Alurista) **34**:22
"Then It Was" (Jordan) **38**:120
"Then the Ermine" (Moore) **49**:126, 130-31, 137
"Theodore Dreiser" (Masters) **1**:343
"Theodore the Poet" (Masters) **1**:345; **36**:201
"Theodotos" (Cavafy) **36**:8
"Theogonien" (Benn) **35**:8
"Theological Cradle Songs" (Viereck) **27**:262
"Theology" (Dunbar) **5**:120, 125, 127
"Theology" (Hughes) **7**:123, 159
"The Theology of Cockroaches" (Alexie) **53**:25
"Theophilos Palaiologos" (Cavafy) **36**:40
"Theophilus" (Robinson) **35**:368
"Theory of Art" (Baraka) **4**:9
"Theory of Evil" (Hayden) **6**:194, 196
"Theory of Flight" (Rukeyser) **12**:207, 218, 225
Theory of Flight (Rukeyser) **12**:202-03, 206, 209-10, 226-27, 235-36
"Theory of Maya" (Tagore)
See "Mayavada"
"A Theory of Prosody" (Levine) **22**:227
"Theory of Truth" (Jeffers) **17**:131, 142, 144
"ther may have been a tunnel thru which my train rolld" (Bissett) **14**:34
"There" (Verlaine) **2**:416
"There Are Birds" (Shapiro) **25**:294
"There Are Blk/Puritans" (Sanchez) **9**:218
"There Are Courtesies That Make You Want to Kill" (Parra)
See "Hay cortesías que merecen palos"
"There Are Delicacies" (Birney) **52**:32, 82
"There Are No Gods" (Lawrence) **54**:185, 187
"There Are Orioles in Woods and Lasting Length of Vowels" (Mandelstam) **14**:141
"There Are So Many Houses and Dark Streets without Help" (Bukowski) **18**:15
"There Are Things I Tell to No One" (Kinnell) **26**:258, 260-61, 280, 292
"There Can Be No Other Apple for Me" (Corso) **33**:36
"There Has to Be a Jail for Ladies" (Merton) **10**:341
"There he is!" (Cavafy) **36**:57
"There I Could Never Be a Boy" (O'Hara) **45**:132, 142, 165
"There is a hill beside the silver Thames" (Bridges) **28**:66-7, 83
"There Is Only One of Everything" (Atwood) **8**:23, 28
"There Never Yet Was Woman Made" (Suckling) **30**:139
"There Once Lived a Poor Knight" (Pushkin)
See "Zhil Na Svete Rytsar' Bednyi"
"There Shines the Moon, at Noon of Night" (Brontë) **8**:75
"There Should be No Despair" (Brontë) **8**:68-9
"There Was a Child Went Forth" (Whitman) **3**:392, 396, 415
"There Was A Dance Sweetheart" (Harjo) **27**:69
"There Was a Lad Was Born in Kyle" (Burns) **6**:76
"There Was a Poor Knight" (Pushkin)
See "Zhil Na Svete Rytsar' Bednyi"
"There Was a Saviour" (Thomas) **2**:390; **52**:258
"There Was a Time" (Thomas) **53**:286-87
"There Was Glass and There Are Stars" (Jarrell) **41**:169
"There was Never Nothing" (Wyatt) **27**:318
"There Was One" (Parker) **28**:362
"There Will Be Rest" (Teasdale) **31**:336, 341, 390
Therefore (Mallarmé)
See *Igitur*
"There's a Better Shine" (Niedecker) **42**:150-51, 167, 169
"There's a Grandfather's Clock in the Hall" (Warren) **37**:304-5
There's a Trick with a Knife I'm Learning to Do: Poems, 1963-1978 (Ondaatje) **28**:327-40
"There's Me" (Baca) **41**:38
"There's Nothing Here" (Muir) **49**:298
"There's Something I Often Notice" (Yevtushenko) **40**:341
"Thermopylae" (Carver) **54**:28
"Thermopylae" (Cavafy) **36**:28, 56, 57, 89
"These" (Williams) **7**:360, 362-63
"Lo These Are Parts of His Ways" (Curnow) **48**:21
"These Are the Young" (Lindsay) **23**:281
"These Images Remain" (Sarton) **39**:324, 345
"These Mornings of Rain" (Walker) **30**:343
"These Pure Arches" (Sarton) **39**:322
"These States: To Miami Presidential Convention" (Ginsberg) **4**:82
"These Streets" (Levine) **22**:224
"These Things that Poets Said" (Thomas) **53**:291
"These Were Her Nightly Journeys" (Sarton) **39**:333
"Theseus and Ariadne" (Graves) **6**:136-37, 144, 146
"Thetis" (H. D.) **5**:267-68
"They" (Sassoon) **12**:241, 249, 263, 275, 277-78, 286
"They All Want To Play Hamlet" (Sandburg) **41**:276
"They Are More on a Corncob" (Guillén)
See "Son más en una mazorca"
"They Are Not Missed" (Toomer) **7**:338-39
"They Are Not Ready" (Madhubuti) **5**:338
"They came at a pace" (Niedecker) **42**:151
"They Clapped" (Giovanni) **19**:141
"They Eat Out" (Atwood) **8**:6
"They Feed They Lion" (Levine) **22**:216, 221, 227
They Feed They Lion (Levine) **22**:211, 213, 215, 217, 223
"They fle from me" (Wyatt) **27**:300, 302, 309, 314, 316, 329-31, 338, 343, 347-48, 355, 357, 362
"They Flee from Me" (Wyatt)
See "They fle from me"
"They Have Come" (Storni)
See "Han venido"
"They Have Put Us on Hold" (Walker) **20**:294
"They Led You Away at Dawn" (Akhmatova)
See "Uvodili tebya na rassvete"
"They Say I Have..." (Silverstein) **49**:342
"They Say it Snowed" (Ammons) **16**:44
"They Say the Sea Is Loveless" (Lawrence) **54**:197
"They Say This Isn't a Poem" (Rexroth) **20**:195-96
"They shall not pass" (Paz)
See "¡No pasarán"
"They Should Have Provided" (Cavafy) **36**:51
"They Take A Little Nip" (Walker) **30**:338
"They Went Home" (Angelou) **32**:27, 29
"They Who Feel Death" (Walker) **30**:345
"They Will Say" (Sandburg) **41**:239, 243, 327, 334, 337, 350, 364, 367-68
"They'd Never Know Me Now" (Masters) **1**:344
"They've Put a Brassiere on the Camel" (Silverstein) **49**:313, 324
"Thick-Lipped Nigger" (Guillén)
See "Negro bembón"
"The Thief" (Kunitz) **19**:150-51, 172, 175
Thieves of Paradise (Komunyakaa) **51**:33, 50, 52, 54-57, 63
"The Thimble" (Kenyon) **57**:23, 43
"Thin Air" (Hass) **16**:215, 217
"The Thin People" (Plath) **1**:388, 406; **37**:184
"Thin Strips" (Sandburg) **41**:298
"The Thing I Am" (Borges) **32**:58
"Things" (Borges) **32**:58, 140
"The Things" (Borges) **32**:58
"Things" (Kenyon) **57**:5, 17, 33
"Things" (Reese) **29**:336
"Things Are What They Seem" (Moore) **49**:105, 110, 134
"Things Ended" (Cavafy) **36**:80
"Things I Say to Myself While Hanging Laundry" (Stone) **53**:224
"Things of August" (Stevens) **6**:313
Things of This World (Wilbur) **51**:231, 237, 272-73, 293, 299, 322, 330, 333
"Things Seen" (Sarton) **39**:342
Things Taking Place (Swenson)
See *New and Selected Things Taking Place*
"Things That Are Worse Than Death" (Olds) **22**:313
Things That I Do in the Dark: Selected Poetry (Jordan) **38**:112, 120-22, 127
"Things That Might Have Been" (Borges) **32**:46, 58, 66, 90
"Things to do with Moonlight" (Curnow) **48**:15-17, 19, 34
"Think No More, Lad: Laugh, Be Jolly" (Housman) **2**:179, 183, 185
"Think of It" (Celan) **10**:98
"Think Tank" (Merrill) **28**:267
"The Thinker" (Williams) **7**:353
"Thinking about El Salvador" (Levertov) **11**:198
"Thinking of Inishere in Cambridge, Massachusetts" (Mahon) **60**:143, 170, 198

"Thinking of Madame Bovary" (Kenyon) **57**:5, 15
"Thinking of Old Tu Fu" (Matsuo Bashō) **3**:10
"Thinking of the Lost World" (Jarrell) **41**:162, 164, 180-81, 189, 208, 217-18
"Third Degree" (Hughes) **1**:248; **53**:119
"The Third Dimension" (Levertov) **11**:159
"Third Elegy" (Rilke) **2**:271
"Third Georgic" (Vergil) **12**:361
"Third Hymn to Lenin" (MacDiarmid) **9**:180-81, 197
"Third Memory" (Yevtushenko) **40**:347
Third Nemean (Pindar)
See *Nemean 3*
Third Olympian (Pindar)
See *Olympian 3*
"Third Psalm" (Sexton) **2**:367
"Third Psalm of Life" (Longfellow) **30**:109
Third Pythian (Pindar)
See *Pythian 3*
The Third Residence (Neruda)
See *Tercera residencia, 1935-1945*
Third Residence (Neruda)
See *Tercera residencia, 1935-1945*
"The Third Sermon of the Warpland" (Brooks) **7**:88-9
Third Snow (Yevtushenko) **40**:341
"Third Song" (Rilke) **2**:273
The Third Symphony (Bely)
See *Vozvrat: Tretiia simfoniia*
Third Voronezh Notebook (Mandelstam) **14**:149, 152, 155
"The Third World" (Ferlinghetti) **1**:186
"Third World Calling" (Ferlinghetti) **1**:183
Third World Poems (Brathwaite) **56**:92
"XIII" (Joyce) **22**:145, 168
"13/16" (Alexie) **53**:34
"Thirteen Ways of Looking at a Blackbird" (Stevens) **6**:293, 326-27
"The Thirteens (Black and White)" (Angelou) **32**:28
Thirteenth Olympian (Pindar)
See *Olympian 13*
"The Thirties Revisited" (Kumin) **15**:202
"XXX" (Joyce) **22**:138, 144-45, 164, 173
"Thirty Delft Tiles" (Doty) **53**:60-61
38 Variations on a Theme by Alison Knowles (Cage) **58**:196-97
Thirty Poems (Merton) **10**:338-39, 350-51
"Thirty Rhymes to Hermit Chang Piao" (Tu Fu) **9**:326
"Thirty Years Under" (Yamada) **44**:330, 333, 345
"XXXV" (Joyce) **22**:138-39, 144, 154, 157, 161, 164
"XXXIV" (Joyce) **22**:139, 145, 157, 161-62, 164-65, 170
"XXXI" (Joyce) **22**:152, 164, 170
"XXXVI" (Joyce) **22**:136, 138, 144-45, 157, 161, 163-64
"36 Mesostics Re and not Re Duchamp" (Cage) **58**:195
Thirty-Six Poems (Warren) **37**:279, 319, 321, 324, 331, 354, 376, 380-81
"XXXIII" (Joyce) **22**:145, 164, 166, 168, 173
"XXXII" (Joyce) **22**:145, 164, 167, 173
"XXXII" (Larkin) **21**:242
"This" (Stone) **53**:259
"This Black Rich Country" (Ammons) **16**:40
This Body Is Made of Camphor and Gopherwood (Bly) **39**:29, 37-41, 43, 45, 99-100
"This Bread I Break" (Thomas) **2**:379, 389; **52**:295-97, 299
"This Bridge" (Silverstein) **49**:323-24
"This Cold Man" (Page)
See "Now This Cold Man"
"This Compost" (Whitman) **3**:410
"This Configuration" (Ashbery) **26**:141
"This Corruptible" (Wylie) **23**:304-305, 308, 311, 316
"This Day" (Levertov) **11**:198-99, 201
"This Do, in Remembrance of Me" (Bryant) **20**:45
"This Florida: 1924" (Williams) **7**:369
"This Frieze of Birds" (Page) **12**:168
"This Grievous Pain" (Storni)
See "Este grave daño"
"This in Which" (Oppen) **35**:301
This in Which (Oppen) **35**:308, 309, 310, 311-17, 321, 322-23, 333, 336, 340, 343, 348-50, 353
"This Is" (Ammons) **16**:54
"This Is A Hymn" (Goodison) **36**:148
"This Is a Photograph of Me" (Atwood) **8**:12, 23
"This is Disgraceful and Abominable" (Smith) **12**:293, 309
"This Is Just to Say" (Williams) **7**:363, 399, 401
"This Is My Carnac" (Thoreau) **30**:192, 235-36
This is My Century: New and Collected Poems by Margaret Walker (Walker) **20**:293
"This Is My Father's Country" (Goodison) **36**:158
"This Is No Case of Petty Right or Wrong" (Thomas) **53**:306-7, 350
"This Is Noon" (Graves) **6**:166
"This Is Not For John Lennon (And This Is Not a Poem)" (Giovanni) **19**:142
"This is the Life" (MacNeice) **61**:178
"this is the tale" (Clifton) **17**:25, 27
"This Is the Track" (Owen) **19**:342
"This Is Their Fault" (Forché) **10**:142
This Journey (Wright) **36**:333, 342, 347-48, 358, 364-66, 368, 370-71, 378, 387, 393, 399-400
"This (Let's Remember) day Died Again and" (Cummings) **5**:107
"This Life" (Dove) **6**:108
"This Lime-Tree Bower My Prison" (Coleridge) **11**:51, 53, 72, 83, 88-9, 97, 104, 107; **39**:127, 161
"This love lost to all" (Char)
See "Cet amour à tous retiré"
"This Moment" (Boland) **58**:18
"This Morning" (Carver) **54**:21-22
"This Morning" (Cervantes) **35**:118
This Music Crept by Me upon the Waters (MacLeish) **47**:175, 210
"This My Song is Made for Kerensky" (Lindsay) **23**:269
"This Near-At-Hand" (Rossetti) **7**:276
"This Occurs To Me" (Ortiz) **17**:225
"This Ol' World" (Alurista) **34**:22
"This Page My Pigeon" (Birney) **52**:22
"This Place Rumord to Have Been Sodom" (Duncan) **2**:127
"This Pleasing Anxious Being" (Wilbur) **51**:332-33, 336
"This Praying Fool" (Kumin) **15**:180
"This Room and Everything in It" (Lee) **24**:243
"This Side of the Truth" (Thomas)
See "This Side of Truth"
"This Side of Truth" (Thomas) **2**:390; **52**:316
"This sun on this rubble after rain" (Brutus) **24**:113
"This, That, and the Other" (Nemerov) **24**:298, 303
This Tree Will Be Here for a Thousand Years (Bly) **39**:46, 53, 69, 85-7, 99
"This Urn Contains Earth from German Concentration Camps" (Lorde) **12**:136
"This Was a Poet" (Dickinson) **1**:96, 102
"This Was My Meal" (Corso) **33**:5, 41, 43
"This Way Is Not a Way" (Snyder) **21**:310
"This Winter" (Mueller) **33**:193
"Thistledown" (Merrill) **28**:228
"Thistles" (Hughes) **7**:121, 137
"Tho I cannot your crueltie constrain" (Wyatt) **27**:321
Thomas and Beulah (Dove) **6**:104, 107, 110-20, 122
"Thomas at the Wheel" (Dove) **6**:111
"Thomas Jefferson" (Niedecker) **42**:107-9
"Thomas Mann" (Szymborska) **44**:294
"Thomas Rhodes" (Masters) **36**:230, 232
"Thomas Trevelyn" (Masters) **36**:190
"Thompson's Lunch Room" (Lowell) **13**:79
"Thorkild's Song" (Kipling) **3**:183
"The Thorn" (Wordsworth) **4**:381, 402, 412, 416-17, 426, 428
"A Thorn Forever in the Breast" (Cullen) **20**:63
"Thorn Piece" (Lowell) **13**:85
"Thoroughgo" (Char)
See "La minutieuse"
"Thorow" (Howe) **54**:38, 40, 48, 52, 58, 95, 97, 112, 125, 130, 135-36
"Those Being Eaten by America" (Bly) **39**:9, 12, 48, 50
"Those Dancing Days Are Gone" (Yeats) **20**:328
"Those eies which set my fancie on a fire" (Raleigh) **31**:201, 219, 249-50, 253
"Those Eyes Which Set My Fancy on a Fire" (Raleigh)
See "Those eies which set my fancie on a fire"
"Those Times" (Sexton) **2**:362-63, 370
"Those Various Scalpels" (Moore) **4**:263-64, 270; **49**:93, 113, 118, 172, 174-76
"Those Who Do Not Dance" (Mistral)
See "Los que no danzan"
"Those Who Fought For the Achaean League" (Cavafy) **36**:8, 17, 58, 60, 84
"Those Who Lost" (Herbert) **50**:17
"Those Who Love" (Teasdale) **31**:379
Those Who Ride the Night Winds (Giovanni) **19**:126-27, 137-38, 142-43
"Those who through their tears" (Castro)
See "Los que a través de sus lágrimas"
"Those Winter Sundays" (Hayden) **6**:194-95
"The Thou" (Montale)
See "Il tu"
"Thou Art Indeed Just, Lord" (Hopkins) **15**:171
"Thou blindmans marke" (Sidney) **32**:239
"Thou didst delight my eyes" (Bridges) **28**:85
"Thou Dusky Spirit of the Wood" (Thoreau) **30**:223
"Thou Famished Grave, I Will Not Fill Thee Yet" (Millay) **6**:242
"Thou Shalt Not Kill" (Rexroth) **20**:181, 187, 193, 205, 218
"Thou Unbelieving Heart" (Kunitz) **19**:155
"Though I regarded not" (Surrey) **59**:297
"Thought and Image" (Muir) **49**:300
"Thought for a Sunshiny morning" (Parker) **28**:362
"A Thought of Columbus" (Whitman)
See "A Prayer of Columbus"
"The Thought-Fox" (Hughes) **7**:120, 158, 166, 168-69
"Thoughts" (Teasdale) **31**:357, 360
"Thoughts about the Christian Doctrine of Eternal Hell" (Smith) **12**:301, 325, 333
"Thoughts about the Person from Porlock" (Smith) **12**:293, 330, 350
"Thoughts fer the Discuraged Farmer" (Riley) **48**:288, 333, 335
"Thoughts in 1932" (Sassoon) **12**:252
"The Thoughts of an Old Artist" (Cavafy) **36**:94-95
"Thoughts of Death" (Brown) **55**:74, 110, 114
"Thoughts on a Breath" (Ginsberg) **4**:76
"Thoughts on His Excellency Major General Lee" (Wheatley) **3**:337
"Thoughts on One's Head" (Meredith) **28**:174, 211
"Thoughts on Saving the Manatee" (Kumin) **15**:211
"Thoughts on the Shape of the Human Body" (Brooke) **24**:56-7
"Thoughts on the Works of Providence" (Wheatley) **3**:332, 339, 358, 361, 363
"Thou-poems" (Stramm)
See "Du-Gedichte"
"The Thousand and One Nights" (Borges) **32**:58

"The Thousand and Second Night" (Merrill) **28**:222, 225-26, 228, 230-32, 234, 250, 252-53
"Thousand League Pool" (Tu Fu) **9**:333
"A Thousand Thousand Times" (Breton) **15**:73
Thread-Suns (Celan)
See *Fadensonnen*
"The Threatened Man" (Borges)
See "The Threatened One"
"The Threatened One" (Borges) **32**:58
"Three" (Corso) **33**:41
"Three" (Gunn) **26**:208
"III" (Joyce) **22**:144, 160, 162, 164, 166
"Three Airs" (O'Hara) **45**:219
"3 a.m. in the High Street" (Abse) **41**:9
"3 A.M. Kitchen: My Father Talking" (Gallagher) **9**:53
"Three Angels" (Dylan) **37**:56
"Three Bushes" (Yeats) **20**:332; **51**:139
"The Three Captains" (Kipling) **3**:157
"The Three Conspirators" (Nemerov) **24**:293
"Three Crows" (Kenyon) **57**:45
"Three Darknesses" (Warren) **37**:365-66, 377-81
"The Three Decker" (Kipling) **3**:161
"Three Desk Objects" (Atwood) **8**:2, 13
"Three Dollars Cash" (Walker) **30**:367
"Three Elegiac Poems" (Berry) **28**:15
"Three Faces" (Swinburne) **24**:329
"Three Floors" (Kunitz) **19**:178
"The Three Gatekeepers of the Jealous Husband" (Dafydd)
See "Tri Phorthor Eiddig"
"Three Ghosts" (Sandburg) **2**:309
"Three Glimpses of Irish Life" (Kavanagh) **33**:157
"The Three Graves" (Coleridge) **11**:117
"Three Green Windows" (Sexton) **2**:363
Three Hundred and Sixty Degrees of Blackness Comin at You (Sanchez) **9**:222
"Three Italian Pictures" (Loy) **16**:313
"Three Kinds of Pleasures" (Bly) **39**:3, 7, 76-8, 82
"The Three Kings" (Zagajewski) **27**:396
"Three Loves" (Corso) **33**:25
Three Material Cantos (Neruda)
See *Homenaje a Pablo Neruda de los poetas espanoles: Tres cantos materiales*
Three Material Songs (Neruda)
See *Homenaje a Pablo Neruda de los poetas espanoles: Tres cantos materiales*
"Three Meditations" (Levertov) **11**:169
"The Three Mirrors" (Muir) **49**:246-47, 249-50
"Three Modes of History and Culture" (Baraka) **4**:16
"Three Moments in Paris" (Loy) **16**:312, 327-28
"Three Mountebanks" (Ransom) **61**:289
"Three Movements and a Coda" (Baraka) **4**:9, 19, 24
"Three Nuns" (Rossetti) **7**:277
"The Three Oddest Words" (Szymborska) **44**:298
"3 of Swords—for dark men under the white moon" (Wakoski) **15**:362, 367
"Three old men" (Illyés)
See "Harom oreg"
"Three Palms" (Lermontov)
See "Tri palmy"
"Three Palm-Trees" (Lermontov)
See "Tri palmy"
"Three Pieces on the Smoke of Autumn" (Sandburg) **41**:313
"Three Poems" (Niedecker) **42**:147, 152
"Three Poems" (Parra)
See "Tres Poesías"
"Three Poems" (Thomas) **52**:316, 322, 324
Three Poems (Ashbery) **26**:108-109, 114-116, 118, 123, 126, 130, 135, 143, 149, 167, 169-171, 173-174
Three Poems (Curnow) **48**:25-26
"Three Poems after Jaccottet" (Mahon) **60**:188
"Three Poems Apart" (MacNeice) **61**:138
"Three Poems from Memory" (Herbert) **50**:18
Three Poems under a Flag of Convenience (Elytis) **21**:131
"Three Poets" (Oppen) **35**:341
"The Three Porters of Eiddig" (Dafydd)
See "Tri Phorthor Eiddig"
"Three Postcards from the Monastery" (Merton) **10**:332
"Three Questions" (Gower) **59**:88
"Three Romances" (Hope) **56**:269, 271, 287
"Three Sentences for a Dead Swan" (Wright) **36**:328, 341, 345-46, 363
"The Three Silences of Molinos" (Longfellow) **30**:51
"Three Small Oranges" (Kenyon) **57**:12, 41, 44
"Three Songs" (Crane) **3**:106
"Three Songs at the End of Summer" (Kenyon) **57**:45
"Three Songs for a Colored Singer" (Bishop) **34**:160
"Three Sonnets" (Sarton) **39**:322
"Three Sonnets for the Eyes" (Bishop) **34**:94, 160-61
"Three Sons Had Abraham" (Amichai) **38**:50
"Three Speeches in a Sick Room" (Wright) **36**:336
"Three Spring Notations on Bipeds" (Sandburg) **41**:285
"Three Stanzas from Goethe" (Wright) **36**:331, 338
"Three Street Musicians" (Abse) **41**:28
"Three Studies on the Subject of Realism" (Herbert) **50**:3, 25, 31
"The Three Susans" (Kenyon) **57**:14-15
The Three Taverns (Robinson) **1**:465-66, 468
"Three Things" (Sarton) **39**:367
"Three Things" (Yeats) **20**:328
"Three Times in Love" (Graves) **6**:172
"Three Times the Truth" (Elytis) **21**:123
"Three Travellers Watch a Sunrise" (Stevens) **6**:295
"Three United States Sonnets" (Cummings) **5**:94
"Three Valentines" (Bishop) **34**:161
"Three Versions of Judas" (Borges)
See "Tres versiones de Judas"
"Three Voices" (Abse) **41**:3
"Three Voices" (Plath) **37**:210
"Three White Vases" (Swenson) **14**:273
"Three Women: A Poem for Three Voices" (Plath) **37**:209-10
"Three Woodchoppers" (Francis) **34**:246
"The Threefold Place" (Muir) **49**:265
"Threefold Time" (Muir) **49**:229
"Threes" (Atwood) **8**:21
"Three-year-old" (Tagore)
See "Tritiya"
Threnodia Augustalis (Dryden) **25**:88-9
"Threnody" (Emerson) **18**:69, 81, 84, 86, 90, 102-3, 112-3
"Threnody" (Parker) **28**:360
"Threnody for a Brown Girl" (Cullen) **20**:57-58, 62, 66
"Threshold" (Char)
See "Seuil"
The Throne of Labdacus (Schnackenberg) **45**:339-43, 345, 347-50
Thrones, 96-109 de los cantares (Pound) **4**:337-38, 352, 353, 357
"Through Corralitos under Rolls of Cloud" (Rich) **5**:401
"Through Nightmare" (Graves) **6**:137, 173
"Through the Boughs" (Carver) **54**:19
"Through the Fences that Surround You, Grita" (Alurista) **34**:23
"Through the Inner City to the Suburbs" (Angelou) **32**:3
"Through the Looking Glass" (Ferlinghetti) **1**:173
"Through the Mouth of the Whippoorwill" (Char)
See "Par la bouche de l'engoulevent"
"Through the Round Window" (McGuckian) **27**:83
"Through the Smoke Hole" (Snyder) **21**:292
"Through These Lashed Rings" (Thomas) **52**:290, 293, 295
"Throughout Our Lands" (Milosz) **8**:187, 194, 214
"Throw Away Thy Rod" (Herbert) **4**:103, 121
A Throw of the Dice Never Will Abolish Chance (Mallarmé)
See *Un coup de dés jamais n'abolira le hasard*
A Throw of the Dice Will Never Abolish Chance (Mallarmé)
See *Un coup de dés jamais n'abolira le hasard*
"The Thrush" (Thomas) **53**:294, 330
"The Thrush in February" (Meredith) **60**:256, 280, 299, 301, 319
"Thrushes" (Hughes) **7**:119, 169
"Thrushes" (Sassoon) **12**:253
"Thrust and Riposte" (Montale)
See "Botta e riposta"
"Thum Ku Klux" (Lanier) **50**:92
"Thunder Can Break" (Okigbo)
See "Come Thunder"
"Thunder in the Garden" (Morris) **55**:340
"Thunder in Tuscany" (Tomlinson) **17**:349-50
"Thunder, Momentarily Instantaneous" (Pasternak) **6**:251
"Thunderhead" (MacLeish) **47**:192
"A Thunder-Storm" (Dickinson) **1**:79
"The Thunderstorm" (Trakl)
See "Das Gewitter"
"Thursday" (Millay) **6**:208, 211
"Thursday: The Bassette Table: Smilinda, Cardelia" (Montagu) **16**:338, 349
"Thurso's Landing" (Jeffers) **17**:141-42
Thurso's Landing, and Other Poems (Jeffers) **17**:122, 124-25, 135, 142
"Thus Truly" (Ignatow) **34**:324
"Thyestes" (Davie) **29**:107
"Thyme Flowering Among Rocks" (Wilbur) **51**:235
"Thyrsis" (Arnold) **5**:7-8, 18-19, 21, 23-4, 33, 36, 45, 47, 52, 55-6
"Ti svelerà" (Ungaretti) **57**:344
"Tiara" (Doty) **53**:72
"Tiare Tahiti" (Brooke) **24**:53, 64, 66, 73-4, 78, 86
"Tic Tac Toe" (Stone) **53**:229
"Tick Tock" (Ignatow) **34**:213, 277
Tide and Continuities (Viereck) **27**:292, 294-96
Tide and Continuities Last and First Poems 1995-1938 (Viereck) **27**:295
"The Tide at Long Point" (Swenson) **14**:247, 249
"Tide Ratio" (Char) **56**:138
"The Tide Rises, The Tide Falls" (Longfellow) **30**:36, 47
"Tidemark" (Ní Chuilleanáin) **34**:349
"Tides" (Teasdale) **31**:336
"Tiempo" (Storni) **33**:244, 302-03;
"Tiempo de esterilidad" (Storni) **33**:261, 294-95, 299, 302, 305;
"Tiempo libre" (Guillén) **35**:228, 229
"Tienanmen, the Aftermath" (Chin) **40**:9
Tiepolo's Hound (Walcott) **46**:302, 322
"Tierra de azules montañas" (Guillén) **23**:125
"Tierra del Fuego" (Zagajewski) **27**:396, 400
"Tierra en la sierra y en el llano" (Guillén) **23**:127
"La tierra se llama Juan" (Neruda) **4**:294
"The Tiger" (Belloc) **24**:24
"The Tiger" (Blake)
See "The Tyger"
"The Tiger" (Borges)
See "El tigre"
"Tightrope Walker" (Goodison) **36**:143

"El tigre" (Borges) **32**:64
"Till de folkhemske" (Ekeloef) **23**:76
"Till Other Voices Wake Us" (Oppen) **35**:301
"Tilting Sail" (Hass) **16**:251
"Timbuctoo" (Tennyson) **6**:358, 389, 407-08, 413, 415-18
"Timbuctu" (Brathwaite) **56**:29
"Time" (Char)
See "Le Temps"
"Time" (Wright) **36**:378
Time (Amichai)
See *Ha-Zeman*
"Time and Life" (Swinburne) **24**:323
"The Time and the Place" (Carman) **34**:208
"Time and Violence" (Boland) **58**:23, 27
"Time as Hypnosis" (Warren) **37**:366
"The Time before You" (McGuckian) **27**:82
"Time Does Not Bring Relief" (Millay) **6**:205
"Time Goes By" (Pavese)
See "Il tempo passa"
"Time in the Rock" (Aiken) **26**:19, 57
Time in the Rock (Aiken) **26**:6, 12, 23, 29, 52
"Time Is Fleeting" (Carducci)
See "Ruit hora"
"Time is Mute" (Ungaretti) **57**:360
"Time Is the Mercy of Eternity" (Rexroth) **20**:181, 208-09, 216-18
"Time Lapse with Tulips" (Gallagher) **9**:37
"The Time of Burning" (Sarton) **39**:328
"A Time of Day" (Curnow) **48**:53
"Time of Disturbance" (Jeffers) **17**:141
The Time of History (Guillén)
See *Clamor*
"Time on Main" (Doty) **53**:69
Time Overflows (Éluard)
See *Le temps déborde*
"Time Passing, Beloved" (Davie) **29**:94, 100, 108
"Time Spirals" (Rexroth) **20**:195, 217-18
"A Time to Dance" (Day Lewis) **11**:126
A Time to Dance and Other Poems (Day Lewis) **11**:126-27, 129
"Time to Kill in Gallup" (Ortiz) **17**:240
"Time-Bomb" (Birney) **52**:7-8, 101
"Timehri" (Brathwaite) **56**:75
"The Time-Piece" (Cowper) **40**:48-9, 51-2, 66, 117, 123
"A Timepiece" (Merrill) **28**:225, 234
"Times at Bellosguardo" (Montale) **13**:147, 152
"Time's Dedication" (Schwartz) **8**:305, 307, 314
Time's Laughingstocks and Other Verses (Hardy) **8**:93, 123
"Times Passes" (Pavese)
See "Il tempo passa"
"Time's Revenges" (Browning) **2**:33
"Times Square Water Music" (Clampitt) **19**:81, 88
"The Times Table" (Frost) **1**:205
Timespace Huracán (Alurista) **34**:4, 15, 26-28, 31
"Timesweep" (Sandburg) **41**:303-4
"Time-Travel" (Olds) **22**:322
"Tin Roof" (Ondaatje) **28**:314
"Tin Roof Blues" (Brown) **55**:70, 110, 153, 156
"Tin Wedding Whistle" (Nash) **21**:268
"Tinder" (Heaney) **18**:202
"The Tingling Back" (Shapiro) **25**:317, 320
"Tinker's Wife" (Kavanagh) **33**:74
"Tinseltown" (Szirtes) **51**:172
"Tintern Abbey" (Wordsworth)
See "Lines Composed a Few Miles Above Tintern Abbey"
"Tippoo's Tiger" (Moore) **49**:149
"Tirade for the Lyric Muse" (Boland) **58**:48, 98
"Tirade for the Mimic Muse" (Boland) **58**:4-5, 12, 29, 44
"Tired" (Silverstein) **49**:329-30
"Tired Memory" (Patmore) **59**:223
"Tiresias" (Tennyson) **6**:361
Tiriel (Blake) **12**:61
"Tirzey Potter" (Masters) **1**:338
"'Tis April and the morning, love" (Clare) **23**:23
"'Tis Now, Since I Sate Down Before" (Suckling) **30**:141
"Tishina" (Pasternak) **6**:286
"Tithonus" (Mahon) **60**:177, 192, 194
"Tithonus" (Tennyson) **6**:366, 411
"Title Divine Is Mine the Wife without the Sign" (Dickinson) **1**:93
"Titmouse" (Emerson) **18**:79, 103-4, 113
"tizoc left us his hair" (Alurista) **34**:34
"Tizzic" (Brathwaite) **56**:10, 15, 76, 88, 100
"Tlön, Uqbar, Orbis Tertius" (Borges) **32**:60, 69
"To—" (Owen) **19**:352
"To—" (Poe) **1**:436, 445
"To —" (Poe) **54**:264
"To a Babe Smiling in Her Sleep" (Harper) **21**:197
"To a Black Dancer in 'The Little Savoy'" (Hughes) **53**:79
"To a Blackbird" (Kavanagh) **33**:83, 92
"To a Blossoming Pear Tree" (Wright) **36**:308, 314, 321, 358, 369, 372, 377, 381-82, 384, 403
To a Blossoming Pear Tree (Wright) **36**:310-11, 314, 318, 320, 322, 347, 354, 356, 358, 363-64, 368-70, 377-78, 381-83, 392, 399, 403
"To a Book" (Wylie) **23**:303
"To a Brother in the Mystery" (Davie) **29**:96, 102
"To a Brown Boy" (Cullen) **20**:52, 62
"To a Brown Girl" (Cullen) **20**:52, 62
"To A Butterfly" (Merrill) **28**:247
"To a Captious Critic" (Dunbar) **5**:125, 127, 135
"To a Certain Lady, in Her Garden" (Brown) **55**:110, 114
"To a Chameleon" (Moore) **49**:89, 114, 118-19, 134, 140
"To a Child" (Kavanagh) **33**:92, 97, 156
"To a Child" (Longfellow) **30**:48
"To a Child Dancing in the Wind" (Yeats) **20**:338
"To a Child Running with Outstretched Arms in Canyon de Chelly" (Momaday) **25**:219
"To a Clergyman on the Death of His Lady" (Wheatley) **3**:357
"To a Comet" (Thoreau)
See "To the Comet"
"To a Common Prostitute" (Whitman) **3**:416
"To a Contemporary Bunkshooter" (Sandburg)
See "To a Contemporary Bunk-Shooter"
"To a Contemporary Bunk-Shooter" (Sandburg) **2**:317, 330; **41**:238, 242, 246, 251, 255, 272, 295, 335, 351
"To a Cuckoo at Coolanlough" (McGuckian) **27**:103
"to a dark moses" (Clifton) **17**:34
"To a Dead Child" (Bridges) **28**:57
"To a Defeated Savior" (Wright) **36**:318, 335-36
"To a Downfallen Rose" (Corso) **33**:40
"To a Dreamer" (Pushkin) **10**:407
"To a Face in a Crowd" (Warren) **37**:287, 319, 330
"To a Fellow Scribbler" (Finch) **21**:168
"To a Fish Head Found on the Beach Near Malaga" (Levine) **22**:215
"To a Freedom Fighter" (Angelou) **32**:28
"To a Friend" (Arnold) **5**:12, 49
"To a Friend" (Herrick) **9**:90
"To a Friend" (Yeats) **20**:321
"To a Friend and Fellow-Poet" (MacDiarmid) **9**:183-84
"To a Friend in the Making" (Moore) **49**:115
"To a Friend in Time of Trouble" (Gunn) **26**:215
"To a Friend Parting" (Warren) **37**:284, 288, 354
"To a Friend Whose Work Has Come to Triumph" (Sexton) **2**:370
"To a Fringed Gentian" (Bryant) **20**:12, 45
"To a Fugitive" (Wright) **36**:335, 373
"To a Gentleman on His Voyage to Great Britain for the Recovery of His Health" (Wheatley) **3**:358
"To a Gipsy Child by the Sea-shore" (Arnold) **5**:38, 49-50
"To a Giraffe" (Moore) **4**:242-43; **49**:145
"To a Guinea Pig" (Shapiro) **25**:269
"To a Highland Girl" (Wordsworth) **4**:404
"To a Husband" (Angelou) **32**:29
"To a Husband" (Lowell) **13**:74
"To a Japanese Poet" (Stryk) **27**:203-4
"To a Jealous Cat" (Sanchez) **9**:223, 232
"To a Lady and Her Children, On the Death of Her Son and Their Brother" (Wheatley) **3**:363
"To a Lady on Her Remarkable Preservation in an Hurricane in North Carolina" (Wheatley) **3**:354
"To a Lady on the Death of Three Relations" (Wheatley) **3**:343, 348
"To a Lady that desired I would love her" (Carew) **29**:3-4
"To A Lady the Forbade to Love Before Company" (Suckling) **30**:130
"To a Lady's Countenance" (Wylie) **23**:321
"To a Little Girl, One Year Old in a Ruined Fortress" (Warren) **37**:295, 297, 300, 307, 347, 360
"To a Louse, on Seeing One on a Lady's Bonnet at Church" (Burns) **6**:65, 79
"To a lovely woman" (Lermontov) **18**:303
"To a Man" (Angelou) **32**:14-17, 29
"To a Man Working His Way Through the Crowd" (Moore) **49**:114
"To a Mountain Daisy, on Turning One Down with the Plough in April, 1786" (Burns) **6**:50, 74
"To a Mouse, on Turning Her Up in Her Nest with the Plough, November, 1785" (Burns) **6**:50, 65, 74, 80, 96
"To a Painter in England" (Walcott) **46**:271
"To a Passing Woman" (Baudelaire)
See "A une passante"
"To a Poet" (Jiménez) **7**:183
"To a Poet" (McKay) **2**:206
To a Polish Mother (Mickiewicz) **38**:158
"To a Poor Old Woman" (Williams) **7**:390, 399
"To a Portrait" (Lermontov) **18**:297
"To a Portrait in a Gallery" (Page) **12**:168
"To a Prize Bird" (Moore)
See "To Bernard Shaw: A Prize Bird"
"To a Republican Friend" (Arnold) **5**:49
"To a Romantic" (Tate) **50**:285, 306
"To a Romantic Novelist" (Tate) **50**:306
"To a Romanticist" (Tate) **50**:228, 285
"To a Sad Daughter" (Ondaatje) **28**:316
"To a Saxon Poet" (Borges) **32**:95
"To a Screen-Maker" (Moore) **49**:104-5, 107
"To a Seamew" (Swinburne) **24**:313, 328
"To a Shade" (Yeats) **20**:348
"to a Sinister Potato" (Viereck) **27**:259, 262, 279
"To a Skylark" (Meredith) **60**:332
"To a Solitary Disciple" (Williams) **7**:357, 378
"To a Sower" (Mistral)
See "A un sembrador"
"To a Steam Roller" (Moore) **49**:114-15, 119-20, 126, 155
"To a Strategist" (Moore) **4**:266; **49**:114
"To a Stray Fowl" (Thoreau) **30**:235
"To a sword in York" (Borges)
See "A una espada en York"
To a Tense Serenity (Char)
See *À une sérénité crispée*
"To a Town Poet" (Reese) **29**:333
"To a Waterfowl" (Bryant) **20**:5-6, 14, 18, 35, 42
"To a Western Bard Still a Whoop and a Holler Away from English Poetry" (Meredith) **28**:174, 187, 207
"To a Winter Squirrel" (Brooks) **7**:82
"To a Wreath of Snow" (Brontë) **8**:67, 73

"To a Young Actress" (Pushkin) **10**:407
"To A Young Friend" (Burns)
See "Epistle to a Young Friend"
"To a Young Girl" (Millay) **6**:217
"To a Young Girl" (Yeats) **20**:330
"To A.D., unreasonable distrustfull of her owne beauty" (Carew) **29**:29
"To Adversity" (Gray)
See "Ode to Adversity"
"To A.L. Perswasions to Love" (Carew) **29**:10, 23-24, 66-68
"To Alchymists" (Jonson) **17**:197
"To Alexander" (Pushkin)
See "Aleksandru"
"To Alexis, in Answer to His Poem against Fruition" (Behn) **13**:26
"To All Brothers" (Sanchez) **9**:224, 232
"To All Brothers: From All Sisters" (Sanchez) **9**:221
"To All Gentleness" (Williams) **7**:354
"To All Sisters" (Sanchez) **9**:224, 231-32
"To all vertuous Ladies in generall" (Lanyer) **60**:5, 17, 52, 90-92, 97, 111-12
"To America" (Johnson) **24**:131, 142, 148, 158, 160
"To Amintas, upon Reading the Lives of Some of the Romans" (Behn) **13**:32
"To an American Poet Just Dead" (Wilbur) **51**:192, 219
"To an Ancestor" (Stone) **53**:215
"To an Ancient" (Frost) **1**:200
"To an Apple" (Ignatow) **34**:305
"To an Athlete Dying Young" (Housman) **2**:180, 183, 185, 191-94, 198, 201
"To an Earth of Dawn" (Bonnefoy)
See "À une Terre d!aube"
"To an Intra-Mural Rat" (Moore) **49**:114, 119
"To an Old Philosopher in Rome" (Stevens) **6**:304, 324, 328
"To Ann Scott-Moncrieff (1914-1943)" (Muir)
See "For Ann Scott-Moncrieff (1914-1943)"
"To Another Housewife" (Wright) **14**:356
"To Antenor on a Paper of mine which J J threatens to publish to prejudice him" (Philips) **40**:273, 297
"To Anthea" (Herrick) **9**:145
"To Anthea Lying in Bed" (Herrick) **9**:137
"To Anthea, Who May Command Him Any Thing" (Herrick) **9**:102
"To Any Dead Officer Who Left School for the Army in 1914" (Sassoon) **12**:268, 277
"To Aphrodite, with a Talisman" (Wylie) **23**:320, 324
"To Art" (Reese) **29**:354
"To Autumn" (Ashbery) **26**:160
"To Autumn" (Glück) **16**:142, 149
"To Autumn" (Keats)
See "Ode to Autumn"
"To Autumn" (Wilbur) **51**:237
"To Bake the Bread of Yearning" (Amichai) **38**:54
"To Bargain Toboggan To-Woo!" (Nash) **21**:265
To Bathurst (Pope)
See *An Epistle to Bathurst*
"To Be a Jew in the Twentieth Century" (Rukeyser) **12**:234
To Be a Poet (Seifert)
See *Býti básníkem*
"To Be Carved on a Stone at Thoor Ballylee" (Yeats) **20**:346, 348
"To Be Dead" (Jarrell) **41**:214
"To Be in Love" (Brooks) **7**:81-2
"To Be Liked by You Would Be a Calamity" (Moore) **4**:250; **49**:114, 120, 122
"to Be of Use" (Piercy) **29**:309
To Be of Use (Piercy) **29**:302, 309-10, 323
"To Be Quicker for Black Political Prisoners" (Madhubuti) **5**:330, 346
"To be Sung" (Viereck) **27**:265
"To Be Sung on the Water" (Bogan) **12**:90, 124
"To Be Written on the Mirror in Whitewash" (Bishop) **34**:67, 109
To Bedlam and Part Way Back (Sexton) **2**:345-47, 349-50, 353, 355, 357-58, 360, 363, 367
"To Become Landscape on Meeting Joseph Sima" (Char)
See "Se recontrer paysage avec Joseph Sima"
"To Beethoven" (Lanier) **50**:77-78
"To Begin With" (Guillén)
See "Por de pronto"
"To Ben Jonson Upon occasion of his Ode of defiance annext to his play of the new Inne" (Carew) **29**:7, 32, 82
"To Bennie" (McKay) **2**:221
"To Bernard Shaw: A Prize Bird" (Moore) **49**:114, 116, 134
"To Billy Sunday" (Sandburg)
See "To a Contemporary Bunk-Shooter"
"To Blk/Record/Buyers" (Sanchez) **9**:209, 217
"To Blossom in Winter" (Char)
See "Eclore en hiver"
"To Blossoms" (Herrick) **9**:145
"To Bring the Dead to Life" (Graves) **6**:143
"To Browning" (Moore) **49**:114
To Burlington (Pope)
See *An Epistle to Burlington*
"To Call up the Shades" (Cavafy) **36**:75
"To Camden" (Jonson)
See "Epigram XIV"
"To Carl Sandburg" (Lowell) **13**:67
"To Carry the Child" (Smith) **12**:320
"To Cedars" (Herrick) **9**:91
"To Celia" (Jonson) **17**:170, 196
"To Celimena" (Philips) **40**:284
"To Certain Censors" (Carducci)
See "A certi Censori"
"To Certain Critics" (Cullen) **20**:66, 83
"To Certain Journeymen" (Sandburg) **41**:313, 338, 365
"To Chaadaev" (Pushkin)
See "Chaadayevu"
"To Change in a Good Way" (Ortiz) **17**:234
"To Charis" (Jonson)
See *A Celebration of Charis in Ten Lyric Pieces*
"To Christ Our Lord" (Kinnell) **26**:239
To . . . Christopher Duke of Albemarle (Behn) **13**:8
"To Chuck" (Sanchez) **9**:224, 233
"To Cipriano, in the Wind" (Levine) **22**:225
To Circumjack Cencrastus (MacDiarmid) **9**:151-53, 158, 171, 175-77, 197
"To Clarendon Hills and H.A.H." (McKay) **2**:222
"To Claudia Homonoea" (Wylie) **23**:324
"To Clio Muse of History" (Nemerov) **24**:262
"To Cole, the Painter, Departing For Europe" (Bryant) **20**:34, 44-5
"To Columbus" (Darío)
See "A Colón"
"To Conclude" (Montale) **13**:146
"To Confirm a Thing" (Swenson) **14**:247, 252, 278
"To Constantia Singing" (Shelley) **14**:177
"To Cooke-ham" (Lanyer) **60**:31, 45, 107
"To Countess Rostopchina" (Lermontov) **18**:297
"To Daddy" (Lowell) **3**:226
"To Daffadills" (Herrick) **9**:101
"To Damon. To Inquire of Him If He Cou'd Tell Me by the Style, Who Writ Me a Copy of Verses That Came to Me in an Unknown Hand" (Behn) **13**:30-1
"To Dante Gabriel Rossetti" (Braithwaite) **52**:107
"To Daphnie and Virginia" (Williams) **7**:360, 363, 392
"To Dean Swift" (Swift) **9**:295
"To Death" (Akhmatova) **55**:9, 38, 43, 56-57, 60, 62
"To Death" (Finch) **21**:179-80
"To Deism" (Wheatley) **3**:354
"To Delmore Schwartz" (Lowell) **3**:219, 222
"To Desire" (Behn) **13**:24
"To Dianeme" (Herrick) **9**:145
"To Dick" (O'Hara) **45**:157
To Disembark (Brooks) **7**:84, 93
"To Dispel My Grief" (Tu Fu) **9**:326
"To Disraeli on Conservatism" (Moore) **49**:114, 118
"To *** Do not think I deserve regret" (Lermontov) **18**:301, 304
"To Doctor Alabaster" (Herrick) **9**:142
"To Don at Salaam" (Brooks) **7**:84, 92
To Dream of A Butterfly (Hagiwara)
See *Chō o yumemu*
"To Earthward" (Frost) **1**:197; **39**:246
"To Edith" (Thoreau) **30**:187
"To Electra" (Herrick) **9**:94
"To Elizabeth Ward Perkins" (Lowell) **13**:90
"To Elsie" (Williams) **7**:382, 384, 411
"To E.M.E." (McKay) **2**:223
"To Endymion" (Cullen) **20**:67, 86
"To Enemies" (Bely) **11**:24
"To Enter That Rhythm Where the Self is Lost" (Rukeyser) **12**:227
"To Eros" (Owen) **19**:352
"To Eros" (Storni)
See "A Eros"
"To Ethelinda" (Smart) **13**:331, 347
"To Evalyn for Christmas" (Shapiro) **25**:286
"To Eve Man's Dream of Wifehood As Described by Milton" (Lindsay) **23**:281
"To Evoke Posterity" (Graves) **6**:143, 152
"To Fausta" (Arnold) **5**:49
"To F.C. in Memoriam Palestine" (Chesterton) **28**:97
"To Find God" (Herrick) **9**:109
"To Fine Lady Would-bee" (Jonson) **17**:197
"To Flood Stage Again" (Wright) **36**:341
"To Flowers" (Herrick) **9**:102
"To Flush My Dog" (Browning) **6**:6-7
"To Ford Madox Ford in Heaven" (Williams) **7**:370
"To Forget Self and All" (Curnow) **48**:3-4
"To France" (Cullen) **20**:66
"To Francis Jammes" (Bridges) **28**:76
"To Free Nelson Mandela" (Jordan) **38**:132
"To Galich" (Pushkin) **10**:407
"To George Sand: A Recognition" (Browning) **6**:26
"To Gerhardt" (Olson) **19**:307
"To Go By Singing" (Berry) **28**:3-4
"To Go to Lvov" (Zagajewski) **27**:381-82, 383-85, 387
"To God" (Herrick) **9**:94-5, 109, 118
"To God, His Good Will" (Herrick) **9**:118
"To God, on His Sicknesse" (Herrick) **9**:144
"To Gurdjieff Dying" (Toomer) **7**:338
"To Hafiz of Shiraz" (Wright) **14**:356, 366
"To Have Done Nothing" (Williams) **7**:383, 389, 410
"To Have Without Holding" (Piercy) **29**:311
"To Heaven" (Jonson)
See *The Forest XV*
"To Hedli" (MacNeice)
See "Dedicatory Poem to Collected Poems, 1925-1948, To Hedli"
"To Helen" (Poe) **1**:420, 424, 426, 428, 431, 438-39, 441, 443-45, 447 **54**:264, 278
"To Helen" (Stryk) **27**:204
"To Helen (of Troy NY)" (Viereck) **27**:294
"To Hell With Commonsense" (Kavanagh) **33**:103
"To Hell With It" (O'Hara) **45**:128
"To Help" (Stein) **18**:313
"To Her" (Pushkin) **10**:408-09
"To Her Father with Some Verses" (Bradstreet) **10**:27, 35
"To Her Most Honoured Father Thomas Dudley" (Bradstreet) **10**:2
"To Her Royal Highness, the Duchess of York, on Her Commanding Me to Send Her Some Things I Had Written" (Philips) **40**:268, 295
"To His Book" (Herrick) **9**:106, 109

"To His Children in Darkness" (Dickey) **40**:176, 178, 184, 187
"To His Closet-Gods" (Herrick) **9**:88
"To His Coy Mistress" (Marvell) **10**:259, 265, 269, 271, 273-74, 277-79, 281-82, 290-94, 297, 304, 310-11, 313
"To His Excellency General George Washington" (Wheatley) **3**:337, 341
"To His Father" (Jeffers) **17**:131
"To His Friend on the Untuneable Times" (Herrick) **9**:89
"To His Girles" (Herrick) **9**:107
"To His Girles Who Would Have Him Sportfull" (Herrick) **9**:107
"To His Grace, Gilbert, Lord Archbishop of Canterbury, July 10, 1664" (Philips) **40**:270
"To His Honor the Lieutenant Governor on the Death of His Lady" (Wheatley) **3**:340
To his lady (Leopardi)
See "Alla sua donna"
"To his Love when hee had obtained Her" (Raleigh) **31**:274
"To His Majesty at His Passage into England" (Philips) **40**:271
"To His Mistresses" (Herrick) **9**:128, 146
"To His Paternall Countrey" (Herrick) **9**:108
"To His Savior, a Child; a Present, by a Child" (Herrick) **9**:120, 143
"To His Saviour, the New Yeers Gift" (Herrick) **9**:95
"To His Saviours Sepulcher: His Devotion" (Herrick) **9**:122
"To His Skeleton" (Wilbur) **51**:283
"To his Son" (Raleigh) **31**:203
"To His Watch" (Hopkins) **15**:167
"To Homer" (Keats) **1**:279, 314
"To Ianthe in Heaven" (Poe) **54**:273
"To Iceland" (Borges) **32**:58, 66
"To Imagination" (Brontë) **8**:54
"To Imagination" (Wheatley)
See "On Imagination"
"To Indianapolis 17 Nov 71" (Brutus) **24**:123
"To Insure Survival" (Ortiz) **17**:225
"To Introduce the Landscape" (Curnow) **48**:12-13
"To Ireland in the Coming Times" (Yeats) **20**:324, 347, 353
"To Ishtar" (Wilbur) **51**:208, 301
"To Ivor Gurney" (Tomlinson) **17**:354-55
"To J. F. H. (1897-1934)" (Muir) **49**:272
"To J. M." (Meredith) **60**:295
"to joan" (Clifton) **17**:18
"To John Goldie, August 1785" (Burns) **6**:70, 78
"To John Keats, Poet: At Spring Time" (Cullen) **20**:62, 66, 86
"To Jos: Lo: Bishop of Exeter" (Herrick) **9**:146
"To Joseph Joachim" (Bridges) **28**:88
"To Joseph Sadzik" (Milosz)
See "Do Jōzefa Sadzika"
"To Juan at the Winter Solstice" (Graves) **6**:137, 144, 146, 168, 171-72
"To Julia" (Herrick) **9**:128, 143
"To Julia, in Her Dawne, or Day-breake" (Herrick) **9**:143
"To Julia, the Flaminica Dialis, or Queen-Priest" (Herrick) **9**:143
"To Julia Walking Away" (Hope) **56**:295
"To . . . K. Charles" (Jonson)
See *The Under-Wood LXIV*
"To K. Charles . . . 1629" (Jonson)
See *The Under-Wood LXII*
"To Keorapetse Kgositsile (Willie)" (Brooks) **7**:83, 92, 105
"To Kevin O'Leary Wherever He Is" (Levertov) **11**:189
"To King Henry the Fourth, in Praise of Peace" (Gower)
See "In Praise of Peace"
"To King James" (Jonson)
See "Epigram IV"
"To Lady Arabella" (Lanyer) **60**:17
"To Lady Crew, upon the Death of Her Child" (Herrick)
See "To the Lady Crew, upon the Death of Her Child"
"To Landrum Guy, Beginning to Write at Sixty" (Dickey) **40**:182
"To Laurels" (Herrick) **9**:127
"To Let Go or to Hold On" (Lawrence) **54**:226
"To Liberty, On Rereading the Works of Vittorio Alfieri" (Cannan)
See "Alla Libertà rileggendo le opere di Vittorio Alfieri"
"To Licinius" (Pushkin)
See "K Liciniju"
"To Live" (Bly) **39**:86
"To Live Merrily, and to Trust to Good Verses" (Herrick) **9**:96, 103-05, 107, 114
"To Live With Such Men" (Char)
See "Vivre avec de tels hommes"
"To Lord Byron" (Keats) **1**:313
"To Lord Harley, on His Marriage" (Swift) **9**:254
"To Lose the Earth" (Sexton) **2**:363
"To Louise" (Dunbar) **5**:121
"To Love" (Aleixandre) **15**:19, 21
"To Love" (Reese) **29**:331
"To Lu Chi" (Nemerov) **24**:257
"To Lucia at Birth" (Graves) **6**:137
"To Lucy, Countesse of Bedford, with Mr. Donnes Satyres" (Jonson)
See "Epigram XCIV"
"To Lyce" (Smart) **13**:348
"To Lycomedes on Scyros" (Brodsky)
See "K Likomedu, na Skiros"
"To Lysander at the Musick-Meeting" (Behn) **13**:30
"To Lysander, on Some Verses He Writ, and Asking More for His Heart than 'Twas Worth" (Behn) **13**:30
"To M" (Teasdale) **31**:368
"To M. L. S." (Poe) **54**:264
"To M.A. at parting" (Philips) **40**:296, 300
"To Madonna Poetry" (Storni)
See "A Madona Poesía"
"To Make a Poem in Prison" (Knight) **14**:48
"To Make Much" (Oppen) **35**:300
"To make seen" (Éluard)
See "Donner àvoir"
"To Marcus Aurelius" (Herbert) **50**:30
"To Marguerite" (Arnold) **5**:19, 64
"To Marguerite—Continued" (Arnold) **5**:13, 42-5, 49, 64
"To Mark Anthony in Heaven" (Williams) **7**:367
"To Mary" (Cowper) **40**:99
"To Mary" (Shelley) **14**:234-36
"To Mary Lady Wroth" (Jonson)
See "Epigram CIII"
"To Matilda Betham" (Coleridge) **11**:58
"To Mæcenas" (Wheatley)
See "Ode to Mæcenas"
"to merle" (Clifton) **17**:18
"To Miss Macartney" (Cowper) **40**:45, 48
"To Mistress Isabel Pennell" (Skelton) **25**:336
"To Mistress Margaret Hussey" (Skelton) **25**:345
To Mix with Time: New and Selected Poems (Swenson) **14**:249-50, 254-55, 257, 260, 266, 268, 274, 278, 281-82, 285
"To Mr. Congreve" (Swift) **9**:250
"To Mr. Creech (under the Name of Daphnis) on His Excellent Translation of Lucretius" (Behn) **13**:8, 31
"To Mr. Delany, Nov. 10, 1718" (Swift) **9**:255
"To Mr. F. Now Earl of W." (Finch) **21**:153, 164
"To Mr. Henry Lawes" (Philips) **40**:268, 296-97
"To Mr R. W. 'If as mine is'" (Donne) **1**:124
"To Mrs. Harriet Beecher Stowe" (Harper) **21**:201, 205
"To Mrs. King" (Cowper) **40**:49
"To Mrs. W. on Her Excellent Verses (Writ in Praise of Some I Had Made on the Earl of Rochester)" (Behn) **13**:8, 31
"To Muscovite Friends" (Mickiewicz)
See "Do przyjaciól Moskali"
"To Music" (Rimbaud)
See "A la musique"
"To My Bones" (Herbert) **50**:4
"To My Brother" (Bogan) **12**:117
"To My Brother" (Cervantes) **35**:113
"To My Brother" (Sassoon) **12**:261, 278
"To My Cup-Bearer" (Moore) **49**:104
"To My Daughter the Junkie on a Train" (Lorde) **12**:146-47, 154
"To My Dead Red-Haired Mother" (Stone) **53**:224
"To My Dear and Loving Husband His Goeing into England" (Bradstreet) **10**:13, 36, 40, 63
"To My Dear Sister Mrs CP on Her Marriage" (Philips) **40**:297
"To my dearest Antenor on his Parting" (Philips) **40**:296
"To my Excellent Lucasia on our Friendship" (Philips)
See "Friendship in Embleme or the Seal To My Dearest Lucasia"
To My excellent Lucasia, on our Friendship (Philips) **40**:281
"To My Fairer Brethren" (Cullen) **20**:52
"To My Father" (Olds) **22**:325
"To my friend G.N. from Wrest" (Carew)
See "Letter to G.N. from Wrest"
"To My Friend Jerina" (Clifton) **17**:29
"To My Friend Whose Parachute Did Not Open" (Wagoner) **33**:326, 369, 371-73
"To My Friend with an Identity Disk" (Owen) **19**:334, 358
"To My Greek" (Merrill) **28**:220, 262-63
"To My Honored Friend, Dr. Charleton" (Dryden) **25**:95
"To my Honoured friend, Master Thomas May, upon his Comedie, The Heire" (Carew) **29**:53
"To My Ill Reader" (Herrick) **9**:89
"To my Inconstant Mistress" (Carew) **29**:3-4, 9, 18, 32-34
"To My Lady Moreland at Tunbridge" (Behn) **13**:8, 29-30
"to my last period" (Clifton) **17**:29, 36
"To my lord Ignorant" (Jonson)
See "Epigram X"
"To my Lucasia in defence of declared Friendship" (Philips) **40**:313
To my Lucasia, in defence of declared friendship (Philips) **40**:281
"To My Mother" (Montale) **13**:112, 149, 152
"To my much honoured Friend, Henry Lord Carey of Lepington, upon his translation of Malvezzi" (Carew) **29**:65, 81
"To My Muscovite Friends" (Mickiewicz)
See "Do przyjaciól Moskali"
"To My Muse" (Jonson)
See "Epigram LXV"
"To My Old Friend, William Leachman" (Riley) **48**:288, 334
"To My Playmate" (Viereck) **27**:263, 278, 281
"To My Prince's Command" (Wang Wei) **18**:366
"To My Rivall" (Carew) **29**:72
"To My Sister" (Roethke) **15**:275
"To my worthy Friend, M. D'Avenant, Upon his Excellent Play, The Just Italian" (Carew) **29**:83
"To my Worthy Friend Master George Sandys, on his Translation of the Psalms" (Carew) **29**:7, 17-18
"To Myself in an Album" (Zagajewski) **27**:389
"To Nannette Falk-Auerbach" (Lanier) **50**:79
"To Natal'ia" (Pushkin) **10**:404
"To Nature" (Hölderlin)
See "An die Natur"

"To Nichori" (Cavafy) **36**:108
"To Night" (Shelley) **14**:171, 177
"To Odoardo Corazzini, killed by the French in the Campaign of Rome, 1867" (Carducci) **46**:5
"To One in Despair" (Carman) **34**:226
"To One in Paradise" (Poe) **1**:432-33, 437, 444, 446; **54**:273
"To One Who Died Young" (Reese) **29**:335
"To One Who Died Young" (Trakl)
See "An einen Frühverstorbenen"
"To One Who Was With Me in the War" (Sassoon) **12**:246
"To Orlov" (Pushkin)
See "Orlovu"
"To Our Friends" (Szymborska) **44**:301
"To Our Friends of the Tiber Valley" (Carducci)
See "Agli amici della Valle Tiberina"
"To Our Mocking Bird Died of a Cat" (Lanier) **50**:79
"To Paolo and Francesca in Purgatory" (Wylie) **23**:326
"To P'ei Ti" (Wang Wei) **18**:362-63, 373-74
"To Penshurst" (Jonson)
See *The Forest II*
"To Perenna" (Herrick) **9**:136-37
"To Perilla" (Herrick) **9**:127-28
"To Pile Like Thunder to Its Close" (Dickinson) **1**:102
"To Pliuskova" (Pushkin) **10**:409
"To Poetry" (Carducci)
See "Alla rima"
"To Posterity" (MacNeice) **61**:183
"To R. B." (Hopkins) **15**:157
"To Raja Rao" (Milosz) **8**:195, 200
"To Remain" (Cavafy) **36**:42
"To Remember" (Ekeloef) **23**:87
"To Remember is a Kind of Hope" (Amichai) **38**:43
"To Return to the Trees" (Walcott) **46**:237, 278, 291
"To Rhea" (Emerson) **18**:102
"To Richard Wagner" (Lanier) **50**:77-78
"To Robert Burns" (Bridges) **28**:65
"To Robert Earle of Salisburie" (Jonson)
See "Epigram XLIII"
"To Robert Southey" (Coleridge) **11**:106
"To Robinson Jeffers" (Milosz) **8**:184, 199, 208
"To Roger Blin" (Stryk) **27**:203, 213
"To Roosevelt" (Darío)
See "A Roosevelt"
"To Rosa Parks of Montgomery who started it all" (Hughes) **53**:150
"To S. M., A Young African Painter, on Seeing His Works" (Wheatley) **3**:336, 338, 344, 362
"To Saxham" (Carew)
See "Address to Saxham"
"To Science" (Poe) **1**:437
"To Secretary Ling-hu" (Wang Wei) **18**:373
"To See a World in a Grain of Sand" (Blake) **12**:36
"To See Him Again" (Mistral)
See "Volverlo a ver"
"To See the Heron" (Tomlinson) **17**:348
"To Sensual Pleasure" (Cavafy) **36**:74
"To Share the Way with . . ." (Char)
See "Faire du chemin avec . . ."
"To Silvia" (Leopardi)
See "A Silvia"
"To Sing a Song of Palestine" (Jordan) **38**:127
"To Sir Edward Dering (the Noble Silvander) on His Dream and Navy" (Philips) **40**:296
"To Sir Horace Vere" (Jonson)
See "Epigram XCI"
"To Sir Joshua Reynolds" (Cowper) **40**:103
"To Sir Robert Wroth" (Jonson)
See *The Forest III*
"To Sleep" (Graves) **6**:137
"To Some Winter Is Arrack" (Mandelstam) **14**:155
"To Speak of Woe That Is in Marriage" (Lowell) **3**:221, 245
"To Spring or Concerning the Antique Fables" (Leopardi)
See "Alla primavera o delle favole antiche"
"To Stand (Alone) in Some" (Cummings) **5**:110
"To Statecraft Embalmed" (Moore) **49**:90, 114-15, 120
To Stay Alive (Levertov) **11**:178-80, 195
"To Stella, Visiting Me in My Sickness" (Swift) **9**:297
"To Stella, Who Collected and Transcribed His Poems, 1720" (Swift) **9**:255
"To Susan Countesse of Montgomerie" (Jonson)
See "Epigram CIV"
"To Swindon From London by Britrail Aloud" (Birney) **52**:33, 79
"To Sylvia" (Herrick) **9**:97
"To T. A." (Kipling) **3**:191
"To The Airport" (Rich) **5**:382
"To the American Negro Troops" (Senghor) **25**:238
"To the Balloil Men Still in Africa" (Belloc) **24**:3, 11
"To the Bitter Sweet-Heart: A Dream" (Owen) **19**:352
"To the Body" (Patmore) **59**:223
"To the Boy Elis" (Trakl)
See "An den Knaben Elis"
"To the Cicada" (Wright) **36**:368, 378
"To the Comet" (Thoreau) **30**:266
"To the Countess of Anglesie upon the immoderately-by-her lamented death of her Husband" (Carew) **29**:60-61
"To the Countess of Bedford" (Lanyer) **60**:17
"To the Countesse of Bedford. 'Madame, reason is'" (Donne) **1**:123
"To the Countesse of Bedford. 'This twilight of'" (Donne) **1**:124
"To the Creature of the Creation" (Wright) **36**:346-47
"To the Cross of Savoy" (Carducci)
See "Alla croce di Savoia"
"To the Cuckoo" (Wordsworth) **4**:403
"To the Daisy" (Wordsworth) **4**:376
"To the Dawn" (Carducci)
See "All'Aurora"
"To the Dead Poets" (Herbert) **50**:18
"To the Dean, when in England, in 1726" (Swift) **9**:255
"To the De'il" (Burns)
See "Address to the De'il"
"To the Diaspora" (Brooks) **7**:84
"To the Dog Belvoir" (Smith) **12**:317
"To the Driving Cloud" (Longfellow) **30**:78
"To the Duke of Wellington" (Arnold) **5**:49
"To the Etruscan Poets" (Wilbur) **51**:278
"To the Evening Star" (Blake) **12**:31
"To the Evening Star: Central Minnesota" (Wright) **36**:316
"To the Excellent Mrs Anne Owen upon receiving the Name of Lucasia and Adoption into our Society December 28 1651" (Philips) **40**:272
"To the excellent Orinda" (Philips) **40**:302
"To the Fair Clarinda Who Made Love to Me, Imagin'd More than Woman" (Behn) **13**:10, 13-14, 20, 22-3, 29
"To the Film Industry in Crisis" (O'Hara) **45**:138, 147, 171, 174, 189, 204-8
"To The Fringed Gentian" (Bryant) **20**:10, 35, 45
"To the German Language" (Mandelstam) **14**:109
"To the Girl Who Lives in a Tree" (Lorde) **12**:154
"To the Governor and Legislature of Massachusetts" (Nemerov) **24**:262, 279
"To the Holy Ghost" (Skelton) **25**:339
"To the Honorable Edward Howard" (Behn) **13**:8
"To the Honorable the Lady Worsley at Longleat" (Finch) **21**:167, 176
"To the honoured Lady E.C." (Philips) **40**:296
"To the House" (Jeffers) **17**:131
"To the Immaculate Virgin, on a Winter Night" (Merton) **10**:339
"To the Immortal Memory of the Halibut on which I dined This Day" (Cowper) **40**:125
"To the Italians" (Carducci)
See "Agli Italiani"
"To the King" (Smart) **13**:342
"TO THE KING, upon His Comming with His Army into the West" (Herrick) **9**:109
"TO THE KING, upon His Welcome to Hampton-Court" (Herrick) **9**:109
"To the Lacedemonians" (Tate) **50**:231, 235, 243-45, 250-51, 255-56, 274, 280, 288, 301
"To the Ladie Anne, countesse of Dorcet" (Lanyer) **60**:33, 112
"To the Ladie Lucie, Countesse of Bedford" (Lanyer) **60**:26, 112
"To the Ladie Susan, Countesse Dowager of Kent, and daughter to the Duchesse of Suffolke" (Lanyer) **60**:15, 52, 82, 112
"To the Lady" (Yamada) **244**:333, 348
"To the Lady Crew, upon the Death of Her Child" (Herrick) **9**:104, 131, 143
"To the Lady E. Boyl" (Philips) **40**:312
"To the Lark" (Herrick) **9**:98
"To the Living" (Sarton) **39**:322
"To the Man after the Harrow" (Kavanagh) **33**:73, 77, 117, 127, 130-2, 147
"To the Master of Sea Bird of Friday Harbor" (Wagoner) **33**:328
To the Memory of . . . George Duke of Buckingham (Behn) **13**:9
"To the Memory of My Dear Daughter in Law, Mrs. Mercy Bradstreet" (Bradstreet) **10**:31
"To the Memory of the most Ingenious and Vertuous Gentleman Mr. Will Cartwright, my much valued Friend" (Philips) **40**:273
"To the Moon" (Leopardi)
See "Alla Luna"
"To the Most Illustrious and Most Hopeful Prince, Charles" (Herrick) **9**:133
"To the Mothers of the Dead Militia" (Neruda)
See "Canto a las madres de los milicianos muertos"
"To the Mountains" (Thoreau) **30**:293
"To the Muse" (Blok)
See "K Muze"
"To the Muse" (Wright) **36**:319, 324, 327-30, 341, 346, 354, 372, 375
"To the Muse of the North" (Morris) **55**:340
"To the Muses" (Blake) **12**:31
"To the New World" (Jarrell)
See "For an Emigrant"
"To the Nightingale" (Finch) **21**:141, 144, 157-61, 175
"To the Noble Palæmon Jeremy Taylor on His Incomparable Discourse on Friendship" (Philips) **40**:267, 296, 300
"To the North" (Sarton) **39**:325
"To the Not Impossible Him" (Millay) **6**:211, 235
"To the Painter of an Ill-Drawn Picture of Cleone, the Honorable Mrs. Thynne" (Finch) **21**:164
"To the Peacock of France" (Moore) **4**:261; **49**:114
"To the Pious Memory of the Accomplisht Young Lady Mrs. Anne Killigrew" (Dryden) **25**:69
"To the Poem" (O'Hara) **45**:178
"To the Poet Who Happens to Be Black and the Black Poet Who Happens to Be a Woman" (Lorde) **12**:136
"To the Poets in New York" (Wright) **36**:301, 341
"To the Poets: To Make Much of Life" (Oppen) **35**:324

"To the Pushkin House" (Blok)
See "Pushkinskomu domu"
"To the Queen of Italy" (Carducci)
See "Alla Regina d'Italia"
"To the Queene" (Herrick) **9**:116
"To the Queene on her arivall at Portsmouth. May. 1662" (Philips) **40**:318
"To the Queenes most Excellent Majestie" (Lanyer) **60**:4, 37, 49, 54
To the Quick (McHugh) **61**:199-200
"To the Rain" (Merwin) **45**:97
"To the Reader" (Baudelaire)
See "Au lecteur"
"To the Reader" (Merrill) **28**:283
"To the Reader of Master William Davenant's Play" (Carew) **29**:84
"To the Right Honorable William, Earl of Dartmouth, His Majesty's Principal Secretary of State for North America" (Wheatley) **3**:337, 341, 343, 347, 350, 352
"To the Right Person" (Frost) **1**:200
"To the Road" (Dunbar) **5**:139
"To the Romantic Traditionists" (Tate) **50**:255, 289
"To the Rose upon the Rood of Time" (Yeats) **20**:343; **51**:149
"To the Sad One" (Borges) **32**:58
"To the Same" (Montagu) **16**:338
"To the Sea" (Larkin) **21**:238, 240
"To the Sea" (Pushkin)
See "K moriu"
"To the Sea" (Teasdale) **31**:341
"To the Second Person" (Skelton) **25**:339
"To the Shore" (Swenson) **14**:263
"To the Sister" (Trakl) **20**:248
"To the Snake" (Levertov) **11**:205
"To the Soul of 'Progress'" (Moore) **49**:113-14, 120
"To the South: On Its New Slavery" (Dunbar) **5**:131
"To the Statue" (Swenson) **14**:264
"To the Stone-Cutters" (Jeffers) **17**:117
"To the truly noble Mr. Henry Lawes" (Philips) **40**:318
"To the Tune of the Coventry Carol" (Smith) **12**:316, 330
"To the Unborn" (Mahon) **60**:177-78
"to the unborn and waiting children" (Clifton) **17**:19
"To the Union Savers of Cleveland" (Harper) **21**:190
"To the University of Cambridge, in New England" (Wheatley) **3**:337, 340-41, 344-45, 353
"To the Unknown Eros" (Patmore) **59**:259, 262, 276
"To the Unknown God" (Hardy) **8**:121
"To the Unseeable Animal" (Berry) **28**:26
"To the Virgin of the Hill" (Mistral)
See "A la Virgen de la colina"
"To the Virgins, to Make Much of Time" (Herrick) **9**:100, 145
"To the Vision Seekers, Remember This" (Rose) **13**:241
"To the Warsaw Critics" (Mickiewicz)
See "O Krytykach i Recenzentach"
"To the Water Nymphs Drinking at the Fountain" (Herrick) **9**:97
"To the White Fiends" (McKay) **2**:212, 216, 218, 229
"To the Wife of a Sick Friend" (Millay) **6**:217
"To the World. A Farwell for a Gentlewoman, Vertuous and Nobel" (Jonson) **17**:172, 212
"To the Young Poets" (Hölderlin)
See "An die jungen Dichter"
"To Thee" (Darío)
See "A ti"
"To Thos. Floyd" (Bridges) **28**:88
"To Those Grown Mute" (Trakl) **20**:258
"To Those of My Sisters Who Kept Their Naturals" (Brooks) **7**:86
"To Time" (Clare) **23**:44
"To Tirzah" (Blake) **12**:7, 34-5
"To Tizengauzen" (Lermontov) **18**:284-85
To Transfigure, To Organize (Pasolini)
See *Trasumanar e organizzar*
"To Urania" (Brodsky) **9**:25, 27
To Urania: Selected Poems 1965-1985 (Brodsky) **9**:20, 23-4, 26, 29, 30
"To Us, All Flowers Are Roses" (Goodison) **36**:154
To Us, All Flowers Are Roses (Goodison) **36**:154
"To V. L. Davydovu" (Pushkin)
See "V. L. Davydovu"
"To Victor Hugo of My Crow Pluto" (Moore) **4**:255, 259; **49**:133, 147, 161
"To Victory" (Carducci)
See "Alla Vittoria"
"To Victory" (Sassoon) **12**:261, 263, 276
"To Virgil" (Tennyson) **6**:370
"To Waken an Old Lady" (Williams) **7**:345, 353, 360, 363
"To Walk on Hills" (Graves) **6**:143
"To W.G.G." (McKay) **2**:226
"To What Listens" (Berry) **28**:9
"To What Serves Mortal Beauty" (Hopkins) **15**:144
"To William Butler Yeats on Tagore" (Moore) **49**:114, 116
"To William E. Channing" (Longfellow) **30**:48
"To William Simpson of Ochiltree, May 1785" (Burns)
See "Epistle to William Simpson of Ochiltree, May 1785"
"To William Wordsworth Composed on the Night after His Recitation of a Poem on the Growth of the Individual Mind" (Coleridge) **11**:52-3, 58, 92, 106
"To Winkey" (Lowell) **13**:64
"To Winter" (Blake) **12**:32
"To Wisshe and Want" (Wyatt) **27**:316-317, 319
"To You" (O'Hara) **45**:150
"To You" (Whitman) **3**:381
"To You, Out There (Mars? Jupiter?)" (Wright) **36**:377
"To You Who Read My Book" (Cullen) **20**:55
To Your Scythe's Content (Char)
See *A Faulx contente*
"Toad dreams" (Piercy) **29**:297
"Toads" (Larkin) **21**:229, 234, 238
"Toads Revisited" (Larkin) **21**:229, 234, 237-38, 244
"A Toast" (MacNeice) **61**:138
"Toast for a Golden Age" (Hope) **56**:266, 306
"Tobacco Shop" (Pessoa)
See "Tabacaria"
"The Tobacconist's" (Pessoa)
See "Tabacaria"
"A Toccata of Galuppi's" (Browning) **2**:37, 88
"A Toccatta of Galuppi's" (Browning) **61**:89
"Todas les efes tenía la novia que yo quería" (Fuertes) **27**:37
"Today" (Baraka) **4**:30
"Today" (Hughes) **53**:149
"Today" (O'Hara) **45**:160, 178, 183-84, 199
"Today" (Reese) **29**:346, 353
"Today and Tomorrow" (Rossetti) **7**:275, 277
"To-day I Climbed" (Thoreau) **30**:236
"Today I Was So Happy, So I Made This Poem" (Wright) **36**:327, 330, 364
"today is a day of great joy" (Cruz) **37**:21
"To-day, this Insect" (Thomas) **52**:228, 230-32
"Todesfuge" (Celan) **10**:96, 102, 115-17, 120-21
Todo asusta (Fuertes) **27**:10, 12
"Todos" (Dalton) **36**:130
"Todtnauberg" (Celan) **10**:98
"Toenails" (Borges) **32**:94
"The Toes" (Carver) **54**:26
"Token Drunk" (Bukowski) **18**:15
"Told" (Levine) **22**:214, 224
"Tolerance" (Hardy) **8**:93
"Tolerance" (Pavese) **13**:205
"The Tollund Man" (Heaney) **18**:195, 202, 204, 210-11
"Tom" (Brathwaite) **56**:49, 82, 99-100
"Tom Fool at Jamaica" (Moore) **49**:126, 128, 134, 136-37, 145, 149
"Tom May's Death" (Marvell) **10**:276
"Tom Merrit" (Masters) **1**:324
"Tom Snooks the Pundit" (Smith) **12**:333
"Tom, Tom the Piper's Son" (Ransom) **61**:279
"th tomato conspiracy aint worth a whol pome" (Bissett) **14**:23, 34
"Tomatoes" (Francis) **34**:242
"Tomb" (Paz) **48**:274
"The Tomb of Edgar Poe" (Mallarmé)
See "Le tombeau d'Edgar Poe"
"Tomb of Eurion" (Cavafy)
See "Tomb of Evrion"
"Tomb of Evrion" (Cavafy) **36**:8, 66
"Tomb of Iases" (Cavafy)
See "Tomb of Iasis"
"Tomb of Iasis" (Cavafy) **36**:8, 13, 65, 75
"Tomb of Ignatios" (Cavafy)
See "Tomb of Ignatius"
"Tomb of Ignatius" (Cavafy) **36**:8, 75
"Tomb of Lanes" (Cavafy)
See "Tomb of Lanis"
"Tomb of Lanis" (Cavafy) **36**:8, 75
"Tomb of Lysias Grammaticus" (Cavafy) **36**:8
The Tomb of Secrets (Char)
See *Le Tombeau des secrets*
"The Tomb of Stuart Merrill" (Ashbery) **26**:145
"The Tomb of the Abbess of Tours" (MacLeish) **47**:131
"Tombeau de Charles IX" (Ronsard) **11**:243-44
"Le Tombeau de tres illustre Marquerite de France, duchesse de Savoye" (Ronsard) **11**:243-44
"Le tombeau d'Edgar Poe" (Mallarmé) **4**:203, 209
"Le tombeau d'Edgard Poe" (Mallarmé)
See "Le tombeau d'Edgar Poe"
Le tombeau des secrets (Char) **56**:127
"Le tombeau d'une mère" (Lamartine) **16**:264, 293
"Tombstone Blues" (Dylan) **37**:51
"The Tombstone-Maker" (Sassoon) **12**:242, 263
"Tom-Dobbin" (Gunn) **26**:226
"Tomlinson" (Kipling) **3**:167, 182
"Tommy" (Kipling) **3**:187
"Tomorrow" (Hughes) **53**:191
"Tomorrow Is My Birthday" (Masters) **36**:195
"Tomorrow's Song" (Snyder) **21**:298
"Tom's Garland" (Hopkins) **15**:134, 138, 171
"Ton portrait" (Césaire) **25**:31
"Ton Soir Mon Soir" (Senghor) **25**:249
"A Tone Poem" (Ashbery) **26**:132
"Tongue" (Herbert) **50**:4
"Tonight slippers of darkness fall" (Abse) **41**:25
"Tonight the Woods Are Darkened" (Warren) **37**:330
"Tonique" (Tzara) **27**:230-31
"Tonu Soy" (Mackey) **49**:66
"Too Blue" (Hughes) **1**:243
"Too Late" (Arnold) **5**:43, 56
"The Too Late Born" (MacLeish) **47**:186
"Tools" (Mistral)
See "Herramientas"
"Toome" (Heaney) **18**:202, 204, 210, 241
"The Toome Road" (Heaney) **18**:246
"To—One word is too often profaned" (Shelley) **14**:233
"A Tooth" (Storni)
See "Un diente"
Topoemas (Paz) **1**:363
Topography and Other Poems (Stone) **53**:215-18, 220, 227-28, 239, 242
"Torch Procession" (Celan)
See "Fackelzug"
The Torch-Bearers (Noyes) **27**:128, 130, 133, 137-8
"The Torch-bearer's Race" (Jeffers) **17**:107
"La Torche du prodigue" (Char) **56**:147

"Torero" (Stryk) **27**:187, 203, 214
"Torero nuestro de cada día" (Fuertes) **27**:38
"La tormenta" (Guillén) **35**:154
"The Torn Sky" (Jordan) **38**:127
"Tornado Blues" (Brown) **55**:71, 74, 151, 160
"Tornado Warning" (Shapiro) **25**:306
"Tornant al pais" (Pasolini) **17**:252, 265
"Tornasol" (Guillén) **35**:158
"Toronto Board of Trade Goes Abroad" (Birney) **52**:16
"Torquemada" (Longfellow) **30**:41, 107
"La torre" (Olson) **19**:268, 293, 309-10
"Torre" (Storni) **33**:239;
The Torrent and the Night Before (Robinson) **1**:459, 474, 484-85
"Torres d' Oeste" (Castro) **41**:95
"Torso" (Brodsky) **9**:8
"Tortilla Host" (Alurista) **34**:40
"Tortoise Gallantry" (Lawrence) **54**:225
"The Tortoise in Eternity" (Wylie) **23**:301, 309
"Tortoise Shout" (Lawrence) **54**:177, 212, 236
Tortoises (Lawrence) **54**:189, 198
"La tortuga de oro..." (Darío) **15**:99
"Torture" (Szymborska) **44**:281
"Torture" (Walker) **30**:343
"The Tortured Heart" (Rimbaud)
See "La coeur volé"
"Tortures" (Szymborska) **44**:281
"Toscani" (Carducci) **46**:50
"The Total Influence or Outcome: The Sun" (Piercy) **29**:305-06
Total Song (Éluard)
See *Chanson complète*
"Totem" (Césaire) **25**:21-2
"Totem" (Plath) **1**:391, 393, 399, 412; **37**:258
"Totem" (Senghor) **25**:224, 230
"The Totem" (Swenson) **14**:249-50
"Totò Merùmeni" (Gozzano) **10**:184-88, 190
Tottel's Miscellany (Surrey) **59**:284, 290, 319, 321, 341
"Tou Wan Speaks to Her Husband, Liu Sheng" (Dove) **6**:107, 109
"Touch" (Gunn) **26**:195, 202, 207, 217, 219
"The Touch" (Sexton) **2**:352
Touch (Gunn) **26**:192, 196-197, 202-203, 207-209, 211-214, 219, 223, 225-226, 231
"Touch Me" (Kunitz) **19**:187
"A Touch of the Hand" (Curnow) **48**:18, 35
"Touch-up Man" (Komunyakaa) **51**:53
"Toujours Miroirs" (Senghor) **25**:251
"The Tour" (Plath) **1**:399-401; **37**:257
"Tour" (Wakoski) **15**:359
"Tour 5" (Hayden) **6**:189, 194
"Touring for Trujillo" (Guillén) **23**:126
"Tourist" (Sarton) **39**:327
"The Tourist and the Town" (Rich) **5**:353, 362
"Tourist Death" (MacLeish) **47**:130, 188
"Tourists" (Amichai) **38**:19, 41, 54
"Tournesol" (Breton) **15**:61-2
"Tous partis" (Char) **56**:146
"De tout ce que j'ai dit de moi que rest-t-il" (Éluard) **38**:68
"Tout Entouré de Mon Regard" (Tomlinson) **17**:321, 339
"Le tout, le rien" (Bonnefoy) **58**:154
A toute épreuve (Éluard) **38**:67
Toute la lyre (Hugo) **17**:65, 86
"Toute une vie" (Péret) **33**:208, 213
"Toward a City That Sings" (Jordan) **38**:119
"Toward an Organic Philosophy" (Rexroth) **20**:215, 217, 221
"Toward Finestère" (Montale)
See "Vento sulla mezzaluna"
"Toward Rationality" (Warren) **37**:284, 288
"Toward Siena" (Montale)
See "Verso Siena"
Toward the Cradle of the World (Gozzano)
See *Verso la cuna del mondo*
"Toward the Empty Earth" (Mandelstam)
See "K pustoi zemle nevol'no pripadaia"
Toward the Gulf (Masters) **1**:330, 332, 335, 342-44; **36**:179, 183
"Toward the Interior" (Wagoner) **33**:364, 367
"Toward the name" (Guillén)
See "Hacia el nombre"
"Toward the Piraeus" (H. D.) **5**:268, 304
"Toward the Solstice" (Rich) **5**:374
Towards a New Poetry (Wakoski) **15**:359
"Towards a New Scotland" (MacDiarmid) **9**:176
"Towards a Personal Semantics" (Jordan) **38**:119-21
Towards a tense serenity (Char)
See *À une sérénité crispée*
"Towards Autumn" (Hacker) **47**:81, 105
"Towards Byzantium" (Yeats) **51**:89, 91-92
"Towards the Slave Quisqueya" (Guillén)
See "Hacia la esclava Quisqueya"
"The Tower" (Yeats) **20**:310, 318, 320, 329, 334, 342; **51**:98, 120, 135-37, 139, 143, 152
The Tower (Yeats) **20**:307, 311, 333, 335; **51**:74, 108, 120, 134-35
"The Tower beyond Tragedy" (Jeffers) **17**:106, 108, 110, 112, 135, 144-46
The Tower of Babel (Merton) **10**:344, 349
Tower of Ivory (MacLeish) **47**:165, 182, 251
"The Tower of Pisa" (Song) **21**:344
"The Tower of Siloam" (Graves) **6**:133
"The Tower Struck by Lightning Reversed; The Overturning of the Tower" (Piercy) **29**:324
"Towers of the West" (Castro)
See "Torres d' Oeste"
"The Town" (Cavafy) **36**:52, 57
"The Town" (Pushkin)
See "Gorodok"
"Town" (Soto) **28**:378, 385
"Town and Country" (Brooke) **24**:56
"The Town Betrayed" (Muir) **49**:264, 289
The Town down the River (Robinson) **1**:462-63, 467, 474, 478, 490
"The Town Dump" (Nemerov) **24**:257, 261, 291-92
"A Town Eclogue" (Swift) **9**:278
Town Eclogues (Montagu)
See *Court Poems*
Town in Tears (Seifert)
See *Město v slzách*
"Town Marshal" (Masters) **36**:230
"Towns in Colour" (Lowell) **13**:79
"The Toys" (Patmore) **59**:209, 222, 264
Toys in a Field (Komunyakaa) **51**:20, 33, 63
"Tracé sur le gouffre" (Char) **56**:153
"Tracking" (Wagoner) **33**:338-39, 345
"Tract" (Williams) **7**:348, 362, 378
"Tractatus" (Mahon) **60**:189, 217-19
"Tractor" (Hughes) **7**:166
"The Trade of an Irish Poet" (Heaney) **18**:201
"The Trade-Off" (Stone) **53**:259
"Tradimento" (Pavese) **13**:202, 226
"Tradition" (Niedecker) **42**:100, 109
"Traditions" (Heaney) **18**:252
"Trafferth mewn Tafarn" (Dafydd ap Gwilym) **56**:208, 220-21, 224, 232, 245, 249
"Trafficker" (Sandburg) **41**:336
"Traficante" (Cisneros) **52**:158-60, 164
"Tragedy" (Graham) **59**:179
"Tragedy of Teeth" (Kipling) **3**:194
"The Tragedy of the Leaves" (Bukowski) **18**:6, 21
"Tragic Books" (Reese) **29**:333, 335
"Tragic Destiny" (Aleixandre) **15**:10
"Traigo conmigo un cuidado" (Juana Inés de la Cruz) **24**:188
"The Trail" (Mistral)
See "La huella"
"The Trail into Kansas" (Merwin) **45**:45
"Train" (Erdrich) **52**:176
"Train Time" (Bogan) **12**:107
"Train to Dublin" (MacNeice) **61**:108, 111, 114-20, 136, 145, 164
"Training" (Owen) **19**:336
"Trainor the Druggist" (Masters) **1**:347
"Trains in the Distance" (MacNeice) **61**:126
Traité du pianiste (Bonnefoy) **58**:150
"Trakat poetycki" (Milosz) **8**:198-99, 204
"Tramontana" (Montale) **13**:105, 126
"Tramontana at Lerici" (Tomlinson) **17**:342
"The Tramp Transfigured" (Noyes) **27**:121, 134
"La trampa" (Parra) **39**:268-69, 282-83
"Las Trampas USA" (Tomlinson) **17**:353
"A Trampwoman's Tragedy" (Hardy) **8**:99
"Trams" (Sitwell) **3**:301
"The Trance" (Muir) **49**:239
"Trane" (Brathwaite) **56**:54-55
"Transaction" (Ammons) **16**:22
"Transcedental Etude" (Rich) **5**:381
"Transcontinental" (Birney) **52**:47-48, 50-52, 58, 92
"Transcription of Organ Music" (Ginsberg) **47**:21, 39
"Transfer" (Brown) **55**:89-90
"Transfer of the the Remains of Ugo Foscolo to Santa Croce" (Carducci)
See "Per il Trasporto delle Relique di Ugo Foscolo in Santa Croce"
"The Transfiguration" (Muir) **49**:198, 229, 233, 262, 264, 274, 284
"Transfigured Life" (Rossetti) **44**:169-70
"Transformation & Escape" (Corso) **33**:37
The Transformation/Transformations (Ovid)
See *Metamorphoses*
"Transformations" (Hardy) **8**:113
"Transformations" (Seifert)
See "Proměny"
"Transformations" (Wright) **14**:339
Transformations (Sexton) **2**:349, 354-55, 362, 364-65, 368
"The Transformed One" (Olds) **22**:326
"Transfusión" (Storni) **33**:250;
"Transgressing the Real" (Duncan) **2**:104
"Transient Barracks" (Jarrell) **41**:172, 189, 203
"Transients and Residents" (Gunn) **26**:220
"Transistors" (Birney) **52**:97
"Transit" (Wilbur) **51**:335
"Transition" (Niedecker) **42**:143
"Transition" (Sarton) **39**:320, 323
"Transitional" (Williams) **7**:392
Transitional Poem (Day Lewis) **11**:123-25, 128-31, 133-35, 137, 143-45, 148, 151
"Tránsito" (Guillén) **35**:154
"Translated from the American" (Alexie) **53**:10, 40
"Translating the Birds" (Tomlinson) **17**:348, 350
"Translation" (Sarton) **39**:321
A Translation of the Psalms of David, Attempted in the Spirit of Christianity, and Adapted to the Divine Service (Smart) **13**:330-32, 341-42, 362
"Translations" (Rich) **5**:397
"Translations" (Stone) **53**:230
Translations, 1915-1920 (H. D.) **5**:304
The Translations of Ezra Pound (Pound) **4**:331
"Translations of the Psalms" (Wyatt) **27**:359
"Translucence" (Erdrich) **52**:186
"The Transmutation" (Muir) **49**:239
Transparence of the World (Merwin) **45**:31
"Transparent Garments" (Hass) **16**:199, 210
Les Transparents (Char) **56**:166, 173, 176
"Transplanting" (Roethke) **15**:295
"Transport" (Meredith) **28**:174
"The Transport of Slaves from Maryland to Mississippi" (Dove) **6**:108
Transport to Summer (Stevens) **6**:301-03
"Transylvania" (Szirtes) **51**:171
"The Trap" (Parra)
See "La trampa"
"The Trap" (Wright) **14**:356
"Trapped Dingo" (Wright) **14**:345
"The Trappist Abbey: Matins" (Merton) **10**:332
"The Trappist Cemetery, Gethsemani" (Merton) **10**:332-33, 342
"Le Trappiste" (Vigny) **26**:401-402, 404
"Trappists, Working" (Merton) **10**:332-33
Trasumanar e organizzar (Pasolini) **17**:273, 286
"Der Traum" (Benn) **35**:69

"Traum" (Stramm) **50**:170-71, 175, 189, 204
"Traum und Umnachtung" (Trakl) **20**:239, 268
"Träumerei am Abend" (Trakl) **20**:239
"Traumig" (Stramm) **50**:171, 173, 188
"Travel" (Brooke) **24**:66
"The Traveler" (Apollinaire)
See "Le voyageur"
"The Traveler" (Jarrell) **41**:146
"The Traveler" (Tate) **50**:230, 243, 256
"A Traveler at Night Writes His Thoughts" (Tu Fu) **9**:324
The Traveler Does Not Return (Nishiwaki)
See *Tabibito Kaerazu*
"TRAVELERS: Lake Superior region" (Niedecker) **42**:110-11, 114-16
"Traveling" (Alexie) **53**:40
"Traveling on an Amtrack Train Could Humanize You" (Sanchez) **9**:234
"Traveling through Fog" (Hayden) **6**:194
"The Traveller" (Curnow) **48**:46
"The Traveller and the Angel" (Wright) **14**:339, 346
"Traveller's Curse after Misdirection" (Graves) **6**:137
"Traveller's Palm" (Page) **12**:181
"Travelling" (Merwin) **45**:48
"Travelling Light" (Wagoner) **33**:337, 344
"Travelogue for Exiles" (Shapiro) **25**:269, 279, 290
"Travels in the South" (Ortiz) **17**:227, 231
"Travels of a Latter-Day Benjamin of Tudela" (Amichai)
See "Mas'ot Binyamin ha'aharon mitudela"
"Travels of the Last Benjamin of Tudela" (Amichai)
See "Mas'ot Binyamin ha'aharon mitudela"
"Traversando la Maremma Toscana" (Carducci) **46**:50, 58, 65, 77, 80
"Traverse" (Char) **56**:120
"A través de los sueños" (Alurista) **34**:28
"Tre donne intorno al cor mi son venute" (Dante) **21**:87
"Treachery" (Cavafy) **36**:56
Tread the Dark (Ignatow) **34**:324-25, 330
"The Treasure" (Brooke) **24**:87-9
"The Treasure" (Jeffers) **17**:117
"Treatise on Poetry" (Milosz)
See "Trakat poetycki"
"The Treble Recorder" (Seifert) **47**:327
"Trébol" (Darío) **15**:89
"Trech a Gais nog a Geidw" (Dafydd ap Gwilym) **56**:232
"The Tree" (Aleixandre)
See "El árbol"
"The Tree" (Finch) **21**:149
"Tree" (Hope) **56**:292
"Tree" (Rukeyser) **12**:224
"The Tree" (Stone) **53**:229
"The Tree" (Teasdale) **31**:360, 370
"Tree at My Window" (Frost) **1**:197, 205; **39**:232
"Tree Burial" (Bryant) **20**:14, 17
"Tree Disease" (Hughes) **7**:120
"Tree House" (Silverstein) **49**:331
"The Tree of Knowledge" (Graham) **59**:155
"Tree of Song" (Teasdale) **31**:322, 356
"Tree Planting" (Tagore)
See "Vriksha-ropan"
"A Tree Telling of Orpheus" (Levertov) **11**:177
The Tree Witch (Viereck) **27**:275-76, 278-80, 282
A Tree Within (Paz)
See *Arbol adentro*
The Tree Within (Paz)
See *Arbol adentro*
"The Trees" (Carruth) **10**:71
"Trees" (Hughes) **7**:120
"Trees" (Nemerov) **24**:266-67
"The Trees" (Sarton) **39**:323, 332
"Trees" (Tsvetaeva)
See "Derev'ya"
"Trees" (Williams) **7**:351
"Trees and Cattle" (Dickey) **40**:162-63, 181, 189, 191
Trees, Effigies, Moving Objects (Curnow) **48**:13, 23, 46-48, 59
"Trees in a Grove" (Meredith) **28**:170
"treez" (Bissett) **14**:24, 33
"La Treizieme" (Nerval) **13**:196; **67**:360
"Trelawnys Dream" (Meredith) **28**:215
"A Trellis for R." (Swenson) **14**:267, 280
The Trembling of the Veil (Yeats) **20**:330
"Tremor" (Zagajewski) **27**:395
Tremor (Zagajewski) **27**:380-81, 383-84, 389, 395, 397, 399
"Tren Fortynbrasa" (Herbert) **50**:36
"Trench Poems" (Owen) **19**:350
"Trenches" (Borges) **32**:121
"Tres Poesías" (Parra) **39**:272, 307
"Tres versiones de Judas" (Borges) **32**:48
"Trespass Into Spirit" (Baraka) **4**:24
The Trespasser (Stryk) **27**:191, 194, 197-98, 215-16, 218
"Trevenen" (Davie) **29**:103, 109
"Tri palmy" (Lermontov) **18**:268, 290-91, 293
"Tri Phorthor Eiddig" (Dafydd ap Gwilym) **56**:208, 225, 227-33, 249
"A Triad" (Rossetti) **7**:272-3, 275, 291
"Tríada" (Borges) **32**:91
"Triage" (Mueller) **33**:192-93
"The Trial" (Abse) **41**:6, 8, 22
"The Trial" (Sassoon) **12**:260
Trial Balances (Bishop) **34**:161
"Trial of a City" (Birney) **52**:8-9, 46-47
Trial of a City and Other Verse (Birney) **52**:7-8, 11, 21-22, 36, 40, 43, 45, 67
"Trial of a Poet" (Shapiro) **25**:277-79
Trial of a Poet (Shapiro) **25**:273-74, 285, 290, 296, 319, 322, 324
"The Trial of Dead Cleopatra" (Lindsay) **23**:280, 286
"Trial-Pieces" (Heaney) **18**:246
"Tribal Scenes" (Song) **21**:345
"Tribe" (Song) **21**:336, 343
"Tribulación" (Mistral) **32**:155, 176
Tribunals (Duncan) **2**:106, 116, 127
"Tribute" (Brutus) **24**:111
"The Tribute" (H. D.) **5**:298, 304
"Tribute" (Merwin) **45**:5
"The Tribute" (Patmore) **59**:231-32
Tribute to the Angels (H. D.) **5**:272, 274-75, 283-84, 286-87, 293-97, 308-09, 313, 315
"The Trick" (Borges)
See "El truco"
"The Trick Was" (Yamada) **44**:347
"Trickle Drops" (Whitman) **3**:406
"Tricks with Mirrors" (Atwood) **8**:21-6
"Trickster 1977" (Rose) **13**:232
"Trieb" (Stramm) **50**:189, 201, 208
"Triebkrieg" (Stramm) **50**:168
"Trillium" (Glück) **16**:171
Trilogie der Leidenschaft (Goethe) **5**:250
Trilogy (H. D.) **5**:281, 283-86, 292-93, 2960-98, 304-07, 310-15
Trilogy (Wakoski) **15**:365
"Trilogy for X" (MacNeice) **61**:127, 138
"Trinchera" (Borges) **22**:92
"The Trinity" (Stone) **53**:257
"Trinity Churchyard" (Rukeyser) **12**:225
"Trinity Peace" (Sandburg) **2**:304
"Trio for Two Cats and a Trombone" (Sitwell) **3**:303, 306
"Triolet" (Brooke) **24**:54
Trionfi (Petrarch) **8**:224-26, 238, 240, 243, 246, 252, 254, 257, 260, 273-78
"Trip to Brundisium" (Horace) **46**:190, 193
"The Triple Fool" (Donne) **1**:125
"The Triple Fool" (Millay) **6**:243
"Triple Time" (Larkin) **21**:227, 236, 242
"Triptych" (Heaney) **18**:246
"A Triptych" (Ignatow) **34**:323
"El triste" (Borges) **22**:80
"Triste, triste" (Laforgue) **14**:86, 88-9
"Los tristes, IV" (Castro) **41**:112
"Tristesse" (Benn) **35**:67
"Tristesse" (Lamartine) **16**:293
"Tristesse d'Olympio" (Hugo) **17**:64, 76-77, 82, 97
"Tristesse d'un étoile" (Apollinaire) **7**:3
"Les tristesses de la lune" (Baudelaire) **1**:44-5
"Tristia" (Mandelstam) **14**:106
Tristia (Mandelstam)
See *Vtoraya kniga*
Tristia (Ovid) **2**:233, 240-42, 244-45, 252-53, 255-59
Tristibus (Ovid)
See *Tristia*
"Tristitia" (Patmore) **59**:262
Tristram (Robinson) **1**:470-72, 474-75, 481, 489; **35**:368
"Tristram and Iseult" (Arnold) **5**:9, 12, 33-4, 42, 49, 64
"Tristram Crazed" (Muir) **49**:239
Tristram of Lyonesse (Swinburne) **24**:307, 309, 310, 313-14, 316, 319, 321-23, 348-50, 352, 355-57
"Tristram's Journey" (Muir) **49**:230, 270, 288
"Tritiya" (Tagore) **8**:415
"Triumph" (Reese) **29**:332
The Triumph of Achilles (Glück) **16**:149, 151-52, 155-57, 159, 163
"Triumph of Charis" (Jonson)
See *A Celebration of Charis in Ten Lyric Pieces*
The Triumph of Life (Shelley) **14**:174, 188, 193, 211
"The Triumph of Life: Mary Shelley" (Mueller) **33**:175, 197
"the triumph of the will" (Schwerner) **42**:196
"The Triumph of Time" (Swinburne) **24**:308, 322, 325, 337-38, 342-43
Triumphal March (Eliot) **5**:168, 185
"Triumphalis" (Carman) **34**:229
Triumphs (Petrarch)
See *Trionfi*
"The Triumphs of Bacchus" (Pushkin) **10**:407
"Trivial Breath" (Wylie) **23**:310
Trivial Breath (Wylie) **23**:302, 307-309, 324-25
"Trofeo" (Borges) **22**:93; **32**:82
Troilus (Chaucer)
See *Troilus and Criseyde*
Troilus and Criseyde (Chaucer) **19**:6-7, 11, 13, 15, 23, 36-9, 42-3, 60-1, 63, 73-5
Troilus and Cryseide (Chaucer)
See *Troilus and Criseyde*
"Trois Ans après" (Hugo) **17**:83
Les trois livres du recueil des nouvelles poesies (Ronsard) **11**:248
"Trois respirations" (Char) **56**:191
"Les Trois Sœurs" (Char) **56**:150, 190-91, 193-95
Troisime livre des odes (Ronsard) **11**:283
The Trojan Horse: A Play (MacLeish) **47**:164, 211
"A Trojan Slave" (Muir)
See "Troy II"
"Trojans" (Cavafy) **36**:7, 28, 57, 73
"Trolling for Blues" (Wilbur) **51**:249, 261, 310-11
"Trompeten" (Trakl) **20**:250, 254-55
"Troop Train" (Shapiro) **25**:263, 268, 288, 295, 297, 324
Tropfblut (Stramm) **50**:204, 208, 214, 221-24
"Trophy" (Borges)
See "Trofeo"
"The Trophy" (Hope) **56**:268
"The Trophy" (Muir) **49**:246
Tropicalization (Cruz) **37**:12, 16, 36
"Trópico" (Storni) **33**:239, 269;
"trópico de Ceviche" (Alurista) **34**:28
"The Tropics in New York" (McKay) **2**:228
"Trostnik" (Lermontov) **18**:304
"Troth with the Dead" (Lawrence) **54**:175, 244
"Troths" (Sandburg) **41**:242, 255
"A troubadour I traverse all my land" (Brutus) **24**:113

"Trouble in a Tavern" (Dafydd)
See "Trafferth mewn Tafarn"
"Trouble in De Kitchen" (Dunbar) **5**:146
"The Trouble is with No and Yes" (Roethke) **15**:277
"The Trouble with 'In'" (McHugh) **61**:200
"The Trouble with Women Is Men" (Nash) **21**:268, 274
"The Troubled Bay" (Cassian) **17**:11, 13
"Troubled Woman" (Hughes) **53**:119
"The Trout" (Char)
See "La Truite"
"Troy" (Muir)
See "Troy I"
"Troy I" (Muir) **49**:214, 230, 243, 255, 258, 264, 278
"Troy II" (Muir) **49**:214, 243, 255-56, 264, 278
Troy Park (Sitwell) **3**:293-94, 298, 301, 303, 307-08, 320
"Troy Town" (Rossetti) **44**:202, 204-5
Troylus and Criseyde (Chaucer) **58**:265-66, 363
"Trozos del poema" (Mistral) **32**:166
"The Truce of the Bear" (Kipling) **3**:171, 182
"Las truchas" (Forché) **10**:134
"Truck-Garden-Market Day" (Millay) **6**:232
"El truco" (Borges) **32**:82
"Truco" (Borges)
See "El truco"
Trudy i dni Lavinii monakhini iz ordena obrezaniia serdtsa (Shvarts) **50**:133-37, 142-43, 159-60
"A True Account of Talking to the Sun at Fire Island" (O'Hara) **45**:117, 133, 141, 164, 189, 229
"The True Beatitude" (Brooke) **24**:57
"True Confessional" (Ferlinghetti) **1**:187
"The True Import of Present Dialogue, Black vs. Negro" (Giovanni) **19**:107, 114-15, 139
"True Love" (Olds) **22**:338
"True Love" (Warren) **37**:375
"True Love at Last" (Lawrence) **54**:185
"True Night" (Snyder) **21**:300
"True Pearl—Belle of the Lo" (Li Ho) **13**:54
"True Place" (Bonnefoy) **58**:123
"True Recognition Often Is Refused" (Schwartz) **8**:292
"True Romance" (Kipling) **3**:161
True Stories (Atwood) **8**:43
"The True Story of Mortar and Pestle" (Chin) **40**:36
"True Story of the Pins" (Ríos) **57**:311
"True Tenderness" (Akhmatova) **2**:14
"The True, the Good, and the Beautiful" (Schwartz) **8**:292
"True Vine" (Wylie) **23**:303, 305, 323
"Truganinny" (Rose) **13**:240
"The Truisms" (MacNeice) **61**:112
"La Truite" (Char) **56**:182
"Trump of Death" (Gower) **59**:88, 91-92, 94, 108-9
"The Trumpet" (Thomas) **53**:266
"Trumpet Player: 52nd Street" (Hughes) **1**:241, 247, 249; **53**:90, 205
"Ein Trupp hergelaufener Söhne schrie" (Benn) **35**:46, 47
"The Trusting Heart" (Parker) **28**:362
"Truth" (Brooks) **7**:61
"The Truth" (Cowper) **40**:47, 50-1, 70-1
"The Truth" (Jarrell) **41**:190, 192, 198
"The Truth" (Jiménez)
See "Paisaje del corozon"
"Truth" (McKay) **2**:215
"The Truth" (Montale) **13**:156
"Truth and Error" (Goethe) **5**:228
"The Truth Is" (Hogan) **35**:245, 255
"Truth Is Not the Secret of a Few" (Ferlinghetti) **1**:186
"Truth Kills Everybody" (Hughes) **7**:160
"The Truth of the Matter" (Hogan) **35**:271
"The Truth of the Matter" (Nemerov) **24**:290
"The Truth the Dead Know" (Sexton) **2**:346, 361
"Try On" (Graham) **59**:187
Tryflings (Ekeloef) **23**:63
"Tryin' on Clothes" (Silverstein) **49**:325, 332
"Trying to Pray" (Wright) **36**:287
"Trying to Sing in the Rain" (Wagoner) **33**:357
"Tsar Sultan" (Pushkin)
See "Skazka o Tsare Sultane"
Tsar-devitsa (Tsvetaeva) **14**:313, 325-26
The Tsar-Maiden (Tsvetaeva)
See *Tsar-devitsa*
Tsuki ni hoeru (Hagiwara) **18**:169, 172-73, 175-82
"Tsung-wu's Birthday" (Tu Fu) **9**:324
"Tsurugai Bridge" (Ishikawa)
See "Tsurugaibashi"
"Tsurugaibashi" (Ishikawa) **10**:213
"Tsutsushimite Kumagori no tame ni sono kokorozashi wo noburu uta ni kotauru rokushu" (Yakamochi) **48**:137, 139
"Tsyganskie stikhi" (Shvarts) **50**:160
Tsygany (Pushkin) **10**:357-61, 365-66, 369, 371, 386-89, 391-92, 398, 410
"Tú" (Borges) **32**:90, 138
"Tú" (Guillén) **23**:134-37
"Il tu" (Montale) **13**:132
"Tu Do Street" (Komunyakaa) **51**:9, 20-21, 39, 42
"Tú me quieres blanca" (Storni) **33**:243, 248-50, 297-98, 305, 318;
"Tú no sabe inglé" (Guillén) **23**:142
"Tu Parles" (Senghor) **25**:250
"tú sabes" (Alurista) **34**:37
"tu Te Languis" (Senghor) **25**:249-50
"Tu ti spezzasti" (Ungaretti) **57**:338
Tucky the Hunter (Dickey) **40**:233-34
"Tuesday: St. James's Coffee-house: Silliander and Patch" (Montagu) **16**:348
"Tulip" (McGuckian)
See "Tulips"
"Tulips" (McGuckian) **27**:79-80, 278
"Tulips" (Page) **12**:176
"Tulips" (Plath) **1**:390, 395, 399-401, 405, 407, 409, 414; **37**:196, 203
Tulips and Chimneys (Cummings) **5**:74-5, 77-8, 86, 91, 93-4, 104
"Tulpen" (Celan) **10**:122-23
"Tumba de Amir Khusrú" (Paz) **48**:232
"Tumblers, Pouters and Fantails" (Moore) **49**:116
"Tumbling-Hair" (Cummings) **5**:104
"Tumi o ami" (Tagore) **8**:414
"A Tune for Festive Dances in the Nineteen Sixties" (Merton) **10**:345
"The Tune of Seven Towers" (Morris) **55**:279-80, 282, 302-3
"El túnel" (Parra) **39**:283
"Tunica Pallio Proprior" (Moore) **49**:105, 121, 134
"tuning flower tones" (Alurista) **34**:28
"Tunk: A Lecture of Modern Education" (Johnson) **24**:141, 163
"The Tunnel" (Crane) **3**:86, 88-90, 106-07, 110-11
"Tunnels" (Komunyakaa) **51**:40
The Tunning of Eleanor Rumming (Skelton)
See *The Tunnynge of Elynour Rummynge*
Tunning of Elinor Rumming (Skelton)
See *The Tunnynge of Elynour Rummynge*
The Tunning of Elynour Rummyng (Skelton)
See *The Tunnynge of Elynour Rummynge*
The Tunnying of Elynour Rummyng (Skelton)
See *The Tunnynge of Elynour Rummynge*
The Tunnyng (Skelton)
See *The Tunnynge of Elynour Rummynge*
The Tunnyng of Elynour Rummyng (Skelton)
See *The Tunnynge of Elynour Rummynge*
The Tunnynge of Elynour Rummynge (Skelton) **25**:330, 332, 338, 342, 347-49, 361-62, 364, 367, 386-88, 390-93
"Il tuo volo" (Montale) **13**:111
"Turbonave Magnolia" (Birney) **52**:34, 97
"Turin" (Gozzano) **10**:177, 180
"The Turkey in the Straw" (Williams) **7**:400
"Turkey Villas" (Guest) **55**:219
"Turkeys Observed" (Heaney) **18**:189, 200
"Turkish Verses" (Montagu) **16**:338
The Türler Losses (Guest) **55**:217, 220-21
Turn (Paz)
See *Vuelta*
"The Turn of the Century" (Szymborska) **44**:319
"The Turn of the Moon" (Graves) **6**:154, 156
Turn of the Offended (Dalton) **36**:120, 124
Turn Off the Lights (Seifert)
See *Zhasněte světla*
Turn Out the Lights (Seifert)
See *Zhasněte světla*
Turn Thanks (Goodison) **36**:158
"Turn Thanks to Miss Mirry" (Goodison) **36**:158
"The Turncoat" (Baraka) **4**:5, 14
"turning" (Clifton) **17**:21
"The Turning" (Graham) **59**:167
"The Turning" (Levine) **22**:212
"Turning" (Rilke) **2**:280-81
"Turning a Moment to Say So Long" (Ammons) **16**:39
"Turning Away from Lies" (Bly) **39**:51
"Turning Away: Variations on Estrangement" (Dickey) **40**:187-88, 199, 202-3
"Turning Fifty" (Wright) **14**:355
"Turning To" (Kumin) **15**:182
"A Turning Wind" (Rukeyser) **12**:213
A Turning Wind (Rukeyser) **12**:211-12
Turns and Movies and Other Tales in Verse (Aiken) **26**:21, 50, 53
"Turquoise Skies Above, and Below" (Quintana) **36**:250
"The Turtle" (Bly) **39**:24
"The Turtle" (Nash) **21**:278
Turtle Island (Snyder) **21**:290-300, 306-08, 310, 316-17, 320, 324-25
"Turtle Mountain Reservation" (Erdrich) **52**:176, 178, 183, 192
"The Turtle Overnight" (Wright) **36**:367, 378
"Turtle Soup" (Chin) **40**:12, 16, 27
Turtle, Swan (Doty) **53**:47, 60, 62
"Tus ojos" (Paz) **48**:183
"Tutecotzimí" (Darío) **15**:92
"Tutto é sciolto" (Joyce) **22**:136
"The Twa Dogs" (Burns) **6**:51, 78, 83-4, 88
"The Twa Herds" (Burns) **6**:85
"Twelfth Morning; or, What You Will" (Bishop) **34**:191
"Twelfth Night" (Belloc) **24**:49
"Twelfth Night, Next Year, a Weekend in Eternity" (Schwartz) **8**:294
"XII" (Joyce) **22**:136, 138, 145, 164, 169, 171
"The Twelve" (Tate) **50**:231, 256
The Twelve (Blok)
See *Dvenadsat*
"Twelve Articles" (Swift) **9**:260
"The 12 boock" (Raleigh) **31**:302, 304
"The Twelve Dancing Princesses" (Sexton) **2**:365
"1200 South / 2100 West" (Cisneros) **52**:157
"Twelve Months After" (Sassoon) **12**:288
"Twelve O'Clock News" (Bishop) **34**:68, 158
"12 O'Clock News" (Bishop)
See "Twelve O'Clock News"
The Twelve-Spoked Wheel Flashing (Piercy) **29**:311, 313
"A Twelve-Step Treatment Program" (Alexie) **53**:30
Twentieth Century Harlequinade (Sitwell) **3**:299-300, 302
"20th-century Fox" (Baraka) **4**:11
"XX" (Joyce) **22**:145, 168
"" (Larkin) **21**:242
Twenty Love Poems and a Despairing Song (Neruda)
See *Veinte poemas de amor y una canción desesperada*

Twenty Love Poems and a Desperate Song (Neruda)
See *Veinte poemas de amor y una canción desesperada*
Twenty Love Poems and a Song of Despair (Neruda)
See *Veinte poemas de amor y una canción desesperada*
Twenty Love Poems and One Song of Despair (Neruda)
See *Veinte poemas de amor y una canción desesperada*
"The 21th: and last booke of the Ocean to Scinthia" (Raleigh) **31**:218, 237, 246, 252, 286, 290
XX Poems (Larkin) **21**:226, 229
Twenty Poems (Neruda)
See *Veinte poemas de amor y una canción desesperada*
Twenty Poems (Trakl) **20**:227
Twenty Poems of Anna Akhmatova (Kenyon) **57**:13, 22
"27 June 1906, 2 p.m" (Cavafy) **36**:53
"26 Points à préciser" (Péret) **33**:203
"XXVIII" (Joyce) **22**:145, 154, 159, 162, 169, 172
"28" (Levine) **22**:224
"Twenty-fifth of Vaisakh" (Tagore)
See "Panchishe vaisakh"
"The Twenty-fifth Year of his Life" (Cavafy) **36**:75, 78
"XXV" (Joyce) **22**:139, 160, 173
"25 Mesostics Re and not Re Mark Tobey" (Cage) **58**:219
Twenty-Five Poems (Thomas) **2**:378, 389; **52**:271
25 Poems (Walcott) **46**:259
"XXIV" (Joyce) **22**:136, 139, 170, 172-73
"Twenty-Four Hokku on a Modern Theme" (Lowell) **13**:66
"Twenty-four Poems" (Schwartz) **8**:302
"Twenty-Four Years" (Thomas) **2**:383; **52**:264
"XXIX" (Joyce) **22**:145, 167, 170, 173
"XXI" (Joyce) **22**:146, 166-68, 170
Twenty-One Love Poems (Rich) **5**:384, 395
"XXVII" (Joyce) **22**:145, 156, 170, 172-73
"XXVI" (Joyce) **22**:136, 139, 168, 171, 173
"Twenty-Third Flight" (Birney) **52**:22-23
"XXIII" (Joyce) **22**:145, 170
"XXII" (Joyce) **22**:138, 145, 170-71, 173
"Twenty-two Rhymes" (Tu Fu) **9**:326
"Twice" (Rossetti) **7**:267, 275
Twice or thrice had I loved thee (Donne)
See "Aire and Angels"
"Twice-Done, Once-Done" (Muir) **49**:245, 250-51
"Twicknam Garden" (Donne) **1**:124, 130, 134
"Twilight" (Apollinaire)
See "Crépuscule"
"Twilight" (Clare) **23**:47
"Twilight" (Kunitz) **19**:147
"Twilight" (Teasdale) **31**:323, 334
"Twilight: After Haying" (Kenyon) **57**:5, 13
"The Twilight Bell" (Ishikawa)
See "Kure no kane"
The Twilight Book (Neruda)
See *Crepúsculario*
"Twilight in Eden" (Carman) **34**:202
"The Twilight of Freedom" (Mandelstam) **14**:106, 147
"Twilight of the Outward Life" (Viereck) **27**:263
"Twilight Reverie" (Hughes) **1**:255
Twilight Songs (Hugo) **17**:45
"Twilights" (Wright) **36**:305, 340, 398
The Twin In the Clouds (Pasternak)
See *Bliznets v tuchakh*
"Twine" (Brathwaite) **56**:96
"The Twins" (Bukowski) **18**:4, 22
"Twister" (Stryk) **27**:211
"II" (Joyce) **22**:138, 165-66
"Two Amsterdams" (Ferlinghetti) **1**:183
"The Two April Mornings" (Wordsworth) **4**:374
"The Two Bobbies" (Carman) **34**:207, 219
"Two Bodies" (Paz)
See "Dos cuerpos"
"The Two Brothers" (Lermontov) **18**:299
"Two Cantos of Mutabilitie" (Spenser) **8**:344, 346, 375, 396; **42**:340-41, 343-44
"Two Children" (Graves) **6**:156
"Two Children" (Guillén) **6**:
See "Dos niños"
"Two Cigarettes" (Pavese)
See "Due sigarette"
Two Citizens (Wright) **36**:304, 306-9, 313-14, 317-18, 346-48, 354-56, 358, 363, 367-68, 370, 376-77, 392, 397-98
"Two Conceits for the Eye to Sing, If Possible" (Tate) **50**:290, 293
"Two days of fever" (Pasolini) **17**:279
"Two Deaths" (Olds) **22**:317
"The Two Deserts" (Patmore) **59**:262, 275-77
"Two Drops" (Herbert)
See "Dwie krople"
"2/18/97" (Graham) **59**:188
"Two Easter Stanzas" (Lindsay) **23**:282
"Two Egyptian Portrait Masks" (Hayden) **6**:185
"Two English Poems" (Borges) **22**:95; **32**:58, 85
"Two Eskimo Songs" (Hughes) **7**:153, 159
Two Figures (Momaday) **25**:201
"Two Figures from the Movies" (Meredith) **28**:187, 210
"The Two Fires" (Atwood) **8**:37
The Two Fires (Wright) **14**:341-49, 353-55, 369
The Two Foscari (Byron) **16**:103
"Two Generations" (Wright) **14**:344, 354
"Two Gentlemen in Bonds" (Ransom) **61**:308, 311
Two Gentlemen in Bonds (Ransom) **61**:267, 274, 289, 305-6, 315
"Two Girls" (Nemerov) **24**:291
"Two Gun Buster and Trigger Slim" (Walker) **20**:273
"Two Hands" (Sexton) **2**:371
"Two Hangovers" (Wright) **36**:326, 340, 396, 398
"Two higher mammals" (Piercy) **29**:303
"Two Horses Playing in the Orchard" (Wright) **36**:326, 338
"Two Hours in an Empty Tank" (Brodsky) **9**:2, 4
"200 B.C." (Cavafy) **36**:35
"Two Hymns" (Ammons) **16**:4
"Two in August" (Ransom) **61**:288
"Two in the Campagna" (Browning) **2**:68
"Two in the Twilight" (Montale)
See "Due nel crepuscolo"
"Two Leading Lights" (Frost) **39**:345
"Two Legends" (Hughes) **7**:159
"Two Little Boots" (Dunbar) **5**:122, 129
"Two Look at Two" (Frost) **1**:194, 229, 231
"Two Lovers" (Eliot) **20**:123
"The Two Lovers" (Marie de France)
See "Les Dous Amanz"
"Two Masks Unearthed in Bulgaria" (Meredith) **28**:182
"Two Meditations on Guanajuato" (Yau) **61**:333
"Two Moments in Venice" (Wright) **36**:321
"Two Monkeys By Bruegel" (Szymborska)
See "Life-Size is Too Large"
"Two Neighbors" (Sandburg) **41**:360
"Two Night Pieces" (Sitwell) **3**:293
"Two of Hearts" (Hogan) **35**:257
"The Two Offers" (Harper) **21**:194
"Two Old Crows" (Lindsay) **23**:281
"2 Pages, 122 Words on Music and Dance" (Cage) **58**:204
"Two Paintings by Gustav Klimt" (Graham) **59**:140, 143-44
"Two Pair" (Nemerov) **24**:302
"The Two Parents" (MacDiarmid) **9**:156, 176
"Two Parted" (Rossetti) **7**:276
"Two Pendants: For the Ears" (Williams) **7**:360, 364, 394
"Two Pewits" (Thomas) **53**:289
"Two Poems" (Madhubuti) **5**:321
"Two Poems" (Niedecker) **42**:148
"Two Poems about President Harding" (Wright) **36**:340, 396
"Two Poems Ending with the Word Blind" (Shvarts) **50**:133
"2 Poems for Black Relocation Centers" (Knight) **14**:46-8
"Two Poems of Going Home" (Dickey) **40**:220
"Two Poets" (Cullen) **20**:68
"Two Postures beside a Fire" (Wright) **36**:341, 393
"Two Preludes" (Swinburne) **24**:323
"The Two Presences" (Bly) **39**:53
"Two Red Roses across the Moon" (Morris) **55**:299, 301
"Two Riddles from Aldheim" (Wilbur) **51**:301
"Two Rivers" (Emerson) **18**:76, 88-89
"The Two Roads" (Gozzano) **10**:177-78
"Two Rondeaus" (Szirtes) **51**:167
"Two Scavengers in a Truck, Two Beautiful People in a Mercedes" (Ferlinghetti) **1**:183, 188
"Two Sisters" (Ní Chuilleanáin) **34**:373
"Two Sisters of Persephone" (Plath) **37**:202
"Two Songs" (Mahon) **60**:138
"Two Songs" (Rich) **5**:365
"Two Songs" (Sarton) **39**:323, 341
"Two Songs for Solitude" (Teasdale) **31**:323
"Two Songs from a Play" (Yeats) **20**:315, 319
"Two Songs of a Fool" (Yeats) **20**:304
"Two Speak Together" (Lowell) **13**:96-7
"Two Stories" (Gallagher) **9**:36
"Two Tales of Clumsy" (Schnackenberg) **45**:337
"The Two Thieves" (Wordsworth) **4**:374, 388
"2527th Birthday of the Buddha" (Komunyakaa) **51**:6, 8
"The Two Towers" (Carducci)
See "Le due Torri"
"Two Tramps in Mud Time" (Frost) **1**:198, 221; **39**:246
"The Two Travellers" (Bryant) **20**:10, 16
"The Two Trees" (Yeats) **20**:317
"221-1424 (San Francisco suicide number)" (Sanchez) **9**:211, 224-25
"221-1424 (San/francisco/suicide/number)" (Sanchez)
See "221-1424 (San Francisco suicide number)"
"Two Versions of 'Ritter, Tod und Teufel'" (Borges)
See "Dos versiones de 'Ritter, Tod und Teufel'"
"Two Views of a Cadaver Room" (Plath) **1**:389; **37**:177, 185-86
"Two Voices" (Ignatow) **34**:277, 324
"The Two Voices" (Tennyson) **6**:360
"Two Voices in a Meadow" (Wilbur) **51**:196, 289
"Two Who Crossed a Line (He Crosses)" (Cullen) **20**:86
"Two Women Talking" (MacLeish) **47**:195
Two Women, Two Shores (McGuckian) **27**:95
"Two Wrestlers" (Francis) **34**:242
"Two Years Later" (Yeats) **20**:338
"Two Young Men, 23 to 24 Years Old" (Cavafy) **36**:50, 76, 78-79, 80
"Two-an'-Six" (McKay) **2**:208-09
"2Cor.: 5.19 God was in Christ reconciling the World to himself" (Philips) **40**:298
"The Two-Days-Old Baby" (Blake)
See "Infant Joy"
Two-Headed Poems (Atwood) **8**:43
Two-Headed Woman (Clifton) **17**:17-18, 23-24, 26-27, 34-35
"Two-Part Pear Able" (Swenson) **14**:247
2000 (Neruda) **4**:287
"Two-Volume Novel" (Parker) **28**:352, 359, 352
"Tyaroye" (Senghor) **25**:235

"The Tyger" (Blake) **12**:6-7, 10, 25, 30, 34-5, 59-64
"The Typical American?" (Masters) **1**:343
"Typists" (Page) **12**:173
"Typists in the Phoenix Building" (Wright) **14**:348
Tyrannus Nix? (Ferlinghetti) **1**:174
"Tyrant of the Syracuse" (MacLeish) **47**:193
"Tyrian Businesses" (Olson) **19**:280, 283
"Tzu-yeh Song # 3" (Li Po) **29**:144
"U nog drugikh ne zabyval" (Lermontov) **18**:302
U samovo morya (Akhmatova) **2**:15
"U tonkoi pnovoloki nad volnoi ovsov" (Tsvetaeva) **14**:319, 321, 323
"Uber Das Werden im Vergehen" (Hölderlin) **4**:147
"Über Gräber" (Benn) **35**:45
"Uccello" (Corso) **33**:41, 43, 47
"Ucieczka" (Mickiewicz) **38**:151-53
"Ugliness" (Mistral)
See "Lo feo"
"Ugolino" (Heaney) **18**:240
"Uh, Philosophy" (Ammons) **16**:6, 13, 36-7
"Ulalume" (Poe) **1**:425-26, 428, 431, 434, 436, 439-40, 442-43, 447, 453; **54**:273, 276, 330-31
"Ultima canto di Saffo" (Leopardi) **37**:102, 110, 142, 169
"A Ultima Nau" (Pessoa) **20**:162
"Ultima Ratio Reagan" (Nemerov) **24**:290
Ultima Thule (Longfellow) **30**:26
"Ultimate Birth" (Aleixandre) **15**:3
"The Ultimate Infidelity" (Gozzano) **10**:180
"The Ultimate Poem Is Abstract" (Stevens) **6**:314
"Ultimate Reality" (Lawrence) **54**:185
"Ultimatum" (Cullen) **20**:57
"Ultimatum" (Larkin) **21**:224-25
"Ultimátum" (Parra) **39**:273
"Ultimatum" (Sassoon) **12**:259
"Ultimi cori per la Terra Promessa" (Ungaretti) **57**:339
"L'Ultimo" (Quasimodo) **47**:297
"El último amor" (Aleixandre) **15**:38
"Ultimo árbol" (Mistral) **32**:183
"Ultimo canto di Saffo" (Quasimodo) **47**:297
"Ultimo sol en Villa Ortúzar" (Borges) **32**:83
"Ultraísmo" (Borges) **22**:93
Ultramarine (Carver) **54**:3, 11, 13, 20-23
"Ultrateléfono" (Storni) **33**:261, 295;
"Ulysses" (Birney) **52**:8, 39
"Ulysses" (Graves) **6**:130, 137
"Ulysses" (Tennyson) **6**:354, 359, 366, 381, 383-84, 398, 409, 411
"Ulysses by the Merlion" (Thumboo) **30**:310, 312-13, 314, 320-21, 329
"Umarli" (Herbert) **50**:6-7
"An Umbrella" (Stein) **18**:334
Umbrella from Piccadilly (Seifert)
See *Deštník z Piccadilly*
The Umbrella from Piccadilly (Seifert)
See *Deštník z Piccadilly*
An Umbrella from Piccadilly (Seifert)
See *Deštník z Piccadilly*
"Umi no ikari" (Ishikawa) **10**:215
"L'umile Itallia" (Pasolini) **17**:294
"Umirajushchij gladiator" (Lermontov) **18**:302
"A un heiniano d'Italia" (Carducci) **46**:73
"A un poeta'" (Guillén) **35**:230
"A un poeta del siglo XIII" (Borges) **22**:82, 85
"A un riche" (Hugo) **17**:94
"A un sembrador" (Mistral) **32**:145
"A un vincitore nel pallone" (Leopardi) **37**:102, 118
"A una Bottiglia di Valtellina del 1848" (Carducci) **46**:52
"A una espada en York" (Borges) **32**:87, 95
"Unable to Hate or Love" (Page) **12**:175
"The Unacknowledged Legislator's Dream" (Heaney) **18**:205
"Un'altra risorta" (Gozzano) **10**:185
"Un-American Investigators" (Hughes) **1**:252; **53**:111
Unattainable Earth (Milosz)
See *Niobjeta ziemia*
"The Unattained Place" (Muir) **49**:230, 265
"Das Unaufhörliche" (Benn) **35**:66
"The Unauthorized Autobiography of Me" (Alexie) **53**:23
"Unbelief" (Pushkin)
See "Bezverie"
"The Unbeliever" (Bishop) **3**:48; **34**:52-53, 156
"The Unborn" (Wright) **14**:352
"An Unborn Child" (Mahon) **60**:138, 181, 186, 192
"Unclassified Poem" (Wang Wei) **18**:387
"Unclassified Poems of Ch'in-chou" (Tu Fu) **9**:332
"Uncle" (Niedecker) **42**:119-22
"Uncle Ananias" (Robinson) **35**:362
"Uncle Bullboy" (Jordan) **38**:127
"Uncle Cal" (Stone) **53**:258
"Uncle Cal on Fashions" (Stone) **53**:258
"Uncle Isidore" (Abse) **41**:25
"Uncle Jim" (Cullen) **20**:64
Uncle Shelby's Story of Lafcadio, the Lion Who Shot Back (Silverstein) **49**:348
"The Uncle Speaks in the Drawing Room" (Rich) **5**:359, 392
"Unclench Yourself" (Piercy) **29**:310
"Uncle's First Rabbit" (Cervantes) **35**:104, 108, 113, 116, 134
"Uncollected Poems" (Crane) **3**:90
"The Uncreation" (Pinsky) **27**:164
"Under" (Guest) **55**:213
"Under" (Sandburg) **2**:300; **41**:225, 314
"Under a Hat Rim" (Sandburg) **41**:313
"Under a Patched Sail" (Moore) **49**:109
Under a Soprano Sky (Sanchez) **9**:238-39, 245
"Under Ben Bulben" (Yeats) **20**:312, 324, 333
"Under Black Leaves" (Merwin) **45**:39-40
"Under Libra" (Merrill) **28**:223, 256
"Under Peyote" (Corso) **33**:22
"Under Saturn" (Yeats) **20**:342
"Under Sedation" (Hope) **56**:276
"Under Sirius" (Auden) **1**:23
"Under St. Paul's" (Davie) **29**:94
"Under Stars" (Gallagher) **9**:37, 58, 60
Under Stars (Gallagher) **9**:37, 42, 54, 58-60
"Under the Bamboo Tree" (Johnson) **24**:151, 170
"Under the Canals" (Wright) **36**:311
"Under the Cupola" (Merrill) **28**:251-52
"Under the Earth" (Aleixandre) **15**:20-2
"Under the Hazel Bough" (Birney) **52**:22
"Under the L.A. Airport" (Ortiz) **17**:229
"Under the Locusts" (Ransom) **61**:294
"Under the Maud Moon" (Kinnell) **26**:247-52, 255, 257, 264, 272
"Under the Migrants" (Merwin) **45**:48-9
"Under the Mistletoe" (Cullen) **20**:85
"Under the Moon's Reign" (Tomlinson) **17**:336, 349
"Under the Oak" (Lawrence) **54**:168
"Under the Old One" (Merwin) **45**:8
"Under the Olives" (Graves) **6**:155-56
"Under the Rose" (Rossetti) **7**:266
"Under the Rowans" (Carman) **34**:208
"Under the Skin of the Statue of Liberty" (Yevtushenko) **40**:369
Under the Skin of the Statue of Liberty (Yevtushenko) **40**:369
"Under the Viaduct" (Dove) **6**:110
"Under the Waterfall" (Hardy) **8**:118
"Under the Weather" (Hope) **56**:277
"Under the Window: Ouro Prêto" (Bishop) **34**:138-39, 141
"Under the Wood" (Thomas) **53**:303-5
"Under Willows" (Rossetti) **7**:285
Under Your Clear Shadow and Other Poems about Spain (Paz)
See *Bajo tu clara sombra y otros poemas sobre España*
"The Underground Stream" (Dickey) **40**:175, 180, 185, 192
"Underkill" (Birney) **52**:28, 43
"The Undermining of the Defense Economy" (Wright) **36**:340
"Underneath 8" (Graham) **59**:186
"Underneath 9" (Graham) **59**:188
"Underneath 13" (Graham) **59**:189
"Underneath (Upland)" (Graham) **59**:184
Undersong: Chosen Poems Old and New (Revised) (Lorde) **12**:153-58
"Understanding" (Cavafy) **36**:91
"Understanding but not Forgetting" (Madhubuti) **5**:337-38, 340
"Understood Not" (Cavafy) **36**:33
"The Undertaking" (Glück) **16**:126, 128, 142
"Undertow" (Sandburg) **41**:267
"Underwear" (Ferlinghetti) **1**:183
The Under-wood (Jonson) **17**:169, 180, 191
The Under-Wood II (Jonson) **17**:171, 194-95, 214
The Under-Wood III (Jonson) **17**:195
The Under-Wood IV (Jonson) **17**:194
The Under-Wood LVI (Jonson) **17**:194
The Under-Wood LVIII (Jonson) **17**:194
The Under-Wood LXII (Jonson) **17**:156
The Under-Wood LXIV (Jonson) **17**:156
The Under-Wood LXIX (Jonson) **17**:153
The Under-Wood LXVIII (Jonson) **17**:156
The Under-Wood LXX (Jonson) **17**:164
The Under-Wood LXXI (Jonson) **17**:162
The Under-Wood LXXII (Jonson) **17**:193
The Under-Wood LXXVI (Jonson) **17**:156
The Under-Wood LXXXVI (Jonson) **17**:191
The Under-Wood XIII (Jonson) **17**:154, 157-59, 211
The Under-Wood XL (Jonson) **17**:194
The Under-Wood XLII (Jonson) **17**:180
The Under-Wood XLIV (Jonson) **17**:194
The Under-Wood XLV (Jonson) **17**:181, 189
The Under-Wood XLVII (Jonson) **17**:153-54, 208
The Under-Wood XV (Jonson) **17**:153, 158, 161-62, 164, 208
The Under-Wood XVI (Jonson) **17**:191
The Under-Wood XXIX (Jonson) **17**:189
The Under-Wood XXVI (Jonson) **17**:153, 172, 192
The Under-Wood XXXI (Jonson) **17**:193
The Under-Wood XXXVII (Jonson) **17**:153-54
"The Underworld" (Hongo) **23**:199
"Undraped Beauty" (Tagore)
See "Vivasana"
"L'Une et l'autre" (Char) **56**:120
"A une femme" (Hugo) **17**:68
"A une raison" (Rimbaud) **3**:260; **57**:232, 275, 282
"A une robe rose" (Gautier) **18**:125, 129
À une sérénité crispée (Char) **56**:108-9, 112, 169, 173
"À une Terre d!aube" (Bonnefoy) **58**:126
"Uneasiness in Fall" (Bly) **39**:85
Unedited Books of Poetry (Jiménez)
See "A Horrible Religious Error"
"Unemployment Monologue" (Jordan) **38**:125
"The Unending Rose" (Borges) **22**:97; **32**:140
The Unending Rose (Borges) **32**:66
"Unendurable Love" (Tagore)
See "Asahya bhalobasa"
"The Unequal Fetters" (Finch) **21**:154, 181
"Unequalled Days" (Pasternak)
See "Edinstvennye dni"
"Unerwidert" (Stramm) **50**:172
"Unexpected Joy" (Blok) **21**:3
"The Unexplorer" (Millay) **6**:235
"The Unfaithful Married Woman" (García Lorca)
See "La casada infiel"
"The Unfaithful Wife" (García Lorca)
See "La casada infiel"
"Unfaithfulness" (Cavafy) **36**:80, 86

"The Unfamiliar Place" (Muir) **49**:230, 242, 288
"Unfinished Ballad" (Wylie) **23**:321
"Unfinished Book of Kings" (Merwin) **45**:18, 22, 28, 49
"Unfinished Portrait" (Wylie) **23**:318, 322, 324
"Unfold! Unfold!" (Roethke) **15**:248, 254, 276, 300-03
"The Unfortunate Lover" (Marvell) **10**:265-66, 271, 300, 302
"The Unfortunate One" (Marie de France)
See "Le Chaitivel"
"UnfortunateCoincidence" (Parker) **28**:360
"Ungathered Apples" (Wright) **36**:279, 336
Ungathered Verse (Jonson) **17**:161
"The Ungrateful" (Stone) **53**:256
"Ungratefulnesse" (Herbert) **4**:119, 133-34
"Unheard" (Char)
See "Ne s'entend pas"
"Unheroic" (Boland) **58**:38, 40, 62
"The Unhistoric Story" (Curnow) **48**:4, 25, 27-29
"The Unicorn" (Silverstein) **49**:319, 346
"Unidad" (Alurista) **34**:42
"Unidentified Flying Object" (Hayden) **6**:196
"L'Union libre" (Breton) **15**:51, 62
"Unión Soviética" (Guillén) **23**:123, 127
"Union Square" (Teasdale) **31**:363, 379
"Union Street: San Francisco, Summer 1975" (Carver) **54**:29
"The Unions at the Front" (Neruda)
See "Los Grernios en el frente"
"L'unique" (Éluard) **38**:69
"A Unison" (Williams) **7**:360
"The United Fruit Company" (Neruda)
See "La United Fruit Company"
"La United Fruit Company" (Neruda) **4**:296
"U.S. 1946 King's X" (Frost) **1**:200
U.S. One (Rukeyser) **12**:203-04, 211
"Unity of Hearts" (Baca) **41**:37
"L'univers solitude" (Éluard) **38**:67, 85
"The Universal Andalusia" (Jiménez)
See "El andaluz universal"
Universal Prayer (Pope) **26**:311
"Universal Sorrow" (Tagore)
See "Vishvashoka"
"The Universe" (Swenson) **14**:258, 268, 281
"UNIVERSITY" (Birney) **52**:76-77
"University" (Shapiro) **25**:279, 283, 290, 297-300, 311, 313, 318
"The Unjustly Punished Child" (Olds) **22**:307
"The Unknown" (Masters) **36**:181, 221, 242
"The Unknown" (Thomas) **53**:271
"The Unknown" (Williams) **7**:369
"The Unknown Bird" (Thomas) **53**:300
The Unknown Eros (Patmore) **59**:204-10, 212-15, 218, 222-25, 259, 261-62, 264-68, 273, 275-77
"Unknown Girl in the Maternity Ward" (Sexton) **2**:349, 355
"The Unknown Neighbor" (Stryk) **27**:201
"Unknown Soldiers" (Masters) **36**:210
"The Unknown War" (Sandburg) **41**:303
"Unknown Water" (Wright) **14**:341, 353
"The Unknown Woman" (Blok) **21**:14
"Unless" (Warren) **37**:312
"The Unlived Life" (Boland) **58**:48
"Unlucky Soldier" (Sarton) **39**:322
"Unmeasured Tempo" (Angelou) **32**:29
"Unnatural Love" (Tate) **50**:274, 300
"Unnatural Powers" (Jeffers) **17**:118
"Unnatural State of the Unicorn" (Komunyakaa) **51**:52-53, 55-56
"Uno" (Storni) **33**:238, 306;
"The Unpardonable Sin" (Lindsay) **23**:280
"Unregierbarkeit" (Enzensberger) **28**:150
"Unresolved" (Levertov) **11**:198
"Unrest" (Bly) **39**:4, 83, 90
"The Unreturning" (Carman) **34**:210, 216
"The Unreturning" (Owen) **19**:343
"Unrhymed Poems" (Lawrence) **54**:184
"Unrhyming Poems" (Lawrence) **54**:207
"Les uns et les autres" (Verlaine) **2**:416
"An Unsaid Word" (Rich) **5**:359, 393
"Unscratchable Itch" (Silverstein) **49**:336
"The Unseen" (Pinsky) **27**:163
"The Unseen Hunter" (Shvarts) **50**:131, 144-45
"Unsere Marine" (Heine) **25**:134
"The Unsettled Motorcyclist's Vision of His Death" (Gunn) **26**:185, 207
"Unsleeping City (Brooklyn Bridge Nocturne)" (García Lorca)
See "Ciudad sin sueño"
"Unsounded" (Rich) **5**:359
"Unspeakable" (McHugh) **61**:205
"Unspeakable" (Stone) **53**:257
"An Unstamped Letter in Our Rural Letter Box" (Frost) **39**:233
"The Unsung Heroes" (Dunbar) **5**:131
"Unsuspecting" (Toomer) **7**:336
"Der Untergand der Titanic" (Enzensberger) **28**:149-51, 158, 160, 164-66
"Untergang" (Trakl) **20**:234, 264-65, 267, 269
"Untergrundbahn" (Benn) **35**:25, 30, 46
"Untitled" (Graham) **59**:169
"Untitled" (Swenson) **14**:274, 285
"Untitled Blues" (Komunyakaa) **51**:33
"Unto a caitife wretch" (Sidney) **32**:235
Unto Dyvers People (Skelton) **25**:374
"Unto the Whole—How Add?" (Dickinson) **1**:103
"Untreu" (Stramm) **50**:172, 175, 189, 202, 209
"Untrimmed Mourning" (Chin) **40**:3
"The Untrustworthy Speaker" (Glück) **16**:157
"Unwilling Admission" (Wylie) **23**:310
"The Unwritten" (Merwin) **45**:77
The Unwritten (Sikelianos)
See "Agraphon"
"Unylyi kolokola zvon" (Lermontov) **18**:302
"Gli uomini che si voltano" (Montale) **13**:133
"L'uomo di pena" (Pasolini) **17**:261
"Up and Down" (Merrill) **28**:222
"Up and Down" (Smith) **12**:316
"Up at a Villa-Down in the City, as Distinguished by an Italian Person of Quality" (Browning) **2**:38
"Up at La Serra" (Tomlinson) **17**:311, 325-26, 341
"Up Branches of Duck River" (Snyder) **21**:297
Up Country: Poems of New England (Kumin) **15**:181-83, 187, 189, 194, 208
"up her can nada" (Birney) **52**:74
"Up Hill" (Rossetti) **7**:261, 298
"Up in the Wind" (Thomas) **53**:291, 327
"The Up Rising" (Duncan) **2**:104
"Up There" (Stone) **53**:259
"Upahar" (Tagore) **8**:407
"The Upas Tree" (Pushkin)
See "Anchar"
"An Upbraiding" (Hardy) **8**:93
"Uplands" (Ammons) **16**:31
Uplands (Ammons) **16**:22, 28, 46, 61
"Upon a Beautiful Young Nymph Going to Bed" (Swift)
See "A Beautiful Young Nymph Going to Bed. Written for the Honour of the Fair Sex"
"Upon a Child. An Epitaph" (Herrick) **9**:129-31
"Upon a Child That Died" (Herrick) **9**:130-31
"Upon a Comely and Curious Maide" (Herrick) **9**:129
"Upon a Dead Man's Head" (Skelton)
See *Uppon a Deedmans Hed*
"Upon a fit of Sickness, Anno 1632" (Bradstreet) **10**:20, 26, 34, 59
"Upon A Mole in Celia's Bosom" (Carew) **29**:43
"Upon a Ribband" (Carew) **29**:9
"Upon A.M." (Suckling) **30**:129, 143
"Upon Appleton House" (Marvell) **10**:260, 265-67, 269, 271-73, 289-91, 294, 298, 303-04, 314-15, 318
"Upon Ben Jonson" (Herrick) **9**:86
"Upon Her Blush" (Herrick) **9**:143
"Upon Himself" (Herrick) **9**:89, 109
"Upon Himselfe Being Buried" (Herrick) **9**:128, 131
"Upon His Kinswoman Mistris Elizabeth Herrick" (Herrick) **9**:131
"Upon His Last Request to Julia" (Herrick) **9**:108
"Upon His Returning Home to Pei-hai, I Respectfully Offer a Farewell Banquet to Reverend Master Kao Ju-Kuei, Gentleman of the Tao after He Transmitted to Me a Register of the Way" (Li Po) **29**:171
"Upon Julia's Clothes" (Herrick) **9**:135-36
"Upon Julia's Recovery" (Herrick) **9**:102
"Upon Julia's Washing Her Self in the River" (Herrick) **9**:143
"Upon Meeting Don L. Lee, in a Dream" (Dove) **6**:104-05, 108
"Upon Mr. Abraham Cowley's Retirement" (Philips) **40**:270, 328
"Upon My Daughter Hannah Wiggin Her Recovery from a Dangerous Fever" (Bradstreet) **10**:34
"Upon My Dear and Loving Husband His Goeing into England" (Bradstreet)
See "To My Dear and Loving Husband His Goeing into England"
"Upon my Lady Carlile" (Suckling)
See "Upon My Lady Carlisle's Walking in Hampton Court Garden"
"Upon my Lady Carliles walking in Hampton—Court garden" (Suckling)
See "Upon My Lady Carlisle's Walking in Hampton Court Garden"
"Upon my Lady Carliles walking in Hampton-Court garden" (Suckling)
See "Upon My Lady Carlisle's Walking in Hampton Court Garden"
"Upon My Lady Carlisle's Walking in Hampton Court Garden" (Suckling) **30**:138
"Upon My Lord Broghill's Wedding" (Suckling)
See "Upon My Lord Brohall's Wedding"
"Upon My Lord Brohall's Wedding" (Suckling) **30**:143, 148, 152-53
"Upon My Lord Winchilsea's Converting the Mount in His Garden to a Terras" (Finch) **21**:176
"Upon My Son Samuel His Going to England, November 6, 1959" (Bradstreet) **10**:26, 34, 36, 63
"Upon occasion of his Ode of defiance annext to his Play of the new Inne" (Carew)
See "To Ben Jonson Upon occasion of his Ode of defiance annext to his play of the new Inne"
"Upon St. Thomas's Unbelief" (Suckling) **30**:156
"Upon the Annunciation and Passion" (Donne) **1**:139
"Upon the Bank at Early Dawn" (Thoreau) **30**:181, 194, 223, 254-55, 267
"Upon the Death of King James the Second" (Finch) **21**:170
"Upon the Death of O.C." (Marvell)
See "Poem upon the Death of O. C."
"Upon the Death of Sir William Twisden" (Finch) **21**:144
"Upon the Death of the Lord Protector" (Marvell)
See "Poem upon the Death of O. C."
"Upon the Dolorous Death and Much Lamentable Chance of the Most Honourable Earl of Northumberland" (Skelton) **25**:339, 372
"Upon the Graving of her Name Upon a Tree in Barnelmes Walk" (Philips) **40**:297
"Upon the Hill and Grove at Billborow" (Marvell) **10**:269

"Upon the Much Lamented, Master J. Warr" (Herrick) **9**:129
"Upon the Nipples of Julia's Breast" (Herrick) **9**:143
"Upon the Roses in Julias Bosome" (Herrick) **9**:143
"Upon This Bank at Early Dawn" (Thoreau)
See "Upon the Bank at Early Dawn"
"Upon Your Held-Out Hand" (Thomas) **2**:406
Uppon a Deedmans Hed (Skelton) **25**:344
"Uprawa filozofii" (Herbert) **50**:5
"Upstream" (Sandburg) **41**:330
"Uptown" (Ginsberg) **4**:47
"The Urals" (Pasternak) **6**:268
"Urania" (Arnold) **5**:43
Urania (Wroth)
See *The Countesse of Mountgomeries Urania*
"An Urban Convalescence" (Merrill) **28**:226, 234, 249, 273
"An Urban Guerrilla" (Curnow) **48**:49
Urbasi (Tagore) **8**:403
"Uriah Heap" (Yevtushenko) **40**:344
"Uriel" (Emerson) **18**:69, 79, 88
Urizen (Blake)
See *The Book of Urizen*
"The Urn" (Olds) **22**:324
The Urn (Bely)
See *Urna*
Urna (Bely) **11**:3-4, 6-7, 24, 32-3
"Urodzony" (Szymborska) **44**:269
"Urtod" (Stramm) **50**:172-73, 198, 205-6, 209
"Urvashi" (Tagore) **8**:409
"Urwanderung" (Stramm) **50**:175
"Úryvek z dopisu" (Seifert) **47**:336
"Us" (Sexton) **2**:352
"U.S.A." (Birney) **52**:58
"The Use of 'Tu'" (Montale) **13**:145
"The Used Side of the Sofa" (Ríos) **57**:325
"Used Up" (Sandburg) **2**:303; **41**:225, 336
"Useless" (Atwood) **8**:27
"Usignolo VI" (Pasolini) **17**:266
"Usignolo VII" (Pasolini) **17**:266
L'usignuolo della Chiesa Cattolica (Pasolini) **17**:252, 262, 264-67, 270, 272, 275, 277, 285, 287
Ustep (Mickiewicz)
See *The Digression*
"Ustica" (Paz) **1**:355, 360-61
"The Usurpers" (Muir) **49**:197, 229, 233, 256, 283, 294-95
"Uswetakiyawa" (Ondaatje) **28**:338
"Utopia" (Enzensberger) **28**:159
"Utopia" (Szymborska) **44**:282, 298
"A Utopian Journey" (Jarrell) **41**:145
"Utopias" (Eliot) **20**:123
"Utopie" (Lamartine) **16**:263, 284
"Utsarga" (Tagore) **8**:409
"Uvodili tebya na rassvete" (Akhmatova) **55**:25, 41, 55
Œuvres (Éluard) **38**:101, 103-7
"Uznik" (Lermontov) **18**:304
"V Al'bom" (Lermontov) **18**:302
"V bol'nitse" (Pasternak) **6**:266, 269, 286-87
"V den' Blagoveshchen'ia" (Tsvetaeva) **14**:322
"V dushe pustynnoi mnogo-mnogo" (Shvarts) **50**:134
"V. Jahrhundert" (Benn) **35**:9, 10, 70
"V. L. Davydovu" (Pushkin) **10**:412
"V lesu" (Pasternak) **6**:280
"V ony dni, ty mne byla kak mat'" (Tsvetaeva) **14**:321
"V starinny gody zhili-byli" (Lermontov) **18**:288
"vaalee daancers" (Bissett) **14**:33
"The Vacant Lot" (Brooks) **7**:69
"Vacation" (Shapiro) **25**:310, 316
"Vacation" (Zagajewski) **27**:389
Vacation Time: Poems for Children (Giovanni) **19**:138
"La Vache" (Hugo) **17**:76, 91
"Vacillation" (Yeats) **20**:333; **51**:84, 147, 152
"The Vagabonds" (Carman) **34**:197, 218
"Vagabonds" (Rimbaud) **3**:261; **57**:229
"Vaguedás" (Castro) **41**:88
Vägvisare till underjorden (Ekeloef) **23**:62, 68-9, 77-8
"Vain and Careless" (Graves) **6**:141, 150
"Vain, vain love" (Cavafy) **36**:52
"Vain Word" (Borges)
See "Vanilocuencia"
"Les vaines danseuses" (Valéry) **9**:392
"Vaishnava kavita" (Tagore) **8**:408
"Vaishnava Poetry" (Tagore)
See "Vaishnava kavita"
"Vaivén" (Paz) **1**:359
Vala (Blake)
See *The Four Zoas: The Torments of Love and Jealousy in the Death and Judgement of Albion the Ancient Man*
Vale (Viereck) **27**:259, 278
Vale Ave (H. D.) **5**:282
"The Vale of Esthwaite" (Wordsworth) **4**:417
"The Valediction" (Cowper) **40**:46
"Valediction" (Heaney) **18**:207
"Valediction" (MacNeice) **61**:106-7, 109, 111, 126, 133, 135, 137, 170-71
"A Valediction: forbidding mourning" (Donne) **1**:124, 126, 130, 135
"A Valediction Forbidding Mourning" (Rich) **5**:371, 395
"A Valediction: of my name, in the window" (Donne) **1**:152
"A Valediction: of the booke" (Donne) **1**:128, 130
"A Valediction: of weeping" (Donne) **1**:124, 130, 153
"A Valedictory to Standard Oil of Indiana" (Wagoner) **33**:333
"Valentine" (Ashbery) **26**:145
"A Valentine" (Poe) **1**:445
"Valentine" (Wylie) **23**:332
"Valentine" (Zukofsky) **11**:349
"Valentine Delivered by a Raven" (Gallagher) **9**:63
"Valentine I" (Bishop) **3**:36
"Valerik" (Lermontov) **18**:283
"Valhalla" (Francis) **34**:244, 246, 259-60
Valhalla and Other Poems (Francis) **34**:241, 244, 258-59, 261
Vallée close (Char) **56**:115-16
"Valley Candle" (Stevens) **6**:338
Valley of Decision (Curnow) **48**:23-25, 29
"The Valley of the Shadow" (Robinson) **1**:490
"The Valley of Unrest" (Poe) **1**:438
"Le vallon" (Lamartine) **16**:268, 276, 283, 290, 298-301
"Valparaiso" (Cisneros) **52**:163
"El vals" (Aleixandre) **15**:8, 14
"Valse d'Automne" (Benn) **35**:26, 66
"Valse triste" (Benn) **35**:8, 25, 26, 27
"Valuable" (Smith) **12**:296
"Values in Use" (Moore) **4**:261; **49**:132, 140
"Valvins" (Valéry) **9**:392
"The Vampire" (Baudelaire)
See "Les métamorphoses du vampire"
"Le Vampire" (Baudelaire)
See "Les métamorphoses du vampire"
"The Vampire" (Kipling) **3**:166
"Van Gogh" (Niedecker) **42**:152
"Van Gogh among the Miners" (Mahon) **60**:179, 199
"Van Gogh in the Borinage" (Mahon) **60**:140, 149, 199
"Van Winkle" (Crane) **3**:100, 109
"Vanaspati" (Tagore) **8**:415
"Vancouver" (Davie) **29**:109
"Vancouver Lights" (Birney) **52**:4-6, 8, 38, 44, 46-47, 49, 66-67, 71-72, 74
"Vandracour" (Wordsworth) **4**:399
"Vanilocuencia" (Borges) **22**:72; **32**:82
"Vanishing Point: Urban Indian" (Rose) **13**:232
"Vanitie" (Herbert) **4**:120
"Vanitie I" (Herbert) **4**:132
"Vanity" (Ungaretti) **57**:359
"The Vanity of All Worldly Things" (Bradstreet) **10**:2, 6, 21
"Vanna's Twins" (Rossetti) **7**:291
"The Vantage Point" (Frost) **39**:231
"The Vanytyes of Sir Arthur Gorges Youthe" (Raleigh) **31**:238
"Vapor Trail Reflected in the Frog Pond" (Kinnell) **26**:263, 290
"Varia" (Castro) **41**:88
"Variable" (Péret) **33**:220
"Variation 1" (Cage) **58**:197
"Variation 4" (Cage) **58**:197
"Variation 5" (Cage) **58**:197
"Variation 6" (Cage) **58**:197
"Variation 7" (Cage) **58**:197
"Variation 9" (Cage) **58**:197
"Variation 10" (Cage) **58**:197
"Variation 12" (Cage) **58**:197
"Variation 15" (Cage) **58**:197
"Variation 16" (Cage) **58**:197
"Variation 19" (Cage) **58**:197
"Variation 21" (Cage) **58**:197
"Variation 25" (Cage) **58**:197
"Variation 26" (Cage) **58**:197
"Variation 29" (Cage) **58**:197
"Variation 30" (Cage) **58**:197
"Variation 31" (Cage) **58**:196
"Variation 32" (Cage) **58**:197
"Variation 34" (Cage) **58**:199
"Variation 36" (Cage) **58**:197-98
"Variation and Reflection on a Poem by Rilke" (Levertov) **11**:206
"Variation and Reflection on a Theme by Rilke (The Book of Hours Book I Poem 7)" (Levertov) **11**:203
"Variation: Ode to Fear" (Warren) **37**:284, 287, 289
"Variation on a Sentence by Laura (Riding) Jackson" (Yau) **61**:335
"Variation on a Theme by Rilke" (Levertov) **11**:202
"Variation on Heraclitus" (MacNeice) **61**:125
"Variations" (Jarrell) **41**:127, 169
"Variations Calypso and Fugue on a Theme of Ella Wheeler Wilcox" (Ashbery) **26**:137, 155
"Variations IV" (Jarrell) **41**:179
"Variations on a Generation" (Corso) **33**:45
Variations on a Sunbeam (Elytis) **21**:120
"Variations on a Theme" (Cullen) **20**:58, 85
"Variations on a Theme by Rilke (The Book of Hours Book I Poem 4)" (Levertov) **11**:203
"Variations on a Time Theme" (Muir) **49**:196, 200
Variations on a Time Theme (Muir) **49**:197, 229, 240-42, 269, 276, 288
"Variations on an Original Theme" (Ashbery) **26**:140
"Variations on Two Dicta of William Blake" (Duncan) **2**:103
"Variations sur le carnaval de Venise" (Gautier) **18**:130
"Vari-Colored Song" (Hughes) **53**:111
Variorum (Yeats)
See *The Variorum Edition of the Poems of W. B. Yeats*
The Variorum Edition of the Poems of W. B. Yeats (Yeats) **51**:87, 143
Variorum Poems (Yeats)
See *The Variorum Edition of the Poems of W. B. Yeats*
Various Poems of All Periods (Valéry)
See *Poésies*
"Various Protestations from Various People" (Knight) **14**:52
"Varsha-mangal" (Tagore) **8**:411
"Varshashesh" (Tagore) **8**:411
"Vasanter Kusumer mela" (Tagore) **8**:406
"The Vase of Life" (Rossetti) **44**:169
"Vashti" (Harper) **21**:185, 191, 209
"El vaso" (Mistral) **32**:176

"Vasundhara" (Tagore) **8**:408
"Vaticinio" (Storni) **33**:239;
Vaudeville for a Princess, and Other Poems (Schwartz) **8**:285, 292-94, 318
"Vaunting Oak" (Ransom) **61**:301
"Vecchi versi" (Montale) **13**:108, 157
"La vecchia ubriaca" (Pavese) **13**:214
"A veces me sucede" (Fuertes) **27**:3
Vecher (Akhmatova) **2**:3, 5-6, 11, 17
Vecherny albom (Tsvetaeva) **14**:305
"Vechernyaya progulka" (Bely) **11**:22
"Veer-Voices: Two Sisters Under Crows" (Dickey) **40**:210-12, 236
"Vegetable Island" (Page) **12**:178
"The Vegetable King" (Dickey) **40**:165, 175-76, 189, 230, 246, 258
"Vegetables I" (Stone) **53**:228, 254
"Vegetables II" (Stone) **53**:229
"Vegetation" (Tagore)
See "Vanaspati"
"Veglia" (Ungaretti) **57**:361-64
"Vegnerà el vero Cristo" (Pasolini) **17**:254
"Vehi tehillatekha" (Amichai) **38**:6, 14
"The Veil" (Graham) **59**:130
"Veillées" (Rimbaud) **57**:173, 243, 250, 253
Veinte poemas de amor y una canción desesperada (Neruda) **4**:276, 282, 284, 291, 299-305, 307
"Veinte siglos" (Storni) **33**:252;
"The veïzades to his love" (Cavafy) **36**:52
Vějíř Boženy Němcové (Seifert) **47**:335
Ve-Lo al Menat Lizkor (Amichai) **38**:17-18, 23
"Velorio" (Cisneros) **52**:158-60, 164
"Velvet Shoes" (Wylie) **23**:301, 305, 307, 314-15, 318-20, 322-23, 330-32
"Vendanges" (Verlaine) **32**:400
"El vendedor de papeles" (Fuertes) **27**:11
"Vendémiaire" (Apollinaire) **7**:10, 36, 44-6
"Vendette della luna" (Carducci) **46**:42, 48
"vending machine" (Enzensberger) **28**:147
"The Vending Machine" (Ignatow) **34**:273
"The Venetian Blind" (Jarrell) **41**:168
Venetian Epigrams (Goethe) **5**:223
The Venetian Glass Nephew (Wylie) **23**:322, 330
"La venganza del minero" (Parra) **39**:303
"Veni vidi vixi" (Hugo) **17**:64
"Venice" (Longfellow) **30**:20
"Venice" (Pasternak) **6**:276
"Venice" (Tomlinson) **17**:331, 334
"Venice, an Italian Song" (Longfellow)
See "Venice"
"The Venice Poem" (Duncan) **2**:105-06
"Venom" (Dickey) **40**:199
"Il ventaglio" (Montale) **13**:108, 128-29
"Ventas" (Guillén) **23**:111
"Vento a Tindare" (Quasimodo)
See "Vento a Tíndari"
"Vento a Tíndari" (Quasimodo) **47**:273-74, 276, 290, 297, 301-2
"Vento e bandiere" (Montale) **13**:164
"Vento sulla mezzaluna" (Montale) **13**:110
"Ventriloquist" (Stone) **53**:257-58
Vents (Perse) **23**:209, 211, 213-18, 221, 223, 232, 234-35, 238-40, 242-43, 247-53, 255, 257
Venture of the Infinite Man (Neruda)
See *Tentativa del hombre infinito*
"Venus" (Darío) **15**:87
"Vénus anadyomène" (Rimbaud) **3**:255; **57**:202-4, 210-11, 243, 257, 292-94
"Venus Anadyomene" (Rimbaud)
See "Vénus anadyomène"
"Venus and the Ark" (Sexton) **2**:355
Venus and the Rain (McGuckian) **27**:77-78, 80-81, 93, 95, 100-104
"Venus and the Sun" (McGuckian) **27**:97
"Venus Transiens" (Lowell) **13**:66, 96
"Venus Tying the Wings of Love" (McGuckian) **27**:103
"Venus's-flytraps" (Komunyakaa) **51**:12, 58
"Veracruz" (Hayden) **6**:193-94
"Verandah" (Walcott) **46**:275, 285, 287
"Le Verbe Être" (Breton) **15**:51
"Le verbe marronner à René Depestre" (Césaire) **25**:29, 33
"La verdad" (Jiménez) **7**:202
"Verdade, Amor, Razão, Merecimento" (Camões) **31**:24
"Verde deriva" (Quasimodo) **47**:302
"Verhalten" (Stramm) **50**:189
"Verlorenes Ich" (Benn) **35**:8, 34
"Vermächtnis" (Goethe) **5**:248
"Vermeer" (Nemerov) **24**:262, 266, 299
"Vermillon" (Char) **56**:156
"Vermont" (Carruth) **10**:73-4, 83
"Vermont Ballad: Change of Season" (Warren) **37**:341, 379
"Vermont Nature" (Stone) **53**:258
"Vernal Equinox" (Lowell) **13**:64
"Vernal Sentiment" (Roethke) **15**:246
"Vernichtung" (Stramm) **50**:170, 205
"Vers dorés" (Nerval) **13**:181
"Vers dorés" (Verlaine) **32**:386
Vers et prose (Mallarmé) **4**:207
"Vers l'Arc en ciel" (Breton) **15**:49
"Vers minuit" (Éluard) **38**:67
"Vers nouveaux et chansons" (Rimbaud) **3**:285
"Versaglia" (Carducci) **46**:71
Verschiedene (Heine) **25**:129-131
Verse (Benn) **35**:6
"Verse about a Red Officer" (Tsvetaeva) **14**:313
"Verses about Russia" (Blok) **21**:9
"Verses about the Beautiful Lady" (Blok) **21**:2-3, 23
The Verses about the Beautiful Lady (Blok)
See *Stikhi o prekrasnoi dame*
Verses Address'd to the Imitator of the First Satire of the Second Book of Horace (Montagu) **16**:338-41
Verses and Sonnets (Belloc) **24**:28-9, 34, 38
"Verses for a Centennial" (MacLeish) **47**:156
"Verses for a Certain Dog" (Parker) **28**:360
Verses from a Tapestry (Seifert)
See *Býti básníkem*
"Verses in the Night" (Parker) **28**:362
"Verses on His Own Death" (Swift) **9**:265
"Verses on the Death of Dr. Swift" (Swift) **9**:258, 279-82, 294-95, 304, 306-08, 310
"Verses on the Death of T. S. Eliot" (Brodsky)
See "Stixi na smert T. S. Èliota"
"Verses on the Unknown Soldier" (Mandelstam)
See "Stikhi o neizvestnom soldate"
"Verses to Czechoslovakia" (Tsvetaeva)
See "Stikhi k Chekhii"
Verses to the Imitator of Horace (Montagu)
See *Verses Address'd to the Imitator of the First Satire of the Second Book of Horace*
"Verses Upon the Burning of Our House" (Bradstreet)
See "Some Verses Upon the Burning of Our House, July 10th, 1666"
"Verses written at Bath on Finding the Heel of a Shoe" (Cowper) **40**:70, 122
"Verses Wrote in a Lady's Ivory Table-book" (Swift)
See "Written in a Lady's Ivory Table-book, 1698"
Versi (Leopardi) **37**:123
"Versi del testamento" (Pasolini) **17**:259
Versification of Donne's Fourth Satire (Pope)
See *Satires of Dr. Donne Versified*
Versifications of Donne (Pope)
See *Satires of Dr. Donne Versified*
"Versilian Shore" (Montale)
See "Proda di Versilia"
"Version I" (Niedecker) **42**:124-25
"Version II" (Niedecker) **42**:124-25
"Verso decorativo" (Storni) **33**:246;
"Verso Finistère" (Montale)
See "Vento sulla mezzaluna"
Verso la cuna del mondo (Gozzano) **10**:177, 184
"Verso la fede" (Gozzano) **10**:184
"Verso Siena" (Montale) **13**:109
"Versos de catorce" (Borges) **32**:57
Versos de salón (Parra) **39**:260, 270-73, 277, 285-87, 292, 295-96, 300-2
Versts (Tsvetaeva)
See *Vyorsty I*
Versty I (Tsvetaeva)
See *Vyorsty I*
Versty II (Tsvetaeva)
See *Vyorsty II*
Versus (Nash) **21**:267, 269
Verteidigung der Wölfe (Enzensberger) **28**:133-38, 140, 143
"Vertigo" (Graham) **59**:130, 138, 151-52, 193-94
"Vertigo" (Rich) **5**:360
"Vertue" (Herbert) **4**:100-01, 110, 113, 132-34
"Vertueux solitaire" (Éluard) **38**:84
"Very late July" (Piercy) **29**:315
"A Very Short Song" (Parker) **28**:346
"A Very Stretched Sennett" (Stone) **53**:222
"Very Tree" (Kunitz) **19**:147, 160
"Very Veery" (Niedecker) **42**:94
"Verzweifelt" (Stramm) **50**:209
"Verzweiflung" (Stramm) **50**:204
"Vespers" (Glück) **16**:170
"Vespers" (Lowell) **13**:64, 67, 97
"The Vestal in the Forum" (Wright) **36**:333
The Vestal Lady on Brattle. (Corso) **33**:2, 8, 14, 35-6, 42, 46-7
"Vestigia" (Carman) **34**:229
"Vestigia nulla retrorsum (In Memoriam: Rainer Maria Rilke 1875-1926)" (MacDiarmid) **9**:156, 176
"Vétérance" (Char) **56**:157
"Les veuves" (Baudelaire) **1**:44, 58-9
"Veve" (Brathwaite) **56**:68, 73-75, 88
"Via Crucis" (Noyes) **27**:136
La via del refugio (Gozzano) **10**:179, 184-85, 188
"Via Portello" (Davie) **29**:95
"Viaje finido" (Storni) **33**:248-50;
"La víbora" (Parra) **39**:268-69, 277, 279, 282-84, 287
"Vibratory Description" (McGuckian) **27**:105
"Vice" (Baraka) **4**:15
"Vice Versa to Bach" (Hughes) **53**:192
"The Vices of the Modern World" (Parra)
See "Los vicios del mundo moderno"
"Los vicios del mundo moderno" (Parra) **39**:268-69, 287-89
"Vicissitude" (Gray)
See "Ode on the Pleasure Arising from Vicissitude"
"Vicolo" (Quasimodo) **47**:274
"A Victim" (Curnow) **48**:29
"The Victim of Aulis" (Abse) **41**:8-9
"The Victims" (Olds) **22**:310, 312, 319, 321, 323
"The Victor Dog" (Merrill) **28**:230
A Victorian Village (Reese) **29**:339
"Victoria's Tears" (Browning) **6**:14, 29
The Victories of Love (Patmore) **59**:205-6, 210-11, 221, 226, 234-35, 240, 242-45, 258-61, 273-74
"The Victorious Sun" (Aleixandre)
See "El sol victorioso"
"Victory" (Dickey) **40**:242, 246-50
Victory: Celebrated by Thirty-eight American Poets (Braithwaite) **52**:106
"Victory in Defeat" (Patmore) **59**:262
Victory Odes (Pindar) **19**:378, 386, 390
"Vida" (Aleixandre)
See "Life"
"La Vida a veces es un río frío y seco" (Fuertes) **27**:16
"Vida de la expresión" (Guillén) **35**:227
"Vida de perros" (Parra) **39**:285-86
"Vida extrema" (Guillén) **35**:230
"Viday" (Tagore) **8**:415
Vides ut alta...Soracte (Horace) **46**:94

"Videshi phul" (Tagore) **8**:415
"La vie" (Éluard) **38**:69
"La Vie dans la mort" (Gautier) **18**:131-32, 155
"La Vie de Chateau" (Hacker) **47**:80
"La vie immédiate" (Éluard) **38**:67, 73
La vie immédiate (Éluard) **38**:68
"Vieira da Silva, Dear Neighbor, Manifold and One . . ." (Char)
See "Vieira de Silva, chère voisine, multiple et une . . ."
"Vieira de Silva, chère voisine, multiple et une . . ." (Char) **56**:146
"Los viejos" (Paz) **48**:179-80, 183
"Viele Herbste" (Benn) **35**:69
"Viennese Waltz" (Wylie) **23**:314, 333
"Viento entero" (Paz) **48**:207-8, 211, 213-14, 274
Viento entero (Paz) **1**:353, 356, 362-63, 369
"El vientre" (Aleixandre) **15**:34
"Vierge folle" (Rimbaud) **57**:236
"La Vierge folle" (Rimbaud) **57**:277
"Le vierge, le vivace et le bel aujourdhui" (Mallarmé) **4**:202, 206
"Vierge Ouvrante" (Ní Chuilleanáin) **34**:362, 367, 373
"Les Vierges de Verdun" (Hugo) **17**:62, 74
"Vies" (Rimbaud) **3**:261-62; **57**:174, 247, 249, 251, 275
"Vies I" (Rimbaud) **57**:284
"Vietnam Addenda" (Lorde) **12**:155
"Vieux de la vieille" (Rimbaud) **57**:252
"Le vieux saltimbanque" (Baudelaire) **1**:44, 58
"The View" (Hölderlin) **4**:178
"The View" (Milosz) **8**:198
"A View across the Roman Campagna" (Browning) **6**:23
"The View from an Attic Window" (Nemerov) **24**:270-71
"View from an Empty Chair" (Gallagher) **9**:50
"View from Charles Bridge" (Seifert) **47**:327
"The View from Kandinsky's Window" (Guest) **55**:185
"View from Rosehill Cemetery: Vicksburg" (Walker) **30**:352
"View from the screen" (Bukowski) **18**:22
"A View of Cracow" (Zagajewski) **27**:381, 385
"A View of Delft" (Zagajewski) **27**:385
"A View of Fujiyama After the War" (Dickey) **40**:175
"View of Teignmouth in Devonshire" (Lowell) **13**:67
"A View of the Brooklyn Bridge" (Meredith) **28**:182, 190
"A View of the Burning" (Merrill) **28**:239
"View of the Mountains from the Kozlov Steppes" (Mickiewicz)
See "Widok gór ze stepów Kozłlowa"
"View of the Pig" (Hughes) **7**:136, 140
"View of the Wilds" (Tu Fu) **9**:332
"View to the North" (Swenson) **14**:288
"View with a Grain of Sand" (Szymborska) **44**:314
View with a Grain of Sand (Szymborska) **44**:286, 293, 295, 303-9, 317
"Viewing the Waterfall at Mount Lu" (Li Po) **29**:145
"The Vigil" (Roethke) **15**:263
"Vigil" (Ungaretti) **57**:374
"Vigil" (Wagoner) **33**:366
"Vigils" (Rimbaud)
See "Veillées"
"Vigil Strange I Kept on the Field One Night" (Whitman) **3**:378
"Vigilance" (Breton) **15**:50-1
"La vigne et la maison" (Lamartine) **16**:268
"Le vigneron champenois" (Apollinaire) **7**:22
"Vignetta" (Carducci) **46**:49
"Vignette" (Kumin) **15**:224
"Vignettes Overseas" (Teasdale) **3**:330-311
"Vihanger gan" (Tagore) **8**:406
VIII (Wylie) **23**:305
"Viking Dublin: Trial Piece" (Heaney) **18**:204
Viktorka (Seifert)
See *Píseň o Viktorce*
"Villa Adriana" (Rich) **5**:362
"Villa on Chung-nan Mountain" (Wang Wei) **18**:368
"The Villa Restaurant" (Vulliamy) **46**:266
"Villa Serbelloni, Bellaggio" (Teasdale) **31**:338
"The Village" (Carruth) **10**:71
"The Village" (Pushkin) **10**:408-09
"The Village" (Walcott) **46**:280
"The Village Atheist" (Masters) **1**:335
"The Village Blacksmith" (Longfellow) **30**:12, 21, 34, 36, 48, 99, 103, 107
"A Village Edmund" (Gunn) **26**:183
"Village in Late Summer" (Sandburg) **41**:284
"A Village Life" (Walcott) **46**:283
The Village Minstrel, and Other Poems (Clare) **23**:25, 38, 42-4
"Village Mystery" (Wylie) **23**:301
"A Village Tale" (Sarton) **39**:328
"The Village Wedding" (Sikelianos) **29**:359, 367-68, 373
"The Villagers and Death" (Graves) **6**:142
"Villanelle" (Hacker) **47**:79
"Villanelle for Fireworks" (Sarton) **39**:323
"Ville" (Rimbaud) **57**:234
"A Villequier" (Hugo) **17**:64, 82-83
"Villes" (Rimbaud) **3**:261, 264-65; **57**:173, 241, 284
"Villes III" (Rimbaud) **57**:241
"Vilota" (Pasolini) **17**:252
"Le vin perdu" (Valéry) **9**:388, 390, 396
"The Vindictives" (Frost) **1**:206
"Vine" (Herrick) **9**:100, 109, 137
"Vine en un barco negre" (Guillén) **23**:120, 127
"The Vineyard" (Kipling) **3**:182
"The Vineyard" (Merwin) **45**:55
Vingt-cinq poèmes (Tzara) **27**:223, 227, 233
"Víno a čas" (Seifert) **47**:333
"Vino, primero, puro" (Jiménez) **7**:187
"Il vino triste" (Pavese) **13**:224
"Vintage" (Hass) **16**:216
"Vinus sai no zenban" (Nishiwaki) **15**:238
Violence (Boland)
See *In a Time of Violence*
"Violences" (Char) **56**:154, 156
Violent Pastoral (Merrill) **28**:253
The Violent Season (Paz)
See *La estación violenta*
"The Violent Space (or when your sister sleeps around for money)" (Knight) **14**:39, 41, 43-4, 52
"Las violetas" (Guillén) **35**:203
"Violets" (Lawrence) **54**:161
"The Violets" (Patmore) **59**:228-29, 232
"The Viper" (Parra)
See "La víbora"
"Le Vipereau" (Char) **56**:152
"Viper-Man" (Davie) **29**:110
"Virgen de plástico" (Fuertes) **27**:23, 30
"A Virgile" (Hugo) **17**:94-95
"Virgilio" (Carducci) **46**:49, 52, 76
"The Virgin" (Jackson) **44**:7, 11-12
"The Virgin" (Philips) **40**:297
"The Virgin" (Thoreau) **30**:180, 198
"The Virgin Carrying a Lantern" (Stevens) **6**:310
"The Virgin Mary to the Child Jesus" (Browning) **6**:29-30
"The Virgin Rides on Venice, and I on Her Back" (Shvarts) **50**:141-43
"Virgin Youth" (Lawrence) **54**:163-65, 174, 220, 231, 233-35
"Virginia" (Eliot) **5**:166
"Virginia" (Lindsay) **23**:280
"Virginia Britannia" (Moore) **49**:91, 98, 128, 134, 141
"Virginia Portrait" (Brown) **55**:108, 112-13, 152
"The Virginians Are Coming Again" (Lindsay) **23**:280, 285
"The Virgins" (Voss) **46**:278
"Virgins Plus Curtains Minus Dots" (Loy) **16**:333
"Virtue" (Herbert)
See "Vertue"
"Virtue" (Wheatley)
See "On Virtue"
"Virtuosi" (Mueller) **33**:193
"Virtuoso Literature" (Wakoski) **15**:346-47
Virtuoso Literature for Two and Four Hands (Wakoski) **15**:346, 355, 361, 365-66
"Le visage mortel" (Bonnefoy) **58**:125
Le Visage nuptial (Char) **56**:141, 171, 201
"Vishvashoka" (Tagore) **8**:417
"Visibile, invisibile" (Quasimodo) **47**:288
The Visibility Trigger (Brathwaite) **56**:71
"The Visible World" (Graham) **59**:151
"A Vision" (Berry) **28**:8-9
"The Vision" (Brathwaite) **56**:64
"Vision" (Bridges) **28**:63, 88
"The Vision" (Burns) **6**:50
"A Vision" (Clare) **23**:22, 25
"Vision" (Gibran)
See "Ru'ya'"
"The Vision" (Masters) **1**:342
"Vision" (Rimbaud) **3**:263
"Vision" (Sassoon) **12**:245
"Vision (2)" (Alexie) **53**:5-7
"Vision And Prayer" (Thomas) **2**:382, 387-88, 390; **52**:279, 290-91, 299, 301, 303-5
"Vision by Sweetwater" (Ransom) **61**:269, 271, 274, 279, 307
"La Vision des montagnes" (Hugo) **17**:66
"Vision: From the Drum's Interior" (Alexie) **53**:11
"Vision in the Repair Shop" (Graves) **6**:143
"A Vision of India" (Kipling) **3**:190
"Vision of Jubal" (Eliot) **20**:123
"A Vision of Poets" (Browning) **6**:7, 26, 38, 41
"Vision of Rotterdam" (Corso) **33**:7, 41
A Vision of Sappho (Carman) **34**:232
"The Vision of Sin" (Tennyson) **6**:359-60, 366, 378
"The Vision of the Archagels" (Brooke) **24**:62, 75-6
A Vision of the Last Judgment (Blake) **12**:40-2
"Vision under the October Mountain: A Love Poem" (Warren) **37**:304
"A Vision upon this Conceit of The Fairy Queen" (Raleigh) **31**:204, 217, 298
"The Visionary" (Brontë) **8**:52
"Visione" (Carducci) **46**:49, 77, 86
"Visions" (Cervantes)
See "Visions of Mexico While at a Writing Symoposium in Port Townsend, Washington"
Les visions (Lamartine) **16**:266, 269, 287
"Visions of Johanna" (Dylan) **37**:47-49, 54-55
"Visions of Mexico While at a Writing Symoposium in Port Townsend, Washington" (Cervantes) **35**:108, 118, 123, 124, 125, 126, 127, 130, 131, 135
Visions of the Daughters of Albion: The Eye Sees More Than the Heart Knows (Blake) **12**:35, 46, 57, 61, 63
"The Visions of the Maid of Orleans" (Coleridge)
See "Joan of Arc"
"Visit" (Ammons) **16**:54
"The Visit" (Baraka) **4**:17
"The Visit" (Nash) **21**:274
"Visit" (Paz)
See "Visita"
"A visit from the ex" (Piercy) **29**:313
A Visit to Sarashina Village (Matsuo Bashō)
See *Sarashina kikō*
"The Visit to the Immortals' Dwelling" (Yakamochi) **48**:105
A Visit to the Kashima Shrine (Matsuo Bashō)
See *Kashima kikō*
"A Visit to the Ruins" (Hope) **56**:278, 285
"Visit to Toronto, with Companions" (Atwood) **8**:40

"Visita" (Paz) **48**:246-49, 251
"The Visitation" (Graves) **6**:172
Visitations (MacNeice) **61**:176, 182
"Visiting a Dead Man on a Summer Day" (Piercy) **29**:307
"Visiting Flannery O'Connor's Grave" (Kumin) **15**:215
"Visiting Hsiang-chi Monastery" (Wang Wei) **18**:378-80
"Visiting Monk Hsüan" (Wang Wei) **18**:388
"Visiting the Ho Family Again" (Tu Fu) **9**:319
"Visiting the Temple of Gathered Fragrance" (Wang Wei) **18**:383, 386
"The Visitor" (Forché) **10**:144, 153
"Visits to St. Elizabeths" (Bishop) **3**:47, 56; **34**:119
"A vista de hombre'" (Guillén) **35**:228
"Vita" (Herbert) **50**:25
Vita d' un uomo: Saggi e interventi (Ungaretti) **57**:337, 343, 350-57
"La vita non è sogno" (Quasimodo) **47**:286
La vita non è sogno (Quasimodo) **47**:284, 286, 289
"Vita Nuova" (Kunitz) **19**:148, 176, 179
La vita nuova (Dante) **21**:48-53, 55, 62, 66, 72-6, 86-92, 94
"La vita solitaria" (Leopardi) **37**:82, 102, 113-17, 124-25, 138-40, 143
"Vital Lightning" (Shvarts) **50**:148
"Vitam quae faciunt beatiorem" (Martial) **10**:243
"Vitzliputzli" (Heine) **25**:167, 170
ViVa (Cummings) **5**:100, 104-07, 110-11
"Viva la Cordillera de los Andes" (Parra)
See "Viva la cordillera de los Andes / Muera la cordillera de la Costa!"
"Viva la cordillera de los Andes / Muera la cordillera de la Costa!" (Parra) **39**:261, 299
"Viva Stalin" (Parra) **39**:311
"Vivaldi, Bird and Angel" (Hope) **56**:301-2
"Vivamus" (Bridges) **28**:59, 63
"Vivasana" (Tagore) **8**:407
"Vivre avec de tels hommes" (Char) **56**:131
V-Letter and Other Poems (Shapiro) **25**:262-67, 269, 285, 288, 292, 295, 297, 307, 309, 316, 319, 322
"Vlez besenok v mokroi sherstke" (Mandelstam) **14**:153-54
"Vmesto predisloviia" (Akhmatova) **55**:13-15, 17-19, 28-29
"Vnov' Ia Posetil" (Pushkin)
See "Vnov' Ya Posetil"
"Vnov' Ya Posetil" (Pushkin) **10**:384, 414-15
"Vnutri gory bezdeistvuet kumir" (Mandelstam) **14**:153
"Vocation" (Levertov) **11**:198
"Voce giunta con le folaghe" (Montale) **13**:112
"Voeu à Phebus" (Ronsard) **11**:256
"The Voice" (Arnold) **5**:49
"A Voice" (Atwood) **8**:14
"The Voice" (Brooke) **24**:56, 76
"The Voice" (Hardy) **8**:88, 117-18, 135
"The Voice" (Levine) **22**:225
"A Voice" (Ní Chuilleanáin) **34**:372
"The Voice" (Roethke) **15**:275
"A Voice" (Sarton) **39**:368
"The Voice" (Silverstein) **49**:343
"The Voice" (Teasdale) **31**:326
"Voice Arriving with the Coots" (Montale) **13**:146, 149
"The Voice as a Girl" (Snyder) **21**:289
"Voice Coming with the Moorhens" (Montale)
See "Voce giunta con le folaghe"
"A Voice from a Chorus" (Blok) **21**:15
"Voice from the Tomb" (Smith) **12**:349
"A Voice from under the Table" (Wilbur) **51**:221, 231, 293
"The Voice of Nature" (Bridges) **28**:67
"The Voice of Rock" (Ginsberg) **4**:55
"The Voice of the Ancient Bard" (Blake) **12**:7
Voice of the Forest (Tagore)
See *Banabani*
"The Voice of the Holy Land" (Sachs)
See "Stimme des Heilegen Landes"
"Voice of the Past" (Bely)
See "Golos proshlogo"
"The Voice of the People" (Belloc) **24**:42
"Voice of the People" (Hölderlin)
See "Stimme des Volks"
"Voices" (Cavafy) **36**:73
"Voices" (Szymborska) **44**:279, 284, 289
"Voices about the Princess Anemone" (Smith) **12**:298, 348-49
"Voices Between Waking and Sleeping in the Mountains" (Wright) **36**:355
"Voices from Kansas" (Kumin) **15**:215
Voices from the Forest (Mueller) **33**:197
"Voices from the Other World" (Merrill) **28**:235, 259
"Voices of the elements" (Enzensberger) **28**:143
"Voices of the Night" (Longfellow) **30**:21-2, 26, 28, 47, 63, 96, 103, 105-06, 108-09
"Voices under the Ground" (Ekeloef) **23**:71, 73, 75
"Voici" (Char) **56**:127
"Voicy le temps, Hurault, qui joyeux nous convie" (Ronsard) **11**:250
"Void in Law" (Browning) **6**:28, 32
"Void Only" (Rexroth) **20**:221
"Voie" (Tzara) **27**:229-31
Les voisinages de Van Gogh (Char) **56**:163, 177, 186-87
"La Voix" (Baudelaire) **1**:73
"Une voix" (Bonnefoy) **58**:119, 131, 167-68, 174
"Voix basses et Phénix" (Bonnefoy) **58**:132, 174
Les Voix intérieures (Hugo) **17**:42, 45, 52, 63, 74, 76, 80, 83, 91-92, 96-97
"Volcanic Holiday" (Merrill) **28**:283, 285
"Volcano" (Walcott) **46**:237, 279
Volcano a Memoir of Hawaii (Hongo) **23**:204-206
"An vollen Büschelzweigen" (Goethe) **5**:247
"Vollmondnacht" (Goethe) **5**:247
"Vol'nost': Oda" (Pushkin) **10**:408-9
"Volontairement" (Éluard) **38**:69
Volshebny fonar (Tsvetaeva) **14**:318
"Volt" (Tzara) **27**:229-31
"Volta" (Brathwaite) **56**:7, 29, 50
"Voltaire" (Jackson) **44**:7, 11
Volume Two (Villa) **22**:347, 353
"Voluntaries" (Emerson) **18**:76-77, 88, 113
"La volupté" (Baudelaire) **1**:71
"Volved" (Castro) **41**:84
"Volverlo a ver" (Mistral) **32**:176
"Von diesen Stauden" (Celan) **10**:122
Von Schwelle zu Schwelle (Celan) **10**:95, 121
"Vooruzhennyi zren'em uzkikh os" (Mandelstam) **14**:154
"Vor einem Kornfeld sagte einer" (Benn) **35**:8, 68
"Voracities and Verities Sometimes Are Interacting" (Moore) **4**:261; **49**:102, 126-27, 129-30, 134
"Vorfrühling" (Stramm) **50**:199, 201, 204, 206
"Vorobyev Hills" (Pasternak) **6**:251-54
Voronezh Notebooks (Mandelstam) **14**:123, 149-50
"Vorstadt im Föhn" (Trakl) **20**:261
"Vospominanie o strannom ugoshchenii" (Shvarts) **50**:136-37
"Vospominanie v Tsarskom Sele" (Pushkin) **10**:409, 421
"Vostok pobledneuskii, vostok onemesvshii" (Bely) **11**:32
"Voto" (Mistral) **32**:159, 173-74
"A Vow" (Ginsberg) **4**:56
"The Vow" (Kinnell) **26**:286
"The Vow" (Lowell) **13**:86-7
"Vowel Sonatas" (Yau) **61**:337
"Vowels" (Rimbaud)
See "Voyelles"
"Vowels 2" (Baraka) **4**:24
"vowl man" (Bissett) **14**:15
Vox Clamantis (Gower) **59**:17, 25, 44, 62, 99, 113-19
"Vox Corporis" (Teasdale) **31**:368-691
"Vox Humana" (Gunn) **26**:200
"Voy a dormir" (Storni) **33**:236, 261, 300;
"Voy hasta Uján" (Guillén) **23**:128
"Le voyage" (Baudelaire) **1**:50, 60, 70, 73-4
"Le Voyage" (Char) **56**:197-98
"The Voyage" (Jonson) **17**:207
"Voyage" (MacLeish) **47**:190
"The Voyage" (Muir) **49**:233
The Voyage (Muir) **49**:210, 224, 229, 232-33, 245, 247, 250-51, 255, 270, 289
"Le voyage à Cythère" (Baudelaire) **1**:65, 72-3
"Un Voyage à Cythère" (Char) **56**:198
"Voyage de découverte" (Péret) **33**:202
"Le Voyage de Tours, ou les amoureux Thoinet et Perrot" (Ronsard) **11**:260-61, 264
"The Voyage of Maeldune" (Tennyson) **6**:359, 369
"Voyage to Cythera" (Baudelaire)
See "Le voyage à Cythère"
Voyage to the Island of Love (Behn)
See *Poems upon Several Occasions, with a Voyage to the Island of Love*
"Voyage to the Moon" (Pinsky) **27**:157
"The Voyage Up River" (Walcott) **46**:322
"Voyage West" (MacLeish) **47**:164, 167, 260
"Voyager" (Mueller) **33**:190
"Voyagers" (Page) **12**:199
"Voyages" (Clampitt) **19**:91
"Voyages" (Crane) **3**:90, 97, 104
Voyages: A Homage to John Keats (Clampitt) **19**:87
"Voyages II" (Crane) **3**:80, 83, 96, 102
"Voyages III" (Crane) **3**:83
"Voyages IV" (Crane) **3**:83
"Voyages V" (Crane) **3**:83
"Le voyageur" (Apollinaire) **7**:48
"Voyant" (Rimbaud) **57**:193
"Les Voyelles" (Rimbaud) **3**:249, 268, 274
"Voyelles" (Rimbaud) **57**:175, 177, 216, 235, 247
"Vozdushnyi korabl" (Lermontov) **18**:291
Vozmezdie (Blok) **21**:10, 17, 25-6, 39, 44
Vozvrat: Tretiia simfoniia (Bely) **11**:3, 8-9, 14-17, 22
"Vpon a Ribband" (Carew)
See "Upon a Ribband"
"Vrai Corps" (Bonnefoy) **58**:173
"Le vrai de la chose" (Laforgue) **14**:76
"Vrai Lieu" (Bonnefoy) **58**:132
"Vrai lieu du cerf" (Bonnefoy) **58**:133-34
"Vriksha-ropan" (Tagore) **8**:416
"Vriksha-vandana" (Tagore) **8**:416
Vrindaban (Paz) **1**:361-63
"Vse Povtoryayv pervyi stikh" (Tsvetaeva) **14**:329
"Vse ushli, i nikto ne vernulsia" (Akhmatova) **55**:52
"Vstrecha" (Pasternak) **6**:280
"Vstuplenie" (Akhmatova) **55**:4, 8, 16, 27, 29, 41, 43, 51
"Vsye eto bylo bylo bylo" (Blok) **21**:15
Vtoraia simfoniia: Dramaticheskaia (Bely) **11**:3-4, 8-11, 13-16, 21, 27, 33
Vtoraya kniga (Mandelstam) **14**:106, 113-18, 121-22, 129, 135, 141, 150, 153, 155
"Vue" (Valéry) **9**:392
"Vuelta" (Paz) **1**:370-72, 374
Vuelta (Paz) **1**:370-71, 374, 376; **48**:188, 192, 228, 233, 245
"La vuelta a America" (Cardenal) **22**:110
"La vuelta a Buenos Aires" (Borges) **22**:94
"Vuelta de paseo" (García Lorca) **3**:139
"Vulcan" (Oppen) **35**:305, 307, 312
"Vulnerant omnes ultima necat" (Cavafy) **36**:53

VV (Cummings)
See *ViVa*
"Vykhozhu odin ja na dorogu" (Lermontov) **18**:303
Vyorsty I (Tsvetaeva) **14**:310, 318
Vyorsty II (Tsvetaeva) **14**:322
"Vysokaya bolesn" (Pasternak) **6**:265
"Vystrel" (Pushkin) **10**:414
Vzmakh Ruki (Yevtushenko) **40**:344, 350
"W drodze do Delf" (Herbert) **50**:5
"W. Lloyd Garrison Standard" (Masters) **36**:231
"W. S. Landor" (Moore) **4**:242, 259; **49**:145
"Wacht" (Stramm) **50**:172, 175
"Wadin' in de Crick" (Dunbar) **5**:144
"Wading at Wellfleet" (Bishop) **3**:49, 57; **34**:117
"Wading in a Marsh" (Wagoner) **33**:361
"Waga Uta" (Yosano Akiko) **11**:302, 306
"Wagner" (Brooke) **24**:53, 56, 64, 83
"The Wagoner" (Pavese) **13**:205
"Waialua" (Song)
See "Easter: Wahiawa, 1959"
The Waif (Longfellow) **30**:46
"Waikiki" (Brooke) **24**:56, 67, 86
"Wail" (Parker) **28**:360
"The Wait" (Borges)
See "La espera"
"Wait" (Hughes) **53**:115
"Wait" (Kinnell) **26**:292-93
"The Waiting" (Borges)
See "La espera"
"Waiting" (Kenyon) **57**:45
"The Waiting" (Olds) **22**:330, 332, 334, 337, 340
"Waiting" (Reese) **29**:333
"Waiting" (Sandburg) **41**:339
"Waiting" (Warren) **37**:313
"Waiting" (Wright) **14**:341
"Waiting by the Gate" (Bryant) **20**:8
"Waiting for Breakfast" (Larkin) **21**:226-27
"Waiting for Father in Pawling, N.Y." (McHugh) **61**:198
"Waiting for It" (Swenson) **14**:263
"Waiting for the Barbarians" (Cavafy) **36**:29, 31, 39, 50, 51, 55, 56-57, 84
Waiting for the King of Spain (Wakoski) **15**:366
Waiting for the Yeti (Szymborska)
See *Wołanie do Yeti*
"The Waiting Head" (Sexton) **2**:350
"Waiting in a Rain Forest" (Wagoner) **33**:337, 342
"Waiting Inland" (Kumin) **15**:208
"Wake" (Brathwaite) **56**:74, 87
"Wake Island" (Birney) **52**:22
"The Wake of the Books" (Kavanagh) **33**:62, 118
"Wake Up" (Carver) **54**:18-19
"The Wakening" (Merwin) **45**:18
"Wake-Up Niggers" (Madhubuti) **5**:329, 338
"The Waking" (Kinnell) **26**:279
"The Waking" (Roethke) **15**:278, 286
"Waking an Angel" (Levine) **22**:213
"Waking Early Sunday" (O'Hara) **45**:133
"Waking from Drunkenness on a Spring Day" (Li Po) **29**:143
"Waking from Sleep" (Bly) **39**:6-7
"Waking in a Newly-Build House" (Gunn) **26**:201
"Waking in a Newly-Built House" (Gunn) **26**:211
"Waking in the Blue" (Lowell) **3**:209, 221
"Waking in the Dark" (Rich) **5**:370, 392, 395
The Waking: Poems, 1933-1953 (Roethke) **15**:249, 261, 263, 282, 284, 309
"Waking this Morning" (Rukeyser) **12**:230
"Waking Up in Streator" (Stryk) **27**:214
"Waking Who Knows" (Oppen) **35**:300, 303
"Walcourt" (Verlaine) **32**:411
"Waldeinsamkeit" (Emerson) **18**:76, 88
Walden; or, Life in the Woods (Thoreau) **30**:207-08, 220, 242, 265
"Wales Visitation" (Ginsberg) **4**:74, 93-4; **47**:17
"The Walgh-Vogel" (Wilbur) **51**:295
"The Walk" (Hardy) **8**:93
"The Walk" (Walcott) **46**:237
"A Walk in Kyoto" (Birney) **52**:23, 34, 45-46, 67-69
"A Walk in Late Summer" (Roethke) **15**:274
"A Walk in the Country" (Kinnell) **26**:257
"Walk Near False Creek Mouth" (Birney) **52**:25
"A Walk on Snow" (Viereck) **27**:260, 277, 282
"Walk on the Moon" (Momaday) **25**:188
"Walk There" (Ignatow) **34**:279
"A Walk to Wachusett" (Thoreau) **30**:246
"A Walk with Tom Jefferson" (Levine) **22**:225-27
"The Walker" (Hope) **56**:270
"Walking" (Ignatow) **34**:313
"Walking among Limnatour Dunes" (Bly) **39**:23
"Walking Down Park" (Giovanni) **19**:140-41, 143
"Walking in a Swamp" (Wagoner) **33**:336-38
"Walking in Broken Country" (Wagoner) **33**:350, 352, 362
"Walking in Paris" (Sexton) **2**:363
"Walking in the Blue" (Sexton) **2**:350
"Walking in the Breakdown Lane" (Erdrich) **52**:178
"Walking in the Snow" (Wagoner) **33**:333
"Walking in the Swamp" (Wagoner)
See "Walking in a Swamp"
"Walking into Love" (Piercy) **29**:308, 311
"Walking into the Wind" (Wagoner) **33**:360
"The Walking Man of Rodin" (Sandburg) **2**:334; **41**:296
"Walking My Baby Back Home" (Thumboo) **30**:328
"Walking on the Prayerstick" (Rose) **13**:233
"Walking Swiftly" (Bly) **39**:38, 42
"Walking Through Broken Country" (Wagoner)
See "Walking in Broken Country"
"Walking to Bell rock" (Ondaatje) **28**:336-37
"Walking to Sleep" (Wilbur) **51**:236, 249, 276, 278, 280, 307, 335
Walking to Sleep: New Poems and Translations (Wilbur) **51**:231, 235, 249, 259, 276, 288, 301, 305
"Walking to the Next Farm" (Bly) **39**:44-45
"Walking to Work" (O'Hara) **45**:227
Walking under Water (Abse) **41**:3, 6, 9-10
"Walking Where the Plows Have Been Turning" (Bly) **39**:58, 63, 103
"Walking-Sticks" (Moore) **49**:129
"The Wall" (Brooks) **7**:82
"The Wall" (Herbert) **50**:26
"The Wall" (Jordan) **38**:121
"The Wall" (Komunyakaa) **51**:54-55
"The Wall" (Montale) **13**:148
"A Wall in the Woods: Cummington" (Wilbur) **51**:336
"Wall Songs" (Hogan) **35**:245, 252
Wallenrod (Mickiewicz)
See *Konrad Wallenrod*
"Die Wallfahrt nach Kevlaar" (Heine) **25**:145
"The Walls" (Cavafy) **36**:46, 52, 53, 54, 56, 73, 74, 112
"Walls" (Hughes) **7**:149
The Walls Do Not Fall (H. D.) **5**:272, 274-76, 293-95, 307, 309, 312, 314-15
"The Walrus and the Carpenter" (Carroll) **18**:51-52
"Walt Whitman" (Whitman) **3**:414
Walt Whitman Bathing (Wagoner) **33**:373-74
"Walter Bradford" (Brooks) **7**:92
"Walter Jenks' Bath" (Meredith) **28**:178, 182, 213
"Walter Rawley of the Middle Temple, in Commendation of the Steele Glasse" (Raleigh) **31**:309, 312-13
"Walter Simmons" (Masters) **36**:182
"The Waltz" (Aleixandre)
See "El vals"
"The Waltzer in the House" (Kunitz) **19**:155
"Wanda" (Vigny) **26**:369, 402
"The Wanderer" (Pushkin) **10**:409
"The Wanderer" (Smith) **12**:326, 349-50, 354
"The Wanderer" (Teasdale) **31**:363, 378-79
"The Wanderer" (Williams) **7**:374, 382, 394
"A Wanderer" (Zagajewski) **27**:381
"The Wanderers" (Morris) **55**:260-61, 306
"The Wanderer's Song" (Hagiwara)
See "Hyōhakusha no uta"
"The Wandering Islands" (Hope) **56**:266, 279-81, 305
"The Wandering Islands" (Walcott) **46**:273
The Wandering Islands (Hope) **56**:265-66, 268-70, 273, 288-89
"The Wandering Jew" (Robinson) **1**:487
"Wandering on Mount T'ai" (Li Po) **29**:166
"The Wanderings of Cain" (Coleridge) **11**:89, 91
"The Wanderings of Oisin" (Yeats) **20**:353; **51**:75, 101, 103
The Wanderings of Oisin, and Other Poems (Yeats) **20**:298, 302, 344, 346
"Wanderschaft" (Trakl) **20**:241
"Wandrers Sturmlied" (Goethe) **5**:237-39, 245, 247
Wang Stream Collection (Wang Wei) **18**:367, 370, 385
"Wang-ch'uan Garland" (Wang Wei) **18**:374
"Wankelmut" (Stramm) **50**:189, 195, 208
"The Want" (Olds) **22**:321, 325-26, 340
The Want Bone (Pinsky) **27**:156, 160, 163-64, 169, 172, 174
"Wanting a Child" (Graham) **59**:132, 178
"Wanting to Die" (Sexton) **2**:364
"Wants" (Larkin) **21**:227, 242, 252
"Wapentake" (Longfellow) **30**:51
"War" (Birney) **52**:44, 58
"War" (Herbert)
See "Wojna"
"War" (Levine) **22**:218
"War" (Niedecker) **42**:99
"War" (Rimbaud)
See "Guerre"
"The War Against the Trees" (Kunitz) **19**:175
War All the Time: Poems, 1981-1984 (Bukowski) **18**:15, 18-19
"War and Memory" (Jordan) **38**:126, 128
"The War Horse" (Boland) **58**:42, 46
The War Horse (Boland) **58**:12-13, 42-44, 91
"War in Ethiopia" (Bishop) **34**:136
"The War in the Air" (Nemerov) **24**:290
"War Machine" (Ondaatje) **28**:327-28, 331
"War Pictures" (Lowell) **13**:76
"War Poems (1914-1915)" (Sandburg) **41**:235-36, 294, 348
"War Song" (Parker) **28**:356
"War Sonnet" (Meredith) **28**:209
War Stories Poems about Long Ago and Now (Nemerov) **24**:287, 289-90
War Trilogy (H. D.)
See *Trilogy*
"War Winters" (Birney) **52**:21, 27, 39, 46, 62
"The War Wound" (Dickey) **40**:181
"The Ward" (Rukeyser) **12**:225
"The Warden of the Cinque Ports" (Longfellow) **30**:50
Ware the Hauke (Skelton) **25**:335, 338, 354, 377, 377-78, 380-81
Ware the Hawk (Skelton)
See *Ware the Hauke*
"Waring" (Browning) **2**:26
"A Warm Place to Shit" (Bissett) **14**:10
"A Warm Small Rain" (Zagajewski) **27**:394
"Warmhearted" (Silverstein) **49**:340
"Warning" (Hughes) **1**:252; **53**:150-52, 161
"Warning" (Meredith) **60**:263
"Warning" (Wagoner) **33**:325, 367
"Warning: Children at Play" (Nemerov) **24**:255
"Warning to Children" (Graves) **6**:139, 143-44, 150
"A Warning to Those Who Live on Mountains" (Day Lewis) **11**:144
"Warnings" (Parra) **39**:310

"Warnings to the Reader" (Parra)
See "Advertencia al lector"
"Warnung" (Goethe) **5**:250
"The Warriors" (Alexie) **53**:23
"The Warriors of the North" (Hughes) **7**:132, 148
"The Warrior's Prayer" (Dunbar) **5**:134
"The Wars" (Ondaatje) **28**:338
"Wars" (Sandburg) **41**:249, 269
"A Warsaw Gathering" (Zagajewski) **27**:381
"Warum gabst du uns die tiefen Blicke" (Goethe) **5**:246
"Was He Married?" (Smith) **12**:333, 352
"Was I never yet" (Wyatt) **27**:356
"Wash" (Ní Chuilleanáin) **34**:349
"Washerwoman" (Sandburg) **2**:329
"Washington Cathedral" (Shapiro) **25**:286, 318
"Washington McNeely" (Masters) **36**:183
"Washington Monument at Night" (Sandburg) **41**:251
"Washyuma Motor Hotel" (Ortiz) **17**:227
"A WASP Woman Visits a Black Junkie in Prison" (Knight) **14**:42, 53
"The Wassaile" (Herrick) **9**:104
"The Waste Land" (Eliot) **31**:99, 120-21, 133
The Waste Land (Eliot) **5**:155-62, 165-67, 173-74, 176, 178-79, 183-89, 191-93, 198, 206-18; **31**:99, 116-17, 120, 123-24, 134, 137-38, 144, 156, 165, 169, 190
The Waste Land (Pound) **4**:353
"Waste Paper Basket" (Tagore) **8**:417
"Waste Sonata" (Olds) **22**:325
"Wasted Energy" (Niedecker) **42**:97, 136-37, 143
Watakushi no Oitach (Yosano Akiko) **11**:309-11
"The Watch" (Swenson) **14**:250
"Watch" (Ungaretti)
See "Veglia"
"Watch Out, Papa" (Hughes) **53**:115
"The Watcher" (Borges)
See "El centinela"
"The Watcher" (Hope) **56**:285-86
"The Watchers" (Braithwaite) **52**:106
"Watchers" (Merwin) **45**:23
"The Watchers" (Thomas) **53**:327
"Watchers of the Sky" (Noyes) **27**:128
"Watchful" (Mistral)
See "Desvelada"
"Watchful, A Tale of Psyche" (Smith) **12**:303-05, 337
"Watching Crow Looking South Towards the Manzano" (Harjo) **27**:64
"Watching Football on TV" (Nemerov) **24**:284
"The Watching of the Falcon" (Morris) **55**:250, 287, 305, 308
"Watching Shoah in a Hotel Room in America" (Zagajewski) **27**:388, 391
"Watching Television" (Bly) **39**:9
"Watching the Dance" (Merrill) **28**:254
"Watching the Needleboats at San Sabra" (Joyce) **22**:137
"The Water" (Carruth) **10**:71
"Water" (Larkin) **21**:244
"Water" (Lee) **24**:247
"Water" (Lowell) **3**:212, 215
"Water" (Wright) **14**:366
"Water and Marble" (Page) **12**:178
"Water Color" (Verlaine)
See "Aquarelles"
"The Water Diviner" (Abse) **41**:2-3, 12
"Water Drawn Up Into the Head" (Bly) **39**:28
"The Water Drop" (Elytis) **21**:130
"Water Element Song for Sylvia" (Wakoski) **15**:345
"the water falls in yr mind nd yu get wet tooo" (Bissett) **14**:16, 33
"The Water Hyacinth" (Merrill) **28**:247
"The Water Journey" (Ní Chuilleanáin) **34**:358
Water Lilies (Jiménez)
See *Ninfeas*
"Water Music" (MacDiarmid) **9**:154, 156, 158, 171, 176
"Water Music for the Progress of Love in a Life-Raft down the Sammamish Slough" (Wagoner) **33**:330, 361
"The Water Nymph" (Lermontov)
See "Rusalka"
"Water of Life" (MacDiarmid) **9**:197-98
"Water Picture" (Swenson) **14**:261, 263; **106**:351
"Water Raining" (Stein) **18**:334, 349
"Water Sign Woman" (Clifton) **17**:29
"Water Sleep" (Wylie) **23**:301
Water Street (Merrill) **28**:220, 225, 228, 234, 238, 240, 244, 247-49, 281
"Water under the Earth" (Bly) **39**:18
"Water Walker" (Wilbur) **51**:188, 192, 224, 279-80
"Watercolor of Grantchester Meadows" (Plath) **1**:388; **37**:185
"Watercolors" (Rose) **13**:238
"The Watercourse" (Herbert) **4**:114
"Watered-Down Love" (Dylan) **37**:66
"Waterfall" (Heaney) **18**:200
"The Waterfall at Powerscourt" (Davie) **29**:110
"Watergate" (Baraka) **4**:30
"The Watergaw" (MacDiarmid) **9**:156, 160, 196
"Watering the Horse" (Bly) **39**:7, 70, 79
"Waterlily Fire" (Rukeyser) **12**:221
Waterlily Fire: Poems, 1935-1962 (Rukeyser) **12**:215-16
"Watermaid" (Okigbo) **7**:232, 239
"Watershed" (Warren) **37**:376
"Watteau" (Walcott) **46**:242
"The Wattle-tree" (Wright) **14**:344, 353
"A Wave" (Ashbery) **26**:159
"The Wave" (MacLeish) **47**:192
"The Wave" (Merwin) **45**:22
"Wave" (Snyder) **21**:304-06, 308
A Wave (Ashbery) **26**:169-170
A Wave of the Hand (Yevtushenko)
See *Vzmakh Ruki*
"Wave of the Night" (Benn)
See "Welle der Nacht"
"Wave Song" (Ekeloef) **23**:53-4
"The Wave the Flame the Cloud and the Leopard Speak to the Mind" (Swenson) **14**:247
Waving from Shore (Mueller) **33**:191-92
"The Waving of the Corn" (Lanier) **50**:56, 105
"Wawóz Malachowskiego" (Herbert) **50**:5
"Waxwings" (Francis) **34**:242
"Waxworks" (Shapiro) **25**:308, 312
"The Way" (Braithwaite) **52**:107
"The Way" (Lowell) **13**:60, 83
"The Way" (Muir) **49**:198, 284, 296
"The Way Ahead" (Thumboo) **30**:301
"The Way Down" (Kunitz) **19**:149, 155, 178
"Way down the Ravi River" (Kipling) **3**:194
"The Way In" (Tomlinson) **17**:319-20, 326
The Way In and Other Poems (Tomlinson) **17**:327, 336, 349, 351-52, 354
"The Way it Was" (Clifton) **17**:23
Way of All the Earth (Akhmatova) **2**:16
"The Way of Parents" (Guillén) **35**:221
"The Way of Refuge" (Gozzano)
See "The Road to Shelter"
The Way of Refuge (Gozzano)
See *La via del refugio*
"The Way of the Wind" (Swinburne) **24**:329
Way Out in the Centre (Abse) **41**:19, 21-2, 31
"The Way the Cards Fall" (Komunyakaa) **51**:36
"The Way Things Are in Franklin" (Kenyon) **57**:20
"The Way Things Work" (Graham) **59**:132-33, 170-71, 176, 181
"The Way through the Woods" (Kipling) **3**:171, 183, 186, 192
"A Way to Love God" (Warren) **37**:309, 363-64, 378
"Way to the West" (Birney) **52**:37-38
"The Way West, Underground" (Snyder) **21**:296
"The Wayfarers" (Brooke) **24**:57
"Way-Out Morgan" (Brooks) **7**:63
"The Ways of Daughters" (Stone) **53**:241, 244
"The Wayside Inn" (Longfellow) **30**:62
Wayside Inn (Longfellow)
See *Tales of a Wayside Inn*
A Wayside Lute (Reese) **29**:330, 335, 339, 346, 349, 352-353
"The Wayside Station" (Muir) **49**:197, 231, 273
The Wayward and the Seeking: A Collection of Writing by Jean Toomer (Toomer) **7**:341
"We" (Ignatow) **34**:345
"We" (Wilbur) **51**:209
We a BaddDDD People (Sanchez) **9**:204, 206-08, 210-13, 216, 218-20, 224-27, 229, 234, 237-38, 240, 242
"We a BadddDDD People (for gwendolyn brooks/a fo real bad one)" (Sanchez) **9**:209, 225, 237
"We Are" (Éluard)
See "Nous sommes"
"We Are" (Kumin) **15**:183
"We are Alive" (Harjo) **27**:57
"We Are All Particles of This" (Stone) **53**:251
"We Are Always Too Late" (Boland) **58**:48
"We Are Human History. We Are Not Natural History" (Boland) **58**:8, 13-14, 48, 84
"We Are Muslim Women" (Sanchez) **9**:228
"We Are Seven" (Wordsworth) **4**:374, 415, 420, 428
"We Are the Only Animals Who Do This" (Boland) **58**:21
"We Are the Women" (Goodison) **36**:142, 153-54
"We Are Transmitters" (Lawrence) **54**:239
"We become new" (Piercy) **29**:301
"We Call Them the Brave" (Moore) **49**:126, 134
"We can work it out. Raza" (Alurista) **34**:29, 45
"We Come Back" (Rexroth) **20**:217-18
"We Did It" (Amichai) **38**:13
"We Encounter Nat King Cole as We Invent the Future" (Harjo) **27**:65, 72
"We English" (Loy) **16**:320
"We Exist" (Graham) **59**:189
"We Fought South of the Ramparts" (Li Po) **29**:176
"We Free Singers Be" (Knight) **14**:40, 46
"We Have Been Believers" (Walker) **20**:272-74, 283, 289
"We knew the world backwards and forwards" (Szymborska) **44**:318-19
"We know him—Law and Order League—" (Niedecker) **42**:136
"We Let the Boat Drift" (Kenyon) **57**:27
"we live in a hundrid yeer old house" (Bissett) **14**:25
"We Lying by Seasand" (Thomas) **2**:404; **52**:243, 334
"We Must Call A Meeting" (Hogan) **35**:266
"We Need th Setting" (Bissett) **14**:10
"We Never Know" (Komunyakaa) **51**:25-26, 35
"We Real Cool" (Brooks) **7**:62, 85, 90
"We Shall Gather Again in Petersburg" (Mandelstam) **14**:116, 121, 157
we sleep inside each other all (Bissett) **14**:6
"We Stood There Singing" (Kumin) **15**:213
"We Too" (H. D.) **5**:268
"We Walk on Pebbled Streets" (Alurista) **34**:48
We Walk the Way of the New World (Madhubuti) **5**:326-27, 336, 343, 345-46
"We Wear the Mask" (Dunbar) **5**:124, 130, 132, 135, 140, 142, 144
"We Who Are Playing" (Lindsay) **23**:286
"We Would Have Been Relieved with Death" (Alurista) **34**:23, 47
"The Weak Monk" (Smith) **12**:333
"A Wearied Pilgrim" (Herrick) **9**:108
"Weariness" (Longfellow) **30**:27
"The Wearing of the Green" (Davie) **29**:107, 109, 120

"The Weary Blues" (Hughes) **1**:236, 246, 248, 261, 269; **53**:80-82, 85-86, 94, 114, 117, 143, 200-203, 205
The Weary Blues (Hughes) **1**:236-37, 242, 244-46, 248, 258, 260, 262-64, 268-70; **53**:79, 85-86, 94, 105-6, 108, 117, 127, 140, 147, 156, 164, 170, 181-82, 189
"Weary in Well-Doing" (Rossetti) **7**:268
"Weary of the Bitter Ease" (Mallarmé)
See "Las de l'amer repos"
"The Weary Pund o' Tow" (Burns) **6**:78
"The Weather in Tohunga Crescent" (Curnow) **48**:13, 20, 29
"The Weather of the World" (Nemerov) **24**:287, 302
"The Weather-Cock Points South" (Lowell) **13**:96
"Weathering Out" (Dove) **6**:111
"Weathers" (Hardy) **8**:124
"The Web One Weaves of Italy" (Moore) **49**:128-29, 137-38
"Webster Ford" (Masters) **1**:344, 346, 348
"The Wedding" (Patmore) **59**:204, 230, 234
"The Wedding Photograph" (Smith) **12**:316, 323
"The Wedding Sermon" (Patmore) **59**:221, 245, 274
"A Wedding Toast" (Wilbur) **51**:279
"Wedding Wind" (Larkin) **21**:227, 247
"Weddings" (Yevtushenko) **40**:341
Weddings (Yevtushenko) **40**:354
The Wedge (Williams) **7**:370, 402
"Wedlock" (Lawrence) **54**:183
"Wednesday at the Waldorf" (Swenson) **14**:267, 276
"Wednesday: The Tete a Tete" (Montagu) **16**:348-49
"The Weed" (Bishop) **3**:37, 45, 75; **34**:52, 144, 160, 162-63, 181, 191
"Weed Puller" (Roethke) **15**:278, 295, 297
"Weekend Glory" (Angelou) **32**:29
"Weeknight Service" (Lawrence) **54**:175
"The Weeping Garden" (Pasternak) **6**:268
"The Weeping Saviour" (Browning) **6**:14
"Weggebeizt" (Celan) **10**:106, 111
"Weiß sind die Tulpen" (Celan) **10**:123
"The weight" (Piercy) **29**:313
"Weight" (Tagore)
See "Bhar"
"A Weightless Element" (Benn) **35**:7
"Die Weihe" (Heine) **25**:157-61, 163-64
"Weinhaus Wolf" (Benn) **35**:34
Die Weise von Liebe und Tod des Cornets Christoph Rilke (Rilke) **2**:266, 268
"Weitere Gründe dafür daB Dichter lügen" (Enzensberger) **28**:165
"weiterung" (Enzensberger) **28**:135
"Welcome Aboard the Turbojet Electra" (Swenson) **14**:268
"Welcome and Parting" (Goethe)
See "Willkommen und Abschied"
"Welcome Back, Mr. Knight: Love of My Life" (Knight) **14**:46
"Welcome Morning" (Sexton) **2**:372
"The Welcome to Sack" (Herrick) **9**:88, 94, 102
"Welcome to the Caves of Arta" (Graves) **6**:153
"The Well" (Levertov) **11**:168, 205-06
"The Well" (Merwin) **45**:32
"The Well" (Tomlinson) **17**:341-42
"Well" (Walker) **30**:343
"Well Said Old Mole" (Viereck) **27**:259
"We'll to the Woods No More, the Laurels Are Cut Down" (Sarton) **39**:328
"Well Water" (Jarrell) **41**:189
"Well, What Are You Going to Do?" (Wright) **36**:359
"Welland River" (Morris) **55**:301-2
"The Well-Beloved" (Hardy) **8**:91
"Welle der Nacht" (Benn) **35**:7, 27, 28, 36
"Wellfleet: The House" (Wilbur) **51**:326
"The Wellspring" (Olds) **22**:338
The Wellspring (Olds) **22**:330, 338-39
"A Well-to-Do Invalid" (Jarrell) **41**:172
"Welsh Incident" (Graves) **6**:143, 150
"The Welsh Marches" (Housman) **2**:159, 179
Welsh Retrospective (Abse) **41**:32-3
"Weltwehe" (Stramm) **50**:173, 175-76, 207, 214
"wer they angels i didnt know" (Bissett) **14**:34
"Werben" (Stramm) **50**:166-68, 189, 194
"We're at the Graveyard" (Ondaatje) **28**:327, 331, 334
"We're Extremely Fortunate" (Szymborska)
See "Wielkie to szczeście"
"We're few" (Pasternak) **6**:252
"We're Not Learnen to Be Paper Boys (for the young brothas who sell Muhammad Speaks)" (Sanchez) **9**:229
"The Wereman" (Atwood) **8**:36
"The Werewolf" (Marie de France)
See "Bisclavret"
Das Werk (Stramm) **50**:181-85, 198-99, 201-2, 204-9
"Wersja wydarzeń" (Szymborska) **44**:308
"An Werther" (Goethe) **5**:250-51
"Werttod" (Stramm) **50**:207
Wessex Poems, and Other Verses (Hardy) **8**:114, 123
"The West" (Housman) **2**:167, 191, 199
"West" (MacNeice) **61**:113
"West" (Oppen) **35**:286, 341
"West and Away the Wheels of Darkness Roll" (Housman) **2**:162
West Indies, Ltd.: Poemas (Guillén) **23**:98-99, 106-107, 114, 133, 137-39
"The West Main Book Store chickens" (Piercy) **29**:315
"The West Wind" (Bryant) **20**:4, 40
"West Wind" (Wright) **14**:342, 354
"Westering" (Heaney) **18**:203
The Western Approaches: Poems, 1973-1975 (Nemerov) **24**:275, 284-86, 303
The Western Borders (Howe) **54**:45
"Western Country" (Merwin) **45**:46
"Western Elegies" (Hope) **56**:292
"The Western Front" (Bridges) **28**:77, 81
"Western Landscape" (MacNeice) **61**:109, 111-12
"Western Purdah, Inc." (Stone) **53**:257
"Western Song" (Trakl)
See "Abendländisches Lied"
West-Östlicher Divan (Goethe) **5**:223, 225, 229, 239, 247, 250
"Westport" (Kinnell) **26**:238, 252
"West-Running Brook" (Frost) **1**:203, 218, 220; **39**:365
West-Running Brook (Frost) **1**:195, 203, 205, 213; **39**:232-33, 253
"Westward" (Clampitt) **19**:95-8
Westward (Clampitt) **19**:93, 95-6
"Wet Casements" (Ashbery) **26**:155
"We've Played Cowboys" (Alurista) **34**:16
"Wha Is That at My Bower-Door" (Burns) **6**:77
"The Whale, His Bulwark" (Walcott) **46**:274
"The Whaleboat Struck" (Ammons) **16**:39
"Whales Weep Not" (Lawrence) **54**:198-201
"The Wharf" (Merwin) **45**:48
what (Bissett) **14**:15
What a Kingdom It Was (Kinnell) **26**:236, 238-39, 252-53, 255, 257, 279, 289
"What a Pretty Net" (Viereck) **27**:259, 179
"What a woman!" (Niedecker) **42**:102, 123
"What Am I without Thee?" (Lanier) **50**:91
"What Are Cities For?" (Jeffers) **17**:132
"What Are Years" (Moore) **4**:243; **49**:100-101, 116, 134
What Are Years (Moore) **49**:98-99, 126
"What Came to Me" (Kenyon) **57**:14
"What Can I Do" (Carver) **54**:12
"What can I Tell My Bones?" (Roethke) **15**:264, 274
"What Can You Do?" (Stone) **53**:229-30, 234
"What Clings like the Odor of a Goat" (Ignatow) **34**:304
"What Declaration" (Jordan) **38**:119
"What Did?" (Silverstein) **49**:311, 344
"What Did You Buy" (Wylie) **23**:330
"What Do I Care" (Teasdale) **31**:323, 359, 379
"What Does Mr. Cogito Think About Hell" (Herbert)
See "Co robia nasi unmarli"
"What Does the Bobwhite Mean?" (Wright) **36**:312
"What Does the King of the Jungle Truly Do?" (Wright) **36**:313
"What else is hell, but losse of blisfull heauen?" (Raleigh) **31**:201
"What, For Us, My Heart . . ." (Rimbaud)
See "Ou'est-ce pour nous, mon coeur . . ."
"What God Is" (Herrick) **9**:94, 141
"What God Is Like to Him I Serve?" (Bradstreet) **10**:34
"What goes up" (Piercy) **29**:315, 317-19, 322
"What Happened" (Duncan) **2**:103
"What Happened Here Before" (Snyder) **21**:298, 325
What Happened When the Hopi Hit New York (Rose) **13**:239
"What Has Happpened to These Working Hands?" (Hogan) **35**:257
"What Have I Learned" (Snyder) **21**:318
"What He Thought" (McHugh) **61**:201
What I Love (Elytis) **21**:131
"What I Saw" (Herbert) **50**:13-14
"What I Should Have Said" (Harjo) **27**:56
"What is Blind" (McHugh) **61**:196
"What Is Called Thinking" (Graham) **59**:151
"What is it, Dear?" (Patmore) **59**:248
"What Is Left to Say" (Mueller) **33**:191
"What is Life?" (Clare) **23**:40
"What is Most Hoped and/or Most Feared: The Judgement" (Piercy) **29**:326
"What Is Said to the Poet About Flowers" (Rimbaud)
See "Ce qu'on dit au poète à propos de fleurs"
"What It Cost" (Forché) **10**:166
"Lo What It is to Love" (Wyatt) **27**:317, 346
"What It's Like" (Kenyon) **57**:44
"What Language Did" (Boland) **58**:50
"What Lips My Lips Have Kissed" (Millay) **6**:225
"What Love Intended" (Boland) **58**:49
"What may it availl me" (Wyatt) **27**:324
"What menythe this?" (Wyatt) **27**:316, 322, 324
What Moon Drove Me to This? (Harjo) **27**:64
"What Must" (MacLeish) **47**:191, 196, 210
"What no perdy" (Wyatt) **27**:304, 328
"What of the Night?" (Kunitz) **19**:175-76, 178
"What One Says to the Poet on the Subject of Flowers" (Rimbaud)
See "Ce qu'on dit au poète à propos de fleurs"
"What Our Dead Do" (Herbert)
See "Co robia nasi unmarli"
"What Ovid Taught Me" (Walker) **30**:350
what poetiks (Bissett) **14**:15
"What rage is this?" (Wyatt) **27**:304
"What Shall I Give My Children?" (Brooks) **7**:76
"What? So Soon" (Hughes) **1**:266; **53**:159-60
"What Stillness Round a God" (Rilke) **2**:275
"What the Bird with the Human Head Knew" (Sexton) **2**:372
"What the Child Sees" (Corso) **33**:50
"What the Dead Man Said About Himself" (Parra)
See "What the Deceased Had to Say About Himself"
"What the Deceased Had to Say About Himself" (Parra) **39**:278, 308, 311
"What the Doctor Said" (Carver) **54**:15, 19
"What the Dog Perhaps Hears" (Mueller) **33**:180
"What the Earth Asked Me" (Wright) **36**:337
"What the End Is For" (Graham) **59**:130, 133-34, 156-57

"What the Fox Agreed to Do" (Bly) **39**:67
"What the Light Was Like" (Clampitt) **19**:102
What the Light Was Like (Clampitt) **19**:85-7, 90-1, 93
"What the Moon Saw" (Lindsay) **23**:268
"What the Old Women See" (McHugh) **61**:191
"What the Rattlesnake Said" (Lindsay) **23**:286
"What the Women Said" (Bogan) **12**:110
"What Then?" (Yeats) **20**:342
"What This Mode of Motion Said" (Ammons) **16**:20
"What vaileth trouth" (Wyatt) **27**:366
"What 'vaileth truth" (Wyatt)
See "What vaileth trouth"
"What Virginia Said" (Tomlinson) **17**:353
"What Voice at Moth-Hour" (Warren) **37**:337
"What Was the Promise that Smiled from the Maples at Evening" (Warren) **37**:348
"What was the Thought" (Warren) **37**:341
"What We Come To Know" (Ortiz) **17**:246
"what we dew if thrs anything" (Bissett) **14**:33
"What We Leave Behind" (Wagoner) **33**:363
"What We Lost" (Boland) **58**:12, 15, 48, 88, 92-93
"What We Take With Us" (Wagoner) **33**:363
"What Were They Like?" (Levertov) **11**:176
"What Why When How Who" (Pinsky) **27**:164
"What Will Remain" (Mahon) **60**:134
What Work Is (Levine) **22**:220-21, 227-28, 231-32
"What Would I Do White" (Jordan) **38**:127
"What Would Tennessee Williams Have Said" (Wakoski) **15**:368
"What Wourde is That" (Wyatt) **27**:314, 342
"What You Might Answer" (Hacker) **47**:98
"What You Need for Painting" (Carver) **54**:21
"What you say . . ." (Cage) **58**:220-22, 224
"Whatever Happened?" (Larkin) **21**:235-36
"Whatever You Now Are" (Warren) **37**:379
"Whatever You Say Say Nothing" (Heaney) **18**:189, 205
"Whatever You Wish, Lord" (Jiménez) **7**:184
"Whatif" (Silverstein) **49**:326, 339
"What's Good for the Soul Is Good for Sales" (Wilbur) **51**:245
"what's got away in my life" (Niedecker) **42**:107
"what's happening" (Alurista) **34**:34, 38
"WHATS HAPPNING OZONE CUM BACK WE STILL LOV YU" (Bissett) **14**:32
"What's Meant by Here" (Snyder) **21**:300
What's O'Clock (Lowell) **13**:66, 76, 84-5, 91, 93-4, 97-8
"What's Real and What's Not" (Baca) **41**:47
"what's so big about GREEN" (Birney) **52**:36, 43, 82, 101
What's So Big about Green? (Birney)
See "what's so big about GREEN"
"What's That" (Sexton) **2**:359
"What's the matter with her?" (Castro)
See "¿Qué tiene?"
"What's the Railroad to Me?" (Thoreau) **30**:236
"What's the Riddle . . ." (Jarrell) **41**:178, 180-81
"What's wrong with marriage?" (Niedecker) **42**:136
Whatsaid Serif: Song of the Andoumboulou: 16-35 (Mackey) **49**:51-61, 63-65, 67-69, 75-80
"Whe' Fe Do?" (McKay) **2**:222-23
"Wheat-in-the-Ear" (Lowell) **13**:96
"The Wheel" (Césaire) **25**:17
"The Wheel" (Hayden) **6**:194-95
The Wheel (Berry) **28**:16
"The Wheel of Being II" (Carruth) **10**:71
"The Wheel Revolves" (Rexroth) **20**:195
"The Wheeling Gospel Tabernacle" (Wright) **36**:376
"Wheesht, Wheesht, My Foolish Heart" (MacDiarmid) **9**:156, 160
"When" (Stone) **53**:259
"When a Boy..." (Corso) **33**:44
"When All My Five and Country Senses See" (Thomas) **2**:392; **52**:247
"When Black Is a Color Because It Follows a Grey Day" (Wakoski) **15**:348
"When Coldness Wraps This Suffering Clay" (Byron) **16**:89
"When de Co'n Pone's Hot" (Dunbar) **5**:117, 122
"When De Folks Is Gone" (Riley) **48**:340
"When de Saints Go Ma'ching Home" (Brown) **55**:102, 108, 110-11, 115, 152, 160, 175-76, 178
"When Death Came April Twelve 1945" (Sandburg) **2**:333; **41**:301-2
"When Ecstasy is Inconvenient" (Niedecker) **42**:98, 144-45
"When First" (Thomas) **53**:266
"When First I Saw" (Burns) **6**:78
"When from Afar" (Hölderlin) **4**:174, 178
"When God Lets My Body Be" (Cummings) **5**:99
"When Golda Meir Was in Africa" (Walker) **30**:343
"When Guilford Good" (Burns) **6**:78
"When Hair Falls Off and Eyes Blur and" (Cummings) **5**:105
"When He Would Have His Verses Read" (Herrick) **9**:87, 96, 102, 109, 139, 145
"When I Am Asked" (Mueller) **33**:197
"When I am Not With You" (Teasdale) **31**:335
"When I Banged My Head on the Door" (Amichai) **38**:41, 53-4
"When I Buy Pictures" (Moore) **4**:251, 266; **49**:96, 160
"When I Came from Colchis" (Merwin) **45**:9
"When I Come" (Francis) **34**:251
"When I consider how my light is spent" (Milton)
See "Sonnet 16 (On his blindness)"
"When I Die" (Brooks) **7**:68
"When I Die" (Giovanni) **19**:113
"When I Have Fears That I May Cease to Be" (Keats) **1**:314
"When I Nap" (Giovanni) **19**:112
"When I or Else" (Jordan) **38**:119-20
"When I Paint My Masterpiece" (Dylan) **37**:56
"When I Roved a Young Highlander" (Byron) **16**:86
"When I Set Out for Lyonesse" (Hardy) **8**:92, 112, 115
"When I Think About Myself" (Angelou) **32**:14, 28
"When I was a Child" (Amichai) **38**:22
"When I Was One-and-Twenty" (Housman) **2**:161, 192
"When I Was Young, the Whole Country Was Young" (Amichai) **38**:53
"When I Watch the Living Meet" (Housman) **2**:184
"When in Rome-Apologia" (Komunyakaa) **51**:18
"When in the Gloomiest of Capitals" (Akhmatova)
See "Kogda v mrachneyshey iz stolits"
"When Jemmy First Began to Love" (Behn)
See "Song to a Scotish Tune (When Jemmy First Began to Love)"
"When Like a Running Grave" (Thomas) **52**:243, 245
"When Like the Sun" (Hope) **56**:301, 306-7
"When Lilacs Last in the Dooryard Bloom'd" (Whitman) **3**:378, 382, 396-97, 410, 418-19, 422
"When Lilacs Last in the Dooryard Bloomed" (Whitman) **3**:378, 382, 396-97, 410, 418-19, 422
"When Love Becomes Words" (Jackson) **44**:8, 11, 43-4
"When Malindy Sings" (Dunbar) **5**:117, 119-21, 134, 146
"When Mrs. Martin's Booker T." (Brooks) **7**:67, 69
"When News Came of His Death" (Ignatow) **34**:310
"When on my night of life the Dawn shall break" (Brooke) **24**:72
"When Once the Twilight Locks No Longer" (Thomas) **2**:402; **52**:227, 237
When One Has Lived a Long Time Alone (Kinnell) **26**:285-87, 293
"When ragyng love" (Surrey) **59**:314-15, 330
"When Rain Whom Fear" (Cummings) **5**:105
"when raza?" (Alurista) **34**:5-6, 32, 38
"When Satan Fell" (Lawrence) **54**:250
"When Serpents bargain for the Right to Squirm" (Cummings) **5**:90, 107
"When She Comes Home Again" (Riley) **48**:290
"When She Wears Red" (Hughes)
See "When Sue Wears Red"
"When Sir Beelzebub" (Sitwell) **3**:303
"When Smoke Stood Up from Ludlow" (Housman) **2**:184
"When Sue Wears Red" (Hughes) **53**:84, 86, 91
"When Summer's End Is Nighing" (Housman) **2**:165, 181
"When the Armies Passed" (Hughes) **53**:149
"When the Dead Ask My Father about Me" (Olds) **22**:323, 326
"When the Dumb Speak" (Bly) **39**:13, 52
"When the Frost Is on the Punkin" (Riley) **48**:288, 314-15, 317-19, 331, 333-34, 340, 350
"When the Guelder Roses Bloom" (Carman) **34**:210, 216
"When the Horizon is Gone" (Merwin) **45**:79, 100-1
"When the Hulk of the World" (Curnow) **48**:45-46
"When the Lamp Is Shattered" (Shelley) **14**:177, 207
"When the Light Falls" (Kunitz) **19**:151, 155
"When the Night Comes Falling from the Sky" (Dylan) **37**:61
"When the Shy Star" (Joyce)
See "IV"
When the Skies Clear (Pasternak)
See *Kogda razglyaetsya*
"When the Tooth Cracks - Zing!" (Warren) **37**:313
"When the Trees Grow Bare on the High Hills" (Muir) **49**:263
"When the War Is Over" (Merwin) **45**:23
"When the Watchman Saw the Light" (Cavafy) **36**:39, 54, 86
"When the Wheel Does Not Move" (Bly) **39**:43
"When the Year Grows Old" (Millay) **61**:213, 222
"When the Yellowing Fields Billow" (Lermontov) **18**:281
"When They Come Alive" (Cavafy) **36**:107
"When They Have Lost" (Day Lewis) **11**:144
"When to my deadlie pleasure" (Sidney) **32**:235
"When Under the Icy Eaves" (Masters) **1**:328; **36**:174
"When Unto Nights of Autumn Do Complain" (Cummings) **5**:104
"When We All..." (Corso) **33**:50
"When We Two Walked" (Thomas) **53**:291
"When We with Sappho" (Rexroth) **20**:203, 216
"When We'll Worship Jesus" (Baraka) **4**:29, 39
"When Will I Return" (Brutus) **24**:116
"When Windesor walles" (Surrey) **59**:352-53, 355-57
"When Winter Fringes Every Bough" (Thoreau) **30**:214, 220, 293
"When Wishes Were Fishes" (Stone) **53**:227
"When You Are Old" (Yeats) **20**:355
"When You Go Away" (Merwin) **45**:9, 18
"When You Have the Earth in Mouthful" (Alurista) **34**:24, 28, 41
"When You Lie Down, the Sea Stands Up" (Swenson) **14**:261
"When you pass the doorway" (Ní Chuilleanáin) **34**:382

"When You Speak to Me" (Gallagher) **9**:36
"When You've Forgotten Sunday" (Brooks) **7**:53, 68
"Whenever I Go There" (Merwin) **45**:22, 42, 49
"Where Are the War Poets?" (Day Lewis) **11**:131
"Where Are We?" (Shvarts) **50**:132
Where Are We Eating? and What Are We Eating? (Cage) **58**:196, 199
"Where Are You From?" (Yevtushenko) **40**:349
"Where can I go, now it's January?" (Mandelstam)
See "Kuda mne det'sia v etom Ianvare?"
"Where Dream Begins" (Sarton) **39**:324
"Where Gleaming Fields of Haze" (Thoreau) **30**:182
"Where He's Staying Now" (Meredith) **28**:179
"Where Is the Moralizer, Your Mother?" (Chin) **40**:9
"Where Is the Real Non-Resistant?" (Lindsay) **23**:281
"Where Knock Is Open Wide" (Roethke) **15**:251, 261, 272, 275-76, 278, 298, 300
"Where nothing grows" (Piercy) **29**:313
"Where Nothing Is Hidden" (Ignatow) **34**:278
"Where, O Where?" (Wylie) **23**:324
"Where Once the Waters of Your Face" (Thomas) **52**:245, 335
"Where Potchikoo Goes Next" (Erdrich) **52**:193
"Where Purples Now the Fig" (Warren) **37**:302
"Where shall I have at myn owne will" (Wyatt) **27**:332, 351-352
"Where Shall the Lover Rest" (Scott) **13**:304
"Where, Tall Girl, Is Your Gypsy Babe" (Akhmatova)
See "Gde, vysokaya, tvoy tsyganyonok"
"Where the Groceries Went" (Carver) **54**:12
"Where the Guelder Roses Bloom" (Carman)
See "When the Guelder Roses Bloom"
"Where the Hayfields Were" (MacLeish) **47**:164-65
"Where the Hell Would Chopin Be?" (Bukowski) **18**:4
"Where the light" (Ungaretti)
See "Dove la luce"
"Where the Peacock Cried" (Sarton) **39**:321
"Where the Picnic Was" (Hardy) **8**:136
"Where the Rainbow Ends" (Lowell) **3**:200, 207
Where the Sidewalk Ends (Silverstein) **49**:306, 309-13, 319, 322-24, 327, 331, 335-36, 338-41, 343, 346-49
"Where the Slow Fig's Purple Sloth" (Warren) **37**:301, 361
"Where the Tennis Court Was" (Montale)
See "Dov'era il tennis"
"Where the Track Vanishes" (Kinnell) **26**:238, 252
Where the Wolves Drink (Tzara) **27**:250
"Where There's a Will There's Velleity" (Nash) **21**:265
"Where They So Fondly Go" (Bukowski) **18**:5
Where Water Comes Together with Other Water (Carver) **54**:20-21
"Where We Live Now" (Levine) **22**:214
"Where We Must Look for Help" (Bly) **39**:42, 82, 85
"Where's Agnes?" (Browning) **6**:24
"Where's the Poker" (Smart) **13**:348
"Wherever Home Is" (Wright) **36**:348
"Whether on Ida's Shady Brow" (Blake) **12**:11
"Whether or Not" (Lawrence) **54**:161
"Which Ane" (Riley) **48**:340
"Which, Being Interpreted, Is as May Be, or, Otherwise" (Lowell) **13**:91
"Whiffs of the Ohio River at Cincinnati" (Sandburg) **41**:288
"While Blooming Youth" (Prior) **52**:205
"While Drawing in a Churchyard" (Hardy) **8**:120-21
"While I Live" (Ignatow) **34**:305
"While Love Is Unfashionable" (Walker) **30**:340, 365
"While Sitting in the Tuileries and Facing the Slanting Sun" (Swenson) **14**:261, 285
"While Someone Telephones" (Bishop) **34**:89
"While the Record Plays" (Illyés) **16**:249, 251
"While We Were Arguing" (Kenyon) **57**:6
"whilst waiting for" (Bissett) **14**:32
"Whimper of Sympathy" (Meredith) **60**:289
"The Whip" (Robinson) **35**:368
"Whip the World" (MacDiarmid) **9**:187
Whipperginny (Graves) **6**:127-28, 131
"The Whipping" (Hayden) **6**:194-96
"Whirligigs" (Kenyon) **57**:45
"The Whirlwind" (Lindsay) **23**:281
"Whiskers, A Philosophical Ode" (Pushkin) **10**:407
Whisper to the Earth (Ignatow) **34**:324-25
"whispered to lucifer" (Clifton) **17**:30
Whispering to Fool the Wind (Ríos) **57**:311-12, 319, 322-25
"Whispers of Heavenly Death" (Whitman) **3**:378
"Whistle and I'll Come tae Ye, My Lad" (Burns) **6**:59
"The Whistle Cockade" (Burns) **6**:82
"Whistle of the 3 A.M." (Warren) **37**:379
Whistle or Hoot (Ignatow) **34**:270
Whistles and Whistling (Ishikawa)
See *Yobuko to kuchibue*
"A Whistling Girl" (Parker) **28**:353, 362
"Whistling Sam" (Dunbar) **5**:122, 146
"Whit Monday" (MacNeice) **61**:140, 144
White (Paz)
See *Blanco*
"White and Green" (Lowell) **13**:60, 69
"White and Violet" (Jiménez) **7**:183
"White April" (Reese) **29**:339
White April (Reese) **29**:335-336, 339, 348, 351
"White Arrow" (Toomer) **7**:336
"White Ash" (Sandburg) **41**:357
"The White Birds" (Yeats) **51**:149
White Buildings (Crane) **3**:81, 84, 87, 90
"The White City" (McKay) **2**:211
"White Coat, Purple Coat" (Abse) **41**:33
White Coat, Purple Coat (Abse) **41**:32
"The white doe" (Borges)
See "La cierva blanca"
The White Doe of Rylstone; or, The Fate of the Nortons (Wordsworth) **4**:394, 402, 407
"White Dwarf" (Ammons) **16**:45
"White Dwarfs" (Ondaatje) **28**:314, 317, 327, 331-32, 334, 336, 338
White Flock (Akhmatova)
See *Belaya staya*
"White Goat, White Ram" (Merwin) **45**:32
"The White Gull" (Carman) **34**:203-04
"White Hawthorn in the West of Ireland" (Boland) **58**:58
"White Horses" (Kipling) **3**:183
"The White House" (McKay) **2**:210, 221, 229
"White Kimono" (Doty) **53**:60
"White Lady" (Clifton) **17**:28
"The White Lilies" (Glück) **16**:170-71
"The White Man's Burden" (Kipling) **3**:192
"White Men Can't Drum" (Alexie) **53**:15
"White Night" (Wright) **14**:372
"The White Ones" (Hughes) **53**:85
"The White Porch" (Song) **21**:331-32, 334, 338, 340-41, 350
"White road, old road" (Castro)
See "Camino blanco, viejo camino"
"White Shoulders" (Sandburg) **2**:303
"White Shroud" (Ginsberg) **4**:86, 90
White Shroud, Poems 1980-1985 (Ginsberg) **4**:86-7, 89-90; **47**:30
"The White Snake" (Sexton) **2**:365
"The White Thought" (Smith) **12**:292, 341, 354
"The White Troops" (Brooks) **7**:73
"The White Van" (Tomlinson) **17**:333
"White Wines" (Stein) **18**:341
"The White Witch" (Johnson) **24**:127, 142, 161, 166
"Whitehaired Girl" (MacLeish) **47**:206
White-Haired Lover (Shapiro) **25**:316, 321-22
The White-Haired Revolver (Breton)
See *Le revolver á cheveux blancs*
"The White-Tailed Hornet" (Frost) **1**:221
"The Whitsun Weddings" (Larkin) **21**:228, 230, 238-39, 255
The Whitsun Weddings (Larkin) **21**:224, 227-28, 230, 233, 235, 240, 244, 253, 255, 259
"Whitsunday" (Herbert) **4**:118
"Who" (Kenyon) **57**:13, 15, 40
"Who Among You Knows the Essence of Garlic" (Hongo) **23**:196-97
Who Are We Now? (Ferlinghetti) **1**:187-88
"Who are We? Somos Aztlán" (Alurista) **34**:45
"Who But the Lord" (Hughes) **1**:241
"Who Cares, Long as It's B-Flat" (Carruth) **10**:85
"Who ever comes to shroud me do not harme" (Donne)
See "The Funerall"
"Who has not walked" (Bridges) **28**:83
"Who Hath Herd" (Wyatt) **27**:317
Who Is the Real Non-Resistant? (Lindsay) **23**:282
"Who Is the Widow's Muse?" (Stone) **53**:258
Who Is the Widow's Muse? (Stone) **53**:220, 224
"Who is this Who Howls and Mutters?" (Smith) **12**:313, 336
"Who Killed James Joyce?" (Kavanagh) **33**:81, 86
"Who Knows" (Dunbar) **5**:130
"Who Know's If the Moon's" (Cummings) **5**:88
"Who list his wealth and ease retain" (Wyatt) **27**:368
Who Look at Me (Jordan) **38**:111, 114
"Who Made Paul Bunyan" (Sandburg) **2**:327
"Who on Earth" (Kinnell) **26**:287
"Who Ordered the Broiled Face?" (Silverstein) **49**:323
"Who Said It Was Simple" (Lorde) **12**:153, 157
Who Shall Be the Sun? (Wagoner) **33**:353
"Who Shall Doubt" (Oppen) **35**:299
"Who Shot Eugenie?" (Smith) **12**:333
"Who so list to hount, I knowe where is an hynde" (Wyatt) **27**:300-01, 303, 309-10, 323, 329-30, 342-44, 348, 356, 358, 360, 363, 367
"Who so list to hounte" (Wyatt)
See "Who so list to hount, I knowe where is an hynde"
"Who Wakes" (Sarton) **39**:358
"Who Was Mary Shelley?" (Niedecker) **42**:134
"Who Watches from the Dark Porch" (Graham) **59**:135
Who Will Know Us?: New Poems (Soto) **28**:402
"Who Will Remember the Rememberers" (Amichai) **38**:56
"Who Will Survive America?/Few Americans/Very Few Negroes/No Crackers at All" (Baraka) **4**:14, 19
"Whoever Finds a Horseshoe" (Mandelstam)
See "Nashedshij podkovu"
"Whoever You Are: A Letter" (Mueller) **33**:174
"A Whole Day Without Debate" (Char) **56**:146
"The Whole Question" (Warren) **37**:376, 378
"Wholesome" (Meredith) **28**:208
"Whom I Write For" (Aleixandre)
See "¿Para quién escribo?"
"Whooping Cranes" (Erdrich) **52**:183, 191
"Whorls" (Meredith) **28**:198
"Who's Out" (Stone) **53**:228
"Whose" (Boland) **58**:38
"Whoso List" (Wyatt)
See "Who so list to hount, I knowe where is an hynde"
"Whoso list to hount, I knowe where is an hind" (Wyatt)
See "Who so list to hount, I knowe where is an hynde"

"Whoso List To Hunt" (Wyatt)
See "Who so list to hount, I knowe where is an hynde"
"Whuchulls" (MacDiarmid) **9**:197-98
"Why" (Carman) **34**:210
"Why Animals Stay Away" (Ríos) **57**:323
"Why Boy Came to Lonely Place" (Warren) **37**:378
"Why Can't I Live Forever?" (Viereck) **27**:258, 276
"Why Come Ye Nat to Courte?" (Skelton)
See *Why Come Ye Nat to Courte?*
Why Come Ye Nat to Courte? (Skelton) **25**:336-37, 342, 348, 350, 356, 374, 379
Why Come Ye Not to Court? (Skelton)
See *Why Come Ye Nat to Courte?*
"why dew magazines lie" (Bissett) **14**:32
"Why Did I Laugh Tonight" (Keats) **1**:279, 305
"'Why Did I Sketch'" (Hardy) **8**:137
"Why do I" (Smith) **12**:337
"Why Do You Sing My Bird" (Ekeloef) **23**:87
"Why East Wind Chills" (Thomas) **2**:379
"Why I Am a Liberal" (Browning) **2**:66
"Why I Am Not a Painter" (O'Hara) **45**:121, 127, 176, 190
"Why I Voted the Socialist Ticket" (Lindsay) **23**:267, 282, 296
"Why I write not of love" (Jonson)
See *The Forest I*
"Why Indian Men Fall in Love with White Women" (Alexie) **53**:24
"Why Kid Yourself" (Stone) **53**:252
"Why So Pale and Wan, Fond Lover" (Suckling) **30**:119, 122, 132-34, 156-59
"Why Some Look Up to Planets and Heroes" (Merton) **10**:334
"Why Sorrow" (Kavanagh) **33**:144, 150, 152, 160
"Why the Classics" (Herbert) **50**:30
"Why We Die" (Swenson) **14**:247
"Why We Tell Stories" (Mueller) **33**:198
"Why You Climbed Up" (Warren) **37**:377
"Whys/Wise" (Baraka) **4**:40
"Wichita Vortex Sutra" (Ginsberg) **4**:50, 53, 66, 82, 85; **47**:48
"The Wide Mouth" (Snyder) **21**:292
"Widok gór ze stepów Kozłowa" (Mickiewicz) **38**:221-22
"The Widow" (Merwin) **45**:20, 22, 25, 34, 43
"Widow" (Mueller) **33**:190
"The Widow at Windsor" (Kipling) **3**:161, 186-87, 191
"Widow La Rue" (Masters) **1**:330, 333
"The Widow o' Windsor" (Kipling)
See "The Widow at Windsor"
"The Widow of Windsor" (Kipling)
See "The Widow at Windsor"
"Widower's Tango" (Neruda) **4**:306
"Widowhood or the Home-Coming of Lady Ross" (Smith) **12**:351-52
"Widows" (Baudelaire)
See "Les veuves"
"The Widow's Lament in Springtime" (Williams) **7**:345, 353, 360, 363
"Widows of the Living and of the Dead" (Castro)
See "As viudas d'os vivos e as viudas d'os mortos"
"The Widow's Party" (Kipling) **3**:160
"The Widow's Resolution" (Smart) **13**:347
"Wie wenn am Feiertage ..." (Hölderlin) **4**:162, 165-66, 169
Wielka liczba (Szymborska) **44**:268-69
"Wielkie to szczeście" (Szymborska) **44**:309
Wiersze zebrane (Herbert) **50**:5-6, 8
"A Wife at Daybreak I Shall Be" (Dickinson) **1**:93
"Wife of Bath's Prologue" (Chaucer)
See "Prologue to the Wife of Bath's Tale"
The Wife of Bath!s Prologue (Chaucer) **58**:230-31, 233-37, 246-49, 252, 256-60, 262, 265-67, 270-75, 277-84, 288-89, 292, 294-95, 299, 305-7, 310, 313, 321-28, 334-37, 339-40, 342-45, 348, 350, 353-55, 362-63, 365, 367-69
"Wife of Bath's Tale" (Chaucer) **19**:13, 15, 29, 33, 60, 63
The Wife of Bath!s Tale (Chaucer) **58**:230-40, 242-44, 250, 252, 255-63, 270, 272-76, 280-84, 299-300, 302-3, 307, 321, 324-28, 334, 336, 342, 354-55, 362-63
"Wife to Husband" (Rossetti) **7**:267
"Wife's Tale" (Chaucer)
See "Wife of Bath's Tale"
"The Wild" (Berry) **28**:14, 37
"Wild Blessings" (Clifton) **17**:29
"Wild Boys of the Road" (Ashbery) **26**:163
"Wild Cherries" (Zagajewski) **27**:389
Wild Cherry (Reese) **29**:335-336, 339, 347-348, 351
"The Wild Common" (Lawrence) **54**:163, 165-66, 175, 179, 188, 191, 221, 231-36
Wild Dreams of a New Beginning (Ferlinghetti) **1**:188
"Wild Flower" (Tagore)
See "Banaphul"
"WILD FLOWRS ABOVE TH TREE LINE" (Bissett) **14**:20
Wild Garden (Carman) **34**:205, 211
"Wild Gardens Overlooked by Night Lights" (Guest) **55**:185
"Wild Grapes" (Frost) **1**:215; **39**:235
The Wild Iris (Glück) **16**:168, 170-71
"Wild Iron" (Curnow) **48**:11, 29
"Wild Life Cameo, Early Morn" (Ferlinghetti) **1**:182-83, 188
"Wild Oats" (Larkin) **21**:230, 234, 244, 247
"The Wild Old Wicked Man" (MacLeish) **47**:214
"A Wild Old Wicked Man" (Yeats) **51**:152
The Wild Old Wicked Man (MacLeish) **47**:193, 197, 214
"Wild Orchard" (Williams) **7**:345
A Wild Patience Has Taken Me This Far: Poems, 1978-1981 (Rich) **5**:385, 389
"Wild Peaches" (Wylie) **23**:301, 305, 314, 329, 333-34
"Wild Plums" (Erdrich) **52**:188
The Wild Rose Flowers (Akhmatova)
See *Shipovnik tsevetyot*
"The Wild Sky" (Rich) **5**:362
"The Wild Swans at Coole" (Yeats) **20**:303, 327; **51**:334
The Wild Swans at Coole (Yeats) **20**:304, 310-11, 314, 326, 328
"Wild Water" (Swenson) **14**:283
"Wild Without Love" (McGuckian) **27**:83
Wild Writing of the Recent Past (Shvarts)
See *Dikopis' poslednego vremeni*
"The Wildebeest" (Bly) **39**:117
"The Wilderness" (Merwin) **45**:23
"Wilderness" (Niedecker) **42**:101
"The Wilderness" (Robinson) **1**:459
"Wilderness" (Sandburg) **2**:302; **41**:240, 251, 270, 296, 303
"The Wildflower" (Williams) **7**:382, 386
"Wildflower Plain" (Wright) **14**:342
"Wildwest" (MacLeish) **47**:146, 189
"Wilfred Owen's Photographs" (Hughes) **7**:133
"Wilia" (Mickiewicz) **38**:149
"Wilk i owieczka" (Herbert) **50**:9
"The Will" (Donne) **1**:126
"The Will" (Merrill) **28**:272
"Will" (Walker) **30**:339
"Will Be" (Pasternak) **6**:252
"Will Boyden Lectures" (Masters) **1**:343
"Will Not Come Back" (Lowell) **3**:226-27
"Will Out of Kindness of Their Hearts a Few Philosophers Tell Me" (Cummings) **5**:93
"Will They Cry When You're Gone, You Bet" (Baraka) **4**:18
The Will to Change: Poems, 1968-1970 (Rich) **5**:365-67, 370-72, 383, 387-89, 391, 399
"Will Waterproof's Lyrical Monologue" (Tennyson) **6**:360
"Will You Perhaps Consent to Be" (Schwartz) **8**:305
"Willful Homing" (Frost) **1**:197
William Blake's Prophetic Writing (Blake) **12**:25
"William Bond" (Blake) **12**:35, 43
William Carlos Williams: Selected Poems (Williams) **7**:357
"William H. Herndon" (Masters) **1**:334; **36**:221
"William Leachman" (Riley) **48**:284
"William Marion Reedy" (Masters) **1**:325, 333, 342
"William McKinley" (Riley) **48**:326
"Williams' influence: Some Social Aspects" (Ignatow) **34**:205
"Willie" (Angelou) **32**:2
"Willie" (Brooks)
See "To Keorapetse Kgositsile (Willie)"
"Willie Brew'd a Peck o' Maut" (Burns) **6**:76
"Willie Wastle" (Burns) **6**:78, 81; **40**:97
"The Willing Mistress" (Behn) **13**:4, 14-16, 18-20, 29
"Willingly" (Gallagher) **9**:58
Willingly (Gallagher) **9**:42-4, 50-1, 53, 56, 58-62
"Willkommen und Abschied" (Goethe) **5**:247, 251
"Willow Waves" (Wang Wei) **18**:364
"Willows" (Stryk) **27**:212-13
"Willowwood" (Rossetti) **44**:166, 203, 238, 256-7, 260, 622
"Willowwood (II)" (Rossetti) **44**:257
"Willowwood (III)" (Rossetti) **44**:257
"Willowwood (IV)" (Rossetti) **44**:257
"Willy Lyons" (Wright) **36**:324, 328, 345, 366, 400
"Wilt thou forgive" (Donne)
See "A Hymne to God the Father"
"Wind" (Carver) **54**:13, 22
"The Wind" (Dafydd ap Gwilym) **56**:215
"Wind" (Hughes) **7**:118, 165
"A Wind" (Kavanagh) **33**:74
"The Wind" (Morris) **55**:238, 279-80, 282
"Wind" (Soto) **28**:370, 373-75, 377-78, 384
"The Wind" (Teasdale) **31**:356
"Wind" (Tomlinson) **17**:328
The Wind among the Reeds (Yeats) **20**:303, 330; **51**:101
"Wind and Flags" (Montale)
See "Vento e bandiere"
"Wind and Gibbon" (Warren) **37**:379
"Wind and Glacier Voices" (Ortiz) **17**:232
"Wind and Mist" (Thomas) **53**:285-88, 290, 292, 341
"Wind and Silver" (Lowell) **13**:94-5
"The Wind and Stream" (Bryant) **20**:15
"The Wind and the Rain" (Frost) **1**:196
"Wind and Water and Stone" (Paz) **48**:190
"Wind and Wave" (Patmore) **59**:208, 212, 271
"Wind at Night" (Zagajewski) **27**:394
"The Wind at Penistone" (Davie) **29**:94, 108, 110
"The Wind Bloweth Where It Listeth" (Cullen) **20**:58
"Wind Chimes in a Temple Ruin" (Birney) **52**:25
"The Wind Coming Down From" (Ammons) **16**:5
"Wind from All Compass Points" (Paz)
See "Viento entero"
"Wind in Florence" (Brodsky) **9**:14
"The Wind in the Dooryard" (Walcott) **46**:237, 240, 289
"Wind in the Hemlock" (Teasdale) **31**:360
"Wind is the wall of the year" (Piercy) **29**:314
"Wind on the Crescent" (Lewis)
See "Vento sulla mezzaluna"
"The Wind Over the Chimney" (Longfellow) **30**:103, 110

"The Wind, the Clock, the We" (Jackson) **44**:73-4, 78
"Wind through St. John's" (Birney) **52**:57-58
"Windfalls" (Kenyon) **57**:45
"A Windflower" (Carman) **34**:210, 216
"Windflower Leaf" (Sandburg) **41**:255
"The Windhover" (Hopkins) **15**:125, 127, 132-33, 144, 160, 168, 169, 171
"Windigo" (Erdrich) **52**:192
The Winding Stair (Yeats) **20**:307, 311, 326-28, 330, 333, 335
The Winding Stair, and Other Poems (Yeats) **51**:73, 94
"Winding Up" (Walcott) **46**:240
"The Windmill" (Bridges) **28**:67
"Window" (Hass) **16**:222
"The Window" (MacNeice) **61**:115, 117, 160
"The Window" (Mahon) **60**:134, 155, 187
"A Window" (Merton)
See "The Blessed Virgin Mary Compared to a Window"
"The Window" (Muir) **49**:197, 245, 247, 252
"Window" (Pinsky) **27**:157, 164, 172
"Window" (Sandburg) **41**:228, 234
"The Window" (Sarton) **39**:321, 358
"A Window Frame" (Curnow) **48**:13, 33
Window in My Face (Dalton) **36**:120
"The Window of the Tobacco Shop" (Cavafy) **36**:74, 81
"The window-pane" (Char)
See "Le carreau"
"Window Poems" (Berry) **28**:5, 39
"The Windows" (Apollinaire) **7**:36
"The Windows" (Herbert) **4**:119, 131
"Windows" (Jarrell) **41**:170
"The Windows" (Mallarmé)
See "Les fenêtres"
"Windows in th Straw" (Bissett) **14**:8
"The Windows of the Tobacco Shop" (Cavafy) **36**:53, 56, 57, 73, 112
"Windows to the Fifth Season" (Elytis) **21**:118
"Windröschen" (Celan) **10**:122
"Winds" (Auden) **1**:23
"The Winds" (Williams) **7**:369
Winds (Perse)
See *Vents*
"The Winds of Downhill" (Oppen) **35**:332
"The Winds of Orisha" (Lorde) **12**:155
"The Wind's Prophecy" (Hardy) **8**:115-17
"The Wind's Way" (Swinburne) **24**:327
"Wind-Song" (Lanier) **50**:101
Windsor Forest (Pope) **26**:315, 319, 321
"The Windy City" (Sandburg) **2**:306, 308, 314; **41**:249, 252, 271, 319-20, 329, 346
"The Wine" (Ashbery) **26**:135-136
"The Wine" (Teasdale) **31**:360
"Wine and Time" (Seifert)
See "Víno a čas"
Wine from These Grapes (Millay) **6**:214, 217, 232
"The Wine Menagerie" (Crane) **3**:81, 90
"Wine: Passages 12" (Duncan) **2**:108
Wine Press (Mistral)
See *Lagar*
"Winged Abyss" (Mackey) **49**:5-6
"The Winged Horse" (Belloc) **24**:11
"Wingfoot Lake" (Dove) **6**:112
"The Wings" (Doty) **53**:53, 63
"Wings" (Hughes) **7**:132, 137
"Wings of a Dove" (Brathwaite) **56**:75-76, 83
"Wings of a God" (Levertov) **11**:176
"Winkel im Wald" (Trakl) **20**:232
"Der Winkel von Hahrdt" (Hölderlin) **4**:148
"The Winning Argument" (Piercy) **29**:309
"Winning His Way" (Stein) **18**:312-14, 316
"The Winnowers" (Bridges) **28**:66-7
"Wino" (Hughes) **7**:123, 132, 137
"Winston Prairie" (Masters) **1**:343
"Winter" (Celan) **10**:129
"Winter" (Clare) **23**:44-5
"Winter" (Darío)
See "Invernal"
"Winter" (Giovanni) **19**:116
"Winter" (Hagiwara) **18**:168
"Winter" (Milosz) **8**:210
"Winter" (Morris) **55**:325
"Winter" (Patmore) **59**:227, 271
"Winter" (Wright) **14**:376
"Winter, a Dirge" (Burns) **6**:52
"A Winter and Spring Scene" (Thoreau) **30**:220
"Winter Boredom" (Carducci)
See "Tedio Invernale"
"A Winter Daybreak above Vence" (Wright) **36**:360, 370
"Winter Dreams" (Goodison) **36**:158
"Winter Encounters" (Tomlinson) **17**:333, 344, 352
"The Winter Evening" (Cowper) **40**:45, 48-9, 52, 77, 140, 142-43
"Winter Evening" (Pushkin)
See "Zimniy Vecher"
"Winter Event" (Cassian) **17**:5
"Winter Festivities" (Pasternak) **6**:266
"Winter Fields" (Clare) **23**:45
"Winter Garden" (Neruda)
See "Jardín de invierno"
"Winter Grace" (Sarton) **39**:323
"Winter Holding off the Coast of North America" (Momaday) **25**:219
"A Winter Holiday" (Carman) **34**:211
"Winter Honey" (Jordan) **38**:44
"Winter in Dunbarton" (Lowell) **3**:218-19
"Winter in the City" (Mickiewicz)
See "Zima miejska"
Winter Insomnia (Carver) **54**:3
"Winter Lambs" (Kenyon) **57**:11, 25, 42
Winter Love (H. D.) **5**:299-300
"Winter Mask" (Tate) **50**:241, 244, 254, 256-57, 259, 295, 336
"Winter Moon" (Hughes) **53**:85
"Winter Morning's Walk" (Cowper) **40**:46, 49, 61, 132
"Winter: My Secret" (Rossetti) **7**:281
"Winter Night" (Sarton) **39**:360
"Winter Night Song" (Teasdale) **31**:365
Winter Numbers (Hacker) **47**:105-8, 112, 115-17
"Winter on the River" (Meredith) **28**:198
"A Winter Piece" (Bryant) **20**:18, 35-7, 39
"Winter Piece" (Tomlinson) **17**:325
"A Winter Poem For Tony Weinberger Written on the Occasion of Feeling Very Happy" (Wakoski) **15**:331
"Winter Privacy Poems at the Shack" (Bly) **39**:115
"A Winter Scene" (Bryant) **20**:15
"The Winter Sea" (Tate) **50**:246
The Winter Sea (Tate) **50**:239-41, 252, 257, 259
"A Winter Ship" (Plath) **1**:389; **37**:176, 180
"Winter Sleep" (Wylie) **23**:309, 329, 332
"Winter Sleepers" (Atwood) **8**:12
"Winter Song" (Owen) **19**:336, 343
"Winter Spring" (Wilbur) **51**:266
"Winter Stars" (Teasdale) **31**:360
Winter Station (Yevtushenko)
See "Zima Station"
"Winter Swan" (Bogan) **12**:95, 106, 122
A Winter Talent and Other Poems (Davie) **29**:93-96, 100, 106, 108-09, 112, 117
Winter Trees (Plath) **1**:396; **37**:184
"The Winter Twilight Glowing Black and Gold" (Schwartz) **8**:295
"Winter Verse for His Sister" (Meredith) **28**:213
"A Winter Visit" (Abse) **41**:21
"The Winter Walk at Noon" (Cowper) **40**:49-51, 132
Winter Words: Various Moods and Metres (Hardy) **8**:89, 96, 124
"Wintergreen Ridge" (Niedecker) **42**:94, 96, 100, 104, 106-7, 109, 132
"Wintering" (Plath) **1**:410, 412-13; **37**:239-41
Wintering Out (Heaney) **18**:188, 192-95, 199, 202-5, 209-11, 215, 238, 241, 252
Wintermarchen (Heine)
See *Deutschland: Ein Wintermärchen*
"Winternacht" (Trakl) **20**:229
"Winterreise" (Hope) **56**:277
"A Winter's Day" (Dunbar) **5**:126
"Winter's gone the summer breezes" (Clare) **23**:23
"The Winter's Night" (Merton) **10**:340, 351
"The Winter's Tale" (Jarrell) **41**:169
"A Winter!s Tale" (Lawrence) **54**:168
"A Winter's Tale" (Plath) **37**:254
"A Winter's Tale" (Thomas) **2**:382, 385, 402; **52**:218-19, 221-22, 224, 272, 279, 286, 312, 314, 322
Winter's Tale (Heine)
See *Deutschland: Ein Wintermärchen*
"Wintry" (Gozzano)
See "A Wintry Scene"
"A Wintry Scene" (Gozzano) **10**:177-78, 180
"Wintry Sky" (Pasternak) **6**:250
"Wir gerieten in ein Mohnfeld" (Benn) **35**:30, 68
"Wir ziehn einen großen Bogen" (Benn) **35**:70
"Wirers" (Sassoon) **12**:267, 285
"Wires" (Tsvetaeva)
See "Provoda"
"Wiretapping" (Montale)
See "Intercettazione telefonica"
"Das wirkliche Messer" (Enzensberger) **28**:159-61, 165
"Wisdom" (Corso) **33**:44
"Wisdom" (Parker) **28**:362
"Wisdom" (Teasdale) **31**:323, 333, 340, 355, 364, 389
"Wisdom" (Yeats) **51**:86
Wisdom (Verlaine)
See *Sagesse*
"Wisdom Cometh with the Years" (Cullen) **20**:52, 62
"The Wisdom of the Eld" (Meredith) **60**:261
"The Wise" (Cullen) **20**:54-55
"The Wise Delights of Love" (Patmore)
See "Deliciæ Sapientiæ de Amore"
"Wise Men" (Hughes) **53**:115
"The Wise Men from the East" (Carman) **34**:208
"Wise Men in Their Bad Hours" (Jeffers) **17**:129
"The Wise Woman" (Teasdale) **31**:389
"The Wish" (Lermontov) **18**:277, 295
"Wish" (Merwin) **45**:22
"Wish" (Mistral)
See "Voto"
"Wish: Metamorphosis to Hearldic Emblem" (Atwood) **8**:32, 39
"The Wish to be Generous" (Berry) **28**:43
"The Wish to Escape into Inner Space" (Swenson) **14**:250
"Wishbones" (Wakoski) **15**:332
"Wishes" (Wright) **14**:355
"wishes for sons" (Clifton) **17**:29, 36
"The Wishing Box" (Plath) **37**:209
"The Wishing Tree" (Heaney) **18**:229, 232
"Wistful" (Sandburg) **41**:298
"Witch Burning" (Plath) **1**:394
"Witch Doctor" (Hayden) **6**:186, 196
"Witch Hazel" (Reese) **29**:330
"The Witch of Atlas" (Shelley) **14**:174, 193, 196, 198
"The Witch of Coös" (Frost) **1**:197, 209, 220; **39**:235
"The Witch of Grafton" (Frost) **39**:235
"Witches are Flying" (Shapiro) **25**:316
"Witching" (Boland) **58**:37, 44-45
"The Witch's Life" (Sexton) **2**:373
"Witch-Woman" (Lowell) **13**:61, 64
"With a Guitar, to Jane" (Shelley) **14**:177, 189
"With a Rose to Brunhilde" (Lindsay) **23**:286
"With All Deliberate Speed" (Madhubuti) **5**:346
"With Eyes At The Back of Our Heads" (Levertov) **11**:168

With Eyes at the Back of Our Heads (Levertov) **11**:168, 205
"With Frontier Strength Ye Stand Your Ground" (Thoreau) **30**:194, 215, 217, 219, 267, 293
"With Garments Flowing" (Clare) **23**:23
"With Happiness Stretch's across the Hills" (Blake) **12**:36
"With Her Lips Only" (Graves) **6**:151
"with liberty and justice for all" (Alurista) **34**:37
"With me" (Guillén) **35**:219
"With Mercy for the Greedy" (Sexton) **2**:346, 348, 351, 370
"With Muted Strings" (Verlaine) **32**:371
"With Official Lu Hsiang Passing Hermit Hsiu-Chung's Bower" (Wang Wei) **18**:358
"With Pale Women in Maryland" (Bly) **39**:14, 103
"With Pencil" (Guillén) **35**:211
"With Rue My Heart Is Laden" (Housman) **2**:180, 184, 192
"With Scindia to Delhi" (Kipling) **3**:182
"With Seed the Sowers Scatter" (Housman) **2**:180
"With the Caribou" (Kumin) **15**:212, 223
"With the Dog at Sunrise" (Kenyon) **57**:27, 35
"With the Door Open" (Ignatow) **34**:276, 305, 327
"With the Gift of a Feather" (Wright) **36**:396
"With the Gift of an Alabaster Tortoise" (Wright) **36**:378
"With the Persuader" (Meredith) **60**:263
"With the Shell of a Hermit Crab" (Wright) **36**:312
"With the World in My Bloodstream" (Merton) **10**:345
"With Trumpets and Zithers" (Milosz)
See "Natrabach i na cytrze"
"With Vengeance Like a Tiger Crawls" (Bukowski) **18**:5
"Within the Circuit of the Plodding Life" (Thoreau) **30**:234, 267
"Within These Caverned Days" (Birney) **52**:8
"Without" (Snyder) **21**:297
"Without a Counterpart" (Gunn) **26**:218
"Without a Nest" (Castro)
See "Sin nido"
"Without Benefit of Declaration" (Hughes) **1**:252; **53**:111
"Without Ceremony" (Hardy) **8**:134-35
"Without End" (Zagajewski) **27**:383
"Without Faith" (Aleixandre) **15**:5
"Without Fear" (Ignatow) **34**:313
"Witness" (Boland) **58**:40
"The Witness" (Tomlinson) **17**:344
A Witness Tree (Frost) **1**:196-97, 203, 205-06; **39**:234
"The Witnesses" (Auden) **1**:22
"The Wits" (Suckling) **30**:148-53, 155
"Wives in the Sere" (Hardy) **8**:90
"The Wizard in Words" (Moore) **49**:161
"Wizards" (Noyes) **27**:135
"Wm. Brazier" (Graves) **6**:143
"Wodwo" (Hughes) **7**:127-28, 155
Wodwo (Hughes) **7**:120-23, 133-34, 136-38, 140-42, 150, 157-60, 163, 171-72
"Woefully arrayed" (Skelton) **25**:330
"Wojna" (Herbert) **50**:5, 7, 9
Wołanie do Yeti (Szymborska) **44**:268, 280, 292, 294, 298, 311, 318
"Wolf" (Mandelstam) **14**:149
"The Wolf and the Sheep" (Herbert) **50**:8
"The Wolf Screamed" (Rimbaud)
See "Le Loup criait . . ."
"Wolfe Tone" (Heaney) **18**:228, 232
"The Wolves" (Tate) **50**:231, 259, 303, 306-7
"Wolves Defended against the Lambs" (Enzensberger) **28**:147, 165
"The Woman" (Carruth) **10**:71
"Woman" (Jarrell) **41**:142, 168-69, 171, 173, 179, 217
"The Woman" (Levertov) **11**:213-14
"A Woman" (Mistral)
See "Una mujer"
"A Woman" (Pinsky) **27**:176
"A Woman Alone" (Levertov) **11**:210
"The Woman and the Sea" (Yevtushenko) **40**:345
"Woman and Tree" (Graves) **6**:149
"The Woman at the Washington Zoo" (Jarrell) **41**:171, 185, 188-89, 191, 194-95, 205, 210
The Woman at the Washington Zoo (Jarrell) **41**:146, 159, 215
"The Woman Changes Her Skin" (Boland) **58**:45, 98
"A Woman Dead in Her Forties" (Rich) **5**:379-80, 394
"The Woman Hanging from the Thirteenth Floor" (Harjo) **27**:64-5
"A Woman Homer Sung" (Yeats) **20**:329
"Woman, I Got the Blues" (Komunyakaa) **51**:33
"A Woman in Heat Wiping Herself" (Olds) **22**:316
"Woman in Kitchen" (Boland) **58**:45
"Woman in Orchard" (Wright) **14**:373
"The Woman in the Ordinary" (Piercy) **29**:309
"Woman of Strength" (Tagore)
See "Sabala"
"The Woman on the Stair" (MacLeish) **47**:190
"A Woman Painted on a Leaf" (Boland) **58**:50, 96
"Woman Poem" (Giovanni) **19**:108
"A Woman Resurrected" (Gozzano) **10**:177-78
"A Woman Speaks" (Lorde) **12**:160
"The Woman Speaks to the Man Who Has Employed Her Son" (Goodison) **36**:154
"Woman to Child" (Wright) **14**:337, 341, 349, 352, 360, 362, 364
"Woman to Man" (Wright) **14**:333, 336-39, 349, 358-60, 363
Woman to Man (Wright) **14**:334, 336-38, 341, 345-47, 349, 352, 358, 363, 365-66, 369
"The Woman Turns Herself into a Fish" (Boland) **58**:45
"A Woman Waits for Me" (Whitman) **3**:372, 387
"The Woman Who Lived in a Crate" (Stryk) **27**:187
"The Woman Who Raised Goats" (Gallagher) **9**:35-6, 59
"A Woman Whose Movements Are a River's" (Paz)
See "Una mujer de movimientos de rio"
"Woman with Girdle" (Sexton) **2**:346, 350
"Woman With the Blue-Ringed Bowl" (McGuckian) **27**:102
"Woman Work" (Angelou) **32**:29
"A Woman Young and Old" (Yeats) **20**:327
"The Womanhood" (Brooks) **7**:54
"Woman's Constancy" (Donne) **1**:125
"Woman's Song" (Wright) **14**:349, 352, 364
"Women" (Bogan) **12**:101
"The Women" (Boland) **58**:7, 15, 80, 92-94
"Women" (Parra) **39**:289
"Women" (Rich) **5**:370
"Women" (Swenson) **14**:279
"The Women" (Walker) **30**:338, 341, 367
"Women" (Yevtushenko) **40**:345
The Women and the Men (Giovanni) **19**:114, 124, 128, 130, 137
"The Women at Point Sur" (Jeffers) **17**:130
The Women at Point Sur (Jeffers)
See *The Women of Point Sur*
"Women Laughing" (Stone) **53**:230
"Women like You" (Ondaatje) **28**:314
"Women Looking for Lice" (Rimbaud)
See "Les Chercheuses de poux"
"The Women of Dan Dance With Swords in Their Hands to Mark the Time When They Were Warriors" (Lorde) **12**:159-60
The Women of Point Sur (Jeffers) **17**:107, 109-11, 116, 124, 135, 144-4
"The Women Speaking" (Hogan) **35**:247
"Women We Never See Again" (Bly) **39**:47, 86
"the women you are accustomed to" (Clifton) **17**:30
"Women's Tug of War at Lough Arrow" (Gallagher) **9**:37
"Wonder" (Hughes) **53**:162
"The Wonder Castle" (Illyés) **16**:234, 250
"The Wonder Woman" (Giovanni) **19**:107, 110, 112
"The Wonderful Musician" (Sexton) **2**:365
"Wonderment" (Szymborska)
See "Zdumienie"
"Wonga Vine" (Wright) **14**:348
"Woo/Dove" (Brathwaite) **56**:89
"A Wood" (Wilbur) **51**:283
"The Wood Dove at Sandy Spring" (MacLeish) **47**:192
"The Wood Pewee" (Francis) **34**:261, 265
"Wood Song" (Teasdale) **31**:325, 340, 356
"The Wood Thrush" (Carman) **34**:229
"Wood-Cock" (Yevtushenko) **40**:347
"Woodcutting on Lost Mountain" (Gallagher) **9**:60
"The Wooden Bird" (Herbert) **50**:4
"Wooden Die" (Herbert)
See "Drewniana kostka"
The Wooden Pegasus (Sitwell) **3**:301-02
"Wooden Steeds" (Verlaine)
See "Chevaux de bois"
"Woodland Peace" (Meredith) **60**:289
"The Woodlot" (Clampitt) **19**:89
"The Woodman" (Clare) **23**:13
"The Woodman" (Patmore) **59**:218
"Woodman and Echo" (Meredith) **60**:299
"The Woodman's Daughter" (Patmore) **59**:218, 225, 240, 258
"Woodnotes" (Emerson) **18**:79, 87-88, 99, 102-3, 108-10
"A Woodpath" (Carman) **34**:208
"The Woodpile" (Frost) **1**:220, 222, 226, 228; **39**:253
"Woodrow Wilson (February, 1924)" (Jeffers) **17**:107
"Woods" (Berry) **28**:43
"The Woods" (Erdrich) **52**:174-75, 192
"Woods" (MacNeice) **61**:118, 126
"The Woods" (Mahon) **60**:145-47
"The Woods of Westermain" (Meredith) **60**:246, 256-57, 262, 287-88, 290-91, 2967-97, 327, 320-30, 333, 339
"The Woodspurge" (Rossetti) **44**:173, 224-29, 231-32
"Woof of the Sun, Ethereal Gauze" (Thoreau) **30**:194, 208, 235, 257, 267, 287, 294
"Wooing" (Bridges) **28**:63, 86
"The Wooing of Hallbiorn" (Morris) **55**:340
"The Wooing of Swanhild" (Morris) **55**:306-8, 331
The Wooing of Swanhild (Morris) **55**:309
"Wooing the Muse" (Hughes) **53**:96-97
"The Word" (Brathwaite) **56**:32
"A Word" (Chesterton) **28**:100
"The Word" (Smith) **12**:354
"The Word" (Thomas) **53**:313, 319, 328
The Word as Archipelago (Char)
See *La Parole en archipel*
"The Word at St. Kavin's" (Carman) **34**:225
"Word Basket Woman" (Snyder) **21**:326
"The Word 'Beautiful'" (Swenson) **14**:250
"The Word Crys Out" (Ammons) **16**:25
"The Word in the Beginning" (Carman) **34**:223
Word Making Man: A Poem for Nicolas Guillen (Brathwaite) **56**:55, 90
"A Word on the Quick and Modern Poem-Makers" (Bukowski) **18**:5
Word over All (Day Lewis) **11**:144, 148
"A Word to the Wise" (Patmore) **59**:204
"Words" (Gunn) **26**:212
"Words" (Levine) **22**:219
"The Words" (Montale)
See "Le parole"
"Words" (Plath) **1**:409; **37**:258
"Words" (Reese) **29**:336

"Words" (Sexton) **2**:372-73
"Words" (Stone) **53**:246, 248
"Words" (Thomas) **53**:271, 330, 332
"Words" (Thumboo) **30**:300, 334
"Words" (Yeats) **20**:329, 331
"Words Above a Narrow Entrance" (Wagoner) **33**:333, 372
"Words for a Wall-Painting" (Shapiro) **25**:304
"Words for Hart Crane" (Lowell) **3**:219, 222
"Words for Maria" (Merrill) **28**:224, 231, 264, 277
"Words for Music Perhaps" (Yeats) **20**:326-29, 331, 333
Words for Music Perhaps, and Other Poems (Yeats) **20**:328, 334
"Words for the Hour" (Harper) **21**:190
"Words for the Wind" (Roethke) **15**:263
Words for the Wind: The Collected Verse of Theodore Roethke (Roethke) **15**:257, 262-64, 267, 282, 284, 286, 288, 309
"Words from a Totem Animal" (Merwin) **45**:34-5
"Words heard, by accident, over the phone" (Plath) **37**:262
Words in Stone (Bonnefoy)
See *Pierre écrite*
Words in th Fire (Bissett) **14**:13-14
"Words in the Mourning Time" (Hayden) **6**:197-98
Words in the Mourning Time (Hayden) **6**:179, 181-83, 193, 195
"Words Like Freedom" (Hughes) **53**:150
"Words of Comfort" (Ammons) **16**:25, 43
"Words of Comfort to the Scratched on a Mirror" (Parker) **28**:361
"The Words of the Poet" (Aleixandre) **15**:6
"The Words of the Preacher" (Kunitz) **19**:149, 170
"Words on a Windy Day" (Stryk) **27**:212
"The Words on Magnet" (Seifert) **47**:332
"Words Rising" (Bly) **39**:67
"Words, Roses, Stars" (Wright) **14**:378-79
"Words to Frank O'Hara's Angel" (O'Hara) **45**:120
"Work" (Hass) **16**:249
"Work" (Komunyakaa) **51**:35
"the work" (Schwerner) **42**:196
"Work Gangs" (Sandburg) **2**:304, 308
"Work in Progress" (MacDiarmid) **9**:199
Work Is Tiresome (Pavese)
See *Lavorare stanca*
"The Work of Creation" (Lawrence) **54**:250
"The Work of Happiness" (Sarton) **29**:332
"Work Song and Blues" (Brathwaite) **56**:38, 82
"Work Wearies" (Pavese)
See "Lavorare stanca"
Work Wearies (Pavese)
See *Lavorare stanca*
"A Worker Reads History" (MacDiarmid) **9**:181
"Workers" (Rimbaud)
See "Ouvriers"
"Worker's Hands" (Mistral)
See "Manos de obreros"
"Worker's Song" (Angelou) **32**:30
"Working Against Time" (Wagoner) **33**:332
"Working for a Living" (Ignatow) **34**:305
"A working man appeared in the street" (Niedecker) **42**:151
"Working on the '58 Willys Pickup" (Snyder) **21**:300
"A Working Party" (Sassoon) **12**:257, 261-62, 277-78, 284
"The Workingman's Drink" (Baudelaire) **1**:47
"The Workman" (Storni)
See "El obrero"
Works (Longfellow) **30**:68
Works (Philips) **40**:280
Works (Pope) **26**:359-60
Works (Sidney)
See "Complete Works of Philip Sidney"
Works, 1735—Poems on Several Occasions (Swift) **9**:256
The Works and Days of Lavinia, a Nun of the Order of the Circumcision of the Heart (Shvarts)
See *Trudy i dni Lavinii monakhini iz ordena obrezaniia serdtsa*
Works II (Pope) **26**:360
The Works of Aphra Behn (Behn) **13**:16, 18
The Works of George Herbert (Herbert) **4**:107
The Works of Horace, Translated into Verse (Smart) **13**:361-62
The Works of Mirabai (Mirabai) **48**:150-69
The Works of Sir John Suckling (Suckling) **30**:120, 125
The Works of William Blake, Poetic, Symbolic, and Critical (Blake) **12**:51
"The World" (Herbert) **4**:100
"The World" (Milosz) **8**:187, 192, 194, 207, 209
"The World" (Rossetti) **7**:277
"The World" (Smith) **12**:328
"The World" (Tagore)
See "Vasundhara"
World Alone (Aleixandre)
See *Mundo a solas*
"The World and I" (Jackson) **44**:86, 104
"The World and the Child" (Merrill) **28**:249
"The World and the Child" (Wright) **14**:352
"The World and the Quietist" (Arnold) **5**:38, 49
"A World in Crystal" (Illyés) **16**:249
"The World Is a Beautiful Place" (Ferlinghetti) **1**:180, 182-83
"The World Is a Wedding" (Schwartz) **8**:303
"A World Is Everyone" (Ekeloef) **23**:80
"The World Is Full of Remarkable Things" (Baraka) **4**:23-4
A World of Difference (McHugh) **61**:190, 200, 205
"The World of Fantasy the Buddha Saw" (Hagiwara) **18**:178
The World of Gwendolyn Brooks (Brooks) **7**:64, 66, 105
"The World of Seven Wells" (Storni)
See "El mundo de siete pozos"
World of the Buddha (Stryk) **27**:181, 194, 198
"The World Outside" (Levertov) **11**:168, 193
"World Soul" (Bely) **11**:24
"The World State" (Chesterton) **28**:100
"A World without Objects Is a Sensible Emptiness" (Wilbur) **51**:188, 206-8, 211, 237, 296, 303, 314, 323
"World World" (Oppen) **35**:317
Worldly Hopes (Ammons) **16**:45-6
"Worlds" (Masters) **1**:333
"Worlds Back of Worlds" (Masters) **1**:343
"The World's Desire" (Masters) **1**:333
"World's End" (Ashbery) **26**:166
"The World's Wonders" (Jeffers) **17**:141
"The World-Soul" (Emerson) **18**:86
Worleys (Reese) **29**:339
"The Worm Turns" (Lawrence) **54**:229
"The Worms of History" (Graves) **6**:137, 142, 144
"The Wormwood Star" (Milosz) **8**:201, 204
"Worsening Situation" (Ashbery) **26**:124
"Worship" (Kavanagh) **33**:120
"Worship" (Ransom) **61**:267
"The Worst Of It" (Sassoon) **12**:248
"Das Wort" (Benn) **35**:35, 58, 61, 62, 63
"Ein Wort" (Benn) **35**:34
"Wortermelon Time" (Riley) **48**:286, 333-34
Worthy It Is (Elytis)
See *The Axion Esti*
"Would Jacob Wrestle with a Flabby Angel?" (Viereck) **27**:286
"Woulda-Coulda-Shoulda" (Silverstein) **49**:343
"The Wound" (Glück) **16**:124, 138, 154
"The Wound" (Gunn) **26**:199, 206-207
"The Wound" (Hardy) **8**:93
"The Wound" (Soto) **28**:375
The Wound (Hughes) **7**:155
"The Wounded Wilderness of Morris Graves" (Ferlinghetti) **1**:165
Woven Stone (Ortiz) **17**:244
"The Wraith" (Roethke) **15**:256, 272
"Wrapt in my carelesse cloke" (Surrey) **59**:315
"The Wrath of Samson" (Vigny)
See "La colère de Samson"
"A Wreath" (Herbert) **4**:127, 130
"Wreath" (Illyés) **16**:250
"Wreath for the Warm-Eyed" (Merrill) **28**:234
"A Wreath for Tom Moore's Statue" (Kavanagh) **33**:75, 86, 90, 94, 121, 156
"The Wreck of the Deutschland" (Hopkins) **15**:129, 131-32, 134, 136-38, 144, 146, 151-52, 156, 170, 172-73
"The Wreck of the Hesperus" (Longfellow) **30**:12, 21, 26, 39, 47-8, 64, 99, 103
"The Wreck of the Nordling" (Corso) **33**:43
"The Wreck of the Thresher" (Meredith) **28**:178, 181, 193-94, 200, 206, 213, 215
The Wreck of the Thresher (Meredith) **28**:175, 178, 191-95, 209, 211, 213, 215
"Wreckage" (Momaday) **25**:221
"The Wrestler's Heart" (Soto) **28**:394, 399
"The Wretched One" (Marie de France)
See "Le Chaitivel"
"Writ in Horace Greeley Square" (Corso) **33**:34-5, 49
"Writ on the Eve of My 32nd Birthday" (Corso) **33**:16, 35
"Writ on the Steps of Puerto Rican Harlem" (Corso) **33**:34
"Write It Down" (Ekeloef) **23**:86
"The Writer" (Wilbur) **51**:236, 250-52, 278, 308-9
"Writer Waiting" (Silverstein) **49**:340
"The Writhing Imperfect Earth" (Lindsay) **23**:281
"Writin' Back to the Home-Folks" (Riley) **48**:302
"Writing" (Cage) **58**:218
"Writing" (Nemerov) **24**:259
"Writing" (Paz)
See "Escritura"
"Writing Again" (Bly) **39**:53, 86
Writing for the Fifth Time through Finnegans Wake (Cage) **58**:189
Writing for the First Time through Finnegans Wake (Cage)
See *Writing through 'Finnegans Wake'*
Writing for the Second Time through Finnegans Wake (Cage) **58**:192, 205
Writing for the Third Time through Finnegans Wake (Cage) **58**:189, 191
"Writing in a Time of Violence" (Boland) **58**:18, 51, 59, 61
"Writing in the Dark" (Levertov) **11**:199
"Writing My Feelings" (Li Po) **29**:179
"The Writing on the Image" (Morris) **55**:262, 329
"Writing on the Sand" (Rossetti) **44**:173
Writing through 'Finnegans Wake' (Cage) **58**:183, 189-90
"Writing to Aaron" (Levertov) **11**:208
Writing Writing (Duncan) **2**:106
Writings and Drawings (Dylan) **37**:59
Writings and Interviews (Ungaretti)
See *Scritti e interventi*
"The Writings Depart" (Breton) **15**:73
Writings through Finnegans Wake (Cage) **58**:183-84, 189, 195
Writings to an Unfinished Accompaniment (Merwin) **45**:30, 33-5, 40, 48-9, 63, 71-2, 75, 77, 79, 83-4, 86, 92, 97
"Written aboard a Boat on the Day of Little Cold Food" (Tu Fu) **9**:320
"Written after Long Rains at My Villa by Wang Stream" (Wang Wei) **18**:392
"Written at Mule Hollow, Utah" (Bly) **39**:65
"Written by Dr. Swift on His Own Deafness" (Swift) **9**:295
"Written in a Hotel" (Szymborska) **44**:300
"Written in a Lady's Ivory Table-book, 1698" (Swift) **9**:251, 295

"Written in Emerson's Essays" (Arnold) **5**:38, 49
"Written in the Mountains in Early Autumn" (Wang Wei) **18**:392
"Written in the Sand at Water Island and Remembered" (O'Hara) **45**:172
"Written on a Big Cheap Postcard from Verona" (Wright) **36**:356, 377
"Written on The Door" (Perse) **23**:229
Written on Water (Tomlinson) **17**:321-23, 327, 333
Written Stone (Bonnefoy)
See *Pierre écrite*
"The Wrong Kind of Insurance" (Ashbery) **26**:134
"Wrong Number" (Bukowski) **18**:4
"Wszelki wypadek" (Szymborska) **44**:270
Wszelki wypadek (Szymborska) **44**:268
"Wunder" (Stramm) **50**:168-69, 189, 199, 201, 208, 217-18
"die würgengel" (Enzensberger) **28**:134
"Wyatt resteth here" (Surrey) **59**:317, 320-21, 326-27, 329-30, 340
Wybór wierszy (Herbert) **50**:39-40
"Wyeth's Milk Cans" (Wilbur) **51**:301, 324, 327
X/Self (Brathwaite) **56**:34-35, 54, 61-62, 71, 92-94
X: Writings, '79-'82 (Cage) **58**:202, 204-6, 208
Xaipe: Seventy-One Poems (Cummings) **5**:82-3, 86, 107-08
"Xango" (Brathwaite) **56**:61, 71
"XCI" (Carman) **34**:228
"XCIII" (Carman) **34**:211
Xenia (Martial) **10**:230
Xenia (Montale) **13**:132-33, 135-36, 138, 165, 167
"Xenia I" (Montale) **13**:144
"Xenia II" (Montale) **13**:144
"Xenion" (Montale) **13**:133-34
"Xenion" No. 7 (Montale) **13**:134
Xénophiles (Breton) **15**:53-4
"XL" (Carman) **34**:224
"XLV" (Carman) **34**:234
"XLVII" (Carman) **34**:209
"Xoanon" (Ekeloef) **23**:67
"X-Ray Photograph" (Hope) **56**:266, 285-86, 294
"XV" (Carman) **34**:211
"XVI" (Shapiro) **25**:285
"XVIII" (Carman) **34**:234
"XXIII" (Carman) **34**:211, 227-28
"XXXII" (Carman) **34**:224
"XXXIV" (Carman) **34**:211, 224
Y and X (Olson) **19**:318
"Y Bardd a'r Brawd Llwyd" (Dafydd ap Gwilym) **56**:211-12
"Y Cariad a Wrthodwyd" (Dafydd ap Gwilym) **56**:246
"Y Cwt Gwyddau" (Dafydd ap Gwilym) **56**:247
"Y Cyffylog" (Dafydd ap Gwilym) **56**:230, 254
"Y Deildy" (Dafydd ap Gwilym) **56**:233, 247, 254-55
"Y Ffenestr" (Dafydd ap Gwilym) **56**:225, 227-30, 233
"Y Gwayw" (Dafydd ap Gwilym) **56**:"The Spear"
"Y la cabeza comenzó a arder" (Storni) **33**:270, 282;
Y Otros poemas (Guillén) **35**:188, 189, 227, 229, 230, 231, 232, 234
"Y Rhew" (Dafydd ap Gwilym) **56**:225, 227, 229-30, 233
"Y Rhugl Groen" (Dafydd ap Gwilym) **56**:247
"Y Wawr" (Dafydd ap Gwilym) **56**:232
"Ya que para despedirme" (Juana Inés de la Cruz) **24**:180
Yabloko (Yevtushenko) **40**:343
"Yacht for Sale" (MacLeish) **47**:143
"The Yachts" (Williams) **7**:360, 368
"Yad elohim ba'olam" (Amichai) **38**:5
The Yaddo Letter (Mahon) **60**:203, 205
"Yadwigha, on a Red Couch, Among Lilies; A Sestina for the Douanier" (Plath) **37**:188-89
"Yalluh Hammer" (Walker) **20**:273, 275-76, 286, 292
"Yam" (Merrill) **28**:259
"Yama no ugoku hi" (Yosano Akiko) **11**:321
"Yamanote Sen" (Hongo) **23**:197
"Yardley Oak" (Cowper) **40**:122
"Los yaruros" (Cardenal) **22**:132
Ya—sibirskoy porody (Yevtushenko) **40**:364
"Yauvan-svapna" (Tagore) **8**:407
"Yawm mawlidi" (Gibran) **9**:78
"Ye Are Na Mary Morison" (Burns) **6**:99
"Ye Goatherd Gods" (Sidney)
See "Yee Gote-heard Gods"
"Ye Know My Herte" (Wyatt) **27**:314-15
"Ye old mule" (Wyatt) **27**:362
"yeah man?" (Bukowski) **18**:14
"The Year" (Patmore) **59**:240
"The Year" (Sandburg) **41**:296
"The Year 1812" (Davie) **29**:109
"The Year 1905" (Pasternak)
See "Devyatsat pyaty god"
"Year at Mudstraw" (Forché) **10**:133
A Year from Monday: New Lectures and Writings (Cage) **58**:182, 194-95, 199, 204, 219
"The Year of 1812" (Mickiewicz) **38**:186
"The Year of Mourning" (Jeffers) **17**:141
"The Year of the Double Spring" (Swenson) **14**:267, 275
"The Years" (Aleixandre) **15**:4
"The Years After" (Quintana) **36**:272
The Years as Catches (Duncan) **2**:104, 109
"The Year's Awakening" (Hardy) **8**:105
"Year's End" (Borges) **32**:139
"Year's End" (Hacker) **47**:104
"Year's End" (Wilbur) **51**:188, 212-13, 257-58, 261
"The Years Go By" (Niedecker) **42**:99
"Years of Indiscretion" (Ashbery) **26**:115, 124
"The Year!s Sheddings" (Meredith) **60**:299
"A Year's Spinning" (Browning) **6**:32
"A Year's Windfalls" (Rossetti) **7**:262
"Yeats in Civil War" (Boland) **58**:42
"Yee Bow" (Masters) **1**:327; **36**:168
"Yee Gote-heard Gods" (Sidney) **32**:245, 260, 303
Yehuda Amichai: A Life of Poetry 1948-1994 (Amichai) **38**:54
"Yell'ham Wood's Story" (Hardy) **8**:91
The Yellow Book (Mahon) **60**:230, 235-36
The Yellow Heart (Neruda)
See *El corazón amarillo*
The Yellow House on the Corner (Dove) **6**:104-09, 116, 118, 122
"Yellow Light" (Hongo) **23**:203
Yellow Light (Hongo) **23**:195, 197, 202-204
"Yellow Ribbons, Baghdad 1991" (Rose) **13**:241
"Yellow Vestment" (Kavanagh) **33**:96
"The Yellow Violet" (Bryant) **20**:4, 35, 40
"Yellowhammer's Nest" (Clare) **23**:5
"Yes" (Ferlinghetti) **1**:187
"Yes" (Gallagher) **9**:64-5
"Yes and It's Hopeless" (Ginsberg) **4**:76, 85
"Yes and No" (Jackson) **44**:70
"Yes, But" (Wright) **36**:349
"Yes, I am lying in the earth, moving my lips" (Mandelstam)
See "Da, ia lezhu v zemle . . ."
"Yes, Think" (Stone) **53**:241, 252, 258
"Yesterday" (Aleixandre) **15**:5
"Yesterday" (Sitwell) **3**:293
"Yesterday" (Thumboo) **30**:328
"Yesterday I Was Called Nigger" (Guillén)
See "Ayer me dijeron negro"
Yesterday the Desert Reigning (Bonnefoy)
See *Hier régnant désert*
"Yesterdays" (Borges) **32**:58
"Yestreen I Had a Pint o' Wine" (Burns) **6**:75
"Yet Do I Marvel" (Cullen) **20**:63, 76
"the yeti poet returns to his village to tell his story" (Clifton) **17**:30
"Les yeux des pauvres" (Baudelaire) **1**:58
Les yeux fertiles (Éluard) **38**:68, 73, 86
"Yeux Glauques" (Pound) **4**:319
Yevgeny Onegin (Pushkin) **10**:357-62, 366, 368-69, 371, 374-83, 386, 391, 400-04, 406, 409
"The Yew-berry" (Patmore) **59**:239-40, 258, 271
"YgUDuh" (Cummings) **5**:98
"Ylang-Ylang" (McGuckian) **27**:83
"Yo" (Borges) **32**:58, 76
"Yo" (Fuertes) **27**:26, 49-50
"Yo cantar, cantar, canté" (Castro) **41**:107, 110-11
"Yo Jehová decreto" (Parra) **39**:275
"Yo no he nacido para odiar" (Castro) **41**:118
"Yo persigo una forma" (Darío) **15**:103-04, 119
"Yo soy aquél" (Darío) **15**:97
Yobuko to kuchibue (Ishikawa) **10**:211
"Yogisha" (Hagiwara) **18**:168, 179, 183
"Yonder Comes Sin" (Dylan) **37**:59
"Yonder See the Morning Blink" (Housman) **2**:179
"Yonec" (Marie de France) **22**:241-45, 258, 260-66, 269-72, 274-75, 299-300, 302-03
"York: In Memoriam W. H. Auden" (Brodsky) **9**:12
The York Road (Reese) **29**:339
"You" (Borges)
See "Tú"
"You" (Cummings) **5**:105
"You All Are State I Alone Am Moving" (Viereck) **27**:258
"You All Know the Story of the Other Woman" (Sexton) **2**:352-53
"You Also, Gaius Valerius Catullus" (MacLeish) **47**:197
"You and I Are Disappearing" (Komunyakaa) **51**:7, 10, 15, 17
"You and Me" (Tagore)
See "Tumi o ami"
"You, Andrew Marvell" (MacLeish) **47**:125-26, 130, 137, 143, 164, 167, 188, 196, 213, 253
"You Are" (Swenson) **14**:274, 283-84
"You are Gorgeous and I'm Coming" (O'Hara) **45**:150, 157
"You Are Happy" (Atwood) **8**:25, 27
You Are Happy (Atwood) **8**:20-4, 29, 31, 33, 41-2
"You Are Like the Realistic Product of an Idealistic Search for Gold at the Foot of the Rainbow" (Moore) **49**:118
"You are old Father William" (Carroll) **18**:49
"You Are Waiting" (Aleixandre) **15**:6
"You Asked About My Life; I Send You, Pei Di, These Lines" (Wang Wei) **18**:391
"You Be Like You" (Celan)
See "Du sei wei du"
"You Bet Travel Is Broadening" (Nash) **21**:273
"You Can Have It" (Levine) **22**:223
You Can't Get There from Here (Nash) **21**:274
"You Cramp My Style, Baby" (Cervantes) **35**:109
"You, Dr. Martin" (Sexton) **2**:359, 365
"You Drive in a Circle" (Hughes) **7**:137
You, Emperors, and Others: Poems, 1957-1960 (Warren) **37**:300, 332, 361, 373, 380-81
"You Frog!" (Hagiwara)
See "Kaeru yo"
"You Get What You Pay For" (Curnow) **48**:14, 20
"You Gote-heard Gods" (Sidney)
See "Yee Gote-heard Gods"
"You Gotta Have Your Tips on Fire" (Cruz) **37**:31
"You Had to Go to Funerals" (Walker) **30**:338
"You Have a Name" (Aleixandre) **15**:5
"you know" (Alurista)
See "tú sabes"

"you know that i would be untrue" (Alurista) **34**:39
"You may not see the Nazis" (Brutus) **24**:118
"You Old Mule" (Wyatt)
See "Ye old mule"
"You Shattered" (Ungaretti)
See "Tu ti spezzasti"
"You sit in the shade of the bare rocks" (Castro)
See "A la sombra te sientas de las desnudas rocas"
"You Speak No English" (Guillén)
See "Tú no sabe inglé"
"You Talk on Your Telephone; I Talk on Mine" (Gallagher) **9**:59
"You Think of the Sun That It" (Ammons) **16**:43
"You want me white" (Storni)
See "Tú me quieres blanca"
You WIll Know When You Get There: Poems, 1979-81 (Curnow) **48**:13, 15, 18, 20
"The Young" (Aleixandre) **15**:5
"Young" (Sexton) **2**:350
"Young Africans" (Brooks) **7**:65, 91, 93
"A Young Birch" (Frost) **1**:200
"The Young British Soldier" (Kipling) **3**:158
Young Cherry Trees Secured Against Hares (Breton) **15**:47
"A Young Child and His Pregnant Mother" (Schwartz) **8**:282, 302, 304
"The Young Cordwainer" (Graves) **6**:144
"The Young Dead Soldiers" (MacLeish) **47**:212, 259
"Young Don't Want to Be Born" (Wright) **36**:310
The Young Fate (Valéry)
See *La jeune parque*
"Young Gal's Blues" (Hughes) **53**:135-36, 140
"The Young Girl at the Ball" (Hope) **56**:301
"Young Girls" (Page) **12**:176
"The Young Good Man" (Wright) **36**:306-7
"Young Heroes" (Brooks) **7**:92-3, 105
"Young Household" (Rimbaud)
See "Jeune ménage"
"The Young Housewife" (Williams) **7**:348, 363, 378, 409
"The Young Lord and the Maiden" (Mickiewicz)
See "Panicz i dziewczyna"
"Young Love" (Marvell) **10**:303-04
"Young Love" (Williams) **7**:382, 410
"The Young Lovers" (Aleixandre) **15**:4-6
"The Young Mage" (Bogan) **12**:100
"Young Man with Letter" (Ashbery) **26**:125
"A Young Man's Exhortation" (Hardy) **8**:108
"Young Man's Song" (Yeats) **20**:331, 333
"Young Maples in Winter" (Graham) **59**:169, 177
"Young Mothers" (Olds) **22**:328
"Young Mothers I" (Olds) **22**:308
"The young night" (Borges)
See "La joven noche"
"A Young Pan's Prayer" (Carman) **34**:222
"A Young Poet, in His Twenty-Fourth Year" (Cavafy) **36**:68, 75, 76, 79
"The Young Princess" (Meredith) **60**:251, 256, 263
"Young Prostitute" (Hughes) **53**:79
"Young Singer" (Hughes) **1**:236, 246
"Young Sorrows" (Heine)
See "Junge Leiden"
"Young Soul" (Baraka) **4**:9
"Young Sycamore" (Williams) **7**:372-77
"The Young Warrior" (Johnson) **24**:127, 166
"Youngest Daughter" (Ransom) **61**:274
"The Youngest Daughter" (Song) **21**:331-32, 350
"Youngsters" (Parra)
See "Jóvenes"
"Your Birthday in the California Mountains" (Rexroth) **20**:204
"Your eyes" (Paz)
See "Tus ojos"
"Your Face on the Dog's Neck" (Sexton) **2**:363
"Your Flight" (Montale)
See "Il tuo volo"
"Your Last Drive" (Hardy) **8**:134
"Your Life and Death My Father" (Amichai) **38**:26, 28
"Your Name in Arezzo" (Wright) **36**:378-79
Your Native Land, Your Life (Rich) **5**:387-89
"Your Tired, Your Poor" (Mueller) **33**:189
"You're" (Plath) **1**:389-90; **37**:256
"You're a Big Girl Now" (Dylan) **37**:56
"You's Sweet to Yo' Mammy jes de Same" (Johnson) **24**:141
"Youth" (Akhmatova) **2**:8
"Youth" (Rimbaud)
See "Jeunesse"
"Youth" (Zukofsky) **11**:368
"Youth and Age" (Coleridge) **39**:175
"Youth and Calm" (Arnold) **5**:42, 51
"Youth in Heaven" (Harper) **21**:209
"The Youth of Man" (Arnold) **5**:19, 49
"The Youth of Nature" (Arnold) **5**:19, 42, 49, 51, 59
"Youthful Picnic Long Ago: Sad Ballad on Box" (Warren) **37**:379
"The Youth's Magic Horn" (Ashbery) **26**:162
"Yr Adfail" (Dafydd ap Gwilym) **56**:231-32
"Ys It Possyble" (Wyatt) **27**:317, 324
Ysopet (Marie de France) **22**:258-59
yu can eat it at th opening (Bissett) **14**:17
"yu know th creaturs ar ourselvs" (Bissett) **14**:34
"yu sing" (Bissett) **14**:30
"yu want th music" (Bissett) **14**:34
"Yube no kane" (Ishikawa) **10**:214
"Yūbe no umi" (Ishikawa) **10**:213, 215
"Yugel'skii baron" (Lermontov) **18**:288
"The Yule Guest" (Carman) **34**:202, 213
"Yule-Song: A Memory" (Braithwaite) **52**:106
"Yvonne" (Char) **56**:157
"Za Ki Tan Ke Parlay Lot" (Lorde) **12**:155
"Zagen" (Stramm) **50**:170, 178, 188, 209
Zahme Xenien (Goethe) **5**:223
"Zakinuv golovu i opustiv glaza" (Tsvetaeva) **14**:319, 322-23
"Zambesi and Ranee" (Swenson) **14**:277
Zapadno-Vostochnyi Veter (Shvarts) **50**:147
"Zaporogue" (Apollinaire) **7**:48
"Ein zärtlich jugendlicher Kummer" (Goethe) **5**:247
"Zarublennyi sviashchennik" (Shvarts) **50**:159
"Zauberspruch" (Celan) **10**:124-25
"Zaveshchanije" (Lermontov) **18**:303
"Zaydee" (Levine) **22**:223
"Zazhigaia svechu" (Shvarts) **50**:163
"Zdumienie" (Szymborska) **44**:270
"Zea" (Wilbur) **51**:332
The Zea Mexican Diary (Brathwaite) **56**:71
"Zebra Question" (Silverstein) **49**:327, 335
"Żeglarz" (Mickiewicz) **38**:231
"Zeitgedichte" (Heine) **25**:131, 134
Zeitgedichte (Heine) **25**:129
Zeitgehöft (Celan) **10**:96, 111
"Der Zeitgeist" (Hölderlin) **4**:166
"Zen Poems of China and Japan: The Crane's Bill" (Stryk) **27**:181
"Zen Poetry" (Stryk) **27**:188
"The Zeppelin Factory" (Dove) **6**:110
"Zero" (Berry) **28**:6
"Zero" (Gallagher) **9**:58
"Zero Hour" (Cardenal)
See "La hora O"
Zero Hour and Other Documentary Poems (Cardenal) **22**:117
"0015 hours Mayday CQ Position 41°46' N orth 50°14' West" (Enzensberger) **28**:155
"Zeroing In" (Levertov) **11**:205
"Zeus over Redeye" (Hayden) **6**:183, 194
"Zeusian toy" (Corso) **33**:46
"Zharenyi anglichanin v Moskve" (Shvarts) **50**:159, 162
Zhasněte světla (Seifert) **47**:316, 325-26, 334
"Zhil Na Svete Rytsar' Bednyi" (Pushkin) **10**:411
"Zhong feng" (Li Po) **29**:188
"Zikade" (Enzensberger) **28**:139
"Zima Junction" (Yevtushenko)
See "Zima Station"
Zima Junction (Yevtushenko)
See *Zima Station*
"Zima miejska" (Mickiewicz) **38**:153, 162
Zima miejska (Mickiewicz) **38**:219
"Zima Station" (Yevtushenko) **40**:349, 340-41, 352-53, 367, 370
Zima Station (Yevtushenko) **40**:365
Ziminiskaya ballada (Yevtushenko) **40**:363
"Zimniy Vecher" (Pushkin) **10**:381
"Zim-Zizimi" (Hugo) **17**:59
"Znayu" (Bely) **11**:32
"The Zodiac" (Dickey) **40**:174
The Zodiac (Dickey) **40**:176-77, 181, 183-84, 207-9, 217, 219, 221-22, 232, 239, 256, 262
"Zoetropes" (Curnow) **48**:46
"Zokudo no, kari ni ai sunawachi hanare, sariyasuku todomarigataki koto wo kanashiburu shi" (Yakamochi) **48**:137;
"Zola" (Robinson) **35**:367
"Zolnierz" (Herbert) **50**:5, 7
Zoloto v lazuri (Bely) **11**:3-6, 22, 26, 31-2
"Zone" (Ammons) **16**:6, 28
"Zone" (Apollinaire) **7**:6, 10-12, 14-15, 21, 41, 44-8
"Zone" (Bogan) **12**:126
"Zoo de verbena" (Fuertes) **27**:16
"Zoo Keeper's Wife" (Plath) **1**:399
"A Zorro Man" (Angelou) **32**:29
"Zov" (Akhmatova) **55**:49
Zovy vremen (Bely) **11**:31-2
"Zueignung" (Goethe) **5**:257
"Zuleika" (Goethe) **5**:228
"Zver'-tsvetok" (Shvarts) **50**:134, 159
Zvezda (Bely) **11**:7, 24, 30, 32
"Zwist" (Stramm) **50**:189, 198, 202, 207